The Revolution in Corporate Finance

The Revolution in Corporate Finance

SECOND EDITION

Edited by
Joel M. Stern
and
Donald H. Chew Jr.

© Basil Blackwell Ltd., 1992 for this collection.
© Stern Stewart Management Services for all individual
articles.

First Edition Published 1982
Second Edition Published 1992
Reprinted 1993

Blackwell Publishers
238 Main Street
Cambridge, Massachusetts 02142, USA

108 Cowley Road, Oxford OX4 1JF, UK

British Library Cataloguing in Publication Data

A CIP catalogue record for this book is available from the
British Library

Library of Congress Cataloging in Publication Data

The Revolution in corporate finance / edited by Joel M.
  Stern and Donald H. Chew, Jr. — 2nd ed.
      p.   cm.
  Essays previously published in the Midland corporate
finance journal and the Chase financial quarterly.
  ISBN 0-631-18554-2
  1. Corporations — Finance. I. Stern, Joel M. II. Chew,
Donald H.
HG4026.5.R48   1992
658.15 — dc20   92-24567
                                              CIP

Printed in the USA

Contents

Acknowledgements

The Editors and Basil Blackwell Ltd. gratefully acknowledge the permission of Chase Manhattan Bank N.A. to reprint the following essays which first appeared in the *Chase Financial Quarterly*: 'Does it Pay to Manipulate EPS?', Ross Watts; The Evidence against Stock Splits', Thomas Copeland; 'The Real Function of Bond Rating Agencies', L. Macdonald Wakeman; 'Deflating Inflation Accounting', Jerold Zimmerman; 'Beta is Dead! Long Live Beta', Jason McQueen; 'The Corporate Uses of Beta', Barr Rosenberg and Andrew Rudd; 'The Corporate Insurance Decision', David Mayers and Clifford Smith; 'Common Stock Repurchases: What Do They Really Accomplish?', Larry Dann; 'The Case for Convertibles', Michael Brennan and Eduardo Schwartz; 'The Future of Floating-Rate Bonds', Bradford Cornell; 'Is Deep Discount Financing a Bargain?', David Pyle; 'The Income Bond Puzzle', John McConnell and Gary Schlarbaum; 'Managing Interest Rate Risk: An Introduction to Financial Futures and Options', Bluford Putnam; 'Can Management Use Dividends to Influence the Value of the Firm?', Merton Miller; 'The Dividend Debate: Twenty Years of Discussion', Patrick Hess; 'How Companies Set Their Dividend Payout Ratios', Michael Rozeff; and to the Midland Bank for permission to reprint the following essays which first appeared in the *Midland Corporate Finance Journal*: 'Tax-Cutting Inventory Management', Garry Biddle; 'Corporate Strategy and the Capital Budgeting Decision', Alan Shapiro; 'A Primer on Arbitrage Pricing Theory', Dorothy Bower, Richard Bower and Dennis Logue; 'A New Approach to Evaluating Natural Resource Investments', Michael Brennan and Eduardo Schwartz; 'The Search for Optimal Capital Structure', Stewart Myers; 'The Capital Structure Puzzle', Stewart Myers; 'The Investment-Financing Nexus: Some Empirical Evidence', Michael Long and Ileen Malitz; 'The Debt-Equity Swap', Harold Bierman; 'An Analysis of Call Provisions and the Corporate Refunding Decision', Alan Kraus; 'Guidelines for Corporate Financing Strategy', Alan Shapiro; 'The Options Pricing Model and the Valuation of Corporate Securities', by Georges Courtadon and John Merrick; 'An Integrated Approach to Corporate Risk Management', Alan Shapiro and Sheridan Titman; 'The Evolving Market for Swaps', Clifford Smith, Charles Smithson and L. Macdonald Wakeman; 'Immunisation and Duration: A Review of Theory, Performance and Applications', Stephen Schaefer; 'An Economic Approach to Pension Fund Management', Thomas Copeland; 'Does Dividend Policy Matter?', Richard Brealey; 'Dividend Cuts: Do They Always Signal Bad News?', J. Randall Woolridge and Chinmoy Ghosh; 'The Market for Corporate Control: A Review of the Evidence', Peter Dodd; 'Observations on the Merger Phenomenon', Baruch Lev; 'The Economic Consequences of Mergers and Tender Offers', Michael Bradley; 'Managerial Incentives in Mergers and their Effect on Shareholder Wealth', David Larcker; 'The Rules for Successful Mergers', J. Fred Weston; 'Comments on M&A Analysis and the Role of Investment Bankers', George Foster; 'The Evaluation of an Acquisition Target', Stewart Myers; 'Why Corporate Raiders are Good News for Stockholders', Cliff Holderness and Dennis Sheehan; 'The Restructuring of Corporate America: A Review of the Evidence', Gailen Hite and James Owers; 'The Corporate Sell-Off', Scott C. Linn and Michael Rozeff; 'The Corporate Spin-Off Phenomenon', Katherine Schipper and Abbie Smith; 'Going Private: The Effects of a Change in Ownership Structure', Harry and Linda DeAngelo and Edward M Rice.

Preface to Second Edition

This new edition attempts to capture some of the developments in the theory and practice of corporate finance that have taken place since the first edition was published in 1986. It accordingly contains significantly expanded sections in the areas of innovative securities, risk management, and corporate restructuring.

In the realm of theory, the award of the 1990 Nobel Prize in Economics to Merton Miller, William Sharpe, and Harry Markowitz was largely, of course, a ceremonial crowning of past achievement. The awards simply confirmed the success of the academic finance profession in transforming the study of corporate finance from what once amounted to an apprenticeship system transmitting folklore among generations—in effect, the old Harvard case-study approach—into a systematic discipline with the predictive power of a hard science.

What is relatively new, however, are the ways in which the theories of "agency costs" and "informational asymmetry" have contributed to an understanding of corporate restructuring and financing decisions that goes beyond the M&M irrelevance propositions. For example, Michael Jensen uses his recently formulated "free cash flow" theory—an extension of his 1976 agency cost article with William Meckling—to provide a remarkably ambitious assessment of the leveraged restructuring of the '80s. And other new articles in this collection by Clifford Smith and by Paul Healy and Krishna Palepu show how the information gap between management and investors causes the stock market to respond negatively to equity and convertible offerings, and positively to dividend increases and share repurchases.

In the "real world," meanwhile, the rate of financial innovation has continued the dramatic acceleration that began with the establishment of futures and stock options in the early 1970s. Extending the successes of these first exchange-traded "derivative" markets, the 1980s gave rise to an astonishing variety of new "risk management" tools: currency, interest rate, and commodity swaps; exchange-traded options on currencies, interest rates, and commodity prices; futures on stock market indexes; and "hybrid" debt securities combining standard debt issues with forward- or option-like features. At the same time, a flourishing junk bond market, besides furnishing capital for promising growth companies, was also making possible an unprecedented wave of leveraged acquisitions, large stock buybacks, divestitures, spin-offs, and multi-billion dollar LBOs—all of which were yoked together under the name of "corporate restructuring."

As the pace of innovation has quickened, moreover, the relationship between theory and practice has become more dynamic. On the one hand, theoretical insights like the M&M (tax-adjusted) capital structure proposition and the Black-Scholes(-Merton) option pricing model helped stimulate the process of innovation. But if theory has affected practice, the flood of new corporate securities, risk management practices, and organizational structures has also acted back upon the theory. Indeed, the 1980s can be viewed as a decade in which Wall Street first adopted and then pushed to their limits principles of financial economics that most businessmen once dismissed as wildly impractical. The experimentation throughout the '80s with corporate securities and structures has provided financial economists with a vast laboratory in which to test the workings of our capital markets. And, as should become clear from the articles in this book, such experimentation is helping finance scholars extend and, in some cases, revise their thinking—which in turn promises to influence corporate practice in the 1990s.

What has all this innovation done for corporate America and general economic growth? Let's begin with the case of corporate restructuring.

Based on the best current research available, the leveraged restructuring movement of the '80s appears to have provided an effective free-market solution to the inefficiencies caused by widespread corporate conglomeration and overinvestment in mature industries. In accordance with Jensen's "free cash flow" theory mentioned above, the widespread substitution of temporary debt capital for more permanent equity—in leveraged takeovers, leveraged buyouts, and leveraged buybacks—has forced excess capital out of companies in mature industries like oil and gas, tobacco, forest products, publishing, broadcasting, tires, food processing, and commodity chemicals. One of the fruits of this restructuring has been impressive growth in the productivity of the U.S. manufacturing sector since 1982; another is the 75% real growth of U.S exports since 1987, a growth rate that has persisted even in the face of the worldwide recession that began in 1989.

Today, of course, the scale of leveraged restructuring in the U.S. is greatly diminished (although the recent $1.4 billion LBO of American Reinsurance by KKR may be signalling a resurgence of at least "voluntary" transactions). The junk bond market has recovered smartly, as most financial economists predicted it would, and the new-issue market is booming.

In the meantime, however, financial innovation has also been proceeding vigorously on the other major front established in the '80s: corporate risk management. The corporate use of futures, swaps, and options, while rising steadily throughout the '80s, has if anything accelerated in the 1990s as corporate treasurers grope toward a better understanding of their economic risks. (As Clifford Smith, Charles Smithson, and Sykes Wilford explain in "Managing Financial Risk," most of these exposures are not reflected on corporate balance sheets, but can have major effects on future cash flows.)

Rather ironically, the regulatory crackdown on one form of financial innovation—LBOs and other HLTs—has provided the impetus for another by contributing greatly to the severity of the "credit crunch." In response to the widening of credit spreads that attended the collapse of the junk bond market, the 1990s have seen a flurry of new "hybrid" debt instruments—that is, debt issues incor-

porating derivatives such as commodity futures and options. Such securities were introduced by Drexel Burnham in the early 1980s as a way of allowing somewhat riskier companies to reduce their interest payments to manageable levels by giving bondholders, in effect, an equity-like participation in corporate profits. In the '90s, as Charles Smithson and I argue in "The Uses of Hybrid Debt in Managing Corporate Risk", many companies are using hybrids to lower their risk profiles and thus avoid the disproportionately higher funding costs now imposed on riskier corporate borrowers. In this sense, financial innovation in the form of new hybrid debt securities is playing a role much like that of junk bonds in the early '80s: They are allowing riskier companies raise capital on economic terms, thus helping them weather the restrictive financing climate of the '90s.

Such securities innovation also provides yet another illustration of Merton Miller's conception of regulatory change as "the grain of sand in the oyster" that irritates the financial system into invention. The continuing proliferation of new forms of hybrid debt into the '90s demonstrates once again the ingenuity of capital markets in circumventing regulatory obstacles to economic growth.

Donald H. Chew
June 26, 1992
New York City

Preface

Over the past 25 years or so, a quiet revolution in the theory of corporate finance has been taking place at select graduate business schools in the U.S. and abroad. Beginning principally with the work of Merton Miller and Franco Modigliani in the late 1950s, the study of finance has been gradually molded through rigorous application of economic logic into the shape of a positive science. (In fact, with the recent award of the Nobel Prize to Modigliani, finance scholarship appears finally to have assumed its rightful standing as a "serious" branch of economic studies.) Now firmly grounded in principles of microeconomic theory, and aided by sophisticated statistical methods and powerful computers drawing on massive data bases, the theory of "modern finance" has made steady progress toward achieving the two major aims of a hard science: internal consistency and predictive power.

Aside from this appropriation of the scientific method, what is "revolutionary" about the modern theory of finance? The revolution in finance is at bottom a change in the theory of valuation, a displacement of older, conventional notions of how the stock market prices securities (even though, of course, many of these discarded theories continue to be propounded daily by Wall Street "authorities"). Financial academics, supported by an extensive body of empirical research, have been challenging much of the accounting-oriented intuition that continues to pass for the collective wisdom of the business community.

The rise of modern finance has brought about a confrontation, in short, between two very different views of the process by which capital markets establish the values of corporate securities. The traditional view holds that stock prices are determined primarily by reported earnings. At its most simplistic, it maintains that investors respond uncritically to financial statements, mechanically capitalizing published EPS figures at standard, industry-wide multiples. We call this the "accounting model of the firm." The rival view, the "economic model," holds that the market value of corporate stock — like the value of a bond or any other investment — is the present value of a company's future expected after-tax *cash flows*, discounted at rates which reflect investors' required returns on securities of comparable risk. According to this view, reported earnings may offer a reasonably good measure of corporate performance, but only insofar as they reflect real *cash* profitability. When earnings seriously misrepresent operating cash flows, accounting statements distort performance and provide an unreliable guide to value. (And dividends, we might add, are probably largely irrelevant — aside from possible tax and "information" effects — to the process of valuation.)

This fundamental difference in theory of value has in turn given rise to two distinct philosophies of corporate management. Corporate executives subscribing to the accounting model view the goal of financial management as the maximization of reported earnings per share. Those who subscribe to the "economic model" argue that public firms should be run largely as if they were private; that is, the public corporation best serves its stockholders by maximizing neither reported earnings nor earnings growth, but after-tax "free cash flow." The sophisticated investors that dominate the market pricing process are accustomed to distinguishing between accounting illusion and economic reality in setting stock prices; and they can be counted on to reward such "value-maximizing" behavior by management.

The crucial assumption underlying the "economic model" is, of course, the sophistication of market investors. And this assumption, which has been formulated and tested by academics as the "efficient markets hypothesis" (EMH), is the central tenet of modern finance. EMH is essentially an extension to capital markets of the "zero profits theorem" which economists have long applied to competitive goods markets. Briefly stated, the principle of market efficiency holds that competition among investors for information about public companies' intrinsic values ensures that the current prices of widely-traded financial assets are "unbiased predictors" of the future value of those securities. This means that a company's future stock price (adjusted for a gradually upward "drift" in which all stocks are expected to participate over time) is equally likely to be higher or lower than today's price. It also implies that new investors can expect a "normal" rate of return on their investment at any given time — no more, no less. (The failure of the vast majority of professional fund managers consistently to outperform the market is forceful testimony to the truth of the efficient markets proposition.)

For corporate management, EMH has three important implications: (1) the market is not likely to be fooled by accounting manipulations; (2) today's stock price reflects the collective wisdom of the marketplace about the future performance of the company (over the long run as well as the short); and unless management has significant inside information, the current price should be viewed as a reliable estimate of the value of the company; and (3) the market's reactions to corporate announcements, such as announcements of acquisitions, divestitures, new securities offerings, or capital expenditure programs, should be viewed as conveying the market's best estimate of the consequences of that transaction on the (long-term) value of the company.

There exists today in the academic finance community a remarkable consensus about the validity of EMH (at least in its so-called "semi-strong" form) — a consensus which is backed by the greater body of academic research in finance conducted over the last two decades. To say this, of course, is not to minimize important remaining disagreements among financial economists about aspects of the theory. The Capital Asset Pricing Model, for example, has not done as good a job in explaining actual corporate returns as its formulators had hoped; and a challenger, known as "arbitrage pricing theory," although far from assuming a usable form, is on the rise. As another example, the widely-accepted DCF valuation framework, which has been under attack in the past few years, is now being supplemented by the use of option pricing theory to evaluate strategic business options. But such disagreements notwithstanding, the relentless testing of the proposition of market efficiency from the late 60s onward has made it — as Michael Jensen has commented — "without doubt the best-documented hypothesis in the social sciences."

But however thoroughly the principles of "modern finance" appear to have prevailed over all rivals in the business schools, they have not captured a strong following in the practicing business community. Nor, we suspect, have its many implications for corporate investment and financing been well understood. The general skepticism is based, in part, on the inevitable unwillingness of experienced practitioners to surrender their intuitive sense of a capricious market to the overly general conclusions of studies whose complex "methodologies" they cannot — or, more likely, will not take the time to — fathom. But another, perhaps more important, reason for this resistance lies in the failure of the academy to state its case in a comprehensible and convincing manner.

To date, the publication of financial studies has been confined largely to academic journals. Unless readers bring to the subject a strong background in economics and quantitative methods, they will find these studies very tough going. And density of presentation aside, such journals do not encourage their contributors to lay significant stress on the practical applications of theoretical developments. As anyone who has gone through a reputable M.B.A. program can tell you, theoretical training in finance, at least as currently structured, is not designed to prepare students for the extensions and modifications of the theory that actual corporate decision-making requires.

Before the lessons of modern finance can be applied to corporate decision-making, the best current research must be identified, rid of its technical obscurities, and presented with a firm eye toward applications. The purpose of this book is further to develop the channel of communication between the academic and business communities, to help close the rift between theory and much corporate practice that now exists, by translating current academic research into practical recommendations for corporate management. Accordingly, the articles printed here reflect an attempt to achieve an ideal balance between theoretical rigor and applicability, analytical precision and compact clarity of expression.

THE SOURCEBOOKS

The Revolution in Corporate Finance represents a gathering up of many of the articles that have been published to date in both the *Chase Financial Quarterly* and the *Midland Corporate Finance Journal*. Before I describe the contents of this book, let me provide a brief history of these publications.

In the fall of 1981, under the aegis of the Chase Manhattan Bank, Joel Stern and I (with the help of Joe Willett) founded a publication called the *Chase Financial Quarterly* in order to supplement our corporate finance advisory work for the Bank. Its purpose, more broadly, was to help bridge what we saw as a "gulf" between modern finance theory and much corporate practice by culling from current research useful prescriptions for corporate policy.

Four issues later, in November of 1982, we and other members of our Chase Financial Policy division left the bank to form Stern Stewart & Co., a private corporate finance advisory firm. We also renewed our publishing efforts by founding, with the sponsorship of the Midland Bank plc, the *Midland Corporate Finance Journal (MCFJ)*. The purpose of the *MCFJ*, like that of its predecessor, was to bring to the attention of senior management the practical import of theoretical developments in finance for a wide range of corporate decisions: capital budgeting, dividend policy, capital structure planning, international performance measurement, acquisition and divestiture pricing, corporate risk management, and executive compensation.

Now beginning its fourth year of publication, the *MCFJ* has achieved a distinction we think unique among financial publications: while making a strong appeal to practicing corporate executives, it has also established a reputation among financial academics as the most creditable corporate finance publication written for the layman. For this reason, besides attracting a growing corporate following, the *MCFJ* is beginning to be used extensively in graduate business schools, especially in Executive Development Programs. The articles are now being assigned in the classrooms at such prestigious institutions as the University of Chicago (where Merton Miller, incidentally, has been using an entire issue of the *MCFJ* as the main text of a course he teaches in corporate policy), MIT's Sloan School, Wharton, Dartmouth's Tuck School, Stanford, Berkeley, UCLA, the University of Virginia, the University of Rochester, and the Harvard Business School.

THE CONTENT

This volume contains 45 articles which are grouped into the following eight sections: (1) Issues in Market Efficiency; (2) The Investment Decision; (3) The Financing Decision I: Capital Structure; (4) The Financing Decision II: The Financing Vehicles; (5) Risk and Liabilities Management; (6) The Dividend Decision; (7) Mergers & Acquisitions; and (8) Corporate Restructuring. Our aim in selecting the topics is to make the articles both as timely, on the one hand, and perennially useful, on the other, by engaging subjects which all corporate financial officers must address at some point in the planning cycle.

Part I, "Issues of Market Efficiency," provides the theoretical groundwork for the articles that follow. In this section we present a series of articles dispelling a number of popular myths: (1) the stock market responds uncritically to accounting numbers and, thus, manipulation of accounting techniques enables management to fool investors and thereby increase stock prices; (2) stock splits *cause* stock prices to rise; (3) changes in bond ratings convey significant new information to the bond markets and

materially affect a company's borrowing costs; and (4) the market requires replacement cost accounting information in order to ascertain the effects of inflation on corporate values.

Part II, "The Corporate Investment Decision," presents a series of articles discussing the strengths and limitations of both current and developing capital budgeting techniques. They also explore the contribution of such quantitative analytical tools to the overall process of strategic planning. Alan Shapiro, for example, presents a corporate finance-based approach to corporate strategy that is far more systematic (and thus, we would suggest, more useful) than Peters' and Waterman's *In Search of Excellence*. Following this attempt to integrate capital budgeting and strategy, we present articles explaining the Capital Asset Pricing Model (CAPM) and its applications. Threatening to unseat the CAPM, however, are two new developments in capital budgeting (explored by the last two articles in the section): Arbitrage Pricing Theory (APT) and the use of options pricing theory to evaluate natural resource investments and strategic operating options.

Parts III and IV deal with two aspects of "The Corporate Financing Decision." Part III offers a series of articles presenting the finance profession's latest thinking on the general question of capital structure: Is there an "optimal" debt-equity mix for a given public corporation; and if so, what are the principal factors that determine that optimum?

Part IV, "The Financing Vehicles," focuses on the specific financing instruments that can be used by corporate treasurers to bring about the desired capital structure. Among the subjects treated in this section are convertibles, OIDs, floating-rate bonds, and income bonds (articles on financial futures and interest rate and currency swaps are included in the section that follows). In each case, the attempt is to separate the real economic motives and benefits of these instruments from the claims of their promoters. Among the popular misconceptions corrected are these: (1) convertibles represent "cheap debt" and the sale of equity "at a premium"; (2) the lower yields required by investors on OIDs represent a real benefit to issuing corporations; (3) floating-rate debt is of necessity "riskier" than fixed-rate debt; and (4) the continued expansion of currency and interest rate swaps is being driven by significant interest rate differences (and thus a form of corporate "arbitraging" of a market inefficiency) among world capital markets.

The subject of Part V is "Risk and Liabilities Management." Finance theorists have for some time maintained that, for public corporations, reducing risks at the corporate level which are diversifiable by investors at the portfolio level does not benefit stockholders. A series of articles — most notably, Alan Shapiro's and Sheridan Titman's "An Integrated Approach to Corporate Risk Management" and David Mayer's and Clifford Smith's "The Corporate Insurance Decision" — presents a relatively new theoretical rationale for managing the total risk (diversifiable as well as non-diversifiable) of the firm. This theoretical framework is used to generate a set of principles to guide financial executives in establishing a comprehensive, centralized approach to risk management. Such a framework weighs the costs and benefits of a variety of available strategies (such as immunization, the subject of one article) and financial instruments (such as financial futures and options, and interest rate and currency swaps, the subjects of two others) for managing the total exposure of the company.

Part VI, "The Dividend Decision," consists of five articles on dividends. The first two are general discussions by Merton Miller and Richard Brealey of the "dividend irrelevance" hypothesis. This argument, which continues in our opinion to be the starting point for any serious discussion of corporate dividend policy, holds as follows: *given* a level of corporate profitability, investors in aggregate are indifferent whether they receive their returns in the form of dividends or capital gains; therefore, aside from possible adverse tax effects, the *level* of the dividend (that is, the yield) has no systematic effect on stock prices. The other three articles offer (1) a concise review of 20 years of research on dividends, (2) a very plausible attempt to explain how companies actually arrive at their dividend payout ratios, and (3) a fascinating study of the market's response to dividend cuts.

Part VII concerns the current controversy on "Mergers and Acquisitions." The available academic research suggests that, on average and over the years, mergers and acquisitions have proven a profitable investment of corporate funds for the buying companies — though acquired firms appear to have received the lion's share of the gains. What these statistical averages conceal, however, is that many acquiring companies have paid too dearly and, in the process, materially harmed their own stockholders. A study by Peter Dodd of the most recent merger wave (1979-1982) suggests that both mergers and tender offers appear to have resulted in significantly *negative* returns, on average, to stockholders of buying companies. The frequent negative market reaction to *buying* firms, together with what appears to be an unprecedented resistance by target managements to "unfriendly" takeovers (or, at least, an astonishing proliferation of new antitakeover strategies) suggests that the market for control may be undergoing some fundamental changes.

The meaning of these changes is explored by Peter Dodd in an ambitious survey entitled "The Market for Corporate Control." Dodd's article is followed by selections from a series of talks delivered at a three-day conference on "Mergers and Acquisitions" sponsored by the finance department of the University of California at Berkeley. The principal focus of the selections are the economic consequences of M & A — more specifically, the effects of mergers and tender offers on stockholders and other corporate security holders. But, supplementing this broad economic perspective, a number of speakers also addressed prescriptive aspects of merger analysis from the corporate perspective: strategic planning, the pricing of acquisition targets, and the structuring of management compensation plans.

Following these selections, we also present an article summarizing the results of the first systematic study of "corporate raiders," one which attempts to explain why such investors as Carl Icahn, Irwin Jacobs, Carl Lindner, and David Murdock are "Good News for Stockholders."

Part VIII, "Corporate Restructuring," offers a series of four articles which present the results of the academic finance community's initial explorations into the "reverse merger" movement: divestitures, spin-offs, stock repurchases, and leveraged buyouts. The findings of this preliminary research suggest that we may be witnessing a new phase in the evolution of the public corporation into a more efficient vehicle for building and storing stockholder wealth. The market's early endorsement of this restructuring also suggests that some forms of corporate organization — most notably, the large, sprawling conglomerate — may now be in the earliest stages of obsolescence.

IN CLOSING

What, then, does the revolution in finance theory have to say to practicing corporate executives? It is important to recognize that to the extent management views its function as the maximization of stockholder value, all financial decisions are based on some theory of capital market pricing. How management decides to use the corporate assets at its disposal, and what it chooses to tell investors, depend fundamentally on its understanding of how the stock market works.

Effective financial management, therefore, is in no small part a matter of achieving a better understanding of how our capital markets work. In fact, we believe that an executive who adopts the perspective of financial markets and views himself as the steward of stockholders' savings has already taken a major step toward achieving the goal of corporate management: the most efficient use of the scarce stockholder capital at its disposal. And, when properly understood and applied, the theory of modern finance can provide corporate decision-makers with a more sensible basis for a number of corporate finance functions: setting corporate goals, evaluating the performance of divisions and subsidiaries, choosing among investment opportunities and financing vehicles, pricing acquisitions and divestitures, structuring incentive compensation schemes, finding the ideal capital structure, and communicating with the investment community.

I would like to close by expressing both Joel's and my gratitude to all the academics who have served on our Advisory Board over the past four years, as well as to our many other contributors, who have made the *Chase Financial Quarterly*, the *Midland Corporate Finance Journal*, and thus this book possible.

Donald H. Chew, Jr.
New York City
February 4, 1986

Part I: Issues of Market Efficiency

INTRODUCTION

In this section we present seven articles bearing witness to the first principle of modern finance, the efficiency of capital markets in processing information and processing securities.

One of the most important corollaries of the efficient markets hypothesis for corporate management is the futility of using accounting manipulations to increase stock prices. Academic research in finance and accounting has produced a large body of evidence attesting to the ability of the stock market to penetrate accounting fictions. Ross Watts, one of the founding editors of the *Journal of Accounting and Economics*, opens this section with an ambitious survey of modern scholarship in accounting. Beginning with the significant turn taken by accounting research in the 1960s, Watts describes the challenge presented by scientific, statistical studies documenting the efficiency of the stock market to the traditional insistence on the need for more and better accounting disclosures.

In "The Evidence Against Stock Splits," Thomas Copeland demonstrates that, contrary to the popular conception, stock splits do not *cause* stock prices to rise. Copeland argues that "there is no sound theoretical explanation why the market should respond positively to a company's announced intention to split its stock, nor is there any creditable empirical evidence that splits benefit stockholders." In fact, by raising average trading costs and reducing liquidity, splits may actually be working against stockholder interests.

In "The Real Function of Bond Rating Agencies," Lee Wakeman argues that bond rating changes do not provide new information to the capital markets. Companies experiencing changes in their bond ratings do see significant changes in the prices of their securities; however, these changes typically occur more than a year before the rating change. But if the rating agencies do not provide timely information to investors about outstanding bond issues, they nonetheless do perform a valuable service for debt issuers. When bonds are first issued, the agencies in effect "certify" the issue, providing investors with an implicit guarantee that the bonds have credit quality. Such a guarantee enables companies to lower the interest cost of their bonds.

In "Deflating Inflation Accounting," Jerold Zimmerman points out that although the SEC requires large companies to disclose "replacement cost" information — purportedly to alert investors

to the impact of inflation on corporate profitability and value — the investors whom the SEC mandate was designed to "protect" do not appear to be using this information in their assessments of companies' market values. The implication of the research is that the market has been adjusting corporate profits for inflation all along, without benefit of replacement cost accounting.

In "Tax-Cutting Inventory Management," Gary Biddle and Kipp Martin estimate that American corporations could save as much as $6 billion annually by switching to LIFO inventory accounting, and perhaps even considerably more by tailoring their ordering policies to control year-end inventory levels. Many (no doubt far too many) financial executives have been reluctant to take advantage of such tax savings because they come at the price of reductions in reported earnings and thus, as many executives believe, lower stock prices. The available research on this issue suggests, however, that the market rewards, not penalizes, companies which switch to LIFO to save taxes. In fact, one of the authors collaborated in a recent study which demonstrated that the larger the expected LIFO tax savings, and thus the larger the reduction in reported earnings, the more positive the market's response to the accounting change.

In "How Investors Interpret Changes in Corporate Financial Policy," Paul Healy and Krishna Palepu attempt to explain why investors react in fairly consistent ways to announcements of three kinds of corporate policy changes: (1) dividend initiations, (2) common stock offerings, and (3) stock splits. As the authors found in their own recent studies, both dividend initiations and stock splits are followed by several years of sustained increases in earnings, thus vindicating the market's initially positive reaction. Announcements of stock offerings, by contrast, presage a period of significantly higher operating risk and share price volatility, thus justifying the generally negative market response.

Since the stock market crash of October 1987, charges of investor irrationality and "excess volatility" have been more widely sounded than ever. And adding fuel to the unfailingly populist clamor of the press, a number of recent academic studies have purported to demonstrate that the market overreacts both to general economic news and to changes in the fortunes of individual companies. In "How

Rational Investors Deal with Uncertainty," Seha Tinic, Keith Brown, and Van Harlow argue that reports of the death of efficient markets theory are greatly exaggerated. Their own recent studies suggest that what appear to be predictable price "corrections" following overreactions by the investing public are better understood as rational responses to abrupt changes in investment risk.

DHC

Does It Pay to Manipulate EPS?

by Ross Watts,
University of Rochester

Introduction

The rise of modern finance has caused some accountants to revise their thinking about the accounting profession: its achievements, its limitations, and, more pointedly, its fundamental purpose. Since the Great Depression, publicly held companies have been required by the SEC to provide investors with increasingly elaborate disclosures. The number and complexity of accounting standards have also greatly increased. The assumption underlying this proliferation and refinement of accounting procedures is that investors are easily misled by accounting numbers, and that financial reporting must be designed to provide investors with reliable guides to the profitability and fair market value of corporations. Under the influence of "efficient markets" theory and evidence, however, a generation of academic accountants has been reexamining and testing some of these fundamental assumptions.

One of the first principles of modern finance is that the economic value of the corporation is the sum of the company's expected *cash flows,* discounted at rates which reflect investors' alternative investment opportunities. Consequently, a company's cash flow rate of return on investment is a more relevant measure of its performance than, say, its rate of growth in EPS. And, as finance theory argues, it is the market's perception of companies' *cash-*generating capacity that most directly governs their stock prices.

To the extent that changes in companies' cash flow prospects are reflected in changes in earnings, accounting earnings may offer a reasonably good substitute for cash flow as a guide to value. But this is only because reported earnings are, on average, highly *correlated* with cash flows. If accounting income does provide a useful proxy for underlying cash flows, we would then expect changes in earnings to be correlated with changes in stock prices. In cases where reported earnings diverge significantly from cash flow measures, however, accounting statements can provide a distorted picture of performance, and an unreliable guide to underlying economic value.

An unsophisticated market — the kind presupposed by much traditional financial scholarship — would be fooled by "cosmetic" earnings, raising the stock prices of companies engaging in accounting manipulations. In a reasonably "efficient" market, however, the dominant price-setting investors would see through accounting illusion to underlying cash flow. Earnings would be important only insofar as they provided investors with information about cash income.

In the face of these relatively new developments in finance theory, the academic accounting profession has been forced to confront questions like the following: Is there a strong relationship between accounting numbers and stock prices? Do announcements of earnings convey timely information to the market; that is, do they tell the market something it doesn't already know? Furthermore, do investors respond mechanically and uncritically to those announcements, or are they really looking through those numbers to cash flow? And finally, if cash is a more relevant guide to market value than accounting earnings, are there other explanations for the prominence of accountants in our corporate culture, other important uses and effects of accounting procedures which could have a major impact on the values of companies?

Corporate compensation committees often compel attention to accounting numbers.

The Strong Hold of EPS

It is probably safe to say that most practicing accountants are not troubled by these issues. And, developments in finance theory notwithstanding, the belief that stock prices are strongly influenced, if not wholly determined, by reported accounting earnings remains a pervasive one in the business community. Quarterly and annual earnings figures are still faithfully reported by the *Wall Street Journal* and other publications. Stock analysts' reports are couched invariably in the language of EPS and price-earnings multiples. Earnings-per-share are forecast, generally with the implicit assumption that the market will mechanically adjust the price to maintain a certain standard multiple. This notion is also embodied in many current valuation models, employed by investment bankers and other financial advisors in pricing acquisitions, divestitures, and new public equity offerings. These popular models establish fair market values simply by assigning prevailing market-wide (or industry-wide) P/E multiples to an annual reported earnings figure.

For many of the above reasons, most financial executives probably also regard EPS as the primary measure of their company's performance. Corporate compensation committees often *compel* attention to accounting numbers by tying managers' bonuses to reported earnings. But this would not explain the apparent conviction of many managers that the stock market is dominated by the common obsession with earnings per share (i.e., accounting income/number of shares) — while ignoring cash.

Many investment bankers and corporate managers believe, for example, that the wave of mergers and acquisitions in the 1960s was the result of a general management scheme to artificially boost earnings per share. In the 1970s, executives' concern with EPS was manifest in their resistance to change to the LIFO method of inventory valuation. Concern about the negative effect of LIFO on reported earnings — and, thus, on stock prices — outweighed the potential tax savings. If it could be shown, however, that managers were needlessly concerned about EPS, then companies failing to switch to LIFO in an inflationary environment passed up not only the additional cash, but also the market's seal of approval in the form of *higher* (not lower) stock prices.

Fifteen years ago, most professors of accounting shared and reinforced management's preoccupation with reported earnings in setting corporate policy. Some estimate of the corporate cash income underlying accounting profits could be obtained, it is true, by sifting through the funds statements that appear farther back in annual reports. To suggest to one's colleagues, however, that the average layman could obtain more than a glimpse of cash flow through the tangled web of accounting procedures would provoke skepticism, if not utter disbelief. Accordingly, the dominant line of reasoning was that the mass of investors, for whom the rites of accounting are tedious and impenetrable mysteries, are compelled by their own ignorance to respond passively to reported earnings. Reported earnings, not cash flow, was believed to be the primary determinant of corporate stock prices.

And, thus, investors were thought to be highly vulnerable to manipulations of financial statements. Concern about this susceptibility to accounting machinations led most academic accountants to accept the idea that government regulation of corporate disclosure was necessary to ensure appropriate stock market valuation.

Probably the best-known spokesman for this point of view was Professor Abraham Briloff, whose "exposes" in *Barron's* of "dirty pooling" and other accounting "cover-ups" (e.g., Penn Central's Leasco's, and McDonald's) created a series of minor sensations in their day. In a book entitled *Unaccountable Accounting* (1972), Briloff quotes a former Executive Vice President of the American Institute of Certified Public Accountants with evident agreement:

In corporate financial reporting...the game plan is to show steadily rising earnings-per-share, thus stimulating investor demand for shares, with consequent rise in their price, and creating a favorable atmosphere for the issuance of new securities in case additional capital is needed.

Briloff himself extends the argument, suggesting that:

where there is a choice of reporting methods...a steady inclination arises to choose the method which will produce the most favorable results.

Briloff concludes his book with a call for increased government regulation, including a new accounting court and federal chartering of corporations. While it is probably more accurate to describe Briloff's position as a "caricature" of academics' attitudes in the 60s, his sentiments were echoed with approval, by colleagues as well as by activist regulators.

Modern Research in Accounting

Today, Briloff's writings are regarded as something of a curiosity, the relic of a past age of scholarship. There is now a broad academic consensus, supported by extensive research conducted at the leading business schools, that the stock market is not systematically misled by accounting earnings. Prices are set, at the margin, by sophisticated investors who recognize the distortions of the accounting process.

A company's stock price, therefore, should be thought of as the market's interpretation of the cash flow implications buried in its financial statements. In academic language, the price is the market's "unbiased estimate," at any given moment, of the value of the company's current and future cash flows. By "unbiased" we mean that there is a roughly 50-50 probability that a company's current stock price is on the high or low side of its future price—the price when those cash flows become known. This does not mean that the market's assessment is right in every case. On average, though, it is right. And the financial executive who bases corporate decisions on superior knowledge of his company's value (unless he has important inside information) is tempting the law of probabilities.

This pronounced change in viewpoint since the 60s is the result of an impressive accumulation, in a growing number of academic accounting and finance journals, of empirical evidence on the relationship between accounting numbers and stock prices. The evidence has been convincing enough to have attracted many converts to modern finance among traditional accounting scholars whose graduate training took place before the 1960s. Charles Horngren, Edmund W. Littlefield Professor of Accounting at Stanford and the author of several best-selling accounting texts, is a notable case of mid-career conversion.

The Early Empirical Work: Ball and Brown (1968)

The impetus for the early empirical research in accounting came, as suggested, from the work in finance. In the late 60s, graduate students studying both accounting and finance noticed that the assumptions on which the leading accounting academics based their prescriptions for accounting standards were inconsistent with the, by then, voluminous evidence attesting to the sophistication of capital markets. This inconsistency led Ray Ball and Philip Brown, while at the University of Chicago, to investigate directly the relationship between accounting earnings and stock prices. The forerunner of a great many other such studies, the Ball and Brown study (1968) provided a new direction for research in accounting.

What distinguished the work of Ball and Brown from the scholarship of their predecessors was its attempt to transform the study of accounting into a "positive" science. The fundamental difference between the new and old scholarship was one both of intent and method. The traditional accounting literature would begin by simply assuming that markets were misled by accounting distortions, and then get on to the real business at hand: devising and prescribing new and more elaborate sets of accounting regulations to remedy supposed market deficiencies.

Beginning with the Ball and Brown study, however, the intent was to determine whether there was any scientific basis for the formal presumption underlying the older research. In place of the traditional prescriptive or "normative" emphasis on "what ought to be," the new research addressed itself to the descriptive or "positive" task of determining "what is." It attempted to provide scientific documentation of the relationship between accounting numbers and stock prices.

Some of the traditional studies, it is true, would begin with perfunctory attempts to justify their proposed improvements of accounting procedures. Perhaps a few real world examples would be chosen to demonstrate investors' "need" for protection from accounting misinformation. A typical example would show the stock market being "misled" by "overstated" earnings. Needless to say, the examples selected *always* supported the contention that current accounting standards were inadequate, and that investors were continually being misled by financial statements. But there would be no attempt to determine whether the example was representative of the experience of most companies, or merely an isolated case.

Ball and Brown studied a sample of 2,340 annual earnings announcements by New York Stock Exchange companies. Their findings, which have since been confirmed by many later studies employing similarly broad samples, suggest that the stock market's reactions to earnings announcements are correct on average — neither too high nor too low. Later studies also conclude that the market is not systematically misled by accounting changes. In confirming these conclusions, the modern empirical literature has pretty thoroughly demolished the theoretical basis of the older work, with its call for more and better accounting disclosures.

The Effect of Earnings on Stock Prices

The modern work on the relationship between stock market prices and earnings can be split into two groups: those that investigate the effect of earnings announcements on stock prices; and those that investigate the stock price effects of *changes* in accounting procedures.

The early empirical research investigating the relationship between earnings announcements and stock prices had two basic aims: first, to determine whether earnings are *associated* with stock price changes over a given period of time; and second, to determine whether earnings *announcements* convey timely information to the market. Unless the information about cash flow is hopelessly obscured by the accounting process, and accounting earnings tell the investor nothing of significance about the market value of companies, we would expect to find a positive association between earnings and stock prices. To the extent that accounting profits are a good indicator of *current* cash income, and also provide some guide to *future* cash flows, we would thus expect to see a strong correlation between yearly changes in earnings and the accompanying stock price changes.

In the case of the market's response to earnings *announcements,* however, the expectations are less clear. There is considerable evidence in the finance literature that announcements and other corporate "events" are anticipated by the stock market. Consequently, some researchers speculated that due to "leakage" of the information or to analysts' ability to predict earnings using other sources (e.g., production data), earnings announcements would have no impact on stock prices. If this were true, the market, by the time of the announcement, would already have "discounted" the effect of the earnings information in the current share price.

The first study to test the association between accounting earnings and stock price changes was Ball and Brown's. They began by splitting their sample of 2,340 annual earnings announcements into two sets: one consisting of all announcements in which a company's current earnings had increased over the preceding year; and the other comprising announcements where annual earnings had declined. They then calculated investors' average, market-adjusted rate of return for holding each sample of stocks over the 12 months up to and including the month of announcement. Their results can be interpreted as follows: If an investor had bought the stock of all companies with increases in annual earnings exactly one year before the actual announcement, his rate of return (dividends plus price appreciation) would have been approximately 7 percent *above* the return on the market portfolio of stocks over the same period. An investor holding the stock of the decreased earnings sample over the year of the decline would have earned about 10 percent *less* than the market. These results have been replicated on other exchanges and in other countries. Brown, for example, found very similar results for Australian companies. In addition, using a more complex classification scheme, Bill Beaver, Roger Clarke, and Bill Wright (all of Stanford) demonstrated that the larger the increase in annual earnings, the larger the associated increase in stock price.

Similar analysis has also been performed for seasonally-adjusted changes in *quarterly* earnings. George Foster of Stanford found that over the three months leading up to and including the quarterly earnings announcement, stock prices of companies with quarterly earnings increases outperformed the market by approximately 2 percent. Companies with decreases in earnings underperformed the market average by 3 percent. The preceding numbers reflect an average of a broad sample of companies.

The results of these and many later studies provide convincing scientific evidence that accounting earnings have a strong correlation with stock prices. During periods when companies perform well by accounting measures, they also, on average, experience increases in stock price. Thus, it would seem the numbers generated by the accounting process offer at least some guide to the market value of corporations. This is, of course, hardly a surprise. But for those theoretically-inclined accountants who believe that markets are "efficient," and that it is only cash flow that fundamentally matters, these findings do provide reassurance that accounting numbers contain useful information about underlying cash profitability.

Accounting numbers do contain useful information about underlying cash profitability.

Do Earnings Announcements Provide 'New' Information to Investors?

Given that accounting numbers are *associated* with stock price changes, the next issue we want to resolve is: Do earnings announcements *cause* the market to change its assessments of companies' value? Or is the market so "efficient" in gathering and processing information that accounting disclosures are largely redundant?

Despite the conclusions of some early researchers to the contrary, it is now apparent that earnings announcements *do* convey information to the market. While much of the stock price change accompanying changes in earnings occurs before the announcement, there is still a significant stock price effect on the day of the announcement. Research has shown that for companies announcing increases in quarterly earnings, the average stock price response on the day of announcement is approximately one percent (after adjusting for the market's overall performance). Announcements of quarter-to-quarter declines are accompanied by a one percent drop in stock prices.

The evidence that earnings changes are associated with stock price changes, and that the market responds to quarterly and annual earnings announcements, is consistent with the claims by the older accountants that the market is misled by accounting manipulations. And, reasoning only from this evidence, one might be tempted to draw the same conclusion. For if stock prices do respond to announced increases in earnings, then might it not pay for corporate managements to "manage" reported earnings?

This argument loses much of its plausibility when we examine the behavior of stock prices *after* earnings announcements. If a large number of financial executives are using accounting methods to "overstate" earnings, and if the market systematically misinterprets these figures, then our sample of companies with increases in earnings should contain a large number of observations in which the earnings increases misrepresented cash flow. The sample's average increase in stock price should then be greater than that justified by the actual improvement in operating cash flows. If this were the case, we would also expect the stock prices of the companies with "overstated" earnings to decline later, when the market discovers its mistake. This pattern

of events would show up in our tests in the following way: in the months and years after the earnings announcement, the average market performance of the same sample of "earnings increased" companies would fall off.

The evidence, however, suggests otherwise. The only way our findings can be made consistent with the stock market being misled is to assume that the market never learns of *any* overstatement.

The Effects of Accounting Changes

We have considerably more direct evidence of the market's ability to see through accounting changes. A number of studies have attempted to measure the stock price effects of changes in accounting procedures.

The earliest of these studies concentrated on detecting the stock price effects of accounting changes which affect reported earnings *without* affecting taxes or cash flows. Consider, for example, the switchback to straight-line from accelerated depreciation. For most companies this accounting change increases reported earnings without affecting taxes (which continue to be calculated using accelerated depreciation). If the market is fooled by accounting, stock prices should increase when the increased earnings are reported. In a reasonably sophisticated market, however, there should be no appreciable price response to purely cosmetic increases in reported earnings caused by fully disclosed accounting changes.

In general, the studies conclude that there is no stock price effect accompanying changes in accounting procedures. We do observe, interestingly, that the stock prices of companies which change accounting procedures have fallen, on average, over the years preceding the change. The implication here is that poorly performing companies are more likely to boost reported earnings through accounting changes. But, if the intention has been to offset a negative market reaction, the attempt has been largely in vain.

Perhaps the strongest evidence against the claim that the market is misled was presented in another study by Ball (1972). He examined the stock price reactions to 108 accounting changes where the effect of the change on reported earnings was disclosed. More specifically, his tests attempted to determine whether the stock price change (over the

It is the poor performers who are more likely to switch accounting methods.

year up to and including the announcement of the first earnings calculated under the new procedure) was related to the effect of the procedure on earnings. In contrast to the earlier finding by Ball and Brown that stock price changes are strongly associated with earnings changes in general, this study found no association between cosmetic earnings increases and changes in market value.

Depreciation and Investment Tax Credit Options

In 1972, Robert Kaplan of Carnegie-Mellon and Richard Roll of UCLA published a study investigating the stock price effects of two accounting changes: the switchback to straight-line depreciation (mentioned earlier); and the switch by many companies in 1964 from the "deferral" to the "flow through" method of accounting for the investment tax credit. Both of these changes increased reported earnings without affecting taxes. But neither change, concluded Kaplan and Roll, had a significant effect on stock prices.

Kaplan and Roll also confirmed Ball's finding that it is the poor performers who are more likely to switch methods. In this case, it seems that the "poorest" performers tried hardest to hide that performance. This became apparent in the pattern of behavior of companies using "flow through." All companies switching to "flow through" would have had deferred credits on their books from prior years. It turns out that those companies which switched *and* chose to bring those credits into income in 1964 (the first year that "flow through" could be used) tended to have had worse stock performance prior to the switch than those companies which switched, but left the deferred credit on the balance sheet. Similarly, those companies which switched back to straight-line depreciation, and *announced* the switchback *prior* to the end of the switch year, had had better stock price performance prior to the switch than those which switched *without* announcing the switch.

The Purchase vs. Pooling Controversy

A more controversial accounting option, one that attracted the censure of some academics, was the availability of two methods for recording mergers and acquisitions. The "purchase" method, employed whenever one company acquires another for cash, involves the amortization of goodwill after the merger. The "pooling" method, used only in security-for-security swaps, does not call for amortizing goodwill. Consequently, while such amortization does not affect a company's taxable income, the use of "pooling" results in higher reported earnings per share. It was once a common claim that the pooling method overstates earnings, thereby misleading the stock market. And it was the widespread use of this method in the 60s that prompted Professor Briloff's now classic exposure of the practice of "dirty pooling."

In place of Briloff's allegations, which were grounded in a handful of anecdotes and casual observations, we now have some creditable scientific evidence on the effects of purchase and pooling on stock prices. The extent to which investors are "fooled" by the choice of "pooling of interests" instead of the purchase method was tested in a study performed at Carnegie-Mellon by Hai Hong, Robert Kaplan, and Gershon Mandelker. This study, published in 1978, began by making the following assumption: if the stock market is systematically deceived by the higher earnings reported in a pooling of interests, share prices of pooling companies will show abnormal increases at the time of announcement of the first earnings after the merger. Using a sample which included 159 mergers (37 purchases and 122 poolings, all involving goodwill) over the 1954-1964 period, the study found no evidence that the market responded to the artificially higher earnings created by poolings.

It could also be argued that the market *anticipates* the positive effect of pooling on earnings, and that the positive market response occurs when the merger is announced. To test this hypothesis, the study also investigated the stock price effect on acquiring companies at the time of the merger announcement. In the two years surrounding the merger, there was no evidence of a positive stock price effect for companies using pooling. In fact, companies using the purchase method *outperformed* the market by 9 percent over the 12 months preceding the merger. This result suggests the same kind of "self-selection bias" found by Ball, and by Kaplan and Roll. Again, it appears that it is largely the poor performers which attempt to inflate their earnings. And again, the evidence says that the market deflates such earnings, zeroing in on cash.

Lifo vs. Fifo

Another prominent issue in the accounting literature concerns the two most popular methods of inventory costing, FIFO and LIFO. The FIFO vs. LIFO question is of special interest because, unlike the other accounting options discussed, the choice of inventory costing method has an effect on taxes as well as reported earnings. In inflationary times, LIFO typically reduces reported earnings, but increases cash flows by reducing taxes. For companies using FIFO, the effect is the opposite: reported earnings are higher, cash is lower.

The change from FIFO to LIFO would thus appear to present the ideal testing-ground for weighing the contending claims of the traditional "earnings per share" advocates and the "efficient markets" supporters for whom cash, not earnings, is the source of economic value. The followers of Briloff would, of course, expect switches to LIFO to be accompanied by lower stock prices. Academics schooled in the principles of modern finance would expect higher prices.

Less sophisticated studies of the FIFO-LIFO switch, performed in the early 1970s, found that companies changing to LIFO experience, on average, significant *increases* in stock price over the 12 months leading up to and including the announcement of the first earnings calculated under LIFO. There is, however, a potential problem with these results: namely, that companies switching to LIFO tend to be those companies experiencing increases in earnings in the year of the switch.

Recently, Gary Biddle and Frederick Lindahl — both associated with the University of Chicago — attempted to correct this problem of selection bias by "controlling for" the stock price effects of contemporaneous increases in earnings. They found that when the tests remove the part of the market increase that can be attributed solely to the earnings increase, there still remains a significantly positive stock market response to companies switching to LIFO. Their results show, furthermore, that the larger the reduction in taxes resulting from the use of LIFO, the greater the increase in stock price attributable solely to the accounting change.

The message of the modern empirical research is thus fairly straightforward: Where earnings fail to present an accurate measure of cash flow performance, it is cash profitability — not accounting profits — that appears to be the market's dominant criter-

ion for assessing economic value. As a consequence, the latitude allowed corporate managers in determining accounting methods does not represent a reliable opportunity to increase stock prices. This suggests, for example, that many companies not currently using LIFO are doing a disservice to their stockholders.

There are a great many other studies of the relationship among stock prices, accounting numbers, and accounting changes. Some of them, it is true, have methodological problems. But their findings, when viewed as a whole, present an impressively coherent body of evidence testifying to the "efficiency" of capital markets. There are, to be sure, some anomalous findings. But, the accumulated empirical research in accounting — combined with the work in finance on stock splits, bond ratings, dividends, and other corporate issues — presents strong testimony to the speed and sophistication with which our capital markets process and interpret information.

Toward a Positive Theory of Accounting

The evidence that the stock market is not systematically misled by accounting changes may answer the criticisms of accounting practice raised by demagogues like Briloff, but it also raises some important questions of its own.

Modern financial and economic theory is grounded in the assumption that investors behave rationally. Why, in an "efficient market" displaying rational expectations, do companies display what appears to be an unwarranted concern with the effects of publicly reported accounting numbers? Clearly, accounting has important *internal* uses: monitoring fixed assets, establishing managerial accountability, measuring performance, allocating capital. But, if accounting methods used for financial reporting are *not* affecting taxes, cash flow, and hence the market values of companies' shares, why do corporate accountants devote so much time and effort to massaging accounting data for public disclosures? And, furthermore, why are they continually attempting to influence the formulation of accounting standards by preparing and submitting position papers to the FASB and the SEC?

Our response to the above questions has been to assume that there are some "real" cash flow effects (other than the tax effect) of accounting procedures which account for the large role played by corporations in deciding public accounting issues.

There are some "real" cash flow effects of accounting procedures.

As financial economists, we are attempting to offer a theory which explains why companies use the accounting methods they do, why they lobby for certain accounting standards and why these standards have evolved as they have.

To understand the evolution of accounting standards, we must go beyond the "normative" assumption that the standards reflect disinterested attempts to realize some set of accounting ideals. More illuminating, we think, is an approach which explains our current accounting standards as the result of the interaction of the various interests of government regulators, academic accounting boards, public accounting firms, and private corporations.

This positive view of the accounting process, then, has led us to focus on more subtle ways in which accounting methods can affect corporate cash flow and, thus, market value. One way is through the regulatory process. As an example, courts and regulatory commissions use the standards set by the Financial Accounting Standards Board as precedents in setting accounting procedures for the rate determination process. And so, for regulated companies, the pricing of its services (and thus its cash flow) is influenced by the methods accountants use to measure the rate base and expected costs.

Another way in which accounting procedures can influence cash flow is through their effect on legislation. At the time of the Arab oil embargo, for instance, oil companies had a strong incentive to show lower reported profits to forestall Congressional interference and possible anti-trust action. Accordingly, they attempted to reduce their reported profitability by publishing industry rates of return on *total assets, instead of stockholder's equity,* as had been done in the past. The change was not disclosed in the published reports.

Corporate contracts specified in terms of accounting measures can also have important effects on management decisions, which in turn affect cash flow. Management compensation contracts are commonly tied to reported earnings, providing incentives for executives to tamper with accounting methods, possibly at the expense of real corporate profitability. A switch to LIFO may be deferred; or profitable acquisitions which reduce accounting returns on investment may be passed by because of their effects on management bonuses. Also, debt contracts have restrictive covenants which use accounting numbers (e.g., times interest earned). A

switch to straight-line depreciation, in this case, can make such covenants less binding.

Although the effects of these accounting considerations are much more difficult to quantify than the tax effect, accounting researchers have attempted to measure the importance of these other potential cash flow effects of accounting changes on stock prices. For instance, FASB Statement No. 19, which restricted the use of the full cost method of accounting by some oil and gas companies, was shown to have a negative impact on the stock prices of those companies.

We have also used these potential cash flow effects to explain the positions corporate executives have taken on proposed accounting standards. When the Accounting Principles Board proposed that general price level accounting be adopted, prominent among the companies backing this proposal were large oil concerns whose accounting earnings would have been decreased by the proposal. On the opposite side of the issue, interestingly, were other large oil companies whose earnings would have been *increased.* In both cases, the positions taken seemed to reflect a desire to avoid the attention of regulators.

This kind of analysis has been expanded to explain the systematic variation in accounting procedures across companies; that is, why companies in certain industries tend to choose one accounting alternative, while companies in other industries select another. These are, in short, the beginnings of an attempt to identify a larger pattern in the accounting behavior of corporations, and to discover the underlying motivation that has given rise to the pattern.

To summarize, the developments in empirical research have taken us a step forward in achieving a scientific understanding of accounting. The aim of the early empirical work was to understand how the capital markets actually respond to accounting numbers. In contrast to the normative focus on improving accounting procedures to make them more meaningful, the modern research questioned the fundamental premise of the prescriptive approach: namely, that financial markets, characterized by naive and gullible investors, would benefit from more and improved accounting disclosure. Over the past 15 years, the hypothesis of "market efficiency" has been continually tested using large samples, and has generally held up well under such testing.

But, now having discarded the old normative

shibboleths, we have been forced to look for new explanations of corporate accounting practices. And, in a more ambitious undertaking, we are seeking a better understanding of the process and pressures out of which our present set of accounting conventions and standards has evolved.

Implications for Policy

The existing empirical work on accounting has several important implications for corporate decision-making:

1. Because the market does not mechanically respond to accounting numbers, manipulating reported earnings through accounting changes to increase the corporation's stock price will, in most cases, be a futile exercise. Financial decisions, furthermore, should not be concerned with negative effects on EPS that have no effect on cash profitability. In cases where management must choose *between* higher reported earnings and higher cash flow, as in the LIFO vs. FIFO decision, maximizing cash is clearly the best guide to maximizing share price.

2. On the other hand, there is some indirect evidence that manipulation of earnings can be helpful in avoiding political scrutiny and opposition. Large corporations can, by adopting accounting procedures which reduce reported profits, also reduce the likelihood that Congress will pass legislation harmful to their interests. Lowering reported profits can also allow companies to divert from themselves some of the attention of the Anti-Trust Division, the F.T.C., and other governing agencies. Lower profits, furthermore, can be beneficial in arguing for tax reductions.[1]

3. Finally, in cases where management bonuses are based on reported earnings, corporate managers may be given incentives to change accounting procedures or manipulate accounting accruals to increase their compensation. Corporate compensation committees should be aware of the effect of these accounting manipulations. Furthermore, they should be especially concerned that tying the bonus to accounting earnings is influencing *investment* decisions in ways that reduce real cash profitability. For example, the executive who is influenced by his contract to reject profitable acquisitions which reduce accounting ROI is working against stockholder interests. The remedy, in such cases, would be to structure a management compensation scheme which focuses not on accounting earnings, but on the source of value: cash flow.

---

1. These observations, of course, beg the question: If the markets are sophisticated enough to see through accounting illusions, why then can't government agencies do the same? The answer lies in a very important difference between the incentives of private investors and public officials to penetrate accounting fictions. In the market, shrewd private investors can capture most of the benefits of their information by trading on it. The political process, however, does not provide the same kind of stimulus for regulators to acquire this information. For this reason, it seems predictable that courts and regulators would continue to respond to accounting deceptions while private markets are aggressively well-informed.

The Evidence Against Stock Splits

by Thomas Copeland,
University of California, Los Angeles

One of the reigning myths on Wall Street, perpetuated by investment bankers, financial analysts, and much of the popular financial press, is that stock splits benefit stockholders by raising the value of their holdings. And thus, for financial managers, stock splits are represented as a handy and effortless way of achieving what finance textbooks tell us is — or should be—the primary goal of management: the maximization of stockholder wealth over the long run.

In an unusually perceptive piece of financial journalism, a 1979 article in *Fortune* went a long way toward debunking the "myth of the stock split." The article began by presenting the popular case for splits as follows:

The day I.B.M. disclosed plans for a four-for-one split late in December, its stocks rose 12-3/4 points. When DuPont announced a three-for-one split in mid-January, its stock was up 11-3/4, and the news was given credit for the market's broad rise that day. Word of a two-for-one split by Mobil late in January was also credited with boosting the company's stock (up 2-1/2 points on the announcement date) and the market as a whole.

The case for stock splits rests on two kinds of flawed evidence: either on scattered, anecdotal, and unsystematic testimony like that offered above; or on long out-dated academic studies which, while rightly documenting the *correlation* of stock price increases with splits, mistakenly identify stock splits as the cause of such price increases.

Modern academic research on the stock split question has shown the popular case to be groundless. There is no sound theoretical explanation why the market should respond positively to a company's announced intention to split its stock, nor is there any creditable empirical evidence that splits benefit stockholders.

The best research reveals that while companies splitting their shares tend to have experienced abnormally high share price increases *prior to the split,* split-up stocks perform, on average, no better than the market during or after the split. Price increases associated with stock splits are maintained throughout the post-split period only when splits are accompanied (shortly before or after) by announcements of dividend increases.

From these findings, we are led to conclude that the positive correlation between stock splits and higher stock prices is attributable to the superior performance of these companies prior to the split and to the above average dividend increases that typically accompany announcements of stock splits. Higher dividends provide investors with signals of management's increased confidence in their companies' future levels of profitability and cash flows. Thus, it is not stock splits *per se* that cause higher stock prices, but rather managements' emphatic statements of continued confidence in the company's future performance conveyed to the market in the form of larger than expected dividend increases.

Stock splits result, on average, in a significant increase in brokerage fees as a percentage of an investor's total dollar investment.

The Myth Examined

Recall that a stock split is nothing more than a paper transaction which multiplies the number of shares outstanding without changing any stockholder's proportional claim on the company's assets, earnings, or dividends. When a stock splits two for one, for example, the stockholder owns twice the number of shares; but per share earnings and dividends (provided they are not increased when the split takes place) simply divide in half, leaving the stockholder with the same percentage interest in the company. Thus stock splits have no "real" or "economic" consequences; that is, they have no effect either on the company's future cash flows or on the stockholder's proportional claim on these cash flows. And both the theory and evidence tell us that, in reasonably sophisticated and efficient capital markets like those in the U.S., Canada, and much of Europe, there is no lasting response by investors to events—like stock splits—which have no economic significance.

If stock splits reflect nothing "real" about the company's future performance, how then do they work their "magic" on the market? There is a strong belief, religiously attested to in the folklore of Wall Street, that there is an "optimal trading range" for security prices — one that enhances the "marketability" or "liquidity" of a company's stock by broadening its stockholder base. This optimal range, generally thought to extend from $20 to $40 per share, is said to represent a strategic balancing of the interests of institutions and wealthy individuals, on the one hand, and small investors, on the other. Wealthy investors and institutions, as the argument correctly maintains, would prefer higher- to lower-priced stocks (other things being equal) because their brokerage commission costs would be lower as a percentage of their total dollar investment. Small investors, however, are supposedly penalized by higher stock prices which deny them the economies of buying stock in round lots.

The purpose of stock splits, according to the popular argument, is to lower (or raise, as in the case of reverse splits) a company's stock price — presumably when it has become "too high" — into this "optimal trading range," thus attracting more small investors, expanding the stockholder base, improving liquidity, and increasing the (split-adjusted) stock price.

Several objections to this line of reasoning come to mind almost immediately. Without belittl-

ing the role of individual savers in the capital formation process, the problems and significance of the "small investor" have been exaggerated. For one thing, the fraction of trading volume accounted for by odd lot trades is negligible. Second, the investor that is put off by the higher per share brokerage costs associated with odd lot purchases has at least two alternatives for obtaining the round lot discount: buying no-load mutual funds and pooling funds through an investment club. Simple logic says that investors will not pay extra (i.e., by bidding up the price of split-up shares) for something (the economies of purchasing in round lots) they can costlessly get for themselves. Finally, if the price of a stock is perceived by the market to be "too high," the market itself obliges by creating round lots of 10 shares, removing the need for either a split or a lower price.

Is there, then, an "optimal trading range" for stock prices? Once again, the best place to turn for an answer is to the empirical evidence. It shows that, although stock splits increase the number of shareholders, they actually impair rather than improve the liquidity of a company's stock. Following splits, the volume of traded shares relative to the number of shares outstanding falls off considerably. We also find, at the same time, that the total commissions paid to brokers trading in split stocks actually increase. Together, these two findings imply that stock splits result, on average, in a significant increase in brokerage fees as a percentage of an investor's total dollar investment. In so doing, they also increase brokerage house revenues, which might provide a clue to the popularity of splits on Wall Street. (The explanation for this has to do with brokerage commission schedules, which will be dealt with later.) Finally, the relative spread between the bid and ask prices of over-the-counter stocks widens substantially following splits, thus providing additional evidence that stock splits burden the investor with higher transactions costs.

The Effect of Stock Splits on Stock Prices

Let's take a closer look at the scholarly evidence on the issue of splits and higher share prices.

In a now largely forgotten study published in the *Harvard Business Review* in 1956, C. Austin Barker pointed the direction for the most current scholarship on the stock split question. Studies prior to Barker's, extending as far back as 1933, had been content to show that stock splits were associated with share price increases, concluding that splits were the cause of such price behavior. Barker's study, however, began by expressing skepticism about the "real effect" of stock splits. "Actually," he argued, "it is illogical for a split-up to affect price — it is simply cutting a loaf of bread in half." Noting that splits were often closely preceded or followed by dividend increases, Barker's study was the first to attempt to separate the "real effect" of stocks splits from the effect of concurrent increases of the dividend. It did so by dividing into two groups a sample of 90 companies that split their shares between 1951 and 1953. Those companies whose splits were accompanied by dividend increases had abnormally high price appreciation; while the other companies, which did not raise their dividends, failed to outperform the market. From these findings, Barker correctly concluded that dividend increases were a more fundamental cause of the price increases attributed to stock splits. However, he also went on to conclude that combining stock splits with dividend increases was an effective means of raising stock prices — a conclusion which has not withstood further scrutiny.

The most widely known and authoritative study of the effect of stock splits on stock prices—one that confirms some of Barker's findings without reaching his conclusions — was published in 1969 by Eugene Fama, Lawrence Fisher, Michael Jensen, and Richard Roll. Their study, henceforth referred to as "FFJR," examined the stock price movements around the announcment dates of all 940 stock splits (involving 622 different companies) which occurred on the New York Stock Exchange during the period 1927- 1959.

In their study, FFJR addressed and solved two significant problems which cast doubt on the validity of earlier studies. The first arose from the fact that splits tend to be cyclical, taking place during or shortly after "bull markets." Because most stock price changes are highly correlated with changes in a general market index like the SP 500, some means had to be developed for isolating the effect of a stock split from the effect of general market conditions on a given company's share price. The second problem, partly resolved in Barker's study, was the need to remove the influence of cash dividend increases to isolate the real effect of splits on prices.

FFJR found stocks earned substantially "above normal" returns in the months preceding the split. However, a close look at the pattern of these returns suggests that they had nothing to do with the split itself. The abnormal performance of the stocks in the sample showed up as early as two-and-a-half years prior to the split—most likely long before the idea of a split was even contemplated.

A far more plausible interpretation of pre-split "abnormal" returns is that we are studying a special set of securities, namely those which were observed to split. But why did they split? Because their price had gone up — presumably because they had had especially good earnings before the split. Thus, the fact that we selected split-up securities — after the fact — virtually guarantees that we will find higher than average returns before the split. In other words, this pre-split stock appreciation suggests that managements decided on stock splits because their stock prices, having gone up, were perceived to be "too high." The underlying cause of this appreciation was thus probably strong earnings performance rather than anticipation of the split.

More significantly, FFJR found no abnormal performance in the share prices of the same stocks either on the split announcement date, or over the 2-1/2 years following the announcement. That is, if an investor had bought all the split securities on their split dates and held them for a period of 30 months, he would not have outperformed the market. Consequently, the splits seem to have had no impact on the total market value of the companies' equity.

Why, then, are increases in stock prices sometimes associated with stock splits? The answer has nothing to do with splits. Price changes are associated with splits because split and dividend change announcements often occur simultaneously or at nearly the same time. FFJR considered this question by dividing their sample of companies into two groups: one having above average dividend increases around the time of the split and the other with lower-than-average dividend increases. They found the class of companies with above average dividend increases had slightly positive abnormal returns following splits. This result is consistent with the hypothesis that split announcements may be interpreted as news about dividend increases. On the other hand, split-up stocks with poor dividend performance experienced lower than normal returns until about a year after the split, by which time it must have been clear that any anticipated dividend increase was not forthcoming.

The Fama, Fisher, Jensen and Roll study concludes that there are no price effects caused by splits. Later studies have confirmed their findings. Although no study has examined stock dividends (which are really just stock splits of less than 1.25 for 1) as a separate issue, it doesn't require any great stretch of the imagination to predict that stock dividends won't have any effect on prices either.

Liquidity Effects Following Stock Splits

If stock splits don't appear to have any "real" or lasting influence on prices, then what of the other arguments? Is there an optimal trading range for stock prices which stimulates trading activity and thus increases the liquidity of a security? One of the first studies to test this hypothesis was Barker's. He found the number of shareholders in split stocks increases relative to non-split stocks of similar growth. However, the question then becomes, does an increase in the number of stockholders necessarily imply higher trading volume and improved liquidity?

Once again, the empirical research on the subject refutes the conventional wisdom. In a study published in 1979, I looked at the direct effect of splits on liquidity by examining a random sample of 25 splits which occurred between 1963 and 1973. Three different aspects of liquidity were examined: 1) the effect of splits on relative trading volume; 2) the effect on total brokerage revenues paid by a round lot investor; and 3) the effect on bid-ask spreads for a sample of OTC firms. The bad news for stockholders is that, measured by any of these three variables, liquidity declines sharply following stock splits.

In the case of a two-for-one stock split, if the total dollar volume level of pre-split trading is to be maintained, the number of shares traded must double following the split. I found, however, that the increase in share volume is less than the proportional increase in shares outstanding following a split, so that dollar trading volume actually declines.

Proportionally lower volume following stock splits is evidence of decreased liquidity, but it is not conclusive because other factors may affect trading volume, for example, changes in the number of shareholders, the rate of new information hitting the market, and transactions costs. If brokerage revenues and bid-ask spreads are also shown to increase as a percentage of the value traded, then we have stronger evidence that liquidity falls following stock splits.

Weekly brokerage fees and taxes paid on a round-trip round lot transaction were simulated using the volume data. Total brokerage fees were estimated to have been 7% higher following the splits even though total dollar trading volume contracted by some 20%.

There is, however, no mystery surrounding the rise in commission charges after stock splits. At most brokerage firms, round-lot commissions are based on the number of shares involved in a trade as well as on the dollar amount of the trade. An investor who buys 100 shares of DuPont at a price of about $135 per share will pay roughly $85 in commissions. After stock splits three-for-one, the same dollar purchase (300 shares at $45 each) will cost about $215 in commissions. As this example illustrates, com-

TABLE 1

Bid-Ask Spreads as a Percentage of the Bid Price						Number of Splits	Year
Before	After	Before	After	Before	After		
1 Day		20 Days		40 Days			
3.62	4.60	...	...	...	...	20	1968
4.64	5.89	4.94	6.01	4.75	5.68	20	1969
5.55	7.58	4.66	5.50	4.80	6.96	13	1970
2.34	3.36	2.46	3.30	3.11	3.24	18	1971
3.64	3.91	2.67	3.56	2.50	3.80	20	1972
3.81	5.59	3.44	5.85	3.46	6.34	20	1973
5.27	10.04	5.34	8.95	5.14	9.00	11	1974
9.52	14.13	9.94	13.38	10.98	13.19	20	1975
6.45	9.26	...	...	...	...	20	1976
4.85	7.03	4.73	6.54	4.95	6.79	Averages	

missions are a much higher percentage of the value traded for low-price stocks than for high-price stocks.

As pointed out in the aforementioned *Fortune* article, even odd-lot investors can lose after a split. At most brokerage houses, an odd-lot trade before a split costs less than does a round-lot of the same dollar value after a split. An investor who buys 50 shares of IBM at the pre-split price of about $300 will pay only about $85 in commissions, plus another $12.50 in odd-lot fees (one quarter point per share). After stock splits four for one, an investor will pay no fee, but he will pay about $170 in commissions for a round-lot trade of 200 shares worth $75 apiece.

In the final part of my study, I analyzed the effect of splits on bid-ask spreads, which represent another form of transactions costs paid by investors. Table 1 presents the pre- and post-split spreads for a sample of 162 OTC splits between 1968 and 1976. The bid-ask spread, as a percentage of the value traded, increases dramatically after a split, and it stays higher at least up to forty trading days after the split. For example, the average bid-ask spread is 4.95% forty trading days before a split and 6.79% forty days afterward.

The results of my study on liquidity can be interpreted in one or two ways: either pre-split liquidity is unusually high and post-split liquidity reflects a more "normal" level, or pre-split liquidity is "normal" and post-split is abnormally low. Either way, stockholders should interpret a split as a message of relatively lower future liquidity. And this, of course, directly contradicts the popular contention that a stock split will improve a stock's liquidity en route to increasing its value.

Summary and Conclusions

The Fama, Fisher, Jensen and Roll study shows that stock splits per se have no effect on the value of the company. My research shows that liquidity is lower following stock splits. Why, then, do managements choose to split their stocks? Who benefits? Who loses?

At present we can only speculate. The evidence of higher brokerage revenues following splits shows a possible benefit to the brokerage industry, but at the expense of shareholders. The benefit to shareholders continues to elude our understanding. Perhaps splits have value as forecasts of anticipated dividend changes. Or perhaps the broadened base of stockholders resulting from splits makes it easier for management to fend off takeovers and thus control the company. None of these ideas has been tested. All that can be said about the real motivation behind splits is that the traditional justifications — improvements in liquidity and increases in stockholder wealth — have no basis in fact.

These are the conclusions which can be drawn from the empirical evidence:

One
● Stock splits are cyclical phenomena. They tend to occur during or shortly after bull markets.

Two
● Stock ownership is more diffuse following stock splits, and this finding may have implications for corporate control.

Three
● Liquidity declines following stock splits. Relative volume is lower, probably because investor transactions costs (in the form of brokerage fees and bid-ask spreads) are higher.

Four
● On average, there are no shareholder wealth effects attributable to stock splits.

Five
● A more fundamental cause of the price increases associated with the announcement of splits are concurrent announcements of higher than expected cash dividends. And even the dividend increases are probably only conveying information about something more fundamental: namely, the improved cash flow and earnings prospects of the company. A comprehensive program of direct financial communication to the investment community may be.a more effective and less costly means of achieving the desired result: higher shareholder returns.

Six
● Stock dividends (stock splits less than 1.25 to 1) are probably a total waste of time and effort. The market will not confuse them with cash dividend changes. They may even be interpreted as a signal of bad news about the future of the company.

The Real Function of Bond Rating Agencies

by L. Macdonald Wakeman
University of Rochester

I've just heard Moody's is going to downgrade our bonds. What do we do?

Nothing.

Nothing? But the price will drop like a stone when the rating change is announced.

No it won't. The market already knows we've been doing badly. Our bond and stock prices have been dropping for the last year. The rating change just reflects the bond's higher risk.

But if a rating change doesn't affect the bond's price, why did we bother to pay for the rating in the first place?

Because having a rating lowered our interest costs when we issued the bonds. The important point is not what rating you have, but whether or not you have a rating.

Wait, you're saying that our rating doesn't matter...and yet it does matter?

Let me try to explain:

Do Bond Ratings Provide New Information?

The belief that bond rating services largely determine the interest rate that a debt issuer must pay is widely held among corporate officers, city managers, and state officials. One company official estimated that the 1978 downgrading of Pacific Telephone's debt by Moody's Investors Service raised its interest cost by approximately $35 million; New York City officials stated in 1972 that the city would have saved $40 million in interest costs if its rating had been raised earlier; and Governor DuPont, after vainly lobbying to prevent the downgrading of his state's bonds in 1977, noted that Delaware would pay a penalty for the lower rating. Financial analysts searching for under- and over-rated issues bolster this belief. So do articles in publications such as *Barrons, The Financial Times, Fortune,* and *The Wall Street Journal* implying that rating agencies determine the debt market's assessment of a bond's risk.

Concern about this concentration of market power has led academics, businessmen, and politicians to suggest that the bond rating industry be reformed, federally regulated, or even nationalized.

But the major assumption underlying these proposals has no basis in fact. Contrary to the popular notion, the bond market does not react to rating changes. Bonds with lower ratings do indeed pay higher interest costs, but to blame the rating is to confuse cause with effect. A bond rating does not actively determine, but simply mirrors the market's assessment of a bond's risk. Hence, a rating change does not *affect,* but merely reflects, the market's altered estimation of a bond's value.

To clarify this point, let's examine the response of the capital markets when a rating change is announced. The most current and carefully done research is unanimous on this point. Neither the company's bond nor its common stock shows any un

17

*Companies experiencing changes in their bond ratings do see
significant changes in the prices of their securities; however, these
changes occur more than a year before the rating change.*

usual behavior — whether on the day of, or during the week and month surrounding the announcement of the rating change. Our conclusion: rating change announcements provide no new information to the capital markets.

What our research shows instead is that bond rating changes convey information that has long been reflected in bond prices. Companies experiencing changes in their bond ratings do see significant changes in the prices of the securities; however, these changes occur, on average, more than a year before the rating change. The evidence is emphatic on this point. The rating agencies downgrade a bond only after the company has done poorly, and after the risk levels of both the company's bonds and common stock have increased. Upgradings come only after it has become clear that the company's performance has enhanced the bond's value.

Nor is there any special effect when bonds are upgraded into, or downgraded below, the "investment grades" (Moody's "Baa" and above). Although the Comptroller of the Currency's ruling in 1936 prohibited federally chartered banks from holding non-investment grade bonds, no "segmentation" in the pricing of bonds resulted then or now. There are no major discontinuities in pricing that would suggest the market makes a sharp distinction between "investment grade" and less than "investment grade" bonds. Furthermore, an analysis of the performance of bonds downgraded from Baa or upgraded from Ba in the 1970's has shown the same reaction to the bond rating change announcement — none.

The evidence raises some interesting questions: what events cause the ratings services to change a bond's rating? And what methods do they use to detect changes in the risk levels of bonds? Three distinct pieces of evidence suggest that the rating services respond to changes reflected in nothing more current than companies' published accounting reports. First, and most obviously, Moody's gives accounting-based explanations (e.g., changes in coverage and leverage ratios) for more than two-thirds of the bond rating changes not resulting from specific events such as mergers or new financing. Second, the monthly distribution of Moody's rating changes is not uniform; instead a significantly larger number of rating changes occur in the months of May and June, shortly after the publication of most companies' annual reports.

The third piece of evidence is provided by studies attempting to "explain" and thus predict ratings and rating changes. Such studies construct models simulating the bond rating process which correctly classify up to 80% of the bonds in their samples using data derived only from published accounting statements.

Armed with such a model, an investor could pursue a strategy of buying underrated issues at "bargain" prices. To test this hypothesis, the studies attempt to use their models to "beat the market" by capitalizing on rating "errors." Their findings show that an investment strategy based on such a systematic attempt to identify and profit from incorrectly rated bonds does not enable an investor to outperform the market. The exercise is pointless because the model's predicted rating is itself based on publicly available information. The "bargain" never existed because the bond prices had already incorporated all relevant information, including published accounting statements, about the companies.

A Rationale for the Existence of Bond Rating Agencies

But if a rating change does not convey new information to the capital markets, what services do the rating agencies provide? Initially they provided investors with data on companies — and, more particularly, with measures of bond risk — at low cost.

Why do investors demand this data? Because collecting the information required to make portfolio choices is costly. With many investors demanding such information, efficient producers of information can expect to gain by reducing the investors' duplication of effort. This point was most directly expressed, and the opportunity seized, by the founder of Moody's Investors Service, who said, "Somebody, sooner or later, will bring out an industrial statistical manual, and when it comes, it will be a gold mine."

Once having compiled such a manual, John Moody had a comparative advantage in producing measures of the relative risks of holding bonds. In 1909 he published the first bond ratings, providing measures which were convenient, comprehensible, and inexpensive.

What information do such measures provide? Though bond ratings do not provide timely information, our studies consistently demonstrate that there is a close relationship between a bond's rating and its level of risk. A bond rating thus incorporates into a single, easily communicated code all the major ingredients of the bond's risk. Although likely to lag behind significant changes in a company's prospects — changes which would warrant a rating change — current bond ratings do contain information about the relative risk of a company's securities.

Over the past 60 years, the rating agencies have acquired a reputation for accurately evaluating and reporting the risks of new bond issues. Having achieved a large measure of credibility and authority, these ratings have been used by some investors to check the performance of trustees and fund managers. For instance, by the 1930's, bond ratings were being used both to circumscribe the discretionary powers of fiduciary trustees (many trust agreements limited investments in debt instruments to bonds with higher ratings), and to monitor their performance (agreements often required trustees to sell bonds that had been downgraded to an unsatisfactory rating). At the same time, courts recognized the rating agencies as "disinterested authorities" and accepted the use of ratings by executives and trustees as evidence of "sound discretion" on their part. More recently, ratings have become recognized inputs to the regulatory process for banks and insurance companies.

The crucial questions, then, are these: if the information provided by bond ratings is not "new," then what is the value of this credibility established by the rating agencies? And who benefits most from the information and assurance provided by published ratings?

The fact that Moody's and Standard Poor's both have long lists of subscribers indicates that there is a demand by investors for such information. However, the additional fact that bond ratings do not appear to influence investors' pricing of bonds — at least, after the initial issue — suggests that investors are not the main beneficiaries of rating services.. They have access to other, more timely sources of information which enable them to price securities without much reliance on current ratings.

If the demand is allegedly coming from investors, why do the issuing companies bear the cost of having their bonds rated? The answer lies partly in an explanation of how the bond market prices securities.

Like all lenders, potential buyers of new bonds recognize that managers (as the representatives of shareholder interests) might have an incentive to take actions — after the bonds are issued — which would reduce the value of those bonds by transferring wealth to the shareholders. (In modern finance literature, this conflict of interest between bond-holders, shareholders, and managers is called the "agency" problem.) In the extreme case, management could simply pay out the proceeds of the debt offering (in the absence of any covenants) to shareholders and liquidate the assets of the company. In less obvious ways, management could reduce the value of the bonds by making significant changes in the investment or financing policies of the company. They could, for instance, acquire riskier companies or undertake riskier projects, thus increasing the risk and lowering the value of the outstanding bonds. On the financing side, they could take on even larger amounts of debt, further leveraging the company's assets. Both of these management actions would reduce the value of the bondholders' claim by making the bonds more risky. Because a bond is a fixed income claim, the bondholder does not share in the increased upside potential associated with a highly leveraged financial policy or a higher-risk investment strategy.

The possibility of such action is recognized by potential bondholders when pricing a bond issue. Unless offered protection from such management behavior, typically in the form of loan covenants, they will expect the worst to happen and require higher returns for holding the bonds. Rather than accept lower prices, management and shareholders will find it in their own interest to have restrictive covenants written (provided they are not too restrictive) which, by offering bondholders protection from such management incentives, will increase the issue price of the bond.

The same argument holds for providing bondholders and shareholders with information about the company. An old and sensible maxim says that investors pay a discount for uncertainty, never a premium. By furnishing investors with detailed financial statements, and by paying a reputable auditor to validate them, management is effectively raising the price it receives for new securities.

The rating agencies, then, by analyzing the company's statements at the time of issue and by offering an independent judgment of the new bond's risk, provide an initial low-cost assessment of the credit standing of the issuing company. Furthermore, the rating services have a comparative advantage in monitoring the changing position of the bond vis-a-vis the company over time. Provided with these services, which in turn offer investors both information and greater assurance about future management actions, companies continue to pay rating agencies to have their bonds rated, and to have their performance monitored. The use of Moody's or S&P's is thus a cost-effective strategy which increases the net proceeds of the debt issue to the issuing company.

Let's summarize our argument about the role of the rating agencies: they attest to the relative quality of the bond issue and to the accuracy of the accompanying information about the issuing company; and they further monitor that bond's risk over the life of the bond. In so doing, the rating agencies enable the bonds to be sold to the public at a higher price than would be otherwise possible. This higher price reflects both economies of scale in the collection of information and the reduction of "agency costs*" incurred when issuing new debt. That the bond rating agencies continue to prosper is strong evidence that the cost to companies of having their bonds rated is more than covered by the increased proceeds from the sale of the bonds.

Another piece of evidence supporting our argument is that private placements are rarely certified by bond rating agencies. In a private placement, the single bondholder (or small group of bondholders) normally has excellent knowledge of the issuer and can monitor the bond's performance inexpensively. There is also no problem of duplication of effort in enforcing covenants. Under these circumstances, there will be little demand for the services of a bond rating agency. Our theory thus implies that the crucial determinant of whether a company should seek a bond rating is not the size of the issue, but rather the number of potential bondholders. The larger the number of potential bondholders, the more valuable to the issuing company will be the information and assurance provided investors by the bond rating agencies.

The Bottom Line on Bond Ratings

What, then, are the implications of our theory and evidence for corporate financial policy?

1. It is in a company's interest to pay for a public issue of new debt to be rated because the greater certainty and assurance provided investors increases the net proceeds to the company at the time of issue.

2. In deciding whether to have its bonds rated, management should regard the number of bondholders as a major variable. The greater the number of potential bondholders, the greater the benefits of having a bond rating.

3. Attempts by investors to predict either ratings or rating changes, even if successful, are pointless because they do not allow an investor to earn above normal profits.

4. Because the markets do not view bond rating changes as conveying timely information, no effort should be made to induce a rating service either to upgrade a bond or to refrain from downgrading a bond. The resources expended would be better devoted to improving the company's performance.

---

*In the finance literature, the "agency costs" of issuing debt are identified as follows: (1) the direct, measurable costs of writing, monitoring, and enforcing covenants; (2) the cost of the opportunities foregone by imposing such covenants, and (3) the costs (in the form of lower proceeds than otherwise from the issue of the bonds) caused by remaining investor uncertainty about managements' future actions.

Deflating Inflation Accounting

by Jerold Zimmerman,
University of Rochester

On March 23, 1976, the Securities and Exchange Commission (SEC) issued Accounting Series Release (ASR) 190. The release required certain large companies[1] to disclose the replacement cost of corporate assets. Specifically, annual disclosure of the replacement cost of inventories, gross productive capacity, cost of sales, and depreciation was mandated. In addition, the SEC required companies to disclose the methods by which the replacement cost estimates were prepared. These replacement cost disclosures were the first formal inflation accounting requirements, and they began to appear in company annual reports in 1976 and SEC form 10-Ks in March 1977.

Financial analysts, academics, and SEC regulators predicted that the disclosure of replacement costs would have a considerable impact on the investment community.

Proponents of the various inflation cost accounting procedures claimed that the use of traditional historical cost accounting seriously misrepresents reported income by failing to adjust for the effects of price changes. They argued, for example, that traditional reported income would be overstated whenever the current replacement cost of a factory exceeded depreciation charges based on historical cost. Furthermore, they claimed that many companies achieved an appearance of profitability by using traditional income numbers when adjustments for inflation would have shown them to be unprofitable. Critics argued that the operations of such companies could not be considered self-sustaining because they were not generating enough current dollars to recover the current, price-adjusted costs; and, thus, they could not replace their assets without investing additional capital. Advocates of inflation accounting also argued that corporate taxes based on historical costs will often, in effect, be taxing a company's capital stock, as well as its income.

Proposals for inflation accounting have not been warmly received by the business community. Corporations generally opposed the early proposals to install various inflation accounting procedures. In complying with the SEC's mandate, several companies offered some unsolicited commentary on the wisdom of the new regulations. The Arkansas Louisiana Gas Company provided the following assessment of replacement costs:

As required by the SEC in its questionable and controversial ASR No. 190, the Company will include in Form 10-K to the SEC the applicable disclosures concerning "replacement cost" as defined. The information is not included in this (annual) report because, in the company's opinion, the disclosure required could be misleading. —1979 *Annual Report*

MAPCO, Inc., in its 1976 Annual Report, offered a somewhat more colorful response:

For the first time, this Annual Report refers to accounting information dealing with "replacement cost accounting" which purports to show that inflation is really consuming a portion of MAPCO's profits as reported on a historical conventional accounting basis. The purported conclusions represent only a portion of the story — and because only a part of the story is set forth, present a misleading, highly distorted picture. In short, the conclusion are hogwash.

Managements object to inflation accounting for the following reasons: (1) the direct costs of collecting, preparing, and reporting inflation adjusted numbers,[2] (2) the possibility of costly litigation over the disclosures, (3) the subjectivity involved in preparing estimates of replacement cost, and (4) the difficulty in interpreting the estimates.

In evaluating the possible costs and benefits of ASR 190, the SEC claimed to have *carefully considered the cost of implementation and weighed it against the need of investors for replacement cost information. It has concluded that the data are of such importance that the benefits of disclosure clearly outweigh the costs of data preparation.*

---

1. Firms had to comply with ASR 190's reporting requirements if they had total inventories and gross property, plant, and equipment aggregating more than $100 million and constituting more than 10% of total assets.

2. W.R. Grace Co. estimated that over 13,000 hours of effort went into their initial 1976 replacement cost disclosures.

The denunciations by management and the public defense by regulators do not provide a scientific basis for assessing the value of inflation accounting procedures.

Although the SEC claims to have carefully considered the costs and benefits, they presented no evidence to support their assertion.

While the denunciations by management and the public defense by regulators are of some interest, they do not provide a scientific basis for assessing the value of inflation accounting procedures. The effectiveness of accounting regulations is, for the most part, an empirical question; that is, it can be resolved only by providing positive evidence either (1) that investors found the replacement cost disclosures useful, or (2) that such disclosures provided some other social benefits that would justify the costs imposed on complying corporations (and thus, ultimately, on consumers, shareholders, and managers).

This article summarizes the findings of a series of studies, all of which demonstrate that there was no significant response by the stock market to replacement cost numbers. These results suggest that investors do not find these disclosures useful. By contrast, the greater part of the research shows that stock (and option) prices are quite responsive to the disclosures of historical cost earnings in both quarterly and annual reports. When placed side by side, these two sets of studies provide strong support for the conclusion that mandatory replacement cost disclosures result in the consumption of valuation resources without creating any measurable benefits.

Studies of Inflation Adjusted Accounting Numbers

Tests of the usefulness of replacement cost disclosures are simplified, to some extent, by the existence of a body of empirical studies which demonstrates that useful investment information can be clearly identified.

Of greatest interest is the evidence from tests attempting to determine the "information content" of conventional earnings announcements. In general, these tests involve two steps. First, researchers construct a "model of expectations" that allows us to classify earnings announcements as conveying "good news" or "bad news." One method of classification is to compare the earnings announcement with what was projected by financial analysts. For example, if the latest analyst's forecast of earnings was $7.15 per share and earnings were $6.90, then the earnings announcement for this

company would be classified as "bad news." Thus, the latest analyst forecast is used as a surrogate or "proxy" for the market's expectations about the company's earnings.

The second step examines the stock price movements surrounding the announcement of earnings. If earnings announcements convey useful information to the market and analyst forecasts provide a reasonably close approximation of the market's expectations, then the market should respond positively to "good news" companies by raising their stock prices, and negatively to "bad news" companies. If the market so distinguishes between "good" and "bad" news contained in earnings reports, then we can conclude that financial statements using historical cost accounting convey information to the market.

A number of studies, covering the period between 1946 and 1980, and dealing with foreign as well as U.S. stock exchanges, consistently find that historical cost accounting earnings — both annual and quarterly—provide information that is used by the market in setting share prices. On the day earnings are announced, "good news" companies' stock prices increase about 2%, on average, while "bad news" companies' fall 2%. Though 2% may not sound like much, remember this is the average over all companies in each group, including many companies whose actual earnings exceeded or fell short of the analysts' forecasts by only a few pennies. It is also important to note that a 2% daily return is an enormous annual return when compounded. These results support the conclusion that the announcement of conventional, historical cost accounting earnings contains timely and relevant information.

Furthermore, although the market does react to traditional accounting numbers, studies also indicate that the market sees through managements' attempts to manipulate reported earnings through accounting changes. If one were to replicate the previously described study, using only those companies whose higher or lower earnings were caused by changes in accounting technique, the difference between the average stock price reactions of the two groups disappears. From these findings, we conclude that accounting changes which have no "real" effects—that is, they don't affect cash flows—do not affect stock prices (assuming the accounting change is disclosed at the time of the earnings change).

In approaching the question—do investors use replacement cost earnings?—the market's response to such information is measured using a strategy

The average price movements of companies required to disclose replacement costs are not appreciably different from those companies not required to do so.

similar to the one described above. Since replacement costs are often disclosed at the same time as historical cost earnings, we must devise some means of separating (or "controlling for") the effect of historical cost earnings from the effect of the replacement cost disclosures that we are trying to isolate and identify.

One simple way to control for the information content of historical cost earnings is to examine the change in stock prices that occurs when Form 10-K (which contains replacement costs) is publicly released. This usually follows the company's preliminary announcement of earnings in *The Wall Street Journal*. Thus, at the time the 10-K is published, the market has already learned of and incorporated historical cost earnings into stock prices. Hence, the price effects of the separate and subsequent disclosures of replacement costs are "uncontaminated" by the price effects of historical cost earnings announcements. The results of the tests, which examined the stock price movements over the period 30 days preceding and 20 days following the filing of the 10-Ks, indicate that average stock price changes are no different from those in other periods when earnings are not released.

Another way researchers have controlled for historical cost earnings is by constructing a "matched sample" pairing individual companies required to disclose replacement costs with companies not required to do so. The companies are also paired or "matched" such that both will have experienced roughly the same percentage differences between actual and forecasted earnings. Because only large companies are required to disclose replacement costs, they are usually matched with smaller companies in the same industry, with approximately the same risk, and with the same proportion of "unexpected" to "expected" earnings. The findings of these tests show that the average price movements (around the date of each company's filing of its 10-K) of companies required to disclose replacement costs are not appreciably different from those companies not required to do so. Hence, we again are led to conclude that investors do not find inflation accounting useful in setting stock prices.

Researchers have also classified companies required to disclose into several "portfolios" according to the magnitude of differences between their replacement cost figures and the corresponding historical costs. If replacement cost disclosures mattered to investors, we would expect the stock price of those companies with the largest differences between historical and replacement cost numbers to show the largest market response. In one test, for instance, the replacement cost disclosures were divided into two groups, one consisting of those companies that reported the greatest differences between replacement and historical cost depreciation, and the other group reporting the smallest differences. As in the above two studies, there was no significant difference in the market's response to the disclosures of the two groups. This is also the result when using finer grades in classfying the sample companies.

In summary, using different methods, slightly different samples, and different computer programs, researchers have uniformly failed to detect differences in stock price performance arising from the disclosure of replacement costs. The fact that stock prices do not seem to have been affected by the disclosures means that there is no systematic evidence that investors (whether institutional or individual) have found the data useful or relevant in setting stock prices. In short, the evidence does not support the SEC's contention that these data are "useful to investors."

Possible Interpretations of the Evidence

One explanation for the absence of any detectable stock price reaction to replacement cost disclosures is that these numbers contain no "new" information. Replacement cost estimates may be so subjective that analysts and investors are unable to draw any inferences from the disclosures. Another possibility is that these disclosures, while reasonably accurate, may not be a timely source of information. Since specific price indexes, which are often used to construct replacement cost numbers, are disclosed well in advance of the accounting numbers, the effect of inflation on the replacement cost of inventories and plant may already be impounded in stock prices. If either of these is a valid supposition, the SEC is wrong in thinking that investors "need" replacement cost disclosures. In the first case, the numbers are unreliable and, thus, useless; in the second case, they are simply redundant.

Proponents of inflation accounting disclosures are quick to answer these charges by pointing out that, even if investors in the stock market do not find these numbers useful, such disclosures have other important uses. For example, replacement costs can be used to bolster the corporate case for income tax

There is no systematic evidence that investors have found replacement cost data useful or relevant in setting stock prices.

cuts in public policy debates. They could also provide corporate managements with a better basis for evaluating their own operating performance, and for allocating capital among divisions. The important point to be made is that these alleged benefits are uncertain, unquantifiable, and impossible to incorporate into the kind of cost-benefit analysis that should serve as the means for evaluating the effectiveness of most proposed regulations. When a host of qualitative, subjectively-determined benefits are allowed to enter into the calculation, cost-benefit analysis becomes just another manipulable tool in the hands of policy makers. And the result is the proliferation of regulations — many of them costly, needless, and socially wasteful.

Still another interpretation of our findings is that investors have not yet learned how to process these numbers. When they do, the claim has it, they will find them useful, and stock prices will respond to the disclosures. The evidence is not encouraging for this view. The first replacement cost disclosures came out in fiscal year 1976. Studies of these and subsequent replacement cost disclosures have failed to detect any learning effect.

Finally it could be argued that some methodological defects common to all the studies prevented the detection of stock price reactions to the disclosures. Given the number of replications by at least six research teams working independently (including one group studying Australian companies complying with Australian inflation accounting rules), this possibility seems highly unlikely.

Some Alternate Reasons for Inflation Accounting

It is also interesting to pose the question: if policy makers knew that investors would not find replacement cost disclosures useful, then is there anything in the political process itself which explains why ASR 190 was adopted? To put the question more directly, who lobbied for inflation accounting?

A number of corporate representatives, financial analysts, and academics supported ASR 190 because they saw it as an opportunity to press for corporate tax relief. Comparing the depreciation expense using historical costs and using replacement costs provides striking confirmation that pre-1982

depreciation and tax laws resulted in the taxing of capital as well as income. Replacement costs also provide companies subject to political scrutiny with the opportunity to argue that "real" corporate profitability is substantially lower than reported, thus diffusing possible political opposition and interference. The fact that most corporations opposed inflation accounting proposals suggests that the corporate concerns previously discussed do not explain the push for replacement cost accounting. The majority of companies felt the costs exceeded the benefits. Investors do not appear to have used the resulting numbers. Who then benefited from this rather costly required disclosure rule?

The SEC felt some pressure from the Nixon White House to prevent the market from being misled about the "real" value of corporate stocks. The fear of being blamed for inaction is probably a major reason why the Commission issued ASR 190. In addition, the financial analyst community, which seems to have an insatiable appetite for data, advocated inflation accounting proposals and strongly endorsed ASR 190. Thus, replacement cost accounting appears to have resulted from a coalition of (1) policy makers trying to avoid blame for some future crisis, (2) security analysts looking to increase the demand for their services, and (3) a few corporate managers hoping for some relief from taxes and political pressures.

In 1979 a revised set of inflation accounting rules were promulgated by the Financial Accounting Standards Board (FASB), a private, independent, non-profit organization charged with setting accounting standards (which are generally then adopted and enforced by the SEC). After several unsuccessful attempts to agree on an inflation procedure in 1974 and 1975, the FASB issued Statement No. 33, *Financial Reporting and Changing Prices*. The FASB was finally able to agree on an inflation accounting procedure, in part because they were preempted by the SEC. Statement No. 33, for all practical purposes, replaced and even expanded ASR 190. Besides being required to provide replacement cost information, companies now have to disclose general price level-adjusted income from continuing operations, purchasing power gains and losses on monetary assets, and a five-year summary of both replacement costs and general price level-adjusted selected data.[3]

---

3. The basic difference between replacement costs and general price level adjustments depends on which price index is used as the adjustment factor. Under the replacement cost convention, specific price indexes (i.e., a copper index to adjust copper, an index of truck prices to adjust trucks, etc.) are used to adjust costs. Under a general price level approach, the consumer price index is used to make all adjustments.

We suspect that as long as "special interests" continue to press for accounting regulations, we shall continue to see the burdens of increasingly elaborate disclosures being imposed upon American corporations.

Implications for Corporate Policy

That the market does not seem to respond to the replacement cost data disclosed in 10-K's should not be taken to imply that managers should rely solely on historical costs, and thus ignore replacement costs, when making decisions. In fact, if the gathering of information were costless, and the objectivity and accuracy of the replacement cost estimates were assured, then there is no question that financial management would benefit by incorporating both the replacement costs *and* the market values of assets into their internal reporting scheme. For instance, using an accurate replacement cost basis for depreciation could be an important means of avoiding the decision to invest additional capital in operations whose profitable appearance is being maintained only by postponing necessary capital expenditures. Similarly, establishing the market value (which may be different from the replacement cost) of net assets employed in a division would provide financial management with a better estimate of capital employed — that is, an estimate of the "opportunity cost" of the funds being tied up in those operations. In cases where the market values of assets and capital employed are far larger than historical costs, using historical costs results in the under statement of these companies' capital investment (again, not in the historical sense, but in the sense of alternative opportunities for using the funds generated from the sale of those assets) and, thus, in the overstatement of ROI. This in turn could lead to decisions to continue operations where divestiture would be the better strategy.

Again, this recommendation — in its strongest form — assumes that the estimation of replacement costs and asset values is both costless and objectively reliable. In the real world, the objectivity and accuracy of such cost and asset value estimates are difficult to guarantee not only because they are by their nature imprecise, but because the managers whose performance is being evaluated according to those estimates often have a strong influence on how the estimates turn out. Unless the company can find a relatively inexpensive means of generating

independent estimates (such as those furnished by insurance companies when insuring corporate assets), the use of inflation-adjusted accounting could provide operating managers with the wrong incentives. Not only will they have an incentive to understate the value of their asset base, but they also may be led to make decisions that artifically boost inflation-adjusted performance without a corresponding improvement in cash flows. Such incentives, and the decisions that result from them, could be working against the best interests of the company.

The vast majority of companies have not incorporated replacement costs into their internal reporting and performance measurement schemes. I suspect that the reasons for the continuing prevalence of historical costs have much to do with the aforementioned incentive problems, as well as with the inherent subjectivity of preparing inflation-adjusted estimates. Accordingly, management's decision whether to incorporate inflation adjustments into its internal measurement and compensation scheme should be based on a careful weighing of the costs (including those associated with counterproductive incentives as well as any additional costs of preparation) against the benefits.

If management finally determines that the costs outweigh the benefits, then the time and effort spent in generating these numbers should be the minimum that allows the company to comply with Statement No. 33. For, if neither the company's investors nor management itself is using inflation-adjusted numbers, it is clearly in the interest of the company's shareholders to minimize the amount being spent on generating these numbers. Management may even want to communicate its views on inflation accounting to the FASB. Statement No. 33 says that "the requirements of this Statement will be reviewed on an ongoing basis and the Board will amend or withdraw requirements whenever that course is justified by the evidence." With the corporate tax relief provided by the Reagan Economic Recovery Tax Act of 1981, much of the impetus for ASR 190 and Statement No. 33 has already been spent. Thus, there appears to be little reason to continue requiring companies to disclose inflation-adjusted numbers. On the basis of the evidence, we conclude that management can only help its investors by pressing for an end to the mandatory disclosure of supplemental inflation-adjusted accounting numbers.

Tax-Cutting Inventory Management

Gary C. Biddle, *University of Washington* and R. Kipp Martin, *University of Chicago*

Few firms take full advantage of the significant tax-cutting opportunities in inventory management. When inventory costs are changing, choosing the appropriate accounting method for inventories can dramatically reduce taxes. Additional savings can be obtained by tailoring inventory ordering policies and production schedules to match the accounting method. Recent advances in accounting research and inventory theory, as well as changes in tax and reporting rules, allow these savings to be captured.

The Determinants of Inventory Tax Savings

Inventory management decisions affect taxes by altering the costs assigned to units sold. Because the cost of goods sold is typically the largest tax-deductible expense for retailing and manufacturing firms, small percentage changes can greatly affect tax liabilities. Taxes are saved by more quickly assigning the larger inventory costs to units sold.

The amount of these potential savings depends on five primary factors:
1. Tax rates;
2. Customer demand;
3. Inventory costs;
4. Accounting method for inventories; and
6. Inventory ordering policies.

While the first three factors cannot be easily controlled, forecasts of each are usually available. The last two factors, the inventory accounting method and inventory ordering policies, are the key components of inventory management.

Tax Rates—Most firms pay close attention to future as well as current tax rates. With 15-year tax loss carryforwards it will generally be advantageous to employ income-reducing inventory policies even if no taxes are currently being paid. Only if there is a danger of losing investment credits or tax-loss carryforwards will it be optimal to ignore tax-cutting opportunities.[1]

Customer Demand—Most firms develop forecasts of customer demand to aid production and procurement planning. While demand can be influenced to some extent by advertising, promotions, and product quality, it is subject to unforeseen random fluctuations. Holding inventories reduces the likelihood that customer orders will go unfilled.

Because taxable earnings are calculated on an annual basis, year-end inventories play an important role in tax calculations. Exhausting year-end inventories, for example, causes all inventory costs to be assigned to units sold. Using demand forecasts to avoid year-end depletions allows lower costs to be held in the balance sheet inventory account, while higher costs are assigned to units sold.

Inventory Costs—If the costs of producing or purchasing inventory never changed, the manner in which they were assigned to units sold would not affect taxable earnings. However, this will rarely be the case. Tax-deductible inventory costs—which include labor costs, material costs, and manufacturing overhead—are typically changing, especially during inflationary periods. Even when general inflation subsides, most firms still experience changes in inventory cost components. The more rapidly these costs are changing, the greater the tax-saving opportunities.

Once forecasts of tax rates, and inventory costs have been obtained, they can be used to select those inventory accounting methods and ordering policies which maximize after-tax cash flows.

---

1. If adopted, the President's recent tax proposals to the Congress (as presented in *The President's Tax Proposals to the Congress for Fairness, Growth and Simplicity* (Commerce Clearing House) May 29, 1985), would lower the top marginal corporate tax rate from 46% to 33%. While this would reduce the tax savings potential of inventory management to firms paying the top marginal rate, substantial advantages would remain. Moreover, because this legislation would also eliminate several major tax breaks, many firms which have been paying little or no taxes would face positive future rates. Their potential savings from inventory management may actually increase.

In 1979 the Internal Revenue Service estimated that if all firms which could have switched that year had done so, approximately $18 billion less in corporate income taxes would have been paid.

EXHIBIT 1
Inventory Cost Flows: Coal Piles, Conveyor Belts and Paint Cans

LIFO

The last-in, first-out (LIFO), first-in, first-out (FIFO) and average cost (AC) methods determine which inventory costs are assigned to units sold and which to units on hand. A useful analogy for LIFO is to view inventory costs as accumulating on a coal pile. At the end of the year costs removed from the top of the pile (who has ever heard of taking coal from the bottom?) are assigned to units sold. Costs assigned to any unsold units remain in the base of the pile, forming a new LIFO cost layer. Thus, the balance sheet inventory account contains accumulated cost layers relating to unsold units from past and present years.

LIFO tax savings can arise during periods of increasing costs because the newest and thus highest costs are the first assigned to units sold, thereby reducing taxable earnings. The older, and thus lower costs can remain in the base of the pile indefinitely. Only if inventories are depleted will these older and lower costs be assigned to units sold.

FIFO

A useful analogy for FIFO is a conveyor belt. Inventory costs move along the belt to be assigned to units sold in the order in which they were incurred. The costs remaining on the belt at year-end are assigned to units in inventory. When the belt starts turning at the start of the next year, these year-end inventory costs are the first assigned to units sold. When costs are increasing it is the oldest and thus lowest costs which are assigned to units sold whereas the newest and thus highest costs are assigned to units in inventory.

Average Cost

A can of paint provides a good analogy for the AC method. During the year new quantities of paint (i.e., costs) are added to the amounts in the can at the start of year (i.e., to the beginning inventory). At year-end the paint is stirred (averaged) to obtain a uniform color (per unit cost). This uniform color (cost) is then applied both to units sold and to those still on hand. The costs assigned to the ending inventory units remain in the bottom of the can as the process is repeated the following year.

Choosing the Right Inventory Accounting Method

The Big Difference Accounting Can Make

The three most widely-used inventory accounting methods are the last-in, first-out (LIFO), first-in, first-out (FIFO) and average cost (AC) cost-flow assumptions. As Exhibit 1 illustrates, LIFO assigns the newest costs to units sold while assigning older costs to year-end inventories. FIFO assigns costs to units sold in the order in which they were incurred. The AC method assigns a weighted average of past and current costs to both units sold and units on hand.

When inventory costs are increasing, LIFO reduces taxable earnings by assigning the newest and thus highest costs to units sold. The magnitudes of the resulting savings are striking.

One study estimates that aggregate savings to firms adopting LIFO in 1974-75 totaled nearly $4 billion. Another study found that LIFO savings for a sample of 311 NYSE firms averaged more than $10 million per firm in the first year alone.[2]

Exhibit 2 reveals the savings realized by General Electric, a long-time LIFO user. In fiscal 1981 the use of LIFO cut GE's taxes by $100 million, more than 6 percent of its after-tax earnings. General Electric's cumulative savings have summed to more than $1 billion since it started using LIFO.

Not surprisingly, many managers have recognized the tax-cutting potential of inventory accounting method choices. Since 1973, over 600 NYSE and AMEX firms have switched from FIFO and AC to LIFO. However, even more firms have passed up available savings. Approximately two-thirds of the inventories in the United States are owned by firms using FIFO.[3] In 1979 the IRS estimated that if all firms which could have switched that year had done so, approximately $18 billion less in corporate income taxes would have been paid.[4] Current estimates indicate potential savings of at least $6 billion annually.[5]

2. *Report on Inventory Methods by the Committee on Tax Policy*, New York State Bar Association Tax Section, December 1975. See also G. Biddle, "Accounting Methods and Management Decisions: The Case of Inventory Costing and Inventory Policy," *Journal of Accounting Research*, Supplement 1980, pp. 235-280.

3. Estimate by the Bureau of Economic Analysis cited in *The President's Tax Proposals to the Congress for Fairness, Growth and Simplicity*, p. 178.
4. T. Copeland and J. Weston, *Financial Theory and Corporate Policy*, Addison-Wesley Publishing Company, 1983, p. 25.
5. *The President's Tax Proposals to the Congress for Fairness, Growth and Simplicity*, p. 175.

Tax savings can be maximized by adopting LIFO for those inventory cost components expected to increase and by adopting FIFO for those expected to decline.

EXHIBIT 2
Saving Taxes with LIFO:
General Electric Corporation-Annual Report 1981

9. Inventories

December 31 (In millions)	1981	1980
Raw materials and work in process	$2,089	$2,082
Finished goods	1,099	961
Unbilled shipments	273	300
	$3,461	$3,343

About 82% of total inventories are valued using the LIFO method of inventory accounting.

If the FIFO method of inventory accounting had been used to value all inventories, they would have been $2,465 million higher than reported at December 31, 1981 ($2,240 million higher at year-end 1980).

LIFO firms will typically disclose the amounts by which their inventory valuations would have differed if FIFO had been used instead. Because all inventory costs are assigned to either units sold or units in inventory, changes in this difference reveal LIFO's impact on reported and taxable earnings. Multiplying this change by the marginal tax rate provides an estimate of LIFO tax savings.

For example, General Electric's inventory footnote indicates that the differences between LIFO- and FIFO-based inventory valuations were $2,465 million and $2,240 million in 1981 and 1980, respectively. This means that using LIFO reduced 1981 earnings by $225 million (= $2,465 - $2,240). Multiplying by an approximate tax rate of 46% implies tax savings in 1981 of over $100 million. Applying the marginal tax rate to the difference between the FIFO- and LIFO-based valuations (which is also the cumulative difference between FIFO- and LIFO-based earnings) reveals cumulative tax savings of over $1 billion.

An estimate of the potential savings for a firm not currently using LIFO can be obtained by multiplying the book value of the beginning-of-year inventory by the marginal tax rate and the rate at which costs are expected to increase.

Which Accounting Method: LIFO, FIFO, or AC?

While many firms would clearly benefit from adopting LIFO, others would not. The conditions under which LIFO, FIFO or AC should be used have recently been examined by the authors.[6] The results prove that as long as inventory purchase/production costs are increasing, the discounted present value of after-tax cash flows will be higher for LIFO than AC, and higher for AC than FIFO. LIFO cash flows are larger even if tax rates are increasing and premiums are paid on purchases made to avoid year-end depletions. In fact, this preference ranking holds for any given ordering policy, even if inventories decline. LIFO's advantages are also inversely related to a firm's inventory turnover ratio; that is, the lower the turnover ratio, the greater the LIFO tax savings.

But if inventory costs are declining, the preference ranking is reversed. Discounted after-tax cash flows are higher for FIFO than AC, and higher for AC than LIFO. As shown in Exhibit 3, Zenith Radio Corporation has recently switched back from LIFO to FIFO for certain electronics inventories whose costs have been declining. The resulting tax savings for the year were approximately $1 million.

These results take on added significance in light of the ability to apply LIFO, AC and FIFO selectively to given divisions, inventories and cost components. Tax savings can be maximized by adopting LIFO for those inventory cost components expected to increase (except for labor and/or overhead alone) and by adopting FIFO for those expected to decline. This, in part, explains why firms rarely adopt LIFO for all inventories. Notice in Exhibit 2 that LIFO is used for only 82 percent of General Electric's inventories.

Switching Inventory Accounting Methods: Cost and Benefits

Lower Reported Earnings

Because virtually all firms face rising costs for some portion of their inventories, the previous results suggest that LIFO should be more widely employed. One reason many firms have been reluctant to adopt LIFO in spite of available tax savings is its effect on reported earnings. Section 472 of the In-

---

6. See our article, "Inflation, Taxes and Optimal Inventory Policies," *Journal of Accounting Research*, forthcoming, Spring 1985. Related articles include S. Sunder, "Optimal Choice Between LIFO and FIFO," *Journal of Accounting Research*, Autumn 1976, pp. 277-300; and D. Morse and G. Richardson, "The LIFO/FIFO Decision," *Journal of Accounting Research*, Spring 1983, pp. 106-127.

A number of studies strongly suggest that enough investors read annual report footnotes (especially those of larger firms) that any information they contain is reflected in stock prices.

EXHIBIT 3
Saving Taxes with FIFO:
Zenith Radio Corporation-Annual Report 1983

NOTE 2-ACCOUNTING CHANGE

In the fourth quarter of 1983 the Company changed its method of valuation for a portion of its inventories to the first-in, first-out (FIFO) method from the last-in, first-out (LIFO) method used in prior years. The electronic parts inventories affected have experienced declining prices during the last few years; therefore, this change was made in order not to value these inventories in excess of replacement cost or net realizable value.

This change has been applied by retroactively restating the financial statements. As a result of adopting the FIFO method for a portion of the inventories, net income for the year ended December 31, 1983 is approximately

$2.4 million or $.11 per fully diluted share ($.12 per primary share) less than it would have been on a LIFO basis.

The effects of the financial statement restatement on net income (loss) and net income (loss) per share were:

Increase (Decrease)	Net Income (In millions)	Per Share Primary	Fully Diluted
1982	$(2.5)	$(.13)	$(.13)
1981	.1	.01	.01
1980	.2	.01	.01
1979	(1.4)	(.08)	(.08)

---

ternal Revenue Code contains a Conformity Rule which requires firms using LIFO for tax purposes also to use LIFO for financial disclosures (but not conversely). Thus, lower LIFO taxes also mean lower reported earnings.[7]

As a result, firms adopting LIFO may need to adjust executive bonuses, debt covenants and other contracts based on reported earnings. However, compensation committees, bondholders and bankers should be happy to make these adjustments because adopting LIFO increases the firm's after-tax cash flows. Similar adjustments may be needed for other inventory accounting method changes.[8]

Stock Price Implications

Some managers may also be concerned about the stock price implications of lower LIFO earnings. They reason that if reported earnings fall, so will investor confidence. The stock price implications of switches to LIFO have been the subject of a number of academic studies.

Shyam Sunder examined the cumulative monthly market-adjusted returns of 119 firms which adopted LIFO over the period 1946-66.[9] For the

portfolio of firms adopting LIFO, cumulative returns generally increased during the fiscal year of the switch (reaching +5.3 percent by the year's end).

Sunder viewed these results as consistent with the hypothesis that, on average, the stock prices of firms adopting LIFO increase because investors overlook the lower reported earnings and instead focus on the expected increase in after-tax cash flows. He cautioned, however, that his results were also consistent with the alternative hypothesis that managers are more likely to adopt LIFO when earnings are up and "business prospects look good." Thus, his results may have been partly attributable to investors reacting to strong earnings rather than to the expected tax savings from changing to LIFO. Sunder was unable to control for this "selection bias" because, prior to 1972, firms typically did not disclose what their earnings would have been under their old accounting method. Subsequent studies have confirmed that firms tend to adopt LIFO when their earnings are up.

Since 1972, Accounting Principles Board Opinion No. 20 has required firms to disclose the earnings effects of changes in accounting methods.[10] These disclosures allowed two subsequent studies—

---

7. The Tax Court's Insilco decision (Insilco Corp. v. Comm'r, 73 T. C. 589 (1979), aff'd without public opinion, 659 F. 2d 1059 (2d Cir. 1981)) appeared to weaken the Conformity Rule by allowing a firm's subsidiaries to use LIFO for tax purposes while using FIFO for consolidated financial disclosures. However, the IRS took a dim view of Insilco and prevailed. The Tax Reform Act of 1984 requires corporations which are financially related (50 percent ownership) or report on a consolidated basis to comply with the Conformity Rule.

8. The President's recent tax proposals to Congress, if adopted, would eliminate the Conformity Rule (effective January 1, 1987). Firms would be permitted to use LIFO for tax purposes and another inventory accounting method for financial disclosures.

9. Shyam Sunder, "Relationship Between Accounting Changes and Stock Prices: Problems of Measurement and Some Empirical Evidence," *Journal of Accounting Research*, Supplement 1973, pp. 1-45. See also Shyam Sunder, "Stock Price and Risk Related to Accounting Changes in Inventory Valuation," *Accounting Review*, April 1975, pp. 305-315.

10. In addition, the SEC requires listed firms to disclose the excess of current over LIFO inventory costs (Regulation S-X, Rule 5-02-66, as interpreted in Accounting Series Releases 141 and 293). But since the IRS did not officially sanction these disclosures until 1973 (Revenue Procedure 73-37 and Revenue Ruling 73-66), it was not until 1972 that LIFO firms started to disclose on a continuing basis the effects of LIFO switches on inventory valuations and, simultaneously, on reported earnings.

The Biddle and Lindahl results suggested that the larger the expected LIFO tax savings, the more positive the market's response.

one by William Ricks and a second by Frederick Lindahl and one of the present authors--to control for earnings performance.[11] Ricks matched 275 firms which adopted LIFO in 1974-75 with 275 non-adopters on the basis of percentage changes in EPS, industry and fiscal year-end. Tests based on differences between the weekly market-adjusted returns of the paired firms suggested a negative market reaction (about -2%) around the time of the preliminary earnings announcements of firms adopting LIFO in 1974.

Biddle and Lindahl regressed the cumulative market-adjusted returns of 311 LIFO adopters on (1) the associated LIFO tax savings relative to the market value of equity, and (2) a measure of unexpected earnings performance (earnings forecast error) relative to the market value of equity. This approach allowed us to take into account both the magnitudes of LIFO tax savings and to control for the "good year" selection bias that complicated earlier studies. Instead of a negative market reaction to LIFO adoptions, the Biddle and Lindahl results suggested that the larger the expected LIFO tax savings, the more positive the market's response.

The most recent study of stock price reactions to LIFO adoptions is consistent with both the Ricks and Biddle-Lindahl findings. Ricks and Biddle, in a study completed within the past year,[12] used the within-group regression approach to examine the relationship between the cumulative market-adjusted returns and the magnitudes of LIFO tax savings for 647 NYSE and AMEX firms which adopted LIFO between June 1973 and September 1980. Analysts' forecasts were employed to provide more precise measures of investors' earnings expectations. Controls were also introduced for firm size effects. Tests based on short (two-day and five-day) event periods confirm a negative market reaction surrounding the preliminary earnings announcements of firms adopting LIFO in 1974. These reactions, which were limited to 1974, appear to be attributable to investors' underestimation of the effect of inflation on

LIFO firms. After carefully controlling for unexpected earnings using analysts' forecast errors, the results also support a positive association between market-adjusted returns and the magnitudes of LIFO tax savings. Thus, it appears that while investors underestimated inflation, they reacted positively to management efforts to offset inflation's effects by adopting LIFO and thereby cutting taxes.

A number of other studies strongly suggest that enough investors read annual report footnotes (especially those of larger firms) that any information they contain is reflected in stock prices. As illustrated in the General Electric footnote (Exhibit 2), estimates of the impact of LIFO on reported earnings are readily available. Because investors will realize that earnings are lower due to LIFO and after-tax cash flows are higher, the stock market is much more likely to reward than to penalize a firm adopting LIFO.

What About Inventory Depletions?

Unanticipated demand or recessionary conditions may cause inventory depletions. Under LIFO, depletions result in old cost layers being assigned to units sold. If inventory costs have been increasing over a long period of time, these old layers may contain very low costs. As a result, inventory depletions in a given year may cause a LIFO firm to report higher earnings, and pay higher taxes, than if FIFO were being used.[13] However, the firm is still better off with LIFO because it has had the use of the money in the meantime.[14] (As an analogy, if someone offered you a million dollars today with the proviso that it be returned if inventories decline, you would surely accept the offer.)

Also, it is important to note that ordering policies can be used to control year-end levels and their effects on earnings and taxes. Indeed, the ordering policies described below explicitly consider the cost/benefit tradeoffs between the costs of holding additional inventory and the benefits of preserving LIFO tax savings.

11. William Ricks, "The Market's Response to the 1974 LIFO Adoptions," *Journal of Accounting Research*, Autumn 1982, pp. 367-387; and Gary Biddle and Frederick Lindahl, "Stock Price Reactions to LIFO Adoptions: The Association Between Excess Returns and LIFO Tax Savings," *Journal of Accounting Research*, Autumn 1982, pp. 551-588.

12. William Ricks and Gary Biddle, "LIFO Adoptions and Stock Price Reactions: Further Evidence and Methodological Considerations," working paper, April 1985.

13. The lower marginal tax rates recently proposed by the President would result in a windfall of sorts for firms currently using LIFO by lowering the cost of LIFO layer liquidations.

14. In fact, simulation experiments presented in our forthcoming article in the *Journal of Accounting Research* suggest that the relative advantage of LIFO over FIFO and AC actually increases with the variability of customer demand. While the generality of this result has not yet been explored, it is clear that it operates at the limit. A firm facing zero demand variance (i. e. , a firm which knows exactly what its demand will be) will hold no inventories and, as a result, will have identical cash flows under LIFO, FIFO, and AC. This assumes that the firm is not motivated to hold inventories for other reasons, such as fixed setup costs for production runs.

Firms which adopt LIFO can continue to use another method for many internal management purposes.

Another way to reduce the likelihood of inventory depletions is to use dollar-value LIFO. This approach allows various inventories to be grouped together in "pools" and accounted for using dollar values rather than physical units. Increases in certain inventories can then substitute for depletions in others, preserving LIFO layers. In addition, new models or product lines can be substituted for discontinued ones without assigning the costs of the discontinued models to units sold. Firms with sales of less than $2 million can include all inventories in a single pool. The Crude Oil Windfall Profit Tax Act of 1980 provides tax refunds for depletions caused by certain government energy policies.

How Costly Is It to Switch Methods?

Adopting LIFO is easy. No prior permission is required; simply file a Form 970 ("Application to Use the LIFO Inventory Method") with your tax return. With extensions of up to eight and one-half months after year-end, the savings can be determined prior to the switch. The only catch is that the IRS reserves the right to adjust the value of the beginning inventory to reflect current costs. Due to the Thor Power Tool Company decision,[15] however, few firms are now carrying undervalued or obsolete inventories. Even if they are, the present value of future tax savings will often offset the initial adjustment.

Abandoning LIFO is not so easy. Permission must be requested (Form 3115) in the first 180 days of the tax year for which the change is to become effective. While it appears that permission will usually be granted (there haven't been many requests), any previous LIFO savings must be repaid. However, this repayment can generally be spread over periods of up to ten (and in some cases twenty) years. Permission is also required for switching between FIFO and AC.

Changing inventory accounting methods may also entail additional administrative costs. Internal reporting procedures and operating policies may have to be modified. But firms which adopt LIFO can continue to use another method for many internal management purposes (e.g., performance evaluation and management compensation) with the conversion to LIFO being made by the comptroller's office at year-end. Recent tax law changes have further reduced the bookkeeping costs of LIFO by allowing firms to estimate inventory costs using government-supplied indexes.

Ordering Policies: Taking Full Advantage of Tax-Saving Opportunities

Once an inventory accounting method has been selected, additional savings can be obtained by tailoring inventory ordering policies to reflect associated tax incentives. Firms which have ignored the tax consequences of inventory ordering and production decisions, as well as firms which have switched inventory accounting methods without modifying inventory ordering policies, may be paying out in taxes cash that could be used for dividends, operating expenditures and investments.

The size and timing of inventory orders and production runs, in conjunction with customer demand, determine year-end inventory levels. These, in turn, influence the costs assigned to units sold. Taxes are reduced by adopting ordering policies and production schedules which result in higher costs being assigned to units sold. The optimal ordering policy differs, however, according to whether the firm is using LIFO, FIFO or AC.

Recently, the authors have derived tax-minimizing ordering policies for each of these three inventory accounting methods.[16] We found, for example, that a firm using FIFO can minimize taxes by using a "base stock" ordering policy. This means that the firm sets a target level (the base stock) for units available for sale to customers which does not depend on the number of units in inventory at the start of the year. During the year orders are placed for the difference between the base stock and beginning inventory levels.

In contrast, a LIFO firm should not use a base

15. 43 AFTR 2d 79-362; aff'g 40 AFTR 2d 77-5799(CA-7); aff'g 64 TC 154 U. S. Supreme Court no. 77-290, January 16, 1979. The Court ruled that it was inconsistent for a firm to take a substantial writedown on an inventory it continued to hold.

16. See our articles, "Inflation, Taxes and Optimal Inventory Policies," *Journal of Accounting Research*, forthcoming, Spring 1985; "An Optimal Inventory Ordering Policy in the Presence of LIFO Tax Incentives," working paper, University of Chicago, 1983; and "A Stochastic Inventory Model Incorporating Intra-Year Purchases and Accounting Tax Incentives," under review, *Management Science*. Related articles include M. Cohen and D. Pekelman, "Optimal Inventory Ordering Policy with Tax Payments Under FIFO and LIFO Accounting Systems," *Management Science*, 1979, pp. 729-743; and M. Cohen and R. Halperin, "Optimal Inventory Order Policy for a Firm Using the LIFO Inventory Costing Method," *Journal of Accounting Research*, Autumn 1980, pp. 375-389.

Simulation experiments indicate that using an ordering policy which considers accounting tax incentives can increase after-tax profits by several percent.

stock policy. A firm on LIFO will maximize after-tax profits by instead using a target level for inventory units available for sale which depends on the quantities and costs of beginning inventory units. This is because during inflationary periods, a LIFO firm can preserve previous tax savings by avoiding the depletion of old LIFO cost layers (see Exhibit 1). Since older inventory costs are generally lower, the incentives to protect these layers increase with the ages and quantities of beginning inventory costs.

In addition, under LIFO (but not under FIFO) it can be optimal to make additional purchases at year-end to protect old cost layers. This is true even if spot market prices or overtime wage rates result in year-end procurement costs which exceed those expected at the start of the next year. It will not always be optimal, however, for a firm to hold larger year-end inventories under LIFO than FIFO. The after-tax costs of year-end purchases, because they are immediately tax deductible, are lower under LIFO. As a result, a firm may set lower initial purchase/production goals. If demand is low, the firm may not order or produce additional units and, as a result, end the year with lower inventory than under FIFO. Similar results hold when the AC method is used.

We have illustrated elsewhere that the appropriate ordering policies for firms using FIFO, LIFO and AC can be obtained with relative ease.[17] They are based on a multi-period dynamic programming model which incorporates stochastic demand, changing inventory costs, and the cost structure of beginning inventories. It also allows additional purchases to be made at year-end. These policies can be easily implemented by personnel familiar with computer-based inventory ordering policy models.

Simulation experiments indicate that using an ordering policy which considers accounting tax incentives can increase after-tax profits by several percent. These opportunities will be particularly important for the many firms which have switched to LIFO in recent years. As their inventories reflect progressively older costs, the potential savings will increase dramatically. Another advantage of using these policies is that because the benefits of holding inventory are measured in after-tax dollars, they

result in lower inventory levels than policies which ignore taxes.[18]

A final advantage of the ordering policies described above is that they smoothly integrate inventory tax incentives into normal purchases and production planning. The U.S. Claims Court recently ruled against a jewelry manufacturer that had purchased gold inventory at year-end for the purpose of protecting old LIFO cost layers and thereby reducing taxes.[19] Over a four-year period the gold purchases during the last two months of each fiscal year exceeded the combined purchases of the preceding ten months. The Court ruled that because the year-end gold purchases were consistently resold at or near the beginning of the next fiscal year, the gold was not acquired for sale or use in the ordinary course of business. Our inventory ordering policies integrate tax incentives into all procurement decisions, thereby avoiding dramatic year-end fluctuations.

Summary

Significant tax-cutting opportunities are available (and they will continue to be available under the recently proposed tax legislation) to firms which (1) select the appropriate inventory accounting method and (2) tailor inventory ordering policies to take advantage of associated tax incentives. Since most firms can expect increases in at least some components of inventory costs, LIFO can be selectively adopted to reduce taxes. As finance theory would predict, the evidence from academic studies suggests that investors look favorably on firms which reduce taxes by adopting LIFO, in spite of lower reported earnings.

Almost all firms, regardless of which inventory costing method they use, could also benefit from modifying their ordering and production policies to take advantage of the tax incentives provided by their specific accounting method. We have developed inventory order quantity models which smoothly integrate tax incentives into normal purchase and production planning.

---

17. See references in footnote 16.

18. The President's recent tax proposals to Congress would allow firms to use LIFO, FIFO, AC and a new inventory accounting method called Indexed FIFO. Under Indexed FIFO firms would get a tax deduction based on a price-level index (such as the Consumer Price Index) applied to the beginning-of-year inventory.

If adopted in its present form, Indexed FIFO, like LIFO, would provide incentives to carefully manage year-end inventory levels. A variant of the models we have developed for LIFO, FIFO and AC could be used to derive the appropriate ordering policies.

19. B. A. Ballou, ClsCt, 85-1 USTC Para 9290, March 29, 1985.

How Investors Interpret Changes in Corporate Financial Policy

by Paul Healy, *Massachusetts Institute of Technology*, and Krishna Palepu, *Harvard Business School*

In May 1987, Apple Computer announced that it would pay $5 million in cash dividends on its common stock (four cents per share) for the first time in its history. On the day of the announcement, the market value of Apple's equity rose by $219 million.

In May 1986, Emhart announced that it intended to issue 2.75 million shares to raise $102 million in new equity. Following the announcement, the market value of its existing equity fell by $23 million.

In February 1989, General Motors declared a 2-for-1 stock split for the first time since 1955, and increased its dividends. The announcement led the market value of GM's equity to increase by $1.3 billion.

Academic research has confirmed what practicing businessmen have long suspected—namely, that changes in corporate financial policies affect stock prices in systematic and thus fairly predictable ways. Announcements of equity offerings are generally accompanied by large decreases in the stock prices of the issuing firms. Dividend increases and stock splits typically lead to significant price increases.

What is relatively new is the explanation for why the market responds in this way. Finance scholars now argue that corporate policy changes affect stock prices because such changes convey information to investors about future performance.[1] Corporate managements, they reason, often have better information than investors about their companies' future profitability, investment opportunities, and business risks. And managers can be expected to use this information when making

decisions about the appropriate level of dividends or financial leverage. For this reason, investors may look to such policy changes to reveal management's expectations about future earnings and investment opportunities. Hence, the effect on stock prices.

Wall Street analysts and corporate executives, however, tend to tell a different story. The conventional wisdom on common stock offerings, for example, is that they decrease stock prices by increasing the supply of a given company's shares. The popular account of stock price reactions to dividend increases is that investors value current income in the form of cash dividends more highly than capital gains. And stock splits are often said to increase stock prices by expanding the number of potential investors.

What each of these popular explanations have in common is their reliance on some form of market malfunction (economists call them "inefficiencies"). For example, it is true that if each company's stock were really unique, an increase in that stock's supply would cause the price to fall. But, as finance theorists have long argued, there are many close substitutes in our capital markets for any individual stock; and thus an increase in the supply of a single company's stock should have no important effect on price. Conversely, given this implied horizontal demand curve for securities, the attempt to increase potential investor "demand" through a stock split should be equally ineffective.

On the dividend question, financial economists have long argued that, apart from tax effects, investors should be indifferent between receiving income in the form of dividends and capital gains. In fact, when dividend tax rates exceeded those on capital

*We are grateful for the helpful comments of Paul Asquith, Gordon Donaldson, Bob Kaplan, and Richard Leftwich.

1. For examples of information-based models see Stewart Myers and Nicholas Majluf, "Corporate Financing and Investment Decisions When Firms Have Information That Investors Do Not Have," *Journal of Financial Economics*, Vol. 13 No. 2

(1984), Merton Miller and Kevin Rock, "Dividend Policy Under Asymmetric Information," *Journal of Finance*, (1985), and Michael Brennan and Thomas Copeland, "Stock Splits, Stock Prices, and Transaction Costs", *Journal of Financial Economics*, Vol. 22 No. 1 (1988).

gains (before the Tax Reform Act of 1986), taxable investors should actually have preferred capital gains to dividends.

In three recent studies, we attempted to discover which version of the story is correct. Do financial decisions influence stock prices because they provide new information to investors, or because capital markets do not work well? In one study, we looked at companies that decided to pay dividends for the first time. In a second study, we investigated publicly traded companies' decisions to issue additional common stock after a long period of financing by debt and retained earnings. The third examined the performance of companies that split their stock.[2]

HOW DO INVESTORS VIEW FIRST-TIME DIVIDEND PAYMENTS?

The vast majority of public companies pay cash dividends.[3] Moreover, they appear to try to maintain a stable, predictable dividend policy. As early as 1956, John Linter's classic study of corporate dividend policy showed that managers consider expected future earnings as well as current earnings in setting dividend policy—presumably because they are very reluctant to cut dividends in the future.[4]

To the extent this model of dividend policy-making reflects actual behavior, we would expect managers to increase dividends only when earnings increases are expected to be sustained in the future. And, if management turns out to be right more often than not, then reasonably astute investors will come to recognize that dividend increases represent managers' forecast of higher earnings.[5] Such implicit forecasts, moreover, will carry considerably more weight than straightforward earnings forecasts because, unlike mere statements, dividend increases are backed up by a commitment to pay out cash.

One of our recent studies attempted to determine whether a special subset of dividend increases—namely, dividend initiations—provided reliable signals of future earnings increases. (We defined dividend initiations as either payments for the first time in a firm's history, or after a hiatus of at least ten years.) We tested this proposition by comparing the earnings growth pattern of 131 NYSE and ASE companies that started (or resumed) dividend payments over the period 1970 to 1979.

As shown in Table 1 and Figure 1, this group of companies report relatively flat earnings until the year before the announcement of the first dividend payment. Then, earnings increase markedly and continue to grow at impressive rates for the next three years.

To give some indication of the size of such changes, the average earnings increases are 43 percent in year 1 (the year before the initiation), 55 percent in year 1, 22 percent in year 2 and 35 percent in year 3.[6] When most companies experience a pattern of large earnings increases like this, the increases typically turn out to be temporary and are reversed in later years.[7] For companies initiating dividends, however, the earnings are sustained through year 4 and thus appear to be relatively permanent.[8]

In short, the actual earnings increases following first-time dividend payments suggest that managers' implicit forecasts of unusual earnings growth are indeed realized. It is not surprising, then, that recent research has also shown that the stock market responds very positively to announcements of dividend initiations. In fact, the average market-adjusted increase in stock price in the two days surrounding the dividend announcement is roughly 4 percent.

Furthermore, it turns out that the larger the *yield* of the initial dividend, the more positive is the immediate stock price reaction to a given company's announcement of a dividend initiation. And, perhaps even more telling, the larger the market's positive reaction to the announcement, the larger are the future earnings increases actually realized by companies initiating the dividend.

This, needless to say, is persuasive evidence that dividend changes provide useful "signals" to investors.

2. Our original research on these issues is presented in the following papers: (1) Paul Healy and Krishna Palepu, "Earnings Information Conveyed by Dividend Initiations and Omissions" *Journal of Financial Economics*, Vol. 21 No. 2 (1988); (2) Paul Healy and Krishna Palepu, "Earnings and Risk Changes Surrounding Primary Stock Offers," *Journal of Accounting Research*, (1990); and (3) Paul Asquith, Paul Healy, and Krishna Palepu, "Earnings and Stock Splits," *The Accounting Review*, (July 1989).

3. In 1987, 76% of NYSE and ASE firms listed on Standard and Poor's Compustat files paid cash dividends.

4. John Linter, "Distribution of Incomes of Corporations Among Dividends, Retained Earnings and Taxes," *American Economic Review*, Vol. 46 (1956). See also Eugene Fama and H. Babiak, "Dividend Policy: An Empirical Analysis," *Journal of the American Statistical Association*, Vol. 63 (1968).

5. Managers could also initiate dividend payments when they forecast that their firms' earnings will be more stable relative to past earnings. In this case, investors will view dividend initiations as a signal of a decrease in the riskiness of the initiating firms.

6. In our original research, we compute earnings performance as earning changes divided by stock prices. Here we convert these values to earnings growth rates by assuming that the average P/E ratio is 10 times.

7. For further evidence on this see L. Brooks and D. Buckmaster, "First-Difference Signals and Accounting Time-Series Properties," *Journal of Business Finance and Accounting* (1980).

8. These findings do not change when we control for industry earnings patterns in years surrounding the dividend initiations.

TABLE 1	Year Relative to Dividend Initiation	Number of Firms	Mean Earnings Growth Rate	Median Earnings Growth Rate
EARNINGS GROWTH RATES IN YEARS SURROUNDING FIRST-TIME DIVIDEND PAYMENTS BY 131 FIRMS IN THE PERIOD 1970 TO 1979*	−4	130	14.9%	17.4%
	−3	129	−7.1	7.6
	−2	128	12.9	10.5
	−1	131	42.7**	28.0
	1	130	55.0**	40.2
	2	130	22.0**	35.9
	3	130	35.0**	28.2
	4	128	3.5	19.5

* In our original research we compute earnings performance as earnings changes standardized by stock prices. Here we convert these values to earnings growth rates by assuming that the average price earnings ratio for the sample firms is ten.
** Significantly different from zero at the 10% level or lower.

FIGURE 1
MEDIAN EARNINGS GROWTH RATES IN YEARS SURROUNDING FIRST TIME DIDIDEND PAYMENTS*

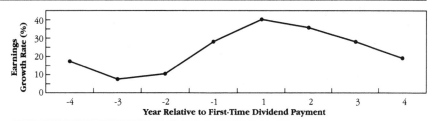

*In our original research we compare earnings performance as earnings changes standardized by stock prices. Here we convert these values to earnings growth ratios by assuming that the average price-earnings ratio for the sample firms is ten.

HOW DO INVESTORS VIEW STOCK OFFERINGS?

Finance theory suggests that corporate management should (if they do not already) determine the mix of debt and equity in their companies' capital structures by balancing the tax benefits of debt financing with the associated costs of financial distress.[9] Companies with high and stable profits are likely to borrow more because they can use interest tax shields without fear of financial distress. Companies with low or volatile profits are likely to borrow less because of the increased threat of financial difficulty.

Studies of actual corporate capital structures tell a somewhat different story about the management decision-making process. These provide strong evidence that, rather than adhering to a stable target ratio that reflects the trade-off between tax benefits and financial distress, managements instead typically fund new investments using retained earnings and, if necessary, external debt financing. Only rarely do they resort to external equity financing; and when they do, it is usually only when they believe that the firm's current debt ratio is too high (or that its debt capacity has been used up) given their expectations about the level or riskiness of future earnings.[10]

Given this reasoning, we might expect managers to make equity offerings when they expect the company's business risk to be higher than previously anticipated, or the level of future earnings to be lower. And, to the extent that managers have better information than investors about the company's future earnings and risk, investors will interpret announcements of equity offerings as "signals" of management's expectations.

Using a sample of 93 seasoned stock offerings over the period 1966 to 1981, we attempted to test whether equity issues convey information about companies' business risk, future earnings, and target

9. See Gordon Donaldson, *Corporate Debt Capacity*, Division of Research, Harvard Business School: Boston (1961), and Harry DeAngelo and Ron Masulis, "Optimal Capital Structure under Corporate and Personal Taxation," *Journal of Financial Economics*, (1980).

10. Publicly listed corporations raise additional capital through equity offerings very infrequently. For a discussion of corporate financing practices see Gordon Donaldson, *Managing Corporate Wealth*, Praeger: New York (1984), and Richard Brealey and Stewart Myers, *Principles of Corporate Finance*, McGraw-Hill: New York (1988).

debt-equity ratios. If a company made multiple offerings less than five years apart, we used only the first offering. The sample therefore comprised firms for which equity offers were relatively rare events. All 93 firms were listed on the NYSE or ASE.

We estimated both the mean and median changes in business risk and leverage for the two years before and the two years after the equity offer. We used two measures of a firm's business risk: (1) asset beta and (2) an index of the firm's earnings volatility.[11]

As shown in Table 2, the average asset betas of the companies issuing equity are stable before the offer, but increase markedly after the offer. On average, asset betas increase by 23 percent (from 0.66 to 0.80) in the year after the equity offer. (This increase is, in a statistical sense, quite reliable.) The asset betas remain at the higher level in year 2, indicating that the beta increase in year 1 is not a temporary phenomenon.

We also found that earnings volatility, an alternative measure of business risk, increases sharply after the equity offer. The earnings volatility index is virtually unchanged in years before the offer, but later more than doubles (from 0.9 to 2.5). These patterns in beta and earnings volatility indicate that the offering firms experience a substantial increase in their business risk after the equity offer announcement.

To examine whether equity offerings signal future earnings declines, we analyzed the post-offer earnings performance as well as revisions in *Value Line* analysts' forecasts. We found no evidence, however, that the offering companies have lower earnings after the equity offer relative to either their pre-offer levels or the earnings of other firms in their industries. Further, analysts do not reduce their earnings forecasts after the announcements of equity issues.

It therefore appears that the managers of the offering firms anticipate future increases in business risk and respond by issuing additional equity to reduce financial leverage. The stated uses of equity-offer proceeds reported in the *Wall Street Journal* and in offer prospectuses indicate that a majority of firms intended to use these proceeds to retire debt and thus reduce leverage

ratios. And subsequent changes in corporate debt ratios suggest that results match intentions. After the equity offering, the average debt-equity ratio decreases by 20% (from 0.95 to 0.76), and remains at the lower level.

The net effect of the increase in business risk combined with the decrease in financial leverage is to increase equity betas. On average, equity betas increase by 8 percent in the offer year (from 1.23 to 1.33). (This increase, moreover, is statistically reliable; and there is no significant change in equity betas in other years.)

The economic significance of this average increase in equity betas of the offering firms can be quantified using a simple valuation model. Start by making the following assumptions: cash flows are constant in perpetuity, the discount rate is determined by the Capital Asset Pricing Model, the market's risk premium is 8%, and the risk-free rate is 10%. Given these assumptions, an expected increase in the equity beta from 1.23 to 1.33 will lead to a stock price decline of 4 percent.[12]

And, in fact, we find that the actual stock price reaction to the announcement of equity offers in our sample is consistent with this prediction. The average, risk-adjusted return is − 3.1 percent in the two days surrounding the offer announcement.[13]

Apparently, then, managers of companies issuing new equity forecast an increase in their companies' business risk, and therefore an increase in the probability of financial distress. They respond by issuing common stock and use the proceeds to retire existing debt, thereby reducing their firms' financial leverage. Investors recognize that managers have superior information and interpret offer announcements accordingly: they revise the offering firms' equity betas upward. And increases in earnings volatility of the offering firms in the years following the offer confirm that managers' forecasts of increased business risk are on average correct.

HOW DO INVESTORS VIEW STOCK SPLITS?

Surveys of managers' views on stock splits show that a vast majority regard splits as a means to keep

---

11. Asset betas measure the sensitivity of a firm's stock returns to market fluctuations after controlling for financial leverage. The asset beta B_a for a firm is estimated as follows:

$$B_a = B_e (1+D/E)$$

where, B_e is the equity beta estimated using the market model, and D/E is the ratio of the book value of debt to the market value equity (financial leverage). See Robert Hamada, "The Effect of Firm's Capital Structure on the Systematic Risk of Common Stocks," *Journal of Business*, Vol. 27 (1972) for a discussion of the relation between asset betas, equity betas, and leverage.

The earnings volatility index is constructed using the variance of changes in EPS as a percentage of stock price across the sample firms. The index for each year is the ratio of the variance in that year to the variance in year −3.

We computed asset betas, earnings volatility indices, and debt-equity ratios also for the offering firms' industries. The industry values are not reported in this paper for brevity, but are used in our tests to confirm that the results for the sample firms are not driven solely by industry-related factors.

12. For Further details on this calculation, see Paul Healy and Krishna Palepu, "Earnings and Risk Changes Surrounding Primary Stock Offers," *Journal of Accounting Research*, (1990).

13. In our sample the average ratio of the offer proceeds to the pre-offer equity value of the firm is 12.5%. Thus, the 3% decline in the stock price of the offer firms translates into a loss of about 25% of the proceeds of the proposed offer.

TABLE 2
CHANGES IN BUSINESS RISK
AND LEVERAGE IN YEARS
SURROUNDING SEASONED
EQUITY OFFERS FOR 93
FIRMS IN THE PERIOD
1966 TO 1981[a]

Variables	Year Relative to Equity Offer				
	−3	−2	−1	1	2
Business Risk:					
Asset Beta					
Mean	0.71	0.67	0.66	0.80	0.83
Median	0.64	0.61	0.62	0.78	0.79
Change in Asset Beta					
Mean		−5.6%	−3.0%	22.7%*	3.8%
Median		−3.1%	−1.6%	24.2%*	1.3%
Earnings Volatility Index	1.0	1.0	0.9	2.5	2.3
Leverage:					
Debt-Equity Ratio					
Mean	1.01	1.05	0.95	0.76	0.80
Median	0.68	0.74	0.72	0.56	0.59
Change in D-E Ratio					
Mean		4.0%	−9.5%	−20.0%*	5.3%
Median		7.4%	−6.8%	−20.8%	1.8%

[a] Two measures of business risk are used: asset betas and an earnings volatility index. Asset betas are unlevered equity betas; the earnings volatility index is the variance of the annual change in earnings as a percent of the stock price before the equity offer in each year relative to the value in year −3. Leverage is the book debt-equity ratio.
* Significant different from zero at the 10% level or lower.

their firm's price within an optimal trading range.[14] Companies typically split their stocks after permanent increases in earnings, since the news of favorable earnings is likely to push their stock prices above the target trading range. By contrast, companies with only temporary increases in earnings are unlikely to split their stock, since their stock prices will not appreciate beyond the target range.

Given this reasoning, we suggest that a company's decision to split its stock could well be determined by its managers' forecasts of whether past or current earnings growth is permanent. If managers have better information than investors about the permanence of earnings growth, investors may infer that past earnings increases are permanent from the announcement of a split.

Using a sample of 121 stock distributions of at least 25 percent over the period 1970 to 1980, we tested whether stock-splitting firms have permanent increases in their earnings. (Since stock splits are often accompanied by explicit or implicit increases in cash dividends and since dividend increases sig-

nal earnings increases, we restricted the sample to firms that did not pay cash dividends at the split date.)[15] None of these firms had made a stock distribution in the prior five years. The sample therefore comprised relatively large and infrequent stock distributions. All the sample firms were listed on the NYSE or ASE.

As shown in Figure 2 and Table 3, companies that split their stocks have large earnings increases for several years before the stock split,[16] as well in the year of the split. In effect, earnings increase by 12 percent two years before the split (year −2), 26 percent in year −1, and 20 percent in year 1.[17] The implied confidence of management about future earnings thus appears to be substantiated; and the earnings of the splitting firms do not decline over the next five years.

While the splitting firms' share prices increase before the split, we find that stock prices do not fully reflect the unusually large earnings increases in these years. Perhaps, without the split, investors would expect such increases to be temporary and reverse

14. H.K. Baker and P.L. Gallagher, "Management's View of Stock Splits," *Financial Management* (1980) report that 94% of the managers surveyed viewed stock splits as a means to keep their firm's price within an optimal trading range. Current finance theories do not address why firms have a preferred trading range. Optimal trading ranges may arise to reduce costs of trading, and to attract a broad and heterogeneous base of stockholders. For further discussion see Josef Lakonishok and Baruch Lev, "Stock Splits and Stock Dividends: Why, Who, and When," *Journal of Finance* (1987).

15. Many firms that split their stock do not decrease their dividend per share proportionally. For these firms the split announcement is accompanied by an increase in the total dividends paid. We have excluded these firms from our sample to isolate earnings changes around stock splits, since we have documented that firms that increase their dividend have large earnings increases.

16. See footnote 6.

17. Pre-split earnings increases are due to both industry- and firm-specific factors. When we controlled for industry earnings patterns in years surrounding the stock splits, we found that the sample firms were in industries that performed well but out-performed their industries in the year before the split.

COMPANIES THAT SPLIT THEIR STOCKS HAVE LARGE EARNINGS INCREASES
FOR SEVERAL YEARS BEFORE THE STOCK SPLIT, AS WELL IN THE YEAR OF THE
SPLIT... THE IMPLIED CONFIDENCE OF MANAGEMENT ABOUT FUTURE
EARNINGS THUS APPEARS TO BE SUBSTANTIATED; AND THE EARNINGS OF
THE SPLITTING FIRMS DO NOT DECLINE OVER THE NEXT FIVE YEARS.

FIGURE 2
MEDIAN PERCENT
CHANGES IN EPS
SURROUNDING
STOCK SPLITS

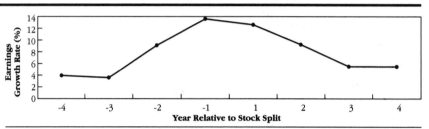

*In our original research we compare earnings performance as earnings changes standardized by stock prices. Here we convert these values to earnings growth ratios by assuming that the average price-earnings ratio for the sample firms is ten.

TABLE 3
EARNINGS GROWTH RATES
IN YEARS SURROUNDING
STOCK SPLITS BY
NON-DIVIDEND PAYING
FIRMS IN THE PERIOD
1970 TO 1980*

Year Relative to Stock Split	Number of Firms	Mean earnings Growth Rate	Median earnings Growth Rate
−4	44	10.5%**	4.1%
−3	61	6.6	3.7
−2	84	12.4**	9.2
−1	100	2.55**	13.7
1	118	20.3**	12.8
2	117	9.1	9.3
3	110	− 6.5	5.6
4	101	21.0	5.5

* In our original research we compute earnings performance as earnings changes standardized by stock prices. Here we convert these values to earnings growth rates by assuming that the average price earnings are for the sample time of ten.
** Significantly different from zero at the 10% level or lower.

themselves in later years—because large earnings increases, as mentioned earlier, are typically followed by declines. A stock split thus may help investors recognize that pre-split earnings increases are permanent.

How does the market respond to announcements of splits? The average market-adjusted stock price increase in the two days surrounding the split announcement is 3.7 percent. Further, the stock price reaction to the split announcement is proportional to earnings increases in *prior* years. That is, firms with higher earnings growth in the two years before the split experience higher stock price reactions to the split announcement.

In short, investors appear to view stock splits as signals that previous earnings increases will be sustained.

CLOSING REMARKS

There are no obvious reasons why corporate policy changes such as stock splits, dividends, and equity offerings should affect stock prices in any consistent or systematic way.

The evidence from our recent research suggests that managers make capital structure, dividend policy, and stock split decisions when they foresee changes in their companies' business risk or earnings levels. Subsequent changes in the actual values of these business fundamentals tend to bear out the implied management forecasts. Sophisticated investors appear to pay attention to such forecasts, and to incorporate them accurately into their own forecasts of future corporate performance.

How Rational Investors Deal with Uncertainty

(Or, Reports of the Death of Efficient Market Theory Are Greatly Exaggerated)

by Keith Brown and Seha Tinic, *University of Texas at Austin*, and Van Harlow, *Salomon Brothers*

M uch academic research in finance in the past quarter century has been devoted to examining the proposition that corporate securities are priced by "rational" investors in an "efficient market." Stated most simply, the proposition says that the intensive pursuit of large returns by stock market investors ensures that, for the vast majority, only modest ones will be had. This argument, which has been refined and tested as the "efficient markets hypothesis" (EMH), could well be described as the foundation of modern financial theory.

* This article is based on our paper, "Risk Aversion, Uncertain Information, and Market Efficiency," *Journal of Financial Economics* 22 (1988), 355-385. The opinions and analyses presented herein are those of the authors and do not necessarily represent the views of Salomon Brothers Inc.

In the 1960s and 1970s, finance scholars amassed a large body of empirical evidence attesting to the efficiency of capital markets. So extensive was this research, and so consistently supportive in its findings, that Professor Michael Jensen of the Harvard Business School has called the EMH the best-documented proposition in all of the social sciences.[1] And, besides dominating academic research for two decades, the EMH and valuation models like the Capital Asset Pricing Model have made significant inroads into Wall Street thinking and practice. Currently, for example, over $150 billion is invested in "index" funds—those which deliberately refrain from active investment strategies and instead attempt simply to mimic the broad market.

Professional money managers, needless to say, have never looked kindly on the EMH. Among many top corporate executives, too—especially those who would like to attribute the bulk of corporate raiders' profits to systematic market undervaluation—the idea of investor rationality arouses skepticism. And when you add to these more or less predictable sources of resistance the heightened political concern about stock market volatility, especially in the wake of the October '87 Crash, proponents of the EMH seem to find themselves in an increasingly defensive position these days.

Much of the criticism, however, stems from a faulty understanding of what the theory really claims for itself. We will begin here by trying to dispel some of the misconception by explaining what economists mean when they speak of an "efficient market."

Efficient markets theory is, at bottom, simply an extension to capital markets of the "zero profits theorem" that economists have long applied to competitive goods markets. Briefly stated, the EMH holds that competition among investors for information ensures that the current prices of widely traded financial assets are "unbiased" predictors of the future values of those securities. The EMH thus does *not* say that today's price is the "right" price, but only that it is an "unbiased" indicator of future value—that is, neither too high nor too low on average. And, therefore, a company's future stock price (adjusted for risk and for general market movements which affect all stocks) is equally likely to be higher or lower than today's price.

For corporate management, then, today's stock price can be understood as the market's collective estimate—although a "noisy" estimate, to be sure—of the present value of the company's future risky cash flows (or, more precisely, the "certainty equivalents" of those flows). And unless one has significant inside information (or can confidently predict the the future direction of the market as a whole), the current price may well be the most reliable estimate of the value of the company *as it is currently being run.*

For investors contemplating purchase of a company's stock, the theory implies that they should expect to earn a "normal" rate of return—nothing more, nothing less—*at any given time* they choose to invest. And, in fact, the well-documented failure of the vast majority of professional fund managers to outperform market-wide averages consistently is one of the strongest pieces of testimony to the efficiency of our financial markets.

RECENT ACADEMIC CHALLENGES: THE OVERREACTION HYPOTHESIS

Over the last few years, however, in addition to the natural skepticism of practitioners, the EMH has begun to face stronger challenges from within the academic community. In the late 1970s, to be sure, a number of "anomalies" were detected that appeared to provide investors with "trading rules" that would allow them to earn consistently above-average returns. For example, one could buy a portfolio of stocks with low P/E ratios or buy a portfolio of small capitalization stocks in December to take advantage of the "January effect." But most of these anomalies may have little bearing on the validity of the EMH. They may instead be the result of flawed models of the relationship between risk and expected returns.

More serious charges against the EMH, however, have arisen from fairly recent studies claiming to have discovered two distinct, but related forms of investor irrationality: (1) "excessive" long-run stock price volatility and (2) short-term investor "overreaction" to the news of dramatic financial events. Because our own research concerns the second of these two issues, we concentrate our attention largely on the question of investor overreaction. (The research on long-run market volatility is summarized very briefly in footnote 6 below.)

Recent studies by Werner DeBondt and Richard Thaler purport to demonstrate that both the market-wide responses to general economic news and the

1. Michael Jensen, "Some Anomalous Evidence Regarding Market Efficiency," *Journal of Financial Economics* 6 (1978), 95-101.

stock price reactions to individual company "events" tend to overshoot their "equilibrium" levels—and then only gradually find their way back to those levels. That is, the market as a whole (and the price of individual stocks as well) systematically exaggerates the economic consequences of major events by raising prices too high when the news is good and cutting prices too sharply when the news is bad. In so doing, the studies argue, capital markets are providing investors with consistently exploitable opportunities for abnormal profits.[2]

In an efficient market, by contrast, prices are expected to respond to major events by moving quickly (if not "instantly") to their new equilibrium levels. How do we know that prices have moved to their proper levels? The answer is that future price movements from these new levels should turn out to be "randomly distributed" around these new levels. In such a market, although investors will certainly overreact in some cases, they learn from their mistakes —because such mistakes, after all, are costly to them. And thus the cases in which investors overreact should be balanced by others in which they "underreact," such that subsequent adjustments, on average, should be roughly equal to zero. This, in effect, was what Eugene Fama found in his classic 1965 study, "The Behavior of Stock Market Prices."[3]

The recent findings of DeBondt and Thaler seem to imply, however, that investors do not learn from their past mistakes and that they consistently misread new information. Formulated as the "Overreaction Hypothesis" (OH), their argument suggests that large movements in stock prices are followed, on average, by large adjustments in the opposite direction. The hypothesis also predicts that the larger the initial price change (that is, the bigger the "surprise" to the market), the larger will be the amount of the initial overreaction, and hence the greater the subsequent price adjustment.

Our Findings

Over the past several years, we have studied this issue of market overreaction and come to a different conclusion. We too observed one of the findings that DeBondt and Thaler reported—the tendency of large stock price declines to be followed by a series of small upward adjustments. But we also made a discovery that contradicts their Overreaction Hypothesis: namely, that large stock price *increases* are also accompanied by small positive (or at least non-negative) adjustments, and not by the negative adjustments predicted by DeBondt and Thaler.[4]

In this article, we present a modified version of the EMH that we call the Uncertain Information Hypothesis (UIH). As noted above, the EMH, at least in its traditional form, starts with the assumption that investors have "complete" information and are thus able to move stock prices quickly to their new proper levels. Our UIH model attempts to extend efficient markets theory by showing how investors would respond "rationally" in situations of major uncertainty—those in which the assumption of complete information clearly does not hold.

As we will argue in the pages that follow, great uncertainty among investors leads, at least initially, to heightened price volatility and thus greater risk for investors. Because investors require higher returns for bearing greater risks, they respond to favorable as well as unfavorable surprise events by setting stock prices, on average, below their expected values. As the uncertainty over the eventual outcome is gradually clarified, subsequent price changes will tend to be positive, on average, regardless whether the initial event was good or bad. In this sense, positive price adjustments following major shocks are better understood as rational responses to increased risk than as chronic overreactions by the investing public.[5]

THE UNCERTAIN INFORMATION HYPOTHESIS

The standard version of the EMH is based on the clearly unrealistic assumption that investors have immediate access to all of the information they need to revise security prices in a definitive, once-and-for-all manner. In the real world, of course, some events are so little anticipated and of such consequence that

2. For the original specification of this proposition, see W. DeBondt and R. Thaler, "Does the Stock Market Overreact?," *Journal of Finance* 40 (1985), 793-805. Subsequent investigations were also performed in J. Howe, "Evidence on Stock Market Overreaction," *Financial Analysts Journal* 42 (1986), 74-77 and W. De-Bondt and R. Thaler, "Further Evidence on Investor Overreaction and Stock Market Seasonality," *Journal of Finance* 42 (1987), 557-581.

3. E. Fama, "The Behavior of Stock Market Prices", *Journal of Business* 38 (1965), 34-105.

4. See K. Brown and V. Harlow, "Market Overreaction: Magnitude and Intensity", *Journal of Portfolio Management* 14 (1988), 6-13.

5. The notion that a short-run pattern of stock price increases following major price declines is consistent with a market comprised of rational, risk-averse investors has some precedent in the finance literature. See R. Merton, "On Estimating the Expected Return on the Market: An Exploratory Investigation," *Journal of Financial Economics* 2 (1980), 225-243.

their ultimate effect on stock prices cannot be immediately determined. In the face of such uncertainty, our theory says, investors effectively form what economists refer to as "conditional probability distributions." Such distributions can be visualized as decision-tree-like diagrams that lay out a number of possible outcomes and assign probabilities to each. By multiplying the value of each possible outcome by its probability, one arrives at an "expected value" for the company's shares. (In the Appendix, we provide a detailed illustration of this process.)

But, as our version of the EMH goes on to say, because of the increased uncertainty and thus greater risk attending such events, investors also *immediately* discount the value of the firm *below* the expected value of this probability distribution. This discount on the shares then disappears gradually, along with the uncertainty that gave rise to it.

For example, upon the unexpected death of a company's talented CEO, the stockholders will quickly mark down the value of the company's shares. But a more precise assessment of the consequences will not be possible until the market learns more about the company's plans for a successor. So, in the immediate aftermath of the announcement, the best that investors will be able to do is to reset stock prices based on a subjective "guess" (or, more precisely, a probability distribution of guesses) about the longer-range effect. And, given investors' aversion to risk, this first guess is more likely to fall below than above the eventual value.

The point of this example is that the unanticipated information affects investors in two ways. First, as the bad news is initially received, projections of the fortunes of the firm in question are immediately revised downward. Second, the level of uncertainty facing investors in this company increases, causing a *further reduction* in the value of the firm's shares. Thus, even if this increase in uncertainty is not permanent, it nevertheless represents a potential source of risk for which investors will demand to be compensated (at least until the source of the risk is removed).

A similar market reaction can be envisioned in the case of unexpectedly good news. Suppose that a company announces it has developed a new technology that promises to reduce its production costs significantly. As in the previous example, to the extent that this information takes investors by surprise, any immediate adjustments to the firm's stock price will be based on a crude forecast of the ultimate consequences of the event. While such an announcement should cause an overall increase in the value of the firm, it might also raise the level of uncertainty about its future performance—which would cause the stock price increase to be less than otherwise.

Of course, we could also have constructed other examples where an event might actually reduce uncertainty. In fact, it is entirely reasonable to suggest that certain news releases—such as the announcement of the jury's verdict in a closely contested trial—might have the effect of decreasing the riskiness of holding corporate shares. Our UIH model simply assumes that major surprises will typically increase the variability and risk of stock returns.

Contrast with the Overreaction Hypothesis

In cases of bad news, then, the pattern of investors' responses predicted by our Uncertain Information Hypothesis will be indistinguishable from that predicted by the Overreaction Hypothesis. That is, the initial decline in stock prices will be followed, on average, by a price increase. The difference between the two theories becomes apparent only in the case of good news. In contrast to the Overreaction Hypothesis, our model predicts what would appear to be an underreaction; that is, an initial price increase followed, on average, by a further increase.

These propositions are demonstrated graphically in Figure 1. For purposes of comparison, Panel A shows the adjustment of stock prices to bad news under the traditional EMH. The arrival of bad news drives the value of the security down from its previous level, P, to P_B; and there is no further adjustment after the initial response. In this case, the stock price moves immediately to its new "intrinsic" value.

In contrast, Panel B shows the pattern of price changes that would accompany unfavorable surprises under the Uncertain Information Hypothesis (and under the Overreaction Hypothesis as well). According to our UIH model, the arrival of bad news would not only decrease the expected cash flows of the security but also increase their systematic risk. With this additional uncertainty, the present value of the "certainty equivalents" of the risky cash flows is P^*_B, which could be significantly less than P_B in a stock market dominated by risk-averse investors. But, as the uncertainty is resolved, the price increases to P_B from P^*_B to reflect the associated reduction of investor risk.

THE UIH ALSO SUGGESTS THAT, TO THE EXTENT INVESTORS' RISK AVERSION
DECREASES WITH HIGHER LEVELS OF STOCK PRICES, THE SUBSEQUENT
UPWARD PRICE ADJUSTMENTS AFTER MAJOR UNFAVORABLE SURPRISES ARE
EXPECTED TO BE GREATER THAN THE ADJUSTMENTS
FOLLOWING FAVORABLE EVENTS.

FIGURE 1
STOCK PRICE CHANGES IN RESPONSE TO UNFAVORABLE AND FAVORABLE UNCERTAIN INFORMATION

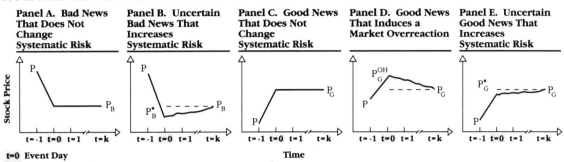

The effect of favorable surprises on stock prices is shown in Panels C, D, and E. In the standard EMH, in which the consequences of the news are immediately and clearly known, the price of the stock increases quickly from P to P_G; and there is no adjustment thereafter. The Overreaction Hypothesis (illustrated in Panel D) predicts that the price will overshoot the mark, rising to P_G^{OH} and then falling back to P_G.

Our UIH model, in contrast to both the standard EMH and the OH, suggests that if the good news also increases the uncertainty about the stock's future cash flows, then the price will initially rise only to P_G^*, and then gradually adjust further up to P_G as the uncertainty is dispelled. As in the case of bad news, this delayed price adjustment is caused by investors' rational demand for higher expected returns to compensate them for the heightened uncertainty.

Although the preceding discussion is couched in terms of favorable and unfavorable surprises affecting the systematic risks of individual stocks, our UIH model is equally relevant to market-wide surprises that affect the values of broad-based stock indexes. The UIH claims that major favorable and unfavorable surprises about the economy will typically increase the risk of holding common stocks in general. Thus, the returns on market portfolios following major shocks would also

be expected to exhibit the same "asymmetric" pattern (i.e., apparent overreaction to bad news, underreaction to good) shown in Panels B and E in Figure 1. Moreover, the UIH also suggests that, to the extent investors' risk aversion decreases with higher levels of stock prices, the subsequent upward price adjustments after major unfavorable surprises are expected to be greater than the adjustments following favorable events.

The heart of our UIH theory, then, can be summarized by the following propositions: (1) on average, stock return variability will increase following the announcements of major unanticipated events; (2) the average price adjustments following the initial market reactions to both "negative" and "positive" events will be positive (or, in the case of the latter, at least non-negative); and (3) to the extent the market's risk-aversion decreases as the level of stock prices increase, post-event price increases will be larger for negative events than for positive ones. The important point here is that the portfolios are priced rationally in both situations, and there are no *ex ante* opportunities for investors to earn riskless profits by "arbitraging" price overreactions or underreactions. Under this scenario, one only has the *illusion* that investors consistently overreact to bad new and underreact to good.[6]

6. It should be noted that the debate between the OH and the UIH is related to another class of market efficiency tests that focus on what is known as "mean reversion" in security prices. The mean reversion hypothesis can be visualized by showing a path of stock prices that swing wildly ("excessively") back and forth across some "trend line" measure of "intrinsic" value. In effect, it suggests a long-run pattern of overreactions followed regularly by "corrections."

Several recent studies have examined this proposition. (See, in particular, E. Fama and K. French, "Dividend Yields and Expected Stock Returns", Journal of Financial Economics 22 (1988), 3-25; J. Poterba and L. Summers, "Mean Reversion in Stock Prices: Evidence and Implications", *Journal of Financial Economics* 22 (1988), 27-60; and E. Fama and K. French, "Permanent and Temporary Components of Stock Prices", Journal of Political Economy 96 (1988), 246-273.)

The general conclusion that has been drawn from the evidence amassed to date is that there appear to be "predictable" return components in security prices. More precisely, it has been shown that from 25 to 45 percent of the variability of stock returns over a three- to five-year time horizon can be predicted from returns in previous periods.

As intriguing as these results are, they can still be "explained" in two different ways: (1) investors are irrational and thus prices often depart from fundamental values in a way that should provide the opportunity for abnormal profits; or (2) both the risks borne and the risk premiums demanded by rational investors change significantly over time in ways as not yet fully understood. Of course, the OH is consistent with the former explanation while the UIH is consistent with the latter.

TABLE 1	Sample	Sample Size	Mean	Standard Deviation	MAX	MIN
DESCRIPTIVE STATISTICS FOR THE TWO SAMPLES OF UNANTICIPATED EVENTS USED TO TEST THE UIH	**Market Index:**					
	Positive Events	36	1.34%	0.40%	2.67%	1.03%
	Negative Events	39	−1.27	0.42	−1.00	−3.47
	Individual Firms:					
	Positive Events	4,788	4.26%	1.77%	22.09%	2.50%
	Negative Events	4,317	−4.06	1.79	−2.50	−30.63

TESTING THE UIH

Defining Unexpected Events

As we have outlined the theory, the UIH attempts to explain investor reactions to major unanticipated events. In devising a test of our theory, the first question that arises is, how do we know when a "major" event has occurred? To avoid introducing any subjective bias on the part of the researcher, we defined "events" using strictly quantitative criteria.

In the case of general market reactions, all daily price movements greater than one percent of a broad market index were considered as events.[7] Over the 24-year period from 1962 through 1985, we found 75 such events: 36 positive and 39 negative.

In the case of individual companies, we deemed as events all daily percentage returns (adjusted for risk and expected return) greater than 2.5 percent by the 200 largest companies in the S&P 500.[8] As expected, there were far more company-specific than market-wide events, even with the difference in the sample criterion. Over the same 24-year period, we found 9,105 events, of which 4,788 were positive and 4,317 were negative. (Table 1 summarizes the statistical characteristics of both samples of events.)

The Effect of Surprises on Volatility

Because the primary prediction of the UIH is that major surprises will tend to increase investor uncertainty, our first task was to compare the level of price volatility before and after the events. To allow for direct comparison of events that took place over a 24-year period, we defined the date of the event to be "Day 0" for all cases in both samples regardless of where it fell in calendar time. Then, a subsequent period running from Day +1 to Day +60 was examined in order to estimate the appropriate measure of "post-event" volatility.

In measuring pre-event (or "normal") volatility, we used different measures for the two different samples. For the sample of market-wide surprises, risk was measured as the variance of the observed stock price returns. We compared the level of post-event variance to the same measure calculated by using all "non-event" days; that is, all days during the 1962-1985 sample period that did not fall in one of the 60-day periods that followed the 75 surprises.

For the sample of individual companies, we measured the stock price "betas" (or covariances) over the period two hundred days prior to the event (Day −200 to Day −1), and then compared those to the betas calculated over the sixty-day period following the event (Day +1 to Day +60).

General Market Volatility. In Panel A of Table 2, we report the results of the return variance analysis on our market-wide sample in the form of three different sets of data: (1) all non-event days; (2) all post-event days following favorable surprises; and (3) all post-event days following unfavorable surprises. As shown there, major surprises appear to affect investor risk precisely as the UIH predicts. The "F-statistics" are measures of the statistical significance of the difference

---

7. More precisely, we determined that an "event" had occurred if the market return on any given day departed from its "expected value" by more than one percent. The expected return to the market index was estimated by the average daily return of an equally-weighted index of all NYSE and ASE companies over the 60 days immediately preceding the event. We chose such a seemingly small number as one percent on the assumption that, because of the natural diversification within the market portfolio, deviations from the expected daily return would not have to be extremely large to be considered a bona fide surprise.

8. Expected returns were estimated differently for the individual firm events than for the market index events. Remember that investors' expected (or, alternatively, "required") returns are a function of risk. And because major surprises change the level of risk, they can be expected to change expected returns as well. Consequently, before calculating the set of abnormal post-event price changes, we first re-estimated expected returns for both the general market index and the individual companies using data from a time period *not affected by* the event.

THESE FINDINGS ABOUT VOLATILITY ARE CONSISTENT WITH THE PRIMARY
PREDICTION OF THE UIH: NAMELY, A LARGE INCREASE IN UNCERTAINTY
(AS REFLECTED IN PRICE VOLATILITY) FOLLOWED BY A GRADUAL
RESOLUTION OF THAT UNCERTAINTY.

TABLE 2
CHANGES IN RISK INDUCED BY UNANTICIPATED EVENTS

Panel A. Marketwide Events

Sample	Number of Observations	Variance	F-Statistic for Difference with (i)
(i) Nonevent Days	1,936	0.00004862	—
(ii) Postevent Days: Positive Events	2,160	0.0006342	1.30***
(ii) Postevent Days: Negative Events	2,340	0.00006515	1.34***

*** denotes significance at the 1% critical level

Panel B. Individual Firm Events

Period	Positive Events	Negative Events
Avg. Beta Coefficient:		
Preevent (Day-200 to-1)	1.00441	1.00875
Postevent (Day +1 to +60)	1.05615	1.07257
Subsequent Days (Day +61 to +260)	1.02472	1.03285
F-Statistics:		
Preevent-Postevent	22.74**	31.87**
Preevent-Subsequent	4.56*	6.09**
Postevent-Subsequent	8.42**	12.34**

** and * denote significance at the 5% and 10% critical levels, respectively

between the non-event risk level and the two post-event risk levels; and they suggest that we can be quite confident in concluding that the events in question are consistently followed by a measurable increase in general market volatility. Our analysis also suggests that, although negative events had a somewhat larger impact on risk than positive ones, the difference was not statistically significant.

Company-Specific Volatility. For the sample of individual company events, the results listed in Panel B of Table 2 are equally striking. As mentioned above, for each of 9,105 events we compared the firm's beta before and after the event. Also, in order to get a better sense of whether these company-specific volatility changes were permanent, we computed a third beta for each event over a time period judged to be well beyond the event itself (from Day +61 to +260).

Two conclusions can be drawn from these findings. First, as with the market-wide sample, unanticipated events result in a sharp increase in the systematic risk of individual firms. The increases averaged 5.2 percent (1.056/1.004) for favorable surprises and 6.3 percent (1.073/1.009) for negative ones. Second, it is also clear that much of this risk increase is temporary. As shown in the column labeled "Subsequent Days," the average betas for both positive and negative events trend back toward

their pre-event levels.[9] Nevertheless, they continue to remain somewhat above their values prior to the surprise. Thus, it appears that unanticipated events have both a permanent and a temporary effect on investors' perception of company risk.

Figure 2 provides a graphic illustration of the increases in total risk (that is, variance as distinguished from covariance (or beta)) that accompany unexpected changes in the stock prices of individual companies.[10] The graph shows the changes in the "cross-sectional" variances computed separately for each of the positive and negative individual companies over the period Day −60 to Day +60. Like the data summarized in Table 2, Figure 2 also demonstrates that much of the increase in risk is only temporary.[11]

These findings about volatility are consistent, then, with the primary prediction of the UIH: namely, a large increase in uncertainty (as reflected in price volatility) followed by a gradual resolution of that uncertainty. Whether investors receive additional compensation for bearing this additional risk, as the UIH also predicts, is the question to which we now turn.

The Effect of Surprises on Prices

Having established that major surprises increase price volatility, we then calculated the daily "abnor-

---

9. Specifically, the level of risk in the Day +61 to +260 interval retains only 39% (=[1.02472 − 1.00441]/[1.05615 − 1.00441]) of the buildup accumulated during the postevent period for positive events and 38% (=[1.03285 − 1.00875]/[1.07257 − 1.00875]) for negative surprises.

10. This method of calculating the volatility for individual securities has the advantage of not being tied to any explicit return-generating relationship, such as

the single index market model. It is apparent from this display, however, that our earlier conclusions are still valid.

11. To be exact, allowing the −60 to Day −5 and (Day +5 to Day +60) intervals to proxy for the portion of the pre-event and post-event periods outside the immediate vicinity of the event, the average cross-sectional variance increased from 0.000339 to 0.000390 for positive surprises and from 0.000357 to 0.000399 for negative ones.

TABLE 3
CUMULATIVE AVERAGE RESIDUALS FOLLOWING UNANTICIPATED EVENTS

Panel A: Marketwide Events

Event Day	Positive Events (N=36)		Negative Events (N=39)	
	CAR (%)	T-Stat	CAR (%)	T-Stat
+ 1	0.014	0.10	0.145	0.96
+ 2	− 0.084	− 0.48	0.454	2.20**
+ 3	0.007	0.03	0.669	2.67**
+ 4	0.194	0.81	0.685	2.33**
+ 5	0.403	1.54	0.630	1.85*
+10	0.493	1.31	1.047	2.23**
+20	1.346	2.53**	.1.360	2.07**
+30	1.360	2.06**	1.550	1.99*
+40	1.183	1.53	1.227	1.47
+50	1.527	1.67	1.349	1.41
+60	0.542	0.54	1.499	1.43

Panel B: Individual Firm Events

Event Day	Positive Events (N=4,788)		Negative Events (N=4,317)	
	CAR (%)	T-Stat	CAR (%)	T-Stat
+ 1	0.118	3.69**	0.045	1.28
+ 2	0.153	3.27**	0.112	2.22**
+ 3	0.095	1.65*	0.139	2.29**
+ 4	0.075	1.13	0.210	3.01**
+ 5	0.080	1.09	0.278	3.59**
+10	0.030	0.29	0.397	3.71**
+20	−0.032	−0.22	0.346	2.33**
+30	−0.048	−0.27	0.281	1.56
+40	0.058	0.29	0.377	1.81*
+50	−0.086	−0.39	0.474	2.05**
+60	−0.134	−0.54	0.542	2.15**

** and * denote significance at the 5% and 10% critical levels, respectively

mal" stock price returns for both sets of surprises (again, market-wide as well as company-specific), and then averaged them "cross-sectionally" over a 60-day period trailing the events. As in the earlier study of volatility, separate averages were calculated for the "good news" and "bad news" subsets of both the market-wide and the company-specific samples. And, finally, these 60 daily average returns were added together to produce "cumulative average returns" (CARs) for each of these four different categories of events.

Table 3 displays a representative portion of the post-event CARs along with their associated significance tests. The complete set of CARs over the 60-day post-event period for each subsample is illustrated in Figure 3. What both exhibits make clear is that, on average, investors did indeed receive additional compensation in the wake of major surprises both favorable and unfavorable. And this point is reinforced by the statistical observation that only the positive CARs in Table 3 (as well as those not listed there) were statistically significant.

What is also clear, however, is that the positive price adjustments were considerably higher after bad news than good. In the cases of good news about individual companies, the CARs pictured in Figure 3 seem to suggest that the uncertainty is resolved very quickly (in as short a period as 5 days), and that stock returns fluctuate randomly around

zero thereafter (in a pattern much like the one predicted by the standard EMH).

The Relationship Between Risk and Return

Having established that major surprises increase both risk and return in the stock market, the final goal of our study was to investigate the strength of the relationship between the two. All models of rational investor behavior assume that investors require greater returns for bearing risk. Consequently, in evaluating the initial price shocks and subsequent adjustments in our samples of events, we would expect to find that the level of increase in the CARs is positively related to the level of increase in volatility.

To test the relationship between risk and return in this case with any degree of precision would have required the use of a formal model of the risk-return relationship—a source of controversy that we wanted to steer clear of. So, we chose instead to run two relatively informal tests that examine certain aspects of this risk-return relationship.

The first of these tests focused on the market-wide surprises. In constructing this experiment, we reasoned that if investors exhibit what is known as "constant relative risk aversion"—that is, if the amount of additional return needed to compensate an added unit of risk remains roughly the same

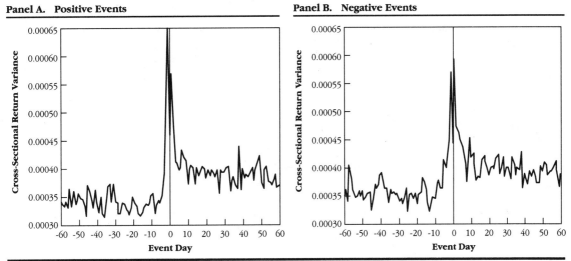

FIGURE 2
STOCK RETURN VOLATILITY BEFORE AND AFTER MAJOR UNANTICIPATED EVENTS

Panel A. Positive Events   **Panel B. Negative Events**

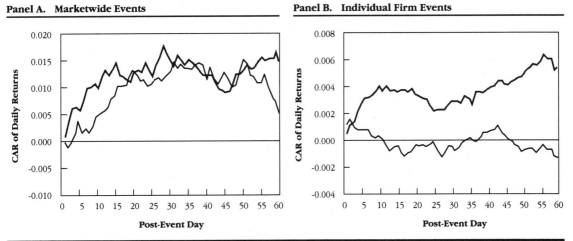

FIGURE 3
CUMULATIVE ABNORMAL RETURNS FOLLOWING UNEXPECTED PRICE-CHANGE EVENTS

Panel A. Marketwide Events   **Panel B. Individual Firm Events**

regardless of the relative level of stock prices—then the expected risk premium on the market index should be directly proportional to the variance of market returns.[12] This, in turn, implies that the percentage increase in post-event expected returns should be roughly equal to the percentage increase in post-event risk.

In fact, as reported in Panel A of Table 4, the increases in post-event returns tended to be somewhat larger than the increases in risk (the "elasticity coefficient" for the whole sample was 1.58). Without a more precisely formulated model of risk and return, however, it is difficult to say whether this represents "excessive" compensation for increased

---

12. See R. Merton, cited in note 5.

OUR FINDINGS DEMONSTRATE RATHER CONVINCINGLY THAT, REGARDLESS OF THE RISK MEASURE USED, POST-EVENT UNCERTAINTY IS AN INCREASING FUNCTION OF THE SIZE OF THE INITIAL PRICE CHANGE. THE LARGER THE INITIAL MARKET REACTION TO A SURPRISE, THE GREATER THE SUBSEQUENT LEVEL OF INVESTOR UNCERTAINTY AND THUS THE HIGHER THE MEASURE OF RISK.

TABLE 4
THE RELATIONSHIP BETWEEN POSTEVENT RISK AND RETURN

Panel A. Risk and Expected Return Changes for Marketwide Events

Sample	% Change In Expected Return	% Change Risk	Ratio
All Events	41.838%	26.523%	1.577
Positive Events Only	49.393	30.440	1.623
Negative Events Only	46.538	33.998	1.369

Panel B. Event Magnitudes and Risk Changes for Individual Firm Events

Sample	Dependent Variable	Estimated Coefficient $\alpha 0$	$\alpha 1$	F-Stat
Positive Events	β	0.8912	3.8733	65.58***
(N = 4,788)	σ_j^2	0.0002	0.0050	299.35***
Negative Events	β	0.9250	−3.6352	53.20***
(N = 4,317)	σ_j^2	0.0002	−0.0054	351.77***

*** indicates significance at the 1% critical level

risk. What is important for our purposes is that the findings in Panel A are consistent with the direction of the relationship that would be expected in an efficient market.

In the case of company-specific surprises, we used regression analysis to determine whether the size of the initial price change was highly correlated with the subsequent increase in risk. Two measures of risk were tested, systematic risk (as measured by a company's beta) and total risk (as measured by total variance).

As reported in Panel B of Table 4, our findings demonstrate rather convincingly that, regardless of the risk measure used, post-event uncertainty is an increasing function of the size of the initial price change. The larger the initial market reaction to a surprise, the greater the subsequent level of investor uncertainty and thus the higher the measure of risk.

In sum, the findings of these two tests, together with the earlier results, provide strong support for our claim that investors "rationally" increase their expected returns to compensate for the increased risk attending major unanticipated events. Now, we attempt to apply our model of investor behavior to the biggest "surprise" in recent stock market history, the October '87 Crash, to see how the claim of investor rationality stands up under extreme uncertainty.

THE UIH AND THE MARKET CRASH OF 1987

On Monday, October 19, 1987, the stock market suffered its largest one-day loss in history, with the S&P 500 losing more than 20 percent of its value.

Explanations for this stunning decline have been many and varied, with blame being cast on everything from order execution procedures on the exchanges and NASDAQ to program trading and portfolio insurance. While we don't presume to be able to shed light on the underlying causes of "Black Monday," we can attempt to use the Uncertain Information Hypothesis to deduce what should have been expected to happen on the days following the crash.[13]

Given the magnitude of the price shock of October 19, the UIH would have predicted the following: (1) volatility in the stock market should increase dramatically; and (2) overall market values should trend upward as the volatility gradually falls toward more normal levels and the general uncertainty disappears. And this is indeed what happened in the wake of the Crash. As shown in Figure 4, the volatility of the S&P 500 market index increased dramatically after October 19, reflecting the substantial increase in the level of investor uncertainty about the market.

The measures of market volatility presented in Figure 4 are not based on direct observations. Traditional estimates of volatility (such as the standard deviations of stock returns) could not be directly calculated in this case because there is only one observation surrounding the event. For this reason we were forced to derive a substitute measure of volatility from changes in other variables. Our surrogate measure of general market volatility was the daily *implied* standard deviation (ISD) of stock price movements using the closest-to-the-money call option on the actual index (that is, the SPX option).[14]

---

13. Because the Crash occurred after the sample period of our original study, an alternative set of data must be considered. Additionally, inasmuch as Black Monday represents a single unanticipated event, the depth of the statistical analysis is obviously quite limited.

14. For a description of this method of volatility estimation, see J. Cox and M. Rubinstein, *Options Markets*, Englewood Cliffs: Prentice-Hall, 1985.

THE STOCK MARKET RATIONALLY RESPONDS TO ANY EVENT WHICH
INCREASES STOCK RISK BY LOWERING THE CURRENT PRICE, AND THEREBY
INCREASING THE LEVEL OF EXPECTED RETURN FOR NEW INVESTORS.
CONVERSELY, WHEN THE PERCEIVED RISK AND VOLATILITY FALL, THEN
INVESTORS LOWER THEIR REQUIRED RATES OF RETURN
AND STOCK PRICES RISE.

FIGURE 4
IMPLIED VOLATILITY OF
THE S&P 500 INDEX
BEFORE AND AFTER THE
STOCK MARKET CRASH
OF OCTOBER, 1987

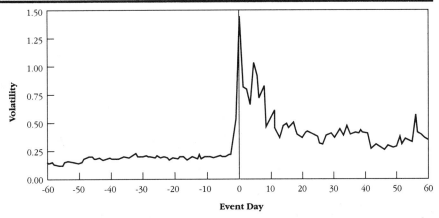

To provide some idea of how much volatility changed with the Crash, the average ISD for the period Day −60 to Day −5 was 18.9% while the comparable figure for the period Day +5 to Day +60 was 43.3%. On the day of the Crash itself, moreover, the ISD went to 145%, more than seven and a half times its pre-Crash value!

In Figure 5, we show the cumulative return as well as the volatility of the S&P 500 index during the 60 days after Black Monday. Once again, the consistently positive sign (excepting a single negative value) on the illustrated pattern of price changes confirms the prediction of the UIH. More important, however, it also appears that the daily returns and risk measures are inversely related; that is, on the days that the volatility measure increases, the S&P tends to fall. (In fact, when the daily realized return is compared to the daily change in the ISD, the estimated correlation coefficient is both negative (−0.544) and significant at the 1% critical level.) And this is exactly the relationship that should exist between these variables in an efficient market. The stock market rationally responds to any event which increases stock risk by lowering the current price, and thereby increasing the level of *expected* return for new investors. Conversely, when the perceived risk and volatility fall, then investors lower their required rates of return and stock prices rise.[15]

CONCLUDING COMMENTS

The efficient markets hypothesis (EMH) is based, in part, on the assumption that reliable information is instantly and costlessly available to investors. In this artificial world of relative certainty, prices are expected to adjust to major events quickly and accurately (or, at least, in an unbiased way, neither systematically overshooting nor undershooting the mark).

In a modification of the EMH called the Uncertain Information Hypothesis (UIH), we discard this assumption of "complete information" and attempt to show how the introduction of uncertainty changes rational investors' responses to new information. In contrast to the EMH, the UIH suggests that in response to surprise events that add greatly to uncertainty (about either the market as a whole or an individual company), both the risk and the required return to stockholders are expected to increase. And thus, whether the news is good or bad, stock prices will immediately trade at a level below their expected value equivalents to reflect the temporary increase in risk. But, as much of the uncertainty disappears over time, required returns should progressively fall back toward normal levels and stock prices should rise to reflect the decrease in risk.

The evidence of our recent study of the market's response to surprises—which examines all 75

15. A far more detailed development of these arguments is given in K. French, W. Schwert, and R. Stambaugh, "Expected Stock Returns and Volatility", *Journal of Financial Economics* 19 (1987), 3-29.

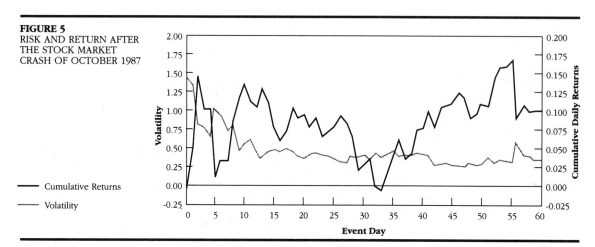

FIGURE 5
RISK AND RETURN AFTER THE STOCK MARKET CRASH OF OCTOBER 1987

— Cumulative Returns

⋯⋯ Volatility

market-wide daily (unexpected) price swings greater than 1 percent and over 9,000 company-specific price movements greater than 2.5 percent over the period 1962-1985—provides strong support for our argument. Our findings demonstrate that regardless of whether the news was good or bad, the average pattern of price adjustments after the initial reaction was significantly positive. Because the volatility of prices was also shown to rise significantly after both good and bad surprises—and then to fall gradually back toward normal levels—these incremental returns to stockholders are interpreted by us as compensating investors for bearing the added risk associated with uncertainty.

While we did find results that could be construed as evidence of market overreaction to large negative shocks, we argue that such apparent overreaction could equally well be viewed as reflecting a large increase in investors' required returns and, thus arguably, in the market-wide risk premium. In fact, we showed that the level of volatility after major surprises is composed of a small permanent as well as a larger transitory component.

What is the import of our findings for efficient markets theory? The main prediction of market efficiency is that the stock market should provide no consistent opportunities for investors to earn more than normal rates of returns (again, adjusted for risk). For this principle to hold, any apparently predictable trend in stock prices—that is, any "trading rule" based on a systematic market "overreaction" to bad news or "underreaction" to good—must turn out, on closer inspection, to be an illusion.

In this case, the illusion is created by the process of averaging the responses by investors (many of which overshoot, while others undershoot their expected stock values) to a large number of events. It is true that if you bought all the individual stocks on the day following a daily price movement of more than 2.5 percent, you would earn what *appears* to be an "excess" rate of return over a very few days. But, if you then adjusted that rate of return for the increased risk of this investment strategy by taking account of the increased price volatility, you would likely discover that you had earned what finally amounts to nothing more than a normal rate of return.

Thus, while we have little doubt that the debate over market efficiency will continue for some time, our research suggests that abandoning the assumptions of investor rationality and market efficiency in favor of loosely formulated alternatives may be premature.

FIGURE 6
PROBABILITY
DISTRIBUTION OF
POSSIBLE STOCK MARKET
OUTCOMES (INCLUDING
UNANTICIPATED EVENTS)

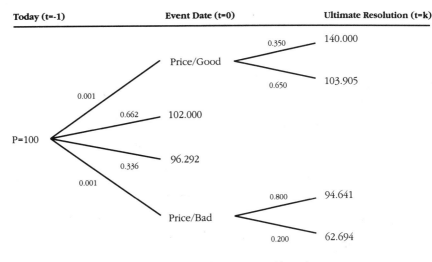

Where: Price/Good = [(.350)(1/140.000) + (.650)(1/103.905)]⁻¹ = 114.211
and: Price/Bad = [(.200)(1/62.694) + (.800)(1/94.641)]⁻¹ = 85.888

APPENDIX ■ THE UNCERTAIN INFORMATION HYPOTHESIS: AN EXAMPLE

We begin by assuming that the stock market is comprised of risk-averse investors whose preferences can be characterized by logarithmic utility function over the terminal value of their wealth.[16] We also assume, for simplicity, that the stock market represents the entire source for investor wealth and that prior to the arrival of any new information (t = −1) the level of a broadly based index of stock is 100. Now, supposing that investors make rational judgements about new information, Figure 6 gives a probability distribution summarizing investors' beliefs about future payoffs to their investments.

The first thing to notice in this display is that investors have allowed for the possible occurrence of four distinct outcomes. Two of these events can be regarded as "normal" in the sense that their impact will be immediately assimilated into market prices (i.e., 102.000 or 96.292). The other two potential outcomes represent "uncertain" surprises. Both of these unexpected events have been structured so that investors can immediately establish: (i) whether they represent good or bad news, and (ii) what the possible eventual effect of the event will be. While these latter two events are treated as being quite unlikely (as evidenced by their assigned probabilities of 0.001), they nonetheless present a practical difficulty for investors trying to evaluate the market at time t = −1 since their resolution, if they do occur, will not be immediate.

To see this, observe from Figure 6 that in the wake of the unexpected good news announcement, investors know only that the ultimate payoff will either be 140.000 (with a 35% probability) or 103.905 (with a 65% probability). Similarly, the unfavorable surprise offers eventual payoffs of 62.694 or 94.641 with 20% and 80% likelihoods, respectively. The challenge that investors face is to establish an economically justifiable value for the market in the face of an uncertain information event.

Stated differently, what will be the prices set immediately after the announcement of a favorable (i.e., Price/Good) and an unfavorable (i.e., Price/Bad) news? The Uncertain Information Hypothesis predicts that rational investors will initially react to the occurrence of these unlikely events

16. Specifically, a logarithmic utility function expresses an investor's level of satisfaction in terms of the value of his or her wealth as follows: U = log (P). This functional form is commonly employed to represent the investor preferences because it exhibits two attributes that are consistent with observed behavior: (i) decreasing absolute risk aversion, and (ii) constant relative risk aversion. For a more detailed explanation, see K. Arrow, *Essays in the Theory of Risk Bearing*, Chicago: Markham Publishing, 1971.

by setting prices so as to maximize the expected utility of their terminal wealth.[17] As indicated at the bottom of the display, these values are equal to 114.211 and 85.888, respectively. Establishing this result has two important consequences. First, since all of the probabilities and potential outcomes (regardless of when they are resolved) are known at time t = −1, investors are able to make the following *unconditional* forecast of the expected return of their stock investment before any event occurs:

$$E(R) = [(.662)(102.000/100) + (.336)(96.292/100)$$
$$+ (.001)(114.211/100) + (.001)(85.888/100)] - 1$$
$$= 0.078\%$$

Using this value, it is also easily confirmed that an unconditional forecast of the standard deviation (i.e., risk) of the stock market is:

$$\sigma = 2.768\%$$

The second consequence of our assumption about investor reaction to uncertain information is apparent upon calculation of revised estimates of E(R) and σ when an unexpected event actually occurs. Specifically, the arrival of the unexpected good news event will prompt investors to initially revalue the index to 114.211 and then compute the following *conditional* forecasts of expected return and risk in the stock market:

$$E(R/Good) = [(.650)(103.905/114.211)$$
$$+ (.350)(140.000/114.211)] - 1 = 2.038\%$$
$$\text{and } \sigma_{Good} = 15.074\%.$$

In the same fashion, following an unfavorable surprise which initially pushes the value of the market index down to 85.888, forecasts of the subsequent return characteristics conditioned on the attendant uncertainty are:

$$E(R/Bad) = [(.800)(94.641/85.888)$$
$$= (.200)(62.694/85.888)] - 1 = 2.752\%$$
$$\text{and } \sigma_{Bad} = 14.878\%$$

The critical aspect of this example—indeed, the main point of the UIH—is that the arrival of unanticipated information has caused the riskiness and, hence, the expected return of the stock investment to increase. This was seen to be true whether the uncertain informational event had a negative (i.e., bad news) or positive (i.e., good news) initial impact. Thus, in the aftermath of such surprises one should expect that market will increase in value. On average, then, the observed pattern of stock prices following unanticipated bad news will superficially resemble the corrections necessitated by the actions of overreactive, irrational investors.

From the above example, however, this interpretation—which is the central prediction of the OH—is clearly incorrect since the initial level of [Price/Bad] was set in rational anticipation of a subsequent stock price movement either up to 94.641 (with 80% probability) or *down* to 62.694 (with 20% probability). Thus, the illusion of overreaction is solely a mathematical artifact caused by averaging realized returns over a large number of negative events. Further, after a favorable surprise, the UIH would predict that the observed pattern of stock returns should, on average, resemble an *underreaction* to the initial event. In any case, the principal point of the example is that seemingly predictable postevent price adjustments need not imply irrationality on the part of investors, particularly if the events increase uncertainty. Thus, empirical results that confirm an increase in risk following substantive unanticipated news events would be consistent with the predictions of the UIH.

---

17. Given the specification of the logarithmic utility function U = log (P), marginal utility can be expressed as U' = (l/P). The UIH predicts that investors will set P_0 equal to $E[(U'(P_1)/E[(U'(P_1)])xP_1]$, or $P_0 = E[1/P_1]^{-1}$. For simplicity, we assume here that the risk-free rate of return is 0.00%.

Issues of Market Efficiency/Selected Bibliography

Arbel, A. and B. Jaggi, "Impact of Replacement Cost Disclosures on Investors' Decisions in the United States," *International Journal of Accounting* 14 (Fall, 1978), 71-82.

Altman, E. I., "Statistical Replication of Bond Quality Ratings: A Worthwhile or Futile Exercise?," Working paper, New York University, 1977.

Ball, R. J, "Changes in Accounting Techniques and Stock Prices," Empirical Research in Accounting: Selected Studies, supplement to Vol. 10 of *Journal of Accounting Research* (1972), 1-38.

Ball, R. J. and P. Brown, "An Empirical Evaluation of Accounting Income Numbers," *Journal of Accounting Research* 6 (Autumn, 1968), 159-177.

Barker, S. A., "Effective Stock Splits," *Harvard Business Review* (January-February, 1956), 72-79.

Barker, S. A., "Stock Splits in a Bull Market," *Harvard Business Review* (May-June, 1957), 101-106.

Bar-Yosef, S. and L. D. Brown, "A Reexamination of Stock Splits Using Moving Betas," *The Journal of Finance* (September, 1977), 1069-1080.

Beaver, W. H., "The Information Content of Annual Earnings Announcements," *Journal of Accounting Research* 6 (1968), 67-92.

Beaver, W. H., "Accounting for Inflation in an Efficient Market," *International Journal of Accounting* (1979), 21-42.

Beaver, W. H., A. A. Christie and P. A. Griffin, "The Information Content of SEC Accounting Series Release No. 190," *Journal of Accounting and Economics* 2 (August, 1980), 127-158.

Beaver, W. H., R. Clarke and W. F. Wright, "The Association Between Unsystematic Security Returns and the Magnitude of Earnings Forecast Errors," *Journal of Accounting Research* 17 (Autumn 1979), 316-340.

Benston, G. J. and M. Krasney, "The Demand for Alternative Accounting Measures," Supplement to the *Journal of Accounting Research* 16 (1978), 1-30.

Biddle, G. C., "Accounting Methods and Management Decisions: The Case of Inventory Costing and Inventory Policy," *Journal of Accounting Research* (Supplement 1980), 235-280.

Biddle, G. C. and F. W. Lindahl, "Stock Price Reactions to LIFO Adoptions: The Association Between Excess Returns and LIFO Tax Savings," Journal of Accounting Research (Autumn, 1982), 551-558.

Biddle, G. C. and R. K. Martin, "Inflation, Taxes and Optimal Inventory Policies," *Journal of Accounting Research* (Spring 1985).

Biddle, G. C. and R. K. Martin, "A Stochastic Inventory Model Incorporating Intra-Year Purchases and Accounting Tax Incentives," *Management Science* (1985).

Brown, P., "The Impact of the Annual Net Profit Report on the Stock Market," *The Australian Accountant* (July, 1970), 277-283.

Cohen, M. and R. Halperin, "Optimal Inventory Order Policy for a Firm Using the LIFO Inventory Costing Method," *Journal of Accounting Research* (Autumn, 1980), 375-389.

Copeland, Thomas E., "Liquidity Changes Following Stock Splits," *The Journal of Finance* (March, 1979), 115-141.

Fama, E. F., L. Fisher, M. D. Jensen and R. Roll, "The Adjustment of Stock Prices to New Information," *International Economic Review* (February, 1969), 1-21.

Foster, G., "Quarterly Accounting Data: Time Series Properties and Predictive Ability Results," *Accounting Review* 52 (January, 1977), 1-21.

Foster, G., *Financial Statement Analysis* (Englewood Cliffs, NJ: Prentice-Hall, Inc., 1978), Chapter 11.

Gheyara, K. and J. Boatsman, "Market Reaction to the 1976 Replacement Cost Disclosures," *Journal of Accounting and Economics* 2 (August, 1980), 107-126.

Gonedes, N. and N. Dopuch, "Capital Market Equilibrium, Information Production, and Selecting Accounting Techniques: Theoretical Framework and Review of Empirical Work," *Studies on Financial Accounting Objectives,* 1974 supplement to the *Journal of Accounting Research,* 48-169.

Hausman, W. H., R. R. West and J. A. Largay, "Stock Splits, Price Changes and Trading Profits: A Synthesis," *Journal of Business* (January, 1971), 69-77.

Holthausen, R. and R. Leftwich, "The Effect of Bond Rating Changes on Common Stock Prices," *Journal of Financial Economics* (1986).

Hong, H., R. S. Kaplan and G. Mandelker, "Pooling vs. Purchase: The Effects of Accounting for Merger on Stock Prices," *Accounting Review* 53 (January, 1978), 31-47.

Johnson, Keith, "Stock Splits and Price Change," *Journal of Finance* (December, 1966), 675-686.

53

Kaplan, R. S., "The Information Content of Financial Accounting Numbers: A Survey of Empirical Evidence," in Abdel-khalik and Keller, eds., *Impact of Accounting Research on Practice and Disclosure* (Durham, NC: Duke University Press, 1978), 134-173.

Kaplan, R. S. and R. Roll, "Investor Evaluation of Accounting Information: Some Empirical Evidence," *Journal of Business* 45 (April, 1972), 225-257.

Kaplan, R. S. and G. Urwitz, "Statistical Methods of Bond Ratings: A Methodological Inquiry," Working paper, Carnegie-Mellon University, 1977.

Melicher, R. W. and D. F. Rush, "Systematic Risk, Financial Data, and Bond Rating Relationships in a Regulated Industry Environment," *Journal of Finance* 29 (1974).

Morse, D. and G. Richardson, "The LIFO/FIFO Decision," *Journal of Accounting Research* (Spring, 1983), pp. 106-127.

Pinches, G. E. and J. C. Singleton, "The Adjustment of Stock Prices to Bond Rating Changes," *Journal of Finance* 33 (1978).

Radcliffe, Robert C. and William B. Gillespie, "The Price Impact of Reverse Splits," *Financial Analysts Journal* (January-February, 1979), 63-67.

Ricks, W. E., "The Market's Response to the 1974 LIFO Adoptions," *Journal of Accounting Research* (Autumn, 1982), 367-387.

Ricks, W. E. and G. C. Biddle, "LIFO Adoptions and Stock Price Reactions: Further Evidence and Methodological Considerations," Working paper, University of Washington, 1985.

Ro., B., "The Adjustment of Security Returns to the Disclosure of Replacement Cost Accounting Information," *Journal of Accounting and Economics* 2 (August, 1980), 159-189.

Sunder, S., "Relationship Between Accounting Changes and Stock Prices: Problems of Measurement and Some Empirical Evidence," *Journal of Accounting Research*, Supplement (1973), 1-45.

Sunder, S., "Stock Price and Risk Related to Accounting Changes in Inventory Valuation," *Accounting Review* (April, 1975), 305-315.

Sunder, S., "Optimal Choice Between LIFO and FIFO," *Journal of Accounting Research* (Autumn, 1976), 277-300.

Wakeman, L. M., "Bond Market Inefficiency: The Evidence Reexamined," Working paper, University of Rochester, 1980.

Wakeman, L. M., "The Function of Bond Rating Agencies: Theory and Evidence," Working paper, University of Rochester, 1981.

Watts, R. L., "Systematic 'Abnormal' Returns After Quarterly Earnings Announcements," *Journal of Financial Economics* 6 (June/September, 1978), 127-150.

Watts, R. L. and J. L. Zimmerman, "On the Irrelevance of Replacement Cost Disclosures for Security Prices," *Journal of Accounting and Economics* 2 (August, 1980), 98-106.

Weinstein, M., "The Effects of a Rating Change Announcement on Bond Prices," *Journal of Financial Economics* 5 (1977).

Part II: The Corporate Investment Decision

INTRODUCTION

One of the major tasks of corporate financial executives is to evaluate investment opportunities. In many corporations, this investment function is separated from the financing decisions typically performed by the corporate treasury, and is instead entrusted to a corporate "planning" or "strategy" group. Perhaps partly as a result of this separation of the investment and financing functions within the corporation, "corporate strategy" has been developed for the most part by practitioners and almost independently of the discipline of financial economics. Quite recently, however, some financial economists have begun making an attempt to bring principles of corporate finance to bear more directly on matters of corporate strategy.

Here we present a series of articles discussing the strengths and limitations of both current and developing quantitative techniques, and their potential contribution to the overall process of strategic planning. In "Corporate Strategy and the Capital Budgeting Decision," for example, Alan Shapiro presents a corporate finance-based approach to corporate strategy that is far more systematic than, say, Peters' and Waterman's *In Search of Excellence*. In so doing, he accounts for the performance of those companies which managed to prosper even in the troubled climate of the '70s. Shapiro's method, which combines a survey of the relevant academic research with a series of illustrations culled from a journal he has been keeping over the past 15 years, is an interesting use of "anecdotal evidence" to give concrete substance to the empirical data.

Following this attempt to integrate capital budgeting and strategy, we present two articles explaining and defending the Capital Asset Pricing Model (CAPM), one of the central theoretical constructs of modern finance. Although it has recently come under considerable criticism, the CAPM offers a practical means for estimating the risks and minimum required rates of return on corporate investments, which of course is a critical part of the capital budgeting process.

In the first of these two articles, Jason McQueen provides a spirited exposition and defense of the model. His most valuable contribution, however, is the clarification of the purpose of theoretical models; his principal aim, to dispel the confusion that surrounds the relationship between models and the economic realities they are intended to represent. Barr Rosenberg and Andrew Rudd follow with a discussion of the corporate applications of the model, including a framework for predicting beta (the measure of investment risk which is the crucial variable in the CAPM). Rosenberg and Rudd's major contribution is the prediction of beta using fundamental operating data — that is, accounting numbers taken from either historical or projected income statements and balance sheets.

In their "Primer on Arbitrage Pricing Theory," Dorothy and Richard Bower and Dennis Logue (all of Dartmouth's Amos Tuck School) provide an introduction to a model of stock risk-return relationships that promises to replace the CAPM as the predominant means of quantifying corporate risk. Unlike the CAPM, which measures risk as sensitivity to a single market index, Arbitrage Pricing Theory (APT) attempts to explain risk in terms of a stock's sensitivity to a number of market-wide factors. Besides providing strategic planners with more precise estimates of both the *kind* and *degree* of risks attending contemplated investments, APT may also be of considerably more use than CAPM to corporate "risk" managers — those whose job it is to estimate a company's vulnerability to changes in a number of macro-economic variables, such as inflation. real interest rates, and rates of growth in GNP.

In "Liquidity and the Cost of Capital," Yakov Amihud and Haim Mendelson discuss the implications for corporate management of a fairly recent research discovery: namely, that liquidity is a major determinant (as important in fact as systematic risk or "beta") of the level of expected stock returns. Less liquid stocks earn proportionately higher rates of return (before transaction costs) over long periods of time, thus representing a higher cost of capital for corporate management. The authors also explore a number of corporate responses designed to reduce the cost of capital by increasing the liquidity of stocks and bonds.

Corporate strategists have long expressed dissatisfaction with the classic discounted cash flow (DCF) technique for evaluating corporate investment opportunities. In "A New Approach to Evaluating Natural Resource Investments," Michael Brennan and Eduardo Schwartz show how corporate planners may benefit from new techniques in capital budgeting: specifically, from the use of commodities futures prices and options pricing models to price commodity-type investments (such as copper mines, oil wells, and timberlands). Although many of the criticisms leveled against DCF arise from an improper understanding and misapplication of the technique, the authors argue that DCF does have an important limitation for corporate strategists: namely, its failure to take account of the value provided by operating options (i.e., the right to close a mine or to stop drilling oil wells when market prices fall).

Presenting an approach they have applied in the analysis of a large Canadian resource project, Brennan and Schwartz demonstrate that the Black-Scholes option pricing model, with subsequent modifications by Robert Merton, can be adapted to evaluate such operating options.

DHC

Corporate Strategy and the Capital Budgeting Decision

Alan C. Shapiro, University of California at Los Angeles

The decade 1974 through 1983 was a dismal one for American business in general. It began with the deepest economic decline since the Depression and ended with national recoveries from back-to-back recessions in the early 1980s. Yet throughout these dark years, 13 companies on the Fortune 500 list of the largest U.S. industrial companies were money-making stars, earning consistently high returns. These firms averaged at least a 20 percent return on shareholders' equity (ROE) over this ten-year span. (To gain some perspective, a dollar invested in 1974 at a compound annual rate of 20 percent would have grown to $6.19 by the end of 1983, a healthy return even after allowing for the effects of inflation.) Moreover, none of these firms' ROE ever dipped below 15 percent during this difficult period.

The 13 were led by a profit superstar, American Home Products, whose ROE not only averaged 29.5 percent during the 1974-83 decade, but also has held above 20 percent for 30 straight years. To appreciate the significance of such a feat, one dollar invested at 20 percent compounded annually would be worth over $237 at the end of 30 years.

What type of firm can achieve such a remarkable record? Far from being the prototypical high-tech firm or a lucky oil company, American Home Products is the low-profile producer of Anacin, Chef Boy-Ar-Dee pasta products, Brach's candy, and Gulden's mustard, in addition to prescription drugs and non-drug products such as cardiovascular drugs, oral contraceptives, and infant formula.

In general, high technology firms were not well represented among the 13, which included just IBM and two pharmaceutical companies, SmithKline Beckman and Merck. IBM, moreover, with an average ROE of 20.5 percent, ranked only 11th out of the 13, far behind such low-tech firms as Dow Jones (26.3%), Kellogg (24.8%), Deluxe Check Printers (24.1%),

and Maytag (23.1%). It was even less profitable than a steel company (Worthington Industries—23.9%) and a chemical firm (Nalco Chemical—21.5%)).

The demonstrated ability of a firm such as Deluxe Check Printers—a firm on the trailing edge of technology, described as a "buggy whip company threatened with extinction by the 'checkless society'"—consistently to earn such extraordinary returns on invested capital must be due to something more than luck or proficiency at applying sophisticated techniques of investment analysis. That something is the knack for creating positive net present value (NPV) projects, projects with rates of return in excess of the required return. The scarcity of this skill is attested to by the fact that aggregate profits of $68.8 billion for the Fortune 500 in 1983 were, in real terms, 22 percent below the $43.6 billion earned in 1974, a recession year. Keep in mind also that the Fortune 500 have been disciplined savers, re-investing over $300 billion of retained earnings in their businesses over the ten-year period. This massive reinvestment alone should have produced considerably higher real earnings than 1974's.

This evidence notwithstanding, it is usually taken for granted that positive NPV projects do exist and can be identified using fairly straightforward techniques. Consequently, the emphasis in most capital budgeting analyses is on estimating and discounting future project cash flows. Projects with positive net present values are accepted; those that fail this test are rejected.

It is important to recognize, however, that selecting positive NPV projects in this way is equivalent to picking under-valued securities on the basis of fundamental analysis. The latter can be done with confidence only if there are financial market imperfections that do not allow asset prices to reflect their equilibrium values. Similarly, the existence of economic rents—excess returns that lead to positive net present values—is the result of monopolistic control over product or factor supplies (i.e., "real market imperfections").

It is the thesis of this article that generating projects likely to yield positive excess returns is at least as important as the conventional quantitative investment analysis. This is the essence of corporate strategy: creating and then taking advantage of imperfections in product and factor markets. Thus, an understanding of the strategies followed by successful firms in exploiting and defending those barriers to

13 Stars of The Decade 1974–1983			
Company		Average ROE 1974–1983	Total return to investors 1974–1983*
American Home Products		**29.5%**	**6.6%**
Dow Jones		26.3%	29.8%
Mitchell Energy		**26.0%**	**26.4%**
SmithKline Beckman		25.4%	19.7%
Kellogg		**24.8%**	**13.3%**
Deluxe Check Printers		24.1%	13.4%
Worthington Industries		**23.9%**	**41.7%**
Maytag		23.1%	14.5%
Merck		**21.9%**	**3.8%**
Nalco Chemical		21.5%	11.4%
IBM		**20.5%**	**11.3%**
Dover		20.3%	26.6%
Coca-Cola		**20.3%**	**2.9%**
Median total return to investors for the 13:		13.4%	
Median total return to investors for the Fortune 500:		13.6%	

*Total return to investors as calculated by *Fortune,* April 30, 1984. It includes both price appreciation and dividend yield to an investor and assumes that any proceeds from cash dividends, the sale or rights and warrant offerings, and stock received in spinoffs were reinvested at the end of the year in which they were received. The return reported is the average annual return compounded over the ten-year period.

Although the 13 have earned extraordinary returns on shareholders' equity capital, Exhibit 1 shows that returns to the shareholders themselves have been less than earthshaking. This is consistent with the efficient market hypothesis, the idea that prices of traded securities rapidly reflect all currently available information. Since the high return on equity capital earned by the 13 is not news to investors—these firms have consistently been outstanding performers—investors back in 1974 had already incorporated these expectations in their estimations of firm values. This means that a firm's expected high ROE is already "priced out" or capitalized by the market at a rate that reflects the anticipated riskiness of investing in the company's stock. As a result, investors will earn exceptional returns only if the firm turns out to do even better than expected, something that by definition is not possible to predict in advance. The fact that the 13's median annual total return to investors (stock price appreciation plus reinvested dividends) of 13.4 percent is almost identical to the Fortune 500's median return of 13.6 percent indicates that investor expectations about the relative performances of both groups of firms were subsequently borne out.

This illustrates the key distinction between operating in an efficient financial market and operating in product and factor markets that are less than perfectly competitive. One can expect to consistently earn excess returns only in the latter markets; competition will ensure that excess returns in an efficient market are short-lived. However, it is evident from the generally dismal performance of the Fortune 500 that it is no mean trick to take advantage of those product and factor market imperfections that do exist.

Only firms that can bring to bear on new projects competitive advantages that are difficult to replicate have any assurance of earning excess returns in the long run.

entry created by product and factor market imperfections is crucial to any systematic evaluation of investment opportunities. For one thing, it provides a qualitative means of identifying, or ranking, ex ante those projects most likely to have positive net present values. This ranking is useful because constraints of time and money limit the number and range of investment opportunities a given firm is likely to consider.

More important, a good understanding of corporate strategy should help uncover new and potentially profitable projects. Only in theory is a firm fortunate enough to be presented, at no effort or expense on its part, with every available investment opportunity. Perhaps the best way to gain this understanding is to study a medley of firms, spanning a number of industries and nations, that have managed to develop and implement a variety of value-creating investment strategies. This is the basic approach taken here.

The first section discusses what happens to economic rents over time, and thus to opportunities for positive NPV projects, in a competitive industry. The second section considers in more detail the nature of market imperfections that give rise to economic rents and how one can design investments to exploit those imperfections. The third section presents the available evidence on the relationship between various competitive advantages and rates of return on invested capital. The fourth introduces a normative approach to strategic planning and investment analysis. The fifth and final section deals with the rationale and means for domestic firms to evolve into multinational corporations.

Competitive Markets and Excess Returns

A perfectly competitive industry is one characterized by costless entry and exit, undifferentiated products, and increasing marginal costs of production. These undifferentiated products, also known as commodities, are sold exclusively on the basis of price. In such an industry, as every student of microeconomics knows, each firm produces at the point at which price equals marginal cost. Long-run equilibrium exists when price also equals average cost. At this point, total revenue equals total cost for each firm taken individually and for the industry as a whole. This cost includes the required return on the capital used by each firm. Thus, in the long run, the actual return on capital in a competitive industry must equal the required return.

Any excess return quickly attracts new entrants to the market. Their additional capacity and attempts to gain market share lead to a reduction in the industry price and a lowering of returns for all market participants. In the early 1980s, for example, the high returns available in the video-game market, combined with the ease of entry into the business, attracted a host of competitors. This led to a red-ink bath for the industry in 1983, followed by the exit of a number of firms from the industry. Conversely, should the actual return for the industry be below the required return, the opposite happens. The weakest competitors exit the industry, resulting in an increase in the industry price and a boost in the overall return on capital for the remaining firms. This process, which is now taking place in the oil refining business, continues until the actual return once again equals the required return.

The message from this analysis is clear: the run-of-the-mill firm operating in a highly competitive, commodity-type industry is doomed from the start in its search for positive net present value projects. Only firms that can bring to bear on new projects competitive advantages that are difficult to replicate have any assurance of earning excess returns in the long run. These advantages take the form of either being the low-cost producer in the industry or being able to add value to the product—value for which customers are willing to pay a high (relative to cost) price. The latter type of advantage involves the ability to convert a commodity business into one characterized by products differentiated on the basis of service and/or quality. By creating such advantages, a firm can impose barriers to entry by potential competitors, resulting in a less-than-perfectly competitive market and the possibility of positive NPV projects.

Barriers to Entry and Positive Net Present Value Projects

As we have just seen, the ability to discourage new entrants to the market by erecting barriers to entry is the key to earning rates of return that consistently exceed capital costs. If these barriers did not exist, new competitors would enter the market and drive down the rate of return to the the required return. High barriers to entry and the threat of a strong reaction from entrenched competitors will reduce the risk of entry and so prolong the opportunity to earn excess returns.

This analysis suggests that successful investments (those with positive NPVs) share a common characteristic: they are investments that involve creating, preserving, and even enhancing competitive advantages that serve as barriers to entry. In line with this conclusion, the successful companies described by Thomas Peters and Robert Waterman in their bestseller, *In Search of Excellence,* were able to define their strengths—marketing, customer contact, new product innovation, low-cost manufacturing, etc.— and then build on them. They have resisted the temptation to move into new businesses that look attractive but require corporate skills they do not have.

A clearer understanding of the potential barriers to competitive entry can help to identify potential value-creating investment opportunities. This section now takes a closer look at the five major sources of barriers to entry—economies of scale, product differentiation, cost disadvantages, access to distribution channels, and government policy—and suggests some lessons for successful investing.[1]

Economies of Scale

Economies of scale exist whenever a given increase in the scale of production, marketing, or distribution results in a less-than-proportional increase in cost. The existence of scale economies means that there are *inherent cost advantages in being large.* The more significant these scale economies, therefore, the greater the cost disadvantage faced by a new entrant to the market. Scale economies in marketing, service, research, and production are probably the principal barriers to entry in the mainframe computer industry, as GE, RCA, and Xerox discovered to their sorrow. It is estimated, for example, that IBM spent over $5 billion to develop its innovative System 360, which it brought out in 1963. In natural resource industries, firms such as Alcan, the Canadian aluminum company, and Exxon are able to fend off new market entrants by exploiting economies of scale in production and transportation.

High capital requirements go hand-in-hand with economies of scale. In order to take advantage of

scale economies in production, marketing, or new product development, firms must often make enormous up-front investments in plant and equipment, research and development, and advertising. These capital requirements themselves serve as a barrier to entry; the more capital required, the higher the barrier to entry. This is particularly true in industries such as petroleum refining, mineral extraction, and mainframe computers.

A potential entrant to a market characterized by scale economies in production will be reluctant to enter unless the market has grown sufficiently to permit the construction and profitable utilization of an economically-sized plant. Otherwise, the new entrant will have to cut price to gain market share, destroying in the process the possibility of abnormal profits. By expanding in line with growth in the market, therefore, entrenched competitors can preempt profitable market entry by new competitors.

Consider, for example, the economics of the cement industry. The low value-to-weight ratio of cement makes the cement business a very regional one; beyond a radius of about 150 to 200 miles from the cement plant, the costs of transport become prohibitive unless cheap water or rail transportation is available. At the same time, the significant economies of scale available in cement production limit the number of plants a given region can support. For instance, suppose that demand in a land-locked region is sufficient to support only one or two modern cement plants. By expanding production and adding substantial new capacity to that already available, a firm can significantly raise the price of market entry by new firms and make plant expansion or replacement by existing competitors look much less attractive. This type of move obviously requires a longer timeframe and the willingness to incur potential losses until the market grows larger.

Scale economies are all-important in the grocery retailing business, on the level of the individual store as well as the city-wide market. Whether a store has $100,000 or $10,000,000 in annual sales, it still needs a manager. In addition, the cost of constructing and outfitting a supermarket doesn't increase in proportion to the number of square feet of selling space. Thus, the ratio of expenses to sales exhibits a significant decline as the volume of sales rises.

---

1. See, for example, Michael E. Porter, "How Competitive Forces Shape Strategy," *Harvard Business Review,* March-April 1979, pp. 137-145 for a good summary and discussion of these barriers to entry and their implications for corporate strategy.

Similarly, whether it has 10 percent or 25 percent of a given market, a supermarket chain has to advertise and supply its stores from a warehouse. The higher the share of market, the lower the advertising cost per customer, the faster the warehouse will turn over its inventory, and the more likely its delivery trucks will be used to capacity. These cost efficiencies translate directly into a higher return on capital.

The relationship between the market dominance of a supermarket chain in a given market and its profitability is evident in the relative returns for firms following contrasting expansion strategies. Chains such as Kroger and Winn-Dixie, which have opted for deep market penetration in a limited geographic area (ranking number 1 or 2 in almost all their major markets), have realized returns on equity that far exceed their equity costs. On the other hand, chains such as A&P and National Tea, which expanded nationally by gaining toe-hold positions in numerous, though scattered markets, have consistently earned less than their required returns.

Computer store chains, to take another example, also enjoy significant economies of scale. These show up in the form of lower average costs for advertising, distribution, and training. Even more important, they receive larger discounts on their products from the manufacturers.

LESSON #1: *Investments that are structured to fully exploit economies of scale are more likely to be successful than those that are not.*

Product Differentiation

Some companies, such as Coca-Cola and Procter & Gamble, take advantage *of enormous advertising expenditures* and *highly-developed marketing skills* to differentiate their products and keep out potential competitors wary of the high marketing costs and risks of new product introduction. Others sell expertise and high-quality products and service. For example, Nalco Chemical, a specialty chemical firm, is a problem-solver and counselor to its customers while Worthington Industries, which turns semifinished steel into finished steel, has a reputation for quality workmanship that allows it to charge premium prices. As indicated in the introduction to this article, both have been handsomely rewarded for their efforts, with average equity returns exceeding 20 percent annually from 1974 to 1983.

Pharmaceutical companies have traditionally earned high returns by developing unique products that are protected from competition by patents, trademarks, and brand names. Three outstanding examples are SmithKline Beckman's Tagamet, for treating stomach ulcers, and Hoffman-La Roche's tranquilizers, Librium and Valium. American Home Products also owes a great deal of its profitability to several patented drugs.

Similarly, the development of technologically-innovative products has led to high profits for firms such as Xerox and Philips (Netherlands). A fat R&D budget, however, is only part of the activity leading to commercially successful innovations. To a great extent, the risks in R&D are commercial, not technical. Firms that make technology pay off are those that closely link their R&D activities with market realities. They always ask what the customer needs. Even if they have strong technology, they do their marketing homework. This requires close contact with customers, as well as careful monitoring of the competition. Studies also indicate that top management involvement is extremely important in those firms that rely heavily and effectively on technology as a competitive weapon. This requires close coordination and communication between technical and business managers.

Failure to heed that message has led to Xerox's inability to replicate its earlier success in the photocopy business. In addition to its revolutionary copier technology, Xerox developed some of the computer industry's most important breakthroughs, including the first personal computer and the first network connecting office machines. But, through a lack of market support, it has consistently failed to convert its research prowess into successful high-tech products.

Service is clearly the key to extraordinary profitability for many firms. The ability to differentiate its computers from others through exceptional service has enabled IBM to dominate the worldwide mainframe computer business with a market share of over 75 percent. Similarly, Caterpillar Tractor has combined dedication to quality with outstanding distribution and after-market support to differentiate its line of construction equipment and so gain a commanding 35 percent share of the world market for earthmoving machinery. American firms, such as the auto companies, that have been somewhat lax in the area of product quality have fallen prey to those Japanese firms for which quality has become a religion.

What may not be obvious from these examples is that it is possible to differentiate anything, even

> *What may not be obvious from these examples is that it is possible to differentiate anything, even commodity businesses.*

commodity businesses such as fast food, potato chips, theme parks, candy bars, and printing. The answer seems to be quality and service as companies like McDonald's, Disney, Frito-Lay, Mars, and Deluxe Check Printers have demonstrated. Cleanliness and consistency of service are the hallmarks of Disney and McDonald's, with both rating at the top of almost everyone's list as the best mass service providers in the world. Similarly, it is said that at Mars plants are kept so clean one can "eat off the factory floor."

High quality work and dependability have helped Deluxe Check Printers flourish in a world supposedly on the verge of doing without checks. It fills better than 95 percent of orders in two days, and ships 99 percent error free.

Frito-Lay's special edge is a highly-motivated 10,000 person sales force dedicated to selling its chips. They guarantee urban supermarkets and rural mom and pop stores alike a 99.5 percent chance of a daily call. Although they get only a small weekly salary, the sales people receive a 10 percent commission on all the Lay's, Doritos, and Tostitos they sell. So they hustle, setting up displays, helping the manager in any way possible, all the while angling for that extra foot of shelf space or preferred position that can mean additional sales income. There are also tremendous side benefits to close contact with the market. Frito can get a market test rolling in ten days and respond to a new competitive intrusion in 48 hours.

A similar level of service is provided by Sysco, a $2 billion firm in the business of wholesaling food to restaurants and other institutional business. It is a very mundane, low-margin business—one where low cost is seemingly all that matters. Yet, behind its slogan, "Don't sell food, sell peace of mind," Sysco earns margins and a return on capital that is the envy of the industry. Even in that business, a large number of customers will pay a little more for personalized service. And in a low-margin business, a little more goes a long way.

Sysco's secret was to put together a force of over 2,000 "marketing associates" who assure customers that "98 percent of items will be delivered on time." They also provide much more, going to extraordinary lengths to produce a needed item for a restauranteur at a moment's notice. Chairman John Baugh summed it up as follows:

The typical food service company picks a case of frozen french fries out of the warehouse and drops it on the restaurant's back porch. Where is the skill in that? Where is the creativity? Service isn't a free lunch. The price tag (and cost) is higher; but even at the lower end of the market, most customers (not all, to be sure) will pay some additional freight for useful service.[2]

Other firms have made their owners wealthy by understanding that they too are *selling solutions to their customers' problems,* not hardware or consumables. John Patterson, the founder of National Cash Register, used to tell salesmen: "Don't talk machines, talk the prospect's business." Thomas Watson, the founder of IBM, patterned his sales strategy on that admonition. Thus, while other companies were talking technical specifications, his salesmen were marketing solutions to understood problems, such as making sure the payroll checks came out on time.

These days, Rolm Corp., a leader in the crowded market for office communications systems, is taking a page out of IBM's book. It has built up a service force of over 3,400 employees whose main job is to reassure customers mystified by the complexities of modern technology, while selling them more equipment. The common strategic vision and approaches of the two firms may help explain why IBM, when it decided to enter the telecommunications business, did so by acquiring Rolm (in 1984) rather than another firm.

The contrast between the approaches followed by IBM and DEC is particularly revealing. DEC has developed excellent narrow-purpose minicomputers, trusting that application solutions can be developed by others to justify advanced technology. That simple strategy—selling machines on their merits to scientists and engineers—worked spectacularly for two decades, turning DEC into the world's second-largest computer company. One consequence of that strategy, however, is that DEC never needed to and never did develop the kind of marketing orientation IBM is noted for.

The advent of the personal computer, which can perform many of the functions of a minicomputer at a fraction of the cost, has underscored the shortcomings inherent in DEC's product- rather than market-oriented strategy. As its traditional business has stagnated, DEC has attempted to reposition itself to

---

2. Quoted in *Forbes,* October 11, 1982, p. 58.

compete in the nimble new world of personal computers. But it has failed thus far to adapt marketing and sales strategies to the new, less technically-sophisticated customers it has tried to attract.

The results are painfully obvious. On October 18, 1983, DEC's stock nose-dived 21 points after it announced that quarterly earnings would be 75 percent lower than the year before. Thus far at least, IBM, and its strategy of utilizing proven technology to market solutions to known problems, has prevailed in the marketplace.

LESSON #2: Investments designed to create a position at the high end of anything, including the high end of the low end, differentiated by a quality or service edge, will generally be profitable.

Cost Disadvantages

Entrenched companies often have cost advantages that are unavailable to potential entrants, independent of economies of scale. Sony and Texas Instruments, for example, take advantage of the *learning curve* to reduce costs and drive out actual and potential competitors. This concept is based on the old adage that you improve with practice. With greater production experience, costs can be expected to decrease because of more efficient use of labor and capital, improved plant layout and production methods, product redesign and standardization, and the substitution of less expensive materials and practices. This cost decline creates a barrier to entry because new competitors, lacking experience, face higher unit costs than established companies. By achieving market leadership, usually by price cutting, and thereby accumulating experience faster, this entry barrier can be most effectively exploited.

Proprietary technology, protected by legally-enforceable patents, provides another cost advantage to established companies. This is the avenue taken by many of the premiere companies in the world, including 3M, West Germany's Siemens, Japan's Hitachi, and Sweden's L. M. Ericsson.

Monopoly control of low-cost raw materials is another cost advantage open to entrenched firms. This was the advantage held for so many years by Aramco (Arabian-American Oil Company), the consortium of oil companies that until the early 1980s had exclusive access to low-cost Saudi Arabian oil.

McDonald's has developed yet another advantage vis-a-vis potential competitors: it has already acquired, at a relatively low cost, many of the best fast-food restaurant locations. Favorable locations are also important to supermarkets and department stores.

A major cost advantage enjoyed by IBM's personal computer is the fact that software programs are produced first for it since it has a commanding share of the market. Only later—if at all—are these programs, which now number in the thousands, rewritten for other brands. Companies that don't develop IBM look-alikes must either write their own software, pay to have existing software modified for their machines, or wait until the software houses get around to rewriting their programs.

Sometimes, however, new entrants enjoy a cost advantage over existing competitors. This is especially true in industries undergoing deregulation, such as the airlines and trucking. In both of these industries, regulation long insulated firms from the rigors of competition and fare wars. Protected as they were, carriers had little incentive to clamp down on costs. And still they were quite profitable. The excess returns provided by the regulatory barrier to entry were divided in effect between the firms's stockholders and their unionized employees.

Deregulation has exposed these firms to new competitors not saddled with outmoded work rules and high-cost employees. For example, new low-cost competitors in the airline industry, such as People's Express and Southwest Airlines, have much lower wages (about half of what big airlines pay) and more flexible work rules (which, for example, permit pilots to load baggage and flight attendants to man reservations phones).

One firm that managed to stay ahead of the game is Northwest Airlines. For years, Northwest has been run as if competition were fierce, while still making the most of the protections of regulations. It gained a reputation for fighting labor-union demands and hammered away to increase productivity. As a result, Northwest's overhead costs are only about 2 percent of total costs, compared with about 5 percent for major competitors. Similarly, its labor costs are about two-thirds the industry average. Consequently, it is the most efficient of the major airlines, which has greatly enhanced its competitive position.

LESSON #3: Investments aimed at achieving the lowest delivered cost position in the industry, coupled with a pricing policy to expand market share, are likely to succeed, especially if the cost reductions are proprietary.

A change in government regulations can greatly affect the value of current and prospective investments in an industry.

Access to Distribution Channels

Gaining distribution and shelf space for their products is a major hurdle that newcomers to an industry must overcome. Most retailers of personal computers, for example, limit their inventory to around five lines. Currently, over 200 manufacturers are competing for this very limited amount of shelf space. Moreover, the concentration of retail outlets among chains means that new computer makers have even fewer avenues to the consumer. This presents new manufacturers with a Catch-22: you don't get shelf space until you are a proven winner, but you can't sell until you get shelf space.

Conversely, well-developed, better yet unique, distribution channels are a major source of competitive advantage for firms such as Avon, Tupperware, Procter & Gamble, and IBM. Avon, for example, markets its products directly to the consumer on a house-to-house basis through an international network of 900,000 independent sales representatives. Using direct sales has enabled Avon to reduce both its advertising expenditures and the amount of money it has tied up in the business. Potential competitors face the daunting task of organizing, financing, and motivating an equivalent sales force. Thus, its independent representatives are the entry barrier that allows Avon consistently to earn exceptional profit margins in a highly competitive industry. Similarly, the sales forces of Frito-Lay, Sysco, and IBM help those firms distribute their products and raise the entry barrier in three very diverse businesses.

Conversely, the lack of a significant marketing presence in the U.S. is perhaps the greatest hindrance to Japanese drug makers attempting to expand their presence in the U.S. Marketing drugs in the U.S. requires considerable political skill in maneuvering through the U.S. regulatory process, as well as rapport with American researchers and doctors. This latter requirement means that pharmaceutical firms must develop extensive sales forces to maintain close contact with their customers. There are economies of scale here: the cost of developing such a sales force is the same, whether it sells one product or one hundred. Thus, only firms with extensive product lines can afford a large sales force, raising a major entry barrier to Japanese drug firms trying to go it alone in the U.S.

One way the Japanese drug firms have found to get around this entry barrier is to form joint ventures with American drug firms, in which the Japanese supply the patents and the American firms provide the distribution network. Such licensing arrangements are a common means of entering markets requiring strong distribution capabilities. Union Carbide, for example, follows a strategy of using high R&D expenditures to generate a diversified and innovative line of new products. Since each new product line requires a different marketing strategy and distribution network, firms like Union Carbide are more willing to trade their technology for royalty payments and equity in a joint venture with companies already in the industry.

LESSON #4: Investments devoted to gaining better product distribution often lead to higher profitability.

Government Policy

We have already seen in the case of the airline, trucking, and pharmaceutical industries that government regulations can limit, or even foreclose, entry to potential competitors. Other government polices that raise partial or absolute barriers to entry include import restrictions, environmental controls, and licensing requirements. For example, American quotas on Japanese cars have limited the ability of companies such as Mitsubishi and Mazda to expand their sales in the U.S., leading to a higher return on investment for American car companies. Similarly, environmental regulations that restrict the development of new quarries have greatly benefited those firms, such as Vulcan Materials, that already had operating quarries. The effects of licensing restrictions on the taxi business in New York City are reflected in the high price of a medallion (giving one the right to operate a cab there), which in turn reflects the higher fares that the absence of competition has resulted in.

A change in government regulations can greatly affect the value of current and prospective investments in an industry. For example, the Motor Carrier Act of 1935 set up a large barrier to entry into the business as it allowed the Interstate Commerce Commission to reject applicants to the industry. The Act also allowed the truckers themselves to determine their rates collectively, typically on the basis of average operating efficiency. Thus carriers with below-average operating costs were able to sustain above-average levels of profitability. It is scarcely surprising, then, that the major trucking companies pulled out all the stops in lobbying against deregulation. As expected, the onset of trucking deregulation, which greatly reduced the entry barrier, has led to lower profits for trucking companies and a significant drop in their stock prices.

LESSON #5: Investments in projects protected from competition by government regulation can lead to extraordinary profitability. However, what the government gives, the government can take away.

Investment Strategies and Financial Returns: Some Evidence

Ultimately, the viability of a value-creating strategy can only be assessed by examining the empirical evidence. Theory and intuition tell us that companies which follow strategies geared towards creating and preserving competitive advantages should earn higher returns on their investments than those which do not. And so they do.

William K. Hall studied eight major domestic U.S. industries and the diverse strategies followed by member firms.[3] The period selected for this study was 1975-1979, a time of slow economic growth and high inflation. These were especially hard times for the eight basic industries in Hall's study. They all faced significant cost increases that they were unable to offset fully through price increases. In addition, companies in each of these industries were forced by regulatory agencies to make major investments to comply with a variety of health, environmental, safety, and product performance standards. To compound their problems, competition from abroad grew stronger during this period. Foreign competitors achieved high market shares in three of the industries (steel, tire and rubber, and automotive); moderate shares in two others (heavy-duty trucks and construction and materials handling equipment); and entry positions in the other three (major home appliances, beer, and cigarettes).

The net result of these adverse trends is that profitability in the eight basic industries has generally fallen to or below the average for manufacturers in the United States. According to Table 1, the average return on equity for these eight industries was 12.9 percent, substantially below the 15.1 percent median return for the Fortune 1000. A number of firms in

these industries have gone bankrupt, are in financial distress, or have exited their industry.

Yet this tells only part of the story. As Table 1 also shows, some companies survived, indeed prospered, in this same hostile environment. They did this by developing business strategies geared towards achieving one or both of the following competitive positions within their respective industries and then single-mindedly tailoring their investments to attain these positions:

1. Become the lowest total delivered cost producer in the industry, while maintaining an acceptable service/quality combination relative to competition.
2. Develop the highest product/service/quality differentiated position within the industry, while maintaining an acceptable delivered cost structure.

Table 2 provides a rough categorization of the strategies employed by the two top-performing companies in each of the eight industries studied. In most cases, the industry profit leaders chose to occupy only one of the two competitive positions. Perhaps this is because the resources and skills necessary to achieve a low-cost position are incompatible with those needed to attain a strongly differentiated position.

At least three of the 16 leaders, however, combined elements of both strategies with spectacular success. Caterpillar has combined lowest-cost manufacturing with outstanding distribution and after-sales service to move well ahead of its domestic and foreign competitors in profitability. Similarly, the U.S. cigarette division of Philip Morris has become the industry profit leader by combining the lowest-cost manufacturing facilities in the world with high-visibility brands, supported by high-cost promotion. Finally, Daimler Benz employs elements of both strategies, but in different business segments. It has the lowest cost position in heavy-duty trucks in Western Europe, along with its exceptionally high-quality, feature-differentiated line of Mercedes Benz cars.

Other examples of the benefits of attaining the low-cost position in an industry or picking and exploiting specialized niches in the market abound. For example, the low-cost route to creating positive NPV investments has been successfully pursued in, of all places, the American steel industry. The strategy has involved building up-to-date mini-mills employing non-union workers who earn substantially less than

---

3. William K. Hall, "Survival Strategies in a Hostile Environment," *Harvard Business Review,* September-October 1980, pp. 75-85.

TABLE 1
Return on Equity in Eight Basic Industries: 1975–1979*

Industry	Return on Equity	Leading Firm	Return on Equity
Steel	7.1%	Inland Steel	10.9%
Tire and rubber	**7.4**	**Goodyear**	**9.2**
Heavy-duty trucks	15.4	Paccar	22.8
Construction and ma-terials handling eq.	**15.4**	**Caterpillar**	**23.5**
Automotive	15.4	General Motors	19.8
Major home appliances	**10.1**	**Maytag**	**27.2**
Beer	14.1	G. Heilman Brewing	25.8
Cigarettes	**18.2**	**Philip Morris**	**22.7**
Average—eight industries	*12.9*	*Average—leading companies*	*20.2*
Median—Fortune 1000	*15.1*		

TABLE 2
Competitive Strategies Employed by Leaders in Eight Basic Industries*

Industry	Low Cost Leader	Meaningful Differentiation	Both Employed Simultaneously
Steel	Inland Steel	National	—
Tire and rubber	**Goodyear**	**Michelin (French)**	
Heavy-duty trucks	Ford, Daimler Benz (German)	—	—
Construction and materials handling equipment	—	**John Deere**	**Caterpillar**
Automotive	General Motors	Daimler Benz	—
Major home appliances	**Whirlpool**	**Maytag**	—
Beer	Miller	G. Heilman Brewing	—
Cigarettes	**R. J. Reynolds**	—–	**Philip Morris**

*From William K. Hall, "Survival Strategies in a Hostile Environment"

members of the United Steelworkers Union. Mini-mills melt scrap, which is cheaper in the U.S. than any-where else, and their modern plant and equipment and simplified work practices greatly reduce their need for labor. Chapparal Steel of Midlothian, Texas, a big—and profitable—mini-mill, has pared its labor costs to a mere $29 on a ton of structural steel. This compares with average labor costs of $75 a ton at big integrated U.S. plants.

The chief disadvantage is that their steelmaking capabilities are limited. They can't, for example, make the industry's bread-and-butter item: flat-rolled steel. But in the product areas where mini-mills do compete—rod, bar, and small beams and shapes—big producers have all but surrendered. So,

too, have foreign mills. In just two years, Nucor Corp's mini-mill in Plymouth, Utah cut the Japanese share of California's rod and bar market from 50 to 10 percent.

Taking a different tack, Armstrong Rubber Co. has specialized in grabbing small market segments overlooked by its rivals. Today, Armstrong ranks second in industrial tires and second or third in both the replacement market for all-season radials and in tires for farm equipment and off-road recreational vehicles. Its niche-picking strategy relies heavily on the design and production innovations arising from its large investments in research and development.

A number of chemical firms, including Hercules, Monsanto, Dow, and Belgium's Solvay, have attempted to lessen their dependence on the production of commodity chemicals and plastics by investing heavily in highly profitable specialty products for such industries as electronics and defense. These specialty chemicals are typically sold in smaller quantities but at higher prices than traditional bulk commodity chemicals. Perhaps the most successful chemical "niche-picker" is Denmark's Novo Industri—one of the world's largest producers of enzymes and insulin, and a pioneer in genetic engineering techniques. Novo's continued success is largely due to its ability to find and exploit small but profitable market niches. For instance, industry analysts credit Novo's success at selling enzymes in Japan to the company's ability to outdo even Japanese purity standards and to concentrate on small specialty markets that Japan's chemical giants can't be bothered with. In fact, most of Novo's markets appear too small for giant chemical firms such as Germany's Hoechst or Du Pont to pursue.

James River Corp. has combined cost cutting with product differentiation to achieve spectacular growth and profits in the paper-goods industry, an industry where many companies are struggling to hold their own. Typically, James River buys other companies' cast-off paper mills and remakes them in its own image. It abandons all or most of the commodity-grade paper operations. It refurbishes old equipment, and supplements it with new machinery to produce specialty products (automobile and coffee filters, airline ticket paper, peel-off strips for Band-Aids, and cereal-box liners) that are aimed at specific markets and provide higher profits with less competition. At the same time, James River cuts costs by extracting wage concessions from workers and dismissing most executives. It also raises the productivity of those employees who stay by allowing many of them to join the company's lucrative *profit-sharing* programs. James River's success in following this two-pronged strategy is reflected in its 1983 net income of $55.1 million, 332 times larger than its 1970 earnings of $166,000.

Designing an Investment Strategy

Although a strong competitive edge in technology or marketing skills may enable a firm to earn excess returns, these barriers to entry will eventually erode, leaving the firm susceptible to increased com-petition. Existing firms are entering new industries and there are growing numbers of firms from a greater variety of countries, leading to new, well-financed competitors able to meet the high marketing costs and enormous capital outlays necessary for entry. Caterpillar Tractor, for example, faces a continuing threat from low-cost foreign competitors, especially Japan's Komatsu, which is second in worldwide sales. To stay on top, therefore, a firm's strategy must be constantly evolving, seeking out new opportunities and fending off new competitors.

Xerox clearly illustrates the problems associated with losing a competitive ege. For many years, Xerox was the king of the copier market, protected by its patents on xerography, with sales and earnings growing over 20 percent annually. The loss of its patent protection has brought forth numerous well-heeled competitors, including IBM, 3M, Kodak, and the Japanese, resulting in eroding profits and diminished growth prospects. Xerox has tried to transfer its original competitive advantage in technology to new products designed for the so-called office of the future. However, its difficulties in closely coordinating its R&D and marketing efforts have led to a series of serious, self-confessed blunders in acquisitions, market planning, and product development. For example, as mentioned earlier, the basic technology for the personal computer was developed by Xerox's Palo Alto Research Center in the early 1970s, but it remained for Apple Computer and IBM to capitalize on this revolutionary product.

More recently, Xerox's 1982 acquisition of Crum & Forster, a property and casualty insurance company, has called into question the company's strategy. It is unclear how Xerox, for whom high technology has been the chief competitive advantage, can earn excess returns in a business in which it has no experience. As we have already seen, firms that stick to their knitting are more likely to succeed than those that don't.

Common sense tells us that, in order to achieve excess returns over time, the distinctive competitive advantage held by the firm must be difficult or costly to replicate. If it is easily replicated, it will not take long for actual or potential competitors to apply the same concept, process, or organizational structure to their operations. The competitive advantage of experience, for example, will evaporate unless a firm can keep the tangible benefits of its experience proprietary and force its competitors to go through the same learning process. Once a firm loses its competitive advantage, its profits will erode to a point where it can no longer earn excess returns. For this reason, the firm's competitive advantage has to be constantly monitored and maintained so as to ensure the existence of an effective barrier to entry into the market. Should these barriers to entry break down, the firm must react quickly either to reconstruct them or build new ones.

Caterpillar has reacted to Komatsu's challenge by attempting to slash its costs, closing plants, shifting productions overseas, forcing union and nonunion workers alike to take pay cuts, eliminating many positions, and pressuring its suppliers to cut prices and speed deliveries. To get lower prices, the company is shopping around for hungrier suppliers, including foreign companies. This is reflected in its philosophy of worldwide sourcing, as described by its director of purchasing: "We're trying to become international in buying as well as selling. We expect our plants, regardless of where they're located, to look on a worldwide basis for sources of supply."[4] For example, German and Japanese companies now supply crankshafts once made exclusively in the U.S.

One important source of extra profit is the quickness of management to recognize and use information about new, lower-cost production opportunities. The excess profits, however, are temporary, lasting only until competitors discover these opportunities for themselves. For example, purchasing the latest equipment will provide a temporary cost advantage, but this advantage will disappear as soon as competitors buy the equipment for their own plants. Only if the equipment is proprietary will the firm be able to maintain its cost advantage. Along the same line, many American electronics and textile firms shifted production facilities to Taiwan, Hong Kong, and other Asian locations to take advantage of lower labor costs there. However, as more firms took advantage of this cost reduction opportunity, competition in the consumer electronics and textiles markets in the U.S. intensified, causing domestic prices to drop and excess profits to dissipate. In fact, firms in competitive industries must continually seize new non-proprietary cost reduction opportunities, not to earn excess returns but simply to make normal profits, or just survive.

Similarly, marketing-oriented firms can earn excess returns by being among the first to recognize and exploit new marketing opportunities. For exam- ple, Crown Cork & Seal, the Philadelphia-based bottle-top maker and can maker, reacted to slowing growth in its U.S. business by expanding overseas. It set up subsidiaries in such countries as Thailand, Malaysia, Ethiopia, Zambia, Peru, Ecuador, Brazil, and Argentina. In so doing, as it turns out, they guessed correctly that in those developing, urbanizing societies, people would eventually switch from home-grown produce to food in cans and drinks in bottles.

Profitable markets, however, have a habit of eventually attracting competition. Thus, to be assured of having a continued supply of value-creating investments on hand, the firm must institutionalize its strategy of cost reduction and/or product differentiation. Successful companies seem to do this by creating a corporate culture—a set of shared values, norms, and beliefs—that has as one of its elements an obsession with some facet of their performance in the marketplace. McDonald's has an obsessive concern for quality control, IBM for customer service, and 3M for innovation. Forrest Mars set the tone for his company by going into a rage if he found an improperly wrapped candy bar leaving the plant. In order to maintain its low-cost position in the structural steel market, Chaparral Steel has teams of workers and foremen scour the world in search of the latest production machinery and methods.

Conversely, AT&T's manufacturing orientation, which focused on producing durable products with few options, was well-suited to the regulated environment in which it operated throughout most of its existence. But such an inward-looking orientation is likely to be a significant barrier to the company's ability to compete against the likes of IBM and other market-oriented, high-tech companies that react quickly to consumer demand. Prior to the breakup of AT&T, the manufacturers at Western Electric, AT&T's manufacturing arm, freely decided which products to make and when. They controlled the factories, supplying telephones to a captive market of Bell companies. AT&T was essentially an order taker, no more needing a sales force than any other utility does. There were no competitors forcing quicker market reaction nor any marketers challenging manufacturers' decisions.

Although AT&T claims that it is now "market-driven," evidence abounds that the company's older, entrenched manufacturing mentality is still dominant. Unless AT&T can change its corporate cul-

---

4. As quoted in the *Wall Street Journal* (August 10, 1971), p.1.

ture—a difficult and demanding task for any company, much less for a giant set in its ways—and marry manufacturing and marketing, it will have a difficult time competing with firms such as IBM in the office automation and computer businesses it has set its sights on.

The basic insight here is that sustained success in investing is not so much a matter of building new plants as of seeking out lower-cost production processes embodied in these plants, coming up with the right products for these plants to produce, and adding the service and quality features that differentiate these products in the marketplace. In other words, it comes down to people and how they are organized and motivated. The cost and difficulty of creating a corporate culture that adds value to capital investments is the ultimate barrier to entry; unlike the latest equipment, money alone can't buy it.

In the words of Maurice R. (Hank) Greenberg, president of American Insurance Group (A.I.G.), a worldwide network of insurance companies that has enjoyed spectacular sucess by pioneering in territory relatively unpopulated by competitors, "You can't imitate our global operation. It's just incapable of being reproduced. Domestically, we have some imitators for pieces of our business, but not the entire business. And in any event, you can only imitate what we've done. You can't imitate what we're thinking. You can't copy what we're going to do tomorrow."[5]

Corporate Strategy and Foreign Investment

Most of the firms we have discussed are multinational corporations (MNCs) with worldwide operations. For many of these MNCs, becoming multinational was the end result of an apparently haphazard process of overseas expansion. But, as international operations become a more important source of profit and as domestic and foreign competitors become more aggressive, it is apparent that domestic survival for many firms is increasingly dependent on their success overseas. To ensure this success, multinationals must develop global strategies that will enable them to maintain their competitive edge both at home and abroad.

Overseas Expansion and Survival

It is evident that if one's competitors gain access to lower-cost sources of production abroad, following them overseas may be a prerequisite for domestic survival. One strategy often followed by firms for whom cost is the key consideration, such as Chapparal Steel, is to develop a global scanning capability to seek out lower-cost production sites or production technologies worldwide.

Economies of Scale. A somewhat less obvious factor motivating foreign investment is the effect of economies of scale. We have already seen that in a competitive market, prices will be forced close to marginal costs of production. Hence, firms in industries characterized by high fixed costs relative to variable costs must engage in volume selling just to break even.

A new term has arisen to describe the size necessary in certain industries to compete effectively in the global marketplace: *world scale.* These large volumes may be forthcoming only if firms expand overseas. For example, companies manufacturing products such as mainframe computers that require huge R&D expenditures often need a larger customer base than that provided by even a market as large as the United States in order to recapture their investment in knowledge. Similarly, firms in capital-intensive industries with significant economies of scale in production may also be forced to sell overseas in order to spread their overhead over a higher volume of sales.

To take an extreme case, L. M. Ericsson, the highly successful Swedish manufacturer of telecommunications equipment, is forced to think internationally when designing new products since its domestic market is too small to absorb the enormous R&D expenditures involved and to reap the full benefit of production scale economies. Thus, when Ericsson developed its revolutionary AXE digital switching system, it geared its design to achieve global market penetration.

Many firms have found that a local market presence is necessary in order to continue selling overseas. For example, a local presence has helped Data General adapt the design of its U.S. computers and software to the Japanese market, giving the company

---

5. Wyndham Robertson, "Nobody Tops A.I.G. in Intricacy—or Daring," *Fortune,* May 22, 1978, p. 99.

a competitive edge over other U.S. companies selling computers in Japan. Data General has also adopted some Japanese manufacturing techniques and quality-control procedures that will improve its competitive position worldwide.

More firms are preparing for global competition. For example, although Black & Decker has a 50 percent market share worldwide in power tools, new competitors like the Japanese are forcing the company to change its manufacturing and marketing operations. Black & Decker's new strategy is based on a marketing concept known as "globalization," which holds that the world is becoming more homogenized and that distinctions between markets are disappearing. By selling standardized products worldwide, a firm can take advantage of economies of scale, thereby lowering costs and taking business from MNCs that customize products for individual markets. Until recently, the latter strategy of customization was the one that Black & Decker followed; the Italian subsidiary made tools for Italians, the British subsidiary tools for Britons.

By contrast, Japanese power-tool makers such as Makita Electric Works don't care that Germans prefer high-powered, heavy-duty drills and that Americans want everything lighter. Instead, Makita's strategy, which has been quite successful, is based on the notion that if you make a good drill at a low price, it will sell from Brooklyn to Baden-Baden. In response, Black & Decker recently unveiled 50 new power tools, each standardized for world production. It plans to standardize future products as well, making only minimal concessions, which require only minor modifications, to cultural differences.

Knowledge Seeking. Some firms enter foreign markets for the purpose of gaining information and experience that is expected to prove useful elsewhere. For instance, Beecham, an English firm, deliberately set out to learn from its U.S. operations how to be more competitive, first in the area of consumer products and later in pharmaceuticals. This knowledge proved highly valuable in competing with American and other firms in its European markets. Unilever, the Anglo-Dutch corporation, learned to adapt to world markets, with impressive results, the marketing skills it acquired in the U.S. through its American affiliate Lever Bros.

In industries characterized by rapid product innovation and technical breakthroughs by foreign competitors, it pays constantly to track overseas developments. The Japanese excel in this. Japanese firms systematically and effectively collect information on foreign innovation and disseminate it within their own research and development, marketing, and production groups. The analysis of new foreign products as soon as they reach the market is an especially long-lived Japanese technique. One of the jobs of Japanese researchers is to tear down a new foreign computer and analyze how it works as a base on which to develop a product of their own that will outperform the original. In a bit of a switch, as pointed out above, Data General's Japanese operation is giving the company a close look at Japanese technology, enabling it quickly to pick up and transfer back to the United States new information on Japanese innovations in the areas of computer design and manufacturing. Similarly, Ford Motor Co. has used its European operations as an important source of design and engineering ideas and management talent.

Designing a Global Expansion Strategy

The ability to pursue systematically policies and investments congruent with worldwide survival and growth depends on four interrelated elements.

1. The first, and the key to the development of a successful global strategy, is to understand and then capitalize on those factors that have led to success in the past. In order for domestic firms to become global competitors, therefore, the sources of their domestic advantage must be transferable abroad. A competitive advantage predicated on government regulation, such as import restrictions, clearly doesn't fit in this category.

2. Second, this global approach to investment planning necessitates a systematic evaluation of individual entry strategies in foreign markets, a comparison of the alternatives, and selection of the optimal mode of entry.

3. The third important element is a continual audit of the effectiveness of current entry modes. As knowledge about a foreign market increases, for example, or sales potential grows, the optimal market penetration strategy will likely change.

4. Fourth, top management must be committed to becoming and/or staying a multinational corporation. Westinghouse demonstrated its commitment to international business by creating the new position of President-international and endowing its occupant with a seat on the company's powerful manage-

ment committee. A truly globally-oriented firm—one that asks, "Where in the *world* should we develop, produce, and sell our products and services?"—also requires an intelligence system capable of systematically scanning the world and understanding it, along with people who are experienced in international business and know how to use the information generated by the system.

Summary and Conclusions

We have seen that rates of return in competitive industries are driven down to their required returns. Excess profits quickly attract new entrants to the market, lowering returns until actual and required returns are again equal. Thus, the run-of-the-mill firm operating in a highly competitive market will be unable consistently to find positive net present value investments—ones which earn excess returns relative to their required returns. The key to generating a continual flow of positive NPV projects, therefore, is to erect and maintain barriers to entry against competitors. This involves either building defenses against potential competitors or finding positions in the industry where competition is the weakest.

The firm basically has two strategic options in its quest for competitive advantage: it can seek lower costs than its competitors or it can differentiate its product in a number of ways, including high advertising expenditures, product innovation, high product quality, and first-rate service.

Each of these options involves a number of specific investment decisions: construction of efficient-scale facilities and vigorous pursuit of cost reduction through accumulated experience, in the case of cost leadership; if product differentiation is the main goal, the focus is on advertising, R&D, quality control, customer-service facilities, distribution networks and the like. The more an investment widens a firm's competitive advantage and reduces the chances of successful replication by competitors, the greater the likelihood that investment will be successful.

Despite our understanding of the subject matter, it is difficult to give a set of rules to follow in developing profitable investment strategies. If it were possible to do so, competitors would follow them and dissipate any excess returns. One must be creative and quick to recognize new opportunities. Nevertheless, without dictating what should be done in every specific circumstance, there are some basic lessons we have learned from economic theory and the experiences of successful firms. The basic lessons are these:

1. Invest in projects that take advantage of your competitive edge. The corollary is, stick to doing one or two things and doing them well; don't get involved in businesses you are unfamiliar with.
2. Invest in developing, maintaining, and enhancing your competitive advantages.
3. Develop a global scanning capability. Don't be blindsided by new competitors or lower-cost production techniques or locations.
4. Pick market niches where there is little competition. Be prepared to abandon markets where competitors are catching up and apply your competitive advantages to new products or markets.

Assuming that a firm does have the necessary resources to be successful internationally, it must carefully plan for the transfer of these resources overseas. For example, it must consider how it can best utilize its marketing expertise, innovative technology, or production skills to penetrate a specific foreign market. Where a particular strategy calls for resources the firm lacks, such as an overseas distribution network, corporate management must first decide how and at what cost these resources can be acquired. It must then decide whether (and how) to acquire the resources or change its strategy.

Beta Is Dead!
Long Live Beta!

by Jason MacQueen,
Quantec, Ltd.

Introduction

The philosophy of natural science as expounded by Karl Popper prescribes a logico-empiricist methodology for invalidating new theoretical models of the observed world, such as those hypothesized in the applied investment field by Harry Markowitz and Bill Sharpe. Their particular paradigm-shift has resulted in a plethora of theoretical investment models, including the Capital Asset Pricing Model (CAPM). Recent papers by Richard Roll, however, have suggested that the CAPM may not be susceptible to invalidation by such methodological tests.

The above paragraph shows quite clearly that it is, in fact, possible to do several things at once. Several imposing names are dropped, lots of long words are used, and a relatively simple statement is made utterly confusing—all in the same paragraph. The next Guiness Book of Records will surely have a new entry in this category, awarded to the author of the 1980 *Institutional Investor (I.I.)* article entitled "Is Beta Dead?," who managed to keep up this kind of thing for seven pages, thereby utterly confusing hundreds of investment managers.

This article attempts to remove some of that confusion. There are three main issues that need to be covered: first, the relationship between theory and reality; second, a review of the particular theories in question, the relationships between them, and how Richard Roll's criticisms affect them; third, and most important, how the practical applications of risk management are affected by these theoretical developments.

About Theories

Modern Portfolio Theory (MPT) developed from the work done by Harry Markowitz in 1952 on Portfolio Selection. In essence, it is based on the single observation that the proper task of the investment manager is not simply to maximize expected return, but to do so at an acceptable level of risk. If this were not so, portfolios would consist solely of managers' favorite stocks, instead of combining different stocks which, although all not equally attractive when considered individually, together offer the maximum expected return for a given level of risk.

This observation itself was not new. The originality of Markowitz's contribution lay in showing how investment risk could be measured and, hence, how mathematics could be used to select the best possible portfolio from all the different combinations of a chosen list of stocks.

There have been many refinements of the theory since. What is now commonly referred to as MPT is no longer a single theory, but several different theories or models, together with their applications. These models may be grouped into three main categories: versions of the Market Model, versions of the Capital Asset Pricing Model (CAPM), and versions of the Efficient Market Hypothesis (EMH).

The most common misconception about MPT is that these three theoretical constructs are all part of the same one and that, therefore, they stand or fall together. While some of the applications depend on two or more of the models, the individual models themselves do not depend heavily on each other. It is thus quite possible that one could be "wrong" while the others were "right."

It is, in any case, a mistake to think in terms of theories being "right" or "wrong" absolutely. All theories are "wrong" in that sense, including, for example, Einstein's Theory of Relativity.

Karl Popper (see first sentence) is a philosopher of science who has pointed out that, even if a particular theory were "right," you could never actually prove it. All you can ever hope to do is prove that it is wrong. If you have a new theory, you keep testing it in as many different ways as possible to see if it doesn't work. As long as it works fairly well, you can assume that it might be right, but you will never know for sure. A good theory is generally reckoned to be one that works quite well most of the time.

Newton's theory about the way planets and stars move was considered to be a good theory for several hundred years. Then some smart engineer invented an extra-powerful telescope with a very accurate scale, and a bored astronomer who had nothing else to do one evening noticed that the orbit of Mercury, the smallest planet around these parts, wasn't quite where it should be. Suddenly, Newton's theory wasn't so hot any more, and we all had to wait a few more years for Einstein to come along and say, "Well, it's nearly right, but if you put in this extra wrinkle here....," and so invent Relativity.

Unfortunately for Einstein, smart engineers and bored astronomers are two a penny these days, even allowing for inflation, and they've already noticed one or two places where his theory is a tiny bit out.

Newton's theory is still taught in schools, and is widely used in many different applications. To give a somewhat gruesome example, it is used for ranging artillery fire. The theory may not be exactly right, but it is certainly right enough to kill people. On the other hand, Einstein's theory was used to plot the flight of the Apollo spacecraft because Newton's theory wasn't good enough to provide the rigorous degree of accuracy required.

This point about a theory being useful without needing to be right was also made about the CAPM in the *I.I.* article mentioned earlier. In that article, Barr Rosenberg[1] was quoted as saying, "While the model is false, it's not very false." All models are false in this sense; what matters is how false they are, and to what extent this affects their application.

The Hard Part

Modern Portfolio Theory itself is about the effects of combining a set of stocks in different ways to get different portfolios. Clearly a portfolio that is 90% Ford and 10% IBM is going to behave differently from one that is 10% Ford and 90% IBM. MPT provides the mathematical framework necessary to work out how different the behavior of these two portfolios will be, given the characteristic behavior of the individual stocks.

According to MPT, there are only two relevant characteristics of common stocks for the purpose of structuring portfolios: risk and return. MPT shows us how to do clever sums (or to get computers to do them for us) and put numbers on these two items. Roughly speaking, these sums can be either fairly complicated (Bill Sharpe — gives investment managers a headache) or very complicated (Harry Markowitz — gives computers a headache). They can also be somewhere in between, or quite complicated (Barr Rosenberg — gives *Institutional Investor* a headache).

The Market Model

The method originally proposed by Markowitz for measuring risk involves comparing every stock against every other stock, which is not really feasible since it requires far too many calculations. In practice, some form of the Market Model is almost always used to simplify the calculation. There is clearly some common factor in the marketplace that affects all stocks to a greater or lesser extent. The Market Model is predicated on the fact that most stocks tend to go up and down together.[2] In mathematical terms, it is expressed simply as a linear equation which measures the degree of co-movement between an individual stock and the market.

There are many variations of the Market Model, such as the Single Index Model, the Multiple Index Model, the Diagonal Model and Rosenberg's Multiple Factor Model (see the following article in this journal). For the purposes of this article, however, the only important things about the Market Model are that:

---

1. Rosenberg is a co-author of "The Corporate Uses of Beta."

2. One result of this common movement is that most market indices, though based on different sets of stocks, nevertheless move very closely together. If there was no common factor, and all stocks moved independently of each other, then the different indices would move independently as well.

There is clearly some common factor in the marketplace that affects all stocks to a greater or lesser extent.

(a) it is based on the observable fact that most stocks tend to go up and down with "the market" to a greater or lesser extent, and
(b) it gives us a practical way of measuring the risk of an individual security or portfolio of securities.

Some form of the Market Model, then, is invariably used to measure investment risk. By comparing the behavior of a stock (or an industry, or a portfolio) against the behavior of the market, we can measure the degree to which that particular asset tends to move with the market ("systematic" risk, as measured by beta), and the extent to which it tends to move independently ("residual" or "unsystematic" risk). Insofar as its price does move with the market, we may also determine whether this movement is an exaggerated or a subdued version of the general market movement; that is, whether an individual stock has a "systematic" risk that is greater or less than the average "systematic" risk of the market.

Time Out

A few caveats are in order at this point. This discussion is not intended to be either rigorous (at least in the mathematical sense) or complete. Of necessity, it provides only the briefest overview of a large and complex body of research. A certain amount of artistic license is being exercised, for the sake of brevity and simplicity. For example, most of the analysis involved in MPT is statistical, so that wherever you see "measure," you should read "estimate."

The situation is further complicated by the fact that MPT has special technical meanings for some fairly common words. An "efficient" portfolio, for instance, is one which maximizes the expected portfolio return at a given level of risk. An alternative, and entirely equivalent, definition is that it minimizes portfolio risk at a given level of expected return. In other words, an "efficient" portfolio offers the best trade-off between risk and expected return.

From the investment manager's point of view, any individual stock should be regarded only as a possible component of a portfolio. As such, part of its total risk would be diversified away, while the rest would contribute to the risk of the overall portfolio. The component of a stock's total risk that is most relevant to the manager is that which cannot be diversified away. In an efficient portfolio, as much unnecessary risk is diversified away as possible; what is

left is usually known as "systematic" or "non-diversifiable" risk. It is this part of the total risk that is measured by beta.

An efficient portfolio is, in a sense, just an extreme case of a "diversified" portfolio. Any spread of investments into different assets constitutes diversification; and provided the risks of the different assets are not completely correlated (a highly unlikely event), the result will be a decrease in the overall level of investment risk. One of the more noteworthy statistical results to come out of the research underlying MPT is that, in a portfolio containing as few as 20 stocks, picked at random, 95% of the unnecessary risk will have been diversified away.

There is, however, a slight catch involved here. We should remember that "risk" should be interpreted as "opportunity for profit or loss." Diversifying away risk also means diversifying away opportunity. This notion is reflected in the use of risk-adjusted performance measurement. An investment should not simply be evaluated in terms of its expected (or achieved) return, but in terms of the risk incurred as well. This is MPT's way of saying that you can't have your cake and eat it, or nothing ventured, nothing gained.

Having got these caveats and definitions out of the way, we can now return to the models.

The Capital Asset Pricing Model

The Capital Asset Pricing Model (CAPM) is a theory about the relationship between stock returns (and, hence, prices) and systematic risk. In simple terms, the CAPM says that return and systematic risk go together; like love and marriage in the song, you can't have the one without the other. It also says that you won't get return for anything else, such as diversifiable risk. In efficient or well-diversified portfolios, therefore, the level of return will be determined directly by the amount of systematic risk, or portfolio beta. If, for instance, a given portfolio has a systematic risk equal to that of the market (i.e., beta = 1.0), that portfolio will fare pretty much as the market does. Higher beta portfolios will outperform low beta portfolios in bull markets, but will suffer proportionately greater losses during downturns.

In terms of risk-adjusted performance, then, the CAPM is somewhat remorseless. Return, it decrees, is doled out in direct proportion to the amount of systematic risk incurred; nothing more,

In a portfolio containing as few as 20 stocks, picked at random, 95% of the unnecessary risk will have been diversified away.

nothing less. One implication that all the highly-paid investment professionals were quick to spot was that this made them all redundant. On a risk-adjusted basis they would not only all be equal but, worse still, the fees they charged for their profound investment insight and consequent superior performance were unjustifiable. All the owner of the capital had to do was to buy a textbook on the CAPM, hire the proverbial college kid to write some computer programs, and then simply decide how much risk he was prepared to take.

This, in essence, is the theoretical rationale for the virtually self-managing "index funds" which have sprung up over the past few years, thereby eliminating the need for the services of a good number of portfolio managers.[3] Needless to say, the CAPM has not gained many adherents in the investment community.

The Theory of Efficient Markets

Lastly, we have the Efficient Market Hypotheses, of which there are three, called the Weak Form, the Stong Form, and the Semi-Strong Form. What these say (more or less firmly, depending on which form you use) is that you can't consistently beat the market, or at least it's very difficult.

The basic idea of the EMH is that when General Motors announces that they've worked out how to get 60 mpg from all their models by installing a $1.35 gizmo, all the smart types in business suits who had worked out that GM stock was worth $46 will get out their calculators and figure that it's now worth $49, give or take an eighth. Had you been possessed of a similar acuteness of faculty, and had you wished to profit from it by trading, the chances are that, by the time you were able to reach your broker, the price would already have risen to $49.

About Alphas

There is, of course, a very good reason why these three theories have become confused in people's minds. To explain this, we will need to look at an equation, although it will be the only one in the article. It is:

$R(i)$ = $A(i)$ + $B(i)$ * $R(m)$ where
$R(i)$ = return on asset i
$A(i)$ = alpha of asset i
$B(i)$ = beta of asset i
$R(m)$ = return on the market

Although it looks simple, this equation can appear in many different forms and with many different meanings. To begin with, it can be looking back, and talking about what has happened in the past; or it can be looking forward, and talking about expectations of the future. Sometimes the "R's" will be replaced by "R-R(f)'s," and sometimes you will see a "+ R(i)" stuck on the end. Different forms of this equation appear in all three of the models, which is why people think they're connected.

The easiest way to explain the differences between the three models is by examining the "A(i)," or alpha. What the equation is saying is that the return on asset 'i' can be broken into two parts: the alpha, which is *not* related to the market; and the beta of the asset multiplied by the market return, which is very definitely related to the market. Alpha is best thought of as an asset's excess rate of return (after due allowance has been made for general market effects). In risk-adjusted terms, individual stocks, or portfolios of stocks, with high positive alphas are the outstanding performers. And the best fund manager is one who achieves consistently positive alphas on his portfolio.

The Market Model doesn't have much to say about alphas, and allows them to be more or less any number. The CAPM says all the alphas should be zero. The EMH says that, with all these smart guys with calculators around, you'll be lucky to find any alphas of a decent size. We should not, of course, forget the real world, which is included in the following table:

THEORY	WHAT THE ALPHAS CAN BE
Market Model	**Just about anything**
C.A.P.M.	**All zero**
E.M.H.	**Mostly very small**
Reality	**Mostly small, some big**

The last line of this table puts all these theories into perspective. They're all wrong.

---

3. An index fund is a portfolio deliberately constructed to mirror the performance of a market index, generally the S&P 500.

Much Ado Abut Nothing Very Much

Presumably, you may say, the *Institutional Investor* article on the demise of beta was supposed to be about something — but what exactly? The story the article was based on is actually more than five years old, and is quite simple.

In 1977 Richard Roll, the noted professor at U.C.L.A., published the first of a series of academic papers showing that there is a bit of a problem with the CAPM. The problem has to do with something else Karl Popper said about theories: namely, that any new theory that someone thinks up should not be given the time of day unless it can be tested.

In the Middle Ages any young priest who wanted to get ahead would think up a new theory about how many angels could balance on the head of a pin. Karl Popper would have said that they were all wasting their time, since there was no way of testing their theories.

What.Richard Roll did was to point out that the CAPM can't be tested either. His reason was that to test it you first need to get hold of "the market," and that can't be done. A lot of so-called testing had already been done using "market proxies" such as the S&P 500. Roll pointed out, quite correctly, that using different proxies gave you different answers; and that, in any case, a proxy was merely a proxy and not what we were supposed to be testing.

The problem with using a proxy is that it is not the efficient market portfolio one would like it to be, but is an inefficient portfolio (i.e., one containing diversifiable risk), representing a subset of the market. Roll showed that one of the mathematical consequences of this was likely to be consistent errors in the betas.

It is worth pointing out that nearly everyone now agrees with this, just as everyone agrees that the CAPM is clearly not true. These errors are fundamentally different from the random errors that arise from the fact that betas are estimated statistically, rather than measured directly. We might also note, en passant, that the gentlemen with calculators continue to work out Discounted Present Values, and that stocks still tend to go up and down together. The validity of EMH and the Market Model, meanwhile, remains unaffected by this controversy over CAPM.

The crucial point is this: beta is supposed to measure the market-related risk of a stock or portfolio. By using the S&P 500 index as a market proxy, we are going to get betas that actually measure S&P 500-related risk. What we were hoping to

do is to separate the total risk of a stock into its diversifiable and non-diversifiable components. By using a proxy that is itself an inefficient portfolio, we run the risk of not separating the total risk into the correct proportions. The S&P 500-related beta could be bigger or smaller than the "real" beta.

The "furious controversy" that the *I.I.* article described is about how important these consistent errors in the betas are. If they are small (and there are good, though complex, reasons why this is likely to be the case), then we do not have much of a problem. If they are large, then we will have to be rather careful in those applications in which it is likely to matter.

No doubt the "furious controversy" will continue to rage in academic circles for some time yet, and when the dust settles it may well turn out that the current version of the CAPM belongs in the same basket as theories about angels and pins. More than likely, though, academics will have thought up a different version of the CAPM that can be tested. And when some subtle variant of the present CAPM is finally vindicated, it is a fairly safe bet that beta will remain (though possibly in a different manifestation) the reigning measure of investment risk.

About Plane Tickets

The average man-(or woman-)in-the-street does not run his (or her) life by needing to understand everything about something before doing it. Millions of people manage to buy plane tickets each year and fly around the place, yet only a handful of them know even the first thing about aerodynamics, metallurgy or structural engineering. Probably no one person knows all there is to know about how planes work. But, to live our lives and go about our business, we don't need to know. It is sufficient to know that a plane works, without needing to know why or how it works.

No doubt in certain academic circles there are furious controversies raging about the theory of wing design or the nature of metal fatigue, which will affect the next generation of supersonic stratospheric airliners. In the meantime, however, the rest of us can still buy plane tickets and fly to Florida for a spot of well-earned rest and relaxation.

As it is with plane tickets, so with betas. The prudent investor envisioned by ERISA can continue to use betas and risk analysis and the rest of MPT, secure in the knowledge that the things work, even while the academics rage.

Is beta dead? One way to answer the question is to calculate (or buy) a few, and then watch what happens as the market goes up and down. The question then becomes fairly simply: do portfolios of high (or medium, or low) beta stocks exaggerate (or match, or dampen) market swings? Answer: yes.

The fact of the matter is that betas do work, more or less well depending mostly on how sensible we've been in calculating them. All betas are relative to one or another market proxy. According to Einstein, everything else is relative too, so this should not be too much of a problem. Naturally something's beta will change if it is measured against different market indices. It will also change if it is measured against hemlines, which many experienced market men believe to be a very reliable market proxy. The point is that it has to be measured against something, and it is therefore up to the user to decide which market proxy is most appropriate.

We know that these theories are not perfectly "right," but we also know that they are not too "wrong." Using MPT can provide valuable information on the risks incurred in different investment strategies. In short, while the model is false, it's not very false, and even a model that is a bit false is a great deal better than no model at all.

Back to the Real World

So far we have looked at MPT in general and betas in particular, and have discovered that although the CAPM leaves something to be desired in the way of theories, it doesn't really matter very much. Indeed, the only real relevance of all this lies in the real world applications.

Besides providing the basis for evaluating the risk-adjusted performance of investment managers, beta and the CAPM have a number of uses in corporate financial management. Insofar as they offer the only reliable, objective means of estimating the risks of corporate investments, they furnish the only reli-

able means of estimating required rates of return (known alternatively as the "cost of capital").

The estimation of required returns yields the discount rate for any discounted cash flow calculation, and is thus an integral step in the corporate capital budgeting process — whether the contemplated investment is an individual project, a prospective acquisition, or the expansion of a division. And, in addition to serving as investment "hurdle rates," these CAPM-generated required rates of return also provide benchmarks for evaluating corporate performance and structuring compensation plans. But this is getting beyond the scope of this article, and into the one which follows...

In short, the appropriate measure of an investment's risk to use for discounting purposes is the non-diversifiable component of the total risk, or our old friend beta. The "furious controversy" mentioned above really boils down to the fact that it is impossible to measure betas precisely, in part because we are obliged to use some market proxy rather than the market itself as our benchmark. For the purists, this may well be a problem, but for the rest of us it's more of a red herring. The crucial question is not "Are they pure as the driven snow?," but "How wrong are they?" The answer is: "Not nearly enough to matter, particularly since there is no sensible alternative."

In practical terms, it is easy enough to test whether betas work as they are supposed to do, and the overwhelming evidence shows that they do. Some fine-tuning may well be possible in the future, as the theories become more refined. But, for the time being, we have a practical tool at hand to enable us to discount for risk, and no real excuse for not using it.

To sum up: Modern Portfolio Theory works quite well most of the time, and is particularly helpful when used sensibly, with an eye to its limitations. No more can be claimed for any theory.

The Corporate Uses of Beta

by Barr Rosenberg and Andrew Rudd,
University of California, Berkeley

Introduction

Of the many analytical methods collectively referred to as Modern Portfolio Theory, the Capital Asset Pricing Model (CAPM) is the most familiar to today's generation of MBA's. The popularity of the CAPM arises from its success in expressing a powerful theoretical insight in a simple, usable form. The primary use of the CAPM is to determine minimum required rates of return from investments in risky assets. The key variable in the CAPM is called "beta," a statistical measure of risk which has become as familiar as — and, indeed, interchangeable with — the CAPM itself. Over the past decade, beta has become the most widely recognized and applied measure of risk in the investment community.

In our view the recognition accorded beta and the CAPM is well deserved. The model captures the essential treatment of risk in capital markets, reflecting the crucial function of those markets in diversifying risk across the society. Although the original methodology and perspective of the CAPM have been refined in the last two decades, we believe the basic concepts underlying the model have stood the test of time.

Beta is an important tool for almost all institutional investors. Indeed, it is hard to find a major investment advisor or pension plan sponsor in the United States who does not use some aspect of Modern Portfolio Theory. By comparison, corporate financial managers have lagged behind in applying the modern analytical tools that have evolved from

the CAPM. Finance theory maintains that the same CAPM-derived expected rates of return that have provided the benchmarks for evaluating the performance of investment managers should also be used by corporate managers as the "hurdle rates" (or discount rates, in discounted cash flow applications) for evaluating corporate investments. These expected rates of return also furnish the standards by which corporate performance should be judged.

Probably the most formidable obstacle to applying the CAPM in corporate investment decisions has been the difficulty of making reasonable judgments about the betas or projects or internal divisions. The prices or values of such "non-trading" assets are not readily observable, and thus the standard statistical estimates of beta cannot be calculated using market data alone. Without such beta predictions, the CAPM is difficult to apply.

This article is concerned with advances in the area of risk prediction that have made it possible to project the relative risks associated with non-trading investments — whether SBU's, subsidiaries, or individual projects. With these advances, the CAPM can be used to obtain required rates of return which can be used in a wide variety of corporate financial decisions: capital budgeting, acquisition and diverstiture pricing, performance comparison among divisions, and structuring management compensation contracts.

Before discussing these topics, we will begin by reviewing the role of the CAPM in determining the appropriate reward for risk.

> *The relevant context for measuring risk is not the individual corporation's portfolio of assets but the cumulative portfolio of the corporation's stockholders.*

The Reward for Risk-Bearing

Financial managers have long realized that some projects were riskier than others, and that these projects required a higher rate of return. A risky investment is, of course, one whose return is uncertain in advance; and in such a case, it is only the *expected* or average rate of return that can be projected.

For example, a project that requires an initial investment of $100 and returns $113 at the end of a year with certainty is a *riskless* project offering an investment rate of return of 13%. Compare this to another project that also requires a $100 investment, but with an uncertain outcome. Suppose the risky project has a 50% probability of success, in which case the investment would be worth $226 (providing an investment return of 226%), and a 50% probability of disaster, in which case the initial investment would be entirely lost (with a rate of return on investment of −100%). The expected value of this project is one half of $226, and so again equals $113. If a company were to invest all of its funds in one or the other of these projects, what manager would not choose the one promising a certain 13%?

To justify undertaking the risky project, a higher payout in the event of success is required. Suppose instead that the success payout were $238. Then, the expected value would be one half of $238, or $119. The excess of this $119 expectation over the $113 obtained from the riskless project would amount to a $6 expected premium on an investment of $100, or a 6% excess rate of return for the project. Faced with the choice between this risky investment and the riskless alternative above, the manager's decision would be more difficult. The important question would then become, "Is this expected excess return of 6% enough to justify taking on the added investment risk?" It is questions like these that the CAPM was designed to answer.

The Portfolio Perspective

The concept of decision-making in the presence of risk is a relatively old one, and was first studied as a formal question in the 1920's. Probably the single most important development in investment theory was Harry Markowitz's insight that because investors are concerned with the return on their entire portfolio of assets, the risk of any individual project is relevant only insofar as it contributes to the risk of that portfolio.[1]

In other words, we cannot evaluate the risk of a project in isolation, but instead must consider each project within the context of all other assets that are held. For a corporation with many divisions, this suggests that the risk of each division should be considered within the context of all divisions. Consider again the case of the risky project above, with its 50% chance of returning $226 and 50% chance of returning nothing. Suppose further that the corporation considering the project is engaged in other risky businesses, such that if this project fails, the other businesses will pay off; and, conversely, if the other businesses fail, this project will succeed. In this case, the project provides a hedge against the risks of the other businesses, and actually *reduces* the risk of the corporation as a whole! Using this corporate-wide framework, such a risk-reducing investment would be chosen instead of the riskless alternative.

The portfolio perspective, in which the risk of each division is evaluated in the context of the whole, is an important advance on the naive "one-at-a-time approach," in which each division is evaluated in isolation. Even the corporate-wide perspective, however, is not broad enough for most corporate applications.[2] For the majority of corporate uses, the relevant context for measuring risk is *not* the individual corporation's portfolio of assets, but rather the cumulative portfolio of the corporation's stockholders — both actual and potential. In this broader perspective, the appropriate criterion for evaluating risk shifts from the corporate portfolio to the portfolio held by all investors, the "market portfolio" of the society.

The Simple Capital Asset Pricing Model

Corporate stockholders typically hold the shares of many companies in their portfolios. The portfolios of institutional investors (mutual fund managers, pension sponsors, investment advisors, trust departments, insurance companies, and the like) include anywhere from a minimum of 30 to 40 to a maximum of several thousand common stocks. From their point of view, the success or failure of a given company is only one of many outcomes that influence the performance of their portfolio.

For such well-diversified investors, then, it is

---

1. Harry M. Markowitz: *Portfolio Selection: Efficient Diversification of Investment,* John Wiley and Jones, New York, 1959.

2. Those uses for the corporate-wide perspective are analyzed in a related article now in preparation.

not the isolated equity risk of the individual corporation that counts, but rather its contribution to the risk of a diversified equity portfolio. The risk of almost all managed equity portfolios looks very much like the risk of the market portfolio of all equities; that is, their risk is very highly correlated with the risk of a market index.[3]

As a result, the individual corporation's contribution to the risk of investors' equity portfolios can be closely approximated by calculating its contribution to the risk of the portfolio of all outstanding equities, or the market portfolio. It is this risk contribution that is measured by a company's beta. The higher the beta, the greater the contribution to the risk of investors' portfolios. And the greater the risk, the higher the return expected by these investors for holding the security.

The simple Capital Asset Pricing Model captures this perspective.[4] According to the simple CAPM, an investment's required rate of return increases in direct proportion to its beta. The CAPM also implies that investors, in pricing common stocks, are concerned exclusively with *systematic* risk. A security's systematic risk, as measure by beta, is the sensitivity (or co-variance) of its returns to movements in the economy as a whole. Assets with high betas exaggerate general market developments, performing exceptionally well when the market goes up and exceptionally poorly when the market goes down.

All common stocks, of course, have additional risk. Such risk is called "residual" because it is the risk that remains after the systematic component has been removed. Residual risk is also sometimes called "diversifiable" because a properly structured portfolio can escape this risk entirely by diversifying it away. The reasoning underlying the CAPM is that, because residual risk can be eliminated cheaply through diversification, capital markets will not reward investors for bearing such risks. Consequently, stocks are priced as if investors' expected (and, on average and over long periods of time, their actual) returns are related only to the systematic risks of their portfolios.

Beta, then, is a measure of exposure to systematic risk only. It is also a measure of *relative* risk, expressing systematic risk exposure in relationship to all other securities and thus to the market as a whole. The market portfolio, by definition, has a beta of 1.0. A beta greater than 1 indicates above-average systematic risk; a beta less than 1, below-average systematic risk. The betas of U.S. common stocks range from about 0.5 to somewhere above 2.0.[5]

At a beta of 1.0, the average level of risk, investors expect an average return. What is an average return? Intuitively, it should be the return on the average investor's portfolio. The average portfolio includes, at least in theory, all assets in the economy in proportion to their value. However, because the returns on this hypothetically all-inclusive "market portfolio" cannot be observed, we are forced to rely on broad stock market indices (often the S&P 500) as a proxy for "the market."[6]

With this as background, the simple CAPM states:

$$E(R) = R_F + B(E(R_M) - R_F)$$

where: $E(R)$ is the required or expected rate of return on the asset,
R_F is the risk-free return,
B is the beta of the asset,
$E(R_M)$ is the expected return on the market portfolio.

In words, the required rate of return is equal to the sum of two terms: the risk-free return and an increment that compensates the investor for accepting the asset's risk. The compensation for risk is expressed as the asset's beta multiplied by the expected excess return of the market, $E(R_M) - R_F$. This expected excess return is sometimes referred to as the "risk premium."

Determining Required Rates of Return

To use the CAPM, three rates of return are needed: the short-term rate (or the rate on whatever maturity corresponds most closely to the term of the investment in question) on government securities, the market rate of return, and the after-tax cost of

3. For example, the equity portfolio held by large pension funds typically have correlations of .98 (where 1.0 represents perfect correlation) or higher with broad-based market indexes.

4. We call it "simple" to contrast it from the extended models that have since been developed. This model had its origin in the work pursued independently by Professors William Sharpe, John Lintner, and Jan Mossin, aimed at understanding how capital asset prices are determined by the give and take of the competitive capital market.

5. A negative beta would identify a common stock as a hedge against the systematic risk of the economy. Because of the extent to which the price of gold

moves against the dollar, gold stocks come closest to having negative betas. Indeed, there may have been a few years in the early 1970s when the betas of gold stocks were actually zero or slightly negative. Since that time, however, they have risen.

6. The market portfolio has holdings in every asset in proportion to the shares outstanding of that asset. Just as the shareholdings in the market portfolio are proportional to shares outstanding, the values of holdings in the market portfolio are in direct proportion to the value of outstanding shares in the market —that is, to the fraction of outstanding common stock value in each company.

Betas calculated against a broad stock market index should provide a good working approximation of the risks of corporate investments.

debt. The first and third of these are determined by market rates of interest and the tax law. Arriving at a figure for the expected excess rate of return on the equity market portfolio (i.e., $E(R) - R_F$) is more difficult.

One approach is to use average historical returns (including dividends plus market appreciation) as a substitute. This typically arrives at a number like 6%.[7]

In addition, surveys of investor opinion have been used to arrive at a consensus of expectations about the market's future performance. The collective response is then used to derive implied rates of return in the market.

An increasing number of services also provide realistic estimates of the required rate of return for equity investment.[8] In recent years, systematic long-term forecasting procedures have been used to project corporate earnings, dividends, and stock prices. The use of these projections (in discounted dividend valuation models) has in turn yielded realistic estimates of expected rates of return.

These alternative methods come up with prospective excess rates of return for the equity market which are, again, in the range of 6%, but often slightly lower.[9]

Extensions of the CAPM

Before illustrating some of the corporate applications of the CAPM, we want to comment briefly on the solidity of its theoretical foundations.

Because the "market portfolio of all assets" is only a theoretical construct whose risks and returns are not practicably calculated, most applications of CAPM use some index of common stocks as a surrogate. As some academics have argued, the errors caused by the failure to use the right benchmark portfolio may be significant. Bonds, real estate, and human capital are all examples of investments whose returns and risks are not reflected in the performance of the S&P 500. And to the extent that

certain corporate projects have characteristics more closely resembling such assets, the use of betas measured against the S&P 500 may not be appropriate.

A similar problem arises from the extension of common stock holdings across national boundaries. The existence of international investment means that the market portfolio of assets held by U.S. investors is not identical to the index of U.S. common stocks. It is our judgment that such problems are not likely to be serious for most corporate uses. In all but a few cases, the application of the CAPM using betas calculated against a broad stock market index should provide a good working approximation of the risks of corporate investments.

Second, problems arise from the unrealistic assumptions of the simple CAPM. Extensions of this model, taking into account a number of subtleties in the investment environment, come up with slightly different formulas for capital asset pricing. These questions will be the subject of academic research for years to come. On balance, though, we favor extensions of the CAPM in which beta remains the dominant determinant of valuation.[10]

Finally, there is the question of which particular definition of the market portfolio of common stocks will be used to define beta. Will it be the Standard & Poor's 500 stock index, a broader-based New York Stock Exchange index, or even the portfolio of all the common stocks in the United States that are publicly traded and meet the SEC requirement to file 10K reports? It seems that the wider the index, the better; and we thus prefer a broader index. But for most applications, the S&P 500 is broad enough.[11]

In sum, the simple CAPM relationship, using either the S&P 500 or a broader-based market-weighted index as the basis for calculating beta, should serve well in most corporate applications. Only in the case of rate regulation, where a company's revenues are set by a regulatory agency in

---

7. The most frequently cited study is R.G. Ibbotson and R. A. Sinquefield, *Stocks, Bonds, Bills and Inflation: The Past (1926-1976) and the Future (1977-2000)* (Charlottesville, VA: Financial Analysts Research Foundation, 1977).

8. The goal is to describe the expectations in the minds of investors since it is these expectations that determine the investor's actions in valuing stocks. A service produces "reasonable" results if investors judge the results to be reasonable. In the 1960s, Value Line pioneered in providing a broad cross-section of long-term earnings and payout forecasts. This was indeed a pioneering effort, but the required rates of return inferred from valuation models applied to these earnings forecasts fluctuated enormously from year to year. In the recent past, however, a number of services have provided forecasts which are sufficiently representative of the consensus to produce expected rates of return that are accepted as plausible by the investor community.

9. For the origins of the Dividend Discount Model, see John Burr Williams, *The Theory of Investment Value,* Cambridge, Mass.; Harvard University Press, 1938.

10. See Barr Rosenberg, "The Capital Asset Pricing Model and the Market Model," *Journal of Portfolio Management* (Winter 1981), pp. 5-16 for a more complete discussion of this question.

11. A definite conclusion can be reached on this subject. As we have complete data on the 10K filing companies, we can evaluate the potential error from more restrictive indexes. Statistical research at BARRA has confirmed that the error implied in the use of the S&P 500 as a market portfolio is tolerable for the definition of beta. See Andrew Rudd and Barr Rosenberg, "The 'Market Model' in Investment Management," *Journal of Finance* (May 1980), pp. 597-607.

If the investment under consideration differs significantly from the company norm, management should evaluate the investment according to its own beta.

line with the CAPM, are refinements of the CAPM likely to have a significant effect.[12]

Capital Budgeting and the Cost of Capital

Perhaps the most common corporate financial decision is the valuation of a capital investment opportunity. In its most general form, we can isolate four steps in the analysis:

(1) Estimation of the investment's after-tax cash flow.
(2) Prediction of the investment's risk.
(3) Estimation of the cost of capital (the expected rate of return demanded by investors for equivalent risk assets).
(4) Calculation of the net present value of the investment by discounting the cash flows using the cost of capital.

Risk assessment and the calculation of expected returns are thus integral steps in the capital budgeting process. They produce the cost of capital that is used to discount expected cash flows back to their present value.

According to the CAPM, then, the relevant measure of risk is beta; and the relationship between risk and required return is the familiar CAPM itself, as specified in the equation above.

How does the computation proceed? Let us consider the example of XYZ Corporation, whose beta as of July 1, 1982, was 0.75.[13] Further, assume the long-run market risk premium is 6% and the risk-free rate is 13%. Putting these numbers into the CAPM equation gives the required rate of return (cost of equity):

$$13\% + 0.75 (6\%) = 17.5\%$$

The CAPM implies that investors who expect the common stock of XYZ to provide an annual rate of return equal to (greater or less than) 17.5% will classify XYZ as fairly (under- or over-) valued.

Notice that this 17.5% figure is the company's cost of **equity** capital only. And while it does represent a minimal standard for the corporate-wide return on equity, it should not be used as a hurdle rate for capital budgeting decisions within XYZ. To obtain the cost of capital for discounting purposes, we have to adjust for the financial leverage of XYZ.

To illustrate, let's assume that XYZ's target capital structure is composed of 65% equity and 35%

debt. Further, the after-tax cost of debt is estimated to be approximately 7.6%. Given these assumptions, XYZ Corporation's overall cost of debt and equity capital (also called the "weighted average cost of capital") is:

$$\begin{vmatrix}\text{equity}\\\text{proportion}\end{vmatrix} \cdot \begin{vmatrix}\text{cost of}\\\text{equity}\end{vmatrix} \cdot + \begin{vmatrix}\text{debt}\\\text{proportion}\end{vmatrix} \cdot \begin{vmatrix}\text{cost of}\\\text{debt}\end{vmatrix} =$$

$$(0.65)(17.5\%) + (0.35)(7.6\%) = 14.0\%$$

What does this 14.0% mean? It is the after-tax return that managers should require from any project that is a "clone" of XYZ. This figure is clearly important in investor relations as well, for it expresses investors' expectations about the company's return on its total capital investment. If, however, the investment under consideration differs significantly from the company norm, management should evaluate the investment according to its own beta, rather than the beta for the company as a whole.

To illustrate this point, let's look at one of XYZ's divisions, a producer of specialized electronic components which we will call "ABC." The most common procedure for applying the CAPM to non-trading assets is known as the "method of similars." This approach estimates the risk of a division or project using the average beta of a sample of companies engaged solely, or largely, in the same line of business.

In the case of ABC, the first step was to identify the division's most direct competitors. ABC was able to identify five direct competitors, but of these only two were publicly-traded. The (value-weighted) average beta for the two competitors was 1.43, suggesting that this branch of the electronics business is substantially riskier than XYZ's other operations. But, because there are only two companies in the sample, this estimate of ABC's beta could be very ·inaccurate.

Consequently, the search for similars was extended to the more general SIC (Standard Industrial Classification) code, adding 15 companies to the sample. The average beta for these 15 companies turned out to be 1.12. And, taking the simple average of 1.12 and 1.43, ABC's beta was estimated to be 1.27.[14]

The cost of equity capital for ABC was then calculated by incorporating the beta estimate into the

---

12. For readings on this subject, see, for example, the articles in the Autumn 1978 issue of *Financial Management*, and the subsequent correspondence.

·13. XYZ is a diversified electronics company, whose name has been deleted to preserve confidentiality. The figures mentioned in the text were derived by a Financial Strategy task force in XYZ.

14. One other assumption is required. Recall that higher leverage increases the beta and, hence, the risk of a company's equity. Thus, to the extent that ABC's debt/equity ratio differs from the average of the companies in the sample, the appropriate beta will also differ. That is, if ABC's leverage is lower (higher) than the sample average, its beta will be lower (higher).

CAPM. As shown below this turned out to be 20.6 %

$$13.0\% + 1.27(6\%) = 20.6\%$$

Hence, 20.6% represents the required rate of return on the equity portion of ABC's financing. If we assume that the debt-equity ratio for ABC is the same as for XYZ, then the weighted average cost of capital for ABC is 17.2%.

$$0.65(20.6\%) + 0.35(7.6\%) = 17.2\%$$

This figure represents the after-tax rate of return that the management of ABC should expect to meet in order to make ABC an economically viable unit. This hurdle rate is substantially higher than the 14.0% figure for XYZ as a whole because of the greater risk inherent in ABC's operations.

This use of the "method of similars" can be extended to a number of other applications — the pricing of mergers and acquisitions, decisions to divest divisions or subsidiaries, the structuring of management compensation contracts, and the evaluation of individual investments. All of these are areas where the CAPM (and, more specifically, the "method of similars") can be used to quantify investment risks and required returns.

Measurement and Prediction of Beta

Now that we have illustrated some of the potential applications of beta and the CAPM, let's return to the more fundamental issue: risk measurement and the prediction of beta.

For publicly-traded companies, beta can be estimated by observing the relationship between that company's stock price and market movements. This estimate can be computed from a regression relationship based on a series of past stock prices and market returns. Simply stated, the beta of the stock is greater (less) to the extent that the excess stock return is greater (less) than the excess return on the market.

Many analysts would be inclined to call this figure a "measurement," rather than an "estimate," of beta. It is important to recognize, however, that beta is an estimate of the *historical* alignment of the stock price with the market. This value in turn is sometimes used as a *prediction* of the future alignment. One potential liability of using historical betas to predict future levels of risk is that the historical alignment may have been strongly influenced by chance events which caused the stock price to move with the market.

The cumulative effect of these chance events gives rise to a problem known as the "estimation error"; such error may cause the historical estimate to misrepresent the underlying systematic relationship between a stock and the general market. This would also make beta unreliable as a predictor of the future level of risk.

There are actually *two* potential sources of error in the prediction. Besides the estimation error discussed above, there is also the possibility that a company's beta may change over time. For example, if a company has recently undergone major changes in its lines of business, its historical beta will be an unreliable guide to its future level of risk.

The Conservative Adjustment of Historical Beta

The individual who had no faith in historical beta as a predictor would, in the absence of any other estimate, be forced to predict that all projects had the same beta — namely, 1.0, the average value. This is a conservative stance, in the sense that it places minimum weight upon past information and draws all predictions toward the average.

A compromise posture (called "Bayesian" because it corresponds statistically to an application of the law named after the statistician Bayes) is to take a weighted average of the historical beta, on the one hand, and the conservative prediction of 1.0, on the other. The basic idea is that there are two balancing considerations for assessing the relative risk of any particular company: one is the historical beta observed for that company; the other is the recognition that this company is one among many and therefore likely to be somewhat similar to the average of all companies. The risk estimates corresponding to these two considerations are, respectively, the historical beta and the average value of 1.0. Each estimate is weighted according to its accuracy as a predictor. The greater the historical estimation error, the less weight that should be placed on the historical beta. The greater the diversity of all firms around the average, the less precise is the average as a predictor for any one firm, and therefore the less weight that should be given to the value of 1.0. An appropriate weighting scheme can be reached by balancing these two considerations.[15]

15. For example, Merrill Lynch uses weights of 0.66 on historical beta and 0.34 on the average value for their predictions of beta. See their booklet entitled, *Security Risk Evaluation Service.*

A compromise posture is to take a weighted average of the historical beta, on the one hand, and the conservative prediction of 1.0, on the other.

Bringing Fundamental Information to Bear

It is natural to ask whether superior prediction of beta can be accomplished by using a third source of information — namely, the fundamental operating and financial characteristics of the company. On the basis of our research, the answer appears to be "yes." For publicly-traded companies, the fundamental approach to risk prediction offers the potential for considerable improvement. In the case of untraded assets like projects or divisions, where price behavior is unavailable, this approach will often be essential. In many cases, if we could not predict these betas on the basis of fundamentals, there would be a strong argument for abandoning the whole effort.

Using econometric methods that are rather complex (and beyond the scope of this article), we have devised a means of predicting betas that relies largely on fundamentals.[16] From a corporate practitioner's point of view, fundamental betas have three advantages over market-generated betas. First, they have a stronger intuitive appeal: the prediction rules for beta coincide with our common sense impression of what it is that makes a company risky. Second, the fundamental prediction rules are ideally suited to the analysis of non-trading investments such as divisions, SBU's, and individual projects. And third, the fundamental betas outperform predictions based only upon historical market co-variability (i.e., historical betas). In other words, prediction rules based on fundamentals alone have proven superior to both historical betas and to Bayesian-adjusted historical betas. Significantly, however, predictions based on both historical price behavior and fundamentals have outperformed either source when used separately.

The Relation of Beta to Fundamentals

Recall that beta measures the relative responsiveness of an individual company's or asset's market value to general market movements. Econometric studies have shown that the industry in which a company operates, together with its earnings performance and balance-sheet characteristics, provide a good indication of the company's exposure to economy-wide developments.[17] On the basis of these studies, we have incorporated balance sheet and income statement characteristics into a single Multiple Factor Model; and this model, as stated, now provides the most accurate forecast of the sensitivity of an investment's value to general economic events. In short, it offers the most reliable means of estimating future betas.

Industry Effects

There are significant and persistent differences in betas between industries. These differences exist independently of differences in the balance-sheet characteristics of the companies in those industries. In other words, these differences are truly related to the business risks of the industries and not to the capital structure or industrial organization typical of companies within the industries. These differences arise because certain industries are more or less exposed to events that typically rock the economy as a whole.

Among the more than 1000 large companies we examined in our studies, industry effects could be observed clearly. For example, we recently tested the predictive performance of a model[18] developed in 1974 to estimate betas. The model was tested by checking the betas of 39 industry groups over the period 1974-1981 against the predictions generated by our model in 1974.

The six industries with the highest betas over the period 1974-1981 were Real Property, Aerospace, Travel & Outdoor Recreation, Energy Raw Materials, Electronics, and Air Transport. The 1974 model predicted four of these six to be the four highest-beta industries. The other two were forecast to be above the median beta.

Similar predictive accuracy was observed at the bottom end of the beta spectrum. The five lowest beta industries in 1974-1981 proved to be Telephone, Energy Utilities, Tobacco, Banks, and Agriculture & Food. Four of these five were forecast by the model to be among the eight lowest. Thus the

16. See Rudd and Clasing, *Modern Portfolio Theory: The Principles of Investment Management* (Dow Jones-Irwin, 1982) for a discussion of beta prediction, as well as the application of the CAPM. See B. Rosenberg and Vinay Marathe, "The Prediction of Investment Risk: Systematic and Residual." *Proceedings of the Seminar on the Analysis of Security Prices*, University of Chicago, November 1975, pp. 82-225; and "Tests of Capital Asset Pricing Hypotheses," *Research in Finance*, edited by Haim Levy (Volume 1, pp. 115-223, 1979) for further details and methodological comments on this subject.

17. For more detailed discussion, see Barr Rosenberg and James Guy, "Prediction of a Beta from Investment Fundamentals," *Financial Analysts Journal*, Part I (May/June 1976, pp. 3-15).

18. Described in B. Rosenberg and V. Marathe, "The Prediction of Investment Risk: Systematic and Residual." *Proceedings of the Seminar on the Analysis of Security Prices*, University of Chicago, November 1975, pp. 82-225, and updated at BARRA.)

predictive ability of our model, which was based on both fundamental and stock market data from 1968-1974, was confirmed by the results in the ensuing years. For interest, we list in Exhibit 1 our current beta predictions for the five highest and five lowest systematically risky industries.

EXHIBIT 1

Highest and Lowest Industry Betas

FIVE HIGHEST	COEFFICIENT
Real Property	1.77
Pollution Control	1.62
Thrift Institutions	1.56
Electronics	1.49
Air Transportation	1.47
FIVE LOWEST	
Telephone, Telegraph	.52
Electric Utilities	.57
Tobacco	.68
Motor Vehicles	.83
Agriculture, Food	.81

Balance-Sheet and Income-Statement Characteristics

A number of fundamental characteristics of companies, as reflected in the income statement and balance sheet, are powerful predictors of differences in beta. The following information reflects our research over the past decade.

1. Growth

Our work over the past decades has shown corporate growth to be a highly significant and consistent predictor of beta. The more pronounced the growth orientation, the higher the beta is likely to be. A growth-oriented strategy implies large capital investment plans. Such investment, especially if long-term, means greater investor uncertainty about the eventual outcome of this capital spending. And this generally translates into higher risk.[19]

Growth orientation can be measured directly by the growth rate of total assets. But another indication of future growth—one which provides an even better gauge of risk — is the extent to which the earnings from the company are retained, rather than being paid out in dividends or transfers. A high

payout ratio implies little growth, while higher earnings retention generally reflects a high level of expected capital investment.

2. Earnings Variability

A second important determinant of beta is the variability of income over time. As demonstrated by both early and recent studies, earnings variation is a good and persistent indicator of the business risk of the company and, hence, of likely future business risk and beta.

3. Financial Leverage

Another key variable in determining beta is financial leverage. At least among industrial companies, for which conventional leverage ratios are meaningful, the greater the financial leverage, the greater the beta. But, this result, although confirming our intuition, must be interpreted with caution. The observed effects are not as large as financial theory would suggest. When highly levered companies are compared with less levered companies, the difference in beta is less than would be expected if a given company levered itself up and was subsequently compared to its previous position. This in turn suggests that differences in leverage reflect not only policy decisions about capital structure, but, more importantly, external factors that affect a company's ability to support debt. Those companies with low business risk and with tax exposures that make the benefits from interest deductions substantial are the ones most likely to have the heaviest debt loads.

Consequently, when we compare highly levered with less levered companies, it is difficult to neutralize differences between business risk and income patterns. The effect of leverage alone on beta is obscured by the imperfectly neutralized effects of these two influences.

4. Size

A final effect on beta, though less important than the others, is company size. As common sense suggests, the stocks of smaller companies are typically perceived by investors as riskier investments. This effect, however, has been partly obscured by the fact that smaller companies trade in thin markets, and this causes historical beta estimates to understate significantly the risks of these companies. But, when a correction is made for this "downward bias" of small company betas, company

---

19. This approach to the problem is explained and tested in Lanstein and Sharpe, "Duration and Security Risk," *Journal of Financial and Quantitative Analysis,* November 1978, pp. 653-668.

size functions as another useful indicator of future risk.

Predicting Beta for a Project or Division of a Corporation

The first step in predicting beta for a project is to determine the industry or industries in which the project will be active. This can usually be accomplished by applying fairly conventional rules. Using SIC classifications, for example, to assign projects to a larger industry group is a common and justifiable practice. When so classified, a project will most often fall into a single industry group. There will be cases, however, where a project spreads across several industries. As examples, a mining venture might be active in precious metals, and in other minerals as well; a small conglomerate might be engaged in business services, as well as in retail. When a project is spread across several industries, especially when the betas in those industries are substantially different, it is useful to allocate the project across those industries. The allocation should be in proportion to the present value of its operations in each industry.

Next, it is important to establish the growth orientation, earnings variation, and financial leverage — all important determinants of beta — associated with the project. These characteristics can be quantified by calculating various "descriptors" akin to financial ratios, based on up to five years of balance-sheet and income-statement data. Reasonably reliable accounting data on divisions and SBU's are generally adequate to estimate these fundamentals. And, even in the case of individual projects, some historical data for comparative purposes should be available — provided the project is not an entirely new venture for the company. The calculation of these fundamental descriptors can then be formalized through computer processing of the accounting data.

One important advantage of predicting betas with fundamentals is that predictions can be based on projections of future descriptors, instead of relying solely on historical data. For example, the growth orientation of a project can be estimated using projected five-year revenues and retention, rather than historical revenues. This approach thus overcomes the problem created by the dearth or absence of good historical data.[20]

To illustrate one application of fundamental risk prediction, consider another division of XYZ Corporation, which we will call "BCD." This division operates in one of the regulated utility industries. In these characteristically low-risk industries, the downward adjustment of beta from the average of all companies (1.0) is quite substantial. For BCD, the industry adjustment is −.15. This adjustment includes the effect of the typical financial leverage in the industry. Assuming that the financing of BCD reflects the industry norm, no further adjustment for the financial leverage of BCD is necessary.

BCD shows all the signs of a relatively low-growth company. The growth rate of total assets in the past five years has been well below the average of all companies, and the payout-ratio has been (and is projected to continue to be) well above average. When the relevant growth descriptors are calculated, the resulting index of growth is well below the average. This low-growth orientation results in a reduction in the beta prediction by an additional .15.

Further, the earnings variation of BCD has been well below average, as indicated by relatively low year-to-year earnings change, the scarcity of extraordinary accounting items, and the relatively low responsivenesss of the division's earnings to earnings fluctuations in the economy as a whole. When these descriptors of earnings variation are quantified using the appropriate set of descriptive formulas, beta is adjusted by another −.05.

The cumulative effect of these fundamental factors is a beta prediction of 0.65 for the division. (These computations are shown in Exhibit 2.) BCD, we should note, was part of a case study we were involved with. This particular division, interestingly,

EXHIBIT 2

Fundamental Beta Prediction for BCD

Average Beta	1.00
Industry Adjustment	−0.15
Financial Leverage Adjustment	0.00
Growth Orientation Adjustment	−0.15
Earnings Variation Adjustment	−0.05
Predicted Fundamental Beta	**0.65**

20. Notice, however, a very important caveat. The projections for future earnings are almost certain to grossly understate the variability of earnings, and hence to lead to an understatement of beta, unless corrections are made. Indeed, if there is no historical data available for variability of earnings, it is quite possibly a good idea to approximate the variability of earnings from the recorded data for similar companies.

is not wholly owned, and the remaining shares are publicly traded. Consequently, its historical beta is available for comparison, and its recent value was 0.60. Thus, in the case of BCD, the findings of the two approaches reinforced one another.

The Fundamental Beta Prediction Compared with the Method of Similars

Both the method of similars and the fundamental prediction rule attempt to estimate future risk using comparative sources of information — whether market or accounting data. In fact, the fundamental prediction rule can be used to support the process of defining similars. The econometric research underlying the fundamental method can be used to identify those financial or operating characteristics having the strongest influence on market betas; and similarities in those characteristics among companies can in turn be used to identify comparable companies in applying the method of similars. If, for example, we found that growth and earnings variability were the two most significant determinants of beta for companies in a certain industry, these two characteristics could be emphasized in defining the set of similar companies.

The great advantage of the method of similars is its simplicity. All that is required is a group of publicly-traded companies whose business risks, on average, are comparable to that of the investment in question. The disadvantage of the method of similars, besides the possibly arbitrary nature of the selection process, is its liability to inaccuracy. The list of similar companies is usually very small, and none of them is likely to be comparable, in all aspects, to the particular project. As a result, the range of uncertainty in the implied prediction can be quite wide.

In contrast to the simplicity of the method of similars, the mathematics supporting the application of the fundamental prediction method are quite complex. The fundamental method attempts to detect and estimate the strength of a systematic relationship between beta and fundamental characteristics by using a variant of linear regression. The estimation method is applied to a vary large data base: typically ten or more years of data on over 1,000 companies. The effect of using such a large body of data is to eliminate or minimize estimation errors through the process of averaging. Because of the large data base and the sophistication of statistical methods, the results are relatively precise.

Once the fundamental prediction rule has been formulated, the additional data requirements for any single application are quite small: descriptors for important fundamental characteristics must be calculated using various ratios that can be derived from standard accounting statements, and these descriptors collectively yield a prediction of beta. The descriptors, such as payout ratio and variance of earnings, can be calculated from historical data or from projections. If neither of these are available, they can be estimated using the published descriptors of similar companies.

These descriptors can be used to identify the unique characteristics of an investment, while the method of similars makes no such attempt to distinguish which characteristics of companies or investments contribute to their total risk profile. The calculation of these descriptors thus results not only in a prediction of beta, but also in a useful description of the investment's distinctive risk characteristics as they might be perceived by institutional investors.

Conclusions

The CAPM is a powerful tool for corporate capital budgeting and performance measurement. Its full potential, however, has not yet been realized, largely for the following reason. To be applied effectively the user must have credible estimates of the risk-free interest rate, the market risk premium, and the individual asset's (project's, division's) beta. The first factor, interest rates, can be observed regularly and therefore do not present a problem. The market risk premium can be estimated from historical data, or projected using a sophisticated statistical technique. Beta estimation, however, has been a major stumbling block in applying the CAPM.

In recent years, betas have been generated by measuring the relationship between a company's stock price movements and movements in a broad-based market index of common stocks. These estimates are more or less satisfactory depending on the magnitude of the estimation error. But, in any case, this does not solve the problem of beta estimation for (non-traded) projects or divisions.

The CAPM has traditionally been applied in estimating required rates of return for non-trading divisions by using the "method of similars." While theoretically valid, this method has the drawback that the selection of comparable companies is often arbitrary; and this potential problem, combined with the fact that the number of similar companies is

The method attempts to detect and estimate the strength of a systematic relationship between beta and fundamental characteristics.

often very small, restricts the number of cases where the method can be used with confidence.

Over the past decade our research has focused on *predicting* beta by analyzing the fundamental characteristics of a company or project. The data required for this procedure can be derived from traditional accounting numbers such as those furnished by historical (or projected) balance sheets and income statements. The method can, therefore, be used to estimate the beta of divisions or even projects. And, even in the case of publicly-traded companies, additional research has confirmed that fundamental analysis outperforms the traditional method of predicting beta. Joint predictions, using both stock market and fundamental data, are best.

In its application to divisions, fundamental prediction is also much less subject to criticism for vagueness or bias than the method of similars. Further, in linking the risk of a division to its tangible operating characteristics, the analysis becomes more intuitively understandable (and, perhaps, easier to apply) for the division manager.

In short, for corporate analysis involving investments in non-trading assets, fundamental risk prediction is likely to provide the following advantages; (a) improved accuracy, (2) the use of explicit formulas, and (3) the direct connection of beta to the operating characteristics of the company, division, or project in question.

Liquidity and Cost of Capital Implications for Corporate Management

by Yakov Amihud, *New York University*, and Haim Mendelson, *Stanford University*

For the past 20 years, finance theory has been dominated by the view that a stock's expected rate of return is determined largely by the level of its risk. There has been much controversy, to be sure, about whether risk is better measured by the single factor "beta," as proposed by the Capital Asset Pricing Model, or by the multiple factors set forth in Arbitrage Pricing Theory. But there has been little serious disagreement with the proposition that risk, however measured, is the primary determinant of investors' required returns on stocks.

In 1986, we published a study demonstrating that portfolios of less-liquid stocks provide investors with significantly higher returns, on average, than highly liquid stock portfolios, even after adjusting for risk.[1] In fact, the liquidity factor appears as important as the risk measures in determining stock returns.

Why does liquidity affect stock returns? The most straightforward answer is that investors price securities according to their returns *net* of trading costs; and they thus require higher returns for holding less liquid stocks to compensate them for the higher cost of trading. Put differently, given two assets with the same cash flows but with different liquidity, investors will pay less for the asset with the lower liquidity.

Some economists have reasoned that, because trading costs represent only a small fraction of the price of a security, the increase in value resulting from increased liquidity cannot amount to more than a "second-order" effect. It is important to realize, however, that the overall effect of trading costs of, say, 4 percent of an asset's value is substantially higher than 4 percent, because these costs will be incurred *repeatedly*—whenever the asset is traded.

*This article is based closely on our paper, "Liquidity and Asset Prices: Financial Management Implications," *Financial Management*, Spring 1988. We thank Don Chew, the editor of this journal, for his comments and suggestions.

1. Amihud, Yakov and Haim Mendelson, "Asset Pricing and the Bid-Ask Spread," *Journal of Financial Economics*, Vol. 17, 1986: pp. 223-249. See also "The Effects of Beta, Bid-Ask Spread, Residual Risk and Size on Stock Returns," *Journal of Finance*, June 1989, pp. 479-486.

Consider a security whose holding period is two years, which is the historical average holding period of NYSE stocks. A trading cost of $0.04 on a $1 stock represents a cost stream of $0.04 every two years. The present value of this cost stream, assuming an 8% discount rate, is equal to

$$.04 + .04/1.08^2 + .04/1.08^4 + .04/1.08^6 + \ldots = .28.$$

Thus, the 4 percent cost per transaction represents a total reduction of 28 percent in the potential market value of the asset (that is, assuming it could be traded costlessly).

We thus suggest that investors require a considerable liquidity "premium" for holding illiquid securities. This finding has important implications for corporate management as well as investors. For corporate management, such liquidity premia on the company's financial claims (stocks and bonds) represent a significantly higher cost of capital, which means that the company must earn a higher return on its capital in order to increase shareholder value. For this reason, providing greater liquidity for the company's claims will reduce investors' required rates of return and increase the value of the claims. To illustrate, in the above example, cutting trading costs from 4 percent to 2 percent would increase the market value of the security by about 20 percent.

Increasing liquidity, however, is also likely to be costly. Thus, management must weigh the benefits of increased liquidity against the costs.

In the pages that follow, we briefly review our evidence on liquidity and stock returns. After pointing out the implications of this research for investors, we examine the costs and benefits of liquidity from corporate management's perspective. In the process, we examine the role of a number of corporate policies and institutional arrangements in increasing the liquidity of corporate shares.

THE EVIDENCE

Our research examined the effect of liquidity on stock prices by looking at the relationship between stock returns and their bid-ask spreads. The bid-ask spread is the difference between the buying and selling prices offered by traders and market makers

in the stock. For example, suppose that the buying price for IBM is 124 7/8 and the selling price is 124 3/4. The bid-ask spread is then 1/8 of a point, or 0.1 percent of the stock price. The bid and ask prices on another actively traded stock, Time Inc., were 127 5/8 and 128 at the opening of trade on June 2, 1989. The bid-ask spread here was thus 3/8 of a point, three times higher than that of IBM.

We estimated the relationship between stock returns and bid-ask spreads using a large sample of New York Stock Exchange stocks during the period 1961-1980. We divided all NYSE stocks into seven groups according to quoted bid-ask spreads. The average spread of the group with the lowest spread was 0.5% compared to 3.2% for the group with the highest spread—a considerable difference. Stocks with high bid-ask spreads are relatively illiquid. Their trading volume is low, they are held by fewer investors, their prices are more volatile and there are fewer dealers making a market in them. Thus, the bid-ask spread (which represents the cost of immediate execution) is a natural measure of a stock's illiquidity.

We found that, on average, an increase of 1 percentage point in the bid-ask spread was compensated by an additional stock yield of 0.21 percent per month (or about 2.5 percent per annum), after adjusting for differences in risk. (The results of our analysis are illustrated in Figure 1.)

How important is this liquidity effect in dollars and cents? Consider a security that generates a perpetual cash flow of $1.00 per month with a bid-ask spread of 2 percent and a required net return of 1.5 percent per month. According to our estimates, the required compensation for a 2 percent spread is about 1.92 percent per month, and the market value of the security will be $1.00/0.0192 = $52.08. If the liquidity of this security can be increased so that its spread is reduced from 2 percent to 1 percent, the required monthly return will decline to about 1.71 percent and its market value will increase to $1.00/.0171 = $58.45, a 12 percent increase in value. Thus, liquidity changes can have a major effect on price.

More recently, we have studied the effect of illiquidity on short-term fixed-income securities.[2] There, too, we found a significant liquidity effect: bonds with higher bid-ask spreads have significantly higher yields to maturity.

---

2. Amihud, Yakov and Haim Mendelson, "Liquidity, Maturity and the Yields on U. S. Treasury Securities," Working Paper, 1989.

EXHIBIT 1
THE ESTIMATED
RELATIONSHIP BETWEEN
EXCESS RETURNS AND
BID-ASK SPREADS FOR
NYSE STOCKS

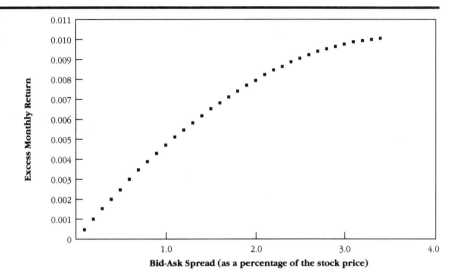

Finally, there is strong evidence on the value of liquidity from the prices of "letter" stocks. Some companies whose stocks are publicly traded also issue "letter" stocks that are not registered with the Securities and Exchange Commission, and thus the trading of these securities is restricted. Restricted stocks are identical in every other respect to their publicly traded counterparts (in terms of dividends, rights in liquidation, voting, etc.), but they can become publicly traded only following a lengthy procedure—all of which renders them quite illiquid. Evidence suggests that letter stocks sell at a discount of about 25% relative to their publicly-traded counterparts. This discount is another demonstration of the value the market assigns to liquidity.

These results have a number of important implications for the individual or institutional investor. First, low-liquidity investments should produce higher average returns to their holders over a long period of time (and perhaps this is the reason for the unusually high long-run returns on illiquid assets such as real estate, artwork, coins, and the like). Privately placed securities, stocks of thinly-traded small firms (especially OTC) and equity in LBO investments also yield relatively higher returns than heavily traded stocks, even after adjusting for risk. These higher returns are not, as some scholars have suggested, an "anomaly" in

an otherwise efficient market. Rather, as proposed earlier, they represent the additional compensation required by investors for the higher costs of transacting.

The observed higher returns on low-liquidity assets are *gross* returns. An investor who is a frequent trader may see these higher returns offset by the higher transaction costs on illiquid assets, and the *net* return may then be lower than on liquid assets whose gross returns are lower. Thus, an investment in a low-liquidity asset will yield a higher net return only for the long-term investor. On the basis of our research, investors can determine, for any given investment horizon, which liquidity-group of securities to hold.

Our research also highlights the importance of developing liquidity-increasing investment vehicles such as mutual funds. Further, our results provide guidance to fund managers by relating the investment horizon, the fund's "load," and the variability and size of its cash flows to its investment policy.

Finally, improvements in trading mechanisms in the capital markets, such as further automation of trading, have also created substantial economic benefits by increasing the liquidity of traded securities.[3] According to our research, continued improvements in securities markets, along with their globalization, should lead to lower required returns and thus to higher stock prices.

---

3. Amihud, Yakov and Haim Mendelson, "Liquidity, Volatility and Exchange Automation," *Journal of Accounting, Auditing and Finance*, 1989, pp. 369-395.

IMPLICATIONS FOR FINANCIAL MANAGEMENT

The value of liquidity implies that corporate management can increase the firm's value by increasing the liquidity of its stocks and bonds.[4] As we have seen, investors require a higher expected return from an asset with lower liquidity to compensate for its higher trading costs. By increasing the liquidity of the firm's financial claims, management can effectively reduce its cost of capital for any level of corporate risk.

Benefits and Costs of Increased Liquidity

Increasing liquidity is clearly not costless. For example, the most obvious method of increasing liquidity—an initial public offering of stock—entails large up-front underwriter fees as well as recurring shareholder servicing and disclosure costs. In addition, there are the "agency costs" that result from the separation of ownership from control, and from the consequent weakening of management incentives to maximize efficiency. Having publicly traded shares also imposes regulations and constraints on management and exposes the information generated inside the firm to competitors.

We have analyzed the trade-off between the benefits and costs of increased liquidity elsewhere. But we will take a moment here to summarize the four major implications that arise from our analysis:

1. The benefits of increasing liquidity are likely to be greater for corporations whose stocks and bonds already enjoy a relatively high level of liquidity. This is because liquid assets are typically held by frequent traders who are more sensitive to changes in liquidity. Low-liquidity assets, by contrast, tend to be held by investors with long planning horizons, who can depreciate the illiquidity costs over longer periods and thus are less sensitive to improvements in asset liquidity.

2. On the other hand, the costs of increasing liquidity are also likely to be an increasing function of the initial level of liquidity. That is, the costs of improving liquidity are likely to be greater when liquidity is already relatively high.

3. Because the benefits of increased liquidity are proportional to the value of the firm, the dollar value of a reduction in cost of capital resulting from greater liquidity will be more beneficial to larger firms, thus reinforcing point 1.

4. In many cases, especially among small, relatively illiquid firms, the costs of increased liquidity are likely to be greater than the benefits.

Investors—especially those with greater need for liquidity—attempt on their own to minimize the costs of illiquidity. While this dampens the illiquidity effect, the empirical evidence demonstrates that this effect is still substantial. Even for highly liquid short-term fixed-income instruments, we found a substantial liquidity effect on the yield to maturity. In letter stocks, the illiquidity discount amounts to about 1/4 of the value of the stock; and, in publicly traded stocks, the liquidity effect is as significant as the risk effect.

CORPORATE METHODS OF INCREASING LIQUIDITY

Now we consider some of the various institutional and contractual arrangements that serve to increase the liquidity of corporate securities.

Going Public

"Going public" through an initial public offering of shares is the most fundamental way of increasing liquidity. By means of this transaction, the firm changes its form of organization from what is legally recognized as a "close" corporation (one in which the claims on its equity value are restricted to a relatively small group of manager-owners) to that of a public corporation (whose equity claims can be transferred without restriction). Holders of the publicly traded common stock of public corporations are not required to have an active role in the corporation and can sell their shares on an exchange. By contrast, the residual claims of the close corporation are illiquid by their very nature. The lower liquidity results from restrictions which increase the costs of finding a qualified buyer, negotiating a price and transferring ownership of the claims.

The costs of going public, as mentioned earlier, include the underwriting costs (which can amount to as much as 10 percent of the gross proceeds of the offering), as well as the cost of registering with the

---

4. Our notion of liquidity should not be confused with corporate liquidity, which relates to its working capital position.

SEC and reorganizing to comply with regulations on public corporations. In addition to these "one-time" costs, there are also recurring costs of public ownership such as shareholder-servicing costs, as well as the legal and accounting costs of satisfying the various reporting requirements, exchange fees, mailings etc. Studies have estimated these recurring costs to run from $100,000 or $200,000 per year, not including management time.[5]

Another important cost of the public corporation is making some information freely available to competitors, which can use it to the corporation's detriment. The publicly available information also enables various parties (such as interest groups) to probe into the corporation's affairs.

Finally, the public corporation bears "agency costs" that arise from the conflict of interest between shareholders and professional managers in the widely held public corporation.[6] For example, LBOs and other forms of the close corporation are reportedly able to establish far more effective managerial compensation schemes (providing extraordinary rewards for extraordinary performance) with less fear of popular and political reaction than can public companies.

The choice of organizational form (private vs. public) thus demonstrates the general trade-off involved in any corporate liquidity-increasing policy. On the one hand, the profitability of the close corporation is expected to exceed that of its public counterpart simply by virtue of stronger incentives for efficiency. On the other hand, the cost of capital of the public corporation is expected to be lower because of its greater liquidity, thus increasing the value to investors of a given level of operating profits.

In considering the decision to be a public corporation or to be privately held, the firm must balance the benefits of lower cost of capital against the costs of dispersed ownership. In some cases, especially for smaller firms without large requirements for new investment, the advantages of private ownership are more likely to outweigh the costs of illiquidity.

The Liquidity of Debt

The bond markets also provide evidence that liquid debt instruments have a lower yield to maturity, thus lowering the corporate cost of capital. Even for highly liquid short-term fixed-income instruments, we found that a reduction in the bid-ask spread from 3 to 0.8 basis points (from 0.03% to 0.008% of total value) is associated with a 40 basis point (0.4%) reduction in the annual yield to maturity on these instruments.[7]

It is well known, moreover, that "on the run" government bonds are more liquid and have lower yields than those that become "off the run." The same applies to corporate bonds. A highly liquid, heavily traded bond, such as an AT&T issue, has a quoted bid-ask spread of about 3/8 of 1 percent. By contrast, bond issues with low liquidity are quoted with spreads as high as 2 or 3 percent.[8] "Junk" bonds, for example, usually have wide bid-ask spreads, suggesting that their high yields are not all due to risk (and therefore do not necessarily imply superior performance). Also important, the returns on privately-placed bonds, which are highly illiquid, exceeded those on publicly-issued corporate bonds by about 50 basis points, on average, during the period 1961-1977.[9]

These results demonstrate the importance of liquidity considerations in corporate debt policy. When issuing corporate debt, it is therefore important to consider not only the design of the debt features and conditions, but also the liquidity of the instrument: Where and how will it be traded? What will be its trading volume? And will any of its features reduce its liquidity?

Public policy decisions can also affect the liquidity, and hence the value, of debt claims. For example, the recent adoption of Rule 144A by the Securities and Exchange Commission, which loosens the restraints on reselling unregistered securities, is expected to bring about an increase in private placement of debt issues that would substitute for publicly-placed bonds.[10]

5. See Schneider, Carl W., Joseph M. Manko and Robert S. Kant, "Going Public: Practice, Procedure and Consequences," *Villanova Law Review*, Vol. 27; November 1981: pp. 1-48; and Borden, Arthur M., "Going Private—Old Tort, New Tort or No Tort," *New York University Law Review*, Vol. 49; 1974: pp. 987-1042.

6. See Jensen, Michael C. and William H. Meckling, "Theory of the Firm: Managerial Behavior, Agency Costs and Ownership Structure," *Journal of Financial Economics*, Vol. 3; October 1976: pp. 306-360.

7. See Amihud and Mendelson cited in Note 2.

8. P. Fabozzi, H. Sauvin, R. Wilson and J. Ritchie, "Corporate Bonds," in R. Fabozzi and I. Pollack, *The Handbook of Fixed Income Securities*, Dow Jones-Irwin, Homewood, Ill, 1989.

9. Holding constant quality, duration and tax treatment. See Zwick, Burton, "Yields on Privately Placed Corporate Bonds," *Journal of Finance*, Vol. 35; 1980: pp. 23-29.

10. See Philip Maher, *Investment Dealers' Digest*, September 4, 1989, pp. 13-20.

The Design of Securities and Standardization of Claims

The design of securities has a large effect on their liquidity and thus on the return required by investors. What may be attractive to some investors may be unattractive to others, resulting in a negative effect on the marketability of the security. Therefore, the advantages of innovative designs of new securities should be weighed against the disadvantages of the lower liquidity that may result.

Sophisticated securities design is particularly apparent in direct investment agreements and in restricted claims in privately placed issues. As one observer has commented, "The list of private deals in 1989 for the most part has been a shopping list of financial engineering... anything that required more explanation to investors than the average investment-grade issue."[11]

By contrast, the rules governing the sharing of the firm's value among investors are remarkably uniform and simple in publicly-issued securities. The capital structure of a typical public corporation contains a variety of short- and long-term debt with fairly familiar features, and one type of equity that provides for the proportional division of the residual value—that which remains after the debt claim is satisfied—among the stockholders.

The preference of issuers of privately placed securities to have customized claims suggests that there may be considerable costs in using standardized claims due to the loss of flexibility. However, securities with unusual contractual provisions are typically far more difficult to trade than securities with a standard contractual form. Non-standard claims require more information and more resources to assess their value, and the very features which make them suitable for the original investors could make them unsuitable for other investors, thus reducing their liquidity. On the other hand, standard claims enjoy greater liquidity in the marketplace. Thus, what offsets the inferiority (and higher costs) of standardization is the higher liquidity of standardized claims.

A case of securities design where liquidity may have played an important role was that of the Unbundled Stock Units (USUs) introduced in 1988. The USUs split the stock into three components—a straight bond, an incremental dividend preferred share, and a warrant or an equity appreciation certificate. The USUs had some tax advantages and also had an appeal to specific clienteles. However, they suffered from a lower liquidity than the underlying shares of stock. There were higher costs in trading the USUs because the trading costs—which are not proportionate to value but include a considerable fixed cost —had to be paid on trades in each of the three components. And due to the relatively thin trading in each component relative to the trading volume in the underlying stock, the market-impact costs of trading in these securities would have been quite high. These illiquidity costs of the USUs may well have contributed to their failure.[12]

Another case in point is the substitution in recent years of publicly traded high-yield bonds for private placements and negotiated bank debt. Privately placed debt allows the custom-tailoring of restrictive covenants and provisions, which in turn allows potentially better control over agency problems and other risks. Also, it removes the need to disclose information which could be used by competitors. These advantages, however, are often outweighed by the marketability of tradable bonds with standard covenants.

In sum, while "financial engineering" and the design of special securities might look beneficial to the issuer, the associated illiquidity costs should also be taken into account because the reduction in liquidity of special securities may increase the return required by investors.

Asset Securitization

Increasing the uniformity of financial claims in order to increase their liquidity is an important motive behind the widespread securitization movement. Securitization involves the pooling and repackaging of individual loans into standard debt securities which are then sold to the public. For example, investment bankers have effectively standardized mortgage investments by pooling them and using them as collateral for liquid debt securities. Commercial banks, investments banks, and finance subsidiaries like GMAC have done much the same with auto loans and

---

11. Philip Maher, cited in note 10.

12. In addition to other factors. See R. Sah and N. Vasavada, "Unbundled Stock Units: What Went Wrong?," *Investment Management Review*, May-June 1989.

credit card receivables. And, in a fairly recent development, commercial banks are issuing debt securities backed by portfolios of corporate and LBO loans. Because of competition between financial intermediaries, at least part of the benefits of increased liquidity are being passed on to the original borrowers in the form of lower interest rates.

Disclosure of Inside Information

A corporation can affect the liquidity of its claims—and consequently its cost of capital—by the amount and quality of the information it releases to investors. The liquidity of a security is reduced when investors suspect that insiders are trading on the basis of privileged information. In that case, market-makers widen the bid-ask spread in order to protect themselves against better-informed traders, and to be compensated for bearing greater risk.[13] Therefore, a commitment by management to make internal information promptly available to the public—say, in the form of accounting reports and special announcements—will reduce the risk of trading against "insiders." This policy should bring about a narrower bid-ask spread, greater liquidity, and thus a lower cost of capital.

By law, publicly traded companies are required to publish periodic accounting reports, and to promptly inform the public of any event which may affect their valuation. But even without these formal requirements, it may well be in the best interest of public companies voluntarily to provide more and better inside information in order to increase the liquidity of their claims. Indeed, consistent with our analysis, most NYSE-listed firms published financial statements long before they were required to do so by the Securities Exchange Act of 1934.

Here, too, there are trade-offs to consider. Making inside information publicly available may not be in the interests of insiders; and, if such information can be used against the firm by competitors, it may not be in the interest of investors either. But, against these potential costs of releasing more information, the corporation should consider the beneficial effect on the liquidity of the corporate claims.

Our argument that liquidity considerations give rise to voluntary corporate disclosure, even at a cost, is also supported by the existence of the bond-rating system. Although companies issuing public debt are under no formal obligation to have their bonds rated, almost all firms voluntarily pay the rating agencies to rate their publicly issued bonds. In the case of private placements, however, companies do not pay to have their debt rated. When such debt is not intended to be traded, the firm derives little benefit from increasing the liquidity of these bonds.

An issuer of debt claims can find an alternative to a full disclosure of information by buying insurance or a guarantee from a financial institution. In this case, the liquidity of the debt claims depends on the financial strength of the insurer, and the issuer has to disclose the information mainly to the insurer rather than to the public. This can be useful for LBO firms whose equity is privately held but have publicly issued debt claims.

Limited Liability

By limiting stockholders' losses to the amount of their investment, the limited liability provision increases the liquidity of stocks. Without limited liability, investors would trade stocks very cautiously, the market would become thin and the bid-ask spreads would be considerably higher since buyers and sellers would set prices to protect themselves.

But there are also costs associated with limiting shareholders' liability. For one thing, like all forms of insurance, the limited liability provision gives rise to the well-known "moral hazard" problem—briefly stated, the tendency for most activities to experience higher losses when the burden of such losses has been transferred from an agent to a third-party insurer. And besides moral hazard, limited liability also spawns a related "agency" or incentive problem. When levered public companies approach insolvency, the insurance policy effectively bestowed upon stockholders gives management (as a representative of stockholders) an incentive to take on ever larger risks because they have claims that resemble call options (that is, an upside without a commensurate downside). This problem, like that of moral hazard, can be illustrated by the extreme case of insolvent S&Ls. In such cases, the existence of deposit insurance (like limited liability) provides

13. See Bagehot, Walter, "The Only Game in Town," *Financial Analysts Journal*, Vol. 27; March/April 1971: pp. 12-14. There is also evidence that an unexpected release of information by the firm causes a widening of its bid-ask spread; see Morse, Dale and Neal Ushman, "The Effect of Information Announcements on the Market Microstructure," *The Accounting Review*, Vol. 58; 1983: 247-258.

the management of failing S&Ls with the incentive to take ever larger risks with depositors' funds to bail themselves out.

Alternative arrangements involving extended stockholder liability could help reduce the moral hazard and agency costs described above. But, in imposing much larger risks on stockholders, extended liability would greatly reduce the liquidity of corporate equities. The fact that public corporations dominate private partnerships and other extended liability vehicles as the major form of American business suggests that the liquidity benefits of limited liability outweigh the costs arising from incentive problems.

Underwriting New Public Issues

A corporation considering the use of an underwriter to issue its securities should take into account (among other things) the liquidity-increasing functions it provides that the corporation cannot perform on its own. First, the underwriter provides "stabilization" of the price of the new issue during the offering period. Then, for some time thereafter, it serves as a market-maker, prepared to step in and provide liquidity as necessary by buying or selling the security.

Another liquidity-increasing service provided by underwriters is the "certification" of the new issue. The underwriting investment bank is an independent agency that takes on the responsibility of providing the public with accurate information about the new issue. It carries out a search process through the firm's records ("due diligence") for any information deemed relevant and publishes a prospectus which details the state of the firm and the expected use of the funds. In effect, the underwriter is a credible outsider that puts its reputation on the line when offering a new issue to its network of investors. At the same time, issuers can protect sensitive information that might compromise their competitive position. This process of certification effectively reduces the bid-ask spread of the new issue and thus increases its liquidity.

Stock Denominations

Liquidity considerations may also explain why companies split their stocks and why stocks are typically issued in relatively small denominations to begin with. For example, instead of having 10 million shares worth $20 each, a company could choose to have only a thousand shares worth $200,000 each. (A somewhat less dramatic version of the latter approach is Warren Buffet's Berkshire Hathaway, whose shares are currently trading at around $8,500.) And the cost savings in servicing the smaller group of shareholders would be considerable.

Lower per share trading ranges may increase liquidity by reducing dealer spreads.[14] This may be related to the fact that block trades incur unusually high liquidity costs. Not only are such blocks difficult to sell at the prevailing market price, but they also incur direct costs that include the underwriter's spread (averaging 5 percent), which is an increasing function of the number of shares sold relative to the issue size, as well as other expenses (averaging 1.7 percent) for offerings registered with the SEC.[15] By issuing shares with smaller denominations, the firm increases the divisibility of its securities, makes small transactions possible, and thus facilitates greater dispersion of ownership. All of these factors may increase the liquidity of the shares.

Listing on Organized Exchanges

Securities markets differ in their method of trading and depth, and this affects the liquidity of the assets traded in them.[16] A company can thus affect the liquidity of its shares of stock by choosing where they will be traded.

Evidence suggests that the desire to increase liquidity may motivate companies to "list" on the large and organized securities exchanges. In particular, firms that listed on the NYSE have experienced significant declines in the spread of their stocks after listing. One study found, for example, that while the pre-listing average OTC median bid-ask spread for their sampled stocks was 3.45 percent

14. Wood, John H. and Norma L. Wood (*Financial Markets* Harcourt Brace, 1985), p. 170) discuss divisibility as a liquidity attribute and suggest that "there is some evidence that divisibility may exert an indirect influence on security returns by affecting dealer spreads." See also W. Baker and P. Gallagher, "Management View of Stock Splits," *Financial Management* 9, 1980, pp. 73-77. They found that the majority of managers questioned cited liquidity as motivating stock splits; but Copeland (see "The Evidence Against Stocks Splits," *Chase Financial Quarterly*, Vol. 1, No. 1) found that stock splits have negative liquidity effects.

15. See Mikkelson, Wayne H. and M. Megan Partch, "Stock Price Effects and Costs of Secondary Distributions," *Journal of Financial Economics*, Vol. 14; 1985: pp. 165-194.

16. See Amihud, Yakov and Haim Mendelson, "Trading Mechanisms and Stock Returns: An Empirical Investigation," *Journal of Finance*, Vol. 42; July 1987: pp. 533-553.

and the average inside (narrowest) spread was 1.73 percent, the post-listing average NYSE spread for the same stocks was 1.24 percent.[17]

This liquidity effect may explain the findings of a number of studies that report increases in the stock prices of firms that apply for listing.[18] In fact, high-spread stocks enjoyed a greater price increase around the time they applied for listing than did stocks with a low spread. This suggests that the increased liquidity due to listing on the NYSE lowered the required return on stocks which had suffered from low marketability.

The link between listing and liquidity is also apparent from the findings of yet another study that the value increases associated with exchange listing were higher in the pre-NASDAQ than in the post-NASDAQ period.[19] This result suggests a narrowing of the differences between the liquidity services provided by the NYSE and the OTC since the implementation of the NASDAQ system.

CONCLUSION

Our recent research has demonstrated that less-liquid securities (stocks and bonds) provide investors with significantly net higher returns than more liquid securities, even after adjusting for risk. These higher returns reflect the "liquidity premium" required by investors for bearing the added trading costs of illiquid securities. For investors who expect to hold their stocks for a long period of time, investing in a portfolio of low-liquidity stocks is likely to provide significantly higher risk-adjusted returns.

For corporate management, such liquidity premia represent significantly higher costs of capital. Thus, increasing the liquidity of corporate stocks and bonds, which reduces investors' required rates of return, can increase the value of the firm *for any given cash flow it generates*.

There are a number of corporate policies designed to increase liquidity. Besides the obvious measures of going public and listing on organized exchanges, management can increase liquidity by properly designing the features of the corporate stocks and bonds, and by providing better information to investors.

As we pointed out, corporate measures to increase liquidity impose significant costs. Among such costs are large underwriters' fees for initial public offerings, recurring shareholder-servicing costs, the release of information which could be used by the firm's competitors, and the costs arising from increased regulation and public scrutiny. In addition, to the extent that increased liquidity means a greater diffusion of ownership, it imposes a most important cost resulting from the further distancing of ownership from control. In the current environment of corporate restructuring, the strengthening of management incentives in private (or recapitalized) companies has clearly proved to be a powerful force for greater efficiency.

This last point is particularly applicable to the recent wave of "going private" transactions, since such moves are the ultimate in reducing the liquidity of the firm's claims.[20] In choosing between the public and private forms of ownership, corporate management has to choose between the value of making the firm's capital claims more liquid—thus reducing its cost of capital—and the benefits of private ownership.[21]

17. See Klemkosky, Robert C. and Robert M. Conroy, "Competition and the Cost of Liquidity to Investors," *Journal of Economics and Business*, Vol. 37; 1985; pp. 183-195.

18. See Ying, Louis K. W., Wilbur L. Lewellen, Larry B. Schlarbaum and Ronald C. Lease, "Stock Exchange Listings and Securities Returns," *Journal of Financial and Quantitative Analysis*, Vol. 10; 1977; pp. 415-435.; Grammatikos, Theoharry and George J. Papaioannou, "Market Reaction to NYSE Listings: Tests of Marketability Gains Hypothesis," *Journal of Financial Research*, 10, Fall 1980, pp. 215-227.

19. See Sanger, Gary C. and John J. McConnell, "Stock Exchange Listing, Firm Value and Security Market Efficiency: The Impact of NASDAQ," *Journal of Financial and Quantitative Analysis*, Vol. 21; March 1986; pp. 1-25.]

20. See Yakov Amihud, "*Leveraged Management Buyouts* and Shareholders' Wealth," In Leveraged Management Buyouts, Dow Jones-Irwin, 1989.

21. Measures undertaken by investors to reduce the cost of illiquidity may have contributed to the recent increase in "going private" transactions. See Jay Light, "The Privatization of Equity," and Michael Jensen, "Eclipse of the Public Corporation," *Harvard Business Review*; September-October 1989.

A Primer on Arbitrage Pricing Theory

Dorothy H. Bower, Richard S. Bower and Dennis E. Logue, *The Amos Tuck School*

Avoiding risk is sometimes an error. Failing to consider risk is always a mistake. This is true in capital budgeting, performance evaluation, strategic planning, and in the setting of operating goals. In all of these corporate decisions, the object is not to minimize the risk of the company's capital investments, but rather to determine whether the promised or the actual returns are sufficient to compensate for the risks incurred. The problem is that measuring risk is not a simple matter.

Financial economists have developed a number of approaches for measuring and pricing risk. The best known is the Capital Asset Pricing Model (CAPM) proposed by William Sharpe and John Lintner.[1] The appeal of this model lies in its postulation of a simple, measurable relationship between risk and expected return. It describes the required or expected return on a real asset or security as the sum of the return on a "risk-free" instrument and a premium for risk. Risk is measured solely by the sensitivity of the asset's or security's return to movements in a broad market index. The risk *premium* depends on that sensitivity and on the spread between the expected return on the broad index and the risk-free rate.

Because CAPM provides such a simple description of risk and return, and because the key variables are easily obtained, alternative models face a stiff challenge. The CAPM, however, does have its shortcomings. Some are evident in the concerns of investment managers who find it difficult to believe that risk is fully captured in sensitivity to a single market index. Contributing further to such doubt is the fact that, although the model's variables can be measured, the measures differ according to the method and the period of measurement selected. Academics, too, have expressed their reservations about the CAPM, objecting that the assumptions of the model are too restrictive. They argue, furthermore, that the model cannot really be tested empirically and that it fails to explain systematic, persistent return differences associated with size, yield, and even the time of year.[2]

Arbitrage Pricing Theory (APT) does not overcome all of these objections, and it has some shortcomings of its own. Nevertheless, it is the first model to challenge CAPM that has a real chance of replacing it. The feature that makes APT of greatest potential value to corporate decision-makers is its attempt to explain the risk-return relationship using several factors instead of a single market index.

While multiple-factor models have been around for many years, none had the theoretical foundation required to challenge CAPM until Stephen Ross presented APT in 1976.[3] Ross began with the idea that returns vary from expected levels because of *unanticipated* changes in production, inflation, term structure, and other basic economic forces. Then, assuming that decision-makers take advantage of all arbitrage opportunities to hold portfolios that offer higher returns, Ross built a model that explained an asset's risk and expected (or required) return in terms of its sensitivity to each of these basic economic factors.

1. See William F. Sharpe, "Capital Asset Prices: A Theory of Market Equilibrium Under Conditions of Risk," *Journal of Finance*, September 1964, 425-442; and John Lintner, "Security Prices, Risk, and Maximal Gains from Diversification," *Journal of Finance*, December 1965, 587-615.

2. See Richard Roll's "A Critique of the Asset Pricing Theory's Tests," *Journal of Financial Economics*, March, 1977, 126-176. Roll is the most widely cited analyst claiming the model cannot be tested. He argues that the return on the true market portfolio cannot be measured and that when tests involving an index of stocks that make up less than the full market are used to measure sensitivity, the tests produce a mechanical relationship that is no test at all. See also Marc Reinganum's "Misspecification of Capital Asset Pricing: Empirical Anomalies Based on Earnings' Yields and Market Values," *Journal of Financial Economics*, March, 1981, 19-46. Reinganum is one of a number of people who find that stock returns vary with company size and dividend yield in ways that are not explained by market sensitivity differences associated with size and yield. Donald Keim, in "Size-Related Anomalies and Stock Market Seasonality: Further Empirical Evidence" (*Journal of Financial Economics*, June, 1983, 13-32), shows that, year after year, stock returns in January are above those in any other month and are not explained by either individual stock sensitivities or market risk premiums.

3. See Ross's articles, "The Arbitrage Theory of Capital Asset Pricing," *Journal of Economic Theory*, 1976, 341-360, and "Return Risk and Arbitrage," in Irwin Friend and James L. Bicksler, *Risk and Return in Finance* (Balinger, Cambridge, 1977).

APT is the first model to challenge CAPM that has a real chance of replacing it.

The theory behind the model has been embellished a bit since Ross first presented it, but its value has not been seriously questioned, and the model has been supported in a number of empirical tests.[4] The quality of the tests has been challenged, however, and not all financial economists have accepted APT.[5] Its application by investors is more a prospect than a realization. But it is a prospect, nevertheless, that now seems very promising. The rise of APT may mean that the CAPM will no longer be used for many applications that require risk measurement.

In this primer we hope to encourage application of APT by illustrating how it works, comparing it to CAPM, and offering an application. We also suggest how APT may gain the intuitive appeal required for a method of risk analysis to be widely applied in investment decision-making.

APT: Idea and Illustration

APT is the product of common sense and algebra. Common sense suggests that investors' expected rates of return from holding stocks are primarily influenced by more than one, but nevertheless by only a few, basic factors. It is also based on the assumption that an investor will not hold a portfolio that will be outperformed under all conditions by an alternative portfolio. Using simple algebra it can be demonstrated that there is a linear relationship between expected return and sensitivity to these basic factors. These, in brief, are the fundamentals of APT.

Numerical Example

Common sense first. Suppose an investor is considering stocks for his portfolio. Assume further that this investor expects that the total monthly return on his portfolio (that is, the sum of dividend yield for the month and the percentage change in portfolio) varies predictably with two, and only two, economy-wide factors: the level of industrial pro-

duction and the rate of inflation.[6] In saying that only two factors determine expected returns, we are assuming that diversification has eliminated the stock portfolio's sensitivity to all other factors.

Suppose, furthermore, that our investor feels that if the industrial production index and inflation are at expected levels, say, 160 and 6 percent, his expected return on the portfolio is 18 percent. If industrial production turns out to be 10 percent higher (lower) than expected in the month (that is, the index is 176 instead of 160), the expected return on his portfolio rises (falls) by 10 percentage points to 28 percent. If inflation varies from expected by 10 percent, say, from 6.0 to 6.6 percent, then the return on his portfolio would vary in the *opposite* direction by 20 percentage points.

The portfolio being considered has now been described in terms of return and sensitivity to basic economic forces. We can summarize this situation in a payoff table in which columns and rows indicate the state of industrial production and inflation, and each block shows return.

Although the table shows payoffs only for unexpected variations of 0, + 10 percent and –10 percent in industrial production and inflation, other conditions could easily be accommodated.

Suppose it were possible to drop one or more stocks from this portfolio and to buy other stocks that would not change the portfolio's sensitivity to industrial production or inflation rates (or introduce any new sensitivity or residual return variation). An investor would certainly substitute those stocks if doing so raised his return. And this process of substitution would in turn yield a new set of payoffs that could be represented in the above table by a higher number in each box.

If investors agreed on the sensitivity of each stock to unexpected variations in the basic factors of production and inflation, and on the return to be expected from each stock, then any number of them would try to carry out the "arbitrage" action of simultaneously selling and buying stocks with the

4. See, for example, Stephen J. Brown and Mark I. Weinstein, "A New Approach to Testing Asset Pricing Models: The Bilinear Paradigm," *Journal of Finance* (June 1983); Nai-Fu Chen, "Some Empirical Tests of the Theory of Arbitrage Pricing," *Journal of Finance* (December 1983); Nai-Fu Chen, Richard Roll and Stephen Ross, "Economic Forces and the Stock Market: Testing the APT and Alternative Asset Pricing Theories," Graduate School of Business, University of Chicago Working Paper No. 119 (December 1983); and Richard Roll and Stephen A. Ross, "An Empirical Investigation of the Arbitrage Pricing Theory," *Journal of Finance* (December 1980).

5. See Phoebus J. Dhrymes, Irwin Friend, and N. Bulent Gultekin, "A Critical Reexamination of the Empirical Evidence on the Arbitrage Pricing Theory," *Journal of Finance* (June 1984).

6. To see why it is logical that the return on a stock portfolio should vary with industrial production and inflation, think of a stock price as the discounted value of the cash flows expected from that stock in the future. If industrial production is above its anticipated level in a month, then cash flow expectations will be revised upward, the price will rise, and the return on the stock will above the expected level. If inflation is above its expected level, however, the discount rate rises, and price and returns fall.

Using simple algebra it can be demonstrated that there is a linear relationship between expected stock returns and their sensitivity to a few basic economic factors.

EXHIBIT 1
Payoff Table

		Inflation	5.4%	6.0%	6.6%
Production	176		48	28	8
	160		38	18	−2
	144		28	8	−12

same sensitivities, but different expected returns. The efforts of those investors would bring expected returns in line with sensitivities. Also, because payoffs would rise if sensitivity increased, arbitrage activity would cause higher expected returns to be associated with greater sensitivity to each basic factor in the economy.

Risk is thus defined in terms of a stock's sensitivity to basic economic factors. Expected return increases with risk and is directly related to sensitivity.

A Further Illustration

Why expected return varies with sensitivity to economic forces in the APT framework should become clearer with a more complete illustration. Again, let us consider only two economic forces, production and inflation. This illustration involves four stocks. The actual realized return on each stock in a given period can be described by the equation:

RETURN = EXPRET + SENSIT(P) x (PROD − EXPPROD)
+ SENSIT(I) x (INFL − EXPINFL)
+ CHANCE

RETURN will be at the expected or required rate (EXPRET, which was 18 percent in the earlier example) in a period if both production and inflation are at expected levels (that is, PROD − EXPROD = 0 and

INFL − EXPINFL = 0) *and* if the chance element in return (CHANCE)—the element that is idiosyncratic or unrelated to any pervasive economic forces—is zero. How the return will vary with unexpected movements in production and inflation is indicated by the SENSIT coefficients.

Could four stocks have the characteristics shown in Exhibit 2?

The answer is no, and the reason is that investors could combine these stocks in a such a way that they would add to their wealth without either taking any risk or making any investment. Given the characteristics in Exhibit 2, an investor could "arbitrage" by buying stocks #1 and #2 and selling short stocks #3 and #4. The arbitrage portfolio is presented in Exhibit 3.[7]

Assume that the chance effect on return has been diversified away by an investor's other security holdings. In this case, that investor bears no risk because his portfolio's sensitivity to both production and inflation variations has been reduced to zero. Net investment is zero because purchases, or positive investments, exactly equal short sales, or negative investments; and the positive return from holding this portfolio is certain.

However, the very activity of buying stocks #1 and #2 and selling stocks #3 and #4 will eliminate

EXHIBIT 2
Characteristics of Four Stocks: Disequilibrium

Stock	Expected Return (EXPRET)	Production Sensitivity (SENSIT(P))	Inflation Sensitivity (SENSIT(I))
#1	13	0.2	2.0
#2	27	3.0	0.2
#3	16	1.0	1.0
#4	20	2.0	2.0

7. To form an arbitrage portfolio—that is, a portfolio with no systematic risk and no investment—three equations must be satisfied:
(1) INV1 + INV2 + INV3 + INV4 = 0: No investment risk
(2) INV1 x SENSIT(P)1 + INV2 x SENSIT(P)2
    + INV3 x SENSIT(P)3 + INV4 x SENSIT(P)4 = 0: No production risk
(3) INV1 x SENSIT(I)1 + INV2 x SENSIT(I)2
    + INV3 x SENSIT(I)3 + INV4 x SENSIT(I)4 = 0: No inflation risk
In these equations INV1 is the investment in stock 1, SENSIT(P)1 is the production sensitivity of stock 1, SENSIT(I)1 is the inflation sensitivity of stock 1, and similar symbols are used for stocks 2, 3, and 4. The unknowns in these equations are INV1, INV2, INV3, and INV4. To get the fourth equation to make a solution possible, it is only necessary to set the level of investment in one of the stocks. We simply set the level of investment in stock 1 at $1, and then solve for the remaining levels of investment in the other stocks to derive the following investment proportions: INV1 = 1.0, INV2 = 0.642857, INV3 = −1.157143, and INV4 = −0.485714.

It seems likely that stocks vary in their sensitivity to economic factors and that unanticipated changes in economic factors do not occur in step.

EXHIBIT 3
Arbitrage Portfolio

Stock	Investment (INV)	Expected Return (INV x EXPRET)	Production Sensitivity (INV x SENSIT(P))	Inflation Sensitivity (INV x SENSIT(I))
#1	+1.000	+13.000	+0.200	+2.000
#2	+0.643	+17.361	+1.929	+0.129
#2	−1.157	−18.512	−1.157	−1.157
#3	−0.486	− 9.720	−0.972	−0.972
PORTFOLIO	0	+ 2.129	0	0

the opportunity for positive, risk-free returns that this arbitrage portfolio is expected to provide. Prices of the stocks purchased will rise and expected returns will fall, bringing the returns on these stocks down to the point where they are in line with the stocks' sensitivities. Conversely, the prices of stocks sold short will fall and expected returns will rise. In this manner, market arbitrage will cause the opportunity to disappear. It is this action that explains why the four stocks will not have the characteristics shown in Exhibit 2.

When all arbitrage opportunities are eliminated, the risk-return characteristics of all stocks must conform to a relationship that takes the following form:

EXPRET = RSKFREERET + PRODPREM x SENSIT(P) + INFLPREM x SENSIT(I).

The expected return on each stock is equal to the risk-free rate, plus the market risk premium on production multiplied by the stock's production sensitivity, plus the market risk premium on inflation multiplied by the stock's inflation sensitivity. The relationship must take this linear form. That is algebra's requirement.

To finish the illustration, suppose that the equilibrium conditions for the market in which these four stocks are traded—the conditions in which arbitrage opportunities no longer exist—are a risk-free rate of 10 percent, a production risk premium

of 5 percent, and an inflation risk premium of 1 percent. The market's risk-return equation would be

EXPRET = 10 + 5 x SENSIT(P) + 1 x SENSIT(I),

and the characteristics of the stocks would be those shown in Exhibit 4.

The expected returns on stocks #1 and #2 are now lower relative to those of stocks #3 and #4 than they were originally. Investment in the four stocks in the same proportions as in the arbitrage portfolio of Exhibit 3 (i.e., +.515 in #1, +.331 in #2, −.596 in #2, and −.250 in #4) has a zero expected return. Arbitrage opportunities no longer exist. Portfolios without any sensitivity to economic forces, such as the one that might be formed by buying $200 worth of stock #3 and selling short $100 worth of stock #4, have the riskless rate, 10 percent, as their expected return. The return differences between stocks are consistent with sensitivity differences. The 6 percent difference in return between stock #4 and stock #3 represents a 5 percent premium for stock #4's one additional unit of production sensitivity plus a 1 percent premium for its one additional unit of inflation sensitivity.

What the riskless rate and risk premiums are in the risk-return relationship of the economy at large depends, of course, on the attitudes of investors, the expected inflation level, the nature and variability of economic factors, and the assets available to investors. The relationship need not remain the same

EXHIBIT 4
Characteristics of Four Stocks: Equilibrium.

Stock	Expected Return (EXPRET)	Production Sensitivity (SENSIT(P))	Inflation Sensitivity (SENSIT(I))
#1	13.0	0.2	2.0
#2	25.2	3.0	0.2
#3	16.0	1.0	1.0
#4	22.0	2.0	2.0

We have done some work, as have Richard Roll and Stephen Ross, which demonstrates that APT and CAPM provide quite different estimates of expected or required returns.

over extended periods, nor must the sensitivities of particular assets to each force remain unchanged. Nevertheless, the APT model requires some stability in these values if it is to be useful in such corporate applications as capital budgeting and performance evaluation. That stability appears to exist; however, even if it did not, APT's prediction that expected return will be a linear function of sensitivity to basic economic factors remains undisturbed.

APT and CAPM

CAPM requires something more than APT to support its prediction that sensitivity to one economic force—the force reflected in the returns to the market portfolio—is the only determinant of expected or required return. The CAPM assumes that for any asset, the return in a given period is generated from the following relationship:

RETURN = EXPRET + (SENSIT(MKT) x
(RETMKT – EXPRETMKT)) + CHANCE.

Unlike APT, CAPM views a single economic force, not several economic forces, as the systematic determinant of actual returns. The risk-return relationship for CAPM is as follows:

EXPRET = RSKFREE + (RSKPREM(MKT)
x SENSIT(MKT)).

The development of the CAPM risk-return relationship is more involved than is that for the APT relationship. But the relationship itself, as formulated in the above equation, is the same one APT would offer if there were only a single pervasive economic force influencing returns.

CAPM's assumption that sensitivity to the market is the only required indicator of risk, and thus the only determinant of expected or required return, may be good enough even if APT provided a better description of how markets behave. The different sensitivities of each asset to the collection of economic forces could "net out," so that sensitivity to a single market index would do as good a job as any multi-factor model in explaining expected return differences among assets. Also, if the unanticipated changes in economic factors were highly correlated, then a stock's sensitivity to any one factor, or

to a market index, could well represent sensitivity to all factors. In either case, the CAPM market return would be a satisfactory proxy for the multiple factors of APT; there would then be neither academic evidence nor practical justification for considering APT as a replacement for CAPM.

It seems more than likely, however, that stocks do vary in their sensitivity to economic factors and that unanticipated changes in economic factors do not occur in step. As evidence of this and as an indication of APT's promise, it is worthwhile to consider how CAPM and APT perform when each is used with the same data.

Corporate Cost of Capital

We have done some work, as have Richard Roll and Stephen Ross, which demonstrates that APT and CAPM provide quite different estimates of expected or required returns.[8] The two models thus have different implications for cost of capital and for the screening rates to be used by corporations in capital budgeting.

Our work used monthly return data for all 942 stocks traded continuously on the New York and American Stock Exchanges during the years 1970 through 1979. Using a set of 815 of these stocks (126 stocks were held out of the sample to test each model's ability to explain returns not included in fitting the model), we estimated both CAPM and APT risk-return relationships. We used these relationships to calculate expected returns for 17 industrial stocks excluded from our initial work.

To derive the CAPM risk-return relationship we regressed monthly returns for each stock against the monthly returns on a market portfolio (specifically, the Center for Research in Security Prices' (CRSP) value-weighted index). This produced an estimate of SENSIT(MKT) for each stock. We then calculated the average annual return for each stock over the ten-year period and regressed average returns against SENSIT(MKT) for the cross-section of 815 stocks. This produced the following CAPM risk-return relationship:

EXPRET = 5.5 + 10.8 SENSIT(MKT)

8. See Richard Roll, and Stephen A. Ross, "An Empirical Investigation of the Arbitrage Pricing Theory," *Journal of Finance*, December 1980, pp. 1073-1103; and Dorothy A. Bower, Richard S. Bower, and Dennis E. Logue, "Equity Screening Rates Using Arbitrage Pricing Theory," in C.F. Lee, ed. *Advances in Financial Planning*, Greenwich, CT: JAI Press, 1984.

As work proceeds, we expect to find more agreement on the number of relevant factors and strong evidence that the number is not so large that it threatens APT's analytic foundation.

The average annual risk-free rate estimate for the period was 5.5 percent, and the risk premium for a stock that moved in step with the market (SENSIT(MKT)=1) was 10.8 percent. (The 10.8 percent for the 70s is a high premium when compared to figures that cover the period from 1926 to 1983.)

The procedure for developing the APT risk-return relationship was considerably more complex. The statistical technique of factor analysis was used to discover basic factors and their movements from month to month.[9] The APT risk-return relationship was as follows:

$$\text{EXPRET} = 6.2 - 185.5\ \text{SENSIT}(1) + 144.5\ \text{SENSIT}(2) + 12.4\ \text{SENSIT}(3) - 274.4\ \text{SENSIT}(4).$$

Unlike the factors in our earlier illustration, the factors in the equation above are unidentified because we derived them from the return data on the 815 stocks rather than specifying them in advance. Although ex-post analysis might show each factor to represent unanticipated changes in a *single* economic variable, the chance of these multiple factors reducing to a single variable is very small. It is more likely that each is a construct representing the movements of several economic variables.

The sensitivity coefficients have an interpretation similar to the "SENSIT(MKT)" variable in the CAPM. They are measures of the relative sensitivity of each security's return to a particular factor. Unfortunately, the analogue to the CAPM market risk premium is not so easily interpreted. In fact, because the factor movements are not expressed as return movements in a portfolio sensitive only to the single factor, they look funny. That is, the sensitivities can be either positive or negative, and they do not conform to intuition as readily as the CAPM. The important thing is that the SENSIT measure, and the risk premium associated with it, are measured on the same scale. If that is the case—and the statistical procedure employed assures that it is—then multiplying a stock's sensitivity values by the associated risk premium will indicate by how much the stock's expected return exceeds the risk-free rate.

We worked with four factors. Other researchers have found more or fewer, depending upon the specific methods used, and this has been a drawback to the acceptance of APT.[10] But this absence of complete agreement about the number and identity of risk factors is not, in our view, a compelling objection. APT has only begun to be tested. As work proceeds, we expect to find more agreement on the number of relevant factors and strong evidence that the number is not so large that it threatens APT's analytic foundation.

Some progress is also being made in estimating factors directly, rather than extracting them from security return data. Work of this type has been done by Chen, Roll and Ross, and is reported in Roll and Ross.[11] The economic variables they find important are industrial production, inflation, interest rate term structure, and the spread between low and high grade bonds. They report that sensitivity to unanticipated changes in these variables provides an explanation of expected return differences among stocks that is not improved by introducing market sensitivity as an additional factor.

One interesting number in the CAPM and APT risk-return relationships is the estimate of the risk-free rate. The APT estimate is 6.2 percent. The CAPM estimate is 5.5 percent. Over the 1970-1979 period the annual average return on 30-day Treasury bills was slightly more than 6.1 percent. APT thus provides the closer estimate.

Seventeen stocks were excluded from the sample used to calculate the risk-return relationships—stocks which are included in calculating the CRSP value-weighted index of all NYSE and AMEX stocks. We computed the CAPM sensitivity coefficients (betas) of these 17 stocks by regressing monthly returns against the CRSP value-weighted index for the 1970–1979 period. Using APT we regressed returns for these stocks against the statistically computed factors derived from the original sample of 815 stocks.

Exhibit 6 shows both the CAPM SENSIT(MKT) and APT SENSIT values for each company. For 14 of 17 stocks, APT's four factors do a better job of explaining return movements through time. The average percent of explained variance, as measured by

9. For details, see Bower, Bower, and Logue, "Arbitrage Pricing and Utility Stock Returns," *Journal of Finance*, September 1984, pp. 1041-1054; and also our article, "Equity Screening Rates Using Arbitrage Pricing Theory," in C.F. Lee, ed. *Advances in Financial Planning*, Greenwich, CT: JAI Press, 1984.

10. Brown and Weinstein, cited in note 4., find three variables. Dhrymes, Friend, Gultekin, cited in note 5., find two to nine factors, depending on portfolio size. Reiganum, cited in note 2, finds three to five factors.

11. The specific articles are: Chen, Roll, and Ross, "Economic Forces and the Stock Market: Testing the APT and Alternative Asset Pricing Theories," Graduate School of Business, University of Chicago, Working Paper No. 119. (December 1983), and Roll and Ross, "The Arbitrage Pricing Theory Approach to Strategic Portfolio Planning," *Financial Analysts Journal*, May-June 1984, 14-26.

The economic variables that Chen, Roll and Ross find important are industrial production, inflation, interest rate term structure, and the spread between low and high grade bonds.

EXHIBIT 6
Comparison of CAPM and APT Sensitivity Estimates.

Company	CAPM		APT				
	SENSIT(MKT)	R^2	SENSIT 1	SENSIT 2	SENSIT 3	SENSIT 4	R^2
American Broadcasting	1.34 (7.23)*	0.32	−0.06 (−7.75)	−0.006 (−0.71)	0.02 (−1.87)	0.01 (1.67)	0.37
American Hosp. Supply	1.47 (9.58)	0.46	−0.05 (−7.27)	0.01 (0.96)	0.04 (5.22)	0.02 (2.74)	0.44
Baxter Travenol Laboratories	1.30 (−7.52)	0.52	−0.04 (−0.59)	−0.004 (5.96)	0.04 (1.85)	0.01	0.46
CBS	1.04 (8.65)	0.41	−0.05 (−4.60)	0.002 (0.31)	0.005 (0.00)	0.01 (0.88)	0.52
Cook Int'l	0.90 (3.12)	0.07	−0.04 (−2.83)	−0.007 (−0.58)	0.05 (3.32)	−0.01 (−0.75)	0.13
Ipco Corp.	2.06 (9.45)	0.45	−0.10 (−10.14)	0.01 (1.11)	0.02 (1.71)	−0.02 (−1.44)	0.49
Matrix Corp.	1.64 (3.42)	0.09	−0.09 (−3.96)	0.03 (1.34)	0.004 (0.19)	0.01 (0.46)	0.11
Metromedia	1.47 (7.73)	0.35	−0.07 (−8.70)	−0.004 (−0.51)	0.02 (−1.82)	0.000 (0.000)	0.41
Napco Ind.	1.44 (6.10)	0.25	−0.07 (−6.10)	−0.02 (−1.68)	0.01 (1.08)	0.003 (0.25)	0.26
Parker Pen	1.36 (6.91)	0.30	−0.07 (−8.41)	0.03 (2.99)	0.005 (0.56)	0.01 (1.37)	0.42
Rollins	1.60 (7.10)	0.36	−0.07 (−7.86)	−0.01 (−1.35)	0.006 (0.57)	0.009 (0.87)	0.36
SPS Tech.	1.36 (5.67)	0.22	−0.07 (−6.50)	0.004 (0.40)	−0.01 (−0.98)	−0.007 (−0.54)	0.27
Storer Broadcasting	1.24 (7.00)	0.31	−0.06 (−6.71)	−0.007 (−0.83)	−0.006 (−0.62)	0.006 (0.67)	0.28
Taft Broadcasting	1.68 (9.63)	0.46	−0.09 (−11.99)	0.002 (0.23)	−0.01 (−1.94)	0.01 (1.37)	0.58
Teleprompter	2.68 (8.58)	0.40	−0.14 (−10.68)	0.007 (0.55)	−0.02 (−1.29)	0.02 (1.40)	0.51
Western Union	1.12 (6.56)	0.28	−0.05 (−7.24)	−0.02 (−2.31)	−0.01 (−1.11)	0.009 (1.16)	0.34
Average		0.32					0.36

*t statistics in parentheses beneath coefficients.

R^2, is .36 for APT and .32 for CAPM. The sensitivities of each of the 17 stocks can be used in the CAPM and APT risk-return relationships—those that were estimated for the other 815 stocks and presented above—to compute what return the market is expecting the firm to earn. This is the required return or screening rate to be considered in making investment decisions.

Exhibit 7 shows these estimates of required return. APT yields lower estimates of required return for 12 of 17 companies than does CAPM, although the average return estimate is the same for the entire sample of 815 companies. The differences, however, are not inconsequential. Using the CAPM, the mean required return for the sample in Exhibit 6 is 23.0 percent. The mean required return using APT is 18.8

Company	CAPM	APT
American Broadcasting Company	21.5%	14.3%
American Hospital Supply	22.9	12.8
Baxter Travenol Laboratories	21.0	11.6
CBA	18.2	13.9
Chris Craft Industries	22.2	17.1
Cook International	16.7	20.2
Ipco Corporation	29.33	2.7
Matrix Corporation	24.7	25.3
Metromedia	22.9	19.2
Napco Industries	22.6	16.4
Parker Pen	21.7	22.6
Rollins	24.3	16.2
SBS Technologies	21.7	22.3
Storer Broadcasting	20.4	15.4
Taft Broadcasting	25.2	21.1
Teleprompter	36.0	28.4
Western Union	19.1	10.8
Average	23.0%	18.8%
Standard Deviation	4.43	6.05

EXHIBIT 7 CAPM and APT Estimates of Expected Return.

percent. In 11 instances, the differences in either direction are at least as large as 4.0 percent. The magnitude of these differences is great enough to suggest that companies should use caution in setting screening rates. It also demonstrates that APT and CAPM produce quite different results.

Performance Compared

APT may provide a different estimate of required return than CAPM, but is there any indication that it performs *better* than CAPM? To us, "performs better" means it provides estimates of expected return that are closer to the "true" expected returns than does CAPM. There is a problem with this concept of performance, however; "true" expected returns are neither known nor knowable. The closest thing to the true expected returns for a given period are the average actual returns that were realized. Our effort to test performance accordingly uses these average actual returns as proxies for the "true" expected returns.

We took a group of 127 stocks that included the 17 industrial stocks listed in Exhibits 6 and 7, and the utility stocks that we held out of our original work. None of these stocks was used in estimating the movements of the four APT factors through time or in estimating the CAPM and APT risk-return relationships shown earlier. For each stock we estimated its CAPM SENSIT(MKT) and its APT SENSIT(1), SENSIT(2), SENSIT(3), and SENSIT(4). We then used these sensitivities in the CAPM and APT risk-return relationships to calculate expected return on each stock for the 1970–1979 period. It is these estimates we compared with average actual returns for each stock.

First we calculated the squares of the differences between average actual and estimated expected returns for each stock using both CAPM and APT estimates. The squares were used to give greater weight to larger differences. Next, we summed the squared differences between actual and CAPM-expected returns, and between actual and APT-expected returns, for the 127 stocks. The APT squared difference for the set of 127 stocks was about 25 percent less than the CAPM difference.

In this test, one that involves predicting expected returns for stocks excluded from the estimation of the risk-return relationship, APT performs better than CAPM. When we included the 127 stocks in estimating the APT and CAPM risk-return relationships and again calculated expected returns and their differences from average actual returns for the same 127 stocks, APT's performance was even better. It produced squared differences that were 50 percent less than those produced by CAPM.

Testing of APT is still in a very early stage, and many questions about the ability to verify the model remain unanswered. But, in all of the performance comparisons with CAPM of which we are aware (whether done by researchers who have hopes for the model, like Chen or by those who question its empirical foundation, such as Dhrymes, Friend, and Gultekin), APT outperformed CAPM.

Conclusion

Arbitrage Pricing Theory is in an early stage of development. At this point, it has not been tested as thoroughly as the Capital Asset Pricing Model. But most tests that have been reported are positive. APT, which explains variation in stock returns using *several* economy-wide variables, seems to perform better than the CAPM, which quantifies risk solely in terms of a single factor: beta, or co-variability with the market. Because APT promises to add to both our understanding of—and our ability to measure—risk, it is a model with a good chance of replacing CAPM as a practical tool of risk analysis for both investors and corporate planners.

Research to identify the real economic forces behind statistically constructed factors has begun. The most promising work of this kind has been done by Nai-Fu Chen, Richard Roll, and Stephen Ross. They have identified growth in industrial production, unexpected changes in the term structure of interest rates, spreads between low and high grade bond portfolio returns, and unexpected inflation as the most important determinants of security returns.

Risk measurement is important in capital budgeting, performance measurement, portfolio selection, and in almost all strategic decisions. Before APT can be widely used by investors or corporate planners, however, the basic factors must be identified more precisely, single factor portfolios developed, and sensitivities to each factor continuously calculated and made easily available to users. In fact, APT needs a factor sensitivity service like Merrill Lynch's "beta book" publication, *Security Risk Evaluation*, which publishes quarterly estimates of CAPM-based risk factors. Such a publication should come as the research progresses and the conviction grows that APT can help in quantifying the risks relevant for investment and corporate managers.

A New Approach to Evaluating Natural Resource Investments

by Michael J. Brennan and
Eduardo S. Schwartz, *University of British Columbia*

The plight of the contemporary capital budgeting analyst may be compared to that of the 19th-century physician. Long on learning, he is short on technique, and such technique as he does possess can be acquired in a matter of weeks by the intelligent layman. For, while understanding of the operation of capital markets has progressed rapidly during the past two decades, significant innovations in corporate capital budgeting techniques have been markedly absent. Such innovations as have been proposed—linear programming, simulation and decision-tree analysis—have failed to win widespread acceptance; and the implementation of corporate capital budgeting rules remains largely a matter of reaching for the discount tables or the pocket calculator.

The object of capital budgeting is to find investment projects whose value exceeds their cost. Setting aside difficulties associated with determination of the cost of projects,[1] the essential problem is that of appraising or valuing the asset which will be created by an investment, be it an oil refinery, a ship or a computer assembly plant. In this sense the task of the financial analyst is not unlike that of the appraiser or realtor who ventures opinions on the value of real properties. It is instructive to note that real estate appraisals typically start from the known prices at which similar properties have changed hands in the recent past and then make marginal adjustments to reflect differences in location, size and so on.

At first blush this approach bears no relation to the procedures followed by financial analysts in appraising investment projects. As is often the case, however, first impressions are misleading. In fact the financial analyst also proceeds by adjustment from the known values of some assets to an estimate of the value of the hypothetical asset—that is, the outcome of the investment project under consideration. The difference is simply that while the realtor makes modest interpolations from the prices of neighbouring properties, the financial analyst typically makes enormous extrapolations from the known values of completely unrelated assets: in fact, from the value of a portfolio of riskless bonds whose time pattern of cash flows corresponds to that of the investment project.

We shall argue that the whole apparatus of the classical discounted cash flow approach to capital budgeting is predicated upon an analogy between a real investment project and a portfolio of riskless bonds. Such an analogy may be appropriate in some contexts—one thinks naturally of public utilities—but it is obviously inappropriate in many other cases (and nowhere perhaps more so than in the realm of natural resource investments, our primary concern in this paper). The challenge to the financial analyst is to choose an asset of known value which is closest in characteristics to the asset whose value is to be determined. Since this choice must contain an element of judgment, capital budgeting is as much a matter of art as of technique. Unfortunately, many text books leave the mistaken impression that capital budgeting is simply a question of mechanical application of the rules of discounting.

In the case of natural resource investments, the relevant asset whose value is known will often be a portfolio consisting of riskless bonds and either the commodity which is to be produced by the investment project—be it gold, oil or lead—or a futures contract on that commodity. This is most easily seen in the case of a gold mine which will produce a known output at a known cost. If the costs are known,

---

1. These may be far from trivial as recent experience with nuclear power plants reveal.

107

While the realtor makes modest interpolations from the prices of neighbouring properties, the financial analyst typically makes enormous extrapolations from the known values of completely unrelated assets.

they can be discounted, like the payments on a Treasury bond, at the riskless interest rate, leaving only the problem of valuing the output. This latter task is simple if there exists a market for forward delivery, or a futures market for the commodity. The present value of an ounce of future production is equal simply to the appropriate current futures price discounted at the riskless interest rate (to reflect the fact that payment is deferred). Indeed it turns out that this discounted futures price for gold is almost exactly equal to the current spot price because of arbitrage considerations which we shall elucidate below. This means that for any commodity which, like gold, is held for investment or speculative purposes, future output can be evaluated at the current spot price without any discounting.

For commodities which are held in inventory for commercial rather than investment purposes, the situation is somewhat more complex, since it is necessary to take account of the net benefits yielded by an inventory of the commodity. The principal benefits of the inventory are, first, production cost savings made possible by avoidance of the interruptions in production which would be inevitable in the absence of an inventory and, second, the ability to take advantage of unforeseen local increases in the demand for the commodity. Collectively these benefits, net of the costs of storage of the inventory, are known as the "convenience yield" of an inventory of the commodity. It is the *marginal* convenience yield, then, or the extra services yielded by an additional unit of inventory, which must be taken into account in valuing future units of production.

It turns out that the present value of a unit of future production of the commodity is equal to the current spot price discounted by the marginal convenience yield. Moreover this marginal convenience yield may be inferred from the relation between the spot and futures prices of the commodity.

Note that this convenience yield approach avoids simultaneously the twin problems of assessing the expected future spot price at which the commodity will be sold, and of assigning a discount rate appropriate to the risk of these revenues. On the other hand it is necessary to estimate the convenience yield, which may itself be a function of the spot price of the commodity. The scope for error in estimating the convenience yield, however, is much less than in estimating future spot prices and discount rates.

Thus far we have assumed that the future output

of the project is known; however, this assumption is unlikely to be the case in most situations. Future output will depend upon a number of factors which are unknown at the time the project is evaluated: most notably, on geological features which will be revealed only as production takes place, and on future market conditions. Depending on actual future prices, production may be changed, or a project shut down or even abandoned with resulting costs of closure, redundancy and so on.

These operating options are extremely difficult to evaluate under the classical present value approach. They may be valued in a quite straightforward manner, however, and the optimal operating policies determined, by treating the project as an *option* on the commodity, and adapting the option pricing paradigm originally developed by Fischer Black and Myron Scholes (1973) and elaborated by Robert Merton (1973). Indeed so flexible is this approach that it is possible to value individual components of the cash flows from a project—for example, to calculate the present value of a royalty, an income tax or redundancy payments—and, even more important, to determine the effect of alternative fiscal arrangements on the optimal operating policies of the projects. However, before we present this new approach to capital budgeting for natural resource investments, it will prove useful to consider in more detail the limitations of the classical discounted cash flow model.

The Classical Discounted Cash Flow Model

The classical Discounted Cash Flow or Present Value procedure for capital budgeting has now almost everywhere replaced cruder payback or accounting rate of return methods. It involves a comparison between the cost of an investment project and the present value of the cash flows the project will generate, which is calculated according to the well-known formula:

$$(1)\ PV = \frac{C_1}{1+K} + \frac{C_2}{(1+K)^2} + \ldots \frac{C_n}{(1+K)^n}$$

where C_t is the cash flow expected in period t and k is the appropriate discount rate. Formula (1) is also the one used to arrive at the value of a bond, where C_t is the coupon payment, C_n is the final repayment of principal and k is the interest rate. This is not fortui-

This approach avoids simultaneously the twin problems of assessing the expected future spot price and of assigning a discount rate appropriate to the risk of these revenues.

tous, since the origin of the formula and its only rigorous justification is precisely in its application to bonds or known cash flows.

The application of the formula to the valuation of real risky assets is made possible by two more or less tacit assumptions or conventions. The first is that uncertain future cash flows can be replaced by their expected values and that these expected cash flows can be treated as given at the outset. The second is that the discount rate is known and constant, and that it depends solely upon the risk of the project. Let us consider the limitations of an approach based on these assumptions and see why the underlying bond analogy may be a poor one for some investment projects, especially in the field of natural resources.

First, the classical approach, by assuming that the cash flows to be discounted are given at the outset, presupposes a static approach to investment decision-making—one which ignores the possibility of future management decisions that will be made in response to the market conditions encountered. Over the life of a project, decisions can be made to change the output rate, to expand or close the facility, or even to abandon it. The flexibility afforded by these decision possibilities may contribute significantly to the value of the project.

To introduce an analogy which we shall develop further below, the classical approach may be likened to valuing a stock option contract while ignoring the right of the holder not to exercise when it is unprofitable. To some extent this drawback of the classical approach may be overcome by employing a scenario or simulation approach in which alternative scenarios—involving for example different price outcomes and management responses—are generated and the resulting cash flows estimated. These cash flows are then averaged across scenarios and discounted to arrive at the present value.

Unfortunately this scenario or simulation approach gives rise to two further problems. First, it requires that the appropriate policy for each scenario be determined in advance. Sometimes this will be possible. For example, if the output rate can be adjusted costlessly, the simple rule of setting marginal cost equal to price may sometimes be optimal.[2] But more generally this will not be possible. If it is costly to close or abandon a project, then the decision to close is itself an investment decision with uncertain

future cash flows depending on commodity prices. The optimal closure policy must therefore be determined simultaneously with the original capital budgeting decision.

Even more fundamentally, the degree of managerial discretion in making future operating decisions will tend to affect the risk of the project under consideration. A project which can be abandoned under adverse circumstances will be less risky than one that cannot; it will be even less risky if part of the initial capital investment can be recovered in the event of abandonment. The classical approach offers no way of allowing for this risk effect except through some *ad hoc* adjustment of the discount rate.

In fact the tacit assumption concerning the discount rate is the second Achilles' heel of the classical approach. Given any set of expected cash flows, there almost always exists some discount rate which will yield the correct present value. But the determination of this discount rate presents an almost insurmountable task, and current procedures cannot be regarded as any more than highly imperfect rules of thumb. Thus these procedures all assume that the discount rate is constant, which is tantamount to assuming that the risk of the project is constant over its life. And this is, of course, highly unlikely. Not only will the risk depend in general upon the remaining life of the project, it will almost certainly depend upon the current profitability of the project through an operating leverage effect. Hence, not only will the discount rate vary with time, it will also be uncertain.

Even if the appropriate discount rate were deterministic and constant, the problems of estimation would still be formidable. In principle the discount rate should depend upon the risk of the project, but how is this risk to be assessed? The generally approved procedure is to use the Capital Asset Pricing Model and to base the discount rate on the beta of the project as estimated from other firms with similar projects. In practice these other firms consist in effect of portfolios of projects, sometimes in unrelated industries, and this makes the assignment of betas to individual projects a hazardous undertaking.[3] Transferring these betas to the project under consideration creates further problems, for a new project is likely to have a cost structure which differs in a systematic fashion from existing, mature projects. The problem is compounded by the consideration, mentioned

2. For an extractive industry even this may not be the case, for it may be better to leave the resource in the ground in the expectation of more favourable prices in the future.

3. Fuller and Kerr (1981) describe well the difficulties of arriving at a beta estimate even for a division of a corporation.

The classical approach presupposes a static approach to investment decision-making—one which ignores the possibility of future management decisions.

above, that the latitude of future operating decisions inherent in a project will affect its risk, and is unlikely to be duplicated in existing projects.

Of course these problems are often ignored in practice and a single corporate discount rate based on the weighted average cost of capital is employed for all projects, regardless of risk. As is well known, however, the price of this simplification is a capital budgeting decision system which contains systematic biases as between projects with different risks and different lives. And, as we have argued, such a decision system will lead to the systematic undervaluation of projects with significant operating options.

A final practical difficulty with the classical approach is the necessity to forecast expected output prices for many years into the future. This problem is particularly acute for natural resource industries, where annual price fluctuations of 25 to 50 percent are not uncommon. Under these conditions a wide range of possibilities for the path of expected future spot prices will appear plausible, and the calculated present value of the project will depend upon some arbitrary selection among them.

The foregoing appears to constitute a fairly strong indictment of the classical discounted cash flow approach to capital budgeting. It would be premature, however, to conclude that the approach is without merit, or that it should be discarded in favour of some even worse approach, such as the old payback rule. The limitations of the classical approach arise because it is based fundamentally on an analogy between a portfolio of riskless bonds and a real investment project. In many cases this analogy may be useful; for example, in situations in which the scope for future managerial discretion is limited, and the fiction of other similar risk projects can be maintained. Moreover, even if these conditions are not satisfied, the bond analogy underlying the classical approach may still be the best method available.

In general the appropriate analogy will depend upon the type of project under consideration. For natural resource projects, as we shall show, a better analogy than the classical model is provided by the option pricing or contingent claims paradigm. This approach treats a natural resource extraction project or mine as an option on the underlying commodity. It will prove helpful first, however, to consider the principles involved in valuing a simple gold mine assuming no scope for future managerial discretion.

A Simple Gold Mine

Consider a gold mine which will produce a known output of 1000 ounces at a cost of $200,000 over each of the next two years. The present value of the mine is simply the difference between the present value of the reserves, which will depend upon the future spot price of gold, and the present value of the costs. Since the costs are certain, the bond analogy applies precisely to them, and they may be discounted at the current bond rate, R, say 10 percent, to yield as follows:

$$(2)\ PV(Costs) = \frac{200,000}{1.1} + \frac{200,000}{1.1^2} = \$347,107.$$

To value the output or revenues of the mine, let us suppose initially there exist futures markets for gold deliverable in one and two years, and that the current futures prices are F_1 and F_2. Now an individual who goes long in a one-year futures contract agrees to take delivery of one ounce of gold in one year in return for a payment of F_1, which will also take place in one year.[4] He is effectively buying gold for future delivery at a *current,* or present value, price of $F_1/(1+R)$, where the discounting reflects the fact that payment is deferred for one year. Similarly, an individual who goes short in a futures contract agrees to make delivery of the gold in one year in return for receiving F_1 at that time. He is effectively selling gold for future delivery at a current or present value price of $F_1/(1+R)$. Thus the futures market reveals to us directly the present value of an ounce of gold deliverable in t years as $F_t/(1+R)^t$.

Now the owner of the gold mine owns nothing but the right to deliver 1000 ounces of gold in one and two years after incurring the necessary extraction costs dealt with above. It follows that the present value of this gold for future delivery is given by the equation:

$$(3)\ PV\ (Revenues) = \frac{1000\ F_1}{1.1} + \frac{1000\ F_2}{1.21}$$

where the interest rate, R, is 10 percent. It follows that the present value of the mine is simply the difference between expressions (3) and (2), and the gold mine is equivalent to a portfolio consisting of gold futures and bonds.

Note that this approach obviates any need either

---

4. We are ignoring the technical distinctions between futures markets and forward markets.

110

The classical approach may be likened to valuing a stock option contract while ignoring the right of the holder not to exercise when it is unprofitable.

to forecast the future spot price of gold, an exceedingly difficult task, or to determine an appropriate discount rate for revenues from sales of gold, which is also a difficult task. Instead, the present value of the mine is expressed solely in terms of observables, the futures prices and the interest rate.

It may be objected that the value of the mine yielded by this approach does not correspond to that obtained by an analyst using his own forecasts of future gold prices. This is quite possible. The value does correspond, however, to the price at which the gold mine could be sold today—a price which depends solely on current market expectations about future gold prices, which in turn are reflected in futures prices. Thus it is important to distinguish between the current market value of the mine, which is what the present value analysis is intended to yield, and deviations between the market's and the analyst's expectations about the future spot price of gold. If the analyst believes that gold is undervalued by the market, then it is quite possible for him to speculate on his hunches in the futures market; but he should not confuse his hunches with his estimate of the current market of the mine.

A second objection that may be made to the foregoing analysis is that there do not exist futures markets for delivery beyond a couple of years, and yet the mine may have a production life of many more years. As we shall see, however, the existence of a futures market is not critical to our analysis. For a commodity which is held for investment purposes, such as gold, the futures price is always equal to the current spot price compounded forward at the interest rate. Thus the futures price for delivery in t years, F_t, may be written as

(4) $F_t = S_o(1+R)^t$

where S_o is the current spot price of gold. Relation (4) permits us to infer what the futures would be, from the current spot price and the interest rate, even if no futures contract of the relevant maturity is actually traded.

To see why relation (4) must hold, consider an individual who is holding gold for investment purposes as part of his portfolio. If the futures price is less than the value given by expression (4), it will pay him to sell his gold at the current spot price, S_o, and enter into a future's contract to repurchase the gold in t years at F_t. The proceeds of the gold sale invested in bonds will yield $S_o(1+R)^t$ at a time t and he will require only F_t to make good on the futures contract,

leaving him with a certain profit $S_o(1+R)^t - F_t$. So long as F_t is below the value implied by (4), it will pay all holders of gold to sell spot and repurchase in the futures market. But since the world stocks of gold must be held by someone, it cannot be profitable for them all to sell gold and repurchase it via a futures market transaction. Thus the futures price cannot be less than the value given by expression (4). Moreover, the futures price cannot exceed this value either, for then unlimited riskless profits would follow from a strategy of purchasing gold to hold in inventory and simultaneously selling futures contracts.

Therefore, the only equilibrium price for gold for future delivery is the compounded value of the current spot price as given by (4). Substituting this value for the futures price in expression (3) for the present value of the mine revenues, we find

(5) PV (Revenues)

$$= \frac{1000 \times S_o(1.1)}{1.1} + \frac{1000 \times S_o(1.1)}{1.1^2}$$

$$= 1000 \times S + 1000 \times S$$

$$= 2000 \times S_o.$$

To express this in words, the present value of the mine revenues is obtained by valuing the future output at the *current spot price* of gold without discounting. Thus, careful reasoning reveals that it is possible to value a gold mine without making any of the hazardous assumptions about future prices of gold which would be required under the classical present value approach. Instead of treating the gold mine as analogous to a portfolio of bonds, as the classical approach does, we recognize that it is more akin to a portfolio of gold and of bonds sold short—with the latter corresponding to the production costs.

Now gold is something of a special case since its high value and imperishability make the costs of storing it in inventory negligible, and since individuals do in fact store it in safety deposit boxes for investment purposes. The situation is somewhat different for most other metals. No one, as far as we know, holds ingots of lead, zinc or aluminum in their safety deposit boxes. Instead these metals are held in commercial inventories by refiners and fabricators who use the metals in their production processes. We consider next how the foregoing analysis must be modified to account for the holding of commercial inventories.

The limitations of the classical approach arise because it is based fundamentally on an analogy between a portfolio of riskless bonds and a real investment project.

A Simple Copper Mine

Let us consider next the example of copper held in inventory not by individual investors, but by manufacturers of copper wire and piping and others who have a commercial interest in the metal. These inventories are held, like inventories of any raw material, because they permit production to proceed smoothly without interruptions caused by shortages of raw materials. Some inventories will continue to be held even if the spot price is expected to decline; the decline in the value of the inventory is offset by the convenience of having the inventory on hand. This benefit of having an inventory on hand is referred to as the *convenience yield* of the inventory. The marginal convenience yield is the benefit yielded by the marginal unit of inventory net of any costs of physical storage, deterioration, etc.

Commercial holders will add to their inventories until the marginal convenience yield, C, is equal to the financial costs of carrying inventory. These costs consist of the interest on the funds tied up in inventory, $S_o \times R$, less the capital gain, $(F_1 - S_o)$, which is realized if a futures contract is entered into to eliminate the inventory price risk:

$$(6) \quad C = S_o \times R + (S_o - F_1)$$

Solving for the one period futures price,

$$(7) \quad F_1 = S_o(1 + R) - C.$$

Comparing expression (7) with the corresponding expression (4) for gold futures, we see that the only difference lies in the convenience yield, C, which tends to reduce the futures relative to the spot price.

The *marginal* convenience yield will depend on the size of the total inventories in the economy. When commercial inventories are large, the benefit of an additional unit of inventory will be correspondingly small. At the same time spot prices will also be low because of the excess supply of the commodity. Therefore it is reasonable to take the convenience yield as proportional to the current spot price, $C = cS$.[5] Substituting into (7) we find that the futures price for delivery in t periods is

$$(8) \quad F_t = S_o(1 + R - c)^t.$$

We are able to use expression (8) to evaluate the revenues from a copper mine in just the same way we could evaluate the revenues from the gold mine. The only difference is that we must value the future output at the current spot price discounted at the convenience yield.[6] For example, if our copper mine will produce 100 pounds of copper in each of the following two years and the convenience yield is 2 percent we find that

$$\text{PV(Reserves)} = \frac{100 \times S_o}{1.02} + \frac{100 \times S_o}{1.02^2} = 194 \times S_o.$$

There is only one remaining problem, and that is the appropriate convenience yield. Fortunately this can be computed from the current spot and futures prices and the interest rate using expression (8).

The Mine as an Option

To this point we have seen how to value a mine whose output rate is predetermined, regardless of the price at which the output can be sold. In practice the owner of a mine generally has the right to choose the optimal output rate, to close the mine, to re-open it, or even to abandon it as circumstances dictate. Because of these decision possibilities, a mine is most appropriately regarded as a complex option on the resources contained in the mine. Just as a stock option gives the holder the right to acquire shares at a fixed exercise price, ownership of a mine confers the right to acquire the output of the mine at a fixed exercise price equal to the variable cost of production. Consequently, a mine may be valued by combining the valuation principles already presented with the option pricing approach pioneered by Black-Scholes (1973) and Merton (1973). The option pricing approach implies that the value of the mine satisfies a certain differential equation subject to a set of boundary conditions which we shall now consider.

The value of the mine will depend upon whether it is currently open and producing or closed and incurring maintenance costs. It will also depend upon the unexploited inventory remaining in the mine. And just as in the case of the fixed output mines already discussed, it will depend upon the current spot price of the commodity. Finally, the mine value will also depend upon an index of operating costs.

To be more specific, we will begin by defining the following symbols:

---

5. More complex relations between the convenience yield and the spot price can also be taken into account.

6. A technical note: this approach is exact only for continuous compounding. In practice discrete compounding makes a negligible difference.

For natural resources projects, a better analogy than the classical model is provided by the option pricing or contingent claims paradigm.

Q — the remaining mine inventory
S — the current spot price of the commodity
OC — an index of mine operating costs
V(Q,S,OC) — the current value of an operating mine
N(Q,S,OC) — the current value of a non-operating mine.

Then we have the following boundary conditions:

Mine Exhaustion: When the inventory in the mine is exhausted, the mine can no longer operate. In this case its value depends solely on the salvage value, which may be negative.

N(Q,S,OC) = Salvage Value

Premature Abandonment: If output prices are sufficiently low, and the cost of maintaining a non-operating mine are sufficiently high, it may pay to abandon a mine even though there is a positive remaining inventory. The abandonment possibility places a floor under the value of the mine so that

N(Q,S,OC) ≥ Salvage Value

Operating Decisions: If the variable costs of operation are constant, and the mine has no influence on the price at which output can be sold, it will always be optimal either to operate the mine at its full capacity rate, q, or to shut it down temporarily. There will generally be costs involved with shutting the mine—redundancy payments and so on. However, the ability to shut down means that the value of an operating mine can never be less than the value of the mine shut less the costs of shutting:

O(Q,S,OC) ≥ N(Q,S,OC) - shutting costs.

Similarly, since a shut mine can always be re-opened at a cost, the value of a non-operating mine cannot be less than the value of an operating mine minus the costs of re-opening, so that

N(Q,S,OC) ≥ O(Q,S,OC) - re-opening costs.

Cash Flows: When the mine is operating it generates a cash flow which is given by

$$q(S(1 - r) - A(OC))(1 - t_c) - t_r O$$

where q is the capacity output rate, r is a royalty rate which is charged on the value of output, $A(OC)$ is the average cash cost of production at the capacity output, t_c is the corporate tax rate, and t_r is the real estate tax rate, which is assumed to be charged on the value of the mine, O. When the mine is shut the cash flow is given by the negative of the maintenance costs and real estate taxes.

Given these conditions the equation for the mine value may be solved simply on a personal computer. The nature of the solution is illustrated in Figure 1, which plots the mine value as a function of the spot price for a given level of mine inventory, Q, and level of operating costs, OC. To understand this figure suppose that the mine is initially shut and that the spot price is between S_1 and S_2. As the spot price rises, the value of the operating mine begins to exceed the value of the mine shut, but not be enough to justify incurring the costs of opening the mine. It is not optimal to open the mine until the spot price reaches S_2, at which point the value of the mine in operation exceeds its value shut by just the amount of the opening costs. Once opened, the mine will remain in operation even if the spot price drops. It will not be optimal to shut the mine unless the price drops to S_1, at which point the value of the shut mine exceeds the value of the operating mine by the amount of the shutting cost. If the salvage value of the mine is zero, it will not be optimal to actually cease maintenance and abandon the mine until the spot price falls to S_0.

Valuing a Gold Mine

To gain some further insight into our valuation procedure and the data inputs required to implement it, we shall consider a specific numerical example. The data for our hypothetical gold mine are presented in Table 1. It is instructive to compare the data required here with those required for a classical discounting analysis. First, we do not require any projections for the price of gold or specification of a "cost of capital" for the mine. We require instead that the convenience yield of gold be specified.[7] Additional data required by this approach, but not by the classical discounting approach, are the standard deviation

---

7. The futures/spot price relation for gold reveals a zero convenience yield.

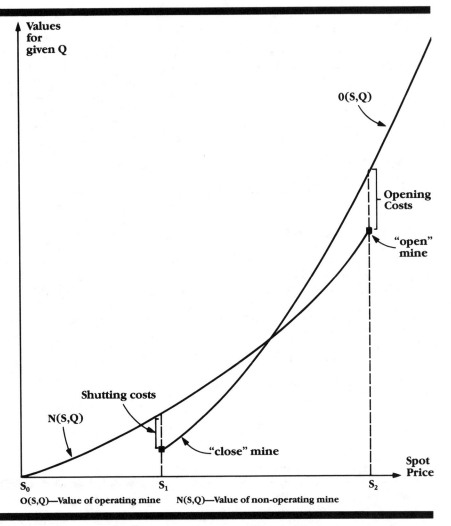

FIGURE 1
The Value of a Mine in Terms of the Current Spot Price of the Commodity

Values for given Q

$O(S,Q)$

Opening Costs

"open" mine

Shutting costs

$N(S,Q)$

"close" mine

Spot Price

S_0 S_1 S_2

$O(S,Q)$—Value of operating mine $N(S,Q)$—Value of non-operating mine

---

Table 1
Data for a Hypothetical Gold Mine

Mine
Capacity Output Rate: 50 thousand ounces per year
Current Mine Inventory: 1 million ounces
Average Production Costs (Current Prices): $250 per ounce
Opening Cost (Current Prices): $1 m
Shutting Cost (Current Prices): $1 m
Annual Maintenance Cost (Current Prices): $1 m per year
Salvage Value: – 0 –
Cost Inflation Rate: 9% per year

Gold
Convenience Yield: 0% per year
Price Risk: 20% per year

Taxes
Real Estate: 2% per year
Income: 48%
Royalty: 2%

Interest Rate: 9% per year

This approach obviates any need either to forecast the future spot price of gold or to determine an appropriate discount rate.

Table 2 Value of Gold Mine for Different Gold Prices	Gold Price $/ounce	Mine Value ($m)		Value of [1] Options ($m)	Risk[2] % per year
		Open	Shut		
	100	–0–	–0–	–	–
	150	**1.08** –	**2.08**	–	**154**
	200	8.65 –	9.65	–	82
	250	**20.02**	**20.85**	**24.36**	**68**
	300	34.86	34.78	17.22	57
	350	**51.82**	**50.96**	**9.75**	**49**
	400	70.04	69.04	9.29	43
	450	**89.05** –	**88.05**	**7.73**	**40**
	500	108.58 –	107.58	6.51	37
	550	**128.47** –	**127.47**	**5.57**	**35**
	600	148.60 –	147.60	4.81	33

– Indicates it is optimal to open mine if currently shut.
– Indicates it is optimal to shut mine if currently open.
[1] Options to open/shut and to abandon.
[2] Standard deviation of rate of return.

or risk of the gold price per unit time,[8] the maintenance costs for a shut mine, the costs of opening and shutting the mine and the salvage value. The reason these data are not required for a classical discounting is that the options of shutdown or abandonment are never explicitly included in this type of analysis.

Table 2 shows the value of the mine when it has a 20-year inventory of production for different gold prices.[9] Note that the value of the mine depends upon whether it is currently open and operating or shutdown. If the mine is currently operating it is optimal to shut it down if the gold price falls below $230. Since the variable cost of production is $250, this implies that it is optimal to maintain production even when the mine is operating at a loss in order to avoid the costs of shutdown and possible subsequent re-opening. On the other hand, if the mine is currently closed, it is not optimal to open it until the gold price has risen to $380, which is substantially above the variable costs of production.

The column "Value of Options" represents the difference between the value of our hypothetical mine when it is open and in production, and the value of an otherwise identical mine which must be operated at full capacity until it is exhausted in 20 years. This comparison is of interest because the assumption of continuous production is implicit in the classical discounting approach. It is clear that the value of the options to shut the mine and subsequently re-open it, or even to abandon it, is a very substantial fraction of the total value of the mine, particularly when the gold price is in the neighborhood of the variable cost of production. Valuation approaches which ignore these operating options are likely to underestimate substantially the value of the mine.

The final column of the table shows how the risk of the mine varies with the price of gold: when the price is low, the operating leverage is high. As the price rises the operating leverage declines and the risk of the mine falls until for very high gold prices it approaches the price risk of gold itself, 20 percent.

While Table 2 shows the value of the complete mine for a range of gold prices, Table 3 shows how, given a particular current gold price of $350, the present values of the different elements of the cash flow combine to yield the value of the mine. This type of analysis is likely to be particularly useful in evaluating cost-saving investments for a given mine. We can see immediately, for example, that a 10 percent saving in operating cost will have a pre-tax present value of $15.9m and an after-tax present value of $15.9m × (1 – .48) = $8.27m.

8. In general the standard deviation of the rate of return on the commodity can be obtained from an historical time series of commodity prices. For those commodities, like gold, on which traded options exist, an implied standard deviation can also be obtained using an appropriate option pricing model [Black and Scholes (1973)].
9. Note that we have neglected the effects of depreciation allowances associated with the investment in the mine. The present value of tax savings due to these allowances should be added to the figures in the table.

TABLE 3 Valuing the Components of Mine Revenue	Gross Revenue	$m. 322.5
	Royalty	6.5
	Net Revenue	316.0
	Operating Cost	159.0
	Taxable Income	157.0
	Corporate Tax	75.4
	After Tax Cash Flow	81.6
	Opening Costs	.3
	Shutdown Costs	.7
	Maintenance Costs	6.9
	Salvage Value	–
	Real Estate Tax	21.9
	Net Cash Flow	51.8

Current gold price: $350 per ounce

The model also makes possible an analysis of the effects of alternative tax and royalty arrangements, taking into account the fact that these not only affect the shares of risk borne by the government and the owner of the mine, but also change the mine owner's optimal policy for operating the mine.

Conclusion

We have argued in this paper that traditional approaches to capital budgeting suffer from some severe limitations. These are particularly acute in the natural resource sector, where output prices are especially volatile. The problems include the forecasting of future output prices, the determination of an appropriate discount rate, and the inability to allow for management flexibility in future operating decisions. The alternative approach we have de- largely overcomes these problems by using the hitherto neglected information contained in futures prices—the convenience yield—and by recognizing that a mine can be treated as a type of option on the underlying commodity.[10] The approach has already been applied with some success to the analysis of a large resource project in Canada.

While our focus here has been on natural resource projects where futures markets for the underlying commodity exist, the basic principles underlying the analysis lend themselves with appropriate modification to applications in other context in which the role of management in influencing future operations and cash flows is significant. This is the typical case, we believe, and while the traditonal analysis views capital investments, like children, as hostages to fortune, our approach recognizes that, like children also, they are often amenable to their progenitors' guidance.

---

10. For a more detailed description of this approach see Brennan and Schwartz (1985).

The Investment Decision/Selected Bibliography

Black F. and M. Scholes, "The Pricing of Options and Corporate Liabilities," *Journal of Political Economy* 81 (1973), 637-657.

Bower, D., R. Bower, and D. Logue, "Arbitrage Pricing and Utility Stock Returns," *Journal of Finance* (September, 1984), 1041-1054.

Bower, D., R. Bower, and D. Logue, "Equity Screening Rates Using Arbitrage Pricing Theory," in C. F. Lee, ed., *Advances in Financial Planning* (Greenwich, CT: JAI Press, 1984).

Brennan, M. and E. Schwartz, "Evaluating Natural Resource Investments," *The Journal of Business* (1985).

Brown, S. and M. Weinstein, "A New Approach to Testing Asset Pricing Models: The Bilinear Paradigm," *Journal of Finance* (June, 1983), 711-743.

Chen, N., "Some Empirical Tests of the Theory of Arbitrage Pricing," *Journal of Finance* (December, 1983) 1393-1414.

Chen, N., R. Roll and S. Ross, "Economic Forces and the Stock Market: Testing the APT and Alternative Asset Pricing Theories," University of Chicago, Working paper, 1983.

Dhrymes, P., I. Friend, and N. B. Gultekin, "A Critical Reexamination of the Empirical Evidence on the Arbitrage Pricing Theory," *Journal of Finance* (June, 1984), 323-350.

Fuller, R. and H. Kerr, "Estimating the Divisional Cost of Capital: An Analysis of the Pure-Play Technique," *The Journal of Finance* 36 (December, 1981).

Ibbotson, R. G. and R. A. Sinquefield, *Stocks, Bonds, Bills and Inflation: The Past (1925-1976) and the Future (1977-2000)* (Charlottsville, VA: Financial Analysts Research Foundation, 1977).

Keim, D., "Size-Related Anomalies and Stock Market Seasonality: Further Empirical Evidence," *Journal of Financial Economics* (June, 1983), 13-32.

Lanstein, R. and W. Sharpe, "Duration and Security Risk," *Journal of Financial and Quantitative Analysis* (November, 1978), 653-668.

Levy, H., "Tests of Capital Asset Pricing Hypotheses," *Research in Finance* 1 (1979), pp. 115-223.

Lintner, J., "The Valuation of Risky Assets and the Selection of Risky Investments in Stock Portfolios and Capital Budgets," *Review of Economics and Statistics* (February, 1965), pp. 13-37.

Lintner, J., "Security Prices, Risk, and Maximal Gains from Diversification," *Journal of Finance* (December, 1965), 587-615.

Markowitz, H. M., *Portfolio Section: Efficient Diversification of Investment* (New York: John Wiley and Jones, 1959).

Modigliani, F. and G. Pogue, "An Introduction to Risk and Return," *Financial Analysts Journal* (March-April and May-June, 1974) 68-80 and 69-86.

Merton, R., "Theory of Rational Option Pricing," *Bell Journal of Economics and Management Science* 4 (1973).

Mossin, J., "Equilibrium in Capital Asset Markets," *Econometrica* (October, 1966), pp. 768-783.

Reiganum, M., "Misspecification of Capital Asset Pricing: Empirical Anomalies Based on Earnings' Yields and Market Values," *Journal of Financial Economics* (March, 1981), 19-46.

Roll, R., "A Critique of the Asset Pricing Theory's Tests," *Journal of Financial Economics* (March, 1977), 126-176.

Roll, R., and S. Ross, "The Arbitrage Pricing Theory Approach to Strategic Portfolio Planning," *Financial Analysts Journal* (May-June 1984), 14-26.

Roll, R., and S. Ross, "An Empirical Investigation of the Arbitrage Pricing Theory," *Journal of Finance* (December, 1980), 1073-1103.

Roll, R., and S. Ross, "Regulation, the Capital Asset Pricing Model, and the Arbitrage Pricing Theory," *Public Utilities Fortnightly* (May 26, 1983), 22-28.

Rosenberg, B. and J. Guy, "Prediction of a Beta from Investment Fundamentals," *Financial Analysts Journal*, Part I (May/June 1976), 3-15.

Rosenberg, B., "The Capital Asset Pricing Model and the Market Model," *Journal of Portfolio Management* (Winter, 1981), 5-16.

Ross, S., "The Arbitrage Theory of Capital Asset Pricing," *Journal of Economic Theory* (1976), 341-360.

Ross, S., "Return, Risk and Arbitrage," in Irwin Friend and James L. Bicksler, *Risk and Return in Finance* (Cambridge: Balinger, 1977).

Rudd, A. and B. Rosenberg, "The 'Market Model' in Investment Management," *Journal of Finance* (May, 1980), 597-607.

Rosenberg, B. and V. Marathe, "The Prediction of Investment Risk: Systematic and Residual." *Proceedings of the Seminar on the Analysis of Security Prices*, University of Chicago, November 1975, 82-225.

Sharpe, W. F., "Capital Asset Prices: A Theory of Market Equilibrium Under Conditions of Risk," *Journal of Finance* (September, 1964), 425-442.

Part III: The Financing Decision 1: Capital Structure

INTRODUCTION

The articles in this section are devoted largely to questions of corporate capital structure: Is there such a thing as an "optimal" capital structure for the public corporation? What are the real benefits and costs of leverage? Does the relative scarcity of triple A-rated companies suggest that corporate America is acquiring a greater appreciation of the value of debt financing? Is the triple A company in fact an anachronism, one that promises to be eradicated once and for all by ever larger corporate takeovers? Do the leveraged buyout and "junk bond" phenomena have any implications for the financing of "blue chip" corporations?

In the 1980s these questions attained a prominence, and indeed perhaps an urgency, that was unprecedented in our corporate history. For, along with the recent wave of corporate restructuring activities—mergers, divestitures, leveraged buyouts, spin-offs, and stock repurchases—we saw a large number of companies undregoing dramatic changes in capital structure. In the leveraged buyout movement, for example, private companies supported debt-to-asset ratios upwards of 90 percent. We saw large public companies, traditionally levered at 50 percent debt-to-equity or lower, resorting to the "junk bond" market to make large acquisitions and, in so doing, raising their debt-to-equity ratios well above one. At the same time, many corporate restructurings included major stock repurchase programs which likely reflected a more explicit, permanent decision to leverage the capital structure.

Critics of the widespread restructuring activity view this apparent leveraging of corporate America as one of its most alarming by-products. A number of other observers, however, have hailed these changes as reflecting a belated recognition by corporate treasurers that the tax advantages of debt financing can add significant value. Still another group views both of the above arguments with skepticism. They contend that although corporate restructuring may have increased the optimal amount of debt in *some* corporate capital structures — in large part because it increases the value of the corporation itself — the principal use of this new debt has been to provide the *means* for executing the restructuring transactions (for example, the use of junk bonds to finance an acquisition).

After the dramatic recapitalizations of the 1980s, often accompanied by large increases in stock prices, it may seem odd to begin this section with Merton Miller's reassessment of the "The Modigliani-Miller Propositions After Thirty Years." For it was Miller who, with Franco Modigliani, formulated in 1958 the now classic "M&M" capital structure "irrelevance" proposition—stated baldly, the argument that a corporation's debt-equity ratio should not affect the value of its shares. A few years after came its equally venerated companion, the M&M dividend irrelevance proposition—the notion that share values are influenced primarily by a corporation's expected earnings power, and not by the percentage of those earnings paid out as dividends.

The empirical import of the M&M propositions—and thus their central message to corporate practitioners—can be seen by turning the propositions "on their heads." That is, if changes in corporate capital structure or dividends do increase stock values, they are likely to do so only for the following reasons: (1) they reduce taxes or transaction costs: (2) they provide a reliable "signal" to investors of management's confidence in the firm's earnings prospects; or (3) they increase the probability that management will undertake only profitable investments.

In this article, after recounting the thinking behind the propositions, Professor Miller goes on to consider the contribution of each of these three factors to an explanation of the leveraged restructuring movement of the '80s. Part of the discussion focuses on the beneficial effect of debt finance on managerial efficiency and corporate reinvestment decisions—especially in companies in mature industries with too much "free cash flow" (for more on this, see the articles by Michael Jensen in later sections). But the greatest stress falls on the tax advantage of debt over equity, an argument put forth by Miller and Modigliani in 1963. In brief, the "tax-adjusted" M&M proposition says that the benefits of substituting tax-deductible interest payments for non-deductible (and thus twice-taxed) dividend payments could push the optimal capital structure toward 100% debt (provided, of course, the offsetting costs of high leverage are not too great).

In "The Search for Optimal Capital Structure," Stewart Myers reviews the corporate capital structure decision in broad terms, presenting academic insights accumulated throughout the 1960s and 1970s. He begins by dispelling the common fallacy that there is "magic" in leverage. When marketing debt or preferred instruments, many investment bankers and other financial advisors begin, as a matter of course, by demonstrating the positive effects of such instruments on EPS and ROE. The catch is that using greater leverage will always cause EPS and ROE to rise, as long as the additional earnings generated from new capital merely exceed the financing payments (which, of course, is hardly tantamount to meeting an acceptable standard of profitability). Because increased leverage means not only higher expected returns but also higher risk for equity investors, it is doubtful that such leveraging of EPS and ROE has any positive effect on stock prices. Thus, in reasonably sophisticated capital markets — the kind financial economists show have been with us for years — the capital structure decision reduces mainly to consideration of market distortions or *imperfections*: taxes, the costs of bankruptcy (or, more precisely, "financial distress"), imperfect information, and conflicts of interest between management and lenders.

But, even this argument has undergone major revision in the past few years. Indeed, Professor Myers's 1984 Presidential Address to the American Finance Association, entitled "The Capital Structure Puzzle," represents a major departure from the thinking on capital structure reflected in his first article. Up to this point, modern financial theory had proposed that the majority of public companies set target capital structures which attempt to balance the tax advantage of debt against some measure of the probability and costs of financial distress. Actual corporate behavior, however, as Myers begins by observing, does not seem to conform to this conception. A much better description of historical American debt ratios is provided by what Myers calls a "modified pecking order theory." This theory argues, in brief, that companies deviate significantly from long-run leverage targets (if they have them at all) owing to a preference to fund investment internally rather than externally, and to use less risky securities such as debt rather than resorting to the public equity markets. He then goes on to offer a new theoretical rationale to explain why this financing "pecking order" might make economic sense — a rationale which explains large and protracted "excursions" from long-run capital structure targets by firms justifiably anxious to protect their "reserve borrowing power."

In "The Investment-Financing Nexus," Michael Long and Ileen Malitz expand upon and provide empirical support for the proposition that investment type is an important determinant of the level of corporate borrowing. Specifically, they demonstrate that companies with relatively high levels of intangible investment, such as expenditures for R&D and advertising, tend to use significantly less debt financing, all else equal, than firms with a large proportional investment in tangible assets.

From discussions of optimal capital structure, we then move on to a series of articles describing transactions for effecting changes in capital structure: debt-equity swaps, stock repurchases, and debt-for-debt refundings.

In "The Debt-Equity Swap," Cornell University's Harold Bierman attempts to identify the real economic consequences, as opposed to the purely cosmetic accounting effects, of a transaction whose vogue appears to have faded with the fall in interest rates. He concludes that although the debt-equity swap may provide some firms with the most efficient means of achieving lower corporate leverage targets, the disproportionate reductions in book leverage and the tax-free accounting income accompanying swaps are not likely to fool the stock market or creditors. There are tax advantages, however, and these are likely to prove the only major real benefits.

In "The Motives and Consequences of Debt-Equity Swaps and Defeasances," Professors John Hand and Patricia Hughes add to the bulk of academic research attesting to the stock market's ability to distinguish artificial from real increases in earnings. The evidence on the timing of swaps and defeasances strongly suggests they were used by corporate treasuries in the 1980s to disguise temporary downturns in operating earnings. But investors, far from being fooled by the accounting treatment, actually responded in systematically negative fashion to announcements of both swaps and defeasances. In the case of swaps, moreover, the larger the reported accounting gain from the swap, the more negative the stock market reaction.

In "Common Stock Repurchases: What Do They Really Accomplish?," Larry Dann examines the most popular rationales for stock repurchases in the light of several recent studies. Stock buybacks have been on the rise among U.S. corporations in the 1980s, and they appear to have been justified by the large accompanying stock price increases. In attempting to sort out the *cause* of such increases, however, Dann cites persuasive evidence that it is the communication of positive information to the market that causes the increase, not the financial effects of the repurchase itself.

In "The Bond Refunding Decision," Alan Kraus of the University of British Columbia discusses call provisions and the corporate bond refunding decision.

The article begins by dismissing the popular rationale for including the call provision in bond agreements: expected interest savings. In a sophisticated market, the corporation pays in advance for such savings in the form of a higher interest rate on callable bonds. The explanation of the almost universal inclusion of the call provision therefore rests on other factors: taxes, operating flexibility, and interest rate risk.

DHC

The Modigliani Miller Propositions after Thirty Years

by Merton Miller,
University of Chicago

I t has now been 30 years since the Modigliani-Miller Propositions were first presented in "The Cost of Capital, Corporation Finance and the Theory of Investment," which appeared in the *American Economic Review* in June 1958. I have been invited, if not to celebrate, at least to mark, the event with a retrospective look at what we set out to do on that occasion and an appraisal of where the Propositions stand today after three decades of intense scrutiny and often bitter controversy.

*This article is a shortened version of an article that appeared in the *Journal of Economic Perspectives* (Fall 1988) and is reprinted here with permission of the American Economic Association, the journal's publisher. The author would like to acknowledge helpful comments on an earlier draft made by George Constantinides, Melvin Reder, Lester Telser, Hal Varian, Robert Vishny, and by the editors of the *Journal of Economic Perspectives*, Carl Shapiro, Joseph Stiglitz, and Timothy Taylor.

THE VIEW THAT CAPITAL STRUCTURE IS LITERALLY IRRELEVANT OR THAT
"NOTHING MATTERS" IN CORPORATE FINANCE, THOUGH STILL SOMETIMES
ATTRIBUTED TO US,...IS FAR FROM WHAT WE EVER ACTUALLY SAID ABOUT
THE REAL-WORLD APPLICATIONS OF OUR THEORETICAL PROPOSITIONS.

Some of these controversies can by now be regarded as settled. Our Proposition I, which holds the value of a firm to be independent of its capital structure (its debt/equity ratio), is accepted as an implication of equilibrium in perfect capital markets. The validity of our then novel arbitrage proof of that proposition is also no longer disputed, and essentially similar arbitrage proofs are now common throughout finance.[1] Propositions analogous to, and often even called, M and M propositions have spread beyond corporation finance to the fields of money and banking, fiscal policy, and international finance.[2]

Clearly Proposition I, and its proof, have been accepted into economic theory. Less clear, however, is the empirical significance of the MM value-invariance Proposition I in its original sphere of corporation finance.

Skepticism about the practical force of our invariance proposition was understandable given the almost daily reports in the financial press, then as now, of spectacular increases in the values of firms after changes in capital structure. But the view that capital structure is literally irrelevant or that "nothing matters" in corporate finance, though still sometimes attributed to us (and tracing perhaps to the very provocative way we made our point), is far from what we ever actually said about the real-world applications of our theoretical propositions. Looking back now, perhaps we should have put more emphasis on the other, upbeat side of the "nothing matters" coin: showing what *doesn't* matter can also show, by implication, what *does*.

This more constructive approach to our invariance proposition and its central assumption of perfect capital markets has now become the standard one in teaching corporate finance. We could not have taken that approach in 1958, however, because the analysis departed too greatly from the then accepted way of thinking about capital structure choices. We first had to convince people (including ourselves!) that there could be *any* conditions, even in a "frictionless" world, where a firm would be indifferent between issuing securities as different in legal status, investor risk, and apparent cost as debt and equity. Remember that interest rates on corporate debts were then in the 3 to 5 percent range, with equity earnings/price ratios—then the conventional measure of the "cost" of equity capital—running from 15 to 20 percent.

The paradox of indifference in the face of such huge spreads in the apparent cost of financing was resolved by our Proposition II, which showed that when Proposition I held, the cost of equity capital was a linear increasing function of the debt/equity ratio. Any gains from using more of what might seem to be cheaper debt capital would thus be offset by the correspondingly higher cost of the now riskier equity capital. Our propositions implied that the *weighted average* of these costs of capital to a firm would remain the same no matter what combination of financing sources the firm actually chose.

Though departing substantially from the then conventional views about capital structure, our propositions were certainly not without links to what had gone before. Our distinction between the real value of the firm and its financial packaging raised many issues long familiar to economists in discussions of "money illusion" and money neutrality. . .

In the field of corporate finance, however, the only prior treatment similar in spirit to our own was by David Durand in 1952 (who, as it turned out, also became our first formal critic).[3] Durand had proposed, as one of what he saw as two polar approaches to valuing shares, that investors might ignore the firm's then-existing capital structure and first price the whole firm by capitalizing its operating earnings *before* interest and taxes. The value of the shares would then be found by subtracting out the value of the bonds. But he rejected this possibility in favor of his other extreme, which he believed closer to the ordinary real-world way of valuing corporate shares. According to this conventional view, investors capitalized the firm's net income *after* interest and taxes with only a loose, qualitative adjustment for the degree of leverage in the capital structure.

That we too did not dismiss the seemingly unrealistic approach of looking through the momentary capital structure to the underlying real flows may

1. Examples include Cornell and French (1983) on the pricing of stock index futures, Black and Scholes (1973) on the pricing of options, and Ross (1976) on the structure of capital asset prices generally. For other, and in some respects, more general proofs of our capital structure proposition, see among others, Stiglitz (1974) for a general equilibrium proof showing that individual wealth and consumption opportunities are unaffected by capital structures; Hirshleifer (1965) and (1966) for a state preference, complete-markets proof; Duffie and Shafer (1986) for extensions to some cases of incomplete markets; and Merton (forth-

coming) for a spanning proof.

Full citations for all articles mentioned are listed in the References section at the end of this article.

2. See, for example, Wallace (1981) on domestic open-market operations; Sargent and Smith (1986) on central bank foreign-exchange interventions; Chamley and Polemarchakis (1984) on government tax and borrowing policies; and Fama (1980),(1983) on money, banking, and the quantity theory.

3. Durand (1959).

well trace to the macroeconomic perspective from which we had approached the problem of capital structure in the first instance. Our main concern, initially, was with the determinants of *aggregate* economic investment by the business sector. The resources for capital formation by firms came ultimately from the savings of the household sector, a connection that economists had long found convenient to illustrate with schematic national income and wealth T-accounts, including, of course, simplified sectoral balance sheets such as:

BUSINESS FIRMS		HOUSEHOLDS	
Assets	**Liabilities**	**Assets**	**Liabilities**
Productive Capital	Debts owed to households	Debts of firms	Household net worth
	Equity in firms owned by households	Equity in firms	

Consolidating the accounts of the two sectors leads to the familiar national balance sheet in which the debt and equity securities no longer appear:

Assets	**Liabilities**
Productive Capital	Household Net worth

The value of the business sector to its ultimate owners in the household sector is thus seen clearly to lie in the value of the underlying capital. And by the same token, the debt and equity securities owned by households can be seen not as final, but only as intermediate, assets serving to partition the earnings (and their attendant risks) among the many separate individual households within the sector.

Our value-invariance Proposition I was in a sense only the application of this macroeconomic intuition to the microeconomics of corporate finance; and the arbitrage proof we gave for our Proposition I was just the counterpart, at the individual investor level, of the consolidation of accounts and the washing out of the debt/equity ratios at the sectoral level. In fact, one blade of our arbitrage proof had the arbitrager doing exactly that washing out. If levered firms were undervalued relative to unlevered firms, our arbitrager was called on to "undo

the leverage" by buying an appropriate portion of both the levered firm's debt and its shares. On a consolidated basis, the interest paid by the firm cancels against the interest received and the arbitrager thus owned a pure equity stream. Unlevered corporate equity streams could in turn be relevered by borrowing on individual account if unlevered streams ever sold at a discount relative to levered corporate equity. That possibility of "homemade leverage" by individual investors provided the second and completing blade of our arbitrage proof of value invariance.

Our arbitrage proof drew little flak from those who saw it essentially as a metaphor—an expository device for highlighting hidden implications of the "law of one price" in perfect capital markets. But whether the operations we called arbitrage could *in fact* substitute for consolidation when dealing with real-world corporations was disputed. Could investors, acting on their own, really replicate and, where required, wash out corporate capital structures—if not completely, as in the formal proof, then by enough, and quickly enough, to make the invariance proposition useful as a description of the central tendency in the real-world capital market? These long-standing and still not completely resolved issues of the empirical relevance of the MM propositions will be the primary focus of what follows here.

Three separate reasons (over and above the standard complaint that we attributed too much rationality to the stock market) were quickly offered by our critics for believing that individual investors could not enforce the corporate valuations implied by Propositions I and II. These lines of objection, relating to dividends, debt defaults, and taxes, each emphasized a different, distinctive feature of the corporate form of business organization. And each in turn will be reexamined here, taking full advantage this time, however, of the hindsight of thirty years of subsequent research and events. . .

■ ARBITRAGE, DIVIDENDS, AND THE CORPORATE VEIL

The law of one price is easily visualized in commodity settings where market institutions deliberately provide the necessary standardization and interchangeability of units. But to which of the many features of an entity as complex as an operating business firm would our financial equilibration extend?

We opted for a Fisherian rather than the

standard Marshallian representation of the firm. Irving Fisher's view of the firm—now the standard one in finance, but then just becoming known—impounds the details of technology, production, and sales in a black box and focuses on the underlying net cash flow. The firm for Fisher was just an abstract engine transforming current consumable resources, obtained by issuing securities, into future consumable resources payable to the owners of the securities. Even so, what did it mean to speak of firms or cash flow streams being different, but still "similar" enough to allow for arbitrage or anything close to it?

Some of the answers would be provided, we hoped, by our concept of a "risk class," which was offered with several objectives in mind. At the level of the theory, it defined what today would be called a "spanning" set; the uncertain underlying future cash flow streams of the individual firms within each class could be assumed perfectly correlated, and hence perfect substitutes. But the characteristics of those correlated streams could be allowed to differ from class to class. Hence, at the more practical level, the risk class could be identified with Marshallian industries— groupings around which so much academic and Wall Street research had always been organized.[4] We hoped that the earnings of firms in some large industries such as oil or electricity generation might vary together closely enough not just for real-world arbitragers to carry on their work of equilibration efficiently, but also to offer us as outside observers a chance of judging how well they were succeeding. Indeed, we devoted more than a third of the original paper (plus a couple of follow-up studies) to empirical estimates of how closely real-world market values approached those predicted by our model. Our hopes of settling the empirical issues by that route, however, have largely been disappointed.[5]

INVESTOR ARBITRAGE WHEN DIVIDENDS DIFFER: THE DIVIDEND-INVARIANCE PROPOSITION

Although the risk class, with its perfect correlation of the underlying real cash streams may have provided a basis for the arbitrage in our formal proof, there remained the sticking point of how real-world market equilibrators could gain access to a firm's operating cash flows, let alone to two or more correlated ones. As a matter of law, what the individual equity investor actually gets on buying a share is not a right to the firm's underlying cash flow but only to such cash dividends as the corporation's directors choose to declare. Must these man-made payout policies also be assumed perfectly correlated along with the underlying cash flows to make the equilibration effective? If so, the likely empirical range of the value-invariance proposition would seem to be narrow indeed.

A second MM-invariance proposition—that the value of the firm was independent of its dividend policy—was developed in part precisely to meet this class of objections. The essential content of the dividend-"irrelevance" argument was already in hand at the time of the original leverage paper and led us there to dismiss the whole dividend question as a "mere detail" (not the last time, alas, that we may have overworked that innocent word "mere"). We stated the dividend-invariance proposition explicitly, and noted its relation to the leverage proof in the very first round of replies to our critics.[6] But because dividend decisions were controversial in their own right, and because considering them raised so many side issues of valuation theory and of practical policy, both private and public, we put off the fuller treatment of dividends to a separate paper that appeared three years after the first one.[7]

That the close connection in origin of the two invariance propositions has not been more widely appreciated traces not only to their separation in time, but probably also to our making no reference to arbitrage (or even to debt or equity) in the proof of the dividend-invariance proposition. Why bring in arbitrage, we felt, when an even simpler line of proof would serve? The dividend invariance proposition stated only that, *given* the firm's investment decision, its dividend decision would have no effect on the value of the shares. The added cash to fund the higher dividend payout must come from somewhere, after all; and with investment fixed, that somewhere could only be from selling off part of the firm. As long as

---

4. Remember, in this connection, that the capital asset pricing models of Sharpe (1964) and Lintner (1965) and their later extensions that now dominate empirical research in finance had yet to come on the scene. For some glimpses of how more recent asset pricing frameworks can accommodate the MM propositions without reference to MM risk classes or MM arbitrage, see Ross (1988).

5. Direct statistical calibration of the goodness of fit of the MM value-invariance propositions has not so far been achieved by us or others for a variety of reasons, some of which will be noted further in due course below.

6. See Modigliani and Miller (1959), especially pages 662-668.

7. See Miller and Modigliani (1961).

the securities sold off could be presumed sold at their market-determined values, then, whether the analysis was carried out under conditions of certainty or uncertainty, the whole operation of paying dividends, again holding investment constant, could be seen as just a wash—a swap of equal values not much different in principle from withdrawing money from a pass-book savings account.

The Informational Content of Dividends

Managerial decisions on dividends thus might affect the cash component of an investor's return; but they would not affect the *total* return of cash plus appreciation, and the total is what mattered. In practice, of course, even changing the cash-dividend component often seemed to matter a great deal, at least to judge by the conspicuous price jumps typically accompanying announcements of major boosts or cuts in dividends. These highly visible price reactions to dividend announcements were among the first (and are still the most frequently mentioned) of the supposed empirical refutations of the MM value-invariance principle. By invoking the dividend-invariance proposition to support the leverage-invariance proposition, we seemed to have succeeded only in substituting one set of objections for another.

But, as we suggested in our 1961 dividend paper, these price reactions to dividend announcements were not really refutations. They were better seen as failures of one of the key assumptions of both the leverage and dividend models, *viz.* that all capital market participants, inside managers and outside investors alike, have the same information about the firm's cash flows. Over long enough time horizons, this all-cards-on-the-table assumption might, we noted, be an entirely acceptable approximation, particularly in a market subject to S.E.C. disclosure rules. But new information is always coming in; and over shorter runs, the firm's inside managers were likely to have information about the firm's prospects not yet known to or fully appreciated by the investing public at large. Management-initiated actions on dividends or other financial transactions might then serve, by implication, to convey to the outside mar-

ket information not yet incorporated in the price of the firm's securities.

Although our concern in the 1961 dividend paper was with the observed announcement effects of dividend decisions, informational asymmetry also raised the possibility of strategic behavior on the part of the existing stockholders and/or their management agents. Might not much of the price response to dividend (and/or other capital structure) announcements simply be attempts by the insiders to mislead the outsiders; and if so, what point was there to our notion of a capital market equilibrium rooted solely in the fundamentals? Our instincts as economists led us to discount the possibility that firms could hope to fool the investing public systematically. But, at the time, we could offer little more support than a declaration of faith in Lincoln's Law—that you can't fool all of the people all of the time.

By the 1970s, however, the concept of an information equilibrium had entered economics, and came soon after to the field of corporate finance as well.[8] In 1978, for example, Stephen Ross showed how debt/equity ratios might serve to signal, in the technical sense, managements' special information about the firm's future prospects.[9] But the extent to which these and subsequent asymmetric information models can account for observed departures from the "invariance" propositions has not so far been convincingly established.[10]

The Interaction of Investment Policy and Dividend Policy

The dividend-invariance proposition, as we initially stated it, highlights still another way in which the corporate form of organization, and especially the separation it permits between ownership and management, can have effects that at first sight at least seem to contradict the MM value-invariance predictions. Recall that the dividend-invariance proposition takes the firm's investment decision as given—which is just a strong way of saying that the level of investment, whatever it might be, is set by management *independently* of the dividend. Without imposing such an "other-things-equal" condition, there would, of course, be no way of separating

---

8. Bhattacharya (1979) noted the formal similarity between Spence's (1973) job-market signalling model and the MM dividend model with asymmetric information.

9. Ross (1977).

10. For a recent survey of results on dividend signalling, see Miller (1987). For a more general survey of asymmetric information models in finance, see Stiglitz (1982).

the market's reaction to real investment events from reactions to the dividend and any associated, purely financial events.

In the real world, of course, the financial press reports single-company stories, not cross-sectional partial regression coefficients. In these single-company tales, the investment decision and the dividend/financing decisions are typically thoroughly intertwined. But if the tale is actually one of cutting back unprofitable investments and paying out the proceeds as dividends, followed by a big run-up in price, then the MM invariance proposition may seem to be failing, but is really not being put to the test. Nor is this scenario only hypothetical. Something very much like it appears in a number of the most notorious of recent takeover battles, particularly in the oil industry where some target firms had conspicuously failed to cut back their long-standing polices of investment in exploration despite the drastic fall in petroleum prices.

In a sense, as noted earlier, these gains to shareholders from ending a management-caused undervaluation of the firm's true earning power can also be viewed as a form of capital-market arbitrage, but not one that atomistic MM investors or arbitragers can supply on their own. Once again, the special properties of the corporate form intrude, this time the voting rights that attach to corporate shares and the majority-like rules (and sometimes supermajority rules) in the corporate charters that determine the control over the firm's decisions. Much of the early skepticism, still not entirely dispelled, about the real empirical force of inter-firm arbitrage (MM-arbitrage included) traces to these properties of corporate shares beyond their purely cash-flow consequences. A particular example of the obstacle they offered to effective capital market equilibrium was that of closed-end investment funds. In 1958, as still today, closed-end funds often sold at a substantial discount to net asset value—a discount that could be recaptured only by the shareholders merely (that word again) by getting enough of them to vote to convert to open-end fund status . . .

[Omitted here from the original is a section entitled "MM Invariance with Limited Liability and Risky Debt."]

■ THE MM PROPOSITIONS IN A WORLD WITH TAXES

We have no shortage of potential candidates for forces that might well lead the market to depart systematically and persistently from the predictions of the original MM value-invariance propositions. One such likely candidate, the third of the original lines of objection, has loomed so large in fact as to have dominated academic discussions of the MM propositions, at least until the recent wave of corporate takeovers and restructurings became the new focus of attention. That candidate is the corporate income tax, the one respect in which everyone agreed that the corporate form really did matter.

The U.S. Internal Revenue Code has long been the classic, and by now is virtually the world's only, completely unintegrated tax system imposing "double taxation" of corporate net income. A separate income tax is first levied directly on the corporation; and, except for certain small and closely held corporations, who may elect to be taxed as partnerships under Subchapter S of the Code, a second tax is then levied at the personal level on any income flows such as dividends or interest generated at the corporate level. Double taxation of the interest payments is avoided because interest on indebtedness is considered a cost of doing business and hence may be deducted from corporate gross income in computing net taxable corporate earnings. But no such allowance has been made for any costs of equity capital.[11]

If the separate corporate income tax were merely a modest franchise tax for the privilege of doing business in corporate form, as was essentially the case when it was introduced in the early years of this century, the extra burden on equity capital might be treated as just one more on the long list of second-order differences in the costs of alternative sources of capital for the firm. But, at the time of our 1958 article, the marginal tax rate under the corporate income tax had been close to and sometimes over 50 percent for nearly 20 years, and it remained there for almost another 30 years until dropped to 34 percent by the recent Tax Reform Act of 1986. The cost differentials of this size were just too big to be set aside in any normative or empirical treatments of real-world capital structure choices.

---

11. Two exceptions should be noted for the record. An undistributed profits tax from which dividends were deductible was in force for two years in the late 1930s. The excess-profits tax during World War II also allowed a deduction not for dividends, but for the "normal profits" of the firm.

Strictly speaking, of course, there is one sense, albeit a somewhat strained one, in which the basic value-invariance does go through even with corporate taxes. The Internal Revenue Service can be considered as just another security holder, whose claim is essentially an equity one in the normal course of events (but which can also take on some of the characteristics of secured debt when things go badly and back taxes are owed). Securities, after all, are just ways of partitioning the firm's earnings: the MM propositions assert only that the sum of the values of all the claims is independent of the number and the shapes of the separate partitions.

However satisfying this government-as-a-shareholder view may be as a generalization of the original model, the fact remains that the government, though it sometimes gives negative taxes or subsidies for some kinds of investment, does not normally buy its share with an initial input of funds that can serve to compensate the other stockholders for the claims on income they transfer to the Treasury. Nor are we talking here of taxation-according-to-the-benefits or of the rights of eminent domain, or even of whether the corporate tax might ultimately be better for the shareholders, or for the general public, than alternative ways of raising the same revenue. For the nongovernment equity claimholders, the government's claim to the firm's earnings is a net subtraction from their own.

THE MM TAX-ADJUSTED LEVERAGE PROPOSITION

Allowing for that subtraction can lead to a very different kind of MM Proposition, though one, as we showed in our Tax Correction article (1963), that can still be derived from an arbitrage proof along lines very similar to the original.[12] This time, however, the value of the firm (in the sense of the sum of the values of the private, nongovernmental claims) is *not* independent of the debt/equity division in the capital structure. In general, thanks to the deductibility of interest, the purely private claims will increase in value as the debt ratio increases. In fact, under conditions which can by no means be dismissed out of hand as implausible, we showed that the value of the private claims might well have no well-defined interior maximum. The optimal capital structure might be all debt!

In many ways this tax-adjusted MM proposition provoked even more controversy than the original invariance one—which could be, and often was, shrugged off as merely another inconsequential paradox from some economists' frictionless dreamworld. But this one carried direct and not very flattering implications for the top managements of companies with low levels of debt. It suggested that the high bond ratings of such companies, in which the management took so much pride, may actually have been a sign of their incompetence; that the managers were leaving too much of their stockholders' money on the table in the form of unnecessary corporate income tax payments—payments which in the aggregate over the sector of large, publicly-held corporations clearly came to many billions of dollars.

We must admit that we too were somewhat taken aback when we first saw this conclusion emerging from our analysis. The earlier modeling of the tax effect in our 1958 paper, which the 1963 paper corrected, had also suggested tax advantages in debt financing, but of a smaller and more credible size. By 1963, however, with corporate debt ratios in the late 50s not much higher than in the low tax 1920s,[13] we seemed to face an unhappy dilemma: either corporate managers did not know (or perhaps care) that they were paying too much in taxes; or something major was being left out of the model. Either they were wrong or we were.

The Offsetting Costs of Debt Finance

Much of the research effort in finance over the next 25 years has been spent, in effect, in settling which it was. Since economists, ourselves included, were somewhat leerier then than some might be now in offering mass ineptitude by U.S. corporate management as an explanation for any important and long-persisting anomalies, attention was naturally directed first to the possibly offsetting costs of leveraging out from under the corporate income tax. Clearly, leveraging increased the riskiness of the shares, as we ourselves had stressed in our original Proposition II and its tax-adjusted counterpart. A sequence of bad years, moreover, might wipe out the firm's taxable income and, given the very ungenerous treatment of losses in our tax law, that

---

12. Modigliani and Miller (1963).
13. See Miller (1963).

IN SUM, MANY FINANCE SPECIALISTS, MYSELF INCLUDED, REMAINED
UNCONVINCED THAT THE HIGH-LEVERAGE ROUTE TO CORPORATE TAX
SAVINGS WAS EITHER TECHNICALLY UNFEASIBLE OR PROHIBITIVELY
EXPENSIVE IN TERMS OF EXPECTED BANKRUPTCY OR AGENCY COSTS.

could reduce, possibly quite substantially, any benefits from the interest tax shields. A run of very bad years might actually find a highly-levered firm unable (or, as the option theorists might prefer, unwilling) to meet its debt-service requirements, precipitating thereby any of the several processes of recontracting that go under the general name of bankruptcy. These renegotiations can be costly indeed to the debtor's estate, particularly when many separate classes of creditors are involved.[14]

The terminal events of bankruptcy are not the only hazards in a high-debt strategy. Because the interests of the creditors and the stockholders in the way the assets are managed need not always be congruent, the creditors may seek the additional protection of restrictive covenants in their loan agreement. These covenants may not only be costly to monitor but may foreclose, if only by the time delay in renegotiating the original terms, the implementation of valuable initiatives that might have been seized by a firm less constrained. Nor should the transaction and flotation costs of outside equity financing be neglected, particularly in the face of information asymmetries. Prudence alone might thus have seemed to dictate the maintenance of a substantial reserve of untapped, quick borrowing power, especially in an era when those managing U.S. corporations (and the financial institutions buying their debt securities) still had personal memories of the debt refinancing problems in the 1930s.

We dutifully acknowledged these well-known costs of debt finance, but we were hard put at the time to see how they could overweigh the tax savings of up to 50 cents per dollar of debt that our model implied. Not only did there seem to be potentially large amounts of corporate taxes to be saved by converting equity capital to tax-deductible interest debt capital, but there appeared to be ways of doing so that avoided, or at least drastically reduced, the secondary costs of high-debt capital structures. The bankruptcy risk exposure of junior debt could have been blunted with existing hybrid securities such as income bonds, to take just one example, under which deductible interest payments could be made in the good years, but passed or deferred in the bad years without precipitating a technical default.

For reducing the moral hazards and agency costs

in the bondholder-stockholder relation, the undoing-of-leverage blade in the original MM proof offered a clue: let the capital suppliers hold some of each—equity as well as debt—either directly or through convertible or exchangeable securities of any of a number of kinds. In sum, many finance specialists, myself included, remained unconvinced that the high-leverage route to corporate tax savings was either technically unfeasible or prohibitively expensive in terms of expected bankruptcy or agency costs.

JUNK BONDS, LEVERAGED BUY-OUTS AND THE FEASIBILITY OF HIGH-LEVERAGE STRATEGIES

A number of recent developments in finance can be seen as confirming the suspicions of many of us academics in the early 1960s that high-leverage strategies to reduce taxes were indeed entirely feasible. Among these, of course, is the now large outstanding volume of what are popularly known as "junk bonds." The very term is a relic of an earlier era in which the distinguishing characteristic of bonds as investments was supposedly their presence at the low-risk end of the spectrum. High-risk, high-yield bonds did exist, of course, but were typically bonds issued initially with high ratings by companies that had subsequently fallen on hard times. The significant innovation in recent years—and it is still a puzzle as to why it took so long—has been in the showing that, contrary to the conventional wisdom, junk bonds could in fact be issued and marketed successfully by design, and not just as "fallen angels."

The designs utilizing new risky-debt securities have often taken the very conspicuous form of "leveraged buyouts" of the outside shareholders by a control group typically led by the existing top management. The device itself is an old one, but had been confined mainly to small firms seeking both to assure their continuity after the death or retirement of the dominant owner-founder, and to provide more liquidity for the entrepreneur's estate. The new development of recent years has been the ability, thanks in part to the market for junk bonds, to apply the technique to a much wider range of publicly-held, big businesses with capitalizations now routinely in the billions, and with new size records

---

14. The perceived complexity of the present bankruptcy code (and perhaps even the very reason for having such a code) reflect mainly the need for resolving conflicts within and between the various classes of creditors. The difficulties parallel those encountered elsewhere in "common pool" problems. (See Jackson (1987)).

being set almost every year.

The debt/equity ratios in some recent LBOs have reached as high as 9 to 1 or 10 to 1 or even more—far beyond anything we had ever dared use in our numerical illustrations of how leverage could be used to reduce taxes. The debtor/creditor incentive and agency problems that might be expected under such high leverage ratios have been kept manageable partly by immediate asset sales, but over the longer term by "strip financing"—trendy investment banker argot for the old device of giving the control and most of the ownership of the equity (except for the management incentive shares) to those providing the risky debt (or to the investment bankers they have designated as monitors). The same hold-both-securities approach, as in our arbitrage proof, has long been the standard one in Japan where corporate debt ratios are, or are at least widely believed to be, substantially higher than for their U.S. counterparts.

Some Possible Non-tax Gains from Leveraging

The recent surge of leveraged buyouts not only shows the feasibility of high-leverage capital structures for reducing corporate income taxes, but also suggests at least two other possible sources for the gains to the shareholder that may accompany a major recapitalization with newly-issued debt. The firm may, for example, already have had some long-term debt outstanding when the additional debt needed to accomplish the buyout was arranged. Even in a world without taxes, the no-gain-from-leverage implication of the original MM invariance proposition might fail if the new debt was not made junior in status to the old, if the old bond covenant was "open ended," as many still are, and if the new bonds were issued under it. Assuming no change in the underlying earning power from the recapitalization, the original creditors would then find the value of their claim diluted. The benefits of this dilution of the old bondholders accrue, of course, to the stockholders, which is why it has often been labeled "theft," particularly by the adversely affected bondholders. (Finance specialists prefer the less emotionally charged term "uncompensated wealth transfer.")

The high debt ratios in LBOs also redirect attention to the assumption, shown earlier to be crucial to the MM dividend-invariance proposition, that the firm's financial decisions can be taken as independent of its real operating and investment decisions. That assumption never sits well and certainly the notion that heavy debt burdens might indeed lead to overcautious business behavior has long been part of the folk wisdom on the dangers of debt. The new wrinkle to the interdependence argument brought in recently by the defenders of LBOs has been to stress the positive *virtues* of having managers face large debt obligations. Managements in such firms must work hard and diligently indeed to achieve any earnings above interest to enhance the value of the residual equity they hold in the firm. By accepting such heavy debt-service burdens, moreover, the managers are making a binding commitment to themselves and to the other residual equity holders against yielding to the temptations, noted earlier, to pour the firm's good money down investment ratholes.[15]

Voluntary Recapitalizations and the MM Dividend Proposition

High debt ratios have been installed in some U.S. firms in recent years, not just by outside-initiated LBOs but through voluntary recapitalizations—sometimes, it is true, merely for fending off an imminent hostile takeover, but sometimes also with the tax benefits very clearly emphasized. Even apart from the tax angles, nothing in the practice of finance these days could be more quintessentially MM than these often highly visible "self takeovers," as some wag has dubbed them. Leverage-increasing recapitalizations of this kind do indeed raise the firm's debt/equity ratio, but because the proceeds of the new bonds floated are turned over to the shareholders, the self takeovers also reunite in a single operation the two Siamese-twin MM propositions, the leverage proposition and the dividend proposition (joined together originally at birth, but soon parted and living separate lives thereafter).

The dividend proposition, as noted earlier, was put forward initially to overcome a line of objection to the leverage proof. But how dividends might actually affect real-world prices raises other issues which in turn have led to as much controversy, and to an

---

15. This view of debt service as a device for reining in managerial discretion is a major strand in what has come to be called the "free cash flow" theory of corporate finance. For an account of that theory, see Jensen (1988).

even larger number of discordant empirical findings, than for the leverage propositions. Once again, moreover, major tax differentials intruded, this time the gap between rates on dividends and capital gains under the personal income tax, with again what seemed in the late 50s and early 60s to be strikingly unorthodox policy implications. Some high-income stockholders clearly would have been better off if the firm paid no dividends and simply reinvested its earnings or bought shares in other corporations. That much every real-world conglomerator and every public finance specialist surely knew.

But the value-for-value presumption of the MM dividend proposition carried within it some further advice. There were better ways to avoid taxes on dividends than pouring the firm's money down ratholes: use the money to buy back the firm's shares! For the taxable shareholders, buybacks at market-determined prices could transform heavily-taxed dividends into less-heavily taxed capital gains and, better yet, into unrealized capital gains for shareholders who choose not to sell or trade their shares. Unlike a declared regular dividend, moreover, an announced share repurchase, whether by tender or by open market purchases, carried no implied commitments about future payouts.

PERSONAL-CORPORATE TAX INTERACTIONS AND CAPITAL MARKET EQUILIBRIUM

These tax-advantaged dividend-substitution properties of share repurchase may also offer a clue as to why the leveraging of corporate America out from under the corporate income tax may have been so long delayed. The point is not so much that share repurchase by itself has been a major vehicle deliberately invoked by corporations to reduce the personal income taxes of their shareholders, though its potential for that purpose certainly has not been lost on corporate treasurers and directors.[16] But the very presence of such a possibility at the corporate level serves as a reminder that the U.S. tax system has not one but two distinct taxes that bear on capital structure choices. Any model of capital market equilibrium must allow for both, and for their interactions.

In particular, under reasonable assumptions, the joint corporate-personal tax gains from corporate leverage, G_L, can be expressed in the following relatively transparent formula:

$$G_L = [1 - \frac{(1 - t_c)(1 - t_{PS})}{(1 - t_{PB})}] \, B_L$$

where B_L is the value of the levered firm's interest-deductible debts, t_c is the marginal corporate tax rate, and t_{PS} and t_{PB} are the marginal investor's personal marginal tax rates on, respectively, income from corporate shares and income from interest-bearing corporate debts.[17] In the special case in which the personal income tax makes no distinction between income from debt or from equity (i.e., $t_{PS} = t_{PB}$), the gain from leverage reduces to $t_c B_L$, which is precisely the expression in the MM tax model.[18] But in the contrasting extreme special case in which (a) the capital gains provisions or other special reliefs have effectively eliminated the personal tax on equity income, (b) full loss offsets are available at the corporate level, and (c) the marginal personal tax rate on interest income just equals the marginal corporate rate ($t_{PB} = t_c$), the purely tax gains from corporate leverage would vanish entirely. The gains from interest deductibility at the corporate level would be exactly offset by the added burden of interest includability under the personal tax—an added burden that, in equilibrium, would be approximated by risk-adjusted interest rate premiums on corporate and Treasury bonds over those on tax-exempt municipal securities.

This somewhat surprising special case of zero net gain from corporate leverage has inevitably received the most attention, but it remains, of course, only one of the many potentially interesting configurations for market equilibrium. Stable intermediate cases are entirely possible in which some gains to corporate leverage still remain, but thanks to the capital gains or other special provisions driving t_{PS} below t_{PB}, or to limitations on loss offsets, those gains at the corporate level are substantially below those in the original MM tax model. The tax gains from lev-

---

16. Most economists, upon first hearing about share repurchase as an alternative to dividend payments, assume that the Internal Revenue Service must surely have some kind of magic bullet for deterring so obvious a method of tax avoidance. It doesn't, or at least not one that will work in the presence of even minimally-competent tax lawyers.

17. See Miller (1977).

18. That special case assumes, among other things, that debt, once in place, is maintained or rolled over indefinitely. For valuing the tax savings when debts are not perpetuities, see the comment on this paper by Franco Modigliani that appears in the same issue of *Journal of Economic Perspectives* (Fall 1988) as this article originally appeared in.

erage might, in fact, even be small enough, when joined with reasonable presumed costs of leverage, to resolve the seeming MM anomaly of gross under-leveraging by U.S. corporations.[19]

THE MM PROPOSITIONS AND THE RECENT TAX REFORM ACT

Any such "Debt and Taxes" equilibrium, however, that the corporate sector might have reached in the early 1980s by balancing costs of debt finance against MM tax gains from leverage must surely have been shattered by the Tax Reform Act of 1986. That act sought, among other things, to reverse the long steady slide, accelerating in the early 1980s, in the contribution of corporate income taxes to total federal tax revenues. But, in attempting to increase the load on corporations, Congress seemed to have overlooked some of the interactions between corporations and individual investors that lie at the heart of the MM propositions and their later derivatives. For shareholders taxable at high marginal rates on interest or dividends under the personal income tax, for example, maintaining assets in corporate solution and suffering the corporate tax hit might make sense, provided enough of the after-corporate tax earnings could be transmuted into long-deferred, low-taxed capital gains by profitable reinvestment in real assets. In fact, over much of the life of the income tax, when shares were held largely by wealthy individuals and hardly at all by pension funds or other tax-exempt holders, the corporate form of organization for businesses with great growth potential may well have been the single most important tax shelter of all.

But the pattern of tax advantages that encouraged the accumulation of wealth in corporate form appears to have been altered fundamentally by the Tax Reform Act of 1986. The Investment Tax Credit and related tax subsidies· to fixed investment have been phased out. The marginal rate on the highest incomes under the personal income tax has now been driven to 28 percent and, hence, below the top corporate rate of 34 percent. The long-standing personal income tax differential in favor of long-term realized capital gains has been eliminated, though

income in that form still benefits from a variety of timing options and from the tax-free write-up of any accumulated gains when the property passes to heirs. The analogous tax free write-up privileges for corporate deaths or liquidations, however, formerly allowed under the so-called *General Utilities* doctrine, have now been cut back by the TRA and some of its recent predecessors, reducing still further the tax benefits of the corporate form.

To finance specialists familiar with the MM propositions, these combined changes suggest that Congressional hopes of substantially increasing the yield of the corporate income-tax—that is to say, their hopes of reinstating the double taxation of corporate profits—may well be disappointed.[20] Our capital markets and legal institutions offer too many ways for averting the double hit. Corporations can split off their cash-cow properties into any of a variety of non-corporate "flow-through" entities such as master limited partnerships or royalty trusts. And, as has been the running theme of this entire section, firms retaining corporate form can always gut the corporate tax with high-leverage capital structures. In fact, under not entirely implausible conditions (notably that the marginal bondholder is actually a tax-exempt pension fund rather than a taxable individual investor, implying that the t_{PB} is zero) the incentive to leverage out from under the corporate tax may now actually be as high or higher than it was back in 1963. The statutory top corporate tax rate has indeed been cut; but with the Investment Tax Credit and Accelerated Depreciation also blown away by the Tax Reform Act of 1986, many capital-intensive corporations may now, for the first time in a very long while, be facing the unpleasant prospect of actually paying substantial corporate taxes.

And perhaps that observation can serve as a fitting note of uncertainty, or at least of unfinished business, on which to close this look back at the MM propositions. The open questions about those propositions have long been the empirical ones, as noted here at many points. Are the equilibria the propositions imply really strong enough attractors to demand the attention of those active in the capital markets either as practitioners or as outside observers? In the physical or biological sciences, one

---

19. For some recent empirical tests of such an intermediate equilibrium using the premium over municipals, see Buser and Hess (1986). Kim (1987) offers a wide-ranging survey of recent theoretical and empirical research on capital market

equilibrium in the presence of corporate-personal income tax interactions.

20. For some recent signs of Congressional concerns on this score, see Brooks (1987) and Canellos (1987).

can often hope to answer such questions by deliberately shocking the system and studying its response. In economics, of course, direct intervention of that kind is rarely possible, but nature, or at least Congress, can sometimes provide a substitute. The U.S. tax system is a pervasive force on business decisions of many kinds, but especially so on the class of financial decisions treated in the MM propositions. Tax considerations have for that reason always figured prominently in the field of finance. Occasionally, the profession may even see changes in the tax regime drastic enough for the path of return to a new equilibrium to stand out sharply against the background of market noise. Whether the Tax Reform Act of 1986 is indeed one of those rare super shocks that can validate a theory remains to be seen.

The Search for Optimal Capital Structure

by Stewart C. Myers,
Massachusetts Institute of Technology

The search for optimal capital structure is like the search for Truth or Wisdom: you will never completely attain either goal. However, there has been progress.

No one has found the formula for optimal capital structure, but we have learned where *not* to look for it. We have accumulated several useful facts and insights. We can identify some of the costs and benefits of debt vs. equity financing. We can say, with reasonable confidence, what kinds of firms ought to borrow relatively more, and what kinds less.

In this paper, I will sketch some of what we know and don't know about firms' choice of capital structure.

First, I will argue that there is no magic in leverage—nothing supporting a *presumption* that more debt is better. Debt may be better than equity in some cases, worse in others. Or it may be no better and no worse. Sometimes all financing choices are equally good.

The case for or against debt financing must therefore be built up from a more detailed look at the firm and capital markets. The smart financial manager ends up asking not general, but specific questions, such as:

1. Is there a net tax advantage to borrowing for my firm?
2. What are the odds that a given capital structure will bring financial embarrassment or distress? What would be the cost of such financial trouble?
3. Is subsidized financing available? If so, are strings attached?
4. Should my firm's existing dividend policy constrain its financing choices? (For example, sticking to a generous dividend payout might force use of debt or new common stock issues.)
5. What are the costs of issuing securities under alternative financing plans?

In this paper, I address the first two questions only—which leaves out lots of fascinating practical and conceptual questions. However, it's worth taking the time to review the main ideas on taxes and financial distress with some care. I conclude below that there is a moderate tax advantage to corporate borrowing, at least for companies that are reasonably sure they can use the interest tax shields. Of course the costs of possible financial distress should limit borrowing. These costs are most important for risky firms—no surprise there—*and* for firms whose value depends on intangible assets. Growth firms should borrow less, other things equal.

I end up proposing a three-dimensional checklist for financial managers. The dimensions are taxes, risk, and asset type. This checklist, and the reasoning underlying it, should help financial managers think more clearly about the problem of optimal capital structure.

Assumptions and Objectives

A warning is necessary before plunging in. The warning is implicit in Brealey and Myers's Fourth Law:[1]

You can make a lot more money by smart investment decisions than by smart financing decisions. The Law does not say financing is irrelevant, only that investment has priority. Financing decisions should be shaped to support the firm's investment strategy, not vice versa.

I will therefore assume the firm's *investment* decision has already been set. I will fix the left hand side of the balance sheet and consider changes only on the right.

Another important preliminary point is to ask what the firm is trying to achieve by its financing decision. The standard objective is this: given the firm's assets and investment plan, find the capital structure that maximizes firm value. Thus, if the only choices are "debt" and "equity," we set up a market value balance sheet,

If capital markets are doing their job, all efforts to increase value by tinkering with capital structure are fruitless.

Market Value Balance Sheet

Assets, tangible and intangible, including growth opportunities	Debt (D)
	Equity (E)
	Market Value of Firm (V=D+E)

and try to find the debt *proportion* that makes the market value of the firm as large as possible.

No Magic in Financial Leverage

The entries on the right hand side of the balance sheet are financial assets—paper claims that have value only because of the real assets (including intangibles and growth opportunities) on the left. Think of the balance sheet this way:

Market Value Balance Sheet

Real assets	Paper assets

The idea is to create value by shuffling the paper assets—by dividing, recasting or recombining the *paper* claims on the firm's *real* assets.

Yet creating true value out of paper sounds like alchemy. Since firm value rests on real asset value, we would not expect purely financial (paper) transactions to change the overall value of the firm.

Of course there could be an effect if the financial transactions were costly, if they affected the firm's tax liability, or if they weakened the firm's incentives to pursue valuable investment opportunities. But set these possible imperfections aside for just a moment. If we ignore the imperfections and reject alchemy, then we must conclude that firm value should not depend on the debt ratio.

Proposition I

In general, if capital markets are doing their job, all efforts to increase value by tinkering with capital structure are fruitless. This is Modigliani and Miller's (MM's) famous Proposition I.

When a firm chooses its capital structure, it sells its real assets to investors as a package of finan-cial claims. Think of the design of the package as a marketing problem. Then you will see plenty of everyday analogies to MM's Proposition. Imagine going to the supermarket with their proposition in mind. You would predict that "The price of a pie does not depend on how it is sliced," or "It costs no more to assemble a chicken—from wings, drumsticks, breasts, etc.—than to buy one whole."

MM's theorem does *not* hold in the supermarket. The slices cost more than the whole pie. An assembled chicken costs more than a chicken bought whole. Whole milk mixed at home from skim milk and cream costs more than whole milk bought at the store.

There are two reasons why the parts cost more than the whole. In the case of chickens, these are:
1. *Costs on the Demand Side.* Consumers are willing to pay extra to pick and choose the pieces they like. It's costly for them to buy whole chickens, cut them up and sell the pieces they don't want.
2. *Costs on the Supply Side.* It's costly for supermarkets to cut up the chickens and sell the pieces separately.

Note that *both* conditions are necessary to explain why the pieces sell for more than the whole. Suppose supermarkets found a way to cut and package the pieces at trivial cost. Then competition would drive out any extra charge for the pieces. Consumers would still be *willing* to pay extra, but they would not have to. On the other hand, suppose there are costs on the supply side, but not on the demand side. (That is, suppose consumers could cut up the chickens and trade in the pieces, costlessly.) Then, consumers would not pay any extra for the pieces offered by supermarkets. Supermarkets would sell only whole chickens.

I apologize for bringing poultry into the world of high finance, but the analogy is almost exact. The firm that uses only common equity financing sells its assets whole. The firm that issues a more complex package of securities sells the assets in pieces. Let's assume investors want the complex package. It will sell at a higher price *only* if there are costs on *both* the supply side and the demand side. It must be costly for the firm to create the complex package, and it must be costly for investors to replicate it.

However, in capital markets, the costs are

---

1. The Fourth Law will appear in the second edition of R.A. Brealey and S.C. Myers, *Principles of Corporate Finance*, New York: McGraw-Hill Book Co.

much lower, relative to the sums involved, than in the grocery store. Suppose a whole chicken costs $2.50 and the corresponding pieces $3.00. The valuation error is $.50—small change. The same percentage valuation error on, say, $250 million of real assets is $50 million, which surely is enough to get managers' and investors' attention.

It's not clear why investors would be willing to pay 20 percent more for levered firms than for unlevered ones. However, if some market imperfection created a clientele willing to pay that much extra for levered firms, then there would be a big profit opportunity for corporate treasurers. Since it costs relatively little to turn an unlevered firm into a levered one, the *supply* of levered firms would expand until the valuation error was wiped out.

The firm is creating and selling paper assets, not real ones. So long as investors value these paper assets by the real assets underlying them, then changes in capital structure won't affect value. To repeat: there is no magic in financial leverage.

Opportunities to Issue Specialized Securities

Under what conditions is this "no magic" result violated? When the firm, by imaginative design of its capital structure, can offer some *financial service* to investors—a service investors find costly or impossible to provide for themselves. The service must be unique, or the firm must be able to provide it more cheaply than competing firms or financial intermediaries.

Thus, you look for an unsatisfied clientele—a group of investors willing to pay a premium for a particular financial instrument. The trouble is that the needs of the obvious clienteles have already been met.

For example, most investors would have difficulty borrowing with limited liability on personal account. There is a *demand-side* cost facing investors who want to borrow with limited liability. Some investors would like to borrow indirectly, with limited liability, through the corporation. This creates a clientele of investors who would be willing to pay a premium for the shares of a levered firm.

These investors would be willing to pay a premium for levered firms' stock, but they don't have to. The costs on the *supply side* are trivial. Firms can create levered equity just by borrowing. The supply of levered equity will therefore expand until the clientele seeking limited liability is satiated. Competition among firms will eliminate any premium.

It's hard to believe that investors would pay a premium for one more garden variety bond, or for the stock of the firm issuing the bond. The only "magic" in capital structure comes as a reward to financial innovation, when firms find ways to create *new* portfolio opportunities for investors, or new ways to provide old opportunities at lower cost.

Financial innovation does occur, of course. It has been going on for generations. We see the result in today's capital markets, which offer an elaborate infrastructure of financial institutions and a remarkably rich menu of traded securities.

Innovation proves that *some* financing decisions matter. If financing were always totally irrelevant, there would be no incentive to innovate, and the menu of securities would not change.

The rewards for financial innovation go mostly to innovators, however, not to followers. The recent introduction of zero-coupon bonds provides a good example. The first corporations who issued zero-coupon bonds obtained very attractive yields. They uncovered a clientele of domestic investors who wanted to "lock-in" long-term interest rates and who could hold the bonds in tax-sheltered accounts. There was also a clientele of foreign investors who could avoid income tax on these bonds' price appreciation. However, the *supply* of zero-coupon bonds expanded rapidly as soon as these instruments' attractiveness was clear. Competition also came from zero-coupon bonds issued by brokerage houses and backed up by Treasury bonds, e.g., Merrill Lynch's TIGRs (Treasury Income Guarantee Receipts). Some of the tax loopholes that contributed to the bonds' initial attractiveness were subsequently closed.[2]

All these changes have eroded the attractiveness of zero-coupon bonds. Issues will no doubt continue, but at yields much less attractive to the firm.

When a firm tries to create value through financial innovation, it competes *in capital markets* with thousands of other firms and financial institutions. This competition implies that investors do not have to pay a premium for standard securities.

Thus, the choice of capital structure should not matter, except for temporary windows of opportu-

2. See David Pyle, "Is Deep Discount Debt Financing a Bargain?," *Chase Financial Quarterly*, Vol. I, Issue 1, 1981.

nity, in which the alert firm may gain by issuing a specialized security. Finding a window does not necessarily call for a move to a higher debt ratio, however. The opportunity might be for a new type of equity, or for a hybrid or convertible instrument.

Leverage and Earnings

Here is one immediate payoff from thinking through MM's "no magic in leverage" proposition: it teaches us *not* to worry about the impact of leverage on earnings per share (EPS).

EPS is the most widely used yardstick of management performance. Normally an increase in EPS is good news, because it signals better operating results. However, sometimes management is tempted to manufacture EPS increases through paper transactions—e.g., by borrowing.

Borrowing increases the book rate of return on equity if the after-tax book rate of return on the firm's assets exceeds the after-tax interest rate. Normally a higher book rate of return on equity means higher EPS. However, this does not make stockholders better off and does not increase the real value of the firm.

Suppose a firm issues debt and retires equity, holding its assets and operating income constant. Suppose it is sufficiently profitable that EPS increases. Are investors really better off?

Increased leverage diverts a larger fraction of the firm's operating income to lenders, and a smaller fraction to stockholders. However, the total going to all investors in the firm must be exactly the same. Lenders and stockholders *considered jointly* receive no more and no less than before.

Stockholders do receive more earnings per dollar invested, but they also bear more risk, because they have given lenders first claim on the firm's assets and operating income. Stockholders bear more risk per dollar invested, and the more the firm borrows the more risk they bear. Lenders accept a lower dollar return per dollar invested because they have a safer claim. If they don't *give up* value by accepting a relatively low rate of return, how can stockholders gain on their side of the transaction? Higher return for higher risk, lower return for relative safety—it ought to be a fair trade. In fact MM *prove* it is a fair trade, provided that investors and financial intermediaries are alert and rational.

Managers who borrow *just* to boost EPS can increase firm value only by systematically fooling investors. Perhaps it's possible to fool some inves-

tors some of the time. It's more likely that these managers are fooling themselves.

Taxes

If there are any useful generalizations about capital structure, they must rest on issues not yet discussed. The first of these is taxes.

Unfortunately, "debt and taxes" is an exceedingly messy subject, one which tends to drive out other equally interesting issues. I will just list the few things we can say with confidence, and then move on.

First, interest is tax deductible. The tax saving from debt financing is greatest for firms facing a high marginal tax rate.

Second, few firms can be *sure* they will show a taxable profit in the future. If a firm shows a loss, and cannot carry the loss back against past taxes, its interest tax shield must be carried forward with the hope of using it later. The firm loses at least the time value of money while it waits. If its difficulties are deep enough, the wait may be permanent, and the interest tax shield is lost forever.

Therefore interest tax shields are worth more to some firms than others. They ought to be worth a great deal to IBM, whose taxable income is relatively high and stable. They ought to be worth very little to Wheeling-Pittsburgh Steel, which has large accumulated tax loss carryforwards and uncertain prospects.

Think of the *expected realizable* value of the tax shield on an extra dollar of promised future interest payments. This amount depends on (1) the probability that the firm will have taxable income to shield and (2) its marginal tax rate if it does have taxable income.

This brings us to the third point: the more the firm borrows, the less the expected realizable value of future interest tax shields. I have plotted this relationship as the top line in Figure 1.

Fourth, there are other ways to shield income. Firms have accelerated writeoffs for plant and equipment. They have the investment tax credit. Investments in research and many other intangible assets can be expensed immediately. So can contributions to the firm's pension fund.

How soon the top line in Figure 1 turns down depends on how profitable it is—i.e., how much income it has to shield—and on how many dollars of *non-interest* tax shields it has. The line *always* turns down if debt is high enough; however, there is

FIGURE 1. The Tax Benefit of Debt Financing

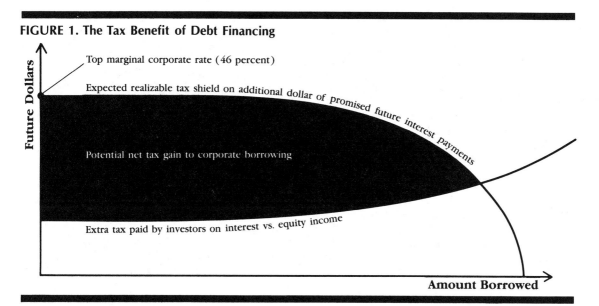

some debt burden which would drive even IBM into the bankruptcy courts.

Fifth, and finally, equity investors get a tax break relative to lenders. This partially, perhaps wholly, offsets the corporate interest tax shield.

In the United States, a corporation's income is taxed twice, first at the firm level and again when the income is passed through to lenders and stockholders. The interest lenders receive is all ordinary income. Stockholders, on the other hand, receive part of their income as capital gains. When a firm borrows in place of equity financing, the Internal Revenue Service loses at the corporate level but usually gains at the investor level (because interest is taxed more heavily than equity income). I have shown the net loss at the investor level as the bottom line in Figure 1. The shaded area between the lines is the potential tax gain to corporate borrowing when both levels are considered.

Here is where we hit trouble. We do not know whether the shaded area in Figure 1 is big, small, or possibly nonexistent. We cannot know until we can fix the position of the two lines that form the upper and lower boundaries of the shaded area.

The upper boundary is not too much of a problem. Most firms, if they had no debt at all, would pay the full 46 percent marginal rate. That gives the starting point on the vertical axis. We also know the general shape of the declining curve. The only question is when the line starts to bend down sharply, but that could be judged case by case.

The bottom boundary's position is a deep mystery, however. Some believe there is not much difference between the effective tax rates faced by debt and equity investors. That would imply a low bottom line and a correspondingly large tax gain to corporate borrowing, perhaps as much as 46 cents per dollar of interest paid. At the other extreme, Merton Miller has presented an ingenious, appealing, but probably oversimplified model,[3] in which the tax rate faced by the *marginal* investor in bonds is about 46 percent higher than the rate that investor would pay on stocks. If that's the way the world works, the tax gain to the firm from corporate borrowing just balances the tax loss to investors. The firm would have to pay such a high interest rate to bribe investors to hold its bonds that it might as well issue equity. There would be no net tax gain to corporate borrowing.

Each of these positions has extreme implications for debt policy. If the net tax gain is very large, firms that pay taxes at the full 46 percent corporate rate ought to borrow very large amounts—a triple-A debt rating would be an extremely expensive luxury. Yet, such firms as IBM and Eastman Kodak do not seem to suffer from their conservative financing.

---

3. "Debt and Taxes," *Journal of Finance*, May 1977.

If the net tax gain is very large, a triple-A debt rating would be an extremely expensive luxury.

On the other hand, if the net tax gain is zero for IBM, as Merton Miller's model implies, then it must be strongly *negative* for Wheeling-Pittsburgh. In other words, Wheeling-Pittsburgh should see Big Money in negative debt: it could set up a money machine by issuing equity to buy the debt of other corporations. If you find these recommendations unacceptable, you are more or less forced into an intermediate view, in which there is a modest net tax advantage for IBM, and a modest disadvantage for Wheeling-Pittsburgh, but not so large as to dominate other factors.

I am not brave enough to take either of these extreme positions. Pending further evidence I conclude that there is a moderate tax advantage to corporate borrowing, at least for companies that are reasonably sure they can use the interest tax shields. For companies that cannot use the interest tax shields there is a moderate tax *disadvantage*.

Trouble

Every corporate treasurer knows that too much borrowing can lead to financial trouble. That one fact is all many care to know. When they start losing sleep over the firm's bond rating, they stop borrowing.

However, there's a lot going on behind the label "trouble." We need to distinguish among the different *kinds* of trouble and to look carefully at the *costs* of trouble.

Financial trouble has its own extensive literature, usually under a more imposing title such as "Costs of Financial Distress." I will offer just a few examples and observations chosen to show the literature's practical implications.

Heartbreak Hotel

Suppose your firm's only asset is a large downtown hotel, mortgaged to the hilt. The recession hits. Occupancy rates fall, and the mortgage payments cannot be met. The lender takes over and sells the hotel to a new owner and operator. You use your firm's stock certificates for wallpaper.

What are the costs of bankruptcy? In this example, probably very little. The value of the hotel is, of course, much less than you had hoped, but that is due to the lack of guests, not to default on the loan. The costs of bankruptcy are only the costs of the default itself. As Richard Brealey and I wrote elsewhere,[4]

Bankruptcies are thought of as corporate funerals. The mourners (creditors and especially shareholders) look at their firm's present sad state. They think of how valuable their securities used to be and how little is left. Moreover, they think of the lost value as a cost of bankruptcy. That is the mistake. The decline in the value of assets is what the mourning is really about. That has no necessary connection with financing. The bankruptcy is merely a legal mechanism for allowing creditors to take over when the decline in the value of assets triggers a default. Bankruptcy is not the cause of the decline in value. It is the result.

The direct bankruptcy costs of Heartbreak Hotel are restricted to items such as legal and court fees, real estate commissions, and the time and talent spent by the lender in sorting things out. The costs are proportionally larger for small firms (there are economies of scale in going bankrupt) and larger for firms with complex capital structures.[5]

Who pays the costs? At first glance it seems that the lender does, because the costs diminish the net value of the assets the lender recoups. Lenders of course realize this and charge an insurance premium every time a new loan is made. The size of the premium depends on the probability of trouble and the costs likely in the event of trouble. Your firm paid this premium when it mortgaged the hotel; these premiums cover bankruptcy costs on average. Thus, *shareholders* end up paying for *expected* bankruptcy costs every time they issue risky debt.

Fledgling Electronics Goes Under

Suppose we repeat the story of Heartbreak Hotel for Fledgling Electronics. Everything is the same, except for the underlying real assets—not real estate, but a high-tech going concern, a growth

---

4. Principles of Corporate Finance, New York, McGraw-Hill Book Co., p. 385.

5. Direct bankruptcy costs would virtually disappear if someone could design a "no fault" system of bankruptcy, in which the assets of the defaulting firm could be transmitted to the creditors by executing a few standard documents. But it is difficult to imagine this working for large firms, which typically have many classes of creditors with conflicting interests. No fault bankruptcy would also undercut another purpose of the law, which is to protect the firm as a going concern for time enough to give reorganization, instead of liquidation, a fair try.

company whose most valuable assets are technology, investment opportunities, and its employees' human capital.

Fledgling is of course more likely to get into trouble for a given degree of financial leverage than a hotel is, but the point here is to contrast what happens *if* a default occurs.

First, you would have a much more difficult time cashing in Fledgling's assets by just selling them off. Many of its assets are intangibles which have value only as part of a going concern.

Could the value of Fledgling, as a going concern, be preserved through default and reorganization? That would require a complete insulation of Fledgling's operating and investment plans from the bankruptcy process. Unfortunately, this is costly and probably infeasible.

Default creates a variety of operating and investment problems. The odds of defections by key employees are higher than if the firm had started out with less debt and had never gotten into financial trouble. Aggressive investment in new products and technology will be more difficult; each class of creditors will have to be convinced that it is in their interest for the firm to raise more money and put the money into risky assets.[6] Special guarantees may have to be given to customers who doubt whether the firm will be around to service its products. Finally, the time that management spends solving these and other problems has its own opportunity cost.

I have taken the extreme cases of the hotel and the electronics firm to make a crucial distinction: some asset values can pass through bankruptcy and reorganization largely unscathed. Other asset values are likely to be considerably diminished. The losses are greatest for the intangible assets that are linked to the health of the firm as a going concern, for example, technology, growth opportunities, and human capital.

The moral is: *think not only of the probability that borrowing will bring trouble. Think also of the value that may be lost if trouble comes.*

The Costs of Avoiding Bankruptcy

Since "You can make a lot more money by smart investment decisions than by smart financing decisions," financing decisions ought to be ar-

ranged to support investment decisions. However, when default or bankruptcy threatens, things can get turned around; the financing side can gain the upper hand. Managers may pass up good investment opportunities in an attempt to conserve cash and keep the firm "alive."

Suppose your hotel, under threat of default, reduces customer services, defers painting guest rooms and cuts corners in the restaurant kitchens. Assume these were sensible outlays—that is, they would have been undertaken if the firm had no debt, other things equal. Then we can say that the threat of default reduces the value of your firm's *real assets*, because it thwarts expenditures that would increase that value.[7] Even if default is avoided, there is still a cost of financial distress, equal to the value lost because of foregone investments.

Fledgling Electronics is liable to the same underinvestment problem, but the value loss could be much greater. A year's delay in painting a room may not permanently undercut that hotel's competitive position, but falling a year behind in technology or product design could wipe out a substantial fraction of Fledgling Electronics' value.

People say "You have to spend money to make money." The threat of default often leads managers *not* to spend as much as they should. The loss in value from good investments passed by is a cost of financial distress even if the firm finally regains its financial health. The extent of loss depends on how valuable the foregone investments are, and on how costly it would be for the firm to catch up. The loss is likely to be greatest for firms whose market value rests primarily on technology, human capital and growth opportunities—another reason why Fledgling Electronics should have a more conservative debt policy than a firm holding tangible assets such as real estate.

Why Should a Firm Ever Pass Up Good Investments?

Some financial economists find it hard to believe that a firm—even firms in financial distress—would ever pass up a positive net present value (NPV) investment. It's clearly in the *joint* interests of all debt and equity securityholders to raise the money to take such investments. There must be

---

6. The funds would probably be raised by giving a new class of creditors a prior claim in the firm's assets.

7. That is, expenditures with positive *net* present value.

The problem is that stockholders will have to share the extra value created by their additional investments with creditors.

some hidden cost.

The costs do exist. They are fundamentally costs of producing and transmitting information. Because information is costly, it is difficult for creditors—or any outside investor—to know what the firm's true risks and prospects are. It becomes difficult for creditors to know when managers are "doing the right thing" for the firm, and when they are acting in their own narrower interests, or in the interests of stockholders. Debt contracts become costly to write and cumbersome for the firm.[8] It becomes costly for creditors to monitor the firm's performance. Finally, it becomes costly to renegotiate the firm's financing.

Consider the following questions with these information costs in mind.[9]

Q: Why don't stockholders and creditors of a firm in financial distress get together and *jointly* advance the funds necessary to undertake all positive-NPV investments?

A: Sometimes they do.[10] However, it's costly for outside investors to find out what the positive-NPV investments really are. (They may suspect managers of trying to raise money to keep the firm alive even if its prospects are not all that great.)

It is also costly and time-consuming to negotiate an agreement in which each class of security-holder makes its share of the sacrifices necessary to allow the firm to take the right investments. Such an agreement may end up being almost as costly and time-consuming as a complete reorganization of the firm's capital structure.

Despite these costs, creditors will make considerable sacrifices for firms they consider worth keeping afloat as going concerns. Think of Chrysler and International Harvester.[11]

However, it's costly to negotiate these sacrifices, sometimes so costly that the sacrifice is not made and good investments are passed by. With either outcome the *overall* value of the firm (i.e., its joint value to all creditors and stockholders) is diminished. This value loss could be avoided by not borrowing so much in the first place.

Q: If joint action by creditors and stockholders is costly, why doesn't the firm just issue stock to finance its positive-NPV investments? For that matter, why doesn't it eliminate the whole problem by issuing stock to pay off the debt?

A: Let's take the second question first. If the firm is in serious financial trouble, its debt is no longer a safe security. The debt's market value has fallen substantially below its par or face value. If the firm issues stock and repays the *face* value of debt, stockholders are buying back the debt for considerably more than it is worth. In other words, paying off the creditors at par is always a negative-NPV investment for stockholders of a firm in financial distress.[12]

Suppose equity is issued not to pay off creditors, but to finance additional *real* investment by the firm. The problem here is that stockholders will have to share the extra value created by these investments with the creditors. Every time the value of the firm increases by one dollar, creditors are better off. Shareholders do not capture the full reward their additional investment creates. When the firm is sound and the debt is safe anyway, the proportion of the extra value captured by creditors is small. However, when the firm is in trouble, the proportion can be substantial. Thus it is often not in the stockholder's interest for firms in financial distress to raise and invest new equity capital, except through a *negotiated* reorganization of the firm's financing—and that, as I have argued before, is costly and time-consuming.

Back to the Underinvestment Problem

All this boils down to a few simple points: First, a firm that falls into financial distress may pass up good investment opportunities, or it (and its security holders) may have to renegotiate its financing in order to avoid passing up the good opportunities. Both possibilities are costly.

Second, firms can reduce the probability of these costs by not borrowing so much in the first place.

Third, *if* the firm lands in financial trouble, the magnitude of loss from underinvestment depends on how good its investment opportunities are. Who

8. Clifford Smith and Jerrold Warner give an excellent description of how debt contracts are written and why they are written as they are. See "On Financial Contracting: An Analysis of Bond Covenants," *Journal of Financial Economics*, June 1979.

9. I discuss these questions more carefully and extensively in "The Determinants of Corporate Borrowing," *Journal of Financial Economics*, November 1977.

10. For example, lenders often allow troubled firms to break covenants and defer debt service. When this is done, stockholders, and often employees, are expected to make sacrifices too: for example, no dividends to stockholders and no bonuses to managers.

11. They may still be forced to decide to let International Harvester sink.

12. Of course, shareholders can always try to buy the debt back at *market* value. Getting creditors to accept this offer is another matter, except as part of a negotiated reorganization.

cares if a firm passes up investment opportunities if the opportunities are worth no more than they cost?

This gives one more reason for Fledgling Electronics, or any firm whose value depends on growth opportunities or intangible assets, to borrow less than a hotel chain. The "underinvestment problem" may explain the low debt ratios in the pharmaceutical industry, where value depends on continued success in research and development, and in consumer-products companies, where sustained, massive investment in advertising is necessary to maintain product recognition and market share. We can also understand why highly profitable growth companies, such as Hewlett-Packard, Digital Equipment Corporation and IBM, tend to use mostly equity financing. Recent empirical research by Michael Long and Ileen Malitz, and by Scott Williamson, confirms that firms whose assets are weighted towards intangible assets and growth opportunities borrow significantly less, on average, than firms holding mostly tangible assets-in-place.[13]

Conclusion

Let me try to sum up this paper's main ideas. The first, most fundamental one is Modigliani and Miller's "no magic in leverage" proposition. The firm markets its *real* assets and *operating* income to investors by issuing a package of financial assets. However, if capital markets are doing their job, one package is as good as another. In particular, there is no presumption that borrowing is a good thing, even if debt is kept to "moderate" levels.

However, there does seem to be some tax advantage to borrowing for firms which make full use of interest tax shields. On the other hand, costs of financial trouble threaten firms that borrow too much. The financial manager should consider not just the probability of trouble, but also the value lost from trouble if it does occur. This value loss is greatest for firms with valuable intangible assets and growth opportunities.

Thus the choice of capital structure, when discussed with the broad brush required by this short paper, boils down to taxes, risk and asset type. For example, a safe, consistently profitable company, with few intangible assets or growth opportunities, ought to find a relatively high debt ratio attractive. A risky growth company ought to avoid debt financing, especially if it has other ways of shielding its income from taxes.

I will cheerfully admit that this three-item checklist of taxes, risk and asset type does not tell the financial manager how much debt to issue. For example, a firm with average risk, lots of unsheltered taxable income, *but* few tangible assets, could use this paper's qualitative arguments to support either a high or low debt ratio. Such a firm would probably decide that any middle-of-the-road debt ratio is OK, and base its financing choices on more down-to-earth considerations, such as issue costs, opportunities for subsidized financing, and so on.

Nevertheless, the checklist does tell the financial manager what's important and what isn't. It gives him or her a *framework* for thinking about optimal capital structure. As always, the financing *decision* finally rests on the manager's shoulders.

13. Both studies hold risk constant. See M. Long and I. Malitz, "Investment Patterns and Financial Leverage," National Bureau of Economic Research, January 1983, and S. Williamson, "The Moral Hazard Theory of Corporate Capital Structure: Empirical Tests," Unpublished Ph.D. Dissertation, MIT, November 1981.

The Capital Structure Puzzle

Stewart C. Myers,
Massachusetts Institute of Technology

This paper's title is intended to remind you of Fischer Black's well-known note on "The Dividend Puzzle," which he closed by saying, "What should the corporation do about dividend policy? We don't know." [6, p.8] I will start by asking, "How do firms choose their capital structures?" Again, the answer is, "We don't know."

The capital structure puzzle is tougher than the dividend one. We know quite a bit about dividend policy. John Lintner's model of how firms set dividends [20] dates back to 1956, and it still seems to work. We know stock prices respond to unanticipated dividend changes, so it is clear that dividends have information content—this observation dates back at least to Miller and Modigliani (MM) in 1961[28A]. We do not know whether high dividend yield increases the expected rate of return demanded by investors, as adding taxes to the MM proof of dividend irrelevance suggests, but financial economists are at least hammering away at this issue.

By contrast, we know very little about capital structure. We do not know how firms choose the debt, equity or hybrid securities they issue. We have only recently discovered that capital structure changes convey information to investors. There has been little if any research testing whether the relationship between financial leverage and investors' required return is as the pure MM theory predicts. In general, we have inadequate understanding of corporate financing behavior, and of how that behavior affects security returns.

I do not want to sound too pessimistic or discouraged. We have accumulated many helpful insights into capital structure choice, starting with the most important one, MM's No Magic in Leverage Theorem (Proposition I) [31]. We have thought long and hard about what these insights imply for optimal capital structure. Many of us have translated these theories, or stories, of optimal capital structure into more or less definite advice to managers. But our theories don't seem to explain actual financing behavior, and it seems presumptuous to advise firms on optimal capital structure when we are so far from explaining actual decisions. I have done more than my share of writing on optimal capital structure, so I take this opportunity to make amends, and to try to push research in some new directions.

I will contrast two ways of thinking about capital structure:

1. A *static tradeoff* framework, in which the firm is viewed as setting a target debt-to-value ratio and gradually moving towards it, in much the same way that a firm adjusts dividends to move towards a target payout ratio.

2. An old-fashioned *pecking order* framework, in which the firm prefers internal to external financing, and debt to equity if it issues securities. In the pure pecking order theory, the firm has no well-defined target debt-to-value ratio.

Recent theoretical work has breathed new life into the pecking order framework. I will argue that this theory performs at least as well as the static tradeoff theory in explaining what we know about actual financing choices and their average impacts on stock prices.

This article first appeared in the *Journal of Finance* (July 1984, Vol. XXXIX No. 3), and is reprinted with the permission of its publisher, the American Finance Association.

We know investors are interested in the firm's financing choices because stock prices change when the choices are announced.

Managerial and Neutral Mutation Hypotheses

I have arbitrarily, and probably unfairly, excluded "managerial" theories which might explain firms' capital structure choices.[1] I have chosen not to consider models which cut the umbilical cord that ties managers' acts to stockholders' interests.

I am also sidestepping Miller's idea of "neutral mutation."[2] He suggests that firms fall into some financing patterns or habits which have no material effect on firm value. The habits may make managers feel better, and since they do no harm, no one cares to stop or change them. Thus someone who identifies these habits and uses them to predict financing behavior would not be explaining anything important.

The neutral mutations idea is important as a warning. Given time and imagination, economists can usually invent some model that assigns apparent economic rationality to any random event. But taking neutral mutation as a strict null hypothesis makes the game of research too tough to play. If an economist identifies costs of various financing strategies, obtains independent evidence that the costs are really there, and then builds a model based on these costs which explains firms' financing behavior, then some progress has been made, even if it proves difficult to demonstrate that, say, a type A financing strategy gives higher firm value than a type B. (In fact, we would never see type B if all firms follow value-maximizing strategies.)

There is another reason for not immediately embracing neutral mutations: we know investors are interested in the firm's financing choices because stock prices change when the choices are announced. The change might be explained as an "information effect" having nothing to do with financing per se—but again, it is a bit too easy to wait until the results of an event study are in, and then to think of an information story to explain them. On the other hand, if one starts by assuming that managers have special information, builds a model of how that information changes financing choices, and predicts which choices will be interpreted by investors as good or bad news, then some progress has been made.

So this paper is designed as a one-on-one competition of the static tradeoff and pecking-order stories. If neither story explains actual behavior, the neutral mutations story will be there faithfully waiting.

The Static Tradeoff Hypothesis

A firm's optimal debt ratio is usually viewed as determined by a tradeoff of the costs and benefits of borrowing, holding the firm's assets and investment plans constant. The firm is portrayed as balancing the value of interest tax shields against various costs of bankruptcy or financial embarrassment. Of course, there is controversy about how valuable the tax shields are, and which, if any, of the costs of financial embarrassment are material, but these disagreements give only variations on a theme. The firm is supposed to substitute debt for equity, or equity for debt, until the value of the firm is maximized. Thus the debt-equity tradeoff is as illustrated in Figure 1.

Costs of adjustment. If there were no costs of adjustment, and the static tradeoff theory is correct, then each firm's observed debt-to-value ratio should be its optimal ratio. However, there must be costs, and therefore lags, in adjusting to the optimum. Firms can not immediately offset the random events that bump them away from the optimum, so there should be some cross-sectional dispersion of actual debt ratios across a sample of firms having the same target ratio.

Large adjustment costs could possibly explain the observed wide variation in actual debt ratios, since firms would be forced into long excursions

1. The finance and economics literature has at least three "managerial" strands: (1) descriptions of managerial capitalism, in which the separation of ownership and control is taken as a central fact of life, for example Berle and Means [5]; (2) agency theory, pioneered for finance by Jensen and Meckling [18], and (3) the detailed analysis of the personal risks and rewards facing managers and how their responses affect firms' financing or investment choices. For examples of strand (3), see Ross's articles on financial signalling [36,37].

2. Put forward in "Debt and Taxes," [27], esp. pp. 272-273. Note that Miller did not claim that all of firms' financing habits are neutral mutations, only that some of them may be. I doubt that Miller intended this idea as a strict null hypothesis (see below).

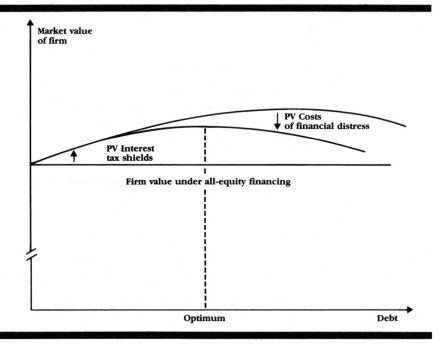

FIGURE 1
The Static-Tradeoff
Theory of Capital
Structure

Market value
of firm

↓ PV Costs
of financial distress

↑ PV Interest
tax shields

Firm value under all-equity financing

Optimum   Debt

away from their optimal ratios. But there is nothing in the usual static tradeoff stories suggesting that adjustment costs are a first-order concern—in fact, they are rarely mentioned. Invoking them without modelling them is a cop-out.

Any cross-sectional test of financing behavior should specify whether firms' debt ratios differ because they have different optimal ratios or because their actual ratios diverge from optimal ones. It is easy to get the two cases mixed up. For example, think of the early cross-sectional studies which attempted to test MM's proposition I. These studies tried to find out whether differences in leverage affected the market value of the firm (or the market capitalization rate for its operating income). With hindsight, we can quickly see the problem: if adjustment costs are small, and each firm in the sample is

at, or close to its optimum, then the in-sample dispersion of debt ratios must reflect differences in risk or in other variables affecting optimal capital structure. But then MM's proposition I cannot be tested unless the effects of risk and other variables on firm value can be adjusted for. By now we have learned from experience how hard it is to hold "other things constant" in cross-sectional regressions.

Of course, one way to make sense of these tests is to assume that adjustment costs are small, but managers don't know, or don't care, what the optimal debt ratio is, and thus do not stay close to it. The researcher then assumes some (usually unspecified) "managerial" theory of capital structure choice. This may be a convenient assumption for a cross-sectional test of MM's Proposition I, but not very helpful if the object is to understand financing behavior.[3]

3. The only early cross-sectional study I know of which sidesteps these issues is MM's 1966 paper on the cost of capital for the electric utility industry[28B]. Their "corrected" theory says that the firm value is independent of capital structure except for the value added by the present value of interest tax shields. Thus tax-paying firms would be expected to substitute debt for equity, at least up to the point where the probability of financial distress starts to be important. However, the regulated firms MM examined had little tax incentive to use debt, because their interest tax shields were passed through to consumers. If a regulated firm pays an extra one dollar of interest, and thus saves T_c in corporate income taxes, regulators are supposed to reduce the firm's pre-tax operating income by $T_c/(1-T_c)$, the grossed-up value of the tax saving. This roughly cancels out any tax advantage of borrowing. Thus regulated firms should have

little incentive to borrow enough to flirt with financial distress, and their debt ratios could be dispersed across a conservative range.

Moreover, MM's test could pick up the present value of interest tax shields *provided* they adjusted for differences in operating income. Remember, interest tax shields are not eliminated by regulation, just offset by reductions in allowed operating income.

Thus regulated firms are relatively good subjects for cross-sectional tests of static tradeoff theories. MM's theory seemed to work fairly well for three years in the mid-1950s. Unfortunately, MM's equations didn't give sensible coefficients when fitted on later data (see for example, Robicheck, McDonald and Higgins [35]). There has been little further work attempting to extend or adapt MM's 1966 model. In the meantime, theory has moved on.

But suppose we don't take this "managerial" fork. Then if adjustment costs are small, and firms stay near their target debt ratios, I find it hard to understand the observed diversity of capital structures across firms that seem similar in a static tradeoff framework. If adjustment costs are large, so that some firms take extended excursions away from their targets, then we ought to give less attention to refining our static tradeoff stories and relatively more to understanding what the adjustment costs are, why they are so important, and how rational managers would respond to them.

But I am getting ahead of my story. On to debt and taxes.

Debt and Taxes. Miller's famous "Debt and Taxes" paper [27] cut us loose from the extreme implications of the original MM theory, which made interest tax shields so valuable that we could not explain why all firms were not awash in debt. Miller described an equilibrium of aggregate supply and demand for corporate debt, in which personal income taxes paid by the marginal investor in corporate debt just offset the corporate tax saving. However, since the equilibrium only determines aggregates, debt policy should not matter for any single tax-paying firm. Thus Miller's model allows us to explain the dispersion of actual debt policies without having to introduce non-value-maximizing managers.[4]

Trouble is, this explanation works only if we assume that all firms face approximately the same marginal tax rate, and that is an assumption we can immediately reject. The extensive trading of depreciation tax shields and investment tax credits, through financial leases and other devices, proves that plenty of firms face low marginal rates.[5]

Given significant differences in effective marginal tax rates, and given that the static tradeoff theory works, we would expect to find a strong tax effect in any cross-sectional test, regardless of whose theory of debt and taxes you believe.

Figure 2 plots the net tax gain from the corporate borrowing against the expected realizable tax shield from a future deduction of one dollar of interest paid. For some firms this number is 46 cents, or close to it. At the other extreme, there are firms with large unused loss carryforwards which pay no immediate taxes. An extra dollar of interest paid by these firms would create only a potential future deduction, usable when and if the firm earns enough to work off prior carryforwards. The expected realizable tax shield is positive but small. Also, there are firms paying taxes today which cannot be sure they will do so in the future. Such a firm values expected future interest tax shields at somewhere between zero and the full statutory rate.

In the "corrected" MM theory [28] any taxpaying corporation gains by borrowing; the greater the marginal tax rate, the greater the gain. This gives the top line in the figure. In Miller's theory, the personal income taxes on interest payments would exactly offset the corporate interest tax shield, provided that the firm pays the full statutory tax rate. However, any firm paying a lower rate would see a net loss to corporate borrowing and a net gain to lending. This gives the bottom line.

There are also compromise theories, advanced by DeAngelo and Masulis [12], Modigliani [30] and others, indicated by the middle dashed line in the figure. The compromise theories are appealing because they seem less extreme than either the MM or Miller theories. But regardless of which theory holds, the slope of the line is always positive. The difference between (1) the tax advantage of borrowing to firms facing the full statutory rate, and (2) the tax advantage of lending (or at least not borrowing) to firms with large tax loss carryforwards, is exactly the same as in the "extreme" theories. Thus, although the theories tell different stories about aggregate supply and demand of corporate debt, they make essentially the same predictions about which firms borrow more or less than average.

So the tax side of the static tradeoff theory predicts that IBM should borrow more than Bethlehem Steel, other things equal, and that General Motors' debt-to-value ratio should be more than Chrysler's.

Costs of financial distress. Costs of financial distress include the legal and administrative costs of bankruptcy, as well as the subtler agency, moral hazard, monitoring and contracting costs which can erode firm value even if formal default is avoided.

---

4. Although Miller's "Debt and Taxes" model [27] was a major conceptual step forward, I do not consider it an adequate description of how taxes affect optimum capital structure or expected rates of return on debt and equity securities. See Gordon and Malkiel [16] for a recent review or the evidence.

5. Cordes and Scheffrin [8] present evidence on the cross-sectional dispersion of effective corporate tax rates.

The expected cost of financial distress depends not just on the probability of trouble, but the value lost if trouble comes. Specialized, intangible assets or growth opportunities are more likely to lose value in financial distress.

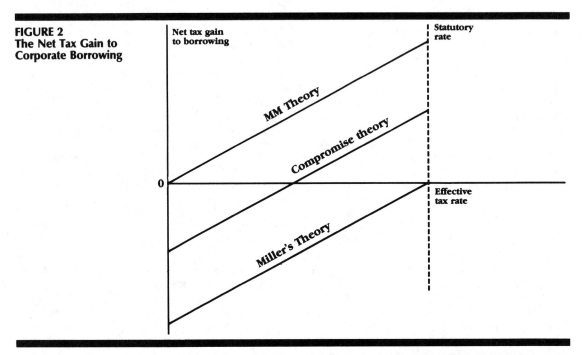

FIGURE 2
The Net Tax Gain to Corporate Borrowing

We know these costs exist, although we may debate their magnitude. For example, there is no satisfactory explanation of debt covenants unless agency costs and moral hazard problems are recognized.

The literature on costs of financial distress supports two qualitative statements about financing behavior.[6]

1. Risky firms ought to borrow less, other things equal. Here "risk" would be defined as the variance rate of the market value of the firm's assets. The higher the variance rate, the greater the probability of default on any given package of debt claims. Since the costs of financial distress are caused by threatened or actual default, firms ought to be able to borrow more before expected costs of financial distress offset the tax advantages of borrowing.

2. Firms holding tangible assets-in-place having active second-hand markets will borrow more than firms holding specialized, intangible assets or valuable growth opportunities. The expected cost of financial distress depends not just on the probability of trouble, but the value lost if trouble comes. Specialized, intangible assets or growth opportunities are more likely to lose value in financial distress.

The Pecking Order Theory

Contrast the static tradeoff theory with a competing popular story based on a financing pecking order:

1. Firms prefer internal finance.

2. They adapt their target dividend payout ratios to their investment opportunities, although dividends are sticky and target payout ratios are only gradually adjusted to shifts in the extent of valuable investment opportunities.

3. Sticky dividend policies, plus unpredictable fluctuations in profitability and investment opportunities, mean that internally-generated cash flow may be more or less than investment outlays. If it is less, the firm first draws down its cash balance or marketable securities portfolio.[7]

4. If external finance is required, firms issue the safest security first. That is, they start with debt, then possibly hybrid securities such as convertible bonds, then perhaps equity as a last resort. In this story, there is no well-defined target debt-equity mix because there are two kinds of equity, internal and ex-

---

6. I have discussed these two points in more detail in [32 and 33]

7. If it is more, the firm first pays off debt or invests in cash or marketable securities. If the surplus persists, it may gradually increase its target payout ratio.

The pecking order hypothesis is hardly new. For example, it comes through loud and clear in Donaldson's 1961 study of the financing practices of a sample of large corporations.

ternal, one at the top of the pecking order and one at the bottom. Each firm's observed debt ratio reflects its cumulative requirement for external finance.

The pecking order literature. The pecking order hypothesis is hardly new.[8] For example, it comes through loud and clear in Donaldson's 1961 study of the financing practices of a sample of large corporations. He observed [13, p. 67] that "Management strongly favored internal generation as a source of new funds even to the exclusion of external funds except for occasional unavoidable 'bulges' in the need for funds." These bulges were not generally met by cutting dividends: Reducing the "customary cash dividend payment...was unthinkable to most managements except as a defensive measure in a period of extreme financial distress" (p. 70). Given that external finance was needed, managers rarely thought of issuing stock:

Though few companies would go so far as to rule out a sale of common under any circumstances, the large majority had not had such a sale in the past 20 years and did not anticipate one in the foreseeable future. This was particularly remarkable in view of the high Price-Earnings ratios of recent years. Several financial officers showed that they were well aware that this had been a good time to sell common, but the reluctance still persisted. (pp. 57-58)

Of course, the pecking order hypothesis can be quickly rejected if we require it to explain everything. There are plenty of examples of firms issuing stock when they could issue investment-grade debt. But when one looks at aggregates, the heavy reliance on internal finance and debt is clear. For all non-financial corporations over the decade 1973-1982, internally generated cash covered, on average, 62 percent of capital expenditures, including investment in inventory and other current assets. The bulk of required external financing came from borrowing. Net new stock issues were never more than 6 percent of external financing.[9] Anyone innocent of modern finance who looked at these statistics would find the pecking order idea entirely plausible, at least as a description of typical behavior.

Writers on "managerial capitalism" have interpreted firms' reliance on internal finance as a by-product of the separation of ownership and control: professional managers avoid relying on external fi-

nance because it would subject them to the discipline of the capital market.[10] Donaldson's 1969 book was not primarily about managerial capitalism, but he nevertheless observed that the financing decisions of the firms he studied were not directed towards maximizing shareholder wealth, and that scholars attempting to explain those decisions would have to start by recognizing the "managerial view" of corporate finance. [14, Ch. 2]

This conclusion is natural given the state of finance theory in the 1960s. Today, it is not so obvious that financing by a pecking order goes against shareholders' interests.

External financing with asymmetric information. I used to ignore the pecking order story because I could think of no theoretical foundation for it that would fit in with the theory of modern finance. An argument could be made for internal financing to avoid issue costs, and if external finance is needed, for debt to avoid the still higher costs of equity. But issue costs in themselves do not seem large enough to override the costs and benefits of leverage emphasized in the static tradeoff story. However, recent work based on asymmetric information gives predictions roughly in line with the pecking order theory. The following brief exposition is based on a forthcoming joint paper by me and Nicholas Majluf [34], although I will here boil down that paper's argument to absolute essentials.

Suppose the firm has to raise N dollars in order to undertake some potentially valuable investment opportunity. Let y be this opportunity's net present value (NPV) and x be what the firm will be worth if the opportunity is passed by. The firm's manager knows what x and y are, but investors in capital markets do not: they see only a joint distribution of possible values (x', y'). The information asymmetry is taken as given. Aside from the information asymmetry, capital markets are perfect and semi-strong form efficient. MM's Proposition I holds in the sense that the stock of debt relative to real assets is irrelevant if information available to investors is held constant.

The *benefit* to raising N dollars by a security issue is y, the NPV of the firm's investment opportunity. There is also a possible cost: the firm may have to sell the securities for less than they are really

---

8. Although I have not seen the term "pecking order" used before.

9. These figures were computed from Brealey and Myers [7], Table 14-3, p. 291.

10. For example, see Berle [4], or Berle and Means [5]

Today, it is not so obvious that financing by a pecking order goes against shareholders' interests.

worth. Suppose the firm issues stock with an aggregate market value, when issued, of N. (I will consider debt issues in a moment.) However, the manager knows the shares are really worth N_1. That is, N_1 is what the new shares will be worth, other things equal, when investors acquire the manager's special knowledge.

Majluf and I discuss several possible objectives managers might pursue in this situation. The one we think makes the most sense is maximizing the "true," or "intrinsic," value of the firm's existing shares. That is, the manager worries about the value of the "old" shareholders' stake in the firm. Moreover, investors who purchase any stock issue will assume that the manager is not on their side, and will rationally adjust the price they are willing to pay.

Define $\triangle N$ as the amount by which the shares are over- or undervalued: $\triangle N = N_1 - N$. Then the manager will issue and invest when

$$y \geqslant \triangle N. \tag{1}$$

If the manager's inside information is unfavorable, $\triangle N$ is negative and the firm will always issue, even if the only good use for the funds raised is to put them in the bank—a zero-NPV investment.[11] If the inside information is favorable, however, the firm may pass up a positive-NPV investment opportunity rather than issue undervalued shares.

But if management acts this way, its decision to issue will signal bad news to both old and new shareholders. Let V be the market value of the firm (price per share times number of shares) if it does not issue, and V' be market value if it does issue; V' includes the value of the newly-issued shares. Thus, if everyone knows that managers will act according to Inequality (1), the conditions for a rational expectations equilibrium are:[12]

$$V = E(x' | \text{no issue}) = E(x' | y < \triangle N) \tag{2A}$$

$$V' = E(x' + y' + N | \text{issue}) = \tag{2B}$$
$$E(x' + y' + N | y \geqslant \triangle N).$$

The total dollar amount raised is fixed by assumption, but the number of new shares needed to

raise that amount is not. Thus $\triangle N$ is endogenous: it depends on V'. For example, if the firm issues, the fraction of all shares held by "new" stockholders is N/V'. The manager sees the true value of their claim as:

$$N_1 = \frac{N}{V'}(x + y + N) \tag{3}$$

Thus, given N, x and y, and given that stock is issued, the greater the price per share, the less value is given up to new stockholders, and the less $\triangle N$ is.

Maijluf and I have discussed the assumptions and implications of this model in considerable detail. But here are two key points:

1. The cost of relying on external financing. We usually think of the cost of external finance as adminstrative and underwriting costs, and in some cases underpricing of the new securities. Asymmetric information creates the possibility of a different sort of cost: the possibility that the firm will choose not to issue, and will therefore pass up a positive-NPV investment. This cost is avoided if the firm can retain enough internally-generated cash to cover its positive-NPV opportunities.

2. The advantages of debt over equity issues. If the firm does seek external funds, it is better off issuing debt than equity securities. The general rule is, "Issue safe securities before risky ones."

This second point is worth explaining further. Remember that the firm issues and invests if y, the NPV of its investment opportunity, is greater than or equal to $\triangle N$, the amount by which the new shares are undervalued(if $\triangle N > 0$) or overvalued (if $\triangle N < 0$). For example, suppose the investment requires $N = \$10$ million, but in order to raise that amount the firm must issue shares that are really worth $12 million. It will go ahead only if project NPV is at least $2 million. If it is worth only $1.5 million, the firm refuses to raise the money for it; the intrinsic overall value of the firm is reduced by $1.5 million, but the old shareholders are $0.5 million better off.

The manager could have avoided this problem

---

11. If the firm always has a zero-NPV opportunity available to it, the distribution of y' is truncated at $y' = 0$. I also assume that x' is non-negative.

12. The simple model embodied in (1) and (2) is a direct descendant of Akerlof's work [1]. He investigated how markets can fail when buyers can not verify the quality of what they are offered. Faced with the risk of buying a lemon, the buyer will demand a discount, which in turn discourages the potential sellers who do not have lemons. However, in Majluf's and my model, the seller is offering not a single good, but a partial claim on two, the investment project (worth y) and the firm without the project (worth x). The information asymmetry applies

to both goods–for example, the manager may receive inside information that amounts to good news about x and bad news about y, or vice versa, or good or bad news about both.

Moreover, the firm may suffer by not selling stock, because the investment opportunity is lost. Management will sometimes issue even when the stock is undervalued by investors. Consequently, investors on the other side of the transaction do not automatically interpret every stock issue as an attempted ripoff–if they did, stock would never be issued in a rational expectations equilibrium.

If the inside information is favorable the firm may pass up a positive-NPV investment opportunity rather than issue undervalued shares.

by building up the firm's cash reserves—but that is hindsight. The only thing he can do now is to redesign the security issue to reduce $\triangle N$. For example, if $\triangle N$ could be cut to $0.5 million, the investment project could be financed without diluting the true value of existing shares. The way to reduce $\triangle N$ is to issue the safest possible securities—strictly speaking, securities whose future value changes least when the manager's inside information is revealed to the market.

Of course, $\triangle N$ is endogenous, so it is loose talk to speak of the manager controlling it. However, there are reasonable cases in which the absolute value of $\triangle N$ is always less for debt than for equity. For example, if the firm can issue default-risk free debt $\triangle N$ is zero, and the firm never passes up a valuable investment opportunity. Thus, the ability to issue default-risk free debt is as good as cash in the bank. Even if default risk is introduced, the absolute value of $\triangle N$ will be less for debt than for equity if we make the customary assumptions of option pricing models.[13] Thus, if the manager has favorable information ($\triangle N > 0$), it is better to issue debt than equity.

This example assumes that new shares or risky debt would be underpriced. What if the managers' inside information is *unfavorable*, so that any risky security issue would be *over*priced? In this case, wouldn't the firm want to make $\triangle N$ as *large* as possible, to take maximum advantage of new investors? If so, stock would seem better than debt (and warrants better still). The decision rule seems to be, "Issue debt when investors undervalue the firm, and equity, or some other risky security, when they overvalue it."

The trouble with this strategy is obvious once you put yourself in investors' shoes. If you know the firm will issue equity only when it is overpriced, and debt otherwise, you will refuse to buy equity unless the firm has already exhausted its "debt capacity"—that is, unless the firm has issued so much debt already that it would face substantial additional costs in issuing more. Thus investors would effectively force the firm to follow a pecking order.

Now this is clearly too extreme. The model just presented would need lots of fleshing out before it

could fully capture actual behavior. I have presented it just to show how models based on asymmetric information can predict the two central ideas of the pecking order story: first, the preference for internal finance, and, second, the preference for debt over equity if external financing is sought.

What We Know About Corporate Financing Behavior

I will now list what we know about financing behavior and try to make sense of this knowledge in terms of the two hypotheses sketched above. I begin with five facts about financing behavior, and then offer a few generalizations from weaker statistical evidence or personal observation. Of course even "facts" based on apparently good statistics have been known to melt away under further examination, so read with caution.

Internal vs. external equity. Aggregate investment outlays are predominantly financed by debt issues and internally-generated funds. New stock issues play a relatively small part. Moreover, as Donaldson has observed, this is what many managers say they are trying to do.

This fact is what suggested the pecking order hypothesis in the first place. However, it might also be explained in a static tradeoff theory by adding significant transaction costs of equity issues and noting the favorable tax treatment of capital gains relative to dividends. This would make external equity relatively expensive. It would explain why companies keep target dividend payouts low enough to avoid having to make regular stock issues.[14] It would also explain why a firm whose debt ratio soars above target does not immediately issue stock, buy back debt, and re-establish a more moderate debt-to-value ratio. Thus firms might take extended excursions above their debt targets. (Note, however, that the static tradeoff hypothesis as usually presented rarely mentions this kind of adjustment cost.)

But the out-of-pocket costs of *repurchasing* shares seems fairly small. It is thus hard to explain extended excursions *below* a firm's debt target by an augmented static tradeoff theory—the firm could

---

13. This amounts to assuming that changes in firm value are lognormally distributed, that managers and investors agree on the variance rate, and that managers know the current value of x' and y' but investors do not. If there is asymmetric information about the variance rate, but not about the firm value at the time of issue, the pecking order could be reversed. See Giammarino and Neave[15].

14. Regulated firms, particularly electric utilities, typically pay dividends generous enough to force regular trips to the equity market. They have a special reason for this policy: it improves their bargaining position vs. consumers and regulators. It turns the opportunity cost of capital into cash requirements.

Firms holding valuable intangible assets or growth opportunities tend to borrow less than firms holding mostly tangible assets.

quickly issue debt and buy back shares. Moreover, if personal income taxes are important in explaining firms' apparent preferences for internal equity, then it's difficult to explain why *external* equity is not strongly *negative*—that is, why most firms haven't gradually moved to materially lower target payout ratios and used the released cash to repurchase shares.

Timing of security issues. Firms apparently try to "time" stock issues when security prices are "high." *Given that they seek external finance*, they are more likely to issue stock (rather than debt) after stock prices have risen than after they have fallen. For example, past stock price movements were one of the best-performing variables in Marsh's study [22] of British firms' choices between new debt and new equity issues. Taggart [39] and others[15] have found similar behavior in the United States.

This fact is embarrassing to static tradeoff advocates. If firm value rises, the debt-to-value falls, and firms ought to issue *debt*, not equity, to rebalance their capital structures.

The fact is equally embarrassing to the pecking order hypothesis. There is no reason to believe that the manager's inside information is systematically more favorable when stock prices are "high." Even if there were such a tendency, investors would have learned it by now, and would interpret the firm's issue decision accordingly. There is no way firms can *systematically* take advantage of purchasers of new equity in a rational expectations equilibrium.

Borrowing against intangibles and growth opportunities. Firms holding valuable intangible assets or growth opportunities tend to borrow less than firms holding mostly tangible assets. For example, Long and Malitz [21] found a significant negative relationship between rates of investment in advertising and research and development(R & D) and the level of borrowing. They also found a significant *positive* relationship between the rate of capital expenditure (in fixed plant and equipment) and the level of borrowing.

Williamson [41] reached the same conclusion by a different route. His proxy for a firm's intangibles and growth opportunities was the difference between the market value of its debt and equity securities and the replacement cost of its tangible assets.

The higher this proxy, he found, the less the firm's debt-to-value ratio.

There is plenty of indirect evidence indicating that the level of borrowing is determined not just by the value and risk of the firm's assets, but also by the type of assets it holds. For example, without this distinction, the static tradeoff theory would specify all target debt ratios in terms of market, not book values. Since many firms have market values far in excess of book values (even if those book values are restated in current dollars), we ought to see at least a few such firms operating comfortably at *very* high book debt ratios—and of course we do not. This fact begins to make sense, however, as soon as we realize that book values reflect assets-in-place (tangible assets and working capital). Market values reflect intangibles and growth opportunities as well as assets-in-place. Thus, firms do not set target market debt ratios because accountants certify the books. Book asset values are proxies for the values of assets in place.[16]

Exchange offers. Masulis [23,24] has shown that stock prices rise, on average, when a firm offers to exchange debt for equity, and fall when they offer to exchange equity for debt. This fact could be explained in various ways. For example, it might be a tax effect. If most firms' debt ratios are below their optimal ratios (i.e., to the left of the optimum in Figure 1), and if corporate interest tax shields have significant positive value, the debt-for-equity exchanges would tend to move firms closer to optimum capital structure. Equity-for-debt swaps would tend to move them farther away.

The evidence on exchanges hardly builds confidence in the static tradeoff theory as a description of financing behavior. If the theory were right, firms would be sometimes above, and sometimes below, their optimum ratios. Those above would offer to exchange equity for debt. Those below would offer debt for equity. In both cases, the firm would move closer to the optimum. Why should an exchange offer be good news if in one direction and bad news if in the other?

As Masulis points out, the firm's willingness to exchange debt for equity might signal that the firm's debt capacity had, in management's opinion, in-

---

15. Jalilvand and Harris[16], for example.

16. The problem is not that intangibles and growth opportunities are risky. The securities of growth firms may be excellent collateral. But the firm which borrows against intangibles or growth opportunities may end up reducing their value.

Market values reflect intangibles and growth opportunities as well as assets-in-place. Thus, firms do not set target market debt ratios because accountants certify the books. Book asset values are proxies for the values of assets in place.

creased. That is, it would signal an increase in firm value or a reduction in firm risk. Thus, a debt-for-equity exchange would be good news, and the opposite exchange bad news.

This "information effect" explanation for exchange offers is surely right in one sense. Any time an announcement affects stock price, we can infer that the announcement conveyed information. That is not much help except to prove that managers have some information investors do not have.

The idea that an exchange offer reveals a change in the firm's target debt ratio, and thereby signals changes in firm value or risk, sounds plausible. But an equally plausible story can be told without saying anything about a target debt ratio. If the manager with superior information acts to maximize the intrinsic value of existing shares, then the announcement of a stock issue should be bad news, other things equal, because stock issues will be more likely when the *manager* receives bad news.[17] On the other hand, stock retirements should be good news. The news in both cases has no evident necessary connection with shifts in target debt ratios.

It may be possible to build a model combining asymmetric information with the costs and benefits of borrowing emphasized in static tradeoff stories. My guess, however, is that it will prove difficult to do this without also introducing some elements of the pecking order study.

Issue or repurchase of shares. The fifth fact is no surprise given the fourth. On average, stock price falls when firms announce a stock issue. Stock prices rise, on average, when a stock repurchase is announced. This fact has been confirmed in several studies, including those by Korwar [19], Asquith and Mullins [2], Dann and Mikkelson [10], and Vermaelen [40], and DeAngelo, DeAngelo, and Rice [11].

This fact is again hard to explain by a static tradeoff model, except as an information effect in which stock issues or retirements signal changes in the firm's target debt ratio. I've already commented on that.

The simple asymmetric information model I used to motivate the pecking order hypothesis does

predict that the announcement of a stock issue will cause stock price to fall. It also predicts that stock price should *not* fall, other things equal, if default-risk debt is issued. Of course, no private company can issue debt that is absolutely protected from default, but it seems reasonable to predict that the average stock price impact of high-grade debt issues will be small relative to the average impact of stock issues. This is what Dann and Mikkelson [10] find.

These results may make one a bit more comfortable with asymmetric information models of the kind sketched above, and thus a bit more comfortable with the pecking order story.

That's the five facts. Here now are three items that do not qualify for that list—just call them "observations."

Existence of target ratios. Marsh [22] and Taggart [39] have found some evidence that firms adjust towards a target debt-to-value ratio. However, a model based solely on this partial adjustment process would have a very low R^2. Apparently the static tradeoff model captures only a small part of actual behavior.[18]

Risk. Risky firms tend to borrow less, other things equal. For example, both Long and Malitz [21] and Williamson [41] found significant negative relationships between unlevered betas and the level of borrowing. However, the evidence on risk and debt policy is not extensive enough to be totally convincing.

Taxes. I know of no study clearly demonstrating that a firm's tax status has predictable, material effects on its debt policy.[19] I think the wait for such a study will be protracted.

Admittedly it's hard to classify firms by tax status without implicitly classifying them on other dimensions as well. For example, firms with large tax loss carryforwards may also be firms in financial distress, which have high debt ratios almost by definition. Firms with high operating profitability, and therefore plenty of unshielded income, may also have valuable intangible assets and growth opportunities. Do they end up with a higher than or lower than average debt-to-value ratio? Hard to say.

---

17. This follows from the simple model presented above. See Myers and Majluf [34] for a formal proof.

18. Of course, we could give each firm its own target, and leave that target free to wander over time. But then we would explain everything and know nothing. We want a theory which predicts how debt ratios vary across firms and time.

19. For example, both Williamson [41] and Long and Malitz [21] introduced proxies for firms' tax status, but failed to find any significant, independent effect on debt ratios.

If the manager with superior information acts to maximize the intrinsic value of existing shares, then the announcement of a stock issue should be bad news because stock issues will be more likely when the manager receives bad news.

Conclusion

People feel comfortable with the static tradeoff story because it sounds plausible and yields an interior optimum debt ratio. It rationalizes "moderate" borrowing.

Well, the story may be moderate and plausible, but that does not make it right. We have to ask whether it explains firms' financing behavior. If it does, fine. If it does not, then we need a better theory before offering advice to managers.

The static tradeoff story works to some extent, but it seems to have an unacceptably low R^2. Actual debt ratios vary widely across apparently similar firms. Either firms take extended excursions from their targets, or the targets themselves depend on factors not yet recognized or understood.

At this point we face a tactical choice between two research strategies. First, we could try to expand the static tradeoff story by introducing adjustment costs, possibly including those stemming from asymmetric information and agency problems. Second, we could start with a story based on asymmetric information, and expand it by adding only those elements of the static tradeoff which have clear empirical support. I think we will progress farther faster by the latter route.

Here is what I really think is going on. I warn you that the following "modified pecking order" story is grossly oversimplified and underqualified. But I think it is generally consistent with the empirical evidence.

1. Firms have good reasons to avoid having to finance real investment by issuing common stock or other risky securities. They do not want to run the risk of falling into the dilemma of either passing by positive-NPV projects or issuing stock at a price they think is too low.

2. They set target dividend payout ratios so that normal rates of equity investment can be met by internally generated funds.

3. The firm may also plan to cover part of normal investment outlays with new borrowing, but it tries to restrain itself enough to keep the debt safe—that is, reasonably close to default-risk free. It restrains itself for two reasons: first, to avoid any material costs of financial distress; and second, to maintain financial slack in the form of reserve borrowing power. "Reserve borrowing power" means that it can issue safe debt if it needs to.

4. Since target dividend payout ratios are sticky, and investment opportunities fluctuate relative to internal cash flow, the firm will from time to time exhaust its ability to issue safe debt. When this happens, the firm turns to less risky securities first—for example, risky debt or convertibles before common stock.

The crucial difference between this and the static tradeoff story is that, in the modified pecking order story, observed debt ratios will reflect the cumulative requirement for external financing—a requirement cumulated over an extended period.[20] For example, think of an unusually profitable firm in an industry generating relatively slow growth. That firm will end up with an unusually low debt ratio compared to its industry's average, *and it won't do much of anything about it*. It won't go out of its way to issue debt and retire equity to achieve a more normal debt ratio.

An unprofitable firm in the same industry will end up with a relatively high debt ratio. If it is high enough to create significant costs of financial distress, the firm may rebalance its capital structure by issuing equity. On the other hand, it may not. The same asymmetric information problems which sometimes prevent a firm from issuing stock to finance real investment will sometimes also block issuing stock to retire debt.[21]

If this story is right, average debt ratios will vary from industry to industry, because asset risk, asset type, and requirements for external funds also vary by industry. But a long-run industry average will not be a meaningful target for individual firms in that industry.

Let me wrap this up by noting the two clear gaps in my description of "what is really going on." First, the modified pecking order story depends on sticky dividends, but does not explain why they are sticky. Second, it leaves us with at best a fuzzy understanding

---

20. The length of that period reflects the time required to make a significant shift in a target dividend payout ratio.

21. The factors that make financial distress costly also make it difficult to escape. The gain in firm value from rebalancing is highest when the firm has gotten into deep trouble and lenders have absorbed a significant capital loss. In that case, rebalancing gives lender a windfall gain. This is why firms in financial distress often do not rebalance their capital structures.

of when and why firms issue common equity. Unfortunately I have nothing to say on the first weakness, and only the following brief comments on the second.

The modified pecking order story recognizes both asymmetric information and costs of financial distress. Thus the firm faces two increasing costs as it climbs up the pecking order: it faces higher odds of incurring costs of financial distress, and also higher odds that future positive-NPV projects will be passed by because the firm will be unwilling to finance them by issuing common stock or other risky securities. The firm may choose to reduce these costs by issuing stock now even if new equity is not needed immediately to finance real investment, just to move the firm *down* the pecking order. In other words, financial slack (liquid assets or reserve borrowing power) is valuable, and the firm may rationally issue stock to acquire it. (I say "may" because the firm which issues equity to buy financial slack faces the same asymmetric information problems as a firm issuing equity to finance real investment.) The optimal *dynamic* issue strategy for the firm under asymmetric information is, as far as I know, totally unexplored territory.[22]

---

22. If the information assymetry disappears from time to time, then the firm clearly should stock up with equity before it reappears. This observation is probably not much practical help, however, because we lack an objective proxy for changes in the degree of asymmetry.

The Investment-Financing Nexus: Some Empirical Evidence

by Michael Long and Ileen Malitz,
University of Illinois at Chicago

For years academicians and practitioners alike have addressed the issue of whether a firm's choice of financing mix affects its value. Traditional arguments have centered on trade-offs between the tax advantages of debt, which imply maximum debt financing, and the increased probability of default, with a resulting increase in expected bankruptcy costs, associated with greater use of debt. Such arguments, however, failed to answer some basic questions: Why did firms issue debt prior to corporate taxation? How could bankruptcy costs, which a study by Jerry Warner found to be quite small, possibly offset the apparently considerable tax savings now available from debt financing?[1] In 1976, Merton Miller provided the explanation that, because of personal taxes on interest income, there may be no corporate tax advantage to debt.[2] But this explanation failed to provide an answer to still another puzzle: What accounts for the differences in capital structure we observe across firms in different industries?

The above theories were all based on the assumption that the firm's decision to invest in real assets was made prior to and completely independently of its choice of financing mix. More recently, however, it has been recognized that when a firm issues risky debt, management's financing decisions may affect its investment decisions; and thus the choice of financing may affect firm value. The purpose of this article is to examine the relationship between investment and financing decisions and to show that the type of investment opportunities a firm faces in part determines its ability to support debt. Specifically, firms with relatively high levels of intangible investment, such as expenditures for research and development (R&D) and advertising, tend to use less debt financing. Conversely, firms undertaking substantial investment in tangible assets such as plant and equipment seem able to support high debt levels. In the pages that follow, we illustrate our thesis by offering contrasting profiles of two companies, Eastman Kodak and Inland Steel. We then present evidence from an aggregate of 545 individual firms representing 39 industries.

Background

In 1961, Franco Modigliani and Merton Miller formally examined the effect of a firm's choice of debt or equity financing on its market value.[3] They showed that if there are no taxes or costs of buying or selling securities, a firm's value depends solely on the level and risk of its future cash flows. Since these cash flows, or earnings, derive solely from the real investments a firm undertakes, its value cannot be affected by its choice of financing as long as the firm's decision to invest is made independently of its decision on how to finance. However, if the firm's capital structure affects its real investment decisions, then the choice of debt or equity financing can affect current and future firm value.

Michael Jensen and William Meckling were among the first to recognize formally this interde-

1. Jerold B. Warner, "Bankruptcy, Absolute Priority, and the Pricing of Risky Debt Claims," *Journal of Financial Economics*, 4: (May 1977) pp.239-276.

2. Merton H. Miller, "Debt and Taxes," *Journal of Finance*, 32: (May 1977), pp.261-276.

3. Franco Modigliani and Merton H. Miller, "The Cost of Capital Corporation Finance and the Theory of Investment," *American Economic Review*, 48: (June 1958), pp.261-297.

If the firm's capital structure affects its real investment decisions, then the choice of debt or equity financing can affect current and future firm value.

pendence of real investment and financing decisions.[4] When a firm issues risky debt, two conflicts of interest are created between shareholders and creditors. The first conflict, discussed by Fischer Black and Myron Scholes in their original options paper, stems from the incentives for managers to shift to higher risk projects and investments.[5] Because of their limited liability, shareholders suffer minimal declines in wealth if the project fails, while they receive all of the gains in wealth if the project is successful. Creditors, of course, can never receive more than their promised return, so that the increased riskiness of the firm's cash flows results in an increased probability of default and a correspondingly lower value of debt.

Stewart Myers examined a second adverse incentive, one which he called "the underinvestment problem." He identified circumstances under which managers, acting in shareholders' interests, might reject investments which would increase firm value because the expected gains would accrue largely to creditors.[6]

Cliff Smith and Jerry Warner noted that both adverse incentives can be controlled by contractual provisions such as sinking funds and limitations on the firm's ability to issue debt and/or pay dividends.[7] For example, a sinking fund reduces the potential for a firm to underinvest. The periodic retirement of debt required by the sinking fund has the effect of reducing the incentive to pass up good investments because there is no one year—including the maturity year—in which a debt payment is large enough to encourage shareholders to default. Similarly, limiting the firm's debt-to-tangible-assets ratio reduces the firm's opportunities to increase risk by investing in high uncertainty R&D or buying high growth firms. Limiting dividends to be paid out of earnings requires the firm to invest the proceeds of new debt. Individual firms will submit to these and other restrictions until the marginal increase in the value of the debt raised from so binding themselves equals the marginal cost of writing and enforcing

covenants, as well as the indirect cost of reducing future managerial flexibility.

Intangible Assets Cannot Support High Levels of Debt

In theory, bond covenants can control adverse managerial incentives. In practice, however, they can be quite costly, and the cost depends on the ability of creditors to monitor and control the firm's actions. This ability depends in turn on the observability of the firms' investment decisions. Firms which are difficult, and thus costly, to monitor are those which invest in intangible assets, such as R&D and advertising. While such investments often produce substantial benefits, both the level of investment and risk of the projects are difficult, if not impossible, to observe.

Adding to the problem is the the often substantial time lag between investment outlay and knowledge of the results. For example, if firms face substantial investments in R&D or advertising, it is a relatively simple matter for them to reduce their expenditures and use those funds to pay higher dividends to shareholders. The results of such underinvestment would take years to be noticed by creditors, by which time firm value might be eroded beyond repair. Potential creditors would shy away from a situation they could neither monitor nor control. Similarly, it is quite simple for a firm to shift R&D expenditures to riskier projects. R&D is one of the most closely guarded industrial secrets. Again, by the time creditors found out what managers had done, it might be too late to salvage enough to guarantee their promised payment.

Finally, and perhaps most important, in cases of financial distress, it is much harder for a firm to cash in on intangible firm-specific assets because such assets have market value only as part of a going concern. As Stewart Myers pointed out in the first issue of this journal, "Think not only of the

4. Michael C. Jensen and William H. Meckling, "Theory of the Firm: Managerial Behavior, Agency Costs and Ownership Structure," *Journal of Financial Economics*, 3: (October 1976), pp.305-360.

5. Fischer Black and Myron Scholes, "The Pricing of Options and Corporate Liabilities," *Journal of Political Economy*, 81: (May/June, 1973), pp.637-659.

6. Stewart C. Myers, "Determinants of Corporate Borrowing," *Journal of Financial Economics*, 5: (November 1977), pp.146-175.

7. Clifford W. Smith and Jerold B. Warner, "On Financial Contracting: An Analysis of Bond Covenants," *Journal of Financial Economics*, 7: (November 1977), pp.117-161.

In cases of financial distress, it is much harder for a firm to cash in on intangible firm-specific assets because such assets have market value only as part of a going concern.

probability that borrowing will bring trouble. Think also of the value that may be lost if trouble comes."[8] This lost value may be much greater for firms with intangible assets than for firms with primarily tangible capital equipment.

In anticipating management incentives to underinvest or increase risk, creditors find it easier to monitor investment decisions if the investments are in tangible assets such as plant and equipment rather than in intangible assets. Creditors would know whether and how much the firm invested, as well as the risk of the investments, since the results are tangible and therefore observable in a relatively short time span. Thus any problematic change in investment policy could be identified in time to prevent further erosion of value. And, in the worst case, that of default on debt, the assets could be sold to provide at least some of the funds to pay off creditors.

For these reasons, we argue that it is the type of investment opportunities a firm faces which, in large part, determines the amount of debt the firm can support. Firms that have tangible investments which are easy to monitor can support more debt than firms which face intangible, unobservable opportunities. This has long been recognized by lenders and firms alike. Debt covenants are all written in terms of tangible assets and specifically exclude intangible assets from calculation of the firm's asset base. It is tangible assets, which generally have a well-defined market value and can be sold in case of default, which provide the general security for creditors. The value of intangible assets, on the other hand, is often nil when apart from the firm as a going concern. Thus such assets provide little or no security for creditors and as such cannot support much debt.

A Tale of Two Firms

To give a better feel for what is actually happening, consider the financing and investment policies of the following two firms: Eastman Kodak and Inland Steel. Eastman Kodak undertakes large amounts of both R&D and advertising, whereas Inland Steel's

expenditures for these items are too immaterial to be reported separately. Thus these two cases provide an excellent example of the hypothesis that the type of a firm's investments influences its choice of capital structure.

Eastman Kodak is well known for its new products and extensive promotion. The company is primarily in photography, which accounts for 80 percent of its revenue. Chemicals provide the other 20 percent. Only 57 percent of its 1983 sales of $10.2 billion were domestic. They earned over $1 billion in each of the last three years (1981-83), paying out just under 50 percent as dividends. At the end of 1982, their market value of equity averaged 170 percent of its stated book value.[9]

Inland Steel is a good example of a large heavy industry firm. It is probably the most modern and automated of any major U.S. steel producer. Its $2.8 billion sales in 1982 accounted for 7.1 percent of the domestic market with all the major product lines closely aligned to steel production and sales. While Inland's aggregate profits over the last three years were $46.2 million, they paid total dividends of $118.8 million.[10] At the end of 1982, Inland's market value was 49 percent of its book value. And despite the fact that its stock was selling well below book value, in January 1983 Inland went to the equity market to raise $56.9 million.

Table 1 reports selected characteristics of both firms and their respective industry averages. All variables are computed as a percentage of invested capital (book value of long term debt and equity plus capitalized R&D and advertising), averaged for the previous 3 years.[11]

Traditional capital structure arguments would suggest that Kodak would have more debt than Inland Steel. Kodak's operating cash flow available to pay interest—that is, earnings before depreciation, interest and taxes—was 16.4 percent of total capital, while Inland Steel's was 3.86 percent (13.6 percent for the three years ending 1981). Kodak is consistently more profitable, has fewer non-interest related tax shields, and has a lower investment in fixed assets (and, thus, lower fixed costs and operating

8. Stewart C. Myers, "The Search for Optimal Capital Structure," *Midland Corporate Finance Journal*, 1: (Spring 1983), pp.6-16.

9. This percentage is slightly overstated, however, because Kodak uses a sum-of-years' digits rather than straight line depreciation and LIFO for most inventory accounting, both of which understate its retained earnings and thus its book value of equity.

10. In September 1985 Inland Steel announced the first suspension of its quarterly dividend in 51 years.

11. We capitalized R&D over a 5 year period and advertising over a 3 year period.

Firms that have tangible investments which are easy to monitor can support more debt than firms which face intangible, unobservable opportunities.

TABLE 1 Characteristics of Eastman-Kodak and Inland Steel: 3 years average ending 1983[1]	Leverage	R&D Expense	Advertising Expense	Net Plant	Capital Expenditures	Profit-ability
Kodak (Photographic	.041	.066	.046	.458	.114	.164
Equipment Industry)	.112	.028	.067	.248	.088	.140
Inland Steel (Blast Furnaces	.390	.000	.000	.888	.055[2]	.039[2]
& Steel Industry)	.337	.001	.005	.626	.121	.136

[1] All variables are as defined in the text.
[2] Inland Steel lost 2.78% in 1982 and earned .63% in 1983. For the three years ending 1981, the average profit was 13.6% and average capital expenditures were 10.8% which is more representative.

leverage) than Inland Steel. However, just the opposite is true. Kodak's leverage, measured as the book value of long-term funded debt to total funded capital, is 4.1 percent. Inland Steel's debt-to-capital ratio is 39.0 percent.

Although both Kodak's and Inland Steel's annual capital expenditures averaged around 10 percent of capital over that three-year period, there is a significant difference in asset type between the two companies. A better measure of tangible investments is provided by net plant (measured as gross plant and equipment less accumulated depreciation) as a percentage of funded capital. Kodak's net plant was 45.76 percent of capital in contrast to Inland Steel's, which was 88.84 percent. Table 1 also shows that Kodak's expenditures on R&D and advertising averaged 11 percent, while Inland Steel had no such expenditures. The contribution of R&D and advertising to Kodak's value is extensive. If Kodak failed to make these intangible investments, its profits would disappear over time. By the time the firm defaulted, the current value of Kodak's trademark, processes, and other intangible assets would be near worthless, causing creditors to suffer losses. Similarly, because of the complexity of and secrecy surrounding R&D, Kodak could shift its R&D into radically new fields with potentially huge, but extremely uncertain payoffs. This would increase bondholders' risk and be virtually undetectable by monitoring. Because of these differences in monitoring, Kodak may well find it less expensive to be almost entirely equity financed rather than to incur monitoring costs of debt.

A word should be said about the relative profitability of the two firms. Traditional finance says that profitable firms can support more debt. In this case, however, we find that a profitable firm such as Kodak has less debt than the less profitable firm, Inland Steel. There are two alternative explanations for this. First, as we have hypothesized, it may be the intangibility of Kodak's assets that has caused management to restrict its use of leverage. An alternative explanation, however, based on Stew Myers and Nicholas Majluf's "pecking order theory," suggests that firms will always find it advantageous to fund investments internally rather than externally. Thus firms with high levels of operating cash flow may have less debt simply because they are not forced to go to capital markets to raise funds.[12]

Industries Are Different Also

We initially identified 63 industries classified by our four-digit Standard Industrial Codes. Because many of these industries consisted of only a few firms, we reduced our sample to 39 industries which had at least eight firms. Table 2 shows the mean leverage, R&D, advertising, net plant, capital expenditures and profitability for the 39 industries grouped into quartiles by leverage. R&D and advertising expenditures are higher for industries with lower leverage, while capital expenditure and net plant are lower. Profitability does not show a clear relationship.

In Table 3 we show the characteristics of the five industries with the lowest financial leverage. Also shown are the ranks (from lowest to highest) of each of the variables. R&D and advertising expenditures show a clearly negative relationship with financial leverage. Of the five industries with the lowest lever-

12. Stewart C. Myers and Nicholas Majluf, "Corporate Financing and Investment Decisions When Firms Have Information That Investors Do Not Have," *Journal of Financial Economics*, 13: (June, 1984), pp.187-221.

R&D and advertising expenditures show a clearly negative relationship with financial leverage.

TABLE 2
Characteristics of Industries by Leverage Quartile

Quartile	Leverage	R&D	Advertising	Net Plant	Capital Exp.	Profitability
1	.136	.044	.042	.273	.083	.182
2	.187	.025	.026	.384	.104	.224
3	.212	.024	.024	.411	.111	.190
4	.307	.010	.008	.589	.132	.194
Mean	.224	.026	.026	.418	.105	.202
Median	.210	.012	.021	.378	.103	.192
Range	.090–.411	.000–.136	.000–.079	.184–.886	.048–.237	.120–.318

TABLE 3
Characteristics of Industries with Highest and Lowest Leverage

Panel A: Five Industries with Lowest Leverage

Industry Number	Industry Name	Leverage	R&D and Advertising	Capital Expenditures	Net Plant	Profit-ability
2844	Cosmetics & Toiletries	.090 (1)	.162 (39)	.064 (4)	.256 (5)	.169 (10)
2830	Drugs	.109 (2)	.132 (38)	.083 (12)	.294 (14)	.205 (22)
3861	Photographic Equipment	.112 (3)	.095 (35)	.088 (16)	.248 (4)	.140 (4)
3721	Aircraft	.134 (4)	.084 (31)	.104 (22)	.326 (17)	.174 (12)
3651	Radio & TV Receiving	.142 (5)	.103 (36)	.076 (6)	.184 (1)	.150 (6)

Panel B: Five Industries with Highest Leverage

Industry Number	Industry Name	Leverage	R&D and Advertising	Capital Expenditures	Net Plant	Profit-ability
2911	Petroleum Refining	.294 (35)	.009 (4)	.237 (39)	.886 (39)	.288 (37)
2200	Textile Mill Products	.308 (36)	.020 (8)	.081 (11)	.403 (23)	.177 (14)
2600	Paper & Allied Products	.322 (37)	.012 (5)	.169 (36)	.793 (37)	.179 (6)
3310	Blast Furnaces & Steel	.337 (38)	.007 (3)	.121 (29)	.626 (36)	.136 (3)
3241	Cement Hydraulic	.441 (39)	.000 (1)	.170 (37)	.858 (38)	.134 (2)

Rank out of 39 Industries from Lowest to Highest in Parentheses.

age, four have the highest intangible investments, while the five industries with the highest leverage show the lowest percentage of intangible assets. Net plant and capital expenditures show a positive, but not quite as strong, relationship with debt financing. Again, profitability shows no clear relationship. For example, the photographic industry has the third lowest leverage and the fourth lowest cash flows, while blast furnaces and steel has the second highest leverage and the third lowest cash flows.

The above results, while suggestive, are not conclusive. Some of our explanatory measures might be interrelated. Therefore, we wanted to look at the ability of the full set of characteristics to explain financial leverage. To test our hypotheses further, we used regression analysis to examine the relationship of leverage to R&D, advertising, net plant and profitability. Using these variables, our regression equation was able to explain 42.1 percent of the differences in leverage across firms. As expected, advertising, R&D were negatively related to leverage while net plant was positively related. Profitability, somewhat surprisingly, was also negatively related to leverage. When we excluded the profitability vari-

TABLE 4	Quartile	Leverage	Adv.	R&D	CE	Profitability	Net Plant
Characteristics of 549	1	.0918	.0594	.0477	.1156	.3320	
Firms by Leverage	2	.1994	.0476	.0446	.1263	.2960	not available
Quartile-Full Sample	3	.2912	.0367	.0332	.1173	.2575	
	4	.4283	.0170	.0208	.1366	.2460	

able, we were still able to explain 37.6 percent of the difference in leverage. Thus, we can't reach any definite conclusions about the validity of the pecking order theory, but we can clearly state that the type of investments by industries exert a strong influence on firm's financing decisions.

Large Sample Analysis

In a recent paper we analyzed 545 manufacturing firms to examine further the relationship between investment type and financing.[13] We grouped our firms into portfolios in order to hold the operating or business risk (as measured by unlevered betas) of all firms constant. The purpose was to eliminate the possibility that firms investing in intangible assets have higher risk than firms investing in tangible assets. If the latter was the case, it is possible that we were really only measuring the tendency of riskier firms to have less debt. Table 4 shows the quartile means for this sample of firms grouped into portfolios with equal operating risk. Advertising, R&D and profitability all decrease as leverage increases.[14]

We also looked at the ability of the full set of characteristics to explain financial leverage, both for portfolios and for the individual firms. For the portfolios we were able to explain 35 percent of the variation in leverage by R&D, advertising and capital expenditures, and 65 percent when we added profitability. For individual firms, the same variables, as well as a measure of operating risk, the corresponding percentages were 21 percent and 31 percent. As expected, companies with higher operating risk had higher average profits and lower leverage ratios. (For this reason, we emphasize our results with equal operating beta portfolios.) Again,

the type of investment appears to be an important factor in financing decisions.[15]

Tax Shields and Leverage

Finally we examined the effect of investment-related tax shields on the power of our model. Merton Miller's aggregate model for corporate debt, which includes personal as well as corporate taxes, suggests that any individual firm would be indifferent to capital structure from a tax perspective. Harry DeAngelo and Ron Masulis were the first to suggest that a firm's financial leverage also depends on the availability of investment-related tax shields, such as depreciation and investment tax credits. They argued that the presence of non-debt tax shields affects the extent to which corporations can gain from the substitution of debt for equity. Because higher financial leverage increases the probability that non-debt tax shields will be lost, they hypothesize that firms with fewer non-debt tax shields would employ more debt in their capital structure.[16]

This argument implies that firms investing heavily in capital equipment, which generates large tax shields, should have less debt. We already observed that the relationships between capital expenditures and net plant and financial leverage was positive. However, we wanted to test directly the effect of other tax shields. We computed the tax shield as depreciation expense times the corporate marginal tax rate plus the change in deferred taxes and added the investment tax credit.

Instead of the expected negative correlation between the alternative tax shield variable and leverage, we found a large positive correlation. This finding does not contradict Miller's "Debt and Taxes" theory, nor does it refute DeAngelo and Masulis's ex-

13. Michael Long and Ileen Malitz, "Investment Patterns and Financial Leverage," *National Bureau of Economic Research* (January 1983).

14. In our research, we also looked at total leverage, including short term debt, and found almost identical results.

15. In his dissertation at MIT, Scott Williamson reached the same conclusion. The effect of a firm's profitability is negative and much stronger, providing some evidence for the pecking order theory.

16. Harry DeAngelo and Ronald Masulis, "Optimal Capital Structure Under Corporate and Personal Taxation," *Journal of Financial Economics*, 8: (March 1980), pp.3-29.

tension of that theory. But there is nonetheless a problem with DeAngelo and Masulis's formulation of their argument: namely, it fails to recognize that advertising and R&D also are investments which must be considered as part of the tax shield. Such investments in fact provide a greater tax shield than capital spending because the entire outlay is expensed for tax purposes in the year incurred instead of being amortized across time.

To incorporate such expenditures into the tax shields, we multiplied them by the tax rates and added to the original tax shields. The correlation of the expanded tax shield measure with leverage was $-.277$, which was statistically significant. Thus there is some evidence that firms with higher tax shields, when defined to include all investment-related tax shields, do have less debt.

Conclusion

We have examined the effect of the type of investments a firm makes on its financing decisions. We suggested that R&D and advertising, because intangible, have little value in cases of financial distress, while investments in plant and equipment support creditors in case of default. For this reason, firms with tangible investments can support more debt than firms with intangible investments. Lenders have long recognized this when writing debt covenants, since all such covenants are based on the firm's *tangible* asset base.

Our survey of the aggregate financing practices of over 500 firms supports our hypotheses. Independent of profitability, operating risk or non-debt related tax shields, the type of investments a firm undertakes was consistently able to provide at least a partial explanation for its use of leverage. We also found that traditional arguments that more profitable firms have more debt are not supported by the evidence. This result may simply reflect a preference by managers for internal funds rather than external finance. Alternatively, intangible investments on average may generate higher returns than tangible investments. If this is the case, then it seems clear that it is the tangibility of the firm's assets and investments, not profitability, which is the more important determinant of financial leverage. Finally, we provided some evidence that non-debt tax shields, when properly measured, also influence the amount of corporate leverage.

The Debt-Equity Swap

by Harold Bierman, Jr.,
Cornell University

In early 1982 a *New York Times* headline read "Debt-Equity Swaps Help Pare Bond Debt." The article described how Mercantile Bancorporation of St. Louis earned a "quick, tax-free $3 million." The transaction also strengthened the firm's balance sheet by reducing the book value of its debt by $8.8 million and increasing its equity base by $5.8 million.

The list of companies that have participated in such stock-for-debt deals is long. It includes the Quaker Oats Company, Midland Ross, Crown Zellerbach, Owens Illinois, Procter & Gamble, Sears, Duke Power, and Western Union.

To students of "modern finance," the popularity of the debt-equity swap has been a little puzzling. In this article, I want to comment both on the professed corporate motives and the principal consequences of these transactions. I consider the following four effects:

1. A reduction in corporate leverage, expressed in terms of the ratio of the *market* value of debt to equity;
2. A disproportionate reduction in balance sheet leverage (i.e., the *book* debt-to-equity ratio) caused by retiring an amount of debt (book value) significantly greater than the amount of stock issued in exchange;
3. An increase in reported earnings without an additional increase in taxes; and
4. A reduction in corporate taxes.

In the language of modern finance, only the first and the last of these effects are likely to be "real"; that is, only they are capable of affecting the cash flow, and thus the market value, of the firm. The second and third—by far the most commonly heard rationales for swaps—are financial illusions caused by accounting conventions; they are fairly transparent distortions of economic reality which, as I shall argue, a reasonably sophisticated market can be expected to see through without much difficulty.

The tax consequences of the debt-equity swap, however, seem to have received little attention. Swaps provide a tax-free mechanism for retiring outstanding bonds to meet sinking fund requirements. There is also a potential tax benefit to corporations from using the debt-equity swap as a vehicle for replacing lower-coupon with higher-coupon debt, thereby increasing the corporate interest tax shield.

The Change in Capital Structure

Let's begin by looking at the effects of a debt-equity swap on capital structure. Any exchange of common stock for debt will decrease a firm's debt-equity ratio, whether that ratio is expressed in terms of the book or the market value of debt. The recent debt-equity swaps, however, magnify this effect by allowing the company to retire an amount of debt (at book or face value) considerably larger than the market value of the stock issued in exchange. Some companies in effect issued $400 worth of common stock to retire a $1000 bond, thus removing a $1,000 liability from their balance sheet. In order to do so, of course, the market value of the bond had to be less than $400 (since investment bankers exact the fee for their services in the form of the difference between the total cost of retiring the bonds and the net proceeds from the stock issue).

How can the market value of the debt be less than $400 when the book value of debt is $1,000? The explanation lies in the accounting convention of carrying debt at par (or issue) value on the balance

163

The elimination of low coupon debt means simply a dollar-for-dollar exchange of debt for stock: there is no magical restoration of the balance sheet.

sheet. Accountants do not adjust the value of debt recorded at issue for subsequent changes in the market interest rate. With the large increase in interest rates over the past ten years, the market value of old, low-coupon debt has fallen considerably, creating a large divergence between the accounting and the market values of corporate debt.

This disparity between accounting and market values gives the financial expert a chance to shine. Or so it would appear. He or she can dramatically improve the reported debt-equity ratio at a modest economic cost (the investment banker's cut), or even at an economic gain (provided there are some tax benefits to a swap).

It would be very surprising, however, if the disproportionate reduction in the book debt-equity ratio from retiring low coupon debt resulted in real benefits to the firm. A 6 percent bond maturing in twenty years is clearly not worth $1,000 when the interest rate is 15 percent. Alert analysts adjust companies' book liabilities for low coupon debt outstanding. And it is difficult to imagine creditors and bond rating agencies not doing the same.

In reality, then, the elimination of low coupon debt thus means simply a dollar-for-dollar exchange of debt for stock: there is no magical restoration of the "balance sheet," merely a change in capital structure, a reduction in the *real* leverage, as distinguished from the accounting leverage, of the firm.

But if a reduction in the *real* target leverage of the firm is the primary motive for a swap, we then have to ask why a debt-equity swap has any distinctive advantage over alternative means of achieving the same effect. Why not simply issue new equity or preferred? The only real difference between these alternatives, ignoring tax consequences, is that a new issue of common or preferred stock increases the size of the firm, while a debt-equity swap merely redistributes the assets of the firm between the categories of debt and equity.

While finance theory argues that the accounting illusions described above should have no effect on the value of the firm, we are less clear about the expected consequences of a real change in capital structure. Ron Masulis of UCLA, for example, has provided evidence of a favorable market response to corporate recapitalizations that *increase* leverage.[1] One possible interpretation of Masulis's results is that debt offers an interest tax shield not provided by common stock. Another possibility, however, is that decisions to increase leverage express management's confidence in the prospects of the company, thus communicating favorable information to the market. If the latter is right, then increased leverage *per se* would not contribute additional value to the firm. At present, our research has been unable to distinguish between these two hypotheses.

A debt-equity swap, as stated, brings about a decrease in corporate leverage. Although such a change reduces the corporate tax shield from interest payments, it also may reduce the risk of future financial embarrassment, or provide increased financing flexibility for companies worried about the level of their debt. In such cases, the debt-equity swap may provide the most efficient means of moving to a less levered capital structure. It also may be the least costly way of circumventing restrictive covenants formulated strictly in book ratios.

Changes in accounting leverage ratios, to the extent that they misrepresent economic reality, probably do not matter much to the market, nor perhaps even to most creditors. For some regulators, however, they may tell a different story. For example, a bank facing regulatory officials requiring a given debt-to-equity ratio would welcome such an opportunity to improve its balance sheet through a swap. In this case, the increase in the equity-debt ratio would be a *real* advantage because of the mechanics of the bank regulatory process.

But this disproportionate improvement in the book debt-to-equity ratio, except in cases of regulation or binding, non-negotiable loan covenants, is not likely to be the primary motivating factor behind the swap. It is not clear that using less debt is desirable and, besides, there are other ways of decreasing the debt-equity ratio. We will have to look elsewhere to determine why it is desirable to decrease the debt-equity ratio by substituting $400 of common stock for debt having a market value less than $400.

Tax-free Increase in Reported Earnings

The retirement of debt by issuing common stock with a market value less than the face amount of the debt gives rise to immediate accounting in-

1. R.W. Masulis, "The Effects of Capital Structure Change on Security Prices," *Journal of Financial Economics*, 8 (1980), pp. 139-178.

come. In an economic sense, however, the increase in stockholder wealth takes place well before this formal accounting recognition of income. In fact, it occurs when interest rates move up and the market value of outstanding bonds goes down. This decline in the value of the bonds represents the capitalized value of the corporate savings in real interest costs over the life of the bond. And, in this sense, the accountants' realization of income from a debt-equity swap effectively transfers future accounting incomes (resulting from low interest costs associated with the outstanding debt) to the present.

Such an increase in reported income, and in the book value of stockholders' equity, has nothing to do with the current profitability of the company. There is no cash inflow associated with a swap; indeed, the difference between the cost of retiring the bonds and the value of the stock issued in exchange (much of which compensates an investment banker for structuring the transaction) represents a net wealth *loss* to stockholders.

To summarize, then, accounting conventions that record changes in the value of debt *not* when it occurs, but only when the debt is retired, open the door for manipulation of income statements and balance sheets. But, once more, such transparently cosmetic accounting effects are likely to fool neither investors nor lenders. Financial analysts will surely adjust for the non-recurring income generated by a debt-stock swap. And academic finance journals are now saturated with testimony to the efficiency of the stock market in responding to accounting fictions.

Consequently, unless the stock market or creditors initially perceive a firm as dangerously overlevered, it is doubtful whether a debt-equity swap will improve a company's stock price. A debt-equity swap may improve a firm's credit rating, but only because of the real reduction in corporate leverage. Thus, we have to continue to look elsewhere for substantive motivations for the swap.

Tax Considerations

If we begin with the widely documented premise of sophisticated equity and credit markets, and its corollary of the futility of accounting manipulation, a rational justification for debt-equity swaps must arise from real economic effects, that is, effects on cash flow. There are some potential tax benefits from a debt-equity swap. And, of course, the less a firm pays the IRS, other things equal, the more cash it has on hand to distribute to stockholders.

Sinking Fund Requirements

A swap is a means of satisfying a bond's sinking fund requirements and, at the same time, eliminating taxes on the retirement of low-coupon, heavily-discounted debt. If the firm attempts to meet those requirements by retiring the necessary bonds with cash, there will be a taxable gain on the purchase. If the sinking fund requirements are satisfied by the bonds acquired in a debt-for-stock swap, however, the accounting income is tax-free.

To illustrate the potential magnitude of this tax benefit, let's consider the following example. Assume a company has outstanding a 6 percent bond issue maturing in 20 years. The current interest rate is now 15 percent for 20-year debt. Using .15 as the discount rate, the current market value of a 6 percent bond with a 15 percent yield-to-maturity is $436.66. (As shown following, the present value of a 20-year annuity, using .15 as the discount rate, is $6.2593 per dollar; and the present value of a dollar due in 20 years is $(1.15)^{-20}$, or $.0611.)

Present value of principal: 1,000 x .0611 = 61.10
Present value of interest: 60 x 6.2593 = 375.56

Present value of old debt 436.66

Assume, furthermore, that in the current year the firm must buy X number of $1,000 bonds for its sinking fund, and that the bonds can be repurchased at the current market price (although, in practice, it will have to pay a premium over market to retire any substantial amounts) of $436.66 per bond. The marginal corporate tax rate is 40 percent.

If the bond is retired in a cash purchase, the accounting gain on retirement of the bonds is $563.34 ($1000–436.66) per bond, and the tax liability is $225.34 (.40 x $563.34) per bond. In effect, the cost of retiring those bonds to the corporation through a cash purchase would be $662 ($436.66 + $225.34) per bond. If a debt-equity swap is arranged, however, the firm would issue only $436.66 of common stock to retire each bond. Thus, the tax savings from the use of a swap to satisfy sinking fund requirements can be significant.

The Tax Effect of a Debt-for-Debt Swap

Apart from sinking fund requirements, the tax advantage of a debt-equity swap is a fairly subtle one. Such an advantage is based on the premise that the firm's reduction in leverage (through a debt-equity swap) is not permanent, and that new higher-coupon debt is eventually issued to replace the retired low-coupon debt. The tax benefit arises from the fact that higher-coupon debt provides a larger interest tax shield than an equivalent amount (in terms of market value) of lower coupon debt. The larger the difference between the coupon rates on the firm's old debt and market rates of interest, the greater the potential tax savings to the firm.

Refinancing low-cost debt with higher-cost debt may sound like folly to most corporate treasurers. Stockholders, of course, benefit from actions which minimize the cost of corporate liabilities, i.e., issuing debt when market rates are lower than higher. But, assuming that prior to a debt-equity swap, a company is positioned at its target capital structure (expressed in terms of the ratio of the market value of its debt to equity), there is a distinct tax advantage to replacing the old issue with an equivalent amount of higher coupon debt. (This also assumes, of course, that interest rates are expected to rise or fall from their current (higher) level with equal probability, and that there is thus no benefit to speculating on interest rates by deferring a bond issue in hope of a fall in rates.)

Acting on the above assumptions, the firm could (1) swap its outstanding low coupon debt for common stock, and (2) replace the old issue with an equivalent amount of new debt (with a higher coupon rate, but the same market value). The debt could then be used to repurchase the common stock just issued, thus keeping the firm's market debt-to-equity ratio unchanged. The use of common stock to retire the debt, instead of cash or a new debt issue, is merely a device that allows the transaction to be nontaxable. That is, so long as an investment banker acts as a principal (by holding the debt and swapping it for common stock), the transaction qualifies as a tax-free exchange.

The tax advantage of such a debt-for-debt swap can be illustrated by returning to our earlier example. Recall that the company has outstanding a 6 percent bond issue maturing in 20 years. The current interest rate is now 15 percent for 20-year debt. The present market value of a 6 percent bond with a 15 percent yield-to-maturity is $436.66.

Present value of principal: 1,000 x .0611 = 61.10
Present value of interest: 60 x 6.2593 = 375.56

Present value of old debt   **436.66**

If the old issue is refinanced with a new issue of 20-year debt, carrying a 15 percent coupon and prin-

cipal of $436.66, the components of the new issue will be as follows:

Present value of principal: 436.66 x .0611 = 26.68
Present value of interest: 65.50 x 6.2593 = 409.98

Present value of new debt   **436.66**

On a pre-tax basis, the firm replacing its old 6 percent debt with new 15 percent debt merely breaks even, and there is no reason to undertake the transaction. If we assume a corporate marginal tax rate of 40 percent, however, the story is different. The after-tax interest rate to the firm is 9 percent (or .15 (1 −.4)). Using the after tax borrowing rate of .09 as a discount rate applied to the after tax cash flows, the present value of the new debt is still $436.66. The after-tax interest cost per year is $39.30 (or $65.50 (1 −.40)), and the present value of a 20-year annuity using .09 as the discount rate is 9.1285.

Present value of principal:
                    436.66 x .17843 = 77.91
Present value of after tax interest:
                    39.30 x 9.1285 = 358.75

Present value of new debt   **436.66**

However, the after-tax present value of the *cost to the firm* of servicing the presently outstanding bond, using the present after-tax borrowing rate, is:

Present value of principal: 1,000 x .17843 = 178.43
Present value of after tax interest:
                    36 x 9.1285 = 328.63

Present value of old debt   **507.06**

Thus, replacing the outstanding 6 percent debt by an equal amount (present value, before tax) of 15 percent debt reduces the after-tax present value of the outstanding debt by $70.40 per bond.

Present value of old debt   507.06
Present value of new debt   436.66

Net Benefit   **70.40**

What is the source of this benefit? The following changes take place when the swap occurs:

a. the payment at maturity changes from $1,000 to $436.66, a saving of $563.34.

b. the after-tax interest payments go from $36 to $39.30 per year.

The firm will pay an extra $3.30 of after-tax interest each year for 20 years and, at the end of 20 years, saves $563.34 in principal. The benefit arises because the firm is able to reduce its principal payment at maturity from $1,000 to $436.66, converting much of that principal into tax-deductible coupon payments.

$563.34 x .17843	= $100.52
−3.30 x 9.1285	= −30.12
Net Benefit	**$ 70.40**

The size of this tax benefit will be reduced, of course, by the transaction costs of the swap and refinancing, and also by any premium over the market value of $436.66 required to retire the bonds.

To summarize, then, provided a firm is comfortable with its present debt-equity ratio, a debt-equity swap provides a tax-free vehicle for refinancing lower-coupon with higher-coupon debt. This substitution of interest for principal payments reduces the corporate tax liability. Of course, if a firm is using a debt-equity swap to effect a permanent reduction of its leverage ratios, then this tax advantage becomes irrelevant. The crucial premise, once again, for a tax advantage from the debt-equity swap is that the firm has reached its target leverage ratio, expressed in market terms—that it wishes to fix (or, at some later point, to restore) the present value of its (pre-tax) liabilities at the current level, and then reduce the after-tax cost of servicing those liabilities by transferring payments from principal to interest.

Other Varieties of Debt Reduction

There is actually a wide variety of securities exchanges that can be used to recapitalize the firm. One is a debt-for-debt swap, in which the new debt can differ in maturity, principal amounts, interest rates, call protection and conversion features from the old debt. This type of swap can also give rise to a reduction in the book value of debt and thus to accounting income. However, the debt-equity swap would once again be a necessary intermediate step to allow such a transaction to be tax-free.

Another strategy used in recent years, known as "in-substance defeasance," was to leave low-coupon debt outstanding, but to invest funds in securities to yield the same or higher returns than the debt is costing. These securities were then pledged to be used to pay the debt at maturity.

Prior to objections by the SEC, firms were leaving the debt and the balancing investment off the statements of financial position, thus improving financial ratios. However, a 1982 announcement of the Financial Accounting Standards Board dampened much of the enthusiasm for "defeasances" by disallowing the reporting of the accounting gain as income, and by requiring the reporting of debt as a balance sheet liability. In 1983, however, the Board reversed its initial proposal. We can expect further announcements from the FASB on the accounting treatment of defeasance transactions.

Summing Up

When market interest rates are significantly higher than rates on outstanding corporate debt, swaps of corporate debt for common stock have a very favorable effect on financial ratios. The convention of recording debt at par value on the balance sheet allows the book (as opposed to market) value of debt to be reduced by an amount considerably larger than the amount of stock issued. This leads to a decrease in the book debt-to-equity disproportionate to the cost of retiring that debt. In addition, the swap transaction gives rise to accounting income and improved earnings per share (provided the stock issue is not dilutive).

Such benefits, however, are largely illusory, at least to the extent that markets are dominated by sophisticated investors. Neither investors nor lenders are likely to be fooled by this kind of financial gimmickry. The real consequences of debt-equity swaps are that they enable management (1) to unlever the firm's capital structure (without changing the size of the firm), but only by the amount of the *market value* of the debt retired; (2) to avoid taxes while meeting sinking fund requirements; and (3), more importantly, provided the firm wishes to maintain its current capital structure (expressed in terms of the market value of debt to equity), to enlarge its interest tax shield by following a debt-equity swap with a new debt issue at the higher market rates of interest, but with the same market value as the older, discounted issue.

The Motives and Consequences of Debt-Equity Swaps and Defeasances:
More Evidence that It Does Not Pay to Manipulate Earnings

by John Hand, *University of Chicago,* and
Patricia Hughes, *University of Southern California*

■

On February 9, 1982, Hammermill Paper registered with the Securities and Exchange Commission to swap as many as 400,000 common shares for $13.4 million of the company's 8.07% promissory notes due February 1, 1997. The resulting swap increased Hammermill's 1st quarter earnings by $3.7 million, accounting for more than a third of its earnings for that period. Between February 9 and 10, the market value of Hammermill's equity fell by 4.5%.

On January 28, 1985, United Airlines announced that its preceding 4th quarter earnings included a $3 million extraordinary gain from the defeasance of $38 million of outstanding notes, and that earnings for all of 1984 included a defeasance gain of $21.5 million, representing 7.6% of UAL's 1984 net income. Between January 28 and 29, the market value of UAL's equity declined by 4.6%.

■

During the period of high interest rates in the early 1980s, many companies availed themselves of two new techniques for retiring discounted debt: debt-equity swaps and insubstance defeasances. These transactions were touted by investment bankers as a means of increasing reported earnings without increasing taxes. They were also held up as a way of achieving reductions of balance sheet leverage. Using debt-equity swaps, for example, companies could retire an amount of (book value) debt significantly greater than the amount of equity issued in exchange.

Skeptics, however, pointed out that such transactions had no economic substance. The increase in earnings did not represent any increase in corporate operating cash flow; and the value to stockholders of reductions in the market price of the debt below par should already have been reflected in corporate stock prices. In a reasonably sophisticated market, they reasoned, transactions designed primarily to project accounting illusions should confer no benefits on stockholders. And, to the extent swaps and defeasances actually impose costs on stockholders or provide "signals" of bad news ahead, they may well end up reducing corporate stock prices.

In this article, we present the findings of our own recent research on swaps and defeasances. This research was designed to answer the following two questions: What were the principal corporate motives for these transactions? And what were the consequences for stockholders?

SOME BACKGROUND

What is a Debt-Equity Swap? In a debt-equity swap, an investment banker purchases a company's bonds in the open market, exchanges those bonds for a new issue of the company's common stock, and then sells the stock to investors. A swap thus combines a new equity issue with a retirement of debt. Because the difference between the book and market values of retired bonds is included in reported earnings, debt-equity swaps increase earnings during periods of high interest rates.

As mentioned above, however, there is no corresponding increase in corporate cash flow. And in fact the reduction in interest tax shields that accompanies debt-equity swaps may actually reduce after-tax operating cash flow. In addition to higher corporate taxes, an additional cost of debt-equity swaps are investment banker fees that average close to 4% of the market value of the newly issued stock.

What Is a Defeasance? In an insubstance defeasance, a company buys U.S. government securities with cash payouts identical in amount and timing to those promised by some of its own outstanding bonds. The government securities are then placed with a trustee who services the company's bonds using the cash flows from the government securities. While the defeased bonds remain outstanding and continue to trade, they are removed from the firm's balance sheet, and the difference between the book value of the defeased bonds and the cost of the government securities is included in earnings.

As in the case of debt-equity swaps, the accounting income from a defeasance does not correspond to an increase in cash flow. Unlike a swap, the interest tax shield from a defeased debt issue remains intact; but because the company also incurs additional taxes on the interest earned on the portfolio of Treasury bonds, the net effect is also likely to be an increase in the total amount of corporate taxes.

Why Did They Come About When They Did? The rise of debt-equity swaps and insubstance defeasances in the 1980s can be seen as the fairly direct consequence of changes in the tax code.

Prior to the 1980s, companies simply bought back their discounted debt in the open market. Such direct repurchases first became popular in the early 1970s, presumably because the rise in interest rates allowed companies to realize large accounting gains by buying back their debt well below par. The practice became so common that, in 1975, the Financial Accounting Standards Board issued FAS #4, which prescribed that gains and losses from early debt retirement be classified as "extraordinary." Until 1981, moreover, the gains arising from the repurchase of discounted debt were essentially tax-free.

The practice of directly repurchasing discounted debt came to an end with the the Bankruptcy Tax Act of 1980, which eliminated this favorable tax treatment. Then, in 1981, with interest rates again on a sharp rise, Salomon Brothers created the debt-equity swap in order to facilitate tax-free retirements of discounted debt. Between August 1981 and June 1984, approximately 290 swaps were performed by 170 different companies.

This movement in turn came to an abrupt halt when a provision in the Deficit Reduction Act of 1984 made the gains from swaps taxable. As a consequence, insubstance defeasances, aided by a ruling from the FASB (#76) that permitted the defeased debt to be removed from the balance sheet, then became the preferred vehicle for retiring debt. The popularity of defeasances, however, was ended by the decline in interest rates that began at the end of 1984. (See Figure 1, which clearly demonstrates that the frequency of these transactions depends critically on the level of interest rates.)

SOME NEW EVIDENCE

Two recently published studies have examined both the corporate motives for and the stockholder consequences of swaps and defeasances. In the first, one of the present writers looked at a sample of 245 debt-equity swaps completed during the three-year period August 1981 to June 1984.[1] In the second, we (along with a third researcher, Steve Sefcik) analyzed data on 80 defeasances executed during the period April 1981-February 1987.[2]

1. John Hand, "Did Firms Undertake Debt-Equity Swaps for an Accounting Paper Profit or True Financial Gain?," *The Accounting Review*, Vol. 64 No. 4 (1989).

2. John Hand, Patricia J. Hughes, and Stephan E. Sefcik, "Insubstance Defeasances: Security Price Reactions and Motivations," *Journal of Accounting and Economics*, Vol. 13 No. 1 (1990).

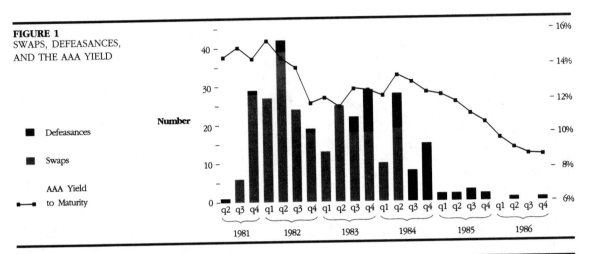

FIGURE 1
SWAPS, DEFEASANCES,
AND THE AAA YIELD

Defeasances

Swaps

AAA Yield
to Maturity

TABLE 1
SWAPS AND DEFEASANCES

Sample Statistics
($ in millions)

Item	Minimum	Median	Maximum
SWAPS			
Face Value of Debt Swapped	1.1	21.1	197.5
Market Value of Equity Issued	0.9	15.1	164.4
Reported Swap Gain	-2.2	4.8	87.3
Coupon on Bonds Swapped	3.75%	8.1%	14.25%
Numbers of Years to Maturity for Bonds Swapped	0.25	15.1	28.2
DEFEASANCES			
Book Value of Debt Defeased	1.8	21.4	550.0
Cost of Riskless Securities	2.2	19.6	550.0
Reported Defeasance Gain	-12.4	0.7	132.0
Coupon on Bonds Defeased	3.0%	7.9%	14.4%
Number of Years to Maturity for Bonds Defeased	0.04	6.2	90.0

Corporate Motives

In the case of both swaps and defeasances, the coupons on the retired debt were in most cases significantly lower than market rates (see Table 1). As suggested earlier, the larger this difference, the greater the opportunity for cosmetic improvements of income statements and balance sheets.

'**Managing' the Income Statement.** The research produced strong evidence that managers used debt-equity swaps to smooth quarterly earnings. In the average swap, quarterly EPS in the quarter the swap was transacted was lower than reported EPS in any of the twelve quarters preceding and twelve quarters following the swap. And, as shown in Figure 2, swaps appear to have been very effective in disguising a temporary downturn in operating earnings.

In the case of defeasances, we chose to focus on trends in annual EPS for only those defeasing

companies that reported defeasance gains greater than the median. Our assumption in so doing was that such firms were most likely to be smoothing earnings. The results of this analysis, as shown graphically in Figure 3, provide strong support for our contention that income "management" was a primary motive for defeasances. Further confirming our suspicions, the research also showed that both swaps and defeasances were concentrated near the ends of the quarters in which they were executed.

'**Managing' the Balance Sheet.** Unlike a debt-equity swap, in which the investment bankers use the proceeds of an equity offering to repurchase the debt, a defeasance requires cash to purchase the portfolio of government securities. How were such defeasances financed? And were they designed to make a permanent change in corporate capital structures?

To answer these questions, we examined the financial statements of 64 defeasing companies and

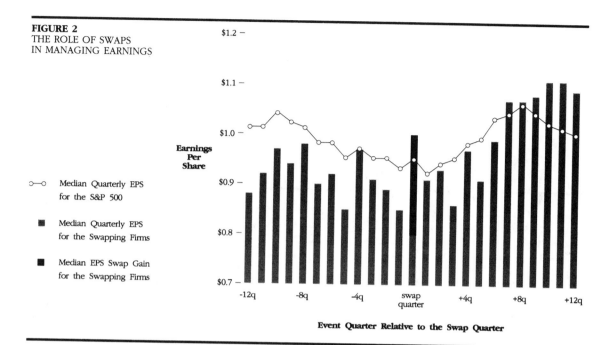

FIGURE 2
THE ROLE OF SWAPS
IN MANAGING EARNINGS

Median Quarterly EPS
for the S&P 500

Median Quarterly EPS
for the Swapping Firms

Median EPS Swap Gain
for the Swapping Firms

Event Quarter Relative to the Swap Quarter

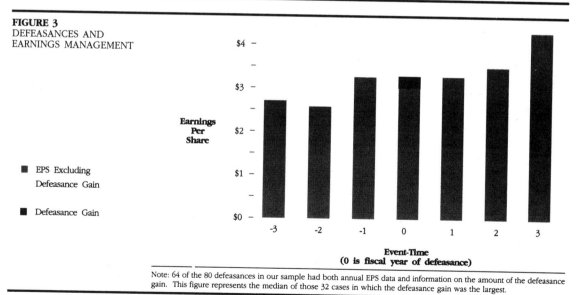

FIGURE 3
DEFEASANCES AND
EARNINGS MANAGEMENT

EPS Excluding
Defeasance Gain

Defeasance Gain

Event-Time
(0 is fiscal year of defeasance)

Note: 64 of the 80 defeasances in our sample had both annual EPS data and information on the amount of the defeasance
gain. This figure represents the median of those 32 cases in which the defeasance gain was the largest.

a control group of other companies matched by
industry, size, and fiscal year-end. Our results, as
summarized in Table 2, show that defeasances were
financed, on average, by some combination of
excess cash and new stock issues. Also not surprising, they were undertaken by companies with

higher debt-equity ratios, possibly either to improve
the look of the balance sheet or to avoid running up
against restrictions in bond covenants.

What was surprising, however, was that one
year after the defeasance, the leverage ratios of
defeasing companies actually *increased* significantly

TABLE 2
DEFEASANCE FINANCING
($ in millions)

		Year Before Defeasance	Year of Defeasance	Year After Defeasance
Cash and Marketable Securities				
	Defeasing Firms	610.4	593.4	643.3
	Matched Firms	324.0	325.3	347.1
Long-term Debt Issued				
	Defeasing Firms	141.4	107.8	164.2
	Matched Firms	156.4	280.9	656.4
Common and Preferred Stock Issued				
	Defeasing Firms	30.5	47.3	22.1
	Matched Firms	32.0	14.7	31.2
Debt/Equity Ratio				
	Defeasing Firms	0.74	0.78	1.14
	Matched Firms	0.64	0.59	0.46

relative to the control group. The fact that many companies followed defeasances with new debt issues suggests that there was no underlying intent to reduce the amount of leverage in the target capital structure. And this reinforces our suspicion that the primary corporate motive for defeasances was simply to boost reported earnings.

The Consequences (Or Did the Stock Market Buy It?)

To determine whether investors capitalized such earnings into stock prices, the research examined the stock market reactions to the initial public release of information about the transactions. In the case of the 245 debt-equity swaps, the price movements were measured over the two trading days surrounding the registration of the transactions with the SEC. In the case of defeasances, we looked at two-day price reactions to announcements of 35 defeasances that appeared in the *Wall Street Journal*.

The Market Response

	Swaps	Defeasances
Mean abnormal return	-1.3%	-0.86%
(t-statistic)	(-7.9)	(-2.4)
% of negative returns	69%	66%

The average stock price reaction to debt-equity swaps was -1.3%. In the case of defeasances, the price movement was -0.86%. In the case of swaps, moreover, the larger the accounting gain from the swap, the more negative the market's response.

Stock market investors, then, do not appear to have been misled by such artificial increases in earnings. In fact, the evidence suggests that investors may have understood the underlying corporate motive for such transactions all too clearly. Anticipating a decline in operating cash flow, they correctly marked down the value of the shares before the lower earnings actually materialized.[3]

Wealth Transfer to Bondholders? Another tenable explanation for the negative market reaction to defeasances concerns its effect on the prices of outstanding bonds. Because the defeasance portfolio is irrevocably dedicated to servicing the defeased bonds, some speculated that a wealth transfer from stockholders to bondholders would result from the reduction in bond default risk. And, in fact, for our 35 public announcements of defeasances, we found the average price response of 24 bond issues to be a positive 1 percent (with a **t** statistic of 3.1). If the total operating value of the firm (debt plus equity) remains unchanged, such increases in bond values represent reductions in the value of the equity.

CONCLUDING COMMENTS

The evidence from our recent research suggests that managers undertake costly debt-equity swaps and defeasances in "bad times" in order to disguise downturns in reported earnings. Stock market investors, far from being fooled by such accounting illusions, respond negatively to these transactions. While reductions in corporate leverage and the associated tax shields partly explain the negative reaction, it also seems likely that investors correctly interpret such attempts to manipulate earnings as a sign of poor operating results ahead.

---

3. The somewhat more negative investor response to debt-equity swaps than to defeasances may have much to do with the fact that swaps involve the issue of new equity. It is now well-documented that announcements of corporate equity offerings reduce stock prices—by 2 or 3 percent, on average.

Common Stock Repurchases: What Do They Really Accomplish?

by Larry Dann,
University of Oregon

Introduction

In the last decade, the repurchase by publicly-held American companies of large quantities of their own common stock has become a commonplace event. A great number of explanations have been offered to account for the popularity of these transactions. But most prominent among them are the following six. Stock buybacks purportedly are being used (1) to increase reported earnings per share, (2) to effect changes in capital structure, (3) to distribute cash to stockholders in a manner that reduces their personal tax obligations, (4) to reduce the company's dividend cash outflow (without cutting dividends per share), (5) to convey to the market management's belief that its stock is undervalued, and (6) to buy out a stockholder that is allegedly interfering with the ability of incumbent management to operate the company most efficiently.

Until recently, systematic evidence on the impact of a common stock repurchase on the repurchasing company's stockholders was not available. Since 1980, however, three studies have been published which analyze the effects of public repurchases — both through cash tender offers and open market transactions — on stockholders' wealth. A fourth study has investigated the stock price impact of privately negotiated repurchases where the ostensible motive was to reduce the threat of a takeover.

In this article, after briefly outlining the different methods of repurchase, I want to examine the conceptual merit of the rationales for stock repurchase cited most frequently by corporate managers and the financial press. Then, I shall consider these rationales in light of the recently reported evidence.

If increasing expected EPS is the only reason for the stock repurchase, the likelihood of a share price increase is small.

Methods of Repurchase

In the United States, corporations can repurchase their own shares in three ways: (1) repurchase tender offers, (2) open market repurchases, and (3) privately negotiated buybacks, generally involving one or, at most, a few large stockholders.

In a repurchase tender offer, the company usually specifies the number of shares it is offering to purchase, the price at which it will buy the shares, and the period of time during which the offer is in effect. The company also generally reserves the right to extend the offer beyond the announced expiration date, and to purchase shares in excess of the number specified. The offer may be conditional on receiving tenders for a minimum number of shares, and may permit the withdrawal of tendered shares prior to the expiration of the offer.[1]

Open market repurchases occur more frequently than repurchase tender offers, but they generally seek to retire a much smaller portion of the company's equity. They are in substance identical to purchases of stock made through a broker by any private investor. Unlike repurchase tender offers, companies are not required to disclose publicly their open market repurchase activities, but open market repurchases must comply with the anti-manipulation and anti-fraud provisions of the Securities and Exchange Act of 1934 as amended. Many companies do, however, make periodic announcements of (1) boards of directors' authorizations to reacquire common stock, (2) management's intentions to repurchase, and (3) the completion of repurchase activity (whether the intention to repurchase was previously announced or not). Further unlike tender offers, which generally are completed within one month of the initial announcement date, open market repurchases often take place over several months or even years.

Privately negotiated repurchases involve buying shares from a stockholder (usually having a sizable holding) through direct negotiation with the company. Private repurchases are less common than either open market or tender offer repurchases. And unlike the public methods of repurchase, either management or the selling stockholder can initiate the negotiation of a private buyback. To a much greater extent than public repurchases, privately negotiated repurchases are often used by managements to maintain control of the company. In many cases, the stockholders involved in such repurchases are dissidents, posing the threat of interference — and, in some cases, takeover — to incumbent management.

The Common Arguments for Stock Repurchase

One popular corporate rationale for stock buybacks is that, by reducing the number of shares outstanding, they raise the market's expectation of future earnings per share. Underlying this argument is the assumption that the market responds mechanically to expected increases in EPS by raising stock prices.

With respect to this "EPS rationale," two points should be noted. First, expected EPS does not automatically increase with a stock repurchase because, unless financed by a new debt offering, repurchases also mean a reduction in corporate assets. To the extent that those assets are efficiently employed and thus contribute proportionately to earnings, a reduction in assets will mean a reduction in earnings. Expected EPS will increase only if the reduction in shares outstanding is proportionately greater than the reduction in expected net income.

Second, even if the repurchase does cause an increase in expected EPS, this increase will be achieved only by increasing the financial leverage of the company and, thus, the financial risk of the common stockholders. Finance theory argues that although repurchases may raise EPS and ROE, these effects will be offset by higher returns demanded by stockholders as compensation for bearing greater risk. The price of the outstanding stock will increase only if the increase in expected return dominates the increase in risk brought about by this financial leveraging of EPS.

In short, if increasing expected EPS is the *only* reason for the stock repurchase, the likelihood of a share price increase is small. A great deal of evidence suggests that investors are not systematically fooled by relatively transparent financial illusions. And the EPS effect of a stock repurchase (indepen-

---

1. With the adoption of SEC Rule 13e-4 in September 1979, shareholders have the right to withdraw tendered shares within the first ten business days of the tender offer. In addition, if the company chooses to purchase less than all shares tendered, shares must be accepted from each tendering shareholder on a pro-rata basis.

Using stock repurchases as substitutes for dividend payments can create problems for managers trying to maximize the wealth of all shareholders.

dent of any other managerial motives or considerations) is just that: a financial illusion.

A second commonly encountered rationale for repurchases is that, by increasing financial leverage, they offer a means of moving the company toward its "optimal" capital structure. Corporate finance theorists have yet to resolve the issue of whether a uniquely optimal capital structure (i.e., one which maximizes the value of the firm) exists for any individual company; and if so, what the determinants of that optimum are. But, even if we assume there is such a thing as an identifiable optimal capital structure, the question remains whether a common stock repurchase is the most efficient (least costly) way of moving toward the target.

New debt issues are, of course, an alternative means of increasing leverage; and a second, less obvious alternative is a direct debt-for-equity exchange. What distinguishes stock repurchases from these debt-increasing alternatives is that repurchases reduce the size of the firm. Managements of mature companies seeking *solely* to increase their debt-to-equity ratios (without shrinking the size of the company) can seemingly do so more efficiently with debt-for-equity exchanges, in which the increase in debt is exactly offset by a decrease in equity. Growing companies can achieve the same result simply by relying on debt as the primary source of new external financing.

Another frequently cited argument for stock buybacks is that they distribute cash to stockholders in a manner that produces lower taxes than an equivalent amount of cash dividends. Reducing stockholder taxes is, to be sure, a legitimate and laudable managerial objective. Using stock repurchases as substitutes for dividend payments, however, can create problems for managers trying to maximize the wealth of *all* shareholders.

The chief difficulty stems from the fact that, in order to induce shareholders with unrealized tax gains to sell their shares, repurchasing firms must offer a premium above the market price. Offering to buy shares at a premium favors shareholders with low tax obligations at the expense of owners with high tax liabilities. As a consequence, there is a danger of paying too high a price for the shares; in so doing, management will effectively be transferring wealth from shareholders retaining their shares (because of their high tax liabilities, which come due when the shares are sold) to those surrendering ownership in the company.

Other kinds of wealth transfers may also result from stock repurchases. Finance theory predicts, for example, that debtholders of repurchasing companies should be harmed by the liquidation of corporate assets that, if retained, would provide greater security for debt claims. In this event, the reduction in the value of the debt would represent a gain to the company's stockholders.

A fourth common argument for stock repurchases is that they allow the company to reduce total dividend payments while maintaining dividends per share. In fact, repurchases undertaken for this reason are generally treated as an investment decision by the repurchaser. Some corporate managers claim that the stock buyback offers an attractive after-tax rate of return on invested cash because, unlike the earnings on most other investments, the dividends "saved" on the reacquired shares are not taxable. But if this differential tax effect is the source of the attractiveness of repurchase, then the "investment" rationale is merely the "stock repurchase as substitute for (present and future) dividend payments" argument in disguise.

The notion that the dividend savings from stock repurchases are a good investment often, however, has nothing to do with the differences in tax treatment. But, apart from tax consequences, the argument that the dividend savings from stock buybacks benefits remaining stockholders has no theoretical support. A company's stock price theoretically reflects the present value of all expected distributable (though not necessarily distributed) cash flows. If the stock is fairly priced, then retiring stock at the current market price to save on dividends (and, more generally, to reduce capital costs) is, by definition, a zero net present value investment; that is, economic value is neither created nor diminished. Consequently, evaluating repurchases as a capital budgeting problem in which the stream of future dividend savings is discounted at the company's cost of equity capital is (again, apart from tax considerations) a futile exercise in circular logic.

What many corporate managers really mean when they say that repurchase is a good investment is that the stock is "cheap," and thus represents a "good buy." Indeed, the belief that the company's shares are undervalued by the market is probably the most popular justification offered by management for stock buybacks. If the stock does prove to be undervalued, then a stock buyback would, of course, represent a good investment (i.e., a positive NPV project) for the company's remaining stockholders. In an efficient market, however, management should not be overly confident about its ability to identify an undervalued situation without possessing important insider information.

Stock repurchases are also thought to be a way of sending a credible signal to investors that management is optimistic about the company's prospects. The fact that management, in the case of repurchase tender offers, is willing to buy back shares at a premium above their market value is believed by many to be an effective means of communicating the confidence of insiders. And the communication of this information alone could lead to higher stock prices.

But, even if there are valid reasons for believing that the current stock price fails to reflect the company's expected future performance, there are good reasons for corporate managers to tread carefully with the stock repurchase decision. First, there may be less costly means of communicating the same message. Investment banker and legal fees, share solicitation fees (in the case of tender offer repurchases), and brokerage fees (for open market purchases) are often substantial. If there is a more efficient vehicle for communicating the company's prospects (such as a continuous program of direct financial communication to investors), the cost savings could be significant. Also, if the company has exceptional investment opportunities on the horizon, then the capital paid out through a stock repurchase may have to be retrieved through another securities offering, which could be expensive.

A second consideration concerns the wealth transfers among stockholders described earlier. The form the repurchase takes — whether tender offer or open market purchase — and the price paid for the shares will determine the size of any wealth transfers between selling and non-selling shareholders. If management, using information not generally available to the investing public, is correct in its conviction that the current market price undervalues the company's stock, then a stock repurchase at the market price effectively benefits remaining stockholders at the expense of those relinquishing their share of the company's future earnings. But, if a premium is paid, and the premium is too high, then a wealth transfer in the opposite direction results: selling stockholders are rewarded at the expense of remaining ones.

In many cases, two or more of these (and, occasionally, other) rationales are offered for repurchase decisions. The intended effects of repurchase may therefore be a combination of the motives con-

sidered above. As a result, the implications of the decision to repurchase shares are often more complicated than any of the rationales, considered individually, suggest.

At this point, let's step back and briefly review the arguments for stock repurchases. First, any effect on earnings per share by a stock buyback that arises *solely* from the reduction in the number of shares outstanding is not likely to have an effect on the price of the common stock or, equivalently, on the value of stockholders' claims. The substitution of stock repurchases for cash dividends probably lowers the personal taxes that most stockholders pay on corporate cash distributions, but not all stockholders benefit equally from these personal tax savings. Indeed, in those cases where the company offers to repurchase shares at a premium over the current price, some stockholders may be harmed by this substitution for dividend payments. Increasing financial leverage and expressing confidence in the company's prospects are also frequently cited as repurchase rationales, but these are sensible only if less costly means of moving toward a target capital structure and communicating perceived undervaluation are not available.

Having presented the most prominent corporate justifications for stock buybacks, and examined them in the light of modern finance theory, I now want to turn to the existing evidence on the effects of stock repurchases.

The Evidence

In independent studies, Ronald Masulis of UCLA, Theo Vermaelen (formerly of the University of British Columbia, now at Catholic University in Leuven, Belgium), and I have investigated the effect of tender offer repurchases on the stock prices of repurchasing companies. Both Vermaelen's study and mine also report stock price effects associated with open market repurchases. In addition, Masulis and I have independently examined the price reactions of actively traded debt and preferred stock to common stock repurchase tender offers.

Although the samples differed, each of our studies revealed a strong positive market response to the announcement of repurchase tender offers. On average, the stock prices of repurchasing companies appreciated by approximately 16 percent over the two days surrounding the announcements. The average price of these tender offers was 22 percent above the market price prevailing shortly before the announcement of the offer.

These offers, furthermore, were not trivial in magnitude. In the typical tender offer, management sought to repurchase slightly over 15 percent of their outstanding shares; and with the repurchase premium factored in, the average repurchase tender offer was designed to distribute to stockholders an amount equal to approximately 19 percent of the market value of equity before the repurchase. Somewhat surprisingly, given that the market price remained below the tender offer price in most cases, only 18 percent of the outstanding shares were tendered in the typical offer.

The 16 percent average price increase at the initial announcement, however, was not a temporary effect; the evidence shows that the higher stock price level was maintained well beyond the expiration of the offer. We also found no perceptible impact of tender offer announcements on the prices of straight bonds and preferred stock. Convertible debt and preferred stock prices, presumably reflecting the increase in common stock prices, rose about 3 percent on average.

In contrast to the findings of our studies of tender offers, the market's response to announcements of open market repurchases was much more subdued, perhaps in part because open market plans are generally of smaller magnitude than tender offers. Whereas the typical tender offer sought 15 percent of outstanding shares, the average open market repurchase plan involved only about 5 percent of the outstanding common stock. The average common stock price increased approximately 3 percent in response to the announcement of an open market repurchase plan.

Interpreting the Evidence

The evidence thus points unambiguously to a positive price effect associated with stock repurchases. Sorting out the most likely *cause* of these price increases, however, is not a simple task. One reason is that, as mentioned earlier, several of the effects (leverage, tax reduction, information, wealth transfers) may operate simultaneously.

There is, however, some additional related evidence which has a bearing on this issue of repurchase effects. By considering these additional findings together with the results just summarized, we can draw some tentative inferences about the predominant forces at work.

The Wealth Transfer Effect

Reasoning from the absence of any appreciable impact of repurchases on the prices of non-convertible debt and preferred stock, we can rule out wealth transfers from these security holders to stockholders as a significant contributor to the stock price increases. The evidence supporting this conclusion should comfort anyone who may have feared that the principal consequence of stock repurchases was enriching common stockholders by expropriating wealth from other classes of security holders. This is hardly surprising, however, because in a reasonably efficient market, we would not expect holders of bonds and preferred stocks to be repeatedly exploited by a corporate practice as common as stock repurchase.

The Tax Effect

It seems doubtful that the tax savings from substituting stock repurchases for dividend payments is an important contributing factor to the positive market response to repurchases. But here the evidence is less conclusive.

To begin with, the actual amount of the tax savings from substituting the average repurchase for an equivalent dividend payment would account only for a fraction of the 16 percent stock price appreciation accompanying the average repurchase tender offer. Vermaelen has pointed out that, for the average company repurchasing (through a tender offer) 15 percent of the value of its outstanding shares as an alternative to a cash dividend of the same amount, the tax savings (assuming the 'representative' marginal investor is taxed at 30 percent on dividends and pays no taxes on the repurchase) should produce only a 4.5 percent gain (15 percent x .30) to non-tendering stockholders. Furthermore, because the tax obligation is not entirely eliminated, but merely reduced and deferred, the actual gain should be even smaller.

Vermaelen's line of reasoning has been countered by the following argument: if the company is expected to continue to substitute stock repurchases for cash dividends in the future, then the stock price at the time of the initial announcement can be expected to capitalize the entire *stream* of present and expected future tax savings.

The credibility of this argument, however, is weakened by several pieces of evidence. First, the vast majority of companies whose repurchase activities have been reported in *The Wall Street Journal*

It seems doubtful that the tax savings from substituting stock repurchases for dividend payments is an important contributing factor.

apparently repurchase shares very infrequently. This is especially true for tender offer repurchases; only one in seven companies buying back their shares over a 15-year period (1962-1976) made more than a single tender offer during that time. Repeat repurchases are somewhat more common using the open market, but even there few companies could be characterized as "regular" repurchasers. (In fact, it would be difficult for firms to become "predictably regular" in their repurchase activity without running afoul of provisions in the Internal Revenue Code that would construe regular stock repurchase distributions as "constructive dividends" and, thus, as ordinary taxable income.)[2]

If companies systematically substituted repurchases for dividends, then the argument that stock prices reflect the capitalized value of the stream of expected tax savings would be a plausible one. But, it is difficult to accept the proposition that investors consistently misinterpret single, non-recurring stock buybacks as signals of continuing repurchasing plans.

Furthermore, our research shows that companies announcing open market repurchase plans did not perform any better than companies that announced only the *completion* of open market repurchase activity *without* having made any earlier public statement about its repurchase plans. (Also, in over half of these "completed repurchase" announcements, companies stated they had no plans for further stock repurchase.) If the market does in fact capitalize an expected stream of future tax savings from repurchases, we would expect a stronger positive response to announcements of the *beginning* of open market repurchase plans. The fact that the market does not distinguish between "completed repurchase" announcements and announcements of forthcoming open market repurchase plans is further evidence that the tax benefits of repurchases are not primarily responsible for the positive stock price impact.

The large premiums in repurchase tender offers also seem inconsistent with a desire to lower investor taxes. The higher the purchase price, of course, the higher the tax liability. Offering large premiums thus reduces any tax advantage gained by substituting stock repurchases for dividends.

There is one additional piece of evidence that may have some bearing on this investor tax savings question. If the tax effect of repurchases is responsible for the positive market response, then we would expect the size of the stock price movement to be positively related to the size (relative to the market value of the company) of the cash payout. The Masulis study reports that there is indeed a positive association between the stock price changes and relative payouts; however, this association is also consistent with other explanations (i.e., the leverage and information hypotheses) of the price impact of repurchases and, therefore, is not conclusive evidence of a personal tax effect.

On the basis of the available evidence, then, the importance, if any, of the personal tax effect of repurchases remains an unresolved issue. In my judgment, however, the bulk of the evidence to date suggests the personal tax savings effect does not contribute in a major way to the stock price increases accompanying repurchase announcements.

The Leverage Effect

The evidence is also mixed concerning the stock price effect of the leverage increases caused by repurchases. Both Vermaelen and Masulis collected information on the way in which companies financed their stock repurchases. They reasoned that if the leverage increase contributes to the positive market response (because of the tax advantage of debt financing), then stock repurchases financed with debt should experience higher rates of return than repurchases financed without the use of debt.

Masulis reported that companies financing their buybacks with more than 50 percent debt experienced larger average stock returns than companies using at most 50 percent debt.

Vermaelen, on the other hand, found that companies using no debt to finance the repurchase experienced larger average stock returns than his sample of all repurchasing firms. He concludes that this evidence does not allow us to distinguish between the stock price effects of increasing leverage and of communicating managerial confidence and undervaluation.

Because the evidence is contradictory here, we cannot with any confidence attribute the stock price

---

2. The IRS concern with regular repurchases suggests that a personal tax savings effect does exist. However, the point being made here is that any such personal tax savings effect is small in relation to the average observed stock price response to a tender offer announcement.

Repurchases may not be the most cost-effective means of communicating managerial confidence.

effect of repurchases to changes in capital structure. The increase in leverage, in many cases, may well be a management decision which primarily reflects insiders' favorable outlook for the company. The confidence expressed by management in further leveraging the company may itself carry positive signals to the market above and beyond the benefits of debt financing.

The Information Effect

This brings us again to the most widely professed motive for stock buybacks: undervaluation of the company's stock. Vermaelen provided one test of the hypothesis that repurchases portend improvements in corporate performance. He reported that earnings per share for tender offer repurchasers, after allowing for the effect of the reduction in shares outstanding, are higher in the years following the repurchase than predictions by sophisticated earnings forecasting models would have led us to expect. Higher than expected earnings after repurchases are consistent, of course, with the claim that repurchases are used to signal that companies are undervalued, or that prospects have improved.

In considering this "information effect" of stock repurchases, however, it is important to keep two things in mind. First, it may be the "signal" about the company's prospects that causes the increase in stock price, *not* the repurchase *per se*. Second, repurchases may not be the most cost-effective means of communicating managerial confidence. Managers acting in their stockholders' interests should use repurchases to convey information only if a more efficient means is not available. Consequently, even if information disclosure is the most plausible explanation of the large and lasting stock price increases that have been documented, the question of why the information is communicated in this fashion, given the costs of a repurchase, remains unanswered.

There is one other curious aspect of tender offer repurchases that warrants mention. Recall that, in the average tender offer, the offer price exceeded the pre-offer market price by 22 percent, and the market price rose by 16 percent in response. Yet, only 18 percent of outstanding shares were tendered.[3]

This finding suggests either there are significant impediments to tendering for the majority of stockholders (because non-tendering stockholders passed on average an apparent opportunity for an additional 6% gain), or there are other important missing factors. One potentially important factor is the extent of managerial ownership or control of the repurchasing company.[4]

In a study that Harry DeAngelo (of the University of Rochester) and I recently completed, we examined the returns to stockholders of companies that privately negotiated repurchases of shares from a substantial (individual or corporate) stockholder —ostensibly to strengthen management's control. A critical distinction between these repurchases and public buybacks is that in public offers the opportunity to tender or sell shares is available to all stockholders.[5] Consequently, although we must be careful about assuming strict comparability between public and privately negotiated repurchases, the results from our study are instructive in the present context.

We divided our sample of privately repurchasing firms into two groups: those companies that repurchased their shares at a premium above the market price, and those that did not. In the case of those private negotiated repurchases where premiums were paid, there was on average a small, but statistically significant, stock price *decline* at the announcement of the repurchase. There was no detectable price response for the companies that did not pay a premium.

These results are pertinent to our earlier discussion of public repurchases in two ways. First, the reason for the repurchase appears to be important. When the repurchase is for the stated purpose of removing a single large holding,[6] there is no positive stock price effect. This is true even though, as in public tender offers, management's demonstrated willingness to pay an above-market price for the company's shares could be construed as a positive information signal. Second, whatever EPS and financial leverage effects exist for public repurchases also exist for privately negotiated buybacks. If these factors were primary contributors to the market's positive response to public repurchases, we would

3. A paper by Ahron Rosenfeld addresses the issue of shareholder response to repurchase tender offers. Instead of simply comparing the tender offer price to the pre-offer market price, he measures the offer premium relative to the sum of (i) the pre-offer market price and (ii) an estimate of the per share value of the new information conveyed by the offer. He finds a strong positive relationship between the size of this "information-adjusted offer premium" and the fraction of outstanding shares that are tendered.

4. Vermaelen reports that the median fraction of insider ownership for his sample of tender offer firms is 8.8 percent.
5. There is an exception. In some tender offers managers and directors voluntarily exclude themselves from eligibility to tender their shares.
6. The average fraction repurchased in the privately negotiated premium repurchases was 11 percent at an average premium of 14 percent above market price.

In the case of those private negotiated repurchases where premiums were paid, there was, on average, a small stock price decline at the announcement of the repurchase.

not expect private repurchases to have such a markedly different effect on the stock price.

This difference between the market reaction to public and private repurchases suggests that management's *perceived* motive for undertaking the repurchase may have the strongest influence on the market. And this, of course, strengthens the hypothesis that the information released by announcements of *public* repurchase tender offers is primarily responsible for the large positive stock price response.

Summary and Conclusions

The conclusions that we can draw from the existing research are less than completely definitive. Nevertheless, the evidence does support at least the following statements:

1. The documented positive effects of announcements of stock repurchases on stock prices are not attributable to the repurchase *per se* (and to the illusory EPS effect), but rather to "real" effects that accompany the repurchase. This has two implications for financial executives considering repurchase. First, it does not make sense to repurchase stock unless the reason for doing so is to bring about some real changes; moving toward a target capital structure, reducing stockholder taxes, or signaling management confidence are the major real effects of repurchases. Second, if management intends to achieve one or more of these objectives through share repurchase, it should first consider whether a less costly means of achieving the same objective is available.

2. The expected personal tax savings from distributing cash through stock repurchase instead of dividends is probably not a major contributing factor to the stock price effects of repurchase tender offers. Also, the relative wealth effects of repurchase on stockholders are not distributed in proportion to existing stockholders' relative ownership positions. That is, it is virtually certain that some stockholders benefit at the expense of the others in a stock repurchase plan. In tender offers, it is most often the non-tendering shareholders who suffer relative to those owners who surrender their shares. The decision to repurchase stock is therefore a delicate one for the manager concerned about acting in the best interests of *all* stockholders.

3. The most plausible *single* explanation of the sizable price effects associated with public repurchases is that investors interpret the repurchase decision as a signal of positive information from management. Exactly what information is being signalled has yet to be identified. But, if new information is the predominant cause of the stock price response, then management should determine whether stock repurchase is the most efficient means of conveying the message. A program of direct and frequent communication of information to investors may be an equally effective and less costly means of ensuring that stock prices reflect management's view of the company's future.

An Analysis of Call Provisions and the Corporate Refunding Decision

by Alan Kraus,
University of British Columbia

Introduction

Almost all publicly-traded corporate bonds, and most preferred stock issues, have call provisions written into their indenture agreements. Such provisions allow the issuer to repurchase the bonds or preferreds at a specified price (generally expressed as a percentage above par value). As a rule, the call privilege cannot be exercised until the "deferred call" period—usually five to ten years from the date of issue—has elapsed. When interest rates fall, corporate treasurers servicing long-term bonds issued at higher rates thus have the option of calling those bonds, and replacing them with a new issue. The purpose of a bond refunding, in such cases, seems to be to reduce current interest costs.

The callability of bond and preferred stock issues raises two questions that corporate treasurers must address. The first is whether to issue callable bonds in the first place, rather than an equivalent but noncallable issue. The second, and more often asked, is: Given that a callable bond or preferred has been issued, when does it make sense to call and refund it?

Why corporations routinely attach call provisions to their bond issues remains an unresolved question in academic finance literature. In the first part of this article, I focus primarily on the "classic" motive: reduction of interest costs. If management, or its financial advisors, has superior ability to forecast interest rates, then it is quite easy to explain why, and under what circumstances, management would choose to attach a call provision to a new issue. But if corporate management has no special foreknowledge of future interest rates, as capital market theory would suggest, then the incentives to make a new bond issue callable are less clear. Tax considerations, restrictive bond covenants, and the reduction of corporate risk are the other possibilities I explore. All in all, though, it appears that no single factor has yet been identified that adequately explains the call provisions observed on virtually all corporate bonds and preferred stock.

In the second part of the article, I offer a relatively simple and straightforward refunding strategy. The conventional wisdom on the bond refunding issue, which reflects most of the available finance literature, has made the refunding decision depend heavily on management's interest rate forecasts. My prescription, grounded in principles of options pricing, finally has nothing to do with management's expertise in forecasting interest rates.

The call provisions on corporate bonds, I will argue, are much like the call options on stocks traded on the Chicago Board Options Exchange. The corporate refunding strategy should be designed to maximize the value of the company's call option on its bond, thus minimizing the value of the outstanding bonds. Ignoring the costs of a new issue, the prescription that comes out of this analysis is very simple: call the bond as soon as its price reaches the call price. When new issue expenses are included in the analysis, the optimal refunding strategy is a little more complicated. The basic principles are the same, however, and a refunding rule can still be stated in fairly simple terms.

The Call Provision

How Much Does It Cost?

As suggested, the most obvious reason for management to include call provisions in indenture agreements is to preserve the option, should inter-

Calling bonds to refinance at a lower interest rate is a "zero sum game" between shareholders and bondholders.

est rates fall, of refinancing high-interest debt at lower rates. The stronger management's conviction that rates will fall, and the steeper the expected fall, the stronger is this motive for including the call provision. It should be recognized, however, that the bond markets are not likely to have significantly different expectations about future rates. To the extent that investors share management's conviction that long-term rates will fall from current levels (which, in most cases, will already be reflected in an inverted yield curve), this motive for including the call provision loses its justification.

As was pointed out a decade ago,[1] calling bonds to refinance them at a lower interest rate is a "zero sum game" between shareholders and bondholders. Any expected gains to the issuer from being allowed to refund a bond at a lower rate are expected losses to (or, more precisely, capital gains foreited by) the bondholders from having to accept a lower rate on their funds. Exercise of the call privilege is the issuer's prerogative and thus will occur only when it benefits shareholders at the expense (in almost all cases) of bondholders. Bondholders, however, are well aware of this possibility and price bond issues accordingly. For this reason, they demand higher rates of interest on callable than on otherwise equivalent noncallable bonds.

Stated most simply, the coupon rate on a *callable* bond issue must be set high enough to make the present value of expected payments to bondholders (based on the probability that the bonds are actually called) the same as if the issue were non-callable.[2] This means that if management and investors hold identical expectations about interest rates, the higher coupon rate that just allows a callable bond to sell at par would make management indifferent between the alternatives of (1) including the call provision and paying a higher rate and (2) issuing a non-callable issue, also at par, but paying a lower rate.

A simple numerical example will illustrate the point. Assume that management plans to issue perpetual bonds of $100 face value with annual coupons, and that a coupon rate of 15 percent would allow a *noncallable* issue to be sold at par. Suppose further that all market participants agree there is a 50 percent chance that, a year from now, the going yield on perpetual, noncallable bonds will have

fallen to 12 percent. If the rate does fall to 12 percent, the noncallable bond with a 15 percent coupon rate will be trading at $125 ($=\$15/0.12$). There is also an equal chance that the going yield will rise to 20 percent, thus causing the same bond to trade at $75 ($15/0.20). Finally, assuming that the current one-year interest rate is also 15 percent, equal to the long-term rate, we can see (below) that the noncallable issue would sell at par:

$$V_{Noncallable} = \frac{\text{First year's coupon} + \text{Expected price at year end}}{1.0 + \text{One-year rate}}$$

$$= \frac{\$15 + (.5)(\$125) + (.5)(\$75)}{1.15} = \$100$$

Suppose instead that management proposes to make the bond callable one year hence, *and only then*, at a call premium of $15 over par. If the noncallable yield next year falls to 12 percent, then all market participants agree the company will exercise its call privilege. In this case, the call provision allows management to retire for $115 ($100 par value plus the $15 premium) a security that would otherwise, in the absence of a call provision, be worth $125 to the bondholders. To put it a little differently, the call privilege enables the company to retire for $115 a security paying $15 per annum, which could then be immediately reissued, in the form of a noncallable bond paying the same $15, for proceeds of $125 (excluding new issue costs). Thus, if rates fall to 12 percent, exercise of the call has the effect of transferring $10 of bondholders' capital gains to shareholders.

Because of this possibility of forfeiting part of their expected gains to shareholders, investors will not pay $100 for the *callable* bond carrying only a 15 percent coupon rate. In fact, under the conditions described above, the market would require a coupon rate of 16.43 percent for the callable bond to be issued at par:

$$V_{Callable} = \frac{\$16.43 + (.5)(\$115) + (.5)(\frac{\$16.43}{0.20})}{1.15} = \$100$$

The issuer's choice here is thus between issuing a noncallable bond with a 15 percent coupon rate and a callable bond requiring payments of 16.43 percent. In this case, the cost of including the call privi-

1. This observation was first made by Stewart Myers in a "Discussion" appearing in the *Journal of Finance*, Vol. 26, No. 2 (1971). Its implications were discussed in my own article, "The Bond Refunding Decision in an Efficient Market," *Journal of Financial and Quantitative Analysis*, Vol. 8, No. 5 (1973).

2. This ignores the effect of differences in default risk among companies, and the risk aversion of investors.

The greater the possibility and magnitude of a fall in rates, the larger the cost of the call provision.

lege is 143 basis points.

Just how large an increment to the coupon rate would be required in an actual issue will obviously depend on a great many factors. There is little evidence on the size of this increment, partly because it is hard to measure directly when virtually all corporate issues are callable. One study of the debt of A.T.&T. and subsidiaries estimated a coupon rate increment of 30 basis points required by tax-exempt investors for callable bonds with yields in the 8 percent range.[3] Given today's higher interest rates, and the much larger variation over time in rates, the required coupon rate increment might well be several times this amount. The greater the possibility and magnitude of a fall in rates, the larger the cost of including the call provision. For example, the more downward sloping the yield curve, the greater the required premium in coupon rate for issuing a callable.

Let's now estimate the value of the call provision from the standpoint of the corporate issuer. To calculate the present value of expected payments on the callable bond, start by assuming that a coupon of $16.43 is made the first year. If rates rise to 20 percent, then the call is not exercised and annual payments of $16.43 continue in perpetuity. If rates fall to 12 percent, the bond will be called for $115. It can then be replaced with a noncallable promising $16.43 per year in perpetuity, which can be sold for $136.92 ($16.43/0.12).

Thus, in the case of a callable bond, the stream of expected payments can be viewed as a series of certain annual payments of $16.43 reduced by a 50 percent chance of a $21.92 ($136.92 − $115) gain to shareholders one year hence. The present value of the stream of expected payments is:

$$V = \frac{\$16.43}{0.15} - \frac{(.5)(\$21.92)}{1.15} = \$109.53 - \$9.53 = \$100$$

This is identical to the present value of payments under the noncallable alternative. Under the conditions described above, management should have no preference between issuing a 15 percent noncallable bond and a 16.43 percent callable bond.

In practice, of course, call provisions extend over many years, so that the comparison facing the

financial manager rests on much more complicated interest rate scenarios than the one in our example. Still, the basic principles are the same.

Valuing the Call Privilege

The call privilege is very similar to the call options on stocks traded by individual investors. In fact, a callable bond can be viewed as a noncallable bond on which the purchaser (the bondholder) has written a call option held by the issuer (the borrowing company).[4] There are two major differences, however, between the corporate issuer's option to call its bonds, and the call options on securities available to individual investors. First, in buying a callable bond issue, all purchasers automatically assume liability for the call option; the option cannot be detached from the underlying security. Second, the company's call option cannot be sold—it can only be exercised or allowed to expire. With these qualifications, then, the value of a callable bond can be expressed as follows:

Callable Bond = Noncallable Bond − Call Option

Continuing with the example from the previous section, recall that the value of the callable, perpetual bond carrying a $16.43 coupon is $100. At the same time, a noncallable, perpetual bond offering a coupon payment of $16.43 per year would have a value of $109.53 ($16.43/0.15) when the yield on such bonds is 15 percent. In this case, then, the value of the call option is $9.53, which is exactly the present value of the expected gain from exercise of the call privilege as calculated in the previous section.

Using the formulation above as a framework for examining the decision to issue a callable bond, I now want to consider reasons why the corporate issuer might place a higher value on the call option than investors who buy the bonds.

1. Call Provisions & Interest Rate Forecasting

As with any option, paying for the call privilege represents a gamble on future events that the buyer of the option takes against the writer of the option. In the case of the call privilege on a bond, the gam-

3. See W.M. Boyce and A.J. Kalay, "Tax Differentials and Callable Bonds," *Journal of Finance*, Volume 34, Number 4 (1979).

4. This view of the call provision is implicit in the analysis by Michael Brennan and Eduardo Schwartz in "Convertible Bonds: Valuation and Optimal Strategies for Call and Conversion," *Journal of Finance*, Volume 32, Number 5 (1977). It has also been discussed by J.B. Yawitz and J.A. Anderson in "The Effect of Bond Refunding on Shareholder Wealth," *Journal of Finance*, Volume 32, Number 5 (1977).

ble is on the future course of interest rates. If bond issuers believe they are more astute than the bond market in general, and if they feel rates are likely to fall significantly before the bond matures, they might be convinced the gamble is loaded in their favor. In this case, they might have good reason to attach a call provision to the issue.

Returning to our earlier illustration, assume once more that investors believe the odds of interest rates going to 12 percent or 20 percent are each one-half. Suppose, however, that management does not share this belief. Instead they assign a 60 percent probability to a rate of 12 percent, and only 40 percent to the chance of its rising to 20 percent. For our perpetual bond paying $16.43 annually and callable at $115, when the rate drops to 12 percent, the value of the bond (without the call provision) rises to $136.92 ($16.43/0.12), and management exercises the call privilege. The shareholders realize a gain, and the bondholders a loss, of $21.92 ($136.92 − $115). In this case, the call option will be valued at $11.44 (.6 × $21.92/1.15) by the issuer and at $9.53 (.5 × $21.92/1.15) by investors.

Thus, if the callable bond is issued at a price between $98.09 ($109.53 − $11.44) and $100, it will be preferred to the noncallable alternative by *both* the corporate issuer and investors. Management will have purchased a call option for less than its perceived value of $11.44, while bondholders receive more than the $9.53 of capital gains they expect to give up through exercise of the call.

Management may also prefer the callable alternative if it believes there is a chance of a greater drop in interest rates than investors foresee—even if management assigns a smaller probability to rates falling than investors. For example, assume investors still believe the chance of rates going to 12 percent is one-half. Suppose management foresees only a 30 percent probability that rates will fall, but believes that if a decline does occur, it will result in a rate of 10 percent. An interest rate at this level would raise the value of the bond (without the call provision) to $164.30 ($16.43/.10), producing a gain to shareholders of $49.30 from exercising the call privilege. The call option will then be valued by the issuer at $12.86 (.3 × $49.30/1.15).

Because investors will still value the call option at $9.53, the callable bond can be issued at any price between $96.67 ($109.53 − $12.86) and $100; and it will again be preferred to the noncallable by both issuer and investors. The point is that the value of

the call option depends on both the chance of interest rates falling and on the magnitude of the fall.

There are several compelling reasons, however, for doubting that callable bonds are issued primarily because of management's confidence in its ability to forecast interest rates. First, although managers possess inside information about their companies' prospects, it is difficult to see why they should have any comparative advantage over the general market in forecasting an economy-wide variable such as the level of interest rates. Indeed, given the structure of incentives, we would expect market investors to be, if anything, better informed than corporate treasurers on interest rate developments.

Second, assuming that corporate management could consistently outperform bondholders in predicting interest rates, this fact would become known over time by bond investors as they watched how, on average, they (the bondholders) lost money on the call provision. In pricing future callable issues, investors would interpret the call provision as a signal of management's expectation that rates were likely to fall below current levels. Having recognized managers' forecasting superiority, investors would insist on further increases in the coupon rate until management would finally see the benefits of including the call provision nullified by the increased cost of the call. Under these circumstances, one would expect new bond issues to be divided fairly evenly between callables and noncallables.

Third, even if issuers proved consistently right in forecasting interest rates and bondholders remained unaware of their own relative forecasting deficiency, we would still expect new issues to be split between callables and noncallables. For, management will place more value than investors on the call privilege only when they are more confident that rates will *fall*. If management were convinced rates could only go higher, there would be no reason to incorporate the call provision. A consistent preference for issuing callables thus rests not only on management's superior forecasting, but also on the belief that, during the period the call is in effect, rates are always likely to fall well below current levels. Neither of these conditions is consistently reliable. That both should hold simultaneously seems highly improbable, to say the least.

2. The Call Provision and Taxes

In our earlier examples, no consideration was given to the effect of taxes paid by either the investor or the issuing company. When taxes are introduced, and provided the bondholder is taxed at a lower marginal rate than the corporation, a callable bond will be preferred to its noncallable equivalent by both the investor and the company.

To illustrate the tax argument, let us assume the investor is a tax-exempt institution, such as a pension fund, while the issuer pays a 50 percent corporate income tax. Coupon and call premium payments are, of course, taxable income to the bondholder and deductible by the issuing company.

Because the investor pays no tax, our example shows that he will be indifferent between the 15 percent noncallable bond and the 16.43 percent callable bond. From the issuer's viewpoint, however, the alternatives must be evaluated using after-tax discount rates applied to after-tax cash flows.

The introduction of taxes does not affect the value of the noncallable bond:

$$V = \frac{\text{After-tax coupon}}{\text{After-tax discount rate}} = \frac{(.50)(\$15)}{(.50)(.15)} = \$100$$

For the callable bond, however, an after-tax calculation from the issuer's standpoint produces a different result. The after-tax value of the $16.43 coupon is $8.21. Because the call premium is tax-deductible to the company, the after-tax value of the $115 call price is $107.50 ($100 + (.50 × $15)). Similarly, if bond yields rise to 20 percent, the after-tax rate is 10 percent; and given that the current one-year interest rate is 15 percent, the one-year after-tax discount rate becomes 7.5 percent. Thus, the after-tax cost of the callable bond to the issuer is calculated as follows:

$$\frac{\$8.21 + (.5)(\$107.50) + (.5)(\$8.21/0.10)}{1.075} = \$95.82$$

The corporate issuer will thus prefer the callable at any price above $95.82 to the noncallable equivalent issued at par. Tax-exempt investors will prefer the callable bond at any price below $100. Thus, at any price within this range, both the issuer and the investor gain from the inclusion of the call provision.

The simplest explanation for this tax advantage is that the call provision, with the associated higher coupon rate, transfers tax-deductible interest costs from later to earlier periods. This increases the present value of the interest tax shield to the company. Whenever the lender has a lower tax rate than the borrower, it is to their mutual advantage to arrange a loan having higher taxable payments at the start and lower taxable payments later.[5]

This tax argument is correct as far as it goes. But as a complete explanation for the almost universal inclusion of call provisions, it has some shortcomings. For one thing, there are certainly bond investors whose marginal tax rates are not lower than those of corporations issuing callable bonds. If callable bonds are priced so that investors with tax rates no lower than the corporate rate are willing to hold them, then the potential tax benefits from debt financing fall entirely to those investors with lower tax rates. Under these circumstances, there is no corporate tax incentive to issue callable instead of noncallable bonds.

What evidence we have,[7] however, suggests that the implied tax rate on corporate bonds is roughly 20 to 30 percent, which, while significantly greater than zero, is still a good deal lower than the statutory corporate rate of 46 percent. Thus, there is probably yet some tax advantage to callable over noncallable bonds.

In the case of preferred stock, however, the tax incentives would appear to favor noncallable over callable issues. Preferred stock dividends are not deductible for corporate taxes; and to the extent that the marginal tax rate of investors pricing preferred issues is positive,[8] companies should benefit by deferring payments to investors through the noncallable alternative. Because the inclusion of call provisions on preferred issues is virtually as automatic as on bond issues, the tax explanation does not fully account for the prevalence of callable bonds.

3. The Call Provision, Bond Covenants, and Operating Flexibility

Because bondholders are not represented on the corporation's board of directors, bond indenture agreements contain various covenants and re-

---

5. This explanation is at the heart of the tax advantage of zero coupon bonds, in which the investor effectively receives all interest payments, and the corporation a large part of its tax shield, in the early years.

6. Indeed, in an address to the American Finance Association in 1976, Merton Miller went so far as to suggest that corporations would continue to issue debt until the tax rate of the marginal bond investor equaled the marginal corporate rate, thus nullifying the tax advantage of debt relative to equity financing.

7. See, for example, David Pyle, "Is Deep Discount Debt Financing a Bargain?" in Chase Financial Quarterly, Vol. 1, Issue 1 (1981).

8. Because preferreds are sold largely to institutional or corporate investors, which are usually either tax-exempt or have an 85 percent exclusion, preferred issues carry rates far below bond issues. Thus, in the case of preferred issues, there is probably no tax-based reason to prefer either option: noncallable or callable.

strictions to persuade bond market investors to hold corporate debt. Such covenants often restrict a company's investment decisions, forbidding mergers or the sale of certain assets. Corporate issuers agree to these restrictions because they reduce investor uncertainty and the negative effects of bondholders' perceived lack of control over management decisions. Imposing such restrictions effectively reduces the interest costs of a new issue.

In certain cases, however, such covenants may prove so restrictive that the cost to the company in foregone opportunities may exceed their savings in capital-raising costs. One plausible motive for including call provisions in the company's debt is to provide a way of getting around such restrictions. Suppose, for example, that a merger opportunity comes along that represents a positive net present value investment. At the same time, however, undertaking such a merger would increase the risk of the bonds, thus reducing their value. If the indenture agreement contains a restriction on mergers, bondholders will invoke the restrictions to prevent the merger. If the bonds are noncallable, the only recourse of the shareholders would be to repurchase all the bonds. This move could be doomed, however, because the bondholders could demand to receive all of the net gain from the merger (say, in the form of convertible bonds) in return for renegotiating the covenants.

If the bonds are callable, however, the call price places an upper limit on what the issuer must pay to redeem the bonds. This flexibility to undertake otherwise restricted investments may partly explain the customary inclusion of call provisions in corporate bond issues.[9] Many deferred call provisions explicitly distinguish between a call for the purpose of refunding the debt at lower interest rates (which cannot be done during the deferment period) and a call for redemption without refunding (which can be done any time). The latter kind of provision seems more clearly intended to preserve management's investment and operating flexibility.

This rationale for the call provision, however, is also far from complete. The call provisions actually included in indenture agreements seem unnecessarily inefficient if management's main purpose is to preserve options to invest or disinvest. Because call prices are generally fixed at a percentage above

face value, calling a bond issue rarely makes sense unless the bonds are trading near or above par. When issues are selling at deep discounts from par, the size of the premium over market necessary to redeem the bonds will offset, in most cases, the gains expected from pursuing the restricted investment opportunity.

Indeed, as interest rates rise above the coupon rate on a callable bond, the value of the call option (in terms both of preserved operating flexibility and expected interest savings) to the company is effectively driven to zero. If call provisions were designed expressly to preserve management's flexibility (regardless of the course of market interest rates), the call price should be specified as a premium *not* over par, but over the discounted value of the coupons and principal on the bond, using as a discount rate the current long-term Government bond rate, or a well-defined long-term yield index. Defined and indexed in this manner, a call provision (solely for the purpose of redemption, not refunding) would make exercise of the call privilege equally attractive regardless of the current level of interest rates. Because call provisions are not written this way, we can conclude that management's desire to preserve investment options, although no doubt important in some cases, does not explain the near universal use of the call provision.

4. The Call Provision and Reduction of Interest Rate Risk

There is still one other potential advantage provided by the call feature on corporate bonds or preferred stock. Although this explanation has received little, if any, attention in the finance literature, it offers another clue to the puzzle—one that gets closest to management's concern about the need to protect the company against exposure to changes in interest rates. Whether such concern is legitimate, however, and whether most large, well-diversified public corporations should actively manage interest rate risk are open questions.[10]

The essence of the argument is that the call provision reduces the sensitivity of the bond's (or preferred's) value to movements in interest rates. Interest rate volatility means greater variability in bond prices, and thus greater risk for bondholders.

9. See Z. Bodie and R. A. Taggart, "Future Investment Opportunities and the Value of the Call Provision on a Bond," *Journal of Finance*, Volume 33, No. 4 (1978).

10. See Bluford Putnam's "Managing Interest Rate Risk: An Introduction to Financial Futures and Options," *Chase Financial Quarterly*, Vol. 1, Issue No. 3.

The call provision may reduce the systematic risk of shareholders as well as bondholders.

Changes in interest rates, especially in real interest rates, also have a major impact on the economy. Increases in real interest rates, such as those experienced during the first year and a half of the Reagan administration, raise all investors' expected returns, thus depressing the value of not only bonds, but corporate assets and stock prices as well. In this sense, stockholders, like bondholders, may be subject to interest rate risk.

My argument is that, by reducing the sensitivity of a bond's value to the systematic risk of interest rate movements, the call provision may reduce the systematic risk of shareholders as well as bondholders.

To see how the call provision reduces the sensitivity of the bond's value to changes in interest rates, recall the earlier formulation:

$$\text{Callable Bond} = \text{Noncallable Bond} - \text{Call Option}$$

As market interest rates rise, the market values of the noncallable bond and the call option held by the company both decline. Thus, the difference between their values—that is, the value of the callable bond—changes less than the value of the noncallable bond.

To return once more to our example, if interest rates one year hence are either 20 percent or 12 percent, the value of the noncallable bond will be either $75 ($15/0.20) or $125 ($15/0.12). Given the same interest rate forecast, however, the value of the callable bond will be either $82.15 ($16.43/0.20) or $115. (Remember the $115 assumes the bond is called when rates fall to 12 percent.) Thus, with the same expectations for interest rates, the value of the noncallable bond will fall or rise by $25; the callable bond's value will fall $17.85 or rise $15.

Assuming that the values of enough companies are sensitive to interest movements such that changes in rates systematically affect the value of the market portfolio, interest rate changes are a component of market-wide, systematic risk. If so, the question becomes: How does a reduction in the systematic risk of a company's bonds affect the risk of its stockholders' investment? The answer depends largely on how the company's operating cash flows (and thus the value of the company's assets) are affected by changes in interest rates and inflation.

If the company's earnings keep pace with interest rates, and thus its real, inflation-adjusted cash flows remain relatively constant over time, then a reduction in the systematic risk of the company's debt represents a reduction in the risk of its equity as well. (In fact, such a company is really not exposed to any systematic interest rate risk.[11]) To see why this is so, recall that the market value of the firm (i.e., the discounted value of expected future cash flows) can be viewed as the sum of the market values of its debt and equity. Formulated in an equation,

$$V_F = \frac{\textbf{Normalized Annual Cashflow}}{\textbf{Cost of Capital}} = V_D + V_E$$

Solving for the value of the equity,

$$V_E = V_F - V_D$$

Holding real operating cash flows constant (and this of course is the crucial assumption), it is clear that the use of a call provision to reduce the sensitivity of the bonds' value to interest changes benefits shareholders by reducing the risk of the equity. Lower risk, other things equal, means higher stock prices.

Conversely, for those companies whose assets contain real, systematic risk due to interest rate movements (that is, their real operating cash flows and hence the value of their assets fall when inflation and interest rates rise), the systematic risk of the equity will actually be increased by making the bonds callable.

The values of companies in industries with high asset turnover (retailing, for example) are generally less sensitive to interest rate movements. Therefore, such companies might have more reason to include call provisions in their bonds. At the other extreme are industries, like mining and heavy manufacturing, with very long-lived assets and a resulting greater sensitivity of total real value to interest rate movements. Companies in these industries would have less reason for including—and indeed perhaps a positive reason for not having—a call provision in their bond agreements.

The Refunding Decision

Most of the voluminous literature dealing with callable bonds has been concerned with the refund-

---

11. In the case of near perfect correlation between interest rates and operating cash flows, floating rate debt is actually the best prescription. Floating-rate debt is an extreme form of the call provision, in the sense that it comes closest to stabilizing the value of the debt at par.

ing question: When does it make sense to call an outstanding bond issue and replace it with another? Even if the decision to include or exclude a call provision in a bond issue is largely irrelevant, once management has chosen to pay the higher cost to make the bonds callable, the refunding decision definitely "matters."[12]

How to Measure the Value of Calling a Bond Issue

In measuring the benefits of a refunding to shareholders, the traditional literature assumes that the refunding will result in debt carrying lower coupon payments, but the same principal. Comparing new debt with lower coupon obligations to an outstanding issue with the same face value assumes, in effect, that management has changed its leverage target—not as measured in book terms, but in terms of the market value of future obligations. As such, the traditional comparison actually reflects the value of interest savings not only from exercise of the call provision, but also from a decrease in the company's market leverage ratio.

Recall that a callable bond is equivalent to a noncallable bond promising the same stream of promised coupons and principal plus a call option on the noncallable bond held by the corporate issuer. The stream of promised coupons and principal is, of course, a liability of the firm. The call option, however, should be viewed as an asset. Therefore, to isolate the value of a refunding from the effect of a change in leverage, it is necessary to assume that when the call option is exercised, the retired debt is replaced with the same stream of promised payments. This effectively fixes the liability leverage ratio, measured in terms of the market value of promised payments.[13]

Furthermore, as suggested earlier, the value of the call provision comes from management's ability to repurchase (at below its market value) a noncallable bond having coupons and principal equal to those of the callable bond. This tells us that the benefit of a refunding should be calculated assuming the retired debt will be replaced with *noncallable* bonds, even when the intended new issue is callable. The value of exercising the call provision, therefore, is the market value of the promised payments of the callable bond (without the call provision) less the call price (and all incremental costs associated with a refunding).

This method for quantifying the benefits of a refunding, as the reader may recall, was illustrated in our earlier numerical example. Remember that if the going yield on (noncallable) bonds falls to 12 percent, the noncallable equivalent value of a callable paying 15 percent rises to $125 ($15/.12). If the call price is $115, the current exercise value of the company's call option on its bonds is $10. To determine the net benefit of a refunding, the value of this call option would then be reduced by the after-tax present value of the expenses of issuing replacement bonds.

Even if the net benefit is positive, however, it does not necessarily follow that the optimal decision is to call the bonds immediately. The reason is simple: the optimal time to "cash in" the call privilege by exercising it is when the value of doing so is *greatest*, not merely when it has become positive.

The Refunding Rule Without New Issue Expenses

In the pages that follow, I am going to concentrate on the question of refunding policy for *publicly-traded* bonds. This will allow us to state a refunding rule which relies on bond prices alone. In the case of private placements, the refunding principle is fundamentally the same. In the absence of directly observable prices, however, management must rely on estimates of yields on equivalent *noncallable* corporate bonds (see previous paragraph) to make the refunding decision.

The guiding principle for the optimal call policy can best be illustrated by returning to the earlier formulation of a callable bond as a noncallable bond combined with a short position (from the bondholder's perspective) in a call option:

Callable Bond = Noncallable Bond − Call Option

Because the callable bond represents a liability of shareholders, maximizing shareholders' value

---

12. See Myers and Kraus, both articles cited earlier and in References.

13. Effectively, the call option has been converted into cash by being exercised. While it is true that the shift in assets from converting the call option into cash may itself represent a change in leverage, this is of secondary significance compared to the change in the present value of promised debt payments.

means minimizing the value of the callable bond. The value of the noncallable is determined largely by market interest rates. Consequently, minimizing the value of the callable bond means adopting that refunding policy which maximizes the value of the company's call option.[14]

This prescription admittedly ignores the costs of issuing replacement bonds. But, it is helpful to begin the analysis by setting aside such costs. In many cases, management may feel that the extra issue expenses associated with a refunding are trivial. For a large bond issue, direct flotation costs may be on the order of 1 percent or less of face value—less than one month's interest cost. Only direct flotation costs are really incremental to a refunding, since duplicate interest payments can be offset by holding the funds in interest-bearing securities.

The optimal refunding policy depends, to a large extent, on how the prices of callable bonds behave as interest rates fall and the bonds trade near the call price. The value of a *noncallable* bond, assuming no risk of default, would depend largely on the current level of interest rates. The value of a *callable* bond also depends primarily on the level of interest rates—at least over a certain range of (higher) interest rates. But, as interest rates fall lower and lower, the price begins to be influenced progressively more by investors' expectations about when the bonds will be called.

Investors' expectations, however, are conditioned by management's past behavior in calling bonds, thus creating a circular chain of causality. The refunding rule I propose relies completely on observable bond prices. Accordingly, it must be based on what refunding policy the bond market is expecting management to follow. To make the truly optimal refunding decision (on the basis of foresight, not hindsight), managers must *know* exactly what investors expect management to do, given the opportunity to refund at a given interest rate. Although far from self-evident at this point, all this will become much clearer as we proceed.

It does not make sense to base a refunding policy on the assumption that bondholders are naive. Bondholders would certainly prefer that corporate treasurers never exercise the call privilege. If such behavior became the rule, then bond prices would continue to rise ever higher above their call price as

interest rates fell ever lower. The bond market, however, recognizes that corporate managements are paid to act in the interests of shareholders, not bondholders. Therefore, we should begin by assuming that, in pricing callable bonds, the market expects management to make refunding decisions designed to increase shareholder wealth—by limiting the value of outstanding bonds.

For those companies whose new issue expenses are relatively trivial, the optimal refunding rule is very simple: call the bonds *as soon as* their price reaches the call price. Such a policy maximizes the value of the corporate option, minimizing the value of outstanding bonds. Furthermore, refunding should be undertaken at the same time the bonds are called under this rule, provided management accepts the market's expectations about future interest rates. If management has different expectations than the market, and is willing to act on them, then this may lead management to modify its *refunding* strategy. Nevertheless, management should still *call* the bonds as soon as their price reaches the call price.

If the bonds are trading below the call price, it is clear that an immediate call is not optimal. In this case, exercising the call privilege would give the bondholders an amount greater than the bonds' market value. But if the callable bonds are trading at the call price, it is not optimal to delay exercising the call privilege as interest rates fall by even a slight amount. As soon as the market realized that management was delaying the call, the bonds would move a bit higher in price. Since the aim should be to minimize the value of the callable bonds, management should prevent this price move by calling the bonds as soon as they trade at the call price.

Suppose interest rates have dropped enough that the bonds are trading at their call price, but management is convinced that rates will soon fall much lower. Wouldn't it be justified in delaying a refunding to obtain a lower interest rate? Ignoring issue expenses, the answer is no: the bonds should be called now and refunded with a new issue. But, at the same time, management should insist that the replacement bonds be callable at any time after issue. This new call option could be purchased at a much lower premium in coupon rate than it is worth *if* management is correct that rates are about

14. This argument was put forth by Brennan and Schwartz, cited earlier, and and by Jonathan Ingersoll in "A Contingent-Claims Valuation of Convertible Securities," *Journal of Financial Economics*, Volume, Number 3 (1977).

to fall. The corporate treasurer who takes this action is essentially speculating *against the market* on interest rates. I doubt that this is a wise course to follow but, in any case, it does not change the rule I have given for the optimal time to call the bonds.

The Refunding Rule With New Issue Costs

As demonstrated earlier, the value of a callable bond to investors includes the present value of the call premium bondholders receive if the bonds are called. This value does not, of course, include the amount of issue expenses connected with the replacement bonds (although, as we shall see, bond prices are definitely affected by the existence of these costs). If such expenses are relatively important, the principle of maximizing the value of the corporate call option should be modified to accommodate these additional costs. With this in mind, maximizing the value of the call privilege to shareholders means minimizing the value of the callable bond plus new issue expenses associated with the refunding.

As a first step, assume management formulates its refunding policy in terms of a critical level of a specific market interest rate. That is, assume management has decided to call and refund outstanding bonds carrying a, say, 14 percent coupon when the yield on 30-year government bonds falls to 8 percent. If the yields on corporate bonds trading *without* the call privilege could be directly observed, then the refunding policy could be formulated in terms of corporate yields: i.e., "Call when the single-A (noncallable) yield falls to 10 percent." But, because virtually all corporate bonds are callable, the yields on noncallable corporate bonds are usually not observable. For this reason, we must use the yields on long-term government bonds as a proxy for "the interest rate."

When bonds are trading well below par, a fall in interest rates generally causes an increase in bond prices roughly equal to the increase in present value of the promised coupons and principal. But, when bonds are trading above par value, and "the interest rate" approaches the critical level at which the market anticipates a call, bond prices will begin to move in a very different pattern. This pattern of interest rate changes and callable bond prices is shown in Figure 1.

The solid curve in the diagram represents the value of the callable bond as the interest rate varies. The dashed curve represents what the market value of the bonds would be, were they not callable.

At all interest rates lower than (to the left of) R_1, the gross benefits of refunding (before new issue costs) are positive. However, the path of callable bond prices above assumes that the market does not expect management to call the bonds until the interest rate falls to R^*.

The first question that arises, then, is: If refunding appears beneficial at interest rates higher than R^*, why would the market expect management to wait for a rate decline to R^* before calling the bonds?

As I emphasized in the previous section, the benefit to shareholders of a refunding comes from repurchasing the stream of promised coupons and principal at less than its market value. In terms of Figure 1, this means that management would surely not want to call the bonds when the interest rate is above (to the right of) R_1. In this range of interest rates, the market value of the stream of coupons and principal is less than the call price. Refunding in this range would mean a loss to shareholders, even before considering the costs of a new issue.

When the interest rate is between R_1 and R_2, though the gross benefit to refunding is positive, the market value of the callable bonds is less than their call price. Exercising the call privilege in this situation would give bondholders an amount greater than the bonds' market value, thus penalizing shareholders. If corporations regularly followed such a policy, the bond market would anticipate such action by bidding up the price of the bonds to their call price as they reached that interest rate (between R_1 and R_2) which triggers their call.

Indeed, it is a fundamental rule of bond market behavior that the price of callable bonds must be bid right to the call price as the interest rate falls to the level the market expects to trigger a call. Notice, though, that the price of the callable bond reaches the call price when the interest rate falls to R_2. Does this mean, then, that the market expects the bonds to be called when the interest rate reaches R_2?

The answer is no. If the market expected the bonds to be called when the interest rate reached R_2, then no one would be willing to pay more than the call price for the bonds. Investors, however, are aware that consideration of issue expenses leads management to delay refunding until the interest rate reaches R^*. Recognizing this, they are willing to

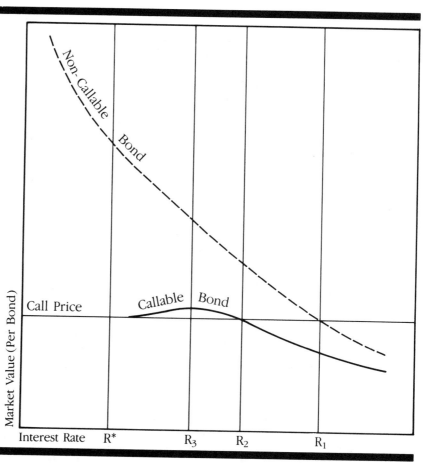

FIGURE 1
Behavior of
Callable Bond Prices

buy the bonds at a price higher than the call price, but lower of course than the present value of the stream of coupons and principal (the dashed curve in Figure 1), when the interest rate falls below R_2. (This pattern is exaggerated in Figure 1 for the sake of clarity.)

If the interest rate then falls far enough to approach R^*, the price of the callable bonds must be bid toward the call price, because that is the amount bondholders will receive when the bonds are called. At first glance, this might cause the reader to wonder why a rational investor would be willing to pay the market price shown in Figure 1 at interest rate level R_3, especially since it appears the bond's price will fall whether the interest rate moves down or back up from R_3. This paradox is easily resolved, however. Though an investor buying the bond at R_3 will sustain a capital loss if interest rates move sharply either way, this possible loss is offset by the

expected gain from receiving a coupon yield (on his purchase price) that exceeds the going interest rate.

As I have argued, then, the effect of extra issue expenses on management's *expected* refunding policy allows callable bonds to trade above their call price. In the absence of such costs, management's refunding objective would simply be to minimize the value of outstanding bonds. This aim would be served, as stated earlier, by calling the bonds when, and only when, their value reaches the call price.

Clearly, this is an easy strategy to implement. A refunding rule modified to take account of new issue costs is not quite as simple. But it, too, can be based largely, if not entirely, on the behavior of market prices. Such a refunding policy would require the same amount of analysis: virtually none.

If management does not wish to rely solely on market pricing, then the correct approach to the refunding decision would be to estimate the critical interest rate, R*, and then simply establish an automatic mechanism for calling the bonds when the rate falls to that pre-specified level. The calculation of this rate, however, is a formidable mathematical task. Not only does it go far beyond the scope of this article, but I know of no work in the finance literature that points to such a calculation having been done in a fully satisfactory way.

Rather than pursuing this path, though, management should seriously consider adopting the refunding policy which relies completely on the market prices of outstanding callable bonds. How would such a policy work? The answer comes directly from the behavior of bond prices suggested by Figure 1. The crucial assumption underlying Figure 1, once again, is that the market expects management to initiate a refunding when the interest rate falls to R*. This expectation will be based, as suggested, on the market's own assessment of when refunding is most advantageous to shareholders, which in turn will be based largely on the company's—and indeed all companies'—past refunding behavior. Given this assumption, then, as interest rates approach R*, the bond price will be bid down toward the call price.

If corporate treasurers have instituted refunding policies that, on average, benefit shareholders, *and* if the market is doing its job in interpreting past corporate policy as a predictor of future policy, then management should take its cue for refunding directly from the market. As Figure 1 illustrates, the bonds' price will rise to and above the call price as interest rates fall below R_2. When further interest rate declines cause the price to converge back on the call price, then that is the bond market's signal that the optimal time for a refunding is now at hand.

Such a refunding policy has the great virtue of simplicity, requiring only the monitoring of the bonds' price behavior. Unlike most of the traditional finance literature, my refunding rule substitutes the collective judgment of the market for management's forecasts of interest rates. When management's view is significantly different from the market's, basing the call decision on intuition about future rates is simply a gamble which the corporate treasurer should not expect to win with regularity. If managers are convinced they have superior predictions about future interest rates, they can act on these beliefs by taking positions in interest rate futures or options on government bonds. The success of these speculative endeavors would be much easier to evaluate.[15]

The market price behavior of callable bonds reflects not only the collective assessment of the direction and probability of future changes in interest rates. In addition, as we have seen, it contains an implicit estimate of the size of corporate refunding costs, and their consequences for the timing of a refunding. As such, bond prices provide management with an unbiased signal when, and when not, to call its bonds. It is doubtful that a corporate staff of analysts can reliably improve on the mathematics of the market.

At the extreme, of course, if *all* bond issuers followed this refunding policy, the policy would be a failure. Investors would catch on to the game, realizing that bonds would never be called as long as they traded above the call price. In this highly improbable case, investors would be willing to bid higher and higher prices for a callable bond as interest rates fell, and the bond would never be called.

In fact, though, corporations do call their bonds. And they can be expected to continue to do so, regardless of the market price of the bonds, if interest rates fall far enough. Investors therefore can never afford to assume bonds will not be called when trading above the call price.

This condition is really all that is necessary to support my recommendation for refunding policy. It is enough simply to ensure that the individual investor will not venture to pay more for the callable bond than he reckons it would be worth, assuming that managers are acting in the shareholder interest. To the extent that investors themselves see bond prices as reflecting the optimal refunding policy, their own pricing behavior actually tends to keep subsequent pricing of bonds consistent with management policy. The more consistent are corporate refundings with investor expectations (e.g., the more often companies call bonds when their price returns to the call price), the stronger and more

---

15. Although these markets involve transactions with much shorter maturities than that of the typical call provision on a corporate bond, the maturities available are certainly sufficient to cover the horizon of any realistic interest rate forecast. Furthermore, such clearly speculative action would have the advantage in accountability of being a clear reflection of management's willingness to act on its own forecasts of interest rates.

*When a bond's price converges back on the call price,
then that is the bond market's signal to call.*

confident are investor expectations. And this strengthening of market expectations increases the probability that this proposed refunding rule, based entirely on market pricing, is indeed the optimal one.

Conclusion

The call provision provides management with a form of insurance against the risk of interest rate changes, and, more specifically, against the risk of being locked into a fixed-interest rate contract. By paying investors a higher coupon rate, management limits the upside potential for bondholders, thus placing a ceiling on a shareholders' liability. As with other forms of insurance, the expected value of the call provision to shareholders (excluding risk preferences) is zero. That is, in a market where investors and management have roughly the same expectations about interest rates, there is no benefit to shareholders (in advance, that is, when all decisions are made, and on an expected value basis) from gambling on the possibility of interest rate declines by including call provisions.

In attempting to solve the mystery of why companies routinely include call provisions in their bond issues, I came to the following conclusions:

1. Paying the price of the call provision in the form of a higher coupon rate may be justified if management, or its financial advisors, knows more about the course of future interest rates than the bond market. But if prescience about interest rates is the only reason for including the call privilege, there will certainly be circumstances when issuers will have compelling reasons *not* to include a call provision on new debt: namely, whenever, the probability of interest rates rising above current levels seems far greater than a decline. For this reason, it is difficult to attribute the almost universal use of the call provision solely to management's faith in its interest forecasts.

2. The call provision may add value by reducing the chances of bondholders blocking desirable investments by the company. If this is a main purpose of the call provision, however, the call price should not be specified as a percentage above par value, but defined with respect to some observable interest rate level, such as long-term government bond yields.

3. The call provision may have a tax advantage to the corporation, especially when the bonds are privately placed with a tax-exempt lender. To the extent that the investor tax rate built into corporate bond yields is not significantly lower than the company's marginal tax rate, this tax advantage disappears. There is no tax advantage, and perhaps a slight tax disadvantage, to including a call provision on a preferred stock issue.

4. The call provision reduces the sensitivity of a bond's value to changes in interest rates, thus reducing the variability of the debt. For companies whose assets are relatively insensitive to interest rate movements, reductions in the risk of the debt directly reduce the risk of the equity. To the degree that all companies are systematically affected by interest rate risk, the call provision thus may lower the company's required return on equity capital.

The optimal refunding strategy can be stated in fairly simple terms, especially when new issue costs are ignored. When modified to take account of the additional costs of refunding, the rule is still simple if based on the collective judgment of the market, as reflected in the movement of bond prices:

1. If issue expenses are ignored, the bond should be called as soon as it trades at the call price.

2. When issue expenses are significant, the bond should be called when interest rates decline sufficiently such that the bond has traded above the call price and then, with a further decline in rates, returned to the call price.

3. If management does not wish to rely solely on market pricing, then it can attempt the very complex mathematical task of estimating the critical interest rate (expressed as a level of, say, 30-year government bonds) at which call is optimal. Or, less ambitiously, for any given rate of interest, it can estimate and then weigh the benefits of a refunding against new issue costs. The latter, of course, is not an optimizing policy.

4. Management's expectations about future interest rates should not influence the refunding strategy. When the price of the callable bond reaches the call price (either on the way up, if refunding costs are minimal, or on the way down, if they are significant), management should not defer the call because they expect a further decline in rates. If the company wishes to serve its shareholder interests by speculating on interest rates, management should take the more direct and accountable step of taking positions in the interest rate futures or government bond options markets.

The Financing Decision 1: Capital Structure/Selected Bibliography*

1.Akerlof, G. A, "The Market for 'Lemons': Quality and the Market Mechanism," *Quarterly Journal of Economics* 84 (August, 1970), 488-500.

2.Asquith, P. and D. W. Mullins, "Equity Issues and Stock Price Dilution," Working Paper, Harvard Business School, May 1983.

3.Barges, A., *The Effect of Capital Structure on the Cost of Capital* (Englewood Cliffs, NJ: Prentice-Hall, Inc., 1963).

4.Berle, A., *The 20th Century Capitalist Revolution* (New York: Harcourt, Brace and World, Inc., 1954).

5.Berle, A. and G. Means, *The Modern Corporation and Private Property*, (New York: MacMillan, 1932).

6.Black, F, "The Dividend Puzzle," *Journal of Portfolio Management* 2 (Winter, 1976), 5-8.

7.Brealey, R. A. and S. C. Myers, *Principles of Corporate Finance*, 2nd Ed., (New York: McGraw-Hill Book Co., 1984).

8.Cordes, J. J. and S. M. Sheffrin, "Estimating the Tax Advantage of Corporate Debt," *Journal of Finance* 38 (March, 1983), 95-105.

9.Dann, L. Y., "Common Stock Repurchases: An Analysis of Returns to Bondholders and Stockholders," *Journal of Financial Economics* 9 (June, 1981), 113-138.

10.Dann, L. Y. and W. H. Mikkelson, "Convertible Debt Issuance, Capital Structure Change and Financing-Related Information: Some New Evidence," *Journal of Financial Economics* 13 (June, 1984).

11.DeAngelo, H., L. DeAngelo, and E. M. Rice, "Minority Freezeouts and Stockholder Wealth," *Journal of Law Economics* (October, 1984).

12.DeAngelo, H., and R. Masulis, "Optimal Capital Structure Under Corporate and Personal Taxation," *Journal of Financial Economics* 8 (March, 1980), 3-29.

13.Donaldson, G., *Corporate Debt Capacity: A Study of Corporate Debt Policy and the Determination of Corporate Debt Capacity* (Boston: Division of Research, Harvard Graduate School of Business Administration, 1961).

14.Donaldson, G., *Strategy for Financial Mobility* (Homewood, Ill: Richard D. Irwin, 1971).

15.Giammarino, R. M. and E. H. Neave, "The Failure of Financial Contracts and the Relevance of Financial Policy," Working Paper, Queens University, 1982.

16.Gordon, R. H. and G. B. Malkiel, "Corporation Finance," in H. J. Aaron and J. A. Pechman, *How Taxes Affect Economic Behavior* (Washington, DC: Brookings Institution, 1981).

17.Jalivand, A. and R. S. Harris, "Corporate Behavior in Adjusting Capital Structure and Dividend Policy: An Econometric Study," *Journal of Finance* 39 (March, 1984), 127-145.

18.Jensen, M. C. and W. Meckling, "Theory of the Firm: Managerial Behavior, Agency Costs and Capital Structure," *Journal of Financial Economics* 3 (October, 1976), 11-25.

19.Korwar, A. N., "The Effect of New Issues of Equity: An Empirical Examination," Working Paper, University of California, Los Angeles, 1981.

20.Lintner, J., "Distribution of Incomes of Corporations Among Dividends, Retained Earnings and Taxes," *American Economic Review* 46 (May, 1956), 97-113.

21.Long, M. S. and E. B. Malitz, "Investment Patterns and Financial Leverage," *National Bureau of Economic Research* (1983).

22.Marsh, P. R., "The Choice Between Equity and Debt: An Empirical Study," *Journal of Finance* 37 (March, 1982), 121-144.

23.Masulis, R. W., "The Effects of Capital Structure Change on Security Prices: A Study of Exchange Offers," *Journal of Financial Economics* 8 (June, 1980), 139-177.

24.Masulis, R. W., "The Impact of Capital Structure Change on Firm Value," *Journal of Finance* 38 (March, 1983), 107-126.

25.Mikkelson, W. H., "Capital Structure Change and Decreases in Stockholders' Wealth: A Cross-Sectional Study of Convertible Security Calls," in B. Friedman, ed., *Corporate Capital Structures in the United States* (National Bureau of Economic Research Conference Volume).

26.Mikkelson, W. H., "Convertible Calls and Security Returns," *Journal of Financial Economics* 9 (June, 1981), 113-138.

27.Miller, M., "Debt and Taxes," *Journal of Finance* 32 (May, 1977), 261-275.

28A.Miller, M., and F. Modigliani, "Dividend Policy, Growth and the Valuation of Shares," *Journal of Business* 34 (October, 1961), 411-433.

*This bibliography is reproduced from Stewart Myers's "The Capital Structure Puzzle" (Journal of Finance 1983) reprinted earlier in this section. The numbering of the sources above corresponds directly to the numerical citations in that article.

28B.Miller, M., and F. Modigliani, "Some Estimates of the Cost of Capital to the Electric Utility Industry, 1954-1957," *American Economic Review* 56 (June, 1966), 333-391.

29.Miller, M. H. and K. Rock, "Dividend Policy Under Information Asymmetry," *Journal of Finance* (September, 1985).

30.Modigliani, F., "Debt, Dividend Policy, Taxes, Inflation and Market Valuation," *Journal of Finance* 37 (May, 1982), 255-273.

31.Modigliani, F. and M. Miller, "The Cost of Capital, Corporation Finance and the Theory of Investment," *American Economic Review* 53 (June, 1958), 261-297.

32.Myers, S., "Determinants of Corporate Borrowing," *Journal of Financial Economics* 5 (November, 1977), 147-176.

33.Myers, S., "The Search for Optimal Capital Structure," *Midland Corporate Finance Journal* 1 (Spring, 1984), 6-16.

34.Myers, S. and N. Majluf, "Corporate Financing and Investment Decisions When Firms Have Information Investors Do Not Have," *Journal of Financial Economics* (1985).

35.Robicheck, A. A., J. MacDonald and R. Higgins, "Some Estimates of the Cost of Capital to the Electric Utility Industry, 1954-1957: Comment," *American Economic Review* 57 (December, 1967), 1278-1288.

36.Ross, S. A., "Some Notes on Financial-Incentive Signalling Models, Activity Choice and Risk Preferences," *Journal of Finance* 33 (June, 1978), 777-792.

37.Ross, S. A., "The Determination of Financial Structure: The Incentive-Signalling Approach," *Bell Journal of Economics* 8 (Spring, 1977), 23-40.

38.Smith, C. and J. Warner, "On Financial Contracting: An Analysis of Bond Covenants," *Journal of Financial Economics* 7 (June, 1979), 117-161.

39.Taggart, R., "A Model of Corporate Financing Decisions," *Journal of Finance* 32 (December, 1977), 1467-1484).

40.Vermaelen, T., "Common Stock Repurchases and Market Signalling: An Empirical Study," *Journal of Financial Economics* 9 (June, 1981), 139-183.

41.Williamson, S., "The Moral Hazard Theory of Corporate Financial Structure: An Empirical Test," Unpublished Ph.D. Dissertation, MIT, 1981.

REFERENCES/THE MODIGLIANI-MILLER PROPOSITIONS AFTER THIRTY YEARS

Bhattacharya, Sudipto, "Imperfect Information, Dividend Policy and the 'Bird in the Hand' Fallacy." *Bell Journal of Economics* 10.1 (Spring 1979): 259-70.

Black, Fischer, and Cox, John, "Valuing Corporate Securities: Some Effects of Bond Indenture Provisions." *Journal of Finance* 31.2 (May 1976): 351-67.

Black, Fischer, and Scholes, Myron, "The Pricing of Options and Corporate Liabilities." *Journal of Political Economy* 81.3 (May-June 1973): 637-54.

Brooks, Jennifer J. S., "A Proposal to Avert the Revenue Loss from 'Disincorporation.'" *Tax Notes* 36.4 (July 27 1987): 425-428.

Buser, Stephen A., and Hess, Patrick J., "Empirical Determinants of the Relative Yields on Taxable and Tax-exempt Securities." *Journal of Financial Economics* 17 (May 1986): 335-56.

Canellos, Peter C., "Corporate Tax Integration: By Design or by Default?" *Tax Notes* 35.8 (June 8 1987): 999-1008.

Chamley, Christopher, and Polemarchakis, Heraklis, "Assets, General Equilibrium and the Neutrality of Money." *Review of Economic Studies* 51.1 (January 1984): 129-38.

Cornell, Bradford, and French, Kenneth, " Taxes and the Pricing of Stock Index Futures." *Journal of Finance* 38.3 (June 1983): 675-94.

Duffie, Darrell, and Shafer, Wayne, "Equilibrium and the Role of the Firm in Incomplete Markets." Manuscript, (August 1986).

Durand, David, "Costs of Debt and Equity Funds for Business: Trends and Problems of Measurement." In Conference on Research in Business Finance. National Bureau of Economic Research. New York. (1952): 215-47.

Durand, David, "The Cost of Capital. Corporation Finance and the Theory of Investment: Comment." *American Economic Review* 49.4 (September 1959): 639-55.

Fama, Eugene, "Banking in the Theory of Finance." *Journal of Monetary Economics* 6.1 (January 1980): 39-57.

Fama, Eugene, "Financial Intermediation and Price Level Control." *Journal of Monetary Economics* 12.1 (January 1983): 7-28.

Hirshleifer, Jack, "Investment Decision under Uncertainty: Choice Theoretic Approaches." *Quarterly Journal of Economics* 79 (November 1965): 509-36.

Hirshleifer, Jack, "Investment Decision under Uncertainty: Applications of the State Preference Approach." *Quarterly Journal of Economics* 80 (May 1966): 611-17.

Jackson, Thomas H., *The Logic and Limits of Bankruptcy Law.* Cambridge. Mass.: Harvard University Press. 1986.

Jensen, Michael C., "Takeovers: Their Causes and Consequences." *Journal of Economic Perspectives* 2 (Winter 1988): 21-48.

Kim, E. Han, "Optimal Capital Structure in Miller's Equilibrium." in *Frontiers of Financial Theory.* Edited by Sudipto Bhattacharya and George Constantinides [Totowa. N.J.: Renan and Littlefleld. 1987]. forthcoming.

Lintner, John. "The Valuation of Risk Assets and the Selection of Risky Investments in Stock Portfolios and Capital Budgets." *Review of Economics and Statistics* 47 (February 1965): 13-37.

Merton, Robert C., "Capital Market Theory and the Pricing of Financial Securities." in *Handbook of Monetary Economics* edited by Benjamin Friedman and Frank Hahn. Amsterdam: North Holland. forthcoming.

Merton, Robert C., "On the Pricing of Corporate Debt: The Risk of Interest Rates." *Journal of Finance* 29.3 (May 1974): 449-70.

Miller, Merton H., "The Corporate Income Tax and Corporate Financial Policies." In *Stabilization Policies*, The Commission on Money and Credit, Prentice-Hall. Inc., New Jersey. (1963): 381-470.

Miller, Merton H., "Debt and Taxes." *Journal of Finance* 32.2 (May 1977): 261-75.

Miller, Merton H., "The Informational Content of Dividends." In *Macroeconomics and Finance: Essays in Honor of Franco Modigliani.* Editors Rudiger Dornbusch. Stanley Fischer and John Bossons. MIT Press. Cambridge. MA. (1987): 37-58.

Miller, Merton H., and Modigliani, Franco, "Dividend Policy. Growth and the Valuation of Shares." *Journal of Business* 34.4 (October 1961): 411-33.

Miller, Merton H., and Modigliani, Franco, "Some Estimates of the Cost of Capital to the Utility Industry, 1954-7." *American Economic Review* 56. 3 (June 1966): 333-91.

Miller, Merton H., and Scholes, Myron S, "Dividends and Taxes." *Journal of Financial Economics* 6.4 (December 1978): 333-64.

Modigliani, Franco, "Debt, Dividend Policy, Taxes, Inflation and Market Valuation." *Journal of Finance* 37.2 (May 1982): 255-73.

Modigliani, Franco, and Miller, Merton H., "The Cost of Capital. Corporation Finance and the Theory of Investment." *American Economic Review* 48.3 (June 1958): 261-97.

Modigliani, Franco, and Miller, Merton H., "The Cost of Capital, Corporation Finance and the Theory of Investment: Reply." *American Economic Review* 49.4 (September 1959): 655-69.

Modigliani, Franco, and Miller, Merton H., "Corporate Income Taxes and the Cost of Capital: A Correction." *American Economic Review* 53.3 (June 1963).

Ross, Stephen, "The Determination of Financial Structure: The Incentive Signalling Approach." *Bell Journal of Economics* 8.1 (Spring 1977): 23-40.

Ross, Stephen, "Return, Risk and Arbitrage." In *Risk and Return in Finance.* Editors Irwin Friend and James Bicksler. Vol. 1. Ballinger. Cambridge MA.(1976): 189-219.

Rubinstein, Mark, "Derivative Assets Analysis." *Journal of Economic Perspectives* 1 (Fall 1987): 73-93.

Sargent, Thomas J., and Smith, Bruce D., "The Irrelevance of Government Foreign Exchange Operations." Manuscript, 1986.

Sharpe, William F., "Capital Asset Prices: A Theory of Market Equilibrium under Conditions of Risk." *Journal of Finance* 19 (September 1964): 425-42.

Spence, Michael, "Job-Market Signalling." *Quarterly Journal of Economics* 87.3 (August 1973): 355-79.

Stiglitz, Joseph, "A Re-Examination of the Modigliani-Miller Theorem." *American Economic Review* 59, 5 (December 1969): 784-93.

Stiglitz, Joseph, "On the Irrelevance of Corporate Financial Policy." *American Economic Review* 64.6 (December 1974): 851-66.

Stiglitz, Joseph, "Information and Capital Markets." In *Financial Economics: Essays in Honor of Paul Cootner.* Editors William F. Sharpe and Cathryn Gootner, Prentice Hall, New Jersey (1982): 118-58.

Stoll, Hans R. "The Relationship Between Put and Call Option Prices," *Journal of Finance* 24 (December 1969): 801-24.

Wallace, Neil, "A Modigliani-Miller Theorem for Open Market Operations." *American Economic Review* 71.5 (June 1981): 267-74.

Part IV: The Financing Decision 2: The Financing Vehicles

INTRODUCTION

The previous section of this book addressed the general question of corporate capital structure: What is the "optimal" debt-equity mix for a given public corporation? This part focuses on the specific financing vehicles that can be used by corporate treasurers to bring about the desired capital structure. Following a general introductory review of various financing instruments, we feature a series of articles analyzing a number of more or less innovative financing vehicles: convertible bonds, zero-coupon bonds, floating-rate bonds, interest rate and currency swaps, income bonds and hybrid debt.

In "Raising Capital: Theory and Evidence," Clifford Smith provides a concise review of academic research bearing on (1) the stock market's response to announcements by public companies of different kinds of securities offerings and (2) the relative efficiency of different methods of marketing corporate securities—that is, rights vs. underwritten offerings, negotiated vs. competitive bid contracts, and traditional vs. shelf registration. Somewhat surprisingly, at least to academics, the research confirms that the average market reaction to security offerings of all kindsòdebt and equity, straight and convertible, and issued by utilities as well as industrials—is "consistently either negative or not significantly different from zero... Furthermore, the market's response to common stock issues is more strongly negative than its response to preferred stock or debt offerings. It is also more negative to announcements of convertible than non-convertible securities, and to offerings by utilities than industrials."

In the first half of the article, Smith evaluates a number of explanations that have been offered to account for these findings. For example, the expected dilutive effect of new equity and convertibles on EPS is dismissed as an "accounting illusion" that should have no effect on economic values. Skepticism is also expressed about the time-honored "price-pressure" argument that maintains that large issues of new securities must be offered at a discount from market prices, even in heavily traded markets like the New York Stock Exchange. In place of these traditional arguments, Smith suggests that the most plausible explanation of the market's systematically negative response to equity and convertibles is a relatively new "information asymmetry" hypothesis. In brief, the argument holds that because of the possibility of inside information and

given the incentives of management as insiders to exploit outside investors by issuing overvalued securities, the mere act of announcing new equity or convertibles often releases a negative signal to the market about the firm's cash flow prospects (at least, relative to those reflected in its current stock price), thus causing stock prices to fall on average.

In the second part of the article, Smith uses this "information asymmetry" argument to explain why firm commitment underwritten offerings predominate over rights offerings, negotiated over competitive bids, and traditional registration over the new shelf registration procedure (although the latter is gaining ground, especially in debt issues). The mere possibility of insider information creates a demand by potential investors for the issuing firm to hire reputable underwriters to "certify" the value of the new securities. The guarantee of quality, as well as the commitment to maintain an after-market, provided to investors is much stronger in the case of firm underwritten offerings, especially those which are negotiated with a single investment banker rather than auctioned through a competitive bid and registered using the traditional rather than the new shelf procedure. In cases where such certification services are unnecessary, however, shelf registration can provide significant savings in transaction costs.

In "Guidelines for Long-term Financing Strategies," Alan Shapiro argues that the aim of corporate treasurers in raising outside capital is to design and issue "positive-NPV securities" — that is, securities which raise more in net proceeds than the present value of the after-tax cost of servicing the liability. In competitive capital markets, this means seeking out financing bargains — created, as a rule, by government-induced "distortions" of those markets — and taking swift advantage of such short-lived "windows of opportunity." The recent rise and fall of OIDs provides a case in point, as does the even more recent opportunity, now largely extinct, for "arbitraging" world capital markets through currency swaps. The lesson to be learned from such case histories is that by exploiting unusual investor preferences, tax peculiarities, and other capital market "imperfections," corporations can endow their securities with special advantages and thereby raise funds at below-market rates.

In "The Case for Convertibles," Michael Brennan and Eduardo Schwartz offer a relatively new explanation for the popularity of convertible financing: namely, that it overcomes the financing problem caused by investor uncertainty about the underlying risks of companies' operations by offering investors in effect a call option on the stock. Besides offering a useful discussion of when to call convertibles, Brennan and Schwartz also put to rest (once and for all, we hope) the popular notion that convertibles are a cheap source of financing.

In "The Future of Floating-Rate Bonds," Brad Cornell of UCLA argues that when there is a great deal of uncertainty about future rates of inflation, fixed interest rates incorporate an "inflation risk premium" in the form of unusually high real interest rates. Floating-rate bonds, by promising investors a relatively constant real rate of return, allow borrowers to eliminate this "inflation risk premium" and issue debt with lower interest costs than fixed-rate debt of the same maturity.

But this, of course, does not mean that all firms should issue floating-rate debt when facing inflation uncertainty and high real rates. The most important consideration for the chief treasurer in deciding whether to issue fixed- or floating-rate debt is the responsiveness of the firm's operating cash flows to inflation. Those companies with operating cash flows that keep pace with inflation will find that the use of floating-rate bonds stabilizes cash flows, and thereby reduces total corporate risk. Conversely, companies in industries that are hurt by inflation will find that floating-rate bonds accentuate the cyclicality of cash flows by matching high interest costs with low operating cash flows in inflationary times, and low interest costs with high operating flows in times of price stability.

In "Is Deep Discount Debt Financing a Bargain?," David Pyle argues that the advantages of deep discount debt financing have not been accurately represented. Only the tax treatment provides real benefits, and even these have been exaggerated by popular analysis which fails to take into account the tax rates of investors implied in the pricing of such bonds. Because the supply of tax-exempt investors is limited, those companies which first issued OIDs got the lion's share of the benefits. As additional OIDs were issued, higher-taxed investors had to be drawn into the market, raising the pre-tax yields required by OID investors relative to those required by current coupon bondholders. This reduction in the supply of tax-favored investors, especially Japanese investors (who were affected by a change in the Japanese tax code), combined with a decline in in-terest rates (which resulted in a smaller amortizable initial discount), effectively erased the tax advantage of OIDs.

In "The Income Bond Puzzle," John McConnell and Gary Schlarbaum of Purdue's Krannert School make a case for the revival of an old, though seldom used security: the income bond. As a hybrid security, income bonds combine the tax advantage of straight debt with the contingency feature of preferred stock. Because the corporate issuer is obligated to pay interest only if earnings are sufficient to cover the payment, income bonds remove the problem of potential bankruptcy costs that may have limited the use of debt in the past. And in an era when increased earnings variability has raised the probability of technical default for many companies, the flexibility that would allow corporate issuers to defer interest payments to more profitable times could be valuable.

In exploring the failure of income bonds to achieve broad acceptance, Schlarbaum and McConnell provide another illustration of the divergence of modern finance theory from the conventional wisdom. Investment bankers have long argued that such bonds are "tainted" by their historical association with railroads undergoing reorganization, and thus discouraged income bond issues by their corporate clients. But, as the article points out, the notion of tainted securities has no theoretical backing. Accordingly, the authors conclude, the present reluctance of investment banks to underwrite income bonds should not be a serious impediment to the renewed use of these instruments, especially as competition intensifies between traditional investment banks and their newly emerging competitors.

In "The Option Pricing Model and the Valuation of Corporate Securities," Georges Courtadon and John Merrick of New York University provide a lucid explanation of the options pricing model devised by Fischer Black and Myron Scholes in the early 70s. The model is now used widely by options traders on the Chicago Exchange (and even has the distinction of having been programmed commercially into a Hewlett-Packard calculator). Besides purely speculative uses, the options pricing model has a number of potential applications to the pricing and valuation of corporate securities. In the remainder of the article, they explore the possibilities of using the model to value corporate debt, both convertible and nonconvertible, and "equity notes" — the "mandatory" convertibles issued in 1982 by Manufacturer's Hanover and Chase Manhattan. A comparison of the model's predictions with the actual prices of Manufacturer's Hanover's equity notes suggests that the model has a good deal of predictive power, and a promising future in pricing (and designing) corporate securities.

In the 1980s, the astonishing growth of the junk bond market provided many smaller companies with an economic alternative to bank loans and private placements. In "The Growing Role of Junk Bonds in Corporate Finance," Robert Taggart and Kevin Perry state the case for junk bonds, showing significant benefits to issuers and investors alike. For investors, they offer in effect a hybrid instrument (part debt, part equity) with an accordingly intermediate risk profile; they also, somewhat surprisingly, have a lower sensitivity to interest rate changes than investment-grade corporates and Treasury bonds. For issuers, they have provided not only a means of amassing large pools of capital for takeovers by "raiders" (which accounts for the regulatory assault on that market), but also what amounts to a tax-deductible, equity-like form of fixed-rate medium-term financing for the normal business operations of "middle market" (and thus the vast majority of American) corporations.

In "The Persistent Borrowing Advantage of Eurodollar Bonds," Wayne Marr and John Trimble report the results of their own recent studies documenting large cost savings by U.S. corporate borrowers in the Eurodollar market. The existence of such a large and persistent borrowing advantage," the authors point out, "runs counter to the conventional wisdom of financial economists that international capital markets are becoming ever more "integrated." And the article goes on to provide an "educated guess" about the real source of these interest savings—one which centers on the value to investors of the "anonymity" conferred by the bearer form of these bonds.

In "The Uses of Hybrid Debt in Managing Corporate Risk," Charles Smithson and I attempt to explain why the 1990s are proving "Hot Times for Hybrids" (to borrow a recent *New York Times* title). In the early 1980s, when interest rates were much higher than they are today, hybrids like Sunshine Mining's silver-linked bond issue were used by riskier companies to help reduce their interest costs to manageable levels. But though rates are much lower today, credit spreads have widened considerably for all but blue-chip borrowers. In many cases, companies are using hybrid debt to lower their risk profile and thus avoid the higher funding costs now associated with being a riskier corporate borrower.

DHC

Raising Capital: Theory and Evidence*

Clifford W. Smith, Jr., *University of Rochester*

Corporations raise capital by selling a variety of different securities. The *Dealers' Digest* (1985) reports that over $350 billion of public securities sales were underwritten between 1980 and 1984. Of that total, 63 percent was straight debt, 24 percent was common stock, 6 percent was convertible debt, 5 percent was preferred stock, and the remaining 2 percent was convertible preferred stock. Besides choosing among these types of securities, corporate management must also choose among different methods of marketing the securities. In issues that accounted for 95 percent of the total dollars raised between 1980 and 1984, the contracts were negotiated between the issuing firm and its underwriter; in only 5 percent of the offers was the underwriter selected through a competitive bid. Shelf registration, a relatively new procedure for registering securities, was employed in issues accounting for 27 percent of the total dollars raised; the remaining 73 percent was raised through offerings using traditional registration procedures.

Despite the critical role that capital markets play in both financial theory and practice, financial economists have only recently begun to explore the alternative contractual arrangements in the capital raising process and the effect of these choices on a company's cost of issuing securities. This article has two basic aims: (1) to examine the theory and evidence concerning the market's response to security offer announcements by public corporations; and (2) to evaluate the different methods of marketing corporate securities (rights versus underwritten offers, negotiated versus competitive bid contracts, traditional vs. shelf registration, etc.), with attention given to the special case of initial public equity offers.

Market Reactions to Security Offer Announcements

A public company seeking external capital must first decide what type of claim to sell. In making that decision, it is important to understand the market's typical reaction to these announcements.

Presented in Table 1 is a summary of the findings of recent academic research on the market's response to announcements of public issues (grouped by industrial firms and utilities) of common stock, preferred stock, convertible preferred stock, straight debt and convertible debt. Perhaps surprisingly, the average abnormal returns (that is, the price movements adjusted for general market price changes) are consistently either negative or not significantly different from zero; in no case is there evidence of a significant positive reaction. Furthermore, the market's response to common stock issues is more strongly negative than its response to preferred stock or debt offerings. It is also more negative to announcements of convertible than non-convertible securities, and more negative to announcements of offerings by industrials than utilities.

I would first like to examine potential explanations of these findings. Let me start by briefly noting a number of arguments that have been proposed to account for at least parts of this overall pattern of market responses, and then go on to consider each in more detail.

EPS Dilution: The increase in the number of shares outstanding resulting from an equity (or convertible) offering is expected to reduce (fully diluted) reported earnings per share, at least in the

---

*This article is based on "Investment Banking and the Capital Acquisition Process," *Journal of Financial Economics* (1986). This research was supported by the Managerial Economics Research Center, Graduate School of Management, University of Rochester.

**TABLE 1
The Stock Market
Response to
Announcements of
Security Offerings**

In the columns below are the average two-day abnormal common stock returns and average sample size (in parentheses) from studies of announcements of security offerings. Returns are weighted averages by sample size of the returns reported by the respective studies listed below. (Unless noted otherwise, returns are significantly different from zero.) Most of these studies appear in the forthcoming issue of the University of Rochester's *Journal of Financial Economics* 15 (1986), but full citations for all can be found in the reference section at the end of this issue.

Type of Security Offering	Types of Issuer	
	Industrial	Utility
Common Stock	$-3.14\%^a$	$-0.75\%^b$
	(155)	(403)
Preferred Stock	$-0.19\%^{c,*}$	$+0.08\%^{d,*}$
	(28)	(249)
Convertible Preferred Stock	$-1.44\%^d$	$-1.38\%^d$
	(53)	(8)
Straight Bonds	$-0.26\%^{e,*}$	$-0.13\%^{f,*}$
	(248)	(140)
Convertible Bonds	$-2.07\%^e$	n.a.^{g}
	(73)	

[a] Source: Asquith/Mullins (1986), Kolodny/Suhler (1985), Masulis/Korwar (1986), Mikkelson/Partch (1986), Schipper/Smith (1986)
[b] Source: Asquith/Mullins (1986), Masulis/Korwar (1986), Pettway/Radcliffe (1985)
[c] Source: Linn/Pinegar (1986), Mikkelson/Partch (1986)
[d] Source: Linn/Pinegar (1986)
[e] Source: Dann/Mikkelson (1984), Eckbo (1986), Mikkelson/Partch (1986)
[f] Source: Eckbo (1986)
[g] Not available (virtually none are issued by utilities)
[*] Interpreted by the authors as not statistically significantly different from zero

near term. New equity is also expected to reduce reported ROE. It has been suggested that such anticipated reductions in accounting measures of performance reduce stock prices.

Price Pressure: The demand curve for securities slopes downward. A new offering increases the supply of that security relative to the demand for it, thus causing its price to fall.

Optimal Capital Structure: A new security issue changes a company's capital structure, thus altering its relationship to its optimal capital structure (as perceived by the market).

Insider Information: Management may possess important information about the company that the market doesn't share. Investors recognize this information disparity and revise their estimate of a company's value in response to management's announced decisions. This effect works through two channels:

Implied Cash Flow Change: Security offers reveal inside information about operating profitability; that is, the requirement for external funding may reflect a shortfall in recent or expected

future cash flows.

Leverage Change: Increases in corporate leverage are interpreted by the market as reflecting management's confidence about the company's prospects. Conversely, decreases in leverage, such as those brought about by equity offers, reflect management's lack of confidence about future profitability.

Unanticipated Announcements: To the extent an offer is anticipated, its economic impact is already reflected in security prices. Thus, market reactions to less predictable issues should be greater, other things equal, than to more predictable issues.

Ownership Changes: Some security offerings accompany actual or expected changes in the ownership or organization of the company, which in turn can influence market reaction to the announcement.

Before considering each of these possibilities at greater length, let me emphasize that some of the above arguments have more explanatory power than others. But no single explanation accounts, to the exclusion of all others, for the complete pattern of market responses documented by the research.

EPS Dilution

Many analysts argue that announcements of new equity issues depress stock prices because the increase in the number of shares outstanding is expected to result in a reduction, at least in the near term, of reported earnings per share. The expected fall in (near-term) EPS causes stock prices to fall.

Underlying this argument is the assumption that investors respond uncritically to financial statements, mechanically capitalizing EPS figures at standard, industry-wide P/E multiples. Such a view is, of course, completely at odds with the theory of modern finance. In an efficient market, the value of a company's equity—like the value of a bond or any other investment—should reflect the present value of all of its expected future after-tax *cash flows* (discounted at rates which reflect investors' required returns on securities of comparable risk). This view thus implies that even if near-term EPS is expected to fall as the result of a new equity offering, the issuing company's stock price should not fall as long as the market expects management to earn an adequate rate of return on the new funds. In fact, if the equity sale is perceived by the market as providing management with the means of undertaking an exceptionally profitable capital spending program, then the announcement of an equity offering (combined perhaps with an announcement of the capital expenditure plan) should, if anything, cause a company's price to rise.

There remains a strong temptation, of course, to link the negative stock price effects of new equity announcements to the expected earnings reduction. But to accept this argument is to mistake correlation for causality. We must look to other events to assess whether it is the expected earnings dilution that *causes* the market reaction, or whether there are other, more important factors at work. I believe that studies of stock price reactions to accounting changes have provided convincing testimony to the sophistication of the market, which contradicts the claims of the EPS dilution argument.[1] Such studies provide remarkably consistent evidence that markets see through cosmetic accounting changes, and that market price reactions generally reflect changes in the expected underlying cash flows—that is, in the long-run prospects for the business. In short, there is no plausible theoretical explanation—nor is there

credible supporting evidence—that suggests that the reductions in expected EPS accompanying announcements of stock offerings should systematically cause the market to lower companies' stock prices.

Price Pressure

In a somewhat related explanation, some argue that the price reduction associated with the announcement of a new equity or convertible issue is the result of an increase in the supply of a company's equity. This price pressure argument is based on the premise that the demand schedule for the shares of any given company is downward sloping, and that new shares can thus be sold only by offering investors a discount from the market price. The greater the proportional amount of new shares, the larger the discount necessary to effect the sale.

Modern portfolio theory, however, attaches little credibility to the price pressure argument—not, at least, in the case of widely-traded securities in well-established secondary markets. The theory says that investors pricing securities are concerned primarily with risk and expected return. Because the risk and return characteristics of any given stock can be duplicated in many ways through various combinations of other stocks, there are a great many close substitutes for that stock. Given this abundance of close substitutes, economic theory says that the demand curve for corporate securities should more closely approximate a horizontal line than a sharply downward sloping one. A horizontal demand curve in turn implies that an issuing company should be able to sell large quantities of new stock without any discount from the current market price (provided the market does not interpret the stock sale itself as releasing negative insider information about the company's prospects relative to its current value).

What does the available research tell us about the price pressure hypothesis? I will simply mention a few studies bearing on this question.

The first serious study of price pressure was Myron Scholes's doctoral dissertation at the University of Chicago. Scholes examined the effect on share prices of large blocks offered through secondary offerings. According to the price pressure hypothesis, the larger the block of shares to be sold, the larger the price decline would have to be to induce increasing

1. For an excellent review of this research, see Ross Watts, "Does It Pay to Manipulate EPS?," *Chase Financial Quarterly* (Spring 1982). Reprinted in *Issues in Corporate Finance* (New York: Stern Stewart & Co., 1983).

numbers of investors to purchase the shares. By contrast, the intrinsic value view suggests that the stock price would be unaffected by the size of the block to be sold. It says that at the right price, the market would readily absorb additional shares.

Scholes found that while stock prices do decline upon the distribution of a large block of shares, the price decline appears to be unrelated to the size of the distribution. This finding suggests that the price discount necessary to distribute the block is better interpreted as a result of the adverse information communicated by a large block sale than as a result of selling pressure. This interpretation was reinforced by the additional finding that the largest price declines were recorded when the secondary sale was made by corporate officers in the company itself—that is, by insiders with possibly privileged information about the company's future.[2]

In another study on price pressure, Avner Kalay and Adam Shimrat recently examined bond price reactions to new equity offers. They reason that if price pressure (and not adverse information) causes the negative stock price reaction, there should be no reduction in the value of the company's outstanding bonds upon the announcement of the stock issue—if anything, the new layer of equity should provide added protection for the bonds and cause their prices to rise. The study, however, documented a significant drop in bond prices, suggesting that the market views an equity offering as bad news, reducing the value of the firm as a whole.[3]

Another recent study of price pressure was conducted by Scott Linn and Mike Pinegar. They examined the price reaction of outstanding preferred stock issues to announcements of new preferred stock issues by the same company. They found that the price of an outstanding preferred stock did not fall with the announcement of an additional new preferred issue, thus providing no support for the operation of price pressure in the market for preferred stock.[4]

In short, there is little empirical evidence in support of price pressure in the market for widely-traded stocks. The observed stock price declines, as I shall suggest later, are more plausibly attributed to negative "information" effects.

Optimal Capital Structure

Financial economists generally agree that firms have an optimal capital structure and a number of researchers have suggested that the price reactions documented in Table 1 reflect companies' attempts to move toward that optimum. This explanation might be useful if we found broad samples of firms experiencing positive market responses to their new security issues. But because the market reaction to most security offerings appears systematically negative (or at best neutral), it is clear that any attempt by firms to move toward a target capital structure is not the dominating factor in the market's response. If we were to use the market's reaction to new security offerings as the basis for any useful generalization about companies' relationship to their optimal structure, we would be put in the embarrassing position of arguing that new security offerings routinely move companies away from, not toward, such an optimum. Thus, I raise this possibility largely to dismiss it.

Information Disparity Between Management and Potential Investors

The documented reductions in firm value associated with security sales—which, after all, are voluntary management decisions—thus present financial economists with a puzzle. One possible explanation is that new security sales are optimal responses by management to changes for the worse in a company's prospects. Alternatively, a company's current market valuation may seem to management to reflect excessive confidence about the future, and it may attempt to exploit such a difference in outlook by "timing" its equity offerings. Investors habituated to stock offerings under such conditions will discount, as a matter of course, the stock prices of companies announcing security offerings. In such circumstances, even if a security sale increases the value of the firm by allowing it to fund profitable projects, it could lead potential investors to suspect that management has a dimmer view of the company's future than that reflected in its current market value.

2. For the published version of Scholes's dissertation, see "Market for Securities: Substitution versus Price Pressure and the Effects of Information on Share Prices," *Journal of Business* 45 (1972), 179-211.

3. Avner Kalay and Adam Shimrat, "Firm Value and Seasoned Equity Issue: Price Pressure, Wealth Redistribution, or Negative Information," New York University working paper, 1986.

4. See Scott Linn and J. Michael Pinegar, "The Effect of Issuing Preferred Stock on Common Stockholder Wealth," Unpublished manuscript, University of Iowa, 1985.

It is now well documented that managers have better information about the firm's prospects than do outside investors.[5] There is also little doubt that outsiders pay attention to insider trading in making their own investment decisions. Given these observations, I believe that the findings in Table 1 are driven in large part by this potential disparity of information between management and the market, and the incentives it offers management in timing the issue of new securities.

Furthermore, I would argue that, as a result of this potential information disparity, new security offerings affect investors' outlook about a company through two primary channels: (a) the implied change in expected net operating cash flow and (b) the leverage change.

Implied Changes in Net Operating Cash Flow. Investors, of course, are ultimately interested in a company's capacity to generate cash flow. Although a new security offering might imply that the company has discovered new investment opportunities, it might also imply a shortfall in cash caused by poor current or expected future operating performance. As accounting students learn in their first year of business school, "sources" must equal "uses" of funds. Consequently, an announcement of a new security issue must imply one of the following to investors: (1) an expected increase in new investment expenditure, (2) a reduction in some liability (such as debt retirement or share repurchase) and hence a change in capital structure, (3) an increase in future dividends, or (4) a reduction in expected net operating cash flow. If new security sales were generally used only in anticipation of profitable new investment or to move capital structure closer to an optimal target ratio, then we should expect positive stock price reactions to announcements of new offerings. But if unanticipated security issues come to be associated with reductions in future cash flows from operations, then investors would systematically interpret announcements of security sales as bad news.

This argument can be generalized to consider other announcements which do not explicitly link sources and uses of funds. Using the above line of reasoning, we would interpret announcements of stock repurchases, increases in investment expenditures, and higher dividend payments as signaling increases in expected operating cash flow and, thus, as good news for investors. Conversely, security

offerings, reductions in investment expenditures, and reductions in dividend payments all would imply reductions in expected operating cash flow.

The academic evidence on market responses to announcements of new securities sales, stock repurchases, dividend changes, and changes in capital spending (summarized in Table 2) is broadly consistent with this hypothesis. As shown in the upper panel of Table 2, announcements of security repurchases, dividend increases, and increases in capital spending are greeted systematically by increases in stock prices. The market responds negatively, as a rule, to announcements of security sales, dividend reductions, and decreases in new investment (an exception has been the oil industry in recent years, in which case the market's response to increases in capital spending has been negative, and positive to announced cutbacks in investment). On the basis of this evidence, the market appears to make inferences about changes in operating cash flow from announcements that ·do not explicitly associate sources with uses of funds.

I should point out, however, that although this explanation helps to explain non-positive price reactions to announcements of all security sales, it provides no insight into the questions of why investors respond more negatively to equity than debt sales, to convertible than non-convertible issues, and to sales by industrials rather than utilities.

Information Disparity and Leverage Changes. Suppose that a potential purchaser of securities has less information about the prospects of the firm than management. Assume, furthermore, that management is more likely to issue securities when the market price of the firm's traded securities is higher than management's assessment of their value. In such a case, sophisticated investors will revise their estimate of the value of the firm if and when management announces a new security issue. Furthermore, the larger the potential disparity in information between insiders and investors, the greater the revision in expectations and the larger the negative price reaction to the announcement of a new issue.

Because debt and preferred stock are more senior claims on corporate cash flows, the values of these securities are generally less sensitive to changes in a company's prospects than is the value of common stock. Thus, this problem of potential insider information that managment faces whenever it issues a

5. See Jeffrey Jaffe's seminal study of insider trading, "Special Information and Insider Trading," *Journal of Business* 47 (1974), 410-420.

TABLE 2
The Stock Market Response to Announcements of Changes in Financing, Dividend, and Investment Policy

In the columns below are the average two-day common stock abnormal returns and average sample size from studies of changes in financing, dividend, and investment policy grouped by implied changes in corporate cash flows. Returns are weighted averages by sample size of the returns reported by the respective studies. (Unless otherwise noted, returns are significantly different from zero.) Full citations for all studies mentioned can be found in the reference section at the end of this issue.

Type of Announcement	Average Sample Size	Two-Day Announcement Period Return
Implied Increase in Corporate Cash Flow		
Common Stock Repurchases:		
Intra-firm tender offer[a]	148	16.2%
Open market repurchase[b]	182	3.6
Targeted small holding[c]	15	1.6
Calls of Non-Convertible Bonds[d]	133	−0.1*
Dividend Increases:		
Dividend initiation[e]	160	3.7
Dividend increase[f]	280	0.9
Specially designated dividend[g]	164	2.1
Investment Increases[h]	510	1.0
Implied Decrease in Corporate Cash Flow		
Security Sales:		
Common stock[i]	262	−1.6
Preferred stock[j]	102	0.1*
Convertible preferred[k]	30	−1.4
Straight debt[l]	221	−0.2*
Convertible debt[l]	80	−2.1
Dividend Decreases[f]	48	−3.6
Investment Decreases[h]	111	−1.1

[a] Source: Dann (1981), Masulis (1980), Vermalen (1981), Rosenfeld (1982)
[b] Source: Dann (1980), Vermalen (1981)
[c] Source: Bradley/Wakeman (1983)
[d] Source: Vu (1986)
[e] Source: Asquith/Mullins (1983)
[f] Source: Charest (1978), Aharony/Swary (1980)
[g] Source: Brickley (1983)
[h] Source: McConnell/Muscarella (1985)
[i] Source: Asquith/Mullins (1986), Masulis/Korwar (1986), Mikkelson/Partch (1986), Schipper/Smith (1986), Pettway/Radcliff (1985)
[j] Source: Linn/Pinegar (1986), Mikkelson/Partch (1986)
[k] Source: Linn/Pinegar (1986)
[l] Source: Dann/Mikkelson (1984), Eckbo (1986), Mikkelson/Partch (1986)
* Interpreted by the authors as not significantly different from zero.

new security is most acute in the case of equity offerings. Similarly, the values of convertible debt and convertible preferred stock are also generally more sensitive to changes in firm value than non-convertible debt and preferred because of their equity component—but less sensitive, of course, than common stock; hence the information disparity should be more problematic for convertible than for straight securities.

The case of utility offerings is somewhat different. In the rate regulation process, managers of utilities generally petition their respective regulatory authorities for permission to proceed with a new security issue. This petitioning process should reduce the price reaction of utilities announcements relative to industrials for three reasons: (1) it could reduce the differential information between manager and outsiders; (2) it could limit managers' discretion as to what security to sell; (3) it could reduce managers' ability to "time" security offerings to take advantage of inside information. Because of this regulatory process, utilies do not face as great a problem in persuading the market to accept its securities at current prices.

Thus, while this information disparity hypothesis does not predict whether the response to announcements of debt and preferred issues will be negative or positive, it does predict that the reaction to common stock sales will be more negative than the response to preferred or debt, more negative to convertible than non-convertible issues, and to industrial than utility offerings.[6]

This second, leverage-related channel through which the information disparity problem operates can be distinguished from the implied cash flow explanation by examining evidence from events that *explicitly* associate sources and uses of funds: namely, exchange offers, conversion-forcing calls of convertible securities, and security sales in which the proceeds are explicitly intended for debt retirement. Research on announcements of these transactions (summarized in Table 3) documents the following: (1) the market responds positively to leverage-increasing transactions and negatively to leverage-decreasing transactions; (2) the larger the change in leverage, the greater the price reaction. Accordingly, debt-for-common offers have larger positive stock price reactions than preferred-for-common offers, and common-for-debt offers have larger negative price reactions than common-for-preferred offers.

In Table 4 the analysis of the two channels is combined to provide additional insight into the information disparity explanation. The events to the upper left of the table tend to have positive stock price reactions, those in the lower right tend to have negative reactions while those along the diagonal tend to be insignificant. Hence, a common stock offering, which implies both a reduction in future operating cash flow and a reduction in leverage, prompts the largest negative market response of all the security offers. A stock

repurchase, by contrast, suggests increases both in operating cash and leverage, and accordingly receives strong endorsement by the market. It seems to provide a credible expression to investors of management's confidence about the company's future performance (at least relative to its current value).

Unanticipated Announcements

Because stock price changes reflect only the unanticipated component of announcements of corporate events, the stock price change at the announcement of a security offering will be larger, all else equal, the more unpredictable is the announcement. For example, debt repayment (either from maturing issues or sinking-fund provisions) requires the firm to issue additional debt to maintain its capital structure. Given a target capital structure and stable cash flows, debt repayment must be matched with a new debt issue; hence the more predictable are principal repayments, the more predictable will be new debt issues. Similarly, the predictability of earnings (and thus internally generated equity) will determine the predictability of a new equity issue. Therefore, one should expect a new debt issue to be more predictable than a new equity issue because principal repayments are more predictable than earnings.

Another reason for the greater predictability of public debt offerings is related to the cost structures of public versus private debt. Flotation costs for publicly-placed debt appear to have a larger fixed component and more pronounced economies of scale than bank debt. Thus, a firm tends to use bank lines of credit until an efficient public issue size is reached; then the firm issues public debt and retires the bank debt. If investors can observe the amount of bank borrowing and the pattern of public debt issues, then more predictable announcements of public bond issues should have smaller price reactions.

Utilities use external capital markets with far greater frequency than industrials, thus making utility issues more predictable. For this reason alone, we would expect utilities' stock prices to exhibit a smaller reaction to announcements of new security sales. In short, the relative predictability of announcements of security offerings helps explain both the observed differences in market reactions to

---

6. But if the evidence across classes of securities is consistent with the information asymmetry hypothesis, some data within security classes is apparently inconsistent. When Eckbo (1986) and Mikkelson/Partch (1986) disaggregate their bond data by rating class, neither study finds higher rated, less risky (and thus less sensitive to firm value) bonds to be associated with smaller abnormal returns. Eckbo also finds more negative abnormal returns to mortgage bonds than non-mortgage bonds. (References for studies are cited in full at the end of this issue.)

TABLE 3
The Stock Market Response to Announcements of Pure Financial Structure Changes:
Exchange Offers, Security Sales with Designated Uses of Funds, and Calls of Convertible Securities

Below is a summary of two-day announcement effects associated with the events listed above. Because each of these transactions explicitly associate sources with uses of funds, they represent virtually pure financial structure changes. (Unless otherwise noted, returns are significantly different from zero.) Full citations for all studies mentioned can be found in the reference section at the end of the article.

Type of Transaction	Security Issued	Security Retired	Average Sample Size	Two-Day Announcement Period Return
Leverage-Increasing Transactions				
Stock Repurchase[a]	Debt	Common	45	21.9%
Exchange Offer[b]	Debt	Common	52	14.0
Exchange Offer[b]	Preferred	Common	9	8.3
Exchange Offer[b]	Debt	Preferred	24	2.2
Exchange Offer[c]	Income Bonds	Preferred	24	2.2
Transactions with No Change in Leverage				
Exchange Offer[d]	Debt	Debt	36	0.6*
Security Sale[e]	Debt	Debt	83	0.2*
Leverage-Reducing Transactions				
Conversion-forcing Call[e]	Common	Convertible	57	−0.4*
Conversion-forcing Call[e]	Common	Preferred	113	−2.1
Security Sale[f]	Convertible Debt	Convertible Bond	15	−2.4
Exchange Offer[b]	Common	Debt	30	−2.6
Exchange Offer[b]	Preferred	Preferred	9	−7.7
Security Sale[f]	Common	Debt	12	−4.2
Exchange Offer[b]	Common	Debt	20	−9.9
		Debt		

[a] Source: Masulis (1980)
[b] Source: Masulis (1983) (Note: These returns include announcement days of both the original offer and, for about 40 percent of the sample, a second announcement of specific terms of the exchange.)
[c] Source: McConnell/Schlarbaum (1981)
[d] Source: Dietrich (1984)
[e] Source: Mikkelson (1981)
[f] Source: Eckbo (1986) and Mikkelson/Partch (1986)
* Not statistically different from zero.

common stock versus debt issues and to the offerings of industrials versus those of utilities.

Changes in Ownership and Control

Some security sales involve potentially important changes in ownership or organizational structure. In such transactions, part of the observed price reaction may reflect important changes in the ownership and control of the firm. For example, equity carve-outs (also known as partial public offerings) are transactions in which firms sell a minority interest in the common stock of a previously wholly-owned subsidiary. In contrast to the negative returns from the sale of corporate common stock reported earlier, equity carve-outs are associated with significant *positive* returns of 1.8 percent for the five days around the announcement.

In this case, the problem of the potential information disparity which appears to plague equity offerings seems to be offset by positive signals to investors. What are these signals? As Katherine Schipper and Abbie Smith argue in the article following this one, equity carve-outs may suggest to the market that management feels the consolidated firm is not receiving full credit in its current stock price for the value of one of its subsidiaries. If such is the information management communicates by offering separate equity claims on an "undervalued" subsidiary, then carve-outs could provide a means of raising new equity capital that neutralizes the negative signal released by announcements of seasoned equity offerings. Also worth noting, the public sale of a minority interest in a subsidiary carries potentially important control implications. For example, the sale of subsidiary stock allows management of the subsidiary to have a

TABLE 4

Implied Cash Flow Change

	Negative	No Change	Positive
Negative	Common Sale	Convertible Bond Sale To Retire Debt Common/Preferred E.O. Preferred/Debt E.O Common/Debt E.O. Common Sale to Retire Debt Call of Convertible Bonds Call of Convertible Preferred	Calls of Non-Convertible Bonds
No Change	Convertible Preferred Sale Convertible Debt Sale Investment Decrease Dividend Decrease	Debt/Debt E.O.	Dividend Increases Investment Increases
Positive	Preferred Sale Debt Sale	Common Repurchase Finance with Debt Debt/Common E.O Preferred/Common E.O. Debt/Preferred E.O. Income Bond/ Preferred E.O.	Common Repurchase

(Leverage Change — vertical axis)

■ Significant Negative Stock Price Reaction
□ Insignificant Stock Price Reaction
▨ Significant Positive Stock Price Reaction

market-based compensation package that more accurately reflects the subsidiary's operating performance. In fact, 94 percent of the carve-outs studied adopted incentive compensation plans based on the subsidiary's stock.[7]

Academic research in general suggests that changes in ownership and organization affect stock prices (see Table 5). The evidence summarized in the upper panel suggests that voluntary organizational restructuring on average benefits stockholders. The research findings summarized in the lower panel suggests that announcements of transactions that increase ownership concentration raise share prices while those that reduce concentration lower share prices. For example, in equity offers where a registered secondary offering by the firm's management accompanied the primary equity, the average stock price reaction was -4.5 percent, almost 1.5 percent more negative than the average response to industrial equity offerings. This is the case, incidentally, in which the information problem becomes most acute: not only is the firm issuing new stock, but man-

agement is using the offering to further reduce its ownership stake—the reverse of a leveraged buyout.

Summing Up The Market's Reaction to Securities Offerings

Table 6 offers a pictorial summary of the various hypotheses and how each contributes to our understanding of the research findings on new security issues. Those arguments focusing on the information gap between management and investors appear to have the most explanatory power. The extent to which announcements are unanticipated helps explain differences in the market's response to debt vs. equity offerings, and to industrial vs. utility issues. And in the special cases when the offer accompanies ownership or organizational changes, there are important additional insights available. The price pressure hypothesis may have some validity, but for widely-traded securities I remain skeptical. The dilutive effects on EPS and ROE of new equity and convertible offerings are

7. See the article immediately following in this journal: Katherine Schipper and Abbie Smith, "Equity Carve-outs." See also the academic piece on which the above article is based, "A Comparison of Equity Carve-outs and Seasoned Equity Offerings: Share Price Effects and Corporate Restructuring," *Journal of Financial Economics* 15 (1986), pp. 153-186.

TABLE 5
The Market Response to Announcements of Organizational and Ownership Changes

In the columns below are summaries of the cumulative average abnormal common stock returns and average sample size from studies of announcements of transactions which change corporate control or ownership stucture. Returns are weighted averages by sample size of the returns reported by the respective studies. (Unless otherwise noted, returns are significantly different from zero.) Full citations for all studies mentioned can be found in the reference section at the end of this issue.

Type of Announcement	Average Sample Size	Cumulative Abnormal Returns
Organizational Restructuring		
Merger: Target[a]	113	20.0%
Bidder[a]	119	0.7*
Spin-Off[b]	76	3.4
Sell-Off: Seller[c]	279	0.7
Buyer[d]	118	0.7
Equity Carve Out[e]	76	0.7*
Joint Venture[f]	136	0.7
Going Private[g]	81	30.0
Voluntary Liquidation[h]	75	33.4
Life Insurance Company Mutualization[i]	30	56.0
Savings & Loan Association Charter Conversion[j]	78	5.6
Proxy Fight[k]	56	1.1
Ownership Restructuring		
Tender Offer: Target[l]	183	30.0
Bidder[l]	183	0.8*
Large Block Acquisition[m]	165	2.6
Secondary Distribution: Registered[n]	146	−2.9
Non-Registered[n]	321	−0.8
Targeted Share Repurchase[o]	68	−4.8

[a] Source: Dann (1980), Asquith (1983), Eckbo (1983), Jensen/Ruback (1983)
[b] Source: Hite/Owers (1983), Miles/Rosenfeld (1983), Schipper/Smith (1983), Rosenfeld (1984)
[c] Source: Alexander/Benson/Kampmeyer (1984), Rosenfeld (1984), Hite/Owers (1985), Jain (1985). Klein (1985), Vetsuypens (1985)
[d] Source: Rosenfeld (1984), Hite/Owers (1985), Jain (1985), Klein (1985)
[e] Source: Schipper/Smith (1986)
[f] Source: McConnell/Nantell (1985)
[g] Source: DeAngelo/DeAngelo/Rice (1984)
[h] Source: Kim/Schatzberg (1985)
[i] Source: Mayers/Smith (1986)
[j] Source: Masulis (1986)
[k] Source: Dodd/Warner (1983)
[l] Source: Bradley/Desai/Kim (1985), Jensen/Ruback (1983)
[m] Source: Holderness/Sheehan (1985), Mikkelson/Ruback (1985)
[n] Source: Mikkelson/Partch (1985)
[o] Source: Dann/DeAngelo (1983), Bradley/Wakeman (1983)
* Interpreted by the authors as not significantly different from zero.

nothing more than accounting illusions; *given* that the security is fairly priced at issue, and that management expects to earn its cost of capital on the funds newly raised, there is no real economic dilution of value caused by a new equity offering. Finally, optimal capital structure theories, at this stage of development, seem to offer little insight into the general pattern of price reactions to new security sales.

Alternative Methods of Marketing Security Offerings

Once having decided on the terms of a security to sell, management then must choose among a number of methods to market the issue. It can offer the securities on a pro rata basis to its own stock-

TABLE 6

		Research Finding		
	Returns ≤ 0	Common ≤ Debt or Preferred	Convertibles ≤ Non-Convertibles	Industrials ≤ Utilities
Optimal Capital Structure	No	No	No	No
Implied Cash Flow Change	Yes	No	No	No
Leverage Change	No	Yes +	Yes	Yes
Unanticipated Announcements	No	Yes	No	Yes
Ownership Changes	Yes*	Yes*	Yes*	No
Price Pressure	No	No	No	No

(left margin label: Potential Explanations)

+ But only for Debt, not Preferred
* In Special Cases

holders through a rights offering, it can hire an underwriter to offer the securities for sale to the public, or it can place the securities privately. If management chooses to use an underwriter, it can negotiate the offer terms with the underwriter, or it can structure the offering internally and then put it out for competitive bid. The underwriting contract can be a firm commitment or a best efforts offering. Finally, the issue can be registered with the Securities and Exchange Commission under its traditional registration procedures; or, if the firm qualifies, it can file a shelf registration in which it registers all securities it intends to sell over the next two years.

Let's look at the major alternatives for marketing securities to provide a better understanding of why certain methods predominate.

Rights versus Underwritten Offerings

The two most frequently used methods by which public corporations sell new equity are firm-commitment underwritten offerings and rights offerings. In an underwritten offering, the firm in effect sells the issue to an investment bank, which resells the issue to public investors (or forms a syndicate with other investment banks to do so). The initial phases of negotiation between the issuing company and the investment banker focus on the amount of capital, the type of security, and the terms of the offering. If the firm and its chosen underwriter agree to proceed, the underwriter begins to assess the prospects, puts together an underwriting syndicate, prepares a registration statement, and performs what is known as a "due diligence" investigation into the financial condition of the company.

In a rights offering, each stockholder receives options (or, more precisely, warrants) to buy the newly issued securities. One right is issued for each share held. Rights offerings also must be registered with the SEC.

Despite evidence that the out-of-pocket expenses of an equity issue underwritten by an investment banker are from three to 30 times higher than the costs of a non-underwritten rights offering,[8] over 80 percent of equity offerings employ underwriters. Perhaps the most plausible rationale for using underwriters is that they are effective in monitoring the firm's activities and thus provide implicit guarantees to investors when they sell the securities. This monitoring function would be especially valuable in

8. See my paper, "Alternative Methods for Raising Capital: Rights versus Underwritten Offerings," *Journal of Financial Economics* 5 (1977), 273-307.

light of the information disparity between managers and outside stockholders discussed in the first part of this article.

Thus, in addition to providing distribution channels between issuing corporations and investors, the investment banker performs a monitoring function analogous to that which bond rating agencies perform for bondholders and auditing firms perform for investors and other corporate claimholders. While such activities are expensive, such monitoring of management increases the value of the firm by raising the price investors are willing to pay for the company's securities.

Negotiated versus Competitive Bid Contracts

The evidence also suggests that competitive bid offerings involve lower total flotation costs than negotiated offers.[9] In fact, it has been estimated that companies which use negotiated contracts can expect their total issue costs to be higher, on average, by 1.2 percent of the proceeds. Nevertheless, the primary users of competitive bids are regulated firms which are required to do so. Companies not facing this regulatory constraint (Rule 50 of the Public Utilities Holding Company Act) appear overwhelmingly to choose negotiated offers.

This behavior may be attributed partly to the fact that the variance of issuing costs has been found to be higher for competitive bid than for negotiated offers. Executives whose compensation is tied to accounting earnings might prefer a more stable, if somewhat lower, bottom line resulting from the use of negotiated offerings. Another potentially important problem with competitive bids is the difficulty in restricting the use of information received by investment bankers not awarded the contract. Hence, companies with valuable proprietary information are likely to find the confidentiality afforded by negotiated bids more attractive.

Probably most important, though, is that the monitoring, and thus the guarantee provided investors, is much more effective in the case of negotiated offerings than in competitive bids. With a negotiated offer, the issuing firm has less control over the terms and timing of the offer; hence, investors have

fewer worries that the issue will be structured to exploit their information disadvantage.

This leads me to generalize about the kinds of companies which are likely to benefit from using competitive bids. The less the potential disparity between management's and the market's estimation of the value of the company, the greater are the likely savings to a company from using the competitive bidding process. For this reason, regulated utilities (those not already subject to Rule 50) stand to benefit more from the use of competitive bids than unregulated firms. Also, in the case of more senior claims such as debt and preferred stock, the informational asymmetry problem is less pronounced, as I have suggested, because the value of the claim is less sensitive to firm value. Thus straight debt, secured debt and non-convertible preferred stock should all be sold through competitive bids more frequently than common stock, convertible preferred stock or convertible bonds. And this is apparently the case.[10]

Shelf versus Traditional Registration

Prior to any public security offering, the issue must be registered with the SEC. Using traditional registration procedures, the issuing firm, its investment banker, its auditing firm, and its law firm all typically participate in filing the required registration statements with the SEC (as well as with the appropriate state securities commissions). The offering can only proceed when the registration statement becomes effective.

In March of 1982, however, the SEC authorized Rule 415 on an experimental basis, and it was made permanent in November 1983. It permits companies with more than $150 million of stock held by investors unaffiliated with the company to specify and register the total dollar amount of securities they expect to offer publicly over the next two years. The procedure is called shelf registration because it allows companies to register their securities, "put them on the shelf," and then issue the securities whenever they choose.

After the securities are registered, management can then offer and sell them for up to two years on a continuous basis. Rule 415 also allows the company to modify a debt instrument and sell it without first

---

9. See Sanjai Bhagat and Peter Frost, "Issuing Costs to Existing Shareholders in Competitive and Negotiated Underwritten Public Utility Equity Offerings," *Journal of Financial Economics* 15 (1986).

10. See the article which appears later in this issue, James R. Booth and Richard L. Smith, "The Certification Role of the Investment Banker in the Pricing of New Issues." The article is based on their study, "Capital Raising, Underwriting and the Certification Hypothesis," *Journal of Financial Economics* 15 (1986).

filing an amendment to the registration statement. Thus, shelf registration allows qualifying firms additional flexibility both in structuring debt issues and in timing all security issues.

Because of the additional flexibility afforded management by the shelf procedure, there is greater opportunity for management to exploit its inside information and issue (temporarily) overvalued securities. Thus, the information disparity problem attending new issues should be especially great in cases of shelf registration. Potential investors anticipating this problem will exact an even larger discount in the case of shelf offerings than in offerings registered through traditional procedures. Hence, stock price reactions to announcements of new offerings registered under Rule 415 could be more negative, other things equal, than those under traditional registration procedures.

It is largely for this reason, I would argue, that shelf registration has been used far more frequently with debt than with equity offerings.

A Special Case: Initial Public Offerings

Private firms that choose to go public typically obtain the services of an underwriter with which to negotiate an initial public equity offering (IPO). IPOs are an interesting special case of security offers. They differ from offerings previously discussed in two important ways: (1) the uncertainty about the market clearing price of the offering is significantly greater than for public corporations with claims currently trading; (2) because the firm has no traded shares, examination of stock price reactions to initial announcements is impossible. The first difference affects the way these securities are marketed; the second limits the ways researchers can study the offerings.

Underpricing

The stock price behavior of IPOs from the time the initial offer price is set until the security first trades in the aftermarket demonstrates unmistakably that the average issue is offered at a significant dis-count from the price expected in the aftermarket. In fact the average underpricing appears to exceed 15 percent. (For a summary of the results of studies of offer prices for initial public equity offerings as well as new issues of seasoned equity and bonds, see Table 7.) Once the issue has begun trading in the aftermarket, however, the returns to stockholders appear to be normal.

In an IPO, as suggested, there is a large amount of uncertainty about the market-clearing price. Furthermore, as some observers have argued, this uncertainty creates a special problem if some investors are considerably more knowledgable than others—for example, institutions relative to, say, individuals (especially since the Rules of Fair Practice of the NASD prohibit raising the price if the issue is oversubscribed). Assume, for the sake of simplicity, that we can divide all potential investors into two distinct groups: "informed" and "uninformed." Under these conditions, if the initial offer price were set at its expected market-clearing price, it is not difficult to demonstrate that uninformed investors would earn systematically below normal returns. If an issue is believed by informed investors to be underpriced, then those investors will submit bids and the issue will be rationed among informed and uninformed investors alike. If the issue is overpriced, however, informed investors are less likely to submit bids and the issue is more likely to be undersubscribed. In this process, uninformed investors systematically receive more of overpriced issues and less of underpriced issues.[11]

Recognizing their disadvantaged position in this bidding process, uninformed investors will respond by bidding for IPOs only if the offer price is systematically below their estimate of the aftermarket price in order to compensate them for their expected losses on overpriced issues. Such a bidding process would also account for the well-documented observation that underpricing is greater for issues with greater price uncertainty.

The above explanation has been tested using data from IPOs in the following way. Given that there is an equilibrium amount of underpricing (i.e., one which has proved to be acceptable to issuers in order to sell the issue), we can hypothesize that an investment banker that repeatedly prices issues below

11. For a systematic formulation of this "informed-uninformed" investor dichotomy and its effects on IPO pricing, see Kevin Rock, "Why New Issues Are Underpriced," *Journal of Financial Economics* 15 (1986).

TABLE 7
The Underpricing of
New Security Issues

Presented below is a summary of estimates of the underpricing of new securities at issuance by type of offering. Underpricing is measured by the average percentage change from offer prices to aftermarket price. Full citations for all studies mentioned can be found in the reference section at the end of this issue.

Type of Offering	Study	Sample Period	Sample Size	Estimated Underpricing
Initial Public Equity Offering	Ibottson (1974)	1960–1969	120	11.4%
Initial Public Equity Offering	Ibbotson/Jaffe (1975)	1960–1970	2650	16.8
Initial Public Equity Offering	Ritter (1984)	1960–1982	5162	18.8
		1977–1982	1028	26.5
		1980–1981	325	48.4
Initial Public Equity Offering	Ritter (1985)	1977–1982		
Firm Commitment			664	14.8
Best Efforts			364	47.8
Initial Public Equity Offering:	Chalk/Peavy (1985)	1974–1982	440	13.8
Firm Commitment			415	10.6
Best Efforts			82	52.0
Equity Carve-Outs	Schipper/Smith (1986)	1965–1983	36	0.19
Seasoned New Equity Offering	Smith (1977)	1971–1975	328	0.6
Seasoned New Utility Equity Offering:	Bhagat/Frost (1986)	1973–1980	552	−0.30
Negotiated			479	−0.25
Competitive Bid			73	−0.65
Primary Debt Issue	Weinstein (1978)	1962–1974	412	0.05
	Sorensen (1982)	1974–1980	900	0.50
	Smith (1986)	1977–1982	132	1.6

this equilibrium level will lose the opportunity for further business. If the investment banker repeatedly overprices (or does not underprice by enough), however, he loses investors.

A recent study by Randy Beatty and Jay Ritter estimated an underpricing equilibrium and then examined the average deviation from that level of underpricing by 49 investment bankers who handled four or more initial public offerings during the period 1977-1981. When they compared the subsequent performance of the 24 underwriters whose average deviation from their estimated normal underpricing was greatest with that of the remaining 25 underwriters, the market share of those 24 firms fell from 46.6 to 24.5 percent during 1981-1982; and five of the 24 actually closed down. For those 25 with the smallest deviation from the estimated underpricing equilibrium, market share goes from 27.2 to 21.0 percent, and only one of the 25 ceases operation. (The remaining 54.5 percent of the business in 1981-

1982 was underwritten by firms which did fewer than four IPOs from 1977-1981.)[12]

As Table 7 shows, security issues by public corporations are also typically underpriced, but much less so than in the case of IPOs. Seasoned new equity issues have been found to be underpriced by 0.6 percent. There is some disagreement about the degree of underpricing of seasoned bonds, with estimates ranging from 0.05 percent to as high as 1.2 percent of the offer price. Seasoned equity issues by utilities, however, appear to be *overpriced* by 0.3 percent.

Best Efforts versus Firm Commitment Contracts

There are two alternative forms of underwriting contracts that are typically used in IPOs. The first is a firm commitment underwriting agreement, in which the underwriter agrees to purchase the whole

---

12. See Randolph P. Beatty and Jay R. Ritter, "Investment Banking, Reputation, and the Underpricing of Initial Public Offerings," *Journal of Financial Economics* 15 (1986).

issue from the firm at a specified price for resale to the public. The second is a "best efforts" agreement. In such an arrangement, the underwriter acts only as a marketing agent for the firm. The underwriter does not agree to purchase the issue at a predetermined price, but simply sells as much of the security as it can and takes a predetermined spread. The issuing company gets the net proceeds, but without any guarantee of the final amount from the investment banker. This agreement generally specifies a minimum amount that must be sold within a given period of time; if this amount is not reached, the offering is cancelled. From 1977-1982, 35 percent of all IPOs were sold with best efforts contracts. Those issues, however, raised only 13 percent of the gross proceeds from IPOs over that period, implying that larger IPOs tend to use the firm commitment method.

The choice between firm commitment and best efforts comes down, once again I think, to resolving the problems created by the information disparity between informed and uninformed investors. The preceding argument for underpricing firm commitments can be contrasted with the incentives in a best efforts contract. Consider that in the case of a best efforts IPO, if the issue is overpriced and the issue sales fall short of the minimum specified in the underwriting contract, the offer is cancelled and the losses to uninformed investors are reduced. Structuring the contract in this manner reduces the problem faced by uninformed potential security holders, and thus reduces the discount necessary to induce them to bid.

Thus, the relative attractiveness of the two types of contracts will be determined, in part, by the amount of uncertainty associated with the price of the issue. The prohibition against raising prices for an oversubscribed issue (imposed by the NASD's Rules of Fair Practice) means that the company has effectively given a free call option to potential stockholders. Thus, relative to a best efforts contract, the expected proceeds to the issuer in a firm commitment IPO are reduced as the amount of uncertainty about after-market prices increases. In a best efforts contract, the firm provides potential investors not only with an implicit call option (because of the rule against raising the price), but also gives them the option to put the shares back to the firm if the issue is undersubscribed. Because of these implicit options

provided investors in best efforts contracts, the greater the uncertainty about the after-market price of an IPO, the more attractive are best efforts contracts to investors; hence, the more likely are issuers to choose that form over a firm commitment.

To summarize, firm commitment offerings are more likely the less the uncertainty about the market-clearing security price. Consistent with this hypothesis, one study found that the average standard deviation of the aftermarket rates of returns for 285 best efforts offerings was 7.6 percent in contrast to a 4.2 percent standard deviation for 641 firm commitment offerings.[13]

Stabilization Activity and the Green Shoe Option

Underwriters typically attempt to stabilize prices around the offer date of a security. In the case of primary equity offers by listed firms, this stabilization is accomplished by placing a limit order to purchase shares with the specialist on the exchange. I believe this activity represents a bonding mechanism by the investment banker—one that promises investors that if the issue is overpriced, they can sell their shares into the stabilizing bid, thereby cancelling the transaction.

The Green Shoe option (so named because it was originally used in an offering by the Green Shoe Company) is frequently employed in underwritten equity offers. It gives the underwriter the right to buy additional shares from the firm at the offer price. This is equivalent to granting the investment banker a warrant with an exercise price equal to the offer price in the issue. The total quantity of shares exercisable under this option typically ranges between 10 and 20 percent of the offer. Obviously, the option is more valuable if the offer price is below the market value of the shares; thus, the Green Shoe option is another potentially effective bonding mechanism by which the investment banker reassures investors that the issue will not be overpriced. That is, if a new offering prospectus contains a Green Shoe provision, potential investors (especially the less-informed) will reduce their forecast of the probability that the issue will be overpriced because the returns to the underwriter from the Green Shoe are lower if the warrant cannot be exercised.

13. See Jay Ritter, "The 'Hot Issue' Market of 1980," *Journal of Business* 57 (1984).

Implications for Corporate Policy

Recent research on the stock market response to new security offers consistently documents a significant negative reaction (on the order of 3 to 4 percent on average) to announcements of new equity issues by industrial companies. Convertible issues, both debt and preferred, also typically are greeted by a negative, though smaller, price change (of roughly 1 to 2 percent). By contrast, the market reaction to straight debt and preferred issues appears to be neutral.

The critical question, of course, is—Why does the market systematically lower the stock prices of companies announcing new stock and convertible offers? Such financing decisions, after all, are voluntary choices by management intended, presumably, to increase the long-run value of the firm by providing necessary funding.

After consideration of several possible explanations, I argue that the primary cause of this negative response is the potential for management to exploit its inside information by issuing overvalued equity (or convertibles, which of course have an equity component). Investors recognize their vulnerability in this process and accordingly reduce their estimate of the firm's value. The result, in the average case, is that the new equity is purchased by investors at a discount from the pre-announcement price.

This theory and evidence has a number of managerial implications. Perhaps the most important is that management should be sensitive to the way the market is likely to interpret its announcement of a new issue. For example, if the company is contemplating a primary equity offering and an executive asks to include a registered secondary in the offer, the board of directors should recognize that this can be a very expensive perk; in such cases the market price typically falls by almost 5 percent upon the announcement. This is probably the surest means of arousing the market's suspicion that insiders have a different view of the company's future than that reflected in the current stock price.

Perhaps the best way for management to overcome this information problem is to state, as clearly as possible, the intended uses for the funds. For example, if management intends to use the proceeds for plant expansion, management should say so—emphatically. We know that the market responds positively, on average, to announcements of increases in capital spending plans (with the exception of the case of oil companies in recent years, where the reverse has been true).[14] Consequently, short of revealing proprietary information which could compromise the firm's competitive position,[15] management should benefit from the attempt to be as forthright as possible in sharing with the investment community its investment opportunities, corporate objectives, capital structure targets, and so forth.

This strategy is not meant to contradict the obvious: namely, that current stockholders benefit when management issues stock or convertibles when the market price proves to have been high; and that debt or preferred stock is better if the company proves to be undervalued (though, in the absence of significant inside information, I would suggest that this can only be determined with hindsight). The problem, however, is that this kind of managerial opportunism may prove an expensive strategy for a firm that wants to maintain its access to capital markets. If management develops a reputation for exploiting inside information, the price discount the market exacts for accepting subsequent new issues could be even larger.

In the second part of the article, I attempt to show how the use of investment bankers as underwriters also helps to solve this financing problem arising from the possibility of insider information. The fact that management may have an incentive to issue overvalued securities causes a demand for "bonding" the firm's actions—that is, investors will offer more for the securities if they are provided a credible promise that they will not be exploited.

In those cases where the information disparity between management and investors is likely to be greatest, and to have the worst potential consequences for new investors (i.e., for equity holders, and especially in the case of smaller firms in less heavily traded markets), the demand for the bonding or certification provided by the banker is also likely to be the greatest. For this reason I have argued that underwritten issues provide stronger guarantees to in-

14. A study by John McConnell and Chris Muscarella ("Corporate Capital Expenditure Decisions and the Market Value of the Firm," *Journal of Financial Economics* 14 (1985)) found that announcements of increases of corporate capital spending were accompanied by a 1 percent increase, on average, of the announcing company's stock price.

15. For example, when Texas Gulf Sulphur discovered substantial mineral deposits in Canada, immediate release of that information would have substantially increased the cost of adjacent mineral rights then under negotiation.

vestors than rights offers; issues with negotiated underwriting contracts are more strongly bonded than competitive bid issues; issues registered using traditional procedures are more strongly bonded than those employing the new shelf registration procedures; and issues containing a Green Shoe option are more strongly bonded than those without. Therefore, for example, an industrial equity issue should more frequently be registered using traditional rather than shelf registration procedures, and sold under a negotiated, firm commitment rather than a competitive bid contract; it is also more likely to include a Green Shoe option. By contrast, a non-convertible debt issue by a utility is more likely to be sold under a competitive bid contract and registered using the new shelf registration procedures.

The above argument is not to deny that shelf registration procedures have significantly lowered the fixed costs of public issues for some industrial companies. In fact it should be especially cost-effective for large, well-established companies, especially in the case of public debt offers.

To take greatest advantage of the potential savings from shelf registration, I believe that management must change some of its practices with respect to debt offerings. Instead of using a line of credit at a bank until a large public issue can be made, qualifying companies could use the shelf registration process to place several smaller issues. In order to retain the additional liquidity in secondary markets associated with larger issues, I expect companies to begin offering multiple issues with the same coupon rate, coupon dates, maturity dates, and covenants—instead of designing all new issues to sell at par.

Guidelines for Long-Term Corporate Financing Strategy

Alan C. Shapiro,
University of Southern California*

Securing the funds to undertake profitable projects is an integral part of the growth program of any company. Therefore, the ability to locate potential sources of funds for capital expenditures, whether from internal reserves or outside institutions, and to arrange them in an attractive financial package become major factors affecting corporate growth. Such, however, is far more easily said than done.

In selecting the right financing mix for funding its worldwide operations, management must consider the availability of different sources of financing and their relative costs and effects on the firm's operating risks. "Right" in this context means that financing arrangement which yields the largest increase in shareholder wealth. Further complicating this task is the abundance of security types and features. Unfortunately, it is not presently within our power (nor will it probably ever be) to identify *the* single financial plan that maximizes the value of the firm. Nevertheless, it is possible to develop a set of reasonable financing guidelines based on our understanding of how financial markets work.

These guidelines derive from three largely separable objectives: (1) minimizing the expected after-tax cost of financing; (2) reducing (or at least managing) the riskiness of corporate cash flows; and (3) minimizing the potential problems, known as "agency costs," caused by managerial incentives to act in ways that harm bondholders or shareholders. In the pages that follow, I present a rationale for pursuing each of these objectives and discuss the strategies and means available to management for achieving them.

Minimizing After-Tax Financing Costs

The overriding objective of all financial management is to sell claims to investors at a price that exceeds the cost to the firm of satisfying those claims. Because the cost to the firm of raising capital is based on investors' required rate of return on securities of comparable risk, this objective translates into raising funds at a below-market rate. Put another way, the firm is trying to create positive net present value financing arrangements.

The value of arranging below-market financing can be illustrated by examining the case of the National Football League's Indianapolis Colts. One of the inducements provided by Indianapolis's city fathers to woo the former Baltimore Colts to the Hoosierdome was a 10-year, $12.5 million loan at 8 percent. How much is this loan worth to owner Robert Isray? That is, what is its net present value?

In return for receiving $12.5 million today, Mr. Isray must pay $1 million in interest annually for the next 10 years, and then repay the $12.5 million principal at the end of 10 years. Given these cash inflows and outflows, we can calculate the loan's NPV just as we would in any project analysis. Note, however, that unlike the typical capital budgeting problem presented in textbooks, the cash inflow occurs immediately and the cash outflows later. But the principle is the same. All we need to know is the required return on this project and Mr. Isray's marginal tax rate.

*This article expands upon the framework presented earlier by Donald R. Lessard and myself in "Guidelines for Global Financing Choices," *Midland Corporate Finance Journal* Spring 1983. Needless to say, the present article is strongly indebted to conversations with (as well as other writings of) my erstwhile collaborator, Don Lessard.

Although some companies have demonstrated a consistent ability to create positive-NPV investment projects, opportunities for designing and issuing positive-NPV securities are typically quite scarce.

The required return is based on the opportunity cost of the funds provided — that is, the rate that Mr. Isray would have to pay to borrow $12.5 million in the capital market. At the time the loan was arranged, in early 1984, the market interest rate on such a loan would have been about 15 percent.

Assuming Mr. Isray's marginal tax rate is 50 percent, then his normal after-tax cost of borrowing is 7.5 percent and the after-tax annual interest payments are $500,000. With this information, we can calculate the NPV of Robert Isray's financing bargain as follows:

$$NPV = \$12,500,000 - \sum_{t=1}^{10} \$500,000/(1 + .075)^t -$$
$$\$12,500,000/(1 + .075)^{10}$$
$$= \$12,500,000 - 9,496,965$$
$$= \$3,003,035.$$

Of course, you don't need a degree in finance to realize that borrowing money at 8 percent when the market rate is 15 percent is a good deal. What the NPV calculations tell you is just how much a particular below-market financing option is worth.

Although some companies have demonstrated a consistent ability to create positive-NPV investment projects, opportunities for designing and issuing positive-NPV securities are typically quite scarce. When it comes to capital investments, the firm often has some type of competitive edge — whether it be in the form of a patent, well-known brand name, special marketing skills, or unique production knowhow. Companies in some product markets may also have few competitors or possess proprietary knowledge about servicing those markets.

By contrast, a company selling securities is competing for funds on a global basis — that is, not only with other firms in its industry but with all firms, foreign and domestic, and with numerous government units and private individuals as well. The fierce competition for funds makes it much less likely that the firm can endow its securities with special advantages. But, as we shall see, the task is not impossible. Marketing skills, tax advantages, and government-induced capital market distortions sometimes enable firms to raise funds at below-market rates.

Financing as a Marketing Problem

Financial securities issued by a firm represent claims against the firm's income and assets. Despite considerable variation among securities, most of these claims can be categorized as either common stock, preferred stock, or debt. These claims are sold to investors for immediate cash. In return, the investors receive some combination of dividends, interest, and principal payments. Firms may also lease assets in return for making lease payments.

The distinguishing features of the basic security types — common stock, preferred stock, and debt — are presented here in abbreviated form, beginning with the least risky security, debt. Corporate debt involves a *contractual* obligation to make periodic payments of interest and principal. If the firm fails to make these payments, the debtholders or creditors can take legal action to collect the money. At the extreme, the firm's creditors could force it to sell off all its assets. Common and preferred stockholders, on the other hand, have only a *residual* claim on the firm's income and assets; that is, their claims are considered only after the firm has met all of its contractual obligations.

The distinction between contractual and residual claims is important for tax purposes as well. Contractual expense obligations such as interest and lease payments are tax deductible. By contrast, preferred and common stock dividends, considered to be payments on residual claims, are not tax deductible.

In the event the firm is unable to meet all its financial obligations, its assets and income must be divided among the various claimants. The division takes place according to the *priority* or *seniority* of the securities it has issued. Debtholders have first claim on the firm's assets and income, followed by preferred stockholders, and finally common stockholders.

The various long-term securities differ also in terms of their *maturity*, or time until repayment of the principal amount. In particular, debt usually has a fixed maturity — whether it be one year or 100 years — whereas common stock and most issues of preferred stock have no maturity date.

As the ultimate owners of the firm, common stockholders have sole *voting power* as long as the firm meets its financial obligations. But if the firm fails to make any of its required interest, principal, or preferred dividend payments, then the debtholders and/or preferred stockholders may get to exercise some degree of control over the firm's affairs.

Because debt is the least risky of the securities discussed here, its cost or required return is the lowest. Next on this risk-cost spectrum of financing vehicles is preferred stock. Higher still are the risks

To the extent that the firm can design a security that appeals to a special niche in the capital market, it can attract funds at a cost that is less than the market's required return on securities of comparable risk.

and cost of common stock. Of course, as the riskiness of the use to which these funds are put rises, so does the required return on each of these securities.

Although it is not obvious from the above discussion, the differences among securities within a given category can be as great as the differences between securities in different categories. Debt and preferred stock may be *convertible* into common stock, while common stock may be classified in terms of voting rights. The greatest diversity exists, of course, among debt securities. Aside from convertibility, some of the possible dimensions along which corporate debt can vary include currency denomination, maturity, tax status, priority of claim, fixed or variable interest coupon, and even whether a coupon exists at all.

The casual observer can be forgiven for failing to understand the underlying causes of this abundance of security types and features. But to a person schooled in marketing, the reasons for such variety are obvious. The vast array of securities in the marketplace exists for the same reasons that M&Ms come in more than one color and that Fords, Chevrolets, and Volkswagens coexist with Mercedes-Benzes and Rolls Royces. Investors have different tastes, preferences, and wealth levels. And whether the market is for cars or financial securities, the better designed the product, the more closely it is tailored to the particular needs and desires of its potential customers, the higher the price it can command. Moreover, as the environment changes, whether in the form of higher oil prices or more uncertain inflation, opportunities arise for astute managers to design new cars or securities that fit the new needs of the marketplace.

Viewed in this light, corporate financing is largely a marketing problem. The firm needs money to finance future investment projects. In lieu of selling some of its existing assets to raise the required funds, it sells the rights to the future cash flows generated by its current and prospective projects. It can sell these rights directly and become an all-equity financed firm. But the firm may get a better price for the rights to its future cash flows by dividing up and repackaging those rights before selling them to the investing public.

Moreover, as Baskin-Robbins has successfully demonstrated, even though plain vanilla may be the most popular ice cream flavor, there's also a market out there for peanut butter ice cream. This suggests another potential source of value creation: to the ex-

tent that the firm can design a security that appeals to a special niche in the capital market, it can attract funds at a cost that is less than the market's required return on securities of comparable risk. Such a rewarding situation is likely to be temporary, however. While the demand for a security that fits a particular niche in the market is not unlimited, the supply of securities designed to tap that niche is likely to increase dramatically once the niche is recognized.

Two examples of the benefits and limitations of designing innovative securities to tap specific financial market segments are provided by zero-coupon bonds and floating-rate securities.

Zero-Coupon Bonds. In 1982, PepsiCo issued the first zero-coupon bond. Although they have since become a staple of corporate finance, zero-coupon bonds initially were a startling innovation. They don't pay interest, but are sold at a deep discount from par. For example, the price on PepsiCo's 30-year bonds was around $60 for each $1000 face amount of the bonds. Investors' gains come in the form of the difference between the discounted price and the face value they expect to receive at maturity.

These securities appeal to those investors who want to be certain of their long-term return. The locked-in return means that investors know in advance how much money they will receive at maturity, an important consideration for pension funds and other buyers who have fixed future commitments. Normal bonds don't provide that certainty because investors can't know at the time they purchase the bond what interest rate they will earn when they reinvest their coupon payments.

But despite the market for such bonds, they were nonexistent until PepsiCo's 1982 zero-coupon issue. The pent-up demand for its $850 million face value offering gave PepsiCo an extraordinarily low cost of funds. The net borrowing cost to the company was under 10 percent, which was almost four percentage points lower than the yield at that time on U.S. Treasury securities of the same maturity.

Zero-coupon bonds, however, did not remain such a low-cost source of funds for long. Once firms saw these low yields, the supply of zero-coupon debt multiplied. The increase in the supply relative to the demand for zeros resulted in a jump in their required yields, negating much of their previous cost advantage.

But the corporate tax advantage of zeros — one which is associated with any issue of original issue discount debt (OID) — remained. The tax advantage to a firm from issuing deep discount debt rather than current coupon debt stems from the tax provision that allows companies to amortize the OID as interest expense over the life of the bond. The firm benefits by receiving a current tax writeoff for a future expense. By contrast, if it issues current coupon debt, the firm's tax writeoff and expense occur simultaneously. The tax advantage of OIDs, which is maximized by issuing zero-coupon bonds, translates into a reduction in the company's cost of debt capital.

The size of this potential tax advantage can be illustrated by considering the General Motors Acceptance Corporation (GMAC) 10-year, zero-coupon notes due in 1991.[1] They were issued at 25.25, giving GMAC a total amortizable discount of 74.75 cents per dollar of par value. Amortized on a straight-line basis over the 10-year life of the issue, this discount provides a yearly tax deduction of approximately 7.5 cents for each dollar of par value. Given the four-to-one ratio of par value to dollars actually raised, this means that each dollar raised yields an annual tax deduction of 30 cents. At GMAC's marginal corporate tax rate of 46 percent, this tax deduction translates into an annual tax savings of about 14 cents ($.46 \times 30$) for each dollar of funds raised. On GMAC's $750 million zero-coupon issue, which provided some $190 million in funds, the annual tax savings amounts to roughly $26 million.

But these tax savings don't tell the whole story. Investors must pay tax on the amortized portion of the discount each year even though they receive no cash until the bond matures. Thus the tax advantage to the firm from issuing OIDs will be offset, in whole or in part, by the higher pre-tax yields required by investors to provide them with the same after-tax yields they could earn on comparable-risk current coupon debt. As a result, corporations issuing OIDs will only realize a tax benefit to the extent that their marginal corporate tax rate exceeds the marginal tax rate of the investors pricing the bonds. At the extreme, if these marginal tax rates are equal, the tax advantage to an issuing corporation will be completely eliminated by the tax disadvantage to the investor.

It will come as no surprise, then, that the initial purchasers of zero-coupon bonds and other OIDs were primarily tax-exempt institutional investors such as pension plans, which sought to lock in higher yields, and Japanese investors, who could treat the discount as a non-taxable capital gain if they sold the bonds prior to maturity. Selling to the tax-exempt segment of the market yielded maximum benefits to the issuers of OIDs because the disparity in marginal tax rates was at its greatest. The supply of tax-exempt institutional money, however, is limited. The Japanese government, furthermore, has threatened to tax zero-coupon bond gains; and Japanese investors have accordingly demanded higher yields to compensate for their possible tax liability.

As additional OIDs are issued, higher-taxed investors must be drawn into the market, raising the pre-tax yields required by OID investors relative to those required by current coupon bondholders. Thus the initial issuers of OIDs received the largest tax benefits, indicating the premium placed on the ability to take advantage quickly of such tax "windows of opportunity." But even though subsequent issuers will receive smaller tax benefits, these benefits will persist as long as the marginal investor tax rate is less than the corporate tax rate.

Floating-Rate Securities. Since the mid-1970s, the overriding fear of many investors has been rising inflation and high interest rates, which sharply eroded the value of older fixed-income securities. So securities dealers and their corporate and other clients sought to make bond issues more palatable to skittish investors by introducing debt instruments with coupons that "float." Because the coupons on the floating-rate securities are periodically adjusted to reflect changes in Treasury-bill yields, the income stream is hedged against rising interest rates and, indirectly, against inflation. The inflation hedge results from the so-called "Fisher effect," which says that if prices start rising (or are expected to rise), nominal interest rates will rise with them, keeping (expected) real rates relatively constant. For purchasers of floating-rate securities, therefore, the harmful impact of inflation on the value of the future dollars they will receive will be offset by their higher interest income. The capital investment is also protected, in theory at least, because the resetting of the coupon should serve to keep the notes selling close to par.

The initial crop of floating-rate notes (FRNs) appeared in 1974, and they were an instant hit. The

---

1. This example appears in David Pyle's article, "Is Deep Discount Debt Financing a Bargain?," *Chase Financial Quarterly*, Fall 1981, pp. 39-61.

The tax advantage of debt can be preserved only if the firm can issue tax-exempt debt or sell debt to investors in marginal tax brackets below 46 percent. Examples of bonds in the respective categories are Industrial Development Bonds (IDBs) and "bearer" bonds.

first major offering, Citicorp notes due in 1989, was enlarged from $350 million to $650 million to meet all the demand. After that reception, other banks, including Chase Manhattan, Mellon, and Crocker, soon issued floaters. The rapid response of the supply of FRNs to market demand quickly dissipated the favorable rates new borrowers could hope to receive.

Once inflation began to cool, in the early 1980s, the "plain vanilla" bond — the old-fashioned fixed-income kind with no trimming — came back into fashion. Again issuers quickly responded to the change in investor tastes. In July 1982, just around the time the bond market rally exploded, only about 46 percent of the bonds sold publicly that month were conventional fixed-income issues. In November of that year, however, 81 percent of the new corporate issues were of the conventional "plain vanilla" kind. As always, those issuers who were first to market with the in-demand securities — in this case, fixed-rate debt — received the best terms and rates.

Tax Factors in Financing

The asymmetrical tax treatment of various components of financial cost, such as the treatment of dividend payments versus interest expense, often means that the differences between before- and after-tax financing costs can diverge sharply. This holds out the possibility of reducing after-tax financing costs by judicious selection of securities. Yet everything is not always what it seems.

For example, many firms consider debt financing to be less expensive than equity financing because interest expense, unlike dividends, are tax deductible. But, as with original issue discount bonds, this comparison is too limited. In the absence of restrictions, the supply of corporate debt could be expected to rise. Yields would also have to rise in order to attract investors from higher and higher tax brackets. Companies would therefore continue to issue debt (and interest rates would continue to rise) up to the point at which the marginal investor tax rate would equal the marginal corporate tax rate.[2] At this point, the necessary yield would be such that there would no longer be a tax incentive for issuing more debt.

The tax advantage of debt can be preserved only if the firm can issue tax-exempt debt or sell debt to investors in marginal tax brackets below 46 percent. Examples of bonds in the respective categories are Industrial Development Bonds (IDBs) and "bearer" bonds.

Industrial Development Bonds. IDBs are issued by states and municipalities, and are therefore tax exempt. But their proceeds are used by private companies, which are responsible for paying interest and principal on the debt. Because the interest from these bonds is exempt from federal income tax to the holder, the sponsoring company will have considerably lower interest cost than with a comparable, fully taxable bond. The power of the lure of lower interest rates is attested to by the fact that some $62 billion of private-purpose tax-exempt debt was issued in 1983. In fact, the Tax Act of 1984 included a provision to limit the use of IDBs so as to stem a tax revenue loss estimated by the Treasury at $8.5 billion a year.

Bearer Bonds. An example of a security designed with investor tax concerns in mind is the bearer bond. Unlike ordinary securities, which must be registered in the name of the purchaser, bearer bonds are unregistered. This feature allows investors to collect interest in complete anonymity and thereby evade taxes. Although U.S. law prohibits the sale of such bonds to U.S. citizens or residents, bonds issued in bearer form are not illegal overseas. As expected, investors are willing to accept lower yields on bearer bonds than nonbearer bonds of comparable risk.

American firms have long taken advantage of the opportunity to reduce their cost of funds by selling bearer bonds abroad. But until 1984, the U.S. government imposed a 30 percent withholding tax on interest paid to foreign investors, largely negating the benefits of issuing bearer bonds. To accommodate foreign investors, U.S. firms raising money abroad issued securities through finance subsidiaries located overseas, thereby exempting from U.S. withholding tax all interest payments by the finance subsidiary to foreign investors. The Netherlands Antilles (N.A.) was a particularly attractive location for such a venture because a bilateral tax treaty between the U.S. and N.A. exempts interest payments by the parent to its N.A. finance subsidiary from U.S. withholding tax.

---

2. This important insight was first presented by Merton Miller in "Debt and Taxes", *Journal of Finance*, May 1977, pp. 261-276.

*The combination of bearer form and no U.S. withholding taxes meant
that highly-rated U.S. companies...could borrow abroad below the cost
at which the U.S. government borrowed domestically.*

The combination of bearer form and no U.S. withholding taxes meant that highly-rated U.S. companies could issue bonds intended for foreign investors (so-called "Eurobonds") at rates considerably below the coupon rates equivalent securities would carry when issued in the United States. Often corporations could borrow abroad below the cost at which the U.S. government borrowed domestically. The arbitrage possibilities inherent in such a situation were made clear by Exxon when, in Fall 1984, it sold zero-coupon Eurobonds and used the proceeds to buy enough Treasury securities to pay off the zeros when they mature. Because the Treasury securities paid a higher yield than Exxon's debt, their price was lower. Exxon pocketed the difference, about $20 million.

Not surprisingly, use of foreign finance subsidiaries grew rapidly. In 1982 and 1983, some $20 billion of Eurobonds were issued by U.S. companies seeking foreign funds to finance their domestic investment projects. The pace has since accelerated. In 1984 alone, American firms raised $20 billion in the Eurobond market. This was helped along by a provision in the Tax Act of 1984 that repealed the withholding tax, enabling American firms to sell bearer bonds overseas directly, without resorting to foreign finance subsidiaries.

What's sauce for the goose is apparently sauce for the gander. Recently, the U.S. Treasury, in an attempt to lower its cost of funds, has issued securities that foreign investors can purchase from U.S. banks and securities firms without revealing their names to the U.S. Treasury. They are not true bearer bonds, however, because the selling institution must certify that the buyer is not an American citizen or resident.

Capital Market Distortions

Sharp-eyed firms are always on the lookout for financing choices that are "bargains" — that is, financing options priced at below-market rates. Bargains result from capital market distortions in the form of concessional financing policies or restrictions imposed on transactions. These distortions grow out of government credit and capital controls, or from subsidies designed to achieve goals other than economic efficiency. For example, the French government has traditionally limited domestic corporate borrowing to hold down interest rates, thereby providing its finance ministry with a lower-cost source of funds to meet budget deficits.

Or overseas investment flows may be restricted, as they were in the United States from 1968-1974 under the Overseas Foreign Direct Investment (OFDI) regulations, in order to conserve foreign exchange. Where the government restricts access to local credit markets or specific credit facilities, the resulting interest rates are usually at a lower-than-equilibrium level on a risk-adjusted basis.

Most governments offer a variety of investment incentives to influence production and export sourcing decisions. For example, new investments located in the Mezzogiorno region of Italy can qualify for cash grants which cover up to 40 percent of the cost of plant and equipment, as well as low interest rate loans.

Closer to home, different U.S. government agencies make low-cost loans available to business for a variety of purposes. These include loans from the Synfuels Corporation, Economic Development Administration (EDA), the Farmers Home Administration (FMHA), the ubiquitous Small Business Administration (SBA), and the Export-Import Bank or Ex-Im Bank.

Small Business Administration. The SBA makes loans available for small business to construct, expand or convert facilities, to install pollution abatement equipment, purchase buildings, equipment materials, or to obtain working capital. By law, however, the SBA may not make a loan if a business can obtain funds on its own. When financing is not otherwise available on reasonable terms, the SBA may guarantee bank loans to a small firm. The SBA may also make direct loans, on its own or in participation with a bank.

The SBA also helps finance small firms through privately-owned small business investment companies (SBICs). These SBA-licensed companies supply venture capital and long-term financing to small firms for expansion and modernization, and may provide management assistance as well. The SBA may purchase, or guarantee, the payment of principal and interest of debentures issued by SBICs to increase the availability of funds for financing small firms.

As might be expected, the demand for low-cost SBA loans on risky investments (otherwise why couldn't the firm get the loan on its own?) vastly exceeds the supply of such loans. Not surprisingly, the Small Business Administration has been rocked periodically by scandals related to the allocation of its low-cost funds.

Organizational capital manifests itself as a set of information and beliefs in the minds of corporate stakeholders—the suppliers, employees, customers, distributors, and others who are necessary to endow the firm's products and projects with value.

Export Financing Programs. In the race for export orders, particularly for capital equipment and other "big-ticket" items requiring long repayment arrangements, most governments of developed nations have attempted to provide their domestic exporters with a competitive edge in the form of low-cost export financing and concessionary rates on political and economic risk insurance. For example, the United States government supplies low-cost export credits through the Export-Import Bank (Ex-Im Bank).

Export credit programs can often be used to advantage by multinational firms. The form of use will depend on whether the firm is seeking to export or import goods or services, but the basic strategy remains the same: shop around among the various export credit agencies for the best possible financing arrangement.

Cross Co., for example, had $40 million of machine-tool orders in 1982 from a Ford Motor Co. unit in Mexico. Cross wanted to put the orders through its Michigan factory. But the British government was willing to provide less expensive export financing than the Ex-Im Bank and so the Cross plant in Great Britain got the order.

Firms engaged in projects with sizable import requirements may be able to finance these purchases on attractive terms from various export financing agencies. To do this, the firm must compile a list of goods and services required for the project and relate them to potential sources by country. Where there is overlap among potential suppliers, the purchaser may be able to extract more favorable financing terms from the export credit agencies involved. Perhaps the best-known application of this strategy in recent years is the financing of the Soviet gas pipeline to Western Europe. By playing off the various European and Japanese export financing agencies against each other, the Soviet Union managed to get extraordinarily favorable credit terms.

Reducing Operating and Financial Risks

After taking advantage of the opportunities available to lower its risk-adjusted financing costs, management should then arrange its additional financing in such a way that the risk exposures of the company are kept at manageable levels. The profitability, and thus the market value, of any company depend to a large extent on its ability to compete. A key element of corporate competitiveness is the firm's ability to capitalize on its organizational assets — its intangible capital, if you will.

There are two main types of organizational capital. One is the wide variety of management and marketing skills that are necessary to inform and coordinate the diverse group of people who develop, produce, sell, buy, enhance, and service a product. The second, and equally important, type of organizational capital is the ability of management to inspire sufficient trust and confidence such that customers, employees, and other stakeholders are willing to develop relationships with the firm. One prerequisite for such confidence is that the firm be seen as financially sound and viable over the long run.

Two important points emerge from this discussion. First, corporate operating cash flows can be affected by perceptions (of non-investor stakeholders) about the financial condition of the firm. Second, shareholder wealth is created, in large part, by exploiting the firm's proprietary knowledge about, and its reputation in, its various product and factor markets.[3]

By extension, the firm's continuing ability to take advantage of future profit opportunities depends on its skill in maintaining the unique package of organizational assets it has accumulated over time. A number of researchers have attempted to identify the nature of the investment in organizational capital, particularly reputation, and the form of market equilibrium that results.[4] I don't deal with these issues here. But, from the perspective of this paper, the significance of organizational capital for corporate financial planning stems from the fact that the firm doesn't directly "own" such capital. Rather, it manifests itself as a set of information and beliefs in the minds of corporate stakeholders — the suppliers, employees, customers, distributors, and others who are necessary to endow the firm's products and projects with value.

Clearly, excessive risk taking, with a corresponding decrease in the firm's survival odds, could adversely affect the firm's relationships with its non-investor stakeholders, thereby jeopardizing

3. This view is expressed by Bradford Cornell and Alan C. Shapiro in "Corporate Stakeholders and Corporate Finance," UCLA working paper, September 1985.
4. See, for example, Benjamin Klein and Keith B. Leffler, "The Role of Market Forces in Assuring Contractual Performance," *Journal of Political Economy*, August 1981, pp. 615-641; and Philip H. Dybvig and Chester S. Spatt, "Does It Pay to Maintain a Reputation?," Yale University working paper, 1983.

The goal of exchange risk management is to offset unanticipated changes in the dollar value of operating cash flows with identical changes in the dollar cost of servicing its liabilities.

this firm-specific capital that has been accumulated over time. The result is that higher total risk can lead to a reduction in a company's operating cash flows by decreasing sales or increasing operating costs.[5]

Thus, to the extent that a particular element of risk contributes materially to the firm's total exposure, management will want to lay off that risk as long as the cost of doing so is not too great. The risks and their relationship to financing arrangements that I discuss are the risks associated with inflation, currency rate fluctuations, political instability, relative price changes (or product market risk), uncertainty over access to funds, and the risk of financial distress associated with financial leverage.

Inflation Risk

As suggested earlier, when there is a great deal of uncertainty about future rates of inflation, floating-rate debt becomes more popular with lenders because the periodic adjustment of interest rates enables them to maintain a relatively constant real return. Thus, floating-rate debt, by eliminating the "inflation risk premium," should be issued with lower interest costs and sell at lower yields than fixed-rate debt of the same maturity. But this does not mean that all firms should take advantage of these lower expected costs and issue only floating-rate debt.[6]

The most relevant consideration for the chief financial officer in deciding whether to issue fixed- or floating-rate debt is the responsiveness of the firm's operating cash flows to inflation. Those companies with operating cash flows that keep pace with inflation — e.g., 10 percent inflation results in a 10 percent increase in operating cash flows — will find that the use of floating-rate bonds stabilizes cash flows, and thereby reduces total corporate risk. Under these conditions, real earnings and real financing costs will remain relatively constant regardless of the rate of inflation. In this category of firms I would include, for example, service firms with minimal fixed assets that can raise prices to keep up with inflation. Conversely, companies in industries that are hurt by inflation will find that floating-rate bonds accentuate the cyclicality of cash flows by matching

high interest costs with low operating cash flows in inflationary times, and low interest costs with high operating cash flows under conditions of price stability. This category would probably include capital intensive firms with large nominal depreciation writeoffs whose real value declines with inflation.

Foreign Exchange Risk

Since the introduction of the floating exchange rate regime in 1973, foreign exchange risk has become of increasing concern to firms doing business internationally. A typical reaction is that of an executive from Volkswagen of America: "I used to call the sales people and ask how sales were doing. Now I call the financial people and ask how the D-Mark [deutsche mark]-to-dollar rate is doing."[7] The unprecedented degree of global economic integration today means that more and more firms are carefully monitoring and managing their currency risks.

If financing opportunities in various currencies are fairly priced, firms can structure their liabilities so as to reduce their exposure to foreign exchange risk at no added cost to shareholders. In the case of contractual items — those fixed in nominal terms — this simply involves matching net positive positions in each currency with borrowings of similar maturity. For example, if Westinghouse sells generating equipment to an English firm for £50 million to be paid in 3 years, it should take out a three-year pound loan such that the principal plus interest owed at maturity equals £50 million.

The goal of exchange risk management is to offset unanticipated changes in the dollar value of operating cash flows with identical changes in the dollar cost of servicing its liabilities.[8] To see how this would work, suppose the pound is worth $1.30 at the time Westinghouse signs the generating equipment contract, which would make the sale worth $65 million. This is also the cost to Westinghouse of repaying its £50 million loan liability. If the pound devalues 10 percent over the next 3 years, to $1.17, Westinghouse will lose $6.5 million on its pound receivables. But it will gain $6.5 million on its loan because it will have to repay only $58.5 million ($1.17 × 50 million) to satisfy a liability originally valued at $65 million. The

5. For a discussion of the adverse consequences of total risk and of strategies for managing such risk, see Alan Shapiro and Sheridan Titman, "An Integrated Approach to Corporate Risk Management," *Midland Corporate Finance Journal*, Summer 1985. See also Clifford W. Smith, Jr. and Rene Stulz, "The Determinants of Firms' Hedging Policies, *Journal of Financial and Quantitative Analysis* (December 1985).

6. For an excellent discussion of floating-rate bonds, see Bradford Cornell, "The Future of Floating-Rate Bonds," *Issues in Corporate Finance* (New York: Stern Stewart & Co., 1984).

7. *Business Week*, February 5, 1972, p. 56.

8. See, for example, Bradford Cornell and Alan C. Shapiro, "Managing Foreign Exchange Risks," *Midland Corporate Finance Journal*, Fall 1983, pp. 16-31.

Perfect hedging against currency risk, of course, is impossible owing to the great uncertainty in estimating the likely effects of currency changes on operating cash flows.

result is a wash, with the exchange loss on its pound receivables being offset exactly by the gain on its pound liabilities.

In the case of non-contractual operating cash flows — those from future revenues and costs — the same financing principle applies. Perfect hedging against currency risk, of course, is impossible owing to the great uncertainty in estimating the likely effects of currency changes on operating cash flows. But often simple rules of thumb will suffice. For example, a firm that has developed a sizable export market should finance the portion of its assets used to create export profits in the currency of the country to which it exports. As a case in point, Volkswagen, which exported almost half its output to the U.S. prior to 1971, should have financed about half of its assets with dollar debt. The failure to do so almost bankrupt Volkswagen following the sharp appreciation of the deutsche mark beginning in August 1971. In 1974 alone, Volkswagen lost over $310 million by lowering its deutsche mark price in an attempt to maintain its market share.

Political Risk

The use of financing to reduce political risks typically involves mechanisms to avoid or at least reduce the impact of certain risks, such as those of exchange controls. It may also involve financing mechanisms that actually change the risk itself, as in the case of expropriation or other direct political acts.

Firms can sometimes reduce the risk of currency inconvertibility by appropriately arranging their affiliate's financing. This includes bank loans secured by deposits in the home country (back-to-back loans), investing parent funds as debt rather than equity (loan repayments are less tightly controlled than dividends), and using local financing to the maximum extent possible. Of course, such arrangements will be most valuable when the banks or local investors face significantly fewer restrictions or smaller risks — especially if the risk in question involves possible discrimination against direct foreign investors. Even if a particular political risk cannot be modified by shifting it from one firm or investor to another, a firm with substantial exposure will benefit by laying off such risks to investors with less exposure. This is the economic basis for commercial political risk insurance.

Another approach used by multinational firms, especially those in the expropriation-prone extrac-tive industries, is to finance their foreign investments with funds from the host and other governments, international development agencies, overseas banks, or even from customers, rather than supplying their own capital. Because repayment is tied to the project's success, the firm (or firms) sponsoring the project can create an international network of banks, government agencies, and customers with a vested interest in the fulfillment of the host government's contract with the sponsoring firm. In such a case, any expropriation threat is likely to upset relations with customers, banks, and governments worldwide.

Kennecott successfully employed this strategy to finance a $259 million copper mine expansion in Chile. First, Kennecott sold a 51 percent stake in its Chilean affiliate to the Chilean government for $80 million. The $80 million was reinvested in the mine and insured with the United States government against the risk of expropriation. Next, Kennecott arranged $110 million in equipment financing from the Ex-Im Bank, which was unconditionally guaranteed by the Chilean state. The Chilean government invested an additional $24 million in the mine. The remaining $45 million in financing was raised by writing long-term contracts for the future output with European and Asian customers, and then selling collection rights on these contracts to a consortium of European banks ($30 million) and a consortium of Japanese banks ($15 million).

Despite the subsequent rise to power of Salvador Allende, a politician who promised to expropriate all foreign holdings in Chile with "ni un centavo" in compensation, Allende was forced to honor all prior government commitments to Kennecott. This included paying Kennecott $80 million plus interest in compensation for the expropriation, as well as releasing Kennecott from any obligations incurred with the Ex-Im Bank, the Asian and European customers of the joint venture, and the European and Japanese bank consortia.

Product Market Risk

Some firms sell their project's or plant's expected output in advance to their customers on the basis of mutual advantage. The purchaser benefits from these so-called "take-or-pay" contracts by having a stable source of supply, usually at a discount from the market price. The seller also benefits by having an assured outlet for its product, which

[In the case of commodity-linked bonds,] the cost to the borrowers fluctuates directly with revenues, providing a hedge against declining commodity prices.

protects the firm against the risk of demand fluctuations, as well as a contract that it can then discount with a consortium of banks.

This technique was used to help finance Kennecott's Chilean copper mine expansion and the Soviet Union's natural gas pipeline to Western Europe. Similarly, in 1981, U.S. Steel Corporation financed a $750 million seamless pipe mill in Fairfield, Alabama by first securing long-term purchase contracts from about a dozen oil companies and oil field equipment suppliers. Those purchase contracts were then used to persuade lenders and equity participants to provide funds for the mill, which U.S. Steel leases and operates. The risk-reducing value of this financing technique became apparent when worldwide oil demand plummeted shortly thereafter and dragged down with it the demand for seamless oil pipe.

Some firms engaged in the extraction and processing of minerals protect against the risk of price fluctuations by issuing commodity-linked bonds. Examples include silver-indexed bonds issued by the Sunshine Mining Company and the oil-linked bonds issued by the Mexican government. The advantage to the issuers are two. First, investors demanded lower coupon rates on these bonds in recognition of their value as inflation hedges because, for example, their face values are indexed to commodities prices that might soar ahead of a general cost-of-living rise. Second, the cost to the borrowers fluctuates directly with revenues, providing a hedge against declining commodity prices. For example, when the price of silver declined, Sunshine Mining Co.'s cost of servicing its silver-linked bonds declined along with its operating revenues.

Similarly, financing linked to production shares (common in the oil industry) shifts product market risks to investors. Another example of a financing technique aimed at shifting market risk occured in 1981 when Oppenheimer & Company, a securities firm, sold a novel $25 million bond. The interest rate was indexed to New York Stock Exchange volume. Even though the rise in volume since then has raised the cost of servicing that debt issue, the higher volume also means that Oppenheimer is making a lot more money from brokerage commissions and other sources.

In all these instances, payments to investors rise and fall with the project's fortunes, thereby stabilizing the company's cash flows. It must be emphasized again that the purpose of the various financing techniques discussed in this section is to protect firms against unexpected changes in sales volume, prices, inflation, exchange rates, and the like. By definition, these changes are unpredictable and, consequently, impossible to anticipate at the time the financing is arranged. No other result would be consistent with the existence of a capital market with numerous well-informed participants.

Securing Access to Funds

A firm's operational flexibility depends, in part, on its ability to secure continual access to funds at a reasonable cost and without onerous restrictions. In this way, the firm can meet temporary shortfalls of cash and also take advantage of profitable investment opportunities without having to sell off assets or otherwise disrupt operations.

The ability to marshall substantial financial resources also signals competitors, actual and potential, that the firm will not be an easy target. Consider the alternative, a firm leveraged to the hilt, with no excess lines of credit or cash reserves. A competitor can move into the firm's market and gain market share with less fear of retaliation. In order to retaliate—by cutting price, say, or by increasing advertising expenditures—the firm will need more money. Since it has no spare cash and can't issue additional debt, it will have to go to the equity market. But, as a recent paper by Myers and Majluf points out, firms that issue new equity are suspect because of the asymmetric information relationship between investors and management (is the firm selling equity now because management knows the stock is overpriced?).[9] The problem of informational asymmetry will be particularly acute when the firm is trying to fend off a competitive attack. Thus, a firm that lacks financial reserves faces a Hobson's choice: acquiesce in the attack or raise funds on unattractive terms.

To ensure adequate financial reserves, a firm can maintain substantial unused debt capacity and liquid assets. It can also diversfy its fund sources and indirectly buy insurance through excess borrowing.

9. Stewart C. Myers and Nicholas Majluf, "Corporate Financing and Investment Decisions When Firms Have Information That Investors Do Not Have," *Journal of Financial Economics*, June 1984, pp. 187-221.

Having these extra financial resources signals competitors, as well as customers and other stakeholders, that the firm is financially healthy and has staying power; temporary setbacks will not become permanent ones.

Diversification of Fund Sources. A key element of corporate financial strategy should be to gain access to a broad range of fund sources to lessen dependence on any one financial market. A further benefit is that the firm broadens its sources of economic and financial information, supplementing its domestic information sources and aiding in its financial decision-making process.

For example, in January 1985, Signal Cos. issued $125 million of Eurodollar bonds even though it had $1.2 billion in cash and very little debt at the time. In the words of its chief financial officer, Signal "wanted access to a large capital market that's separate from the U.S. Next time, we may come to this market for $500 million and we'll know we can do a major offering at a substantial savings [to a comparable U.S. financing]."[10]

Similarly, in 1977, Natomas sold a $30 million Eurobond issue even though it could have obtained funds at a lower cost by drawing on its existing revolving credit lines or by selling commercial paper. According to Natomas, the key purpose of this Euroissue was to introduce the company's name to international investors as part of its global financial strategy.[11] Each lead underwriter was handpicked by the company with an eye to its overall financing needs. For example, a Swiss bank was picked as the issue's lead manager because Natomas felt that European banks, and Swiss banks in particular, have greater placing power with long-term investors than do U.S. underwriters operating in Europe. In addition, these European institutions were expected to serve Natomas as a source of market and economic information to counterbalance the input it already was receiving from U.S. banks.

This latter benefit of dealing with several financial institutions at once has been described by Richard K. Goeltz, Vice President-Finance of Joseph E. Seagram & Sons, Inc., as follows:

By being a major client at a number of high-quality firms rather than only one, we are able to avail ourselves of the knowledge, ingenuity and expertise of different groups of skilled professionals. No one bank is omniscient and omnipotent; we must be able to draw on the resources of many organizations.[12]

The threat of domestic credit controls has accelerated the trend toward global diversification of financing sources. For example, after the Federal Reserve Board tightened credit in October 1979 and proposed a voluntary ceiling on loan growth in March 1980, many anxious corporate treasurers feared that mandatory credit controls might be close at hand. So large numbers of them arranged to borrow abroad, far from the Fed's reach.

Monsanto, for example, negotiated a short-term credit line of nearly $200 million with eight European banks; Dow Chemical maintained about $1 billion in unused credit lines with foreign banks; and Ford Motor opened a $1 billion credit line with a group of banks, including some European banks. In the event the U.S. imposed formal controls, these firms planned to tap their foreign credit lines and repatriate the funds back home. According to John Rolls, Monsanto's treasurer, "To us, this credit line is insurance. We probably won't need it, but it's a good idea to have it."[13]

Similarly, Japanese firms such as Pioneer are issuing securities in the U.S. to familiarize American investors with their names. The purpose is to protect against the periodic credit controls imposed by the Bank of Japan by enabling them to turn to the American market.

Excess Borrowing. Related to the strategy of diversifying fund sources, most firms have lines of credit with a number of banks which give them the right to borrow up to an agreed-upon credit limit. Unused balances carry a commitment fee, normally on the order of 0.5 percent per annum. In order not to tie up funds unnecessarily, most banks periodically review each credit limit to see whether the customer's account activity level justifies that credit line. Some firms are willing to borrow funds that they do not require (and then place them on deposit elsewhere) in order to maintain their credit limit in the event of a tight money situation. In effect, they are buying insurance against the possibility of being out of the money market. One measure of the cost of this policy is the difference between the borrowing rate and the deposit rate, multiplied by the average

---

10. *Wall Street Journal*, January 23, 1985, p. 38.

11. "Diversifying Sources of Financing." *Business International Money Report*, September 23, 1977, pp. 297-298.

12. "Citibank Treasurers' Conference," June 28, 1984, p. 5. This is the text of a speech by Mr. Goeltz.

13. Anthony Ramirex, "Dodging the Fed," *Wall Street Journal*, April 17, 1980. p. 44.

amount of borrowed funds placed on deposit. Another cost may be considerable banker ill will if a corporation borrows when money is tight and does not use the money "productively."

Financial Leverage and Financial Distress

To the extent that risk affects the firm's sales and cost of doing business, and to the extent that financial leverage contributes to this risk, firms should voluntarily restrict the amount of debt in their capital structures. Reduced financial leverage is a way to signal a low-risk image to the firm's non-investor stakeholders, and thereby convince them of its intention to remain in business. This is an especially important consideration for those firms with a high ratio of intangible to tangible assets and with valuable reputations tied to their perceived longevity.

Minimizing Agency Costs

The recognition that ownership and control are largely separated in the modern corporation has important implications for financial strategy and, in particular, the selection of an appropriate debt-equity mix. Given this separation, there is little reason to believe that managers, who serve as agents for the owners, will always act in the best interest of the shareholders. The agency conflict between managers and outside shareholders derives from two principal sources.[14] The first is management's tendency to avail itself of some of the firm's resources in the form of various perquisites. The second important conflict arises from the fact that, as a manager's equity interest falls, his or her willingness to work hard and take risks in launching new products or businesses will suffer. It is this entrepreneurial spirit that is the driving force in any firm, and any business that lacks it will eventually decline. Thus, as outside equity accounts for a larger share of corporate ownership, there is a corresponding decrease in managerial incentive, resulting in higher agency costs. (In fact, I suspect that the role of leveraged buyouts in strengthening management incentives to perform is one of the major forces behind the proliferation of LBO's in recent years.)

With respect to debt, there is a similar incentive problem. Managers, as the agents of the shareholders, sometimes have incentives to expropriate the wealth of bondholders by taking certain actions after the debt has been sold that have not been anticipated by bondholders at the time they bought the firm's debt. In a highly leveraged firm, for example, well-diversified owners may be tempted to engage in highly risky projects where they will benefit greatly if successful. If these investments pay off, the owners gain handsomely; if the investments are unsuccessful, the bondholders bear most of the costs. On the other hand, if management's income is largely derived from the firm, management may be unduly risk averse, passing up profitable opportunities that the firm's shareholders would benefit from.

The net result of these agency problems is that the amounts and riskiness of future cash flows may not be independent of a firm's ownership structure. But as long as investors anticipate these agency costs, which they should in an efficient market, it is the firm and its managers — not outside investors — who bear the wealth effects of this divergence of interests in their attempts to raise capital. Recognizing that managers will at times make decisions at odds with the objective of share price maximization, outside investors will take these agency costs into account when valuing the firm's equity issues. Similarly, the negative effects of conflicts of interests between the firm's bondholders and its managers (as representatives of shareholders' interests) will be jointly borne by the managers and shareholders.

With respect to raising equity capital, suppose that in the absence of such agency costs investors would be willing to pay $100 for a share of stock. If agency costs are expected to reduce the value of the firm by, say, $15, outside investors will be willing to pay only $85 per share. In this way, the firm, and not outside investors, ends up bearing all anticipated agency costs.

Similarly, when the firm issues debt, potential bondholders will take into account the possible ways in which they can be hurt by the conflicts of interest that can arise between their interests and those of management (again, acting as representatives of shareholders' interests). As in the case of outside equity, in an efficient bond market, the firm will bear all the negative wealth effects of the agency costs of issu-

14. These insights first appeared in Michael Jensen and William Meckling, "Theory of the firm: Managerial Behavior, Agency Costs, and Ownership Structure," *Journal of Financial Economics*, October 1976, pp. 305-360.

Although the constraints imposed by lenders can avoid many of the potential agency cost associated with debt financing, they can also prove costly to shareholders by greatly reducing the firm's operating and investment flexibility.

ing debt. Debtholders will pass these costs along to the firm by discounting more heavily the cash flows promised in the loan agreement. Suppose, for example, that the firm promises to pay $100 in principal plus a $10 coupon in one year. If the risk-free interest rate is 10 percent, the bond will sell for $100, assuming that the risk of default is nil. But if there is, say, a 5 percent chance of complete default stemming entirely from agency problems — then the expected value of the money to be collected next year is $104.50 ($110 × .95). The price that an investor would be willing to pay today for this bond is thus only $95 ($104.50/$1.10), assuming there is no systematic risk (that is, no risk other than that associated with management's behavior). The net result is that an increase in the effective interest rate — in this case, from 10 percent to 15.79 percent — is necessary to compensate investors for this anticipated conflict of interest.

The fact that agency costs are borne by management and its shareholders means that firms wanting to raise capital in efficient markets have a strong incentive to minimize such costs and, in so doing, to reduce their costs of equity and debt. Thus management resorts to several different devices to provide, in effect, a "guarantee" to stockholders and bondholders that it will act in the interest of all investors. These include offering incentives to managers, such as stock options, to act in accordance with shareholder wealth maximization; bearing monitoring costs in the form of audits and other surveillance methods; and incorporating various restrictive covenants in bond and bank loan agreements.[15] If the firm violates any of these covenants, it can be declared in default on its debt and the loan becomes payable immediately. If the firm doesn't pay up or renegotiate the loan, it can then be forced into bankruptcy by its creditors.

Although the constraints imposed by lenders can avoid many of the potential agency cost associated with debt financing, they can also prove costly to shareholders by greatly reducing the firm's operating and investment flexibility. For example, lenders may veto certain high-risk projects with positive net present values because of the added risk they would have to bear without a corresponding increase in their expected returns; these returns are limited to

principal plus interest payments, no matter how profitable the firm's investments turn out to be.

The tightness of the restrictions varies but, in general, it depends on the perceived level of the firm's business and financial risk. Business risk, in turn, depends on how logical and well-articulated the firm's business strategy is. Financial risk is largely a function of the firm's business risk relative to its level of debt financing. This suggests the possibility that a well-prepared financial manager can favorably influence the types of restrictions that are imposed on the firm.

Negotiating Debt Restrictions

In negotiating the terms of a loan or bond issue, management must first identify unduly restrictive covenants and then try to minimize their effect. The most useful tool to determine whether restrictions are too tight is the financial forecast. Suppose, for example, that the bank wants to impose a limit on a firm's long-term debt-equity ratio of .8 to 1; the firm forecasts that next year's profits will be $6 million, long-term debt $20 million, and equity $27 million (including the $6 million in forecasted profit). A drop greater than $2 million in the firm's anticipated net income will cause a default. The importance of this debt ratio restriction, therefore, depends on the likelihood of such an earnings decline.

Once the most onerous restrictions are recognized, the financial manager can try to relax or eliminate them through negotiation. Part of the negotiation process involves attempting to convince lenders that such restrictions are unnecessary (that is, the lenders will still achieve their objectives with the remaining covenants) or even self-defeating (they are likely to reduce the firm's profitablility and, hence, its ability to repay its debts).[16]

Perhaps the most convincing aid in negotiating less restrictive covenants is competition. By shopping around among banks or other lenders, the firm can find out what their requirements are. Armed with this knowledge, the financial manager can then attempt to influence the lender to propose more acceptable terms. Failing that, the firm can consider borrowing from a less risk-averse or more understanding source, provided one exists.

15. For a discussion of bond covenants and how they are designed to control agency problems, see Clifford Smith and Jerold Warner, "On Financial Contracting: An Analysis of Bond Covenants," *Journal of Financial Economics*, 7 (June 1979), pp. 117-161.

16. For a more extensive discussion of how to negotiate restrictions on debt, see Jasper H. Arnold III, "How to Negotiate a Term Loan," *Harvard Business Review*, March-April 1982, pp. 131-137.

Banks Loans Versus Bonds

Problems of agency bear on the choice of using bank loans versus bond issues as well. Ordinarily, commercial banks are not considered to be part of the capital market. But the growth of floating-rate notes (FRNs) is increasingly blurring the distinction between syndicated bank loans (primarily Eurodollar credits) and bonds. Indeed, many of the participants on the borrowing and investing sides are identical for FRNs and bank credits. On the basis of similar economic and contractual terms for both instruments, many firms opt for the bank credit. Richard Goeltz, the VP-Finance of Seagram's cited earlier, explains this preference as follows:

There is an important advantage in dealing with individual bankers rather than an amorphous capital market. One can explain a problem or a need to account officers at a few institutions. Direct communications with the purchasers of FRN's are almost impossible. These investors, as is the case for most public issues, have litttle feeling of commitment to the borrower or sense of continuity...If the borrower can modify the terms and conditions of the former more easily and inexpensively than the latter, then the bank loan will be less costly, even if the effective interest rates are identical.[17]

Thus, the advantages of a bank credit are twofold: First, the firm can more readily custom-tailor a set of terms and conditions in face-to-face negotiations with its bankers than by trying to deal with a number of smaller investors that it never meets. Second, renegotiating certain covenants in response to changing circumstances is less cumbersome with a bank loan. These advantages stem from the personal nature of the relationship between borrower and lender. This implicitly assumes that bankers, who deal directly with the borrower, have lower costs of monitoring client activities than do bondholders.

If the room for discretion on the part of the bank over the years reduces the implicit cost of a bank credit compared with that of a bond, then the same logic should apply when judging a private placement and publicly-issued bond. Privately-placed debt is sold directly to a limited number of institutional investors like life insurance companies or pension funds. Such placements are especially valuable to firms with unusual requirements because of the ability to deal directly with the ultimate investor. By contrast, a public debt issue is sold to a potentially large number of unknown investors. Such issues usually contain fairly straighforward terms and conditions, thereby reducing the need for direct negotiation with the investor.

Summary and Conclusions

This article has attempted to provide a framework for firms to use in arranging their financing mix and choosing appropriate financing vehicles. The problem has been broken down into three largely separable objectives: minimizing after-tax financing costs, managing risks, and minimizing the agency costs caused by the incentives managers sometimes have to act in ways that harm bondholders or stockholders.

The primary emphasis is on taking advantage of financing choices that are "bargains" — that is, financing options priced at below-market rates. Bargains can result from the creative packaging and marketing of claims issued by the firm. More likely, they will be the result of distortions in capital markets due to tax asymmetries or government intervention; either of these may cause differences to exist in the risk-adjusted after-tax costs of different sources and types of funds.

Once the firm has taken advantage of any bargains available, it can then arrange additional financing in such a way as to reduce operating risks resulting from economic or political factors. Finally, we saw how the agency costs associated with the separation of ownership and control can influence the choice of capital structure and the use of public versus private sources of funds.

---

17. "The Corporate Borrower and the International Capital Markets," manuscript dated March 6, 1984, p. 5.

The Case for Convertibles

by Michael Brennan and Eduardo Schwartz, *University of British Columbia*

The Convertible Security

Until fairly recently, the popularity of convertible securities was something of a mystery to financial economists. To those well-versed in the literature of "efficient markets," there seemed no convincing reason why convertible bonds — which, after all, represent nothing more than straight debt securities combined with options on the company's stock — should provide issuing companies with financing benefits. Why, the question was asked, should sophisticated investors be willing to pay more (thus costing the corporate issuer less) for these securities in combination than for separate offerings of straight debt and straight equity?

The characteristic response from the business schools was to attribute the use of convertibles to a widespread, but relatively harmless delusion entertained by corporate treasurers and fostered (unwittingly or otherwise) by their financial advisors. This popular delusion, which continues to captivate a good number of investment bankers and their corporate clients, is that convertible bonds (or preferreds) are a cheap source of capital because (1) they carry coupon rates below the market rates of interest on straight debt (or preferred) and (2) they allow companies to sell stock at a premium over the current price.

The astute corporate treasurer has probably long suspected that such an apparent "free lunch" is tainted. And if he has had any exposure to theoretical finance and the modern conception of "cost of capital," his suspicions will have been confirmed. For there is general agreement—among academics, at least—that the real economic cost of convertibles to the issuing corporation is not reflected by the explicit interest rate (just as the dividend yield on common fails to represent the corporate "cost of equity"). The real cost of a convertible bond is considerably higher than the coupon rate; and, because of the conversion rights, it is also higher than the company's borrowing rate on straight and, for that matter, on subordinated debt. In fact, because of its hybrid nature — part debt, part equity — the cost of convertible debt is best thought of as a weighted average of the explicit interest charges, and the implicit opportunity costs associated with the conversion or equity option.

A New Explanation

It is probably true to say that the slow spread of the "gospel" of modern finance has had a modest success in dispelling the popular illusions surrounding convertibles. And that many corporate managers now perceive convertibles to be more expensive than they look. To the perplexity of academics, however, the popularity of convertibles has shown little sign of abating. Consequently, as "positive" financial economists, we have been faced with the task of finding a *convincing* explanation for the corporate use of convertibles — one that is consistent with rational investors and sophisticated financial markets.

In this article, after first examining the conventional arguments more closely, we offer a relatively new rationale for the use of convertibles. Instead of relying on the naivete of corporate financial officers or the marketing facility of investment bankers, our explanation centers largely on an important feature of convertibles: *the relative insensitivity of their value to the risk of the issuing company.* This insensitivity makes it easier for the bond issuer and purchaser to agree on the value of the bond — even when they disagree on the risk of the company — and, thus, to come to terms. It also protects the bondholder against the adverse consequences of management policies which would increase the risk of the company.

The market, as a general rule, exacts a premium for bearing additional uncertainty. Companies un-

The actual call policies of corporations depart significantly from this apparent optimal policy.

able to provide investors with assurance about the level and stability of their risks may be forced to bear interest costs on straight debt that are considerably higher than management's expectations would warrant. The advantage of a well-designed convertible, as we will argue, is that its value is not much affected by changes in company risk; and that investors are willing to provide funds on better terms when their uncertainties about risk are allayed.

The available evidence, moreover, supports our theory by suggesting that the companies issuing convertibles tend to be those for which uncertainty about risk is likely to be greatest; that is, the companies for which the costs of straight debt appear prohibitively (and needlessly) expensive. For large, mature corporations with strong credit ratings, however, there still appears to be no good reason for issuing convertibles.

The Call Question

In the third section of this article, we explore the issue of when companies should call their convertibles. The call provision, which is a feature of most corporate bonds, takes on added significance in the case of convertibles because of the holders' rights to convert into common stock.

But, if our theory is now better able to account for the corporate decision to issue convertibles, some mystery still surrounds the call decision — both the conventional corporate practice, and the market's response to the announcement of calls. Our theory provides a fairly simple rule for the corporation to follow in exercising its call option: namely, to call a convertible as soon as the conversion price exceeds the call price, while providing enough of a margin to ensure conversion.

The actual call policies of corporations, however, depart significantly from this apparently optimal policy. Convertible securities, whether bonds or preferred, are not generally called until their premium over the call price is significantly larger. Moreover, when corporations actually do call their convertibles their stock prices tend to decline, which seems to suggest that the decision to call convertibles is in general a mistake.

We provide answers to both of the questions: Why do companies delay so long in forcing conversion? Why does the market respond negatively when they finally do? But neither are completely satisfying. We can account for companies' actual call be-

havior only as the result of a common, but misguided concern with the effects of conversion on reported (undiluted) earnings per share. In response to the second of these puzzles, our best guess is that the market has come to associate forced conversions with companies anticipating hard times. As a result, announcements of convertible calls may be conveying negative information about management's outlook for the company.

In the final part of the article, we present the outlines of a model we have recently devised for the pricing and valuation of convertible securities. Our model, which incorporates the insights of the Black-Scholes Options Pricing Model (now widely used by professional option traders on the Chicago Exchange), permits analysis of the contributions of various features to the value of convertibles.

In designing a convertible bond contract, the corporate treasurer (and/or his investment banker) faces the complex problem of juggling conversion and call price schedules, coupon rates, maturity and other bond characteristics. The potential application of our model is to assess the value of a convertible with a given set of features or, alternatively, to estimate the effect of a change in one or more provisions on the value of the bond. It is also useful in arriving at decisions to force conversion.

The Common Misconception

The idea that the convertible offers a cheap source of finance stems from arguments of the following kind. Suppose, as might reasonably be the case, that if a company can float senior debt at 14 percent, it can also issue a convertible debenture with a conversion premium of 15 percent carrying a coupon rate of only 11 percent. The 15 percent conversion premium means that if the current stock price is $40, the bondholder has the right to convert into common at $46, or 15 percent above the current stock price.

Now if, as the conventional argument runs, the company performs poorly and the stock price does not rise, the bondholders will not find it advantageous to exercise their conversion option. The issuing company will then have obtained debt financing at a cost of 11 percent, or 300 basis points below the going rate for senior debt. On the other hand, if the firm prospers and the share price rises, bondholders will convert. For each $1000 raised, the company will have to issue 21.74 ($1000/$46) shares. In this case, management will in effect have sold common stock at the conversion price of $46, or 15 percent above the stock price at the time the funds were raised.

Thus, whether the bond is converted or not, the company will have done better with convertibles than with the alternative source of funds. Or so it seems.

The argument is beguiling because it involves sleight of hand. Notice that it compares the convertible with straight debt only when the company performs poorly, but compares the convertible with common stock when the firm performs well. This is similar to the argument that it is best to buy fire insurance on only 50% of the value of your house. If the house burns down, 50% insurance is better than none; and if the house does not burn down, 50% insurance is cheaper than full insurance.

This argument is clearly fallacious since it neglects to point out that 50% insurance is worse than full insurance if the house burns down, and more expensive than no insurance if the house does not burn down. Similarly, the convertible will turn out to be more expensive than common stock if the company does poorly, because the debt will still have to be serviced. If the company does very well, the convertible will have been more expensive than straight debt, for then the convertible bond purchasers will participate in the stockholders' profits.

It is clear that the case for the convertible cannot be made on the basis of this "heads you win, tails you also win" kind of argument. The convertible bondholder is perhaps best thought of as a kind of fair-weather stockholder and foul-weather bondholder. To compensate for the fact that he is not the ideal type of business partner, the convertible purchaser accepts less advantageous terms for the debt or stock with which he will finally end up: thus is the convertible coupon below the straight debt coupon, and the conversion price above the current stock price.

A somewhat stronger case can be made for the cost advantage of the convertible if it is assumed that the company's stock is significantly overpriced or underpriced. Suppose, for example, that the stock at $40 is so overpriced that management can be *sure* that the bond will not be converted. By issuing the convertible, the company would then be selling 14 percent debt at a cost of only 11 percent.

This is certainly an attractive proposition. But how often can management be sure that the conversion option is worthless, unless they are fraudulently concealing information about the company?

Moreover, in such circumstances, it would almost certainly be better to sell the overpriced stock itself.

Suppose, on the other hand, that the stock is so underpriced that management can be *sure* that the bondholders will convert. Then, by issuing the convertible, the company is in effect selling stock at the higher conversion price. In these circumstances, however, it would be even better to issue straight debt, retiring it with proceeds of a stock issue after the stock price has risen.

In general, arguments for convertibles based on the assumed mispricing of the common stock come down to nothing more than the observation that the convertible is a hybrid security—part stock, part bond. Therefore, if the stock is undervalued and so a costly source of funds, the convertible will be less undervalued. But straight debt, in this case, will be even less undervalued. If the stock is overvalued, the convertible will also be overvalued and therefore a less costly source of funds than straight debt. Common stock, however, will be even less costly. In short, the argument that the company's stock is improperly valued does not provide a sensible justification for issuing convertibles.

Why, Then, Convertibles?

If the traditional argument for convertibles does not deserve serious attention, is there another explanation for their popularity? And, furthermore, is this explanation consistent with the financing behavior of companies in American capital markets?

The institutional explanation of convertibles is that certain financial institutions are restricted as to the amount of common stock they can hold, and that convertibles provide a means by which such institutions can increase their equity position. There may be an element of truth in this. But the further suggestion that such institutions bid up the price of convertibles so that companies can reduce their financing costs by appealing to this restricted segment of the market is unlikely to be true.

A more reasonable account of capital market behavior would show that firms in aggregate supply enough convertibles to satisfy the demand of this segment of the market, so that there are no "scarcity rents"—or, in this case, major cost reductions—to be had. After all, chocolate manufacturers do not expect to make more money on sugarless chocolate because diabetics are prohibited from consuming the regular kind. By the same logic, this preference for convertibles by some institutions should not provide any significant cost reduction to companies issuing them.

A more convincing rationale for convertibles — one that has received a good deal of support in the academic finance community — centers on the effect of changes in risk on the value of securities. Recall that, as a general rule, the higher the risk associated with a company's operations (and the greater the market's uncertainty about that risk), the higher the interest cost that a company will be forced to pay. At least, on its straight debt. In the case of convertibles, however, higher risk may not mean a correspondingly greater burden of financing costs for the issuing company. That is, the use of convertibles may effectively shelter companies of high and indeterminate risk from prohibitively high costs of straight debt capital.

To see why this is true, note that a convertible is roughly equivalent to a package of straight debt and warrants. Instead of issuing a $1,000 bond which is convertible into 21.74 shares at a conversion price of $46, a corporation could issue a package of one $1,000 straight bond and 21.74 warrants with an exercise price of $46; and the consequences would be almost identical. Such bond-warrant combinations are indeed a quite popular alternative to convertible bonds.

How, then, would warrants in combination with a debt offering affect investors' perception of the risks involved in holding such securities? Although there are exceptions to this rule, companies with higher operating and financial risk tend to have more volatile stock prices. As noted earlier, companies with higher risk and, hence, greater price volatility pay higher rates for straight debt. And increases in the market's perception of a company's risk will cause a reduction in the value of its straight bonds.

The effect of increased risk and volatility on a warrant, however, is the opposite. Remember that the holder of a warrant profits from increases in the stock price above the exercise price, but is protected against declines below the exercise price. That is, there is an "asymmetry" in the return to the warrant which *increases* as the spread of possible future stock prices widens. In other words, as the risk and price volatility of the company increases,

the value of the warrant increases. For instance, a warrant on the shares of an electronics company will be worth considerably more than a warrant (with the same conditions) on a utility's shares.

In the case of a convertible security, then, the effect of an increase in risk on the cost of a straight debt offering is offset, to an extent, by its effect on the value of the warrant. As a result, the value of an appropriately designed convertible security (or its equivalent package of straight debt and warrants) will be largely unaffected by the risk of the issuing firm.

Practically, this means that two companies at different points along the risk spectrum, facing very different costs of straight debt, could issue convertibles with nearly identical maturities, conversion premiums, and coupon rates. Such a case is illustrated in Table 1. Note that while the terms of the

TABLE 1

Coupon Rates Required on New Issues of Straight and Convertible Debt

	Company Risk	
	Medium	High
Convertible Debt	11%	11.25%
Straight Debt	14%	16%

convertible debt sold by the medium- and high-risk companies are almost identical, the proportions of the convertible's value which are accounted for by the straight debt element and by the conversion feature will be quite different. For the higher-risk company, less of the convertible's value will be accounted for by the straight debt component, and correspondingly more by the conversion or warrant element.[1]

We are not suggesting, in this example, that convertibles offer higher-risk companies a "free lunch." We are arguing, however, that the inclusion of warrants in a debt package provides a kind of financing "synergy" which allows companies with high and uncertain risk to raise capital on more advantageous terms.

Consider the further case of a company whose managers believe it to be one of medium risk, but which is perceived by the market to be high risk.

---

1. This example is not meant to suggest that because the terms of the two convertible issues are nearly identical, the cost of the convertible is identical for the two companies. Remember that convertible debt is a hybrid security, partly straight debt and partly (a call option on the company's) equity. The opportunity cost of a convertible debt issue should thus be thought of as a weighted average of the company's cost of debt and equity capital. For the higher-risk company in this

example, the fact that it has both a higher cost of straight debt and a higher implicit cost of equity suggests that its convertible will have a higher implicit cost. But, more important, the fact that a much greater portion of the value of its convertible rests in the warrant or equity component means that the convertible holder has been promised a more substantial equity stake in the higher-risk company: this, of course, translates into a higher opportunity cost of capital.

Facing a 16 percent coupon rate, when companies of what it deems comparable risk are paying only 14 percent, the management of such a company may find straight debt prohibitively expensive. Although convertible debt will also appear expensive, because the company must pay 11 1/4 percent coupon instead of the 11 percent it considers reasonable, the effect of the divergence in risk assessment between management and the market is much less for the convertible than for the straight debt.

In such a situation, management will undoubtedly prefer to issue the convertible. Notice that the role of the convertible in this situation is independent of any mispricing of the stock. Even if the market and management agree that the stock is correctly priced, the convertible is still useful in resolving their disagreement over the risk of the company's operations.

The relevant risk is not only the risk of the company's existing operations, but also the risk of any future operations in which the firm may become involved over the life of the bond. It has been pointed out that the management of a company with straight debt outstanding will have an incentive to increase the risk of the firm, since the downside risk is borne by the bondholders while the upside returns accrue solely to the stockholders. In reasonably sophisticated capital markets, purchasers of straight debt issued by companies for which this behavior is a real possibility will demand a correspondingly higher coupon rate to compensate for this anticipated future risk. In this case also, the cost of straight debt will look high relative to the risk of the company's existing operations.

Because of their option on the firm's equity, however, purchasers of a convertible issue are likely to be much less concerned by the prospect of increases in the future risk of the company. For although an increase in risk would reduce the straight debt value of their bonds, it would also increase the value of the warrant element. Consequently, when there is doubt about the future policies of the company, the convertible is likely to be the preferred instrument. It should also be noted that because the convertible holders are protected against this type of expropriation, managements issuing convertible rather than straight debt reduce their own incentive to increase the risk of the firm simply to transfer wealth from the bondholders to the existing stockholders.

For the reasons offered above, convertibles are most likely to be used by companies which the market perceives as risky, whose risk is hard to assess, and whose investment policy is hard to predict.

The Evidence

The data on the corporate use of convertibles seem to be consistent with our theory. In a recent doctoral dissertation (1978), Wayne Mikkelson found that highly-levered and high-growth companies were more likely to issue convertibles. High leverage is certainly related to risk, and it is high-growth firms whose future investment is hardest to predict. Mikkelson also found that the longer the term of the issue, the more likely it was to contain a conversion feature. This is also consistent with the theory because longer maturities involve greater risks of a shift in companies' investment policies.

Interestingly enough, Mikkelson also found that convertibles are much more frequently offered publicly than placed privately. This is evidence against the institutional explanation of convertibles, which would have the demand for them coming primarily from institutions. It is also consistent with the stress our theory lays on uncertainty in risk assessment, since it is undoubtedly easier for the financial institutions involved in private placements to assess the risks of individual companies than for the public at large.

A more recent study by Donald Chew provides further confirmation of Mikkelson's findings. In an attempt to identify some of the financial characteristics which distinguish companies issuing convertibles from those issuing straight debt only, this study reported that over the period 1977-1980, convertible issuers tended to have higher market and earnings variability, and more highly-levered capital structures. They were also, on average, considerably smaller, younger, and growing more rapidly. All of these characteristics translate fairly directly into greater investor uncertainty about risk, and higher potential rewards associated with the conversion privilege.

Conversion and Call Policies

Having offered a corporate motivation for issuing convertibles, we now want to consider the question of conversion — first from the perspective of investors, and then from the standpoint of management formulating call policies for convertible issues.

A rational bondholder will not convert his bond as long as the coupon on the bond exceeds the dividends on the shares into which the bond is convertible — not unless the conversion privilege is about to expire or change adversely. By postponing conversion the bondholder continues to enjoy a greater income, and literally keeps his options open. Indeed, even if the dividend foregone exceeds the bond coupon, the investor may yet decide to postpone conversion because of the greater flexibility he retains.

The issuing company can, of course, induce bondholders to convert simply by raising the dividend on the common stock sufficiently high. At some point the opportunity cost of foregoing the higher dividend will ensure that bondholders voluntarily choose to convert.

If the bond is callable, and if the conversion value of the bond exceeds the call price, the bondholders can also be induced to convert by calling the bond for redemption. For example, if each $1000 bond is convertible into 25 shares of stock, and the share price is $50, the conversion value of the bond is 25 x $50 = $1250. Suppose that each bond is callable at $1100. If the company calls the bond, the bondholder may either redeem the bond at the call price of $1100 or convert the bond into common stock with market value of $1250. Faced with these alternatives, the bondholders will have no difficulty in deciding to convert the bond; and the company would be said to have "forced conversion" by calling the convertible.

When should a company call its convertibles? Assuming that management's objective is to maximize the value of the common stock, the appropriate policy — at least, in theory — is to call as soon as the value of the convertible reaches the call price. This will typically occur when the conversion value of the bonds is equal to the call price. Such a call policy minimizes the value of the convertible by putting the lowest possible lid on its value. That is, by forcing conversion or redeeming the issue, management effectively limits the value of the convertible by eliminating the warrant component — and the flexibility it provides the investor. Because the convertible represents a liability of the existing stockholders, acting to minimize its value increases the value of the common stock.

There are a couple of considerations which would make the proposed call policy somewhat impractical. First, bondholders typically must be given 30 days notice of call. Secondly, management may wish to avoid the costs associated with issuing new securities if the bonds are redeemed rather than converted into stock. The effect of these considerations on the optimal policy is to delay the call until the conversion value is sufficiently above the call price — high enough such that management can be reasonably assured that fluctuations in the stock price during the call notice period will not cause the investors to redeem rather than to convert the bonds.

A study by Jonathan Ingersoll of the University of Chicago has shown that using this modification of the original rule, the optimal timing for calling a convertible would be when the conversion value were, at most, 6-8 percent above the call price.

The actual call policies of corporations, however, do not even approximate this proposed optimal policy. In a 1965 survey of corporations with convertibles outstanding, Eugene Brigham of the University of Florida found that only 23 percent planned to force conversion as soon as conversion could be assured (the optimal policy); another 23 percent planned to encourage conversion by raising dividends; and the remaining 54 percent had no clear plans to force conversion. Ingersoll confirmed Brigham's results, finding that the median company among all firms calling convertibles between 1968 and 1975 waited until the conversion value of its bonds was 43.9 percent higher than the call price.

It is difficult to explain such behavior on a rational basis. It has been suggested that by forcing conversion, the company loses the advantage of the tax deductibility of interest payments on the bonds. While, in principle, this tax advantage could be regained by making a new issue of bonds and retiring stock, this kind of recapitalization involves additional underwriting costs. (Mikkelson found that only 23 of his 113 corporations forcing conversion replaced the debt.)

This tax-based rationalization of corporate call policies is further weakened by Ingersoll's finding that companies calling their convertible preferreds behaved in roughly the same way: the median corporation delayed call until the conversion value exceeded the call price by 38.5 percent. There is no corporate tax advantage associated with preferred shares.

Alternative explanations rely on notions of fair play and management concern with (undiluted) earnings per share. It is argued that it is unfair to deprive the bondholders of the full benefit of their conversion privilege; and that if the company enforces its call rights, it may experience difficulty in selling convertibles in the future. The idea, however, that corporate treasurers are constrained by these misdirected scruples (which, after all, will reward convertible holders only at the expense of the existing stockholders) seems far-fetched. Furthermore, the supposedly adverse consequences for future issues can be avoided by placing appropriate restrictions on the call privilege for those issues. Some convertibles, for example, restrict the corporation's right to call to periods during which the conversion value of the bonds exceeds the call price by a stated percentage. In the absence of such provisions, though, self-imposed restrictions on the use of the call privilege seem just silly.

Another motive for deferring conversion is management's concern with the effect on reported (undiluted) earnings per share. Conversion of outstanding bonds or preferreds will typically reduce this figure, spreading the company's earnings over a larger number of shares. To the extent that management believes the market value of its shares responds to announcements of accounting transactions without any economic consequences, they may wish to postpone this formal declaration that all future cash flows are now to be divided among a larger group of stockholders. In a reasonably sophisticated market, however, investors will have already anticipated the conversion, recognizing that fully diluted EPS provides a better guide to the value of the company's stock. Consequently, we remain a bit skeptical of the idea that excessive concern with the effect of reduced EPS on stock prices accounts for the widespread tendency to put off conversion.

There is, however, another reason for managers' heeding reported earnings per share — one consistent with rational behavior: namely, their compensation may be tied to this figure. If such is the case, then tying the bonus to undiluted EPS is creating the wrong incentive for financial managers, rewarding actions which detract from instead of contribute to stockholder value.

It is interesting to note, however, that management's alleged concern with the stock price implications of forcing conversion seems to find justification in Mikkelson's puzzling discovery that announcements of convertible bond calls are accompanied, on average, by a 2 percent *drop* in stock prices. In the case of forced conversions on preferred issues, the average market response is a negative ⅓ percent. It is unlikely that these negative reac-

tions are attributable to a systematic error by the market in interpreting the reported earnings figures.

Mikkelson tentatively attributes this market response to the tax effect discussed earlier; that is, the negative response reflects the market's recognition of the loss of the interest tax shield associated with the bonds. Some indirect support for this position is provided by a study[2] demonstrating a *positive* stock price response to companies that issue debt to retire stock, which is essentially the reverse of converting outstanding bonds. The problem with this explanation is that it implies that managements systematically make financial decisions which are contrary to the interests of their shareholders; and we are reluctant to rest with such a conclusion.

A more palatable explanation, and the one that we favor, would attribute Mikkelson's findings to an "information effect." That is, the market may have become conditioned to associate convertible calls with unfavorable events having nothing to do with the conversion. For example, if managements, in anticipation of difficult times, have a tendency to clear the decks of fixed and semi-fixed obligations by forcing conversion, the market would then come to recognize forced conversions as unfavorable auguries, and mark down the stock prices accordingly.

In summary, corporate call policies and their effects remain obscure. Managers seem to delay too long in exercising their call privilege. Yet the stock price tends to decline when they do exercise it. We have suggested that the delay may be due to management's concern with the negative effect on reported EPS. The negative stock price reaction to the announcement of a call may be attributable to tax effects or to information effects. We favor the information hypothesis because, unlike the tax hypothesis, it does not imply that managers are acting against the shareholder interest. At this point, however, we do not have the evidence to make any confident choice among these alternatives.

Pricing a Convertible Issue

At the outset, we stated that most of the existing models for valuing convertibles (and thus for pricing new convertible issues) are inadequate. Such models have been based on simplistic analyses which assume the future is known with certainty.

2. Masulis, R., 1980, "The Effects of Capital Structure Change on Security Prices: A Study of Exchange Offers, *Journal of Financial Economics*, Vol. 8, pp. 139-178.

The conversion option gives the bondholder the right to wait until current uncertainties are at least partially resolved.

The price of the company's stock is assumed to grow at a given rate; and on the basis of this assumption, conversion is assumed to take place a pre-determined number of years after the security is issued.

The problem with such models is their failure to reflect the essential feature of the convertible: the conversion *option* gives the bondholder the right to wait until current uncertainties are at least partially resolved before deciding to be treated as a fixed claim holder or as an equity investor. By assuming that the future evolution of the bond is known with certainty, conventional valuation techniques assume away the *raison d'etre* of the security. Recent advances in the theory of option pricing have enabled us to construct a richer model, which takes account of future uncertainties.

Our own research, in combination with the work on options conducted by Fischer Black of M.I.T. and Myron Scholes of the University of Chicago, has led to the development of a more realistic means of valuing and analyzing convertible securities. Our model relies on a fundamental principle underlying the Black-Scholes Options Pricing Model: namely, that the expected rate of return on a convertible security should be equal to the expected rate of return on an equivalent risk portfolio consisting of bonds and the company's common stock. Unlike the older certainty models, which are essentially static in nature, our model is a dynamic, continually-adjusting formula which enables the user to determine the effect of changes in several key variables on the value of the convertible.

Our valuation model takes the form of a fairly complicated differential equation, which yields the value of convertible securities only with the aid of a computer. But though the equation itself would probably have little meaning for readers unfamiliar with quantitative methods, a simplified account of what the model says about how convertibles are valued by investors can be compressed into a sentence or two.

The major determinants of a convertible's value are: the coupon rate on the bond (or the preferred dividend); the current level of interest rates (including the company's current yields on straight debt and preferred); the conversion price; the level *and* the volatility of the company's stock price; the dividend yield on the stock; the call provisions; and the maturity of the issue. The general relationships between a convertible's value and the major variables are these: The lower the coupon rate relative to the company's borrowing rates on straight securi-

ties, the lower the price of the convertible. The higher the stock price relative to the conversion price, and the greater the volatility of the underlying stock price, the higher the value of the convertible. Also, the lower the call price, and the sooner the call can be exercised, the lower the value. And, finally, the higher the common dividend, the lower the value of the convertible (since higher dividends mean less price appreciation).

There is nothing exceptional about the identification of these determinants, and the direction in which they affect convertible prices. The virtue of our model lies rather in its improved ability to analyze and quantify the effects of changes in these crucial variables on the price of a given security.

For the sake of illustration, consider the example described in Table 2. Given the bond characteristics summarized in this table and a measure of the risk (and volatility) of the company's common stock — and further assuming that both the investor and management follow the optimal conversion and call policies outlined earlier — our model estimates the value of the bond at $997 per $1000 of par value.

In Table 3, the results of a sensitivity analysis show the effect of changes in various parameters and bond characteristics on the value of the bond. For example, removal of the company's right to call the bond would increase its value by 3.5 percent, or $35 per $1000. On the other hand, also removing the conversion privilege, which would make the bond a straight non-callable bond, would reduce its value by 21.1 percent.

Note the relative insensitivity of the bond value to the risk of the firm. In this case, a 10 percent increase in risk results in a 1 percent increase in the value of the convertible. This supports the rationale for convertibles we offered above: they are likely to be especially attractive to an issuing company which is perceived as more risky by the market than by management. Such a company would be burdened by a penalty coupon rate on a straight bond issue, whereas it may actually benefit from the higher risk perceived by the market if it issues a convertible.

Table 3 also contains the kind of information which would be most valuable to an issuer in designing a convertible, because it enables management to determine the relative costs and benefits of various improvements and concessions in the basic terms of the issue. For example, a 6.4 percent reduction in the conversion price from $54 to $50.54 could be granted in return for a 10 percent reduction (6.4% x 5.0/3.2) in the coupon rate.

Convertibles are likely to be especially attractive to an issuing company which is perceived as more risky by the market than by management.

TABLE 2

Basic Characteristics of a Convertible Issue

Financial Markets

Treasury Bill Rate	15%
10 year Government Rate	11.46%

The Issuing Firm

Capitalization	1 million shares of common stock No Senior Debt
Stock Price	$44.02
Dividend/Share	$ 2.08

The Convertible Issue

Issue Size	$6 million
Coupon Rate	8%
Conversion Price	$54
Maturity	10 years
Callable after 5 years	
Recovery in Bankruptcy	⅔ of par value

TABLE 3

Bond Value Sensitivity Analysis

	Bond Value	Effect of Change on Bond Value
Basic Characteristics	$ 997	
Non-callable	1032	3.5%
Non-callable, non-convertible	787	−21.1
Stock Price: 10% increase	1045	4.9
Firm Risk: 10% increase	1007	1.0
Coupon Rate: 10% increase	1028	3.2
Conversion Price: 10% decrease	1047	5.0
Call Period Deferred: 1 year increase	1005	0.8
Call Price: 10% increase	1005	0.8

As the variety of possible bond contracts continues to increase, effective analysis of the alternative possibilities demands a valuation model of this type.

Conclusion

1. We have shown the fallacy in the conventional argument that convertibles are a cheap source of funds. That convertibles allow companies to borrow at below market rates and to sell stock at premiums over the present price does not mean that they provide cost advantages to the issuer. The real opportunity cost of convertible debt, reflecting its hybrid character, should be thought of as a weighted average of the company's cost of straight debt and the considerably higher cost associated with the conversion or equity option.

2. The most plausible rationale for the continuing popularity of convertibles lies in their insensitivity to company risk. This allows them to be issued on terms that look fair to management, even when the market rates the risk of the issuer higher than does management of the issuing company.

This rationale receives strong support from the available evidence. Companies issuing convertible bonds—over the last few years, at least—tend to be characterized by higher market and earnings variability, higher business and/or financial risk, stronger growth-orientations, and shorter corporate histories than their straight debt counterparts. Such companies stand to benefit most from convertible financing.

3. Although our theory suggests that management should force conversion of convertibles soon after the value of the security rises above the call price, companies tend to delay calling their convertibles well beyond this point. We surmise that this may be due to management's misguided preoccupation with reported earnings-per-share.

4. When a convertible call is announced, the company's stock price tends to drop. Although a tax-based explanation of this market response has been offered, we favor the "information" hypothesis suggesting that convertible calls are interpreted by the market as management's effort to clean up the balance sheet in the face of impending difficulties.

5. We offer a brief introduction to the Brennan-Schwartz valuation model for pricing convertible securities. By incorporating some of the insights of the Black-Scholes Options Pricing Model, the model represents a significant advance over the older static models of convertible pricing.

The Future of Floating-Rate Bonds

by Bradford Cornell
University of California, Los Angeles

The day-to-day functioning and efficiency of our economy are based, to a large degree, on the existence and continuing stability of many conventions. We all agree, for instance, to measure lengths and distances in units of (the metric invasion from Europe notwithstanding) inches, feet, and miles. By the same token, we measure the value of goods and services in terms of dollars. One of the most vexing consequences of inflation is that it undermines our basic unit of economic value. During the 1980 presidential campaign Ronald Reagan made political hay by waving a bill the size of a business card and calling it "the Carter dollar." Though the former President was not entirely to blame, Reagan's point was well taken. By the end of 1980 the purchasing power of the dollar was less than one-fifth what it was at the end of World War II.

Imagine the confusion that would have resulted if our units for measuring distance had shrunk at a similar rate. New York and Los Angeles would be over 15,000 miles apart and Chrysler's new K-car would be getting one hundred and twenty-five miles per gallon. What's more, blueprints would have to be adjusted each year, tool calibrations changed, speed limits revised, and maps redrawn.

If the future rate of decline in the unit of measurement were known with confidence, then these problems would not be too severe because all the adjustments could be made in advance. But consider the effect of an unexpected, random shrinkage — like that the purchasing power of the dollar has undergone recently—in our unit of distance. In this event prior adjustment would be impossible and a new method of measuring distance would have to be devised to avoid chaos.

Random inflation has a similar disconcerting effect on our financial markets. Each year, for instance, we know that inflation will produce a tax increase, but we don't know how large it will be. Where unexpected inflation proves especially disruptive, however, is in its effects on traditional financial contracts between borrowers and lenders. Just as blueprints cannot be based on an unstable and unpredicable measure of distance, financial contracts cannot be based on an erratically shrinking measure of value. If the rate of inflation becomes sufficiently unpredictable, both borrowers and lenders will become increasingly reluctant to bind themselves into conventional long-term fixed-interest rate contracts. Such a development, when carried to its final term, would lead to the disappearance of long-term fixed-rate debt markets in the U.S. Two basic financing options would remain: (1) exclusive reliance on short term debt or (2) the introduction of long-term indexed contracts, that is, floating-rate bonds. (Commodity-backed debt securities represent yet another financing approach to the condition of uncertain inflation; however, the principle of indexation underlying their effectiveness is fundamentally the same as that of floating-rate bonds.)

I also want to suggest that, even though our conventional corporate bond market is as yet far from defunct, there are some strong arguments for the use of floating rate debt under current capital market conditions.

It is important, at the outset, to keep in mind a clear distinction between the *level* and the *variability* of inflation. Confusion often arises because the two have historically gone hand in hand. Countries such as Brazil and Argentina, which have experienced high rates of inflation, have also had variable rates of inflation. In the United States as well, the rise in the level of inflation has been accompanied by an increase in its volatility. Because of this perceived, though not necessarily causal relationship, changes in financial contracting caused by

240

Just as blueprints cannot be based on an unstable and unpredictable measure of distance, financial contracts cannot be based on an erratically shrinking measure of value.

the increasing variability of the rate of inflation are often mistakenly attributed to the rising level of inflation. The distinction is important because a high but predictable rate of inflation will not cause a major shift to indexed contracting. On the other hand, a rate of inflation that is comparatively low on average, but highly variable, will lead to an increased reliance on floating-rate bonds.

Inflation and Indexed Bonds: Some Theory and Evidence

Any account of the major developments in interest rate theory begins inevitably with the American economist Irving Fisher, whose classic Theory of Interest (1930) has continued to provide the foundation for later enlargements of our theoretical framework. Applying principles of economic analysis combined with his own observation of capital markets, Fisher argued that, in a world where future rates of inflation are known by lenders and borrowers with complete certainty, interest rates would be made up of two components: (1) a relatively constant real rate of return and (2) an inflation premium equal to the annual expected rate of inflation over the life of the security. Formulated as an equation, Fisher's theory states:

$$i = r + E(p)$$

where i = the market or nominal rate of interest
r = the expected real interest rate, or expected real rate of return
$E(p)$ = The expected rate of inflation

All financial contracts thus contain, in the rate of interest, an implied rate of inflation anticipated by both borrowers and lenders. And all interest rates, in an economy experiencing a relatively stable and predictable level of inflation, will vary directly with changes in the expected rate of annual inflation.

It was not until the early 1970s that academic researchers devised a statistical method for testing the applicability of Fisher's theory to real capital markets, where actual borrowers and lenders are faced with an uncertainty about future rates of inflation. In a pathbreaking series of empirical studies, Eugene Fama, Professor of Finance at the University of Chicago, attempted to confirm the validity of Fisher's hypothesis by examining the returns on one-to-six month Treasury bills during the period 1953-1971. Fama found that the real or inflation adjusted returns were fairly constant over the entire period, and that nominal Treasury bill rates were reasonably accurate predictors of *actual* inflation over the duration of the bill.

Subsequent studies by Hess and Bicksler (1977) and Nelson and Schwert (1977), using more powerful statistical tests, were not fully consistent with Fama's original findings. Hess and Bicksler interpret their results as a rejection of the view that real returns are constant. Nelson and Schwert, more cautiously, offer two alternative explanations for similar findings: either (1) the *expected* real rate of return is variable or (2) the market is "inefficient" in its predictions of inflation; that is, the inflation premiums built into market interest rates by investors systematically either under - or over-estimate the actual rates of inflation experienced during the period.

Unfortunately, the statistical methods employed in the above tests did not enable the researchers to determine which of these explanations was correct. However, our own recent experience with interest rates would suggest that expected or required real rates of return have not been constant. In fact, at present, they appear to be climbing steadily toward ever higher historical highs. With the annualized rate of change in the CPI running at under 10% over the past year or so, Treasury bills appear to be earning real returns of nearly 6% (Fama's study of the period 1953-1971 estimated their average real return at close to 0%); 30-year Government bonds, which have historically earned real returns of 2-3% (and which theoretically reflect the market's consensus about long-term inflation), are yielding near a record high of almost 15%; and those fixed rate conventional mortgages which are still available are carrying average rates close to 18%, which would seem to be providing an astonishingly high real return for a secured loan.

Recent work by Lee Wakeman of the University of Rochester and Sanjai Bhagat of the University of Washington offers a plausible explanation of this apparent "unhinging" of interest rates from the expected level of inflation. Wakeman and Bhagat found that under conditions of uncertain inflation, a third term, representing an "inflation risk premium," should be added to the Fisher equation. In the modified equation,

$i = r + E(p) + $ **Inflation Risk Premium.**

As specified here, market interest rates are made up of a constant expected real rate, an inflation premium for the expected *level* of inflation, and an additional "inflation risk" or uncertainty premium which is largely a function of the *variability* of inflation and interest rates. The third term represents the "risk," attending even a nominally "riskless" security such as government bond, which is due to random changes in the purchasing power of the dollar. Recognizing this increased uncertainty or "inflation risk," rational investors now appear to be demanding a premium for bearing this relatively new (at least in the U.S.) kind of risk. What may now appear to be unprecedentedly high real rates of return may actually prove — as the results of this last study suggest — to have been relatively normal real rates of return combined with unprecedentedly high "inflation risk" premiums. All of which has come about, predictably, in the aftermath (or perhaps in the midst) of a period of the most volatile interest rates in our history.

The Rise of Floating-Rate Bonds?

Though uncertainty about future inflation has only recently been incorporated into models of interest rate formation, inflation risk is not new to American investors. They have grown accustomed to the fact that actual inflation rates can differ sharply from the rates they anticipated. In the l960s, as a prime instance of this divergence of inflationary reality from expectations, real estate lenders and borrowers clearly did not foresee the double-digit inflation of the 70s when they entered into 30-year mortgage contracts specifying an interest rate of only 7%. Currently, in the mortgage market, we are witnessing the consequences of increased "inflation risk:" while homeowners continue to receive a large windfall from financial contracts extending as far back as thirty years, lenders (most notably S and L's) remain strapped with portfolios of unprofitable loans and net worths which, in many cases, are negative when loans are carried at market value. Under these circumstances, it is not difficult to understand why mortgage bankers are demanding rates near 18% — even while inflation appears to be under 10% — for conventional fixed-rate mortgages. Nor would it have been hard to predict the fairly recent introduction and proliferation of adjustable - and variable-rate mortgages by mortgage bankers anxious to preserve the purchasing power of their principal.

These developments in real estate financing represent the most visible and dramatic version of changes that could come to pass in the market for long-term corporate bonds. Like mortgage bankers,

pension-fund managers and individual bondholders have been made painfully aware that long-term fixed-rate investments are a gamble — by *both* borrowers and lenders — on future rates of inflation. (In academic language, "inflation risk" is "symmetric;" that is, under a fixed-rate contract, "inflation risk" is borne both by borrowers and lenders.) When inflation turns out higher than anticipated, borrowers win at the expense of lenders; when inflation is lower than expected, lenders profit at the expense of borrowers.

Recent research in financial economics tells us, as might be expected, that for a given cost of funds or return on investment, borrowers and lenders attempt to minimize the "risk" or variability associated with that cost or return. This means that *both* borrowers and lenders will attempt to avoid gambling on inflation by minimizing their exposure to the uncertainty of future interest rate movements *unless* paid a premium for bearing "inflation risk."

Since both borrowers and lenders are exposed to inflation risk, they cannot both receive a premium. As the modified version of Fisher's model shows, borrowers will be able to induce investors to lend funds at fixed rates only by offering higher real rates of return which incorporate the premium for inflation uncertainty. Thus, in an economy with high and variable inflation, fixed-rate borrowers must not only bear their own exposure to inflation risk, but must also pay a premium to investors in the form of real rates of interest higher than those required under conditions of relatively stable inflation.

Given the possibility of still more volatile inflation, we can easily conceive of an impasse in long-term corporate bond markets in which investors find the long-term commitment too risky and corporate treasurers find the real rates of interest too costly. At this point, long-term fixed-rate financing would disappear to be replaced by increasing reliance on shorter maturities, and by floating-rate notes and bonds.

The Role of Floating-Rate Bonds

Although the similarity may not be immediately apparent, short-term financing and floating-rate financing are related strategies for reducing the borrowing company's exposure to "inflation risk." Recall that "inflation risk" arises because the actual rate of inflation diverges from the expected rate. If the maturity of a security is short enough, the divergence will be small. When the security matures,

We can easily conceive of an impasse in long-term corporate bond markets in which investors find the long-term commitment too risky and corporate treasurers find the real rates of interest too costly.

the funds can be "rolled over" or borrowed again at a new rate which reflects a revised or updated set of inflationary expectations. If inflationary expectations and interest rates are not changing too rapidly, inflation risk can be largely eliminated by continuously rolling over short-term debt.

Floating-rate debt provides, in effect, for an automatic rollover of funds through a periodic adjustment of the interest rate. These adjustments are generally tied to an "index" such as the CPI, the three- or six-month Treasury bill rates, or an average of short-term or long-term government securities. As an example, Citibank's floating-rate 15-year notes, issued in 1974, were set at 1% above the three-month Treasury bill rate and adjusted semiannually. Gulf Oil's 1979 30-year debentures, to cite another instance, carry a coupon rate that floats 35 basis points over an average of rates on 30-year government bonds.

The effect of such periodic adjustments of interest rates is to provide investors with the assurance that the purchasing power of their principal will remain reasonably constant. Our theory predicts that, granted this assurance, investors will reduce their required real rates of return by roughly the amount of the "inflation uncertainty premium." It was essentially this argument that Stanley Fischer, Professor of Finance at M.I.T., used to justify his contention (1975) that floating-rate or "index" bonds — in an economy experiencing unpredictable inflation — will be issued with lower interest costs and sell at lower yields than fixed-rate bonds of the same maturity.

By effectively guaranteeing the investor a fixed real return and the borrower a fixed real cost of funds, floating-rate bonds would eliminate the "inflation risk premium." Our theory further predicts that if inflation becomes more volatile, floating-rate notes and bonds—by removing the growing wedge of uncertainty between borrowers and investors which now threatens the future of our fixed-rate debt markets—could become the prevalent form of long-term corporate debt financing in the U.S.

Some Evidence: International and Domestic

International capital markets provide an interesting test and confirmation of our theory. In Argentina, Brazil, and Israel — three highly inflationary economies—the standard deviation of the inflation rate is approximately 50% per year. As our theory predicts, long-term fixed-rate financing is no longer available in the capital markets of these countries.

At the other extreme is the American experience of the 1950's and early 1960's, when inflation remained within a range of 0-4% per year. Under these conditions, as we would expect, long-term fixed-rate financing was almost universally employed by companies to fund long-term assets and growth.

Today the U.S. occupies a position somewhere between these two extremes. Most recent research —some of which has been reviewed in these pages — provides strong evidence that most of the variation in U.S. interest rates, at least since 1960, can be attributed to changes in the market's expectations about inflation. Our theory thus implies that reliance on long-term fixed-rate debt should have been on the decline during the latter part of the 1970s.

The evidence is abundant. Conventional 30-year mortgages appear to be on the way out. Federal and state banking authorities have been swamped by the variable-rate innovations that mortgage bankers have been devising to protect themselves against inflation. Commercial banks are coming to rely almost exclusively on floating-rate loans tied to the prime rate. In the Eurodollar market, we are seeing a form of implicit indexation incorporated into lending agreements. The common practice of Eurobanks is to designate both a *commitment* period, the length of time during which funds are made available to borrowers, and a *pricing* period, the time over which the interest rate remains fixed. While the commitment period may be as long as 10 years, the pricing period is rarely longer than three months. To keep the pricing problem from becoming too cumbersome, interest rates are usually set at a given differential over the London Interbank Rate, LIBOR. When the pricing period ends, the interest rate is automatically adjusted to maintain a constant premium over LIBOR. This procedure is essentially the equivalent of a corporate floating-rate note being sold to the Eurobank. In the domestic market, of course, the practice is effectively the same, with the prime rate substituting for LIBOR.

As additional evidence of the decline in fixed-rate financing, the average maturity of corporate debt has fallen dramatically, indicating that corporate treasurers continue to balk at paying historically high real rates while, at the same time, bearing unprecedented inflation risk (i.e., the risk that inflation and rates could fall sharply). And though floating rate bonds are still something of an oddity in today's markets, recent articles in *Business Week* and *Harvard Business Review* describing a "wave of adjustable-rate debt" attest to an increasing corporate interest in long-term indexed securities.

In spite of these developments, the long-term corporate bond market in the U.S., while far from flourishing, is not yet moribund. Its future viability depends largely on the success of Reagan's economic program in bringing down and stabilizing the rate of inflation. The number of new corporate issues has been greatly reduced by the increasing variability of past inflation, and the resulting uncertainty about future inflation and interest rates. As suggested earlier, the apparently all-time high real interest rates now demanded by investors can be explained as incorporating a relatively new "inflation risk premium." Further increases in inflation volatility and uncertainty, and the accompanying increases in *real* rates of return required by investors, could signal the end for conventional corporate bonds.

The Fixed vs. Floating Decision: from Theory Back to Practice

As long as the fate of the U.S. corporate bond market remains an open question, American companies will continue to have the option of choosing between fixed - and floating-rate bonds. In approaching this financing decision, corporate treasurers must cope with some practical problems which our theory fails to address.

The conventional rationale for using fixed-rate financing is that it ensures the predictability of future interest payments. While this view has merit, especially for the financial planner who is attempting to estimate future outlays for funding his company's growth, it should also be recognized that fixed rates provide certainty only about "nominal" as distinguished from "real" interest costs. Floating rates, which tend to move with the underlying rate of inflation, ensure a fixed real cost of debt. In a highly inflationary economy like that of Israel or Argentina, it is the relative certainty about "real costs" which constitutes the primary advantage of floating-rate debt.

To illustrate the practical problems, consider the hypothetical case of a corporate treasurer facing the fixed vs. floating decision. Assume that 30-year rates for single-A credits are in the 17-18% range. In

order to provide a sense of urgency, assume further that the company is supporting an unusually large amount of short-term bank debt with rates in excess of 20%, and that this build-up in short-term debt represented a conscious "bridge-financing" strategy based on management's conviction that a sharp fall in long-term rates was imminent. In light of recent experience, however, management is beginning to doubt its conviction that rates are about to fall. And thus, the corporate treasurer is giving serious thought to a long-term issue. What are the relevant considerations in choosing between fixed and floating rates?

In earlier pages, we argued that issuing floating-rate bonds would induce lenders to accept a lower average rate of interest over the life of the loan than that required on a fixed-rate issue. This argument, however, is subject to some qualification. First, it is difficult to design an indexed security whose return is perfectly correlated with changes in interest rates. In practice, therefore, the prices of floating-rate bonds vary within a fairly narrow range around par value. The difficulty in designing a continuously-adjusted indexed security which always sells at par value means that some inflation risk remains. The market's willingness to lower its required real rate of return for an indexed issue will thus depend, at least partly, on the treasurer's success and ingenuity in designing such an issue. Finally, it should be recognized that floating-rate bonds, because of their scarcity, may still be seen as suspect. The corporate bond market's relative unfamiliarity with such issues may also qualify our credible, though as yet untested, proposition that floating-rate bonds could be issued with lower rates under today's conditions. Nonetheless, recent research continues to confirm the sophistication and efficiency of our capital markets in pricing all kinds of securities.

Another practical issue involved in the fixed vs. floating decision concerns the *proper use* of the treasurer's expectations about the future direction of interest rates. Fixed-rate debt will result in an unexpected loss to the issuing company if inflation and interest rates go down. On the other hand, if the treasurer shares the other half of the market's skepticism about "Reaganomics" and thus believes that interest rates and inflation will move higher, then long-term, fixed-rate borrowing, even at current rates, could turn out to be the best strategy. The treasurer should bear in mind, however, that in efficient capital markets the long-term interest rates

Companies whose performance benefits from rising inflation will find that floating-rate financing stabilizes earnings, and thus reduces the perceived risk or variability of the business.

reflect the current consensus about the future level of interest rates. The corporate treasurer who decides the fixed vs. floating question on the basis of his interest rate "intuition" is betting he knows something that the market does not. Modern empirical research says that his chances of winning such a bet are not much better than 50%. Consequently, though some intuition about future interest rates will inevitably influence the treasurer's financing decision, he should not weight his intuition too heavily in assessing the pros and cons of floating rate debt. Senior management must decide whether speculation on interest rates is a legitimate function of corporate finance.

The most important consideration, however, is likely to be how the treasurer's company fares in an environment of sharply rising or falling rates of inflation. To the extent that the company's prices, revenues, and earnings are highly correlated with rates of inflation and interest, the use of floating-rate financing will stabilize or "hedge" its bottom-line earnings. This strategy is clearly illustrated in the case of Citicorp, whose $650 million issue in 1974 was the first floating-rate offering in the post-World War II era. For Citicorp, as for other banks and financial institutions whose floating-rate issues account for the greatest share of that market, the issuance of floating-rate notes was part of a comprehensive strategy to fund interest-sensitive assets (i.e., loans tied to prime and LIBOR) with interest-sensitive liabilities of similar maturities. Such a strategy assures the bank of a fixed interest spread or gross profit margin. For this reason, floating-rate notes and bonds are likely to become increasingly popular long-term financing vehicles for finanncial institutions whose revenues and operating earnings move in lock-step with inflation.

For industrial companies, the reasoning is the same. Those companies whose performance benefits from rising inflation will find that floating-rate financing stabilizes earnings, and thus reduces the

perceived risk or variability of the business. Conversely, companies in industries which are hurt by inflation will find that floating·rates accentuate the cyclicality of profits by matching high interest costs with low operating earnings in inflationary times, and low interest costs with high operating earnings under conditions of price stability.

Unfortunately, in many cases, the degree of correlation between an individual company's level of profitability and the rate of inflation may not be predictable. In dealing with such uncertainty, the treasurer may not want to expose the company to the risk that an inflation-induced reduction in profits will be associated with higher interest by using floating rates. (Remember, however, that "inflation risk" is "symmetric"; and by insulating his company from the possibility of higher inflation, the treasurer is also denying it the equal and opposite possibility of benefiting from lower than expected future inflation.) If, on the other hand, the treasurer is reasonably confident that his company's earnings (before interest) increase with the rate of inflation, issuing floating-rate bonds will reduce the variability of future earnings, as well as reducing the average *real cost* of debt relative to the cost of fixed-rate financing.

The Future

The Reagan administration claims to be bringing inflation under control. By 1984, they say, the days of high and variable inflation will be over. If they are right, then investment bankers and corporate treasurers need not concern themselves with the intricacies of floating-rate bonds. If, however, the rate of inflation continues to rise and become more variable, as it has in the past twenty years, then floating-rate bonds will become the predominant long-term instrument. It would be wise, therefore, for financial managers to prepare themselves for this possibility.

Is Deep Discount Debt Financing a Bargain?

by David Pyle
University of California at Berkeley

Introduction

Between mid-March and mid-July of 1981, 16 U.S. corporations raised almost $2 billion in debt funds by selling public issues of original issue discount (OID) bonds. Proceeds from these sales of OIDs accounted for nearly 30% of all corporate (excluding utilities)[1] debt financing during this period. Although prior to 1981 deep discount financing had been confined to private placements by lower-rated credits, the list of companies that have issued public OID debt is made up of major American corporations, with bond ratings ranging from A to Aaa. (For a listing of these issues, see Table 1.)

Among the 21 issues that have come out since the first public OID offering on March 10, most (17) were long-term (20-30 year) bonds with coupon rates set within the narrow range of 6 to 7-1/2 percent. Three of the issues were intermediate-term (7-10 year) zero coupon notes; and a single issue was convertible. My discussion of OIDs will focus on the non-convertible varieties: low coupon and zero coupon.

Why are companies using deep discount debt financing? More importantly, what are the real as distinguished from the alleged benefits of using this innovative debt instrument? The consensus among Wall Street analysts seems to be that OID debt

financing is a bargain because it lowers the issuing company's cost of debt capital. Their argument proceeds along two general lines. The first observes that OID bonds have been sold with lower yields-to-maturity than current coupon bonds issued by the same company. This reduction in yield is offered as evidence of a reduction of the company's cost of capital.

The second line of argument concerns the tax advantage of issuing OID debt rather than current coupon debt. The source of this advantage is the tax provision that allows companies to deduct a ratable proportion of the initial discount. The incremental tax savings from the amortizing the discount are said to provide a further reduction (i.e., in addition to the reduction provided by the interest deductibility of current coupon debt) of the company's after-tax cost of debt.

I will argue that the yield advantage of OIDs has been misrepresented by the investment banking community. Only the tax effect of OID financing is likely to provide the company with a real advantage — one which translates into a reduction of overall cost of capital. And, though this tax advantage is likely to be significant, the conventional argument supporting such an advantage is simplistic and thus somewhat misleading. In later pages, I will present some complexities of the tax effect which qualify the popular argument.

---

1. One of the earliest OID issues was a private placement by General Telephone of Florida. However, no public issues of OID utility bonds had been made when this paper was written. A recent news letter (*Corporate Financing Week,* August 3, 1981) reported that investment bankers are trying to help utilities find ways to overcome regulators' resistance to this financing innovation. As noted in Standard and Poor's "Perspective," dated June 15, 1981, utilities will be less interested in this financing approach if any tax savings that result must be passed on to their customers.

Only the tax effect is likely to provide a real advantage–one which translates into a reduction of overall cost of capital.

TABLE 1 Original Issue Discount Debt Issue	1981 Issued Date	Rating	Amt (Mil)	Issued Price	Ask Price	Trade Date	Estimated OID Rate Tax (Td)
Martin Marietta 7-11	**3/10**	**A**	**175**	**53.835**	**55**	**3/13**	**(.129)**
Transamerica Finl 6½-11	3/19	A	200	48.067	48	3/20	(.211)
Northwest Ind Inc 7-11	**3/18**	**A**	**125**	**52.75**	**52⅜**	**3/20**	**(.207)**
GMAC OID Debs 6-11	4/1	Aaa	400	44.51	44¾	4/3	(.226)
Eaton Corp OID Debs 7-11	**4/8**	**A**	**200**	**48.80**	**48⅞**	**4/10**	**(.202)**
City Svc OID Debs 7-11	4/9	A	300	49.941	49⅝	4/16	(.185)
ALCOA OID Debs 7-11	**4/22**	**A**	**250**	**48.362**	**48⅞**	**4/23**	**(.194)**
JC Penny Nts 0-89	4/22	A	100	33.247	33¼	4/23	(.313)
JC Penny OID Debs 6-06	**4/16**	**A**	**200**	**42.063**	**42⅜**	**4/23**	**(.200)**
ITT Finl Sr OID 6-½-11	4/29	A	200	41.89	42	5/1	(.233)
A-D-M OID 7-11	**5/12**	**A**	**250**	**46.246**	**47¾**	**5/15**	**(.200)**
Borg-Warner Accep 6-01	5/27	A	125	42.553	45	5/29	(.188)
Assoc Corp No.Am. 6-01	**6/17**	**A**	**150**	**45.125**	**44¾**	**6/19**	**(.204)**
GMAC Disc Nts 0-91	6/24	Aaa	750	25.245	25½	6/26	(.307)
General Foods OID 6-01	**6/23**	**Aa**	**150**	**47.58**	**47½**	**6/26**	**(.213)**
General Foods OID 7-11	6/23	Aa	200	51.624	50½	6/26	(.223)
IBM Cr Corp O-Cpn 0-88	**6/30**	**Aaa**	**150**	**39.164**	**39⅞**	**7/2**	**(.328)**
Dana Corp OID Cvt 5⅞-06	7/1	A	150	50	50¼	7/2	—
Phillip Morris OID 6-01	**7/9**	**A**	**250**	**42.8**	**43½**	**7/10**	**(.205)**
ITT Corp OID 6½-01	7/1	A	150	46.479	45½	7/10	(.226)
ITT Corp OID 7½-11	**7/1**	**A**	**150**	**50.218**	**48½**	**7/10**	**(.239)**

Source: "BOND Market Roundup," Salomon Brothers.

The Yield Advantage

The yield advantage of OID debt is largely, if not completely, illusory. Consider, for example, the case of Archer-Daniels-Midland (ADM), which floated two thirty-year bond issues on the same day: one carried a 7% coupon rate and was priced to yield 15.35%; the other had a 16% coupon, and was issued near par to yield 16.08%. To argue that the 73 basis-point difference between yields constitutes an advantage of OID over current coupon bonds is to ignore important differences in the features of the two issues. The most notable difference is that OIDs, which are typically callable at par, provide investors with protection from early redemption (because they are issued at such deep discounts from par value). By contrast, most current coupon bonds — icluding the ADM 16% bonds—give investors only a 10-year exemption before the issuing company is allowed to exercise its call privileges.

By simply lengthening this exemption period and providing investors with comparable call protection, the issuing company could sell non-callable current coupon bonds at yields lower than those on callable current coupon bonds. In fact, on the basis of some empirical studies, the 73 basis-point differential between the two ADM bonds could be attributed entirely to the difference in call provisions. For example, a study by Boyce and Kalotay (1979) estimated the value of a call on Bell Systems bonds to be about 30 basis points when long-term corporate bonds were yielding 8%. Judging from these results, a call value of 70 basis points or more in a 16% market does not seem out of line.

Another difference between OID bonds and current coupon bonds, which makes the direct comparison of yields even less meaningful, is in their cash flow profiles. This difference is greatest for zero coupon notes, where all of the cash flows are received by the investor at the date of maturity. For the low coupon bonds, the shift in the timing of cash flows (relative to that of current coupon debt) toward the maturity date is less pronounced. For instance, in the case of the ADM 7 percent bonds, the annual cash flow to the investor is roughly $0.15 per dollar invested as compared to slightly over $0.16 for holders of the (callable) ADM 16 percent issue. The final principal repayment per dollar invested, however, is over $2 for the 7 percent OIDs as compared to $1 for the par bonds.

When the term structure of interest rates is inverted (as it was throughout the period OIDs have been issued), this cash flow bias of OIDs toward the date of maturity causes the yield-to-maturity of OID bonds to be lower than the yield on current coupon bonds. As in the case of increased call protection, this reduction in yield, which merely reflects differences in the timing of cash flows received by the investor, does not represent a financing bargain for the issuing company.

Unless the term structure of rates is perfectly flat, there will always be yield differences which complicate the task of comparing OIDs and par bonds. Such differences, again, do not reflect any difference in the present value of the cost to the issuing company of servicing these bonds.

The Tax Advantage

The argument for a tax advantage from issuing OID debt, however, deserves serious attention. Current U.S. tax law permits companies using OIDs to deduct as interest expense a ratable proportion of the initial discount from par every year. The total discount is amortized on a straight-line basis over the life of the issue.

The potential advantage of this tax provision can be illustrated by considering the GMAC 0s due in 1991. The issue price was 25.25, which gives GMAC a total amortizable discount of 74.75 cents per dollar of par value. Amortized on a straight-line basis over the 10-year life of the notes, this discount provides a tax deduction of roughly 7.5 cents on each dollar of the face value of the issue. On each dollar of funds raised, this represents an annual tax deduction of 30 cents. At a marginal corporate tax rate of 46%, the amortization of the discount over the 10-year life of the notes reduces tax payments by roughly 14 cents per year for each dollar of funds raised. Thus, on GMAC's $750 million OID issue, which raised some $190 million in debt capital, the annual tax savings from amortizing the initial discount amount to some $26 million.

These tax savings, however, do not correctly represent the real tax advantage of OID financing. There is an offsetting factor which could cause the tax benefits to be overstated. OID bondholders are required to pay taxes on the same amortized discount which corporations use to reduce taxes. The extent of the tax advantage of OIDs will be offset, either partially or completely, by any taxes which OID bondholders pay on the amortized portion of the discount.

As I will show later, for there to be a tax advantage from issuing OID instead of current coupon debt, the marginal investor tax rates implied in the prices of OID's must be less than the marginal corporate tax rate. When the spreads between the implied investor tax rates and the corporated tax rates narrow, the tax savings to companies from issuing debt are offset by the higher pre-tax yields required by investors to provide them with a given after-tax return.

While OID debt would thus have the strongest appeal to tax-exempt (i.e., institutional) investors, we cannot assume that the pricing of OID debt is such that taxed investors are not drawn into the market.[2] Part of the analysis that follows attempts to estimate the investor tax rates implied by the actual prices of OIDs in the market. My research suggests that the implicit tax rates built into the pricing of OID notes and bonds are considerably below the corporate statutory rate of 46%, providing evidence that there is a tax advantage of issuing OID instead of current coupon debt. But because the implied tax rates are greater than zero, the tax advantage of OID financing has been exaggerated.

Demand Effects: What are the Attractions of OID Debt for Investors?

Before analyzing the potential tax advantage of OIDs, I want to examine more closely some of the features which are said to be stimulating investors' demand for OIDs, and which are thus believed to be providing the issuing companies with a cost advantage relative to the use of current coupon debt.

Call Protection

One of the advantages claimed for OID financing, as mentioned earlier, is the yield reduction gained by offering investors greater call protection. But whether the increased call protection of OID

---

2. In contrast with the view expressed by Livingston (1979), there is no reason to believe that the value of a long-term zero coupon bond would be negative, since the return on that bond for a non-taxed holder would approach infinity as the price approached zero. Even though such bonds might not be held by a taxed investor their pricing by non-taxed investors would imply a tax rate at which they could be held by a taxed investor.

debt provides an economic advantage to the borrowing company depends on the value the company places on the call provision associated with their current coupon bonds.

When issuing callable par bonds, the company makes the decision to pay for conventional call privileges (and the financing flexibility they provide) in the form of higher yields-to-maturity and lower issue prices. Only if the borrowing company places less value on the foregone call privileges than the yield investors are willing to sacrifice for increased call protection is there a real advantage to the company from this feature of OIDs. I know of no convincing argument why companies should treat the value of the call provision differently from investors.

While it is true that foregoing conventional call privileges reduces the cost of issuing debt, it does so by transferring risk from bondholders (who, in the event of an unexpected fall in rates, will have locked in their return) to the company and its shareholders (who, in the same event, will be prevented from refinancing at lower rates). Thus, such a reduction in the cost of debt is offset by an increase in financial risk, and in the company's cost of equity. The company's overall weighted average cost of capital remains unchanged.

If offering more call protection to bondholders were really advantageous (e.g., by reducing the company's overall cost of capital), borrowing companies could obtain roughly the same cost reduction by simply issuing current coupon bonds *without* the customary call provisions. The fact that only $200 million of non-callable current coupon debt was issued over the time period in question suggests that the increased call protection provided by OID debt — and the accompanying yield reduction — is not an important explanation of the recent OID debt phenomenon.

Reinvestment Risk

Another alleged attraction of OID debt is that, by paying a lower or no coupon, it substantially reduces the "reinvestment risk" faced by the lender or investor. This is a doubtful proposition at best.

It is not at all persuasive for low coupon OIDs, which account for about 85% of the funds raised through deep discount debt offerings. Consider again the two simultaneous issues by Archer-

Daniels-Midland. The annual cash flow before taxes per dollar invested from the ADM 7 percent OID bonds is $0.1513, while the comparable figure for the ADM 16 per cent OID bonds is $0.1608.[3] The investor holding the OIDs will be forced to reinvest almost the same amount as the holders of the current coupon issue. Hence, the protection from reinvestment risk provided by low coupon OIDs is negligible.

In the case of zero coupon OIDs, the popular argument for providing investors with protection from reinvestment risk must be considered more carefully. For, here the need to reinvest funds is entirely eliminated. But while this feature of zero coupon OIDs may be attractive to lenders seeking a guaranteed yield-to-maturity, it is important to recognize that every reinvestment advantage to the lender will be matched by an equal and opposite disadvantage to the borrower. If rates fall more sharply than expected, the investor holding zero coupon OIDs will avoid receiving coupon income that can only be reinvested at lower rates. At the same time, however, the company will have lost the opportunity to service those bonds with funds having (as a result of lower interest rates) a lower opportunity cost. Again, I know of no good argument for treating lender reinvestment gains and borrower reinvestment losses differently.

One last word on the question of reinvestment risk: the argument that locking in the yield-to-maturity is an advantage to the lender seems based on the assumption that future rates of interest are more likely to decline (i.e., to decline more sharply than is predicted in the present term structure of interest rates) than to increase. Neither the theory nor the evidence of modern finance provides any basis for this assumption; and thus neither supports the contention that the reduction of reinvestment risk provides a real advantage to the lender. If rates go up, locking in a yield-to-maturity will have proven to be a disadvantage since investors will not be able to reinvest at the higher rates. Lenders, therefore, are not likely to reduce their required rate of return for a guaranteed yield-to-maturity.

Price Leverage of OIDs

A related argument holds that OID debt provides greater speculative opportunities for investors. But, as illustrated in the ADM case above, cash

---

3. Recall that the coupon on the 16s is higher than that on a comparable, non-callable bond.

When the personal tax rate built into corporate bond yields becomes sufficiently large, the tax advantage is completely negated.

flows per dollar invested in low coupon OID bonds are similar to the cash flows from funds invested in current coupon bonds. Therefore, the price volatility of long-term, low coupon OID bonds will not be much different from that of comparable current coupon bonds.

A more aggressive version of the OID price leverage argument contends that the relative volatility will be greater for price increases than for price decreases. To be sure, the price volatility of zero coupon bonds will be greater than the volatility of a comparable current coupon bond. And thus, for zero coupon bonds (or for long-term OID bonds with lower coupon rates), total return gains and losses from a change in the level of interest rates would be larger than for comparable current coupon bonds. However, if returns are measured properly, it is not true, as some analysts have claimed, that the difference in gains on OID bonds would be consistently greater than the difference in losses for a given percentage change in the level of rates.[4]

Although the price volatility of zero coupon bonds will be higher than that of comparable current coupon bonds, the effect of the greater price volatility for bondholders is clearly symmetric with its effect on shareholders; that is, any benefit to bondholders from such price volatility translating into a lower cost of debt (which, again, is highly improbable) will be offset by an increase in shareholders' required return. It should be noted, however, that zero coupon bonds do offer opportunities for interest rate speculation to some investors (e.g., pension funds) that are often precluded from using interest rate futures markets; such investors may be willing to pay a premium for this speculative opportunity.

Transaction Costs

To the extent that investors in OID bonds can avoid the transactions costs associated with the reinvestment of interest payments or with immunization programs, a company's use of OIDs would have the effect of reducing those investors' required rates of return and, thus, the interest cost of such issues to the company. Avoiding the transactions

costs due to coupon payments would also provide an advantage to the issuing company. But, again, while these advantages might be significant for zero coupon OIDs, they would not be important for the low coupon debt that has predominated among OID issues.

Swaps

One of the special uses of low coupon OIDs is to replace old, deep-discounted bonds (bonds issued at par that have gone to discount) in the portfolios of tax-exempt investors. Old discounted issues contain a potential asset—namely, the capital gains tax savings—which has value only for a taxed investor. For this reason, in a bond market that includes taxed investors, a bond that has gone to deep discount will sell at a premium relative to (i.e., at a lower yield than) a newly issued OID bond with the same coupon. A swap of the deep-discounted bond for an OID bond with the same coupon rate provides a gain for the tax-exempt investor. It also allows institutions to avoid the realization of book losses which, in many cases, is prevented by actuarial restrictions.

These par for par swaps appear to have been one of the major reasons for the private placements of OID bonds that occurred before the first public issue by Martin Marietta. In the case of the public issues, the fact that there are a large number of old intermediate-term deep discount bonds in the 6 to 7-1/2 percent range may partly explain the clustering of OID coupons in the same range.

The Tax Advantage of OID Debt

The suggestion that there is a tax advantage to a corporation from issuing debt rather than equity would probably appear obvious to most corporate financial officers. It is not as well known that the tax deductibility of interest by the corporation is not a sufficient condition for such an advantage. The tax advantage of debt relative to equity also depends on the personal rate of taxation on interest income relative to both the marginal corporate tax rate and the tax rate on share income.

---

4. Analyses of the gains and losses on OID debt relative to current coupon debt for given changes in the level of interest rates have been based on holding period rates of return. These analyses are only valid for an instantaneous rate change of the assumed size. A more useful approach would be to compare log price relatives over the period. The alleged asymmetry in price volatility is likely to disappear with this alternative approach.

The same condition that provides a tax advantage from using current coupon debt instead of equity results in an additional tax advantage from the use of OID relative to current coupon debt.

A simple example should illustrate the point. Suppose that the tax rate on share income is zero and the tax rate for the marginal holder of corporate bonds is greater than zero. Under such a condition, for a taxed investor to hold a company's bonds, the interest rate on the bonds would have to be sufficiently greater than the (risk-adjusted) required return on shares so that the marginal investor would be as well off *after taxes* as with common stock.

Because investors are concerned about after-tax rates of return, investor tax rates are an important determinant in the setting of (pre-tax) interest rates. The yields-to-maturity on all debt securities contain an implied investor tax rate. For instance, if a tax-exempt 30-year bond is yielding 12%, and a taxable corporate bond of comparable risk is yielding 15%, the implicit tax rate of the marginal investor holding those corporate bonds is 20%. If, however, the marginal holder of the same bonds were in the 50% tax bracket, then the yield would have to rise to 24% in order to induce him to hold those bonds. From this example, it should be clear that the advantage of the tax deductibility of interest to the corporation can be offset by the taxability of interest to investors. When the personal tax rate built into corporate bond yields and prices becomes sufficiently large, the tax advantage of debt financing is completely negated by the increase in investors' required pre-tax return (i.e., the coupon rate) on those bonds.

In an article entitled "Debt and Taxes" (1977), Merton Miller argued that, in a world where the corporate use of debt was not limited by factors such as the costs of bankruptcy and concerns about financing flexibility, companies would continue to issue debt until the tax advantage was fully exploited.[5] The supply of corporate debt would increase—and yields would rise—to the point where there would no longer be a tax incentive for issuing more debt. To view it from the demand side, corporate debt would continue to attract all investors in increasingly higher tax brackets until the marginal personal tax rate on interest income would be as large as the marginal corporate tax rate.

The same condition that provides a tax advantage from using current coupon debt instead of equity results in an *additional* tax advantage from the use of OID relative to current coupon debt. That is, if the personal tax rates implied in the yields of OID and par bonds are equal to each other and less than the company's marginal tax rate, OID bonds will provide a greater tax advantage than current coupon bonds.[6]

Another important determinant of the size of the incremental tax advantage of OIDs — as will become clear later—is the extent to which the marginal investor tax rates implied in the prices of OIDs are less than the tax rates implied in the pricing of comparable current coupon bonds. If the tax rates pricing OIDs become sufficiently larger than the rates pricing par bonds (even when investor tax rates are less than the corporate tax rates), the incremental tax advantage of OIDs will be eliminated.

There is one other condition which must be satisfied for the tax advantage of OID's to be as stated. Financing with OID debt must not impose more financial risk on the company's shareholders than current coupon debt financing. It is widely believed that OIDs, especially the zero coupon variety, add greater financial risk to the issuing company by deferring the repayment of interest as well as principal. That GMAC, for instance, must repay $3.96 in 1991 for every $1 borrowed on its zero coupon notes in 1981 is said to increase the default risk of these bonds. If such a contention were true, then this increased risk would also increase the risk of the common equity, which could offset the effect of the tax advantage to the company.

Contrary to the popular view, OID financing *per se* does not impose more financial risk on the company (or on OID bondholders) than does current coupon debt. Under reasonable assumptions about a company's dividend and investment policies, including the reinvestment of tax savings from the use of OID debt, it can be demonstrated that although OID financing requires a much larger final repayment, the potential increase in default risk associated with this larger payment at maturity will be neutralized by the accumulated and reinvested tax savings which can be used to fund the final payment. Thus, I can find no legitimate support for the notion that OID financing results in an uncompensated increase in the financial risk of the issuing company.

---

5. In the context of the marginal comparison made above, a non-tax factor would limit corporate debt supply if it induced anticipated after-tax costs for shareholders from the issuance of more debt without a commensurate increase in the after-tax return perceived by lenders.

6. If instead of constant tax rates we assume that future tax rates may vary from today's tax rates, a similar proposition holds involving a weighted average of the anticipated future tax rates. The most critical tax factor for the tax efficiency of OID debt is the anticipated spread between the marginal corporate rate and the marginal personal tax rate on interest income over the life of the OID bond.

Measuring the Tax Advantage

Wall Street analysts generally estimate the tax advantage of conventional debt financing by calculating the annual tax savings to the company. Expressed as an equation, the tax advantage is represented as follows:

FORMULA I

$$VTS = C_p \cdot T_c \cdot B$$

where **VTS** is the annual tax savings from using current coupon debt instead of equity

C_p is the annual coupon rate on a current coupon bond

T_c is the marginal corporate tax rate (assumed constant over time)

B is the face value of the bond issue

These annual savings are then usually discounted at the company's borrowing rate to obtain an estimate of the present value of the tax savings to the company.

The problem with this formulation of the tax advantage is that it ignores the effects of personal taxation on the required yields of current coupon bonds. Only if the tax rate implied in the pricing of the company's bonds is equal to the tax rate implied in the pricing of its shares will the above equation correctly represent the real tax advantage of debt financing.

The importance of personal taxes can be illustrated by returning to the case in which the marginal tax rate on share income is zero while the marginal tax rate pricing a company's bonds is positive. In this case, the equation for the annual tax savings as viewed by the company's shareholders becomes:

FORMULA 2

$$VTA = C_p \cdot (T_c - T_p) \cdot B$$

where **VTA** is the annual tax savings (adjusted for marginal investors' tax rates) of current coupon debt financing

T_p is the tax rate of the marginal investor which is implicit in the price and current yield of the bond.

This equation incorporates the offsetting effect of positive investor tax rates on the advantage of corporate interest deductibility. Recall Miller's argument that, as companies exploit this tax advantage, the supply of bonds will increase and the tax rate pricing them will be driven up until the tax advantage is eliminated. In the above case, as the equation makes clear, this could occur when the marginal personal tax rate pricing bonds is equal to the marginal corporate tax rate $(T_p = T_c)$.

In presenting the tax advantage of (low coupon) OID relative to current coupon debt financing, the popular Wall Street analysis typically estimates the present value of the annual tax savings from deducting the amortized discount. The value of these savings is then translated into an equivalent yield reduction (roughly 50 to l00 basis points on a long-term issue).

As suggested earlier, this kind of analysis is incomplete because of its failure to account for positive investor tax rates implied in the prices of both OID and current coupon debt securities. The real tax advantages of *OID debt over current coupon debt*, which must also take into account the tax advantage that could have been obtained raising the same amount of funds with current coupon debt, can be estimated by using the following equation:[7]

FORMULA 3

$$VOID = D(T_c - T_d) + [Cd(T_c - T_d) \cdot B^1] - [C_p(T_c - T_p) \cdot B]$$

where **VOID** is the annual incremental tax advantage of the OID bond relative to current coupon debt.

D is the total annual discount amortization from the OID bond with face value B^1 (or raising an amount of funds equal to B)

T_d is the marginal tax rate pricing the OID bond.

C_d is the annual coupon rate on the OID bond.

B^1 is the face value of the OID issue

B is the face value of a current coupon issue which would raise the same amount of funds as the OID issue

The first term of the equation represents the annual tax savings (adjusted for OID investor tax rates)

---

7. If the marginal tax rate for share income is positive, the tax advantage of debt will be greater than that given by the equation. I will assume zero taxes on share income throughout the rest of this article. Since the major objective will be to compare the tax benefits of OID bonds with those of current coupon bonds, this assumption is not critical.

from amortizing the discount. The second and third terms represent, respectively, the tax savings from the interest deductions using OIDs and the tax savings foregone by not raising the same amount of funds with (non-callable) current coupon bonds.

This equation leads to the following conclusions about the real tax advantage of OID debt relative to current coupon debt financing:

1. The greater the spread between the corporate tax rate and the personal tax rate implied in the pricing of the OID bonds, the larger the tax advantage of OID financing. The incremental tax advantage of OID debt disappears when the corporate tax rate is equal to the personal tax rate.

2. The greater the spread between the tax rates implied in the pricing of current coupon bonds and those implied in the pricing of comparable OIDs, the greater the incremental tax advantage of OID debt financing. For a given marginal tax rate pricing OIDs, an upper limit on the tax advantage exists if the marginal tax rate pricing current coupon bonds is as large as the corporate tax rate $(T_p = T_c > T_d)$. A conservative estimate of the incremental tax advantage can be calculated under the assumption that the marginal tax rates pricing OID and par bonds are equal. $(T_d = T_p < T_c)$.

3. For a given term structure of interest rates, the tax advantage of OID debt increases with the level of rates.

4. Although this is not immediately apparent from the above equation, the lower the OID coupon rate, and thus the larger the initial discount, the larger will be the incremental tax advantage. This statement is also true for zero coupon bonds, where the tax advantage is greatest.

Using a variant of the above equation (see Appendix 2), I calculated estimates of both an upper and lower limit of the incremental tax advantage of each of the twenty non-convertible OID issues listed in Table 1. These limits, as suggested, reflect two extreme assumptions about the variable "T_p", the tax rate pricing comparable current coupon bonds. In estimating the upper limit, I assumed the marginal tax rate pricing par bonds was equal to the corporate tax rate $(T_p = T_c > T_d)$. If the tax rate on share income is assumed to be zero, this condition results in the maximum spread between the implied tax rates of OID and current coupon bondholders

(since companies would not issue current coupon debt when T_p becomes larger than T_c).

In estimating the lower value of the OID tax advantage, I made the assumption that the marginal tax rates pricing OIDs and par bonds were equal ($T_p = T_d < T_c$).While it is possible for the implied tax rate pricing OID bonds to be greater than that of current coupon bonds, my estimates of implied OID investor tax rates (see Table 2) make this possibility seem unlikely.

To use Formula 3, one needs a means of estimating the implied investor tax rates (T_d) on OIDs. Furthermore, in order to derive the present value of the incremental tax savings, one also needs an estimate of investors' after-tax discount rates.

Market discount rates (after-tax) for calculating the present value of the annual tax savings from the use of OIDs were estimated by using the yields on municipal bonds of comparable risk.[8] By using these discount factors together with the market prices of OID bonds, I calculated estimates of the implied personal tax rates of the marginal investors holding those bonds. (See the last column of Table 2.) For low coupon OIDs the implied investor tax rates range from 13% to 24%, with the average tax rate estimated at 20.5%. For zero coupon notes, the implied tax rates are somewhat higher, ranging from 31% to 33%.

One must use some care in interpreting these estimates of investor tax rates. The important thing to recognize is that these estimates do not necessarily represent the tax rate of the marginal holder of a given OID issue.[9] In some cases, they may instead reflect a complex relationship between the actual tax rates of OID investors and the tax rates pricing available current coupon bonds. (For a more detailed interpretation of these tax estimates, the ambitious reader is referred to Appendix 1.)

Having estimated implicit tax rates and discount factors, my next step was to calculate upper and lower limits on the present value of the incremental tax advantage (assuming a marginal corporate tax rate of 46%) for each of the OID issues in the sample. As the results in Table 2 show, the incremental tax savings on OID debt are impressive. Under the more conservative assumption, the estimated present value of annual tax savings from using OID debt amounts to nearly $200 million on the $2 bil-

---

8. Salomon Brothers new issue, municipal bond scales were used to obtain estimates of the present value of after-tax flows at future dates. Prime general obligation yields were used to obtain estimates of the after-tax requied return on Aaa corporate bonds, medium grade general obligation yields for Aa corporates, and good grade general obligation yield for A corporates. One should note that some analysts would not agree with the use of municipal bond rates as estimates of the incremental tax savings.

9. As suggested earlier, even if OID bonds are being held by non-taxed investors, the pricing of such bonds may be consistent with their being held at the margin by a taxed investor.

TABLE 2
Present Value of After-Tax Debt Service Cost Savings: OID vs. Current Coupon Debt

Present Value of Savings per $1 of Debt Funds		Total Raised (Millions)	Lower Limit on Total Savings on Issue	Estimated OID Rate Tax (Td) (Millions)	Issue
Upper Limit	Lower Limit				
.47	.10	94.2	9.4	(.129)	**Martin Marietta 7-11**
.41	.10	96.1	9.6	(.211)	Transamerica Finl 6-½-11
.39	.08	65.9	5.3	(.207)	**Northwest Ind Inc 7-11**
.39	.10	178.0	17.9	(.226)	GMAC OID Debs 6-11
.41	.09	97.6	8.8	(.202)	**Eaton Corp OID Debs 7-11**
.41	.09	149.8	13.5	(.185)	City Svc OID Debs 7-11
.43	.10	120.9	12.1	(.194)	**ALCOA OID Debs 7-11**
.21	.10	33.2	3.3	(.313)	JC Penney Nts 0-89
.44	.14	84.1	11.8	(.200)	**JC Penney OID Debs 6-06**
.40	.11	83.8	9.2	(.233)	ITT Finl Sr OID 6-½-11
.44	.12	115.6	13.2	(.200)	**A-D-M OID 7-11**
.46	.16	53.2	8.	(.188)	Borg-Waner Accep 6-01
.43	.13	67.7	8.8	(.204)	**Assoc Corp No. Am. 6-01**
.29	.16	189.3	30.3	(.307)	GMAC Disc Nts 0-91
.39	.11	71.4	7.9	(.213)	**General Food OID 6-01**
.37	.07	103.2	7.2	(.233)	General Foods OID 7-11
.15	.06	58.7	3.5	(.328)	**IBM Cr Corp O-Cpn 0-88**
.43	.14	107.0	15.0	(.205)	Phillip Morris OID 6-01
.37	.10	69.7	7.0	(.226)	**ITT Corp OID 6-½-01**
.35	.07	75.3	5.3	(.239)	ITT Corp OID 7-½-11
TOTAL		**1914.7**	**197.5**		

Weighted Average of the present value of cost savings per $1 raised = .10

lion in OID funds raised between mid-March and mid-July. This represents an average tax savings of roughly 10 cents on every dollar of debt raised or, equivalently, a 10% reduction in the issuing company's cost of debt capital. If we consider the upper limit, the estimated incremental tax savings on the long term OID debt is between 35 and 47 cents on every dollar of funds raised.

In reading Table 2, one should recognize that the tax savings on OID bonds of different maturities cannot be directly compared. The effect of different maturities on my estimates is best illustrated by the three zero coupon issues. The incremental tax savings from these issues were estimated to be between 6% and 15% for the 7-year issue, 10% and 21% for the 8-year issue, and 16% to 29% for the 10-year issue.

A rough comparison between the tax advantage of a 10-year zero coupon issue and the tax advantage of a 30-year low coupon OID can be made by setting the present value of the incremental tax savings from a sequence of three 10-year issues against the savings on the 30-year bond. On this basis, the tax savings from the sequence of three GMAC 10-year zero coupon notes (priced like the GMAC 0s of 1991) would be between 24 cents and 48 cents on each dollar raised, as compared to 10 to 30 cents from the GMAC 6s of 2011. And, if adjusted for the effect of shorter maturities, the estimates in Table 2 would show a decided tax advantage from issuing zero coupon OIDs instead of the 6 to 71/2% coupon OIDs that have predominated among public OID issues.

Conclusions

1. The only significant advantage from issuing OIDs is the tax advantage. And even the tax advantage, though substantial, has been exaggerated by popular analysis, which fails to account for positive tax rates implied in the actual prices of OID bonds. The tax advantage of OID financing exists only insofar as the marginal corporate tax rate is greater than the implied investor tax rates pricing that debt.

2. The incremental tax savings from an OID bond of

a given maturity increase as the coupon on that bond becomes smaller. This conclusion is not apparent from Table 2 because the estimates do not control for the effect of the different maturities of the issues. Using these controls, however, the analysis does show the incremental tax savings on the Transamerica Financial 6½s to be greater than those on the Northwest Industries 7s, and the tax savings on the Phillip Morris 6s, to be greater than those on the ITT Corp 6½s.

The tax advantage of zero coupon OIDs is greater than that of low coupon OIDs because of the larger tax deductions provided by the larger initial discounts. And though direct comparisons in the Table between the tax advantages of zero coupon and low coupon bonds are not meaningful, a crude comparison would proceed along the following lines: If GMAC had issued a 10-year OID note with a 7% coupon that was priced by the same marginal tax rates as their zero coupon issue, the 7% notes would have sold at 64% of par. The approximate range of the present value of the incremental tax savings of the 7% notes would have been 3 to 16 cents on each dollar of funds raised, as opposed to 10 to 29 cents on the zero coupon notes. In short, if GMAC had issued 10-year OID notes with a 7% coupon, the incremental tax savings would have been about half of those obtained using a zero coupon issue.

3. The use of zero (and lower) coupon OIDs may be constrained by the amount of taxable income that a company can generate.[10] Consider the tax income implications of the GMAC 0s of 1991. With $190 million of zero coupon notes, GMAC must generate $57 million in taxable income each year to use its entire tax shelter. If GMAC had instead issued $190 million in current coupon notes at 16%, the company would have had to generate only $30.4 million in annual taxable income to offset its interest payments, and thus benefit fully from the debt tax shelter. For the typical low coupon 30-year OID bond in my sample, the required taxable income is less than 20 cents per dollar of debt funds raised, which is not very different from the required taxable income on a comparable current coupon bond. Thus, limits on anticipated future taxable income may explain the scarcity of zero coupon issues. This taxable income effect also suggests that we will find OID bonds, and especially zero coupon bonds, being issued by companies with relatively predictable future taxable income.

The Future of OID Debt

As suggested earlier, the existence of a tax advantage from issuing OID debt depends on the implied investor tax rates being lower than the marginal corporate tax rate. If there were an unlimited pool of tax-exempt investors available to purchse OIDs, we could confidently predict that the tax savings of OIDs would continue to represent a significant tax advantage to companies.

As companies continue to bring OID issues to market, the demand by tax-exempt investors will have to be supplemented by investors with increasingly higher tax rates, pushing up pre-tax yields and offsetting the corporate tax savings. This process, especially in the case of zero coupon OIDs, could continue — at least theoretically — until the tax incentive for issuing more OIDs is exhausted. This, however, seems only a remote possibility.

Nevertheless, investment bankers and financial analysts have suggested that the yield differentials between OIDs and current coupon issues are beginning to narrow. This observation, if correct, suggests that the supply of tax-exempt and low-taxed OID investors may be somewhat limited. As companies are forced to move along the demand curve for OIDs from tax-exempt toward taxed investors, the yields required by OID holders may rise relative to those required by current coupon holders. Thus, the companies that have already issued OIDs may have exploited the largest real tax benefits.

But, even with this narrowing in yield differentials, the present tax treatment of OIDs continues to provide issuing companies with significant tax advantages. Barring a major decline in corporate tax rates, or a sharp contraction in the available supply of tax-exempt (and low-taxed) investors, these tax advantages can be expected to persist. In short, OID debt seems here to stay unless its tax advantage provokes a change in the tax law.

---

10. The question of an optimal policy as a function of a company's future income prospects is being pursued in current research.

The Income Bond Puzzle

by John McConnell and Gary Schlarbaum,
Purdue University

Income bonds should be used more extensively by corporations than they are. Their avoidance apparently arises from a mere accident of economic history — namely, that they were first employed in quantity in connection with railroad reorganizations, and hence they have been associated from the start with financial weakness and poor investment status. But the form itself has several practical advantages... Chief among these is the deductibility of the interest paid from the company's taxable income.

— Benjamin Graham

... Income bonds, in sum, are securities that appear to have all the supposed tax advantages of debt, without the bankruptcy cost disadvantages. Yet, except for a brief flurry in the 1960s, such bonds are rarely used.

The conventional wisdom attributes this dearth to the unsavory connotations that surround such bonds. As an investment banker once put it to me: "They have the smell of death about them." Perhaps so. But the obvious retort is that bit of ancient Roman wisdom: pecunia non olet (money has no odor).

— Merton Miller

Introduction

The 1980's promise to be an exciting decade for American capital markets. Recent descriptions of our financial environment have featured such problems as capital shortages, inflation at unprecedented rates, and more than the usual amount of volatility and uncertainty in the credit markets. It is a time of financial innovation; deep discount bonds,

GNMA pass-through securities, and financial futures and options are only a few of the new financing instruments that are now being developed and introduced at an unusually rapid pace. It is also a time of financial crisis, in which several very large publicly-held firms have failed or approached the brink of failure.

In such an environment, it is important for the practicing financial manager to be familiar with the full array of financial instruments at his disposal. Our intention in this article is to draw attention once again to a frequently advocated, but infrequently used class of corporate security: the income bond.

Before investigating this income bond "puzzle," let's first review the features of the income bond.

Characteristics of Income Bonds

Income bonds are hybrid instruments which combine the features of straight debt securities and preferred stock. Like straight debt, income bonds are a contractual obligation of the issuer; they give the holder a claim on the company's earnings that ranks ahead of all equities, preferred and common. At the same time, however, they represent a contingent claim: interest is payable only if earned. And, because the income bond is in fact a debt instrument, the interest payments are tax deductible to the corporate issuer.

That the payment of coupon interest depends on the level of the issuer's reported accounting earnings, is, of course, the most important characteristic distinguishing income bonds from other debt instruments. If sufficient accounting earnings are available after the deduction of operating expenses, allowable fixed asset depreciation, and interest payments with a prior claim on income, then the interest due on the income bonds *must* be paid. But if reported earnings (after deduction of the various allowed expenses) are not sufficient to cover contingent interest payments, the corporation may pass the payment with no change in the ownership structure of the company.

Thus, when a contingent interest payment is omitted, the bond technically is not in default, and bondholders obtain no additional control over the company (except for the possible future claim to accumulated interest). In contrast, when an interest payment is omitted on a fixed-interest bond, it is considered to be in default, and the bondholders may force the company into bankruptcy.

It is also worth noting, however, that income bonds can take on many of the characteristics of more conventional forms of debt. They may be callable, convertible into common stock, or subordinated to other classes of debt securities. They may contain sinking fund provisions. Also, and perhaps most important, the income bond, like preferred stock, may contain a provision for the accumulation of missed interest payments. As in the case of the dividend payments on both preferred and common stock, the interest payments associated with income bonds are "declared" by the board of directors. As a consequence, unlike other corporate bonds, income bonds trade "flat," or without accrued interest.

An Historical Perspective

Income bonds were first employed extensively in the railroad reorganizations that followed the panics of 1873, 1884, and 1893. After this period, income bonds were rarely used until the depression years of the 1930's. The Interstate Commerce Commission decreed that income bonds had no place in well-balanced capital structures and, in one extreme case, required the substitution of preferred stock for an income-bond issue.

During the 1930's companies with large funded debts and cyclical incomes found it necessary to reduce the fixed-income segment of their capital structures; income bonds were useful for this purpose, and were issued by both public utility and industrial firms. Around 1940, the ICC relaxed its position on income bonds, allowing for a marked increase in their use, mostly by railroads undergoing reorganization. And, in a dramatic departure

from the prior decades, a number of solvent railroads issued income bonds in the early 1950's.

In a 1955 article published in the *Harvard Business Review*, Sidney Robbins surveyed the use of income bond financing by solvent corporations, and identified four or five industrial companies that had used them. Robbins noted that while income bonds afford virtually all the benefits of other debt instruments, they do not present the danger of "default risk" associated with conventional debt. That is, income bonds offer management greater flexibility when they need it most—when earnings are down. Other writers have also argued that income bonds offer all the advantages of preferred stock while providing the tax advantage of debt.

In the decade following Robbins' article, another handful of industrial companies floated small income bond issues. In fact, the president of Sheraton Corporation wrote a letter to the editor of the *Harvard Business Review* indicating that Sheraton had become interested in income bonds as a direct result of Robbins' article. (Sheraton ultimately sold $35 million of income bonds.)

In addition, several more railroads issued income bonds after publication of Robbins' article and, in 1961, Trans World Airlines completed an income bond financing. But, as characterized by Robbins, the use of income bonds remained "sparse and intermittent."[1]

One notable exception to the general neglect of income bonds was the financing strategy of Gamble-Skogmo. In the mid-1960's, this large and prominent retail company built its financing program around the use of income bonds. The company first issued $15 million of income bonds in 1966, and thereafter entered the market every year through 1976. By 1976 Gamble-Skogmo had over $200 million of income bonds outstanding. Indeed, by 1974, the company had more income bondholders than common and preferred stockholders.

From the cases of Gamble-Skogmo, TWA, and the railroads, it is clear that income bonds have had a number of strong advocates among practitioners of corporate finance. Further, the writings of Robbins and other financial observers (see epigraph) are evidence of an income bond following among finance theorists.

Why, then, have income bonds not been used more frequently? There is a considerable amount of reluctance on the part of investment bankers, issu-

---

1. Robbins, S., 1974. *An Objective Look at Income Bonds*, Boston: Envision.

Income bonds have had a number of strong advocates among practitioners of corporate finance.

ers, and investors that must be overcome before income bonds will be used extensively. Gamble-Skogmo, it should be noted, encountered such strong resistance from investment bankers that it had to form its own securities company to distribute its income bonds. But surely, in a competitive environment, if companies had been serious about pursuing income bond financing, they would have found investment bankers willing to accommodate them.

The Possible Explanations

The most widely accepted explanation of the general reluctance to issue income bonds is that the bonds were tainted by their association with the reorganization of bankrupt railroads. Because these securities carry the "smell of death," those investors — the argument seems to imply — that can be induced to hold income bonds will demand rates of return higher than the returns justified by the actual level of risk of holding such bonds. In other words, income bonds will be persistently undervalued relative to other securities, forcing the company to pay an abnormally high price for its capital.

Another possible explanation involves the tax deductibility of the interest payments made to income bondholders. There has never been a definitive ruling on what is necessary to establish that income bonds are indeed debt. Thus, there remains a fear that the tax laws may be changed such that income bond payments will be treated like preferred stock dividends.

A third explanation for the scarcity of income bonds is the potential for "deadweight costs" associated with this form of financing. Because the computation of earnings is crucial in determining whether income bondholders will receive interest payments, conflicts between stockholders and income bondholders can arise over the company's accounting methods. The concern is that, in the resolution of such conflicts, the company may incur substantial legal fees.

In the remainder of this article, we examine each of these proffered solutions to our income bond puzzle. The first and most complicated part of our analysis investigates whether the returns actually earned by the holders of income bonds have been "too high"—that is, higher than the returns we would have expected, given the relative risk of holding the bonds. Using past experience as the best guide to the future, we offer evidence on the *histori-*

cal risks and returns to income bondholders as our best estimate of the prospective cost of income bond financing to corporations.

In subsequent sections, we look more closely at the tax considerations, and the alleged "deadweight costs" associated with income bonds. In the final section of our article, we offer some additional evidence which suggests that the stock market responds favorably to the substitution of income bonds for preferred stock in corporate capital structures.

Returns and Pricing of Income Bonds

Bond Sample and Selection Procedure

In attempting to determine whether income bondholders receive returns that are "too high" for their level of risk, we followed the procedure described below.

First, we compiled a sample of 53 income bonds issued by public corporations, whose historical price quotes and records of interest payments over a fairly long period of time were available. This constituted the minimum information necessary to reach statistically reliable conclusions.

Using month-end price quotes combined with the "declared" interest payments, we calculated monthly rates of return for our income bond portfolio over the period January 1956 through December 1976. (In the Appendix we have listed the name of each issuing company in our sample, the original issue and maturity dates of each bond, the coupon rates, the dates on which each bond entered and left the sample, and the reason given by the company for issuing the bond.)

After measuring the actual returns of our income bond portfolio, we measured its risk. As specified by the Capital Asset Pricing Model (the last two articles in this issue provide a detailed elaboration of CAPM) the "normal" or "expected" rate of return of any security, or portfolio of securities, is directly proportional to its risk. Consequently, once we have measured the portfolio's risk, establishing expected rates of return for income bonds is fairly straightforward.

In the final stage of our analysis we compared the actual returns earned by income bondholders to the risk-adjusted expected returns. Any difference between these two we called the "abnormal" return. If income bonds truly have the "smell of death about them," and thus are systematically underpriced at

We calculated monthly rates of return for our income bond portfolio over the period January 1956 through December 1976.

issue, we would expect income bondholders to have earned significantly positive abnormal returns. If the abnormal returns were negative, however, then we would conclude that income bonds have been a cheap source of capital relative to conventional stock and bond financing.

Preliminary Results

In order to make our results more intelligible it would probably be helpful to explain briefly our procedures for measuring the risks and expected returns of income bonds.

If we imagine all corporate securities ranging along a spectrum of risk (and expected return), we would expect to find straight senior secured debt at the lower extreme; and corporate equities and, even riskier, common stock warrants at the upper extreme. Investors' average risk and returns on income bonds would be expected to fall somewhere in between these extremes. Because of the more uncertain claim represented by income bonds, they should (all else equal) be more risky than a randomly selected portfolio of fixed-interest, high-grade corporate bonds. We would also expect the income bond portfolio to be considerably less risky than a randomly selected portfolio of common stocks.

Because investors are rewarded, on average, according to the level of risk they bear, we expect riskier assets to yield higher rates of return. Thus, we would expect the common stock portfolio to provide higher average returns than income bonds, which, in turn, should provide higher average returns than the portfolio of high-grade corporate bonds.

How, then, do we measure the risk of income bonds? Perhaps the most intuitively appealing measure of a security's risk is the variability of its price. Higher variability means, of course, a higher probability of very large returns, but also a higher probability of substantially negative returns. A common statistical measure of the variability of a series of returns is the standard deviation. The broader the spread, or the more variable the returns, the higher the measured standard deviation.

The standard deviations of the returns earned by these three classes of securities (i.e., portfolios of income bonds, common stocks, and fixed-interest bonds) is consistent with our expectations (see Table 1). Over the period 1956-1976, the variability of income bond returns was greater than the variabil-

TABLE 1

Sample Statistics, Monthly Returns: 1956-1976

Statistic	Income Bond Portfolio	Common Stock Portfolio	Portfolio of High-Grade Fixed-Interest Corporated Bonds
Average Monthly Rates of Return	.54%	.74%	.32%
Standard Deviation of Monthly Rates of Return	2.80%	4.08%	1.87%
Lowest Monthly Rate of Return	−5.53%	−11.70%	−4.76%
Highest Monthly Rate of Return	14.83%	16.42%	8.85%

ity of high-grade corporate bond returns, but less than that of common stocks.

Further, if we provisionally accept the standard deviation of returns as a measure of risk, the estimated average monthly returns of the three classes of securities can be compared to determine whether the income bond returns are too high relative to returns on straight debt and equity.

The results recorded in Table 1 confirm our expectations. The average monthly return for the common stock portfolio was 0.74 percent, for income bonds, 0.54 percent, and for fixed-interest, high-grade corporate bonds, 0.32 percent. As expected, the portfolio with the highest risk, common stocks, also had the highest average return. Income bonds, the intermediate risk portfolio, provided returns almost exactly mid-way between common stocks and straight debt (the lowest risk portfolio).

Thus, at least on a preliminary basis, there is nothing to suggest that the returns on income bonds are extraordinarily high.

Risk-Adjusted Returns on Income Bonds

We also used a more technically precise measure of risk to test whether income bonds provided abnormally high returns over the period 1956-76. Where the prior analysis ranked the three portfolios' returns according to their total risk (i.e., total variability of returns), we then assessed whether the income bond returns were normal for their level of *systematic* risk (i.e., co-variability with the market).[2]

Briefly, our procedure was to estimate the systematic risk (known as "beta") of the income bond portfolio.[3] Using the Capital Asset Pricing Model, we generated an estimate of expected or "normal" returns for income bonds using the alternate (systematic) measure of risk. The actual returns provided by the income bond portfolio were then compared with the "normal" return to estimate "abnormal" rates of return.

To repeat our earlier hypothesis, if income bonds provide returns to investors that are too high — implying an extraordinarily high corporate cost —the estimated abnormal rates of return should be systematically positive. If, on the other hand, income bonds are priced to provide returns commensurate with their level of risk, the series of abnormal monthly returns should be distributed randomly around zero, with an average abnormal return not significantly different from zero.

Our estimate of the average abnormal return on the income bond portfolio was only −0.07 percent which, in a statistical sense, is not reliably different from zero. The same calculations for the portfolio of fixed-interest, high-grade corporate bonds are shown in the second column of Table 2. The average abnormal return for this bond portfolio is a positive 0.39 percent per month, which also is not reliably different from zero.

The results in Table 2 thus support our assertion that the market properly assessed the risk of, and investors earned a fair return on, income bonds over the period 1956 to 1976. Our results do not support the contention that income bonds are priced to provide returns that are too high for their level of risk; that is, given their level of risk to investors, income bonds were not systematically underpriced by the market. If anything, the (slightly) negative abnormal returns suggest that income bonds earned returns that were too low over the test period.

Tax Considerations

We now turn our attention to the fear that a change in the tax law will remove the tax deductibility of interest payments on income bonds.

First, it should be noted, companies that have issued income bonds have been able to deduct the

TABLE 2

Estimates of Abnormal Returns the Bond Portfolios: 1956-1976

Statistic	Income Bond Portfolio	Portfolio High-Grade Corporate Bonds
Average Monthly Abnormal Rates of Return	−.07%	.39%
t-Statistic for the Average	−.32	1.22
Standard Deviation of Abnormal Rates of Return	3.61%	5.11%
Lowest Monthly Abnormal Rate of Return	−13.86%	−12.83%
Highest Monthly Abnormal Rate of Return	16.83%	22.68%

interest payments for tax purposes. We confirmed this for each of the companies in our sample, either by conversations with the corporate treasurer or controller, or examination of corporate annual reports and published accounts of the bond issue.

There is always, of course, the possibility that the government will terminate the tax deductibility feature; however, a close examination of tax rulings suggests that, as long as income bonds have certain characteristics common to all debt instruments, interest deductions for tax purposes will be permitted. This point is illustrated by a particular incident which occurred while the Internal Revenue Act of 1954 was being drafted. As reported by Robbins:

"In an effort to eliminate the possibility that spurious evidences of indebtedness would obtain a tax deduction, the original version of the 1954 act incorporated language that might have ended this income bond privilege. But when this condition was brought to their attention, the legislators were quick to redraft the measure. They indicated that 'there is many a slip twixt the cup and the lip' and that there was no intention to disallow the interest deduction in the case of true debt. The general rule continues to be embodied in Section

---

2. Recall that systematic risk measures only the instrument's sensitivity to overall economic conditions. A detailed discussion of why this is appropriate appears in Barr Rosenberg, Andrew Rudd, "The Corporate Uses of Beta," later in this volume.

3. The beta estimates for the income bond and fixed-interest bond portfolios were, respectively, 0.29 and 0.15. This is consistent with our prior expectations.

4. Robbins, S., 1955. "A Bigger Role For Income Bonds," Harvard Business Review 33 (November-December): pp. 112-113.

163(a) of the Internal Revenue Code of 1954, which allows a deduction for all interest paid or accrued within the taxable year on indebtedness."[4]

Unfortunately, neither the U.S. Congress nor the tax courts have defined precisely what features are necessary to establish that income bonds are indeed debt, and not a preferred stock equivalent. From tax court cases and IRS rulings, however, experts on the question have identified two important characteristics. First, the bonds must have a fixed maturity. (This can, however, be fairly distant. An extreme case is the bond issued by Elmyra & Williamsport Railroad, with maturity set for the year 2862. A 30- to 50-year maturity is more typical.) Second, contingent interest payments cannot be discretionary. This is generally interpreted to mean that interest payments must be paid if earned, and omitted payments must be cumulative and due, in any event, on the maturity date of the debt.

Conversations with the treasurers and tax attorneys of our sample of corporations issuing income bonds indicate that, in some instances, two other tests may be applied in lieu of the accumulation of omitted interest: income bondholders must rank equally with the corporation's other creditors in liquidation; and the bonds must have been issued in an "arms-length" transaction.

In short, provided income bonds retain the essential characteristics of valid debt obligations, interest deductions can be expected to continue to be allowed by the IRS. Concern about changes in the tax law should not deter companies from issuing income bonds.

Potential Deadweight Costs of Income Bonds

The final explanation offered for the scarcity of income bonds is that they impose deadweight costs on the issuing company similar to the bankruptcy costs associated with fixed-interest bonds. Bankruptcy proceedings typically involve fees for lawyers, trustees, auctioneers, referees, accountants, and appraisers. Also, the time management devotes to the restructuring of the company's operations must be considered part of the expected costs of bankruptcy.

Income bonds, of course, largely eliminate the potential for such bankruptcy costs. But their critics have noted another problem that can arise from the conflict of interest between income bondholders and common stockholders. Remember that interest payments to income bondholders depend on the level of reported accounting earnings which, typically, are under the control of stockholders (or, more generally, managers acting on their behalf).

For any given level of performance, it is in the stockholders' interest to depress reported accounting earnings to avoid the contingent interest payments on income bonds. Consequently, income bondholders cannot be certain whether an interest payment was omitted because earnings were "truly" insufficient or because stockholders employed some form of accounting trickery. As a result, if contingent interest payments are passed, bondholders may have an incentive to initiate court proceedings against the company. And, of course, such proceedings involve lawyers, accountants, and the other third parties who demand proper compensation for their services.

While we could not measure these costs directly, we did discover two court cases concerned with this specific issue. In both cases the courts ruled in favor of the income bondholders and ordered payment of previously omitted contingent interest.

The first case, involving the Central of Georgia Railway, occurred over the period 1907-1910. The source of contention was the accounting methods used in determining the earnings available for the payment of contingent interest. The second, and more recent, case occurred in 1971-1973 when the Chicago, Milwaukee, St. Paul, and Pacific Railroad Company omitted contingent interest payments on three of its outstanding bond issues. Class-action suits were filed on behalf of each of the three sets of income bondholders.

The Chicago-Milwaukee case concerned two primary points of issue. The first involved the way in which subsidiary earnings were computed and whether or not such earnings (or losses) should be included when determining the parent company's net earnings available for contingent interest payments. The second point concerned the carry-forward of accumulated losses in determining net earnings available. The bondholders alleged that the Company, in each case, had used improper accounting procedures which depressed reported earnings.

On both points the court found in favor of the bondholders. As a result the Railroad was obliged to pay about $4.1 million (less court-approved attorney's fees and various other costs) to the bondhold-

If a company's earnings are perceived to be highly volatile, a relatively higher coupon rate will be required by investors.

ers. In addition, the Railroad agreed to alter its accounting practices as requested by the class-action suits.[5]

We should note again that the omission of a contingent interest payment does not, by itself, generate deadweight costs. In fact, such missed payments, even those resulting from accounting manipulations, are easily priced in the capital market. When the income bonds are initially issued, investors weigh the likelihood of actually receiving the interest payments and price the bonds accordingly. If a company's earnings are perceived to be highly volatile (or its management somewhat "unorthodox" in its accounting practices), a relatively higher coupon rate will be required by investors. Management, therefore, probably has an incentive to reduce investor uncertainty in cases where such uncertainty is a major problem. But, on an expected value basis, the possibility of missed interest payments does not represent a loss to either income bondholders or stockholders. The deadweight loss to stockholders arises only from the cost of the court proceedings over the missed payments.

These costs appear to us to be relatively small, however, especially when compared to the potential bankruptcy costs associated with fixed-interest obligations. And, more important, there are ways for the company to circumvent this problem of investor uncertainty. The most direct way is to minimize (or completely eliminate) the incentive for stockholders to conceal earnings. This can be done by making missed interest payments cumulative, and by compounding such payments at an interest rate comparable to the firm's cost of capital (i.e., its current investment opportunity rate).[6] By inserting such provisions, and thus making the returns to income bondholders more certain, companies issuing income bonds will reduce the coupon rate required by investors at the time the bonds are offered, and largely eliminate the incentive of income bondholders to recover missed interest payments through legal action.

In short, there are fairly inexpensive ways of reducing the expected costs of court proceedings (and investor uncertainty). Hence, this argument does not explain the corporate neglect of income bonds.

Exchange of Income Bonds for Preferred Stock: The Effect on Stock Values

We have seen that none of the reasons popularly offered for the scarcity of income bonds stands up to close scrutiny. We now switch our focus from the negative to the positive: is there empirical support for the alleged benefits of income bond financing? More precisely, is there any evidence that the market rewards companies for using income bonds?

In a recent paper, we attempted to test what happens to stock prices when companies issue income bonds to retire preferred stock.[7] Briefly, our test involved a comparison of each company's common and preferred share price just before, and immediately after, the announcement of their intention to exchange income bonds for outstanding preferred stock.

If the market viewed the income bonds favorably, we should detect abnormally positive returns (arising from an increase in the stock price) at the time of announcement; negative stock returns would indicate an adverse reaction from the market. Similarly, returns that are "normal" for the systematic risk of the stocks would suggest neutrality, or indifference toward income bonds.

Our sample included 22 companies completing income bonds-for-preferred stock exchanges between 1954 and 1965. The value of the preferred stock involved in the average exchange, as a percent of the market value of the outstanding common stock, was 87.8 percent. The exchange offers thus represented, on average, a significant recapitalization of the sample companies.[8]

We analyzed both monthly and daily rates of return around the time of announcement.

The results of our monthly analysis indicated little impact on value. The common stocks of those companies exchanging income bonds for preferred stock had a positive, but small and not statistically significant, abnormal return. In the case of the preferred stocks the abnormal return was negative, but again small in absolute value and not significant statistically.

The results of our study of *daily* returns, however, were more telling. In measuring daily returns,

---

5. Additional details are available in the annual reports for 1975, 1976, and 1977 of the Chicago, Milwaukee, St. Paul, and Pacific Railroad, and in the *Wall Street Journal*.

6. Two of the three bonds that were the source of contention in the Chicago-Milwaukee case did not have a provision for accumulating missed interest

payments. Further, none of the income bonds in our sample had a compounding feature.

7. McConnell and Schlarbaum, 1981, "Evidence on the Impact of Exchange Offers on Security Prices: The Case of Income Bonds," *Journal of Business*, January.

we computed the average rates of return separately for the common and preferred stocks for the day of the exchange offer announcement, and for the five days preceding and following the announcement date. These results are presented in Table 3.

For the common stocks, we found an average abnormal return of 1.45 percent on the day of the first published announcement, and 0.73 percent on the announcement day plus one. While the announcement-day return is not extraordinarily large, it is, in statistical jargon, significantly different from zero. (The return on the day after announcement is not.) Thus, we can say with great confidence, this is not the result of random chance.

For the sample of preferred stocks we found an abnormal return of 1.01 percent on the announcement day and 1.47 percent on the day after. Neither of these can be attributed to random chance either.

There are two important points to note here. First, we again were not able to find any evidence consistent with the hypothesis that income bonds are somehow "tainted." If this were true we would have found negative abnormal returns to shareholders around the announcement date. Second, and more important, we did find a clear, albeit small, market preference for income bonds. In sum, the theory and evidence, while contradicting the popular objections to income bond financing, provide

TABLE 3

Average Daily Returns for Common and Preferred Stocks of Companies Issuing Income Bonds: Five Days before and after the Day of Announcement

Day	Common Stocks	Preferred Stocks
−5	−.31%	−.90%
−4	.39	−.22
−3	−.72	.56
−2	1.14	−.16
−1	.11	.76
0 (Announcement Day)	1.45	1.01
+1	.73	1.47
+2	−.64	−.28
+3	−1.09	−.18
+4	.22	−.04
+5	.04	.14

8. Because railroad companies were disproportionately represented in our sample, we had to adjust our estimates of the sample's overall rate of return to isolate out events affecting only the railroad industry.

fairly strong support for more extensive use of income bonds in corporate capital structures.

Summary and Conclusions

1. Our research indicates that income bonds are priced fairly by investors; they offer a "normal" rate of return for their risk and, therefore, do not represent an expensive source of financing. We did not find any evidence that income bonds have the "smell of death."

2. While it is possible that new legislation will terminate the tax deduction of interest payments associated with income bonds, the existing tax rulings suggest that this is unlikely. Further, all companies that have used income bonds have been able to deduct the interest payments for tax purposes.

3. It is fairly easy and inexpensive to avoid potential "deadweight" costs resulting from the stockholder/income bondholder conflict over accounting earnings. The company can accumulate and compound, at a rate reflecting the company's cost of capital, all missed interest payments. Because this makes the bondholder's return more certain, the company will also reduce the required coupon rate at the initial offering.

4. A close investigation indicates that companies using income bonds have benefited from doing so; that is, shareholders take note of the advantages of income bonds and price them into the company's shares.

Thus, there appear to be no good reasons for the present neglect of income bonds. Given the instrument's unique characteristics, we think they can provide financial managers with increased flexibility in structuring their company's financing. Indeed, for those companies which view conventional debt financing as placing unacceptable constraints on their financing flexibility, income bonds may allow them to secure the tax advantage of debt without the attendant concern of meeting periodic interest payments, or facing the consequences of not doing so.

The failure of income bonds to gain acceptance thus remains a puzzle to us. But, in response to the same financial pressures that are giving rise to other financial innovations, the attention of investment bankers and their corporate clients will, of necessity, be directed once again to the largely unexploited benefits of income bond financing. A competitive market for financial advisors and financing instruments should ensure it.

APPENDIX A

List of Income Bonds in Sample

Issuing Company	Coupon Interest Rate	Year Issued	Year Matures	Date Entered Sample	Date Left Sample	Purpose
American Steel & Pump Corp.	**4.00**	**1954**	**1994**	**12/55**	**12/70**	**Refund short-term debt**
Armour & Co.	5.00	1954	1984	12/55	12/76	Exchange for preferred stock
Atchison, Topeka & Santa Fe Railway Co.	**4.00**	**1895**	**1995**	**12/55**	**12/76**	**Reorganization**
Boston & Maine Railroad	4.50	1940	1970	12/55	12/76	Exchange for long-term debt
Budget Finance Corp.	**6.00**	**1960**	**2010**	**5/62**	**12/76**	**Exchange for preferred stock**
Central of Georgia Railway	4.50	1948	2020	12/55	12/76	Reorganization
Chicago & Eastern Illinois Railroad Co.	**5.00**	**1954**	**2054**	**12/55**	**12/76**	**Exchange for preferred stock**
Chicago & Great Western Railway Co.	4.50	1938	2038	12/55	12/76	Reorganization
Chicago, Indianpolis & Louisville Railroad Co.	**4.00**	**1943**	**1983**	**12/55**	**12/76**	**Reorganization**
Chicago, Indianapolis & Louisville Railroad Co.	4.50	1943	2003	12/55	12/76	Reorganization
Chicago, Milwaukee, St. Paul & Pacific Railroad Co.	**4.50**	**1944**	**2019**	**12/55**	**12/76**	**Reorganization**
Chicago, Milwaukee, St. Paul & Pacific Railroad Co.	5.00	1955	2055	12/55	12/76	Exchange for preferred stock
Chicago, Rock Island & Pacific Railroad Co.	**4.50**	**1955**	**1995**	**12/55**	**12/76**	**Exchange for preferred stock**
Chicago, Terre Haute & Southeastern Railway Co.	2.75 + 1.50*	1946	1994	12/55	12/76	Refund long-term debt
Curtis Publishing Co.	**6.00**	**1956**	**1986**	**11/56**	**4/69**	**Exchange for preferred stock**
Delaware, Lackawanna & Western Railroad Co.	5.00	1945	1993	12/55	7/76	To facilitate merger
Denver, Rio Grande & Great Western Railroad Co.	**3.00 + 1.00***	**1943**	**1993**	**12/55**	**12/76**	**Reorganization**
Denver, Rio Grande & Western Railroad Co.	4.50	1943	2018	12/55	12/76	Reorganization
Denver & Salt Lake Railroad Co.	**3.00 + 1.00***	**1947**	**1993**	**12/55**	**12/76**	**Refund long-term debt**
Elmyra & Williamsport Railroad Co.	5.00	1863	2862	12/57	2/67	To facilitate merger
Erie Railroad Co.	**5.00**	**1955**	**2020**	**12/55**	**12/76**	**Exchange for preferred stock**
General Baking Co.	6.00	1966	1990	1/67	12/76	Exchange for preferred stock
General Cigar Co.	**5.50**	**1957**	**2015**	**7/57**	**12/76**	**Exchange for preferred stock**
Gulf, Mobile & Ohio Railroad Co.	5.00	1940	2015	12/55	12/76	Reorganization
Gulf, Mobile & Ohio Railroad Co.	**4.00**	**1947**	**2044**	**12/55**	**12/76**	**Reorganization**
Gulf, Mobile & Ohio Railroad Co.	5.00	1957	2056	1/58	12/76	Exchange for preferred stock
Lehigh Valley Railroad Co.	**4.00**	**1949**	**2003**	**12/55**	**7/76**	**Reorganization**
Lehigh Valley Railroad Co.	4.50	1949	2003	12/55	7/76	Reorganization
Lehigh Valley Railroad Co.	**5.00**	**1949**	**2003**	**12/55**	**7/76**	**Reorganization**
Maine Central Railroad Co.	5.50	1959	2008	10/59	2/69	Exchange for preferred stock
Minneapolis, St. Paul & Sault Ste. Marie Railroad Co.	**4.50**	**1944**	**1971**	**12/55**	**11/70**	**Reorganization**
Minneapolis, St. Paul & Sault Ste. Marie Railroad Co.	4.00	1944	1991	12/55	12/76	Reorganization
Missouri-Kansas-Texas Railroad Co.	**5.50**	**1958**	**2033**	**1/59**	**12/76**	**Exchange for preferred stock**
Missouri Pacific Railroad Co.	4.75	1955	2020	3/56	12/76	Reorganization
Missouri Pacific Railroad Co.	**4.75**	**1955**	**2005**	**3/56**	**12/76**	**Reorganization**
Missouri Pacific Railroad Co.	5.00	1955	2045	3/56	12/76	Reorganization
Monon Railroad Co.	**6.00**	**1958**	**2007**	**4/58**	**12/76**	**Exchange for preferred stock**
New York, Chicago & St. Louis Railroad Co.	4.50	1955	1989	12/55	12/76	Exchange for preferred stock
New York, Susquehana & Western Railroad Co.	**4.50**	**1953**	**2019**	**12/55**	**1/76**	**Reorganization**
Norfolk & Western Railway Co.	5.85	1965	2015	1/67	12/76	Exchange for preferred stock
Peoria & Eastern Railway Co.	**4.00**	**1890**	**1990**	**12/55**	**7/76**	**Reorganization**
Pittsburgh Brewing Co.	5.00	1958	1992	8/58	7/70	Exchange for preferred stock
St. Louis-San Francisco Railway Co.	**5.00**	**1956**	**2006**	**9/56**	**12/76**	**Exchange for preferred stock**
St. Louis-Southwestern Railway Co.	4.00	1891	1989	12/55	12/76	Reorganization
Southern Indiana Railway Co.	**2.75 + 1.50***	**1946**	**1994**	**12/55**	**12/76**	**Exchange for long-term debt**
Sheraton Corp.	6.50	1956	1981	4/61	12/76	Expansion and Construction
Sheraton Corp.	**7.50**	**1959**	**1989**	**1/59**	**12/76**	**Expansion**
Trans World Airlines	6.50	1961	1978	5/61	12/76	. . .
Virginian Railway Co.	**6.00**	**1958**	**2008**	**12/58**	**12/76**	**Exchange for preferred stock**
Wabash Railroad Co.	4.00	1941	1981	12/55	12/76	Reorganization
Wabash Railroad Co.	**4.25**	**1941**	**1981**	**12/55**	**12/76**	**Reorganization**
Western Pacific Railroad Co.	5.00	1954	1984	12/55	12/76	Exchange for preferred stock
Wisconsin Central Railroad Co.	**4.50**	**1954**	**2029**	**12/55**	**12/76**	**Reorganization**

*Fixed plus contingent interest.

The Option Pricing Model and the Valuation of Corporate Securities

by Georges R. Courtadon and
John J. Merrick, Jr., *New York University*

The authors would like to thank Arthur Djang and Henry Bethe of Chase Manhattan for their helpful discussions and provision of the equity note data set.

Without question, the most exciting breakthrough in the theory of finance in the last decade has been the development of the Black-Scholes option pricing model. In the early 1970s, Fischer Black and Myron Scholes devised a formula which computes the "fair value" of a call option on a stock as a complex, but *exact* function of five factors: (1) the stock's current value, (2) the option's exercise price, (3) the option's time to expiration, (4) the prevailing interest rate, and (5) the volatility of the underlying stock's rate of return. Of these five factors, only the volatility of the stock's rate of return cannot be directly observed; and even this "unobservable" factor can be estimated by various means. If it should happen that the current market price of the call is either above or below its calculated "fair value," Black and Scholes provide a perfectly hedged investment strategy for accumulating *riskless* profits by exploiting the option's mispricing.

As one might have expected, the Black-Scholes arbitrage trading strategy has generated enormous interest among options traders. Perhaps less widely appreciated, however, is the fact that the *method* developed by Black and Scholes in formulating their option pricing model is broadly applicable to the valuation of a variety of corporate securities. In Black and Scholes's seminal paper, "The Pricing of Options and Corporate Liabilities" (1973), this general application of the option pricing model was foreshadowed in their use of the model to analyze the "fair value" of both corporate debt and equity. Subsequent contributions by other researchers have applied the Black-Scholes method to the valuation of convertible bonds and other contingent claims, such as loan commitments and deposit insurance.[1]

The purpose of this article is to outline the basic elements of the option pricing model, and then to identify and demonstrate some of its potential applications to the design and pricing of corporate securities—most notably, convertible securities. We also show the effectiveness of the option pricing model in valuing "equity notes," the new corporate securities issued within the past year by Manufacturer's Hanover and Chase Manhattan.

---

[1]. Further treatment of the application of option pricing to general corporate claims pricing can be found in Merton (1974) and Geske (1979). Applications to the pricing of convertible bonds can be found in Ingersoll (1978) and Brennan and Schwartz (1977), (1980). Applications to the valuation of safety covenants imposed by bondholders can be found in Black and Cox (1976) and Mason and Bhattacharya (1981). Applications to valuation of loan commitments and deposit insurance can be found in Bartter and Rendleman (1979), Hawkins (1982) and Merton (1977), (1978).

*The payoff of a call option **at expiration** can be **exactly duplicated** by a carefully constructed portfolio composed of stock and debt.*

The Option Pricing Model

The Black-Scholes arbitrage technique for the pricing of options and other contingent claims can be illustrated through the following simple example. Suppose that the market price of a stock currently is $50 per share and that, at the end of one time period, it will either rise to $55 or fall to $45.[2] Suppose further that a call option contract for 100 shares of this stock, with a one-period maturity and an exercise price of $50 per share, is also trading. Finally, suppose that it is possible to borrow and lend funds at an interest rate of 5 percent per period, that there are no restrictions on the use of funds from short sales of stock, and that transactions costs are negligible.

Using this information alone, we can show that *all investors*—regardless of whether they are "bullish" or "bearish" on the underlying stock—*must agree* that the current "fair" value of the call option is $3.5714 per share ($357.14 per 100 share call contract). This "fair" value is the value of the call at which no profitable arbitrage opportunities exist, given the conditions listed above.

To understand why all investors must agree that the current fair market value of the call contract is $357.14, let us return to the assumption that the value of the call at expiration will be either of two, and only those two, possible values. If the stock's price at the expiration of the call turns out to be the "high" value of $55, the call will be "in-the-money" and its market price will be $5 per share. This reflects the value of being able to purchase a $55 stock for the exercise price of $50. If, instead, the stock takes on its "low" value of $45, the option will expire worthless since there is no value to exercising an option which allows the purchase of a $45 stock for $50.

The key insight of the Black-Scholes approach is that the payoff structure of this particular call option contract *at expiration* can be *exactly duplicated* by a carefully constructed portfolio composed of a specific number of stock shares and a certain amount of one-period debt.

In this particular case, the position which, if undertaken today, will duplicate that of the call con-

tract is a long position of 50 shares of stock levered by a one-period borrowing of $2,142.86. This portfolio has a current net value of $357.14 (equal to the value of the 50 shares of stock, $2,500, less the current borrowing of $2,142.86).

To verify that this particular portfolio has exactly the same payoff structure as our option contract, we reason as follows: if the stock price at expiration turns out to be its high value of $55, the stock component of the duplicating portfolio will be worth $2,750 (50 shares @ $55 per share) which, net of the $2,250 ($2,142.86 x 1.05) that must be repaid on the loan, leaves a total end-of-period value of $500. If, instead, the stock's price turns out to be its low value of $45, the total value of the duplicating portfolio will be $0; that is, the stock's value of $2,250 will be exactly offset by the payment due on the loan. Because the payoff structure of this portfolio exactly duplicates that of our call option contract, these two assets are essentially identical and therefore their values must obey the "law of one price." Since the beginning-of-period value of the portfolio is $357.14, the call contract should sell for $357.14.

If the market price of the call contract should happen to differ from the call's "fair value" of $357.14, riskless profits can be made by following the investment strategy below:

(A) If Call Contract Price > $357.14	**Sell (write) the "overpriced" Call Contract and Buy the Duplicating Portfolio.**

(B) If Call Contract Price < $357.14	**Buy the "underpriced" Call Contract and Short the Duplicating Portfolio.**

In both cases the investor would immediately pocket the difference between the call's market price and its "fair" price and suffer no net future cash flow commitment. As a specific example, suppose our call contract was priced in the market at $367. Since $367 is greater than the "fair" price of

---

2. For expositional purposes, we will base most of our initial discussions within a simplified "two state" option pricing framework. Additional details on this technique can be found in Cox, Ross and Rubinstein (1980), Rendleman and Bartter (1979), Rubinstein and Leland (1981) and Sharpe (1981). Extending this simplistic framework to more complex, more realistic conditions is not only possible, but quite practicable.

TABLE 1

TABLE 1
Arbitrage Strategy When Call is Overpriced
Call price of $367 is greater than the "fair" price of $357.14

Beginning-of-Period Action	Cash Flow	Offsetting End-of-Period Action	Cash Flow if Stock Price is	
			$55	$45
Write 1 Call Contract	$ 367	Buy 1 Call Contract	($ 500)	$ 0
Buy 50 Shares of Stock	(2,500)	Sell 50 Shares of Stock	2,750	2,250
Borrow $2,142.86	2,142.86	Repay Loan	(2,250)	(2,250)
Net Cash Flow	**$ 9.86**		**$ 0**	**$ 0**

$357.14, our strategy is to sell (write) the call contract and buy the duplicating portfolio. Table 1 outlines the cash flows of this investment plan for both the beginning and end-of-period initial and offsetting transactions.

Note that our investment strategy generates a net current cash inflow of $9.86 per call contract and will have a net future cash flow of zero *regardless* of whether the stock finishes the period at $55 or $45 per share. The $9.86 represents the difference between the call contract price of $367 and the "fair" price of $357.14.

The existence of this "free" $9.86 per position will certainly arouse interest among arbitrageurs seeking to profit from such option mispricing. In fact, we would expect that the investment strategy described in Table 1 would be continually implemented until the call price fell to its fair value of $357.14, or $3.5714 per share of the underlying stock.

As a second example, suppose that the call's market price was $347—less than its fair value of $357.14. Strategy (B), in which we *buy* the underpriced call and *short* the duplicating portfolio, is then appropriate. We would buy the call option contract, short 50 shares of the underlying stock, and lend $2,142.86. This set of transactions would generate a certain cash flow of $10.14 at the beginning of the period, with no net future cash flow commitments. Consequently, we would expect market forces to drive the call contract's price up to the "no arbitrage" point of $357.14, or $3.5714 per share of the underlying stock.

Our ability to calculate the call option's fair price in the example above depends on the possibility of constructing a levered position in the underlying stock (i.e., the "duplicating portfolio") that gives exactly the same payoffs as the call option. Thus, the following questions arise: (1) is it always possible to construct such a duplicating portfolio?

and (2) if it is indeed possible, how precisely must the portfolio be proportioned to ensure a value at expiration identical to that of the call (i.e., why were 50 shares of stock included—half as many shares of stock as controlled through the call contract being duplicated—why not 40 or 60 shares instead)?

The answer to the first question depends upon the assumptions about the stock price "probability distribution," that is, about the possible movements of the underlying stock price over the period. In our example above, we assumed the stock price followed a *binomial* distribution: only *two* possible end-of-period outcomes were allowed to occur, $55 and $45. Loosely speaking, if the number of possible stock price outcomes is equal to the number of distinct assets to be included in the duplicating portfolio (in our case, two), then it will be possible to form a portfolio which exactly duplicates the end-of-period payoffs of a call option contract.

We saw that the duplicating portfolio for the call option contract considered above involved a long position of 50 shares of stock and one period borrowings of $2,142.86. The 50 shares of stock represent one-half as many shares as are controlled through the call option contract being duplicated. The ratio of stock shares to option controlled shares is called the *hedge ratio*. It is the precise proportion of stock-to-options that completely insulates the arbitrageur from the risk of stock price changes.

In general, the proper proportions of stock and borrowings necessary to form the duplicating portfolio within the binomial model depend upon the two possible end-of-period stock prices and the two possible end-of-period option prices (per share of stock). Let S^H and S^L be the possible high and low values for the end-of-period stock price. Further, let C^H and C^L denote the end-of-period option contract values per share of stock when the stock finishes at S^H and S^L, respectively. The proper hedge ratio can be solved as:

$$h = \frac{C^H - C^L}{S^H - S^L}$$

In our example above, $S^H = \$55$, $S^L = \$45$, $C^H = \$5$ and $C^L = \$0$, so that:

$$h = \frac{5 - 0}{55 - 45} = \frac{5}{10} = \frac{1}{2}$$

Thus, we should hold 50 shares of stock long (short) when we write (buy) a call option contract for 100 shares of stock (one-half as many stock shares as controlled through the option contract). Given the one-period interest rate, R, the total amount of (beginning-of-the-period) borrowings, B, necessary to duplicate the 100 share option contract can be expressed as:

$$B = \frac{100}{1 + R} [hS^L - C^L]$$

In our example,

$$B = \frac{100}{1.05} [\tfrac{1}{2}(45) - (0)] = \$2142.86$$

For completeness, the option contract's "fair" value is:

$$C^{FAIR} = 100(\tfrac{1}{2})(\$50) - \$2142.86 = \$357.14$$

Perhaps the most surprising feature of this option pricing technique is that, in developing the "fair price" for the option, we did not need to specify explicitly the investor's *expectation* as to where the stock would be upon the expiration of the option. All we needed to know was the *range* of possible values. Thus, both "bulls" (those believing the stock will finish at $55) and "bears" (those believing the stock will finish at $45) will *agree* on the current fair value of the option *relative* to the current stock price.

Beyond the Binomial Model

For practical purposes, the model's suggested "fair" option contract value of $357.14 must be viewed with some skepticism because the binomial stock price model is obviously an unrealistic description of stock price movements over a week, a day, or even an hour's time. For these time intervals, there are obviously more than two possible end-of-period stock price outcomes. But, as we consider shorter and shorter period lengths, say, a minute or, better yet, a microsecond, a version of the binomial process which states that the stock price will move either slightly up or slightly down during the next

microsecond could provide an adequate characterization of observed stock price movements. Given a beginning-of-day stock price, such a process, with continuous iterations, could explain virtually *any* end-of-day stock price realization.

This version of the binomial stock price process is known as a *diffusion* process. It assumes that stock prices move "smoothly" over time without any sudden "jumps." By restricting the end-of-microsecond stock price movements to be either slightly up or slightly down, it is again possible to construct a duplicating portfolio for the call option as above. But because the relevant trading interval of a microsecond is shorter than the life of the option, our arbitrage position must be continually reevaluated over time—because the components of the duplicating portfolio change continually, both as the stock price changes and as the option's expiration date approaches.

For the more general diffusion process model of stock price movements, Black and Scholes provide a formula to calculate the "fair" option contract price. They also provide a formula to calculate (and to update continually) the hedge ratio used in a dynamic arbitrage trading strategy. The complexity of their formulas reflect a more complex and realistic description of future stock price movements than the simple binomial model presented above. The essence of their argument, however, remains the same.

Specifically, then, as pointed out at the beginning of this article, the Black-Scholes model also solves for a call option's fair price as a function of five inputs: (1) the current stock price, (2) the option's exercise price, (3) the option's time to maturity, (4) the interest rate and (5) the volatility of the stock's rate of return. In the Black-Scholes model, the volatility variable serves for the diffusion process the function that the range of possible end-of-period stock prices served for the binomial model: namely, as a measure of stock price risk.

Table 2 provides the calculated Black-Scholes prices of call options on stock XYZ for varying exercise prices, times to maturity, and volatilities. In this example, XYZ stock is currently selling at $50 a share and is assumed not to pay any dividends over the life of the options under consideration.[3]

These calculated option values reveal a number of important regularities. First, call options are always worth more than the value obtainable by exercising them immediately—that is, the difference between the current stock price and the option's

Options on stocks with high volatility are more valuable than those on stocks with low volatility.

TABLE 2
Calculated Black-Scholes Values
Stock Price = $50
Interest Rate = 8 percent (annualized)

Volatility	Exercise Price	Time to Maturity		
		1 month	4 months	7 months
.2	45	5.32	6.50	7.61
	50	1.31	2.97	4.21
	55	0.08	1.00	2.00
.3	45	5.48	7.19	8.62
	50	1.88	4.07	5.64
	55	0.35	2.04	3.49
.4	45	5.77	8.05	9.79
	50	2.45	5.18	7.09
	55	0.75	3.15	5.00

exercise price. Second, options on stocks with high volatility are more valuable than those on stocks with low volatility. Third, on an absolute dollar basis, the options most affected by a change in volatility are the at-the-money, long-time-to-maturity options. Those most affected on a percentage basis by a change in volatility are the deep-out-of-the-money, short-time-to-maturity options.

Of the five Black-Scholes inputs, only the stock's volatility is not observable and, hence, must be estimated. As shown above, the volatility estimate is crucial since volatility has a large effect on the option's calculated value. For example, suppose a call option with one month to expiration and an exercise price of $50 is currently selling for $1.50. Using a volatility estimate of .2, the option will appear overpriced in the market. But if the actual volatility is .3, the option is actually being underpriced in the market. (See the Table 2 calculations.)

Some help in estimating stock volatility can be derived from historical stock return data. Such historical measures are not infallible, however, because the volatility of a stock can change over time. A main product line of the growing number of option advisory services is the provision of estimates of the "true" volatilities of particular stocks listed for option trading.[4] But such services notwithstanding, the estimation of the proper volatility input remains the most serious problem in the use of the Black-Scholes model to identify option mispricing.

Of course, the valuation techniques we have used to price a call option can also be used to value a *put* option. A put option contract confers the right (but not the obligation) to *sell* 100 shares of a stock for the put's exercise price on or before a specified expiration date. At expiration, the put will be "in-the-money" if the stock price turns out to be less than the exercise price; it will be worth the difference between the put's exercise price and the (lower) stock price. If, instead, the stock price happens to be greater than or equal to the put's exercise price, the put will be "out-of-the-money" and will expire worthless.

Using the binomial price process described earlier, the fair value of a 100-share put option contract on the stock with one period to expiration and an exercise price of $50 per share is $119.05 ($1.1905 per share of the underlying stock). The $119.05 is equal to the value of the put option contract's duplicating portfolio, which consists of a short position of 50 shares of stock and one-period five percent lending of $2,619.05. The formulas for the hedge ratio (h^p) and the lending position (L^p) in the put's duplicating portfolio can be solved as:

---

3. The original Black-Scholes model is applicable only to European options on nondividend-paying stocks. However, the model can be modified to take into account the effects of dividend payouts on the stock and to approximate the subsequent value of the possible early exercise of American options.

4. Alternatively, some "free" advice on stock volatilities can be gleaned from an analysis of the "implied volatilities" of a number of different options on a given stock. For a discussion of the use of implied volatilities for Black-Scholes trading, see Chiras and Manaster (1978).

$$h^P = \frac{P^H - P^L}{S^H - S^L} = \frac{0 - 5}{55 - 45} = -\tfrac{1}{2}$$

and

$$L^P = \frac{100}{1 + R}[P^L - h^P S^L] = \frac{100}{1.05}[5 - (-\tfrac{1}{2})(45)]$$

$$= \$2{,}619.05$$

where P^H (\$0) and P^L (\$5) are the alternative expiration date values of the put per share of the underlying stock as the stock price takes on its high (\$55) and low (\$45) values, respectively. Thus, the put contract's no-arbitrage (fair) value is:

$$P^{FAIR} = 100 h^P S + L^P = 100(-\tfrac{1}{2})(\$50) + \$2{,}619.05$$

$$= \$119.05$$

Deviations of the market price of the put contract from \$119.05 would imply the existence of profitable arbitrage strategies along the lines of those studies for call options. Further, as in the case of call options, a more complex Black-Scholes put option pricing formula based on a diffusion process assumption for stock price movements can be developed and applied.[5]

Applications of the Model to the Valuation of Corporate Securities

As noted in the introduction, the duplicating portfolio method used in formulating the option pricing model is applicable to the valuation of a variety of corporate claims. In this section, we will review how this method has been applied to the pricing of both nonconvertible and convertible corporate debt. We will then present a new application of this pricing technique to the case of equity notes.

Nonconvertible Debt

Suppose we want to calculate the fair market value of a firm's total outstanding debt. Let us consider a firm with a total current asset market value of \$8 million, whose capital structure consists of one million shares of common stock and a nonconvertible debt issue. For simplicity, assume that the debt issue is composed of discount bonds with an aggregate face value of \$6 million and one year until maturity.

Given the limited liability provisions of the equity position, the actual end-of-year payment to the bondholders depends upon the end-of-year market value of the firm's assets. Continuing in the spirit of the binomial option pricing model, suppose further that the end-of-year asset value of the firm will be either \$12 million or \$3 million, depending upon whether a new product under development is given a warm reception by consumers. If the product succeeds and the value of the firm turns out to be \$12 million at the end of the year, then the scheduled \$6 million debt repayment will be funded by the shareholders of the firm. If, however, the firm's product is not well received and the value of the firm's assets turns out to be \$3 million, then the firm will default on its \$6 million debt repayment obligation. In this scenario, assume that the firm is liquidated and that all bondholders take *pro rata* shares of the \$3 million liquidation value with no residual value for the stockholders. Thus, the total end-of-year payoffs to the bondholders will be either \$6 million or \$3 million.

Given the *contingency* of the bond's end-of-year payoff on the realized asset value of the firm, we can value the firm's debt issue in a straightforward manner using the duplicating portfolio technique. A general set of formulas for the fair price of a contingent claim X for a firm with a binomial end-of-year asset values can be expressed as follows:

$$X^{FAIR} = h^x V - M$$

$$h^x = \frac{X^H - X^L}{V^H - V^L}$$

$$M = \frac{1}{1 + R}[h^x V^L - X^L]$$

where V is the current market value of the firm's assets; where X^H, X^L, V^H, and V^L are the respective values of the contingent claim (in this case, nonconvertible discount debt) and the firm's assets in the high and low firm asset value states; and where h^x and M are the proper proportion of the firm's assets and the proper current riskless money market position, respectively, in the duplicating portfolio.[6]

In our nonconvertible debt example, $X^H = \$6$ million, $X^L = \$3$ million, $V^H = \$12$ million and $V^L = \$3$ million so that $h^x = \frac{6 - 3}{12 - 3} = .333$ and $M = \frac{1}{1.05}[.333(3) - 3] = -1.905$. Thus, the duplicating portfolio for our firm's debt issue is a one-third

---

5. Exact solution for European puts can be derived. Only approximate solutions for American puts are possible due to the problem of early exercise.

6. A positive value for M constitutes a one-period borrowing of M dollars; a negative value for M constitutes extending a one-period loan of M dollars. The call and put option formulas are just specific applications of this general solution.

share of the firm's total existing assets (obtained by purchasing a one-third share of the firm's outstanding equity and debt) and one-year riskless lending of $1.905 million at the market interest rate of five percent. Because this portfolio and the pure debt position in the firm have the same one-year-ahead payoffs, they must have identical current market values to avoid arbitrage. Thus, the aggregate fair value of the firm's outstanding debt is $4.57 million:

$$X^{FAIR} = (.333)(8) - (-1.905) = \$4.57 \text{ million.}$$

Note that the current market value of the firm's debt issue is substantially below $5.71 million, the value at which *riskless* one-year $6 million face discount debt yields five percent interest. The $1.14 million differential reflects the premium necessary to compensate the firm's bondholders for bearing the risk of a possible default by the firm should its end-of-period asset value turn out to be "low."

Indeed, the firm's bondholders can view their investment as a combination of riskless one-year $6 million face debt and a short position in a one-year put option contract on the value of the firm's assets with an exercise price of $6 million. The short put position is implied since the bondholders of the firm implicitly have granted stockholders, through the limited liability provision, the right to "put" to them the assets of the firm (worth $3 million in the "low" firm value state) in exchange for the $6 million cash par value.[7]

The $1.14 million discount on the firm's *risky* debt relative to the cost of *riskless* five percent debt is, in fact, the *fair premium* for writing a put on the value of the firm's assets with an exercise price of $6 million with one-year to expiration.

Convertible Debt

A convertible bond obligates the issuing firm either to redeem the bond at par value upon maturity or, at the option of the bondholder, to permit the bondholder to purchase newly-issued equity at a prespecified price in lieu of the cash par value payment. This prespecified price is called the bond's *conversion price* because it determines the number of new shares of stock into which the bond can be "converted." If the (fully-diluted) market price of

the firm's stock at the maturity date of the bond is higher than the conversion price of the bond, the bond will be converted because the converted stock position is of greater market value than the bond's original par value. If the stock price at maturity is lower than the bond's conversion price, the bondholder will choose the cash par value redemption alternative since conversion in this case would imply a purchase of the firm's stock at a price greater than the price an investor would otherwise face in the open market. In this latter case, of course, the bondholder also bears the risk that the firm may default on its redemption of the bond at par value.

Thus, the convertible bond offers participation in the high payoffs to equity in states of the world in which the value of the firm is "high." At the same time, it offers the "insurance" aspect of a straight bond in states where the value of the firm turns out to be "low."

To show the difference between the valuation of convertible and nonconvertible debt, consider a firm identical to that used in the above example. The only difference is that, besides the one million outstanding shares of stock, it is financed with a convertible instead of a straight debt bond issue, having a par value of $6 million. The conversion price, we will assume, is $5.50 per share. The maturity date payoff to the convertible issue is contingent on the end-of-year value of the firm's assets.

Again, let us consider two possible end-of-period firm asset values, $12 million and $3 million. If the value of the firm turns out to be $3 million, the current stockholders default on repayment of the $6 million par value, and holders of the convertible issue receive total claim to the $3 million in assets. If the value of the firm instead turns out to be its high value of $12 million, the bondholders can either accept the $6 million cash par value redemption payment or exercise their option to purchase $6 million worth of newly-issued equity at the conversion price of $5.50 a share (thereby creating 1.091 million ($6 million/5.5) new shares).

The decision to convert or not convert depends, of course, upon whether the market value of the 1.091 million new shares of stock received (valued at their fully-diluted price) exceeds the unconverted cash redemption value. If the bond is con-

---

7. Conversely, the shareholder's *equity* can be viewed as a *call* option on the value of the firm's assets with an exercise price equal to the par value of the debt. For expositions, see Black and Scholes or Bookstaber (1981). Thus traded stock options on leveraged firms actually are "options-on-options." See Geske (1979).

A convertible bond can be viewed as a combination of nonconvertible debt and a call option contract.

verted, the number of shares outstanding will grow to 2.091 million, but the entire $12 million asset value of the firm will be available to the shareholders. The fully-diluted price of the firm's stock would be about $5.74 per share. Thus, the aggregate value of the 1.091 million shares in the converted position would be $6.26 million. Since this sum is $0.26 million greater than the unconverted value of $6 million, the optimal policy for bondholders in the "high" firm value case is to convert.

Given that the maturity value of the convertible will be either $6.26 million (if V^H occurs) or $3 million (if V^L occurs), we can use our general contingent claim valuation formulas to calculate the current fair value of the convertible issue. Substituting $6.26 million for X^H, $3 million for X^L, $12 million for V^H, and $3 million for V^L, we determine that a portfolio equal to 36.23 percent of the firm's assets, combined with $1.82 million in riskless one-year lending at five percent interest, will duplicate the cash flows of the convertible issue. Since this portfolio currently is valued at $4.72 million, the current fair value of the convertible issue also is $4.72 million.

Note that the value of the convertible issue is $0.15 million greater than that of a nonconvertible $6 million discount debt issue of an otherwise identical firm. This differential reflects the value of the call option on the company's assets effectively conferred by convertible debt. *In fact, a convertible bond can be viewed as a combination of nonconvertible debt and a call option contract on a certain proportion of the firm's value.*

The call option contract has an expiration date corresponding to the maturity of the convertible, and an exercise price per share equal to the convertible's conversion price. Furthermore, it delivers a proportion of the firm's value equal to the ratio of the number of shares of stock due the convertible bondholders at the conversion price to the number of shares of stock in the fully-diluted firm. In the current example the aggregate implicit call option contract is written on 52.18 ($1091/2091$) percent of the firm's value, has an exercise price equal to the $6 million face value of the bond, and a time to expiration of one year. The fair value of such a call option contract is $0.15 million—exactly the difference between the fair values of the convertible and nonconvertible issues.

Finally, because a convertible bond can be viewed as a nonconvertible bond plus a special call option contract and because a nonconvertible bond

itself is actually (as we saw) a combination of a riskless bond and a short put option on the assets of the firm, a convertible bond ultimately should be valued as a call option plus a risk-free bond and a short put option position.

Equity Notes

A most recent application of the duplicating portfolio technique for the valuation of corporate securities is the case of equity notes. The equity note is perhaps best described as a "mandatory convertible" instrument. In its most basic form, it is a fully-collateralized stock purchase contract *obligating* the bearer to buy a specified number of new shares in the issuing firm at some future date (usually ten years from the date of initial issue). The collateral is the par value of an attached coupon-bearing note maturing at the date of the future stock sale. At that date, the note is exchanged for the specified number of stock shares. Because this simple version of the equity note guarantees the future delivery of a fixed number of stock shares, it exhibits the same risk as an equity position and thus will be priced essentially as fully-diluted equity—with one exception: it substitutes *certain* coupon payments on the note for *uncertain* dividend payouts on the stock until the stated stock purchase date.

The equity notes actually issued are structured somewhat differently from the "basic" form to partially mitigate the inherent stock price risk. The number of shares received by the investor at maturity in lieu of the par value of the attached note varies with the actual market price of the stock at that date. The contract specifies two boundary maturity date stock prices: a ceiling price and a floor price. If the actual market price of the stock turns out to be equal to or above the ceiling price, the investor uses the full par value of the note to purchase the firm's shares at the ceiling price (i.e., the investor receives the number of newly-issued shares equal to the ratio of the par value of the note to the ceiling price of the stock purchase contract). If the actual maturity date market price of the stock is between the ceiling price and the floor price, the investor receives the number of shares which, at the going market price, have a market value equal to the par value of the bond. Finally, if the stock price is less than the floor price, the investor receives the number of shares equal to the ratio of the par value of the note to the floor price of the contract (i.e., the investor uses the note's full par value to purchase stock at the floor price of the contract). Under this set-up, the investor receives stock with an aggregate market value greater than, equal to, or less than the par value of the bond as the maturity date stock price turns out to be greater than the ceiling price, between the ceiling and floor prices, or less than the floor price.

While the investor can choose to receive the stock at any time prior to maturity, the provisions of the equity notes observed to date make this event unlikely. This is because the coupons foregone by converting typically exceed the dividends gained, and, more importantly, because the sliding schedule of stock purchase prices is effective only on the equity note's maturity date. Prior to the maturity date, the purchase price is the ceiling price.

To provide a concrete example of the valuation of an equity note issue, we will once again examine a firm with the same asset value as above. In this case, the firm's capital structure will consist of one million outstanding shares of common stock and a $6 million par value zero-coupon equity note issue maturing in one year. For comparative purposes, we will assume that the ceiling price for the equity note is set at $5.50 per share (identical to the conversion price of the convertible issue discussed earlier). The floor price is assumed to be $4.00 per share. This price structure implies that the total number of new shares to be exchanged for the note issue at maturity can range from 1.091 million (if the maturity date stock price is greater than or equal to $5.50 per share) to 1.5 million (if the stock price is less than or equal to $4.00 per share).

As in our previous applications of the duplicating portfolio pricing technique, we begin by identifying the possible end-of-year payoffs to the equity note which, once again, are contingent upon whether the value of the firm's assets turns out to be $12 million or $3 million. If the firm happens to be worth $12 million at maturity, the value of the equity of the fully-diluted firm will be greater than $5.50 per share so that, under the terms of the collateralized stock purchase agreement, a total of 1.091 million new shares of the firm's stock would be issued to the holders of the equity note issue. The market value of each of the new total of 2.091 million shares of the firm's stock would be about $5.74 ($12 million of asset value divided among 2.091 mil-

lion shares). The total value accruing to the original holders of the equity note issue thus would be $6.26 million (1.091 million shares valued at $5.74 per share).

If, instead, the end-of-year value of the firm assets turns out to be $3 million, the value of the firm's fully-diluted equity will be less than $4 per share so that a total of 1.5 million newly-issued equity shares would be transferred to the equity note holders. The market value of each of the new total of 2.5 million outstanding shares of the firm's stock would be $1.20 ($3 million of asset value divided among 2.5 million shares). The total value accruing to the original holders of the equity note issue would be $1.8 million (1.5 million shares valued at $1.20 per share).

Given that the value of the equity note issue at maturity will be either $6.26 million or $1.8 million, we can find the duplicating portfolio for the equity note just as we did for nonconvertible and convertible bonds. In our equity note example, $X^H = \$6.26$ million and $X^L = \$1.8$ million so that $h^X = \frac{6.26 - 1.8}{12.3} = .496$ and $M = \frac{1}{1.05}[.496 (3)-1.8] = -\$0.30$.

Thus, the equity note's duplicating portfolio is a 49.6 percent share of the firm's total existing assets combined with one-year riskless lending of $0.30 million at five percent interest. The current market value of this duplicating portfolio, and thus the current fair value of the equity note, is $4.27 million:

$$X^{FAIR} = (.496)(8.0)-(-.30) = \$4.27 \text{ million.}$$

Note that the $4.27 million fair market value of this $6 million par value equity note is less than the $4.72 million fair value of a $6 million par value convertible issue of an otherwise identical firm. The $0.45 million premium on the convertible over the equity note reflects the fact that the value of the convertible in the "low" firm asset value state is higher than that of the equity note ($3 million versus $1.8 million).

In general, the difference in value between a convertible bond and a comparable equity note will reflect the difference between the values of the short put positions implicit in the two instruments.[8] The implied put position of a convertible is a put on the assets of the firm. The implied put of an equity note is a put on only a certain proportion of the

8. By comparable issues we mean that the coupon streams are identical, the ceiling price of the equity note equals the conversion price of the convertible, and that both are viewed in the context of otherwise identical firms whose only other capital structure component is equity.

The model allows us to quantify the effects of changes in the underlying specifics of the equity note on its fair value.

firm's assets. This proportion is determined by the fraction of total shares in the diluted firm which are delivered to the equity note holders at the floor price. In this example, this floor proportion is 60 percent of a firm's assets.

From our previous analysis we know that the implied put position of the convertible is worth $1.14 million. It is straightforward to show that the fair value of the implied put position of the equity note is $1.59 million.[9] *Indeed, the difference between these implied put option values is the $0.45 million differential between the convertible and the equity note derived above.*

The foregoing analyses of the nonconvertible debt, convertible debt and equity note issues highlight the fact that the option pricing model can be applied to corporate claim valuation problems in general. While our specific examples were couched in the "unrealistic" binomial model for end-of-year firm asset values, a more realistic diffusion process assumption can also be used. Diffusion-based valuation models for these corporate claims can be derived to improve upon our binomial models, just as the Black-Scholes option pricing model was an improvement over the binomial option pricing model. (And in the next section, we will demonstrate the application of such a diffusion model to the pricing of an actual equity note issue.)

The basic idea that certain contingent claims contain option-like components also becomes useful in practice when alternative structurings of a security are being considered. For example, we might want to redesign the above equity note issue such that investors would value it essentially as a convertible bond. Our analysis implies, however, that this would occur only if the short put option position implicit in the equity note was identical to that implicit in the convertible. This would happen only if the number of newly-issued shares granted the equity note holders was large enough to dilute completely the value of the original stockholders' one million share position, such that the equity note holders would acquire the total value of the firm's assets. This condition would be approached only if the floor price of the equity note were set very close to zero.

Empirical Analysis of an Equity Note Issue

In order to test the applicability of the option pricing model to the valuation of equity notes, we used a diffusion-based model to value the equity notes issued by Manufacturer's Hanover Corporation (MHC) in April, 1982. The issue has a face value of $100 million, matures on April 15, 1992, and carries a 15⅛ percent coupon payable semiannually. The contract ceiling and floor prices are $55.55 and $40.00, respectively. These contract prices imply that the number of MHC shares to be purchased on April 15, 1992 for the $1,000 face value of each note can range from 18 (at the ceiling price) to 25 (at the floor price). On the day prior to issue, MHC stock closed at $31.75. Thus, the ceiling and floor prices in this collateralized stock purchase agreement were set at premiums of 74.96 percent and 25.98 percent, respectively.

In this analysis, we assume that the total value of MHC's outstanding stock plus its equity notes follows a diffusion process. We will refer to this total value as the firm's value. This is a simplification which allows us to side-step an explicit analysis of the other components of MHC's capital structure. Note, however, that this simplification is still sophisticated enough to capture the essential co-determination of equilibrium stock and equity note values subject to the ultimate uncertainty about their total value.

While the financial theory underlying our model is cast within the same contingent claims framework set forth earlier, the specifics of diffusion-based equity note valuation are too complex to be solved analytically. In practice, we can solve for our fair equity note values only with the aid of a computer. The computer solves a system of difference equations approximating a complex differential equation, which in turn characterizes the equity note's value in a diffusion-based contingent claims analysis. In general, the model allows us to quantify the effects of changes in the underlying specifics of the equity note on its fair value. The model also allows us to compute the fair value of the MHC issue at alternative points in its trading life.

9. Use $X^H = 0$, $X^L = 4.2$, $V^H = 12$ and $V^L = 3$ in the general contingent claim formulas above to solve for this put's value. To derive $X^L = 4.2$, observe that this put's low state value is the difference between the $6 million "exercise price" (par value) and *sixty percent* of the $3 million asset value. Sixty percent is the "floor proportion" determined by the ratio of the 1.5 million equity note-related shares to the total of 2.5 million outstanding shares in the fully-diluted firm.

Thus, we are able to test how well the model explains the actual market prices of this specific issue. Table 3 presents the results of a comparison between actual market prices of the MHC equity note issue and our model's predicted prices for the two-month period between July 1, 1982 and August 30, 1982.

Columns 2 and 3 present the market values of MHC common stock (per share) and the MHC equity note (per one dollar of face value), respectively. Column 4 presents the aggregated value of MHC's stock and its equity notes (in billions of dollars). Columns 5 through 6 report the calculated fair equity note values given the firm value's (column 4), the time left to maturity of the equity note, the rate of interest, the specifics of the issue (par value, coupon stream, ceiling and floor prices, etc.), the stock's dividend stream, and *two* alternative values of volatility.

The volatility input required by the model is the annualized standard deviation of the percentage change in the aggregate market value of MHC stock and equity notes. Ideally, we would want to estimate this volatility directly by examining the historical data on the aggregate market value of these two claims. However, since there is no significant trading history for the equity note issue prior to the start of our sample period, we impute this volatility estimate from an historical estimate of the volatility of the return to MHC common stock. For weekly data over the first six months of 1982, this imputed volatility was found to be .22. A slightly higher volatility estimate of .25 is obtained when the historical sample is lengthened to include the data from 1981.[10] We examine the model's equity note values for *both* of these volatility estimates.

We use a riskless interest rate of 13.95 percent in calculating the July model prices, and 13.06 percent in calculating the August model prices. These rates are the average yields on 10-year Treasury notes for the months of July and August, respectively.

Finally, we must make some projection as to the likely dividend stream to be paid on MHC stock over the period ending April 15, 1982, given the information available to the market in July, 1982. The 1982 first quarter MHC dividend amounted to $2.92 per share on an annualized basis. We assume that the market expected dividends to grow at a 7.35 percent compounded annual rate over the equity note's life. This dividend growth rate is the actual percentage dividend increase for 1982 over 1981.

Of the two alternative model price series constructed, the series based upon a volatility input of .22 most closely tracks the actual equity note prices observed in the market.[11] For this volatility estimate, while the model underprices the market values by $1.20 per $100 of face value on average, the root mean squared deviation of the model price from the market price is just 1.6 percent of the average market equity note price. To be sure, significant differences between the model's price and the actual market price do occur on certain days. But most of the larger percentage discrepancies appear when the firm's value is low relative to its average value. In these cases, model prices show greater downward movement in response to the decrease in firm value than market prices tend to show. We do not observe an equivalent phenomenon for higher than average firm values because of the model's general tendency towards underpricing.

One reason for this "undershooting" problem may be the simplifying assumption invoked in our specification of the model. The model's performance would certainly be improved if our measure of firm value were expanded to include a more complete picture of MHC's total asset value. The equity note valuation procedure could be fine-tuned through the incorporation of a more exact total asset value, along with the added rational pricing restrictions. It remains nonetheless a fact that our simple format—using only the market values of the stock and the equity notes itself—explains actual equity note prices within 1.61 percent on average.

The "Components" of an Equity Note

As discussed above, investors can view an equity note position as the sum of three components: a long position in a call option on a certain proportion of the firm's value, a long position in a certain nonconvertible bond, and a short position in a put option on another proportion of the firm's value. The call option contract has an exercise price equal to the par value of the equity note, and its expiration date is the same as the equity note's maturity date. The proportion of the firm value con-

---

10. The .22 and .25 firm value volatilities are imputed from estimated stock return volatilities of .23 and .26, respectively. In the imputation procedure we assume that the equity note displaced an equivalent amount of riskless debt in the capital structure.

11. Of course, the .25 volatility-based model would fit the market data more closely than the .22 volatility-based model, if the assumed dividend growth rate were sufficiently low.

Table 3 Model Versus Market Equity Note Values July 1, 1982 – August 30, 1982	Date	Market Stock Price ($/Share)	Market Equity Note Price ($/$1 of Face)	Firm Value ($ Billions)	Model Equity Note Values ($/$ of Face)	
					Vol = .22	Vol = .25
	7/01	26.875	0.940	1.026	.919	.917
	7/02	26.625	0.935	1.017	.914	.912
	7/06	26.625	0.935	1.017	.913	.911
	7/07	26.750	0.935	1.021	.915	.913
	7/08	26.625	0.935	1.017	.913	.911
	7/09	27.125	0.935	1.034	.921	.919
	7/12	28.000	0.950	1.066	.936	.934
	7/13	27.250	0.935	1.039	.922	.921
	7/14	26.875	0.935	1.026	.916	.914
	7/15	26.875	0.935	1.026	.915	.914
	7/16	27.125	0.935	1.034	.919	.918
	7/19	27.250	0.935	1.039	.921	.919
	7/20	28.125	0.945	1.070	.936	.934
	7/21	28.750	0.940	1.091	.946	.945
	7/22	28.625	0.940	1.087	.944	.942
	7/23	28.500	0.940	1.083	.941	.940
	7/26	28.125	0.940	1.070	.934	.933
	7/27	28.250	0.940	1.074	.936	.935
	7/28	28.000	0.940	1.066	.932	.930
	7/29	28.250	0.940	1.074	.936	.934
	7/30	28.125	0.940	1.070	.934	.932
	8/02	28.625	0.950	1.089	.957	.955
	8/03	28.625	0.955	1.089	.957	.955
	8/04	28.375	0.955	1.080	.953	.951
	8/05	28.125	0.955	1.072	.948	.946
	8/06	27.500	0.955	1.050	.937	.935
	8/09	27.500	0.945	1.049	.936	.934
	8/10	27.750	0.950	1.059	.941	.939
	8/11	27.125	0.945	1.037	.929	.927
	8/12	27.125	0.955	1.038	.930	.928
	8/13	27.375	0.960	1.047	.934	.932
	8/16	27.625	0.960	1.056	.938	.936
	8/17	29.125	0.975	1.109	.964	.962
	8/18	29.000	0.975	1.105	.961	.960
	8/19	27.000	0.950	1.033	.926	.924
	8/20	28.250	0.955	1.077	.947	.945
	8/23	28.750	0.950	1.094	.955	.953
	8/24	28.625	0.950	1.089	.952	.951
	8/25	28.250	0.950	1.077	.946	.944
	8/26	28.250	0.950	1.077	.946	.944
	8/27	26.625	0.940	1.019	.917	.915
	8/30	26.250	0.945	1.007	.910	.908

Root Mean Squared Deviation
(in percent of average market price): 1.61   1.77

Firm Value is aggregate market value of stock plus equity notes (cum accrued interest).
Vol. is the measure of volatility applied (see text).

trolled in this call option is equal to the ratio of the number of shares of stock due the equity note holders at the ceiling price to the number of shares of stock in the fully-diluted firm. The bond component is a special security which has a riskless maturity date par value, but a risky coupon stream. The maturity date, par value, and coupon structure of this bond correspond to that of the equity note. Finally, the put option is written on the proportion of the firm's value determined by the number of shares due the equity note holders at the floor price in the fully-diluted firm. The put's exercise price and expiration date are identical to that of the call.

To complete our analysis, we will show how our model distributes an equity note's total fair value among these three primary component securities at alternative firm asset values. Table 4 presents the component calculations for the MHC equity note issue as of July 23, 1982. Here we present the breakdown of the model equity note value into its implicit call, bond, and put positions—not only for the actual value of the firm on that date (the asterisked row), but also for other possible values of the firm. Our results are based on the .22 volatility parameter along with the other background assumptions used above.

Row 3 of Table 4 computes the total fair equity note value of $94.1 million on July 23, 1983 (based on the actual firm value of $1.083 billion) as the sum of the values of its three component parts. At this level of firm value, the equity note's value is dominated by its straight bond value. The net effect of the implicit long call and short put positions represents only $8.1 million (just about eight percent of face value). If the value of the firm were substantially higher or lower, this result would change. As the value of the firm rises the equity note's value increases for three reasons: first, the call option becomes more valuable as it now has a greater chance of finishing in-the-money; second, the implicit bond position is more valuable since there is less of a chance of default on the risky coupon stream; and third, the short put position is less of a drag since it is more likely to finish out-of-the-money.

Analogous effects on these component values for a decrease in firm value also can be seen. As the value of the firm falls, the call and the bond becomes less valuable and the short put becomes more of a drag. At some point between firm values of $1.2 billion and $1.5 billion, the two option positions would completely offset each other and the equity note would be priced (for the moment) as if it were a bond with a risky coupon stream, but riskless par value.

TABLE 4 The Underlying Components of Equity Note Value[12] July 23, 1983	Firm Value ($ Billions)	Model Value of Equity ($/Share)	Model Value of Equity Note ($/$1 of Face)	Component Values ($/$ of Face)					
				Call	+	Bond	–	Put	
	0.5	12.56	.620	.001	+	.872	–	.253	
	0.8	20.72	.799	.014	+	.990	–	.205	
	*1.083	28.50	.941	.059	+	1.022	–	.140	
	1.2	31.72	.999	.088	+	1.027	–	.116	
	1.5	39.99	1.143	.182	+	1.032	–	.070	
	2.5	67.53	1.628	.607	+	1.034	–	.013	
	4.0	108.81	2.366	1.333	+	1.034	–	.002	

12. The implicit call contract is a contract on the ceiling proportion of the firm's value, $(n^c/n^c + N)$ V, where n^c is the number of new shares issued in exchange for the equity note at maturity, N is the existing number of shares and V is the value of the firm. In the MHC example, $(n^c/n^c + N) = .0495$. The implicit bond position is a nonconvertible bond with a secured par value, a coupon rate of 15⅛ and a maturity identical to that of the equity note. The implicit put option is a contract on the floor proportion of the firm's value, $(n^f/n^f + N) = V$, where n^f is the number of new shares issued in exchange for the equity note at maturity and N and V are as defined above. The floor proportion in the MHC example is $(n^f/n^f \div N) = .0675$. Column 4 + Column 5 – Column 6 may not equal Column 3 because of rounding errors.

Closing Remarks

This article discusses the potential application of the Black-Scholes option pricing model to the valuation of corporate securities. After outlining the basic elements of the option pricing model, we reviewed how a general contingent claims framework has been used to value corporate debt, both non-convertible and convertible.

We next explained the model's revelance to the pricing of a relatively new corporate security: the equity note. We then went on to apply the contingent claims model to the valuation of Manufacturer's Hanover's outstanding equity note issue. The model was able to explain market equity note prices within 1.61 percent on average, though certain "large" but short-lived discrepancies did appear during the two-month sample period studied. Finally, we broke down the fair value of this equity note into its three component values: a long call option, a long bond, and a short put option. We then showed how each component contributes to the total equity note value as the total value of the firm changes.

The analysis presented here for the MHC equity note issue touches on just a few of the possible uses of the option pricing model for the valuation of corporate claims. The method is useful not only for determining whether a particular security is under- or over-valued, but also for simulating the effects of changes in the features of the issue, or changes in the value of the firm, on the value of the security. In designing securities, trade-offs between features of the issue—e.g., coupon rates, conversion premiums, maturity—can be analyzed in a systematic fashion and the net effects on value determined precisely.

In summary, the contingent claims valuation framework is applicable to the pricing of all corporate securities for which the two following conditions obtain: (1) the security's value can be expressed as a function of the total asset value of the firm, and (2) the total value of the firm can be modelled as a smoothly changing random variable. Applications of this valuation framework to alternative corporate claims are distinguished only by the background work necessary to analyze the differences in the payoff streams of the securities being valued.

The Growing Role of Junk Bonds in Corporate Finance

by Robert Taggart, *Boston University*, and
Kevin Perry, *Baring Asset Management*

T he growing volume of newly-issued "junk" bonds has been among the most controversial of recent developments in corporate finance. Preferring to call them "high yield" bonds, their promoters extol them as an essential cog in the revitalization of American industry.[1] Their critics, by contrast, denounce them as "securities swill" and have called for restrictions on investment in junk bonds by financial institutions and on the the issuance of junk bonds in hostile takeover attempts.[2]

What are junk bonds, and why have they aroused such heated and conflicting emotions? What are the capital market conditions that have fueled the growth in junk bonds? What factors should a corporate treasurer consider in deciding whether to issue junk bonds? The present article seeks to shed light on these questions.

---

1. Because of its more widespread popular usage, the term "junk bonds" is used throughout this article.

2. See Felix G. Rohatyn, "Junk Bonds and Other Securities Swill," *The Wall Street Journal*, April 18, 1985.

THE TOTAL AMOUNT OF JUNK BONDS OUTSTANDING HAS BEEN
ESTIMATED AT ABOUT $125 BILLION BY THE END OF 1986, AND AT
ABOUT $137 BILLION BY THE MIDDLE OF 1987. THIS REPRESENTS MORE
THAN 20 PERCENT OF THE ENTIRE CORPORATE BOND MARKET.

TABLE 1 NEW ISSUES OF JUNK BONDS ($ BILLIONS)	Year	(1) Newly-Issued Public Straight Junk Bonds[1]	(2) Exchange Offers and Private Issues Going Public[2]	(3) Total Junk Bond Issuance n(1) + (2)m	(4) Total Public Bond Issues by U.S. Corporations[2]	(5) (1) as % of (4)	(6) (3) as % of (4)
	1987	28.9	n.a.	n.a.	219.1	13.2	n.a.
	1986	34.3	11.3	45.6	232.5	14.8	19.6
	1985	15.4	4.4	19.8	119.6	12.9	16.6
	1984	14.8	0.9	15.8	73.6	20.1	21.5
	1983	8.0	0.5	8.5	47.6	16.8	17.9
	1982	2.7	0.5	3.2	44.3	6.1	7.2
	1981	1.4	0.3	1.7	38.1	3.7	4.5
	1980	1.4	0.7	2.1	41.6	3.4	5.0
	1979	1.4	0.3	1.7	25.8	5.4	6.6
	1978	1.5	0.7	2.1	19.8	7.6	10.6
	1977	0.6	0.5	1.1	24.1	2.5	4.6

1. From Drexel, Burnham Lambert (1987). 1987 figure from *Investment Dealer's Digest*.
2. From *Federal Reserve Bulletin*. 1987 figure from *Investment Dealer's Digest*.

RECENT GROWTH OF THE JUNK BOND MARKET

Junk bonds are those rated below Ba by Moody's or below BBB − by Standard and Poor's. That is, they are bonds with below investment grade ratings. Unrated corporate bonds are usually included in the junk bond category as well.

Under their broadest definition, junk bonds include private placements and public issues, convertible and straight debt, low-rated municipal bonds and even low-rated preferred stock. For the most part, however, this article focuses on the largest segment of the market: public, straight debt issued by U.S. corporations.

Junk bonds have existed ever since the first bond ratings were published by John Moody in 1909. In fact, junk bonds were a significant source of corporate funds throughout the pre-war period, accounting for 17 percent of total rated, publicly issued straight corporate debt during the years 1909-43. Downgradings during the Depression swelled the supply of junk bonds so that they grew from 13 percent of total corporate debt outstanding in 1928 to 42

percent in 1940.[3]

Junk bonds were less widely used as a source of corporate funds in the early postwar years. Between 1944 and 1965, for example, they accounted for only 6.5 percent of total corporate bond issues,[4] and from the mid-sixties to the mid-seventies they were used even less frequently. By 1977, junk bonds accounted for only 3.7 percent of total corporate bonds outstanding and most of these were "fallen angels" or bonds initially issued with investment grade ratings and subsequently downgraded.[5]

In 1977, however, the market began to change, as newly-issued junk bonds started to appear in larger volume. Although this has been widely heralded as the birth of the new-issue junk bond market, it is perhaps more accurately viewed as a resurgence of the flourishing market of the prewar years. In either case, the growth of new issues, as documented in Table 1, has been impressive, particularly since 1983.[6]

Between cumulative new issues and additional fallen angels, the total amount of junk bonds outstanding has been estimated at about $125 billion by the end of 1986, and at about $137 billion by the middle of 1987.[7] This represents more than 20 percent of

---

3. As reported by Thomas R. Atkinson, *Trends in Corporate Bond Quality* (New York: National Bureau of Economic Research, 1967).

4. Ibid.

5. As reported by Edward I. Altman and Scott A. Nammacher, *Investing in Junk Bonds* (New York: John Wiley & Sons, 1987).

6. It is true that new issues of junk bonds were much reduced in the wake of the stock market crash of October 1987. After running slightly ahead of the 1986 pace for the first three quarters of 1987, new issues of junk bonds totaled only $4.4 billion in the fourth quarter, compared with $8.7 billion for the comparable period

in 1986. Often overlooked, however, is the fact that corporate debt issues in general were much reduced in the fourth quarter of 1987. Thus junk bond issues still represented 11.7 percent of total corporate debt issues for the fourth quarter of 1987, not much different from their share for 1985 and 1986.

7. The 1986 estimate was provided by Drexel Burnham Lambert ("The Case for High Yield Securities," April 1987) and the 1987 estimate by Edward I. Altman, in "Analyzing Risks and Returns in the High Yield Bond Market," forthcoming in *Financial Markets and Portfolio Management*, Zurich, Switzerland.

OVER THE PERIOD 1977 TO 1986, JUNK BONDS HAD A LOWER STANDARD
DEVIATION OF MONTHLY RETURNS THAN DID EITHER HIGH-GRADE
CORPORATES OR LONG-TERM TREASURIES (2.86 PERCENT VERSUS 3.73
PERCENT AND 4.02 PERCENT RESPECTIVELY).

TABLE 2
ESTIMATED OWNERSHIP
OF JUNK BONDS
DECEMBER, 1986

Type of Investor	Estimated Holdings ($ Billions)	% of Total
Mutual Funds	40	32
Insurance Companies	40	32
Pension Funds	15	12
Individuals	15	12
Thrift Institutions	10	8
Other (Foreign Investors, Securities Dealers, etc.)	5	4
Total	125	100

Source: Rasky (1986)

the entire corporate bond market. Approximately one-third of all junk bonds outstanding consisted of fallen angels as of year-end 1986.[8]

On the investor side, the junk bond market is primarily institutional. More than 50 mutual funds now specialize in holding junk bonds and these, together with other nonspecialized mutual funds, hold nearly one-third of junk bonds outstanding. The estimated ownership distribution of junk bonds as of December, 1986, is shown in Table 2.

INVESTMENT CHARACTERISTICS OF JUNK BONDS

Presumably, the attraction that junk bonds hold for investors is a high expected return. Expected returns are impossible to measure, and realized returns are an imperfect proxy because of their substantial variation from year to year. Over longer periods, however, junk bonds do seem to offer higher average realized rates of return. For the period 1977 to 1986, for example, a study by Marshall Blume and Donald Keim calculated an annualized compound monthly rate of return of 11.04 percent for an index of junk bonds, compared with 9.6 percent for an index of AAA- and AA-rated corporate bonds and 9.36 percent for an index of long-term Treasury bonds.[9]

In exchange for these higher returns, investors in junk bonds can expect to bear higher levels of risk. Their lower ratings, of course, suggest a higher risk

of default.[10] In addition, junk bonds tend to have fewer restrictive covenants than other bonds, and they are frequently subordinated. Thus junk bondholders have less flexibility to accelerate the bankruptcy process in the event that the borrower's condition deteriorates, and they stand lower in the line of creditors if bankruptcy does occur.

Measured default rates are, in fact, higher for junk bonds than for corporate bonds generally. For the period 1970 through 1986, a recent study by Ed Altman calculates the junk bond default rate (that is, par value of defaulting junk bonds divided by total junk bonds outstanding) as 2.22 percent, compared with 0.20 percent for all straight, public corporate debt. Influenced by the LTV and Texaco bankruptcies, the junk bond default rate was 3.39 percent for 1986 and 4.69 percent for 1987 (through August 31).[11]

The default rate, however, is probably not the best measure of the risk of holding junk bonds. Losses on defaulting bonds are rarely equal to their entire par value. For the period 1974 to 1986, for example, the weighted average default loss was 1.10 percent, compared with a default rate of 1.67 percent for the same period. In addition, junk bonds and investment grade bonds have different sensitivities to interest rate changes and to fluctuations in the value of the issuing firm's assets.

The importance of these additional factors is illustrated by Blume and Keim's finding that, for the period 1977 to 1986, their junk bond index had a lower standard deviation of monthly returns than did

8. See Susan F. Rasky, "Tracking Junk Bond Owners," *The New York Times*, December 7, 1986.

9. Marshall E. Blume and Donald B. Keim, "Lower Grade Bonds: Their Risks and Returns," *Financial Analysts Journal* 43 (July/August, 1987), pp. 26-33. A similar return relationship prevailed during 1987, even though junk bonds were hurt by the October stock market crash. The return on the Drexel Burnham Lambert Composite Index of high yield bonds was 5.41 percent for all of 1987, as

opposed to −0.35 percent for comparable-duration treasury bonds (for the fourth quarter alone, analogous return figures were 2.73 percent for junk bonds versus 6.73 percent for treasuries)

10. In the Blume and Keim return calculations, default losses are already recognized to the extent that bonds in default are retained in the index as long as they have quoted market prices.

11. See Altman (1988), as cited in note 7.

their indices of either high-grade corporates or long-term Treasuries (2.86 percent versus 3.73 percent and 4.02 percent respectively).[12] Thus, after the fact, junk bonds actually had lower total risk than did their investment-grade counterparts. This seemingly paradoxical result may be attributed to two factors.

First, since junk bonds have higher coupon rates, they have shorter "durations" than investment grade bonds. That is, the weighted average of the times at which cash is received over the life of the bond is shorter for a junk bond.[13] This in turn implies that junk bond values are less sensitive to interest rate fluctuations than the values of investment grade bonds. Since the 1977-86 period was one of substantial interest rate fluctuations, this factor may have dominated the relative variability of realized bond returns.

Second, junk bonds are typically protected by smaller equity cushions than investment grade bonds, and thus are more sensitive to fluctuations in the value of the issuing firm's assets. The value of the assets in turn reflects the present value of the operating cash flows they generate. As a result, the variability of junk bond returns is more heavily influenced by sector, industry, and firm-specific factors than is that of investment grade bonds. However, much of the risk stemming from these fluctuations may be diversifiable. Thus the risk of a large portfolio or index may be substantially less than the average risk of the individual bonds.

Taken as whole, the investment characteristics of junk bonds are unlike those of either high grade bonds or common stocks. Their lower sensitivity to interest rate changes and the diversifiability of a substantial portion of their risk make them unlike high-grade bonds. Like common stocks, junk bond values move up and down with the value of the issuing firms' assets. Unlike common stocks, however, this upward movement is truncated for junk bonds beyond a certain point. This is because most junk bonds are callable; and if the issuing firm's creditworthiness improves dramatically, it will find it advantageous to call the bonds and refinance at a lower rate.

In the final analysis, investing in junk bonds may be most akin to a covered call option strategy, whereby a portfolio manager buys common stocks but also writes call options on those stocks. If the stocks fail to appreciate, the portfolio manager still receives the premium income from having written the call options. If the stocks do appreciate, however, the portfolio's upside potential is limited, because the stocks will be called away.

In a similar fashion, junk bonds' high current yield affords the investor some protection against the possibility that the firm's assets will decline in value. If, on the other hand, the firm's fortunes improve substantially, the junk bondholders participate to some degree, but that participation is limited by the fact the firm will ultimately call the bonds away.

CAPITAL MARKET CONDITIONS AND THE RISE OF THE JUNK BOND MARKET

Capital Markets in the 1970s and '80s

It is natural to wonder why junk bonds suddenly regained a significant share of the total corporate debt market after having been relatively dormant for a number of years. Several key factors emerged in the 1970s and '80s that brought about fundamental changes in the overall capital market environment. These same factors were conducive to the growth in junk bonds.

The first factor has been increasing competition on an international scale. Industry boundaries and firms' market shares have become more fluid; and the financial services, transportation, communication and energy industries, as well as major segments of U.S. manufacturing, have all undergone extensive restructuring. Deregulation has been a factor in several of these industries. In banking, for example, the erosion of interest rate ceilings has forced banks to compete on a broader scale in financial markets. It could be argued that these and other moves toward deregulation have often been a response to, rather than a cause of, increased competitive pressure. Whatever their source, these pressures have generated substantial capital market activity in the form of mergers and divestitures, issues and repurchases of securities, and the start-ups of new firms and liquidation of old ones. Regulatory changes that have given financial institutions greater flexibility should also be mentioned. For example,

---

12. Blume and Keim (1987), cited in note 9.

13. Over the period 1978-83, for example, Altman and Nammacher (1987), cited in note 5, calculated an average duration of 8.53 years for bonds in the Shearson-Lehman Long-Term Government Bond Index versus 6.64 years for their junk bond

index. For further discussion and applications of the duration concept, see Stephen Schaefer, "Immunization and Duration. A Review of Theory, Performance and Applications." *Midland Corporate Finance Journal* 2 (Fall, 1984), pp. 41-58).

TABLE 3
COMPOSITION OF
CREDIT MARKET
DEBT RAISED BY
U.S. NONFINANCIAL
CORPORATIONS

Period	1977-83	1984-86
Total Credit Market Debt Raised ($ Billion)	$565.4	$535.1
Proportion of Credit Market Debt Accounted for by (%):		
Bank Loans	40.6%	32.7%
Commercial Paper	4.4	5.0
Finance Co. Loans	11.0	11.6
Tax-Exempt Bonds	12.9	6.5
Corporate Bonds	25.9	43.7
Mortgages	2.1	0.5
Other	3.0	0.0
Total	100.0	100.0
Note: Credit Market Debt as % of Total Sources of Funds	23.3	36.3

Source: Federal Reserve Flow of Fund Accounts

the ERISA standards of 1973 for pension fund investments essentially replaced the "Prudent Man" rule with a rule of reasonable compensation for risks incurred. This allowed pension fund to compete more broadly for investment opportunities.

A second important factor has been uncertain inflation and interest rate volatility. As exemplified by the response to the Federal Reserve's switch from interest rate to money supply targets in October 1979, the prices of fixed income securities have become more variable. This has spurred investors to seek protection against sudden changes in rates and has induced them to increase their portfolio turnover. For corporations, changing inflation rates have contributed to sharp fluctuations in the availability of internal funds relative to total financing needs. Thus many firms have found themselves moving in and out of the capital markets more frequently, and facing highly variable conditions when doing so.

The third important factor in changing capital market conditions is at least partially motivated by the first two. Securities issuers have greatly expanded the range of their potential sources of funds. In part, the increasingly global nature of competition in many industries has led to raising funds on an international scale as well. This is exemplified by the growth of the Eurobond markets, in which U.S. corporations raised an average of $28.4 billion in both 1986 and 1987, up from just $300 million in 1975. In addition, the need to move in and out of markets more frequently has led to an emphasis on reducing the costs of external financing. Since 1982, corpo-

rations have taken advantage of the shelf registration rule (Rule 415) to cut their underwriting costs. They have also sought to raise funds in public markets, where possible, circumventing more costly borrowing through financial intermediaries.

This disintermediation has been especially apparent in recent years, as indicated in Table 3. As the corporate bond market has expanded, the share of corporate debt financing accounted for by bank loans has declined. Although it is less apparent in the table, use of the commercial paper market by the most creditworthy corporations has also eroded banks' traditional lending relationships with their prime customers. These developments, combined with competition from foreign banks and other financial institutions, have turned prime lending into more of a low-margin commodity business. The banks have thus been forced to turn to lower grade credits in an attempt to maintain their profitability.

The Influence of Capital Market Conditions on the Junk Bond Market

The same factors that have molded capital market developments more generally have been important contributors to the recent growth of the junk bond market. Let us consider in turn the impact of these factors on investors, underwriters, and issuers of junk bonds.

Hurt by unexpected inflation during the 1970s, investors have sought higher returns and greater flexibility. Thus junk bonds, with their premium yields and shorter durations, grew more attractive by the late 1970s. This attractiveness was enhanced by the widely-noticed performance of Keystone's B4 Fund, a pioneer junk bond fund that inspired the start-up of other such funds.

Investors also found that traditional loss-protection measures were inadequate in a rapidly changing environment. High credit quality, for example, offered little protection against volatile interest rates. Similarly, restrictive covenants in bond indentures proved insufficient to guard against the losses imposed by massive corporate restructurings.[14] As a result, investors have increasingly emphasized liquidity relative to credit quality or contractual provisions. Despite their higher default risk and fewer restrictive covenants than other corporate bonds, junk bonds' attractiveness to investors has thus been greatly enhanced by the development of a liquid secondary market.

In this sense, the rise of the junk bond market has paralleled the "securitization" phenomenon more generally. Because little or no secondary market existed, mortgages, auto loans, and other receivables were formerly held to maturity by their originators or by specialized intermediaries. Increasingly, however, they have been packaged as asset-backed securities, and a more active secondary market has developed. In a similar vein, junk bonds are akin to medium or long-term loans that might formerly have been originated and held by commercial banks and insurance companies. With the development of a secondary market, however, they are now more widely traded.

Changing capital market conditions have also rapidly eroded the stigma that was formerly attached to junk bond underwriting and trading. As in commercial banking, prime-quality underwriting has become more of a low margin business as worldwide competition, shelf registration and issuer pressure have all combined to squeeze profits. This has in turn sparked a search for new opportunities. Merger and acquisition advising is one such opportunity that has been pursued by many securities firms. Providing investment banking services to below-investment grade companies, which comprise about 95 percent of all U.S. corporations, is another natural target.

The latter opportunity was especially attractive to Drexel Burnham Lambert in the late 1970s, since it did not have a strong investment grade client base. It did, however, have a well established junk bond trading operation under the direction of Michael Milken. Thus it had already developed a network of investors and an expertise in secondary market-making.

When Drexel Burnham began underwriting junk bonds in 1977, it was therefore able to provide investors with the liquidity they needed to make these securities attractive. Drexel quickly became, and remains today, the leading underwriter of junk bonds; but other firms have recognized the potential profitability of the business and have entered the market as well.

Junk bonds also afforded Drexel Burnham a way to enter the lucrative merger and acquisition business and thus to participate in the restructuring boom. The firm began financing leveraged buyouts with junk bonds in 1981 and hostile takeover bids in late 1983. Drexel was able to capitalize on its established investor network to mobilize large amounts of funds within very short periods. Again, competitors have followed suit or have come up with alternative means of raising cash quickly, such as committing their own capital in the form of "bridge loans."

Finally, capital market conditions of recent years have also enhanced the appeal of junk bonds for issuers. Junk bond underwriting spreads are high, typically falling in the three to four percent range, compared with less than one percent for investment grade issues.[15] Still, there are reasons to believe that junk bond financing can offer cost advantages to issuers.

Investors, for example, appear to be willing to accept lower expected returns in exchange for greater liquidity.[16] Hence, investors' ability to trade their bonds in a secondary market can lower the cost of junk bond financing relative to negotiated debt, for which secondary trading is thin or nonexistent. This should be particularly the case in recent years, as volatile market conditions have dictated increased investor emphasis on liquidity.

In addition, rapidly changing financing needs and competitive situations have necessitated flexibility for issuing corporations. In this respect, the implicit cost of junk bond financing may have been less than that of other sources in recent year. For exam-

14. See S. Prokesch, "Merger Wave: How Stock and Bonds Fare," *The New York Times*, January 7, 1986.

15. As reported by Henny Sender, "Don't Junk the High-Yield Market Yet," Institutional Investor 21 (March, 1987).), pp. 163-66.

16. See Yakov Amihud and Haim Mendelson, "Asset Pricing and the Bid-Ask Spread," *Journal of Financial Economics* 17 (December, 1986), pp. 223-49.

ple, junk bonds have allowed lower-grade firms to raise larger amounts of money in a shorter period than would be possible from negotiated sources. Junk bonds also tend to have fewer restrictive covenants and more liberal call provisions than many types of negotiated debt. Recent market conditions have apparently created a willingness on the part of some investors to make these concessions in exchange for greater liquidity. In fact, it could be argued that investors' demand for liquidity has greatly facilitated the placement of junk bonds from the largest leveraged buyouts.

THE ROLE OF JUNK BONDS IN CORPORATE FINANCIAL POLICY

Given that junk bonds have established a solid position in the corporate debt market, we now examine their role in corporate financial policy. When should a corporation consider issuing junk bonds?

Stewart Myers' "pecking order" theory provides a useful starting point.[17] Myers notes that a firm's managers typically know more about its true value than other capital market participants. If the managers act in the interests of their existing shareholders, they will thus try to issue securities at times when they know them to be overvalued. Recognizing this incentive, however, market participants will then interpret securities issues as a sign that they are overvalued. That in turn reduces the amounts they are willing to pay for the securities.

This problem of unequal information gives rise to a pecking order of sources of funds. Internally generated funds are unaffected by the problem, since their use entails no new securities issues. The closer a company's debt securities are to being riskless, the less severe is this problem as well. This is because the value of riskless securities will be unaffected by revisions in the estimated value of the company's assets. Riskier securities such as equity, however, will clearly be affected by investors' perceptions of firm value. Since the mere fact of their issuance is likely to lead to downward revisions in their value, managers will be reluctant to issue these securities.

The pecking order, then, implies the following rules for financial policy: (1) Use internal funds first,

until these have been exhausted; (2) to the extent that external funds must be relied upon, issue debt first, the less risky the better; (3) issue common stock only as a last resort, after all debt capacity has been exhausted.

Junk bonds occupy an intermediate position in this pecking order. They are more susceptible to the investor information problem than investment grade debt, but less so than common stock. For a firm that needs large amounts of external financing for its current investment plan, junk bonds can allow the firm to fully use its available debt capacity and thus avoid an equity issue.

At what point is debt capacity used up? While it is difficult to identify a given firm's optimal debt ratio with any precision, finance theory does suggest certain characteristics that will lead some firms to have higher debt capacities then others.[18]

The first of these is the firm's tax-paying status. The tax-deductibility of interest is one of the potential advantages of debt. Firms pay for this advantage, however, because the more debt they issue in the aggregate, the more they bid up the returns on debt securities relative to equity. Thus firms that already have large tax shields (for example, from depreciation and loss carry forwards) relative to their cash flow would find little tax benefit from additional debt, even though they would be implicitly paying for this benefit. For such firms, debt capacity is likely to be relatively low.[19]

A second important determinant of debt capacity is the riskiness of the firm's assets. The costs of bankruptcy and of resolving conflicts of interest among security holders are closely related to the perceived probability of default. The fact that a company's bonds are rated below investment grade is, of course, itself an indication that perceived default risk is relatively high. Hence, issuers of junk bonds should carefully weigh the potential costs of bankruptcy and claimholder conflicts against the dilution that might be entailed by an equity issue. In particular, a firm that plans to return to the debt markets on a regular basis in the future should be wary of increasing its debt ratio suddenly and sharply through the issuance of junk bonds today. To the extent that this undermines the value of its already outstanding

---

17. See "The Capital Structure Puzzle," *Journal of Finance* 39 (June, 1984), pp. 575-92. Reprinted in *Midland Corporate Finance Journal* 3. Fall 1985, pp. 6-18).

18. For a discussion of these characteristics, see Stewart C. Myers, "The Search for an Optimal Capital Structure," *Midland Corporate Finance Journal* 1 (Spring, 1983), pp. 6-16.

19. Since the new tax law reduces nondebt tax shields by eliminating the Investment Tax Credit and lengthening allowable depreciation schedules, it may tend to increase debt capacity for many firms.

bonds, the firm can expect investors to extract a penalty yield or more stringent covenants the next time it returns to the market.

A third factor affecting a firm's debt capacity is the composition of its assets. A firm whose value stems largely from assets already in place is likely to have a greater debt capacity than one for which future investment opportunities comprise a substantial portion of current market value. This is because debt that is issued now can weaken the firm's incentive to undertake those future investments. The riskier is the firm's currently outstanding debt, the more the future projects will tend to bolster the bondholders' position. Because they must share the value of these projects, however, equityholders' willingness to undertake them will be less than if they captured the entire value themselves. In the face of this potential problem, firms with significant future growth opportunities will tend to rely less heavily on debt financing today.

The foregoing analysis suggests that the ideal junk bond issuer is a firm that can take full advantage of the interest tax shields, that does not have a potential for severe bankruptcy costs or conflicts among security holders, and that has a total market value that is largely attributable to assets in place. One such firm would be the prototypical leveraged buyout candidate: a firm with a mature business that generates a high but relatively steady level of cash flows. Another might be a younger firm that has already cleared the hurdles of developing its product and establishing a market position but that now needs capital to finance its major expansion phase.

One other factor should also be considered by the potential junk bond issuer. The arguments advanced above concerning debt capacity and the pecking order of funds sources do not distinguish between public and private debt. Hence the issuer must decide whether it is better to rely on the public market or to negotiate a private agreement with a financial institution. The more highly the issuer values the flexibility entailed by call provisions and less restrictive covenants, the more the choice will tend toward public debt. The public market will also be favored the more investors are willing to make yield concessions in exchange for the possibility of secondary trading.

PUBLIC POLICY ISSUES

If junk bonds are simply one possible choice in an entire spectrum of funds sources, why have they aroused such controversy in pubic policy circles? The general economic conditions described earlier--especially worldwide competitive upheaval and uncertain inflation combined with interest rate volatility--have been accompanied by many painful dislocations. Although total employment has expanded, the wave of restructurings has brought plant closings and loss of jobs in a number of industries and localities. Changes in control have extended the threat to job security to the most senior executive ranks. Competition and volatile market conditions have also aroused fears over the safety of the financial system. These developments have in turn generated heated debate over such issues as industrial policy and the regulation of financial institutions. And because they are a highly visible product of the same economic forces that have caused these dislocations, junk bonds have become enmeshed in the same policy debates.

However, the true contribution of junk bonds to these perceived policy problems may be more symbolic than real. Their very label tends to surround junk bonds with the unsavory aura that makes them a convenient target. Their real influence is less easy to detect.

Consider, for example, the role of junk bonds in financing mergers and acquisitions. This has been the subject of several congressional hearings and various restrictions on junk bond financing of hostile takeover bids have been proposed.[20] Sometimes lost amidst the furor, though, is the fact that junk bonds account for only a small fraction of all merger and acquisition financing. The peak occurred in 1986, when junk bond issues were related to 7.8 percent of the $190 billion in total merger financing (*Mergers and Acquisitions*, 1987). This was up from 4.3 percent in 1985 and 2.6 percent in 1984. Merger and tender offer transactions have accounted for at most 41 percent of public junk bond issue proceeds in any given year, this occurring in 1986.

It cannot be denied that the availability of the junk bond market has strengthened the credibility of takeover threats, allowing larger amounts of funds to

---

20. To date, the only restriction actually imposed has been the Federal Reserve Board's 1986 determination that a shell corporation, set up for the purpose of making a takeover bid, is subject to margin requirements under Regulation G. The impact of this ruling is limited, however, by numerous stated exceptions. See M. Langley and J.D. Williams, "Fed Board Votes 3-2 to Restrict the Use of 'Junk' Bonds in Takeovers," *The Wall Street Journal* (January 9, 1986).

be raised in a shorter time period than was previously thought possible. Nevertheless, merger-related activity does not absorb a majority of the proceeds from junk bond issues, and bank loans are a far bigger source of merger financing than junk bonds.

The junk bond market has also been discussed frequently in conjunction with the recent insider trading charges, and revelations connected with the Boesky scandal have apparently triggered some decreases in junk bond prices, at least temporarily.[21] While the SEC has recommended that charges be brought against Drexel Burnham and several of its employees, however, no systematic involvement of junk bond market participants in insider trading has been established as yet. Furthermore, as with mergers and acquisitions generally, the issue is broader than junk bonds. Tender offers can create opportunities for insider trading, but it is not clear why offers that will be financed with junk bonds are more susceptible to such opportunities than others.

Consider finally the connection between junk bonds and the safety of the financial system. Some have argued that junk bonds represent part of a general weakening of corporate financial strength in recent years. However, it is at least debatable whether such weakening has in fact occurred.[22] When measured in market value terms, the ratio of debt to total capital for U.S. nonfinancial corporations has actually declined by more than 20 percent since 1974. Even if it were conceded that U.S. corporations have relied too heavily on debt financing, it should be noted that junk bond issues account for only six percent of the total credit market debt that companies have raised during the period 1977-1986.

It has also been argued that junk bond invest-

ments can weaken the safety of financial institutions. Acting on these arguments the state of New York has recently moved to limit unapproved junk bond investments by insurance companies.[23] Given their default risk, it is of course true that an ill-conceived junk bond investment program can lead to trouble. But the number of ways to make risky investments is almost unlimited. They include, for example, issuing short-term debt and investing in long-term Treasury securities that are free of default risk. Limiting junk bond investments, but not other investments, is unlikely to significantly enhance the safety of financial institutions.

CONCLUSION

The rapid growth of the junk bond market has been impressive, but controversial. Most of the controversy stems from the fact that the market's development has coincided with the rise of such emotional policy issues as industrial restructuring and corporate control. It has been argued here, however, that the junk bond market is a product of the same forces — international competition, volatile capital market conditions, and the search for new funds sources — that have given rise to these policy issues. It is a symptom rather than a cause of those forces.

For the corporate treasurer, the development of this market represents a significant financial innovation. It allows companies that do not qualify for investment grade bond ratings to tap the public market and thus to take advantage of investors' willingness to pay for liquidity. For such firms, access to the junk bond market can be an important alternative to privately negotiated debt.

---

21. Estimates of these price decreases range from one to four percentage points (see Randall Smith, "Junk Bonds Lag Market Since Boesky Case, But Exact Gap Proves Difficult to Measure," *The Wall Street Journal*, December 4, 1986). Much of these losses, however, appear to have been recouped within about two months (see Randall Smith, "Junk Bonds Retain Strength and Discount Latest Fallout From Insider Trading Scandal," *The Wall Street Journal*, February 18, 1987).

22. See, for example, Robert A. Taggart, Jr., "Corporate Financing: Too Much Debt?," *Financial Analysts Journal* 42 (May/June, 1986), pp. 35-42.

23. See Johnnie L. Roberts, "New York Limits Assets Insurers Put in Junk Bonds," *The Wall Street Journal*, June 1

The Persistent Borrowing Advantage of Eurodollar Bonds

by Wayne Marr, *Clemson University,* and
John Trimble, *University of Tennessee*

Between 1975 and 1988, the volume of U.S. corporate borrowing in the Eurodollar bond market grew at the astonishing rate of 63 percent annually. In 1975 U.S. firms borrowed approximately $30 million overseas, which accounted for less than one percent of total U.S. corporate borrowing. In 1987 they borrowed nearly $17 billion overseas, which represented roughly 17 percent of total U.S. corporate borrowing. This amount, moreover, was sharply down from the 1985 high of $42 billion, accounting for 42 percent of total corporate borrowing.

What is behind this huge increase in overseas borrowing? According to the chief financial officers of U.S. companies, it is extraordinarily favorable borrowing rates. Many CFOs, in fact, report interest cost savings between 25 and 100 basis points in the Eurodollar as compared with the domestic market.[1]

---

1. See W. Cooper, "Some Thoughts About Eurobonds," *Institutional Investor*, February 1985, pp. 157-158; S. Lohr, "The Eurobond Market Boom," *The New York Times*, December 31, 1985, p. 31; F. G. Fisher, *The Eurodollar Bond Market*, London, Euromoney Publications Limited, 1979; R. Karp, "How U.S. Companies are Catching the Eurobond Habit," *Institutional Investor* (August 1982), pp. 208-212; M. S. Mendelson, *Money on the Move*, New York, McGraw-Hill, 1980; Orion Royal Bank Limited, *The Orion Royal Guide to the International Capital Markets*, London, Euromoney Publications Limited, 1982; Securities Industry Association, *The Importance of Access to Capital Markets Outside the United States* (May 1983); and D. W. Starr, "Opportunities of U.S. Corporate Borrowers in the International Bond Markets," *Financial Executive* (June 1979), pp. 50-59.

Though intermittent, such savings have been available often enough to provide a significant advantage. And, harder to believe, the reported savings at times have been much larger than 100 basis points. On September 11, 1984, for example, Coca Cola issued $100 million of seven-year Eurodollar bonds priced at 80 basis points below comparable U.S. Treasury notes.[2] And, while interest cost savings as large as Coca Cola's are clearly an aberration, recent academic research provides support for claims in the financial press of substantial corporate savings in the Eurobond market.[3]

The existence of such a large and persistent borrowing advantage runs counter to the conventional wisdom of financial economists that international capital markets are becoming ever more "integrated." Expressed in simplest terms, the "integration" of two financial markets implies that the free flow of capital across boundaries should erase all but minor and momentary borrowing cost differences. Thus, if markets are truly integrated, the domestic and international yields in the primary market for domestic and Eurodollar bonds should be roughly equal.

How, therefore, does one explain the significant cant Eurobond savings that have recently been documented by academic studies? In this article we attempt to provide an "educated guess" about the real source of the savings—one which reflects fairly recent trends in international banking as well as other well-known features of the Eurobond market.

THE EURODOLLAR BOND MARKET

Historical Development

The recent availability of low-cost Eurobond financing has presented U.S. companies issuing debt with a new option: selling their bonds in international capital markets. A Eurobond is underwritten by an international syndicate of commercial banks or investment banks and sold principally, at times exclusively, in countries other than the country in whose currency the bond is denominated. Eurodollar bonds are dollar-denominated Eurobonds.

The first dollar-denominated Eurobond was sold in 1957 by Petrofina, a Belgian petroleum company. The dollar volume of Eurobonds began to grow in the early 1960s when the U.S. government enacted a series of measures designed to restrain the outflow of funds from the United States and to improve the country's balance of payments.[4] As a result, many American firms found it advantageous during this period (1963-74) to finance their international operations by selling securities overseas. By 1974, the government's capital control programs were dropped but the Eurodollar bond market still continued to grow.

Historically, most Eurobond issuers have been well-known financial institutions or industrial firms with extensive overseas holdings, such as American Express and Mobil Oil. Today, this is no longer true. Many lesser-known and smaller-sized firms have become Eurobond issuers. Between 1977 and 1984, more than 400 industrial firms sold straight debt in the Euromarket, totaling more than $41 billion.[5]

Eurobond Characteristics

Eurodollar bonds sold by domestic firms are similar in most respects to their domestic bonds. The majority of bonds are fixed-rate, unsecured, straight debt (i.e., no special features other than the call or sinking fund provisions) and are listed on a major exchange (U.S. or European). Most of the differences between domestic and Eurodollar bonds are attributable to the fact that they are designed for a different clientele of investors. In the U.S. market, corporate bonds are purchased primarily by life insurance companies and pension funds which, historically, have desired long-term debt instruments. The Eurobond market initially was dominated by individual investors who purchased securities through anonymous bank accounts and who preferred short-term maturities. In recent years, the market has become more institutional, with large participation by central banks and insurance companies. Such institutions, however, still prefer short-term maturities because of liquidity needs and foreign exchange risk. As a result, most Eurobonds issued by industrial companies have maturities of between three and ten years.

Other features that distinguish Eurodollar from

2. See W. Cooper, "Some Thoughts About Eurobonds," *Institutional Investor*, February 1985, pp. 157-158.

3. See M. W. Marr and J. L. Trimble "Domestic versus Euromarket Bond Sale: A Persistent Borrowing Cost Advantage," University of Tennessee Department of Finance Working Paper, 1988.

4. The federal government's capital control programs consisted of the Foreign Direct Investment Program, the Interest Equalization Tax, and the Voluntary Foreign Credit Restraint program.

5. See S. Lohr, "The Eurobond Market Boom," *The New York Times*, December 31, 1985, 31.

domestic bonds include annual (instead of semi-annual) coupon payments, no registration requirement, and smaller issue sizes. Annual coupon payments lower the yield for a Eurobond as compared with an identical bond issued in the United States. Also, most Eurobonds are in bearer form as compared with the registered form prevalent in the United States. Bearer bonds provide the holders with anonymity and the potential to avoid tax liabilities resulting from coupon income or capital gains. Such anonymity also allows investors to hide illicit or politically sensitive activities such as drug trafficking and covert arms sales. Finally, the typical Eurobond issue is smaller than the typical domestic bond issue. Whereas domestic issues have raised an average of a little over $100 million, the average Eurodollar bond issue has been around $85 million.

THE EURODOLLAR BOND BORROWING ADVANTAGE

Besides cost considerations, there could be other reasons why U.S. companies choose to issue Eurobonds. They may wish, for example, to broaden the market for their securities and attract investors who would not otherwise purchase securities registered in the United States. Or they may wish to avoid the disclosure requirements of regulations. But surely the predominant reason for the large volume of Eurodollar bonds is that U.S. companies perceive some cost advantage to borrowing overseas.[6]

In two recent studies we found that, in fact, Eurodollar bonds have offered issuers remarkable savings relative to comparable domestic bonds. Using a sample of 229 new debt issues sold by U.S. public utility firms between January 1979 and December 1983, we found that the average gross yield on 38 Eurodollar bond issues was approximately 58 basis points less than yields on 191 comparable domestic issues.[7] In a more recent study we found an even larger 104-basis-points saving for 118 industrial firms issuing Eurodollar bonds (relative to 198 domestic issues) during this same period. These are indeed significant savings. For a typical $100 million bond issue, for example, 104 basis points translates into a reduction in debt service cost of $1.04 million dollars a year.

WHY THE EUROBOND ADVANTAGE?

Why has a borrowing cost advantage in Eurodollar bonds persisted? The answer to this question surely lies in the forces that govern, and the linkages between, the primary and secondary markets for domestic and Eurodollar bonds. These forces appear to consist of temporary as well as more permanent elements. For while the Eurobond advantage has existed in long periods throughout the past 14 years, it does not appear to have been continuously present; at times domestic bonds have had a clear cost advantage. But, clearly, the trend on the whole has favored the Euromarket sale.

In this section, we suggest an explanation for the persistence of the savings that is rooted in these forces and is consistent with the facts concerning the domestic and Eurodollar bond markets. In the final analysis, however, much of the information that would answer our question is not available to the public (and thus to researchers like us). Our explanation, accordingly, should be viewed as at best an educated guess.

Privately, some observers have suggested that during the last decade money from investors in oil-producing states has gone principally to Eurobonds because such investors generally prefer anonymity. Because these investors are "segmented" from other investors in world financial markets, such an increase in demand could conceivably have caused a persistent differential in the *secondary-market* prices of Eurobonds relative to domestic bonds. But it does not explain how this differential in secondary-market prices would necessarily translate into a borrowing advantage for U.S. firms. Eurobond underwriters could price the Eurodollar issues only slightly below domestic bonds and then keep the balance of the secondary-market price differential for themselves. Which leads us to the following question: Why do only U.S. companies (and not, say, German or English firms) appear to be getting the lion's share of the cost savings from Eurobond offerings?

In addition, Ingo Walter has shown that the market for financial anonymity (of which the Eurobond market is a large part) is very complex.[8] Like most markets, the forces which govern price movements

6. Two empirical studies have documented the savings. They are D. S. Kidwell, M. W. Marr, and G. R. Thompson, "Eurodollar Bonds: Alternative Financing for U.S. Companies," *Financial Management* (Winter 1985), pp. 18-27, (a correction to the above study appears in *Financial Management* (Spring 1986), pp. 78-79); and, M. W. Marr and J. Trimble, "Domestic versus Euromarket Bond Sale: A Persistent Borrowing Cost Advantage," University of Tennessee Working Paper, 1988.

7. *Ibid.*

8. Ingo Walter, *Secret Money*, Lexington, Mass.: Heath and Co., Lexington Books.

arise from both the demand and the supply sides. Consider the sources of demand. Half of the Euromarket's demand for bonds comes from institutional investors, many of which are likely to have legitimate preferences for anonymity. The other half is from retail investors, some of whom no doubt require anonymity for legitimate business and personal motives. Another part of the retail demand stems, however, from the desire to hide illicit activities. These investors include participants in international drug trafficking, fraud, insider trading, tax evasion, capital flight, and covert government operations such as arm sales and state-sponsored terrorism.

Thus, it is easy to see how, in the last decade, increases in the demand for financial secrecy could have come with equal force from sources other than investors in oil-producing states. But, without better information, we cannot determine with any confidence the extent to which retail demand for Eurodollar bonds is being driven by any particular source.

An explanation of the Eurobond puzzle must therefore provide answers to two fundamental questions: What might have caused a differential in secondary-market prices? And why would underwriters share a Eurobond price rise with U.S. borrowers? We will begin by addressing the second question first.

Why Would Underwriters Share A Price Differential?

Why Banks Might. Underwriting relationships with wealthy corporate clients generate large profits for underwriting institutions. Consequently, competitive banks are generally looking for opportunities to penetrate or increase their share of such underwriting markets. Of course, some banks will have stronger motives than others. For example, some U.S. commercial banks, apparently in anticipation of the repeal of the Glass Steagall Act, have sought entry into the Eurobond underwriting market by offering competitively low rates.[9]

Also, according to Walter, Swiss banks steadily lost international underwriting business to more competitive banks in London during the last decade.

In addition, he notes that the ability of the Swiss to compete in their traditional underwriting areas has been hampered by competition from a greater number of suppliers of financial secrecy and by unfavorable changes in Swiss tax laws.[10] To the extent Walter is right, it would be understandable if Swiss banks were to seek new markets in which to compete in international banking. And, in fact, the predominant lead manager of the syndicates underwriting Eurodollar bonds in the U.S. is Credit Suisse First Boston, a Swiss bank affiliate that is also typically involved in distributing these bonds.

Why the U.S. Market? There are six attractive features of the U.S. market. First, there is an abundance of wealthy corporations. Second, the dollar is an accepted international currency. Third, during much (1980-85) of the period we are considering, the dollar's value was rising against most other world currencies. Fourth, Euromarket investors prefer to invest in top credit quality U.S. corporations, and thus the bonds are relatively easy to distribute to retail investors in the Euromarket. Fifth, the U.S. capital market is the largest in the world and is relatively free of capital controls. Sixth, in the 1980s, U.S. interest rates (fueled by expansionary policies) were high relative to those in other developed countries.

How Would a Price Differential Be Shared? Historically, the relationship between underwriting fees in the Euromarket and the domestic market has been relatively stable, running at roughly 2.67 times.[11] A large portion of this difference in the underwriting fees arises because proportionately more Eurobonds are distributed to retail investors than in the U.S. The selling concession, a component of the underwriting fee which goes to the banks in the selling syndicate to compensate them for their retail effort, is thus much larger in the Euromarket than in the U.S. market.

Euromarket merchant banks are the only banks with established distribution networks to investors seeking anonymity. And, as such, they have the ability to exact gains from these investors which other banks do not. Therefore, when the demand from secrecy-seeking investors increases relative to the supply of bearer bonds, those merchant banks in the selling syndicate stand to profit from two sources.

---

9. But this is not the result of a price rise in the secondary market. Such competitive market pricing, moreover, is not the dominant reason for the Eurodollar bond borrowing advantage. There are too few banks pricing competitively for that to be true. See M. W. Marr, R. J. Rogowski, and J. L. Trimble, "The Competitive

Effects of Commercial Bank Entry in Eurodollar Bond Underwriting," Working Paper, Tulane University School of Business Administration.

10. Walter, cited in note 8.

11. See Marr and Trimble, cited in note 3.

One is from selling more Eurobonds at higher prices to secrecy-seeking investors; the other is from the associated increase in volume of secrecy-related banking services, also a particularly high-margin business. Thus, when demand is strong, a lead manager of a Eurodollar bond issue will be offered the highest prices by affiliate banks offering financial anonymity to their clients. In this way, the lead manager can choose to distribute a greater share of the issue to investors seeking anonymity. Their profits will rise, as a result, and the proceeds could be used to help fund a desired long-range investment such as pricing bond underwritings to penetrate the U.S. market.

What Has Been Happening to the Eurobond Advantage?

During the 1977-83 period, the price of Eurodollar bonds was increasing relative to that of domestic bonds because demand was increasing faster than supply. Three causes contributed to this increase in relative demand.

High U.S. interest rates. Between 1977 and 1981, the demand for Eurodollar bonds by all foreign investors increased because U.S. interest rates were rising relative to other world interest rates. U.S. rates, fueled by an increasing money supply, rose in fact to extraordinarily high levels. By 1980 the prime rate had risen above 20 percent. As a result, foreign capital flowed into the U.S. market, causing domestic interest rates to rise.

Rising U.S. dollar. After 1980 the demand for Eurodollar bonds from all foreign investors continued to increase because the dollar rose in value against other world currencies. Under a tighter monetary policy, inflation subsided. As a result, domestic interest rates fell and the value of the U.S. dollar began a rise against most European currencies which lasted through 1985. Consequently, Eurodollar bonds were attractive to Euromarket investors during this period principally because of the gains in currency conversion.

Secrecy-seeking investors. It is likely that the demand for Eurodollar bonds also increased between 1977 and 1984 as a result of an increase in demand from investors seeking anonymity. A number of developments during this period could have spurred the demand for financial secrecy. State-sponsored terrorism emerged as a signficant political phenomenon; arms sales to revolutionary and counter-

revolutionary groups were on the rise; increased social acceptance of cocaine by middle-class society increased cocaine demand and international drug trafficking; and increases in the number of countries and banks offering financial secrecy, aided by technological improvements and innovations in financial services, increased the possibilities for capital flight.

Regulation of the U.S. Market

Even given all the factors above, the development of the Eurodollar borrowing alternative could not have occurred if there were a largely unrestricted flow of capital flow between the U.S. and Eurodollar bond markets. From the point of view of Euromarket investors, the registration requirement on registered bonds, which is the norm in the U.S., are obstructions to the free flow of capital. But, from the point of view of the Internal Revenue Service (IRS), bearer bonds, which are the norm in Europe, are a threat to ensuring tax compliance by U.S. citizens.

Until 1984 the only instrument of U.S. policy bridging these markets was a 1948 treaty between the U.S. and the Netherlands Antilles. This treaty, which applies to affiliates of U.S. issuers, exempts foreign investors from the 30 percent withholding tax that U.S. citizens have to pay on the coupon income from bonds. In 1984 the exemption was extended to Eurobonds issued from within the U.S., but the treaty (though seemingly now ineffectual) remained in effect. Under either arrangement domestic corporations could, and may still, sell new-issue bearer bonds to Euromarket but not to U.S. investors. U.S. investors, however, may legally purchase these bonds after they have been "seasoned" in the secondary market.

THE FUTURE

Will the borrowing advantage in Eurodollar bonds continue? If our assessment of the situation is correct, that will depend on the rate at which the demand from anonymity-seeking investors grows and on the inclination of Eurobond underwriters to share a price gain with U.S. firms. Intuition tells us that secrecy demand will likely fluctuate with political and market conditions and that the incentive to penetrate the U.S. market will at some time reach a saturation point. Hence, a major borrowing advantage probably will not persist indefinitely. At the same time, however, Eurodollar bonds will likely remain a viable bor-

IN 1984 THE U.S. TREASURY, IN AN ATTEMPT TO CAPTURE SOME OF THE LOW INTEREST RATES IN THE EUROMARKET, OFFERED A REGISTERED ISSUE AT THE BEHEST OF THE IRS. THE ISSUE FAILED TO SELL, HOWEVER, UNTIL IT WAS MODIFIED TO A "PARTIALLY" BEARER FORM ACCEPTABLE TO EUROMARKET INVESTORS.

rowing source for U.S. firms.

Perhaps as important for the persistence of this borrowing advantage, however, is the possibility of change in government policy. The growth in the Eurodollar bond market is a symptom of changing times. Financial markets are becoming more international and this is likely to create pressures for change in government regulation of financial markets.

The Netherlands Antilles treaty (and its post-1984 counterpart, the repeal of withholding tax for foreign investors) is a critical link between secrecy-seeking investors in the Euromarket and corporate borrowers in the U.S. It gives U.S. borrowers a substitute financing source. This dampens pressures on domestic interest rates but at the expense of greater interdependency with Euromarket interest rates.

Because the capital movements promoted by the Antilles treaty and related U.S. policies have only recently become important, the corresponding policy issues are just beginning to surface. This seemed evident in June 1987 when the U.S. Treasury outraged major institutional investors and industry groups in the U.S. and in Europe by attempting to terminate the Antilles treaty. Apparently unaware that many Eurobond indentures carry special call provisions which trigger with any change in the market, including termination of the Antilles treaty, the Treasury moved to terminate the treaty on the grounds that it was unnecessary because the 30 percent withholding tax on Eurobonds had been terminated in 1984. After discovering that U.S. pension funds and insurance companies held Eurobonds in their portfolios and would lose millions of dollars if the treaty was terminated, the Treasury dropped their termination proposal.

An issue that likely will surface continually in the coming years concerns the trade-off between maintaining tax compliance of U.S. citizens on the one hand and promoting free capital movement on the other. Although this is not a new issue, the specific question is gaining renewed importance in policy implementation. And a recent conflict between the Treasury and the IRS indicates that there are important issues yet to be resolved (as well as suggesting the strength of investor demand for anonymity in the Euromarket). In 1984 the U.S. Treasury, in an attempt to capture some of the low interest rates in the Euromarket, offered a *registered* issue at the behest of the IRS. The issue failed to sell, however, until it was modified to a "partially" bearer form acceptable to Euromarket investors. And these so-called targeted Treasury bonds are still being offered in limited quantities.

There also are difficult welfare issues attending government policies that promote capital movements between these two markets. The issues arise because some segments of the domestic economy gain at the expense of others. For example, by bridging the domestic and Eurodollar bond markets, the Antilles Treaty promotes foreign investment in dollar bonds. Foreign investment causes the value of the dollar *vis-a-vis* other currencies to rise, which in turn causes our exports to become less competitive and our imports more competitive. But failing to bridge these markets generates even greater costs because the financial markets would be less integrated and thus less efficient worldwide. As a result, domestic interest rates would generally be higher than otherwise. Also, although U.S. citizens presently are prohibited from buying Eurodollar bonds until they are seasoned in the secondary market, the incentive to escape withholding taxes is strong and likely to increase as the technology of banking makes the Euromarket more accessible to U.S. residents.

The Uses of Hybrid Debt in Managing Corporate Risk

by Charles Smithson, *Chase Manhattan Bank*, and Donald Chew, *Stern Stewart & Co.*

T he corporate use of hybrid debt securities—those that combine a conventional debt issue with a "derivative" such as a forward, swap, or option—increased significantly during the 1980s. And, while many of the more esoteric or tax-driven securities introduced in the last decade have disappeared, corporate hybrids now seem to be flourishing. In so doing, they are helping U.S. companies raise capital despite the restrictive financing climate of the '90s.

Hybrid debt, to be sure, is not a new concept. Convertible bonds, first issued by the Erie Railroad in the 1850s, are hybrid securities that combine straight debt and options on the value of the issuer's equity.[1] What is distinctive about the hybrid debt instruments of the 1980s is that their payoffs, instead of being tied to the issuing company's stock price, are linked to a growing variety of *general economic variables*. As illustrated in Figure 1, corporate hybrids have appeared that index investor returns to exchange rates, interest rates, stock market indices, and the prices of commodities such as oil, copper, and natural gas.

The recent wave of corporate hybrids began in 1973, when PEMEX, the state-owned Mexican oil producer, issued bonds that incorporated a *forward contract* on a commodity (in this case, oil). In 1980, Sunshine Mining Co. went a step further by issuing bonds incorporating a commodity *option* (on silver). In 1988, Magma Copper made yet another advance by issuing a bond giving investors a *series of commodity options* (on copper)—in effect, one for every coupon payment.

Other new hybrids, as mentioned, have had their payoffs tied to interest rates, foreign exchange rates, and the behavior of the stock market. In 1981, Oppenheimer & Co., a securities brokerage firm, issued a security whose principal repayment is indexed to the volume of trading on the New York Stock Exchange. Notes indexed to the value of equity indexes appeared in 1986, and inflation-indexed notes (tied to the CPI) were introduced in 1988.

---

1. The date for the introduction of convertible bonds is reported by Peter Tufano in "Financial Innovation and First-Mover Advantages," *Journal of Financial Economics*, 25, pp. 213-240.

FIGURE 1 ■ DEVELOPMENT OF HYBRID SECURITIES: 1973-1991

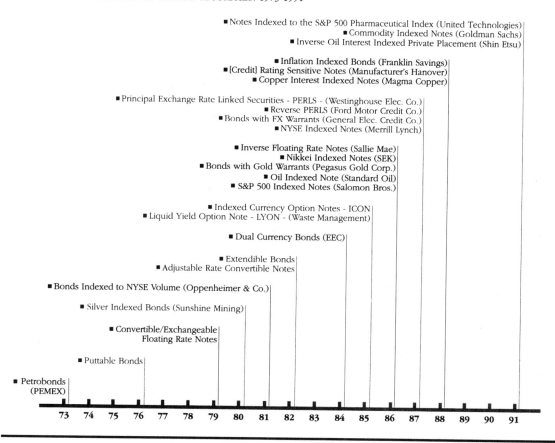

The 1980s also saw new hybrids with payoffs that, like those of convertibles, are tied to company-specific performance. For example, the Rating Sensitive Notes issued by Manufacturer's Hanover in 1988 provide for increased payments to investors if Manny Hanny's creditworthiness declines. And the LYON™ pioneered and underwritten by Merrill Lynch in 1985 grants investors not only the option to convert the debt into equity, but also the right to "put" the security back to the firm.

The pace of hybrid innovation peaked around 1987. But hybrids are now staging a comeback. As the title of a recent *Wall Street Journal* article put it, 1991 was "A Boom Year for Newfangled Trading Vehicles."[2] The past year witnessed the introduction of notes indexed to a subset of a general equity index, Goldman Sachs' notes indexed to a commodity index, private placements incorporating options on commodities, and a boom in convertible debt.

Why do companies issue, and investors buy, such complex securities? Before the development of derivative products in the 1970s, investors may have been attracted by the prospect of purchasing a "bundle" of securities—say, debt plus warrants—that they could not duplicate themselves by purchasing both of the components separately. And this "scarce security" or "market completion" argument also holds for some of today's debt hybrids (especially those that provide longer-dated forwards and options than those available on organized exchanges).

2. December 26, 1991, p. C1. The *Journal* article dealt more with exchange-traded products than with hybrids.

LYON™ is a trademark of Merrill Lynch & Co.

By hedging a variety of financial and operating risks and thereby increasing the
expected stability of corporate cash flows, hybrids may lower the issuer's overall
funding costs.

But, because active exchanges now provide low-cost futures and options with payoffs tied to all variety of interest rates, exchange rates, and commodity prices, markets are becoming increasingly "complete," if you will. Given the existence of well-functioning, low-cost markets for many of the components making up the hybrid debt instruments, we have to ask the following question: Is there any reason investors should be willing to pay more for these securities sold *in combination* rather than separately?

In this article, we argue that hybrid debt offers corporate treasurers an efficient means of managing a variety of financial and operating risks—risks that, in many cases, cannot be managed if the firm issues straight debt and then purchases derivatives. By hedging such risks and thereby increasing the expected stability of corporate cash flows, hybrids may lower the issuer's overall funding costs.[3] At the same time, though, part of the present corporate preference for managing price risks with hybrids rather than derivative products stems from current restrictions on the use of hedge accounting for derivatives, as well as tax and regulatory arbitrage opportunities afforded by hybrids.

PRICE VOLATILITY: THE NECESSARY CONDITION FOR HYBRIDS

The stability of the economic and financial environment is a key determinant of the kinds of debt instruments that dominate the marketplace. When prices are stable and predictable, investors will demand—and the capital markets will produce—relatively simple instruments.

In the late 1800s, for example, the dominant financial instrument in Great Britain was the *consol*: a bond with a fixed interest rate and no maturity— it lasted forever. Investors were content to hold infinite-lived British government bonds because British sovereign credit was good and because inflation was virtually unknown. General confidence in price level stability led to stable interest rates, which in turn dictated the use of long-lived, fixed-rate bonds.

But consider what happens to financing practices when confidence is replaced by turbulence and

uncertainty. As one of us pointed out in an earlier issue of this journal, in 1863 the Confederate States of America issued a 20-year bond denominated not in Confederate dollars, but in French Francs and Pounds Sterling. To allay the concern of its overseas investors that the Confederacy would not be around to service its debt with hard currency, the issue was also convertible at the option of the holder into cotton at the rate of six pence per pound. In the parlance of today's investment banker, the Confederate States issued a *dual-currency, cotton-indexed* bond.[4]

The Breakdown of Bretton Woods and the New Era of Volatility

Throughout the 1950s and most of the 1960s, economic and price stability prevailed in the U.S., and in the developed nations generally. Investment-grade U.S. corporations responded predictably by raising capital in the form of 30-year, fixed-rate bonds (yielding around 3-4%). But, toward the end of the '60s, rates of inflation in the U.S. and U.K. began to increase. There was also considerable divergence among developed countries in monetary and fiscal policy, and thus in rates of inflation. Such pressures led inevitably to the abandonment, in 1973, of the Bretton Woods agreement to maintain relatively fixed exchanged rates. And, during the early 1970s and thereafter, the general economic environment saw higher and more volatile rates of inflation along with unprecedented volatility in exchange rates, interest rates, and commodity prices. (For evidence of such general price volatility, see Figure 2.)

In response to this heightened price volatility, capital markets created new financial instruments to help investors and issuers manage their exposures. Indeed, the last 20 years has seen the introduction of (1) futures on foreign exchange, interest rates, metals, and oil; (2) currency, interest rate, and commodity swaps; (3) options on exchange rates, interest rates, and oil; and (4) options on the above futures and options. Flourishing markets for these products in turn helped give rise to corporate hybrid debt securities that effectively incorporate these derivative products.

3. For preliminary evidence of the impact of issuing hybrid debt on the firm's cost of capital, see Charles Smithson and Leah Schraudenbach, "Reflection of Financial Price Risk in the Firm's Share Price," Chase Manhattan Bank, 1992.

4. Waite Rawls and Charles Smithson, "The Evolution of Risk Management Products," *Journal of Applied Corporate Finance*, Vol. 1 No. 4 (1989).

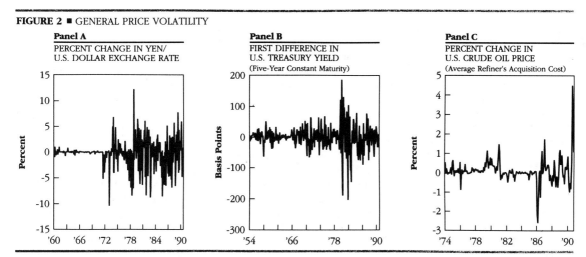

FIGURE 2 ■ GENERAL PRICE VOLATILITY

Panel A

PERCENT CHANGE IN YEN/
U.S. DOLLAR EXCHANGE RATE

Panel B

FIRST DIFFERENCE IN
U.S. TREASURY YIELD
(Five-Year Constant Maturity)

Panel C

PERCENT CHANGE IN
U.S. CRUDE OIL PRICE
(Average Refiner's Acquisition Cost)

USING HYBRIDS TO MANAGE COMMODITY RISK

Unlike foreign exchange and interest rates, which were relatively stable until the 1970s, commodity prices have a long history of volatility. Thus, it is no surprise that hybrid securities designed to hedge commodity price risks came well before hybrids with embedded currency and interest rate derivatives.

As mentioned earlier, the Confederacy issued a debt instrument convertible into cotton in 1863. By the 1920s, commodity-linked hybrids were available in U.S. capital markets. A case in point is the gold-indexed bond issued by Irving Fisher's Rand Kardex Corporation in 1925. Similar to the PEMEX issue described earlier, the principal repayment of this gold-indexed bond was tied directly to gold prices.[5] Fisher realized that he could significantly lower his firm's funding costs by furnishing a scarce security desired by investors—in this case, a long-dated forward on gold prices. And Fisher's successful innovation was imitated by a number of other U.S. companies during the '20s.

Like so many of the financial innovations of the 1920s, however, that wave of hybrid debt financings was ended by the regulatory reaction that set in during the 1930s.[6] Specifically, the "Gold Clause"

Joint Congressional Resolution of June 5, 1933 virtually eliminated indexed debt by prohibiting "a lender to require of a borrower a different quantity or number of dollars from that loaned." And it was not until October 1977, when Congress passed the Helms Amendment, that the legal basis for commodity-indexed debt was restored.

Hybrids with Option Features

The hybrids issued by Rand Kardex and PEMEX represent combinations of debt securities with forward contracts; that is, the promised principal repayments were designed to rise or fall directly with changes in the prices, respectively, of gold and oil. In the case of PEMEX, moreover, this forward-like feature reduced the risk to investors that the issuer wouldn't be able to repay principal; it did so by making the *amount* of the principal vary as directly as possible with the company's oil revenues.

Unlike the PEMEX and Rand Kardex issues, Sunshine Mining's 15-year silver-linked bond issued in 1980 combined a debt issue with a *European option*[7] on silver prices. In this case, the promised principal repayment could not fall below a certain level (the face value), but would increase proportionally with increases in the price of silver price above $20 per ounce at maturity.[8] Because most of

5. See J. Huston McCulloch, "The Ban on Indexed Bonds," *American Economic Review* 70 (December 1980), pp. 1018-21.

6. See Merton Miller's account of financial innovation in the 1920s and 1930s in the first article of this issue.

7. European options can be exercised only at maturity, as distinguished from American options, which can be exercised any time before expiration.

the commodity-linked hybrids that followed the Sunshine Mining issue in the '80s contain embedded options rather than forwards, let's consider briefly how the embedding of options within debt issues manages risk and lowers the issuer's cost of capital.

How Hybrids with Options Manage Risk. Corporate bondholders bear "downside" risk while typically being limited to a fixed interest rate as their reward. (In the jargon of options, the bondholder is "short a put" on the value of the firm's assets.) Because of this limited upside, they charge a higher "risk premium" when asked to fund companies with more volatile earnings streams. Like the forward contract embedded in the PEMEX issue, options also provide bondholders with an equity-like, "upside" participation. In return for this upside participation, bondholders will reduce the risk premium they charge. Indeed, the greater the expected volatility of the commodity price in question, the more valuable is that embedded option to the bondholders.[9]

Unlike hybrids with forwards, hybrids with embedded options provide investors with a "floor"— that is, a minimum principal repayment or set of coupons. And, though options therefore effect a less complete transfer of risk than in the case of forwards (in the sense that the firm's financing costs don't fall below the floor in the event of an extreme decline in commodity prices), investors should be willing to pay for the floor in the form of a reduced base rate of interest. To the extent they lower the rate of interest, option-like hybrids reduce the probability of default, thus reassuring bondholders and the rating agencies.

A good example of corporate risk management with options was a 1986 issue of Eurobonds with detachable gold warrants by Pegasus Gold Corporation, a Canadian gold mining firm. In effect, this issue gave investors two separable claims: (1) a straight debt issue with a series of fixed interest payments and a fixed principal repayment; and (2) European options on the price of gold. By giving bondholders a participation in the firm's gold revenues, the inclusion of such warrants reduced the coupon rate on the bond—which in turn lowered the issuer's financial risk.

Probably the most newsworthy hybrid in 1986, however, was Standard Oil's *Oil-Indexed Note*. This hybrid combines a zero-coupon bond with a European option on oil with the same maturity. The issue not only aroused the interest of the IRS, but also succeeded in rekindling regulatory concerns about the potential for "speculative abuse" built into hybrid securities.[10]

Commodity Interest-Indexed Bonds. The commodity hybrids mentioned thus far are all combinations of debt with forwards or options with a single maturity. In effect, they link only the principal repayment to commodity prices, but not the interim interest payments. But, in recent years, hybrids have also emerged that combine debt with a *series of options* of different maturities—maturities that are typically designed to correspond to the coupon dates of the underlying bond.

In 1988, for example, Magma Copper Company issued *Copper Interest-Indexed Senior Subordinated Notes*. This 10-year debenture has embedded within it 40 option positions on the price of copper—one maturing in 3 months, one in 6 months, ..., and one in 10 years. The effect of this series of embedded option positions is to make the company's quarterly interest payments vary with the prevailing price of copper, as shown below:

Average Copper Price	Indexed Interest Rate
$2.00 or above	21 %
1.80	20
1.60	19
1.40	18
1.30	17
1.20	16
1.10	15
1.00	14
0.90	13
0.80 or below	12

In 1989, Presidio Oil Company issued an oil-indexed note with a similar structure, but with the coupons linked to the price of natural gas. And, in 1991, Shin Etsu, a Japanese chemical manufacturer,

---

8. From the perspective of 1991, during which the silver price has averaged $4.00 per ounce, this exercise price of $20 per ounce may seem bizarre. But keep in mind that this bond was issued in early 1980. During the period October 1979–January 1980,the price of silver averaged $23 per ounce.

9. For a discussion of how the equity option embedded in convertibles could make convertible bondholders indifferent to increases in the volatility of corporate

cash flow, see Michael Brennan and Eduardo Schwartz, "The Case for Convertibles," *Chase Financial Quarterly* (Fall 1981). Reprinted in *Journal of Applied Corporate Finance* (Summer 1988).

10. See James Jordan, Robert Mackay, and Eugene Moriarty, "The New Regulation of Hybrid Debt Instruments," *Journal of Applied Corporate Finance*, Vol. 2 No. 4 (Winter 1990).

issued a hybrid with a similar structure; however, the issue was a private placement and the coupon payment floated *inversely* with the price of oil.

The Case of Forest Oil:
The Consequences of Not Managing Risk

It was Forest Oil, however, and not Presidio, that first considered issuing natural gas-linked debt. But Forest's management was confident that natural gas prices would go higher in the near future and thus decided that the price of the natural gas-linked debt would turn out to be too high. Unfortunately, the company's bet on natural gas prices ended up going against them. Natural gas prices since the issue was contemplated have fallen dramatically, and the company has been squeezed between high current interest costs and reduced revenues. Indeed, the squeeze has been so tight that Forest has been forced to restructure its debt.

USING HYBRIDS TO MANAGE FOREIGN EXCHANGE RISK

As Figure 2 suggests, exchange rates became more volatile following the abandonment of the Bretton Woods agreement in 1973. As a result, many companies have experienced foreign exchange risk arising from transaction, translation, and economic exposures.

The simplest way to manage an exposure to foreign exchange risk is by using a forward foreign exchange contract. If the firm is long foreign currency, it can cover this exposure by selling forward contracts. Or if it has a short position, it can buy forwards.

Dual Currency Bonds. Similar to PEMEX's oil-indexed issue, the simplest FX hybrid debt structure is a *Dual Currency Bond*. Such a bond combines a fixed-rate, "bullet" (that is, single) repayment bond and a long-dated forward contract on foreign exchange. For example, in 1985, Philip Morris Credit issued a dual-currency bond in which coupon payments are made in Swiss Francs while principal will be repaid US Dollars.

PERLs. A variant of the dual currency structure is the *Principal Exchange Rate Linked Security*. In 1987, Westinghouse Electric Company issued *PERLs*

wherein the bondholder received at maturity the principal the USD value of 70.13 million New Zealand dollars. The issuer's motive in this case was likely to reduce its funding costs by taking advantage of an unusual investor demand for long-dated currency forwards. Earlier in the same year, and presumably with similar motive, Ford Motor Credit Company issued *Reverse PERLs*. In this case, the principal repayment varied inversely with the value of the yen.[11]

Creating a Hybrid By Adding Options

As in the case of commodity-linked hybrids, forward-like FX hybrids seemed to have given way to structures containing warrants or other option-like features. In 1987, for example, General Electric Credit Corporation made a public offering made up of debt and yen-USD currency exchange warrants.

Bonds with Principal Indexed (Convertible) to FX. Like bonds with warrants, convertible bonds are made up of bonds and equity options. But there is one important difference: In the case of bonds with warrants, the bondholder can exercise the option embodied in a warrant and still keep the underlying bond. With convertibles, the holder must surrender the bond to exercise the option. Sunshine Mining's Silver-Indexed Bonds and Standard Oil's Oil Indexed Notes are similar constructions. The bondholder can receive either the value of the bond or the value of the option, but not both.

When this debt structure appeared with an embedded foreign currency option, the hybrid was called an *Indexed Currency Option Note* (or *ICON*). This security, which was first underwritten by First Boston in 1985, combines a fixed rate, bullet repayment bond and a European option on foreign exchange.[12]

USING HYBRIDS TO MANAGE INTEREST RATE RISK

Some companies have significant exposures to interest rates. Take the case of firms that supply inputs to the housing market. When interest rates rise, the revenues of such firms tend to fall. The use of standard, floating-rate bank debt in such cases would likely increase the probability of default.

---

11. See Michael G. Capatides, *A Guide to the Capital Markets Activities of Banks and Bank Holding Companies*, (Browne & Co.), 1988, p. 132.

12. In his article in this issue, "Securities Innovation: An Overview," John Finnerty notes that ICONs "were introduced and disappeared quickly."

Corporate hybrids reduce shareholder-bondholder conflicts by reducing current
interest rates, shifting debt service payments to periods when firms are better able to
pay, stabilizing cash flow, and thereby reducing the likelihood of financial distress.

Creating a Hybrid with Embedded Swaps

To manage interest rate risk, such companies may be best served by a debt instrument wherein the coupon payment actually declines when interest rates rise. Such an *Inverse Floating Rate Note*—or a *Yield-Curve Note*, as it was called when first issued by the Student Loan Marketing Association (Sallie Mae) in the public debt market in 1986—can be decomposed into a floating-rate, bullet repayment note and a plain vanilla interest rate swap for twice the principal of the loan.

Creating a Hybrid By Adding Options

Just as bondholders can be provided options to exchange their bonds for a specified amount of a commodity or foreign currency, hybrid securities have been issued that give bondholders the option to exchange a bond (typically at maturity) for another bond (typically with the same coupon and maturity).

Convertible/Exchangeable Floating Rate Notes. These hybrids, which give the holder the right to convert to (or exchange for) a fixed-rate bond at a pre-specified interest rate, first appeared in 1979. Such notes contain embedded "put" options on interest rates; that is, investors are likely to exercise their conversion or exchange rights only if interest rates fall below a certain level.

Extendible Notes. The same, moreover, is true of extendible notes, which give the holder the right to exchange the underlying bond for a bond of longer maturity. Such bonds first appeared in 1982.

USING HYBRIDS TO REDUCE CONFLICTS BETWEEN BONDHOLDERS AND SHAREHOLDERS

In "normal" circumstances—that is, when operations are profitable and the firm can comfortably meet its debt service payments and investment schedule—the interests of bondholders and shareholders are united. Both groups of investors benefit from managerial decisions that increase the total value of the firm.

In certain cases, however, corporate managements find themselves in the position of being able to increase shareholder value *at the expense of bondholders*.[13] For example, as happened in a number of leveraged recapitalizations, management could reduce the value of outstanding bonds by increasing debt or adding debt senior to that in question. (In professional circles, this is known as *event risk*; in academic parlance it is the *claims dilution problem*.) Or, if the firm were in danger of insolvency, management could choose—as did some S&L executives—to invest in ever riskier projects in desperate attempts to save the firm (the *asset substitution problem*). Finally, a management squeezed between falling revenues and high interest payments could choose to pass up value-adding projects such as R&D or, if things are bad enough, basic maintenance and safety procedures (the *underinvestment problem*).[14]

Corporate debtholders are well aware that such problems can arise, and they accordingly protect themselves by lowering the price they are willing to pay for the debt. For corporate management, such lower prices translate into higher interest payments, which in turn further raise the probability of financial trouble.

Hybrids reduce these shareholder-bondholder conflicts by reducing current interest rates, shifting debt service payments to periods when firms are better able to pay, stabilizing cash flow, and thereby reducing the likelihood of financial distress. In so doing, they also raise the price of the corporate debt to investors and lower the overall corporate cost of capital.

Using Hybrids to Reduce the Claims Dilution Problem (or Protect Against "Event Risk")

Puttable Bonds. Introduced in 1976, these bonds give their holders the option to "put" the bond back to the issuer. Such an option would be exercised only if interest rates rise or the issuer's credit

13. For the seminal discussion of the effect of conflicts between shareholders and debtholders (and between management and shareholders as well) on the behavior of the firm, see Michael C. Jensen and William H. Meckling, "Theory of the Firm: Managerial Behavior, Agency Costs, and Capital Structure," *Journal of Financial Economics* (1976), pp. 305-360.

14. For an account of the underinvestment problem, see Stewart Myers, "The Determinants of Corporate Borrowing," *Journal of Financial Economics* (1977).

For a more detailed examination of these sources of shareholder/debtholder conflict, see Clifford W. Smith and Jerold B. Warner, "On Financial Contracting: An Analysis of Bond Covenants," *Journal of Financial Economics*, 7 (1979), pp. 117-161.

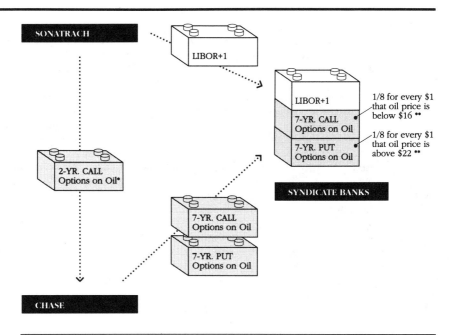

FIGURE 3
OIL-LINKED CREDIT-
SENSITIVE SYNDICATE

SONATRACH

LIBOR+1

LIBOR+1

7-YR. CALL
Options on Oil

1/8 for every $1
that oil price is
below $16 **

7-YR. PUT
Options on Oil

1/8 for every $1
that oil price is
above $22 **

SYNDICATE BANKS

2-YR. CALL
Options on Oil*

7-YR. CALL
Options on Oil

7-YR. PUT
Options on Oil

CHASE

*During the first two years, if the price of oil exceeds $23, Sonatrach will pay a supplemental coupon to Chase.
**In the first year, the syndicate receives additional interest if the price of oil falls outside the range of $16-$22. In year 2, the
range widens to $15-$23, then to $14-$24 in year 3, and to $13-$25 in years 4 through 7.

standing falls. In this sense, puttable bonds give bondholders both a call option on interest rates and an option on the credit spread of the issuer.[15] Such put options thus protect bondholders not only against increases in interest rates, but also against the possibility of losses from deteriorating operating performance or leveraged recapitalizations. In the wake of the widely publicized bondholder losses accompanying the KKR buyout of RJR Nabisco in 1989, the use of put options to protect against such "event risk" enjoyed a new vogue.

Floating Rate, Rating Sensitive Notes. These notes, issued by Manufacturer Hanover in 1988, contain explicit options on the issuer's credit standing. In this security, Manufacturer's Hanover agreed to pay investors a spread above LIBOR that increased with each incremental decline in the bank's senior debt rating.

From the standpoint of risk management, however, there is an obvious flaw in the design of this security. Although it may partially compensate investors for increases in risk, it actually increases the probability of default instead of reducing it. The security increases the corporate debt service burden precisely when the issuing firm can least afford it— when its credit rating has fallen and, presumably, its operating cash flow declined.

A hybrid structure designed to overcome this problem was a syndication of oil-indexed bonds created by Chase Manhattan for Sonatrach (the state hydrocarbons company of Algeria) in 1990. As illustrated in Figure 3, the transaction was structured so that Chase accepted two-year call options on oil from Sonatrach and then transformed those two-year calls into seven-year calls and puts that were passed on to the syndicate members. Investors were compensated for a below-market interest by a payoff structure that would provide them with higher payoffs in the event of significantly *higher or lower* oil prices.

---

15. Extendible notes also provide bondholders with an option on the firm's credit standing. But, unlike puttable debt, it represents the opportunity to benefit from increases in the firm's credit standing, or decreases in the spread. In the case of extendible notes, if the credit spread of the issuer decreases, the right to extend the maturity of the note (at the old credit spread) has value.

The combination of the put and conversion features are especially useful in controlling the asset substitution, or risk-shifting, problem. For this reason, the LYONs structure should be particularly attractive to issuers with substantial capital investment opportunities and a wide range of alternative investment projects.

For the issuer, however, the security requires higher payments to Chase *only in the event of higher oil prices*. If the price of oil declines, although the syndicate members receive a higher yield, the increase comes from Chase, not Sonatrach.

Using Hybrids to Reduce the Asset Substitution and Underinvestment Problems

Convertibles. At the outset, we noted that convertible bonds contain embedded options on the company's equity. By providing bondholders with the right to convert their claims into equity, management provides bondholders with the assurance that they will participate in any increase in shareholder value that results from increasing the risk of the company's activities—whether by leveraging up or undertaking riskier investments. By lowering current interest rates and thus reducing the likelihood of financial trouble, convertibles also reduce the probability that financially strapped companies will be forced to forgo valuable investment opportunities.[16]

Convertibles (and debt with warrants, their close substitutes) are also potentially useful in resolving disagreements between bondholders and shareholders about just how risky the firm's activities are. The value of convertibles are risk-neutral in the following sense: Unexpected increases in company risk reduce the value of the bond portion of a convertible, but at the same time increase the value of the embedded option (by increasing volatility). It is largely because of this risk-neutralizing effect—and for their role in reducing the "underinvestment problem" mentioned below—that convertible issuers tend to be smaller, newer, riskier firms characterized by high growth and earnings volatility.[17]

The Case of LYONs

While a number of bonds are puttable or convertible, the Liquid Yield Option Note (LYON) introduced by Merrill Lynch in 1985 is both puttable and convertible. The combination of the put and conversion features are especially useful in controlling the asset substitution, or risk-shifting, problem just described.[18] For this reason, the LYONs structure should be particularly attractive to issu-

ers with substantial capital investment opportunities and a wide range of alternative investment projects (with varying degrees of risk).

It is thus interesting to note that the LYON structure was first used to fund companies where the asset substitution problem was acute. Take the case of Waste Management, the first issuer of LYONs. Although Waste Management is today a household name among even small investors, in 1985 the company could best be viewed as a collection of "growth options." As such it posed considerable uncertainty for investors.

THE ECONOMIC RATIONALE FOR ISSUING A HYBRID SECURITY

We are still left with a fundamental question: Given the well-functioning, low-cost markets for derivative products available today, why should a corporate issuer ever prefer the "bundled" hybrid to simply issuing standard debt and buying or selling the derivatives. We now discuss the following three reasons why corporate management might choose hybrids:

(1) If the firm issuing the hybrid can provide investors with a "play" not available otherwise—that is, a derivative instrument not available in the traded derivatives markets—the issuing firm will consequently be paid a premium for "completing the market."

(2) The hybrid may enable the issuer to take advantage of tax or regulatory arbitrages that would lower the cost of borrowing.

(3) By embedding a risk management product into a hybrid, the issuer may be able to obtain hedge accounting treatment, which may not be allowed if the derivative was bought or sold separately.

Using Hybrids to Provide Investors with a "Play"

The most straightforward reason for issuing a hybrid is to provide investors with a means of taking a position on a financial price. If the issuer provides a "play" not otherwise available, the investor will be willing to pay a premium, thereby reducing the issuer's cost of funding. (And, if the hybrid provides

---

16. More technically, the underinvestment problem arises from the fact that, in financially troubled firms, an outsized portion of the returns from new investments must go to help restore the value of the bondholders' claims before the shareholders receive any payoff at all. This has also been dubbed the "debt overhang" problem.

17. For an exposition of this argument, see Michael Brennan and Eduardo Schwartz, "The Case for Convertibles," *Chase Financial Quarterly* (Fall 1981). Reprinted in *Journal of Applied Corporate Finance* (Summer 1988).

18. As described at length in the next article in this issue, the put feature also enabled Merrill Lynch to tailor the security for its network of retail investors.

investors with a "scarce security" not otherwise obtainable, it may also provide corporate issuers with a hedge they can't duplicate with derivative products.)

The "play" can be in the form of a forward contract. Perhaps the best example of such is dual currency bonds, which provided investors with foreign exchange forward contracts with longer maturities than those available in the standard market. The forward contracts embedded in dual currency bonds have maturities running to 10 years, whereas liquidity in the standard foreign exchange forward market declines for maturities greater than one year, and falls very significantly beyond five years.

The "play," however, has more commonly been in the form of an option embedded in the bond—generally an option of longer maturity than those available in the standard option market. Sunshine Mining's Silver Indexed Bond fits this category, as do Standard Oil's Oil Indexed Note and the gold warrants issued by Pegasus Gold Corporation. In 1986 long-dated options on stock market indices were introduced with the development of hybrid debt in which the principal was indexed to an equity index. While the first such debt issues were indexed to the Nikkei, Salomon Brothers' "S&P 500 Index Subordinated Notes (SPINs)" have probably received more public attention. A SPIN is convertible into the value of the S&P 500 Index, rather than into an individual equity. Since then, debt has been issued that is indexed to other equity indices (for example, the NYSE index) or subsets of indices. For example, in 1991, United Technologies issued a zero-coupon bond indexed to the S&P Pharmaceutical Index.

Using Hybrids to "Arbitrage" Tax and/or Regulatory Authorities

Hybrid debt has also been used to take advantage of asymmetries in tax treatment or regulations in different countries or markets. One classic example is a case of "arbitrage" reported in *Business Week* under the provocative title, "A Way for US Firms to Make 'Free Money'." The "free money" came from two sources:

(1) A difference in tax treatment between the U.S. and Japan—the Japanese tax authorities ruled

that income earned from holding a zero-coupon bond would be treated as a capital gain, thereby making interest income on the zero non-taxable for Japanese investors. In contrast, U.S. tax authorities permitted any U.S. firm issuing a zero coupon bond to deduct from current income the imputed interest payments.

(2) A regulatory arbitrage—The Ministry of Finance limited Japanese pension funds' investments in non-yen-dominated bonds issued by foreign corporations to at most 10% of their portfolios. The Ministry of Finance also ruled that dual currency bonds qualified as a yen issue, thus allowing dual currency bonds to command a premium from Japanese investors.

Consequently, U.S. firms issued zero-coupon yen bonds (to realize the interest rate savings from the tax arbitrage), and then issued a dual currency bond to hedge the residual yen exposure from the yen zero, while realizing a further interest savings from the regulatory arbitrage.

Tax-Deductible Equity. Perhaps the most thinly disguised attempt to issue tax-deductible equity was the *Adjustable Rate Convertible Debt* introduced in 1982.[19] Such convertibles paid a coupon determined by the dividend rate on the firm's common stock; moreover, the debt could be converted to common stock at the current price at any time (i.e., there was no conversion premium). Not surprisingly, once the IRS ruled that this was equity for tax purposes, this structure disappeared.

On a less aggressive level, hybrid structures like Merrill Lynch's LYON take advantage of the treatment of zero coupon instruments by U.S. tax authorities—that is, zero coupon bonds allow the issuer to deduct deferred interest payments from current income (although the holder of the bond must declare them as income). Given the impact of the IRS ruling on adjustable rate convertible debt, it is not surprising that a great deal of attention has been given to the tax status of the LYON.

Using Hybrids to Obtain Accrual Accounting Treatment for Risk Management

If a U.S. company uses a forward, futures, swap, or option to hedge a specific transaction (for example, a loan or a purchase or a receipt), it is

19. This point is made by John Finnerty in his article in this issue.

Except for the highest-rated companies, most firms today face *non-price* credit restrictions that have greatly enlarged credit spreads. Many such companies are using hybrid debt to lower their risk profile and thus avoid the higher funding costs now associated with being a riskier borrower.

relatively simple to obtain accrual accounting treatment for the hedge. (Changes in the market value of the hedging instrument offset changes in the value of the asset being hedged, so there is no need to mark the hedging instrument to market.)

If, however, the firm wishes to use one of the risk management instruments to hedge expected net income or an even longer-term economic exposure, the current position of the accounting profession is that the hedge position must be marked to market. Some companies have been reluctant to use derivatives to manage such risks because this accounting treatment would increase the volatility of their reported income—*even while such a risk management strategy would stabilize their longer-run operating cash flow.*

With the use of hybrids, by contrast, which contain embedded derivatives, the firm may be able to obtain accrual accounting treatment for the entire package. Accountants are accustomed to valuing convertible debt at historical cost; and, given this precedent, they can extend the same treatment to hybrids.[20]

CONCLUDING REMARKS

Beginning in 1980 with Sunshine Mining's issue of silver-linked bonds, U.S. corporations have increasingly chosen to raise debt capital by embedding derivatives such as forwards or options into their notes and bonds. In the early '80's, such hybrids typically provided investors with payoffs (at first only principal, but later interest payments as well) indexed to commodity prices, interest rates, and exchange rates. But, in recent years, companies have begun to issue debt indexed to general stock market indices and even subsets of such indices.

Critics of such newfangled securities view them as the offspring of "supply-driven" fads. According to this view, profit-hungry investment banks set their highly-paid "rocket scientists" to designing new securities that can then be foisted on unsuspecting corporate treasurers and investors.

As economists, however, we begin with the assumption that capital market innovations succeed only to the extent they do a better job than existing products in meeting the demands of issuers and investors. The evidence presented in these pages, albeit anecdotal, suggests that hybrid debt is a capital market response to corporate treasurers' desire to manage pricing risks and otherwise tailor their securities to investor demands. In some cases, especially those in which hybrids feature long-dated forwards or options, hybrids are furnishing investors with securities they cannot obtain elsewhere.

Like the remarkable growth of futures, swaps, and options markets beginning in the late '70s, the proliferation of corporate hybrids during the '80s is fundamentally an attempt to cope with increased price volatility. The sharp increase in the volatility of exchange rates, interest rates, and oil prices—to name just the most important—during the 1970s provided the "necessary condition" for the rise of hybrids.

But another important stimulant to hybrids has come from other constraints on companies' ability to raise debt. In the early '80s, for example, when interest rates were high, hybrid debt was used by riskier firms to reduce their interest costs to manageable levels. Given the current level of interest rates today, most companies would likely choose to borrow as much straight debt as possible. But except for the highest-rated companies, many firms also now face *non-price* credit restrictions that have greatly enlarged credit spreads. In some such cases, companies are using hybrid debt to lower their risk profile and thus avoid the higher funding costs now associated with being a riskier corporate borrower. In other cases, hybrids are providing access to debt capital that would otherwise be denied on any terms.

---

20. See J. Matthew Singleton, "Hedge Accounting: A State-of-the-Art Review," *Journal of Banking and Finance*, 5 (Fall 1991), pp. 26-32.

The Financing Decision 2: The Financing Vehicles/Selected Bibliography

Black, F. and J. Cox, "Valuing Corporate Securities: Some Effects of Bond Indenture Provisions," *Journal of Finance* 31 (1979), 351-367.

Black, F. and M. Scholes, "The Pricing of Options and Corporate Liabilities," *Journal of Political Economy* 81 (May-June, 1973).

Bierman, H. and B. Brown, "Why Corporations Should Consider Income Bonds," *Financial Executive* 35 (October, 1967).

Brennan, M. and E. Schwartz, "Convertible Bonds: Valuation and Optimal Strategies for Call and Conversion," *Journal of Finance* 32 (1977), 1699-1715.

Brennan, M. and E. Schwartz, "Analyzing Convertible Bonds," *Journal of Financial and Quantitative Analysis* 15 (1980), 901-929.

Boyce, W. M. and A. J. Kalotay, "Optimum Bond Calling and Refunding," *Interfaces* 9 (November, 1979).

Cornell, B., "Monetary Policy, Inflation Forecasting and the Term Structure of Interest Rates," *Journal of Finance* 33 (March, 1978), 117-127.

Courtadon, G. and J. J. Merrick, Jr., "The Valuation of Equity Notes," New York University, October, 1983.

Cox, J., S. Ross and M. Rubinstein, "Option Pricing: A Simplified Approach," *Journal of Financial Economics* 7 (1979), 229-263.

Dann, L. and W. Mikkelson, "Convertible Debt Issuance, Capital Structure Change and Financing-Related Information: Some New Evidence," *Journal of Financial Economics* 13 (June, 1984).

Fama, E. F., "Short-term Interest Rates as Predictors of Inflation," *American Economic Review* 65 (June, 1975), 265-282.

Fama, E. F., "Inflation Uncertainty and the Expected Return on Treasury Bills," *Journal of Political Economy* 84 (June, 1976), 472-448.

Fama, E. F., and M. R. Gibbons, "Inflation, Real Returns and Capital Investment," *Journal of Business* (1981).

Fischer, S. "The Demand for Index Bonds," *Journal of Political Economy* 83 (March, 1975), 509-534.

Fisher, I., *Theory of Interest* (New York: Macmillan Co. 1930).

Garbade, K. and P. Wachtel, "Time Variation in the Relationship between Inflation and Interest Rates," *Journal of Monetary Economics* 4 (November, 1978), 755-765.

Geske, R., "The Valuation of Corporate Liabilities as Compound Options," *Journal of Financial and Quantitative Analysis* 12 (1979), 541-552.

Halford, F. A., "Income Bonds: The Sleeping Giant," *Financial Analysts Journal* 20 (January-February, 1964), pp. 73-79.

Hess, P. J. and J. L. Bicksler, "Capital Asset Prices Versus Time Series Models as Predictors of Inflation," *Journal of Financial Economics* 2 (December, 1975), 341-360.

Ingersoll, J., "A Contingent-Claims Valuation of Convertible Securities," *Journal of Financial Economics* 4 (May, 1977).

Ingersoll, J., "An Examination of Corporate Call Policies on Convertible Securities," *Journal of Finance* 32 (1977) 463-478.

Jensen, M. C. and W. Meckling, "Theory of the Firm: Managerial Behavior, Agency Costs and Capital Structure," *Journal of Financial Economics* 3 (October 1976), 11-25. Kraus, A., "The Bond Refunding Decision in an Efficient Market," *Journal of Financial and Quantitative Analysis* 8 (1973).

Livingston, M., "A Note on the Issuance of Long-Term Pure Discount Bonds," *Journal of Finance* 34 (March, 1979).

Logue, D. and T. Willet, "A Note on the Relation between the Rate and Variability of Inflation," *Economica* 43 (May, 1976), 151-58.

Mason, S. and S. Bhattacharya, "Risky Debt, Jump Processes and Safety Covenants," *Journal of Financial Economics* 9 (1981), 281-307.

Masulis, R. W., "The Effects of Capital Structure Change on Security Prices: A Study of Exchange Offers," *Journal of Financial Economics* 8 (June 1980), 139-177.

Maxfield, G., and Lyons, M. M., "Bonds--Income Bonds--Rights of Bondholders and Deductibility of Interest for Federal Tax Purposes," *Michigan Law Review* 56 (June, 1958), 1334-52.

McConnell, J. J. and G. G. Schlarbaum, "Another Foray Into the Backwaters of the Market," *The Journal of Portfolio Management* 7 (Fall, 1980), 61-65.

McConnell, J. J. and G. G. Schlarbaum, "Returns, Risks, and Pricing of Income Bonds, 1956-76 (Does Money Have an Odor?)," *Journal of Business* 54 (January, 1981), 33-64.

McConnell, J. J. and G. G. Schlarbaum, "Evidence on the Impact of Exchange Offers on Security Prices: The Case of Income Bonds," *Journal of Business* 54 (January, 1981), 65-86.

Merton, R. C., "The Theory of Rational Option Pricing," Bell *Journal of Economics and Management Science* 4 (Spring, 1973).

Merton, R. C., "On the Pricing of Corporate Debt: The Risk Structure of Interest Rates," *Journal of Finance* 29 (1974), 449-470.

Merton, R. C., "An Analytic Derivation of the Cost of Deposit Insurance and Loan Guarantees: An Application of Modern Option Pricing Theory," *Journal of Banking and Finance* 1 (1977), 3-11.

Mikkelson, W. H., "Convertible Calls and Security Returns," *Journal of Financial Economics* 9 (June 1981), 113-138.

Miller, M., "Debt and Taxes," *Journal of Finance* 32 (May 1977), 261-275.

Modigliani, F. and R. Sutch, "Innovations in Interest Rate Policy," *American Economic Review* 56 (May, 1966), 178-197.

Modigliani, F. and R. Sutch, "Debt Management and the Term Structure of Interest Rates," *Journal of Political Economy* 73 (August, 1967), 583-600.

Nelson, C. R., and G. W. Schwert, "On Testing the Hypothesis That the Real Rate of Interest is Constant," *American Economic Review* 67 (June, 1977), 478-486.

Rendleman, R. J., Jr. and B. J. Bartter, "Two State Option Pricing," *Journal of Finance* 34 (1979), 1093-1110.

Robbins, S., "A Bigger Role for Income Bonds," *Harvard Business Review* 33 (November-December, 1955), 100-114.

Robbins, S., *An Objective Look at Income Bonds* (Boston: Envision, 1974).

Rubinstein, M. and H.E. Leland, "Replicating Options with Positions in Stock and Cash," *Financial Analysts Journal* (July-August, 1981).

Schaefer, S. M., "The Problem with Redemption Yields," *Financial Analysts Journal*, 33 (July/August, 1977).

Smith, C. and J. Warner, "On Financial Contracting: An Analysis of Bond Covenants," *Journal of Financial Economics* 7 (June 1979), 117-161.

Wakeman, L. M., and S. Bhagat, "The Fisher Equation under Uncertainty," forthcoming *Journal of Monetary Economics* (1986).

Part V: Risk and Liabilities Management

INTRODUCTION

In "Managing Financial Risk," Charles Smithson, Clifford Smith, and Sykes Wilford provide an introduction to the four basic instruments for managing financial risks: forwards, futures, swaps, and options. After demonstrating the close relationships among these four "financial building blocks," the article goes on to demonstrate the potential for combining these to achieve virtually any desired risk position. The framework also lends itself to the analysis and pricing of complex hybrid securities by breaking them down into the basic components.

Finance theorists have for some time maintained that reducing risks at the corporate level which are diversifiable by investors at the portfolio level does not benefit stockholders. In "An Integrated Approach to Corporate Risk Management," Alan Shapiro and Sheridan Titman present a relatively new theoretical rationale for managing a company's *total risk* — that is, those risks which can be managed by investors through diversification of their portfolios as well as "non-diversifiable" or market risk. The authors then use this theoretical framework to generate a set of principles to guide financial executives in establishing a comprehensive, centralized approach to risk management — one which considers the costs and benefits of a variety of available strategies and financial instruments for managing the total exposure of the company.

But if, in some cases, there are good reasons for actively managing the total corporate exposure to a variety of risks, there also seems little doubt that many corporations are hedging some risks which are better borne by capital markets. In "The Corporate Insurance Decision," for example, David Mayers and Clifford Smith suggest that recent changes in the insurance industry are the result of corporate management's increasing awareness of its ability to self-insure. Insurance companies, as the article points out, have long provided services other than risk transference; and, for many large, widely-held corporations, it is principally these non-risk functions that are now at the source of the corporate demand for insurance.

The relatively new, but rapidly growing market for swaps also affords corporate treasurers a low-cost means of managing interest rate and currency risks. In "The Evolving Market for Swaps," three academic economists (two of which were employed by money-center banks when this article was written) collaborate in an attempt to explain the rise and proliferation of a variety of swap instruments — most notably, currency and interest rate swaps. The popular account of the origination of swaps is that they provided a corporate treasurer with substantial interest savings by drawing on other companies' "comparative advantages," if you will, in raising funds in certain segments of worldwide capital markets. By swapping, the advantaged company could effectively share its advantage with the less privileged company, and each would obtain funding at lower costs than otherwise.

The problem with this argument, at least as an explanation of the continuing expansion of the swaps market, is that this very process of "arbitraging" interest rate differences among world financial markets should soon eliminate further opportunities to do so; that is, the demand for loans in low-interest rate markets can be expected to raise rates until such opportunities disappear. A more plausible explanation of the continuing expansion of the swaps market is that swaps provide companies with a low-cost means of (1) taking advantage of tax and regulatory differences in various markets and (2) of managing interest rate and currency exposures. They also provide a way of creating securities that do not exist (such as long-dated foreign exchange contracts and interest rate futures, Swiss T-bills, etc.) The authors also suggest that any swap, for purposes of design and pricing, can be broken down into a series of corresponding forward contracts; and this suggestion, besides holding out the possibility of a simple means of pricing complicated "non-standardized" swaps, also points the way to a variety of as yet undevised swaps (tied to commodity prices, stock exchange indices, etc.) that could be designed by innovative corporate treasurers and their investment bankers.

In "Immunization and Duration," Stephen Schaefer of the London Business School provides a concise and elegant history of developments in the theory and practice of bond immunization. Immunization is a specific form of asset/liability management whereby one constructs and manages a portfolio of assets (generally bonds) such that, regardless of interest rate changes, the value of the assets remains as close as possible to the value of the liabilities being hedged. In reviewing the various immunization strategies now available, Dr. Schaefer's principal conclusion is that, for most purposes, the conventional, single-factor measure of "duration" (a measure of an asset's sensitivity to interest rate changes) proposed over 30 years ago seems to provide as good a basis for immunization as any of the more sophisticated models since devised.

Laurie Goodman (a Wall Street practitioner who also holds a Ph.D. in Economics from Stanford) provides a useful catalogue and illustration in " The Uses of Interest Rate Swaps in Managing Corporate Liabilities." Besides locking in new-issues costs and hedging interest rate exposures by converting floating-rate debt to fixed-rate (and vice versa), swaps have also been widely used to create lower-cost "synthetic" debt issues. For example, by issuing callable debt and then effectively selling the call provision through sale of a swap option (or "swaption")—or by issuing puttable debt and then buying an offsetting interest rate cap—issuers have apparently wound up with straight fixed-rate debt issues at significantly lower costs.

In "Forward Swaps, Swap Options, and the Management of Callable Debt," Keith Brown and Donald Smith address a special problem in corporate debt management: Namely, if interest rates have fallen sharply after the issuance of callable debt, but the call protection has several years yet to run, how can management preserve the value of the company's in-the-money call option on interest rates?

The swap market now appears to provide for more cost-effective alternatives to the large bond repurchases and futures-based hedging strategies sometimes used to accomplish the same end.

In proposing "An Economic Approach to Pension Fund Management," Thomas Copeland views the corporate pension fund not as a separate entity, but as part of an "augmented" corporate balance sheet. Adopting this "economic" perspective on the pension fund, as opposed to the conventional "accounting" framework, gives very different answers to questions such as: How do pension fund liabilities affect stock prices? What are the real effects of changing the actuarial assumptions of the plan, and thereby reducing corporate contributions and increasing reported earnings? What is the optimal mix of pension plan investments? To quote from Copeland's introduction, *Some of the answers will surprise you. First, in most cases it pays to overfund a defined benefit plan and invest one hundred percent of its assets in bonds. Second, changing the fund's actuarial assumptions in order to decrease current contributions is not likely to affect the market value of the firm's equity. Such manipulations are chicanery at best and stupidity at worst. Third, it never pays to invest pension fund assets in real estate, municipal bonds or other investment vehicles which are used primarily as tax shelters.*

DHC

Managing Financial Risk

by Clifford Smith, *University of Rochester*, and Charles Smithson and D. Sykes Wilford, *Chase Manhattan Bank*

T here is no doubt that the financial environment is a lot more risky today than it was in the 1950s and 1960s. With changes in some macroeconomic institutional structures—notably, the breakdown of the Bretton Woods agreement in 1972—have come dramatic increases in the volatility of interest rates, foreign exchange rates, and commodity prices.

Such increased volatility will not come as "news" to most corporate executives. Since the 1970s, many CEOs and CFOs have watched the profitability of their firms swing widely in response to large movements in exchange rates, interest rates, and commodity prices. What may be news, however, are the techniques and tools now available for measuring and managing such financial risks.

Recognition of the increased volatility of exchange rates, interest rates, and commodity prices should lead managers of the firm to ask three questions:

1. To what extent is my firm exposed to interest rates, foreign exchange rates, or commodity prices?
2. What financial tools are available for managing these exposures?
3. If my firm is significantly exposed, how do I use the financial tools to manage the exposure?

It is with these three questions that the following discussion deals.

*This article is an abbreviated version of Chapters 2, 3, and 19 of *Managing Financial Risk*, forthcoming Ballinger/ *Institutional Investor Series*. This material is used with the permission of the publisher.

IDENTIFYING AND MEASURING FINANCIAL RISK

The Risk Profile

U.S. savings and loans (S&Ls) are a widely cited example of firms subject to interest rate risk. Because S&Ls typically fund long-lived assets (e.g., 30-year fixed-rate mortgages) with liabilities that reprice frequently (passbook deposits), their value is negatively related to interest rates. When interest rates rise, the value of S&Ls' assets declines significantly, but the value of their liabilities changes little. So, the value of shareholders' equity falls.

The resulting relation between interest rates and the value of S&Ls is portrayed graphically in a *risk profile* in Figure 1.

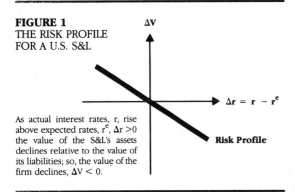

FIGURE 1
THE RISK PROFILE
FOR A U.S. S&L

As actual interest rates, r, rise above expected rates, r^e, $\Delta r > 0$ the value of the S&L's assets declines relative to the value of its liabilities; so, the value of the firm declines, $\Delta V < 0$.

The negative slope reflects the inverse relation between the financial price—i.e., interest rates—and the value of the S&L. The precise measure of the exposure is reflected by the slope of the line; and it is a measure of the slope that the techniques described below will provide.

But before considering the size of the exposure, the first question is: How do we go about identifying such exposures? In the case of S&Ls, the exposure to interest rates is apparent from the firm's balance sheet; the mismatch of maturities between assets and liabilities is obvious. Many companies, however, have economic or "operating" exposures that are not reflected on their balance sheets. Take, for example,

the vulnerability of building products firms to increases in interest rates. Increases in interest rates decrease the demand for building products. As sales and thus cash inflows decline—and to the extent that its costs and liabilities are fixed—the value of a building products firm declines.

We can make a similar observation about foreign exchange risk. In some instances, exposures are apparent. For example, a U.S. importer orders product from Germany and is expected to pay in Deutsche Marks (DM) for the products when they are delivered in 90 days. If, during those 90 days, the price of a DM rises—that is, the value of the dollar declines—the U.S. importer will have to pay more for the product. In this case, an increase in the price of the foreign currency leads to a decrease in the value of the importer.

Since 1972, firms have become adept at dealing with such transaction exposures.[1] However, a firm's exposure to foreign exchange rate risk can be more subtle; even firms that have no foreign receipts or payments may still be exposed to foreign exchange risk. If the dollar is strong, the dollar price of foreign products to U.S. consumers becomes cheaper and foreign firms make inroads into the U.S. market, thereby decreasing net cash flows to the U.S. producers and thus reducing their value. The reverse is true when the value of the dollar falls. Obvious for firms like automakers, this economic or competitive (or "strategic") risk is receiving more attention by the managers of other U.S. firms as well.[2]

Not surprisingly, the same relations appear with respect to commodity price risk. The exposures can be apparent: For example, as the price of oil rises, the costs for an airline rise; so rising oil prices are linked to falling firm values. Or, the exposures can be subtle. For example, a primary input in aluminum production is electric energy. Aluminum manufacturers in Iceland use electricity generated by that country's abundant geothermal energy. As the price of oil rises, the costs of competitors rise while the costs of Icelandic producers remain unchanged, thus improving the competitive position and increasing the value of Icelandic firms. It is when oil prices fall and competitors' costs decline that Icelandic producers worry.[3]

Financial price risk, then—whether caused by changes in interest rates, foreign exchange, or com-

1. A transaction exposure occurs when the firm has a payment or receipt in a currency other than its home currency. A translation exposure results when the value of foreign assets and liabilities must be converted into home currency values.

2. A case in point is Kodak, which has begun to manage "overall corporate

performance in the long run." See Paul Dickens, "Daring to Hedge the Unhedgeable," *Euromoney Corporate Finance*, August 1988.

3. For this useful story about Icelandic aluminum producers, we are indebted to J. Nicholas Robinson of Chase Manhattan Bank.

TABLE 1
CALCULATION OF THE
VALUE & DURATION OF
THE BUSINESS LOAN

	(1)	(2)	(3)	(4)	(5)	(6)
	Time to Receipt (Years)	Cash Flow	Discount Rate	PV	Weight	Weight × Time
	0.5	90	7.75%	86.70	0.22	0.11
	1.0	90	8.00%	83.33	0.21	0.21
	1.5	90	8.25%	79.91	0.20	0.31
	2.0	90	8.35%	76.66	0.19	0.38
	2.5	90	8.50%	73.40	0.18	0.45
				400.00 Present Value		1.45 Duration

modity prices—consists of more subtle economic exposures as well as the obvious balance sheet mismatches and transactional exposures. And the *risk profile* mentioned earlier, in order to provide a useful measure of a firm's overall economic exposure, must reflect the total effect of both kinds of price risk.

The question that naturally arises, then, is: How do you determine the slope of the risk profile? That is, how do you estimate the change in firm value expected to accompany a given change in a financial price ($\Delta V / \Delta P$)?

Quantifying Financial Risk: A Special Case

Financial institutions, particularly banks, were the first to devote significant attention to quantifying financial exposures. Our S&L example is admittedly an extreme case of interest rate exposure, even for a financial institution. Nevertheless, because some mismatch between the maturities of assets and liabilities almost inevitably occurs in the normal course of their business, all financial institutions generally face some degree of interest rate risk. To measure this exposure to interest rates, financial institutions rely on two techniques: gap and duration.

GAP: The method most financial corporations use to measure their exposure to interest rate changes is called the "maturity gap" approach.[4] The approach gets its name from a procedure designed

to quantify the "gap" between the market values of rate-sensitive assets (RSA) and rate-sensitive liabilities (RSL)—that is, GAP = RSA − RSL.[5] The financial institution determines the "gapping period"—the period over which it wants to measure its interest rate sensitivity—say, 6 months, one year, five years, and so forth. Then, for each of these periods, it measures its gap as defined above. In the context of a gap model, changes in interest rates affect a financial institution's market value by changing the institution's Net Interest Income (NII). Hence, once the GAP is known, the impact on the firm of changes in the interest rate can be calculated as follows:

$$\Delta NII = (GAP) \times (\Delta r)$$

Duration: Some financial institutions use an alternative to the GAP approach called "duration analysis" to measure their interest rate exposure.[6] In essence, the duration of a financial instrument provides a measure of when on average the present value of the instrument is received.

For example, let's look at the duration of a business loan with a maturity of 2.5 years and a sinking fund. Because part of the value is received prior to maturity, the duration of the instrument is clearly less than 2.5 years. To find out how much less, we need to ask the question "When on average is the present value received?"

4. For a discussion of the maturity gap model, see Alden L. Toevs, "Measuring and Managing Interest Rate Risk: A Guide to Asset/Liability Models Used in Banks and Thrifts," Morgan Stanley Fixed Income Analytical Research Paper, October 1984. (An earlier version of this paper appeared in *Economic Review*, The Federal Reserve Bank of San Francisco, Spring, 1983.)

5. The assets and liabilities that are "rate sensitive" are those that will reprice during the gapping period.

6. For a discussion of duration, see George G. Kaufman, "Measuring and Managing Interest Rate Risk: A Primer," *Economic Perspectives*, Federal Reserve Bank of Chicago. See also Stephen Schaefer, "Immunisation and Duration: A Review of the Theory, Performance, and Applications," *Midland Corporate Finance Journal*, Vol. 2 No. 3, Fall 1984.

Table 1 provides an illustration. Columns 1-4 provide the present value of the bond. To determine *when* the present value will be received, on average, we need to calculate the weighted average time of receipt. Column 5 provides the weights. Multiplying these weights (column 5) by the times the cash flows are received (column 1) and summing gives the duration of this business loan—1.45 years.

The use of duration effectively converts a security into its zero-coupon equivalent. In addition, duration relates changes in interest rates to changes in the value of the security.[7] Specifically, duration permits us to express the percentage change in the value of the security in terms of the percentage change in the discount rate $(1 + r)$ and the duration of the security, as follows:[8]

$$\frac{\Delta V}{V} = \frac{\Delta (1 + r)}{(1 + r)} \times D$$

For example, if the duration of a security is 1.45 years, and the discount rate increases by 1 percent (that is, if $\Delta (1 + r)/(1 + r) = 0.01$), the market value of the 2.5 year business loan will decrease by 1.45 percent. The concept of duration, moreover, can be extended to provide a measure of the interest rate exposure of an entire bank or S&L.

Quantifying Financial Price Risk: The General Case

While gap and duration work well for financial institutions, these techniques offer little guidance in evaluating the interest rate sensitivity of a nonfinancial institution; and, neither gap nor duration is useful in examining a firm's sensitivity to movements in foreign exchange rates or commodity prices. What is needed is a more general method for quantifying financial price risk—a method that can handle firms other than financial institutions and financial exposures other than interest rates.

To get a measure of the responsiveness of the value of the firm to changes in the financial prices, we must first define a measure of the value of the firm. As with interest rate risk for financial institutions, this value measure could be a "flow" measure (gap analysis uses net interest income) or a "stock" measure (duration uses the market value of the portfolio).

Flow Measures. Within a specific firm, estimation of the sensitivity of income flows is an analysis that can be performed as part of the planning and budgeting process. The trade press suggests that some firms have begun using simulation models to examine the responsiveness of their pre-tax income to changes in interest rates, exchange rates, and commodity prices.[9] Beginning with base case assumptions about the financial prices, the firm obtains a forecast for revenues, costs, and the resulting pre-tax income. Then, it considers alternative values for an interest rate or an exchange rate or a commodity price and obtains a new forecast for revenues, costs, and pre-tax income. By observing how the firm's projected sales, costs and income move in response to changes in these financial prices, management is able to trace out a risk profile similar to that in Figure 1.

In making such an estimation, two inherent problems confront the analyst: (1) this approach requires substantial data and (2) it relies on the ability of the researcher to make explicit, accurate forecasts of sales and costs under alternative scenarios for the financial prices. For both these reasons, such an approach is generally feasible only for analysts within a specific firm.

Stock Measures. Given the data requirements noted above, analysts outside the firm generally rely on market valuations, the most widely used of which is the current market value of the equity. Using a technique much like the one used to estimate a firm's "beta," an outside observer could measure the historical sensitivity of the company's equity value to changes in interest rates, foreign exchange rates, and commodity prices.

For example, suppose we wished to determine the sensitivity of a company's value to the following financial prices:

● the one-year T-bill interest rate;
● the Deutsche Mark / Dollar exchange rate;
● the Pound Sterling / Dollar exchange rate;
● the Yen / Dollar exchange rate; and
● the price of oil.

---

7. Note the contrast with the gap approach, which relates changes in the interest rate to changes in net interest income.
8. The calculations in Table 1 are based on the use of MacCauley's duration. If we continue to apply MacCauley's duration (D), this equation is only an approximation. To be exact, modified duration should be used. For a development

of this relation, see George G. Kaufman, G.O. Bierwag, and Alden Toevs, eds. *Innovations in Bond Portfolio Management: Duration Analysis and Immunization* (Greenwich, Conn.: JAI Press, 1983).
9. See for instance, Paul Dickens, cited in note 2.

TABLE 2

MEASUREMENTS OF
EXPOSURES TO
INTEREST RATE,
FOREIGN EXCHANGE
RATES, AND OIL PRICES

Percentage Change In	Chase Manhattan		Caterpillar		Exxon	
	Parameter Estimate	T Value	Parameter Estimate	T Value	Parameter Estimate	T Value
Price of 1-Year T-Bill	2.598*	1.56	− 3.221**	1.76	1.354	1.24
Price of DM	− 0.276	0.95	0.344	1.07	− 0.066	0.35
Price of Sterling	0.281	1.16	− 0.010	0.38	0.237*	1.50
Price of Yen	− 0.241	0.96	0.045	0.16	− 0.278**	1.69
Price of WTI Crude	0.065	1.21	− 0.045	0.77	0.082***	2.33

*   Significant at 90% single tailed
**   Significant at 90%
*** Significant at 95%

We could estimate this relation by performing a simple linear regression as follows:[10]

$$R_t = a + b_1\left(\frac{\Delta P_{TB}}{P_{TB}}\right)_t + b_2\left(\frac{\Delta P_{DM}}{P_{DM}}\right)_t + b_3\left(\frac{\Delta P_{\pounds}}{P_{\pounds}}\right)_t + b_4\left(\frac{\Delta P_y}{P_y}\right)_t + b_5\left(\frac{\Delta P_{OIL}}{P_{OIL}}\right)_t$$

where R is the rate of return on the firm's equity; $\Delta P_{TB}/P_{TB}$ is the percentage change in the price of a one-year T-bill; $\Delta P_{DM}/P_{DM}, \Delta P_{\pounds}/P_{\pounds},$ and $\Delta P_y/P_y$ are the percentage changes in the dollar prices of the three foreign currencies; and $\Delta P_{OIL}/P_{OIL}$ is the percentage change in the price of crude oil. The estimate of b_1 provides a measure of the sensitivity of the value of the firm to changes in the one-year T-bill rate; b_2, b_3, and b_4 estimate its sensitivity to the exchange rates; and b_5 estimates its sensitivity to the oil price.[11]

To illustrate the kind of results this technique would yield, we present three examples: a bank, Chase Manhattan, an industrial, Caterpillar, and an oil company, Exxon. For the period January 6, 1984 to December 2, 1988 we calculated weekly (Friday close to Friday close) share returns and the corresponding weekly percentage changes in the price of a one-year

T-bill rate, the dollar prices of a Deutsche Mark, a Pound Sterling, and a Yen, and the price of West Texas Intermediate crude. Using these data, we estimated our regression equation. The results of these estimations are displayed in Table 2.

Given the tendency of banks to accept short-dated deposits to fund longer-dated assets (loans), it is not surprising that our estimates for Chase Manhattan indicate an inverse exposure to interest rates. Although only marginally significant, the positive coefficient indicates that an increase in the one-year T-bill

TABLE 2.A

Bank	Estimated Sensitivity	T-Value
Bank of America	3.2	1.5
Bankers Trust	2.2	1.4
Chase	2.6	1.6
First Chicago	3.0	1.6
Manufacturers Hanover	3.2	1.9

---

10. In effect, this equation represents a variance decomposition. While it is a multifactor model, it is not related in any important way to the APT approach suggested by Ross and Roll. Instead, it is probably more accurate to view the approach we suggest as an extension of the market model. In its more complete form, as described in Chapter 2 of our book *Managing Financial Risk*, the regression equation would include the rate of return to the market ("beta") as well as the percentage changes in the financial prices, and would thus look as follows:

$$R_t = a + \beta R_{m,t} + b_1 PC(P_{TB}) + b_2 PC(P_{DM}) + b_3 PC(P_{\pounds}) + b_4 PC(P_y) + b_5 PC(P_{OIL})$$

This more complete model is based on a number of earlier studies: French/Ruback/Schwert (1983) ("Effects of Nominal Contracting on Stock Returns," *Journal of Political Economy*, Vol. 91 No. 1) on the impact of unexpected inflation on share returns, Flannery/James (1984) ("The Effect of Interest Rate Changes on Common Stock Returns of Financial Institutions," *Journal of Finance* Vol. 39 No. 4) and Scott/Peterson (1986) ("Interest Rate Risk and Equity Values of Hedged and Unhedged Financial Intermediaries," *Journal of Financing Research* Vol. 9 No. 6)

on the impact of interest rate changes on share prices for financial firms, and Sweeney/Warga (1986) ("The Pricing of Interest Rate Risk: Evidence from the Stock Market," *Journal of Finance* Vol. 41 No. 2) on the impact of interest rate risk on share prices for nonfinancial firms. This model does exhibit the problems of measuring the reaction of firm value to changes in exchange rates, which are described by Donald Lessard in "Finance and Global Competition: Exploiting Financial Scope and Coping with Volatile Exchange Rates," *Midland Corporate Finance Journal* (Fall 1986).

For expositional purposes, we use in this paper the shorter form of the equation. This abbreviated model is acceptable empirically given the small correlations which exist between the percentage changes in the financial prices and the market return.

11. These coefficients actually measure elasticities. Further, had we used the percentage change in the quantity, (1 + one-year T-bill rate), instead of the percentage change in the price of the one-year T-bill, the coefficient b_1 could be interpreted as a "duration" measure.

THE DATA REFLECT THE FACT THAT, AS CATERPILLAR HAS MOVED ITS
PRODUCTION FACILITIES, THE FIRM HAS CHANGED FROM BEING
POSITIVELY EXPOSED TO THE YEN TO BEING NEGATIVELY EXPOSED TO
THE YEN.

TABLE 2.B

	1984	1985	1986	1987	1988
Parameter Estimate for Percentage Change in Price of Yen	1.72	0.15	0.33	−1.08	−0.85
T-Value	1.59	0.31	0.65	1.08	1.53

TABLE 2.C

	1984	1985	1986	1987	1988
Parameter Estimate for Percentage Change in Price of Oil	0.80	0.15	0.09	0.05	−0.01
T-Value	3.94	0.85	2.79	0.37	0.17

rate (or a decrease in the price of the T-bill) is expected to lead to a decrease in the bank's value.

Additional information can be obtained by comparing the coefficient estimates among firms in the same industry. For example, we can compare the estimated sensitivity of Chase's value to the one-year T-bill rate to the sensitivities of other banks as shown in Table 2.A.

In contrast to the bank's inverse exposure, Caterpillar appears to have a positive exposure to the one-year T-bill rate. That is, the negative regression coefficient indicates that increases in the one-year T-bill rate (or decreases in the price of the T-bill) lead to increases in the value of the firm.

Even more surprising, though, given much that has been written about Caterpillar's exposure to foreign currency changes, is the lack of any significant exposure to the yen. This result is more understandable if we break up this 5-year span into shorter intervals and look at Caterpillar's sensitivity to the price of the yen on a year-by-year basis. (See Table 2.B.) The data reflect the fact that, as Caterpillar has moved its production facilities, the firm has changed from being positively exposed to the yen (such that an increase in the value of the dollar would harm Caterpillar) to being negatively exposed to the yen (an increase in the value of the dollar now helps Caterpillar).

Unlike the other two firms, the estimate for Exxon's exposure to interest rates is not statistically significant (not, at least, to the one-year T-bill rate). Exxon does exhibit the expected positive exposure to the price of oil. But our estimates also reflect the

now common view, reported in the financial press and elsewhere, that Exxon's exposure to the price of oil has been declining over time—both in size and consistency (as measured by statistical significance). (See Table 2.C.) Given its international production and distribution, as well as its international portfolio of assets, Exxon also exhibits marginally significant exposures to foreign exchange rates. Our estimates suggest Exxon benefits from an increase in the value of the pound but is harmed by an increase in the value of the yen.

Measuring Corporate Exposure: Summing Up

The purpose of this first section, then, has been to outline a statistical technique (similar to that used to calculate a firm's "beta") that can be used to provide management with an estimate of the sensitivity of firm value to changes in a variety of financial variables. Such measures can be further refined by using information from other sources. For example, the same regression technique can be used, only substituting changes in the firm's periodic earnings and cash flows for the changes in stock prices in our model. There are, however, two principal advantages of our procedure over the use of such accounting numbers: (1) market reactions are likely to capture the entire capitalized value of changes in firm value in response to financial price changes; and (2) regression analysis using stock prices, besides being much faster and cheaper, can be done using publicly available information.

WE TREAT FORWARDS, FUTURES, SWAPS, AND OPTIONS NOT AS FOUR
UNIQUE INSTRUMENTS AND MARKETS, BUT RATHER AS FOUR
INTERRELATED INSTRUMENTS FOR DEALING WITH A SINGLE PROBLEM:
MANAGING FINANCIAL RISK.

THE TOOLS FOR MANAGING FINANCIAL RISK: A BUILDING BLOCK APPROACH[12]

If it turns out that a firm is subject to significant financial price risk, management may choose to hedge that risk.[13] One way of doing so is by using an "on-balance-sheet" transaction. For example, a company could manage a foreign exchange exposure resulting from overseas competition by borrowing in the competitor's currency or by moving production abroad. But such on-balance sheet methods can be costly and, as firms like Caterpillar have discovered, inflexible.[14]

Alternatively, financial risks can be managed with the use of off-balance-sheet instruments. The four fundamental off-balance-sheet instruments are forwards, futures, swaps, and options.

When we first began to attempt to understand these financial instruments, we were confronted by what seemed an insurmountable barrier to entry. The participants in the various markets all seemed to possess a highly specialized expertise that was applicable in only one market to the exclusion of all others (and the associated trade publications served only to tighten the veil of mystery that "experts" have always used to deny entry to novices). Options were discussed as if they were completely unrelated to forwards or futures, which in turn seemed to have nothing to do with the latest innovation, swaps. Adding to the complexities of the individual markets was the welter of jargon that seems to have grown up around each, thus further obscuring any common ground that might exist. (Words such as "ticks," "collars," "strike prices," and "straddles" suddenly had acquired a remarkable currency.) In short, we seemed to find ourselves looking up into a Wall Street Tower of Babel, with each group of market specialists speaking in different languages.

But, after now having observed these instruments over the past several years, we have been struck by how little one has to dig before superficial differences give way to fundamental unity. And, in marked contrast to the specialized view of most Wall Street practitioners, we take a more "generalist" approach—one that treats forwards, futures, swaps, and options not as four unique instruments and markets, but rather as four interrelated instruments for dealing with a single problem: managing financial risk. In fact, we have come up with a little analogy that captures the spirit of our conclusion, one which goes as follows: The four basic off-balance-sheet instruments—forwards, futures, swaps, and options—are much like those plastic building blocks children snap together. You can either build the instruments from one another, or you can combine the instruments into larger creations that appear (but appearances deceive) altogether "new."

Forward Contracts

Of the four instruments, the forward contract is the oldest and, perhaps for this reason, the most straightforward. A forward contract obligates its owner to buy a specified asset on a specified date at a price (known as the "exercise price") specified at the origination of the contract. If, at maturity, the actual price is higher than the exercise price, the contract owner makes a profit equal to the difference; if the price is lower, he suffers a loss.

In Figure 2, the payoff from buying a forward contract is illustrated with a hypothetical risk profile. If the actual price at contract maturity is higher than the expected price, the inherent risk results in a decline in the value of the firm; but this decline is offset by the profit on the forward contract. Hence, for the risk profile illustrated, the forward contract provides an effective hedge. (If the risk profile were positively instead of negatively sloped, the risk would be managed by selling instead of buying a forward contract.)

Besides its payoff profile, a forward contract has two other features that should be noted. First, the default (or credit) risk of the contract is two-sided. The contract owner either receives or makes a payment, depending on the price movement of the underlying

12. This section of the article is adapted from Charles W. Smithson, "A LEGO Approach to Financial Engineering: An Introduction to Forwards, Futures, Swaps, and Options," *Midland Corporate Finance Journal* 4 (Winter 1987).

13. In this paper we do not address the question of why public corporations hedge. For a discussion of the corporate decision whether or not to hedge financial price exposures, see Alan Shapiro and Sheridan Titman, "An Integrated Approach to Corporate Risk Management," *Midland Corporate Finance Journal* 3 (Summer 1985). For other useful theoretical discussions of the corporate hedging decision, see David Mayers and Clifford Smith, "On the Corporate Demand for Insurance," *Journal of Business* 55 (April 1982) (a less technical version of which was published as "The Corporate Insurance Decision," *Chase Financial Quarterly* (Vol.

1 No. 3) Spring 1982); Rene Stulz, "Optimal Hedging Policies," *Journal of Financial and Quantitative Analysis* 19 (June 1984); Clifford Smith and Rene Stulz, "The Determinants of Firms' Hedging Policies," *Journal of Financial* and *Quantitative Analysis* 20 (December 1985).

For some empirical tests of the above theoretical work, see David Mayers and Clifford Smith, "On the Corporate Demand for Insurance: Some Empirical Evidence," working paper, 1988; and Deana Nance, Clifford Smith, and Charles Smithson, "The Determinants of Off-Balance-Sheet Hedging: An Empirical Analysis," working paper 1988.

14. See "Caterpillar's Triple Whammy," *Fortune*, October 27, 1986.

FIGURE 2
PAYOFF PROFILE
FOR FORWARD
CONTRACT

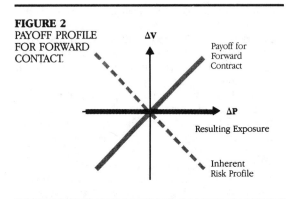

asset. Second, the value of the forward contract is conveyed only at the contract's maturity; no payment is made either at origination or during the term of the contract.

Futures Contracts

The basic form of the futures contract is identical to that of the forward contract; a futures contract also obligates its owner to purchase a specified asset at a specified exercise price on the contract maturity date. Thus, the payoff profile for the purchaser of a forward contract as presented in Figure 2 could also serve to illustrate the payoff to the holder of a futures contract.

But, unlike the case of forwards, credit or default risk can be virtually eliminated in a futures market. Futures markets use two devices to manage default risk. First, instead of conveying the value of a contract through a single payment at maturity, any change in the value of a futures contract is conveyed at the end of the day in which it is realized. Look again at Figure 2. Suppose that, on the day after origination, the financial price rises and, consequently, the financial instrument has a positive value. In the case of a forward contract, this value change would not be received until contract maturity. With a futures contract, this change in value is received at the end of the day. In the language of the futures

markets, the futures contract is "marked-to-market" and "cash settled" daily.

Because the performance period of a futures contract is reduced by marking to market, the risk of default declines accordingly. Indeed, because the value of the futures contract is paid or received at the end of each day, Fischer Black likened a futures contract to "a series of forward contracts [in which] each day, yesterday's contract is settled and today's contract is written."[15] That is, a futures contract is like a sequence of forwards in which the "forward" contract written on day 0 is settled on day 1 and is replaced, in effect, with a new "forward" contract reflecting the new day 1 expectations. This new contract is then itself settled on day 2 and replaced, and so on until the day the contract ends.

The second feature of futures contracts which reduces default risk is the requirement that all market participants—sellers and buyers alike—post a performance bond called the "margin."[16] If my futures contract increases in value during the trading day, this gain is added to my margin account at the day's end. Conversely, if my contract has lost value, this loss is deducted from my margin account. And, if my margin account balance falls below some agreed-upon minimum, I am required to post additional bond; that is, my margin account must be replenished or my position will be closed out.[17] Because the position will be closed before the margin account is depleted, performance risk is eliminated.[18]

Note that the exchange itself has not been proposed as a device to reduce default risk. Daily settlement and the requirement of a bond reduce default risk, but the existence of an exchange (or clearinghouse) merely serves to transform risk. More specifically, the exchange deals with the two-sided risk inherent in forwards and futures by serving as the counterparty to all transactions. If I wish to buy or sell a futures contract, I buy from or sell to the exchange. Hence, I need only evaluate the credit risk of the exchange, not of some specific counterparty.

The primary economic function of the exchange is to reduce the costs of transacting in futures

15. See Fischer Black "The Pricing to Commodity Contracts," *Journal of Financial Economics* 3 (1976), 167-179.

16. Keep in mind that if you buy a futures contract, you are taking a long position in the underlying asset. Conversely, selling a futures contract is equivalent to taking a short position.

17. When the contract is originated on the U.S. exchanges, an "initial margin" is required. Subsequently, the margin account balance must remain above the "maintenance margin." If the margin account balance falls below the maintenance level, the balance must be restored to the initial level.

18. Note that this discussion has ignored daily limits. If there are daily limits on the movement of futures prices, large changes in expectations about the underlying asset can effectively close the market. (The market opens, immediately moves the limit, and then is effectively closed until the next day.) Hence, there could exist an instance in which the broker desires to close out a customer's position but is not able to immediately because the market is experiencing limit moves. In such a case, the statement that performance risk is "eliminated" is too strong.

FIGURE 3

Panel A: An Interest Rate Swap

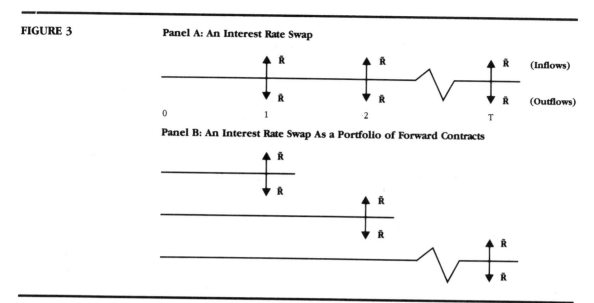

Panel B: An Interest Rate Swap As a Portfolio of Forward Contracts

contracts. The anonymous trades made possible by the exchange, together with the homogeneous nature of the futures contracts—standardized assets, exercise dates (four per year), and contract sizes—enables the futures markets to become relatively liquid. However, as was made clear by recent experience of the London Metal Exchange, the existence of the exchange does not in and of itself eliminate the possibility of default.[19]

In sum, a futures contract is much like a portfolio of forward contracts. At the close of business of each day, in effect, the existing forward-like contract is settled and a new one is written.[20] This daily settlement feature combined with the margin requirement allows futures contracts to eliminate the credit risk inherent in forwards.

Swap Contracts[21]

A swap contract is in essence nothing more complicated than a series of forward contracts strung together. As implied by its name, a swap contract obligates two parties to exchange, or "swap," some specified cash flows at specified intervals. The most common form is the interest rate swap, in which the cash flows are determined by two different interest rates.

Panel A of Figure 3 illustrates an interest rate swap from the perspective of a party who is paying out a series of cash flows determined by a fixed interest rate ($\bar{R}$) in return for a series of cash flows determined by a floating interest rate ($\tilde{R}$).[22]

Panel B of Figure 3 serves to illustrate that this swap contract can be decomposed into a portfolio of

19. In November of 1985, the "tin cartel" defaulted on contracts for tin delivery on the London Metal Exchange, thereby making the exchange liable for the loss. A description of this situation is contained in "Tin Crisis in London Roils Metal Exchange," *The Wall Street Journal*, November 13, 1985.

From the point of view of the market, the exchange does not reduce default risk. The expected default rate is not affected by the existence of the exchange. However, the existence of the exchange can alter the default risk faced by an individual market participant. If I buy a futures contract for a specific individual, the default risk I face is determined by the default rate of that specific counterparty. If I instead buy the same futures contract through an exchange, my default risk depends on the default rate of not just my counterparty, but on the default rate of he entire market. Moreover, to the extent that the exchange is capitalized by equity from its members, the default risk I perceive is further reduced because I have a claim not against some specific counterparty, but rather against the exchange. Therefore, when I trade through the exchange, I am in a sense purchasing an insurance policy from the exchange.

20. A futures contract is like a portfolio of forward contracts; however, a futures contract and a portfolio of forward contracts become identical only if interest rates are "deterministic"—that is, known with certainty in advance. See Robert A. Jarrow and George S. Oldfield, "Forward Contracts and Futures Contracts," *Journal of Financial Economics* 9 (1981), 373-382; and John A. Cox, Jonathan E. Ingersoll, and Stephen A. Ross, "The Relation between Forward Prices and Futures Prices," *Journal of Financial Economics* 9 (1981), 321-346.

21. This section is based on Clifford W. Smith, Charles W. Smithson, and Lee M. Wakeman, "The Evolving Market for Swaps," *Midland Corporate Finance Journal* Winter (1986), 20-32.

22. Specifically, the interest rate swap cash flows are determined as follows: The two parties agree to some notional principal, P. (The principal is notional in the sense that it is only used to determine the magnitude of cash flows; is is not paid or received by either party.) At each settlement date, 1, 2,..., T the party illustrated makes a payment $\bar{R} = \bar{r}P$, where $\bar{r}$ is the T-period fixed rate which existed at origination. At each settlement, the party illustrated receives $\tilde{R} = \tilde{r}P$, where $\tilde{r}$ is the floating rate for that period (e.g., at settlement date 2, the interest rate used is the one-period rate in effect at period 1).

forward contracts. At each settlement date, the party to this swap contract has an implicit forward contract on interest rates: the party illustrated is obligated to sell a fixed-rate cash flow for an amount specified at the origination of the contract. In this sense, a swap contract is also like a portfolio of forward contracts.

In terms of our earlier discussion, this means that the solid line in Figure 2 could also represent the payoff from a swap contract. Specifically, the solid line in Figure 3 would be consistent with a swap contract in which the party illustrated receives cash flows determined by one price (say, the U.S. Treasury bond rate) and makes payments determined by another price (say, LIBOR). Thus, in terms of their ability to manage risk, forwards, futures, and swaps all function in the same way.

But identical payoff *patterns* notwithstanding, the instruments all differ with respect to default risk. As we saw, the performance period of a forward is equal to its maturity; and because no performance bond is required, a forward contract is a pure credit instrument. Futures both reduce the performance period (to one day) and require a bond, thereby eliminating credit risk. Swap contracts use only one of these mechanisms to reduce credit risk; they reduce the performance period.[23] This point becomes evident in Figure 3. Although the maturity of the contract is T periods, the performance period is generally not T periods long but is instead a single period. Thus, given a swap and a forward contract of roughly the same maturity, the swap is likely to impose far less credit risk on the counterparties to the contract than the forward.

At each settlement date throughout a swap contract, the changes in value are transferred between the counterparties. To illustrate this in terms of Figure 3, suppose that interest rates rise on the day after origination. The value of the swap contract illustrated has risen. This value change will be conveyed to the contract owner not at maturity (as would be the case with a forward contract) nor at the end of that day (as would be the case with a futures contract). Instead, at the first settlement date, part of the value change is conveyed in the form of the "difference check" paid by one party to the other. To repeat, then, the performance period is less than that of a forward, but not as short as that of a futures contract.[24] (Keep in mind that we are comparing instruments with the same maturities.)

Let us reinforce the two major points made thus far. First, a swap contract, like a futures contract, is like a portfolio of forward contracts. Therefore, the payoff profiles for each of these three instruments are identical. Second, the primary difference among forwards, futures, and swaps is the amount of default risk they impose on counterparties to the contract. Forwards and futures represent the extremes, and swaps are the intermediate case.

Option Contracts

As we have seen, the owner of a forward, futures, or swap contract has an *obligation* to perform. In contrast, an option gives its owner a *right*, not an obligation. An option giving its owner the right to buy an asset at a pre-determined price—a call option—is provided in Panel A of Figure 4. The owner of the contract has the right to purchase the asset at a specified future date at a price agreed-upon today. Thus, if the price rises, the value of the option also goes up. But because the option contract owner is not obligated to purchase the asset if the price moves against him, the value of the option remains unchanged (at zero) if the price declines.[25]

The payoff profile for the party who sold the call option (also known as the call "writer") is shown in Panel B. In contrast to the buyer of the option, the seller of the call option has the *obligation* to perform. For example, if the owner of the option elects to exercise his option to buy the asset, the seller of the option is obligated to sell the asset.

Besides the option to buy an asset, there is also the option to sell an asset at a specified price, known as a "put" option. The payoff to the buyer of a put is illustrated in Panel C of Figure 4, and the payoff to the seller of the put is shown in Panel D.

Pricing Options: Up to this point, we have considered only the payoffs to the option contracts. We have side-stepped the thorniest issue—the valuation of option contracts.

---

23. There are instances in a which bond has been posted in the form of collateral. As should be evident, in this case the swap becomes very like a futures contract.

24. Unlike futures, for which all of any change in contract value is paid/received at the daily settlements, swap contracts convey only part of the total value change at the periodic settlements.

25. For continuity, we continue to use the $\Delta V, \Delta P$ convention in figures. To compare these figures with those found in most texts, treat ΔV as deviations from zero ($\Delta V = V - 0$) and remember that P measures deviations from expected price ($\Delta P = P - P_e$).

BLACK AND SCHOLES TOOK WHAT MIGHT BE DESCRIBED AS A
"BUILDING BLOCK" APPROACH TO THE VALUATION OF OPTIONS...THEY
DEMONSTRATED THAT A CALL OPTION COULD BE REPLICATED BY A
CONTINUOUSLY ADJUSTING PORTFOLIO OF TWO SECURITIES: FORWARD
CONTRACTS AND RISKLESS SECURITIES.

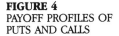

FIGURE 4
PAYOFF PROFILES OF
PUTS AND CALLS

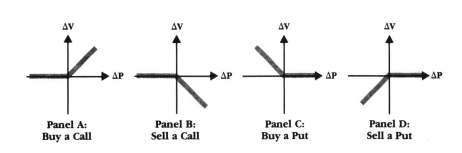

The breakthrough in option pricing theory came with the work of Fischer Black and Myron Scholes in 1973.[26] Conveniently for our purposes, Black and Scholes took what might be described as a "building block" approach to the valuation of options. Look again at the call option illustrated in Figure 4. For increases in the financial price, the payoff profile for the option is that of a forward contract. For decreases in the price, the value of the option is constant—like that of a "riskless" security such as a Treasury bill.

The work of Black and Scholes demonstrated that a call option could be replicated by a continuously adjusting ("dynamic") portfolio of two securities: (1) forward contracts on the underlying asset and (2) riskless securities. As the financial price rises, the "call option equivalent" portfolio contains an increasing proportion of forward contracts on the asset. Conversely, the replicating portfolio contains a decreasing proportion of forwards as the price of the asset falls.

Because this replicating portfolio is effectively a synthetic call option, arbitrage activity should ensure that its value closely approximates the market price of exchange-traded call options. In this sense, the value of a call option, and thus the premium that would be charged its buyer, is determined by the value of its option equivalent portfolio.

Panel A of Figures 5 illustrates the payoff profile for a call option which includes the premium. This figure (and all of the option figures thus far) illustrates an "at-the-money" option—that is, an option for which the exercise price is the prevailing ex-

pected price. As Panels A and B of Figure 5 illustrate, an at-the-money option is paid for by sacrificing a significant amount of the firm's potential gains. However, the price of a call option falls as the exercise price increases relative to the prevailing price of the asset. This means that if an option buyer is willing to accept larger potential losses in return for paying a lower option premium, he would then consider using an "out-of-the-money" option.

An out-of-the-money call option is illustrated in Panel C of Figure 5. As shown in Panel D, the out-of-the-money option provides less downside protection, but the option premium is significantly less. The lesson to be learned here is that the option buyer can alter his payoff profile simply by changing the exercise price.

For our purposes, however, the most important feature of options is that they are not as different from other financial instruments as they might first seem. Options do have a payoff profile that differs significantly from that of forward contracts (or futures or swaps). But, option payoff profiles can be duplicated by a combination of forwards and risk-free securities. Thus, we find that options have more in common with the other instruments than was first apparent. Futures and swaps, as we saw earlier, are in essence nothing more than portfolios of forward contracts; and options, as we have just seen, are very much akin to portfolios of forward contracts and risk-free securities.

This point is reinforced if we consider ways that options can be combined. Consider a portfolio constructed by buying a call and selling a put with the

26. See Fischer Black and Myron Scholes, "The Pricing of Options and Corporate Liabilities," *Journal of Political Economy* 1973. For a less technical discussion of the model, see "The Black-Scholes Option Pricing Model for Alterna-tive Underlying Instruments," *Financial Analysts Journal*, November-December, 1984, 23-30.

FIGURE 5

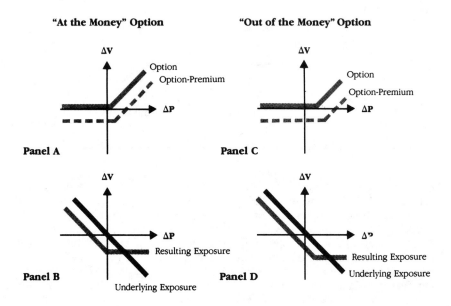

"At the Money" Option

ΔV

Option
Option-Premium

ΔP

Panel A

ΔV

ΔP
Resulting Exposure

Panel B

Underlying Exposure

"Out of the Money" Option

ΔV

Option
Option-Premium

ΔP

Panel C

ΔV

Δᵖ

Resulting Exposure
Underlying Exposure

Panel D

same exercise price. As the left side of Figure 6 illustrates, the resulting portfolio (long a call, short a put) has a payoff profile equivalent to that of buying a forward contract on the asset. Similarly, the right side of Figure 6 illustrates that a portfolio made up of selling a call and buying a put (short a call, long a put) is equivalent to selling a forward contract.

The relationship illustrated in Figure 6 is known more formally as "put-call parity." The special import of this relationship, at least in this context, is the "building block construction" it makes possible: two options can be "snapped together" to yield the payoff profile for a forward contract, which is identical to the payoff profile for futures and swaps.

At the beginning of this section, then, it seemed that options would be very different from forwards, futures, and swaps—and in some ways they are. But we discovered two building block relations between options and the other three instruments: (1) options can be replicated by "snapping together" a forward, futures, or swap contract together with a position in risk-free securities; and (2) calls and puts can be combined to become forwards.

The Financial Building Blocks

Forwards, futures, swaps, and options—they all look so different from one another. And if you read the trade publications or talk to the specialists that transact in the four markets, the apparent differences among the instruments are likely to seem even more pronounced.

But it turns out that forwards, futures, swaps, and options are not each unique constructions, but rather more like those plastic building blocks that children combine to make complex structures. To understand the off-balance-sheet instruments, you don't need a lot of market-specific knowledge. All you need to know is how the instruments can be linked to one another. As we have seen, (1) futures can be built by "snapping together" a package of forwards; (2) swaps can also be built by putting together a package of forwards; (3) synthetic options can be constructed by combining a forward with a riskless security; and (4) options can be combined to produce forward contracts—or, conversely, forwards can be pulled apart to replicate a package of options.

THE COMPANY MIGHT WANT TO MINIMIZE THE EFFECT OF UNFAVORABLE
OUTCOMES WHILE STILL ALLOWING THE POSSIBILITY OF GAINING FROM
FAVORABLE ONES. THIS CAN BE ACCOMPLISHED USING OPTIONS.

FIGURE 6

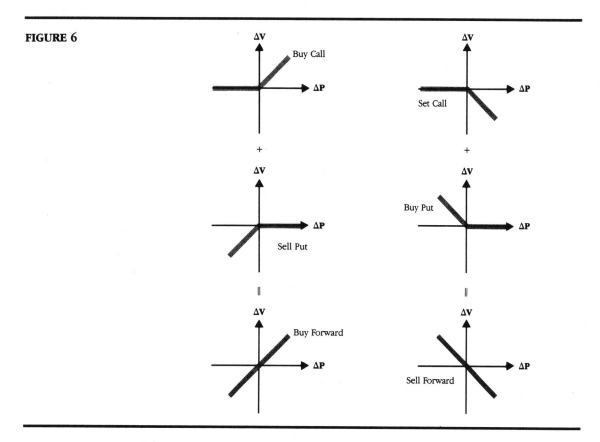

Having shown you all the building blocks and how they fit together in simple constructions, we now want to demonstrate how they can be used to create more complicated, customized financial instruments that in turn can be used to manage financial risks.

ASSEMBLING THE BUILDING BLOCKS

Using The Building Blocks to Manage an Exposure

Consider a company whose market value is directly related to unexpected changes in some financial price, P. The risk profile of this company is illustrated in Figure 7. How could we use the financial building blocks to modify this inherent exposure?

The simplest solution is to use a forward, a futures, or a swap to neutralize this exposure. This is shown in Panel A of Figure 8.

But, the use of a forward, a futures, or a swap

FIGURE 7

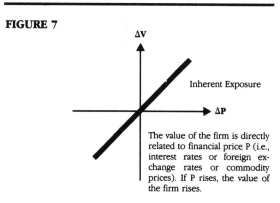

The value of the firm is directly related to financial price, P (i.e., interest rates or foreign exchange rates or commodity prices). If P rises, the value of the firm rises.

eliminates possible losses by giving up the possibility of profiting from favorable outcomes. The company might want to minimize the effect of unfavorable outcomes while still allowing the possibility of gaining from favorable ones. This can be accom-

FIGURE 8

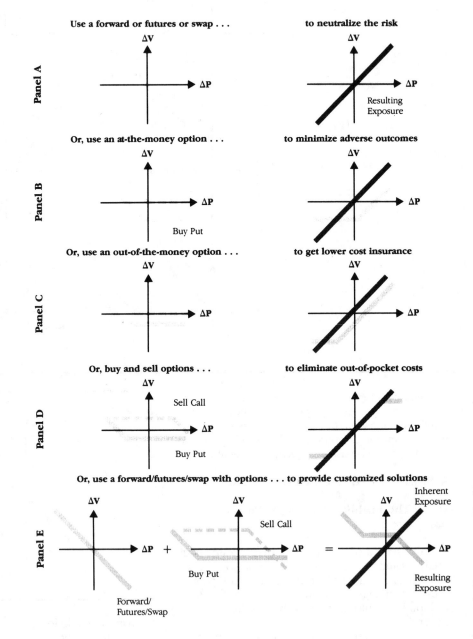

plished using options. The payoff profile of an at-the-money option (including the premium paid to buy the option) is shown on the left side of Panel B. Snapping this building block onto the inherent exposure profile gives the resulting exposure illustrated on the right side of panel B.

A common complaint about options—especially at-the-money options—is that they are "too expensive." To reduce the option premium, you can think about using an out-of-the-money option. As Panel C of Figure 8 illustrates, the firm has thereby given up some protection from adverse outcomes in return for paying a lower premium.

But, with an out-of-the-money option, some premium expense remains. Panel D illustrates how the out-of-pocket expense can be *eliminated*. The firm can sell a call option with an exercise price chosen so as to generate premium income equal to the premium due on the put option it wishes to purchase. In building block parlance, we snap the "buy-a-put" option onto the inherent risk profile to reduce downside outcomes; and we snap on the "sell-a-call" option to fund this insurance by giving up some of the favorable outcomes.

Panel E reminds us that forwards, futures, and swaps can be used in combination with options. Suppose the treasurer of the company we have been considering comes to you with the following request:

I think that this financial price, P, is going to fall dramatically. And, while I know enough about financial markets to know that P could actually rise a little, I am sure it will not rise by much. I want some kind of financial solution that will let me benefit when my predictions come to pass. But I don't want to pay any out-of-pocket premiums. Instead, I want this financial engineering product to pay me a premium.

If you look at the firm's inherent risk profile in Figure 7, this seems like a big request. The firm's inherent position is such that it would lose rather than gain from big decreases in P.

The resulting exposure profile shown on the right side of Panel E is the one the firm wants: it benefits from large decreases in P, is protected against small increases in P (though not against large increases) and receives a premium for the instrument.

How was this new profile achieved? As illustrated on the left side of Panel E, we first snapped a forward/futures/swap position onto the original risk profile to neutralize the firm's inherent exposure. We then sold a call option and bought a put option with exercise prices set such that the income from selling the call exceeded the premium required to buy the put.

No high level math was required. Indeed, we did this bit of financial engineering simply by looking through the box of financial building blocks until we found those that snapped together to give us the profile we wanted.

Using the Building Blocks to Redesign Financial Instruments

Now that you understand how forwards, futures, swaps, and options are all fundamentally related, it is a relatively short step to thinking about how the instruments can be combined with each other to give one financial instrument the characteristics of another. Rather than talk about this in the abstract, let's look at some examples of how this has been done in the marketplace.

Combining Forwards with Swaps: Suppose a firm's value is currently unaffected by interest rate movements. But, at a known date in the future, it expects to become exposed to interest rates: if rates rise, the value of the firm will decrease.[27] To manage this exposure, the firm could use a forward, futures, or swap commencing at that future date. Such a product is known as a *forward* or *delayed start* swap. The payoff from a forward swap is illustrated in Panel C of Figure 9, where the party illustrated pays a fixed rate and receives floating starting in period 5.

Although this instrument is in effect a forward contract on a swap, it also, not surprisingly, can be constructed as a package of swaps. As Figure 9 illustrates, a forward swap is equivalent to a package of two swaps:

Swap 1—From period 1 to period T, the party pays fixed and receives floating.

Swap 2—From period 1 to period 4, the party pays floating and receives fixed.

Forwards with Option-like Characteristics: The addition of option-like characteristics to forward

---

27. For example, the firm may know that, in one year, it will require funds which will be borrowed at a floating rate, thereby giving the firm the inverse exposure to interest rates. Or, the firm may be adding a new product line, the demand for which is extremely sensitive to interest rate movements—as rates rise, the demand for the product decreases and cash flows to the firm decrease.

FIGURE 9

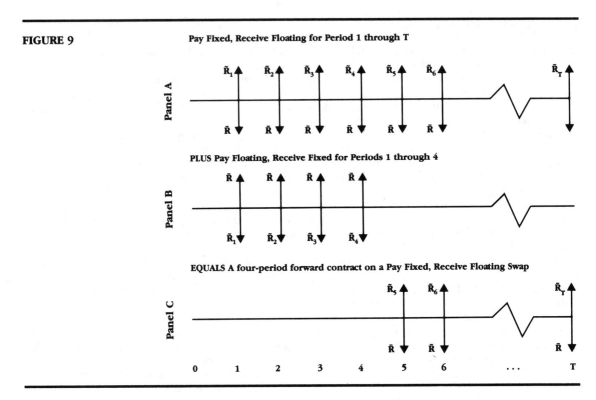

Pay Fixed, Receive Floating for Period 1 through T

PLUS Pay Floating, Receive Fixed for Periods 1 through 4

EQUALS A four-period forward contract on a Pay Fixed, Receive Floating Swap

contracts first appeared in the foreign exchange markets. To see how this was done, let's trace the evolution of these contracts.

Begin with a standard forward contract on foreign exchange. Panel A of Figure 10 illustrates a conventional forward contract on sterling with the forward sterling exchange rate (the "contract rate") set at $1.50 per pound sterling. If, at maturity, the spot price of sterling exceeds $1.50, the owner of this contract makes a profit (equal to the spot rate minus $1.50). Conversely, if at maturity the spot price of sterling is less than $1.50, the owner of this contract suffers a loss. The owner of the forward contract, however, might instead want a contract that allows him to profit if the price of sterling rises, but limits his losses if the price of sterling falls.[28] Such a contract would be a call option on sterling. Illustrated in Panel B of Figure 10 is a call option on sterling with an exercise price of $1.50. In this illustration we have assumed an

option premium of 5 cents (per pound sterling).

The payoff profile illustrated in Panel B of Figure 10 could also be achieved by altering the terms of the standard forward contract as follows:

1. Change the contract price so that the exercise price of the forward contract is no longer $1.50 but is instead $1.55. The owner of the forward contract agrees to purchase sterling at contract maturity at a price of $1.55 per unit; and

2. Permit the owner of the contract to break (i.e. "unwind") the agreement at a sterling price of $1.50.

This altered forward contract is referred to as a *break forward* contract.[29] In this break forward construction, the premium is effectively being paid by the owner of the break forward contract in the form of the above market contract exchange rate.

From our discussion of options, we also know that a call can be paid for with the proceeds from selling a put. The payoff profile for such a situation is

---

28. This discussion is adapted from Warren Edwardes and Edmond Levy, "Break Forwards: A Synthetic Option Hedging Instrument," *Midland Corporate Finance Journal* 5 (Summer 1987) 59-67.

29. According to Sam Srinivasulu in "Second-Generation Forwards: A Comparative Analysis," Business International Money Report, September 21, 1987, break forward is the name given to this construction by Midland Bank. It goes under other names: Boston Option (Bank of Boston), FOX—Forward with Optional Exit (Hambros Bank), and Cancelable Forward (Goldman Sachs)

FIGURE 10

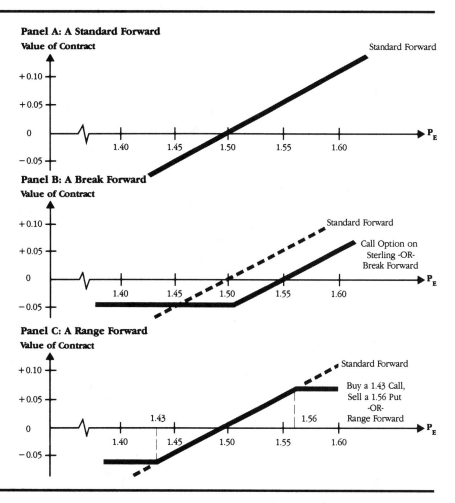

Panel A: A Standard Forward

Panel B: A Break Forward

Panel C: A Range Forward

illustrated in Panel C of Figure 10. In this illustration, we have assumed that the proceeds of a put option on sterling with an exercise price of $1.56 would carry the same premium as a call option on sterling with an exercise price of $1.43.[30]

A payoff profile identical to this option payoff profile could also be generated, however, simply by changing the terms of a standard forward contract to the following:

● at maturity, the buyer of the forward contract agrees to purchase sterling at a price of $1.50 per pound sterling;

● the buyer of the forward contract has the right to break the contract at a price of $1.43 per pound sterling; and

● the seller of the forward contract has the right to break the contract at a price of $1.56 per pound sterling.

Such a forward contract is referred to as a *range forward*.[31]

Swaps with Option-like Characteristics: Given that swaps can be viewed as packages of forward contracts, it should not be surprising that swaps can also be constructed to have option-like

---

30. These numbers are only for purposes of illustration. To determine the exercise prices at which the values of the puts and calls are equal, one would have to use an option pricing model.

31. As Srinivasulu, cited note 29, pointed out, this construction also appears under a number of names: range forward (Salomon Brothers), collar (Midland Montagu), flexible forward (Manufacturers Hanover), cylinder option (Citicorp), option fence (Bank of America) and mini-max (Goldman Sachs).

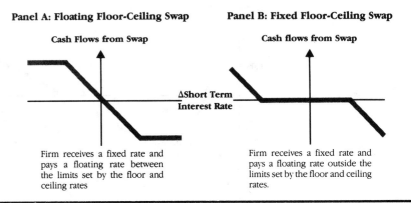

FIGURE 11
PAY-OFF PROFILE FOR
FLOOR-CEILING SWAPS

Panel A: Floating Floor-Ceiling Swap

Cash Flows from Swap

ΔShort Term
Interest Rate

Firm receives a fixed rate and
pays a floating rate between
the limits set by the floor and
ceiling rates

Panel B: Fixed Floor-Ceiling Swap

Cash flows from Swap

Firm receives a fixed rate and
pays a floating rate outside the
limits set by the floor and ceiling
rates.

characteristics like those illustrated for forwards. For example, suppose that a firm with a floating-rate liability wanted to limit its outflows should interest rates rise substantially; at the same time, it was willing to give up some potential gains should there instead be a dramatic decline in short-term rates. To achieve this end, the firm could modify the interest rate swap contract as follows:

As long as the interest rate neither rises by more than 200 basis points nor falls more than 100 basis points, the firm pays a floating rate and receives a fixed rate. But, if the interest is more than 200 basis points above or 100 basis points below the current rate, the firm receives and pays a fixed rate.

The resulting payoff profile for this floating floor-ceiling swap is illustrated in Panel A of Figure 11.

Conversely, the interest rate swap contract could have been modified as follows:

As long as the interest rate is within 200 basis points of the current rate, the firm neither makes nor receives a payment; but if the interest rate rises or falls by more than 200 basis points, the firm pays a floating rate and receives a fixed rate.

The payoff profile for the resulting fixed floor-ceiling swap is illustrated in Panel B of Figure 11.

Redesigned Options: To "redesign" an option, what is normally done is to put two or more options together to change the payoff profile. Examples abound in the world of the option trader. Some of the more colorfully-named combinations are *straddles, strangles,* and *butterflies.*[32]

To see how and why these kinds of creations evolve, let's look at a hypothetical situation. Suppose a firm was confronted with the inherent exposure illustrated in Panel A of Figure 12. Suppose further that the firm wanted to establish a floor on losses caused by changes in a financial price.

As you already know, this could be done by purchasing an out-of-the-money call option on the financial price. A potential problem with this solution, as we have seen, is the premium the firm has to pay. Is there a way the premium can be eliminated?

We have already seen that buying an out-of-the-money call can be financed by selling an out-of-the-money put. However, suppose that this out-of-the-money call is financed by selling a put with precisely the same exercise price—in which case, the put would be in-the-money. As illustrated in Panel B of Figure 12, the proceeds from selling the in-the-money put would exceed the cost of the out-of-the-money call. Therefore, to finance one out-of-the-money call, one would need sell only a fraction of one in-the-money put.

In Panel B, we have assumed that the put value is twice the call value; so, to finance one call, you need sell only 1/2 put. Panel C simply combines the payoff profiles for selling 1/2 put and buying one call with an exercise price of X. Finally, Panel D of Figure 12 combines the option combination in Panel C with the inherent risk profile in Panel A.

Note what has happened. The firm has obtained the floor it wanted, but there is no up-front premium.

---

32. For a discussion of traditional option strategies like straddles, strangles, and butterflies, see for instance chapter 7 of Richard M. Bookstaber, *Option Pricing and Strategies in Investing* (Addison-Wesley, 1981).

FIGURE 12

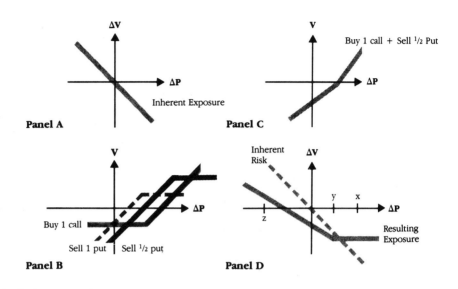

At the price at which the option is exercised, the value of the firm with the floor is the same as it would have been without the floor. The floor is paid for not with a fixed premium, but with a share of the firm's gains above the floor. If the financial price rises by X, the value of the firm falls to the floor and no premium is paid. If, however, the financial price rises by less, say Y, the value of the firm is higher and the firm pays a positive premium for the floor. And, if the financial price falls, say, by Z, the price it pays for the floor rises.

What we have here is a situation where the provider of the floor is paid with a share of potential gains, thereby leading to the name of this option combination—a *participation*. This construction has been most widely used in the foreign exchange market where they are referred to as *participating forwards*.[33]

Options on Other Financial Instruments

Options on futures contracts on bonds have been actively traded on the Chicago Board of Trade since 1982. The valuation of an option on a futures is a relatively straightforward extension of the traditional option pricing models.[34] Despite the close relation between futures and forwards and futures and swaps, the options on forwards (*options on forward rate agreements*) and options on swaps (*swaptions*) are much more recent.

More complicated analytically is the valuation of an option on an option, also known as a *compound option*.[35] Despite their complexity and resistance to valuation formulae, some options on options have begun to be traded. These include options on foreign exchange options and, most notably, options on interest rate options (caps), referred to in the trade as *captions*.

Using the Building Blocks to Design "New" Products

It's rare that a day goes by in the financial markets without hearing of at least one "new" or "hybrid" product. But, as you should have come to expect from us by now, our position with respect to "financial engineering" is that there is little new under the sun. The "new" products typically involve nothing more than putting the building blocks together in a new way.

33. For more on this construction, see Srinivalsulu cited in note 29 and 31.
34. Options on futures were originally discussed by Fischer Black in "The Pricing of Commodity Options," *Journal of Financial Economics* 3 (January-March 1976). A concise discussion of the modifications required in the Black-Scholes formula is contained in James F. Meisner and John W. Labuszewski,

"Modifying the Black-Scholes Option Pricing Model for Alternative Underlying Instruments," *Financial Analysts Journal* November/December 1984.
35. For a discussion of the problem of valuing compound options, see John C. Cox and Mark Rubinstein, *Options Markets* (Prentice-Hall, 1985) 412-415.

FIGURE 13
USING A SWAP TO
CREATE A REVERSE
FLOATING RATE LOAN

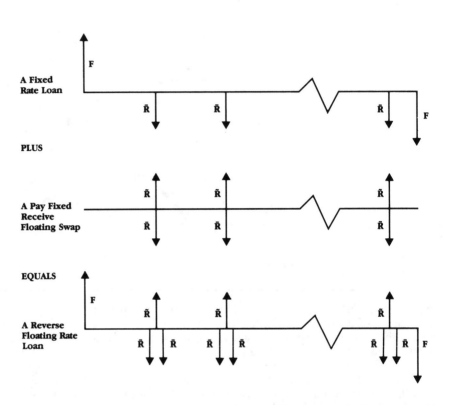

Reverse Floaters: One example of a hybrid security is provided in Figure 13. If we combine the issuance of a conventional fixed rate loan and an interest rate swap where the issuing party pays fixed and receives floating, the result is a reverse floating-rate loan. The net coupon payments on the hybrid loan are equal to twice the fixed rate ($\bar{r}$) minus the floating rate ($\tilde{r}$) times the principal (P), or

$$\text{Net Coupon} = (2\bar{r} - \tilde{r})P = 2\bar{R} - \tilde{R}$$

If the floating rate ($\tilde{r}$) rises, the net coupon payment falls.

Bonds with Embedded Options: Another form of hybrid securities has evolved from bonds with warrants. Bonds with warrants on the issuer's shares have become common. Bond issues have also recently appeared that feature warrants that can be exercised into foreign exchange and gold.

And, in 1986, Standard Oil issued a bond with an oil warrant. These notes stipulated that the principal payment at maturity would be a function of oil prices at maturity. As specified in the Prospectus, the holders of the 1990 notes will receive, in addition to a guaranteed minimum principal amount, "the excess...of the Crude Oil Price...over $25 multiplied by 170 barrels of Light Sweet Crude Oil." What this means is that the note has an embedded four-year option on 170 barrels of crude oil. If, at maturity, the value of Light Sweet Oklahoma Crude Oil exceeds $25, the holder of the note will receive (Oil Price − $25) x 170 plus the guaranteed minimum principal amount. If the value of Light Sweet Oklahoma Crude is less than $25 at maturity, the option expires worthless.[36]

The building block process has also been extended to changes in the timing of the options

36. Note that this issue did have a cap on the crude oil price at $40. Hence, the bondholder actually holds two options positions: long a call option at $25 per barrel and short a call option at $40 per barrel.

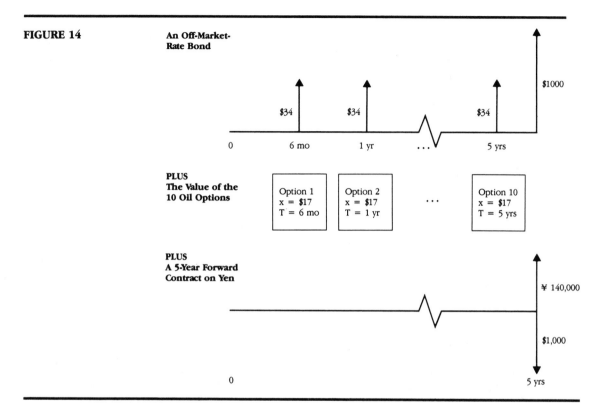

FIGURE 14

An Off-Market-Rate Bond

$34 $34   ... $34 $1000

0   6 mo   1 yr   ...   5 yrs

**PLUS
The Value of the
10 Oil Options**

| Option 1
x = $17
T = 6 mo | Option 2
x = $17
T = 1 yr | ... | Option 10
x = $17
T = 5 yrs |

**PLUS
A 5-Year Forward
Contract on Yen**

¥ 140,000

$1,000

0   5 yrs

embedded in the bond. For a traditional bond with an attached warrant, there is only one option exerciseable at one point in time. More recent bonds have involved packages of options which can be exercised at different points in time.

The first time we saw this extension was in Forest Oil Corporation's proposed *Natural Gas Interest Indexed Debentures.* As set forth in the issue's red herring prospectus of July 1988, Forest Oil proposed to pay a stipulated base rate plus four basis points for each $0.01 by which the average gas spot price exceeds $1.76 per MMBTU (million British Thermal Units). In effect, then, this proposed 12-year "hybrid" debenture is a package consisting of one standard bond plus 24 options on the price of natural gas with maturities ranging from 6 months to 12 years.[37]

And, if we want to get a little fancier, we can consider the possibility of an *Oil Interest-Indexed, Dual-Currency Bond.*[38] Assume that the maturity of this issue is 5 years, with the semi-annual coupon payments indexed to the price of crude oil and the final principal repayment indexed to the value of yen. More specifically, assume that, for each $1000 of principal, the bondholder receives the following: (1) the greater of $34 or the value of two barrels of Sweet Light Crude Oil at each coupon date; and (2) 140,000 yen at maturity.

How would we value such a complicated package? The answer, again, is by breaking it down into the building blocks. As shown in Figure 14, this oil-indexed, dual currency bond consists of three basic components: (1) a straight bond paying $34 semi-annually; (2) 10 call options on the price of oil with an exercise price of $17 per barrel ($34/2) maturing sequentially every six months over a five-year period; and (3) a five-year forward contract on yen with an exercise price of 140 yen/dollar. As it turns out, then, this complicated-looking bond is nothing more than a combination of a standard bond, a series of options, and a forward contract.

37. As reported in the Wall Street Journal on September 21, 1988, Forest Oil withdrew its Natural Gas Indexed Bond in favor of a straight issue. However, in November of 1988, Magma Copper did issue senior subordinated notes on which the coupon payments were linked to the price of copper in much the same way as Forest's coupons would been linked to the price of natural gas.

38. Unlike the other structures discussed, this one has not yet been issued.

CONCLUDING REMARKS

The world is more volatile today than it was two decades ago. Today's corporate risk manager must deal with the potential impact on the firm of significant month-to-month (and sometimes day-to-day) changes in exchange rates, interest rates, and commodity prices. Volatility alone could put a well-run firm out of business, so financial price risk deserves careful attention. As this summary has demonstrated, there now exist techniques and tools for accomplishing this task.

This article makes three major points:

First, there are simple techniques that allow management (and outsiders as well) to identify and measure a firm's exposures. Besides managing "one-off" exposures (such as interest rate exposures from floating-rate borrowings or foreign exchange transaction and translation exposures), many firms are now recognizing their economic exposures. To measure such economic exposures, we have introduced the concept of the *risk profile*. Using this concept, we have proposed simple methods for quantifying the extent of an individual firm's exposures to interest rates, foreign exchange rates, and commodity prices. In the case of a financial firm's exposure to interest rate risk, the techniques of "gap" and "duration" analysis can be applied directly. For the more general case, we demonstrate how simple regression analysis (the same technique used in calculating a firm's "beta") can be used to measure a variety of exposures.

Second, the tools for managing financial risk are more simple than they appear. These financial instruments can be viewed as building blocks. The basic component is a forward contract. Both futures and swaps are like bundles of forward contracts; forwards, in fact, can be combined to yield futures and swaps. The primary differences between these two instruments are the way they deal with default risk and the degree of customization available.

Even options, moreover, can be related to forward contracts. An option on a given asset can be created by combining a position in a forward contract on the same asset with a riskless security; in short, forwards and T-bills can be combined to produce options.[39] Finally, options can be combined to create forward positions; for example, buying a call and shorting a put produces the same position as buying a forward contract.

Third, once you understand the four basic building blocks, it is a straightforward step to designing a customized strategy for managing your firm's exposure. Once the exposure is identified, it can be managed in a number of ways:

● by using one of the financial instruments—for example, by using an interest rate swap to hedge a building products firm's exposure to rising interest rates;

● by using combinations of the financial instruments—for example, buying a call and selling a put to minimize the out-of-pocket costs of the hedge; or

● by combining financial instruments with a debt instrument to create a hybrid security—for example, issuing an oil-indexed bond to hedge a firm's exposure to oil prices.

Our final point in all of this is very simple. Managing financial price risk with "financial engineering" sounds like something you need a degree from Caltech or M.I.T. to do. Designing effective solutions with the financial building blocks is easy.

---

39. This is most often referred to as a synthetic option or as dynamic option replication.

330

An Integrated Approach to Corporate Risk Management

Alan C. Shapiro and Sheridan Titman,
University of California at Los Angeles

In determining their risk management policy, many firms solicit the opinions of investment bankers and commercial lenders. They also pay attention to the yields and ratings on their debt since this gives them direct evidence on how the market perceives their current risk profile. Firms also rely on industry standards in deciding how much debt to issue and how much insurance to purchase.

These approaches are useful because they give the firm access to potentially valuable information about what a "normal" risk profile would look like. But relying too heavily on the opinions of lenders or industry standards doesn't take into account the unique attributes of a particular firm. In many cases, there are no firms whose business breakdown and product market strategy are similar enough to be directly comparable. Even where there is a well-defined industry, this doesn't mean that the risk profiles of other companies are optimal for their current circumstances. For example, there is some evidence that individual debt ratios are, to a large extent, a product of random historical events.[1] Moreover, the potential costs of financial distress to a firm may be quite large, even if the risk to a lender is not that great. If these costs of financial distress are high enough, the fact that, for example, lenders are willing to provide additional funds doesn't mean that the firm should borrow more.

Corporate managements seem to recognize the costs associated with a high risk profile because they engage in a wide variety of risk-reducing behavior. They buy insurance to protect against property and casualty losses and product liability suits. They use commodity and financial futures and forward contracts to guard against fluctuations in interest rates, foreign exchange rates, and the prices of specific products. They shun risky products, sometimes even when the promised returns are high. And, in many cases, they restrict the amount of financial leverage they employ, even when there may be substantial tax advantages to borrowing.

Typically, these decisions—such as how much fire insurance to buy, whether to hedge a particular foreign exchange risk, and how much leverage to incorporate within the company's capital structure—are made independently of one another, presumably because each deals with a different source of risk. But because each of these decisions affects the total risk of the firm (albeit with different costs and consequences), there are clearly benefits to integrating risk management activities into a single framework. To do this properly, however, requires answers to two major questions: (1) What factors should management consider in deciding the firm's optimal risk profile? (2) What are the relevant tradeoffs involved in choosing among the various risk-reducing or hedging mechanisms available? (For example, should one reduce corporate risk by lowering the debt-equity ratio or by taking out a larger product liability policy?)

Unfortunately, modern financial theory offers little guidance in such matters. Indeed, the theory of risk in modern finance, as embodied by the capital asset pricing model (CAPM) and the more recent

---

1. Some academics have suggested that corporate capital structures are determined in large part by companies' current investment requirements and their past profitability (and thus the availability of internal funds); to the extent this is true, actual debt ratios may be more the product of random economic events than any conscious management adherence to a capital structure "target." See Stewart C. Myers, "The Capital Structure Puzzle," *Journal of Finance* (July, 1984), pp.575-592; also Sheridan Titman and Roberto Wessels, "The Determinants of the Capital Structure Choice," UCLA working paper, 1984.

arbitrage pricing theory (APT), seems to regard as irrelevant, if not actually wasteful, a range of corporate hedging activities designed to reduce the total risk, or variability, of the firm's cash flows. Both the CAPM and the APT demonstrate that, under reasonable circumstances, diversifiable risks are not "priced" by sophisticated investors and, hence, do not affect the stock market's required rates of return. Systematic or "market" risks (those which cannot be diversified away by investors) are priced; but because the price of risk is the same for all market participants, there is no gain to shareholders from "laying them off" to financial markets. Consequently, as this reasoning goes, the expected net present value of buying insurance or a futures or forward contract should be zero in an efficient market. In this light, management decisions to insure or hedge assets appear, at best, "neutral mutations" (having no effect on the value of the firm). At worst, such actions, to the extent they are costly, are viewed as "irrational behavior" penalizing corporate stockholders.

The purpose of this article is to present and expand upon a relatively new justification for corporate hedging practices—"new," that is, in the academic finance literature. We begin by offering a rationale for actively managing *total* corporate risk that is consistent with both the premise of shareholder wealth maximization and the exclusive focus of asset pricing models on systematic risk. We then go on to use this theoretical framework to generate a set of principles to guide corporate management in establishing a coherent, centralized approach to risk management. Such an approach considers the costs and benefits of a variety of available risk-reducing tools and strategies for managing the total exposure of the company.

Why Total Risk Matters

Modern finance theory holds that the value of a firm is equal to its expected future cash flows discounted at the appropriate interest rate. Financial economists have concerned themselves almost exclusively with the effect of risk on market discount rates, for the most part ignoring its effect on expected cash flow. According to both the CAPM and APT, sophisticated investors require higher rates of return on securities imposing greater risk; but because such investors diversify their asset holdings, they require risk premiums only for bearing system-

atic (or non-diversifiable) risk. This systematic or "market" risk, generally measured by "beta" under the CAPM, is the sensitivity of a firm's stock price to market-wide price movements. As measured using APT, systematic risk is measured by the sensitivity of market prices to a number of economic factors, such as changes in real interest rates, unexpected fluctuations in GNP growth, and unanticipated changes in inflation.

Finance theory thus implies that stock market investors are concerned not with the total variability of the firm's cash flows (which we shall refer to hereafter as "total risk"), but only with the *co-variability* of those flows with the performance of the economy as a whole. Finance theorists have therefore maintained that reducing risks at the corporate level which are diversifiable at the portfolio level does not benefit stockholders. Consequently, the argument goes, most company-specific risks, provided they do not significantly raise the prospect of bankruptcy, can be managed more efficiently by stockholders.

Recent scholarship, however, has argued that although total risk may not affect investors' required returns, large unsystematic risks, if unmanaged, can substantially reduce the value of the firm. In terms of the DCF model of firm value, diversifiable risks may not raise investors' discount rates (the denominator), but they can significantly lower the level of the firm's expected cash flows (the numerator). If this is the case, then reducing total risk can increase expected cash flows, thereby increasing the value of the firm. Given these assumptions, which we think quite reasonable, corporate hedging makes economic sense.

How does higher total risk lower expectations about future cash flows? Firms with higher *total* risk, all else equal, are more likely to find themselves in financial distress. Financial difficulties in turn are likely to disrupt the operating side of the business, reducing the level of future operating cash flows. Perhaps most important, financial distress can give rise to management incentives that conflict with the interests of other parties who do business with the firm; and the adverse effect of such incentives on sales and operating costs is compounded by the risk-aversion of customers, managers, employees, suppliers, and other corporate stakeholders. In addition, variability in corporate earnings can affect a firm's ability to take full advantage of tax credits and writeoffs.

Financial difficulties are likely to disrupt the operating side of the business, reducing the level of future operating cash flows.

The Adverse Incentive Problem

Financial distress, or the threat of bankruptcy, affects management incentives in three fundamental ways. First, managers are more likely to choose high-risk investments that benefit shareholders at the expense of bondholders. Second, they have a tendency to exit promising lines of business or liquidate the entire firm when they would otherwise continue to operate. Third, they may have an incentive to produce goods of inferior quality and provide a less safe work environment for their employees.

A number of finance theorists discuss how the possibility of bankruptcy leads firms to choose possibly suboptimal investment projects that expropriate wealth from their creditors.[2] They demonstrate that if bankrupcty is likely, the firm's stockholders have an incentive to invest in very risky projects, even if they have negative net present values. This is because the bondholders, rather than the stockholders, bear most of the downside risk from these investments, while the stockholders enjoy most of the gain from the upside potential.

Similarly, one of the present authors shows that financial distress, or the threat of bankruptcy, has an important impact on the firm's liquidation decision and, therefore, on its sales and costs.[3] Managers of financially sound firms, as representatives of stockholder interests, generally will not choose to liquidate the firm because stockholders, as the firm's most junior claimants, receive liquidation proceeds only after other claimants are paid in full. Also, because they will lose their jobs if the firm fails, managers have a more direct incentive to keep the firm in business. As the firm progresses through stages of financial distress toward bankruptcy, however, the firm's creditors exert increasing influence on management decisions; and creditors' priority claim to any liquidation proceeds gives them a much stronger incentive to liquidate the firm. The possibility that a financially distressed firm may be liquidated is shown to reduce the current sales and raise the operating costs of high-risk firms by raising concerns of customers, suppliers, and employees.

Because both stockholders and managers have strong incentives to avoid bankruptcy and liquidation, management may take actions under the threat of financial distress they would not otherwise take. For example, a firm having difficulty raising cash may be tempted to lower the quality of its products and services; they may also cut corners on safety for their employees. These temptations will be especially strong in cases where quality or safety is difficult to monitor from the outside, and where the damage may not come to light immediately. Or, a firm facing financial distress may be tempted to conserve cash by cutting back on research and development, advertising and promotional expenditures, and various forms of working capital such as inventory and receivables.

Thus, while a healthy firm has a strong incentive to produce high-quality products and to take other actions that ensure its long-term viability, these normal incentives are likely to change if the firm is suffering financial distress. Under the threat of bankruptcy, the long-run value of a strong reputation may be less important than generating enough cash to make it through the next day. The cost savings associated with cutting quality levels may be particularly attractive to firms facing creditors threatening to take over and possibly liquidate the firm.

Potential customers and other stakeholders anticipate these changes in management incentives and actions. As a result, they become increasingly reluctant to do business with firms in financial distress, as well as with high-risk firms likely to face financial distress in the future. Such expectations of consumers, suppliers, and even employees will adversely affect the firm's future sales, operating costs, and financing costs. In short, the expectation alone of financial distress reduces the expected value of doing business with the firm.

The Effect on Sales

The incentive of companies in financial distress to produce lower quality products will scare off potential customers. This may, in part, explain Chrysler's difficulty in attracting customers when they were on the verge of bankruptcy. In response to this

2. See, for example, Michael Jensen and William Meckling, "Theory of the Firm: Managerial Behavior, Agency Costs and Ownership Structure," *Journal of Financial Economics* 3 (1976), pp.305-360; Stewart Myers, "Determinants of Corporate Borrowing," *Journal of Financial Economics* 9 (1977), pp.138-147; and Dan Galai and Ron Masulis, "The Option Pricing Model and the Risk Factor of Stock," *Journal of Financial Economics* 3 (1976), pp.53-81.

3. See Sheridan Titman "The Effect of Capital Structure on a Firm's Liquidation Decision," *Journal of Financial Economics* 13 (1984), pp.137-183.

Reducing total risk can aid a firm's marketing efforts by providing greater assurance to potential customers that the company will be around in the future to service and upgrade its products.

customer hesitancy, Chrysler decided to offer 5-year service warranties on its new cars. This service contract, which may have been very costly to Chrysler, would probably have been unnecessary if Chrysler were not in such financial straits. Certainly, none of its competitors matched its generous terms.

But product quality is not consumers' only worry; service is a major concern as well. If the original supplier goes out of business, parts and repairs may become a problem. This is particularly important where there are economies of scale in producing parts and providing service. The volume of parts for the aftermarket is likely to be far lower than the volume required for the production of new units. Hence, if the firm goes out of business, production volume will drop precipitously, raising the cost and the price of spare parts. Spare parts will also be more difficult to locate. Similarly, the value of investing in specialized training and equipment to repair a particular product will diminish if the product's sales outlook becomes shaky. This means fewer qualified mechanics and more difficulty in finding those who are around. (The problems roughly parallel those that might befall the owner of a Maserati Biturbo whose car breaks down in an obscure town in the middle of nowhere.)

Thus, reducing total risk can aid a firm's marketing efforts by providing greater assurance to potential customers that the company will be around in the future to service and upgrade its products. Purchasers of long-lived capital assets are especially concerned about the seller's survival. Potential buyers of Chrysler cars, for example, were understandably nervous about purchasing a product which they might have difficulty getting serviced if Chrysler went bankrupt. Clearly, it is comforting to know that the manufacturer will be there to service the equipment and supply new parts as old ones wear out.

At present, with a shakeout under way in the personal computer business, and with several companies dropping by the wayside, shoppers are more worried about producers' staying power. IBM is exploiting buyers' fears about its competitors' longevity with the message, "What most people want from a computer company is a good night's sleep." The widespread concern about whether companies will be around to service and update their machines threatens further to erode the market shares of smaller producers.

In general, whenever customers face large (fixed) costs to switching suppliers, the suppliers have an incentive to present a low-risk image. Switching costs arise when buyers must spend substantial amounts of money tailoring the product to their particular needs, which is often the case in the purchase of a computer or factory automation equipment. These costs come in the form of specific product adaptations, necessary investments in specialized ancillary equipment, and time spent learning how to operate a supplier's equipment or software.

The importance of having a secure position in the marketplace is evident in the case where outside suppliers provide complementary products or services that add value to the firm's product. If a supplier must bear a fixed cost to adapt its product to work with a new brand, it will first make an assessment of the brand's viability in the marketplace. For example, software programs are produced for computers with the largest market share first; only later, if at all, are they rewritten for other brands.

Risk hurts sales for another reason as well. Most firms diversify among suppliers in order to reduce disruption to operations in the event that any one supplier is unable to meet its commitments. It takes time to line up new suppliers, ascertain that their products meet required quality standards, negotiate prices and credit terms, establish new shipping routines, and make all the other adjustments necessary to fit a new supplier into the production schedule. The problem of finding new sources of supply becomes more acute during periods of shortage, such as those caused by price controls. Because financial distress can jeopardize a firm's ability to serve as a stable source of supply, riskier suppliers, all else equal, will gain a smaller share of orders. This is true of suppliers of commodity-type products as well as those of specialized products.

For example, when Wheeling-Pittsburgh Steel Corp. filed for bankruptcy in April 1985, customers reduced their orders, the company was forced to discount prices on some products, and suppliers changed their credit terms to cash-on-delivery. One buyer of Wheeling-Pittsburgh's output interviewed by the *Wall Street Journal* said that he wasn't looking for another supplier because his company had multiple sources. But, he added, "If I were single-sourced, I'd have been on the phone two months ago looking for other suppliers."[4]

---

4. *The Wall Street Journal*, April 18, 1985, p.4

Even if a firm facing financial distress intends to be conscientious in dealing with its creditors, it will have difficulty in assuring them of its intentions.

Risky firms become victims of lost consumer confidence. Customers aren't as willing to do business with a firm that might be going out of business. To some extent, this fear is self-fulfilling as lost sales worsen the firm's financial position and result in a further reduction in sales. Thus, the riskier a firm, the lower its sales are likely to be. Those customers that continue to do business with a risky firm will reduce the price they are willing to pay for the firm's products by an amount equal to their expected damages. As a result, both the unit sales volume and the price received by a firm can be affected by the (perceived as much as the actual) level of its total risk.

As sales decline, distribution will suffer as well, especially for products that cannot just be plugged in, eaten, or worn. Distributors must then invest in training programs so that their salespeople understand and are able to demonstrate the uses of the company's latest products. This fixed cost, in combination with scarce shelf space, limits the number of product lines retailers are willing to carry. The resulting decline in sales further hinders the firm's ability to take advantage of economies of scale, making it less competitive still.

Changes in total risk affect the probability of bankruptcy and, therefore, the possibility that a company will quit a business. Consequently, any action taken by a firm that decreases its total risk will improve its prospects for survival and, hence, its sales outlook.

The Effect on Operating Costs

A firm's cost of doing business is, in part, a function of its suppliers' view of the company's long-run viability. A firm struggling to survive is unlikely to find suppliers bending over backwards to provide it with specially developed products or services, particularly if those products or services are unique and suitable for use only by the firm in question. In general, the value of investing in a long-term relationship with a customer will depend on whether the customer is expected to survive in the long run. The lower the likelihood of future survival, the more of these relationship costs the customer will have to bear up front in the form of higher prices or less closely-tailored services and products.

Lower-risk firms also have an easier time attracting and retaining good personnel. In the event of liquidation, employees must bear search costs, espe-

cially where the job provides firm-specific training and skills not easily transferred elsewhere. Higher level managers bear the stigma of being associated with a failure. The more difficult it is for potential future employers to determine the extent of an individual manager's culpability in the corporate failure, the higher the cost attached to this stigma.

The Effect on Financing Costs

The potential for myopic behavior on the part of the firm extends to its dealings with creditors as well. A company that expects to remain in business will generally be very protective of its credit reputation. The value of a good credit reputation, however, is lower for firms that may not survive to reap the long-run benefits. Such firms have an incentive to borrow money under false pretenses and mistreat creditors in order to delay the onset of bankruptcy. Because creditors understand this change in incentives, risky firms will find it more difficult to borrow and obtain credit under favorable terms. Moreover, even if a firm facing financial distress intends to be conscientious in dealing with its creditors, it will have difficulty in assuring them of its intentions.

Firms extending trade credit will have a difficult time imposing sufficiently stringent conditions to assure themselves of repayment. Rather than putting up with the associated risks and problems, they are likely just to cut off trade credit for riskier firms. The potential loss of supplier credits presumably is costly since firms seem to prefer it to most other sources of funds, possibly because it is such a flexible form of financing. (The alternative of negotiating bank loans or other financing every time additional credit is needed imposes a variety of transaction costs on the firm that may be avoided with supplier credits.)

Excessive variability in cash flows could also affect the firm's ability to borrow. Just as a firm facing financial distress cannot be trusted to maintain product quality, so it cannot be trusted to honor its obligation to its creditors. Because of the option-like character of equity shares, shareholders have an incentive to select high-risk projects which increase their wealth by reducing the value of the firm's liabilities. As pointed out earlier, equity holders receive *all* of the upside potential from high-risk investments, whereas bondholders share in the downside losses.

Consequently, the riskier a firm is perceived to be, the more stringent the restrictions lenders will

The riskier a firm is perceived to be, the more stringent the restrictions lenders will impose on its operating policies and investment projects. These restrictions can prove especially costly for high-growth firms.

impose on its operating policies and investment projects. These restrictions can prove especially costly for high-growth firms with financing requirements that exceed internally generated cash flow. Moreover, with a risky firm, the interest rate necessary to compensate lenders for the threat that stockholders will yield to temptation may be so high, and the restrictive debt covenants so tightly drawn, as to virtually guarantee that the firm will be unable to pay back its new debts. The result is a drying up of new credits. This could cause the firm to forgo attractive projects, especially if the alternative is an equity issue requiring disclosure of valuable information to competitors.[5]

Decreasing total risk can reduce or eliminate some of the more onerous debt restrictions and covenants. Investment and operating policies with fewer restrictions on them should increase expected future cash flows and shareholder wealth.

The Problem of Risk Aversion

We have already seen one example of how total risk could change the value of the firm as a going concern. Specifically, creditors might push into bankruptcy and liquidation a firm that would otherwise survive. Recognition of this possibility will be reflected in the form of lower sales and higher operating costs.

Less evident is the likelihood that even in a 100 percent equity-financed firm, the firm's value as a going concern will be reduced by large risk exposures. The income streams of most managers and employees are probably not well (or easily) diversified. Consequently, most people will be concerned about the total risk of their job-derived income. The close connection between corporate and personal risk means that a riskier firm must pay employees more to induce them to commit their human capital to the firm. Similarly, suppliers, distributors, and other corporate stakeholders will demand to be compensated for bearing added risk. As a result, higher total risk increases the cost of maintaining the organization.

Competition, however, will limit (to the level set by efficient firms) a high-risk company's ability to meet demands for higher compensation. A highly risky firm, therefore, will have difficulty maintaining

its organization. The case of AM International is a good illustration of the organizational problems posed by financial distress. After disastrous investments in high-technology businesses, AM International filed for Chapter 11 protection in 1982. The unsettled conditions at the firm, both before and after entering bankruptcy, led to a rapid turnover of managers, with a high cost. As the president of one of AM's divisions commented, "When you are constantly shifting direction, there is no civility, no culture, none of those things that make good companies."[6] The Multigraphics Division had seven presidents in as many years. And 40 executives paraded through the division's six vice-president slots in one four-year period.

The reduction in value caused by such disorder is especially great for those firms whose principal assets are not physical but intangible—assets, for example, that take the form of organizational skills and assets inseparable from the firm itself. One such skill involves knowledge about how best to service a market, including new product development and adaptation, quality control, advertising, distribution, after-sales service, and the general ability to read changing market desires and translate them into salable products. Other valuable organizational assets whose worth would suffer from financial distress—aside from managers with their firm-specific human capital—could include a network of independent distributors or suppliers of specialized products, such as software.

Similarly, many firms are in industries that require salespeople to develop close relationships with their customers. Financial distress, which increases a salesman's personal risk, will cause him—whether he is a high-technology sales engineer or a stockbroker—to jump ship, taking customers with them and further eroding the value of the firm. For example, when Cordis, a medical technology firm, found itself in a battle with the Food and Drug Administration (FDA) over the safety of its pacemakers, it suffered serious damage to its sales force, whose members found their commission income plummeting. Many salespeople switched to Cordis's competitors. Because of the complexity of pacer technology, salespeople tend to have close relationships with the physicians they supply and thus can take their customers along when they

5. This point was made in by Donald Lessard and Alan Shapiro in "Guidelines for Global Financing Choices," *Midland Corporate Finance Journal* (Winter 1983), pp.68-80.

6. *Business Week*, December 3, 1984, p.169.

The close connection between corporate and personal risk means that a riskier firm must pay employees more to induce them to commit their human capital to the firm.

switch companies. Needless to say, the cost to the company from desertion amongst their sales force was considerable.

Moreover, even a temporary increase in risk can do permanent damage to the firm if some stakeholders leave in response to their perception of added personal risk. In order to reconstitute the organization, the firm must bear a variety of fixed costs associated with replacing those risk-averse stakeholders. These costs—which include the costs of hiring and training new managers, salespeople and other employees, adding new distributors, and finding new suppliers—reduce the value of the firm as an ongoing entity. When disintegration of the organization has progressed far enough, cash flows will turn negative. At this point, shareholders will have no choice but to liquidate the firm. A creditor-financed firm will likely be liquidated prior to this point.

Tax Effects

As the variability of operating profits increases, so does the probability that a firm will be unable to make full use of its tax credits and depreciation and interest expense tax deductions.[7] To the extent the resale market in these tax benefits is imperfect (as measured by the discount taken when the tax benefit is sold), an increase in total risk will lead to a reduction in expected corporate cash flows. If the tax credit or tax loss is carried forward, the relevant cost is the reduction in the present value of the tax benefit. By reducing its total risk, a firm can increase the expected value of its tax credits and tax writeoffs and thereby increase its expected future cash flows.

Why Total Risk Matters: Summing Up

The negative feedback effect of large corporate exposure to risk on expected cash flow should now be evident. As total risk goes up, the firm's cost of doing business rises, reducing its prospects for survival. The combination of risk aversion and poorer corporate prospects weakens the bonds between the firm and the individuals who comprise the extended organization; and an exodus begins. Distributors switch to other brands, suppliers

reorient their production facilities, and firms supplying complementary services and specialized products tailor their products for competing brands. Recognizing this, customers buy less; and the firm's best employees either demand higher salaries or leave, taking their firm-specific knowledge elsewhere. This adds to the firm's risk, which, in turn, further affects the firm's sales and cost of doing business. Thus, there is a natural progression from increased total risk to increased risk of bankruptcy and liquidation. Furthermore, even if liquidation is unlikely, total risk will lower the firm's value by an amount equal to the added cost of organizational maintenance.

To summarize the arguments above, the true cost of higher corporate risk is the reduction in the value of the firm's tangible and intangible assets caused by the presence (or probability) of financial distress. In general, the greater the value added by the organization to the firm's products or services and the more expensive it is to reconstitute that organization, the greater this cost is likely to be.

Characteristics of Firms With High Costs of Financial Risk

Based on the previous discussion, it is possible to identify specific characteristics of firms for which financial distress is especially costly. Such companies would therefore be likely to benefit most from active management of total corporate risk. Some of these characteristics are industry-specific, based on product type, while others are firm-specific. Industry-specific product characteristics include the following:

● *Products that require repairs.* This is illustrated by Lee Iacocca's response to suggestions that Chrysler declare bankruptcy: "Our situation was unique... It wasn't like the cereal business. If Kellogg's were known to be going out of business, nobody would say:'Well, I won't buy their cornflakes today. What if I get stuck with a box of cereal and there's nobody around to service it'?"[8]
● *Goods or services whose quality is an important attribute but is difficult to determine in advance.* One such service is air transportation. In fact, airline

7. This effect was first pointed out by Harry DeAngelo and Ron Masulis in "Optimal Capital Structure Under Corporate and Personal Taxation," *Journal of Financial Economics* 8 (1980), pp.3-29.

8. *Fortune*, November 26, 1984, p.224.

Firms with substantial growth opportunities will often prefer to maintain a continuous research and development program, and to fund substantial advertising and other marketing expenditures, in both good times and bad.

companies in financial difficulty have been hurt by the common belief that they are more likely to cut corners on safety, thereby increasing the risk of an accident.

- *Products for which there are switching costs.* Such products would include computers or office and factory automation equipment.
- *Products whose value to customers depends on the services and complementary products supplied by independent companies.* As we saw earlier, many firms require third parties to distribute, sell, service, upgrade, and otherwise add value to their products. Being a low-risk firm helps persuade independent firms to enter into such a symbiotic relationship.

Firm-specific factors include the following:

- *High-growth opportunities.* Firms having more positive net present value projects available than they can finance with internally-generated funds will jeopardize their access to outside financing by the appearance of being risky. Otherwise, prospective investors could be scared off by the previously-discussed management incentive problems.
- *Substantial organizational assets.* Firms whose principal assets are intangible—in the form of managers and employees with firm-specific human capital, outside distributors, suppliers, brand names, a reputation for quality and reliability—will have a higher cost of financial distress than firms with mostly physical assets. These intangible assets will rapidly depreciate in value if the firm experiences, or seems likely to experience, financial distress. As firm risk increases, the value of a reputation for quality products diminishes, and managers and other stakeholders are increasingly likely to sever their ties with the firm.
- *Large excess tax deductions.* Companies such as Chrysler and U.S. Steel cannot take full advantage of their available tax losses, much less the interest on additional debt. Thus, they have less incentive to load up on debt.

Determining the Firm's Risk Profile

A company's optimal risk profile should be determined by trading off the costs of the firm bearing all (or some) of its risks against the costs of somehow hedging or otherwise reducing those risks. In deciding on an appropriate risk profile, management should conduct a comprehensive analysis of all of its significant exposures. The principal focus of this analysis should be on the risk of *cash insolvency*—that is, the probability of running out of cash before meeting debt servicing charges—given a particular risk profile. Cash insolvency is critical because the inability to meet principal, interest, and lease payments may lead to financial insolvency and, ultimately, to bankruptcy.

However, the analysis can and should be extended to examine the firm's capacity, under various risk scenarios, to service fixed charges of any kind. For example, those firms that perceive large costs to cutting preferred and common stock dividends will treat these as a fixed cost. Strategic factors also enter here. Firms with substantial growth opportunities will often prefer to maintain a continuous research and development program, and to fund substantial advertising and other marketing expenditures, in both good times and bad.

The Worst Case Scenario

Unfortunately, the difficulty of performing a thorough cash flow analysis may lead firms to limit themselves to using rules of thumb, usually based on various coverage ratios. But coverage ratios do not tell a financial manager what is most important: the probability of cash insolvency associated with alternative risk profiles. This requires a series of cash budgets prepared assuming (1) different economic conditions and (2) the levels of usage of different risk-reducing mechanisms. To do this properly, the financial manager must specify a range of likely future economic scenarios and how the firm's cash flows will be affected by these developments, with a probability attached to each scenario. Moreover, it is necessary to determine other possible sources of cash besides the cash flow from operations. This includes liquid assets that can be drawn down, accounts payable that could be stretched, expenditures that could be deferred, and assets that could be sold. The end result is a series of net cash flows that are or can be generated under each of the different economic scenarios. Based on the associated probabilities, the financial manager can then examine these cash flows and see whether a particular risk profile exposes the firm to too much financial risk.

A useful place to begin determination of an appropriate risk profile is to analyze what happens to a firm's cash flows under a "worst case scenario." This could mean a general or industry recession when sales are severely depressed, but it could be any combination of adverse circumstances. For example, a company with a sizable export market, such as Rolls Royce, might be most concerned with a possible appreciation in the value of its home currency, while a pharmaceutical company like Johnson & Johnson might be especially concerned with the effects of a product recall.

In 1961, Gordon Donaldson presented a framework for evaluating corporate debt capacity that can be easily adapted (and, in fact, may actually be better suited) to the task of quantifying total corporate risks.[9] In order to use Donaldson's method for this purpose, management would begin by identifying the various sources of risk to which the firm is exposed. Then, for each of these categories of risk, net cash flows can be calculated assuming the worst happens; and, at the end of this process, management will have an estimate of the cash balance the firm can reasonably expect to have at the end of the recession (or some firm-specific catastrophe). Specifically, this means estimating

$$CB_r = CB_o + NCF_r$$

where

CB_r = the cash balance at the end of a recession
CB_o = the cash balance at the start of a recession
NCF_r = the net cash flow during the recession.

By doing this calculation for a range of possible net recessionary cash flows, this information can be used to construct a probability distribution of the ending cash balance, CB_r.

The next step in this analysis is to compare these cash flows to fixed charges. Then for each increment of debt, insurance, forward contracts and the like, the firm could determine the probability of cash insolvency based on the probability distribution of CB_r.

Suppose, for example, that a firm normally maintains $1 million in cash and marketable securities. This is the cash balance that would be on hand at the start of a recession or the onset of some other adverse circumstances. Assume that such an economic decline, when it comes, is expected to last for two years. To show the effects of additional debt on the firm's risk profile, assume it borrows an additional $5 million, with annual debt servicing charges of $1.5 million. Its cash balance at the end of the economic decline will be

$$CB_r = \$1,000,000 - (2 \times \$1,500,000) + NCF_r.$$
$$= -\$2,000,000 + NCF_r$$

Hence, the probability of cash insolvency under this financing plan equals the probability that net cash flow under adverse conditions will fall below $2 million. Management must then decide how high a probability of cash insolvency it is prepared to tolerate. (This judgment should not be based on its own preferences alone, but rather on what would add most value to shareholders.)

Cash Inadequacy

Thus far, our analysis of the firm's risk profile has been in terms of the probability of cash insolvency. But long before reaching this point, the firm could be in serious financial trouble. More important, as we saw earlier, this financial distress can prove very costly for certain types of firms, especially those with substantial amounts of organizational assets.

This means that the risk analysis should be extended to deal with the case of *cash inadequacy*, defined by Donaldson as the inability to fund all desired, but not absolutely essential, expenditures.[10] This category would include items such as dividends, an R&D program, expenditures to upgrade plant and equipment, and advertising and other marketing costs. By this point, the company is cutting into muscle and bone; and this will affect its ability to sustain whatever competitive advantage it has. The result will be lower expected future operating cash flows, which will be reflected in a lower stock price today.

Table 1 shows the various ways in which firms can mobilize financial resources in the event of a liquidity problem.[11] These financial resources can be categorized into uncommitted reserves, reductions of planned expenditures, and liquidation of assets. The first category includes excess cash and marketable securities, unused lines of credit, and other sources of liquidity that can be readily

---

9. *Corporate Debt Capacity* (Boston: Division of Research, Harvard Business School), 1961.

10. Donaldson, *Corporate Debt Capacity.* See earlier citation.
11. The mobilization of financial resources is discussed by Donaldson in *Strategy for Financial Mobility* (Homewood, Ill.: Richard D.Irwin), 1971.

TABLE 1
Inventory of Financial Resources

Resources	Available for use within		
	One quarter	One year	Three years
Uncommitted reserves			
Instant reserves			
Surplus cash	$_____		
Unused line of credit	$_____		
Negotiable reserves			
Additional bank loans	$_____		
Issue of long-term debt		$_____	
Issue of new equity			
Preferred stock		$_____	
Common stock		$_____	
Reduction of planned outflows			
Volume related			
Change in production schedule	$_____		
Scale related			
Marketing program		$_____	
R&D budget		$_____	
Administrative overhead		$_____	
Capital expenditures		$_____	
Value related			
Dividend payments		$_____	
Liquidation of assets			
Sales of assets			
Land and real estate		$_____	
Equipment		$_____	
Accounts receivable		$_____	
Inventory		$_____	
Sales of business units			$_____
Total financial resources available	$_____	$_____	
		$_____	$_____
			$_____

Source: Donaldson (1971), "Strategy for Financial Emergencies," *Harvard Business Review* (November–December), p. 72.

accessed. If these sources prove insufficient, the firm can then begin cutting certain non-essential expenditures. Provided the firm is already operating in an efficient manner, these cuts will trade off future cash flows for current cash. Finally, the firm can sell off some of its assets. Again, if the firm was already being run in a lean manner, these asset sales will harm future profitability. The costs associated with these various forms of cash inadequacy and insolvency must be traded off against the costs of reducing risk.

Methods of Reducing Total Risk

There are many ways in which firms can reduce their total risk, though some are clearly less costly than others. Depending on the methods used, a firm's cost of achieving a given level of risk reduction can vary widely. Management thus has an incentive to select carefully the most cost-effective method of dealing with total risk.

The methods for managing corporate risk can

A policy of avoiding risky investments ignores the the extent to which a firm can control risk in other ways. After all, companies are in business to take risks, provided such risks promise to be compensated through adequate returns.

be broken down into two basic categories:"financial" and"real." The principal risk-reducing techniques that can be categorized as financial include lowering the firm's debt-equity ratio, buying or selling forward or futures contracts, and buying insurance. Real adjustments include the adoption of production processes that reduce the degree of operating leverage, avoidance of high-risk projects, and abandonment of existing high-risk products (such as those subject to large liability suits for which no adequate insurance is available).

Restricting the Debt-Equity Ratio

The finance literature is replete with references to the effect of debt financing on the firm's total risk. By restricting its debt ratio, the firm will reduce its degree of financial leverage, thereby decreasing the probability of financial distress and bankruptcy. In the limit, the all-equity firm would virtually eliminate the probability of bankruptcy (though there would still be a positive probability of voluntary liquidation).[12]

The fact that we see very few all-equity financed firms suggests that this risk-reducing technique is not costless. In particular, because interest payments come out of before-tax income whereas dividends are paid out of after-tax income, debt may be a less expensive source of financing, at least up to a certain point. Hence, the loss of the interest tax shield provided by debt serves as a disincentive to firms to lower their total risk by means of debt reduction. At the same time, however, the tax advantage of debt gives firms an incentive to use other methods of reducing total corporate risk, enabling them to add still more debt to their capital structures. This may allow them to increase their debt tax shield without significantly raising the probability of financial distress.

Futures and Forward Contracts

A futures or a forward contract calls for delivery, at a fixed future date, of a specified quantity of a given commodity—be it foreign exchange or orange juice—with the price fixed at the time the contract is set. With a forward or futures contract, a firm can lock in its future cost of inputs or sales revenue. For example, an orange juice manufacturer can hedge against the possibility of price fluctuations in its basic raw material by buying orange juice futures. Similarly, a copper mining firm can lock in the revenues from a new mine by selling the output in advance through use of a copper futures contract.

The cost of a forward or futures contract is simply the cost of executing the transaction. In the case of a forward contract, the cost is the spread between the bid and ask price. With a futures contract it is the opportunity cost of the margin amount plus the trading commissions. In a large, active, and well-organized market, such as the foreign exchange market, these costs are likely to be minimal. In other words, the net present value of a futures or forward contract traded in such a market is close to zero. (But, at the same time, the benefits to the corporation from reducing total risk could be substantial.)

Insurance

Buying insurance is a standard approach to hedging corporate risk. The basic problem with insurance is the large load embedded in its price; that is, insurance rates include a premium over and above the expected losses associated with the policy in order to cover marketing and claims servicing costs, as well as the implicit costs of moral hazard and adverse selection.[13]

Insurance firms do have a comparative advantage in some areas of risk management, such as efficiency in claims service and evaluating safety projects. In addition, the purchase of insurance can act as a signal to debt holders and other claimants that the firm's investment decisions will be geared toward maximizing the value of the firm rather than the value of the firm's equity.[14]

Those firms for which the cost of risk is not that great, based on the characteristics described in Section 2, will choose to self-insure more of their risks. But it should be emphasized that the decision not to insure risks with an insurance company is not the same as choosing to self-insure. The firm has many other means available to reduce risk. It should use

---

12. There will still be a positive probability of bankruptcy since even all-equity financed firms rely on trade credit.

13. Moral hazard involves the possibility that having an insurance policy will adversely effect (from the insurance company's standpoint) the purchaser's behavior, while adverse selection involves the possibility that the highest-risk firms choose the highest coverage.

14. The comparative advantages of insurance contracts and insurance companies are discussed at length by David Mayers and Clifford Smith in "The Corporate Insurance Decision," *Chase Financial Quarterly* (Spring, 1982), pp.47-65.

*An investment with a negative NPV when evaluated standing
alone may have a positive NPV when account is taken of the
beneficial effects of risk reduction on the firm's other project
cash flows.*

insurance only when the costs of insurance compare favorably with the costs of other risk-reducing techniques.

Avoiding High Risk Projects

The easiest way to manage risk is to avoid it, which firms can do by screening out high-risk projects. The ease of this approach, however, masks potentially high opportunity costs. The real issue is the degree of risk a company is willing to tolerate and the return required to bear it. A policy of avoiding risky investments ignores the potentially high returns available and the extent to which a firm can control risk in other ways. After all, companies are in business to take risks, provided such risks are recognized, intelligently managed, and promise to be compensated through adequate returns.

In judging the value of undertaking an investment, however, it must be recognized that a project that adds excessive risk to the firm's overall project portfolio may cause financial trouble, and thereby jeopardize all its other activities. An example of this is the case of the Johns Manville Corporation. The high risk associated with its asbestos division resulted in huge product liability suits and increased uncertainty about the financial viability of the firm. Many other firms are very concerned about the huge product liability suits directed against Johns Manville, A. H. Robbins (the Dalkon shield), and other companies. Their response more often than not is to avoid making those products that may subject them to similar liability lawsuits in the future. Again, however, as pointed out above, the opportunity cost of such a policy may be very great.

While some firms may choose to drop overly risky projects or products, there are less drastic steps that can be taken. Since it is the project's contribution to the riskiness of the firm's portfolio of projects—and not simply the risk of the project itself—that matters, one alternative is to choose projects with cash flows that are negatively correlated, thereby hedging or insuring the cash flows of the other projects. Conversely, firms could avoid choosing projects with returns that are highly correlated because of the added likelihood of bankruptcy.

The latter strategy is not costless, however. Investments with differing cash flow patterns are most likely to be those in businesses outside of management's area of expertise, which of course increases the probability that the investments selected will

have negative net present values. But, even an investment with a negative NPV when evaluated standing alone may have a positive NPV when account is taken of the beneficial effects of risk reduction on the firm's other project cash flows.

Firms can also reduce the correlation among project returns without venturing into new businesses by diversifying internationally. The relevant issue is whether diversification is the least costly form of risk reduction. For example, firms can also reduce total risk by designing their projects to have lower operating leverage, a subject we turn to now.

Reducing the Degree of Operating Leverage

Just as reducing the degree of financial leverage lowers total risk, so too does reducing the degree of operating leverage. And for the same reason: it reduces the ratio of fixed to variable costs. For example, if workers can be laid off or fired with relative ease, the more labor-intensive the production process selected, the higher the variable cost-fixed cost ratio, and so the lower the firm's risk. But, if a more capital-intensive production process has lower expected costs, the benefits of risk reduction can come at a high price. Similarly, a firm may forgo the opportunity to take advantage of economies of scale because of the attendant increase in its degree of operating leverage; it may choose instead to build a scaled-down plant that has higher unit costs but involves less risk. In both cases, however, competitors who select the more efficient process will have a cost edge they can use to great advantage.

Long-term sales contracts provide a possible solution to this dilemma. By entering into such a contract, particularly of the "take-or-pay" variety with a minimum floor price, the firm can take advantage of the lower expected cost of the large-scale, capital-intensive process while at the same time reducing its total risk. But if a long-term contract involves simply a transfer of risk to customers, they will demand a price discount for bearing this risk. Under plausible circumstances, however, both the producer and the purchaser can realize risk-reduction benefits from long-term sales contracts. The producer has a guaranteed outlet for its goods while the customer has a stable source of supply.

In some instances, it is not possible to reduce the degree of operating leverage by altering the labor-to-capital ratio. For example, as long as an

The risk of the firm can be reduced by converting a portion of a worker's income from a strictly contractual claim into a residual or equity claim.

airplane is in service, it requires a full crew; that is, its ratio of labor to capital is fixed. As another example, labor is a fixed cost for many Japanese firms because they provide lifetime employment for their workers. Thus, changing the labor-to-capital ratio does not change a Japanese firm's degree of operating leverage.

The alternative in these instances is to convert a portion of the worker's income from a strictly contractual claim into a residual or equity claim. This can be done by tying a substantial portion of the worker's expected income to the firm's profitability. Thus, for example several airlines facing financial difficulty have lowered pay levels while offering higher expected bonuses; others have given their employees stock in lieu of higher pay. Similarly, in Japan, most employees receive on the order of one-third their annual income in the form of a year-end bonus tied to the firm's profitability during the year.

Tradeoffs Among Risk-Reducing Mechanisms

Choosing among the various risk-reducing techniques described in the previous section involves several considerations. We begin this section by offering a few basic principles of risk management:

● First, since the management of total risk entails real costs, the firm should be prepared to pay a positive price to reduce risk.

● Second, the optimal level of risk—the firm's risk-bearing capacity—is found at the point at which the cost of reducing an additional unit of risk is just equal to the benefit from that incremental degree of risk reduction.

● Third, the firm should take advantage of any opportunities to reduce risk at a zero net cost. Needless to say, the firm should seize any risk-reduction bargains; that is, any opportunities to reduce risk at a below-market price. Such bargains are generally to be found, for example, in the form of government-subsidized insurance, such as political risk insurance or export credit insurance.

● Fourth, the firm must bear in mind that real adjustments to reduce risk usually entail real costs, whereas some financial adjustments, such as the use of forward or futures contracts, may be undertaken at a minimal cost.

● Fifth, the firm must take into account the compara-

tive advantages in risk bearing of different institutions. A large multinational industrial firm may have sufficient diversity of operations to self-insure risks ordinarily transferred to an insurance company.

● Sixth, the firm should take into account the effect that reducing one form of risk can have on another form of risk.

The last point, especially, bears some elaboration. Suppose, for example, General Electric sells jet engines to Lufthansa with payment due in one year and set in deutsche marks. GE can hedge its currency risk on this transaction by selling an equivalent amount of deutsche marks forward for dollars for one year. But this does not mean that all risk is eliminated. By transforming a deutsche-mark denominated contract into a U.S. dollar-denominated contract, use of the forward contract is substituting exposure to inflation risk for exposure to currency risk. Without hedging, GE will know how many deutsche marks it will receive in one year, but it won't know the dollar value of those deutsche marks. By hedging, GE will lock in a dollar price for its receivable, but it will not know the purchasing power of those future dollars.

The choice of hedging or not hedging, therefore, depends on which is the bigger risk, inflation risk or currency risk. For most countries with moderate inflation, the answer will surely be currency risk. But for hyperinflationary countries such as Brazil or Mexico, the future purchasing power of the local currency will be less certain than the future purchasing power of the dollar or other strong currency. In this situation, currency risk will be less of a concern than inflation risk.

Similarly, hedging one end of a transaction without hedging the other could result in more risk than not hedging. Suppose Trader Joe buys 4,000 bottles of French champagne to be delivered and paid for in 90 days. The French franc (FF) price is FF100 per bottle which, at the current spot rate of FF1 = $.11, is equivalent to $11 a bottle. If the 90-day forward rate is $.105, Trader Joe can lock in a dollar cost of $10.50 per bottle.

But suppose Trader Joe buys French francs forward to pay for its purchase and the franc depreciates to $.09, while the price of French champagne remains at FF100 per bottle. Trader Joe will now be facing competition from other wine importers whose cost per bottle is only $9.00, $1.50 below its own cost. This competitive pressure will drive down the price at which Trader Joe can sell its champagne.

Total cash flows of the two firms joined together will exceed the sum of their cash flows operating independently--not because of any synergistic effects but because customers perceive less risk in buying the new product or service.

Thus, if it hedges its future purchases of champagne, Trader Joe's dollar profit margin will be hurt by a franc depreciation.

Of course, it will benefit from an appreciation of the franc. The important point, though, is that hedging in this case actually increases the variability, and hence the risk, of Trader Joe's profit margin. The reason is that hedging will fix Trader Joe's dollar cost while its dollar price will vary in line with the dollar value of the franc. By not hedging, Trader Joe's dollar cost and dollar revenue will move in unison, thereby preserving a relatively constant dollar margin.

Reducing the Costs of Risk

An alternative approach to risk management is to reduce the costs associated with risk. There are several ways of doing this, each of which can be used in conjunction with any of the risk-reducing mechanisms discussed previously.

Merger with a Larger, More Financially Stable Company

A small firm with an innovative product but in a precarious financial position can strengthen its marketing effort by linking up with a larger, less risky company. Potential customers will realize that the company's prospects have improved and worry less about whether its product will be serviced and upgraded in the future. Thus, total cash flows of the two firms joined together will exceed the sum of their cash flows operating independently—not because of any synergistic effects but because customers perceive less risk in buying the new product or service. Additionally, mergers lead to lower total risk because of diversification, which may benefit the acquiring firm's existing marketing efforts.

Product Compatibility

Another possibility is to produce equipment compatible with the leading manufacturer's product line. Then, even if the original producer becomes financially distressed, there will still be a large support network. Service and spare parts should be readily available and there should be a ready secondary market for the product. This strategy, however, forces companies to compete on the basis of production cost, hurting those firms with a competitive

advantage in the design and development of novel products. For example, if Apple Computer had followed the strategy of IBM-compatibility, it would never have brought out its innovative Macintosh personal computer. Also, those so-called "plug compatible" companies (those producing IBM-compatible equipment) have faced enormous risks because their destinies are largely controlled by IBM.

Off-the-Shelf Components

In line with the previous discussion, the firm can use off-the-shelf components and other readily available product inputs to reduce the cost to its suppliers of financial distress. In the event the firm goes out of business at a later date, the alternative of using specialized inputs could impose heavy costs on suppliers, in the form of plant and equipment and inventory unsuitable for other uses. On the other hand, the decision to stick to off-the-shelf items could prove costly since it limits the firm's design options.

Training Programs

As pointed out earlier, a major cost of financial distress to employees is that the value of their firm-specific human capital will be greatly diminished should they be forced to seek employment elsewhere. Firms can reduce this cost by providing opportunities to their employees to develop their human potential so it is applicable to a wider variety of circumstances. For example, Procter and Gamble's reputation for providing employees with a postgraduate education in consumer marketing has enabled it to attract top-flight talent. The portability of this knowledge is evidenced by the large numbers of P & G alumni holding top marketing positions in other firms (though such a policy, by making its employees more mobile, is likely to result in increased turnover with all its attendant costs).

Using Manufacturers' Representatives

Salespeople who specialize in only one product line face a good deal of personal risk in the event something happens to that line. They will demand to be compensated for bearing this risk. An alternative to hiring in-house salespeople is to use manufacturers' representatives who handle a variety of products and lines. This diversification reduces their personal risk and lowers the amount of compensation they demamd. The cost of using manufacturers' reps, of course, is that the firm's products may not be adequately represented and serviced.

Summary and Conclusions

The basic message of this paper is that corporate cash flows are influenced by the firm's risk profile. Its revenues, operating costs, financing costs, taxes, and future investment opportunities will all be affected by the likelihood of financial distress, which in turn is a function of total risk. Consequently, even though finance theory maintains that reducing total risk will not lower the firm's required rate of return, it should lead to an increase in corporate cash flows.

For this reason, firms should carefully consider hedging and other risk-reducing activities. Because these activities may be costly, however, it is necessary to balance their costs against the benefits of risk reduction. In particular, the optimal level of risk—the firm's *risk capacity*, if you will—is found at the point at which the cost of reducing an additional unit of risk is just equal to the benefit from that incremental degree of risk reduction. In other words, the firm's risk capacity is defined as the amount of risk it *should* bear, as distinguished from the amount of risk it *could* support.

The risk capacities of firms vary widely given the different natures of the markets they operate in and the strategies they pursue. Some of the characteristics of firms for which financial risk is most costly are industry-specific, based on product type, while others are firm-specific. Industry-specific product characteristics that indicate a high cost of financial distress include the following:

- Products that require periodic repairs.
- Goods or services whose quality is difficult to determine in advance.

- Products for which there are switching costs.
- Products whose value to customers depends on the services and products supplied by independent companies.

Firm-specific factors include the following:

- High-growth companies.
- Substantial amounts of organizational assets.
- Large excess tax deductions.

Firms with high costs of financial distress have relatively low risk capacities and should use the various risk-reducing techniques suggested in this paper. These techniques can be characterized as either"financial" or"real." Financial techniques include limiting the use of debt, buying insurance, and buying or selling forward or futures contracts. Real adjustments include adopting production processes that reduce the degree of operating leverage, avoiding high-risk projects, abandoning existing high-risk products, and choosing projects that lead to internal diversification. Conversely, firms without these characteristics, such as utilities and oil companies, have high risk capacities and, hence, can afford to be more highly leveraged, undertake riskier projects, and self-insure.

In choosing these risk-reducing techniques the firm should take advantage of any opportunities to reduce risk at a zero cost. One consideration that should be borne in mind is that real adjustments to reduce risk usually entail real costs, whereas some financial adjustments, such as the use of forward or futures contracts, may be undertaken at minimal cost. Moreover, the firm should take into account the effect that reducing one form of risk can have on another form of risk. For example, entering into a fixed-price contract eliminates relative price risk but may introduce a significant exposure to inflation risk. It is these kinds of interdependent exposures that an integrated approach for managing corporate risks can recognize and deal with.

The Corporate Insurance Decision

by David Mayers, *UCLA*, and
Clifford Smith, *University of Rochester*

Introduction

In 1980, American corporations paid more than $49 billion in property and liability insurance premiums. When set against the roughly $63 billion in corporate dividend payments during the same year, these insurance purchases seem particularly significant. Yet, in spite of the magnitude of these numbers, there has been little careful analysis of the decisions leading to such large expenditures. The finance and economics literature has devoted scant attention to the topic. There is, to be sure, a large separate body of academic insurance literature which purports to explain the corporate demand for insurance. But the approach of this insurance literature, we will argue, is fundamentally flawed.

We think there are useful answers to the question of why companies buy insurance, answers consistent with economic logic and the theory of modern finance. But these answers are less obvious than those that have been furnished by recognized authorities on insurance. Our approach also provides explanations of some fairly recent developments in corporate insurance: the appearance of retroactive liability coverage, in which companies purchase additional coverage *after* major disasters; the use of "claims only" insurance contracts, whereby insured companies pay for the services of an insurance company while bearing themselves the risk of losses through claims; and the growing trend toward self-insurance, reflected both in the use of higher deductibles and the establishment of captive insurance companies.

But, before examining the competing arguments for corporate insurance, let's take a careful look at what an insurance policy does.

The Economics of Insurance

Insurance does not eliminate risk; it is a contract which simply transfers risk from the policyholder to an insurance company. In return, the insurance company, of course, demands a premium. The real cost of insurance, called the "loading fee," is the difference between the premium and the expected payoff. As that difference increases, insurance becomes less attractive.

Let's begin by assuming that the decision to purchase insurance, whether by corporations or by individuals, is *solely* a decision to transfer risks from the policyholders to an insurance company. From the perspective of financial economics, this decision is justified only when the insurance company has a comparative advantage in bearing the risks in question. Such an advantage can derive from several sources: (1) from the reduction of risk achievable by pooling a large portfolio of risks, for which the expected loss is highly predictable; (2) from superior access to capital markets; and (3) from expertise acquired through specialization in evaluating and monitoring certain kinds of risks.

Now, we relax our initial assumption to allow that companies might be buying insurance for reasons other than to transfer risk. The expected payoff of the policy generally contains two components: (1) the monetary indemnity the insurer pays if a loss occurs, and (2) any services provided by the insurer

Companies might by buying insurance for reasons other than to transfer risk.

under the policy.[1] The distinction between monetary indemnity and service provision is important because, in types of insurance where relatively more services are provided, a larger difference exists between the premium and the expected indemnity. In other words, because a significant portion of the premium paid is used to provide the services rendered in conjunction with the policy, a relatively smaller portion will be used to satisfy claims. Thus, a fourth source of insurance companies' comparative advantage would be their specialization and economies of scale in providing services such as claims administration and settlement.

Only the last two are the exclusive province of insurance companies; and thus, only they are likely to constitute the principal comparative advantage of insurance companies over the large, widely-held corporations they insure. And the fact that some of the largest corporations have chosen to develop their own insurance expertise — or to form their own insurance captives — suggests that, in many cases, even these two advantages are not that significant.

The Important Difference between Individual and Corporate Insurance

Before proceeding further with the question of the corporate demand for insurance, we want to consider first the simplest case: the purchase of insurance by individuals. Why do individuals buy insurance? Most people are "risk averse."[2] Insurance contracts allow them to hedge risks, reducing uncertainty. And it is not hard to see that, relative to the risk-bearing capacity of insurance companies, the ability of most individuals to self-insure against large risks is severely limited. The private assets of individuals are not protected by the "limited liability" clause which shelters the other assets of corporate stockholders. Thus, decisions by individuals to pay premiums to insure their hard assets and human capital are economically "rational" choices based primarily on insurance companies' advantages in averaging,[3] and thus "diversifying away," such risks.

Private or closely-held corporations are likely to purchase insurance for the same reason — namely, their limited ability to bear certain risks relative to the risk-bearing capacity of insurance companies. The owners (who are also, of course, "risk-averse") of such companies often have a large proportion of their wealth invested in the firm; and, whether out of a desire to maintain control or some other motive, they do not fully diversify their own holdings. So, for many closely-held and private companies, logic and experience tell us that the companies' owners will self-insure only where they have specialized expertise and, thus, their own kind of comparative advantage.

The case of large, widely-held corporations, however, presents some important differences which the standard insurance literature has failed to acknowledge. The conventional wisdom says, in effect, that because the owners of corporations (their stockholders and bondholders) are risk averse, a prudent financial manager should attempt to minimize the corporate owners' exposure to risk. This prescription does not necessarily imply that all risks should be insured. For example, the standard theory rightly holds that a large national car rental agency, like Hertz, should not purchase collision insurance on its automobiles. With its large fleet of cars, Hertz can eliminate its collision risk, just as an insurance company does, by pooling its risks and averaging its losses. The purchase of collision insurance by Hertz would thus not only be needless duplication, but the payment of the "loading fees" built into the premiums would represent an outright loss to the company.[4]

But, in the case of a large corporation with a smaller fleet of more expensive vehicles, the conventional rationale for corporate insurance — which, again, holds that the underlying source of the corporate demand for insurance is risk-aversion — would argue *for* insuring those corporate assets. Because such a company does not have the ability to eliminate its collision risks by averaging, the owners are exposed to risk. Such risks, so the reasoning goes, are better borne by insurance companies; and

---

1. Insurance companies provide a range of administrative services associated with claims management. For example, for claims resulting from property losses, claims management is frequently accomplished through a nation-wide network of independent adjusters who are employed to negotiate certain types of settlements. The decisions are then reviewed by the claims department of the insurance company.

2. In the financial economics literature, risk aversion refers to an individual who prefers the average outcome, or the "expected value," of a gamble to taking a chance on the distribution of possible outcomes, some higher and some lower than the average outcome. Thus, a risk averse individual would pay to get out of a

risky situation. There are, of course, different degrees of risk aversion; individuals displaying greater aversion to risk than the average stockholder might prefer holding government bonds to stocks. But, as a consequence of bearing less risk, they also have a lower expected return on their investment.

3. The essence of averaging is that by holding a portfolio of a large number of approximately equal-sized, but unrelated risks, the size of the loss on the portfolio of risks is virtually guaranteed. Thus there is no uncertainty with regard to the loss on the portfolio. Risks that can be eliminated by averaging are referred to as "insurable" risks.

4. In insurance jargon, the insurance premium would be actuarially unfair.

By combining many securities in a portfolio, investors can effectively eliminate most insurable corporate risks.

thus the corporation should purchase collision insurance.

The conventional explanation, however, is inadequate because it fails to recognize that the company's stockholders and bondholders have the incentive and the ability to diversify their own portfolios of corporate securities; and in so doing, they can and do eliminate precisely the kinds of risks that are insurable through an insurance company.

Stockholders and bondholders, on average, hold a lot of different securities because they are aware of the benefits of diversification. As the owners of corporate assets, they bear risks in many dimensions: some are insurable risks and some are not. By combining many securities in a portfolio, investors can effectively eliminate most insurable corporate risks by "averaging across" many securities—just as Hertz averages its automobile collision risk. The theory of finance tells us that because stockholders and bondholders can cheaply eliminate insurable risks by diversifying their own holdings, the corporate purchase of insurance for the sole purpose of reducing investors' exposure to risk is redundant; and, furthermore, it imposes needless costs on the company's stockholders.

One of the cardinal principles of modern finance is that, on average and over long periods of time, investors both expect and receive rewards commensurate with the risks they bear. As the bulk of the academic evidence also shows, however, average returns on investment correlate most strongly with what is known as "systematic" or "non-diversifiable" risk. The measure of this risk, known as "beta," is a measure of the sensitivity of individual stock prices to market-wide and general economic developments; and such risk cannot be reduced or eliminated by investors' diversification of their holdings. Nor, of course, is a company's "systematic" risk likely to be reduced by purchasing insurance—because insurable risks, to the extent they have no discernible correlation with broad economic cycles, are completely "diversifiable" for investors.

The capital markets, as logic would suggest, do not reward companies for eliminating "diversifiable" risks: Why should investors pay a premium for managements' reducing exposures to risk which rational investors have already eliminated through their own diversification? By reducing or eliminating diversifiable—and thus most insurable—risks, a company does not reduce the market's perception of its required rate of return or "cost of capital."

Thus, the prices of its stocks and bonds are not likely to be affected by the presence or absence of insurable risks. Consequently, just as in the Hertz case, the purchase of insurance by a corporation for the sole purpose of reducing insurable risks for the stockholders and bondholders would be redundant. It would also be a waste of stockholder funds because the premium charged for the insurance will not be actuarially fair.

For the widely-held corporation, then, where the owners have the incentive and the means to provide their own kind of self-insurance through diversification, the logic of modern finance says that corporations should not purchase insurance—not, at least, for the conventional reasons.

A Rationale for Corporate Insurance

At the same time, however, we believe there are important incentives that provide for a *rational* corporate demand for insurance, incentives which have nothing to do with investors' aversion to risk. In the remainder of this article, we will argue that this demand derives from the ability of insurance contracts to provide corporations with: (1) low-cost claims administration services; (2) assistance in assessing the value of safety and maintenance projects; (3) an improvement in their incentives to undertake investments in such projects; (4) a means of transferring risk away from those of the company's claimholders who are at a disadvantage in risk-bearing; and (5) a reduction of the company's expected tax liability. We also briefly analyze the special case of regulated companies, which have some additional incentives for buying insurance.

Efficiency in Claims Settlement.

Examining more closely the services provided under insurance contracts can provide a partial answer to the question of why corporations purchase insurance. Most obviously, insurance companies develop a comparative advantage in processing claims, an advantage which derives from specialization and from economies of scale. Accordingly, we would expect the corporate demand for insurance to be explained, at least in part, by insurance companies' relative expertise and efficiency in providing low-cost claims administration services.

The most striking confirmation of our argument is the existence of special "claims only" insurance contracts. Under the terms of a "claims only" contract, the insurance company provides only claims management services, while the firm pays all the claims.[5] There is no transfer of risk between the insured and the insuring company. We would expect such policies to be used by companies experiencing a large number of claims. In such cases, a "claims only" policy not only allows the insured company to pool and average its own risks; it also reduces the average cost of settling claims by enabling the insured company to pool and average its own risks; it also reduces the average cost of settling claims by enabling the insurance company to use its network of claims administrators more intensively.

One of the problems that could arise from a "claims only" arrangement is that the insurance company would lose its incentive to negotiate the best possible settlement, because it no longer has to pay the indemnity. But when claims are numerous, the insured company should be in a good position to review and evaluate the settlement record. This in turn should enable the insured to monitor the insurer's effectiveness in holding down the costs of claims. By contrast, in those cases where claims are relatively infrequent, it would be more difficult for the insured company to monitor the efficiency of the claims settlement procedure. In such cases, we expect to see standard policies where the insurer provides both claims administration and the indemnity.

Liability insurance provides another example of claims settlement services provided by the insurance companies. A liability insurance policy not only indemnifies the policyholder if a valid claim is presented, it also provides legal representation when the insured is faced with a suit. If the suit is for less than the policy limit—as is the case in most suits — the policyholder has little incentive to engage quality legal services. We suspect that it is largely because of these incentives, as well as insurance companies' greater familiarity with claims negotiations and settlements, that providing legal representation has become a standard part of liability insurance contracts.

In the unusual case where the suit greatly exceeds the limit on coverage, the roles—and thus the incentives — are reversed. Because the insurance company's liability is limited under the policy, it has less incentive to negotiate an efficient settlement.

Consider, for example, the following case reported in the *Wall Street Journal:*

When the fire hit the MGM Grand Hotel in Las Vegas last November 21, killing 85 persons, the hotel's owner had $30 million in liability insurance. Since then the hotel company has increased its liability coverage to nearly $200 million. Significantly, the new insurance is backdated to November 1, or 20 days before the catastrophic blaze.[6]

We believe that the incentives described above help to explain the purchase of retroactive liability coverage by MGM Grand. By retroactively increasing the coverage limit, MGM effectively restores the normal structure of incentives, so that the insurance company's lawyers have a stronger interest in negotiating an efficient settlement.

Efficiency in Project Evaluation.

Insurance companies also develop a comparative advantage in evaluating safety projects. As a simple illustration, insurance companies that sell boiler insurance also — as would be expected — provide inspection services. These inspections require a highly specialized engineer to inspect the boiler and its component parts. Although the company could obtain these services through an independent consultant, insurance companies are generally better suited for the task. And by agreeing to indemnify the firm for any losses, the insurance company, in effect, guarantees the quality of the inspection. This combining of insurance and inspection services provides the strongest incentive for the inspector to do a careful job.

To minimize property and casualty losses, insurance companies also generally prescribe safety projects. Such projects, of course, impose additional costs on the insured company. But a competitive market for insurance effectively restrains insurers from over-prescribing safety projects. At the same time, of course, those insurance companies which systematically under-prescribe such projects will not long survive the effects of continuing higher indemnity payments. In short, a competitive market provides insurance companies with the incentive to prescribe what should be the optimal level (based on expectations, of course, and not hindsight) of

---

5. "Claims only" policies represent only one extreme of a spectrum of insurance policies which allow the insured company to maintain a degree of self-insurance. More often employed are policies which provide retrospective rating. This type of policy continually adjusts the premium to reflect actual claims experience over the life of the policy. In a year with higher-than-expected claims, the company is required to pay higher premiums; while in a year with low claims, the

company receives a rebate. So that the insured company is effectively bearing most of the risk of claims losses. Typically, however, the policy specifies a maximum on the additional premiums (and rebates), so that the insurance company continues to bear the risk of very large losses.

6. Tim Metz, "Why Insurers and Insured Like the Idea of Covering Disasters After They Happen," *Wall Street Journal*, May 12, 1981.

The combining of insurance and inspection services provides the strongest incentive for the inspector to do a careful job.

safety and maintenance investment for the insured and the insurer alike.

Besides maintaining a comparative advantage in prescribing the proper level of loss prevention measures, insurance contracts also simplify the insured company's project choice decisions by quoting a schedule of premiums associated with various levels of loss prevention. With insurance, the insured company simply asks if the cost of a safety project is less than the present value of the reduction in insurance premiums. If so, it should be undertaken.

Improvement of Investment Incentives.

Corporations often enter into contracts requiring the maintenance of insurance coverage. Bond covenants, for example, frequently require companies to purchase insurance. The conventional explanation of such requirements is that bondholders will not invest without such a provision.

We have a different explanation: namely, that in buying an insurance policy, the company provides a different kind of assurance to lenders — one which effectively guarantees or "bonds" a set of investment decisions by the corporation which gives the bondholders more protection. Such an assurance in turn lowers the borrowing costs to the company, while also providing the best possible incentives for the company's investment in maintenance and safety projects.

Before elaborating this point, let's take a closer look at the relationship between stockholder and bondholder interests. In the case of profitable companies with abundant cash flows, the interests of these two classes of the company's owners would appear to be fairly consonant. What's good for the one is, for the most part, good for the other.

However, in the case of financially distressed companies — or even those with relatively higher probabilities of someday facing financial distress — the interests of bondholders and stockholders can diverge sharply. In such cases, financial managers intent on maximizing stockholder wealth may have incentives to take actions which will reduce the value of the bonds while increasing the value of the stock. Actions that increase the variability of the firm's cash flows, e.g., undertaking riskier invest-

ments or taking on increased financial leverage, will tend to have this effect. By so increasing the variability of the company's future cash flows, management will have, of course, increased the probability of both large gains and large losses. The effect of the increase in the probability of large gains benefits only the stockholders (because the bondholder's is a fixed-income claim) and the effect of the increase in the probability of large losses falls mainly on the bondholders (because stockholders are protected by limited liability.)

Consider the case of a company with a large amount of debt outstanding. Assume also that the covenants on its existing debt have not required the purchase of insurance. How do these two conditions together influence the company's decision to invest in safety projects such as, say, a sprinkler system? Our theory says that a company carrying a large enough burden of debt would actually have a rational incentive to pass up good investments — like safety projects — which reduce the expected variability of cash flows. The company's failure to undertake such investments will decrease the value of its bonds by increasing the *expected* variability of cash flows. Our theory further tells us that, in reasonably sophisticated markets, potential bondholders will anticipate such actions by management; and without the stipulation of insurance by the covenants, they will place a lower value on the bonds when they are initially sold.[7]

By purchasing insurance, the company hedges any losses the bondholders would suffer if it did not invest in the sprinkler system, thus eliminating the bondholders' problem. But also, and perhaps more importantly, the stockholders' incentives are changed by the insurance contract. Having committed itself to carry insurance, the company now will choose to undertake any investment in safety and maintenance projects that is justified by the reduction in its insurance premiums. And lenders, provided with this assurance, will require a lower rate of interest from the company. By allowing mandatory insurance to be included in the indentures, companies are securing a reduction in their borrowing costs that is greater than the cost of the insurance "loading fees." For both of these reasons, then, it may be in the best interest of the company

---

7. If, at the time the bonds were offered, the company had another means of convincing potential bondholders that it would make the safety and maintenance investments (even in the absence of insurance), then the rate of interest on the bonds would also be lower.

and its stockholders to include some kinds of insurance coverage in its debt covenants.

Because the potential conflict of interest between bondholders and stockholders is also greater the riskier the bonds, the use of a debt covenant requiring insurance should be more valuable in riskier debt issues. For this reason, we would expect the covenants in private placements to contain more restrictive insurance provisions than those on public issues. Insurance provisions should also be employed more frequently in privately-placed than public issues because, with only a small number of parties involved, it is cheaper to administer and enforce more detailed insurance requirements.

Insurance covenants are also regularly included in other corporate contracts. For example, subcontracting agreements between corporations generally include provisions requiring the subcontractor to maintain an acceptable level of insurance coverage. In the event that an independent subcontractor were sued for a liability claim, the subcontractor might renege on the contract and declare bankruptcy. The subcontractor's failure to complete the project could impose large costs on the company, as well as increasing its own potential liability. The purchase of insurance by the subcontractor effectively bonds the promise that he makes not to default on the performance of his job.

In each of the aforementioned examples — claims administration, the evaluation of safety projects, and the improvement of investment incentives and guarantees — the insured company is paying primarily for a set of services which the insurance company offers at a lower cost than can be obtained elsewhere. The pure insurance aspect of the contract, the transference of risk, is secondary, if not completely irrelevant.

Riskshifting within the Corporation.

For large corporations with diffuse ownership, the risk aversion of the stockholders—as we argued earlier—does not provide a rational justification for the corporate purchase of insurance. Stockholders are equally capable of diversifying the kinds of risks that insurance companies are able to minimize by pooling. In the case of the closely-held company, as we also suggested, the owners' risk aversion and limited ability to achieve full diversification can provide an incentive for insurance purchases.

Up to this point, we have viewed the corporation only from the perspective of its investors and owners, the bondholders and stockholders. In reality, of course, the corporation is a vast network of contracts among various parties which have conflicting as well as common interests in the company. In addition to bondholders and stockholders, the managers, the employees, the suppliers, and even the customers all have a vested claim and interest — a form of investment (whether of physical or human capital) — in the company's continuation as a viable economic entity. Management and labor are likely to have a substantial investment of human capital in the company. The profitability of suppliers depends partly on the fortunes of the company buying its products. And even the buying decisions of customers, both actual and potential, can be influenced by their perceptions of the company's prospects.

Like the owners of private or closely-held companies, the corporation's managers, employees, suppliers, and customers may not be able to diversify away insurable risks; and such risks, if not insured against, can affect their future payoffs under their respective contracts. Because they are also "risk-averse," these individuals will require extra compensation to bear any risk not assumed by the owners or transferred to an insurance company. Employees, for example, will demand higher wages from a company where the probability of layoff is greater. Managers will demand higher salaries (or perhaps even an equity stake in the company) where the risks of failure, insolvency, and financial embarrassment are great. Suppliers will be more reluctant to enter into long-term contracts with companies whose prospects are uncertain, thus making the terms of those contracts more unfavorable. And customers, concerned about the company's ability to fulfil warranty obligations or service their products in the future, may be reluctant to buy those products.

Because of the limited liability clause, the amount of risk that can be allocated to the stockholders is limited by the capital stock of the company. Companies in service industries, for instance, are often thinly-capitalized. And for such companies, where the claims — and thus the risks — of managers and employees are likely to be very large relative to the claims of investors, there may be substantial benefits from shifting those risks to an insurance company. To the extent that the purchase of insurance reduces the possibility of layoffs, plant closings, or even bankruptcy, such corporations could — by transferring such risks to an insurance

There is no obvious reason to prefer the tax effects of insurance to those of self-insurance.

company — be providing themselves with significant reductions in required wages and salaries. To provide a simple illustration, the purchase of business interruption insurance covering the company's ordinary payroll would reduce the risk borne by employees that, say, a fire will cause a plant to shut down. The justification for the purchase of insurance, in this case, is that the cost of the insurance is more than covered by the reduction in employees' extra compensation required for otherwise bearing such risks themselves.

The Tax Advantage

One of the alleged benefits of corporate insurance is that insurance premiums are tax-deductible expenses, while reserves set aside for losses by self-insuring companies are not.[8] And though casualty losses sustained by companies which self-insure *are* tax-deductible, the conventional argument for a tax advantage from buying insurance rests on the premise that the guaranteed annual tax shield provided by premium payments is more valuable than the random tax shield provided by unforeseen future losses. This premise, in turn, seems to be based on the notion that the company can somehow exploit the time value of money by getting its tax deductions "up front" instead of in the uncertain future.

In some cases, such a strategy will result in a tax advantage; that is, the losses will take place far enough in the future that the tax savings to the insuring company — compounded at the interest rate reflecting the opportunity cost of those savings — will turn out to be significantly greater than the time-adjusted value of the tax shield created by uninsured losses. It is important to recognize, however, that decisions are made in the present, and on the basis of expected future probabilities. And on this basis, there is no obvious reason to prefer the tax effects of insurance to those of self-insurance. Remember that an insurance premium incorporates an insurance company's estimate of the expected level and timing of future losses. And thus, ignoring the effect of "loading fees" (and assuming that a company's marginal tax rate would not be reduced by a large casualty loss), the *expected* tax shields from buying insurance and self-insurance are identical.

As an example of the confusion which surrounds this tax issue, let's return to the case of MGM Grand's purchase of retroactive liability coverage. According to the *Wall Street Journal* article, cited earlier:

> ... *MGM Grand, meanwhile, gets a tax break by insuring, rather than assembling a big cash reserve against losses. Premiums are tax deductible as a business expense right now while casualty reserves can't be written off until claims are paid. In MGM Grand's case, that could be years from now.*

It is true that by buying the retroactive insurance, MGM did get a large tax deduction; and that the tax deduction is more valuable the earlier it is used. But what this argument fails to recognize is that if MGM had chosen to self-insure, it could have earned a normal rate of return on its capital prior to the date of any settlement. There will be no reason to prefer getting the tax savings up front to retaining and investing the so-called reserves. The income earned on those reserves, on an expected value basis, should exactly offset the value of getting the tax savings up front.

There are provisions in the tax code which, by reducing the expected tax shield from self-insurance, could favor the purchase of insurance. There is a three year carry-back and a seven year carry-forward provision. If an uninsured loss exceeds the sum of the most recent four years' earnings, the additional loss must be carried forward; and if the loss exceeds the earnings over the eleven-year period, the excess casualty loss is lost. Furthermore, when a company employs the carry-back provisions, the current year's tax must be totally offset before any of the previous year's taxes can be used.[9] Finally, if the uninsured loss forces the company into bankruptcy and liquidation, any loss carry-forward will be lost.

Thus, if MGM did not expect claims losses in any single year to be large enough to push the company into a lower marginal tax bracket (thus reducing the value of the random tax shield from deducting claims losses), then the *expected* values of the tax shields from insurance and self-insurance should be equal. If, however, the company did expect very large losses to fall within a given year, then there would have been a tax advantage from buying the insurance.

---

8. FASB #5 not only prohibits companies from deducting self-insurance reserves from taxable income, it also excludes them from published income statements. Thus, self-insurance reserves have no effect on reported earnings. The maximum required disclosure is a footnote to the accounting statement.

Moreover, neither Generally Accepted Accounting Procedures nor the IRS requires that "reserves" for uninsured losses actually be funded.

9. This is offset by the fact that the IRS pays interest on the tax refund.

To the extent, then, that the magnitude of potential losses is large relative to the company's expected annual taxable earnings, the expected value of the tax shield from insurance can be greater than the random tax shield provided by uninsured losses. This conclusion would suggest that the tax advantage of buying insurance is likely to be most significant for smaller companies with less diversified operations. For large companies with geographically dispersed operations, the tax benefits of insurance should not be important. (We would not expect Hertz to purchase collision insurance for tax purposes either). Finally, because uninsured losses do provide a (random) tax shield, companies which have other tax shields (e.g., investment tax credits, high interest expense) would be expected to buy more insurance because of the reduced value of the expected tax deductions from self-insurance.

Regulated Companies: A Special Case

The prices of the products or services of regulated companies are established by regulatory commissions with the intention of allowing those companies to earn a "fair" rate of return for their stockholders. At the risk of oversimplifying the rate regulation process, regulators set prices which are expected to generate revenues covering the sum of expected costs, taxes, depreciation, plus a normal rate of return on the rate base. Insurance premiums are allowed as part of expected costs. If a regulated company does not insure against a particular hazard, in order for it to earn a "fair" rate of return for its stockholders, the rate commission (or the company itself) must include an expected loss estimate in computing expected costs; and this expected cost figure used in establishing allowed revenues and prices must accurately reflect the probability and magnitude of potential uninsured losses. As the rate-setting is currently administered, however, such expected costs from uninsured losses are not allowed.

Also, because uninsured casualty or liability losses are insurable risks, the regulators — like the stock market itself — would not compensate an uninsured, regulated company for bearing such risks by allowing them a higher return on its equity base.[10]

This regulatory process provides incentives for regulated companies to buy insurance. First, because regulated companies are allowed revenues to cover the cost of expected losses *only* if they insure, they have a strong incentive to insure against all insurable risks. Second, the "loading fees" (the insurance company's expected profit after paying indemnities and providing associated ervices) reflected in the premiums are costs which are shifted by the regulatory process from the firm's owners to its customers. In an unregulated, competitive industry, where output prices and revenues are determined in the market — regardless of whether an individual company insures — insurance loading fees cannot be passed on to the consumer.[11] Third, because of its specialization, an insurance company is expected to have a comparative advantage in assessing the amount of expected losses. Regulators, in effect, "subcontract" this assessment by having the insurance company reflect its assessment of expected losses in the insurance premium. For all of the above reasons, we would expect a regulated company to buy significantly more insurance than a comparable, but unregulated company.

Compulsory Insurance Laws

Some forms of corporate insurance coverage are required by law. Workmen's compensation laws have been enacted in every state in the U.S. These laws essentially impose on employers the responsibility of providing no-fault insurance to their workers for job-related accidents. Although self-insurance is allowed in all but five states, to qualify for self-insurance under the law, the firm must demonstrate that it has sufficient size and diversification of risks. Some states (Massachusetts, New York and North Carolina) have adopted compulsory liability insurance statutes which require some companies to purchase insurance policies. Such regulation also has the effect of increasing the likelihood that other companies will buy insurance to protect themselves against the specific hazards addressed in those regulations.

Conclusion

Our purpose in this article has been to identify and analyze a set of incentives which justify the purchase of insurance by corporations. In so doing, we have provided a theory which attempts to explain, first, why large, widely-held companies should *not*

---

10. Recall from earlier the capital market compensates only for uninsurable ("non-diversifiable") risks, not insurable ("diversifiable") risks.

11. One exception to this rule is where insurance makes warranties or product guarantees more valuable. Recall our discussion of risk-shifting.

insure against some risks; and second, why they *should* insure against others.

We believe the majority of corporations are probably making the right insurance decisions; but perhaps, in many cases, for the wrong reasons. By asking the right questions, by focusing on the important issues, corporate managers can make fewer and less expensive mistakes.

The value of any theory lies, of course, in the strength of its correspondence with events we can observe in the "real world"; that is, in its ability to explain why things are being done as they are, and to predict how they will be done in the future. We think that our theory, besides being more consistent internally, does a better job of explaining recent developments in the insurance industry than the rationale for corporate insurance that has prevailed in the insurance literature.

Industry observers have noted a pronounced tendency toward corporate self-insurance. This trend has taken several forms: the increasing use of "claims only" policies, the creation of captive insurance companies, and the use of higher deductibles. In each of these developments, corporations are not using insurance to transfer risk from their investors to the insurer — as the conventional explanation holds—but for other reasons: for special insurance services like claims administration; for tax benefits (as in the formation of offshore insurance captives); and to provide assurances (in the case of "stop loss" contracts with higher deductibles) not so much to investors as to employees, managers, and suppliers — that very large property and casualty losses will not threaten the solvency of the company, or the continuity of its operations.

Part of this corporate trend toward self-insurance can be attributed to companies' increasing awareness of their ability to pool their own risks and average expected losses. And this, as we said earlier, is consistent with the conventional explanation of the corporate demand for insurance. We suspect, however, that another part of this movement reflects decisions, using an increasingly sophisticated framework for risk management, to allow companies' investors to bear insurable corporate risks themselves. In making such decisions on the correct basis (that is, except in special cases, from the point of view of well-diversified stockholders and bondholders), risk managers will be conserving corporate cash which can be put to better uses.

How can we summarize the implications of our theory for corporate risk management? All risks should not be insured, even though the owners of the company, the stockholders and bondholders, are individually risk averse. The fact that investors have access to capital markets and the ability and incentive to diversify their portfolio holdings can make the corporate purchase of insurance a waste of stockholder funds. Insurance companies, as we have seen, may have an advantage in providing certain kinds of claims services. There also may be tax benefits, though these may have been exaggerated because of a failure to focus on companies' *expected* tax liabilities.

In deciding whether to purchase insurance, it may also be important to focus on the set of contracts through which stockholders, bondholders, customers, suppliers, managers, employees and insurers interact. Some insurance contracts may help remedy a possible conflict of interest between bondholders and stockholders, especially in the case of companies with higher-risk investments and highly levered capital structures. Others may be valuable to the company by transferring risks away from managers, employees, and suppliers—groups which are at a relative disadvantage in bearing some insurable corporate risks. These solutions cannot, of course, be used indiscriminately, but must be applied carefully to specific corporate situations.

The Evolving Market for Swaps

Clifford W. Smith, Jr.,
University of Rochester
Charles W. Smithson,
Chase Manhattan Bank
Lee Macdonald Wakeman,
Chemical Bank

A recent advertisement extols swaps as "a tool no financial manager can ignore."[1] While this statement has the hyperbolic ring of Madison Avenue prose, it is nevertheless quite clear that the swaps market — a relatively new and rapidly developing market — has become increasingly important. As with other evolving markets in the past, there exists confusion about certain economic implications of this market, especially among some corporate treasurers to whom these instruments are being marketed. Questions that deserve consideration include: (1) How does the swaps market relate to other financial markets? (2) How (and why) did the swaps market evolve? (3) What goes into the pricing of a swap, particularly the evaluation of credit risk? (4) What direction might the swaps market be expected to take in the future? Our paper focuses on these questions; and, in so doing, it proposes a general analytical framework that should prove helpful in evaluating both the broad variety of swaps now available, and those that are yet to be devised.

Analysis of Swap Transactions

As its name implies, a swap is normally defined as an exchange. More specifically, it is an exchange of cash flows over time between two parties (generally referred to as the "counterparties"). The first swaps developed from parallel loans arranged between two companies in different countries, a form popular in the 1970s. To illustrate a parallel loan, suppose a British company makes a loan denominated in pounds to a US company, which in turn makes a loan of equal value denominated in dollars to the British company. As illustrated in Figure 1, these loans have parallel interest and principal repayment schedules. By entering into this parallel loan agreement, the British company is able to transform a debt incurred in pounds into a fully-hedged US dollar liability. There are, however, two potentially important problems with parallel loans: (1) default by one party does not release the other from making its contractually obligated payments; (2) although the loans effectively cancel one another, they remain on-balance-sheet items for accounting and regulatory purposes. Early in the 1980s a new transaction known as a "currency swap" was devised to overcome these problems; and because of its success, it effectively displaced the use of parallel loans.

The Currency Swap. A currency swap involves the same pattern of cash flows as a parallel loan. Indeed, without any modification, Figure 1 could be used to illustrate the cash flows for a fixed currency swap where firm A pays a fixed interest rate in dollars and receives a fixed rate in pounds, while the counterparty, firm B, pays fixed-rate pounds and receives fixed-rate dollars. (In this context, the short arrows in Figure 1 denote the cashflows exchanged during the term of the agreement, while the long arrows denote the initial exchange of principals at time 0 and the reexchange at maturity, time T.) Alternatively, a swap transaction could be illustrated by looking at the cash flows paid and received over time by one of the counterparties. Figure 2 illustrates the position of the British firm A in this fixed currency swap.

Although a swap is defined as an "exchange" of cash flows, there need not be an actual exchange of payments. Instead, at specified intervals, only the net

1. Bankers Trust Company, "The International Swap Market," Advertising Supplement to *Euromoney Corporate Finance*, September 1985.

FIGURE 1
Cash Flows in a Parallel
Loan Agreement

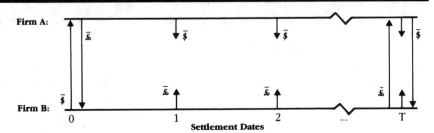

The British firm A simultaneously borrows dollars from American firm B and loans an equivalent amount denominated in pounds to firm B at time 0. During the term of the loan, firm A makes interest payments in dollars to firm B, while firm B makes interest payments in pounds to firm A. At maturity (time T̄) the two firms make their final interest payments and return the principals. Firm A returns dollars and firm B returns pounds.

FIGURE 2
Cash Flows from a Fixed
Currency Swap

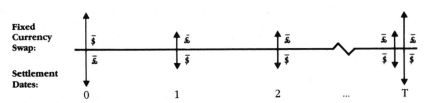

Fixed
Currency
Swap:

Settlement
Dates:

The British firm A pays interest at a fixed dollar rate ($̄) and receives interest at a fixed pound rate (£̄) The long arrows denote the initial exchange of principal and the reexchange at maturity; the short arrows denote the cash flows exchanged over the course of the agreement.*

cash flows could be exchanged, and the party that would have received the lower of the cash flows could simply pay the other the difference in the two cash flows. In the case of currency swaps, the counterparties do exchange interest payments; however, the exchange is conditional in the sense that if one party defaults, the other is released from its obligation. In currency swaps, moreover, the counterparties generally exchange the principals at an agreed-upon rate of exchange and then reexchange at the end of the agreement; but this exchange also need not occur. The principal could instead be "notional," as is generally the case in interest rate swaps (which we take up later).

By thus converting the older parallel loan transaction into a conditional exchange of the cash flows, the currency swap reduces the probability and magnitude of default. Furthermore, as implied

above, current regulatory and accounting practice treats swap contracts as off-balance-sheet items. Thus, as stated earlier, the currency swap accomplishes the goals of its predecessor, the parallel loan agreement, while eliminating the major remaining problems with that transaction.

Swaps as Packages of Forward Contracts. One of the major themes of this paper, to which we shall return throughout, is the fundamental similarity between swaps and forward contracts. In fact, it is our contention that any swap can be decomposed into a series of forward contracts.

Again consider Figure 2, which illustrates the cash flows in a fixed currency swap — one in which the firm pays fixed-rate interest in one currency and receives fixed-rate interest in another. The cash flows for the counterparty receiving pounds and paying dollars at time 1 are equivalent to those from holding

*In this figure and in similar figures to follow, we adopt the convention of showing inflows above the line and outflows below the line.

a long position in pounds in a pound-dollar forward contract. This also applies to each settlement date between 2 and T; hence this currency swap for firm A is equivalent to a package of T long forward contracts in pounds. The positions are reversed for the counterparty.

We believe this decomposition of swaps into forward contracts is the most productive way of evaluating swaps, particularly the pricing of swaps. Simple swaps have been standardized and are now quoted virtually as commodities; and for such swaps this method of analysis will seem roundabout. But, as we will demonstrate, for more complicated swaps, where the timing of cash-flow exchanges differ or where the principal changes, decomposition of cash flows into forward contracts is the simplest, most effective analytical approach.

Currency Coupon Swaps. In a currency swap, as we have seen, the counterparties agree on the timing of the exchanges, the principal amounts of the currencies that will be exchanged, the interest rates (which reflect credit market forward prices) that will determine the future cash flows, and the exchange rates used to calculate the net cash flows. The earliest currency swaps were fixed currency swaps, which specified fixed interest rates in both currencies. Soon after came a variant of the fixed currency swap called the currency coupon swap. In such an arrangement, the interest rate in one currency is fixed and the other is floating.

Interest Rate Swaps. The interest rate swap, which was introduced shortly after currency swaps, is a special case of the currency coupon swap — one in which all the cash flows are denominated in a single currency. Figure 3 illustrates a simple interest rate swap. The primary difference between Figures 2 and 3 is that the exchanges of principal flows at time 0 and T net to zero because they are of the same amount and denominated in the same currency.

Basis Rate Swaps. To this point, we have described swaps in which both interest rates are fixed (fixed currency swaps) and swaps in which one interest rate is fixed and one is floating (simple interest rate swaps and currency coupon swaps). In a basis rate swap, both interest rates are floating. The primary effect of such swaps is to allow floating-rate cash flows calculated on one basis to be exchanged for floating rate cash flows calculated on another. For example, it permits firms to make conversions from one-month LIBOR to six-month LIBOR, or from LIBOR to US commercial paper rates. A basis rate swap is equivalent to

pairing two simple interest rate swaps such that the flows are converted from floating to fixed, and then converted from fixed to floating (but on a different basis).

Commodity Swaps. A swap is, in effect, an exchange of net cash flows calculated to reflect changes in designated prices. So far, we have considered only two prices, interest rates and exchange rates. However, swaps defined in prices other than interest rates and foreign exchange rates are also possible. Once a principal amount is determined and that principal contractually converted to a flow, any set of forward prices can be used to calculate the cash flows (and thus the difference checks).

Consider, for example, the possibility of swaps denoted in commodities such as oil and wheat. The counterparties could agree to some notional principal and to the conversion of this principal to flows using a fixed dollar interest rate and the US price of wheat. Such a swap is analytically no different from a currency swap where forward prices of wheat replace the forward currency prices. In addition, neither firm need be in the wheat business; the difference checks are paid in dollars, not wheat. Moreover, in a swap in which the firm elects to pay with wheat, it can receive either fixed or floating rates in any currency or commodity.

Swaps with Timing Mismatches. In addition to differences resulting from the price used to calculate the cash flows (i.e., interest rates, foreign exchange rates, and commodity prices), swaps can differ in the timing of the cash flows. At the simplest level, it could be that one party is paying on a monthly basis while the other is on a quarterly schedule. More significant differences in the timing of the cash flows include so-called "zero" swaps — swaps in which one party makes no payment until maturity — and customized swaps in which the payments from one party vary, either in terms of timing or amount.

Swaps with Option-Like Payoffs. We have stressed the similarity of swaps to forward contracts. Indeed, the payoff profile for a simple swap contract is identical to that of a forward contract. Fig. 4 presents a simple case in which the firm pays a floating interest rate and receives a fixed rate. This firm has positive net cash flows when the short-term interest rate is below that existing at the contract origination date.

Swaps can also be constructed so as to have option-like provisions which limit the range of outcomes. For example, suppose that a firm with a

Swaps defined in prices other than interest rates and foreign exchange rates are clearly possible. Once a principal amount is determined and that principal converted to a flow, any set of forward prices can be used to calculate the net cash flows.

FIGURE 3
Cash Flows in an
Interest Rate Swap

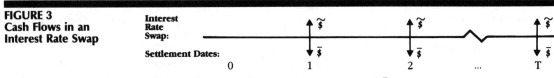

The firm illustrated pays a fixed dollar interest rate ($\bar{\$}$) and receives interest computed on a floating dollar rate ($\tilde{\$}$). The counterparty pays floating and receives fixed.

FIGURE 4
Payoff Profile of an
Interest Rate Swap
for Firm Paying Floating
Rate and Receiving
Fixed Rate

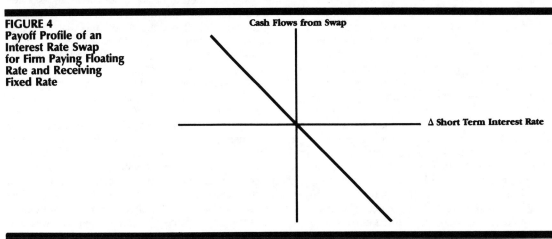

FIGURE 5
Pay-off Profile for
Floor-Ceiling Swaps

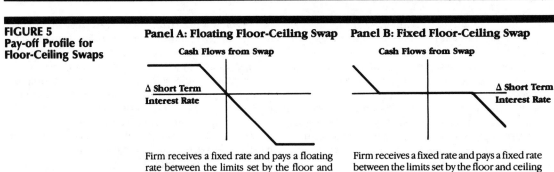

Panel A: Floating Floor-Ceiling Swap

Firm receives a fixed rate and pays a floating rate between the limits set by the floor and ceiling rates.

Panel B: Fixed Floor-Ceiling Swap

Firm receives a fixed rate and pays a fixed rate between the limits set by the floor and ceiling rates.

floating-rate liability wanted to limit its outflows should interest rates rise substantially and was willing to give up some potential gains should there instead be a dramatic decline in short-term rates. To achieve this end the firm could modify a simple interest rate swap contract to read as follows: As long as the interest rate neither rises by 200 basis points nor falls more than 100 basis points, the firm pays a floating rate and receives a fixed rate; but, if the interest is more than 200 basis points above or 100 basis points below the current rate, the firm receives and pays a fixed rate. The resulting payoff profile for this floating floor-ceiling swap is illustrated in Panel A of Figure 5. (It is also the payoff profile for a "spread.")[2]

---

2. Note also that if the floor and ceiling rates are equal, this side of the contract is equivalent to a fixed rate obligation since a long call plus a short put with the same terms equals a long forward contract.

Conversely, the contract could have been modified as follows: As long as the interest rate is within 200 basis points of the current rate, the firm receives and pays a fixed rate; but if the interest rate rises or falls by more than 200 basis points, the firm pays a floating rate and receives a fixed rate. The payoff profile for the resulting fixed floor-ceiling swap is illustrated in panel B of Figure 5.

Given the range of swaps described above, we agree with the market participant who noted that "the future potential structures....are limited only by the imagination and ingenuity of those participating in the market."[3]

Development of the Swaps Market

The swaps market is still relatively new. As we noted, its origins can be traced to the parallel loan products of the 1970s. However, a market for swaps did not exist in any meaningful sense until the 1980s. Currency swaps are slightly older than interest rate swaps; their public introduction was the World Bank-IBM transaction in August 1981. US dollar-denominated interest rate swaps started in 1982. While not as old as the currency swaps market, the US interest rate swaps market is now the largest of the swaps markets.

Given the growth in swaps that has occurred, there are two questions we want to consider in this section: (1) Since swaps are so similar to forward contracts, WHY did this market evolve? (2) In order to provide a framework for looking at the future of this market, what path has the evolution of this market followed so far — HOW did this market evolve?

Why Did the Swaps Market Evolve?

Trade journals and market participants agree that the growth of the swaps market has resulted from the ability to receive "significant cost savings" by combining a bond issue with a swap.[4] Using swaps, the firm ends up with lower borrowing costs than it could have obtained with a single transaction. For example, with the use of swaps, companies have obtained funding at LIBOR minus 75-100 basis points. Obviously, a satisfying explanation of why the swaps market evolved must identify the source of this cost saving.

Financial Arbitrage. The popular argument seems to be that the cost savings is based on some kind of financial arbitrage across different capital markets. That is, prices in various world capital markets are not mutually consistent; and firms can lower their borrowing costs by going to foreign capital markets with lower rates, borrowing there, and then swapping their exposure back into their domestic currency, thereby ending with cheaper funding than that obtainable from simply borrowing at home.

The problem with this argument, however, is that the very process of exploiting this kind of opportunity should soon eliminate it. The opening and expansion of a swap market effectively increases the demand for loans in low-rate markets and reduces the demand in higher-rate markets, thereby eliminating the supposed rate differences. Moreover, if this were the only economic basis for swaps, the benefits to one party would come at the expense of the other. Thus, in reasonably efficient and integrated world capital markets, it seems difficult to attribute the continuing growth of the swaps market simply to interest rate differences, and thus financial arbitrage, among world capital markets.

Tax and Regulatory Arbitrage. Swaps allow companies to engage in what might be termed tax and regulatory arbitrage. Prior to the existence of a well-functioning swap market, a firm issuing dollar-denominated, fixed-rate bonds generally did so in US capital markets and thus had to comply with US securities regulation. Moreover, the issuing firm, as well as the security purchasers, were generally faced with the provisions of the US tax code. The introduction of the swap market allows an "unbundling," in effect, of currency and interest rate exposure from the regulation and tax rules in some very creative ways. For example, with the introduction of swaps, a US firm could issue a yen-denominated issue in the Eurobond market, structure the issue so as to receive favorable tax treatment under the Japanese tax code, avoid much of the US securities regulation, and yet still manage its currency exposure by swapping the transaction back into dollars. Unlike the classic financial arbitrage de-

3. Bankers Trust Company, "The International Swap Market," cited earlier.
4. As an example of the popular literature on swaps, see Tanya S. Arnold, "How to Do Interest Rate Swaps," *Harvard Business Review*, September-October 1984, pp.96-101.

scribed above, there is no reason for opportunities for tax or regulatory arbitrage to disappear (barring changes, of course, in the various tax and regulatory codes).

To illustrate the manner in which tax and regulatory arbitrage induces swaps, consider the way one US firm used swaps to take advantage of special tax and regulatory conditions in Japan:

(1) Until recently, zero coupon bonds received extremely favorable treatment under the Japanese tax code: taxes were not due until maturity, and at maturity the difference between the purchase price and the face value of the bond was taxed at the capital gains rate.

(2) The Ministry of Finance limited the amount a pension fund could invest in non-yen-denominated bonds issued by foreign corporations to at most 10% of their portfolio.

In response to these conditions, a US firm issued a zero coupon yen bond plus a dual currency bond with interest payments in yen and principal repayment in dollars. The zero coupon yen bond permitted the firm to take advantage of the tax treatment of yen zeros. The Ministry of Finance ruled that the dual currency bonds qualified as a yen issue for purposes of the 10% rule, even though the dual currency bond has embedded within it a dollar-denominated zero. Hence, by issuing the dual currency bond, the US firm was able to capitalize on the desire of Japanese pension funds to diversify their portfolios internationally, while at the same time adhering to the regulation imposed by the Ministry of Finance.

The same US firm also, however, wanted to transform its resulting yen exposure to a US dollar expo-

FIGURE 6
Cash Flows in a Dual Currency Bond Issue Plus a Zero Coupon Yen Issue Combined with a Fixed Currency Swap and Spot Currency Transaction

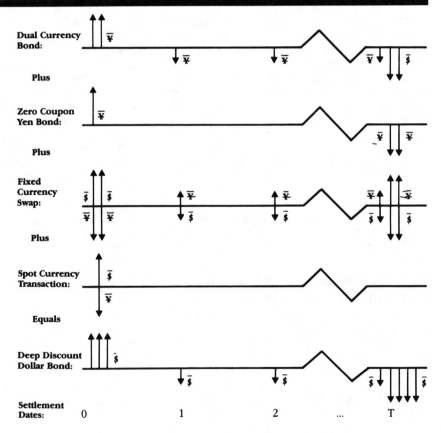

The final cash flows are equivalent to those of a deep discount dollar bond.

The swap market can be used as a way of synthetically "completing" the financial markets.

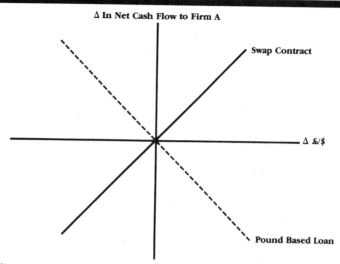

FIGURE 7
Payoff Profile of a Currency Swap Used to Hedge the Financial Risk Exposure from its Underlying Business

Δ In Net Cash Flow to Firm A

Swap Contract

Δ £/$

Pound Based Loan

The dashed line represents the exposure of the firm's net cash flow to changes in the £/$ exchange rate without hedging. The payoff profile for the swap is the solid line. Thus, after the swap, the firm is completely hedged against changes in this exchange rate.

sure. To transform the bond issues, the firm used a currency swap together with a spot $/¥ transaction. (There is less liquidity in non-standard, annuity-type swaps. By combining the principal repayment of the yen zero with the coupon payments of the dual currency bond, a standard, bond-type swap could be used to hedge.) The resulting cash flows are solely in dollars (see Figure 6). Indeed, the swap transaction has created a synthetic deep discount dollar bond, and the rates were such that the firm lowered its total borrowing costs. By using the swap transaction, the firm capitalized on both the favorable regulatory ruling concerning dual currency bonds and the favorable tax treatment of zero coupon bonds, while retaining a fixed dollar interest rate exposure.

Exposure Management. Swaps also allow firms to lower the transactions costs of managing their exposure to interest rates, currency prices, or commodity prices. As we noted, a fixed currency swap can be used by a firm to transform a debt incurred in pounds into a dollar liability. This transformation is illustrated in Figure 7. The payoff profile for a loan incurred in pounds relative to changes in the £/$ exchange rate is shown as the

dashed line. The payoff profile for the swap is shown as the solid line. Viewed in this context, the swap contract behaves like a conventional long-dated foreign exchange forward contract; losses on the dollar-based loan resulting from exchange rate changes will be offset by gains on the swap contract.

For example, consider the case of a firm just entering a foreign market. Although well-known at home, the company might have difficulty placing debt in the foreign credit market where access to information about the firm is more expensive. In this case, it might be less expensive to issue debt in domestic capital markets and swap into the foreign currency exposure.

Conversely, suppose a firm's cash flow exposure in Deutschemarks declines, reducing the amount of DM-denominated debt desired in the firm's balance sheet. Without swaps, the firm would have to call outstanding DM bonds to manage its exposure, an expensive alternative if German interest rates have risen. With access to a liquid swap market, the firm may have a lower-cost means of reducing its DM-denominated liabilities.[5]

Completing Markets. Finally, the swaps

5. For discussions of corporate motives for hedging, see David Mayers and Clifford Smith, "The Corporate Insurance Decision," *Chase Financial Quarterly* (Spring 1982), and "Corporate Insurance and the Underinvestment Problem," Working Paper, The University of Rochester Managerial Economics Research Center, 1985. See also Clifford Smith and Rene Stulz, "The Determinants of Firms' Hedging Policies," *Journal of Financial and Qualitative Analysis,* December 1985; and Alan Shapiro and Sheridan Titman, "An Integrated Approach to Corporate Risk Management," *Midland Corporate Finance Journal* (Summer 1985).

market contributes to the integration of financial markets by allowing market participants to fill gaps left by missing markets. An obvious gap filled by the swaps market is the forward market in interest rates. Until recently, there were no forward interest rate contracts available. But, because an interest rate swap behaves like a series of forward contracts, a swap could be used in place of the missing forward contract. Hence, the swap market can be used as a way of synthetically "completing" the financial markets.

Less obvious is the manner in which currency and interest rates swaps have been used to fill gaps in the international financial markets. For example, there is no Swiss Treasury Bill market. Currency and interest rate swaps, however, can be used to create this market synthetically.

In sum, there are four primary reasons WHY the swaps market evolved: (1) classic financial arbitrage opportunities; (2) profit opportunities from regulatory and tax arbitrage; (3) lower transaction costs for some types of financial risk exposure management; and (4) financial market integration. It appears that the first of these is significantly less important today than when swaps markets first opened. Spreads which were initially available have been substantially reduced by the very process of financial arbitrage which produced the original cost savings. As one market observer has commented,

"...at the outset of the market, a 'AAA' issuer could reasonably expect to achieve 75-100 basis points below LIBOR on a bond/swap; under current conditions, this same issuer might expect only 25-30 basis points below...Many issuers now find it more cost-effective to approach the floating rate note market than the bond/swap market."[6]

But if the opportunities for classic financial arbitrage have been eroded by competition, the other three factors remain important and can be expected to stimulate further activity in swaps.

How Did the Swaps Market Evolve?

A picture of the historical development of the swaps market can be obtained by looking either at the evolution of the products or at changes in the market's participants. Both tell the same story. We first look at the products.

As we noted, currency swaps were the first to appear. The earliest swaps were done on a one-off basis, which involved a search for matching counterparties — matching not only in the currencies, but also in the principal amounts desired. These early swaps were custom-tailored products. Because the deals were all one-off, they involved a great deal of work by the financial institution arranging the swap; but — and this is a crucial point — they involved virtually no direct exposure for the intermediary. In the language of the market participants, the early swaps required "creative problem solving" rather than capital commitment from the intermediary.

As interest rate swaps began to appear, the movement toward a more standardized product began. With the US dollar interest rate swaps, there were fewer areas in which counterparties might not match than had been the case for currency swaps. The product had become more homogeneous; and because the product had become more homogeneous, there was less demand for one-off deals. Instead of requiring an exactly matching counterparty, the intermediary could bundle counterparties.

With the move toward homogeneity and the reduced reliance on an identifiable counterparty, markets for swaps — in particular, interest rate swaps — began to look more and more like markets for commodities. Increased competition forced down the spreads. And, with the increased competition, an extensive search for a counterparty or group of counterparties was unprofitable for the intermediary. Instead, the intermediaries began to accept swap contracts without a counterparty, taking the risk into their own books and either matching it internally with an offsetting position or hedging it with government securities or instruments in the financial futures market.

Hence, the evolution of the products offered in the swaps market paralleled that of most markets; swaps evolved from a customized, client-specific product to a standardized product. With the customized product, the role of the intermediary had been one of problem solving. As the product became more standardized, the role of the intermediary changed considerably, with less emphasis on arranging the deal and more on transactional efficiency and capital commitment.

Looking at the participants in the swaps market, the dominant intermediaries in the early stage of development were investment banks. As the market

---

6. Bankers Trust Company, "The International Swap Market," cited earlier.

evolved, the entrants into this market were more highly capitalized firms, in particular commercial banks. This evolution fits precisely with that of the products. In the early stages the emphasis was on the intermediary arranging the transaction rather than accepting risk from the transaction; thus investment banks were the natural intermediaries. But, as the swaps became more standardized, it became essential for the intermediary to be willing and able to accept part or all of a potential transaction into its books. Hence commercial banks, with their greater capitalization, became a more significant factor.

As we noted, the path the swaps market followed in its evolution is similar to that other markets have taken — most notably, the development of the options market. Prior to 1973, the market for put and call options in the U.S. was an over-the-counter market. Members of the Put and Call Dealer's Association would write options, but only on a one-off basis. Each option was virtually unique because (1) the maturity date was set 181 days from the date the contract was written and (2) the exercise price was set as a function of the prevailing stock price (usually at the stock price). The result was that, for options, there was little volume, little liquidity, and virtually no secondary market. The growth of the options market occurred after the Chicago Board Options Exchange standardized the contracts (maturity dates and exercise prices) and developed an active secondary market. Dealing with a homogeneous product rather than individual customized deals, market makers were able to manage their risks by managing bid-ask spreads to maintain a neutral exposure rather than hedging each transaction on a one-off basis. While over-the-counter options are still offered, the real liquidity in the options market is in exchange-listed options. The options market evolved by moving from an individualized, custom-made product to one resembling a commodity.

While swaps have not evolved to the point of becoming exchange-traded instruments (a point to which we will return in our final section), the paths of evolution — particularly the major factors —have been similar. As was the case with options, contract standardization has played a major role. One market observer put it well by noting that "swaps have become a high volume, lower margin business, rather than the personalized, corporate financial deal of the past."[7] As we have pointed out, the standardization has been more pronounced for interest rate swaps, which may go a long way in explaining why this market has grown more rapidly than that for currency swaps.

Also paralleling the development of options markets, the growth of the swap market corresponded to the liquidity available through the secondary market. While positions can be traded, the secondary market in swaps normally involves the reversing(unwinding) of a position. The simplest method to unwind a swap would involve a cancellation of the agreement, with a final difference check determined on the basis of the remaining value of the contract. However, since this simple "unwind" could result in taxable income, the more common method of unwinding a swap is by writing a "mirror" swap to cancel out the original. Most market observers indicate that this market is sufficiently deep to decrease risks in the primary market, particularly for short-term swaps. Indeed, a 24-hour market now exists for dollar interest rate swaps of up to 12-year maturities and amounts to $500 million.

Pricing Swaps

The pricing of a swap transaction is the aspect of the swap market that has received the most attention, especially that part of pricing which concerns credit risk. The pricing of a swap involves more, however, than just that single dimension. In fact swap pricing can be viewed as having three major components: forward prices, transaction costs, and the credit risk inherent in the transaction.

Forward Prices. Central to any swap agreement is the forward price — whether it be the forward interest rate, the forward exchange rate, or the forward price of a commodity — embodied in the exchange. Earlier we demonstrated that a swap contract is fundamentally a series of forward contracts.[8] In this view, the forward rate embodied in a swap contract must be the same as the forward rates employed in other corresponding financial contracts such as bonds and futures. And the empirical evidence bears this out: the difference between the two-year swap rate and the forward rate implied by Eurodollar futures declined from over 50 basis points in

7. K. Henderson Schuyler, "The Constraints on Trading Swaps," *Euromoney*, May 1985, pp.63-64

8. Floor-ceiling swaps also involve options.

1982 and 1983 to less than 20 basis points in 1984; the remaining 20 basis points essentially reflect the difference in transaction costs and credit risk. This development also confirms our expectation that once the initial financial arbitrage opportunities discussed earlier are exhausted, the forward rates for swaps must conform to the market's view of the future as reflected in the prevailing term structure.

The forward rate component of the pricing of a swap, then, is determined neither by the intermediary nor by the swap market. It is determined by competition from other credit market instruments. Because a swap is a package of forward contracts, the forward rates reflected in the swap must conform to the market's view of the forward rate, or financial arbitrage will be profitable.

Transaction Costs. This component would be reflected in the bid/ask spread for a risk-free transaction plus any origination fees that are charged.[9] The primary determinant of the bid/ask spread is the demand for liquidity. Put another way, the bid/ask spread is determined not by the market maker but, like the forward rate component, by competition in the market. The bid-ask spread, in short, is a market-determined price which reflects the costs of market-making activities.[10]

Credit Risk. In contrast to the preceding components, both of which are independent of the counterparties, the credit risk premium is determined by the specific credit risk of the intermediary and/or the counterparties. The premium added to the bid/ask spread to reflect nonperformance risk depends on characteristics of the counterparty and of the intermediary arranging the swap; it must therefore reflect an appropriate compensation for the probability of default.

It has been argued by some observers that credit risk in a swap contract is priced "too low" relative to the pricing of credit risk in the loan market. To attempt to evaluate such a statement, we examine the determinants of the credit risk premium.

In a loan, the lender has at risk not only the obligated interest payments, but also the loan principal. In a swap the intermediary has at risk only the net cash flow difference at each settlement date. The difference in exposure implies that, for equal levels of nonperformance risk, the credit-risk premium associated with a swap would be far smaller than for a loan of comparable size.

As with a loan, the exposure of the intermediary issuing the swap contract to this firm — or, more precisely, its portfolio exposure to similar firms — is a determinant of the credit-risk premium. However, one element is significantly more important in the case of a swap contract. If the counterparty is arranging the swap as a hedge and if the counterparty has outstanding lines of credit with the intermediary, the swap decreases expected nonperformance losses of the loan. A counterparty which uses a swap to hedge its financial exposure is reducing its overall probability of financial distress.[11] The probability of default for a swap, and therefore the risk premium, depend critically on whether or not the swap has been arranged as a hedge.

Consider the situation in which the swap is a hedge. During periods when the firm would be in financial distress, the swap contract would be in the firm's favor; the firm would be receiving difference checks. For example, consider a firm that experiences some financial difficulty if short-term interest rates rise. Suppose that this firm has entered into an interest rate swap to hedge its interest rate exposure. When short-term interest rates rise, the firm does indeed experience a decline in operating cash flow from its core business; but, at the same time, the firm is receiving inflows from the swap contract. In such a situation, even a firm in financial distress would have no incentive to default on the swap contract.

Therefore, if the swap is a hedge, the probability of default on the swap contract, as well as the probability of default on other liabilities such as loan contracts, are both reduced by this active financial risk exposure management; and the credit risk premiums attached to swap contracts should reflect this difference.

By contrast, if the swap had been used *not* to create a hedge, but rather to speculate on

---

9. In this paper, we do not differentiate between transaction costs reflected in the bid/ask spread and those reflected in up-front origination fees. In essence, we assume that the firm is indifferent about the manner in which it receives its fee for transaction costs.

10. See Harold Demsetz, "The Cost of Transacting," *Quarterly Journal of Economics*, 1968, pp.33-53; and Jack Treynor, "The Only Game In Town," *Financial Analysts Journal*, March-April 1971, pp.12-22.

11. Another way of looking at this is that a hedge can make the cost of credit endogenous. It may be advantageous to negotiate swaps and lines of credit simultaneously, since a swap used as a hedge could reduce the cost of the credit line.

If the US decided to place burdensome regulations on swaps, the principal effect on swap activity would be to change the location of swap transactions.

FIGURE 8
A Currency Coupon Swap from Fixed-Rate Pounds to Floating-Rate Dollars Viewed as a Combination of a Fixed Currency Swap from Pounds to Dollars Plus an Interest Rate Swap from Fixed-Rate Dollars to Floating-Rate Dollars

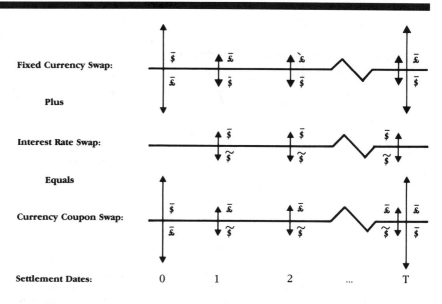

movements in financial markets, the probability of default on the swap is higher and the risk premium should be correspondingly greater. In the same way, if the swap is acting as a reverse hedge, the swap would increase the intermediary's exposure.

The above argument suggests that the credit risk assigned to a swap contract should not be based solely on a credit review of the counterparty. The credit risk associated with a swap contract depends on the exposure of the intermediary to firms similar to the one seeking a swap contract and on whether or not the swap acts as a hedge.

We have purposely not dealt with more technical aspects of credit risk, such as the degree to which risks change if a swap is unwound, the credit risk implications of trading swap positions, and the legal standing of swap contracts in a bankruptcy. (Some of these will be considered in the next section.) Instead, our objective has been to point out what we think are the special features in evaluating the credit risk of a swap: (1) there is no principal at risk so we have "settlement risk" rather than "credit risk" per se; and (2) whether the swap is used as a hedge is an important factor. On the basis of what we have seen, we tend to be more optimistic than many observers about the probability of defaults. One piece of evidence consistent with our view is the fact that in June of 1985, Citicorp determined that it had been

overcautious, and thus reduced its assessment of credit risk, in its pricing of swaps.

Pricing Restrictions from Arbitrage. Our major emphasis has been on viewing swaps as packages of forward contracts. We believe that the approach of pricing swaps by breaking them down into a set of fundamental cash flows is by far the most general, and thus the least restrictive, framework for evaluating new products; it is also likely to be the most flexible in solving pricing problems for very tailored swaps. At the same time, however, we have suggested that complicated swaps can also be decomposed into more simple swaps. For example, as Figure 8 demonstrates, a currency coupon swap is equivalent to a fixed currency swap plus a simple interest rate swap. The idea of unbundling swaps into other swaps can be important in identifying arbitrage opportunities within the market. For example, the cost of a currency coupon swap should be compared to the cost of a simple interest rate swap plus a fixed currency swap. Because they are equivalent transactions, the sum of the prices of the least costly alternative for each component is the best guide to pricing the complex swap.

Moreover, from the perspective of the intermediary, swap decomposition is important for exposure management by the intermediary. Again considering a currency swap, it may be easier to find

365

counterparties for a currency coupon swap by looking for separate counterparties for the interest rate and the currency swap components.

The Future of the Swap Market

We do not purport to be able to predict the future for this market. Indeed, we subscribe to the adage that "he who lives by the crystal ball ends up eating ground glass." Certain factors, however, are likely to have the largest impact on the future evolution of this market. In this section, we will point out those factors we think are most important and suggest possible outcomes.

Liability of the Intermediary. Much of what we have read in the trade journals and heard from the market participants involves conjecture about the swap market "after the first major default." This reflects uncertainty about the legal standing of swap contracts and, more significant, a good deal of controversy over the liability borne by the intermediary (both the current level and the appropriate level).

At one extreme, there are those who argue that the intermediary should assume no liability. Proponents of this view recommend making swaps more like exchange-traded instruments. Suggestions include marking swaps to market with callable margins (or with variable fees) and collateralization (with or without a clearing house).

At the other extreme are those who argue that the intermediary should always retain part of the risk. Arguing against the move toward exchange trading, proponents of this position note that, because swaps are like bundles of forward contracts, credit risk of the counterparties is an important element; and the intermediary (who has a comparative advantage in assessing the credit risk) is effectively a counterparty to each side of the contract.

Secondary Market. As we noted, the growth of the secondary market has made possible much of the growth of the swaps market, and future growth depends on the existence of an active secondary market. Whether a still broader secondary market should be encouraged inevitably throws us back on the earlier question of the liability of the intermediary. Proponents of making swaps exchange-traded instruments point out that marking to market or collateralizing permit contract standardization as well as providing effective guarantees against contractual default. Furthermore, if contracts are effectively bonded, as would be the case with marking to market or collateralizing, the secondary markets can be more anonymous.

Opponents of the move toward exchange trading for swaps point out that secondary markets can be active even if the assets are not homogeneous. For example, there exists an active secondary market for mortgaged-backed securities. In this market, performance is guaranteed by mortgage insurance and the reputation of the originating institution. And it is argued that similar mechanisms are also possible in the swaps market.

Regulation. As might be expected, the divisions evident in the preceding issues are also evident when it comes to questions concerning appropriate regulation of this market. One group argues that additional contractual guarantees are necessary if abuses in this market are to be avoided. Hence, in this view, regulation should take the form of codifying the contractual guarantees — for example, requiring that the contracts be marked to market or collateralized. Those taking the opposite position argue that this market is an simply an extension of credit markets and that imposing liability on the financial intermediary is the best way to limit potential abuses.

Besides this controversy over how to regulate, there is also the issue of who should regulate swaps. There are differences in regulatory bodies across countries, and also multiple regulatory bodies within the same country, that need to be considered. (For example, in the United States, the interested regulatory authorities include the Federal Reserve, the SEC, and the Financial Accounting Standards Board.) Under such circumstances, effective regulation will be difficult if not impossible because it requires coordination both within and among countries. If the US, for example, decided to place burdensome regulations on swaps, the principal effect on swap activity would be to change the location of swap transactions. Even if a group of the major countries acted in concert, the economic incentives for swaps discussed earlier suggest that there would be strong motive for some country to supply a favorable legal environment.

The future of the swaps market, then, appears to turn on whether that market moves further in the direction of becoming a widely-traded exchange. While we are not comfortable in predicting the direction the market will actually take, we are confident that the future composition of this market, both the users and the intermediaries, will depend

While the market will continue to develop a more homogeneous set of products with greater liquidity, there will continue to exist a subset of swaps which are custom-tailored.

strongly on the resolution of the above uncertainty. If swaps move further toward exchange trading, investment banks will be the major beneficiary. Removing the liability for the intermediary by marking to market or collateralizing would diminish the emphasis on capital commitment; and if so, investment banks might well regain the dominance they enjoyed in the earliest stages in the evolution of this market. On the other hand, if the intermediary continues to bear risk (or if the liability for the intermediary is increased), commercial banks will be the beneficiary.

The degree to which the swap market moves toward exchange trading will also determine the users of this market. With credit risk borne by the intermediaries, entry to the swaps market may well be denied to lesser credits. Hence, the predominant users of swaps will be the best credit risks. If the swaps market moves toward exchange trading, however, this composition will change. Lesser credit risks will be able to enter the swap market. Furthermore, to the extent that collateralization or some other form of bonding raises the cost of a swap transaction, the best credits will be expected to exit the market, refusing to pay the implicit insurance premium.

Because of the considerable dispute about the appropriateness of moving further toward exchange trading, there is no consensus about the future form of the swaps market. But there are issues where a consensus is possible. Most observers agree, for example, that while the market will continue to develop a more homogeneous set of products with greater liquidity, there will continue to exist a subset of swaps which are custom-tailored. The commercial banks should dominate in the homogeneous swaps market, which will be characterized by high volume, low spreads, and a significant capital commitment. Investment banks should continue to have a comparative advantage in the customized end of the market.

Immunisation and Duration:
A Review of Theory,
Performance and Applications

Stephen M. Schaefer,
London Business School

It is with pleasure that I acknowledge the helpful comments of Richard Brealey and David Pyle.

Introduction

The 1970s were a volatile period in many financial markets and, in particular, fixed income markets. In the U.S. Treasury market, for example, the variability of long rates of interest was between two and three times the average variability over the previous 50 years.[1] Bond markets had apparently become almost as volatile as stock markets and, among other changes, there was a surge of interest among money managers in techniques for managing interest rate risk.

The main tools which have emerged for this task are duration and immunisation. *Duration* is a measure of the interest rate sensitivity of an asset's value and, as such, it links the variability of interest rates and the variability of rates of return on bonds. *Immunisation* is a strategy or technique by which one constructs and manages a portfolio of (component) bonds such that its value is always as close as possible to the value of another asset (the target).[2]

Immunisation can be applied in a number of ways. Both the concept and the name of the strategy came from the work of F. M. Redington who, in the early 1950s, developed immunisation as a means for life insurance companies to ensure that the value of their assets remains in line with the value of their liabilities. A more recent application uses a long-term (say, five-year) pure discount bond as the target. In this case immunisation is used to manage a portfolio of conventional bonds so as to mimic the return on an asset (the pure discount bond) which does not actually exist in the market. In both cases the operational core of the strategy is to equalize the *duration* of assets and target.

Immunisation is a hedging strategy analogous to those used by manufacturers and producers in commodity markets. And just as the main benefit from hedging in, say, the cocoa futures market accrues to cocoa growers and manufacturers of chocolate bars, so the attraction of hedging interest rates is greatest to those firms with most exposure to interest rate movements—most notably, financial institutions. Apart from the important exception of pension fund management, non-financial corporations are unlikely to find these concepts of routine applicability.

The purpose of this article is to review recent thinking on the question, "How to immunize?" Although I will largely pass over the prior issue of "Why and when to immunize?," it is worth emphasising at the outset that merely because a firm has the opportunity to hedge a particular risk, it is not necessarily in the interest of the firm's shareholders to do so. It should also be pointed out that even if a company decides not to immunise, the concept of duration is potentially useful since it allows management to calculate the extent of its exposure to interest rate risk. In short, duration and immunisation have a role to play in measuring *and* controlling the effects of changes in interest rates.

---

1. See, for example, J. Nelson and S. M. Schaefer, "The Dynamics of the Term Structure and Alternative Portfolio Immunization Strategies," in G. O. Bierwag, George G. Kaufman and Alden Toevs, eds, *Innovations in Bond Portfolio Management: Duration Analysis and Immunization* (Greenwich, CT: JAI Press) 1983.

2. Although, for the sake of clarity, we refer to "bonds," these techniques are generally applicable to any interest rate dependent claims, e.g. bond futures, options, etc. See Section IV.

The conventional single-factor measure of duration proposed by Redington some 30 years ago appears to provide as good a basis for immunisation as any of the more sophisticated models since devised.

A brief overview of the article may be useful: Section I presents the basic theory of immunisation as put forward by Redington in the 50s. Because the crucial assumption underlying this approach concerns the way the yield curve moves over time, Section II provides some empirical evidence on this issue and also discusses the implications of changes in the yield curve for the construction of more sophisticated, generally "multi-factor," immunizing portfolios. Section III reviews the empirical evidence on the effectiveness of alternative immunisation strategies, and Section IV discusses some applications of immunisation.

The main conclusion of this article is that, for most purposes, the conventional single-factor measure of duration proposed by Redington some 30 years ago appears to provide as good a basis for immunisation as any of the more sophisticated models since devised—even though recent measures are more successful in capturing actual shifts in the yield curve. This is fortunate for practitioners because the data requirements for calculating Redington's duration measure are relatively simple. It also means that those readers pressed for time may feel some justification in simply skimming section II (by far the longest and most technical part of the article), which describes the recent "multi-factor" versions, and which also shows *why* Redington's simple approach works relatively well.

I. Theory of Immunisation

Funding Liabilities: Matching Cash Flows Versus Hedging Present Values

Let us consider, as Redington did, an insurance company with a known stream of nominal liabilities. The problem is to fund these liabilities in such a way that they can be met regardless of what subsequently happens to interest rates.

The most obvious solution would be to purchase an asset with cash flows that exactly match those of the liabilities.[3] The drawback of this approach is that it may be difficult, expensive or even impossible to achieve a perfect match.

The solution Redington devised was to break the problem down into a number of smaller problems. Instead of asking: "How can I choose my assets to be sure of meeting *all* of my future liabilities?," he asked: "How can I choose my assets so that if I am just solvent today—in the sense that my assets and liabilities have identical market values—I can be sure of being solvent tomorrow no matter what happens to interest rates in the interim?" If the problem of how to maintain solvency over a short period—say, a week—can be solved, then the same problem can be solved for the next week, so that we shall be solvent in two week's time. This argument is then repeated up until the time the last of our liabilities is discharged.

Interest Rate Sensitivity of Asset Values

The solution to Redington's problem depends principally on the sensitivity of asset and liability present values to interest rate changes. It is well known that, all else equal, the value of a long-term asset is more sensitive to interest rate changes than that of a short-term asset. This is illustrated in Exhibit 1, which shows the relation between an asset's present value and the discount rate. (We shall leave aside for the moment the important issue of precisely which interest rate or rates should be used for discounting.) Panel (a) illustrates this relation for a short-term asset and here the curve is relatively flat. Panel (b) shows the same curve for a long-term asset and here the curve is steeper. In both cases the curves slope downwards (which will always be the case so long as the cash flows under consideration are positive), and the slope of the curve measures the interest rate sensitivity of the asset's present value. The steeper the slope the more sensitive is the asset's value to a change in the discount rate.

In Exhibit 2 we plot curves for both liabilities and assets in order to identify the effect of interest rate changes on net worth (which is represented in the graph by the vertical distance between the two lines). Suppose that initially, when the discount rate is i_0, the fund is just solvent; that is, the value of assets and liabilities are exactly equal. Thus, in each case, the two curves coincide when the discount

---

3. Portfolios constructed so as to match a particular set of cash flows are often called "dedicated portfolios." See S. D. Hodges and S. M. Schaefer, "A Model for Bond Portfolio Improvement," *Journal of Financial and Quantitative Analysis*, Vol. 12 No. 2, pp. 243-260.

rate equals i_0. In panel (a) the asset curve is steeper than the liability curve, indicating that the assets have a longer term than the liabilities. Here the manager cannot be confident of maintaining solvency because, if interest rates were to rise, the value of the assets would be expected to fall below the value of the liabilities. In panel (b) the situation is reversed; the liabilities have a longer term than the assets and, again, solvency is not guaranteed.

If the asset and liability cash flows were per-fectly matched, then the two curves would coincide, as in panel (c). In this case, solvency is guaranteed, but we still face the problem of feasibility described earlier. The case which is of most interest here is illustrated in panel (d), where not only are the asset and liability values coincident at i_0, but the slopes of the two curves—that is, the interest rate sen-sitivities—are also equal. Here, for *small* changes in interest rates, solvency is maintained whether rates move up or down.

EXHIBIT 1
Short and
Long-Term Assets.

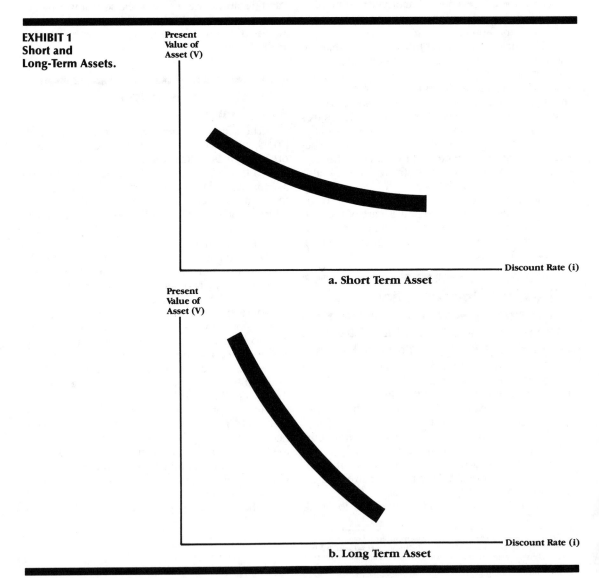

Present
Value of
Asset (V)

Discount Rate (i)

a. Short Term Asset

Present
Value of
Asset (V)

Discount Rate (i)

b. Long Term Asset

Duration and Conditions for Immunisation

The important lesson from panel (d) is that it identifies the parameter which is relevant for hedging: the slope of the curve which relates an asset's present value to the discount rate or, in other words, the sensitivity of its present value to a change in the interest rate. For a stream of cash flows X_1 at time 1, X_2 at time 2 and so forth, it is easy to show that this sensitivity is given by the following formula:

$$(1) \quad G = -\frac{1}{(1+i)}\left[\frac{PV(X_1).1 + PV(X_2).2 + .. PV(X_T).T}{V_0}\right].$$

In equation (1) $PV(X_t)$ represents the present value

EXHIBIT 2
Discount Rates.

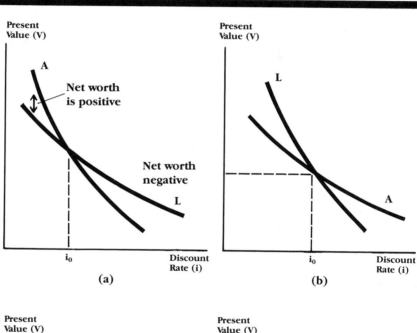

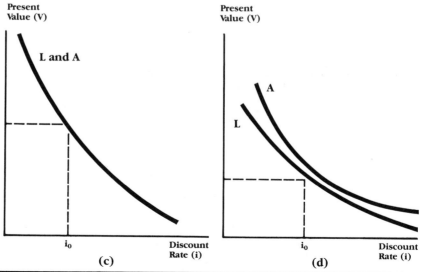

of the cash flow X_t discounted at interest rate i, and G is the slope of curve divided by the initial value of the fund V_0.[4] Thus G measures the *percentage* change in value per 1 percent change in the discount rate.[5]

The expression in square brackets is interesting because it can be interpreted as the *weighted average term to maturity* of the stream (the weights reflect the fraction of total value represented by each cash flow). This weighted average maturity is also known as the stream's *duration*, and can be written as follows:

$$(2)\ D = \frac{PV(X_1).1 + PV(X_2).2 + .. PV(X_T).T}{V_0}$$

where $PV(X_t) = X_t/(1 + i)^t$ is the present value of cash flow X_t, and $V_0 = PV(X_1) + PV(X_2) + \dots PV(X_T)$, is the total present value of the stream.

Redington's solution to the problem of how to ensure solvency without exactly matching cash flows was thus to choose a portfolio of assets which satisfied the following conditions: not only the present value, but also the *duration*, of assets must equal those of the liabilities. Redington called a fund which meets these two conditions "immunised."

It is important to recognise that, at least in principle, this solution holds good for only a short time. A change in interest rates, or simply the passage of time, will change the duration of both assets and liabilities, and this means that continuous adjustments to the portfolio will generally be required to re-establish immunisation. How frequently this needs to be done in practice to ensure "reasonable" hedging is a matter of balancing the benefits of achievable improvements in accuracy with the costs of portfolio revision.

Immunisation: An Example

It may be useful at this stage to have an example of how an immunised fund is constructed. We shall suppose that the liabilities consist of a cash outflow of $100 for each of the next five years. The asset portfolio is to be constructed from two bonds: a one-year bond with a 6 percent coupon and a four-

year bond with an 8 percent coupon. The interest rate is currently 10 percent.

Exhibit 3 shows the calculations of present value and duration both for the liability stream and for the two bonds. (The durations are calculated using equation (2).) To determine the correct amount of each bond to buy it is useful to express the immunisation condition in terms of investment proportions:

$$(3)\quad \begin{aligned} W_1 + W_2 &= 1 \\ W_1 D_1 + W_2 D_2 &= D^* \end{aligned}$$

where W_1 and W_2 are the proportions of total value invested in the two bonds, D_1 and D_2 are the durations of the bonds (assets), and D^* is the duration of the liabilities. As panel (d) of Exhibit 3 shows, W_1 and W_2, the investment *proportions*, are 0.293 and 0.707 respectively. Because the present value of the liabilities is $379.07, this means that the *amounts* invested are 0.293 x $379.07 = $111.21 in bond one and 0.707 x $379.07 = $267.86 in bond two.

Finally, Exhibit 4 shows how the value of the assets and liabilities would change if the discount rate falls to 9.5 percent and rises to 10.5 percent. For a half percent change in the interest rate, whether up or down, asset and liability values remain equal.

Exhibit 4 also illustrates another aspect of our earlier analysis. Equation (1) gives the percentage change in value for a one percent change in the discount rate. Using the formula for duration (equation 2) we see that equation (1) can be rewritten as:

$$(4)\quad G = \frac{D}{(1+i)}.$$

From Exhibit 4 we see that the values of both the liability stream and the asset portfolio decline from $383.97 at a discount rate of 9.5 percent to $374.29 at 10.5 percent—a fall of $9.69 or 2.6 percent. From equation (4) the fall is predicted to be equal to the duration (2.81 years at 10 percent) divided by one plus the interest rate; that is, 2.81/1.1 or 2.6 percent. Thus, even if a manager decides not to immunise, duration provides a convenient way of computing the change in value that will occur when interest rates change.

---

4. In equation (1) the interest rate i is a discretely compounded rate with compounding interval equal to the period between the cash flow dates 1,2, ... T. If a continuously compounded rate is used, equation (1) is unchanged except that the term 1/(1 + i), which multiplies the square brackets, is absent.

5. A "1%" change in the interest rate means a change from 8% to 9% rather than 8% to 8.08%.

EXHIBIT 3
Immunisation Example:
Calculation of
Durations, Present
Values, and Portfolio
Proportions

a. Liabilities

Time	Cash Flow	Discount Factor	PV of Cash Flow	PV of Cash Flow x Time
1	100	0.9091	90.91	90.91
2	100	0.8264	82.64	165.29
3	100	0.7513	75.13	225.39
4	100	0.6830	68.30	273.21
5	100	0.6209	62.09	310.46
Total	——	——	379.07	1065.26

$$\text{Duration} = \frac{1065.26}{379.05} = 2.81 \text{ years.} \quad PV = 379.07$$

b. One Year Bond with 6% Coupon

Time	Cash Flow	Discount Factor	PV of Cash Flow	PV of Cash Flow x Time
1	106	0.9091	96.36	96.36

Duration = 1 Year   PV = 96.36

c. Four Year Bond with 8% Coupon

Time	Cash Flow	Discount Factor	PV of Cash Flow	PV of Cash Flow x Time
1	8	0.9091	7.27	7.27
2	8	0.8264	6.61	13.22
3	8	0.7513	6.01	18.03
4	108	0.6830	73.77	295.58
			93.66	333.58

$$\text{Duration} = \frac{333.58}{93.66} = 3.56 \text{ years.} \quad PV = 93.66$$

d. Computation of Portfolio Proportions, W_1 and W_2

$W_1 + W_2 = 1$

$1 \times W_1 + 3.56 \times W_2 = 2.81$

Solution: $W_1 = 0.293, W_2 = 0.707$

EXHIBIT 4
Immunisation Example.
Values of Assets and
Liabilities for Small
Changes in Interest
Rates.

a. Number of Bonds Held (at 10% Discount Rate)

Bond	(i) Amount Invested ($)	(ii) Price Per $100 Nominal	(iii) = (i)/(ii) Units Held
1-Year	111.21	96.36	1.154
4-Year	267.86	93.66	2.860

b. Present Values

Asset	Present Value at	
	9.5%	10.5%
Liability Stream	383.97	374.29
1-Year Bond	96.80	95.93
4-Year Bond	95.19	92.16

c. Present Values of Asset Portfolio and Liability Stream

Discount Rate	Asset Portfolio*	Liability Stream
9.5%	383.97	383.97
10.5%	374.29	374.29

*Notes: The asset portfolio value is computed as the sum of the number of units of each bond held (panel a) times the unit value (panel b).

Now the Bad News

The procedure described in the previous section appears to provide a complete solution to the problem of funding liabilities in the face of changing interest rates. Unfortunately, as we shall now see, our success is more apparent than real.

The problem which has been overlooked concerns the discount rate. For an individual bond, formulae (1) and (2) are correct provided we interpret the discount rate, i, as the bond's yield-to-maturity. This means, however, that in working out the example in Exhibits 3 and 4, we have implicitly assumed that the yields-to-maturity for the two bonds and for the liability stream change by exactly the same amount when interest rates change. If these yields were to shift by different amounts, then the ratio of percentage changes in value would no longer be proportional to the durations, and the fund would not be immunised.

Is it reasonable to assume that yields-to-maturity on different assets will always change by the same amount? The answer, unfortunately, is no. There are two reasons for this. The first is that yields-to-maturity are complex averages of the underlying "spot rates," or zero coupon yields.[6] In general, a given shift in the spot rate curve will result in the yields to maturity on different assets changing by differing amounts. The second reason is that discount rates for different maturities, whether we are talking about spot rates or yields-to-maturity, are imperfectly correlated. Thus if short-term rates go up by one percent, not only is it true that long rates typically move by less than one percent, but the movement in the long rate is only partially determined by the movement in the short rate.

This second problem is important because it means that there is more than one "factor" which determines the yield curve and that immunising, or hedging, against one factor only cannot eliminate all risk. This situation can be redeemed, as we shall see in the next section, by generalising Redington's approach to accommodate more than one factor. However, before moving on, it should be said that despite the fact that actual interest rate movements clearly violate Redington's assumptions, in practice his simple approach performs quite well.

II. Multi-Factor Immunisation

The Statistical Properties of Shifts in the Yield Curve

Although he never said so explicitly, Redington's approach is based on a very simple model of the way spot rates (that is, zero coupon yields) move. That model can be stated as follows:

(5) $\quad \Delta y_t = \Delta y_t^*.$

According to this equation, the shift in spot rate at any maturity t (Δy_t), is equal to the shift at some reference maturity t* (Δy_t^*). We are free to choose t* arbitrarily, so let us suppose that y_t^* is the yield on a long-maturity, zero-coupon bond. We shall write this as y_L. In this case equation (5) would simply say that the shift in the spot rate for all maturities equals the shift in the long rate. Equivalently, equation (5) says that the spot rate curve never changes its shape, but makes only parallel shifts.

The fact that short rates tend to fluctuate more than long rates can be accommodated by making the shift in y_t *proportional to*, rather than equal to, the shift in y_L, such that

(6) $\quad \Delta y_t = c_t \Delta y_L,$

where c_t measures the sensitivity of the t-period rate to a shift in the long rate. If the variability of rates declines with maturity, then the c_t's are all greater than one and decline towards unity as maturity increases. This modification changes the appropriate measure of duration since, if c_t is greater than one, Redington's duration formula (2) will tend to understate the price sensitivity of short bonds relative to long bonds.[7] But because formula (6) still involves only one factor, nothing else is changed and immunisation can be achieved by choosing a portfolio which satisfies the conditions described earlier (equation (3)), with appropriately modified duration measures.

Accommodating less than perfect correlation between short and long rates, however, requires the introduction of at least one more factor into equation (5), a rather more fundamental change. The simplest model of this kind relates the shift in spot

---

6. For a discussion of the relationship between spot rates and yields-to-maturity on bonds, see my article, "The Problem with Redemption Yields," *Financial Analysts Journal*, Vol. 33.

7. A duration measure along these lines has been proposed by C. Khang in his article, "Bond Immunization when Short-term Interest Rates Fluctuate More than Long-term Rates," *Journal of Financial and Quantitative Analysis*, Vol. 14 No. 5, pp. 1085-1090.

EXHIBIT 5
Proportion of Term-Structure Variation (R²) "Explained" by Different Rates.

Explanatory Variables	Maturity (Years)				
	1	3	5	10	13
Long	0.22	0.33	0.35	0.79	1.0*
Short	1.00*	0.67	0.35	0.24	0.22
Long/Short	1.00*	0.72	0.48	0.79	1.0*

Notes: 1. Rates used: Short: 1-year; Long: 13-years
2. Regressions use estimates of spot rates for the period 1930–1979 (US Treasury Data)
3. (*) denotes value determined by construction

rate at a given maturity to the shifts in two reference rates: say, the long rate and the short rate:

$$(7) \quad \Delta y_t = g_t \Delta y_r + c_t \Delta y_L$$

where g_t measures the sensitivity of the t-period rate to shifts in the short rate and c_t, as before, its sensitivity to shifts in the long rate. If equation (7) were to hold exactly it would mean that if we knew how much the long and short rates had moved, we should know exactly how the whole of the term structure had moved.

While the data don't support this description exactly, equation (7) fits the actual behaviour of interest rates much better than either equations (5) or (6). Exhibit 5 provides support for this claim; it shows the R²s which are obtained when equations of the form (6) and (7) are estimated using linear regression.[8] (The data used are estimates of spot rates for U.S. Treasury securities over the period 1930 to 1979.) The first row shows the R² for regressions which use the long rate as the single independent variable (or index). In this case, the long rate explains only 22 percent of the variation of the short (one-year) rate and 33 percent of the variation of the three-year rate. Using the short rate as the single index produces similar results. But, as might be expected, when both rates are included a substantially higher fraction of total variation is explained.

It appears, then, that two factors explain shifts in the spot rate curve much better than one, and it is natural to conclude that hedging strategies which are based on two factors will be similarly superior. We shall see, however, that this conclusion is not always justified.

For some purposes it is convenient if the factors employed in a two-factor model of the term structure are uncorrelated. Clearly the long and short rate do not satisfy this condition. But recently,

Ayres and Barry (1979, 1980) noticed that the correlation between changes in the long rate and changes in the *spread* between the short rate and the long rate is very close to zero. Other authors have subsequently confirmed their findings.[9]

If we reformulate equation (7) in terms of the long rate and the spread, we arrive at the following:

$$(8) \quad \Delta y_t = b_t \Delta S + c_t \Delta y_L$$

where ΔS is the change in the spread, equal to $(\Delta y_r - \Delta y_L)$ and b_t measures the sensitivity of changes in the t-period rate to changes in the spread. The c_t's are the same as defined earlier, although their numerical values in equation (8) will, of course, differ from their values in equation (7). Because equation (8) involves merely a redefinition of the variables in (7), its explanatory power must be identical.

Duration and Immunisation with Several Factors

With one factor—say, the long rate—immunisation requires that the price sensitivity of both assets and liabilities to the long rate be equal. With two factors—say, the long rate and the spread—the price sensitivities to both factors must be equal. This adds another constraint to the problem and, for this condition to be satisfied, the portfolio must generally include three rather than two assets.

The mathematical form of these price sensitivities also differs from that of conventional duration (equation 2). If shifts in the spot rate curve are as described by equation (8), then the relevant duration measure for the long rate (known as "long rate duration") is given by:

$$(9) \quad D_L = \frac{PV(X_1).1.c_1 + PV(X_2).2.c_2 + \ldots PV(X_T).T.c_T}{V_0}$$

---

8. These data are abstracted from Nelson and Schaefer, cited earlier.

9. See, for example, Nelson and Schaefer, cited earlier, and my "Discussion" in the *Journal of Finance*, Vol. 35 No. 2, pp. 417-419.

While similar to the formula for conventional (Redington) duration, equation (9) includes a c_t term for each payment which reflects the sensitivity of the spot rate for that payment to shifts in the long rate. Similarly, the duration measure associated with the spread is:

$$(10) \quad D_S = \frac{PV(X_1).1.b_1 + PV(X_2).2.b_2 + \ldots PV(X_T).T.c_T}{V_0}$$

Like conventional measures of duration, the duration measures in equations (9) and (10) have the convenient feature that portfolio duration can be calculated as simply a weighted average of the durations of individual assets, with the weights reflecting the proportions of those assets in the portfolio.[10] (We have already used this fact in deriving equation (3)). The immunising conditions for the two-factor model (8) are therefore:

$$(11) \quad \begin{array}{llll} W_1 & + W_2 & + W_3 & = 1 \\ W_1 D_{1S} & + W_2 D_{2S} & + W_3 D_{3S} & = D_S^* \\ W_1 D_{1L} & + W_2 D_{2L} & + W_3 D_{3L} & = D_L^* \end{array}$$

In equation (11) D_{iS} is the "spread duration" of asset i, D_S^* is the spread duration of the liabilities, and D_L^* is the long rate duration of the liabilities. The first equation constrains the sum of the portfolio proportions to unity. The second equation sets the spread duration of the asset portfolio equal to the spread duration of the liabilities. The third equation does the same for long rate duration. (If *three* factors were necessary to describe shifts in the yield curve, then equation (11) would have four equations and the asset portfolio would contain four bonds, and so forth).

Implementing Multi-Factor Immunisation

What data are required to compute immunising portfolio holdings as the solution to equations (3) and (11)? In both cases the only coefficients not equal to unity are durations. In the case of conventional immunisation (3), the duration measures are the standard ones defined by equation (2). The data needed to compute these are: (i) the stream of cash flows, (ii) the payment dates of the cash flows, and (iii) the discount factors corresponding to the payment dates. (These discount factors should ideally be calculated using spot rates rather than yields-to-maturity, but the distinction is unlikely to be critical

here.) In the case of two-factor immunisation, the durations are defined by equations (9) and (10). And, in addition to data items (i)–(iii) above, the interest rate sensitivities $b_1, \ldots b_T$ and $c_1, \ldots c_T$ are required. These must be derived from estimates of spot rates.

These parameters will usually be estimated from the following multiple regression equation (which is simply equation (8) with the addition of an intercept term and an error term):

$$(12) \quad \Delta y_t = a_t + b_t \Delta S + c_t \Delta y_L + u_t$$

where a_t is a constant term and u_t is the disturbance term. Exhibit 6 shows the results of estimating equation (12) using spot rates estimated from the prices of U.S. Treasury securities. The striking feature of these results is that the estimates of c_t are all very close to unity (they range from 0.95 to 1.04 with a mean value of 0.99), while the estimates of b_t decline uniformly from unity (by construction) at the short end to zero (again by construction) at the long end.

The significance of the c's being close to unity is that this is the value which is implicitly assumed in conventional duration. Comparing the formula for conventional duration (2) with that for long-rate duration in the two-factor model (9), we see that the latter collapses to the former when each of the c_t's is unity. Empirical estimates of long rate duration will therefore be very close to conventional duration. The difference between a conventional immunisation strategy and the two-factor strategy considered here thus depends almost entirely on the relationship between conventional duration and spread duration.

The unit sensitivity to changes in the long rate also emerges if the following simple regression is estimated:

$$(13) \quad \Delta y_t = a_t + c_t \Delta y_L + v_t$$

Empirical estimates of equation (13) reveal that the coefficient associated with the long rate is largely unaffected when the change in the spread is excluded from the regression. This confirms Ayres and Barry's idea that changes in the long rate and changes in the spread are uncorrelated. Our model of term structure changes therefore comprises two independent parts: first, a shift in the long rate, which affects all shorter rates by an equal amount, and second, a shift in the spread between the long and short rates, which has a diminishing effect as maturity increases.

---

10. In formulae (9) and (10), the parameters (b) and (c) are the sensitivities of *continuously-compounded* spot rates to shifts in the long rate and the spread.

EXHIBIT 6
Sensitivity of Spot Rates to Long Rate and to Spread.

Estimates of the Regression:
$$\Delta Y_t = a_t + b_t \Delta S + c_t \Delta Y_l + u_t.$$

Maturity (Years)	b_t	c_t
1	1.000*	1.000*
2	0.743	1.036
3	0.542	1.026
4	0.391	0.997
5	0.269	0.970
6	0.200	0.953
7	0.163	0.950
8	0.131	0.962
9	0.100	0.983
10	0.100	1.005
11	0.043	1.022
12	0.019	1.022
13	0.000*	1.000*

Note: An asterisk (*) denotes that the value of the estimate is determined by construction. The estimates reported are simple averages of the corresponding estimates for five ten-year subperiods between 1930 and 1979.

EXHIBIT 7
Immunisation Example with Two-Factor Model: Calculation of Spread Durations.

a. Liabilities

Time	Cash Flow	Discount Factor	PV of Cash Flow	B_t	PV of Cash Flow x Bt x Time
1	100	0.9091	90.91	1.000	90.91
2	100	0.8264	82.64	0.743	122.81
3	100	0.7513	75.13	0.542	122.16
4	100	0.6830	68.30	0.391	106.82
5	100	0.6209	62.09	0.269	83.51
Total	——	——	379.07	——	526.22

$$\text{Spread Duration} = \frac{526.22}{379.67} = 1.39$$

b. One Year Bond with 6% Coupon

Time	Cash Flow	Discount Factor	PV of Cash Flow	B_t	PV of Cash Flow x Bt x Time
1	106	0.9091	96.36	1.000	96.36

Spread Duration = 1.0

c. Four Year Bond with 8% Coupon

Time	Cash Flow	Discount Factor	PV of Cash Flow	B_t	PV of Cash Flow x Bt x Time
1	8	0.9091	7.27	1.000	7.27
2	8	0.8264	6.61	0.743	9.82
3	8	0.7513	6.01	0.542	9.77
4	108	0.6830	73.77	0.391	115.37
Total	——	——	93.66	——	142.24

$$\text{Spread Duration} = \frac{142.24}{93.66} = 1.52$$

EXHIBIT 8		Asset Holding (% age)	
Immunisation Example:		Two Factor	Conventional
Immunising Portfolio	**Asset**	Model	Immunisation
Under Two-Factor	One-Year Bond	0.327	0.293
Model Compared with	Four-Year Bond	0.697	0.707
Conventional Solution.	Cash	–0.024	Nil*

*Note: Under conventional immunisation the cash holding is constrained to zero.

Two-Factor Immunisation: The Example Reconsidered

How much does the immunising portfolio under the two-factor model differ from the conventional immunising portfolio computed earlier? The substantial difference between long rate sensitivities (the c_t's) and spread sensitivities (the b_t's) might lead one to suppose that the portfolio differences are also large. To investigate this issue the immunising portfolio for the example considered in Section II is recomputed for the two-factor (long rate/spread) model.

Exhibit 7 uses equation (10) and the estimates of b_t from Exhibit 6 to calculate spread durations for the assets and liabilities of our earlier example. Since the b_t's are all less than or equal to unity, we know that an asset's spread duration will be less than its conventional duration. Thus, from Exhibit 7, the spread duration for the five-year annuity is found to be 1.39, as compared with a conventional duration of 2.81. The four-year bond has a spread duration of 1.52 compared with a conventional duration of 3.56. Only in the case of the one-year bond are the spread and conventional durations equal. This occurs because the one-year rate is used as the short rate in our definition of the spread and, as Exhibit 6 shows, this fixes the estimate of b_t at unity. To calculate the immunising portfolio, the long rate durations are also required. Because the estimates of c_t in Exhibit 6 are so close to unity, long rate durations are assumed to be equal to the conventional durations computed earlier.

Finally, one other asset must be included in the portfolio because, as mentioned earlier, three assets are required to hedge against two factors. The choice of the third asset is largely arbitrary, but if cash is chosen—that is, overnight borrowing or lending—equation (11) is simplified. The duration of cash is always zero no matter which index is used. This means that if asset 3 is cash, both D_{3S} and D_{3L} are zero and W_3 appears only in the first equation. With this simplification we can solve (11) by first determining W_1 and W_2 as the solution to the following two equations:

(14) $\quad W_1 D_{1S} + W_2 D_{2S} = D_S^*,$
$$W_1 D_{1L} = W_2 D_{2L} = D_L^*,$$

and then calculating the cash holding W_3 as a residual:

(15) $\quad W_3 = 1 - W_1 - W_2$

The solution to equations (14) and (15) is shown in Exhibit 8. The resulting portfolio is strikingly similar to the conventional solution. In fact the two-factor solution is essentially *the same* as the conventional solution with one minor exception. In the former, 2.5 percent of the value of the portfolio is borrowed short and invested in the one year bond. For all practical purposes this difference is trivial and there is no doubt that, as regards hedging effectiveness, these two portfolios would be empirically indistinguishable.

The similarity between the two portfolios is, at first sight, surprising. However, Exhibit 9, which presents a graph of spread durations plotted against conventional durations (both calculated for conventional par bonds with a yield of 10 percent), reveals the reason. Over a substantial range—that is, for values of conventional duration above two years—the relationship between the two duration measures is almost linear. Therefore, any portfolio which equates the conventional durations of assets and liabilities will also result in the spread durations being approximately equal.[11] But, while this is clearly true for our example, we must remember that duration also depends on the cash flow pattern of the stream involved. The same would not necessarily be true for all cash flow patterns.

---

11. This important fact was first pointed out by Michael Brennan and Eduardo Schwartz in their article, "Duration, Bond Pricing and Portfolio Management," in G. O. Bierwag, G. G. Kaufman and Alden Toevs (Eds.), *Innovations in*

Bond Portfolio Management: Duration Analysis and Immunization, Greenwich, CT: JAI Press.

EXHIBIT 9
Spread Duration.

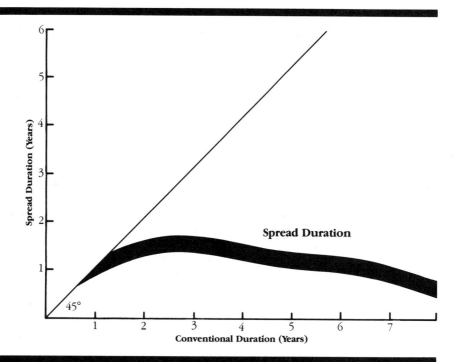

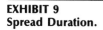

III. The Empirical Evidence

Although the basic ideas of immunisation have been understood since Redington's work in 1952, the first serious test of immunisation was performed nearly 20 years later by Fisher and Weil (1971), and ten more years elapsed before further tests were carried out by Brennan and Schwartz (1983), Ingersoll (1983), Nelson and Schaefer (1983) and others.[12]

What does it mean to "test" immunisation? Immunisation is the attempt to hedge one asset against another or, in some cases, to replicate one asset's payoffs with another's. Fisher and Weil attempted to form portfolios of coupon-bearing bonds that replicated long-term pure discount bonds. Nelson and Schaefer used coupon-bearing bonds to replicate other coupon-bearing bonds. If an immunisation strategy works perfectly, then the return on a "rep-licating" portfolio is identical to the return on the asset which is replicated. If the strategy works only imperfectly, then there will be a difference in the returns; the smaller this difference, of course, the better the immunisation strategy.

Unfortunately, there is no one obvious or natural way to design a test of immunisation. The relatively small number of tests which have been performed use several different approaches and the results of these cannot easily be compared. Similarly, it is not possible to answer the broad question: "How well does immunisation work?" because the answer depends entirely on how the test is constructed. The closer the *cash flow* streams of the immunising portfolio and the stream of the asset to be replicated, the better *any* immunisation strategy will work.

What, then, do the empirical tests of immunisation tell us? They certainly show that immunisation

12. A recent book edited by Bierwag, Kaufman, and Toevs (*Innovations in Bond Portfolio Management: Duration Analysis and Immunization* (Greenwich, CT: JAI Press, 1983)) includes these three papers as well as a number of other recent contributions in this area. See also the recent survey article, also by Bierwag, Kaufman, and Toevs, "Duration: Its Development and Use in Bond Portfolio Management," *Financial Analysts Journal* (July/August), pp. 15-35.

Conventional immunisation, which is by far the simplest approach to implement, appears to perform as well as any of its more sophisticated rivals.

EXHIBIT 10
Results of Alternative Immunisation Strategies: 1930-1979.

Target Bond has 10 Years to Maturity and Immunising Portfolio Contains Bonds with 5 and 15 Years to Maturity.*

	Mean Returns (% per Annum)			Standard Deviation of Difference (% p.a)	Percentage of Target Variance Remaining
Strategy	Target Bond	Immunising Portfolio	Difference		
Maturity	3.495	3.351	0.144	1.791	11.76
Duration	3.495	3.327	0.168	1.640	9.85
Short Rate	3.495	3.270	0.225	1.854	12.59
Long Rate/ Spread	3.495	3.324	0.171	1.668	10.20

*Note: The third asset in the case of the long rate/spread strategy was a 2-year bond.

does not work exactly. There are always errors, remaining differences in return between the immunising portfolio and the target asset. And, in many cases, these differences are not negligible. But the tests do not allow us to say how large the errors are without being specific about the cash flow characteristics of the assets and liabilities used in the tests.

But, notwithstanding this inconclusiveness about *absolute* performance, the tests do provide some useful conclusions about the *relative* performance of alternative strategies. For example, in this article two strategies have been discussed: conventional immunisation and a two-factor approach. Other (principally single factor) approaches have been suggested and tested. The empirical results strongly suggest that there is little difference in performance among these different strategies. Perhaps most important, conventional immunisation appears to do as well as any other.

This finding is of practical importance because conventional immunisation is by far the simplest approach to implement. Unlike two-factor immunisation, it requires no prior statistical analysis of the term structure. It is, of course, quite possible that some situations may arise when more sophisticated strategies outperform conventional immunisation, but these have not shown themselves in the tests carried out to date.

Exhibit 10 shows the results of Nelson and Schaefer's study published in 1983. It investigated the accuracy with which a portfolio containing five-year and fifteen-year coupon bearing bonds (the

"component bonds") would have replicated the return on a ten-year coupon-bearing bond ("the target"). The target and the component bonds were reselected at six-month intervals so that they had always approximately the same maturity, and every six months the returns on the target and on the immunising portfolio were measured. The measure of immunising effectiveness employed was the variance of the difference between these returns expressed as a percentage of the variance of the return on the target asset.

Results for four strategies are reported. In the first, called "Maturity," the portfolio was constructed so that its weighted average maturity was equal to the maturity of the target. The second, "Duration," was a conventional duration strategy. The third, "Short Rate," was, like conventional duration, a single factor strategy; but it used durations based on the sensitivity of the term structure to the short rate. The "Long Rate/Spread" strategy used was similar to that described above, but defined the spread as the difference between the long rate and the five-year rate.

The key results in Table 10 are those in the fifth column; this gives the measure of immunising effectiveness described above. The lower this number the better the strategy's performance. The results show that conventional duration had the best performance with the "Long Rate/Spread" strategy doing almost as well. The naive maturity strategy did not do much worse, while the "Short Rate" strategy had the worst performance.[13]

Nelson and Schaefer also report results for sev-

---

13. It is important not to overestimate the differences between the performance of the different strategies. For example, the measures of hedging effectiveness of 9.81% and 10.20% for conventional duration and the two-factor strategy, respectively, imply correlation coefficients between the target asset and the immunising portfolio of 0.950 and 0.948, respectively.

eral different subperiods, and for target assets and portfolios with different maturities, but the character of their results remained the same: they found relatively little difference between the performance of the alternative strategies. Such differences as there were tended to favour the conventional duration and long rate/spread strategies—which had about the same performance—over a naive maturity strategy or a strategy based on the short rate. The results of tests reported by Brennan and Schwartz (1983), Bierwag, Kaufman and Toevs (1983) and Ingersoll (1983) are broadly similar.

To sum up, the empirical results obtained so far suggest that conventional immunisation performs as well as its more sophisticated rivals. Thus, at least for the time being, there is no great incentive for practitioners to go beyond what Redington proposed 30 years ago.

IV. Applications

Guaranteed Investment Contracts

Probably the most widespread application of immunisation to date has been in the management of portfolios designed to mimic long-term pure discount bonds. Claims on these portfolios, sometimes marketed as "guaranteed investment contracts" (GICs), are generally sold by one financial intermediary, such as a bank or an insurance company, to another, usually a pension fund.

To construct a GIC we simply treat the liability stream in our earlier examples as a pure discount bond. An immunising portfolio which replicates a pure discount bond with a maturity (and therefore, for a pure discount bond, a duration) of T years has portfolio proportions W_1 and W_2 which satisfy the following conditions:

$$(16) \quad W_1 + W_2 = 1$$
$$W_1 D_1 + W_2 D_2 = T$$

Often a given financial transaction can be carried out in several different ways and, in this case, some of the alternative approaches to creating long-term pure discount bonds may be preferable to immunisation. It seems likely that much of the demand for GICs is a demand for a security to be held to maturity, rather than as part of a strategy to hedge a fluctuating pattern of liabilities. If GICs are held to maturity, intermediaries may prefer to issue long-term pure discount bonds directly, rather than engage in a dynamic hedging strategy (which is not only less reliable but almost certainly involves higher transaction costs). As recent experience has shown, long-term pure discount securities can be created relatively simply by buying conventional bonds and "unbundling"—that is, selling each of the cash flows (whether a coupon payment or a repayment of principal) as a separate pure discount bond.[14] This is also a hedging strategy of sorts; but, because it is static and involves no trading once the position is initially established, its execution is much simpler than the corresponding immunisation strategy.

Managing Interest Rate Risk in Financial Intermediaries

The more interesting and productive applications of immunisation are those where the liability stream changes over time. In such cases, no simple static policy can substitute for immunisation and any hedging strategy must consequently involve trading. There are many types of institutions for which problems of this type arise. Good examples are life insurance companies (Redington's original application) and pension funds with fixed liabilities. Others are commercial or investment banks, which typically offer a number of interest-rate dependent products and services; market making in bonds, trading in bonds, interest rate swaps and trading in interest rate futures are examples. The list may also include products such as forward exchange contracts and currency swaps, where interest rate uncertainty represents only part of the risk. Each of these activities involves exposure to interest rate risk, but it is not always obvious how to calculate the overall exposure or how to adjust one's position in one area (such as interest rate swaps) in order to offset risk in another (such as a holding of bonds in inventory).

The problems of correctly aggregating risk may lead managers to limit their interest rate exposure in each area *individually* and, where a risk exists in a particular area, to undertake an offsetting transaction in the same area whenever possible. For example, when a bank engages in an interest rate swap with a client who wishes to pay a floating interest rate in exchange for a fixed rate, it is not uncommon

---

14. These are CAT's, TIGR's, etc.

By calculating the overall duration of a bank's assets and liabilities, management can measure the extent of its overall exposure to interest rate changes.

for the bank to try to find (as quickly as possible) a client "on the other side" who wishes to pay a fixed rate for the same period of time in exchange for a floating rate.

If opportunities to hedge in this way were freely available, then banks would lose nothing by pursuing this approach exclusively. In practice, however, such opportunities are restricted; and in an effort to hedge one transaction, a bank may either take on another relatively unprofitable investment to hedge the first, or refuse a profitable opportunity which is on the same side as the first.

The concepts of duration and immunisation can be used to contribute to the solution of this problem in two ways. First, by calculating the overall duration of a bank's assets and liabilities across its various product and service areas, management can measure the extent of the bank's overall exposure to interest rate changes. Then, if management decides that the level of interest rate exposure is too high, immunisation techniques can be used to reduce that exposure to a comfortable level.

An Example

Consider a bank which engages in only two activities: bond trading (for which it must maintain an inventory of bonds) and interest rate swaps. Just before the close of business on a particular day, it holds an inventory of one 10-year bond with a 10 percent coupon, and has also engaged in one five-year interest rate swap. The bank's position is summarised in Exhibit 11. Management wishes to know what degree of exposure the bank has to interest rate changes and what action can be taken to eliminate this risk. For simplicity, and also because this will probably be adequate in practice, we shall use conventional immunisation rather than a two-factor approach.

To simplify the analysis further, we also assume that the floating interest rate which the bank receives on the swap is adjusted in such a way that, when we include the payment of principal, the present value of this side of the transaction is constant and therefore has zero duration. In this case the fixed rate payments have exactly the same interest rate sensitivity as a bond with a 10 percent coupon and five years to maturity. Since the bank is paying rather than receiving fixed rate money, it is effectively short one five-year bond.

To aggregate the risks over the three positions, we calculate the sensitivity of the total value of the portfolio to a change in the discount rate as a value-weighted sum of the durations. For the aggregate position this exposure equals $0.160mm; which is to say, a rise in the discount rate of 1 percent would

EXHIBIT 11 Immunising Combined Swap and Bond Position.	**a. Asset Holdings and Durations**		
	Asset	Amount	Duration
Bond	10 Year (10%)	+10.0 mm	6.76
Swap	5 Year Floating	+12.0 mm	0.0
	5 Year Fixed (10%)	−12.0 mm	4.17

b. Interest Rate Sensitivity of Initial Position

(i) Asset	(ii) Amount	(iii) Duration	(iv) = (ii) x (iii) x 0.01/(1+i) Sensitivity
Bond	+10.0	6.76	0.615
5 Yr Float	+12.0	0.0	0.0
5 Yr Fixed	−12.0	4.17	−0.455
Net Position	+10.0	——	0.160

c. Interest Rate Sensitivity of Revised Position

(i) Asset	(ii) Amount	(iii) Duration	(iv) = (ii) x (iii) x 0.01/(1+i) Sensitivity
Bond	+7.4	6.76	0.455
5 Yr Float	+12.0	0.0	0.0
5 Yr Fixed	−12.0	4.17	−0.455
Net Position	+7.4	——	0.0

reduce aggregate value by $160,000. If the standard deviation of changes in the discount rate over a month is, say, 12 basis points, then the standard deviation of wealth changes over the same period would be $160,000 x 0.12 = $19,200.

At this stage it is also simple to determine the transactions which are necessary to immunise the overall position. The sensitivity of the unhedged position is $160,000 for a 1 percent change in the discount rate. If the bond inventory of $10mm could be reduced by $2.6mm, then the interest rate sensitivity of the remaining balance would be 0.455 (i.e., (10.0 − 2.6) x 6.76 x 0.01/1.1), and the overall sensitivity would be zero.[15] Clearly the same result would be produced in many other ways—for example, by selling bond futures or writing a call option on a bond. In each case the sensitivity of the position taken must be a positive $160,000 for each 1 percent rise in the discount rate.

Options and Duration

Options on government bonds are already traded in the U.S. and, at the time of this writing, it seems quite likely that similar instruments will shortly be introduced in the UK. Option writers and traders will often wish to hedge their positions by taking positions in either cash instruments or futures. Similarly, as mentioned in the previous example, options on bonds provide an alternative vehicle for hedging both cash bonds and other interest-rate dependent claims (swaps, for example).

We are accustomed to thinking of duration as a weighted average time to maturity. But, while this is a useful interpretation in the case of a bond, it is much less helpful in the case of an option on a bond. Duration is first and foremost a price elasticity, measuring the sensitivity of present value to a change in the discount rate.[16] Viewed in this way, the duration of an option on a bond is no more mysterious than the duration of the bond itself. Indeed it turns out that the following simple relation exists between the two:

(17) **Duration of Option on Bond** = **Option Elasticity** x **Duration of Underlying Bond**

In equation (17) the "option elasticity" is the price elasticity of the option with respect to the price of the underlying bond, i.e.

(18) **Option Elasticity** $= \dfrac{\beta}{V} \dfrac{\delta V}{\delta B}$

where B is the price of the underlying bond and V is the price of the option. In option terminology, the partial derivative, $\delta V/\delta B$, is known as "hedge ratio".

It may be useful to provide some idea of the magnitude of an option's duration. Using the Black-Scholes model,[17] and assuming that the discount rate is 10 percent and that the standard deviation of the rate of return on long-term bonds is 10 percent per annum, a three month at-the-money call option is worth around 3.5 percent of the bond's value and the hedge ratio is approximately 0.7. This means that, in this case, the option's elasticity is 20. Thus, if the underlying bond has a duration of, say, 6.76 years (as in the example described earlier) then, using equation (17), the option has a duration of 20 x 6.76, or approximately 135 years.

In the previous section the net interest rate sensitivity of the combined bond and swap position was eliminated by selling part of the bond inventory. If options are available then an alternative strategy is to sell a call (or buy a put). Consider, for example, the call option described above with a price of 3.5 percent, a hedge ratio 0.7 and a duration of 135 years. To neutralise a net sensitivity of + $160,000 per 1 percent change in the interest rate, it is necessary to sell call options to the value of

$$\dfrac{0.160 \times (1 + i)}{135 \times 0.01} = \$0.13mm.$$

If the proceeds are invested in cash then the net sensitivity is, once again, zero. Notice that, even though the dollar value of the option transaction is much smaller than previously ($0.13mm compared to $2.6mm), the dollar value of the bonds on which the option is written is actually greater at $3.725mm ($0.13mm x 100/.035). However, the option value changes by only $0.70 for each $1 move in the bond price. Therefore the value of the option position has the same interest rate sensitivity as a bond position of 3.725 x 0.7 = $2.6mm, the amount of bonds sold in the earlier example.

---

15. In the calculation of value sensitivities, we divide by 1.1 since the discount rate used is discretely compounded: see equation (4).

16. Technically, duration is a semi-elasticity rather than an elasticity, i.e., it is $(1/V) \times (\delta V/\delta i)$ rather than $(i/V) \times (\delta V/\delta i)$.

17. See Fischer Black and Myron Scholes's, "The Pricing of Options and Corporate Liabilities," *Journal of Political Economy*, Vol. 81, pp. 637-659. The Black-Scholes model would not seem to be particularly well suited to the problem of valuing options on bonds. But, the work of Brennan and Schwartz, as described in their article, "Alternative Methods for Valuing Debt Options" (*Finance* Vol. 4 No. 2) suggests that it provides reasonable values, at least for short-term options on long-term bonds.

Conclusion

The attention that immunisation techniques are currently attracting appears to have two causes. The first is the historically high level of interest rate volatility. The second, which may well stem from the first, is the proliferation of interest-rate dependent contracts and products, such as interest rate futures, options on bonds, and interest-rate swaps. Both users and suppliers of these products need to know how to hedge their positions and thus, wittingly or unwittingly, they find themselves involved in immunisation.

It will not have escaped the attention of well-informed readers that the techniques for hedging interest rate risk described here could be, and have been, applied to hedging many other risks. The basis of an immunising portfolio is the sensitivity of asset prices to changes in interest rates. In this respect immunisation is exactly parallel to the Black-Scholes continuous hedging strategy in option pricing, where the portfolio proportions depend on the sensitivity of the option price to a change in the underlying stock price. Thus, immunisation should not be seen as an isolated hedging technique, but rather as a particular application of an approach which is widely used.

The most prominent conclusion of this article is that the simplest measure of interest rate sensitivity, known as "conventional duration" and formulated by Redington in the early 1950s, appears to perform the task of immunising bond portfolios as well as the more sophisticated alternatives which have been proposed since then. What is most remarkable about this result is that a technique whose underlying assumptions appear to have so little correspondence with interest rate data should turn out to perform so well. The use of multi-factor measures of duration, which do a much better job of predicting actual interest rate movements, theoretically should, but nevertheless fails to, improve upon conventional duration as the basis for immunisation.

As we have seen, the solution to this puzzle has two parts. First, the sensitivity of spot rates to shifts in the long rate is very close to unity, and this in turn implies that long-range duration and Redington's duration are practically identical. Second, spread duration for typical bonds is almost linearly related to long-rate duration and, therefore, any portfolio which equates the long-rate durations of two assets also equates their spread durations to a close approximation.

While this is undoubtedly the explanation for the empirical results reviewed in section III, there is a caveat. The approximately linear relationship between the two duration measures holds much less well for short maturities. It is quite possible that, in the case of shorter maturities, careful empirical analysis would uncover at least a measurable difference between the hedging performance of one- and two-factor strategies.

The Uses of Interest Rate Swaps in Managing Corporate Liabilities

by Laurie Goodman, *Eastbridge Capital*

A s a result of the high and volatile interest rates of the early 1980s, companies began to emphasize active management of their liabilities as well as their assets. Issuers started to realize that the type of debt used and its maturity could make a considerable difference in their funding costs. At the same time, a number of new risk management products—futures, options, swaps, and caps—made it possible for corporate treasurers to manage their liabilities more actively. They began to understand that debt could be readily transformed to take advantage of changing market conditions. Rates on floating-rate debt could be fixed by using futures or swaps, floating debt could be capped, fixed rates could be transformed into floating rates, and issuers could hedge the cost of a new issue by fixing or capping the rate. Corporate treasurers also discovered that the cheapest way to issue a given variety of debt was not always the most straightforward. Issuers have sometimes found opportunities to make initial debt offerings in one form and then, with the use of risk management products, to convert that debt into the desired form, thereby producing a lower all-in cost of funds.

In this article, I shall discuss the corporate uses of one of the most widely used risk management products: interest rate swaps. The principal roles that swaps have assumed in corporate liability management can be summed up in the following three:

1. reducing the cost of current issuance,
2. locking in the cost or spread on an expected future issue, and
3. hedging the corporate exposure to interest rates by altering the cash flows on an existing liability.

In the process of allowing corporations to manage interest rate exposures and reduce funding costs, the growth of the interest rate swap market has contributed significantly to the further integration of the fixed-rate and floating-rate debt markets. As a result of corporate attempts to exploit pricing differences between these markets, many of the financing "arbitrage" opportunities described below are no longer available. For example, while the combination of floating debt with a swap has at times been considerably cheaper than issuing fixed debt, the disparities are not nearly as great as they were reported to be five years ago. Thus, while some of the funding techniques presented here may still be used on a fairly regular basis, most should probably be regarded as "window-of-opportunity" arbitrages that appear only from time to time—and are thus available to only the most opportunistic corporate treasurers.[1]

---

1. This article considers the economics of various swap transactions, but does not address tax and accounting issues. An issuer would want to take these into account before making a final decision as to what form the debt will take.

EXHIBIT 1 **EXHIBIT 1** USING SWAPS AND SWAPTIONS TO TRANSFORM DEBT

Transformed Debt	Original Debt				
	(1) Floating Rate	**(2)** Fixed rate Non-callable Non-putable	**(3)** Callable Fixed Rate Debt	**(4)** Putable Fixed Rate Debt	**(5)** Non-Conventional
(1) Floating rate debt	X	Vanilla Swap	Callable Swap	Putable Swap	FROG + yield Curve Swap
(2) Fixed rate non-callable non-putable debt	Vanilla Swap	X	Callable Swap + Vanilla Swap or Swaption	Putable Swap + Vanilla Swap	Inverse Floater + Vanilla Swap or FROG + yield curve swap + vanilla swap
(3) Callable fixed rate debt	swaption + vanilla swap	swaption	X	not economical	not economical
(4) Putable fixed rate debt swaption + vanilla swap	swaption	two swaptions	X	not economical	
(5) Non-conventional debt	not economical	not economical	not economical	not economical	X

This exhibit shows how swaps can transform one type of debt to another. The original form of the debt is given in the colums, the transformed debt in the rows. The entry in the cell shows the swap requirements that are necessary to accomplish the transformation. Thus, callable fixed rate debt (Column 3) can be transformed into floating rate debt (Row 1) via a callable swap (Column 3, Row 1). An "X" indicates no transformation is necessary. "Not economical" means the transformation has never made sense economically—the transformed debt has never been cheaper than the original.

REDUCING THE COST OF A CURRENT ISSUE

By using the swap market, companies have obtained their desired financing at a lower cost than issuing the desired debt directly. For example, if a firm wants to issue fixed-rate noncallable debt, it has at least five choices:

1. issue the fixed-rate debt directly;

2. issue floating-rate debt and swap the floating-rate debt into fixed-rate debt;

3. issue callable fixed-rate debt and enter into a callable swap or write an option on a swap;

4. issue putable fixed-rate debt and enter into a putable swap; or

5. issue an unconventional instrument and enter into a swap to obtain the equivalent of a fixed-rate bond.

Exhibit 1 illustrates each of these funding strategies, as well as a number of others. For example, to obtain fixed-rate noncallable debt (row 2), any of the original debt issues listed in the top row can be transformed by adding the features of the cell that intersects the applicable column and row 2. Thus, an issue of callable fixed-rate debt (column 3) can be transformed into noncallable fixed-rate debt (column 3, row 2) by entering into a callable swap or writing an option on a swap (also known as a "swaption").

The choice among the five alternatives outlined above will depend primarily on which is cheapest for the issuer. Although the development of competitive markets over time should limit the cost differences among such financing alternatives, issuers should nonetheless consider all possibilities to ensure their achieving the lowest cost of funds in fixed-rate *noncallable* debt. That is, pricing inefficiencies arise from time to time, and thus issuers should examine all of the alternatives across row 2 to be sure of gaining the lowest-cost means to this method of funding.

In addition, many issuers will want to investigate the other funding opportunities that are available, while bearing in mind the necessary trade-offs. For example, issuers should weigh the cost of issuing fixed-rate noncallable debt against the cost of issuing callable fixed-rate debt in order to evaluate the cost of purchasing the right to call the debt. They might also want to see how much issuing a put bond might lower the required coupon on an issue. In terms of Exhibit 1, after finding the lowest-cost funding method in each row, issuers may also want to compare the various rows as alternative financing strategies. Thus, an issuer interested in ending up with some form of fixed-rate debt should compare the low-cost entry in row 2 with those in rows 3, 4, and 5.

As we proceed in this article, we will first look at the various ways of creating straight fixed-rate debt with no embedded options. Then we will consider ways of creating floating-rate debt, callable fixed-rate debt, and putable fixed-rate debt. All the techniques discussed in these pages, I should point out, have been used in the market. Some, though, have been used only sparingly, and thus seem to have been appropriate only for a special set of market conditions. The "arbitrage" financing techniques in the first part of this article are all premised on some kind of market mispricing. As the swap market further integrates the fixed and floating debt markets, the cost reductions achieved by issuing synthetic debt should become increasingly hard to find.

Creating Synthetic Optionless Fixed-Rate Debt

The interest rate swap market provides a variety of ways to create noncallable fixed-rate debt using original debt of another form. Such synthetic fixed-rate debt is most often created in one of two ways: (1) if the original bond is a floater, it can be combined with a conventional (or "plain vanilla") swap to convert floating payments to fixed; or (2) if the original bond is callable, it can be combined with the sale of a callable swaption. Less frequent variations use putable bonds and unconventional bonds as the original underlying instrument.

Transforming Floating-Rate Debt Into Synthetic Fixed-Rate Debt. Companies with credit ratings lower than AA have taken advantage of opportunities to achieve cheaper fixed-rate financing by using floating-rate debt plus swaps instead of conventional fixed-rate issues. These opportunities arise from sizeable differences in the relative credit spreads between the fixed-rate market and the floating-rate market. Firms with a lower credit rating often pay a smaller spread over a more highly rated borrower in the floating market than in the fixed market.

To illustrate how swaps have been used to take advantage of this disparity, assume that an issuing firm would have to pay a fixed rate of 200 basis points over a 10-year Treasure (T_{10}). Alternatively, it could issue a floating-rate note (FRN) at LIBOR + 50 bp. Assume also that the swap rate it faces is T_{10} + 70 bp. The firm could arrange LIBOR-based financing and swap the proceeds for fixed at an interest rate equal to the 10-year Treasury + 70 bp. By so doing, the firm would obtain "synthetic" fixed financing of T_{10} + 120 bp, calculated as follows:

Instrument	Action	Cash Flow
FRN	Firm pays	LIBOR + 50 bp
Swap	Firm receives	(LIBOR)
	Firm pays	T_{10} + 70bp
Synthetic Fixed	Net payment	T_{10} + 120 bp

When this net payment is compared with an original fixed-rate issue of T_{10} + 200 bp, the net saving is 80 bp.[2]

If the firm issues a floating-rate note as illustrated above, the payment on the synthetic fixed-rate instrument is locked in. Typically, however, the firm chooses to issue floating-rate debt in which the credit spread is reset each period. Examples of this include short-term issues in the Euromarket and commercial paper market. In these instances, the firm has not actually locked in a rate beyond the first period. The borrowing rate can be

---

2. For a much more detailed and precise attempt to calculate the cost savings from this kind of financing "arbitrage," see the next article in this issue ("Swaps at Transamerica: Analysis and Applications," by Robert Einzig and Bruce Lange). Among other important points made by Einzig and Lange, this article demonstrates that creating synthetic fixed-rate debt with swaps sometimes imposes considerable refunding and basis risk that is often ignored in popular accounts of the benefits of swaps.

EXHIBIT 2
USING CALLABLE SWAPS
TO CREATE SYNTHETIC
NON-CALLABLE DEBT

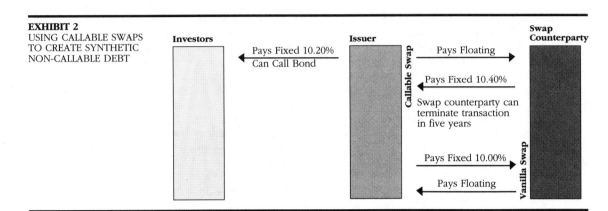

decomposed into two parts—a base interest rate and a credit spread. As the base interest rate rises, the rate received on the swap (and paid on the commercial paper) will also rise. Changes in the firm's credit standing are unhedged. Thus, if the firm-specific credit spread narrows (the firm's credit quality improves), then the firm will achieve a lower cost for subsequent periods. If the firm-specific credit risk widens, the firm will end up with a higher cost for subsequent periods. If a firm expects its credit spread to remain constant or to narrow, a series of short-term borrowings will be preferable to a floating-rate note. In choosing that option, however, the firm is bearing the risk that its credit spread will widen.

Corporate treasurers should be aware that short-term borrowings usually have a lower credit spread than floating-rate notes, as credit spreads generally increase with maturity. Thus, when a corporate treasurer is comparing the cost of a commercial paper issue plus a swap to a fixed-rate financing, the cost savings will appear to be misleadingly large, as he has not locked in the credit spread. The cost of doing so is the cost differential between a floating-rate note and short-term borrowings.[3]

Transforming Callable Debt Into Noncallable Debt Using Callable Swaps. Callable swaps have often been used together with callable bonds to create synthetic noncallable debt. The reason: Bond investors may demand less for the call option inherent in a callable bond than such an option will bring in the swap market.[4] An issuer generally pays a premium to investors (in terms of a higher interest rate than otherwise) for the right to call the original bond after a stated period of time, say, 10 years. In essence, the issuer has purchased a call option. Having purchased this call option, the issuer is thus in a position to *sell* an equivalent call option—but in the form of an option to call (or terminate) an interest rate swap. In this way, some issuers have been able to obtain noncallable debt at lower cost.

The mechanics of this transaction, which can best be illustrated by means of a simple example, actually involve entering into two swaps. Say that a firm issues a 10-year note that can be called at par after five years. The note is sold to yield 10.20%. This option may add 20 bp to the cost of the debt. In other words, if the firm issued a non-callable bond, it would pay only 10.00%. But as we shall see, the issuer will ultimately be better off by issuing the callable debt.

Along with the callable issue, the firm executes two transactions in the swap market. It enters into a callable swap—a swap with an option to call or terminate the

3. Actually, many firms may make a deliberate decision to use short-term financing rather than a floating-rate note. There are two possible reasons for this. First, short-term financing plus a swap allows a firm to achieve a fixed base interest rate plus a floating credit spread. There is no other combination of instruments available which can achieve this result. (See Marcelle Arak, Arturo Estrello, Laurie Goodman, and Andrew Silver, "Interest Rate Swaps: An Explanation," *Financial Management*, Summer 1987 for a complete explanation.) Second, short term paper plus a swap fixes an interest rate while avoiding agency costs. If a firm has only long-term debt (either fixed rate or floating rate notes), the firm would have an incentive to shift toward more risky projects because bondholders share the downside, but not the upside. Short-term debt requires the firm to go to the markets each period to be re-evaluated and hence saves these agency costs. This argument is developed by Larry R. Wall, "Interest Rate Swaps, an Agency Theoretic Model with Uncertain Interest Rates," *Journal of Banking and Finance* (in press).

4. There is considerable anecdotal support, as well as some academic evidence, that corporate bond investors have "underpriced" the option they give corporations on the typical bond. Investors might, however, rationally charge less than "fair value" for granting such an option. A failure by corporate management to exercise the option efficiently (by exercising as soon as the bond price exceeds the call price by an acceptable margin) would cause investors to underestimate its true value. (For a discussion of the optimal bond refunding strategy, see Alan Kraus, "An Analysis of Call Provisions and the Corporate Refunding Decision," *Midland Corporate Finance Journal*, Vol. 1 No. 1 (Spring 1983).

The amount of refunding activity in the last 7-8 years would suggest underpricings of the call option by bond market investors should become increasingly scarce over time. Moreover, the growth of markets for callable swaps and swaptions (those with surrogate call provisions) should further act to erase large call pricing disparities between the swaps and bond markets.

swap after five years. The firm pays the floating rate and receives a fixed rate of 10.40%. For illustrative purposes, we further assume that the fixed rate on a vanilla swap is 10.00%, which means that the counterparty to the callable swap is willing to pay 40 bp per annum for the right to terminate the swap after five years. Because the swap counterparty will terminate the swap only if rates decline—that is, if it can enter into a new swap and pay less than 10.40%—the counterparty has effectively purchased a call on the debt.

The net effect is that the issuing firm pays a net floating rate of interest of LIBOR minus 20 bp. In order to transform the debt into fixed rate, the issuer can then enter into a plain vanilla swap in which it agrees to receive floating and pay fixed. Assuming the fixed interest rate is 10.00%, the firm ends up with a net interest cost of 9.80% (10.20% on the bond less 10.40% on the swaption plus 10.00% on the vanilla swap), which is 20 bp less than it would have cost to issue the non-callable debt directly. (This series of transactions is illustrated in Exhibit 2.)

Let's also look at the transactions from the perspective of the issuer and the swap counterparty under different interest rate scenarios:

Scenario	Issuer	Swap Counterparty	Result
Interest rates are higher after five years.	No action on bond.	No action. Both swaps remain outstanding.	Issuer has ended up with 10-year fixed rate money.
Interest rates are lower after five years.	Bond is called. Issuer funds floating.	Swap in which issuer pays floating and receives fixed is called. Swap in which issuer pays fixed and receives floating remains outstanding.	Issuer has ended up with 10-year fixed rate money.

Thus, a callable swap is simply a swap in which the fixed payer (the counterparty) has the right of early termination without penalty. In either scenario, the issuer has achieved 10-year fixed rate financing.

Other variants of this structure are, of course, possible. For example, rather than receiving 10.40% per annum on the callable swap, the bond issuer could receive 10% plus 2.00%-2.25% of the par value of the bond as an upfront fee. In this case, the firm is paying the same 10.20% to issue debt as initially, but has traded away its call option for a fee of 2.00%-2.25%.

Transforming Callable Debt Into Noncallable Debt Using Swaptions.

Thus far we have discussed how to achieve fixed-rate financing by transforming callable debt into noncallable debt using callable swaps. The same result can be achieved using "swaptions." A swaption is an option providing a counterparty the right, but not the obligation, to enter into an interest rate swap at a future date. A callable bond and a swaption can be used to create fixed-rate funding to the call date and synthetic fixed-rate financing from the call date to the maturity date. As with the use of callable swaps described above, the use of swaptions to convert callable into noncallable debt is likely to be undertaken only if and when the call feature is priced more cheaply by the bond market than by the swap market.

In order to create five-year noncallable debt, one funding technique uses callable debt with a final maturity of five years and a "back-end fixed" swaption—that is, an option to enter into a swap to pay fixed and receive floating extending from the call date to the maturity date on the notional amount of the debt. If the call can be exercised after year 3, the swaption would allow the issuer to pay fixed from year 3 to year 5. Alternatively, an issuer could achieve the same result by issuing longer maturity (10-year) debt with a call in five years and a "back-end floating" swaption to enter into a swap to pay floating and receive fixed for the balance of the 10-year maturity. A "back-end fixed" swaption simply means that the issuer pays fixed and receives floating if the swaption is exercised. With a "back-end floating" swaption, the issuer pays floating and receives fixed.

Let's look at an example of callable debt and a "back-end fixed" swaption. Assume an issuer wants five-year fixed-rate funding. He can create it by issuing a five-year bond, callable at par after three years, and selling a back-end fixed swaption. This swaption provides the buyer with the option to enter into a two-year interest rate swap commencing in three years. The back-end fixed swaption would commit the issuer to pay fixed and receive floating if desired by the counterparty. We show the results below:

Scenario	Swap	Issuer	Result
Interest rates are higher after three years.	The swaption is not exercised.	The issuer does not call the bond.	Issuer has five-year fixed rate money.
Interest rates are lower after three years.	The swaption is exercised. The issuer pays fixed and receives floating for years four and five.	The issuer calls the bond and funds floating for years four and five.	Issuer has five-year fixed rate money.

Note that, under either scenario, the issuer has obtained five-year fixed-rate money.

TO THE EXTENT INVESTORS ARE WILLING TO PAY MORE FOR
THE PUT FEATURE THAN THE PRICE OF THE PUT IN THE SWAP MARKET,
A PUT BOND CAN BE COMBINED WITH A PUTABLE SWAP TO
CREATE INEXPENSIVE NONCALLABLE DEBT.

EXHIBIT 3
USING PUTTABLE SWAPS
TO CREATE SYNTHETIC
NON-CALLABLE DEBT

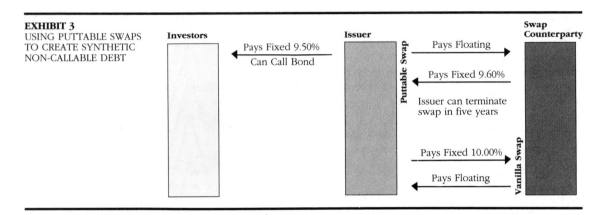

An issuer could also obtain noncallable debt by issuing a 10-year note callable at par after five years and selling a "back-end floating" swaption. This swaption would allow the buyer the option to enter into a five-year swap, commencing in five years. The back-end floating swaption would commit the issuer to pay floating and receive fixed. Here are the results under the two interest rate scenarios:

Scenario	Swap	Issuer	Result
Interest rates are higher after five years.	The swaption is exercised. Issuer pays floating and receives fixed from years 6-10.	The issuer does not call the bond.	Issuer has five-year fixed-rate money. Over years 6-10, the issuer has floating money.
Interest rates are lower after five years.	The swaption is not exercised.	Issuer calls the bond.	Issuer has five-year fixed-rate money.

Again, the issuer has achieved fixed-rate funding for five years under either interest rate scenario.

One advantage of this structure is that if the swaption is exercised, and the issuer does not call the bond, he still has the call option. That is, the swaption does not extinguish the call on the bond. This option can be exercised if rates move down in the future.

In all of these alternatives, the issuer obtains synthetic noncallable debt. The choice among these alternatives will depend on how costly the embedded call option is relative to the back-end fixed swaption, the back-end floating swaption, and the callable swap.

Transforming Putable Debt Into Optionless Debt

Putable swaps paired with put bonds have occasionally been used by issuers wanting to issue noncallable debt as cheaply as possible. They are used less frequently than callable swaps. With a put bond the investor purchases the right to put the bond back to the issuing firm—an option which becomes more valuable to the investor as interest rates rise. For example, assume a firm issues a 10%, 10-year bond with a put that can be exercised after five years. If after five years rates had risen to 12%, the investor would put the bond back to the issuer and reinvest at the 12% rate. Naturally, from an investor's perspective, a 12% reinvestment rate is preferable to the 10% rate implicit in the bond. If rates fall, the put bond remains outstanding.

To the extent investors are willing to pay more for the put feature than the price of the put in the swap market, a put bond can be combined with a putable swap to create inexpensive noncallable debt. With a put bond, as suggested above, the issuer writes an option. He can then buy a putable swap to offset the exposure created by the put in the bond. But, once again, this would make sense only if the issuer can realize more by selling the put option on the bond than he must pay for the put on the swap he purchases.

This funding strategy, as illustrated in Exhibit 3, is achieved by using two swaps. In the putable swap, the issuer receives a fixed rate and pays a floating rate. The fixed rate the issuer receives is lower than the rate on a vanilla swap, reflecting the fact that the issuer can terminate the swap if rates rise. The issuer will terminate the swap if he can receive a higher rate than 9.60% at the expiration of the option—in other words, if interest rates have risen. The vanilla swap converts the then-floating rate payments of LIBOR less 10 bp into fixed payments. The issuer pays an effective interest rate on the noncallable, nonputable debt of 9.90%—9.50% on the bond less 9.60% on the swaption plus 10.00% on

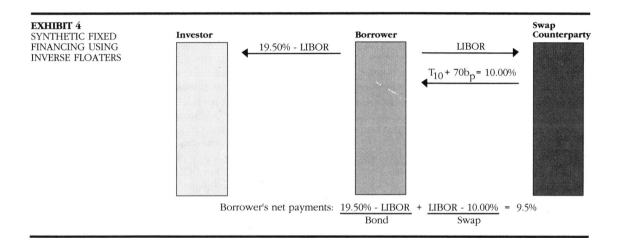

EXHIBIT 4
SYNTHETIC FIXED
FINANCING USING
INVERSE FLOATERS

Investor ← 19.50% - LIBOR ← Borrower

Borrower → LIBOR → Swap Counterparty

$T_{10} + 70b_p = 10.00\%$

Borrower's net payments: $\dfrac{19.50\% - LIBOR}{Bond} + \dfrac{LIBOR - 10.00\%}{Swap} = 9.5\%$

the vanilla swap. This is 10 bp cheaper than optionless debt with the same characteristics.

Under our alternative interest rate scenarios:

Scenario	Issuer	Swap Counterparty	Result
Interest rates are higher after five years.	Bond is put to issuer.	Swap for issuer to pay floating and receive fixed is terminated. Swap for issuer to pay fixed and receive floating remains standing.	Issuer has 10-year fixed-rate money.
Interest rates are lowest after five years.	No action.	Both swaps remain outstanding.	Issuer has 10-year fixed rate money.

Note that a putable swap is a swap in which the fixed-rate receiver (in this case, the issuer) has the option to walk away from the swap.

Creating optionless debt from put bonds is an arbitrage-driven transaction—that is, it is done only if the optionless debt can be created synthetically more cheaply than it can be issued directly.

Transforming Unconventional Debt

Inverse Floaters Into Fixed-Rate Debt. Another, less frequently used method of obtaining fixed-rate financing is through the use of an inverse floating rate security. An inverse floater is an instrument that pays a pre-specified interest rate minus LIBOR. This is generally coupled with a swap in which the issuer receives fixed and pays floating.

We can illustrate this transaction with an example viewed from the issuer's perspective (see Exhibit 4). We assume the floater pays 19.50% minus

LIBOR. The swap spread in this example would be $T_{10} + 70$ bp or 10.00%.

Instrument	Action	Cash Flow
FRN	Firm pays	19.50% – LIBOR
Swap	Firm receives	(10.00%)
	Firm pays	LIBOR
Synthetic Fixed	Net payment	9.50%

Using an inverse floater plus a vanilla swap, the issuer has locked in a coupon payment of 9.5%. The coupon payments on a new fixed-rate issue would be 10.0%. Thus, the borrower has saved 50 bp over a traditional bond.

With this sort of funding strategy, a cap is necessary to protect against very high rates. Without a cap, if LIBOR happened to rise above 19.5%, the investor would owe the issuer money. Obviously, the issuer could not logistically collect from the investor. Thus, the issuer can buy a cap that will enable him to be paid if rates go above 19.50%. This cap is far out of the money, and the protection is very inexpensive.

This structure attracted a great deal of interest when introduced in 1986. Investors initially did not realize that it was equivalent to holding a long position in *two* fixed-rate bonds and a short position in a floating-rate instrument. They could easily recreate this position by purchasing a fixed-rate bond and entering into a swap in which the investor received fixed and paid floating. Investors showed interest in the security because they were convinced short rates would drop. When LIBOR rates fell, the coupon on an inverse floater increased. But once investors realized how easily this strategy could be replicated, it was priced fairly and there were no new issues.

Transforming FROGS Into Fixed-Rate Debt.
There is one other kind of unconventional debt that has been transformed into fixed-rate debt. FROGS are floating-rate notes with coupons based on the 30-year treasury rate that are reset quarterly or semi-annually. They have typically been combined with "yield curve" swaps in order to produce floating-rate debt. In a yield curve swap, floating payments are exchanged at two different points of the yield curve. This debt can then be transformed into fixed-rate debt with a vanilla swap.

To see how this works, assume that a firm issues a FROG that pays the 30-year Treasury rate, reset every six months (UST), minus 115 bp. The issuer enters into a yield curve swap in which he pays six-month LIBOR and receives the 30-year Treasury rate, reset every six months, less a fixed spread (say 105 bp). (This is called a "yield curve" swap because floating-rate payments indexed to the short end of the market are being exchanged for floating rate payments indexed to the long end of the yield curve.)

As shown below, the issuer has essentially locked in floating-rate financing:

Instrument	Action	Cash Flow
FROG	Firm pays	UST − 115 bp
Swap	Firm receives	(UST − 105 bp)
	Firm pays	LIBOR
Synthetic Floating	Net payment	LIBOR − 10 bp

This synthetic floating-rate instrument can be converted to fixed-rate payments by means of a vanilla swap in which the issuer pays the three-year Treasury rate (T_3) + 70 in exchange for LIBOR (as shown below).

Instrument	Action	Cash Flow
Synthetic Floating	See above	LIBOR − 10 bp
Vanilla Swap	Firm receives	(LIBOR)
	Firm pays	T_3 + 70 bp
Synthetic Fixed	Net payment	T_3 + 60 bp

FROGs, in fact, were initially created out of the desire to locate counterparties for yield curve swaps. Firms were enticed to issue FROGs and swap for LIBOR funding—a transaction that generated sub-LIBOR financing for the issuer.

FROGs were very popular investments in mid-1988 as a yield curve strategy, in large part because the average spread between 30-year Treasuries and LIBOR during 1983-87 was 125 bp. At 115 basis points (which was 10 basis points less than historical levels), these notes became very attractive. Moreover, investors who preferred (or were required) to purchase only short-term securities were able to obtain a short-term instrument reset off a long-term rate—a combination not previously available.

Ex-post, however, FROGs have turned out not to be attractive investments. If the yield curve had steepened, FROGs would have performed well. With the yield curve flattening and inverting in 1989, FROGs have performed poorly and no new issues have come to market since late 1988.

Creating Floating-Rate Debt

We now consider funding alternatives that have enabled issuers to create synthetic floating-rate debt. The two most common alternatives are as follows: (1) a fixed rate optionless bond plus a vanilla swap and (2) a callable bond plus a callable swap. Less commonly used alternatives include put bonds combined with putable swaps and FROGs combined with yield curve swaps. We examine each of these in turn.

Synthetic Floating Using Vanilla Swaps

Companies with well-known names and high credit ratings have taken advantage of very inexpensive fixed-rate financing in the Eurobond market.[5] In fact, many of these entities have been foreign banks that actually prefer floating-rate financing because their loan portfolio is primarily floating rate. To see how an issuer might create synthetic floating-rate assets, we start by assuming that the firm can raise 10-year fixed-rate funds at only 50 bp over the 10-year Treasury (T_{10}) bond rate. The swap rate is LIBOR against T_{10} + 70 bp. Using the swap market, the firm can create synthetic floating-rate debt at LIBOR minus 20 bp. If the firm issued the debt directly, it would issue at LIBOR. This is illustrated below:

Instrument	Action	Cash Flow
Fixed Rate Bond	Firm pays	T_{10} + 50 bp
Swap	Firm receives	T_{10} + 70 bp
	Firm pays	LIBOR
Synthetic Fixed	Net payment	LIBOR − 20 bp

5. For a discussion of the cost savings from Eurobond financing, see Wayne Marr and John Trimble, "The Persistent Borrowing Advantage in Eurodollars: A Plausible Explanation," which appeared in the Summer 1988 issue of this journal.

Thus, the firm ends up paying LIBOR minus 20 bp for its funds, 20 bp less than the cost of issuing new floating rate debt at LIBOR flat.

Transforming Callable Debt into Floating-Rate Debt. Issuers can create synthetic floating-rate financing by using a callable bond and a callable swap. The rate on this financing will be less than on a straight floating-rate issue whenever the issuer is able to purchase a call option from investors (the call option that is embedded in the debt) for substantially less than the swap market is willing to pay for the call option.

The mechanics of this transaction are similar to those described in the previous section for transforming callable debt into noncallable debt. The firm issues callable debt and enters into a callable swap (as illustrated earlier in Exhibit 2). The difference in this case is that there is no vanilla swap.

Let us consider the payoffs from this combination under different scenarios. If rates are higher at the call date than they were at the time of issue, neither the bond nor the swap will be called, and the issuer will obtain floating funding until maturity. If rates are lower at the call date than at issue, the issuer will call the bond. The counterparty will terminate the swap. Thus, if rates go down, the issuer will have floating money until the call date.

The issuer, then, has issued floating-rate funding for a period either to call or to maturity. If interest rates are lower, the issuer has locked in floating rate debt for only the time until the call. If interest rates go up, he locks in floating-rate money until maturity—a desirable situation.

Transforming Putable Debt into Floating-Rate Debt. Putable debt can be transformed into floating-rate debt by pairing a put bond with a putable swap. This is similar to transforming putable debt into optionless fixed-rate debt (as illustrated in Exhibit 3). In this case there is no need for the vanilla swap.

Let us now consider the payoffs from this combination under different scenarios. Assume a firm issues 10-year money, putable at the investor's option after year 5. If rates turn out to be higher at the put date than at the issue date, the bond will be put and the swap in which the issuer pays floating and receives fixed will be terminated. The issuer can raise new floating rate money during years 6-10 at par. Thus, the issuer has floating money over the 10-year period. If rates decline, the bond remains outstanding and the swap remains outstanding. The net result

here is also floating-rate money over the 10-year period.

Transforming FROGs Into Floating-Rate Debt. FROGs are frequently transformed into floating-rate rather than fixed-rate debt. This is done by pairing a FROG with a yield curve swap. The issuer pays the long-term Treasury rate less a spread on the FROG. Again, the long-term rate is reset every six months. The issuer then enters into a yield curve swap in which he pays six-month LIBOR and receives the long-term Treasury rate, reset every six months, less a spread.

Creating Callable Debt

Issuers with access to the U.S. long-term fixed-rate debt markets have generally not found it economical to replicate callable debt. However, there are certain issuers, such as U.S. savings and loan associations, that have been unable to borrow economically in these markets. These issuers have occasionally used the swap market to transform fixed- and floating-rate debt into long-term callable debt. In other instances, issuers that do have access to the corporate market prefer instead to issue debt using a medium-term note strategy, with which they can bring a small issue or an odd amount to market. Medium-term notes are noncallable.

Long-term callable debt can be created from long-term noncallable fixed-rate debt by purchasing a back-end floating swaption. If rates decline, the swap will be activated and the issuer will pay floating and receive fixed. Consider an issuer of five-year noncallable debt who has purchased a back-end floating swaption for years four and five. If rates remain high, the issuer will have five-year debt. If rates decline, the issuer will have three-year fixed-rate debt.

A floating-rate issue can be transformed into fixed-rate debt through combination with a vanilla swap and then be made callable by purchasing a back-end floating swaption.

Creating Putable Debt

We now consider a synthetic alternative to a put bond issued in the marketplace. The most common synthetic put bond is constructed by combining a callable bond issue with the sale of both a back-end fixed swaption and a back-end floating swaption. By holding both these options, the swap counterparty has a one-time right either (1) to make the issuer pay the fixed-rate versus receiving floating (by exercising the back-end fixed swaption) or (2) to make the issuer receive fixed (by exercising the back-end floating swaption) and pay floating.

The swap counterparty, to repeat, purchases two options. The effect of one (the back-end fixed swaption) is to cancel the embedded option on the call, and the effect of the other (the floating swaption) is to create the put that is inherent in a putable bond.

Let us use the example of a five-year issue, callable in three years. At the end of three years, the results under alternative interest rate scenarios are shown below:

Scenario	Swap	Issuer	Result
Interest rates rise higher after three years.	Issuer caused to receive fixed and pay floating for years four and five.	No action.	Issuer has ended up with three-year followed by two-year floating-rate money.
Interest rates are lower after three years.	Issuer caused to pay fixed and receive floating for two years.	Issuer calls issue, funds floating-rate.	Issuer has ended up with five-year rate money.

As with a regular put bond, if rates fall the issuer has ended up with five-year fixed-rate money. If rates rise the issuer has ended up with three years of fixed funding and two years of floating funding.

The major difference between a synthetic put bond and a real put bond is that, with a synthetic put bond, the issuer has to raise funds in the floating-rate market if rates fall. With a real put bond, the issuer has to borrow in the floating rate market if rates rise. This is important to some issuers, such as banks and finance companies, that are more concerned about funding in a higher-rate than in a lower-rate environment.

Note that whatever cost savings can be achieved by using a synthetic rather than a straightforward put bond depend upon investors' pricing the call option for less than the swap market. By contrast, swap counterparties will pay full value for that call and a further significant premium for the right to buy the put.

A less commonly used variation on the synthetic put bond has been accomplished by issuing fixed-rate noncallable debt and selling a back-end fixed swaption. This eliminates the arbitrage opportunity in the call option. Assume the debt is issued for a five-year period, and the back-end fixed swaption can be exercised at the end of year three. The swaption will be exercised and the issuer will have received fixed and paid floating for years four and five if rates are lower.

This transaction could also be done by using floating-rate debt as the initial issue. Such debt could then be transformed into fixed debt by means of a five-year swap. It could then be further transformed into a synthetic put bond with a back-end fixed option.

LOCKING IN THE COST OF A FUTURE ISSUANCE

While the major use of swaps centers on altering the character of a current bond issue, issuers also apply strategies involving the swap market to expected future issuances. For example, a company that expects rates to rise may want to lock in a fixed cost on a future issuance by using a forward swap (also known as a "delayed start" swap). A corporate treasurer who expects interest rates to remain steady or decline while credit spreads widen may wish to lock in a generic credit spread by means of a "spread lock." We examine each of these in turn.

Forward Swaps

A forward swap is exactly like a regular interest rate swap transaction, except that the accruals begin on a future date—normally the expected date of the bond issuance. A forward swap is usually combined with a floating-rate issue in order to lock in a fixed rate.

Consider the following example. A firm enters into a three-month forward swap agreeing to pay the current five-year Treasury rate plus 75 bp. In return, the firm will receive six-month LIBOR. The notional amount of the swap will be the same as that of the anticipated debt issue. In three months the firm issues floating-rate debt. Six months after the issuance, the first payments are exchanged. The firm pays the fixed rate available at the time the swap was entered into and receives six-month LIBOR. The LIBOR payment is used to pay the interest on the floating-rate debt.

The net cost of the issuance will be the fixed rate on the swap plus the difference between six-month LIBOR and the floating rate at which the firm issues its debt. If the firm issues floating-rate debt at six-month LIBOR + 25 bp, its all-in funding cost will be the five-year Treasury yield plus the 75 bp swap spread plus the 25 bp margin on the floating-rate debt. Note that the only component not locked in is the margin on the floating-rate debt.

If the firm later issues floating-rate debt off a different index from LIBOR, it can realize cost savings but will incur basis risk. If, for example, the firm issues floating-rate debt at the commercial paper rate, the cost of funds to the firm will be less than the five-year Treasury yield plus 75 bp, reflecting the fact that the commercial paper rate is below LIBOR.

Forward swaps are most attractive for issuers that like the current level of interest rates and expect a rate increase in the future, but do not currently need funding. Entering into a forward swap locks in the rate without forcing the issuer to fund immediately.

Spread Locks

A spread lock allows an issuer to fix the credit spread without fixing the base rate. Thus, a spread lock can be viewed as a tool to hedge the general level of corporate spreads. A spread lock is most effective when a firm knows it will have to come to market within a relatively short time—two or three months.

In a spread lock, the issuer agrees to enter into a swap deal at a specified spread to Treasuries but delays fixing the base Treasury rate for a period ranging up to two or three months. In other words, the issuer must fix the base interest rate by the end of the period, but may choose to fix the rate anytime within that period. When the base rate is eventually fixed, the pre-specified swap spread is added to arrive at the fixed rate payable on the swap. If Treasury rates fall over near term, the firm is able to take advantage of the decline.

To see how a spread lock would work, assume that a firm wants a spread lock for the next two months. At the end of the two-month period—or earlier if Treasury rates look attractive in the interim—the firm issues floating-rate debt and takes down the swap (in which it pays fixed and receives floating). Assume that the fixed swap spread is 80 bp and its issuing rate is LIBOR + 25bp. The firm will, on net, pay the Treasury rate prevailing at the time the swap is taken down plus 105 bp (80 + 25).[6]

A spread lock will be used if the firm does not expect rates to rise, but is concerned that credit spreads may widen. Issuers should note, however, that the spread lock does not hedge their firm-specific credit spread, but rather a general credit market spread.

MANAGING CORPORATE INTEREST RATE EXPOSURES BY ALTERING THE CASH FLOWS ON AN EXISTING LIABILITY

Companies can also use swaps to alter the cash flow on an existing liability, in a variety of ways: (1) by entering into a swap in order to fix the payment on an existing floating liability; (2) by entering into a swap in order to turn an existing fixed payment security into a floating-rate liability, and (3) by entering into a forward swap to lock in attractive interest rates after the call date on existing debt with in-the-money call options.

Fixing a Payment on a Floating-Rate Issue

A firm can convert a floating rate issue into a fixed-rate instrument by using a swap in which the issuer receives floating and pays fixed. The fixed rate is the then-prevailing fixed rate. Thus, when interest rate levels look attractive and a firm feels vulnerable to higher rates, it can lock its floating debt into a fixed rate through the use of the swap market.

Converting an Existing Fixed-Rate Bond

Similarly, a firm that has initially issued fixed-rate debt can also convert that debt to floating rate through the swap market. In this instance, the firm pays floating and receives fixed. If market rates have changed, the fixed rate at which the firm issued the debt is different from the prevailing fixed rate. The firm can either receive the fixed rate prevailing in the swap market, or match its own funding cost with an upfront payment if rates have declined or with an upfront receipt if rates have risen.

This is not, it is important to note, a means of escaping high-coupon debt in a declining rate environment. It does, however, provide a way for the firm to benefit from a further future reduction in rates.

To give an example, we assume that three years ago a firm issued fixed-rate 10-year noncallable debt at 11%. The firm now wishes to convert this debt to floating-rate debt. The swap market is such that the firm currently would have to pay LIBOR to receive 70 bp over the rate on seven-year Treasury notes (T_7+70 bp, or 9.70%). If the firm entered into a market swap, its cash flows would be as follows:

---

6. A spread lock is typically offered at a 2-4 bp premium over the straight swap. The premium exists because of the swap counterparty's hedging cost. The swap counterparty will short Treasury securities and invest the proceeds in short-term instruments until the swap is taken down. The negative carry during the hedge period is figured into the quoted spread. Thus, 150 bp of negative carry for two months is $0.25 per $100 par, or 2.5 bp for a seven-year issue.

Instrument	Action	Cash Flow
Bond	Firm pays	11.00%
Swap	Firm receives	(9.70%)
	Firm pays	LIBOR
Synthetic Floater	Net payment	LIBOR + 130 bp

Note that the firm is paying LIBOR + 130 bp. The large increment over LIBOR reflects the fact that the firm has above-market (11%) noncallable debt outstanding. It cannot escape this obligation. If rates decline further, however, the LIBOR financing will prove more attractive than the fixed rate financing. If rates increase, the reverse will be true.

Alternatively, the firm could enter into an off-market swap in which it pays an upfront amount in order to pay LIBOR and receive 11% on the swap. The upfront payment would reflect the 130 bp per annum, capitalized into an upfront sum, as shown below:

Instrument	Action	All-in Cost per Annum
Bond	Firm pays	11.00%
Swap	Firm receives	(11.00%)
	Firm pays	LIBOR
	Firm pays upfront $6.50	130 bp
Synthetic Floater	Net payment	LIBOR + 130 bp

Note the present value of the all-in costs is roughly the same if the firm accepts a market swap or an off-market swap.

If rates have risen and the issuer is convinced they have peaked, it may want to swap an outstanding fixed-rate issue into a floating-rate obligation. This allows the issuer to benefit from lower rates in the future. The issuer could opt for a swap at market rates, or for an off-market swap in which it accepts a below-market rate on the swap plus an upfront payment.

To give an example, let's assume that three years ago a firm had issued 8.00% debt for 10 years. In the swap market, this firm could pay LIBOR and receive $T_7 + 70$ bp, or 9.70%. If the firm agreed to a swap at now-current rates, its cash flows would be as follows:

Instrument	Action	Cash Flow
Bond	Firm pays	8.00%
Swap	Firm receives	(9.70%)
	Firm pays	LIBOR
Synthetic Floater	Net payment	LIBOR − 170 bp

The net payment of LIBOR minus 170 bp reflects the fact that the firm had below-market debt on its books.

If the firm wanted an off-market swap, the all-in cost would be as follows:

Instrument	Action	All-in Cost
Bond	Firm pays	8.00%
Swap	Firm receives	(9.70%)
	Firm pays	LIBOR
	Firm receives $8.50 upfront	(170 bp)
Synthetic Floater	Net payment	LIBOR − 170 bp

In both cases, the firm's all-in cost is the same. With an off-the-market swap, the firm is compensated for accepting a below-market rate on the swap.

Thus, if converting fixed-rate debt to floating-rate debt is designed only to take advantage of an expected fall in rates, any fall or rise that has already occurred will be built into the price of the swap. Nonetheless, if further changes in rates are anticipated, a review of outstanding liabilities is in order.

Locking in Attractive Interest Rates on Existing High-Coupon Debt

Forward swaps can be used to lock in future rates on outstanding callable debt. To see how this can be done, assume that a firm has 14.00% debt outstanding, originally issued in 1984. The debt matures in 10 years, or 1994. It is callable in 1991. If the notes were currently callable, the issuer would call the bond and refinance with lower-cost debt. However, since the notes are not callable for some years, the company must leave the bonds outstanding until the call date and continue to pay the 14.00% coupon.

If the company feels that interest rates will rise by 1991 and eliminate some or all of the benefits of today's relatively low interest rates, the issuer can execute a forward swap. Essentially, this would lock in current forward rates. In other words, the firm can enter into a three-year swap effective two years from now in which it agrees to pay fixed and receive floating. We will assume here that the firm can lock in a 10% fixed rate on this swap.

This strategy leaves the company with a great deal of flexibility on the call date. If interest rates turn out to be lower than 14% on the call date, the firm could refinance on a floating-rate basis. The floating payments on the debt would be offset by payments on the swap. The firm's all-in cost would be the 10% fixed rate plus (minus) its issuing cost above (below) LIBOR.

If the firm wanted to refinance at a fixed rate, the forward swap could be sold. The cash settlement to (or by) the issuer will be equal to the present value of the difference between the forward rate swap and the market rate for new swaps with a three-year maturity. If rates turn out to be higher than 10%, the issuer will receive a payment. If rates prove to be lower than 10.0%, the issuer will pay the cash settlement from the sale of the swap.

There is a third alternative, as well. Say the firm wants to refinance with a fixed rate, but rates are lower and the issuer is reluctant to buy out the forward swap. As an alternative, it could enter into an offsetting spot transaction. To see how this might work, assume the fixed rate is 9%, and the firm has locked in a 10% forward swap. The forward swap can be offset on the call date as follows:

Instrument	Action	Cash Flow
Original Bond	Called	
New Bond	Firm pays	9.00%
Forward Swap	Firm receives	(LIBOR)
	Firm pays	10.00%
New Swap	Firm receives	(9.00%)
	Firm pays	LIBOR
Fixed + Swap	Net payment	10.00%

Note that the firm has locked in the 10% rate. The rate on the new bond is 9.00%, and the 1% per annum loss on the forward swap takes the form of a higher net payment.

So far we have assumed that the interest rates on the call date are below 14% and that the issue will be called. The forward swap does not affect the company's ability to leave the issue outstanding if rates are above 14% on the call date. In this instance, if the issuer chooses to leave the issue outstanding, it could sell the forward swap. The windfall profit on the forward swap would be the difference between the then-current market rates for a three-year period. Thus, the forward swap locks in the "intrinsic value" of the call option.[7] It does not, however, extinguish the option. And it can gain further value in the future if rates rise sufficiently.

CONCLUSION

The primary corporate uses of interest rate swaps are to reduce corporate exposures to interest rate movements by altering the cash flow pattern of outstanding debt, to reduce the cost of a current issuance by "arbitraging" disparities between debt and swap markets, and to lock in the cost or spread of an expected future issue. Historically, much of the corporate use of swaps has centered on reducing the cost of a current issue. Prior to the introduction of swaps, companies had to issue debt into the ultimately desired form. For example, companies wanting long-term fixed-rate noncallable debt had to include all the desired features in the issue itself. There was no way to transform callable debt into noncallable or putable debt.

With swaps, however, debt can be easily and inexpensively transformed from one form into another. Issuers have sometimes been able to obtain the desired form of debt synthetically at a lower cost than by a direct issuance. This arises, in part, because the swap market allowed issuers to take advantage of differential pricing between the new issue bond market and the swap market. Call options, for example, appear to be cheaper in the bond market than in the swap market. Floating-rate issues can be less expensive than fixed-rate issues for lower-rated issuers. In addition, certain new structures can give investors their desired risk-return trade-off while allowing the issuer to end up with what looks like conventional debt.

Issuers can also lock in the cost of a future issue through a forward swap. Spread locks can be used to lock in generic credit spreads. Finally, the swap market allows issuers to transform floating rates on outstanding debt into fixed rates, and fixed rates into floating (although off-market swaps are generally necessary to equate cash flows on a new swap with those on the old debt).

Swaps, in short, are highly versatile and cost-effective instruments for managing corporate liabilities. They have transformed liability management into a more active undertaking, one that involves not only evaluating what is desirable for current issuances, but also re-evaluating past issues and anticipating those of the future.

---

7. The "intrinsic value" is the value of the option if exercised immediately.

Forward Swaps, Swap Options, and the Management of Callable Debt

by Keith C. Brown, *University of Texas at Austin*, and Donald J. Smith, *Boston University*

C ompanies issuing intermediate- to long-term fixed-rate bonds generally choose to attach call provisions to those issues. Such a call provision gives management the *option* to buy back the bonds (usually at a slight premium over par) after a specified period of "call protection." After the call protection period, if interest rates have fallen below the rate on the outstanding issue, management can reduce its cost of funds by calling and refunding the issue with lower-cost debt.[1]

A good deal of academic work has been devoted to the problem of when a corporation should call its outstanding bond issues. The consensus to date is that it is optimal to exercise the refinancing option as soon as the bond trades in the market at a price sufficiently greater than its contractual call price to cover the transactions costs of refunding.[2] This decision rule and the supporting analysis are based, of course, on the assumption that it is possible to call the bond whenever it is advantageous to the issuer—that is, the bond is no longer "call-protected."

The problem this paper addresses is somewhat different: What if interest rates have fallen significantly since the bond was originally placed, but the call provision cannot be exercised for several more years?

A callable bond that is still in its deferment, or protection, period contains what amounts to a European-style, but unmarketable option. It is like a European option, which cannot be exercised until maturity, in the sense that its exercise must be deferred to a future "call" date. Further, since it is attached to the underlying bond, it cannot be sold directly as a separate instrument.

The option's current value to the issuer—that is, the value of the option if exercised today—is roughly equivalent to the difference between the price of the callable bond and the price of the same issue if it were noncallable. Alternatively, the intrinsic value of the option can be thought of as the present value of the cost savings that management could achieve by retiring the issue at the date of first call and then issuing a (noncallable) fixed-rate issue at today's lower interest rates.[3]

As the holder of this surrogate call option on interest rates, management has three choices: (1) it can wait until the protection period ends, thus risking future increases in rates (which would reduce the current value of the call option) while benefiting from further declines; (2) it can take steps to preserve the value of the option until it can be exercised by hedging against future increases in rates; or (3) it can attempt to find a way to effectively "sell" the option to a third party.

Taking the first approach, management can capture part of the value of the call feature immediately by refunding the entire outstanding debt

1. Financial theorists have argued that, in a capital market free from "imperfections," the inclusion of such covenants would be a matter of indifference to issuers. That is, in a world without taxes, transaction costs, and informational "asymmetries," the cost of the call to issuers in the form of higher interest rates required by bond market investors should equal the expected benefits.

However, several recent studies have presented cogent explanations for the pervasiveness of callable bonds based on the tax and informational asymmetries that exist between the firm's various agents and investors. See, for instance, Z. Bodie and B. Taggart, "Future Investment Opportunities and the Value of the Call Provision on a Bond," *Journal of Finance* 33 (September 1978), pp. 1187-1200, A. Barnea, R. Haugen and L. Senbet, "A Rationale for Debt Maturity Structure and Call Provisions in the Agency Theory Framework," *Journal of Finance* 35 (December 1980), pp. 1223-1234 and I. Brick and B. Wallingford, "The Relative Tax Benefits of Alternative Call Features in Corporate Debt," *Journal of Financial and Quantitative Analysis* 20 (March 1985), pp. 95-105.

2. On this point, see A. Kraus, "The Bond Refunding Decision in an Efficient Market," *Journal of Financial and Quantitative Analysis* 8 (December 1973), pp. 793-806. For a less technical version of the same, see "The Corporate Refunding Decision," *Midland Corporate Finance Journal* (Stern Stewart & Co., publisher), Vol. 1 No. 1 (Spring 1983).

3. Assuming a common coupon rate and maturity date.

through a tender offer or open market repurchase program while issuing new noncallable bonds as replacements. There are, however, major uncertainties in implementing such a bond repurchase program. In the case of a tender offer, management fixes the repurchase price (typically at a significant premium over market), but has no direct control over the quantity of bonds that are actually tendered.[4] With a direct market repurchase, by contrast, management faces considerable uncertainty about the average price necessary to buy back the outstanding bonds, especially in the case of large debt issues. Moreover, to the extent management is forced to pay a price above the call premium, such buyback strategies effectively give away much of the current option value—which derives from the firm's right to retire the debt at a fixed price over par.[5]

Over the last few years, investment and commercial banks have promoted the use of interest rate swaps with delayed starting dates (or "forward swaps") and options on swaps ("swaptions") as ways of reducing the uncertainty attending the above refunding strategies. As a number of scholars have pointed out, an interest rate swap is essentially a series of over-the-counter forward contracts, wherein two counterparties agree to exchange fixed for floating payments based on a notional principal amount.[6] Because of their forward-like structure, swaps are ideal vehicles for hedging "symmetric" interest rate risks—for example, situations in which an increase in rates leads to a proportionate decrease in the value of the asset and vice versa. Companies seeking to realize the current value of their embedded call options, presumably to protect against rises in market rates between now and the call date, can use either a forward swap or a swap option in a hedging scheme similar to those using exchange-traded futures and options on futures.

The key difference between the use of swaps and exchange-traded instruments in call management is that swaps are flexible, negotiated contracts that can be tailored by a market-maker to match the dates and amount of the targeted call provision. That flexibility can be used to improve the hedge by reducing its basis risk. Further, it allows callable debt

management strategies for deferment periods extending beyond the relatively short delivery dates of available futures contracts. In sum, the swap-based hedging techniques described in this paper represent advances over both traditional capital market refunding strategies and the use of exchange-traded financial futures and options.

FORWARD SWAPS AND CALLABLE DEBT

Forward swaps can be used to manage callable debt in two different ways. First, management can preserve the value of an (in-the-money) option to call its own debt by entering into an "on-market" forward swap—that is, a delayed-start swap agreement at the prevailing market (forward) swap rate set to begin at the date of first call. This would effectively "lock in" the current level of interest rates until the call exercise date. Alternatively, it can choose a forward swap rate different from the current rate (thus creating an "off-market" forward swap) and thereby capture immediately (or "monetize") the present value of the bond's call option.

Preserving the Value of the Call With an On-Market Forward Swap

Let us start by assuming that if rates have fallen significantly since a callable bond was originally issued, management would choose to sell the call option (thereby locking in current rates) if it could indeed be separated from the host bond. The problem arises from the fact that the embedded call cannot be separated and sold as such.

This is a classic hedging problem: rates could rise or fall by more than is generally expected during the time until the call date. If rates rise, the call option loses value; if rates fall, the call gains value. Management's concern is that interest rates might rise prior to the call date, reducing or even wiping out the value of the option. If management is uncomfortable with the uncertainty of these outcomes, a negatively correlated position in another instrument can be acquired to serve as a hedge. The objective

4. Bond tender offers are, on average, only 76% successful at obtaining the desired number of outstanding instruments. See J. Finnerty, A. Kalotay and F. Farrell, *Evaluating Bond Refunding Opportunities*, Hagerstown: Ballinger Publishing (1988).

5. Note that exercising an option that could be sold on the market captures only the "intrinsic value" and forgoes the remaining "time value." This approach can lead to a deadweight loss in the option's value due to the extinguishment of

the benefits associated with potential exercise features. See M. Livingston, "Measuring the Benefit of a Bond Refunding: The Problem of Non Marketable Call Options," *Financial Management* 16 (Spring 1987), pp. 38-40.

6. For a background discussion on the swap market, see C. Smith, C. Smithson and L. Wakeman, "The Evolving Market for Swaps," *Midland Corporate Finance Journal* Vol. 3 No. 4 (Winter 1985).

THE DESIGN FLEXIBILITY AND EASE OF OPERATIONAL MANAGEMENT OF
INTEREST RATE SWAP CONTRACTS CAN ALSO BE USED TO REDUCE THE
BASIS RISK IN THE HEDGING STRATEGY THAT OFTEN ATTENDS THE USE OF
FINANCIAL FUTURES.

EXHIBIT 1	**Years**			
MARKER EVENTS IN THE CALL MANAGEMENT PROBLEM	0	2	4	7
	Original Issue Date	Current Date	Call Date	Maturity Date

of the hedge is to smooth the range of future payoffs, if not indeed to "lock in" the future value of the asset. (It should be noted, however, that one can only hedge against unexpected changes because the forward rates used in hedging already reflect market expectations.)

The most obvious means of hedging the interest rate risk is to take a short position in a financial futures contract. The short position would gain when interest rates rise and thus futures prices fall. An alternative would be to buy a put option on the futures contract. The put option, which upon exercise allows the holder to acquire a short position in the futures contract at the strike price, would also appreciate in value as rates rise.

The problem with exchange-traded futures and futures options, however, is often the absence of a suitable contract. The call date on the bond can be several years away, but liquidity in the futures market (and indeed the availability of the futures option) usually is limited to the nearest delivery months. Also, futures contracts require frequent managerial attention to deal with the margin account and daily mark-to-market valuation and settlement.

Forward interest rate swaps, by contrast, are over-the-counter, directly negotiated instruments that represent the hedging equivalent of financial futures contracts. In particular, as we shall demonstrate later, a "pay-fixed" forward swap is functionally equivalent to a short position in futures in terms of reducing the interest rate risk in the future value of the call option. Moreover, the design flexibility and ease of operational management of interest rate swap contracts can also be used to reduce the basis risk in the hedging strategy that often attends the use of financial futures.

A Simple Case. A numerical example will be useful to illustrate the use of forward swaps to preserve the call rate. Suppose that two years ago a corporation issued $100 million in seven-year 12% coupon bonds at par value. Assume also that the bonds pay coupons semi-annually, the issue was originally callable at par in four years, and two years remain in the call protection period. (See Exhibit 1.)

Now suppose that an on-market, $100 million notional principal forward swap is available such that the corporation could pay 10.25% and receive six-month LIBOR for three years, starting two years from now. This forward swap is simply a deferred-start transaction. The deferral period corresponds to (and is set to equal) the time remaining in the call protection period; and the maturity (or "tenor") of the swap corresponds to the remaining maturity on the underlying bonds as of the call date. There is no initial cash settlement on the transaction, hence the term "on-market" swap. (As we will discuss later, an "off-market" swap would require an initial payment from one counterparty to another.)

This on-market forward swap agreement will appreciate in value if interest rates rise over the next two years by more than had been generally expected (as reflected in the forward swap rate). The gain on the swap, like that on a comparable short position in interest rate futures, would offset the decline in the value of the call option. Unlike the use of futures, however, the timing of the forward swap can be set to match exactly the call and maturity dates—an outcome that would only occur by coincidence with standardized, exchange-traded futures.

Pricing Forward Swaps. The fixed rates on forward swaps are determined by the rates available in the current swap spot market—that is, for swaps that begin at once. Suppose that a company could simultaneously enter a five-year, pay-fixed swap at 9.75% and a two-year, receive-fixed swap at 9.00%, both versus six-month LIBOR. As illustrated in Exhibit 2, that combination of swaps effectively constructs a three-year, pay-fixed (since the initial LIBOR flows cancel) swap that is deferred for two years. Unless the two-year and five-year fixed rates are identical (which is highly unlikely), there will be a remaining fixed rate payment or receipt during the initial "stub" period.

Pricing the forward swap, then, is basically an exercise in the time value of money. The problem is to transfer the first four cash payments forward in time and spread them evenly amongst the latter six. In practice this is done using implied forward rates

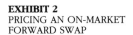

EXHIBIT 2
PRICING AN ON-MARKET
FORWARD SWAP

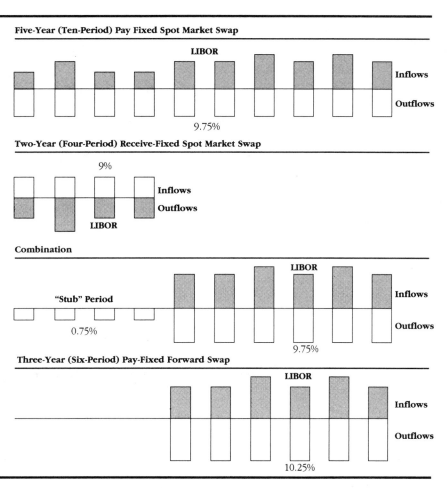

Five-Year (Ten-Period) Pay Fixed Spot Market Swap

LIBOR

Inflows

Outflows

9.75%

Two-Year (Four-Period) Receive-Fixed Spot Market Swap

9%

Inflows

Outflows

LIBOR

Combination

LIBOR

"Stub" Period

Inflows

Outflows

0.75%

9.75%

Three-Year (Six-Period) Pay-Fixed Forward Swap

LIBOR

Inflows

Outflows

10.25%

derived from a zero-coupon swap yield curve. Here, and in the continuation of this example that follows, we simply assume that the result of that exercise is a forward swap fixed rate of 10.25%.

The effectiveness, and inherent risks, of this forward swap hedging strategy can be demonstrated by considering the various decisions that must be made at the call date in two years. First, management must decide whether to call the underlying debt. It is reasonable to assume that it will do so only if the fixed-rate cost of funds for the remaining three years turns out to be lower than 12%. Second, if the debt is called, management must decide if it will refinance with fixed- or floating-rate debt. Third, it must decide if it will retain the swap or close it out by entering into an offsetting, receive-fixed swap. If management wants to continue with fixed-rate funding, then

the second and third decisions are not independent: If the swap is closed out, the firm can just issue fixed-rate notes; but if the swap is retained, management will have to issue LIBOR-based floating-rate debt to obtain a net fixed-rate cost of funds.

A Digression on The Relationship between Swap and Bond Spreads. At this point it is necessary to introduce some notation to describe the relevant market rates prevailing at the call date in two years. Following market conventions, we decompose all fixed rates into the Treasury yield (T) for a comparable maturity (in this case, three years) and a spread over that Treasury yield. For example, the three-year fixed-rate cost of funds is denoted $T + BS$, where BS stands for "bond (market) spread." In a similar fashion, the fixed rate on a three-year swap (versus six-month LIBOR) is denoted $T + SS$, where

EXHIBIT 3
CALL VALUE PRESERVATION
USING AN ON-MARKET
FORWARD SWAP

	Treasury Yield (T)			
	9%	10%	11%	12%
Refunding Fixed Rate (T + BS)	9.75%	10.75%	11.75%	12.75%
Decision	Call	Call	Call	Not Call
Value of the Call Option	$1,125,000	$625,000	$125,000	0
Swap Fixed Rate (T + SS)	9.50%	10.50%	11.50%	12.50%
Gain on the Forward Swap	− $375,000	$125,000	$625,000	$1,125,000
Total Gain	$750,000	$750,000	$750,000	$1,125,000
Present Value	$3,822,034	$3,761,539	$3,702,522	$5,467,406

Numerical Example Assuming BS = 0.75%, CS = 0.25%, and SS = 0.50%
Value of the Call Option (as an Annuity) = (12% − Refunding Fixed Rate) × ($\frac{1}{2}$) × $100 Million,
Gain on the Forward Swap (as an Annuity) = (Swap Fixed Rate − 10.25%) × ($\frac{1}{2}$) × $100 Million
Total Gain = Value of the Call Option plus the Gain on the Forward Swap
Present Value (as of the Call Date) of the Total Gain per Semi-Annual Period for Six Remaining Semi-Annual Periods, Discounted at the Refunding Fixed Rate

SS means "swap (market) spread." The reset rate for a three-year floating rate note is LIBOR + CS, where CS stands for "credit (market) spread."[7]

When the swap market is "in equilibrium," the general relationship between these three spreads is that SS = BS − CS—that is, the swap spread equals the bond spread minus the credit spread. We assume that the corporation at the call date in two years can either issue fixed-rate debt at T + BS or floating-rate debt at LIBOR + CS. Then suppose that it issues fixed-rate debt and also enters a swap agreement to receive a fixed rate of T + SS and to pay LIBOR. Its net "synthetic" floating-rate cost of funds would be LIBOR + (BS − SS) since the fixed Treasury yield (T) cancels out. In equilibrium, that floating rate should equal the explicit floating rate of LIBOR + CS; and simple algebra tells us that BS − SS = CS.[8]

The Effectiveness of Forward Swaps as a Hedge. Exhibit 3 shows the results of the forward swap hedge assuming four different interest rate outcomes. On the call date, Treasury yields are allowed to range from 9% to 12% (while bond credit and swap spreads are assumed to remain fixed, and in equilibrium, at BS = 0.75%, CS = 0.25%, and SS = 0.50%).

For example, if the three-year Treasury yield turns out to be 10% at the time of the call date, the corporation is assumed (1) to call and refund its 12% debt with a three-year fixed-rate note at 10.75% and (2) to close out its pay-fixed 10.25% forward swap by entering into a three-year receive-fixed swap at 10.50%. As shown in Exhibit 3 (third row, second column), the value of exercising the call option expressed as a six-period (three-year) annuity turns

---

7. BS and CS represent the issuing corporation's marginal risk relative to the Treasury yield and LIBOR in the fixed- and floating-rate markets, respectively. Those spreads depend largely on default risk, but also reflect any differing degrees of marketability, taxation, and so forth. Note that there is no particular reason for BS to equal CS since the former is expressed relative to risk-free Treasuries and the latter to "bank-risk," or LIBOR.

8. This discussion abstracts from the bid-ask spread on swaps in practice. Since the swap market-maker, typically a commercial or investment bank, will need to cover the credit risk inherent in the transaction as well as other hedging and regulatory (e.g., capital adequacy) costs, it will always quote a higher receive-fixed rate than its pay-fixed rate. The bid-ask spread has narrowed markedly in recent years as testimony to the competitiveness of the swap market and now ranges between 4-10 basis points.

out to be $625,000 per period (or [12.00% − 10.75%] × 1/2 × $100 million). The value of the forward swap hedge is also positive because management is able to close out the 10.25% pay-fixed forward swap with a 10.50% receive-fixed swap; and the per period savings are $125,000 per period ([10.50% − 10.25%] × 1/2 × $100 million) for the six remaining semi-annual periods. The sum of the two sources of gain, the call and the hedge, is an annuity of $750,000. The present value of that annuity, as of the call date, is $3,761,539, calculated using the 10.75% fixed rate cost of funds as the discounting factor.

The salient features of the call rate preservation strategy are apparent in this simulation exercise. As shown in Exhibit 3, the payoffs on closing out the pay-fixed forward swap are negatively correlated with the value of the call option. For the given values of BS, CS, and SS, the strategy "locks in" the future gain for varying levels of market rates. (Actually, the "locked in" value is a nominal annuity, the present value of which depends on the level of the rate used for discounting.) Notice, however, that although the net gain is constant when it is optimal to call the existing debt (that is, when the refunding rate is less than the existing rate), the gains rise when it is not optimal to call (i.e., when rates rise above 12%). This means that the forward swap strategy, in effect, "overhedges" the risk.

This "overhedging" arises from the use of a symmetric-payoff instrument like a futures contract or swap agreement to hedge an "asymmetric" or one-sided risk exposure. This asymmetric exposure in turn arises from the fact that management's option to call its bond has a minimum value of zero. (Remember that the issuer effectively paid for the call right in the form of a higher interest rate when it issued the bonds.) If the refunding rate exceeds 12%, the call option value falls to zero but is never negative; but the value of the forward swap hedge continues to rise proportionately with increases in rates above 12%.

If management wanted to eliminate (or at least minimize) this overhedging effect, then it would have to substitute the use of an asymmetric (or option-like) hedging instrument to offset its one-sided exposure. As we will show later in this paper, call monetization strategies using swap options instead of swaps can be used to accomplish this end.

The Problem of Basis Risk. The forward swap hedge, as illustrated in Exhibit 3, immunizes the corporation against changes in future Treasury yields. But, it is important to recognize that the amount of the future gain—and thus the effectiveness of the hedge—depends on the corporation's future refunding rates. Specifically, it depends on the firm-specific risk spreads represented by BS and CS, as well as on the swap spread SS.

Suppose that the credit standing of the corporation deteriorates at the time of the call date, such that BS rises to 0.95% while SS remains at 0.50%. The value of the call option falls for any level of T, while the payoff on closing out the swap hedge is unchanged. This shift in the bond spread relative to the swap spread lowers the net gain either as a future annuity or as a present value.

This type of basis risk is common in hedging programs. In effect, such hedging programs reduce general market interest rate risk while continuing to bear some spread risk. The assumption underlying these strategies is that the variance in the spread over Treasuries will be much less than the variance in the Treasury yield itself. Nevertheless it should be clear that the hedge does entail risk. As a worst-case scenario, suppose that the combined Treasury yield and swap spread remain less than 10.25%, and thus the forward swap can only be closed out at a loss, while the bond spread rises such that the call option value falls to zero. The corporation would be worse off for having hedged than not.

To assess the level of basis risk, it is instructive to break the annuity gain of $750,000 per period in our example into two components: a non-random part that depends on the existing coupon rate vis-a-vis the forward swap rate, and a random part that depends on the bond and swap spreads at the future call date. The first part is $875,000 per period, calculated as (12% − 10.25%) × 1/2 × $100 million. That amount is known with certainty at the current date when the hedging strategy is undertaken since both rates are observable. The second part, in general, is (SS − BS) × 1/2 × $100 million. In Exhibit 3, where it is assumed that SS = 0.50% and BS = 0.75%, this second amount is −$125,000 per period. Adding the two gives the annuity gain of $750,000. The key point here is that (SS − BS), the difference between the swap and bond market spreads over Treasuries, is the source of basis risk in the hedging program. (In a later section, we will examine some empirical evidence attesting to the size and variance of these spreads.)

Basis Risk Also Affects The Call Decision. Up to this point, we have assumed that when the call

EXHIBIT 4
PRICING AN OFF-MARKET
FORWARD SWAP

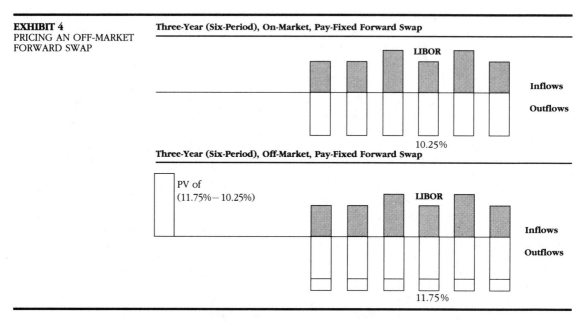

date arrives, the decision whether to call or not is made simply by comparing the current three-year fixed rate to the existing coupon rate; that is, if T + BS is less than 12%, management calls the bonds. Management also, however, has two other alternatives. It can call the debt and refund in the floating-rate market at LIBOR + CS and retain the swap to pay 10.25% and receive LIBOR. That alternative yields a net fixed-rate cost of funds of 10.25% + CS (since the LIBOR-based cash flows cancel). Or, it can choose not to call, maintain the 12% debt and close out the swap. That entails receiving T + SS while paying 10.25%; and the net cost of funds would be 12% + [10.25% − (T + SS)].

Given this analysis, the decision to call or not depends on a comparison of 10.25% + CS to 12% + [10.25% − (T + SS)]. Simplifying that comparison, the decision rule becomes to call if T + SS + CS is less than 12%. If swap markets are in equilibrium (and thus BS = SS + CS), then the two decision rules—one based on the fixed spread and one on the floating-plus-swap spread—will yield identical call decisions. If swap markets are not in equilibrium, then the two rules could produce conflicting decisions.

The importance of this last result is that there can be circumstances when a corporation appears to be making a sub-optimal call decision if only the fixed-rate cost of funds is observable. For instance, suppose that T = 11.30%, BS = 0.75%, CS = 0.20%,

and SS = 0.40% on the call date. The fixed-rate refunding alternative of 12.05% would indicate that the call option has a value of zero and that calling the debt would be irrational. At the same time, however, the (likely short-lived) disequilibrium in the swap market would allow the firm to call the debt, refund at LIBOR + 0.20%, and pay 10.25% on the forward swap, obtaining a net fixed rate of 10.45%. That strategy generates a six-period annuity gain of $775,000 per period, whereas not calling the debt and simply closing out the swap by agreeing to receive the current swap fixed rate of 11.70% against the payments of 10.25% generates an annuity gain of only $725,000. Naturally, in an efficient capital market one would not expect disequilibrium conditions like this to persist.

In summary, the future value of the firm's embedded call option depends on future interest rates. That risk exposure can be hedged in principle by short positions in financial futures contracts or by the use of pay-fixed forward swaps. While the forward swap can lock in some of the current value of the call option—although only the amount that reflects the generally expected level of future rates—there is still basis risk. In this context, the basis risk is represented by the relationship between the (fixed-rate) bond spread, the (floating-rate) credit spread, and the swap market spread. Unexpected changes in those spreads can reduce the effectiveness of the hedge.

EXHIBIT 5
CALL MONETIZATION USING
AN OFF-MARKET FORWARD
SWAP

	Treasury Yield (T)			
	9%	10%	11%	12%
Refunding Fixed Rate (T + BS)	9.75%	10.75%	11.75%	12.75%
Decision	Call	Call	Call	Not Call
Value of the Call Option	$1,125,000	$625,000	$125,000	0
Swap Fixed Rate (T + SS)	9.50%	10.50%	11.50%	12.50%
Gain on the Forward Swap	− $1,125,000	− $625,000	− $125,000	$375,000
Total Gain	0	0	0	$375,000
Present Value	0	0	0	$1,822,469

Numerical Example Assuming BS = 0.75%, CS = 0.25%, and SS = 0.50%
Value of the Call Option (as an Annuity) = (12% − Refunding Fixed Rate) × ($^1/_2$) × $100 Million,
Gain on the Forward Swap (as an Annuity) = (Swap Fixed Rate − 11.75%) × ($^1/_2$) × $100 Million
Total Gain = Value of the Call Option plus the Gain on the Forward Swap
Present Value (as of the Call Date) of the Total Gain per Semi-Annual Period for Six Remaining Semi-Annual Periods,
Discounted at the Refunding Fixed Rate

Monetizing the Call Value with an Off-Market Forward Swap

The use of an on-market, pay-fixed forward swap effectively locks in the future value of the call option, subject to the basis risk mentioned above. That future value, as we have seen, is an annuity that reflects the difference between the existing coupon rate and the forward swap rate multiplied by the principal. For instance, in Exhibit 3, the annuity (or semi-annuity) is a cost savings of $750,000 per period for six remaining semi-annual periods.

Call monetization, by contrast, refers to strategies that transform this deferred annuity into a single current cash payment that is equal to the present value of the series of payments. To return to our earlier example, management could monetize the value of the call by entering into a pay-fixed forward swap at 11.75% for three years instead of using the on-market

forward swap with a fixed rate of 10.25%. Of course, the corporation would be willing to pay the higher fixed rate only if it receives something in return—in fact, an immediate payment for the present value of the annuity represented by the difference between the rates. That annuity is $750,000 ([11.75% – 10.25%] × 1/2 × $100 million) for six semi-annual periods.

The actual amount of cash that the corporation will receive upon agreeing to the off-market forward swap will depend on the discount factors used to calculate the present value. Typically, a commercial bank is the counterparty to these swaps. The bank should view this off-market transaction as a combination of an on-market forward swap and a loan agreement. The on-market swap calls for no immediate exchange of cash; however, the bank is effectively lending the corporation a specific amount now and later expects to be repaid in six installments of $750,000. Based on this reasoning, the appropriate

---

9. Notice that if the corporation enters an off-market forward swap to pay fixed at less than 10.25%, it would effectively be making a deposit to the bank. Then, the bank's lower deposit rates would be used for discounting, thereby raising the amount of the requisite immediate payment.

discount factors are the bank's lending rate for zero-coupon transactions ("bullet" loans) maturing in 2 1/2 to 5 years (See Exhibit 4).[9]

The Effectiveness of an Off-Market Forward Hedge. The implications of hedging the call value with an off-market, forward swap are apparent in Exhibit 5 (which, like Exhibit 3, also assumes BS = 0.75%, CS = 0.25%, and SS = 0.50%, and T ranging from 9% to 12%). The structure by design has transferred the future gain of $750,000 per period to the current date. In cases when it would be optimal to call the debt (for example, when Treasury yields turn out to be 9, 10, or 11%), the value of the call option is completely offset by the loss on the forward swap. If rates rise to 12% or higher (and thus the call option's value falls to zero), there is a gain on the forward swap, thus leading to the same asymmetric outcome associated with the use of on-market swaps. As explained earlier, this overhedging phenomenon arises from the use of forward-based instruments with symmetric payoffs to hedge one-sided risks.

This strategy also contains the same basis risk that attends the use of on-market forward swaps: namely, that which results from possible changes in the relationship between the swap spread and the bond spread (SS − BS). The future annuity gain would be reduced for any level of T, and even could be negative, if BS turns out to be higher than 0.75% or SS lower than 0.50%.

For example, assume that on the current date the expected future values for BS, CS, and SS are 0.75%, 0.25%, and 0.50%, as in Exhibits 3 and 5. These expectations would likely be based on current spreads and the assumption of swap market equilibrium. In this case, the off-market forward swap rate of 11.75% is simply the one that makes the expected annuity gain zero (at least, over that range of interest rates when the call would be exercised). The corporation could have chosen any number of other forward rates—12%, for instance, to match the existing coupon rate.

In short, the choice of a different forward rate merely transfers the certain portion of the annuity gain from a future value to a present value, but it does not remove the basis risk.

SWAP OPTIONS AND CALLABLE DEBT[10]

Another way of monetizing the current value of the bond's embedded call option is through the use of swap options (also known as "swaptions"). In contrast to hedges with off-market forward swaps, the use of swaptions has the advantage of reducing the overhedging problem that affects forward swap-based hedging schemes. But these benefits are also accompanied by one new drawback: because the strategy requires the callable debt issuer to sell a swap option, the swaption holder must decide when to exercise the option, thereby introducing—as we shall see—another dimension of risk into the problem.

Because the market for options on swaps is not as well developed as the swap market itself, it might be helpful to begin this section with a brief description of the product. Broadly speaking, in exchange for a front-end premium, the holder of a swap option has the right, but not the obligation, to enter into a swap on or before a specific exercise date. The agreement also specifies which counterparty pays the fixed rate. By convention, the holder of the right to enter into a pay-fixed swap is said to own a call option; and the holder of the right to enter a receive-fixed swap is said to have a put. Finally, the swaption contract also designates the amount of notional principal, the level of the fixed rate (i.e., strike rate) and the particular index used to represent the floating rate (e.g., six-month LIBOR).

To extend the example of the previous section, assume once again that the firm holds an option to call its original $100 million of 12% debt and that it would like to convert this asset into cash today. But, because the call feature is·attached to the bond, it cannot be sold separately nor can it be exercised for another two years. What can be sold today is an option on a swap market transaction.

Monetizing the bond option in this context involves selling a swap option having terms set as closely as possible to those of the original debt issue. Specifically, the firm would sell a put option (i.e., the right to receive the fixed rate) on a three-year swap, exercisable in two years with a strike rate of 12% and notional principal of $100 million. In this case, the two-year expiration date on the swaption matches that on the bond option while the three-year swap tenor matches the difference between the bond's call date and its maturity.

Like the off-market forward swap strategy discussed earlier, the sale of a swap option converts the benefits of the call into an immediate receipt of cash.

---

10. The discussion in this section is an expanded version of a portion of our article "The Swap-Driven Deal," *Intermarket* 6 (March 1989), pp. 15-19.

EXHIBIT 6
SEMI-ANNUAL FUNDING
COST WITH THE SWAP
OPTION-BASED CALL
MONETIZATION STRATEGY

Treasury Yield (T)	Bond Spread (BS)	Swap Spread (SS)		
		0.25%	0.50%	0.75%
10.5%	0.50%	$6,125,000	$6,000,000	$5,875,000
	0.75%	6,250,000	6,125,000	6,000,000
	1.00%	6,375,000	6,250,000	6,125,000
11.0%	0.50%	$6,125,000	$6,000,000	$5,875,000
	0.75%	6,250,000	6,125,000	6,000,000
	1.00%	6,375,000	6,250,000	6,125,000
11.5%	0.50%	$6,125,000	$6,000,000	$6,000,000
	0.75%	6,125,000	6,000,000	6,000,000
	1.00%	6,125,000	6,000,000	6,000,000
12.%	0.50%	$6,000,000	$6,000,000	$6,000,000
	0.75%	6,000,000	6,000,000	6,000,000
	1.00%	6,000,000	6,000,000	6,000,000

In this display, the funding cost is calculated as: **(Funding Rate)** × **(1/2)** × **($100 million)** where Funding Rate = Min[12%, (T + BS)] + Max[0, 12% − (T + SS)].
Decisions: (i) Call option on bond is exercised if (T + BS) < 12%, (ii) Swap option is exercised if (T + SS) < 12%.

The swap option strategy, however, is complicated by an unknown that does not present itself with the forward swap hedge. In the case of the swaption hedge, when the call date arrives two years later, there are two decisions to be made (or two options that can be exercised) by two different parties: (1) management may decide to call and refinance its original debt; and (2) the swap option holder must decide at that point whether to enter into a receive-fixed swap on the designated terms.

The complicating factor is not the presence of two separate parties in the decision process, but rather the fact that their decisions will be based on movements in two different interest rates. As in the case of forward swaps, the firm's decision to refund at the call date will be determined by the prevailing level for three-year fixed-rate debt in relation to the 12% coupon it is currently paying. On the same call date, the swaption holder will evaluate the economic merits of entering into a three-year swap to receive the fixed rate of 12% based on the prevailing three-year swap rate.

Generally speaking (that is, if interest rates are the only factor), a firm that has chosen to monetize its debt option through the sale of a swaption faces four different possible outcomes:

1. The bond is called if (T + BS) < 12%
   The swap option is exercised if (T + SS) < 12%,
2. The bond is called if (T + BS) < 12%
   The swap option is not exercised if (T + SS) ≥ 12%,
3. The bond is not called if (T + BS) ≥ 12%
   The swap option is exercised if (T + SS) < 12%,
4. The bond is not called if (T + BS) ≥ 12%
   The swap option is not exercised if (T + SS) ≥ 12%.

Whether the options are exercised either independently or simultaneously depends once again on the relationship between BS and SS. Thus, as with the forward swap-based alternative, the basis risk between the bond and swap market yields becomes an important factor.

The Effectiveness of the Hedge Using Swaptions. In Exhibit 6, we have calculated the semi-annual funding cost to the firm employing this swap option-based monetization strategy under several representative interest rate outcomes. For purposes of this analysis, we also assume that if management chooses to call its original debt, it will issue new three-year fixed-rate debt having a coupon rate of (T + BS). Also, if the swap option holder chooses to exercise its contract, the firm—which would then be forced into paying a 12% fixed swap rate in exchange for LIBOR—will counterbalance its position with an offsetting receive-fixed swap at (T + SS).[11]

---

11. Under these assumptions, the post-call date funding cost can be expressed in an annual percentage rate as follows: Min[12%, (T + BS)] + Max[0, 12% − (T + SS)].

EXHIBIT 7
PAYOFF DIAGRAMS
ILLUSTRATING THE
RELATIONSHIP BETWEEN
FORWARD SWAPS AND
SWAP OPTIONS

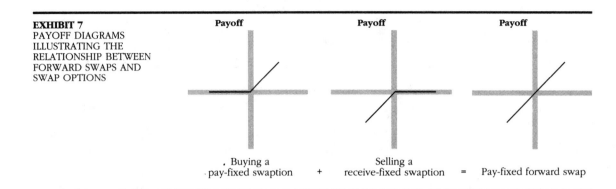

| Buying a pay-fixed swaption | + | Selling a receive-fixed swaption | = | Pay-fixed forward swap |

The most intriguing thing about the display is that it indicates that the firm's funding cost could be either higher, lower, or the same as its present expense depending on the relationship between the credit spreads in the swap and bond markets. More precisely, notice that the semi-annual funding cost will remain at its current level of $6 million if the prevailing rates in both markets exceed 12% at the call date. In this case, neither option will be exercised and so the firm simply will continue to repay its original debt issue. Alternatively, notice that even when (T + BS) and (T + SS) are both below 12%—implying that both options will be exercised—the funding cost will still be $6 million *as long as the swap and bond spreads are equal.*

On the other hand, whenever SS < BS, the funding cost to the firm will increase any time it is optimal to exercise the swap option (i.e., when (T + SS < 12%). And, as we have suggested, it can be profitable to exercise the swap option even when it doesn't make sense to refund the bond. Conversely, if BS < SS, the funding cost may be reduced below the $6 million level. The important point here, once again, is that while the sale of the swaption can provide a hedge against general movements in Treasury yields, it does not protect the firm against changes in the relationship between BS and SS.

Management may be justified in having some confidence in the stability of the spread differential, in which case its assessment of the amount of basis risk would be relatively low. For instance, in the preceding examples we assumed that the initial spreads were SS = 0.50% and BS = 0.75%. Without

reason to believe otherwise, the company might expect this differential of –0.25% to continue through the call date. In such a case, a conservative firm might actually set the strike rate on the swaption it sells 25 basis points lower (i.e., at 11.75%). This decision would result in a lower premium received, but reduce the firm's exposure to future changes in the spread differential.

Before leaving the subject of swaptions, it is instructive to compare the front-end premiums generated by the sale of swaptions to the cash payments accompanying the use of off-market forward swaps. By extending the well-known "put-call-futures" parity relationship, we can show that entering into the pay-fixed side of a three-year off-market swap two years forward at the rate of 11.75% is equivalent to the following transactions: (1) buying a pay-fixed option that can be exercised in two years on an 11.75% three-year swap; and (2) selling a receive-fixed option on the same swap.[12] (The pay-off diagrams illustrating put-call parity are shown in Exhibit 7.) Because both of these options carry the same strike rate, which is greater than the assumed on-market forward swap rate of 10.25%, only the latter option will be in-the-money upon issue.

What this exercise reveals is that the forward swap monetization strategy effectively requires the firm to purchase an out-of-the-money pay-fixed swap option that it does not really need to hedge changes in the value of its call provision. As demonstrated earlier, the off-market forward swap overhedges the firm's call option relative to the sale of a swaption. And, because the forward swap strategy involves the purchase of this

---

12. For a detailed discussion of the theoretical foundations for this result, see H. Stoll, "The Relationship Between Put and Call Option Prices," *Journal of Finance* 24 (December 1969), pp. 801-824 and E. Moriarty, S. Phillips and P. Tosini, "A

Comparison of Options and Futures in the Management of Portfolio Risk," *Financial Analysts Journal* 37 (January/February 1981), pp. 61-67.

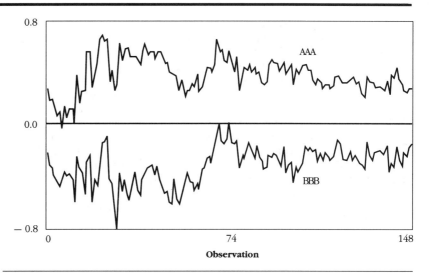

In this display, Observations 1, 74 and 148 refer to the calendar dates January 10, 1986, June 5, 1987 and November 4, 1988, respectively.

unnecessary option, the premium the firm receives from the use of forward swaps must always be less than that generated by the sale of swaptions.

THE BASIS RISK IN SWAP-BASED STRATEGIES

In the previous sections, we have demonstrated that all of the swap-based approaches to callable debt management provide an explicit hedge against unanticipated movements in Treasury rates during the protection period. What we have also emphasized, however, is that the general level of interest rates is not the only factor determining the effectiveness of the hedging strategy. The difference between swap and bond credit spreads (i.e., SS − BS) at the call date—which, of course, is not known at the time the initial decision is made—will also play a significant role. This source of uncertainty, which we call basis risk, arises from the issuing firm's attempt to "sell" its debt option through a parallel transaction in the swap market.

To get a better sense of the extent to which this credit spread differential changes over time, we analyzed several different series of weekly swap and bond yields from Salomon Brothers' *Bond Market Roundup* during the period spanning January 10, 1986 to November 4, 1988.[13] To calculate bond market spreads, we used the average yield-to-maturity (i.e., T + BS) on seven-year utility bond indices in two different Standard & Poor's credit rating classes: AAA and BBB. These data were then adjusted by subtracting the yield on seven-year Treasury bonds in order to isolate the bond credit spread component. Each of these adjusted series was then compared to weekly quotes of the fixed-rate credit spread (SS) for seven-year U.S. dollar interest rate swaps using three-month LIBOR as the floating rate. Exhibit 8 shows the resulting spread differential series for the 148 observations in the data set.

As the graph rather strikingly illustrates, the relationship between the swap and bond markets, as measured by (SS − BS), has not been stable over time. For the AAA and BBB rating classes, the range between the maximum and minimum values was 72 and 84 basis points, respectively. This represents a considerable degree of volatility considering that the historical bond yield differential between the two credit grades is typically only about 150 basis points.[14] Consequently, even if it is assumed that the credit rating of the firm doesn't change during the

---

13. We are indebted to Dave Hartzell for furnishing us with this data.

14. See J. Bicksler and A. Chen. "An Economic Analysis of Interest Rate Swaps." *Journal of Finance* 41 (July 1986), pp. 645-655.

call protection period, movements in this basis risk component can generate considerable uncertainty about the ultimate effectiveness of the hedge.

There is also another potential complication in that changes in the spread differential documented in Exhibit 8 appear to vary considerably across the two credit grades. (In fact, the correlation between the spread differentials for AAA-rated and for BBB-rated debt in this sample was only 0.258.) This means that if the credit quality of the firm should deteriorate after any of the swap-based management strategies are initiated, the degree of basis risk volatility at the beginning of the hedge will be an unreliable indica-tion of what it can expect on the call date.

CONCLUDING COMMENTS

The events of the last several years have created a tremendous demand for new tools and strategies designed to manage a corporation's exposure to interest rate movements. Interest rate swaps are among the most prominent of the new products introduced by investment and commercial banks during the past decade. Although the ability of swaps to transform current cash flows has received a great deal of recent attention, little has been written about some of their more creative uses.

In this paper, we explain how interest rate swaps with delayed starting dates can be used to preserve the value of the call option built into a seasoned callable debt issue. We also demonstrate how such instruments offer protection against movements in the underlying term structure of Treasury rates. In so doing, however, they leave the firm exposed to potentially volatile movements in the risk premium differential between swap and credit markets. Finally, we also show how the basic hedge, as well as one involving options on swaps, can be modified to allow the company, in effect, to detach the call feature from the original bond and sell an otherwise unmarketable asset.

Perhaps the most critical advantage of the swap-based hedging strategies—at least, relative to the exchange-traded financial futures and options that can be used to accomplish the same end—is that swaps and swaptions can be tailored to meet the exact requirements of the end user. This kind of flexibility is one of the primary by-products of the ongoing search in our capital markets for innovative solutions to traditional problems. On the downside, however, it must also be recognized that the more specialized the structure, the less liquid it is likely to be. The lack of liquidity, in turn, makes the default potential of the financial intermediary a concern that must be carefully evaluated. Further, our evidence on bond and swap spread volatility indicates that, over the past three years, the basis risk inherent in these strategies would have been large and unpredictable.

An Economic Approach to Pension Fund Management

Thomas E. Copeland,
University of California at Los Angeles

Corporate pension plan liabilities have grown rapidly during the last three decades. For many companies, pension liabilities are larger than the book value of all tangible assets. In 1980, private pension plans totaled $434 billion, and were growing at a rate of 12.5 percent per year. ERISA (the Employment Retirement Income Security Act of 1974) has dictated that all defined benefit pension plans are a senior "debt" obligation of the firm. Thus, as every chief financial officer knows, corporate pension fund management requires serious, thoughtful attention.

This article focuses on the economics of pension fund management. It addresses such questions as: How do pension fund liabilities affect stock prices? What are the real effects of changing the actuarial assumptions of the plan? What is the optimal mix of pension plan investments? How should pension fund portfolio performance be measured? When, if ever, is it optimal to voluntarily terminate a defined benefit pension plan? How can termination be legally accomplished? Should the firm self-manage its pension plan, use professional portfolio managers, or enter into a contract with an insurance company?

Some of the answers will surprise you. First, in most cases it pays to overfund a defined benefit plan and invest one hundred percent of its assets in bonds. Second, changing the fund's actuarial assumptions in order to decrease current contributions (as well as the present value of the pension fund liabilities) is not likely to affect the market value of the firm's equity. Such manipulations are chicanery at best and stupid at worst. Third, it never pays to invest pension fund assets in real estate, municipal bonds or other investment vehicles which are used primarily as tax shelters. These, and other arguments, make up the substance of what follows.

How to View Your Pension Fund: A Market Value Approach

Broadly speaking, there are two basic ways of viewing the process by which investors establish the values of companies. One, known as the "accounting model of the firm," holds that stock prices are determined largely by reported earnings. In its most simplistic form, this view holds that the market responds uncritically to financial statements, capitalizing a published EPS figure at a standard, industry-wide multiple.

The rival view, sometimes called the "economic model" of the firm, holds that the value of the corporation equals the present value of all future expected *cash flows*, discounted at a rate which reflects investors' alternative investment opportunities. According to this view, accounting earnings may offer a reasonably good substitute for cash flow as a guide to value—but only insofar as changes in earnings correspond to changes in companies' cash flow profitability. When reported earnings seriously misrepresent the operating cash profitability of a business, accounting statements distort real performance, and provide an unreliable guide to value.

Proponents of the accounting model, which underlies much of the older finance scholarship, assume in effect that the market is regularly fooled by "cosmetic" earnings. Accounting manipulation is believed to be a profitable corporate exercise, leading a gullible market to place higher values on corporate shares. Financial economists, however, assume a reasonably sophisticated market—one that is dominated by investors accustomed to seeing through accounting illusion to the reality of after-tax cash flow. In this view, earnings are important only insofar as they provide investors with a good proxy for cash income.

411

Now, what are the implications of these two models for pension fund management? The accounting and the economic models of firm value offer two very different ways of looking at your pension fund. The view of the fund which you choose to adopt will greatly influence your decisions.

The accounting model of the firm, at least under current accounting conventions (although there is pressure for change), maintains in effect that the public corporation has two separate balance sheets: one for the corporation and another for the pension fund. Although ERISA has declared pension fund liabilities the most senior obligation of the corporation, unfunded pension liabilities do not appear on the corporate balance sheet. They appear only as a footnote in the annual report. And although the Financial Accounting Standards Board (FASB) has proposed changes which would record unfunded pension liabilities on the right-hand side of the balance sheet, resistance to the proposal has been stiff, and such changes could be slow in coming.

The economic model of the firm, by contrast, says that pension fund assets and liabilities are an inseparable part of the firm; in the market's view, there is only one balance sheet. Because of the materiality of pension obligations, investors have strong incentives to ferret out the details of pension liabilities regardless of whether they appear in a footnote, as part of the firm's balance sheet, or not at all. Bond rating agencies are clearly aware of the effect of pension funding requirements. In its *Credit Overview*, Standard and Poor's confirms this position: "Pension obligations represent a significant financial responsibility which must be considered in judging the relative ability to make complete and timely debt service payment." They state further: "By treating the deficiency of plan assets versus accumulated benefits as quasi-debt, S&P believes that a company's capital structure and future flexibility can be more properly evaluated." There is also evidence that investors discount the shares of companies having a substantially unfunded pension liability. Martin Feldstein, the current chairman of the President's Council of Economic Advisors, and Stephanie Seligman conducted a study that concluded that a company's share value was marked down $1.84 for every dollar increase in unfunded pension liability.

For the above reasons, and in view of the abundance of other evidence testifying to the success of the market in penetrating accounting fictions, I recommend that management use the economic model of the firm as the basis for virtually all decisions concerning its pension fund. All my subsequent arguments stem from this premise of a reasonably sophisticated market.

Now, let's look a little more closely at the economics of the pension fund, and at the effect of pension liabilities on the market value of the firm's equity. The economic model of the firm states that the market value of shareholders' wealth is equal to the market value of the firm, V, minus the market value of its liabilities, including *pension fund obligations*. This is illustrated in Equation 1, where S is the market value of shareholders' wealth and PFL and B are pension and debt liabilities, respectively. Pension liabilities, PFL, are placed before debt, B, because ERISA has made them senior obligations of the firm.

$$S = V - PFL - B \qquad (1)$$

The key question then, is how do various managerial decisions about pension fund strategy affect the market value of shareholder's wealth?

The Effect of Changing Actuarial Assumptions

In 1973 U.S. Steel increased its reported profits by $47 million by "reducing" its pension costs. This was accomplished by recognizing some appreciation in its $2 billion pension fund. Presumably cash was then diverted from pension contributions to other uses. In the fourth quarter of 1980 Chrysler changed its assumed discount rate on its employee pension plan from 6 percent to 7 percent. Pension costs were reduced and $50 million was added to profits. Also in 1980, Bethlehem Steel raised the assumed discount rate for its pension benefits from 7 percent to 10 percent.[1] This three percent increase had the effect of decreasing the net present value of accumulated pension plan benefits by $713 million (22.5 percent of the total benefits). Before the change pension plan net assets totaled $1.952 billion and the plan was underfunded by $1.215 billion. After the change underfunding fell to $502 million, a 58.7 percent decline. Accounting Trends and Tech-

1. FASB Statement No. 36 allows companies to use a different interest rate assumption for disclosure in the annual report than for funding purposes, e.g., Bethlehem used 7% for funding and 10% for disclosure. See Regan (1982).

As long as the firm is making profits, pension contributions are "shared" with the government because more contributions mean lower taxes.

niques, an annual survey of reporting practices of 600 companies showed that roughly 30 percent of the companies sampled voluntarily changed their pension fund accounting assumptions at least once between 1975 and 1980.

Remember, we are interested in the market value of pension fund liabilities and how it is affected by accounting changes. The market value of the *real* pension fund deficit, it turns out, does not have any necessary relationship to the accounting or "book" fund deficit. To see why this is true, let's consider Equation 2 below, which represents the market value of the pension fund deficit:

$$PFL = -\text{Market value of}$$
$$\text{pension fund assets} \quad (2)$$
$$- [PV \text{ (expected contributions)}] (1-T)$$
$$+ PV \text{ (expected pension fund benefits from past and future service)}$$

There are two major sources of a pension fund's asset value. First is the value of stocks, bonds, mortgages, etc., currently held by the pension fund. Second is the present value of the expected pension fund contributions. Expected contributions to the fund are multiplied by one minus the corporate tax rate $(1-T)$ to reflect the fact that pension fund contributions are tax deductible by the firm. As long as the firm is making profits, pension contributions are "shared" with the government because more contributions mean lower taxes.[2] Expected contributions include 1) "normal" costs; 2) "experience" costs (those caused by a decline in the market value of securities in the fund, by unexpected changes in employee turnover, or by changes in actuarial assumptions about the discount rate), which are amortized over a period not to exceed 15 years; and 3) supplemental liabilities (resulting from increased benefits or unfunded past service costs), which must be amortized over a period not to exceed 30 years. Balancing the pension fund assets is the pension fund liability: the present value of all pension defined fund benefits currently expected to be paid to employees.

The main difference between the book value of the pension fund deficit and its market or true economic value, PFL, is reflected in differences in the discount rates; that is, in the expected rates of return. This can be illustrated by rewriting Equation 2 to show the present value of the pension fund as a function of the appropriate *market-determined* discount rate.

$$PFL = -\text{Market value of}$$
$$\text{pension fund assets} \quad (3)$$
$$- \sum_{t=1}^{N} \frac{E(\text{contributions in year T})(1-T)}{[1+k_b(1-T)]^t}$$
$$+ \sum_{t=1}^{N} \frac{E(\text{benefits in year t})}{(1+k_b)^t}$$

The expected pension benefits are discounted at the current pre-tax cost of senior debt, k_b, because ERISA has made the payment of pension benefits a senior obligation of the firm, second only to tax liabilities.[3] Pension contributions are also discounted at the same rate, k_b. Prior to ERISA, the expected benefits would have been discounted at the cost of junior or subordinated debt, k_j, which is higher than k_b, the cost of senior debt. Thus, ERISA had the effect of increasing the present value of the pension benefit liability. By increasing the present value of pension deficits, PFL, ERISA effectively transferred wealth from shareholders to pension beneficiaries. This transfer was especially large for plans which were seriously underfunded.

Let's now return to our original question about the effects of changing actuarial assumptions on the economic value of the pension liability. The real effect of a change in actuarial assumptions depends almost entirely on the cash flow consequences.[4] If the *actuarial* discount rate assumption is raised (while market interest rates remain unchanged), then the *accounting* present value of accumulated benefits will decrease; and, as a result, so will the

---

2. If one considers Social Security to be a pension plan, then recent changes in the Social Security tax law which requires nonprofit organizations to pay Social Security for their employees are burdensome. Because nonprofit organizations have no tax shelter, they must bear the full cost of Social Security expenses.

3. Some have argued that promised pension benefits are subordinated to other debt claims in spite of ERISA because other debt comes due before pension obligations. Pension beneficiaries cannot force the firm into bankruptcy while debt holders can. The existence of large unfunded pension deficits will, in our opinion, cause debt holders to force bankruptcy sooner than they might if there were no pension obligations. Nevertheless, pension liabilities will still be senior claims at the time of bankruptcy.

4. Accounting numbers may affect cash flows by tripping bond covenants stipulated in terms of accounting numbers. These covenants in turn could limit the operating and/or financing flexibility of the firm, thus affecting its future real, cash profitability.

Changing the actuarial assumptions in order to reduce pension contributions and the book value of the pension deficit is likely to be an exercise in futility.

"normal costs" which have to be paid into the fund. This in turn decreases the expected future annual contributions into the fund. And if you look back at Equation 3, this means that the present value of those expected contributions declines because, even though the actuarial rate may have been adjusted, the market-determined discount rate, k_b, has not changed. And because the market rate has not changed, the present value of expected benefits does not go down, but remains unchanged. Thus, *the real net effect of raising the actuarial discount rate is to increase the market value of pension liabilities.*

However, tax effects aside (and we will return to them later), *there is no net effect on the value of the firm as a whole* because the cash flow not put into pension fund contributions may be used either to decrease other liabilities or to increase assets. Either way the increased pension liability is exactly offset by the present value of those funds retained.[5]

Thus, we see that changing the actuarial assumptions in order to reduce pension contributions and the book value of the pension deficit is likely to be an exercise in futility from the shareholders' point of view. But this is the best that can happen because we have assumed the firm merely trades one tax shelter for another. The outcome can be considerably worse. If the funds generated by cutting pension contributions are used in ways which do not directly increase the company's tax shield (e.g., repaying the principal on debt), the effect may be to increase taxable income, increase taxes, and decrease net cash flows to shareholders. By increasing accounting profits, the firm may sacrifice the tax shield from the pension contribution. The net effect (assuming the firm is paying taxes) is to benefit the IRS at the expense of shareholders.

Finally, changing actuarial assumptions for disclosure in the annual report but not for funding purposes is chicanery at best and stupid at worst. If taxes are based on income reported in the annual report, the effect of such a manuever is to increase tax liabilities without decreasing cash contributions to the pension fund. If taxes are based on actual contributions, then at best managers think they can somehow fool the market place.

Determining the Mix of Assets
1. The shareholders' position as a call option.

Before turning to the effect of ERISA and taxes on the mix of pension fund investments, let's build a more complete understanding of their risk and return characteristics. Before the passage of ERISA, corporate pension liabilities were not guaranteed. They were analogous to (subordinated) risky debt. The shareholders' position, even if the firm had no debt per se, was equivalent to a call option on a levered firm.[6]

For illustration, suppose we have a one-period world. All of our employees will retire at the end of the year and their defined benefit is D dollars. At that time, if the value of the firm exceeds the pension benefits (i.e., if V>D), the shareholders get to keep the difference (i.e., S = V − D). But, if the value of the firm is less than the promised benefits (i.e. if V<D), the shareholders get nothing and the employees receive less than the promised benefit.

The shareholders' position is identical to a call option on the value of the firm, with an exercise (or striking) price equal to the defined benefit, D. They win if their option finishes in-the-money (V>D) and lose if it finishes out-of-the-money (V<D).

Considerable insight into pension fund asset mix can be provided by this simple option pricing approach. For example, what happens to shareholders' wealth if the pension trustees change the mix of pension assets from a well-diversified portfolio of equity to being 100 percent invested in shares of the firm?[7] The effect would be to increase the correlation between the value of the firm and the value of the pension assets. Consequently, the variance of the underlying portfolio of assets increases; and the value of shareholder's wealth, S, which is a call option on the assets, will also increase. Thus, the effect of any decision which unexpectedly increases the combined risk of the firm and the pension assets is to shift wealth to shareholders away from pension beneficiaries. The only mitigating circumstance is that employees may be able to demand higher wages to compensate them for the higher risk they must bear when pension

---

5. One sometimes hears that pension contributions can be legitimately cut if the funds are alternatively used to invest in positive net present value projects. This argument confuses the investment decision (take the profitable project) with the way is financed (cut pension contributions). The project can be financial either by cutting pension contributions, which increases pension liabilities or by borrowing which increases debt liabilities. Either way, the effect on shareholders' wealth is the same.

6. For a more complete presentation of pension fund liabilities as options see Sharpe (1976) and Treynor, Priest and Regan (1976).

7. This situtation is not unusual. For example, at one point in time Sears' pension fund had over 50% of its assets invested in Sears' stock.

The optimal strategy from the point of view of share-holders of nearly bankrupt firms is to put all of the pension assets into very risky stocks.

assets are invested in the firm's own stock. Or they might require pension fund insurance.[8]

2. ERISA and the PBGC

Now let's look at the effect of government pension fund insurance on the pension fund asset mix, but maintain our assumption that there are no taxes. The Pension Benefit Guarantee Corporation (PBGC) insures pension fund liabilities. Corporations contribute a fixed insurance premium per employee each year into PBGC. (It is currently $3 per employee per year.) In the event that an underfunded pension plan is terminated, the firm is liable for up to 30 percent of its net worth. The PBGC guarantees the remainder of the pension liability.

If the PBGC were a privately owned insurance company, it would charge premiums based on the probability of corporate default on a pension fund. However, as a government organization, it charges all firms exactly the same insurance premium regardless of the extent of pension plan underfunding or the likelihood of bankruptcy. One implication, of course, is that firms with overfunded pension funds are paying too much to the PBGC relative to those with badly underfunded pension plans. Another is that firms threatened with bankruptcy can decide to change their pension plan asset mix to maximize the value of the call option which represents their shareholders' wealth. If they go bankrupt, shareholders receive nothing. And although the PBGC can claim 30 percent of the firm's net worth, 30 percent of nothing is still nothing. The PBGC claim on equity is worthless in Chapter 10 bankruptcy. Consequently, the optimal strategy from the point of view of shareholders of nearly bankrupt firms is to put all of the pension assets into very risky stocks. If they are lucky the risky portfolio may do well and even result in overfunding of the pension fund. If they are not, then they end up with nothing, which is where they would have been anyway, and the PBGC has to pay off the pension beneficiaries. Given that the PBGC undercharges for pension fund insurance for underfunded plans, there is the distinct possibility that corporations facing potential bankruptcy can "game" the PBGC by shifting pension plan assets to being 100 percent invested in risky stocks.

An interesting case history of a company in trouble is International Harvester. In May of 1982 the *Wall Street Journal* reported that International Harvester Company's pension fund abruptly switched at least $250 million of stock holdings into bonds, chiefly U.S. government issues. Pension industry executives suggested that the company was pursuing a strategy which would let it reduce pension contributions. As of October 31, 1981, Harvester's combined pension assets totaled $1.35 billion.

What are the real economic consequences of Harvester's decision? First, since the company had negative earnings, it is not likely that the tax consequences of the decision were important.[9] Second, by changing the actuarial assumptions of the plan either 1) by realizing gains on the stocks which were sold or 2) by raising the fund rate of return assumption due to the shift from stocks to bonds, Harvester could reduce its planned cash contributions to the fund. We earlier saw that the change in actuarial assumptions has at best no effect on shareholders' wealth, and a negative effect (tax increases) at worst. And if we view the stockholders' claim as a call option on a highly levered firm, a shift from stocks to bonds (in the absence of tax benefits) decreases shareholders' wealth and benefits pension beneficiaries (as well as debt holders of the firm). Although we have insufficient information to draw a definite conclusion about the Harvester decision, it looks like the net effect was to diminish shareholders' wealth.[10]

3. Tax Consequences

For most firms, pension fund contributions reduce taxes because they are immediately deductible. At the same time, the pension plan pays no taxes on its earnings. Hence, the rapid growth of pensions is largely attributable to the fact that they are a form of tax-deferred compensation.

Pension assets should be invested in those securities which have the most favorable pre-tax rates of return. Obvious examples of securities which pension managers should *not* invest in are those which are used as tax shelters by investors with high marginal tax rates such as municipal bonds or real estate.

Perhaps the most interesting tax implication of

---

8. This was pointed out by William Sharpe (1976). For more on the economics of insuring portfolios of risky assets, see Gatto, Geske, Litzenberger and Sosin (1980).

9. The next part of this section provides the only rational tax explanation for why Harvester shareholders may have benefited from switching pension assets to bonds.

10. Raising the discount rate and increasing earnings may have helped Harvester to satisfy bond covenants, which are often expressed in terms of accounting net worth. In this sense, it may have preserved some valuable operating flexibility.

Because an overfunded pension plan is an asset of the firm, the pre-tax return on debt held in a corporate pension fund is passed through the firm to its shareholders.

the pension fund asset mix is that pension plan should be *fully funded and invested totally in bonds* as opposed to equities.[11]

There are two separate tax arguments. The first is that, because an overfunded pension plan is an asset of the firm, the pre-tax return on debt held in a corporate pension fund is passed through the firm to its shareholders in the form of higher share prices.[12] The implication is that the return on debt held in the pension fund is taxed at the lower personal tax rate on equities. Shareholders will pay less taxes than if the debt were held in their personal portfolios. Consequently, shareholders are better off if the pension funds of corporations are invested in bonds while their personal portfolios are invested in equities. This conclusion is based on the fact that pension plan earnings are not taxed and that, for most investors, bond income is taxed at a higher rate than capital gains. It does not depend on any theoretical tax advantage from funding pension assets with corporate debt.

The second reason for investing pension assets in bonds is the potential value of the tax shelter created when the firm borrows to invest pension assets in bonds.

To illustrate this argument, I am going to offer an example which compares two pension investment strategies, the first with all pension assets in stock and the second with all assets in government bonds. For the sake of simplicity, let's assume we live in a one-period world with two equally likely states of nature. If the economy is good, stocks will yield a 100 percent rate of return while bonds yield 10 percent. If the economy is bad, bonds will still yield 10 percent (that is, 10 percent is the risk-free rate of return) while stocks yield -50 percent. Note that the expected (or average) return on stocks is 25 percent while bonds are expected to yield only 10 percent. Even though the stock portfolio promises a significantly higher rate of return over time, I can demonstrate that the bond investment strategy is better for shareholders.

Table 1 shows a beginning-of-period market value balance sheet which combines the firm and pension fund assets and liabilities for each of the two pension investment strategies: all stock and all bonds. The firm's defined benefit pension plan promises to pay $220 million at the end of the period. The present value of this liability is $200 million and it appears on the liability side of the corporate balance sheet. On the asset side, the current market value of pension assets is $200 million (ei-

TABLE 1 **Beginning Balance Sheets for Two Pension Investment Strategies**	100% Stock Strategy			
Assets			**Liabilities**	
Pension Plan			Pension Plan	
Bonds, B	0		PV of Benefits, PFB	200
Stock, S	200		Corporate	
Corporate, A	800		Debt, D	300
			Equity, E	500
	1000			1000

	100% Bond Strategy			
Assets			**Liabilities**	
Pension Plan			Pension Plan	
Bonds, B	200		PV of Benefits, PFB	200
Stocks, S	0		Corporate	
Corporate, A	800		Debt, D	400
			Equity, E	400
	1000			1000

11. For proof of this proposition, the reader is referred to Tepper and Affleck (1974), Black (1980) and especially to Tepper (1981). In order for shareholders (rather than employees) to receive the higher pre-tax return, the fund must be overfunded.

12. The last section of this article discusses ways that shareholders can gain access to the assets of overfunded pension plans.

TABLE 2		State of Nature	
Payoffs for the 100% Stock Pension Investment Strategy		**Good Economy**	**Bad Economy**
	Sell stock and receive	$400 million	$100 million
	Payoff defined benefits	−220	−220
	Cash to the firm	180	−120
	less taxes at 50%	− 90	60
	Net cash to shareholders	90	− 60

ther in bonds or in stocks). The pension plan is fully funded because the present value of its assets equals that of its liabilities.

If we employ the 100 percent stock investment strategy for our pension plan, the end-of period payoffs are as shown in Table 2.

In the good economy, we see that the pension fund stocks can be sold for $400 million at the end of the year. After paying the $220 million of pension benefits, shareholders are left with $180 pretax and $90 after taxes. In the "bad economy" they suffer a $60 million loss. The expected (or average) gain in shareholders' wealth is thus $15 million. But remember that they are exposed to a great deal of risk.

The alternate pension investment strategy is to invest $200 million in bonds. In this case, the end-of-period payoff would be exactly $220 million in either economy, the pension benefits would be paid off, and there would be no gain or loss to shareholders. Their expected gain is zero, but they take no risk at all.

However, in order to make a valid comparison of the stock and bond strategies, we need to hold shareholders' risk constant. Then we can compare after-tax expected returns to see which strategy is better, given equivalent risk.

If you look again at the two balance sheets shown in Table 1, you can see that the risk for shareholders has actually been equalized by making offsetting changes in the capital structures of the two firms.[13] If you compare only the asset sides of the balance sheets, the $200 million of bonds is less risky than $200 million of stock. But, in order to offset this decline in the risk of the assets caused by

the 100 percent bond strategy, we have increased the firm's financial leverage by borrowing $100 million and using the proceeds to repurchase $100 million in equity.[14] The resulting payoffs are given in Table 3.

In the "good economy" the bonds are sold for $220 million and the proceeds are used to pay off the defined benefits. Next, the $100 million of re-purchased equity is reissued for $200 million (because the company's stock is also assumed to appreciate by 100 percent in the good economy). Half of the $200 million is used to repay the $100 million of borrowing, and $10 million pays the required interest. Note that the interest payments are tax deductible. If the firm is in a 50 percent tax bracket, then taxes are reduced by $5 million more than otherwise.

Therefore, the net cash available to shareholders in the favorable state of nature is $95 million with the 100 percent bond investment strategy, but was only $90 million with the 100 percent equity strategy. The bond strategy also dominates the equity strategy in the unfavorable state of nature ($ − 55 million versus $ − 60 million). Hence, our example demonstrates the superiority of the bond strategy from the shareholders' point of view. We have increased their return in both states of nature without changing their risk: the range of possible payoffs is $150 million in either case. To repeat, regardless of whether the actual return on stock investments is higher or lower than on the bonds, the bond strategy is preferable.

To summarize, then, we have seen that investing all pension fund assets in bonds benefits shareholders in two ways. First, the pretax bond rate of return is passed through the firm to its shareholders

---

13. It really doesn't make any difference, in our example, how risk is measured. Shareholders' risk is equivalent whether you use the range, the variance or the beta to measure risk.

14. In practice it is not necessary for corporations to actually repurchase shares in order to implement the 100% bond pension investment plan. What is important is that when pension assets are invested in bonds rather than stock, the risk of the corporate asset portfolio is lower. Hence, there is greater debt capacity from the point of view of lenders. More borrowing provides a debt tax shield.

TABLE 3		State of Nature	
Payoffs for the 100%		**Good Economy**	**Bad Economy**
Bond Pension	Sell bonds and receive	$220 million	$220 million
Investment Strategy	Payoff defined benefits	220	220
		0	0
	Sell stock (book value =		
	$100 million)	200	50
	Payoff extra bonds	–100	–100
		100	– 50
	Less interest on bonds	– 10	– 10
		90	– 60
	Plus tax shield on interest	5	5
	Net cash to shareholders	95	– 55

in the form of higher share prices, which in turn are taxed at the lower capital gains rate. This argument applies even if there is no gain to leverage. The second reason for favoring bonds over equity is that there may be a gain to firms which can carry more debt without increasing shareholders' risk— a gain to leverage. We have seen that firms which choose to invest pension assets in bonds actually experience lower total asset risk than firms which put pension assets in stock. The lower risk means a greater debt capacity. If the firm uses this debt capacity and if there is a valuable tax shield created by the deductibility of interest payments, then there is a gain to leverage from investing pension assets in bonds while borrowing to hold shareholders' risk constant.[15]

Recent empirical evidence by W. R. Landsman (1984) covering a large sample of firms for the years 1979 through 1981 shows that on average each dollar contributed to the assets of defined benefit pension funds results in a $1.12 increase in the value of shareholders' equity, other things being held constant. This is the first statistically significant evidence that there is, indeed, a clear tax advantage resulting from pension assets held by the firm.

Measuring Pension Plan Portfolio Performance

If your firm decides to hire a pension plan management firm for a substantial fee, the natural question is: what are you getting for your money? The answer comes in two parts. First, how do you calculate the rate of return on monies invested in the pension fund? Second, once you have determined the rate of return, was it higher than could have been expected given the riskiness of the portfolio of investments? Was it a positive risk-adjusted rate of return?

The first consideration for measuring pension fund return is that it must be a total market value return—one which includes all dividends, coupons and capital gains. Second, it must be a *time-weighted return*; that is, it must properly account for the timing contributions to and disbursements from the fund.[16] In order to illustrate the difference between time-weighted returns and *dollar-weighted returns*, consider the following example. Two funds have all of their assets continuously invested in the Standard & Poor's 500 Index for a two-year period. They both begin with $10 million. As shown in Table 4, Fund A receives an additional $10 million contribution at the end of the first year while Fund B disburses $1 million.

The only difference between the funds is their pattern of receipts and disbursements. If we use a dollar-weighted return measure, we find that in two years Fund A appears to have a 200 percent return,

dollar-weighted return on Fund A
$$= \frac{\$30MM - \$10MM}{\$10MM} = 200\%$$

---

15. The gain to leverage is most likely to be valuable for those firms which have higher effective tax rates because their tax shelters from other sources (such as investment tax credits, depreciation, research and development expenses, or tax carry-back and carry-forward) are limited.

16. The recommendations of the Bank Administration Institute have become a standard for performance measurement. In cooperation with the University of Chicago, they have devised two ways for estimating time- weighted returns.

TABLE 4
Fund Balances for Two Pension Funds

End of Year	Return on S&P 500	Beginning Cash	Deposit	Ending Cash
			Fund A	
0	—	$10MM	—	—
1	–50%	$ 5	$10MM	$15
2	100%	$15	$ 0	$30
			Fund B	
0	—	$10MM	—	—
1	–50%	$ 5	$–1	$ 4
2	100%	$ 4	$ 0	$ 8

TABLE 5
Time-Weighted Returns for Two Pension Funds

End of Year	Return on S&P 500	Fund Balance	Number of Shares	Price per Share	New Deposit	Shares	Time-Weighted Returned
Fund A							
0	—	$10MM	10	$1.0MM	—	—	—
1	–50%	$ 5MM	10	.5MM	$10MM	20	–50%
2	100%	$30MM	30	1.0MM	$10MM	10	100%
3	50%	$60MM	40	1.5MM	—	—	50%
Fund B							
0	—	$10MM	10	$1.0MM	—	—	—
1	–50%	$ 5MM	10	$ .5MM	– 1MM	–2	–50%
2	100%	$ 8MM	8	$1.0MM	$21MM	21	100%
3	50%	$43.5MM	29	$1.5MM	—	—	50%

while Fund B appears to have a two-year return of minus 20 percent

dollar-weighted return on Fund B
$$= \frac{\$8MM - \$10MM}{\$10MM} = -20\%.$$

A time-weighted return, similar to that used by many mutual funds, begins by dividing the fund into "shares." In Table 5 we have divided the initial $10 million investment into 10 shares each worth $1 million.[17] By the first year both funds have declined to $5 million because the S&P 500 went down 50 percent. Each share has declined in price to $.5 million. When money is deposited or disbursed, we compute the number of "shares" involved. For example, in year 1 a deposit of $10 million to fund A represents 20 new shares at $.5 million each. Thus in period 2, Fund A has 30 shares and $15 million. When the market goes up 100 percent, Fund A

finishes the year with $30 million and 30 shares worth $1 million each. The time-weighted return is computed by using the hypothetical share prices. For example the year 2 return for Fund A is

time-weighted returned
$$= \frac{\text{(end-of-period share price)} - \text{(beginning share price)}}{\text{beginning share price}}$$
$$= \frac{1.0MM - .5MM}{.5MM} = 100\%.$$

Since both funds were continuously 100 percent invested in the S&P 500 Index, we know that they must have had exactly the same return. The time-weighted return calculations shown in the last column of Table 5 show that the returns for both funds are indeed identical.

Having correctly measured the time-weighted returns it is necessary to evaluate the risk-adjusted performance of portfolio managers. It is not very

17. The number of "shares" is arbitrary. Usually the initial investment is divided by enough shares so that each is worth one dollar.

TABLE 6 Hypothetical Pension Fund Returns	Year	Hypothetical Pension Fund Returns	S&P 500 Index	90-day T-Bill Rate
	1973	40.9%	29.1%	7.0%
	1974	−15.0	−22.9	7.8
	1975	− 8.0	4.0	5.8
	1976	22.0	18.5	5.0
	1977	−10.0	− 3.7	5.3
	1978	−20.0	− 2.2	7.2
	1979	10.0	7.1	10.1
	1980	25.0	15.5	11.4
	1981	7.0	7.9	14.0
	Arithmetic Average	5.66%	5.92%	8.18%
	Standard Deviation	20.48%	14.94%	3.05%
	Beta	1.22	1.00	.02

hard to invest in the Standard & Poor's 500 Index. The difficult task, the task which should be rewarded, is to select a portfolio which has the same risk but higher returns. The capital asset pricing model (CAPM) and the arbitrage pricing model (APM) provide a sound theoretical basis for measuring risk-adjusted returns. The data given in Table 6 show the rates of return on a hypothetical pension portfolio and on the S&P 500 Index from 1973 to 1981, a nine-year interval.

Most pension fund managers report their performance by comparing their portfolio returns with the Standard & Poor's 500 Index without making any adjustment for their portfolio's risk.[18] Figure 1 illustrates a typical presentation.

The gross rates of return (before management

**FIGURE 1
Typical Version
of Pension Fund
Performance**

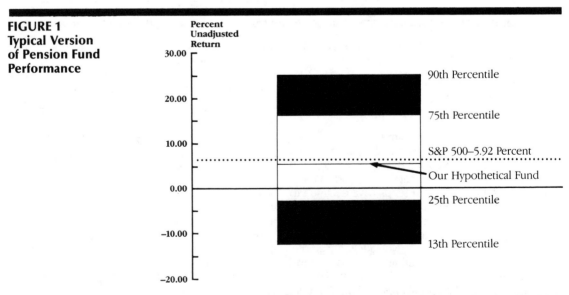

18. Bond portfolios are usually compared with the Lehman Brothers government and corporate bond index which is a weighted average of the rates of return on government and corporate bonds.

fees and brokerage expenses) on a pension fund (5.66% in our example) are compared with the distribution of S&P 500 returns, or with the actual performance of other managed funds over the same time interval.[19] Our hypothetical pension fund has earned just about the "average" rate of return and is in the 49th percentile.

Unfortunately, it is meaningless to compare gross rates of return which have not been adjusted for risk. At present, the handiest means of adjusting returns for risk is to use the capital asset pricing model (CAPM). The CAPM calculates expected or required returns on investment as a direct function of the investment's systematic or portfolio risk and the level of interest rates. The measure of risk is called beta. A perfectly riskless asset has a beta of zero and the market portfolio (in this case the S&P 500 Index) has a beta which is defined to be 1.0. The CAPM says that the predicted risk-adjusted rate of return will be equal to the risk-free rate, R_f, plus a risk premium which is equal to the amount of risk, β_j, times a market risk premium which is equal to the difference between the market rate of return, R_m, and the risk-free rate.

$$R_j = R_f + (R_m - R_f)\beta_j \qquad (4)$$

Our pension portfolio had a beta of 1.22. In other words, it was 22 percent riskier than the S&P 500 Index. Substituting the appropriate numbers from Table 6 into Equation 4, we would conclude that the predicted return was

$$R_j = 8.18\% + (5.92\% - 8.18\%)1.22$$
$$= 5.42\%$$

The actual rate of return was 5.66 percent. Hence our pension fund managers earned a positive risk-adjusted rate of return of 0.24 percent, equal to the difference between the fund's actual return, R_j, and the rate of return which could have been earned in the market place for portfolios of equivalent risk, R_j.

Between 1973 and 1981 the S&P 500 Index actually did worse, on average, than the lower risk 90-day Treasury Bill portfolio. Those are the breaks of the game. In the long run, however, we expect riskier stock portfolios to outperform low-risk bond portfolios; and they have. However, in shorter time intervals, riskier portfolios can and do underperform bonds. That's what happened in our example. Nevertheless, our pension managers did better than they were expected to do and should be rewarded, even though their gross rate of return was less than the lower-risk S&P 500 Index.[20]

A few rules of thumb for managing and evaluating pension funds are:

- Keep bond and stock funds separate. This makes it easier to evaluate their performance.
- Keep a record of time-weighted returns.
- Evaluate pension fund managers' performance by having them subtract all management and brokerage fees from the fund's gross rate of return. Then compare this net return with the risk-adjusted return expected for portfolios of equivalent risk.
- Give the fund manager guidelines for the percentage of the fund which should be invested in bonds or stocks. In so doing, keep in mind the effect your decision will have on the risk of the pension fund and on the value of shareholders' wealth *after taxes.*

Voluntary Termination of Defined Benefit Pension Plans

In June of 1983 Occidental Petroleum voluntarily terminated four defined benefit pension plans for salaried employees in its oil and chemicals divisions, and replaced them with defined contribution plans. All employees covered by the terminated plans received a lump sum payment covering their vested benefits. Because the defined benefit plans were overfunded by approximately $294 million (at the end of 1982), the voluntary termination boosted Occidental's after-tax net income (and cash flow) by approximately $100 million. This increase represented 64 percent of 1982 earnings.

A recent issue of *Fortune* magazine (December 26, 1983) reported that since 1980, 128 companies have carried out 138 fund reversions where defined benefit plans were cancelled. The excess assets, which reverted to use in operating and capital budgets, amounted to $515 million. The Pension Benefit Guarantee Corporation (PBGC), which has to ap-

19. A.G. Becker Inc. is the usual source of the distribution of managed funds' gross rates of return.

20. Of course, one year of abnormal performance might be attributable to luck rather than skill.

prove any cancellations, is currently considering applications which would free well over $1 billion more in excess assets. Furthermore, an estimated $150 billion in excess assets sits untapped in other private pension plans.

These examples clearly demonstrate that if underfunded defined benefit plans are liabilities of the shareholders, then overfunded plans are shareholder assets. Although the firm owns the excess assets in the fund, it is restricted greatly in its ability to use them.[21] ERISA states that any residual assets in a terminated plan revert to the employer only if the pension plan explicitly provides for such a distribution upon termination. In some cases, the PBGC has contended that excess assets should go to plan beneficiaries. Consequently, firms must be careful about the process of terminating overfunded pension plans. A company can't simply draw off the excess and keep the old plan going. Also, ERISA requires evidence that the plan became overfunded through "actuarial error"—meaning that the assets increased more rapidly than anticipated. This is a way of discouraging the practice of heavy pension contributions in good years followed by attempts to reclaim the money when profits are down. It should also be noted that ERISA has made it more difficult to borrow against the assets in the pension fund.

Usually firms do not consider voluntary termination of underfunded plans because the PBGC can lay claim to 30 percent of their net worth. However, two questions arise. How is net worth to be measured? And, can a subsidiary with negative net worth terminate its pension plan and relinquish the unfunded liabilities to the PBCG? In answer to the second question, the PBGC has denied subsidiaries the right to terminate their plans so long as the parent company shows adequate net worth. Furthermore, the PBGC has argued that in determining net worth it can look beyond book value and use other information to establish the value of the firm as a going concern. Consequently, voluntary termination of underfunded plans is an unlikely strategy.

Most companies replace their defined benefit with defined contribution plans, thereby shifting the uncertainties of pension performance from themselves to their employees. The company simply promises to pay a fixed percentage of each employee's salary or wages into the defined contribution plan. Benefits upon retirement depend on the return on the pension investments. Sometimes the defined contribution plans are coupled with the 401K tax deferred savings plan authorized by the Internal Revenue Act of 1978. Employee contributions to the plan reduce their tax liabilities and earn tax-free returns until retirement. One drawback, from the company's perspective, is that its contribution to the plan is vested immediately under the 401K plan, whereas it would not be immediately vested under most defined benefit pension plans. Also, don't forget that overfunding a defined benefit plan provides tax benefits that are not available with defined contribution plans.

Insurance Company Contracts

About 39 percent of all non-government pension plans were invested with insurance companies. The usual insurance company contract provides "guaranteed" rates of return for a fixed period of time. For example, you may be guaranteed an 8 percent return for a ten-year period. The insurance companies can provide the guarantee because they invest your pension fund contributions in ten-year government bonds which, if held to maturity, yield exactly 8 percent. The catch is that you cannot withdraw your pension plan assets if interest rates change. When market rates of interest rose rapidly during the late 1970s and early 1980s, many firms suddenly realized that a "guaranteed" rate of return was very different from a riskless return. Market rates of interest of 14 percent on long- term bonds were not unusual, but those companies whose pension assets were committed to insurance company contracts found they were locked into an 8 percent return. This is the hard way to learn about opportunity cost.

If your company is large enough to provide its own pension fund accounting for employees, then there is no difference between contributing pension funds to an insurance company plan and directly investing in 8 percent ten-year bonds yourself. Just bear in mind that long-term bonds are riskier than short-term bonds or money market assets. Some companies have decided to "immunize" their defined benefit pension liabilities by purchasing long-term bonds which mature with the same pattern as employee retirements. They know for sure that the maturing bonds will pay promised benefits.[22]

---

21. For a more complete exposition, the reader is referred to Bulow, Scholes and Manell (1982).

22. A discussion of bond immunization will appear in Vol. 2, No. 3 of this journal, which will come out in the Fall of 1984.

Summary and Conclusions

The rapid growth of pension funds in the last two decades has made pension fund management one of the primary responsibilities of corporate financial officers. Financial executives must be familiar with accounting regulations governing pension fund reporting practices, with government regulation of defined benefit plans under ERISA, and with the implications of a wide range of managerial decisions. In this article, I discuss the economic implications of changing the pension fund actuarial assumptions, the choice of asset mix, the problem of measuring pension fund portfolio performance, the implications of voluntary termination of defined benefit plans, and the option of investing pension plan assets with guaranteed insurance company plans.

The most important conclusions are these:

- Unfunded pension fund liabilities are equivalent to senior debt of the firm. Shareholders take this fact into account when trading the firm's common stock, bond rating agencies consider it as an integral part of their evaluations, and ERISA guarantees that it is true.

- Changes in actuarial assumptions which increase reported income and reduce pension fund contributions have, at best, no effect on the value of the firm. If the cash flow from reduced contributions is used to pay off debt principal, the effect is to decrease shareholders' wealth. Although earnings increase, after-tax cash flows decrease.

- Firms facing bankruptcy and having underfunded pension plans might consider placing all of the pension assets in stocks in order to maximize the chance that the pension can become overfunded. There is nothing to lose.

- Most profitable firms will want to fully fund or even overfund their pension plans and invest 100 percent of the pension assets in bonds in order to maximize the tax benefits accruing to shareholders.

- Overfunded defined benefit plans can be terminated, with all excess cash going to the firm, by converting them into defined contribution plans.

Risk and Liabilities Management/Selected Bibliography

Alchian, A. A. and Demsetz, H., "Production, Information Costs, and Economic Organization," *The American Economic Review* 62 (1972), 777-795.

Arnott, R., and M. Gersovitz, "Corporate Financial Structure and the Funding of Private Pension Plans," *Journal of Public Economics* (1980).

Arrow, K. J., *Essays in the Theory of Risk-Bearing* (North Holland: Amsterdam, 1974).

Ayres, H. R. and Barry, J. Y., "The Equilibrium Yield Curve for Government Securities," *Financial Analysts Journal* (May/June, 1979) 31-39.

Bagehot, W. (pseud.), "Risk and Reward in Corporate Pension Funds," *Financial Analysts Journal* (January/ February 1972).

Barnow, B., and R. Ehrenberg, "The Costs of Defined Benefit Pension Plans and Firm Adjustments," *Quarterly Journal of Economics* (November 1969).

Bierwag, G. O., G. G. Kaufman and A. Toevs, (eds.), *Innovations in Bond Portfolio Management: Duration Analysis and Immunization* (Greenwich, CT: JAI Press, 1983).

Bierwag, G. O., G. G. Kaufman and A. Toevs, "Duration: Its Development and Use in Bond Portfolio Management," *Financial Analysts Journal* (July/August), 15-35.

Black, F., "The Investment Policy Spectrum: Individuals, Endowment Funds, and Pension Funds," *Financial Analysts Journal* (January/February 1976.)

Black, F., "The Tax Consequences of Long-run Pension Policy," *Financial Analysts Journal* (July/August 1980).

Bulow, J., M. Scholes, and P. Manell, "Economic Implications of ERISA," Working paper, Graduate School of Business, University of Chicago, March 1982.

Coase, R. H. , "The Problem of Social Cost," *Journal of Law and Economics* 2 (1960), 1-44.

Donaldson, G., *Corporate Debt Capacity* (Boston: Division of Research, Harvard Business School, 1961).

Donaldson, G., *Strategy for Financial Mobility* (Homewood, Ill.: Richard D. Irwin, 1971).

Ehrbar, A. F., "How to Slash Your Company's Tax Bill," *Fortune*, (February 23, 1981), pp. 122-124.

Fama, E. F., "Agency Problems and the Theory of the Firm," *Journal of Political Economics* 38 (1980), 288-307.

Feldstein, M., "Do Private Pensions Increase National Savings?," *Journal of Public Economics* (1978), 277-293.

Feldstein, M., "Private Pensions and Inflation," *American Economic Review*, (1981), 424-428.

Feldstein, M., "Private Pensions as Corporate Debt," in *The Changing Roles of Debt and Equity in Financing U.S. Capital Formation*, edited by B. Friedman (Chicago, Ill.: University of Chicago Press, 1982).

Feldstein, M., and S. Seligman, "Pension Funding, Share Prices, and National Saving," NBER Working Paper No. 509.

Fisher, L. and R. L. Weil, "Coping with the Risk of Interest Rate Fluctuations: Returns to Bondholders from Naive and Optimal Strategies," *Journal of Business* 44 (October, 1971), 408-431.

Gatto, M., R. Geske, R. Litzenberger, and H. Sosin, "Mutual Fund Insurance," *Journal of Financial Economics* (September 1980).

Greenbaum, M., "The Market has Spotted Those Pension Problems," *Fortune*, (December 1, 1980), pp. 143-146.

Hodges, S.D. and Schaefer, S.M., "A Model for Bond Portfolio Improvement," *Journal of Financial and Quantitative Analysis* 12 (1977), 243-260.

Khang, C., "Bond Immunization when Short-term Interest Rates Fluctuate More than Long-term Rates," *Journal of Financial and Quantitative Analysis* 14 (1979), 1085-1090.

Klein, B., Crawford, R. G., and Alchian, A. A., "Vertical Integration, Appropriate Rents, and the Competitive Contracting Process," *Journal of Law and Economics* 21 (1978), 297-326.

Lucas, T., and B. Hollowell, "Pension Accounting: The Liability Question," *Journal of Accountancy* (October 1981).

Mayers, D. and Smith, C. W., "Contractual Provisions, Organizational Structure, and Conflict Control in Insurance Markets," *Journal of Business* (1981).

Merton, Robert C., "On Consumption-Indexed Public Pension Plans," Working paper, Sloan School of Management, MIT, 1982.

Miller, M., and M. Scholes, "Pension Funding and Corporate Valuation," Working paper, Graduate School of Business, Unversity of Chicago, 1981.

Myers, S. C., "The Application of Finance Theory to Public Utility Rate Cases," *Bell Journal of Economics and Management Science* 3 (1972), 58-97.

Myers, S. C., "Determinants of Corporate Borrowing," *Journal of Financial Economics* 9 (1977), 138-147.

Nichols, W., and M. Morris, "The Rate of Return Assumption: Insights from the New FASB No. 36, Disclosure," *Financial Analysts Journal*, (September/October 1982), 10-11, 15.

Norby, W., "Employers' Accounting for Pensions," *Financial Analysts Journal* (March/April 1982), 14-15.

Redington, F. M., "Review of the Principles of Life Office Evaluation," *Journal of the Institute of Actuaries* 78 (1952), 286-315.

Regan, P., "Reasons for the Improving Pension Figures," *Financial Anaylsts Journal* (March/April 1982), 14-15.

Schaefer, S. M., "The Problem with Redemption Yields," *Financial Analysts Journal* 33 (1977).

Schaefer, S. M., "Discussion," *Journal of Finance* 35 (1980), 417-419.

Sharpe, W., "Corporate Pension Funding Policy," *Journal of Financial Economics* (June, 1976).

Tepper, I., "Optimal Financial Policies for Trusteed Pension Plans," *Journal of Financial and Quantitative Analysis* (June 1974).

Tepper, I., and A. R. P. Affleck, "Pension Plan Liabilities and Corporate Financial Strategies," *Journal of Finance* (December 1974).

Tepper, I., and R. D. Paul, "How Much Funding for Your Company's Pension Plan?," *Harvard Business Review* (November/December 1978).

Tepper, I., "Taxation and Corporate Pension Policy," *Journal of Finance* (March 1981), pp. 1-13.

Tepper, I., "The Future of Private Pension Funding," *Financial Analysts Journal*, (1982), pp. 25-31.

Titman, S., "The Effect of Capital Structure on a Firm's Liquidation Decision," *Journal of Financial Economics* 13 (1984), 137-183.

Titman, S. and R. Wessels, "The Determinants of the Capital Structure Choice," UCLA working paper, 1984.

Treynor, J., W. Priest, and P. Regan, *The Financial Reality of Pension Funding Under ERISA* (Homewood, Ill.: Dow Jones-Irwin Inc., 1976).

Treynor, J., "The Principles of Corporate Pension Finance," *Journal of Finance* (May 1977).

Westerfield, R., "Pension Plan Asset Mix and Corporate Shareholder Value: An Overview and Preliminary Work," Working paper, The Wharton School, University of Pennsylvania, December 1981.

Part VI: The Corporate Dividend Decision

INTRODUCTION

Over the past fifteen or twenty years, the question of the effect of dividends on stock prices has been a controversial one. Until quite recently, in fact, the academic finance profession collectively had come up with no convincing rationale for corporate dividend payments. Up to this point, there were only two positions on the dividend question that were seriously defended by financial economists: (1) dividends are "irrelevant" (that is, investors in the aggregate care only about their total returns, and the level of total stockholder returns is unaffected by management decisions to pay out part of that return in the form of dividends); and (2) higher dividends actually lead to lower stock prices because taxable investors pay higher taxes on dividends than on capital gains.

Of course, there has never been any doubt that large announced dividend increases are generally accompanied by increases in stock price, and that dividend cuts can send prices plummeting. But the reigning interpretation of this phenomenon has been that such changes in dividend policy convey information to the market *only* about the firm's future *earnings* power. The positive market response to announcements of higher dividends thus says nothing about a preference by investors for dividends per se over capital gains. And this "information effect" has accordingly been interpreted as being consistent with the dividend "irrelevance" proposition.

A third school, however, has recently proposed a positive economic rationale for corporate dividends by elaborating the role of dividends in providing information. Proponents of this relatively new line of reasoning observe that management often has significant inside information about its company's prospects that it cannot (or chooses not to) divulge to investors; and the mere possibility of this information "gap" between management and stockholders causes stock prices to be lower than they otherwise would under conditions of perfect certainty. Corporate dividends, this argument goes, may be management's most cost-effective means of overcoming the investor uncertainty resulting from this potential "informational asymmetry." In periodically and predictably raising the dividend, management effectively binds itself to make a series of future payments to stockholders; and this commitment, which is costly in terms of management's future flexibility (we all know how reluctant managements are to cut the dividend), provides investors with the as-surance that management is not sitting on some important piece of negative information.

A potential problem with this argument, however, is that it doesn't convincingly explain why dividend changes are the most efficient (least costly) way of communicating management's confidence. The fact that almost all successful companies pay dividends would suggest, at least to a "positive" economist, that dividends must have some value for investors that they don't get through capital gains. But, given that there are some very successful companies that have never paid a dividend, and have declared their intention of never paying a dividend, one is led to wonder whether investors really value dividends, or whether they have just been strongly "conditioned" by *management's* behavior to receive them. If the latter is the case, then presumably the process of market conditioning can be reversed by companies persuasively communicating their intention to put their costly equity capital to more profitable uses.

This section on dividends is fittingly introduced by Professor Merton Miller of the University of Chicago, whose 1961 paper (written with Franco Modigliani of M.I.T.) on "Dividend Policy, Growth and the Valuation of Shares" continues to stand as the central pronouncement of "modern finance" on the subject. In "Behavioral Rationality in Finance: The Case of Dividends," Merton Miller addresses the "puzzle" of corporate dividend behavior that has vexed the academic community for the last 25 years. The "puzzle" is this: Given the strongly preferential treatment given capital gains relative to ordinary (dividend) income from 1945 until the Tax Reform Act of 1986, why have American companies persisted in paying, and why do investors seem to want, ever more dividends? Miller defends the "rationality" of U.S. corporate dividend policy by noting that dividend payouts in the post-World War II era have been significantly lower (in response, it appears, to the increasing personal income tax burden) than in the 1920s and early 1930s. And, lest you think this has little application to the current tax environment in which there is no capital gains differential, Miller also cites an impressive body of evidence documenting the responsiveness of stock prices and corporate dividend-paying behavior to major changes in tax regimes (in Canada and the U.K., as well as a short-lived tax on retained earnings levied on U.S. corporations in the 1930s).

In "Does Dividend Policy Matter?," Richard Brealey discusses the dividend irrelevance proposition, as well as the tax arguments against dividends, and the import of each for corporate policy. Although large, unexpected *changes* in dividends can have dramatic effects on stock prices, and thus should probably be avoided, the *level* of the dividend may be a matter of complete indifference to investors in aggregate. Indeed, as the theory and supporting evidence suggest, if dividend yield has any systematic influence on stock prices at all, it is probably a negative one.

In "The Dividend Debate: Twenty Years of Discussion," Patrick Hess provides an historical overview of the relevant academic research, tracing the developments in theory and evaluating the empirical evidence that has accumulated since the publication of the Miller-Modigliani paper 20 years ago. In so doing, Hess provides a persuasive restatement of the "M&M dividend irrelevance" argument.

In "How Companies Set Their Dividend Payout Ratios," Michael Rozeff attempts to take the theory beyond the Miller-Modigliani dividend "irrelevance" argument by offering positive rationales for the corporate practice of paying dividends. Rozeff's study provides some suggestive evidence that the separation of ownership from control in the large public corporation creates a demand for dividends by stockholders. He also presents a model, based on a measure of stockholder dispersion as well as the risk and capital requirements of the firm, which does a reasonably good job of explaining actual corporate dividend payout ratios.

The real crux of the dividend controversy comes down to the question: Does management dare cut the dividend to provide equity capital for funding profitable growth? In the final article in the section, Randy Woolridge and Chinmoy Gosh argue that dividend cuts can be good news for stockholders. Announcements of dividend cuts generally evoke a response little short of panic by investors.

But, as the authors argue, this may be largely the effect of management's past conditioning of the market to expect dividend cuts only as a matter of desperation. For companies with very promising investments and high dividend payout ratios, cutting the dividend may offer the cheapest source of finance, especially if access to equity capital is very costly.

In what may turn out to be some of the most suggestive empirical work to date in support of the dividend "irrelevance or worse" proposition, the authors attempted to distinguish between possible differences in management motives for dividend cuts by isolating a special case from the broader sample: those cases where management announced it was cutting the dividend to provide internal funding for significant growth opportunities. And while the market did not appear to discriminate, except in one or two cases, between these motives when responding to *announcements* of the cuts, there were nevertheless some interesting findings: for example, (1) the sample of all dividend-cutting firms outperformed the market by 10 percent in the *year* following the cut; (2) the special sample of "growth-motivated" dividend-cutting firms outperformed by the market by roughly 9 percent in the quarter following the announcement, and by 16 percent over the following year; (3) when dividend cuts were accompanied by declarations of stock dividends, the market's negative reaction was strongly muted and, for a special case of companies, completely offset; and (4) in one case where a company combined the announcement of a dividend cut with that of a stock repurchase program, the market's response was positive. Shortly after this article first went to print (in the summer of 1985), as if to reinforce the burden of this study, Litton Industries announced the complete cessation of its dividend together with an exchange offer of debt for shares at a large premium — and the market has responded very favorably.

DHC

Behavioral Rationality in Finance: The Case of Dividends*

Merton H. Miller,
*University of Chicago***

Introduction

As the title suggests, this paper attempts to get to the specifics of the behavorial rationality theme of this conference by focusing on an area in the main core of finance—namely, the demand for and supply of dividends—where, by common consent, the essentially "rationalist" paradigm of the field seems to be limping most noticeably. Important and pervasive behavior patterns on both the paying and the receiving ends have despairingly been written off as "puzzles" even by theorists as redoubtable as Fischer Black.[1] Behavorists have homed in on precisely these same dividend-related soft spots in the current body of theory.[2] We seem to have, in sum, an ideal place to look for signs of an imminent "paradigm shift" in the behavorial direction of precisely the kind envisioned by some of the other contributors to this conference.

The dividend-related difficulties and supposed anomalies at issue here are more than just the parochial concern of finance specialists. The finance model of the firm, after all, *is* the standard economists' model of the firm, but with some of the components grouped differently[3]...The two models of the firm, the finance model and the price theory model, are variations on a single theme; moreover, the anomalies burdening any one class of users must be of some concern to the other classes as well.

How much concern should we show at this point about our dividend anomalies? Less, I will argue here, after a fresh look at the evidence, than I and others in finance may once have thought.[4] This is not to say that we do not have our share and more of still-unsolved problems. Finance, after all, is one of the newer specialty areas in economics. But I do not see us in such disarray, even on the much-mooted dividend issues, that we must think of abandoning or even drastically modifying the basic economics/finance paradigm on which the field has been built.

The first task of the paper will be to sketch out briefly what the supposed dividend anomalies are all about. Their perception as anomalies will then be shown to a considerable extent to be traceable to a misinterpretation of the basic model, to a misreading of the empirical record, and perhaps also to exaggerated expectations of what our models can hope to accomplish.

EDITOR'S NOTE: This paper was written in 1985, on the occasion of a University of Chicago conference on "The Behavioral Foundations of Economic Theory," and thus well before the recent tax changes were enacted into U.S. law. Its focus, accordingly, is on past dividend policies and their interpretation rather than on likely future policies. Nevertheless, the economic logic and supporting evidence remain undisturbed and, indeed, bear directly on unexpected changes in U.S. corporate dividend policy over the next few years.

*This article is a slightly condensed version of a paper of the same title published in the *Journal of Business* Vol. 59 No. 2 (October 1986), pp. S451-468; and it is reprinted here with permission of the University of Chicago Press.

**The author wishes to acknowledge helpful comments on an earlier version of this paper that have been received from Nai-fu Chen, Jean-Marie Gagnon, Gur Huberman, Kose John, James Poterba, and especially Melvin Reder.

1. See especially his much-cited 1976 article, "The Dividend Puzzle," *Journal of Portfolio Management* 2 (Winter): 72-77.

2. See especially H. Shefrin and M. Statman, "Explaining Investor Preference for Cash Dividends," *Journal of Financial Economics* 13, no. 2 (June, 1984): 253-82.

3. Deleted from original at this point: "The finance version, focusing on the interaction between the firm and the capital markets, subsumes the details of optimizing output, product pricing, and factor-input combinations into a single intertemporal 'transformation function' of current resource inflows into future resource outflows. The firm in finance becomes, as it were, simply an abstract engine that 'uses money today to make money tomorrow,' as Alfred P. Sloan, that most quintessential of finance-oriented business executives once (almost) described his General Motors Corporation. The firm's objective function, reflecting the specifically intertemporal statement of the firm's problem, must go beyond the familiar rubric of maximizing 'profits' to maximizing 'the net present value of future cash flows.'" The relation between the finance and economics model of the firm is discussed at length by Eugene Fama and Merton H. Miller in *The Theory of Finance* (New York: Holt, Rinehart & Winston, 1972), Chapter 3.

4. See, for example, the introduction to Merton Miller and Myron Scholes, "Dividends and Taxes," *Journal of Financial Economics* 6, no. 2 (December, 1978): 333-64.

The Dividend Anomalies

The dividend anomalies at issue here are mainly tax-related. They are instances in which a substantial body of corporate managers, presumably acting on behalf of their shareholders, appears to have been responding (or, more precisely, failing to respond) over long periods to large and persistent incentives in the tax system.

Recall the essential tax facts [see Editor's Note]. Under U.S. law, the net income of the large, publicly held corporations that are our main concern is first subject to tax at progressive rates that quickly reach 46 percent. Marginal rates at these levels (and higher) were first reached during World War II and have been maintained with only minor changes over the entire period since then. Any dividends paid by the corporation out of its current or accumulated past after-tax earnings are subject to tax (with the inevitable minor exceptions) at the regular progressive rates under the personal income tax.[5] These rates currently peak at 50 percent, their low point for the postwar era; but the maximum has reached as high as 92 percent in the years during and immediately following World War II. The dividends received would also be taxable under state income taxes as well.

By contrast, the portion of the after-corporate tax profits not paid out in dividends, but retained in the firm, is not directly subject to personal income tax.[6] The earnings retained by the corporation may still be reached by the tax system, but by a somewhat more indirect route. The retained earnings increase the value of the shares—or at least that is the presumption in the model whose anomalies are being probed. Should the share subsequently be sold at a price greater than its original cost, the price appreciation will constitute a taxable capital gain. The rates applied to such gains are hard to describe briefly; but, for individual holders, the rates on realized capital gains are never higher than those on ordinary income and are typically lower. For securities owned for more than a minimum holding period—which has varied from six months to one year in the post-World War II era—the statutory rate on gains has rarely been more than half the regular rates and then only for taxpayers who have triggered one of the minimum-tax provisions that Congress tends to enact in its periods of loophole-closing frenzy. The maximum rate on capital gains was capped for much of the postwar era at 25 percent, so the maximum gap between the top rate on ordinary income and on capital gains could have been as much as 67 percentage points! Remember, that is for *realized* gains only. Shares not sold during one's lifetime but held for one's estate escape the capital gains tax altogether.

Our tax law, in sum, thus places a substantial penalty on dividends as opposed to retained earnings/capital gains. Why, then, in the face of these penalties, do firms continue to pay them? Before the modern finance model was developed, economists and public finance specialists may have presumed that firms had no better alternative. Investment in projects at declining rates of profitability could proceed until the marginal return on internally financed investments had been driven to equality with the stockholders' after-tax dividend return. But thereafter, paying out the funds and taking the dividend tax hit would dominate further pouring of funds into low-return rat holes.

In the finance model, however, there are better alternatives to dividend payouts than wasteful real investments[7]....In such a setting, the firm is pictured as taking any internally generated funds remaining after profitable real investment opportunities have been exhausted and using them not for paying tax-disadvantaged dividends but for the purchase of securities, either its own or those of other firms (or governments). On these financial investments the firm will presumably earn not a rat-hole return but the same market, risk-adjusted return that serves as its own capital budgeting cutoff. The firm's share-

---

5. For tax years after 1981, the first $100 of dividends ($200 on a joint return) could be excluded from income. Special provisions, which expired at the end of 1985, were also made for the dividend reinvestment plans of utilities. Prior to 1936, dividends were exempt from the low, flat-rate normal tax but fully subject to the progressive surtaxes.

6. Small, closely held corporations, but only such, may elect to be taxed as partnerships under subchap. S of the Internal Revenue Code. In this case, no corporate income tax is levied and the entire net profit of the corporation, whether distributed or not, is taxed as ordinary personal income to the shareholders.

7. Deleted from original at this point: "The technological concavity in the opportunity set imposed by the law of diminishing returns on real investment can be bypassed, as it were, for any one firm by adjoining the essentially linear technology of transactions in securities in well-functioning capital markets. The production function in the finance model of the firm is only weakly concave, not strictly concave."

The critical role of external securities in the dividend supply function was first noted explicitly in my 1961 paper with Franco Modigliani, "Dividend Policy, Growth, and the Valuation of Shares," *Journal of Business* 34, no. 4 (October): 411-33. That was indeed a major thrust of our paper, though somewhat obscured perhaps by the more controversial and provocative material on the valuation of shares. Our point, however, is also a fairly direct implication of the standard Fisherian model of the finance firm, as can clearly be seen from our discussion in ch. 2 of Eugene Fama and Merton Miller, *The Theory of Finance* (New York: Holt, Rinehart & Winston, 1972).

The anomaly plaguing the current finance model...rests essentially on the belief that firms are systematically failing to benefit their shareholders by converting high-taxed dividends to low-taxed capital gains.

holders, moreover, whatever their tax status, would, if they are behaving rationally, also seem to be unanimous in favoring such a strategy.[8] Some of the shareholders, like pension funds and university endowments, are themselves tax-exempt and hence have no incentive to shun dividends. But, by the same token, they would seem to have no tax incentive to oppose the efforts of their taxable brethren to improve their lot by transforming the firm's return from fully taxable dividends to untaxed or at least lower-taxed capital gains. (It may be a weak-inequality form of unanimity, but it is still unanimity.)[9]

Such, then, is the anomaly plaguing the current finance model of the dividend-paying firm. It rests essentially on the belief that firms are systematically failing to benefit their shareholders by converting high-taxed dividends to low-taxed capital gains. Most nonspecialists will suspect that the most likely route for resolving the anomaly is on the cost-of-conversion side. Surely, they will presume, there can be no free lunches in conversions. They will certainly be correct with respect to one of the main financial strategies for conversion suggested by the underlying model—namely, buying the securities of other firms and (and governments). It may be instructive, therefore, to get at least that class of distractions out of the way before turning to the more serious issues raised by the other conversion strategy of buying back the firm's own securities.[10]

The Costs of Avoiding Cash Payouts by Buying Outside Securities

A first look at the finance model can all too easily lead one to the belief that even investing in government bonds normally would be better (and

never worse) for the shareholders than paying out cash dividends. Not so, however. In fact, holding significant amounts of government bonds or other purely financial instruments is not even a feasible alternative for corporations under U.S. tax laws.

The infeasibility is more than just a matter of Internal Revenue Code section 532, which imposes a penalty tax for "improper accumulation of surplus." That provision has indeed been part of the code almost from its inception, and its purpose has been precisely to keep shareholders from avoiding the personal income tax on dividends by piling up cash in the corporation. But few firms have ever been caught in its meshes.[11]

The moral to be drawn from this lack of bite, however, is precisely the opposite of that usually drawn, which is that the section is a toothless tiger, not even worth mentioning as a deterrent to cutting back on dividends. Clearly, from the section's existence and history we know that both Congress and the Internal Revenue Service are aware of the potential for dividend tax avoidance via corporate hoarding as well as of the steps that would have to be taken to close off that route. That they have not troubled to do so suggests that the route is not being sufficiently traveled to make an effort via section 532 worthwhile.

Section 532 has been rendered largely superfluous for publicly held corporations by another and much more fundamental tax provision, the corporation income tax itself. Under that tax, the interest earned on any government bonds in the corporate hoards would be taxable in principle at the full marginal corporate rate of 46 percent.[12] Hence any pension fund or other institutional holder offered a choice between receiving an immediate cash dividend or having the corporation invest the cash in government bonds would not be indifferent, or anywhere close to it, even though the institution itself

---

8. Not quite. Nothing in our tax law ever seems that clear-cut. Corporations holding shares in other corporations are permitted to exclude 85% of intercorporate dividends received. The effective minimum tax on intercorporate dividends is about 7%, which is substantially below the corporate capital gains tax. Corporate holdings of shares for investment purposes, however, are predominantly in the form of preferred stocks. Corporate shareholding is worth a mention but is not a major part of the story to be developed here.

9. Another qualification should be entered for the record. Where a firm has adopted a dividend reinvestment plan (DRIP) with a significant price discount (frequently as high as 5%) on the shares acquired, its institutional investors would no longer be neutral between dividends and capital gains but would strongly prefer dividends. By reinvesting the dividends and then immediately selling off the shares so acquired, they pick up a substantial quasi-arbitrage profit. Relative to the issues of concern here, however, DRIPs are of too recent an origin and too limited a scope to play any major explanatory role.

10. Although the emphasis in this paper will be on the conversion opportunities available to firms, individuals too have methods for converting dividends to capital gains. In principle, as shown in a paper I co-authored with Myron Scholes

("Dividends and Taxes," *Journal of Financial Economics* 6, no. 2 (December): 333-64), these tactics could make the corporate conversion possibilities redundant; but, in practice, these techniques are likely to be availed of only by the small (but possibly important) minority of stockholders who regularly buy stocks on margin.

11. The penalty will not be invoked if the firm can show that its accumulations have a "valid business purpose," and proving that presents little challenge to even a moderately competent tax lawyer. In the past few years, the Internal Revenue Service has begun to put some additional muscle behind its enforcement efforts and to reach firms substantially larger than had earlier been the case. But the firms affected have all been closely held or at least clearly controlled by a dominant shareholder. No publicly traded firm with widely dispersed ownership (of the kind that the finance model is concerned with) has even been hit by sec. 532. The similarly motivated personal holding company penalties are also confined to closely held corporations.

12. The inevitable qualification: the IRS will tolerate a limited amount of stashing away of tax-free investments by "overfunding" the firm's pension fund.

was tax-exempt and subject to no tax on either dividends or capital gains. Nor are institutional investors the only body of shareholders disadvantaged when a taxable corporation uses otherwise available funds to purchase securities that those investors could acquire directly. Taxable shareholders can also be hurt if the numbers are such that the front-end bite of the dividend tax on the dollars paid out turns out to be less than the present value of the stream of additional corporate tax payments incurred on the funds invested. Precisely where that boundary lies need not be spelled out in detail. The present concern is simply whether observed corporate dividend behavior can be regarded as anomalous relative to the standard finance model because investment in securities by the firm would be a uniformly or even weakly superior alternative to paying dividends. Merely establishing that a cutoff exists means that the answer is no.[13]

To dispose of a dividend-related anomaly by invoking a tax argument is never entirely satisfactory even when, as here, the anomaly itself is tax-induced. The dividend policies of firms and individuals today are similar, at least in broad outline, to those found before the present tax system and in countries with tax regimes very different from our own. It is worth emphasizing, therefore, that the tax case against corporate hoarding is offered here in the sense of sufficiency, not necessity. No shortage exists of other costs and drawbacks to a policy of holding securities at the corporate level beyond the liquidity needs of

the business. Too much of the benefits would accrue to the firm's creditors and, more to the point, the treasures might attract raiders, as the story of the Rhine Maidens and their ring reminds us. Indeed, much of the presumed motivation of the acquirers, and certainly much of their rhetoric, in recent highly publicized takeover struggles, has focused precisely on getting unproductive assets out of corporate solution and into the hands of the shareholders.[14] Hoarding, in sum, is not a feasible alternative to dividends. With that established, we can turn now to some dividend-conversion strategies available to the firm that make the tax anomaly less easy to shrug off.

Share Repurchase and the Supply of and Demand for Dividends

Rather than buy government securities or securities of other firms, a firm, in this country at least, always has the option of purchasing its own securities.[15] This route can get excess funds out of corporate solution, thus avoiding the class of difficulties just seen but without creating dividends, which are taxable as ordinary income under the personal income tax.

At first sight, the policy of share repurchase may seem to benefit only those shareholders who choose to take the other side of the firm's offer to buy. But that is not so. The policy of share repurchase, like the quality of mercy, is twice blessed. It blesses not only

---

13. The argument in this section about the purely tax disadvantages of financial investment relative to dividends was first made in the finance literature, as far as I am aware, by David Emanuel ("Debt and Taxes, Dividends and Taxes, and Taxes," Mimeographed. Dallas: University of Texas (1983)). Essentially the same point could have been made, though in a less transparent way, in terms of standard finance "capital structure" models. In a so-called before-tax equilibrium world (as in Modigliani and Miller (1963), for example), any investment in taxable, interest-bearing securities would be "negative leverage" and hence would, ceteris paribus, lower the value of the shares. In an "after-tax equilibrium" world (as in Miller (1977)), holding of taxable securities by the firm would deprive the tax-exempt and low-bracket shareholders of the "bondholders' surplus" that they could earn with the funds on their own. Investments by corporations in preferred stock of other taxable corporations are less tax disadvantageous to institutional and low-bracket holders than investments in interest-bearing securities, thanks to the 85% exclusion on intercorporate dividends received. Hence the great popularity in recent years of new instruments such as ARPs (adjustable rate preferreds) and MARs (multiple adjustable rate preferreds) as temporary abodes for cash. To the extent, however, that yields adjust and issues recapture some of the tax benefits, as appears to be the case, the corporate buyers are paying what Scholes, Mazur, and Wolfson (see "A Model of Implicit Taxes and their Effect on Empirical Estimates of Income Tax Progressivity," Mimeographed. Stanford, Calif.: Stanford University (1984)) have dubbed an "implicit tax" over and above the nominal 7% (i.e., .46 x .85). For holdings of common stock by corporations, the implicit tax on the dividends is smaller. Some would argue, as we shall see, that it is substantially negative because dividends sell at such a substantial discount. Even if true, however, it would clearly be a self-referencing paradox to imagine every cash-rich dividend-paying corporation to be avoiding payment of dividends by investing in the dividend-

paying shares of other cash-rich corporations. Of course, cash-rich firms could purchase the shares of cash-poor corporations. Indeed, some, but only some, of the seeming merger wave of recent years has been so motivated. But merger activity that eliminates one firm's securities from the capital markets is perhaps more appropriately treated as real investment than as financial investment. (I have benefited from discussions of these issues with my colleague Gur Huberman but absolve him from responsibility for any errors.)

14. Interestingly enough, the raiders have been zeroing in on hoards of passive investment funds even when held in tax-exempt form in overfunded pension plans (see, for example, L. Asinof, "Excess Pension Assets Lure Corporate Raiders," *Wall Street Journal* (September 22, 1985). For a discussion of some moral hazard problems in overfunding pension plans, see also R. A. Ippolito, "The Economic Function of Underfunded Pension Plans," *Journal of Law and Economics* 28, no. 3 (October, 1985): 611-51.) Recent spin-offs of developed oil field properties into limited partnerships (not subject to corporate income tax) offer additional examples of efforts to get what amounts to passive "investment income" out of corporate form and attendant tax burdens.

15. The qualification is made because the frequently heard, conventional wisdom is that corporate law in Great Britain and in most European countries rules out share repurchase. Perhaps so, if taken literally; but one suspects that there must be other, equivalent tactics that permit a business to reduce in size. In Belgium, the explicit restrictions appear to apply only to self-tenders, not to open-market purchases. In Canada, Jean-Marie Gagnon of Laval University in Quebec, commenting on an earlier version of this paper, notes that share repurchase very definitely is permitted under Canadian law, subject, however, to the standard restrictions on actions damaging to the firm or its creditors. He suspects that a misinterpretation of those restrictions may be the source of the folk belief that share repurchase is somehow illegal.

those who sell but also those who do not. In fact, the nonsellers are thrice blessed because their benefit takes the form not of realized, but of unrealized capital gains.[16] Note also that when allowance is made for the taxes, stayers under the buy-back plan might be better off than under a dividend plan, even if the firm had to pay the sellers a premium over the market price, as is often the case when the firm tenders for the shares. The gain from nontaxability more than offsets the loss from dilution.[17]

Share repurchase is thus clearly superior to corporate hoarding as a method of transforming current dividends into current capital gains. But it is not a costless alternative to paying dividends. Brokerage fees must be incurred, and, in the case of tenders, often underwriting expenses must be paid as well. Still, transaction costs of this kind seem small when compared with the statutory tax differentials between dividends and capital gains. So much so, in fact, that it might be daunting to a behavorial theorist of the firm to venture even a boundedly rational explanation of why dividends continue to be paid (at least by firms other than public utilities).[17a]

Remember, however, that in the finance model of the supply of dividends, whose possibly anomalous status is our concern, the tax differentials under the personal income tax do not enter the firm's objective function directly. The managers of large, widely held corporations are not pictured there as solving dividend decision problems by performing "thought experiments," as we here have been doing, about what might or might not be in the best interests of this or that group of the shareholders (though they may well tend to couch their explanations in those terms). Rather, as with constructing any other supply function in the theory of the firm, the managers are assumed to be responding to the

signals conveyed to them by market prices. The process is a bit harder to visualize for dividends, perhaps, because the price of dividends relative to capital gains is not quoted directly, as such, in the columns of the *Wall Street Journal*. But that price can be *inferred*, at least within tolerable limits, from the stock prices and dividend yields reported there and from the analyses, formal and informal, performed on that and other relevant data by financial analysts within and outside the firm.

For the finance model of dividend supply to be held anomalous, therefore, or at least as requiring important structural modifications (including, quite possibly, the grafting on of major elements from the behavorial theory of the firm), it would be sufficient (and, in my view, also necessary) to show that the observed market price of dividend return can confidently be placed too far below the observed market price of capital gain return to be plausibly attributed to the likely cost of converting current dividends to current capital gains. The feeling that empirical research has established that dividends have, in fact, long been selling at a substantial discount appears to be the major contributor to the sense of unease within the profession about the status of the model. It is important, therefore, to be clear about what has and what has not been shown about the market price of dividends relative to capital gains.

The Empirical Record

The conventional impression that academic empirical research has shown a large and long-standing price penalty on dividends is perhaps nowhere so neatly capsulized as in a "box score" table added to the last edition of Brealey and Myers's excellent textbook

16. For nonspecialists, perhaps the following numerical example may help sort things out. Suppose, to keep things simple, there were no taxes to complicate calculations, and suppose a firm with 1 million shares outstanding had set aside $4 million for return to the shareholders. Suppose further that, after it announced the setting aside of $4.00 per share, the *cum-dividend* price of each share at this time were to be $44. After the dividend was paid, each shareholder would have $4.00 in cash plus an *ex-dividend* share worth $40, ceteris paribus. Imagine now that, instead of paying the dividend, the firm had used the same $4 million to buy 90,909 shares at the predistribution price of $44. The nonselling shareholders receive no cash, of course, but each of their shares now represents a larger fraction of the firm. In fact, each will be worth $44 ($40,000,000/909,091). Thus every stockholder winds up with the same net worth of $44 per share no matter which policy the firm follows in disposing of the cash. The only difference is in how the net worth is divided between cash and shares (a uniform $4.00 in cash and $40 in shares for every holder under the dividend route vs. $44 in cash for the sellers and $44 in stock for the stayers under the buy-back route).

17. But the premium cannot be set too high or the procedure becomes self-defeating. If everyone tenders and is prorated, the cash distribution is "proportional" and will be treated as a dividend for tax purposes. Under present rules, a reduction in fractional interest in the corporation of 20% or more is required to assure any stockholder that payments received in a share self-tender offer are not deemed to be merely disguised dividends. These restrictions do not apply to open-market repurchases and are moot, of course, even under self-tenders for nontaxable institutional shareholders. But that does not mean that such investors will be indifferent between dividends and self-tenders. A tender offer at a premium above market (but not so far above to get even the taxable holders to tender) may well be better for them than a dividend after all costs have been taken into account.

17a. Public utility managements have found a policy of high dividends combined with frequent external equity financing to be a useful strategy for forcing their regulators to keep utility rates high enough to continue attracting new funds from investors. Investors realize this, of course, and hence utility stocks historically have tended to attract a clientele that strongly prefers cash dividends to plow-back induced capital gains.

18. Richard Brealey and Stewart Myers, *Principles of Corporate Finance*. 2d ed. New York: McGraw-Hill, 1984, p. 348.

> *[According to a study by Marshall Blume,]* the relation between
> *risk-adjusted returns and dividend yields was U-shaped. The market*
> *appeared to demand a return premium both from those firms paying*
> *the most in dividends and from those paying the least.*

on corporate finance.[18] Ten separate statistical studies of the average cross-sectional relation between risk-adjusted stock returns and dividend yields are summarized therein. In eight of the ten studies, the regression coefficient representing the return premium for dividends—or, equivalently, the price discount for dividends—was substantial both in absolute size (equivalent, say, to an effective "tax differential" on dividends over capital gains of from 25 percent to as high as 56 percent) and relative to its reported standard error. There were only two exceptions to the modal result.[19] One was the classic study by Black and Scholes.[20] If the results of the Black-Scholes study had to be expressed as a single point estimate, then it too would have been a dividend discount on the order of 20 percent. But the essential message of the paper, stressed repeatedly by the authors themselves, was that with the data and techniques then available, the differential in the weight on dividends relative to capital gains could not be pinned down in size or even in sign.

The other study departing from the general trend was one by Miller and Scholes.[21] In that study, however, our concern was not to provide the best estimate of the dividend coefficient but to show that the dividend coefficient reported in another and very influential study (Litzenberger and Ramaswamy (1978))[22] was sensitive to seemingly small adjustments in the definition of dividend yield used. In addition, and more to the present point, we showed that what Scholes and I called the "short-run measure" of dividend yield used by Litzenberger and Ramaswamy was, for a variety of reasons, inappropriate for measuring the market price obtainable for dividends supplied. On that score, at least, some-

thing approaching a consensus has emerged, and virtually all recent cross-sectional empirical work on the dividend issue has relied on so-called long-run measures of dividend yield, in the same spirit as the original Black-Scholes study, though with some improvements in detail.[23]

One of the most provocative of these post-Black-Scholes studies is that of Marshall Blume.[24] Blume showed that, looking solely at firms that were actually paying dividends, there did indeed appear to be a substantial average cross-sectional dividend yield premium—an excess return so large, in fact (as Blume noted), as to be beyond plausibility as a compensation solely for tax differentials. But the cross-sectional scatters showed that the relation between risk-adjusted returns and dividend yields (which, when properly scaled, is the sought-for measure of the market price for dividends) was U-shaped. The market appeared to demand a return premium both from those firms paying the most in dividends and from those paying the least (i.e., zero).

Attempting to account for puzzling extreme observations can sometimes turn up important neglected aspects of the problem under study, and such indeed proved to be the case with Blume's "U." Donald Keim noticed that the firms at the two ends of the U—the zero-dividend firms and the highest-dividend firms—were primarily small companies.[25] What made that observation so interesting was the rapidly building mountain of research on the so-called small-firm effect.

The small-firm effect is the finding—by now amply documented both here and abroad—that small firms, even after adjustment for the standard CAPM-based measures of risk, appear to earn signifi-

---

19. There is even one very small piece of evidence often cited in support of the position that the relative price of dividends may actually be *higher* rather than lower than that of capital gains. This is the case of Citizens' Utility as reported by John Long ("The Market Valuation of Cash Dividends: A Case to Consider," *Journal of Financial Economics* 6, no. 3 (June/September, 1978): 235-64). The company was allowed by the Treasury to issue two class of shares, one paying cash dividends and the other dividends in stock, with the stock dividend shares convertible to the cash dividend shares. The ratio of the stock dividend to the cash dividend was subject to change (and hence to some uncertainty at the time of purchase). But after making reasonable adjustments, Long concludes that the cash dividend shares were selling at a premium relative to the stock dividend shares. It is difficult, however, to know how much weight to place on observations on a stock so thinly traded. For an updated look at Citizens' Utility that comes to somewhat different conclusions, see J. Poterba, "The Citizens' Utility Case: A Further Dividend Puzzle," Working Paper no. 339. Cambridge: Massachusetts Institute of Technology, 1985.

20. F. Black and M. Scholes, "The Effects of Dividend Yield and Dividend Policy on Common Stock Prices and Returns," *Journal of Financial Economics* 1, no. 1 (May, 1974): 1-22.

21. M. Miller and M. Scholes, "Dividends and Taxes: Some Empirical Evidence," *Journal of Political Economy* 90, no. 6 (December, 1982): 1118-41.

22. R. Litzenberger and K. Ramaswamy, "The Effect of Personal Taxes and

Dividends on Capital Asset Prices," *Journal of Financial Economics* 7, no. 2 (June, 1979): 163-95.

23. The use of short-run measures of dividend yield makes a test essentially one of the size of the momentary cum-dividend/ex-dividend (cum-ex) differential. The substantial body of literature attempting to use the direct, cum-ex route to establish the discount for dividends has established that the differential is certainly affected by taxes but that transactions costs, dividend "arbitrage" games, and the distortion of the normal patterns of transactions around ex days make it impossible to draw any reliable inferences about the price of dividends over the longer intervals that are relevant for the supply curve of dividends. For an account of the current state of the cum-ex experiments, see B. Grundy, "Trading Volume and Stock Returns around Ex-dividend Days," Mimeographed. Chicago: University of Chicago, Graduate School of Business, 1985.

24. Marshall Blume, "Stock Returns and Dividend Yields: Some More Evidence," *Review of Economics and Statistics* 62 (November, 1980): 567-77.

25. Donald Keim, "Further Evidence on Size Effects and Yield Effects: The Implications of Stock Return Seasonality," Mimeographed. Chicago: University of Chicago, Graduate School of Business, 1982. Many of these high-yield firms, of course, are likely to be once-large firms that have recently become smaller because of adverse business conditions, but have not yet adjusted their dividends to their new, lower level of earnings.

> *We may not be able to say as much as we would like about the long-run equilibrium price of dividends; but...evidence is accumulating that the quantity of dividends does vary appropriately in response to significant exogenous shocks to demand or supply.*

cantly higher rates of return than do large firms.[26] These higher returns, moreover, appeared to have a marked seasonal pattern: they occurred mostly in January.[27] The same was true of the dividend-yield return premiums on each arm of Blume's U. What, therefore, were all the dividend studies measuring? Dividend effects? Small-firm effects? January effects? All of the above? None of the above?

Since Keim's work, the focus of empirical research has shifted to seeking more powerful econometric methods for isolating the separate contributions of these effects. The search, however, has yet to produce much in the way of results[28]...

Until recently, at least, we could hope that these difficulties would someday be overcome and that eventually we would get a sharp enough fix on the market price of dividends to determine whether the aggregate corporate supply of dividends has really been in the long-standing disequilibrium relative to the predictions of the standard, value-maximizing model of the firm. My colleagues Nai-Fu Chen, Bruce Grundy, and Robert Stambaugh, however, have been devoting their not inconsiderable econometric prowess to this task and have reluctantly concluded that the estimating equations are too sensitive even to small variations in the risk measure to establish confidently whether dividends sell at a discount relative to capital gains.[29] We are back to Black and Scholes!

This inconclusiveness is certainly not the best that one could have hoped for; but it is also not the worst. At least, it puts to rest the charge that the corporate sector has systematically failed to respond to the price signals being sent by the market. No clear and steady signal to management to reduce dividends is coming through the noise.[30]

But we can actually do somewhat better than this. We may not be able to say as much as we would like about the long-run equilibrium *price* of dividends; but, as will be shown in the next section, evidence is accumulating that the *quantity* of dividends brought to market does vary appropriately in response to significant exogenous shocks to demand or supply.[31] After all, comparative statics—explaining and predicting the economy's adjustment to change—is why we build maximizing models in the first place.

The Response to Shocks

The most promising place to look for experiments testing the dividend supply and demand model is along the fault line between the corporate and personal income taxes. While a method of integrating the two taxes that is not open to serious attack on economic or political grounds has yet to be found (and, indeed, may not exist), the possibility is always on the tax policy agenda. When such switches in tax regime are implemented, drastic, order-of-magnitude changes can occur in the relative demand price of dividends, the supply price of dividends, or both.

In the United States, such changes in regime have unfortunately (or perhaps fortunately) been rare. A deduction at the corporate level for part of dividends paid was a feature of the recent Treasury tax reform bill, but it remains unlikely that academic researchers will ever have the benefit of observing that particular comet. Aside from these periodically proposed and usually aborted integration schemes (which would not leave even a trace for an event study) and some trivial relief under the personal income tax such as the flat $100 dividend exclusion

26. For a recent survey, see G. W. Schwert, "Size and Stock Returns and Other Empirical Regularities," *Journal of Financial Economics* 12, no. 1 (June, 1983): 3-12.

27. Donald Keim, "Size-related Anomalies and Stock Return Seasonality: Further Empirical Evidence," *Journal of Financial Economics* 12, no. 1 (June, 1983): 13-32.

28. Deleted from original at this point: "This should not be entirely surprising in view of the higher degree of collinearity between each of the intertwined effects and between each of them and the CAPM-based risk measure. There is the further complication that the true functional form of the relation between returns and the variables may not be the linear one to which we are effectively restricted. If, then, we happen to turn up a significant coefficient for one or more of our variables, how can we be confident that we are seeing genuine economic contributions and not mere correlations of the variable with residuals induced by the misrepresentation of the functional form?"

29. N.-F. Chen, B. Grundy, and R. Stambaugh, "Changing Risk, Changing Expectations and the Relation between Expected Return and Dividend Yield," Mimeographed. Chicago: University of Chicago, Graduate School of Business, 1985.

30. If the tax penalty on dividends does not show up in the price of dividends, where can it have gone? The answer to be offered in this paper (and proposed earlier by Black and Scholes, though in somewhat different terms) is that the quantity of dividends supplied has adjusted. The current equilibrium price of dividends, at the intersection of demand and supply, is now not easily distinguished from the price of capital gains, suggesting that the fabled "marginal shareholder" is a tax-exempt institution, or at least someone with a low cost of switching between dividends and capital gains.

31. Soon we may also have at least some indirect evidence as to whether the market for dividends is so far out of equilibrium as to generate substantial arbitraging side flows between "clienteles," i.e., between those who might have high relative demand prices for dividends and those who might have low cost of switching between dividends and capital gains. Recent Treasury rulings have permitted one firm, the Americus Trust, to purchase shares of ordinary corporations and reissue them in two pieces, one giving rights (essentially) to the dividends and the other (essentially) to the capital appreciation. The two pieces can be recombined at any time and turned in to the trust for a single underlying share. At present, only two stocks are involved, AT&T and Exxon, but more are promised. A separation of dividends and capital gains has long been available, though less efficiently, via so-called dual funds. The aggregate holdings of all such funds, however, represent only a tiny fraction of corporate shares outstanding.

(which, of course, affects no decisions at the margin), I am aware of only one major, detectable change of regime in the United States since the income tax took its modern form during World War I. I refer to the Undistributed Profits Tax of 1936. This now-all-but-forgotten piece of New Deal legislation levied a tax on corporate profits remaining after corporate income taxes (then at a rate of 11 percent in the top bracket), interest on U.S. government securities, and payment of taxable cash dividends. The rates of the undistributed profits tax were progressive, starting at 7 percent of undistributed profits and reaching a maximum rate of 27 percent when 100 percent of after-tax income was retained.

The tax was in force for only two years, 1936 and 1937. It was still technically on the books in 1938, but by then it had been virtually emasculated.[32] During the two years of 1936 and 1937, when the cost of not paying dividends was increased so sharply, the flow of cash dividends paid surged dramatically. A study undertaken shortly after the incident, while memories were still fresh, puts the extra flow of dividends (beyond what might normally have been expected at that stage of the business cycle) at about 33 1/3 percent.[33] A collapse of equivalent magnitude occurred in 1938, when the tax was, mercifully, put to death.

Although the episode of the Undistributed Profits Tax exhausts the list of major regime changes in the United States, the set of instructive experiments can be expanded substantially by drawing on experience from abroad. In 1973, for example, Canada abandoned its long-standing policy, common to all tax systems adapted from the old British model, of exempting from tax all capital gains and losses (except for brokers and others in the business of dealing in securities). The same Canadian statute also reduced effective tax rates on dividends so that the combined effect (though not uniform across all income levels) amounted on balance to a substantial tipping of the scales in favor of dividend income.

For the period immediately after the shift, Khoury and Smith report a significant increase in the rate of growth of dividends on the part of a repre-

sentative sample of Canadian firms.[34] They also find significant differences, in the predicted direction, between the dividend payout policies before and after the tax change of their Canadian sample relative to a matched sample of comparable U.S. firms.

In Great Britain, as many as five distinct changes in tax regime can be discerned in the post-World War II era as Labour and Conservative governments alternated their tenure in office. The direction of change in the relative burdens on dividends and capital gains was not always uniform across all income levels; also, dividend responses by firms were inhibited over part of the period by direct controls on dividends.[35] Still, a study by Poterba and Summers was able to document reasonably clear signals of the appropriate kind being sent to management by changes in stock prices in the period following the changes and of an appropriate adaptation of dividend flow to those signals when firms had the freedom to do so.[36]

Although changes in tax regime provide the most dramatic and hence informative experiments, changes in the rate structure, if sudden enough and drastic enough, can be almost as effective. In the United States, for example, the transition of the income tax from a minor nuisance to a major engine of income redistribution was a matter of only a few years. Surtax rates on ordinary income, which would include dividends, surged upward in the mid-1930s and were ratcheted up again during the the rearmament period of the late 1930s and the war years of the early 1940s. The adustments of corporate payout policies (and of individual portfolio strategies) to the new environment was masked for a while by concern with other, even more massive tax effects on corporate profits--notably, those coming from the excess-profits tax and the carryback of postwar losses and unused credits against wartime taxes. But by the early 1950s, the increased reliance on retained earnings by U.S. corporations, compared with their payout practices in the 1920s and early 1930s, was widely noted among economists. In fact, it is worth remembering that the classic dividend

---

32. See D. L. Rolbein, "Noncash Dividends and Stock Rights as Methods for Avoidance of the Undistributed Profits Tax," *Journal of Business* 12, no. 3 (July, 1939): especially pp. 221-22, n.3.

33. See G. E. Lent, *The Impact of the Undistributed Profits Tax, 1936-37.* New York: Columbia University Press, 1948.

34. N. T. Khoury and K. V. Smith, "Dividend Policy and the Capital Gains Tax in Canada," *Journal of Business Administration* 8, no. 2 (Spring, 1977): 19-37.

35. The United Stated too has long been known to institute dividend controls. Under the Nixon price controls of 1973-74, dividend growth was to be

"voluntarily" restricted by firms to 5%. A noticeable bulge in share repurchases occurred during this period. In fact, some cynics regarded the spectacle of leading corporate officials standing at the side of Arthur Burns and calling for voluntary dividend restrictions as a classic example of the Brer Rabbit tactic of pleading not to be thrown into the briar patch.

36. J. M. Poterba and L. H. Summers, "The Economic Effects of Dividend Taxation," in E. Altman and M. Subrahmanyam (eds.), *Recent Advances in Corporate Finance.* Homewood, Ill.: Irwin, 1985.

study of John Lintner (1956) was undertaken precisely in response to the then-controversial issue of whether there had indeed been a fundamental shift in the corporate propensity to save.[37] Lintner concluded that there had not been a shift. But a subsequent, much more detailed study by John Brittain (1966) showed quite convincingly that a downward shift in corporate dividend payout policies had occurred and that it could not be attributed to any of the proposed explanatory factors other than the change in the tax environment.[38] Poterba and Summers, moreover, report that the shift first noted by Brittain appears to have been a permanent one. They find no signs in the period after Brittain's study of any return to prewar payout patterns.[39]

Although major tax changes of the kind discussed above are likely to provide the most direct demonstrations of the comparative statics of the finance/dividend model, they are certainly not the only detectable shocks to which the underlying demand curves and supply curves are subject. We seem, in fact, to be undergoing just such a major shock at the moment in the form of a dramatic reduction in the cost of going back and forth between cash and securities.

These costs of getting in and out of cash are important to the model if only because they are presumed to be a major part of what justifies our speaking of a demand curve for dividends. The direct and indirect costs of converting shares to cash, if high enough, create a demand for cash dividends, even on the part of taxable investors, that would support a nonzero equilibrium supply of dividends by the corporate sector. With the coming of discount brokers, however, and with new financial instruments such as Cash Management Accounts that can make a portfolio of stocks the virtual equivalent of a checking account, the liquidity benefits of dividend-paying shares are fast eroding. The demand curve for cash dividends would thus appear to be shifting to the left.[40] Furthermore, casual observation of corporate share repurchase activity (especially, but not only, in connection with well-publicized take-overs and recapitalizations) suggests that supply too is adjusting--but slowly. In the last

analysis, it may well be this slowness to adjust, as well the seemingly endless persistence on both sides of the market of long-outmoded habits of thought about dividends, that is at least partly responsible for the concern within the profession about the predictive power of the underlying model.

Some of what appears to be sluggishness in corporate dividend policies relative to model predictions can be traced to the failure, in the short run, of the model's strong information assumptions. The equilibrium conditions in the model are worked out under essentially "double dummy" rules in which all the players are presumed to know each other's cards. Over the long pull, disclosure policies, both mandatory and voluntary, may make this a reasonable enough approximation. But in the shorter run-- and certainly at the time that any single particular dividend in the temporal sequence is under active consideration--management can be presumed to know more than outside investors about the current and immediate prospects of the firm. Under these conditions of asymmetric information, dividend decisions can take on an additional strategic dimension that, on balance, tends to inhibit changes in policy. That inhibition is likely to be particularly strong where, as at present, the objective conditions seem to be suggesting a fall in the demand for dividends. Passing or cutting the dividend has often been taken by the market as a bad-news signal despite the most elaborate educational preparation by the management and its public relations support teams. Many, indeed, are the corporate treasurers who have wished to be the *second* major firm in their industry to slash dividends.

Taking these strategic and information-related elements more formally into the basic model is clearly desirable and is, in fact, currently the focus of much research.[41] But developments of the underlying apparatus in these directions should not be taken as implying any systematic drawing away from the rationality postulate. If anything, signaling models and other models in information economics tend, in some ways, to place even greater demands on the rationality assumption than the valuation models from which they are taken.[42]

37. J. Lintner, "The Distribution of Incomes of Corporations among Dividends, Retained Earnings and Taxes," *American Economic Review* 46 (May, 1956): 97-113.

38. J. Brittain, *Corporate Dividend Policy*, (Washington, D.C.: Brookings, 1966).

39. Poterba and Summers (1985, p. 270), cited in note 36.

40. It was thus somewhat ironic that dividend relief was included among the administration's and Ways and Means Committee tax reform proposals. The technological improvements and regulatory changes that have lowered the cost of security transactions by individuals have also done so for corporations. Reductions at that level have reduced the cost of both increasing dividends (by outside finance) and decreasing dividends (by share repurchase) so that the net effect remains unclear.

In the shorter run...management can be presumed to know more than outside investors about the current prospects of the firm. Under these conditions, dividend decisions can take on an additional strategic dimension that, on balance, tends to inhibit changes in policy.

Conclusion: What Role for Behavorial Models of Dividends?

The purpose of this paper has been to show that the rationality-based market equilibrium models in finance in general and of dividends in particular are alive and well—or at least in no worse shape than other comparable models in economics at their level of aggregation. The framework is not so weighed down with anomalies that a complete reconstruction (on behavioral/cognitive or other lines) is either needed or likely to occur in the near future.

Having tried to establish that, let me conclude on a more conciliatory note by freely conceding again that, at the most micro-decision level, behavioral/cognitive elements are very much a part of the picture.[43] If the concern is primarily with the fine details of specific cases (as it may well often tend to be in many business school finance classes), they cannot be ignored. It was not a lack of command over standard theoretical tools that led John Lintner to encapsulize his months of observation of actual dividend decisions in the neat little behavioral model we have all come to call the Lintner model.[44] (I assume it to be a behavioral model, not only from its form, but because no one has yet been able to derive it as the solution to a maximization problem, despite 30 year of trying!) Nor should we be surprised to find evidence of "satisficing," "organizational slack," "rules of thumb," or "bounded rationality" in the making of individual dividend decisions. Corporate treasurers have many

other, and often vastly more important, problems to contend with on a day-to-day basis, particularly in the volatile and takeover-jittery capital markets of recent years. The amounts of money involved in a quarterly dividend are typically not large in relation to corporate cash and financing flows (though crises do occasionally arise), and many corporate officers find it convenient under normal conditions to defer (or to pretend to defer) to the judgment of the firm's directors, who have the technical responsibility for declaring the dividend. Policy reviews and changes do occur, but only fitfully and at a pace that all recently hired M.B.A.'s are bound to regard as maddeningly slow.

The behavioral/cognitive elements in decisions involving dividends (including, perhaps, even some of the cognitive, cash-preference illusions imagined by Shefrin and Statman[45]) are also likely to loom larger for individual investors who hold modest amounts of stock directly and who, unlike institutional and other large investors, do not rely heavily on professional portfolio advisers. For these investors, stocks are usually more than just the abstract "bundles of returns" of our economic models. Behind each holding may be a story of family business, family quarrels, legacies received, divorce settlements, and a host of other considerations almost totally irrelevant to our theories of portfolio selection. That we abstract from all these stories in building our models is not because the stories are uninteresting, but because they may be too interesting and thereby distract us from the pervasive market forces that should be our principal concern.

Author's Note:

How the new tax law will affect corporate dividend policies is difficult to say at this point because so many changes were made at once and because they don't all push in the same direction. Certainly, lowering the top rate of taxation on dividends and raising the top rate on capital gains tilts against retaining cash earnings for investment in the corporation. But it doesn't follow that paying the cash out as dividends will be the best alternative. For many companies it may pay to recapitalize with debt, pay the cash out as

interest, and so at least avoid paying the still-heavy corporate income tax. For others, given the diminution of the traditional capital-gains offset to the heavy penalty of double taxation of corporate earnings, it may even pay to abandon the corporate form of organization altogether. About all we can confidently predict as of now is that capital structure, dividend policy, and organizational form will continue to be major issues in finance in both academia and in practice.

—**Merton Miller**

41. For a survey of some recent efforts, see my paper, "The Informational Content of Dividends," in J. Bossons, R. Dornbusch, and S. Fischer (eds.), *Macroeconomics: Essays in Honor of Franco Modigliani*, (Cambridge, Mass.: MIT Press, forthcoming 1987).

42. The same strong thread of rationality also runs through another and even larger current stream of research in finance, i.e., the literature on agency theory

and optimal contracting.

43. See my article, "Debt and Taxes," *Journal of Finance* 32, no. (May, 1977): especially pages 272-273.

44. Lintner, 1956, cited earlier in note 37.

45. Sheffrin and Statman, cited earlier in note 2.

Does Dividend Policy Matter?

by Richard A. Brealey,
The London Business School

Several paragraphs in this article have been loosely adapted from *Principles of Corporate Finance*, by Richard Brealey and Stewart Myers, Copyright McGraw-Hill Book Co., 1981.

Six years ago, Fischer Black, Professor of Finance at M.I.T., wrote an article entitled "The Dividend Puzzle." The puzzle referred to was that despite considerable debate and research, there is little agreement among economists, managers and investors about the stock price consequences of, and thus the corporate motives for, paying cash dividends. Does a high payout increase the stock price, reduce it, or make no difference at all?

Defining Dividend Policy

Part of the reason for this continuing controversy is that different people mean different things by dividend policy. So let me start by explaining what I mean by the term.

A company's dividend decisions are often mixed up with other financing and investment decisions. Some companies finance capital expenditures largely by borrowing, thus releasing cash for dividends. In this case, the higher dividend is merely a by-product of the borrowing decision. Other companies pay low dividends because management is optimistic about the company's future and wishes to retain earnings for expansion. In this case, the dividend is a by-product of management's capital budgeting decision.

It is therefore important to begin by isolating the effects of dividend policy from those of other financial management decisions. The precise question we should ask, then, is: "What is the effect of a change in cash dividends, given the firm's capital-budgeting and borrowing decisions?" If we fix the firm's investment outlays, borrowing, and operating cash flow, there is only one source of additional dividend payments: a stock issue. For this reason, I define dividend policy as the trade-off between retaining earnings on the one hand, and paying out cash and issuing new shares on the other.[1]

We know that the value of the firm depends on a number of factors. It may be affected by the plant and equipment that it owns, how much debt it issues, how hard the managers work and so on. If we want to know whether dividend policy as such is important, we should hold these other factors constant and ask whether, given the firm's investments, capital structure and management incentives, the level of payout makes any difference.

No financial manager can avoid taking a view on this question. If you are involved in the company's dividend decision, you have an obvious interest in how that decision will affect your shareholders. If you are concerned with capital investment appraisal, you need to know whether the firm's cost of capital depends on its payout policy. (For example, if investors prefer companies with high payouts, management should be more reluctant to take on investments financed by retained earnings.) And, if you have responsibility for the pension fund, you will want to know whether it is better to invest more in high- or low-payout stocks.

Why Dividend Policy May *Not* Matter

There is now substantial agreement among academic economists that, as defined above, dividend policy is largely irrelevant apart from possible tax effects.[2] The reason for this, stated most simply, is that the money for new investments must come from somewhere. Once you have fixed on a sensi-

---

1. This trade-off may seem artificial at first, for we do not see companies scheduling a stock issue with every dividend payment. But there are many firms that pay dividends and also issue stock from time to time. They could avoid the stock issues by paying lower dividends. Other companies restrict dividends so that they *do not* have to issue shares.

2. The irrelevance of dividend policy in perfect markets was demonstrated by Merton Miller and Franco Modigliani in "Dividend Policy, Growth and the Valuation of Shares," *Journal of Business* 34 (October 1961), 411–432.

ble debt policy, any increase in dividends must be matched by a corresponding issue of equity. So management's choice, as we have observed, is between retaining earnings or simultaneously paying them out as dividends and issuing stock to replace the lost cash. To suggest that you can make shareholders better off by paying them money with one hand and taking it back with the other is rather like suggesting that you can cool the kitchen by leaving the refrigerator door open. In each case, you are simply recycling.

Of course, a higher payout could affect the share price if it was the only way that the shareholder could get his hands on the cash. But, as long as there are efficient capital markets, a shareholder can always raise cash by selling shares. Thus, the old shareholders can "cash in" on their investment either by persuading management to pay a higher dividend or by selling some of their shares. In either case there will be a transfer of value from old to new shareholders. Because investors do not need dividends to get their hands on cash, they will not pay higher prices for the shares of firms with a high payout. Therefore, firms ought not to worry about dividend policy.

Just as a high payout policy does not in itself raise firm value, so a low payout policy also cannot affect value. The argument is essentially the same. If you hold capital expenditure constant and pay lower dividends, then you will have more cash than you need. In the United States you can hand this cash back to the shareholders by repurchasing the shares of your own company. In countries where this is not permitted, you can hand the cash back by purchasing the shares of other companies.

Of course, all this ignores the costs involved in paying dividends and buying or selling shares. For example, if the company needs the cash, it is likely to be somewhat cheaper to retain it than to pay it out and make a stock issue. But these are matters of fine tuning and should not absorb large amounts of management time.

Some Common Misunderstandings

Some people find it difficult to accept the notion that, apart from tax considerations, dividend policy should not affect the value of the firm. For example, in the UK in 1975 the Diamond Commission received submissions from both the investment community and the trade unions about the effect of dividend control. The representatives of the investment community pointed out that the value of a share is equal to the discounted value of the expected stream of dividends. Therefore, they claimed, legislation that holds down dividends must also hold down share prices and increase companies' cost of capital.

The trade union representatives also thought that dividend policy is important. They argued that dividends are the shareholders' wages and so it was only equitable that the government's incomes policy should include control of dividends. Both sides ignored the secondary effects of dividend control. If a company raises its dividend, it must replace the cash by making a share issue. So the old shareholder receives a higher current dividend, but a proportion of the future dividends must be diverted to the new shareholders. The present value of these foregone future payments is equal to the increase in the current dividend.

Another common misunderstanding is the so-called "bird-in-the-hand" fallacy. Dividends, it is suggested, are more predictable than capital gains because managers can stabilize dividends, but cannot control stock price. Therefore, dividend payments are safe cash in hand while the alternative capital gains are at best in the bush.

But, the important point to remember, once again, is that as long as management's dividend policy does not influence its investment and capital structure decisions, a company's *overall* cash flows are the same regardless of its payout policy. The risks borne by its stockholders are likewise determined only by its investment and borrowing policies. Thus, it seems odd to suggest that while dividend policy has no effect on the firm's total cash flow, it nevertheless can still affect its risk.

The actual effect of a dividend increase is not to decrease the fundamental riskiness of the stock, but to transfer ownership and, hence, risk from "old" to "new" stockholders. The old stockholders—those who receive the extra dividend and do not buy their part of the stock issue undertaken to finance the dividend—are in effect disinvesting; that is, their stake in the firm is reduced. They have indeed traded a safe receipt for an uncertain capital gain. But the reason their money is safe is not because it is special "dividend money," but because it is in the bank. If the dividend had not been increased, the stockholders could have achieved an equally safe position just by selling shares and putting the money in the bank.

If the current shareholder receives a higher dividend, a proportion of future dividends must be diverted to new shareholders.

The old shareholder who receives and banks his dividend check has a safer asset than formerly, whereas the new shareholder who buys the newly issued shares has a riskier asset. Risk does not disappear; it is simply transferred from one investor to another, just as it is when one investor sells his stock to the other.

A third common objection to the dividend irrelevance argument is that many investors for reasons good or bad like high dividends. This may well be the case just as many people like to own motor cars, television sets and so on. But it does not mean that you can get rich by going into the dividend-manufacturing business any more than you can do so by going into the car or television business. A high-payout policy will only increase the stock price if there are not enough high-payout companies to satisfy the clientele for such stocks.

Why Dividend Policy *Seems* to Matter

If there is such widespread agreement that dividend policy does not matter aside from the tax consequences, why do so many managers believe it to be important? The obvious explanation is that the economists have got it wrong again. But I suspect that the real reason is that the economists and managers are talking about different issues.

For example, although I have suggested that low-payout stocks sell for as high a price as high-payout stocks, I also believe that the stock price is likely to rise if the dividend is unexpectedly increased. In other words, *unexpected changes* in a company's dividend matter even though the expected *level* of dividends does not. The reason for this has mostly to do with how managements typically set dividend policy.

Studies of corporate dividend policy suggest that most companies have a conscious or, at least, some subconscious long-term target payout rate.[3] If management attempted to adhere to a target every year, then the level of the dividend would fluctuate as erratically as earnings. Therefore, they try to smooth dividends by moving only partway toward the target payout in each year. They also take into

account expected future earnings, as well as current earnings, in setting a long-run target. From long experience, investors are aware of this, and thus often interpret a large dividend increase as a sign of management's optimism about the company's prospects.

Thus, because unanticipated dividend changes convey information to the market about the outlook for profits, it makes sense to establish a reasonable set of investor expectations and to take these expectations into account when you decide on the annual payment.

A second reason that managers believe that the dividend decision is important is because they assume that it will affect the investment decision. In other words, they will say things like "If we pay this high dividend, then we won't have enough money to go ahead with our capital expenditure program." They are, therefore, implicitly rejecting the alternative of an equity issue. For example, many companies are reasonably tolerant of appropriation requests that can be financed out of retained earnings, but seem to impose much more stringent criteria on expenditure proposals that would involve a new issue of stock. In these cases the dividend decision feeds back on the investment decision and, therefore, it makes sense to take account of investment opportunities when setting the dividend level.

In both of these examples dividend policy appeared to matter. But in fact it was not the dividend policy as such that was important, but the company's investment policy and investors' expectations of future earnings.

Dividends and Taxes

The only serious challenge to those who believe that dividend policy does not matter comes from those who stress the tax consequences of a particular dividend policy.

If there were no taxes, investors would have no incentive to prefer one particular group of stocks. So they would hold well-diversified portfolios that moved closely with the market. But the fact that investors pay taxes at different rates on investment

3. In the mid-1950s John Lintner conducted a series of interviews with corporate managers about their dividend policies. The results are presented in an article entitled "Distribution of Incomes of Corporations among Dividends, Retained Earnings, and Taxes," *American Economic Review*, 46: 97–113 (May 1956). Lintner came to the conclusion that the dividend payout depends largely on two variables: the firm's current earnings and the dividend for the previous year (which in turn depends on that year's earnings and the prior year's dividend). The current dividend is thus generally a weighted average of past earnings, placing the heaviest weights on more recent years.

A more recent study by Eugene Fama and Harvey Babiak confirmed these results, demonstrating that the probability of a dividend increase depends largely on how consistently earnings have risen over the two or three years prior to the dividend change. See E. F. Fama and H. Babiak, "Dividend Policy: An Empirical Analysis," Journal of the American Statistical Association, 63: 1132–1161 (December 1968).

Unexpected changes *in a company's dividend matter even though the expected* level *of dividends does not.*

income provides an incentive for them to hold different portfolios. For example, the millionaire who is highly taxed on his dividend income has an incentive to slant his portfolio towards the low-payout stocks, even though this results in a less well-diversified portfolio. This extra demand by highly taxed investors for low-yield stocks will cause their prices to rise. As a result, tax-exempt investors such as pension funds will be induced to slant their portfolios towards the high-yielding stocks even though this causes their portfolios also to be less well-diversified. In between these two extremes is the investor with an "average" rate of tax. He has no incentive to slant his portfolio towards one particular group of stocks and will, therefore, invest in a well-diversified portfolio of high- and low-yielders.

The investor who pays tax at the average rate will be prepared to hold a well-diversified portfolio of both high- and low-yielders only if they offer him equal returns after tax.[4] But, if the returns are to be equal *after* tax, the high yielders must offer a higher return *before* tax. Thus, given two stocks which promise equal total returns (dividends plus capital gains) to investors, the stock that provides more of its return in the form of dividends will have a higher pre-tax expected return, and thus a lower stock price, than the one whose return is expected mostly in the form of capital gain.

The tax argument against high payouts is persuasive, but its advocates have so far failed to answer an important question: If generous dividends lead to generous taxes, why do companies continue to pay such dividends? Would they not do better to retain the earnings and avoid stock issues or, if they have excess cash, would it not be preferable to use it to repurchase stock? It is difficult to believe that companies are really foregoing such a simple opportunity to make their shareholders better off. Maybe there are offsetting advantages to dividends that we have not considered, or perhaps investors have ways to get round those extra taxes.

Merton Miller and Myron Scholes are among those who believe that the tax laws allow investors to avoid paying extra taxes on dividends.[5] For example, they point out that you can offset interest on personal loans against investment income. Such a strategy increases the risk of one's portfolio. But this

increase in risk can be avoided or neutralized by channeling the borrowed funds through tax-exempt institutions like insurance companies or pension funds. As an example, one could eliminate taxes on investment income without any increase in risk by using the personal loan to pay the premiums on a life insurance policy.

It is hard to know how literally to take Miller and Scholes's argument. There is no doubt that wealthy people are aware of the tax advantages of saving through insurance policies and pension plans. But the "average" tax rate on dividends is clearly not zero. So the puzzle has not entirely gone away: If taxes on dividend income do reduce the value of high-payout stocks, why do firms pay such high dividends?

The Empirical Evidence

The obvious way out of such a dilemma is to look at the evidence and test whether high-yielding stocks offer higher returns. Unfortunately, there are difficulties in measuring these effects.

One problem is to disentangle the effect of dividend yield from the effect of other influences. For example, most economists believe that risky stocks offer higher expected returns, and many believe that small company stocks also do so. Researchers have developed techniques for removing the effect on return of differences in risk, but there has been little attempt to disentangle the possible influences of yield and company size.

With the benefit of hindsight, we know some stocks have high yields because the dividend turned out to be higher than expected; others provided low yields because the dividend was lower than expected. Clearly what we want to measure is whether stocks that offer a higher *expected* yield also have a higher expected total return. To do that, however, it is necessary to estimate the dividend yield investors expected.

A third problem is that nobody is quite sure what is meant by a high dividend yield. For example, utility stocks are generally regarded as offering high yields. But are their yields high throughout the year, or only in the dividend month, or on the dividend day? Except at the time of the dividend pay-

---

4. Michael Brennan showed that two stocks with equal risk should offer the same expected returns net of the average rate of tax. This average tax rate is a complicated average whose weight depends on each investor's wealth and aversion to risk.

5. See M.H. Miller & M. Scholes. "Dividends and Taxes," *Journal of Financial Economics*, 6 (December 1978) 333–364.

If the returns of high- and low-yielding stocks are to be equal after tax, the high yielders must offer a higher return before tax.

TABLE 1 Some Tests of the Effect of Yield on Returns	Test	Test Period	Interval	Implied Tax Rate Percent	Standard Error of Tax Rate
	Brennan (1970)	1946–65	Monthly	34	12
	Black & Scholes (1974)	1936–66	Monthly	22	24
	Litzenberger & Ramaswamy (1979)	1936–77	Monthly	24	3
	Litzenberger & Ramaswamy (1982)	1940–80	Monthly	14–23	2–3
	Rosenberg & Marathe (1979)	1931–66	Monthly	40	21
	Bradford & Gordon (1980)	1926–78	Monthly	18	2
	Blume (1980)	1936–76	Quarterly	52	25
	Miller & Scholes (1981)	1940–78	Monthly	4	3
	Stone & Bartter (1979)	1947–70	Monthly	56	28
	Morgan (1982)	1946–77	Monthly	21	2

ment, utility stocks effectively have zero yield and are thus perfect holdings for the highly taxed millionaire. The millionaire could avoid all taxes by selling the stock to a securities dealer just before the dividend date, and buying it back after. Since the securities dealer is taxed equally on dividends and capital gains, he should be quite content to hold the stock over the ex-dividend date. Thus, as long as investors can pass stocks freely between one another at the time of the dividend payment, we should not expect to observe any tax effect by dividends on stock prices. But if there are costs to avoiding taxes in this way, then any yield effect should become stronger as the ex-dividend day approaches.

A fourth problem is that most empirical studies have looked for a straight-line relationship between yield and return. But if there are any asymmetries in the tax system, that may not be the case. For example, if investors do not receive a tax refund on stocks that are sold short, there could be stocks traded only among millionaires and other stocks traded only by pension funds. In this case, there would be no single tax rate that clears the market and the relationship between yield and return would no longer be a straight-line one.[6] Stocks with above-average yields might be owned by pension funds, and priced to give the same expected pre-tax returns. By contrast, stocks offering below-average yields might all be owned by taxpayers, and priced to offer the same expected after-tax return.

Given these difficulties in measuring the relationship between yield and return, it is not surprising that different researchers have come up with somewhat different results. Table 1 summarizes the results of some of these empirical tests. Notice that in each of these tests the estimated tax rate was positive. In other words, over long periods of time, high-yielding stocks appeared to have offered higher returns, thus implying lower prices, than low-yielding stocks.

But if, at this point, the dividends-are-bad school can claim that the weight of evidence is on its side, the contest is by no means over. Not only are

---

6. Michael Brennan, for example, in an unpublished working paper entitled "Dividends and Valuation in Imperfect Markets: Some Empirical Tests," argues that the relationship is not linear.

Over long periods of time, high-yielding stocks appeared to have offered higher returns, thus implying lower prices.

many of the empirical problems unsolved, but the standard errors in Table 1 show that the estimated tax rate is not always significantly different from zero.

Summary and Conclusion

It is difficult to summarize the dividend puzzle, and harder still to draw firm conclusions.

Almost no academic economist believes that paying out higher percentages of corporate earnings leads to higher stock prices. There is an important school which argues that taxes reduce the value of high-payout stocks. And, although there are unresolved problems of method, empirical tests of the issue to date provide tentative confirmation of an adverse tax effect on stock prices from higher dividends.

In setting the target payout, therefore, one should not dismiss entirely the tax argument against generous dividends. At the very least, management should adopt a target payout that, on the basis of its future capital requirements, is sufficiently low to minimize its reliance on external equity. In addition, the target payout should probably recognize that surplus funds can better be used to repurchase stock than to pay dividends.

There is little doubt, however, that sudden *changes* in dividend policy can cause dramatic changes in stock price. The most plausible reason for this reaction is the information investors read into dividend announcements. It is therefore important to define the firm's target payout as clearly as possible and to avoid unexpected changes in dividends. If it becomes necessary to make a sharp change in the level of the dividend, or in the target payout ratio, management should provide as much forewarning as possible, and take considerable care to ensure that the action is not misinterpreted.

The Dividend Debate: 20 Years of Discussion

by Patrick Hess
Ohio State University

The First Decade

In 1961 Merton Miller and Franco Modigliani published a theoretical paper on the subject of "Dividend Policy, Growth and the Valuation of Shares."[1] The central argument of the paper, now well-known as the "M & M dividend irrelevance" proposition, set off one of the longest and most intractable controversies in the literature of finance. Since the first sounding of the M & M argument 20 years ago, the issue of the impact of dividends on stock prices has been the subject of intensive academic investigation. And if we can judge from the findings of the most recent research, the dividend controversy promises to be with us a while longer.

Briefly stated, the M & M "irrelevance" proposition says that in a world without taxes, transactions costs, or other market "imperfections,"[2] a company's dividend policy should have no effect on its market value. An assumption crucial to the argument is the *independence* of a company's investment policy from its dividend policy; that is, the "irrelevance" argument holds only if the company's investment decisions are not influenced by management's insistence on maintaining or raising the company's dividend.

Given the company's investment decisions, its dividend policy affects only the level of outside financing required (in addition to retained earnings) both to fund new investment and pay the dividend. Under these assumptions, each dollar of current dividends paid means one less dollar in future dividends for current stockholders. To put it another way, each additional dollar of dividends represents a dollar of capital gains lost.

The basic contention underlying the M & M proposition is that the investment decisions responsible for a company's future profitability are the only important determinants of its market value. And thus, the insistence on subordinating the dividend decision to investment decisions turns out to be not only their crucial assumption, but also their principal recommendation to management.

Accepted Doctrine

Needless to say, the conclusions of Miller and Modigliani presented a strong challenge to the conventional wisdom of the time. Then it was almost universally accepted, by finance theorists and corporate managers alike, that investors preferred dividends to capital gains; and that companies could increase or, at least, "support" the market value of their shares by choosing a generous dividend policy.

Perhaps the most popular and durable of the arguments for dividends — one whose grip on the imagination of the investment community does not seem to have loosened with time — is the "bird in the hand" theory. This notion holds that, because stock prices are highly variable, dividends represent a more reliable form of return than capital gains. And the greater certainty associated with dividends leads investors to place a higher value on dividends than on an equivalent amount of uncertain and riskier capital gains.

Among the best known spokesmen for this dividend orthodoxy were the investment analysts, Benjamin Graham and David Dodd. In their now classic *Security Analysis: Principles and Techniques* (1951), Graham and Dodd wrote, "The considered and continuous verdict of the stock market is overwhelmingly in favor of liberal dividends as opposed to niggardly ones. The common stock investor must take this judgment into account in the valuation of stock for purchase. It is now becoming a standard practice to evaluate common stock by applying one

---

1. Miller, M. and F. Modigliani, 1961, "Dividend Policy, Growth and the Valuation of Shares," *Journal of Business,* October, 411-433.

2. A working definition of a perfect capital market allows for costless access by all investors.

multiplier to that proportion of the earnings paid out in dividends and a much smaller multiplier to the undistributed balance."[3]

In a more sophisticated and analytical version of the "bird in the hand" argument, Myron Gordon (1959) argued that investors will discount the expected stream of future dividends at a lower rate than expected capital gains. This proposition was formalized into the "Gordon Valuation Model," which places premium prices on stocks offering higher dividend growth.[4]

At first glance, Gordon's argument appears to make good sense, especially in light of the well-documented fact that higher dividend stocks tend to be lower on the risk spectrum of common stocks. And, other things being equal, less risky companies sell at premiums to higher-risk companies with the same expected future cash flow.

But the question we have to ask is: Do higher dividends *cause* this reduction in risk; that is, do they in any way *affect* the market's perception of the risk of a company's stock? Or is it rather the riskiness of a company's operations that influences the level of dividends?

There are good reasons and some empirical support[5] for believing that companies in riskier operations *consciously choose* to limit their dividend payouts. It is fairly well established that riskier companies tend to be relatively immature and more growth-oriented.[6] To the extent that such companies are reluctant to resort to external financing (although, excepting the flotation costs, there seem to be no good reasons for this reluctance), they will choose to retain earnings to fund their growth. Or, in the case where these prospective earnings are highly uncertain, managements may keep the dividend low to avoid having to cut it if the investment turns out badly. Stated another way, risky companies with high operating or financial leverage may choose lower dividends because higher dividends would represent an additional commitment, effectively burdening the company with even higher fixed costs.[7] The important thing to recognize is that the line of causation is *from* higher risk *to* lower dividends, and not the reverse.

So, if dividend payments *per se* do not influence market values, then where have the "bird in the hand" proponents gone wrong? The "bird in the hand" is, at bottom, an argument about investment policy, not dividends. What it's really saying is that companies paying lower dividends tend to have riskier investments; or that there is greater uncertainty about how those investment decisions will be made in the future. And for these reasons—and not the low dividends—the market discounts the earnings of low-dividend companies more heavily.

In discounting future capital gains more heavily than future dividends, Gordon's argument actually rests on the causal relationship between a higher risk investment policy and lower market values — not on some intrinsic value of dividends independent of the company's investment prospects. To clarify this point, remember that future dividends must be paid out of future earnings. How, then, is it possible for investors to be any more certain of future dividends than future earnings? The answer, of course, is that *given a company's investment policy,* they can't.

Investors discount future earnings according to the perceived operating and financial risk of the company, regardless of whether those earnings will be retained or distributed.

Early Empirical Tests

By the mid 1960's Miller and Modigliani's dividend "irrelevance" proposition was generally accepted as logically consistent. The existing body of empirical evidence, however, almost uniformly supported the pro-dividend school of thought. Most of the studies of dividends had demonstrated a strongly positive correlation between dividend-payout ratios and price-earnings ratios. That is, on average, companies with higher dividend-payout ratios tend to have higher P/E ratios, and vice versa.

Faced with this contradiction between the theory and the evidence, the academic finance profession had two explanations to choose from: either (1) Miller and Modigliani had "assumed away" some important piece of reality that might make dividends "relevant," or (2) the existing empirical work

---

3. Graham, B. and D. L. Dodd, *Security Analysis: Principles and Techniques*, 3d. ed., McGraw-Hill Book Company, New York, 1951.

4. Gordon, M. J., "Dividends, Earnings and Stock Prices," *Review of Economics and Statistics*, 41: 99-105 (May 1959).

5. See Michael Rozeff's article later in this issue.

6. See Rosenberg, B. and V. Marathe, "The Prediction of Investment Risk:

Systematic and Residual Risk" or Rosenberg, and J. Guy, "Prediction of Systematic Risk from its Fundamental Determinants," *Financial Analysts Journal*, 1976.

7. This is true only to the extent that management refuses to consider cutting the dividend.

8. An insightful discussion of these tests is contained in Friend, I. and M. Puckett, 1964, "Dividends and Stock Prices," *American Economic Review,* September, 656-82.

was seriously flawed. [8] At present, while M&M's irrelevance proposition has not received complete assent, the early empirical work has been pretty thoroughly discredited.

There are several sources of statistical "bias" in these studies which cast doubt on their conclusions. Probably the most serious problem arises from the fact that dividend-payout ratios and P/E ratios tend to move together whether companies are doing well or poorly. While many companies set target dividend payout ratios, very few attempt to adhere strictly to those targets, which would require actual cuts in the dividend whenever earnings decline from the previous year. Instead they generally attempt to maintain a steady, but gradual growth in per share dividends, allowing the payout ratio to rise or fall within certain limits. So that if a company's earnings are unexpectedly good in a particular year, the percentage of its earnings paid out in dividends will actually fall; and if earnings fall sharply, the payout ratio rises. Neither of these effects, of course, represents a conscious choice of dividend policy by management.

Empirical studies have shown that roughly the same thing happens to P/E ratios. Because investors tend to capitalize a "normalized" level of earnings in setting stock prices, a company's P/E ratio will actually go down (relative to the change in the market-wide average) when the company has an exceptionally good year. Investors will not fully adjust the price of the shares to reflect the higher level of earnings because those earnings are not expected to continue. And, for the same reason, P/E's tend to rise when earnings are unusually low.

Thus, whenever a company experiences fluctuations in the level of its earnings, dividend-payout and P/E ratios will tend to move together. This correlation is a purely statistical phenomenon, one we would expect to observe even in the absence of any causal relationship between dividends and stock prices.

Another serious problem faced by the early studies was that of controlling for the different risks of common stocks. An important determinant of a company's P/E ratio, as the reader might have gathered from the earlier discussion, is the risk associated with holding its shares. Other things being equal (including, most importantly, the expected level of future cash flows) we would expect riskier stocks to have lower P/E's. This is the point overlooked by defenders of the "bird in the hand" thesis.

We have already indicated that higher risk companies tend to pay low dividends and lower risk companies, high dividends. If differences in risk are not taken into account, the statistical method will blindly associate low dividend payouts with lower than average P/E's. Disciples of Gordon interpret this relationship as support for their position. The correct message, however, is that investors perceive the higher risk company as having lower "quality" or less predictable earnings — hence, the "lower P/E." Thus, risk is one of the important variables driving the correlation between dividend-payout and P/E ratios.

When these older studies were conducted, our present methods for measuring the risks of common stocks were not yet available. Earlier risk measures, if used at all, were based on ad hoc reasoning rather than rigorous financial analysis. As a result, the older studies were forced either to ignore risk completely, or to represent it with an arbitrary measure. This failure or inability to control for risk seriously undermines our confidence in the validity of the older empirical work.

The Second Decade

By the beginning of the 1970's, the consensus of academic researchers was that no strong conclusion about dividends and stock prices could be drawn from the existing studies. Ten years after its inception, the Miller and Modigliani "irrelevance" argument was still without any empirical support. But, at the same time, it had not yet been contested by anything which would pass for rigorous scientific evidence.

During the second decade of the dividend controversy, the focus of academic interest in the dividend question changed dramatically. The issue which came to the forefront of the research was, specifically, the tax effect of dividends on stock prices.

Along with this shift in the focus of the argument came a major shift in the alignment of the two major contending positions on dividends. What had been, in the 1960's, a debate primarily between pro-dividend advocates and the "efficient markets" supporters of M&M dividend "irrelevance" became, in the 70's, an opposition largely between the M&M camp and a relatively new *anti-dividend* group. The pro-dividend forces, while maintaining their powerful presence in the business world, became an all but silent minority in the business schools.

Companies responding to some specific investor preference cannot increase their stock prices by adjusting the dividend policy.

The main argument of the "anti-dividend" school is, as suggested, a tax argument. It holds that the higher marginal rate of taxation (for most individuals) on dividends relative to capital gains has a negative effect on stock prices. Dividends received by investors are taxed as ordinary income, and until this year could be taxed at rates as high as 70 percent.

The retention of earnings, as the M&M proposition holds, results in capital gains equal (on a pretax basis to the investor) to the dividends that could otherwise have been distributed. Capital gains have two apparent tax advantages over ordinary income. First, 60 percent of long-term capital gains is tax-exempt, thus reducing the maximum effective tax rate to 20 percent (40% x 50%). Second, capital gains are taxed only when realized, thus allowing for the use of tax-deferral and timing strategies. Both of these features reduce the effective capital gains tax below the statutory maximum of 20 percent. To the extent that the investor intends never to realize holding gains, they are tax-free indefinitely.

These apparent tax advantages of capital gains over dividends led many academic researchers to speculate that investors might actually have an "aversion" to dividends; and that, in order to hold higher-dividend stocks, they would have to receive higher pre-tax returns to achieve the same after-tax return available on low-dividend stocks. Higher expected pre-tax returns, holding other things constant, would translate into lower stock prices for companies with generous dividend policies.

Thus, within a decade, the academic thinking on dividends had almost completely reversed itself.

The anti-dividend argument is, of course, fairly vulnerable to its own *reductio ad absurdum:* namely, that no company should pay cash dividends. The payment of dividends by the leading lights of American industry is almost as perennial as the issuance of annual reports. Is it possible that such a flagrant tax disadvantage has been systematically overlooked by financial managers accustomed to dealing with much more esoteric tax issues? Moreover, is it plausible that high-dividend paying companies could increase their stock prices by simply reducing their dividend payouts?

A 1974 study by Fischer Black (of MIT) and Myron Scholes (of the University of Chicago) began by expressing strong skepticism about the logic of the tax case against dividends, especially in its more exteme forms. In establishing the theoretical basis for their research, Black and Scholes took what is called a "positivist" approach to the dividend question by assuming that if most companies are paying dividends, investors must derive some benefits from dividends that offset the negative tax consequences. Some investors, they suggested, may require current income for "consumption purposes." Though selling part of their holdings is always an alternative, these transactions are costly, and dividends may be the least costly way of providing the necessary income. Some investors may be trying to reduce the risk of their common stock portfolios; and because dividend-paying stocks tend to be less risky, dividends could be furnishing them with a more reliable guide to choosing stocks of a desired level of risk.

These are by no means revolutionary arguments. But they were incorporated into a larger conception of investor behavior which was less familiar and more complex. Black and Scholes reasoned that each investor performs a kind of implicit calculus which weighs the benefits of receiving dividends against the tax disadvantage. Thus, we find that certain investors prefer higher dividends and other investors lower dividends. This difference in investor preferences, however, does not mean that companies responding to some specific investor preference for, or aversion to, dividends can increase their stock prices by adjusting the dividend policy.

What explains this seemingly paradoxical conclusion? The answer, briefly, is that competition among companies ensures that investors' demands for dividends will be met.[9] As Black and Scholes elaborate this point,

If corporations are generally aware of the demands of some investors for high dividend yields, and the demands of other investors for low dividend yields, then they will adjust their dividend policies to supply the levels of yield that are most in demand at any particular time. As a result, the supply of shares at each level of yield will come to match the demand for that yield, and investors as a group will be happy with the available range of yields. After equilibrium is reached, no corporation will be able to affect its share price by changing its dividend policy.[10]

9. A similar argument is presented in Miller, M., 1977, "Debt and Taxes," *Journal of Finance*, May, 261-275.

10. Black, F. and M. Scholes, 1974, "The Effects of Dividend Yields and Dividend Policy on Common Stock Prices and Returns," *Journal of Financial Economics*, May, 1-24.

Investors tend to "sort themselves out" across different securities by buying stocks which provide their preferred level of dividends. If a company cuts its dividends, those investors with stronger preferences for dividends will move into other stocks with higher payouts. But, at the same time, other investors with different preferences will take their place. Provided that the dividend cut is not communicating bad news about a company's prospects, this substitution of investor "clienteles" should leave stock price unchanged.

This, in brief, is the M & M "irrelevance" proposition applied to a world with taxes and transactions costs.

The Modern Empirical Studies

Black and Scholes (1974)

Unlike the pioneering paper by Miller and Modigliani, the Black-Scholes study was not purely theoretical. Besides providing a forceful argument for the irrelevance of dividend policy in a world *with* taxes and transactions costs, their study furnished what are now regarded as the first rigorous empirical tests on dividends and stock prices.

While the earlier studies focused primarily on the correlation between dividend payout ratios and P/E's, Black and Scholes attempted to examine the relationship between *dividend yield* and *total stock returns* (dividends plus price appreciation/initial price). Three hypotheses were proposed and tested: dividend "preference," "neutrality," and "aversion." If investors prefer dividends to capital gains, higher dividend yields would imply *higher* stock prices and thus *lower* expected returns. Dividend "aversion" would imply lower prices for high dividend stocks, and thus higher *expected* returns. Finally, dividend "neutrality" would suggest no discernible relation between dividend yields, stock prices, and expected returns.

Because it may not be obvious why the association of higher returns with higher dividend stocks would imply an *aversion* and *not* a *preference* for dividends, it is probably worth a brief digression to explain this point.

One of the cornerstones of modern portfolio theory is that investors *expect* to earn returns commensurate with the risks they bear. The higher the risks, the higher the market's "expected" or "required" rate of return. How, then, do we know the market's *expected* rate of return on stocks, both in

general and for individual securities? We are unable, of course, to observe directly individual investors' expectations. Historical or actual returns, however, can serve as a reliable substitute for expected returns.

To see why this is true, begin by thinking of actual returns as having two components: (1) an expected return and (2) an unexpected deviation (whether positive or negative) from that expected return. The unexpected part of the total actual return is, by definition, completely random and thus unpredictable. If there were some predictable pattern to these deviations, sophisticated investors looking for such opportunities would exploit, and thus eliminate, this pattern. That is, investors collectively learn from their past mistakes, and they adjust their expectations accordingly.

The idea, then, is that present or future deviations from an expected return are "independent" of past abnormal returns; that is, over long periods of time, actual returns tend to fall on the high or low side of the so-called expected return with a roughly 50-50 probability. In modern portfolio theory, this is known as the "random walk."

What does this "independence" or "randomness" of deviations tell us about expected returns? Simply this: we can say with considerable confidence that, on average and over long periods of time, the positive and negative deviations or "errors" cancel each other out. For this reason, long-term average *historical* rates of return (for stocks of a given level of risk) provide a reasonably accurate measure (when adjusted for current inflation) of investors' *expected* or *required* rates of return.

So, if the findings of Black and Scholes show that investors have actually earned higher total returns on higher-dividend stocks, we would interpret this to mean that investors "require" higher rates of return, presumably to compensate for the higher tax rate on dividends. Higher "required" or "expected" rates of return, holding risk and all else constant, would mean lower stock prices (i.e., the entry price for the new investor has to fall to provide him with the higher pre-tax return).

Conversely, if the results show lower returns associated with high-dividend stocks, this would mean that investors are satisfied with a lower total return, presumably because dividends are more valuable than capital gains. And lower expected rates of return, holding all else equal, would mean higher stock prices.

One of the important advances of the Black-Scholes study, then, is the substitution of this dividend yield-total return relationship for the "spurious" correlation between dividend payout and PE's which all but invalidated the earlier tests. Its other major improvement in testing methods was its procedure for controlling for risk; that is, in neutralizing the effects of differences in risk on the total returns of individual stocks. The point of controlling for risk, as suggested earlier, is to help isolate the effect of dividend yield on total return.

Controlling for risk, of course, requires a means of estimating the risks of individual securities. A description of how risks are currently measured—requiring another brief digression—should provide greater insight into the methods of the tests.

As stated before, investors' expected returns are a function of the risk of their investment. The higher the risk, the higher the expected return. This relationship has been formalized in the Capital Asset Pricing Model (CAPM):

Expected Return	=	Risk-Free Rate	+	Risk Index Beta	×	Market Risk Premium

Or, expressed in symbols:

$$E(R_S) = RF + \beta \times [E(RM) - RF]$$

Where,

$E(R_S)$ = the expected return for security,,

RF = the risk-free interest rate,

$E(R_M)$ = the expected return on the market portfolio,

β = the beta for security,.

Though it has come under fire recently, the Capital Asset Pricing Model has been shown to be a reasonably good approximation of the market-wide average relationship between risks and returns. What it says, in brief, is that the expected rate of return on a stock is a function of the risk-free return available to investors (generally estimated by the yields on government securities, which in turn are a function of the rate of inflation), a market-wide average risk "premium" (the average historical difference between the overall market return and the risk-free rate) and the risk of that stock relative to the market.

The measure of risk is called "beta," which technically defined, is the statistical "covariance" of a stock's returns with the general market return. In less technical terms, beta reflects the sensitivity of a

company's performance (as reflected in changes in its stock price) to general developments in the economy (as reflected in changes in, say, the S & P 500). The greater the sensitivity, the greater the risk; and thus the higher the expected return.

Let's return, then, to the central question posed by the Black-Scholes study: Once we remove the effect of differences in risk on stock returns, does dividend yield help to explain the return behavior of common stocks; or, stated another way, does there exist a difference in total returns that can be attributed solely to differences in dividend policy? To answer this question, Black and Scholes introduced an additional term into the traditional Capital Asset Pricing Model, intended to reflect the effect of dividend yield on returns:

Expected Return of Security	=	Risk-Free Rate	+	Risk Index (Beta) of Security	×	Market Risk Premium	+	Dividend b x yield of Security

Where **"b"** = the coefficient on the dividend yield variable.

To the extent that this new dividend yield term adds statistical "explanatory power" to the original model, dividend yield can be said to have a "systematic" effect on expected stock returns.

Their next question, then, was: How do we use this modified Capital Asset Pricing Model to test the "dividend yield effect?" Simply stated the tests used a method called "linear regression" which attempts to quantify the relationship(s) between two or more variables. In the case of Black and Scholes, the variables in question were dividend yields, betas, and stock returns. The strength of the correlation between dividend yield and total return is measured by a dividend yield "coefficient" (represented by "b"). For example, if "b" turns out to be "significantly" greater (less) than zero, then we would infer a strong positive (negative) association between dividend yields and total returns. If "b," however, is not reliably different from zero, we would conclude that there is no "systematic" or predictably consistent effect of dividend yields on stock returns.

The Data

Black and Scholes began by classifying all common stocks on the New York Stock Exchange into 25 portfolios (for every year between 1931 and 1966) on the basis of both dividend yield and risk. This was accomplished in two steps: first, breaking down the stocks by dividend yield into five different

Comparisons among five diversified portfolios, each having the same risk and different dividend yields, do not reveal any significant connection between dividends and stock returns.

groups, ranging from highest to lowest; and second, further dividing each of these groups into five risk classifications. The result was 25 different portfolios of securities with widely different risks and yields. This procedure was repeated for each of the 35 years tested in order to capture changes in risk and yield.

This elaborate classifying procedure enabled Black and Scholes to hold the risk of securities constant, while permitting only dividend yield to vary. At the same time, while holding risk constant within individual portfolios, it also allowed them to test whether the dividend yield had a different effect on stocks at different *levels* of risk.

The Results

Applying the regression model described, Black and Scholes found that the effect of dividend yield was not reliably different from zero, whether over the entire period 1936-1966, or in any of the shorter sub-periods tested. For the period 1935-1966, the annualized dividend yield "coefficient" was 0.0108, which means, in very imprecise language, that only 1% of annual average stock returns can be attributed to the effect of dividend yield. This does not mean, however, that dividend yield actually caused this 1% difference. In fact, judging from this coefficient, we would argue that the yield effect is so small that it cannot be distinguished from the effect of random chance. Over shorter periods, measures of the dividend yield effect ranged from 0.24% to 2.16% of average annual returns. While the latter may seem quite high, it occurs only over a short seven year period, 1940-1947. And because random influences are relatively more important in shorter periods of time, the probability of this result being explained by chance is over 73%.

To summarize the findings of the Black-Scholes study, comparisons among five diversified portfolios (at each of five different levels of risk), each having the same risk and different dividend yields, do not reveal any significant connection between dividends and stock returns. The findings thus suggest that there is no clear-cut relationship between dividends and stock prices.

Final scientific proof is, of course, beyond the reach of empirical studies in finance — as it is even in the most precise of the natural sciences. Because of the remaining uncertainty that attends any use of the "scientific method," the conclusions of serious studies are always stated in tentative terms. And

Black and Scholes's is no exception. In the typically cautious idiom of the profession, they profess themselves "unable to reject" their original hypothesis that the market is "neutral" toward dividends.

The message of the Black and Scholes study is that corporations cannot influence the prices of their shares by pursuing a high-yield or a low-yield dividend policy. And, therefore, companies should not pass up good investment opportunities to pay high dividends.

The Black-Scholes study is significant for two reasons: first, it was the first empirical study of the issue of dividends and stock prices to gain general — though far from complete — acceptance among the academic finance community. And this was, in large part, because of the sophistication of its methods. Second, it was also the first study to provide empirical support for the M&M dividend "irrelevance" proposition. For both of these reasons, this pioneering study remains one of the major contributions to the "modern finance" literature.

Litzenberger and Ramaswamy (1979)

In 1979, Robert Litzenberger (of Stanford University) and Krishna Ramaswamy (of Columbia) published a study of dividends and stock returns which presented a strong challenge to the Black-Scholes findings and the "irrelevance" proposition.

Litzenberger and Ramaswamy began with the premise that the differential tax treatment of dividends should result in an "aversion" to dividends by investors, resulting in higher (pre-tax) *expected* returns and lower stock prices. Stated another way, dividend "aversion" means that investors will value a dollar of dividends less than a dollar of capital gains, causing higher-dividend stocks to sell at a relative discount to their lower-dividend counterparts.

Litzenberger and Ramaswamy argued that the Black-Scholes statistical method was not sensitive enough to detect the dividend tax effect on stock returns. Their criticism of Black-Scholes's methods focused largely on the definition of dividend yield. In defining yields, Black and Scholes used the previous year's dividend, and then divided this annual dividend by the previous year's closing share price.

Litzenberger and Ramaswamy, by contrast, updated their yields every month. They argued that, if there is a dividend tax effect on stock prices, these effects will be more pronounced in those months in which stocks go *ex-*dividend than those in which they trade with the *(cum-)* dividend. Why? Because investors receive their dividends in the ex-dividend month.

Accordingly, their test separated the dividend yields and total returns in ex-dividend months from the returns in cum-dividend months. Using this modification of the Black-Scholes methods, Litzenberger and Ramaswamy tested the following hypothesis: Do dividends help explain the ex-month returns of common stocks? If investors have an "aversion" to dividends, then we would expect to see a strong positive correlation between dividend yields and total returns in ex-dividend months. That is, high yields should be accompanied by higher total returns in ex-dividend than in cum-dividend months.

Like Black and Scholes, Litzenberger and Ramaswamy constructed a regression model which is a variant of the Capital Asset Pricing Model. But, where Black and Scholes introduced an additional term to measure the difference in returns attributable to yield differences, the later study incorporated a term measuring the implied difference in effective tax rates caused by different dividend yields. Their sample, like Black and Scholes's, included all NYSE stocks; but it covered the somewhat longer period, 1936-1977.

The findings of Litzenberger and Ramaswamy were, at least on the surface, quite surprising. Over the entire 42 year period, the average dividend tax effect—which, again, was intended to measure the difference in investors' *effective* tax rates on dividends and capital gains—was approximately 23%, much too high to be attributed to chance alone. Thus, where the Black-Scholes study concluded that one dollar of dividends is worth a dollar of capital gains, the Litzenberger-Ramaswamy result implied that a dollar of dividends was worth only 77 cents of capital gains. On the basis of these conclusions, companies could substantially increase their share values by *reducing* dividends.

Needless to say, this radical difference between the findings of the Litzenberger-Ramaswamy and the Black-Scholes studies was received by academic researchers with some skepticism. Both studies were consistent with state of the art statistical methods, yet the studies reached vastly different conclusions. So, the obvious question was: What had gone wrong?

Miller and Scholes (1981)

In 1981, Merton Miller and Myron Scholes challenged the validity of the Litzenberger-Ramaswamy study, criticizing its definition of a monthly dividend yield. In nearly a third of the ex-dividend months included in the Litzenberger-Ramaswamy study, a dividend was both declared and paid in the same month. A good deal of evidence has been accumulated showing that announcements of *unanticipated* dividend changes are accompanied by strong price reactions. For this reason, argued Miller and Scholes, any extraordinary change in share price could not be attributed solely to the tax consequences of the dividend paid.

In their own study, Litzenberger-Ramaswamy had attempted to eliminate this "information effect" of dividends by using the following procedure: If a dividend was not announced before the ex-month, the previous regular dividend payment was used as a surrogate for the *expected* level of the current dividend. If a dividend was announced before the ex-month, then the announced dividend was used to represent the expected level.

Taking a "rational expectations" approach (as described by Merton Miller earlier in this issue), Miller and Scholes showed that this method does not correct the problem. As the time of the dividend announcement approaches, the market forms some expectations about the level of the dividend to be declared. To the extent that the declared level of the dividend differs from the market's expectation, dividend announcements will convey "information" about a company's prospects. In so doing, they will affect stock prices in a way (up for higher than expected dividends, down for lower) that the methods of Litzenberger and Ramaswamy would interpret as a tax effect. Because the earnings prospects of companies are liable to change drastically between quarterly dividend announcements, the market's expectations could also be highly variable. And a model which naively assumes that the previous dividend is a reliable substitute for the expected current dividend will create some serious measurement problems.

To illustrate one kind of error that can result from this model of expectations, consider the following case. If the market expects good news in the form of a higher dividend, which in turn could be signalling an improvement in the company's prospects, we would expect the share price to rise *prior* to the announcement month. As a result of the price rise, the dividend yield (dividends/price) will fall. Now, if the expected dividend increase does not materialize, or is not as large as generally expected, the market will interpret this announcement as conveying bad news, the stock price will fall, and the ex-month return will also be lower.

In such a case, the regression method will associate the lower dividend yield with a lower monthly stock return. This in turn will be interpreted as evidence supporting the tax effect hypothesis. But, while this association is *consistent* with the Litzenberger-Ramaswamy differential tax hypothesis, the underlying *cause* of this correlation is clearly the negative information released by a lower than expected dividend—not the tax effect.

Thus, the strong positive correlation between yields and returns that Litzenberger and Ramaswamy have interpreted as the negative tax effect of dividends on stock prices could be, as Miller and Scholes argued, the effect of the "information" communicated by dividend announcements. In order to test this alternative interpretation, Miller and Scholes actually repeated the Litzenberger-Ramaswamy regressions, *removing all the cases where the dividend was declared and paid in the same month.* When these monthly observations (which, again, accounted for 35-40 per cent of the Litzenberger-Ramaswamy sample) were excluded from the regression, the estimate of the differential tax rate between dividends and capital gains fell quite dramatically — from 23%, in the Litzenberger-Ramaswamy test, to under 4%, which is not reliably different from zero.

Miller and Scholes interpret their results as a confirmation of their suspicion that the negative tax effect detected by Litzenberger and Ramaswamy was actually caused by the information content of dividends. Once the information effect is removed, there appears to be no systematic relationship between dividends and stock prices. Together with the Black-Scholes study, the 1981 Miller-Scholes findings represent another strong empirical argument for the M & M "irrelevance" proposition.

Hess (1981)

My own work takes a somewhat different approach to the dividend question. Throughout most of the 1970's, the academic dividend controversy has centered largely on the question of the tax effect: namely, does the differential tax on dividends relative to capital gains have an effect on stock prices? There could, however, be other more convincing explanations and profitable avenues of research that we have yet to explore.

My research, accordingly, begins by taking a step back to ask the question: Are the measures of the dividend yield effect on stock returns by existing studies *really* measuring the presence or absence of a dividend *tax* effect? Neither my research nor anyone else's that I'm aware of has supplied a clear answer to this question.

My work does, however, take a modest step in that direction by asking a somewhat different question from that posed by the existing studies: Are dividend yield effects on stock returns roughly the same for *individual* securities as they are for the broad "cross-sectional" averages detected by the earlier tests? In all of the studies discussed—Black-Scholes, Litzenberger-Ramaswamy, and Miller-Scholes—the tests are based on the assumption that if differential tax rates on dividends and capital gains affect share prices, the effect should be roughly the same for all securities. The purpose of my work, then, was to extend the existing research by testing for the constancy or similarity of the dividend yield effect (whether a tax effect or otherwise) across *individual* stocks.

Using a technique known as "time-series" regression (which examines the behavior of a relationship between variables over time), I examined the relationship between dividend yield and the monthly stock returns of two samples (the Dow Jones 30 and a sample of utility stocks) of individual securities over the period 1926-1980. Based on my analysis of the entire 55 year period, I was forced to conclude that the effect of dividend yield on return varies widely among different stocks, and thus that there is no consistent or systematic dividend yield effect across individual securities.

My tests suggest that no clear-cut conclusions can be derived from the relation between stock returns and dividend yields. My estimates of the yield effect are certainly far too complicated to be explained by the differential tax thesis of Litzenberger and Ramaswamy. In this sense, my work reinforces the findings of the Miller-Scholes study. In so doing, it lends further empirical support to the original M & M proposition with which we began: namely, that a company cannot predictably affect the price of its shares by changing its dividend policy.

Concluding Comments

After 20 years of academic discussion, the dividend news is both good and bad. The bad news is that academic researchers have been unable to isolate the effect of corporate dividend policy on stock prices. On the basis of our studies, there is no clear way in which a corporation could use its dividend policy to influence the value of its shares.

The good news is that the bad news isn't as bad as it sounds. The failure of academic researchers to establish a systematic or causal connection between dividend yields and stock returns means that corporate treasurers can relegate dividend policy to its rightful position in the hierarchy of corporate decisions. And this position is far below the corporate investment decision. In other words, the important message of the research is what it *doesn't* say; it doesn't say that management is justified in passing up profitable investments to satisfy some perceived investor "demand" for "dividend growth."

How Companies Set Their Dividend-Payout Ratios

by Michael Rozeff,
University of Iowa

Introduction

Most of the academic finance literature on dividends has concerned itself with the question: Should companies pay dividends? Or, alternatively, can management influence their stock price by their choice of a dividend policy? The impression left by this literature is that there is no best dividend policy for a company. Stated in stronger terms, there seems to be no good reason why one dividend policy isn't as good as another, or why companies should be paying dividends at all.

This conclusion rests primarily on two considerations. First, the logic of "perfect" capital markets —where there are assumed to be no costs of buying or issuing securities, no taxes, no "information effects" of dividends, and no conflicts of interest between corporate managers and security holders — maintains that a company's dividend policy should not affect its market value. Second, the existing evidence suggests that this logic can be extended to the "real world" by demonstrating that high- and low-dividend stocks have not provided investors with systematically different returns.

In this article, which is based on a study completed last year, I will present a theoretical argument why dividend policy *might* matter to corporations, and some empirical evidence that it *does*. In so doing, I take a somewhat less frontal approach to the dividend question than past studies. My study never directly raises the issue whether companies *should* be paying dividends. Nor do I attempt to measure the effect of alternative dividend policies on stock prices and returns. Instead, I begin by recognizing that most successful companies pay dividends, and that most boards of directors regard the dividend decision as an important one. Furthermore, the press reports dividends regularly, heralding signifi-

cant changes. Because it does not seem sensible to attribute such persistent behavior solely to the "irrationality" of investors and managements, my work tacitly assumes that there are good reasons for companies to pay dividends, and for investors to pay heed to dividend announcements.

My study begins by observing that the percentage of earnings distributed as dividends (the dividend payout ratio) varies widely among corporations, and then attempts to answer the following series of questions: Are there some identifiable financial characteristics that clearly distinguish companies paying high dividends from those which have chosen to pay out smaller portions of their earnings? If so, could those distinguishing characteristics have a major influence on management's choice of dividend policy? Or could they be pointing to other more fundamental considerations which affect the corporate dividend decision?

After identifying some of the potentially important determinants of dividend payout ratios, my study goes on to measure statistically the "explanatory power" of each of the variables of interest. On the basis of these tests, which reveal a fairly consistent pattern in the actual dividend behavior of American corporations, I offer a theory or "model" describing an interaction of market pressures and conscious managerial considerations that appears to be shaping corporate dividend policy.

The purpose of this article, then, is to relate briefly the reasoning, methods, and findings of my recent study. Before describing my own tests, however, I want to provide a short review of other studies which have attempted to account for *differences* in dividend policy among corporations.

The Existing Studies

Several studies have documented the contention that companies requiring large amounts of capital for investment and expansion are likely to choose lower dividend payout ratios. Most notable among these was a study by Robert Higgins of the University of Washington, which demonstrated that higher funds requirements have a negative influence on the dividend level. Unless a company is able to finance all new investment with retained earnings, higher dividend payout ratios mean larger external financing requirements. The flotation costs of new debt or equity issues, especially for smaller, riskier, and less established companies, could act as a deterrent to raising the dividend.

A second and related factor, also supported by Higgins' study, is the level of companies' debt financing. Another study, by George McCabe of the University of Nebraska, has shown that new long-term debt has a negative influence on the amount of dividends paid. For more highly leveraged companies, higher dividends could be viewed by some managements as increasing their burden of fixed costs. Such companies, accordingly, may intentionally keep their payouts lower to avoid the possibility of having to cut or pass a dividend. For a similar reason, companies with riskier operations, and thus less stable or predictable operating earnings, may also choose lower dividend payout ratios.

The study by McCabe, along with other studies by Allen Michel, and by the team of Phoebus Dhrymes and Mordecai Kurz, have provided some evidence that a company's industry may be an important determinant of its dividend payout ratio. The aforementioned study by Higgins, however, failed to detect any consistent effect of industry on corporate dividend policy.

The three factors discussed above — anticipated growth and investment, a high level of financial leverage, and a high level of business risk — are all possibly important reasons why companies might *restrict* their dividend payout. If corporate managements were basing dividend policy on these factors alone, the dividend decision would be a decision only by default, a matter of calculating the company's requirements for future funds relative to the level and variability of future earnings. The dividend payout, in this case, would be a passive variable, the end result or "residual" of the company's investment policy. What is missing from the existing research is a convincing *positive* reason for paying higher dividends.

The Agency Costs of Equity: A Rationale for Corporate Dividends

The next question we want to ask, then, is: Do dividend payments have some positive effect on (rational) investors which would cause companies to *increase* their payout ratios? Without entangling ourselves in the academic dispute over the "information effect" of dividends on stock prices, I want to offer what I think is a plausible explanation why some corporations choose to pay out higher percentages of their earnings, significantly higher than other companies in the same industry.

As Miller and Modigliani have demonstrated, under the conditions known as "perfect capital markets," there is no good reason for corporate managements to prefer one dividend policy to another. Differences in dividend policy should not affect the value of the firm. In my study, I attempt to take a step beyond the dividend irrelevance theorem by asking if there are any so-called market "imperfections" which could be stimulating a demand for dividends by investors.

One of the central assumptions of the Miller-Modigliani proposition, and of modern finance as well, is that the interests of management and stockholders are reasonably consonant, if not inseparable. Corporate managements, therefore, are assumed to act so as to maximize stockholder wealth. This in turn implies that the market values of companies with more diverse ownership will not differ, other things equal, from companies which are owned and run largely by insiders.

There are two market mechanisms which support this assumption: first, the market for "corporate control" should ensure that companies not being run to maximize stockholder wealth (companies which, as a result, are selling at lower market values than otherwise) will attract take-over bids by more efficient and capable managements; second, a competitive labor market for corporate managers also should be operating such that managers who are not acting in the interests of stockholders are replaced. If both of these markets were functioning perfectly, without cost or other "friction," the ownership structure of companies would not be an important corporate concern. There are some good reasons, however, to believe that the "imperfections" in these market mechanisms may be significant.

The most forceful challenge to this standard assumption of the modern finance literature has come from the "agency cost" argument originated by Michael Jensen and William Meckling, both of the

University of Rochester. In an article published in 1976, entitled "Theory of the Firm: Managerial Behavior, Agency Costs, and Ownership Structure," Jensen and Meckling argued that the separation of ownership and control may explain much corporate behavior that does not appear "rational" under the assumptions of perfect markets. More precisely, they argued that "agency costs" result from the potential conflict of interest between "agents" (managers) and "principals" (stockholders/owners). That is, "agency costs" arise whenever owner-managers sell off portions of their stock holdings to "outside" security holders who have no voice in management. The measure of these "agency costs" is the difference between the market value of the company when 100 percent owned by management, and its value when less than 100 percent owner-managed.

What, then, do "agency costs" have to do with dividend policy? Although Jensen and Meckling did not explore the implications of their "agency costs" argument for dividend policy, they demonstrated that corporate managers take actions designed to minimize the implicit costs associated with the separation of ownership and control. These actions include the external auditing of the company's accounts and activities, the establishment of supervisory and control functions by boards of directors, the acceptance of covenants in lending agreements which contractually limit management's decision-making powers, and the structuring of incentive compensations contracts to bring the interests of managers and outside equity holders into closer harmony. These "bonding," "monitoring," and "auditing" functions help to control management behavior, thus reducing the potential conflict between managers and security holders. They are worthwhile if the costs of carrying out these functions are more than offset by an increase in the value of a company with substantial outside ownership.

My argument is that dividend payments serve a function similar to the "bonding" and "monitoring" devices described above. In the process of providing additional information to investors about the actions and intentions of management, dividends reduce the "agency costs" associated with outside ownership.

The typical analysis of dividend policy assumes that dividends paid out to stockholders will be replaced by new security issues to finance existing and future investment. My study assumes that stockholders recognize that the company is financing the dividend with new offerings, and that these offer-ings are costly. Nevertheless, they find this process desirable because they are thus able to observe the terms on which new funds are raised, and perhaps the identity of the new suppliers of funds. Also, because it is very likely that fresh lenders and equity suppliers will not supply funds unless they receive new information about the uses intended for the funds, the current shareholders may gain new information about management's intentions through this process.

The alternative to this admittedly roundabout process by which shareholders learn of the market's current evaluation of the company's investment program is that management retain the investment capital and provide "equivalent" information to the current owners using more direct means — security analysts presentations, policy declarations, shareholder letters, etc. I suspect, however, that informing shareholders by these alternative means may not be nearly as convincing and effective as the information provided by the process of paying dividends and then retrieving these funds through market offerings.

A Model of the Dividend Decision Process

The existing finance literature contains several attempts to incorporate some of these isolated factors (discussed earlier) into a coherent "model" of how companies set dividend policies. The two most useful theoretical approaches are those offered by John Lintner's classic 1956 study and, again, by the Higgins study. Basing his conclusions on a series of interviews with corporate managers in the 1950's Lintner suggested that companies, on average, do set target payout ratios. But because managements are extremely reluctant to cut the dividend, the target ratio is not strictly maintained, but used only as a rough guide. If the company insisted on paying out the targeted percentage of earnings every year, then any year-to-year decline in earnings would require a *cut* in the level of the dividend. To avoid this possibility, the level of the dividend is almost always adjusted *gradually* to the current level of earnings. Unusual year-to-year increases in earnings are thus accompanied by less than proportional increases in the dividend, while a decline in earnings (unless signalling the beginning of a drastic change in the company's longer-term prospects) will generally result not in a dividend cut, but in the continuation of the old level, a smaller than customary increase, or even perhaps a continuation of a charted rate of dividend growth.

The model proposed by Higgins assumes that companies' dividend policies reflect their attempt to maintain a targeted debt/equity ratio without relying excessively on external financing. Thus, besides the company's target capital structure, its planned level of new investment relative to its operating cash flow is the major variable influencing the dividend decision. In Higgins' model, target dividend payouts result from a process which balances two offsetting considerations: (1) a desire to avoid or minimize the flotation costs associated with new equity offerings (caused by paying higher dividends); and (2) an opposing attempt to minimize the costs of carrying "excessive current assets" (resulting from too low a payout policy). The theoretically "optimal" payout ratio is thus, according to Higgins, a largely "residual" dividend policy (i.e., one which pays out only what remains of operating cash flow after new investment has been fully funded) which minimizes the *sum* of the costs of new equity financing and carrying excess securities. Finally, the higher rate of taxation on dividends than capital gains is also incorporated into the model as a negative influence on the level of dividends.

My study presents a third model of the dividend decision-making process which is close in spirit to that of Higgins, but ignores the possible effect of taxes. I argue that any rational shareholder would wish management to minimize the transactions costs associated with raising funds by external security issues. This factor, by itself, argues for the retention of earnings and the restriction of the dividend payout to excess funds that are neither currently being used, nor are expected to be used, for capital investment. The offsetting consideration is the role of higher dividends in reducing the "agency costs" arising, as suggested earlier, from the separation of ownership and control.

In my proposed model, the dividend decision thus calls for a strategic balancing of two conflicting aims: reducing the largely explicit costs associated with external financing; and and reducing the implicit costs arising from the potential conflict of interest between management and stockholders. The "optimal" or ideal dividend payout is the one which minimizes the sum of the explicit transactions costs of raising new capital and the agency costs caused by remaining investor uncertainty about management behavior.

A third factor which may be important in determining dividend policy is the company's operating and financial leverage. Other things equal, if a company has relatively high operating and financial leverage, its dependence on external finance is increased. Consider two companies with identical funds available (before dividend payments) for reinvestment over a three year period, but with significant differences in operating and/or financial leverage. Suppose company A with low leverage generates a cash pattern of $4 each year while company B with high leverage generates −$2, +$4, and +$10 (which means the same average or expected level of $4 per year). B will have to borrow in the first year and incur financing costs. Whatever dividend payout ratio A finds optimal, I hypothesize that, other things equal, B will pay out a lower fraction of earnings in order to lower its dependence on external financing. Leverage produces fixed charges. Dividend payments may be viewed by management as substitutes for these charges. Because company B, with its higher fixed charges, must rely more on costly external financing, the opportunity cost of its dividends is higher than company A's. Hence, it will choose to pay lower dividends.

To summarize, then, my theory suggests that companies' dividend payout ratios are influenced primarily by three considerations: the transactions costs of external finance, the agency costs of outside ownership, and the financing constraints created by higher operating and financing leverage. The first and third are both arguments for restricting the dividend payout; and both rest on the assumption that raising new securities is far from a costless activity for corporations. These two closely related concerns are balanced by the positive role of higher dividends in mitigating the "agency" problem—the implicit loss in value caused by the separation of ownership from control.

Empirical Tests and Findings

Designing the Tests

The next stage of my study was to provide empirical support for my theory by examining, with the aid of statistical methods, the actual dividend decisions of a broad sample of American corporations. Because it is not possible to observe, much less to measure, the effect of these offsetting considerations on the actual formulation of companies' dividend policies, the biggest problem in devising such a test was to find observable, quantifiable "variables" which would serve as good measures of transactions costs, agency costs, and operating and financial leverage. Having once found these surrogates, the tests then became a matter of measuring the strength of the statistical "correlation" between the surrogate variables and companies' dividend payout ratios.

In order to test the strength of this correlation, I used a technique known as "multiple regression analysis." This procedure attempts to describe, in a simple mathematical formula, the relationship between the central variable of interest (known as the "dependent" variable) and a number of "independent" variables. The dependent variable was the company's target dividend payout ratio. I measured a company's target dividend payout ratio by calculating the average of its actual payout ratios over the seven year period, 1974-1980. I chose seven years because it appears to be a period long enough to smooth out the usual fluctuations in earnings, but not so long that a large number of companies would have significantly changed their dividend policy during this time.

As surrogates for the transactions costs of a company's required external financing, I used two variables. The first was the growth rate of the company's revenues over the five-year period 1974-1979. The second was Value Line's *forecast* of the growth of sales revenue over the next five years, 1979-1984.

The reasoning behind the choice of these variables is straightforward. If a company's past growth has been rapid, the generation of those increased sales has probably required, other things equal, substantial new investment. In such a case, the company would tend to retain funds in order to avoid external financing with its attendant costs. Similarly, if rapid growth is anticipated in the future, then a prudent management will conserve on funds by establishing a lower payout ratio now. Hence, I argue that a company's dividend payout ratio will be, on average, negatively related to both past and predicted growth in revenues.

As also suggested earlier, companies with higher operating and financial leverage will also choose lower dividend payouts to reduce the costs of external finance. A natural surrogate for operating and financial leverage is the company's risk index or "beta coefficient" (the covariance of a company's total monthly stock returns with market-wide returns). For the reasons discussed earlier, we would expect to see a strong *negative* correlation between companies' betas and their dividend payout ratios.

Measuring the effect of "agency costs" on a company's dividend policy was more difficult. The role of higher dividends, remember, is to reduce the implicit loss in value associated with "outside" stockholder's loss of control over management decisions. Therefore, the larger the proportion of the stock owned by outsiders, the higher the potential agency costs, and thus the higher the expected level of dividends. That is, if outside equity holders own a larger share of the equity, they will demand a higher dividend as a kind of monitoring mechanism.

For this reason, I chose the percentage of stock held by *insiders* (as reported by Value Line) as a *negative* surrogate for the level of the agency costs of outside ownership. The lower the percentage of insiders, the more significant the problem of "agency." My prediction, accordingly, was that companies with large proportional inside ownership would have lower dividend payout ratios, and vice versa.

The fraction of stock held by outsiders, however, may not be the only (or the best) measure of the demand for dividends caused by outside ownership. To the extent that the larger proportion of outside shares may be concentrated in the holdings of a small number of stockholders, those outside stockholders may be able to exert considerable influence over the behavior of management. This situation would mean lower agency costs and lower dividend payouts, *even* in the presence of a large *proportional* outside ownership.

To allow for this possiblity, I also attemped to use the *dispersion* of ownership among outside stockholders as a measure of agency costs. That is, the actual *number* of stockholders may influence the dividend decision, with greater dispersion of ownership leading to higher dividends. Hence, I expected the dividend payout to be positively related to the number of shareholders in the company.

In order to test my predictions, I compiled a sample of 1,000 companies representing 64 industries. I intentionally excluded regulated companies because their financing policies may be significantly affected by their regulatory status. I also omitted foreign companies and oil exploration firms because their accounting practices may significantly influence the observed dividend payout ratio. My tests are thus based on a broad sampling of data on non-financial, unregulated companies, and the results of the regression analysis (described below) can be viewed as typical of major unregulated American corporations.

Results

The results of my statistical regressions provide strong support for the model outlined earlier. All of the proposed variables were strongly correlated (in the predicted directions) with the dividend payout ratio. Higher past and forecast growth rates, higher "betas," and higher proportional inside ownership were all strongly associated with lower dividend payout ratios. Larger numbers of stockholders were associated with a larger dividend payout.

My tests also showed a company's industry does not help explain its payout ratio. The apparent significance of the industry effect found in past studies results from the fact that the other variables are often similar within a given industry. These similarities, and not the specific industry *per se,* are the *fundamental* reason why companies in the same industry often have similar dividend policies.

The results of my regression analysis can be interpreted as follows: Holding all else equal,

(1) a company forecasting an annual growth rate of 7 percent can be expected to have a payout ratio that is 11 percentage points higher than a company with an expected growth rate of 20 percent;

(2) a company with a low beta of 0.75 can be expected to have a payout ratio roughly 13 percentage points higher than a company with a relatively high beta of 1.25;

(3) a tenfold increase in the number of a company's shareholders from 500 to 5,000 typically raises the dividend payout ratio by six percentage points; another tenfold increase, from 5,000 to 50,000 shareholders, would raise the expected payout by another six points;

(4) a company in which insiders own virtually none of the stock typically has a dividend payout that is five percentage points higher than that of a company with roughly 50 percent inside ownership of the stock.

When all of these factors are incorporated into a single model, they provide a respectable prediction of individual companies' average or targeted dividend payout ratios. For example, on the basis of the above results, the model predicts that Deere & Co. would be expected to have a target dividend payout ratio of 39 percent. Its actual payout over the last seven years has averaged 35 percent. One of the potential uses of this model, then, is to ascertain whether the dividend payout ratio of an individual company is in line with current market practice.

The most encouraging part of these findings is the strength of their support for my "agency cost" rationale for higher dividends. I don't want to claim, however, that this is the only explanation of the significance of these surrogate variables. Consider, for instance, the association between high inside ownership and low dividends; and then remember that dividends are taxed at higher rates than capital gains. If a director holds only 100 shares of stock, presumably a small fraction of his wealth, his decision on the dividend is less likely to be influenced by tax considerations than if, say, 50 percent of his wealth were invested in the shares of the company. To the extent that the holdings of insiders represent a significant portion of their wealth, the tendency of companies with large proportional inside ownership to pay lower dividends may simply reflect management decisions to avoid taxes.

This, of course, is only part of the story. Because we also find that the number of shareholders is positively associated with higher dividends, a consistent tax story would have to argue that a larger number of shareholders implies lower marginal investor tax brackets, and vice versa. If this were true, then the larger the number of shareholders, the less the tax aversion to dividends by those shareholders, and thus the higher the expected dividend payout. Attempts to distinguish this and related theories from the agency costs explanation of dividends must be left for future research.

Summary and Conclusion

Dividend policy continues to be an area of some mystery among financial economists, with many questions unanswered, some questions answered in conflicting ways, and some questions yet to be asked. My theory is based on the existence and, indeed, the importance of two market "imperfections": the transactions costs associated with issuing new securities and the agency costs that result from outside ownership of the corporation. While higher dividends increase the flotation costs associated with new debt or equity offerings, they may also provide investors with additional information about management's intentions which would partly correct the "agency" problem. The ideal or optimal dividend policy is that which perfectly balances these two offsetting considerations, thus minimizing the combination of transactions and agency costs.

In support of this theory of how companies choose (whether consciously or implicitly) their dividend payout ratios, my study furnishes empirical evidence consistent with the following propositions:

(1) Companies establish lower dividend payout ratios when they are experiencing, or expect to experience, higher revenue growth, presumably because this growth entails higher investment expenditures. This evidence supports the view that investment policy influences dividend policy. I argue that the reason why investment policy influences dividend policy is that raising external capital is costly.

(2) Companies with higher financial and operating leverage (as reflected by higher "betas") establish lower dividend payout ratios. This evidence supports the view that dividend payments are "quasi-fixed" charges which are substitutes for other fixed charges. I argue that companies with higher fixed charges pay lower dividends to avoid the costs of external financing.

(3) Companies establish higher dividend payouts when insiders hold a lower fraction of the equity and/or a greater number of stockholders own the outside equity. This evidence supports the view that there is a demand for dividends based on stockholders' perceived lack of control over, and information about, management decisions.

(4) Once the more basic factors above have been considered, industry factors do not help to explain dividend payout ratios. This evidence supports the view that if industry rules of thumb are used to establish dividend payout ratios, they are at best surrogates for the other more fundamental variables.

It seems safe to conclude that dividend payout ratios are not "randomly distributed" among companies. In other words, there appears to be a predictable pattern of dividend behavior among corporations. This pattern could in turn be reflecting decisions by corporate managements that are both consistent and "rational"; that is, they *conserve* stockholder wealth.

Further progress in understanding the determinants of dividend policy would be better served by moving away from a focus on perfect capital markets. Although internally consistent, and thus the logical starting point for a company formulating its dividend policy, the Miller and Modigliani proposition cannot illuminate how a company actually settles on a dividend policy. This will be accomplished only by concentrating our attention on those market "imperfections" which much of the literature has ignored.

Dividend Cuts: Do They Always Signal Bad News?

J. Randall Woolridge and Chinmoy Ghosh,| *Pennsylvania State University*

The relationship between corporate dividend policy and stock prices has long been something of a mystery to financial economists. Since the formulation of the "dividend irrelevance" proposition by Merton Miller and Franco Modigliani in 1961, the dominant thinking in the business schools has been that the level of a company's dividend payout, whether expressed as a dividend payout ratio or a dividend "yield," should have no effect on the value of a company's shares.[1] Simply stated, the M & M argument says that in a world without taxes, transactions costs, or other market "imperfections," the only important determinants of a company's market value are the expected level and risk of its cash flows. Provided management's investment decisions are not affected by its insistence on maintaining or raising the level of cash dividends, a company's dividend policy affects only the amount of outside financing required to fund new investment. Under these conditions, a dollar paid out in dividends means a dollar of capital gains forgone.

The most serious challenge to this "dividend irrelevance" argument has come from academics focusing on the tax disadvantage of dividends relative to capital gains.[2] Their argument, in brief, is that the taxation of dividends as ordinary income raises stockholders' required rates of return on higher-yield stocks, thereby causing those shares to sell at a discount relative to their lower-yield counterparts. In response to this argument, however, financial economists have argued that the abundance of tax shelters, the reduction of personal marginal income tax rates and the increasing domination of the market by tax-exempt institutions may largely neutralize any potential tax disadvantage of dividend payments, thus leaving the dividend irrelevance position undisturbed.[3]

But if the level of the dividend payment appears to be a matter of indifference to investors in aggregate, there is little doubt that changes in dividend policy affect stock prices, and often dramatically so. Even the most casual observer of the stock market will tell you that large dividend increases are good news, and dividend cuts bad news, for stockholders.

But, as Miller and Modigliani pointed out in their paper, the market's response to the announcement of dividend changes says little, if anything, about the market's preference for dividends per se. Instead, the commonly observed, strongly positive relationship between dividend announcements and security price movements is really caused by the information about future earnings that management conveys to the market through announced changes in dividend policy.

This proposition has since become known as the "dividend information" hypothesis.[4] Moreover, it has been explored in a number of recent theoretical papers which attempt to explain how and why dividend changes signal information to the market.[5]

1. "Dividend Policy, Growth, and the Valuation of Shares," *Journal of Business*, October, 1961, pp.411-433.

2. In an article published in 1970, Michael Brennan incorporated personal taxes in a valuation framework and argued that investors would expect higher returns on stocks with higher dividend yields (see "Taxes, Market Valuation and Corporate Financial Policy, *National Tax Journal*). His theoretical work was extended by Robert Litzenberger and Krishna Ramaswamy, who also performed an empirical study supporting this view (see "The Effect of Personal Taxes and Dividends on Capital Asset Prices: Theory and Empirical Evidence," Journal of Financial Economics, 1979).

3. See Merton Miller and Myron Scholes, "Dividends and Taxes: Some Empirical Evidence," *Journal of Political Economy* (1982).

4. For empirical work supporting the dividend information hypothesis, see R.R.Pettit, "Dividend Announcements, Security Performance, and Capital Market Efficiency," *Journal of Finance* (1972); J.Aharony and I.Swary, "Quarterly Dividend and Earnings Announcements and Stockholders' Returns: An Empirical Analysis," *Journal of Finance* (1980); and J.R.Woolridge, "The Information Content of Dividend Changes," *Journal of Financial Research* (1982); and J.R.Woolridge, "Dividend Changes and Security Prices," *Journal of Finance* (1983b). (Continued on following page.)

If the level of the dividend payment appears to be a matter of indifference to investors in aggregate, there is little doubt that changes in dividend policy affect stock prices, and often dramatically.

Such models, like the original M & M argument, are based on the assumptions that transactions costs (including the cost of issuing equity) are immaterial, and that the company's investment decisions are unaffected by its decision to retain earnings or pay them out in the form of dividends. Unlike the pioneering M & M work, however, the more recent work is premised on a so-called "informational assymetry." In plain English, managers often have information about the company's future that is unavailable to investors; investors suspect this and accordingly may be paying less (or more) for the company's shares than if they had the same information. By binding themselves to make a series of payments to their stockholders, managers use dividend policy to convey their confidence (or lack thereof) about the prospects of the firm; the market knows this from long experience with management's behavior, and it responds accordingly to the dividend signal.

Let's look a little more closely at the reasoning behind this argument. In a world of "imperfect" information—especially one in which management has the capacity to know significantly more than investors about the company's future plans and opportunities—it can be costly to provide investors with assurances that management is not misrepresenting its view of the company's prospects. The announcement of a dividend increase, so this argument runs, although costly in terms of reducing management's financing flexibility, may be the most cost-effective means of overcoming this information "gap" between management and investors, especially because managements have typically been so reluctant to cut the dividend. (In fact, dividend changes are probably such an effective signal because higher dividends can be so costly to management in terms of higher fixed charges and reduced financing flexibility.) Conversely, because of this historical reluctance to cut the dividend, the announcement of a dividend cut communicates management's loss of confidence (regardless of whether this is management's intention or not) in the firm's future earnings capability.

An Alternative Hypothesis: Dividend Cuts May Be Good News

Under certain conditions, however, it can be argued that the signal sent to the market by a dividend cut is a *positive* one—the opposite of that posited by the traditional dividend information hypothesis. Specifically, if a company has lots of profitable investment opportunities, but little available cash, and if its cost of external financing is substantial, the value of that company's shares may be increased by reducing current dividends and increasing investment. At the same time, if a company has a limited supply of profitable investment opportunities, shareholders may be better off if the excess cash is paid out to them in the form of higher dividends. In both of these situations, the signal sent to the market about internal investment opportunities and prospective company performance would be the opposite of that predicted by the conventional model of dividend changes; under this alternative hypothesis, dividend increases signal reduced investment opportunities and lower future earnings while dividend cuts are interpreted as signs of opportunities.

In this paper we explore this alternative dividend information hypothesis and present some supporting empirical data on companies cutting their dividends. We also report evidence on companies instituting stock dividends in place of cash dividends, and describe the interesting case of one company which announced, simultaneously, a major dividend cut and a stock repurchase program. As mentioned, the theoretical models cited above all assume that management's investment decision is not affected by the decision to maintain or raise the current level of the dividend. Our work attempts to identify and analyze special situations where managers are explicitly signaling to the market that dividends are being reduced to provide funds for new investment—investment which, in some cases, might not

Pettit found a strong positive relationship between dividend changes and stock price changes, and that the size of the stock price reaction depended heavily on the size of the dividend change.

Aharony and Swary improved upon Pettit's methodology by considering only those cases where dividends and earnings announcements were separated by more than 10 days. Their results revealed that dividends convey information over and above that conveyed by earnings announcements and the effect was found to be present for earnings reports both following and preceding dividend announcements.

Woolridge observed that in order to measure the effects of dividend changes on stock prices, it was important to distinguish between anticipated and unanticipated changes in dividends. Dividend forecasts by Value Line were used as

an estimate of the expected dividend. Though his results were essentially similar to those of Pettit and Aharony and Swary, the significant finding was that the announcement of dividend changes anticipated by the market had no effect on stock prices. In addition, Woolridge shows that changes in bond and preferred stock prices were also significantly positively correlated with unanticipated dividend changes.

5. See S.Bhattacharya, "Imperfect Information, Dividend Policy, and the 'Bird in Hand' Fallacy," *The Bell Journal of Economics* (1979); Avner Kalay, "Signalling Information Content, and the Reluctance to Cut Dividends," *Journal of Financial and Quantitative Analysis* (1980); and Merton Miller and Kevin Rock, "Dividend Policy under Asymmetric Information: Part I," unpublished manuscript, University of Chicago (1982).

In order to disarm investors' skepticism and thus blunt the typical adverse market reaction to announcements of dividend cuts, management must carefully educate the market about its prospects.

otherwise be undertaken.

One critical assumption underlying our argument, of course, is that raising equity capital can be costly, especially for those firms undertaking a new business strategy.[6] Companies with promising investment opportunities, especially those reporting relatively lower earnings, may face major difficulties in convincing the market to share their vision of the future. In the remainder of this paper, we will argue that if profitable investment opportunities exist and if external financing is costly (whether in terms of underwriting fees, aftermarket performance, or potential dilution because management feels its shares are "undervalued"), stockholder wealth may be increased by management's decisions to reduce cash dividends to provide lower cost funding for new investment. Under such circumstances, a dividend cut accompanied by some alternative, but effective signal of future growth opportunities could convey positive information to the market, resulting in an increase, not a decline, in stock prices.[7]

Two Cases of Companies Cutting Their Dividend

In the overwhelming majority of cases, companies have cut or passed dividend payments because of poor earnings performance. Because of this association, the market has in effect been "conditioned" by management's behavior to interpret dividend cuts as bad news and stock prices fall, often dramatically, upon the announcement of the cut.

Instances of dividend cuts motivated *solely* by the need to fund investment opportunities are very rare, perhaps non-existent (no doubt because of management's sensitivity to the market "condition-

ing" described above). But there have been a number of cases in the last decade or so where dividend cuts seem to have been motivated, at least in part, by investment opportunities—or so at least management has claimed in announcements accompanying the cuts.

Because of the conditioning process described above, however, investors are likely to view any dividend cut with some skepticism, regardless of how convincingly management makes its case for the future. In order to disarm this skepticism and thus blunt the typical adverse market reaction to announcements of dividend cuts, management must carefully educate the market about its prospects. The very different reactions of the stock market to the recent dividend cut announcements of Gould Inc. and ITT illustrate this point.

The Case of Gould: How to Prepare the Market for a Dividend Cut

On December 6, 1983, Gould cut its quarterly dividend from $.43 to $.17 per share, a 60 percent drop. Management stated that its decision was made with the intent to "conserve cash that can be used to finance the growth of its electronics businesses." As further stated in the accompanying press release, "The Board set the new dividend in light of the company's transition to a high-technology electronics firm." Moreover, this announcement was preceded by a statement several months earlier that management was in the process of reviewing the company's dividend policy to determine its consistency with the new business strategy.

The signal to the market about the firm's investment opportunities was heeded by investors. On the day of the announcement, the stock closed up $.50 to

6. Stewart Myers, in "The Capital Structure Puzzle" (*Journal of Finance*, 1984), points out that if investment projects have to be financed by external funds, the "assymetry" between management's and shareholders' information about the expected profitability of the investments may lead to an underpricing of risky new issues.Current stockholders would therefore suffer a loss of wealth if the investment turned out to be worth more than the market gave the company credit for in pricing the new shares.In its attempt to avoid such consequences, management ought to finance growth from internal funds. Given this logic, a dividend cut may thus be interpreted as a good signal.

Another implication of Myers's analysis is that, due to this market tendency to underprice because of uncertainty, management would resort to external financing only for those investment opportunities about which they had least confidence.In fact, a number of recent studies--all demonstrating a pronouncedly negative market response to the announcement of seasoned common stock issues--are consistent with Myers's argument: Paul Asquith and David Mullins, "Equity Issues and Stock Price Dilution," working paper, Harvard Business School (1983); A.N.Korwar, "The Effect of New Issues of Equity: An Empirical Examination," working paper, UCLA (1981); and Wayne Mikkelson and Megan Partch,

"Stock Price Effects and Costs of Secondary Distributions," *Journal of Financial Economics* (1985).The significantly negative market reaction to seasoned equity issues represents of course a cost to the issuing firm.And this is in addition to the underwriter's fee, which can be substantial for smaller equity issuers.

7. While this proposition has not been tested, a similar issue has been addressed in a recent paper by Arjun Divecha and Dale Morse, "Market Responses to Dividend Increases and Changes in Payout Ratios," *Journal of Financial and Quantitative Analysis* (1983).This study groups companies increasing their dividends into two different samples: one consisting of firms that also increased their payout ratios and the other of firms decreasing their payout ratios.Their results showed that the groups of firms *decreasing* payout ratios at the time dividends were increased recorded *higher* abnormal returns than the firms *increasing* their payout ratios.The authors attributed their results to the market's interpretation of the reduced payout ratio as a sign of access to profitable growth opportunities. A potential problem with this conclusion, however, is that the dividend payout ratio falls, of course, as earnings increase; and the superior market performance of lower payout firms could be attributed to the higher earnings which caused the payout ratio to fall.

> *For companies with very promising investments and high dividend payout ratios, cutting the dividend may offer the cheapest source of finance.*

$28 7/8. The stock price rose another 8 points in the following months—a period when the market was essentially flat.

Gould's situation is not unique in the current business environment. Many firms are seeking to reposition themselves strategically to re-enter a high-growth cycle in sales and earnings. Such a transformation typically requires a substantial investment in research and development combined with costly acquisitions. (In the Gould case, the company had been making the transition from the relatively slow-growth electrical business to the high-technology, high-growth electronics field over a four-year period. The move had been made at the expense of doubled research and development costs and numerous acquisitions.) As a result, reported earnings often suffer during this transition, adding to investor uncertainty about the outcome of the company's investments, and perhaps reducing the company's market value.

Such a combination of factors can make external financing very costly. And, to the extent decisive action is required to exploit the profit potential from such investment opportunities, management must quickly find the most economical means of funding such investment. For companies with very promising investments and high dividend payout ratios, cutting the dividend may offer the cheapest source of finance.

The Case Of ITT: How NOT to Cut the Dividend

After the stock market closed on July 10, 1984, ITT announced a 64 percent cut in its quarterly dividend payment (from $.69 to $.25 per share). Rand Araskog, ITT Chairman, explained that the company's dividend-to-earnings ratio had become "inconsistent with the intensely competitive high-technology environment." He also said that the directors approved the dividend cut to save $232 million and to "continue its current rate of investment in high-technology products and services at over $2 billion annually."

The market, however, treated ITT's announcement harshly. The day following the cut, ITT's common closed down $9 7/8 to $21 1/8, a 32 percent decline.

Analysts offered several reasons for the adverse market reaction. Several analysts noted that while ITT is a leader in the telecommunications equip-

ment business, this division generates only 1/3 of the firm's revenues. Other commentators pointed to what they saw as an erratic strategic planning process—one which had given rise to a sprawling conglomerate selling, among other products, "Hostess Twinkies, Burpee Seeds, and street lights."

Perhaps most important, however, was the fact that the ITT decision to cut its dividend appeared to take the investment community completely by surprise. This observation by a number of commentators seems further supported by the fact that, within several months after the announcement, ITT's stock price recovered much, although not all (on a market-adjusted basis), of this 32 percent drop.

Our strong suspicion, based in large part on the evidence we present below, is that much of the market's consternation at ITT's dividend reduction could have been avoided by preparing investors for this radical change in the company's dividend policy.

Some New Evidence on Dividend Cuts

Virtually all studies of stock price reactions to announcements of dividend reductions show a pronouncedly negative market response. None of these studies, however, has attempted to take into account possible differences in management's motive for cutting the dividend.

We recently completed a study of the stock market's response to announcements by NYSE-listed firms (as reported in the *Wall Street Journal*) of 408 dividend cuts and omissions over the period 1971 to 1982. In an effort to distinguish between different motives for reducing the dividend, we divided our total sample into three categories: (1) those dividend cuts and omissions accompanied by a simultaneous announcement of an earnings decline or a loss; (2) those coming after a *prior* announcement of earnings decline or loss; and (3) those accompanied *either* by a simultaneous (or immediately prior) announcement of higher earnings and/or a statement by management of significant future investment or growth opportunities.

Category (3), although it may include cases of management attempting to mislead the market, is intended to isolate those cases where management's decision to cut the dividend was essentially "voluntary"—that is, those where management's intent was not simply to ensure future solvency, but to

Much of the market's consternation at ITT's dividend reduction could have been avoided by preparing investors for this radical change in the company's dividend policy.

conserve capital in anticipation of a major investment program. Several examples follow:

(A) McGraw-Hill, on October 26, 1972, reduced its quarterly dividend from $.15 to $.12, because, to quote the Chairman, "...the years ahead will be ones of very substantial growth in the economy and in our business. Conservation of our resources at this time will position us to participate fully in this growth."

(B) Carpenter Technology, on February 11, 1972, cut its dividend from $.30 to $.20 "in order to provide adequate working capital for the period ahead and for renewed growth."

(C) Zenith Radio Corporation, on November 24, 1981, halved its quarterly dividend to $.075 per share to help maintain spending programs and "...to help generate working capital to finance the growth of new businesses and new products."

(D) Dayco Corporation, on February 25, 1975, reduced its quarterly dividend from $.285 to $.125 to satisfy "...the need to conserve funds for planned capital investment and expanded working capital needs."

(E) Ford Motor Company, on April 11, 1975, cut its quarterly dividend from $.80 to $.60 to help the company, according to Henry Ford II, "revamp its future products" and "...to conserve sufficient cash to finance products that can add to profitability in future years."

The Results

Table 1 presents the average changes in market value (adjusted for overall market movements) for the three dividend cut/omission categories during five time periods around the announcement dates: 1) one year prior to the announcement, 2) 60 trading days before the announcement, 3) a three-day announcement period, 4) 60 days after the announcement, and 5) one year after the announcement. As expected, the sample sizes for categories (1) and (2) are very large (180 and 212, respectively) compared to the only 16 cases comprising category (3). The average percentage reductions in the dividend, by category, were 56, 49, and 42 percent, respectively.

First, let's consider the market's response to these three groups over the periods prior to and including the announcement of the dividend cut. During the *year prior* to the dividend reduction announcement, the average, market-adjusted change in market value for companies in categories (1) and (2) was about -19 percent. For category (3) the stockholders' return was -11.6 percent, which reflects the fact that many of the companies we identified as making "growth-induced" dividend cuts were also probably experiencing earnings problems. For the *quarter prior* to the dividend cut, the adusted returns were approximately -7 percent for all three categories(-7.07%, -7.44% and -7.69%, respectively).

TABLE 1 Average Market-Adjusted Returns Around Dividend Reductions	Periods Around Announcement Date				
Category	Prior Year Day −251 to Day −2	Prior Quarter Day −61 to Day −2	Announcement Period Day −1 to Day +1	Quarter After Day +2 to Day +61	Year After Day +2 to Day +251
Simultaneous Announcement of earnings decline or loss N = 176	−19.51%	−7.23%	−8.17%	+1.80%	+10.23%
Prior Announcement of earnings decline or loss N = 208	−18.49%	−7.58%	−5.52%	+1.07%	+11.38%
Simultaneous Announcement of investment or growth opportunities or higher earnings N = 16	−11.61%	−7.69%	−5.16%	+8.79%	+15.97%

Much, if not all, of the announcement-period losses following dividend cuts appear to have been recouped shortly after the announcement period.

During the three day announcement period, the average return for category (1) was lower- (−8.17%) than the average return for categories (2) and (3) (which were -5.52% and -5.16%, respectively). The lower announcement-period returns for category (1) are not surprising because these announcements include simultaneous announcements of lower earnings. The fact that the negative returns for category (3) companies are smaller in an absolute sense than the average returns to companies in the other two categories may be attributable to the signal of investment opportunities. Nonetheless, these results do not indicate that the positive signal is sufficiently strong to offset the negative connotations associated with dividend reductions—not, at least, at the time of the announcement.

Much, if not all, of these announcement-period losses, however, appear to have been recouped shortly after the announcement period. During the *quarter following* the dividend cut or omission, the returns indicate that, on average, the stocks of categories (1) and (2) performed at least as well as the market. Those companies in category (3), however, far outperformed both the general market and the rest of the sample of dividend-cutting firms. In fact, their market-adjusted return of a positive 8.79 percent—relative to 1.8 percent and 1.1. percent for categories (1) and (2)—suggests that the market previously discounted the growth prospects which prompted the dividend cut and therefore overreacted to the dividend reduction.

Over the *year after* the dividend cut, the stock

TABLE 2A Common Stock Returns Associated with Announcements Accompanied With Investment/Growth Signals			Average Market-Adjusted Stock Returns				
Company/Date	Prior Dividend	New Dividend	Prior Year	Prior Quarter	Ann. Period	Quarter After	Year After
Alcan Aluminum Jan. 30, 1975	0.350	0.300	−13.6%	−5.1%	−14.3%	+13.6%	+6.3%
McGraw Edison April 24, 1975	0.375	0.300	+1.8%	+1.6%	−10.2%	+26.1%	+61.7%
RTE Corp. May 27, 1975	0.060	0.030	−11.3%	−16.4%	−3.8%	−1.0%	−4.0%
Zenith Radio Nov. 24, 1981	0.150	0.075	−30.0%	−7.9%	−10.2%	+24.6%	+21.1%
Ford Motor April 11, 1975	0.800	0.600	−13.9%	−13.3%	+1.9%	+3.3%	+32.8%
International Harv. May 21, 1971	0.450	0.350	−8.8%	−12.9%	+1.9%	+2.3%	+14.4%
Emery Air June 9, 1982	0.250	0.125	−44.4%	−24.4%	−6.0%	+36.9%	+65.4%
Sunshine Dec. 11, 1974	0.150	0.120	+42.0%	+18.2%	−13.8%	+21.0%	−8.9%
Alpha Portland Nov. 15, 1971	0.100	0.000	−17.32	−6.9%	−0.6%	+14.9%	+8.1%
Springs Mills August 18, 1972	0.250	0.150	+3.2%	−4.4%	−12.4%	−4.5%	+5.7%
McGraw Hill Dec. 26, 1972	0.150	0.120	−27.5%	−9.0%	−4.7%	−6.8%	−33.1%
Dayco Feb. 25, 1975	0.250	0.000	+27.2%	+15.2%	−21.0%	−8.3%	+25.7%
Carpenter Tech. Feb. 11, 1972	0.300	0.200	−9.0%	+17.1%	−13.3%	+17.5%	+23.3%
Foxboro July 30, 1970	0.100	0.000	−12.8%	−42.8%	+12.5%	−0.3%	+44.9%
Acme Cleveland Feb. 27, 1975	0.250	0.125	−28.1%	−22.4%	+4.2%	+8.8%	+13.7%
Ford Motor July 11, 1980	1.000	0.300	−43.9%	−6.3%	+7.3%	−7.6%	−21.6%

prices of companies in all three categories significantly outperformed the market, with the category (3) firms again faring the best (15.97%). Companies in categories (1) and (2) also saw their market value appreciate by over 10 percent. The obvious suggestion here is that, at least for this sample of companies, the market systematically overreacted to the dividend announcements. But we take up this point later.

To return to the performance of our sample of 16 "growth-induced" dividend cuts, we have compiled some additional data on the earnings as well as the market performance of these companies around the announcement date. (See Tables 2A, 2B, and 2C.) The earnings performance of these 16 firms after the dividend cut appears, on the whole, to have vindicated management's professions of optimism about the future. Although the earnings results vary highly

TABLE 2B
Earnings Performance Following Dividend Cut/Omission Announcements Accompanied With Investment/Growth Signals

Company/Date	Prior Dividend	New Dividend	Quarterly Earnings Growth After Dividend Cut (%)						
			Div. Qtr.	+1Q	+2Q	+3Q	+4Q	+6Q	+8Q
Alcan Aluminum Jan. 30, 1975	**0.350**	**0.300**	**−16**	**−51**	**−91**	**−87**	**−117**	**42**	**575**
McGraw Edison April 24, 1975	0.375	0.300	70	84	93	385	57	52	02
RTE Corp. May 27, 1971	**0.060**	**0.030**	**−1300**	**−133**	**300**	**650**	**275**	**250**	**014**
Zenith Radio November 24, 1981	0.150	0.075	−35	−76	−139	−300	−69	442	490
Ford Motor April 11, 1975	**0.800**	**0.600**	**−186**	**−36**	**017**	**663**	**410**	**−25**	**47**
International Harv. May 21, 1971	0.450	0.350	3	12	107	121	44	24	16
Emery Air June 9, 1982	**0.250**	**0.125**	**125**	**−43**	**−15**	**−50**	**17**	**−35**	**−95**
Sunshine December 11, 1974	0.150	0.120	−95	−19	−15	−81	1000	96	68
Alpha Portland Nov. 15, 1971	**0.100**	**0.000**	**200**	**2300**	**80**	**114**	**143**	**37**	**33**
Springs Mills August 18, 1972	0.250	0.150	22	30	92	72	33	24	30
McGraw Hill Dec. 26, 1972	**0.150**	**0.120**	**13**	**22**	**300**	**14**	**07**	**38**	**04**
Dayco February 25, 1975	0.250	0.000	10	−04	07	27	45	72	19
Carpenter Tech. Feb. 11, 1972	**0.300**	**0.200**	**750**	**111**	**78**	**450**	**353**	**38**	**27**
Foxboro July 30, 1970	0.100	0.000	18	−15	60	157	30	−30	−63
Acme Cleveland Feb. 27, 1975	**0.250**	**0.125**	**−09**	**133**	**−27**	**−35**	**−55**	**−20**	**−79**
Ford Motor July 11, 1980	1.000	0.300	−191	−682	−651	−168	113	−10	240

TABLE 2C
Median Earnings Growth Rates Following Dividend Cut/Omission Announcements Accompanied With Investment/Growth Signals

	Quarterly Earnings						
	Div. Qtr.	+1Q	+2Q	+3Q	+4Q	+6Q	+8Q
Median Quarterly Earnings Growth Rate*	7.0%	−9.5%	38.5%	49.5%	44.5%	37.5%	23.0%

* Computed as the Percentage Change in Quarterly Earnings over the Same Quarter of the Previous Year, Averaged Over All 16 Firms.

The market's response to the announcement of stock dividend substitutions is strikingly different from its strongly negative response to dividend cuts alone.

TABLE 3 Average Market-Adjusted Returns Around Dividend Reductions-Stock Dividend Announcements	Periods Around Announcement Date				
Category	Prior Year Day −251 to Day −2	Prior Quarter Day −61 to Day −2	Announcement Period Day −1 to Day +1	Quarter After Day +2 to Day +61	Year After Day +2 to Day +251
(1) Simultaneous/prior Announcement of Earnings Decline or Loss N=42	−10.90%	−3.11%	−2.14%	+1.03%	+6.99%
(2) Simultaneous Announcement of Investment or Growth Opportunities or Higher Earnings N=8	+9.02%	+1.84%	+1.49%	−2.39%	+6.51%

from company to company, the median earnings growth figures (in Table 2C) demonstrate that, on average, earnings grew in all but one quarter (+1Q) for these 16 firms over the two years *following* their decision to cut dividends. One year after the dividend reduction, the quarterly earnings of the median firm in the sample were up 44.5 percent. Moreover, 13 of the 16 companies reported higher quarterly earnings a year after the dividend reduction, and 12 had higher quarterly earnings two years down the road.

Mixed Signals I: Substituting Stock for Cash Dividends

What happens when companies cut their dividend and pay stock dividends instead?

Stock dividends are generally considered to be worthless to stockholders. While they provide stockholders with additional shares, each stockholder's proportional ownership of the company remains unchanged. But this logic notwithstanding, many firms regularly declare and pay stock dividends. Also, several recent studies have concluded that stock dividends signal positive information to the market.[8]

In a study we completed in 1983, we identified and analyzed 50 cases where companies simultaneously cut or omitted cash dividends and instituted stock dividends. As in the case of straight cash dividend reductions, most of these decisions appeared to be a response to earnings problems. In eight cases, however, it seemed reasonable to conclude that stock dividends were being substituted for cash dividends in order to provide financing for future growth. Two examples follow:

(A) Hecla Mining Company, on May 1, 1970, omitted its quarterly cash dividend of $.175 and paid a 2 percent stock dividend in order "...to conserve funds that the company needs to finance preproduction at the Arizona Copper Properties."

(B) Food Fair Stores Inc., on February 2, 1972, reduced its annual cash dividend from $.90 to $.20 and instituted a stock dividend of 4.0% "...to conserve cash for Food Fair's expansion program."

The Results

Table 3 presents the average market-adjusted returns around the announcement dates of 42 "earnings-induced" (category (1)) and eight "growth-induced" (category (2)) substitutions of stock for cash dividends. The market's response to the *announcement* of stock dividend substitutions is strikingly different from its strongly negative

8. M.S.Grinblatt, R.W.Masulis and S.Titman report, in "The Valuation Effects of Stock Splits and Stock Dividends" (*Journal of Financial Economics*, 1984), that for a sample of 84 pure stock dividend announcements during the period 1967-1969, the average two-day return around the announcement was 5.87 percent. Similar price behavior was displayed by a subsample of stocks that paid no dividends in the three years prior to the announcement of stock dividends, a result that prompted the authors to conclude that stock dividends have positive

"information content" about the company's prospects.

J.R.Woolridge, in "Stock Dividends as Signals" (*Journal of Financial Research*, 1983), analyzed a sample of 317 pure stock dividend announcements since 1964 and found an average return of 1.65 percent over a three-day period surrounding the announcement day.He also attributes his results to the positive "signaling effect" of stock dividends.

Several recent studies have shown that common stock repurchases by firms send a positive signal to investors and result in significant increases in stock values.

TABLE 4A **Common Stock Returns Associated with Dividend Cut/ Omission Announcements Accompanied With Stock Dividend and Investment/Growth Signals**				Average Market-Adjusted Common Stock Returns				
Company/Date	Prior Dividend	New Dividend	Stock Dividend	Prior Year	Prior Quarter	Ann. Period	Quarter After	Year After
Chock Full of Nuts March 27, 1970	0.150	0.000	0.020	−25.90%	5.4%	−1.9%	−6.1%	32.30%
Chock Full of Nuts May 20, 1974	0.100	0.000	0.030	15.30%	9.5%	15.4%	−19.9%	2.50%
Food Fair December 6, 1972	0.100	0.000	0.020	−45.50%	−3.1%	−1.9%	−11.1%	−7.20%
Hamilton Watch October 4, 1968	0.250	0.000	0.010	42.90%	5.9%	−4.1%	−7.8%	−33.90%
Hecla Manufacturing May 1, 1970	0.175	0.000	0.020	18.10%	−14.3%	0.9%	20.2%	−14.50%
Parker Pen February 14, 1974	0.125	0.000	0.050	20.10%	7.4%	0.0%	+3.1%	32.40%
Sun Oil September 28, 1973	0.250	0.230	0.060	29.90%	0.0%	7.7%	21.5%	21.70%
Stouffer Foods September 16, 1966	0.125	0.000	0.040	17.30%	3.9%	−4.2%	−18.9%	18.70%

response to dividend cuts alone. For example, the announcement period returns for category (1) companies substituting stock dividends were much less negative (-2.14%) than the corresponding returns for the straight dividend reductions (reported in Table 1). Even more surprising, the average announcement period return was actually a *positive* 1.49 percent for the eight category (2) companies substituting stock for cash dividends (although only 3 of the 8 had positive returns). These results are especially revealing given that the average dividend reduction (81% and 82% for categories (1) and (2), respectively) was much larger in these stock dividend cases.

Thus, it appears that the positive signal provided by stock dividends helps to offset some, if not indeed all, of the negative news conveyed to the market by a cut in cash dividends. Also, as in the case of straight dividend cuts, both samples outperformed the market during the year following the cut (by 6.99% and 6.51%, respectively).

The significantly better announcement day returns for those cases where dividends cuts were accompanied by stock dividends provide another insight into the market's interpretation of management signalling. Economic theory postulates that the value of information conveyed through a signaling mechanism is directly related to the cost of providing the signal. Stock dividends impose costs on the firm, in the form of registration and handling costs (amounting perhaps to over $1 million for a large firm). And stock dividends, accordingly, may be viewed by the market as a stronger signal about the firm's prospective performance and investment opportunities than simply a direct statement by management to the financial community.

Mixed Signals II: A Dividend Cut Combined with a Stock Repurchase

Several recent studies have shown that common stock repurchases by firms send a positive signal to investors and result in significant increases in stock values.[9] Stock repurchases, especially through tender offers, are generally made at significant premiums over the current market value; and management's willingness to pay a premium to buy back the company's shares seems very effective in communicating management's confidence about the future to the market.

On July 24, 1984, Whittaker Corporation sent mixed signals to the market by slashing its quarterly dividend from $.40 to $.15 per share and, at the same time, announcing a stock repurchase plan. The

9. Stock market reactions to announcements of stock repurchase plans have been analyzed by two studies: Larry Dann, "Common Stock Repurchases: An Analysis of Returns to Bondholders and Stockholders" (*Journal of Financial Economics*, 1981), and Theo Vermaelen, "Common Stock Repurchases and Market Signalling: An Empirical Study" (*Journal of Financial Economics*, 1981).Both studies reveal that stock prices rise, on average, on the announcement of these plans.The authors attribute the large positive response to the market's interpretation of such decisions as signals of management confidence about the future.

The average stockholder wealth increase reported by these studies is around 16 percent.Moreover, these returns to stockholders are even larger on an after-tax basis because they are taxed as capital gains rather than ordinary income (which would be the case if the cash was paid out in the form of higher cash dividends, the most common substitute for a stock repurchase plan).

Even those firms whose dividend cuts appear to be dictated by earnings declines also significantly outperform the market (on average, by 10 percent) in the year following the cut.

company also reported an 11 percent decline in quarterly earnings due to the loss of a large contract with Saudi Arabia. The Chairman stated that the company's financial position "is healthy and adequate to support both the stock repurchase and a planned aggressive expansion program." He also stated that the plan was not cosmetic or geared to holding up the stock price and that "...the capital structure of the company is such that, at these prices, it is wise for us to reduce the equity we have out there."

In trading on the NYSE, Whittaker's shares closed at $18.625, up $.125 for the day, and have subsequently gone up another 25 percent, significantly outperforming the market.

Analysts greeted the company's move with mixed reviews. Carol Neves of Merrill Lynch speculated that the repurchase plan was intended to prevent the stock from being vulnerable to a takeover and that the stock would have been under much more pressure from sellers concerned about the dividend cut if not for the plan to buy back shares. David Moore of Donaldson, Lufkin, and Jenrette was much more positive. He called the repurchase plan an "astute management move" because, in his opinion, the stock "...is a better buy than 90 percent of the acquisitions out there."

The positive market response to Whittaker's simultaneous announcement of a dividend cut and a stock repurchase plan provides additional evidence consistent with the hypothesis that the market must perceive some cost to management in sending a signal to the market. A stock repurchase has the opposite effect of a dividend cut, in that it requires a major capital *outlay* by management. Consequently, combining a stock repurchase with a dividend cut won't be useful for managements seeking an immediate internal source of funding for new investment.

It seems very effective, however, in assuring investors that the dividend reduction is not the result of the management's doubts about the company's *ability* to make future dividend payments. Therefore, for companies intending to make a smooth transition toward a longer-term reduction in their overall payout to investors, combining dividend cuts with a stock repurchase may be the most effective means of breaking the market's habitually negative association of management pessimism with dividend cuts.[10]

Discussion of Results

Our results indicate that, during the announcement period, the adverse effects of a dividend reduction far outweigh, on average, the management's positive signal of profitable investment opportunities. This finding lends credence to the belief that "actions speaks louder than words." Higher dividends, because they impose future financing constraints, effectively "bond" management's expression of confidence in the future in a way that statements alone probably cannot.

However, those companies cutting their dividend to provide the lowest-cost financing for growth opportunities (to the extent our study has been successful in identifying them) appear to recover most of their losses as early as the first quarter following the announcement. In fact they substantially outperform the market over the following year (and show strong earnings performance over the next two years), suggesting a vindication of management's statements about future profitable investments.

At the same time, however, we have seen that even those firms whose dividend cuts appear to be dictated by earnings declines also significantly outperform the market (on average, by 10 percent) in the year following the cut. This market response to the "control" group suggests that, although investors may place some faith in managment statements to the market, much of the rebound in stock prices after dividend cuts may simply be the result of an initial "overreaction" by the market.

How do we account for this apparent "overreaction" to dividend cuts? Is this evidence of a glaring market inefficiency? Does it represent an opportunity for investors seeking abnormal returns? Or is there some other explanation consistent with a stock market dominated by sophisticated investors continually attempting to profit from decisions made by their less sophisticated counterparts?

Our initial response is to argue that the market's negative reaction to dividend cuts, based on management's historical behavior, is a rational one. That is, investors have become conditioned to respond negatively by managements that have cut the dividend only as a matter of last resort, perhaps only when firms face financial distress.

---

10. Shortly after this article went to print, Litton Industries announced the complete cessation of its dividend together with an exchange offer of debt for shares at a large premium over market. Its stock price has since appreciated by over 25 percent.

*Because dividend cuts have often been a desperate measure
by firms trying to stave off bankruptcy, the market responds
initially by assuming the worst. Only later is the uncertainty
about the firm's prospects resolved.*

Furthermore, there may be certain clienteles of investors for whom the prospect of bankruptcy is more intimidating than others. Consider the import of dividend cuts for, most notably, institutional investors. For many institutional investors, the negative implications of a dividend reduction may dominate the positive investment opportunity signal for several reasons:

(1) Due to their fiduciary responsibilities, institutional investors, and especially pension funds, may be especially concerned with the perceived change in risk (and the possibility of bankruptcy) of a firm which has decided to cut or eliminate its cash dividend;

(2) It is commonly alleged that institutional investment managers "window dress" their portfolios. Window dressing refers to the practice of "cleaning up" investment portfolios prior to required disclosures to investors. Holding the common stocks of firms which have cut dividends (for whatever reasons) may reflect poorly on the stock selection ability of portfolio managers. Consequently, these securities may be sold for window dressing purposes;

(3) Institutional investment managers may plan to use the cash received in the form of dividends to meet expected liabilities. Since most institutions are not taxed on dividend income and would be required to sell shares (and absorb transactions costs) in the absence of cash dividend distributions, cash dividends may represent the least cost method for these managers to generate cash for operational purposes.

(4) Some institutions can invest only in dividend-paying stocks.

Due to any or all of these special concerns of certain institutional investors, they may mechanically react to dividend cut announcements by selling their shares, thereby driving down the prices of these stocks. Such institutional selling may in turn provide buying opportunities for other investors less concerned with "fiduciary responsibilities" or other artifical constraints.

The problem with this argument is that once this general market "overreaction" becomes a well-established trend (and, remember, our data only cover the most recent 10 or so years), then professional investors can be expected to catch on fairly quickly, and buy up the stocks of those companies suffering a severe market reaction to a dividend cut.

This very process of "arbitrage" by sophisticated investors should itself ensure that market overreaction can not be overly drastic or prolonged.

Perhaps the most plausible explanation, then, is that the announcement of a dividend cut creates a great deal of uncertainty among investors. Because dividend cuts have often been a desperate measure by firms trying to stave off bankruptcy, the market responds initially by assuming the worst. Only later is the uncertainty about the firm's prospects—and perhaps in many cases, about its very survival—resolved. As an analogy, companies on the verge of bankruptcy are highly risky; and the returns from holding a portfolio of firms in or near bankruptcy are accordingly very high. Therefore, the 10 percent average return in the year following announcements of dividend cuts may simply be a "normal" rate of return to investors bearing a very large amount of uncertainty and, hence, risk.

Some of this reasoning would also apply to the exceptional post-announcement appreciation (on average, 16 percent) of our category (3) firms. We might have expected the market to exercise more discrimination, and to react less negatively to the announcement itself. But, as mentioned earlier, most of these "growth-induced" dividend cuts also followed periods of low earnings and poor market performance, thus making it difficult for investors to distinguish between these cases and the "earnings-induced" cuts with which they have become all too familiar.

The puzzle posed by this apparent market "overreaction" will only be resolved by further research. The fact that the sample of category (1) and (2) dividend cuts are drawn only from a 10-year period restricts the amount of confidence we can place in these results. And, of course, the sample of 16 firms announcing "growth-induced" cuts is far too small to support any general conclusions about the market's response to dividend signaling. But the fact that the market has responded positively to some carefully crafted announcements of dividend cuts, and that some managements have displayed a seemingly greater willingness to cut the dividend to provide a source of finance, suggests that the market's traditional perception of dividend changes may be subject to change. This will happen as more companies cut the dividend to finance new investment, and then back their statements with successful performance. In fact, we wouldn't be surprised if this reversal of traditional expectations is now under way.

The fact that the market has responded positively to some carefully crafted announcements of dividend cuts, suggests that the market's traditional perception of dividend changes may be subject to change.

Conclusion

To conclude, we will briefly run through the major results of our study on the market's response to dividend cuts:

(1) The common stock of dividend-cutting firms tends to underperform the market significantly in the quarter preceding the reduction;

(2) In general, the market reacts very negatively to dividend cut announcements, even when they are accompanied by statements citing the need for funds to undertake profitable investment opportunities;

(3) In the quarter following dividend cuts, firms which have cut the dividend perform, on average, at least as well as the market. But those firms which appeared to use a dividend cut to finance future growth outperformed the market by almost 9 percent, on average, in the quarter following the announcement, and by 16 percent in the year following the announcement. Moreover, even those firms cutting the dividend primarily because of lower earnings outperformed the market by 10 percent, on average, in the year following the announcement; and

(4) Other signaling mechanisms, such as simultaneous announcements of stock dividends or stock repurchases, appear to offset much of the negative market reaction to the announcement of cash dividend cuts.

The lesson for management, therefore, seems to be as follows: companies wishing to cut dividends to conserve cash for investment may be able to offset at least part of the market's habitually negative response to dividend cuts. However, the ability of the market to overcome its past conditioning depends in large part on management's effectiveness in communicating its investment opportunities. Also, those signals that appear costly (that is, those that involve a greater commitment by management, such as that provided by a stock repurchase) are much more likely to elicit a favorable market response.

The vastly superior post-announcement performance of companies cutting dividends to finance investments suggests that while the immediate investor reaction is unfavorable, a dividend cut is not likely to have a lasting effect on a company's market value. In fact, those companies announcing the dividend cut as part of an investment package outperformed the market by over 3 percent, on average, from the time of the announcement through the first quarter following the announcement. And, on the basis of this evidence, we are brought full circle to the Miller-Modigliani "dividend irrelevance" proposition with which we began. The market, it seems, does not really have a preference for dividends per se over capital gains. (And the fact that the average of all our sample companies forced by poor earnings to cut dividends significantly outperformed the market in the year following the dividend cut suggests that the market may even have an *aversion* to higher-dividend stocks.) Thus, managers need not be overly concerned with the market's reaction (not in the long- to intermediate-term, at least) to dividend cuts if they have promising investment opportunities.

Nevertheless, better financial communication to the investment community may minimize the immediate adverse stock market reaction to the announcement of the dividend cut. Investors, to be sure, are much more likely to respond to a substitute signal for dividend increases when they see that providing that signal imposes some cost on management. A stock repurchase, for example, is probably so effective in neutralizing the standard negative market reaction to dividend cuts because, like higher dividends, it has such a high cost to management in terms of reduced financing flexibility.

At the same time, however, there is clearly a potential cost to management in simply making statements to the investment community about its prospects and intentions. For if it fails to deliver on its promises, the company forfeits its credibility. And for the simple reason that management has a strong incentive to maintain good investor relations, the market may respond to a carefully structured series of statements from management explaining its dividend policy, preferably as part of the firm's overall investment and financing strategy. (Also, to the extent there are clienteles of investors with different dividend preferences, such statements should also provide the market with sufficient advance notice to allow investors to adjust their portfolios.)

In short, unless the Gould case is an anomaly, management may find that improved direct financial communication to the market is a far less costly method of communicating with the investment community than the conventional approach of regular, periodic increases in the dividend—especially if the company has significant investment opportunities and access to equity capital is costly.

Aharony, J. and I. Swary, "Quarterly Dividend and Earnings Announcements and Stockholders Returns: An Empirical Analysis," *Journal of Finance* (1980).

Berk, I., "Electric Utility Dividend Policy and Stock Market Recognition," *Public Utilities Fortnightly* (July 21, 1977), 36-38.

Bhattacharya, S., "Imperfect Information, Dividend Policy, and the 'Bird in Hand' Fallacy," *The Bell Journal of Economics* (1979).

Black, F., "The Dividend Puzzle," *Journal of Portfolio Management* 2 (Winter 1976).

Black, F. and M. Scholes, "The Effects of Dividend Yield and Dividend Policy on Common Stock Prices and Returns," *Journal of Financial Economics* (1974).

Blume, M. E., "Stock Returns and Dividend Yields: Some More Evidence," *Review of Economics and Statistics* (November, 1980), 567-577.

Bradford, D. F. & R. H. Gordon, "Taxation and the Stock Market Valuation of Capital Gains and Dividends," *Journal of Public Economics* 14 (1980), 109-136.

Brennan, M. J., "Taxes, Market Valuation and Corporate Financial Policy," *National Tax Journal* 23 (December, 1970), 417-427.

Dhrymes, P., and Kurz, M., "Investment, Dividends, and External Finance Behavior of Firms," in R. Ferber (ed.), *Determinants of Investment Behavior* (New York: Columbia University Press, 1967).

Fama, E. F., "The Empirical Relationships Between the Dividend and Investment Decisions of Firms," *American Economic Review* 64 (June, 1974), 304-318.

Fama, E. F. and H. Babiak, "Dividend Policy: An Empirical Analysis," *Journal of the American Statistical Association* (December, 1968), pp. 1132-1161.

Feldstein, M. and J. Green, "Why Do Companies Pay Dividends?" (National Bureau of Economic Research, Conference Paper No. 54, October, 1980).

Friend, I. and M. Puckett, "Dividends and Stock Prices," *American Economic Review* (September, 1964), 656-82.

Gonedes, N., "Corporate Signaling, External Accounting, and Capital Market Equilibrium: Evidence on Dividends, Income, and Extraordinary Items," *Journal of Accounting Research* 16 (Spring, 1978), 26-79.

Grinblatt, M. S., R. W. Masulis and S. Titman, "The Valuation Effects of Stock Splits and Stock Dividends," *Journal of Financial Economics* (1984).

Hakansson, Nils, "To Pay or Not to Pay Dividends," *The Journal of Finance* 37 (May 1982).

Hamada, R. F., "The Effect of the Firm's Capital Structure on the Systematic Risk of Common Stocks," *Journal of Finance* 26 (May, 1971), 435-452.

Hess, P., "The Ex-Dividend Behavior of Stock Returns: Further Evidence on Tax Effects," *Journal of Finance* (May, 1982).

Higgins, R. C., "The Corporate Dividend-Saving Decision," *Journal of Financial and Quantitative Analysis* 7 (March, 1972), 1527-1541.

Jensen, M. C. and Meckling, W. H., "Theory of the Firm: Managerial Behavior, Agency Costs and Ownership Structure," *Journal of Financial Economics* 3 (October, 1976).

Kalay, A., "Signalling Information Content, and the Reluctance to Cut Dividends," *Journal of Financial and Quantitative Analysis* (1980).

Laub, M., "On the Informational Content of Dividends," *The Journal of Business* 49 (January, 1976), 73-80.

Lev, B., "On the Association Between Operating Leverage and Risk," *Journal of Financial and Quantitative Analysis* 9 (September, 1974), 627-641.

Lintner, J., "Distribution of Incomes of Corporations Among Dividends, Retained Earnings and Taxes," *American Economic Review* 46 (May, 1956), 97-113.

Litzenberger, R. H. & K. Ramaswamy, "The Effect of Personal Taxes and Dividends on Capital Asset Prices: Theory and Empirical Evidence," *Journal of Financial Economics* 7 (June, 1979), 163-195.

Litzenberger, R. H. & K. Ramaswamy, "Dividends, Short Selling Restrictions, Tax-Induced Investor Clienteles and Market Equilibrium," *Journal of Finance* 35 (May, 1980), 469-482.

McCabe, G. M., "The Empirical Relationship Between Investment and Financing: A New Look," *Journal of Financial and Quantitative Analysis* 14 (March, 1979), 119-135.

Michel, A., "Industry Influence on Dividend Policy," *Financial Management* 8 (Autumn, 1979), 22-26.

Miller, M. H. & F. Modigliani, "Dividend Policy, Growth and the Valuation of Shares," *Journal of Business* 34 (October, 1961), 411-432.

Miller, M. H., "Dividends and Taxes," *Journal of Financial Economics* 6 (December, 1978), 333-364.

Miller, M. H., "The Information Content of Dividends," Proceedings of Conference in Honor of Franco Modigliani, MIT Press, 1986.

Miller, M. H., "Behavioral Rationality: The Case of Dividends," *Journal of Business*, forthcoming 1986.

Miller, M. H. & M. Scholes, "Dividends and Taxes: Some Empirical Evidence," *Journal of Political Economy* 90 (1982).

Miller, M. H. and K. Rock, "Dividend Policy under Assymetric Information," *Journal of Finance* (September, 1985).

Morgan, I. G.., "Dividends and Capital Asset Prices," *Journal of Finance* 37 (September, 1982), 1071-1086.

Pettit, R. R., "Dividend Announcments, Security Performance, and Capital Market Efficiency," *Journal of Finance* (1972).

Sharpe, W. F. and H. B. Sosin, "Risk, Return and Yield: New York Stock Exchange Common Stocks 1928-1969," *Financial Analysts Journal* (March/April 1976) 33-42.

Stone, B. K. and B. J. Bartter, "The Effect of Dividend Yield on Stock Returns: Empirical Evidence on the Relevance of Dividends," W.P.E.-76-78, Georgia Institute of Technology, Atlanta, Georgia.

Watts, R., "The Information Content of Dividends," *The Journal of Business* 46 (April, 1973), 191-211.

Woolridge, J. R., "The Information Content of Dividend Changes," *Journal of Financial Research* (1982).

Woolridge, J. R., "Stock Dividends as Signals," *Journal of Financial Research* (1983).

Woolridge, J. R., "Dividend Changes and Security Prices," *Journal of Finance* (1983).

Part VII: Mergers & Acquisitions

INTRODUCTION

The 1980s saw an unprecedented wave of corporate acquisitions, divestitures, spin-offs, split-ups, buybacks, ESOPs, partial public offerings, limited partnerships, and leveraged buyouts—all of which have been yoked together under the name of "corporate restructuring." In "The Takeover Controversy: Analysis and Evidence," Jensen uses his "free cash flow" theory of takeovers to provide a remarkably ambitious and coherent explanation of the 1980s' restructuring wave. His argument leads to conclusions like the following:

- mergers in a wide range of mature or shrinking industries (most notably oil and gas, but also forest products, minerals, tobacco, broadcasting, food processing, and financial services) reduced waste and curbed unprofitable reinvestment, thereby creating value for shareholders and promoting the national interest;
- the use of large amounts of debt to finance acquisitions, leveraged buyouts, and large stock buybacks increased corporate efficiency;
- junk bonds played a major role in the restructuring process by reducing the effectiveness of sheer size as a deterrent to takeover;
- the stock market, contrary to the frequent claims of management and the press, is quite capable of taking the long view in assessing corporate performance (even though management often does not);
- the capital markets brought about the dismemberment of inefficient conglomerates through takeovers, divestitures, spinoffs, and LBOs;
- golden parachutes, when properly structured, can be used to unify management and stockholder interests;
- the practice of greenmail should, and could have been quite easily, prevented by corporate boards; and
- court decisions to uphold poison pills and otherwise ban takeovers undermined the contractual agreement between management and stockholders that is at the heart of the corporate form of organization.

In the article entitled "The Market for Corporate Control," the University of Chicago's Peter Dodd reviews the accumulating body of academic research on the stock price effects of not only mergers and tender offers, but also of a range of transactions in which control of the corporation is established, traded, challenged, or defended; these include proxy fights, standstill agreements, targeted buybacks, "antitakeover" amendments, and golden parachutes. The evidence suggests that, on average and over the years, mergers and tender offers have proven a profitable investment of corporate funds, though stockholders of acquired companies—no surprise here—have received the lion's share of the total gains from these transactions. The research also documents that acquired companies tend to have underperformed, and acquiring companies outperformed, the market over the years prior to acquisitions, thus supporting Dodd's conception of the market for corporate control as a means of channeling assets to more efficient users or higher-valued uses.

What these statistical averages conceal, however, is that many acquiring companies have paid too dearly and, in the process, materially harmed their own stockholders. In fact, on the authority of Dodd's just completed study of the most recent merger wave (1979-1982), both mergers and tender offers appear to have resulted in significantly negative returns, on average, to stockholders of buying companies. These somewhat disturbing results, together with what appears to be an unprecedented resistance by target managements to "unfriendly" takeovers (or, at least, an astonishing proliferation of new antitakeover strategies) leads Dodd to speculate that the market for control may be undergoing some fundamental changes. He closes with the suggestion that the recent spate of corporate raidings and proxy fights, in which institutions have backed the cause of dissident stockholders for the first time in our corporate history, may well reflect a resurgence of the market for corporate control. This supposition is bolstered, furthermore, by Dodd's own study of proxy fights (with Jerry Warner), which provides strong evidence that the mere possibility of a challenge to incumbent management can be beneficial to stockholders.

Following Dodd's summary of the academic evidence, we present our transcription of a series of presentations at a recent University of California-Berkeley conference on "Mergers and Acquisitions." The principal focus of the conference was the economic consequences of M & A — more specifically, the effects of mergers and tender offers on stockholders and other corporate security holders. But, supplementing this broad economic perspective, a number of speakers also addressed prescriptive aspects of merger analysis from the corporate perspective: strategic planning, the pricing of acquisition targets, and the structuring of management compensation plans.

In "Observations on the Merger Phenomenon," Baruch Lev provides a general overview of the issues, a summary of the research findings, and a fairly controversial interpretation of that research. Lev expresses strong doubt about the validity of the traditional academic assumption that corporate management acts in the best interest of its stockholders, especially in M & A transactions. The frequent negative market reaction to *buying* firms together with the widespread resistance to takeovers by target management — both matters of intense academic and regulatory debate — furnish the grounds for Lev's skepticism about the genuineness of management's service to its stockholders. Also casting doubt on the value of the conglomerate merger movement to acquiring companies' stockholders is the market's decidedly positive response to divestitures and spin-offs.

In an analysis of "Managerial Incentives in Mergers," David Larcker further fuels a controversy by presenting evidence that the predominance in acquiring companies of "short-term accounting-oriented compensation plans" may be partly responsible for the significant numbers of mergers—especially in the 70s—that were unfavorably received by the market.

The evidence pointing to the inefficiency of conglomerates begs the question: Why in the 1960s did the stock market appear to encourage the building of conglomerate empires? In "Divestitures: Mistakes or Learning?," Fred Weston provides evidence that the conglomerate movement of the 1960s may once have served a valuable purpose. Professor Weston takes issue, for example, with Michael Porter's sweeping indictment of "corporate strategy"—an attack based on the frequency with which American corporations have acquired and then divested the same units. Some of these divestitures surely represent corporate "mistakes," as Weston concedes; but many others reflect a valuable and "dynamic interaction" between corporate management and capital markets in which management attempts to apply its perceived comparative advantages in a continually changing business and economic environment.

George Foster offers some entertaining anecdotal evidence buttressing Lev's position. He begins by recounting the history of the Chock Full O'Nuts-Rheingold merger, goes on to cite (from a Berkshire Hathaway annual report) the compressed M & A wisdom of Warren Buffett, and concludes with a brief commentary on the controversial role of investment bankers in these transactions.

Moving from the descriptive to the prescriptive side of merger analysis, Stewart Myers illuminates some of the pitfalls of DCF capital budgeting techniques in the evaluation of acquisition targets. Expressing skepticism about target undervaluation as a rationale for merger, Professor Myers argues that acquisitions can be justified only when the expected synergistic "benefits" from the combination exceed the "costs" of merger (defined as the amount of the acquisition premium which represents a transfer of value from the buying to the selling company's stockholders). Such an approach, he concedes, may be overly conservative because some merger benefits may elude measurement — especially in those cases where an acquisition would offer the acquirer some strategic or "real" option. While DCF analysis itself is shown to be a highly fallible tool for M & A analysis, the evaluation of strategic or "real" options is a far less exact science. But though yet in its infancy, the valuation of strategic opportunities promises to be one of the "greatest growth areas" in finance. (For a longer discussion of the use of options pricing theory in evaluating strategic options, see the Brennan-Schwartz article in Part II.)

In the final article, "Why Corporate Raiders Are Good News for Stockholders," Cliff Holderness and Dennis Sheehan present the findings of what, to our knowledge, is the first systematic empirical test of the "stockholder wealth effects" of the activities of specific individual investors. In the first part of their two-part study, the authors document a significantly positive market response on average to announcements of holdings by six of the most notorious of the so-called "corporate raiders" (Carl Icahn, Victor Posner, Irwin Jacobs, Carl Lindner, David Murdock and the late Charles Bluhdorn). If such investors had a tendency to reduce the long-term value of their target firms after acquiring an interest (as the term "raider" suggests), we would expect a negative response to such announcements.

The second part of the study, which examines the market performance of the target firms over a two-year period following their original stock purchases, appears to confirm the rightness of the market's initial response. Stockholders in those firms substantially outperformed the market, regardless of whether the target was eventually acquired or not.

How does the presence of dissident stockholders increase the value of a company? Holderness and Sheehan offer two explanations: (1) the so-called "raiders" improve the quality of management's service to its stockholders, either through active participation in running the target firm (and while such investors rarely take a hand in the day-to-day operations, the authors provide suggestive evidence that these "raiders" are far more than passive investors) or merely by holding out the threat of takeover; or (2) the investors are adept at identifying undervalued corporate assets. They go on to speculate, however, that "perhaps the most plausible explanation for the undervaluation of assets is a failure by management to put the assets at its disposal to their highest-valued use...'Corporate raiders' may be the catalyst necessary to allow potential asset values to be realized." While such an explanation may not be universally appropriate, it does seem a plausible account of, say, Boone Pickens's forays into the oil patch and the Bass brothers' recent restructuring of Walt Disney.

DHC

The Takeover Controversy: Analysis and Evidence*

Michael C. Jensen,
*University of Rochester and
Harvard Business School*[1]

Introduction

The market for corporate control is fundamentally changing the corporate landscape. Transactions in this market in 1985 were at a record level of $180 billion, 47 percent above the $122 billion in 1984. The purchase prices in 36 of the 3,000 deals exceeded a billion dollars in 1985, compared with 18 in 1984.[2] These transactions involve takeovers, mergers, and leveraged buyouts. Closely associated are corporate restructurings involving divestitures, spinoffs, and large stock repurchases for cash and debt.

The changes associated with these control transactions are causing considerable controversy. Some argue that takeovers are damaging to the morale and productivity of organizations and therefore damaging to the economy. Others argue that takeovers represent productive entrepreneurial activity that improves the control and management of assets and helps move assets to more productive uses.

The controversy has been accompanied by strong pressure on regulators and legislatures to enact restrictions that would curb activity in the market for corporate control. In the spring of 1985 there were over 20 bills under consideration in Congress that proposed new restrictions on takeovers. Within the past several years the legislatures of New York, New Jersey, Maryland, Pennsylvania, Connecticut, Illinois, Kentucky, and Michigan have passed antitake-over laws. The Federal Reserve Board entered the fray early in 1986 when it issued its controversial new interpretation of margin rules that restricts the use of debt in takeovers.

Through dozens of studies, leading financial economists have accumulated considerable evidence and knowledge about the effects of the takeover market. Since most of the results of the work completed prior to 1984 are well summarized elsewhere,[4] I focus here on current aspects of the controversy and on new results. In a nutshell, the previous work tells us the following:

- Takeovers benefit target shareholders—premiums in hostile offers historically exceed 30 percent on average, and in recent times have averaged about 50 percent.
- Acquiring-firm shareholders on average earn about 4 percent in hostile takeovers and roughly zero in mergers.
- Takeovers do not waste credit or resources; they generate substantial gains—historically 8.4 percent of the total value of both companies. Recently the gains seem to have been even larger.
- Actions by managers that eliminate or prevent offers or mergers are most suspect as harmful to shareholders.
- Golden parachutes for top-level managers do not, on average, harm shareholders.
- The activities of takeover specialists such as Icahn,

* This article is a somewhat shortened version of Michael C. Jensen's "The Takeover Controversy: Analysis and Evidence," which will appear in the forthcoming volume, *Takeovers and Contests for Corporate Control* (Oxford University Press, 1987), edited by John Coffee, Louis Lowenstein, and Susan Rose-Ackerman. It is printed here with permission of the publisher.

1. Michael Jensen holds a joint appointment as Professor of Business Administration, Harvard Business School, and LaClare Professor of Finance and Business Administration and Director of the Managerial Economics Research Center at the University of Rochester's Graduate School of Management. This research is supported by the Division of Research, Harvard Business School, and the Managerial Economics Research Center, University of Rochester.

2. W. T. Grimm, *Mergerstat Review* (1985).

4. A detailed summary of this evidence is available in Michael C. Jensen and Richard S. Ruback, "The Market for Corporate Control: The Scientific Evidence," *Journal of Financial Economics* 11 (April, 1983); and in Michael C. Jensen, "Takeovers: Folklore and Science", *Harvard Business Review* (November/December, 1984). See also Paul J. Halpern,, "Empirical Estimates of the Amount and Distribution of Gains to Companies in Mergers," *Journal of Business*, V. 46, No. 4 (October, 1973) pp. 554-575.

Posner, Steinberg, and Pickens, on average, benefit shareholders.[5]

• Takeover gains do not come from the creation of monopoly power.

This paper analyzes the controversy surrounding takeovers and provides both theory and evidence to explain the central phenomena at issue. The paper is organized as follows. Section 2 contains basic background analysis of the forces operating in the market for corporate control—analysis which provides an understanding of the conflicts and issues surrounding takeovers and the effects of activities in this market. Section 3 discusses the conflict between managers and shareholders over the payout of free cash flow and how takeovers represent both a symptom and a resolution of the conflict. Sections 4, 5, and 6 discuss the relatively new phenomena of, respectively, junk-bond financing, the use of golden parachutes, and the practice of greenmail. Section 7 analyzes the problems the Delaware court is having in dealing with the conflicts that arise over control issues and its confused application of the business judgment rule to these cases.

The following topics are discussed:

• The reasons for takeovers and mergers in the petroleum industry and why they increase efficiency and thereby promote the national interest.

• The role of debt in bonding management's promises to pay out future cash flows, to reduce costs, and to reduce investments in low-return projects.

• The role of high-yield debt (junk bonds) in helping to eliminate mere size as a takeover deterrent.

• The effects of takeovers on the equity markets and claims that managers are pressured to behave myopically.

• The effects of antitakeover measures such as poison pills.

• The misunderstandings of the important role that "golden parachutes" play in reducing the conflicts of interests associated with takeovers and the valuable function they serve in alleviating some of the costs and uncertainty facing managers.

• The damaging effects of the Delaware court decision in Unocal vs. Mesa that allowed Unocal to make a self-tender offer that excluded its largest shareholder (reverse greenmail).

• The problems the courts are facing in applying the model of the corporation subsumed under the traditional business judgment rule to the conflicts of interest involved in corporate control controversies.

The Market for Corporate Control — Background

The Benefits of Takeovers

The market for corporate control is creating large benefits for shareholders and for the economy as a whole. The corporate control market generates these gains by loosening control over vast amounts of resources and enabling them to move more quickly to their highest-valued use. This is a healthy market in operation, on both the takeover side and the divestiture side.

Gains to target firms. Total benefits created by the control market have been huge, as reflected in gains of $40 billion to stockholders of acquired firms in 260 tender offers alone in the period from January 1981 through May 1985.[6] This figure does not include the gains from other control transactions such as mergers, leveraged buyouts, or divestitures. Nor does it include the gains from reorganizations such as those of Phillips, Unocal and others that have been motivated by takeover attempts. (The Phillips, Unocal and ARCO reorganizations created gains of an additional $6.6 billion.) One study estimates the total premiums received by shareholders of target firms to have been approximately $75 billion in $239 billion of merger and acquisition deals in 1984 and 1985.[6a]

Gains to bidding firms. The evidence on the returns to bidding firms is mixed. The data indicate that prior to 1980 shareholders of bidding firms earned on average about zero in mergers (which tend to be voluntary) and about 4 percent of their equity value in tender offers (which tend to be hostile).[7] These differences in returns are associated with the form of payment rather than the form of the

---

5. Clifford G. Holdnerness and Dennis P. Sheehan, "Raiders or Saviors? The Evidence on Six Controversial Investors," *Journal of Financial Economics* 14 (December, 1985); and Wayne H. Mikkelson and Richard S. Ruback, "An Empirical Analysis of the Interfirm Equity Investment Process," *Journal of Financial Economics* 14 (December, 1985).

6. As estimated by the Office of the Chief Economist of the SEC and provided to the author in private communication.

6a. John D. Paulus, "Corporate Restructuring, 'Junk,' and Leverage: Too Much or Too Little?" (Morgan Stanley, February 1986).

7. See Jensen and Ruback [1983, Tables 1 and 2], cited earlier in note 4.

Major changes in energy markets have required a radical restructuring of and retrenchment in that industry; and takeovers have played an important role in accomplishing these changes.

offer (tender offers tend to be for cash and mergers tend to be for stock).[8]

Although there are measurement problems that make it difficult to estimate the returns to bidders as precisely as the returns to targets,[12] it appears the bargaining power of target managers, coupled with competition among potential acquirers, grants much of the acquisition benefits to selling shareholders. In addition, federal and state regulation of tender offers appears to have strengthened the hand of target firms; premiums received by target-firm shareholders increased substantially after introduction of such regulation.[13]

Causes of Current Takeover Activity

The current high level of takeover activity seems to be caused by a number of factors:
- the relaxation of restrictions on mergers imposed by the antitrust laws;
- the withdrawal of resources from industries that are growing more slowly or that must shrink;
- deregulation in the financial services, oil and gas, transportation, and broadcasting markets that is bringing about a major restructuring of those industries;
- and improvements in takeover technology, including a larger supply of increasingly sophisticated legal and financial advisers, and improvements in financing technology (for example, the strip financing commonly used in leveraged buyouts and the original issuance of high-yield non-investment-grade bonds).

Each of these factors has contributed to the increase in total takeover and reorganization activity in recent times. Moreover, the first three factors (antitrust relaxation, exit, and deregulation) are generally consistent with data showing the intensity of takeover activity by industry. For example, the value of merger and acquisition transactions by industry in the period 1981-84 (see Table 1) indicates that acquisition activity was highest in oil and gas, followed by banking and finance, insurance, food processing,

and mining and minerals. For comparison purposes, the last column of the table presents data on industry size measured as a fraction of the total value of all firms. All but two of the industries, retail and transportation, represent a larger fraction of total takeover activity than their representation in the economy as a whole.

Many areas of the U.S. economy have been experiencing slowing growth and, in some cases, even retrenchment—a phenomenon that has many causes, including substantially increased competition from foreign firms. This has increased takeover activity because takeovers play an important role in facilitating exit from an industry or activity. Major changes in energy markets have required a radical restructuring of and retrenchment in that industry; and, as discussed in detail below, takeovers have played an important role in accomplishing these changes. Deregulation of the financial service market is consistent with the high ranking in Table 1 of banking and finance and insurance. Deregulation has also been important in the transportation and broadcasting industries. Mining and minerals has been subject to many of the same forces affecting the energy industry, including the changes in the value of the dollar.

Takeovers Provide Competition for Top-level Management Jobs

The market for corporate control is best viewed as a major component of the managerial labor market. It is the arena in which different management teams compete for the rights to manage corporate resources.[14] Understanding this is crucial to understanding much of the rhetoric about the effects of hostile takeovers.

Managers formerly protected from competition for their jobs by antitrust constraints that prevented takeover of the nation's largest corporations are now facing a more demanding environment and a more uncertain future.

The development of innovative financing

8. See Yen-Sheng Huang and Ralph A. Walkling, "Differences in Residuals Associated with Acquisition Announcements: Payment, Acquisition Form, and Resistance Effects" (Manuscript, Georgia Institute of Technology and Ohio State University, November, 1985).

12. See B. Espen Eckbo, "Do Acquiring Firms Gain From Merger?" (unpublished manuscript, University of British Columbia, June, 1985). Eckbo concludes that the zero returns to U.S. bidding firms is due to difficulties in measuring the gains to bidding firms when the bidder is substantially larger than the

target firm. In his sample the average Canadian bidder was approximately the same size as the average target while the average U.S. bidder is approximately 8 times the size of the average Canadian target. See also Jensen and Ruback [1983, pp 18ff.], cited earlier in note 4.

13. See Gregg Jarrell and Michael Bradley, "The Economic Effects of Federal and State Regulation of Cash Tender Offers," *Journal of Law and Economics* 23 (1980), pp. 371-407.

14. See Jensen and Ruback [1983], cited earlier in note 4.

When the internal processes for change in large corporations are too slow, costly, and clumsy to bring about the required restructuring or management change, the capital markets are doing so through the operation of the market for corporate control.

TABLE 1
Intensity of Industry Takeover Activity: 1981–1984

Intensity of industry takeover activity as measured by the value of merger and acquisition transactions in the period 1981–84 (as a percent of total takeover transactions for which valuation data are publicly reported) compared to industry size (as measured by the fraction of overall corporate market value).

Industry classification of seller	Percent of total takeover activity*	Percent of total corporate market value**
Oil and gas	26.3%	13.5%
Banking and finance	8.8	6.4
Insurance	5.9	2.9
Food processing	4.6	4.4
Mining and minerals	4.4	1.5
Conglomerate	4.4	3.2
Retail	3.6	5.2
Transportation	2.4	2.7
Leisure and entertainment	2.3	.9
Broadcasting	2.3	.7
Other	39.4	58.5

*Source: W. T. Grimm, *Mergerstat Review* (1984), p. 41.
**As of 12/31/84. Total value is measured as the sum of the market value of common equity for 4,305 companies, including 1,501 companies on the NYSE, 724 companies on the ASE plus 2,080 companies in the Over-The-Counter market. Source: *The Media General Financial Weekly,* (December 31, 1984), p. 17.

vehicles, such as high-yield, non-investment-grade bonds ("junk" bonds), has removed size as a significant impediment to competition in this market. Although they have not been widely used in takeovers yet, these new financing techniques permit small firms to obtain resources for acquisition of much larger firms by issuing claims on the value of the venture (that is, the target firm's assets) just as in any other corporate investment activity. It is not surprising that many executives of large corporations would like relief from this new competition for their jobs, but restricting the corporate control market is not the efficient way to handle the problems caused by the increased uncertainty in their contracting environment.

Takeovers Provide External Control

The internal control mechanisms of corporations, which operate through the board of directors, generally work well. On occasion, however, they break down. One important source of protection for investors in these situations is the takeover market. Other management teams that recognize an opportunity to reorganize or redeploy an organization's

assets and thereby create new value can bid for the control rights in the takeover market. To be successful, such bids must be at a premium over current market value. This gives investors an opportunity to realize part of the gains from reorganization and redeployment of the assets.

The Market for Corporate Control Is an Agent for Change

Takeovers generally occur because changing technology or market conditions require a major restructuring of corporate assets. In some cases takeovers occur because incumbent managers are incompetent. When the internal processes for change in large corporations are too slow, costly and clumsy to bring about the required restructuring or management change in an efficient way, the capital markets are doing so through the operation of the market for corporate control. In this sense, the capital markets have been responsible for bringing about substantial changes in corporate strategy in recent times.

Managers often have difficulty abandoning strategies they have spent years devising and im-

Some firms in the oil industry have to go out of business. This is cheaper to accomplish through merger and the orderly liquidation of marginal assets of the combined firms than by a slow, agonizing death in a competitive struggle in an industry with overcapacity.

plementing, even when those strategies no longer contribute to the organization's survival. Such changes often require abandonment of major projects, relocation of facilities, changes in managerial assignments, and closure or sale of facilities or divisions. It is easier for new top-level managers with no ties with current employees or communities to make such changes. Moreover, normal organizational resistance to change commonly lessens significantly early in the reign of new top-level managers. For example, the premium Carl Icahn was able to offer for TWA, and his victory over Texas Air in the battle for control of TWA, were made possible in part by the willingness of the TWA unions to negotiate favorable contract concessions with Icahn—concessions that TWA itself was unable to attain prior to the takeover conflict. Such organizational factors that make change easier for newcomers, coupled with a fresh view of the business, can be a major advantage to new managers after a takeover. On the other hand, lack of detailed knowledge about the firm also poses risks for new managers and increases the likelihood of mistakes.

Takeovers are particularly important in bringing about efficiencies when exit from an activity is required. The oil industry is a good example. Changing market conditions mandate a major restructuring of the petroleum industry, and none of this is the fault of management. Management, however, must adjust to the new energy environment and recognize that many old practices and strategies are no longer viable. It is particularly hard for many managers to deal with the fact that some firms in the oil industry have to go out of business. This is cheaper to accomplish through merger and the orderly liquidation of marginal assets of the combined firms than by a slow, agonizing death in a competitive struggle in an industry with overcapacity. The end of the latter process often comes in the bankruptcy courts, with high losses and unnecessary destruction of valuable parts of organizations that could be used productively by others.

In short, the external takeover market serves as a court of last resort that plays an important role in (1) creating organizational change, (2) motivating the efficient use of resources, and (3) protecting shareholders when the corporation's internal controls and board-level control mechanisms are slow, clumsy, or defunct.

Divestitures Are the Subject of Much Erroneous Criticism

If assets are to move to their most highly valued use, acquirers must be able to sell off assets to those who can use them more productively. Therefore, divestitures are a critical element in the functioning of the corporate control market, and it is thus important to avoid inhibiting them. Indeed, over 1200 divestitures occurred in 1985, a record level.[15] Labeling divestitures with emotional terms such as "bustups" is not a substitute for analysis or evidence.

Moreover, it is important to recognize that divested plants and assets do not disappear; they are reallocated. Sometimes they continue to be used in similar ways in the same industry, and in other cases they are used in very different ways and in different industries. But in all cases they are moving to uses that their new owners believe are more productive. This process is beneficial to society.

Finally, it is useful to recognize that the takeover and divestiture market provides a private market constraint against bigness for its own sake. The potential gains available to those who correctly perceive that a firm can be purchased for less than the value realizable from the sale of its components provide incentives for entrepreneurs to search out these opportunities and to capitalize on them by reorganizing such firms into smaller entities.

The mere possibility of such takeovers also motivates managers to avoid putting together uneconomic conglomerates and to break up existing ones. This is now happening. Recently it has appeared that many firms' defenses against takeovers have led to actions similar to those proposed by potential acquirers. Examples are the reorganizations occurring in the oil industry, the sale of "crown jewels," and divestitures brought on by the desire to liquidate large debts incurred to buy back stock or to make other payments to stockholders. Unfortunately, the basic economic sense of these transactions is often lost in a blur of emotional rhetoric and controversy.

The sale of a firm's crown jewels, for example, benefits shareholders when the price obtained for the division is greater than the present value of the future cash flows to the current owner. A takeover bid motivated by the desire to obtain such an underused division can stimulate current managers to re-

---

15. W. T. Grimm, *Mergerstat Review* (1985).

It is important to recognize that divested plants and assets do not disappear; they are reallocated...to uses that their new owners believe are more productive. This process is beneficial to society.

examine the economics of the firm's current structure and to sell one or more of its divisions to a third party who is willing to pay even more than the initial offerer. Brunswick's sale of its Sherwood Medical Division to American Home Products after a takeover bid by Whittaker (apparently motivated by a desire to acquire Sherwood) is an example of such a transaction. The total value to Brunswick shareholders of the price received for selling Sherwood to American Home Products plus the remaining value of Brunswick without Sherwood (the proceeds from the sale of Sherwood were distributed directly to Brunswick's shareholders) was greater than Whittaker's offer for the entire company.[16]

Managers May Behave Myopically But Markets Do Not

It has been been argued that growing institutional equity holdings and the fear of takeover cause managers to behave myopically and therefore to sacrifice long-term benefits to increase short-term profits. The arguments tend to confuse two separate issues: 1) whether *managers* are shortsighted and make decisions that undervalue future cash flows while overvaluing current cash flows (myopic managers); and 2) whether *security markets* are shortsighted and undervalue future cash flows while overvaluing near-term cash flows (myopic markets).

There is little formal evidence on the myopic managers issue, but I believe this phenomenon does occur. Sometimes it occurs when managers hold little stock in their companies and are compensated in ways that motivate them to take actions that increase accounting earnings rather than the value of the firm. It also occurs when managers make mistakes because they do not understand the forces that determine stock values.

There is much evidence inconsistent with the myopic markets view and none that supports it:

• Even casual observation of the equity markets reveals that the market values more than current earnings. It values growth as well. The mere fact that

price/earnings ratios differ widely among securities indicates the market is valuing something other than current earnings. Indeed, the essence of a growth stock is one that has large investment projects yielding few short-term cash flows but high future earnings and cash flows.

• The continuing marketability of new issues for start-up companies with little record of current earnings—the Genentechs of the world—is also inconsistent with the notion that the market does not value future earnings.

• A recent study provides evidence that (except in the oil industry) stock prices respond positively to announcements of increased investment expenditures, and negatively to reduced expenditures.[17] This evidence is inconsistent with the notion that the equity market is myopic.

• The vast evidence on efficient markets indicating that current stock prices appropriately incorporate all currently available public information is also inconsistent with the myopic markets hypothesis. Although the evidence is not literally 100 percent in support of the efficient market hypothesis, there is no better documented proposition in any of the social sciences.[18]

The evidence indicates, for example, that the market appropriately interprets the implications of corporate accounting changes that increase reported profits but cause no change in corporate cash flows.[19]

Additional evidence is provided by the 30 percent increase in ARCO's stock price that occurred when it announced its major restructuring in 1985. This price increase is inconsistent with the notion that the market values only short-term earnings. Even though ARCO simultaneously revealed that it would have to take a $1.2 billion write-off as a result of the restructuring, the market still responded positively.

• Recent versions of the myopic markets hypothesis emphasize increasing institutional holdings and the pressures institutional investors face to show high returns on a quarter-to-quarter basis. It is argued that these pressures on institutions are a major cause of pressures on corporations to generate high current

16. See the analysis in Jensen [1984, p. 119], cited in note 4.

17. John J. McConnell and Chris J. Muscarella, "Corporate Capital Expenditure Decisions and the Market Value of the Firm," *Journal of Financial Economics* 14, No. 3 (1985).

18. For an introduction to the literature and empirical evidence on the theory of efficient markets, see E. Elton and M. Gruber, *Modern Portfolio Theory and Investment Analysis*, (New York: Wiley, 1984), Chapter 15, p. 375ff. and the 167 studies referenced in the bibliography.

19. Examples are switches from accelerated to straight-line depreciation techniques and adoption of the flow-through method for reporting investment tax credits. Here the evidence indicates that "security prices increase around the date when a firm first announces earnings inflated by an accounting change. The effect appears to be temporary, and, certainly by the subsequent quarterly report, the price has resumed a level appropriate to the true economic status of the firm." See R. Kaplan and R. Roll, "Investor Evaluation of Accounting Information: Some Empirical Evidence," *Journal of Business*, (April, 1972), 225-257.

*I believe this phenomenon [myopic managerial behavior] does occur.
Sometimes it occurs when managers hold little stock in their companies
and are compensated in ways that motivate them to take actions that
increase accounting earnings rather than the value of the firm.*

earnings on a quarter-to-quarter basis. The institutional pressures are said to lead to increased takeovers of firms (because institutions are not loyal shareholders) and to decreased research and development expenditures. It is argued that because R&D expenditures reduce current earnings, firms making them are therefore more likely to be taken over, and that reductions in R&D are leading to a fundamental weakening of the corporate sector of the economy.

A recent study of 324 firms by the Office of the Chief Economist of the SEC finds substantial evidence that is inconsistent with this version of the myopic markets argument.[20] The evidence indicates the following:

• increased institutional stock holdings are not associated with increased takeovers of firms;

• increased institutional holdings are not associated with decreases in research and development expenditures;

• firms with high research and development expenditures are not more vulnerable to takeovers;

• stock prices respond positively to announcements of increases in research and development expenditures.

Those who make the argument that takeovers are reducing R&D spending also have to come to grips with the aggregate data on such spending, which is inconsistent with the argument. Total spending on R&D in 1984, a year of record acquisition activity, increased by 14 percent according to *Business Week's* annual survey of 820 companies. (The sample companies account for 95 percent of total private-sector R&D expenditures.) This represented "the biggest gain since R&D spending began a steady climb in the late 1970s."[21] All industries in the survey increased R&D spending with the exception of steel. Moreover, R&D spending increased from 2 percent of sales, where it had been for five years, to 2.9 percent.

An Alternative Hypothesis

There is an alternative hypothesis that explains the current situation, including the criticisms of management, quite well.

Suppose that some managers are simply mistaken—that is, their strategies are wrong—and that the financial markets are telling them they are wrong. If they don't change, their stock prices will remain low. If the managers are indeed wrong, it is desirable for the stockholders and for the economy to remove them to make way for a change in strategy and more efficient use of the resources.

Free Cash Flow Theory of Takeovers[22]

More than a dozen separate forces drive takeover activity, including such factors as deregulation, synergies, economies of scale and scope, taxes, managerial incompetence, and increasing globalization of U.S. markets.[23] One major cause of takeover activity are the agency costs associated with conflicts between managers and shareholders over the payout of corporate free cash flow. Though this has received relatively little attention, it has played an important role in acquisitions over the last decade.

Managers are the agent of shareholders, and because both parties are self-interested, there are serious conflicts between them over the choice of the best corporate strategy. Agency costs are the total costs that arise in such cooperative arrangements. They consist of the costs of monitoring managerial behavior (such as the costs of producing audited financial statements and devising and implementing compensation plans that reward managers for actions that increase investors' wealth) and the inevitable costs that are incurred because the conflicts of interest can never be resolved perfectly. Sometimes these costs can be large and, when they are, takeovers can reduce them.

Free Cash Flow and the Conflict Between Managers and Shareholders

Free cash flow is cash flow in excess of that required to fund all projects that have positive net values when discounted at the relevant cost of capital. Such free cash flow must be paid out to share-

20. Office of the Chief Economist, Securities and Exchange Commission, "Institutional Ownership, Tender Offers, and Long-Term Investments," April 19, 1985.

21. "R&D Scoreboard: Reagan & Foreign Rivalry Light a Fire Under Spending", *Business Week*, July 8, 1985), p. 86 ff.

22. This discussion is based on my article, "Agency Costs of Free Cash Flow,

Corporate Finance and Takeovers," forthcoming in *American Economic Review*, (May, 1986).

23. Richard Roll discusses a number of these forces in "Empirical Evidence on Takeover Activity and Shareholder Wealth," (presented at the Conference on Takeovers and Contests for Corporate Control, Columbia University, November, 1985).

> *Free cash flow [that which cannot be profitably reinvested by management inside the firm] must be paid out to shareholders if the firm is to be efficient and to maximize value for shareholders.*

holders if the firm is to be efficient and to maximize value for shareholders.

Payment of cash to shareholders reduces the resources under managers' control, thereby reducing managers' power, and potentially subjecting them to the monitoring by the capital markets that occurs when a firm must obtain new capital. Financing projects internally avoids this monitoring and the possibility that funds will be unavailable or available only at high explicit prices.

Managers have incentives to expand their firms beyond the size that maximizes shareholder wealth.[24] Growth increases managers' power by increasing the resources under their control. In addition, changes in management compensation are positively related to growth.[25] The tendency of firms to reward middle managers through promotion rather than year-to-year bonuses also creates an organizational bias toward growth to supply the new positions that such promotion-based reward systems require.[25a]

The tendency for managers to overinvest resources is limited by competition in the product and factor markets, which tends to drive prices toward minimum average cost in an activity. Managers must therefore motivate their organizations to be more efficient to improve the probability of survival. Product and factor market disciplinary forces are often weaker in new activities, however, and in activities that involve substantial economic rents or quasi-rents.[26] In these cases, monitoring by the firm's internal control system and the market for corporate control are more important. Activities yielding substantial economic rents or quasi-rents are the types of activities that generate large amounts of free cash flow.

Conflicts of interest between shareholders and managers over payout policies are especially severe when the organization generates substantial free cash flow. The problem is how to motivate managers to disgorge the cash rather than invest it at below the cost of capital or waste it through organizational inefficiencies.

Some finance scholars have argued that financial flexibility (unused debt capacity and internally generated funds) is desirable when a firm's managers have better information about the firm than outside investors.[26a] Their arguments assume that managers act in the best interest of shareholders. The arguments offered here imply that such flexibility has costs: financial flexibility in the form of free cash flow, large cash balances, and unused borrowing power provides managers with greater discretion over resources that is often not used in the shareholders' interests.

The theory developed here explains (1) how debt-for-stock exchanges reduce the organizational inefficiencies fostered by substantial free cash flow, (2) how debt can substitute for dividends, (3) why "diversification" programs are more likely to be associated with losses than are expansion programs in the same line of business, (4) why mergers within an industry and liquidation-motivated takeovers will generally create larger gains than cross-industry mergers, (5) why the factors stimulating takeovers in such diverse businesses as broadcasting, tobacco, cable systems and oil are essentially identical, and (5) why bidders and some targets tend to show abnormally good performance prior to takeover.

The Role of Debt in Motivating Organizational Efficiency

The agency costs of debt have been widely discussed,[27] but the benefits of debt in motivating managers and their organizations to be efficient have largely been ignored. I call these effects the "control hypothesis" for debt creation.

24. See Gordon Donaldson, *Managing Corporate Wealth*, (Praeger: 1984). Donaldson, in a detailed study of 12 large Fortune 500 firms, concludes that managers of these firms were not driven by maximization of the value of the firm, but rather by the maximization of "corporate wealth." He defines corporate wealth as "*the aggregate purchasing power available to management for strategic purposes during any given planning period.* ... this wealth consists of the stocks and flows of cash and cash equivalents (primarily credit) that management can use at its discretion to implement decisions involving the control of goods and services." (p. 3, emphasis in original) "In practical terms it is cash, credit, and other corporate purchasing power by which management commands goods and services." (p.22).

25. Where growth is measured by increases in sales. See Kevin J. Murphy, "Corporate Performance and Managerial Remuneration: An Empirical Analysis," *Journal of Accounting and Economics* 7, Nos. 1-3 (April, 1985), pp. 11-42. This positive relationship between compensation and sales growth does not imply, although it is consistent with, causality.

25a. See George Baker, "Compensation and Hierarchies" (unpublished, Harvard Business School, January, 1986).

26. Rents are returns in excess of the opportunity cost of the resources committed to the activity. Quasi-rents are returns in excess of the short-run opportunity cost of the resources to the activity.

26a. See Stewart C. Myers and Nicholas S. Majluf, "Corporate Financing and Investment Decisions When Firms Have Information That Investors Do Not Have,' *Journal of Financial Economcics* 13 (1984), pp. 187-221.

27. See Michael C. Jensen and William H. Meckling, "Theory of the Firm: Managerial Behavior, Agency Costs and Ownership Structure," *Journal of Financial Economics*, V. 3 (1976), pp. 305-360; Stewart C. Myers, "Determinants of Corporate Borrowing," *Journal of Financial Economics*, V. 5, No. 2 (1977), pp. 147-175; and Clifford W. Smith, Jr. and Jerold B. Warner, "On Financial Contracting: An Analysis of Bond Covenants," *Journal of Financial Economics*, V. 7 (1979), pp. 117-161.

The control function of debt is more important in organizations that generate large cash flows but have low growth prospects, and it is even more important in organizations that must shrink.

Managers with substantial free cash flow can increase dividends or repurchase stock and thereby pay out current cash that would otherwise be invested in low-return projects or otherwise wasted. This payout leaves managers with control over the use of future free cash flows, but they can also promise to pay out future cash flows by announcing a "permanent" increase in the dividend.[28] Because there is no contractual obligation to make the promised dividend payments, such promises are weak. Dividends can be reduced by managers in the future with little effective recourse to shareholders. The fact that capital markets punish dividend cuts with large stock price reductions is an interesting equilibrium market response to the agency costs of free cash flow.[29]

Debt creation, without retention of the proceeds of the issue, enables managers effectively to bond their promise to pay out future cash flows. Thus, debt can be an effective substitute for dividends, something that is not generally recognized in the corporate finance literature.[30] By issuing debt in exchange for stock, managers bond their promise to pay out future cash flows in a way that simple dividend increases do not. In doing so, they give shareholder-recipients of the debt the right to take the firm into bankruptcy court if they do not keep their promise to make the interest and principal payments.[31] Thus, debt reduces the agency costs of free cash flow by reducing the cash flow available for spending at the discretion of managers.

Issuing large amounts of debt to buy back stock sets up organizational incentives to motivate managers to pay out free cash flow. In addition, the exchange of debt for stock also helps managers overcome the normal organizational resistance to retrenchment that the payout of free cash flow often requires. The threat of failure to make debt-service payments serves as a strong motivating force to make

such organizations more efficient. Stock repurchase for debt or cash also has tax advantages. Interest payments are tax-deductible to the corporation; the part of the repurchase proceeds equal to the seller's tax basis in the stock is not taxed at all, and that which is taxed is subject to capital-gains rates.

The control hypothesis does not imply that debt issues will always have positive control effects. For example, these effects will not be as important for rapidly growing organizations with large and highly profitable investment projects but no free cash flow. Such organizations will have to go regularly to the financial markets to obtain capital. At these times the markets will have an opportunity to evaluate the company, its management, and its proposed projects. Investment bankers and analysts play an important role in this monitoring, and the market's assessment is made evident by the price investors pay for the financial claims.

The control function of debt is more important in organizations that generate large cash flows but have low growth prospects, and it is even more important in organizations that must shrink. In these organizations the pressures to waste cash flows by investing them in uneconomic projects are most serious.

[The original paper contains a section here entitled "Evidence from Financial Transactions in Support of the Free Cash Flow Theory of Mergers," which appears in the "Appendix" to this article.]

The Evidence from Leveraged Buyout and Going-Private Transactions

Many of the benefits of going-private and leveraged buyout transactions seem to be due to the control function of debt. These transactions are creating a new organizational form that competes

---

28. Interestingly, Graham and Dodd, in their treatise, *Security Analysis*, placed great importance on the dividend payout in their famous valuation formula: V = M (D + .33E),(p.454). V is value, M is the earnings multiplier when the dividend payout rate is a "normal two-thirds of earnings," D is the expected dividend, and E is expected earnings. In their formula, dividends are valued at three times the rate of retained earnings, a proposition that has puzzled many students of modern finance (at least of my vintage). The agency cost of free cash flow that leads to overretention and waste of shareholder resources is consistent with the deep suspicion with which Graham and Dodd viewed the lack of payout. Their discussion (chapter 34) reflects a belief in the tenuous nature of the future benefits of such retention. Although they do not couch the issues in terms of the conflict between managers and shareholders, the free cash flow theory explicated here implies that their beliefs, sometimes characterized as "a bird in the hand is worth two in the bush," were perhaps well founded. See Chapters 32, 34, and 36 in Benjamin Graham and David L. Dodd, *Security Analysis: Principles and Technique* (New York, McGraw-Hill, 1951).

29. See Guy Charest, "Dividend Information, Stock Returns, and Market Efficiency-II, *Journal of Financial Economics* 6, (1978), pp. 297-330; and Joseph Aharony and Itzhak Swary, "Quarterly Dividend and Earnings Announcements and Stockholder's Returns: An Empirical Analysis," *Journal of Finance* 35 (1980), pp. 1-12.

30. Literally, principal and interest payments are substitutes for dividends. However, because interest is tax-deductible at the corporate level and dividends are not, dividends and debt are not perfect substitutes.

31. Two studies argue that regular dividend payments can be effective in reducing agency costs with managers by assuring that managers are forced more frequently to subject themselves and their policies to the discipline of the capital markets when they acquire capital. See Frank H. Easterbrook, "Managers' Discretion and Investors' Welfare: Theories and Evidence," *Delaware Journal of Corporate Law*, V. 9, No. 3 (1984b), pp. 540-571; and Michael Rozeff, "Growth, Beta and Agency Costs as Determinants of Dividend Payout Ratios", *Journal of Financial Research*, V.5 (1982), pp. 249-59.

successfully with the open corporate form because of advantages in controlling the agency costs of free cash flow. In 1984, going-private transactions totaled $10.8 billion and represented 27 percent of all public acquisitions.[36] The evidence indicates premiums paid averaged over 50 percent.[37]

Desirable leveraged buyout candidates are frequently firms or divisions of larger firms that have stable business histories and substantial free cash flow (that is, low growth prospects and high potential for generating cash flows)—situations where agency costs of free cash flow are likely to be high. Leveraged buyout transactions are frequently financed with high debt; ten-to-one ratios of debt to equity are not uncommon. Moreover, the use of strip financing and the allocation of equity in the deals reveal a sensitivity to incentives, conflicts of interest, and bankruptcy costs.

Strip financing, the practice in which risky nonequity securities are held in approximately equal proportions, limits the conflict of interest among such security holders and therefore limits bankruptcy costs. A somewhat oversimplified example illustrates the point. Consider two firms identical in every respect except financing. Firm A is entirely financed with equity, and Firm B is highly leveraged with senior subordinated debt, convertible debt, and preferred as well as equity. Suppose Firm B securities are sold only in strips—that is, a buyer purchasing X percent of any security must purchase X percent of all securities, and the securities are "stapled" together so they cannot be separated later. Security holders of both firms have identical unlevered claims on the cash flow distribution, but organizationally the two firms are very different. If Firm B managers withhold dividends to invest in value-reducing projects or if they are simply incompetent, strip holders have recourse to remedial powers not available to the equity holders of Firm A. Each Firm B security specifies the rights its holder has in the event of default on its dividend or coupon payment—for example, the right to take the firm into bankruptcy or to have board representation. As each security above equity goes into default the strip holder receives new rights to intercede in the organization. As a result, it is quicker and less expensive to replace managers in Firm B.

Moreover, because every security holder in the highly levered Firm B has the same claim on the firm, there are no conflicts between senior and junior claimants over reorganization of the claims in the event of default; to the strip holder it is a matter of moving funds from one pocket to another. Thus, Firm B need never go into bankruptcy. The reorganization can be accomplished voluntarily, quickly, and with less expense and disruption than through bankruptcy proceedings.

Securities commonly subject to strip practices are often called "mezzanine" financing and include securities with priority superior to common stock yet subordinate to senior debt. This seems to be a sensible arrangement. Because of several other factors ignored in our simplified example, IRS restrictions deny tax deductibility of debt interest in such situations and bank holdings of equity are restricted by regulation. Riskless senior debt need not be in the strip because there are no conflicts with other claimants in the event of reorganization when there is no probability of default on its payments.

It is advantageous to have top-level managers and venture capitalists who promote the transactions hold a larger share of the equity. Top-level managers frequently receive 15 to 20 percent of the equity, and venture capitalists and the funds they represent generally retain the major share of the remainder. The venture capitalists control the board of directors and monitor managers. Managers and venture capitalists have a strong interest in making the venture successful because their equity interests are subordinate to other claims. Success requires, among other things, implementation of changes to avoid investment in low-return projects in order to generate the cash for debt service and to increase the value of equity. Finally, when the equity is held primarily by managers or generally by a small number of people, greater efficiencies in risk bearing are made possible by placing more of the risk in the hands of debt holders when the debt is held in well-diversified institutional portfolios.

Less than a handful of these leveraged buyout ventures have ended in bankruptcy, although more have gone through private reorganizations. A thorough test of this organizational form requires the passage of time and another recession.

Some have asserted that managers engaging in a

36. By number. See W. T. Grimm, Mergerstat Review (1985), Figs. 36 and 37.

37. See H. DeAngelo, L. DeAngelo and E. Rice, "Going Private: Minority Freezeouts and Stockholder Wealth," *Journal of Law and Economics*, V. 27, No. 2 (October, 1984), pp. 367-401; and Louis Lowenstein, "Management Buyouts,"

Columbia Law Review, V. 85 (May, 1985), pp. 730-784. Lowenstein also mentions incentive effects of debt but argues tax effects play a major role in explaining the value increase.

buyout of their firm are insulating themselves from monitoring. The opposite is true in the typical leveraged buyout. Because the venture capitalists are generally the largest shareholder and control the board of directors, they have both greater ability and incentives to monitor managers effectively than directors representing diffuse public shareholders in the typical public corporation.

Evidence from the Oil Industry

The oil industry is large and visible. It is also an industry in which the importance of takeovers in motivating change and efficiency is particularly clear. Therefore, detailed analysis of it provides an understanding of how the market for corporate control helps motivate more efficient use of resources in the corporate sector.

Reorganization of the industry is mandatory. Radical changes in the energy market from 1973 through the late 1970s imply that a major restructuring of the petroleum industry had to occur. These changes are as follows:
• a ten-fold increase in the price of crude oil from 1973 to 1979;
• reduced annual consumption of oil in the U.S.;
• reduced expectations of future increases in the price of oil;
• increased exploration and development costs;
• and increased real interest rates.

As a result of these changes the optimal level of refining and distribution capacity and crude reserves fell over this period, and since the late 1970s the industry has been plagued with excess capacity. Reserves are reduced by reducing the level of exploration and development, and it pays to concentrate these reductions in high-cost areas such as the United States.

Substantial reductions in exploration and development and in refining and distribution capacity meant that some firms had to leave the industry. This is especially true because holding reserves is subject to economies of scale, whereas exploration and development are subject to diseconomies of scale.

Price increases created large cash flows in the industry. For example, 1984 cash flows of the ten largest oil companies were $48.5 billion, 28 percent of the total cash flows of the top 200 firms in Dun's Business Month [1985] survey. Consistent with the agency costs of free cash flow, management did not pay out the excess resources to shareholders. Instead, the industry continued to spend heavily on exploration and development even though average returns on these expenditures were below the cost of capital.

Paradoxically, the profitability of oil exploration and drilling activity can decrease even though the price of oil increases if the value of reserves in the ground falls. This can happen when the price increase is associated with reductions in consumption that make it difficult to market newly discovered oil. In the late 1970s the increased holding costs associated with higher real interest rates, reductions in expected future oil price increases, increased exploration and development costs, and reductions in the consumption of oil combined to make many exploration and development projects uneconomic. The industry, however, continued to spend heavily on such projects.

The hypothesis that oil-industry exploration and development expenditures were too high during this period is consistent with the findings of the earlier-mentioned study by McConnell and Muscarella.[38] Their evidence indicates that announcements of increases in exploration and development expenditures by oil companies in the period 1975-1981 were associated with systematic decreases in the announcing firms' stock prices. Moreover, announcements of decreases in exploration and development expenditures were associated with increases in stock prices. These results are striking in comparison with their evidence that exactly the opposite market reaction occurs with increases and decreases in investment expenditures by industrial firms, and with SEC evidence that increases in research and development expenditures are associated with increased stock prices.[38a]

Additional evidence of the uneconomic nature of the oil industry's exploration and development expenditures is contained in a study by Bernard

---

38. John J. McConnell and Chris J. Muscarella, "Corporate Capital Expenditure Decisions and the Market Value of the Firm," *Journal of Financial Economics*, V. 14, No. 3 (1985).

38a. Office of the Chief Economist, Securities and Exchange Commission, "Institutional Ownership, Tender Offers, and Long-Term Investments," April 19, 1985.

Wall Street was not undervaluing the oil; it was valuing it correctly, but it was also correctly valuing the wasted expenditures on exploration and development that oil companies were making.

Picchi of Salomon Brothers. His study of rates of return on exploration and development expenditures for 30 large oil firms indicated that on average the industry did not earn "even a 10% return on its pretax outlays" in the period 1982-84. Estimates of the average ratio of the present value of future net cash flows of discoveries, extensions and enhanced recovery to expenditures for exploration and development for the industry ranged from less than .6 to slightly more than .9, depending on the method used and the year. In other words, even taking the cost of capital to be only 10 percent on a pretax basis, the industry was realizing on average only 60 to 90 cents on every dollar invested in these activities. Picchi concludes:

For 23 of the [30] companies in our survey, we would recommend immediate *cuts of perhaps 25%-30% in exploration and production spending. It is clear that much of the money that these firms spent last year on petroleum exploration and development yielded subpar financial returns—even at $30 per barrel, let alone today's $26-$27 per barrel price structure."[39]*

The waste associated with excessive exploration and development expenditures explains why buying oil on Wall Street was considerably cheaper than obtaining it by drilling holes in the ground, even after adjustment for differential taxes and regulations on prices of old oil. Wall Street was not undervaluing the oil; it was valuing it correctly, but it was also correctly valuing the wasted expenditures on exploration and development that oil companies were making. When these managerially imposed "taxes" on the reserves were taken into account, the net price of oil on Wall Street was very low. This provided incentives for firms to obtain reserves by purchasing other oil companies and reducing expenditures on non-cost-effective exploration.

High profits are not usually associated with retrenchment. Adjustment by the energy industry to the new environment has been slow for several reasons. First, it is difficult for organizations to change operating rules and practices like those in the oil industry that have worked well for long periods in the past, even though they do not fit the new situation. Nevertheless, survival requires that organizations adapt to major changes in their environment.

Second, the past decade has been a particularly puzzling period in the oil business because at the same time that changes in the environment have required a reduction of capacity, cash flows and profits have been high. This is a somewhat unusual condition in which the average productivity of resources in the industry increased while the marginal productivity decreased. The point is illustrated graphically in Figure 1.

As the figure illustrates, profits plus payments to factors of production other than capital were larger in 1985 than in 1973. Moreover, because of the upward shift and simultaneous twist of the marginal productivity of capital schedule from 1973 to 1985, the optimal level of capital devoted to the industry fell from Q_1 to Q_2. Thus, the adjustment signals were confused because the period of necessary retrenchment coincided with substantial increases in value brought about by the tenfold increase in the price of the industry's major asset, its inventory of crude oil reserves.

The large cash flows and profits generated by the increases in oil prices both masked the losses imposed on marginal facilities and enabled oil companies to finance major expenditures internally. Thus, the normal disciplinary forces of the product market have been weak, and those of the capital markets have been inoperative, during the past decade.

Third, the oil companies' large and highly visible profits subjected them to strong political pressures to reinvest the cash flows in exploration and development to respond to the incorrect, but popular, perception that reserves were too low. Furthermore, while reserves were on average too high, those firms which were substantially short of reserves were spending to replenish them to avoid the organizational consequences associated with reserve deficiencies. The resulting excessive exploration and development expenditures by the industry and the considerable delays in retrenchment of refining and distribution facilities wasted resources.

In sum, the stage was set for retrenchment in the oil industry in the early 1980s. Yet the product and capital markets could not force management to change its strategy because the industry's high internal cash flows insulated it from these pressures.

The fact that oil industry managers tried to invest funds outside the industry is also evidence that they could not find enough profitable projects within the industry to use the huge inflow of resources

---

39. Bernard J. Picchi, "The Structure of the U.S. Oil Industry: Past and Future" (Salomon Brothers Inc.) July, 1985, emphasis in original.

Partly as a result of Mesa's efforts, firms in the [oil] industry were led to merge, and in the merging process they paid out large amounts of capital to shareholders, reduced excess expenditures on exploration and development, and reduced excess capacity in refining and distribution.

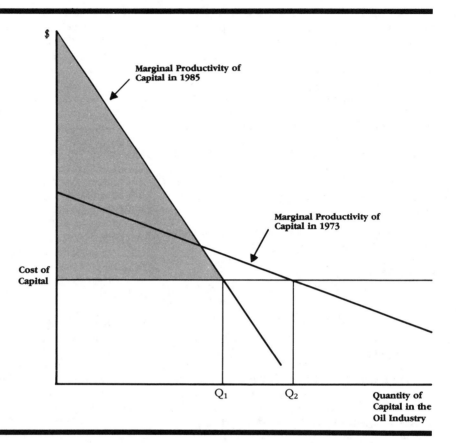

efficiently. Unfortunately these efforts failed. The diversification programs involved purchases of companies in retailing (Marcor by Mobil), manufacturing (Reliance Electric by Exxon), office equipment (Vydec by Exxon), and mining (Kennecott by Sohio, Anaconda Minerals by ARCO, Cyprus Mines by Amoco). These acquisitions turned out to be among the least successful of the last decade, partly because of bad luck (e.g., the collapse of the minerals industry) and partly because of a lack of managerial expertise outside the oil industry.

The effects of takeovers. Ultimately the capital markets, through the takeover market, have begun to force managers to respond to the new market conditions. Unfortunately, there is widespread confusion about the important role of takeovers in bringing about the difficult but necessary organizational changes required in the retrenchment.

Managers, quite naturally, want large amounts of resources under their control to insulate them from the uncertainties of markets.[40] Retrenchment requires cancellation or delay of many ongoing and planned projects. This affects the careers of the people involved, and the resulting resistance means that such changes frequently do not get made without the major pressures associated with a crisis. A takeover attempt can create the crisis that brings about action where none would otherwise occur.

T. Boone Pickens of Mesa Petroleum perceived early that the oil industry must be restructured. Partly as a result of Mesa's efforts, firms in the industry were led to merge, and in the merging process they

---

40. See Gordon Donaldson, *Managing Corporate Wealth* (Praeger: 1984).

Horizontal mergers for cash or debt in declining industries generate gains by encouraging exit of resources (through payout to shareholders) and by substituting existing capacity for investment in new facilities by firms that are short of capacity.

paid out large amounts of capital to shareholders, reduced excess expenditures on exploration and development, and reduced excess capacity in refining and distribution.

The result has been large gains in efficiency. Total gains to the shareholders in the Gulf-Chevron, Getty-Texaco and Dupont-Conoco mergers, for example, were over $17 billion. Much more is possible. A study by Allen Jacobs estimates that, as of December l984, the total potential gains from eliminating the inefficiencies in 98 petroleum companies amounted to roughly $200 billion.[41]

Recent events indicate that actual takeover is not necessary to bring about the required adjustments:

• The Phillips restructuring plan, in response to the threat of takeover, has involved substantial retrenchment and return of resources to shareholders; and the result was a $1.2 billion (20%) gain in Phillips' market value. It repurchased 53 percent of its stock for $4.5 billion in debt, raised its dividend 25 percent, cut capital spending and initiated a program to sell $2 billion of assets.

• Unocal's defense in the Mesa tender offer battle resulted in a $2.2 billion (35%) gain to shareholders from retrenchment and return of resources to shareholders. It paid out 52 percent of its equity by repurchasing stock with a $4.2 billion debt issue and will reduce costs and capital expenditures.

• The voluntary restructuring announced by ARCO resulted in a $3.2 billion (30%) gain in market value. ARCO's restructuring involves a 35 to 40 percent cut in exploration and development expenditures, repurchase of 25 percent of its stock for $4 billion, a 33 percent increase in its dividend, withdrawal from gasoline marketing and refining east of the Mississippi, and a 13 percent reduction in its work force.

• The announcement of the Diamond-Shamrock reorganization in July 1985 provides an interesting contrast to the others and further support for the theory because the company's market value *fell* 2 percent on the announcement day. Because the plan results in an effective increase in exploration and capital expenditures and a reduction in cash payouts to investors, the restructuring does not increase the value of the firm. The plan involved reducing cash

dividends by $.76/share (−43%), creating a master limited partnership to hold properties accounting for 35 percent of its North American oil and gas production, paying an annual $.90/share dividend in partnership shares, repurchasing 6 percent of its shares for $200 million, selling 12 percent of its master limited partnership to the public, and *increasing* its expenditures on oil and gas exploration by $100 million per year.

Free Cash Flow Theory of Takeovers

Free cash flow is only one of approximately a dozen theories to explain takeovers, all of which are of some relevance in explaining the numerous forces motivating merger and acquisition activity.[41a] The agency cost of free cash flow is consistent with a wide range of data for which there has been no consistent explanation. Here I sketch some empirical predictions of the free cash flow theory for takeovers and mergers, and what I believe are the facts that lend it credence.

The positive market response to debt creation in oil and other takeovers is consistent with the agency costs of free cash flow and the control hypothesis of debt.[41b] The data is consistent with the notion that additional debt has increased efficiency by forcing organizations with large cash flows but few high-return investment projects to pay out cash to investors. The debt helps prevent such firms from wasting resources on low-return projects.

Acquisitions are one way managers spend cash instead of paying it out to shareholders. Therefore, free cash flow theory predicts which kinds of mergers and takeovers are more likely to destroy rather than to create value. It shows how takeovers are both evidence of the conflicts of interest between the shareholders and managers and a response to the problem. The theory implies that managers of firms with unused borrowing power and large free cash flows are more likely to undertake low-benefit or even value-destroying mergers. Diversification programs generally fit this category, and the theory predicts they will generate lower total gains. The major benefit of such diversifying transactions may be that they involve less waste of resources than if the funds had been invested

41. Allen Jacobs, "The Agency Cost of Corporate Control: The Petroleum Industry," (MIT, unpublished paper, March, 1986).

41a. See Roll, 1986, cited earlier.
41b. See Robert Bruner, "The Use of Excess Cash and Debt Capacity as a Motive for Merger," (unpublished, Colgated Darden Graduate School of Business, December, 1985).

internally in unprofitable projects.[41c]

Low-return mergers are more likely to occur in industries with large cash flows where the economics dictate retrenchment. Horizontal mergers (where cash or debt is the form of payment) within declining industries will tend to create value because they facilitate exit; the cash or debt payments to shareholders of the target firm cause resources to leave the industry directly. Mergers outside the industry are more likely to have low or even negative returns because managers are likely to know less about managing such firms.

Oil fits this description and so does tobacco. Tobacco firms face declining demand as a result of changing smoking habits, but they generate large free cash flow and have been involved in major diversifying acquisitions recently—for example, the $5.6 billion purchase of General Foods by Philip Morris. The theory predicts that these acquisitions in non-related industries are more likely to create negative productivity effects—though these negative effects appear to be outweighed by the reductions in waste from internal expansion.

Forest products is another industry with excess capacity and acquisition activity, including the acquisition of St. Regis by Champion International and Crown Zellerbach by Sir James Goldsmith. Horizontal mergers for cash or debt in such an industry generate gains by encouraging exit of resources (through payout) and by substituting existing capacity for investment in new facilities by firms that are short of capacity.

Food-industry mergers also appear to reflect the expenditure of free cash flow. The industry apparently generates large cash flows with few growth opportunities. It is therefore a good candidate for leveraged buyouts, and these are now occurring; the $6.3 billion Beatrice LBO is the largest ever.

The broadcasting industry generates rents in the form of large cash flows on its licenses and also fits the theory. Regulation limits the overall supply of licenses and the number owned by a single entity. Thus profitable internal investments are limited and the industry's free cash flow has been spent on organizational inefficiencies and diversification programs, making these firms takeover targets. The CBS debt-for-stock exchange and restructuring as a defense against the hostile bid by Turner fits the theory, as does the $3.5 billion purchase of American Broadcasting Company by Capital Cities Communications. Completed cable systems also create agency problems from free cash flows in the form of rents on their franchises and quasi-rents on their investment, and are thus likely targets for acquisition and leveraged buyouts.

Large cash flows earned by motion picture companies on their film libraries also represent quasi-rents and are likely to generate free cash flow problems. Similarly, the attempted takeover of Disney and its subsequent reorganization is consistent with the theory. Drug companies with large cash flows from previous successful discoveries and few potential future prospects are also likely candidates for large agency costs of free cash flow.

The theory predicts that value-increasing takeovers occur in response to breakdowns of internal control processes in firms with substantial free cash flow and organizational policies (including diversification programs) that are wasting resources. It predicts hostile takeovers, large increases in leverage, the dismantling of empires with few economies of scale or scope to give them economic purpose (e.g. conglomerates), and much controversy as current managers object to loss of their jobs or changes in organizational policies forced on them by threat of takeover.

The debt created in a hostile takeover (or takeover defense) of a firm suffering severe agency costs of free cash flow need not be permanent. Indeed, sometimes it is desirable to "over-leverage" such a firm. In these situations, levering the firm so highly it cannot continue to exist in its old form yields

41c. Acquisitions made with cash or securities other than stock involve payout of resources to (target) shareholders, and this can create net benefits even if the merger creates operating inefficiencies. To illustrate the point, consider an acquiring firm, A, with substantial free cash flow that the market expects will be invested in low-return projects with a negative net present value of $100 million. If Firm A makes an acquisition of Firm B that generates zero synergies but uses up all of Firm A's free cash flow (and thereby prevents its waste) the combined market value of the two firms will *rise* by $100 million. The market value increases because the acquisition eliminates the expenditures on internal investments with negative market value of $100 million. Extending the argument, we see that acquisitions that have *negative* synergies of up to $100 million in current value will still increase the combined market value of the two firms. Such negative-synergy mergers will also increase social welfare and aggregate

productivity whenever the market value of the negative productivity effects on the two merging firms is less than the market value of the waste that would have occurred with the firms' investment programs in the absence of the merger. The division of the gains between the target and bidding firms depends, of course, on the bargaining power of the two parties. Because the bidding firms are using funds that would otherwise have been spent on low- or negative-return projects, however, the opportunity cost of the funds is lower than their cost of capital. As a result, they will tend to overpay for the acquisition and thereby transfer most, if not all, of the gains to the target firm's shareholders. In extreme cases they may pay so much that the bidding-firm share price falls, in effect giving the target-shareholders more than 100 percent of the gains. These predictions are consistent with the evidence.

The abolition of mere size as a deterrent to takeover...has made possible the realization of large gains from reallocating larger collections of assets to more productive uses.

benefits. It creates the crisis to motivate cuts in expansion programs and the sale of those divisions that are more valuable outside the firm. The proceeds are used to reduce debt to a more normal or permanent level. This process results in a complete rethinking of the organization's strategy and structure. When it is successful, a much leaner, more efficient, and competitive organization results.

Some Evidence from Merger Studies

Consistent with the data, free cash flow theory predicts that many acquirers will tend to perform exceptionally well prior to acquisition. That exceptional stock price performance will often be associated with increased free cash flow which is then used for acquisition programs. The oil industry fits this description. Increased oil prices caused large gains in profits and stock prices in the mid-to-late 1970s. Empirical evidence from studies of both stock prices and accounting data also indicates exceptionally good performance for acquirers prior to acquisition.[42]

Targets will tend to be of two kinds: firms with poor management that have done poorly before the merger, and firms that have done exceptionally well and have large free cash flow that they refuse to pay out to shareholders....In the best study to date of the determinants of takeover, Palepu [1986] finds strong evidence consistent with the free cash flow theory of mergers. He studied a sample of 163 firms that were acquired in the period 1971-1979 and a random sample of 256 firms that were not acquired. Both samples were in mining and manufacturing and were listed on either the New York or American Stock Exchange. He finds that target firms were characterized by significantly lower growth and lower leverage than the nontarget firms, although there was no significant difference in their holdings of liquid assets. He also finds that poor prior performance (measured by the net-of-market returns in the four years before the acquisition) is significantly related to the probability of takeover, and, interestingly, that accounting measures of past performance such as

return on equity are unrelated to the probability of takeover. He also finds that firms with a mismatch between growth and resources are more likely to be taken over. These are firms with high growth (measured by average sales growth), low liquidity (measured by the ratio of liquid assets to total assets) and high leverage, and firms with low growth, high liquidity, and low leverage. Finally, Palepu's evidence rejects the hypothesis that takeovers are due to the undervaluation of a firm's assets as measured by the market-to-book ratio.[42a]

High-Yield ("Junk") Bonds

The last several years have witnessed a major innovation in the financial markets with the establishment of active markets in high-yield bonds. These bonds are rated below investment grade by the bond rating agencies and are frequently referred to as junk bonds, a disparaging term that bears no relation to their pedigree. They carry interest rates that are 3 to 5 percentage points higher than the yields on government bonds of comparable maturity. High-yield bonds are best thought of as commercial loans that can be resold in secondary markets. By traditional standards they are more risky than investment-grade bonds and therefore carry higher interest rates. An early study finds the default rates on these bonds have been low and the realized returns have been disproportionately higher than their risk.[43a]

High-yield bonds have been attacked by those who wish to inhibit their use, particularly in the financing of takeover bids. The invention of high-yield bonds has provided methods to finance takeover ventures like those companies use to finance more traditional ventures. Companies commonly raise funds to finance ventures by selling claims to be paid from the proceeds of the venture; this is the essence of debt or stock issues used to finance new ventures. High-yield bonds used in takeovers work similarly. The bonds provide a claim on the proceeds of the venture, using the assets and cash flows of the target

42. See the following two papers which were presented at the Conference on Takeovers and Contests for Corporate Control, Columbia University, November, 1985: Ellen B. Magenheim and Dennis Mueller, "On Measuring the Effect of Acquisitions on Acquiring Firm Shareholders, or Are Acquiring Firm Shareholders Better Off After an Acquisition Than They Were Before?"; and Michael Bradley and Gregg Jarrell, "Evidence on Gains from Mergers and Takeovers." See also Paul R. Asquith and E. Han Kim, "The Impact of Merger Bids on the Participating Firms' Security Holders," *Journal of Finance*, 37, 1209-1228; Gershon Mandelker, "Risk and Return: The Case of Merging Firms," *Jour-*

nal of Financial Economics, V. 1, No. 4 (December, 1974), pp. 303-336; and T.C. Langetieg, "An Application of A Three-Factor Performance Index to Measure Stockholder Gains from Merger" *Journal of Financial Economics*, V. 6 (December, 1978), pp. 365-384.

42a. Palepu (1986), presented at the Conference on Takeovers and Contests for Corporate Control, Columbia University, November, 1985.

43a. Marshall E. Blume and Donald B. Keim, "Risk and Return Characteristics of Lower-Grade Bonds" (unpublished paper, The Wharton School, December, 1984).

The Federal Reserve System's own data are inconsistent with the reasons given for its restrictions on the use of debt.

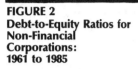

FIGURE 2
Debt-to-Equity Ratios for Non-Financial Corporations: 1961 to 1985

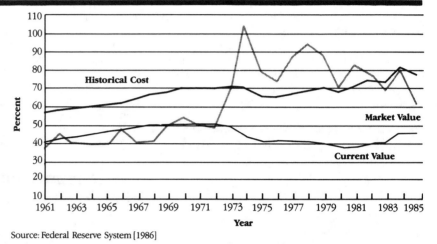

Source: Federal Reserve System [1986]

plus the equity contributed by the acquirer as collateral. This basic structure is the common way that individuals purchase homes; they use the home plus their down payment as collateral for the mortgage. There is nothing inherently unusual in the structure of this contract, although those who would bar the use of high-yield bonds in takeover ventures would have us believe otherwise.

Some might argue that the risk of high-yield bonds used in takeover attempts is "too high." But high-yield bonds are by definition less risky than common stock claims on the same venture. Would these same critics argue that stock claims are too risky and thus should be barred? The risk argument makes logical sense only as an argument that the transactions costs associated with bankruptcy are too high in these ventures or that the promised yields on the bonds are too low and that investors who purchase them will not earn returns high enough to compensate for the risk they are incurring. This argument makes little sense because there is vast evidence that investors are capable of pricing risks in all sorts of other markets. It is inconceivable they are peculiarly unable to do so in the high-yield bond market.

In January 1986 the Federal Reserve Board issued a new interpretation of the margin rules that restricts the use of debt in takeovers to 50 percent or less of the purchase price. This rule reintroduces size as an effective deterrent to takeover. It was apparently motivated by the belief that the use of corporate debt had become abnormally and dangerously high and was threatening the economy.

This assessment is not consistent with the facts. Figure 2 plots three measures of debt use by nonfinancial corporations in the U.S. The debt/equity ratio is measured relative to three bases: market value of equity, estimated current asset value of equity, and accounting book value of equity measured at historical cost.

Although debt/equity ratios were higher in 1985 than in 1961, they were not at record levels. The book value debt/equity ratio reached a high of 81.4 percent in 1984, but declined to 78 percent in 1985. The fact that debt/equity ratios measured on an historical cost basis are relatively high is to be expected, given the previous decade of inflation. Maintenance of the same inflation-adjusted debt/equity ratio in times of inflation implies that the book value ratio must rise because the current value of assets in the denominator of the inflation-adjusted ratio is rising. The current value ratio, which takes account of inflation, fell from 50.7 percent in 1970 to 46.5 percent in 1985. The market-value ratio rose from 54.7 percent in 1970 to 80.5 percent in 1984 and plummeted to 60.8 percent in 1985. The 1985 market-value ratio was 45 percentage points below its 1974 peak of 105.2 percent. In short, the Federal Reserve System's own data are inconsistent with the reasons given for its restrictions on the use of debt.

High-yield bonds were first used in a takeover bid in early 1984 and have been involved in relatively few bids in total. In 1984, only about 12 percent of the $14.3 billion of new high-yield debt was associated with mergers and acquisitions. In 1985, 26 per-

496

When correctly implemented they [golden parachutes] help reduce the conflicts of interest between shareholders and managers at times of takeover and therefore make it more likely that the productive gains stemming from changes in control will be realized.

cent of the $14.7 billion of new high-yield debt was used in acquisitions.[44] Some of the acquisitions, however, such as the Unocal and CBS offers (both unsuccessful), have received intense attention from the media; and this publicity has fostered the belief that high-yield bonds are widely used in takeovers. Nevertheless, high-yield bonds are an important innovation in the takeover field because they help eliminate mere size as a deterrent to takeover. They have been particularly influential in helping to bring about reorganizations in the oil industry.

Historical default rates on high-yield bonds have been low, but many of these bonds are so new that the experience could prove to be different in the next downturn. Various opponents have proposed regulations or legislation to restrict the issuance of such securities, to penalize their tax status, and to restrict their holding by thrifts, which can now buy them as substitutes for the issuance of nonmarketable commercial loans. These proposals are premature. Policymakers should be wary of responding to the clamor for restrictions by executives who desire protection from the discipline of the takeover market and by members of the financial community who want to restrict competition from this new financing vehicle.

The holding of high-yield bonds by thrifts is an interesting issue that warrants further analyis. The recent deregulation of the banking and thrift industries presents many opportunities and challenges to the thrifts. Elimination of restrictions on interest paid to depositors has raised the cost of funds to these institutions. Thrifts have also received the right to engage in new activities such as commercial lending. Survival requires these institutions to take advantage of some of these new business opportunities.

The organizational costs of developing commerical lending departments in the 3,500 thrifts in the country is substantial. Thousands of new loan officers will have to be hired and trained. The additional wage and training costs and the bad-debt losses that will be incurred in the learning phase will be substantial. High-yield bonds provide a promising solution to this problem. If part of the commercial lending function can be centralized in the hands of investment bankers who provide commerical loans in the form of marketable high-yield debt, the thrifts can substitute the purchase of this high-yield debt for their commercial lending and thereby avoid the huge investment in such loan departments.

The Legitimate Concerns of Managers

Conflicts of Interest and Increased Costs to Managers

The interests of corporate managers are not the same as the interests of corporations as organizations, and conflicts of interest can become intense when major changes in the organization's strategy are required. Competition causes change, and change creates winners and losers, especially in that branch of the managerial labor market called the takeover market.

Managers' private incentives sometimes run counter to overall efficiency. The costs of takeovers have fallen as the legal and financial skills of participants in the takeover market have become more sophisticated, as the restrictions on takeovers imposed by antitrust laws have been relaxed, and as financing techniques have improved. Except for new regulatory constraints on the use of debt, this means that the largest of the Fortune 500 companies are now potentially subject to takeover. The abolition of mere size as a deterrent to takeover is desirable because it has made possible the realization of large gains from reallocating larger collections of assets to more productive uses.

This new susceptibility to takeover has created a new contracting environment for top-level managers. Many managers are legitimately anxious, and it will take time for the system to work out an appropriate set of practices and contracts reflecting the risks and rewards of the new environment. Some of the uncertainty of top-level managers formerly insulated from pressures from the financial markets will fade as they learn how their policies affect the market value of their companies.

The Desirability of Golden Parachutes

Unfortunately, a major component of the solution to the conflict of interest between shareholders and managers has been vastly misunderstood. I am referring to severance contracts that compensate managers for the loss of their jobs in the event of a

---

44. Source: Drexel Burnham Lambert, private correspondence.

change in control—what have been popularly labeled "golden parachutes."

These contracts are clearly desirable, even when judged solely from the viewpoint of the interests of shareholders; but they are also efficient from a social viewpoint. When correctly implemented they help reduce the conflicts of interest between shareholders and managers at times of takeover and therefore make it more likely that the productive gains stemming from changes in control will be realized. The evidence indicates that stock prices of firms that adopt severance-related compensation contracts for managers on average rise about 3 percent when adoption of the contracts is announced.[45] There is no easy way to tell how much of this could be due to the market interpreting the announcement as a signal that a takeover bid is more likely and how much is due to the reduction in conflict between managers and shareholders over takovers.

At times of takeover, shareholders are implicitly asking the top-level managers of their firm to negotiate a deal for them that frequently involves the imposition of large personal costs on the managers and their families. These involve substantial moving costs, the loss of position, power and prestige, and even the loss of their jobs. Shareholders are asking the very people who are most likely to have invested considerable time and energy (in some cases a life's work) in building a successful organization to negotiate its sale and the possible redirection of its resources.

It is important to face these conflicts and to structure contracts with managers to reduce them. It makes no sense to hire a realtor to sell your house and then penalize him for doing so. Yet that is the implication of many of the emotional reactions to control-related severance contracts. The restrictions and tax penalties imposed on these severance payments by the Deficit Reduction Act of 1984 are unwise interferences in the contracting freedoms of shareholders and managers; and they should be eliminated. Moreover, it is important to eliminate the misunderstanding about the purpose and effects of these contracts that has been fostered by past rhetoric on the topic so that boards of directors can get on with the job of structuring these contracts.

Golden parachutes can also be used to restrict takeovers and to entrench managers at the expense of shareholders. How does one tell whether a particular set of contracts crosses this line?

The key is whether the contracts help solve the conflict-of-interest problem between shareholders and managers that arises over changes in control. Solving this problem requires extending control-related severance contracts beyond the chief executive to those members of the top-level management team who must play an important role in negotiating and implementing any transfer of control. Contracts that award severance contracts to substantial number of managers beyond this group are unlikely to be in the shareholders' interests. The contracts awarded by Beneficial Corp. to 234 of its managers are unlikely to be justified as in the shareholders' interests.[46]

It is particularly important to institute severance-related compensation contracts in situations where it is optimal for managers to invest in organization-specific human capital—that is, in skills and knowledge that have little or no value in other organizations. Managers will not so invest where the likelihood is high that their investment will be eliminated by an unexpected transfer of control and the loss of their jobs. In such situations the firm will have to pay for all costs associated with the creation of such organization-specific human capital, and it will be difficult to attract and retain highly talented managers when they have better opportunities elsewhere. In addition, contracts that award excessive severance compensation to the appropriate group of managers will tend to motivate managers to sell the firm at too low a price.

No simple rules can be specified that will easily prevent the misuse of golden parachutes because the appropriate solution will depend on many factors that are specific to each situation (for example, the amount of stock held by managers, and the optimal amount of investment in organization-specific human capital). In general, contracts that award inappropriately high payments to a group that is excessively large will reduce efficiency and harm shareholders by raising the cost of acquisition and by transferring wealth from shareholders to managers. The generally appropriate solution is to make the control-related severance contracts pay off in a way that is tied to the premium earned by the stockholders. Stock op-

45. See R. Lambert and D. Larcker, "Golden Parachutes, Executive Decision-Making, and Shareholder Wealth", *Journal of Accounting and Economics*, V. 7 (April, 1985), pp. 179-204.

46. Ann Morrison, "Those Executive Bailout Deals," *Fortune*, (December 13, 1982).

Greenmail is the Trojan horse of the takeover battle in the legal and political arenas...Management can easily prohibit greenmail without legislation: it need only announce a policy that, like Ulysses tying himself to the mast, prohibits it from making such payments.

tions or restricted stock appreciation rights that pay off only in the event of a change in control are two options that have some of the appropriate properties. In general, policies that encourage increased stock ownership by managers and the board of directors will provide incentives that will tend to reduce the conflicts of interests with managers.

Targeted Repurchases

The evidence indicates takeovers generate large benefits for shareholders. Yet virtually all proposals to protect shareholders from asserted difficulties in the control market will harm them by either eliminating or reducing the probability of successful hostile tender offers. These proposals will also block the productivity increases that are the source of the gains.

Most proposals to restrict or prohibit targeted repurchases (transactions pejoratively labeled "greenmail") are nothing more than antitakeover proposals in disguise. Greenmail is an appellation that suggests blackmail; yet the only effective weapon possessed by a greenmailer is the right to offer to purchase stock from other shareholders at a substantial premium. The "damage" to shareholders caused by this action is difficult to find. Those who propose to "protect" shareholders hide this fact behind emotional language designed to mislead. Greenmail is actually a targeted repurchase, an offer by *management* to repurchase the shares of a subset of shareholders at a premium, an offer not made to other shareholders.

Greenmail is the Trojan horse of the takeover battle in the legal and political arenas. Antitakeover proposals are commonly disguised as anti-greenmail provisions. Management can easily prohibit greenmail without legislation: it need only announce a policy that, like Ulysses tying himself to the mast, prohibits management or the board from making such payments.[47]

Problems in the Delaware Court

Delaware courts have created over the years a highly productive fabric of corporate law that has benefited the nation. The court is having difficulty, however, in sorting out the complex issues it faces in the takeover area. The court's problems in settling conflicts between shareholders and management over control issues reflect a fundamental weakness in its model of the corporation, a model that has heretofore worked quite well. The result has been a confusing set of decisions that, in contrast to much of the court's previous history, appears to make little economic sense.[49]

Altruism and the Business Judgment Rule

The Delaware court's model of the corporation is founded in the business judgment rule—the legal doctrine that holds that unless explicit evidence of fraud or self-dealing exists the board of directors is presumed to be acting solely in the interests of shareholders....The courts must not apply the business judgment rule to conflicts over control rights between principals and agents. If the business judgement rule is applied to such conflicts, the courts are effectively giving the *agent* (management) the right unilaterally to change the control rights. In the long run, this interpretation of the contract will destroy the possibility of such cooperative arrangements because it will leave principals (stockholders) with few effective rights.

Recently the courts have applied the business judgment rule to the conflicts over the issuance of poison pill preferred stock, poison pill rights, and discriminatory targeted repurchases, and have given managers and boards the rights to use these

47. Three excellent studies of these transactions indicate that when measured from the initial toehold purchase to the final repurchase of the shares, the stock price of target firms rises. Therefore, shareholders are benefited, not harmed, by the whole sequence of events. (See Clifford Holderness and Dennis Sheehan, "Raiders or Saviors: The Evidence on Six Controversial Investors," *Journal of Financial Economics* (December, 1985), Wayne H. Mikkelson, and Richard S. Ruback, "An Empirical Analysis of the Interfirm Equity Investment Process," *Journal of Financial Economics*, V. 14 (December, 1985), and Wayne H. Mikkelson and Richard S. Ruback, "Targeted Repurchases and Common Stock Returns", (unpublished manuscript, June, 1986).) There is some indication, however, that the stock price increases might represent the expectation of future takeover premiums in firms in which the targeted repurchase was not sufficient to prevent ultimate takeover of the firm. If so, it may well be that, much as in the final defeat of tender offers found by Bradley, Desai and Kim (Michael Bradley,

Michael, Anand Desai and E. Han Kim, "The Rationale Behind Interfirm Tender Offers: Information or Synergy?" *Journal of Financial Economics*, V. 11 (April, 1983), pp. 183-206), all premiums are lost to those shareholders in firms for which the repurchase and associated standstill agreements successfully lock up the firm. The evidence on these issues is not yet sufficient to issue a final judgement either way.

49. See, for example, Moran v. Household Intl, Inc., 490 A.2d 1059 (Del.Ch.1985) aff'd. 500 A.2d 1346 (Del.1985) (upholding poison pill rights issue), Smith v Van Gorkom, 488 A.2d 858, (holding board liable for damages in sale of firm at substantial premium over market price), Unocal v Mesa, 493 A.2d 946, 954 (Del. 1985) (allowing discriminatory targeted repurchase that confiscates wealth of largest shareholder), Revlon Inc. v MacAndrews & Forbes Holdings Inc., 506 A.2nd 173, 180 (Del. 1986), (invalidation of Revlon's lockup sale of a prime division to Forstmann Little at a below-market price).

Rights issues like Household's and Crown Zellerbach's harm shareholders. They will fundamentally impair the efficiency of corporations that adopt them, and for this reason they will reduce productivity in the economy if widely adopted.

devices.[52] In so doing the courts are essentially giving the agents (managers and the board) the right unilaterally to change critical control aspects of the contract—in particular the right to fire the agent. This has major implications for economic activity, productivity, and the health of the corporation. If the trend goes far enough, the corporation as an organizational form will be serioiusly handicapped.

Poison Pills

Poison pill securities change fundamental aspects of the corporate rules of the game that govern the relationship between shareholders, managers, and the board of directors. They do so when a control-related event occurs, such as a takeover offer or the acquisition of a substantial block of stock or voting rights by an individual or group. The Household International version of the poison pill rights issue is particularly interesting because it was a major test case in the area.

When the Household International board of directors issued its complicated right to shareholders, it unilaterally changed the nature of the contractual relationship with Household's shareholders in a fundamental way. The right effectively restricts the alienability of the common stock by prohibiting shareholders from selling their shares, without permission of the board, into a control transaction leading to merger at a price that involves a premium over market value of less than $6 billion. Since Household had a market value of less than $2 billion at the time, this was a premium of over 300 percent—more than 6 times the average takeover premium of 50 percent common in recent times—a premium that is difficult to justify as in the shareholders' interests.

The November 1985 Delaware court decision upholding the Household International rights issue will significantly restrict hostile takeovers of firms that adopt similar provisions. Before that decision, 37 pills of various forms had been adopted. Over 150 corporations adopted pills in the seven months following that decision.[53] Unlike most other antitakeover

devices, this defense is very difficult for a prospective acquirer to overcome without meeting the board's terms (at least one who desires to complete the second-step closeout merger). An SEC study analyzed the 37 companies introducing pills between June 1983, when Lenox introduced the first one, and December 1985. Eleven of these 37 firms experienced control changes: five experienced a negotiated change in control while the pill was in effect (Revlon, Cluett Peabody, Great Lakes, Int., Lenox, and Enstar), two were taken over by creeping acquisitions (Crown Zellerbach and William Wright), two were taken over after their pills were declared illegal (AMF and Richardson Vicks), one (Superior Oil) was acquired after the pill was withdrawn in the face of a lawsuit and proxy fight by its largest holder, and one (Amsted) has proposed a leveraged buyout. The SEC study finds that "Announcements of [twenty] poison pill plans in the midst of takeover speculations have resulted in an average 2.4 percent net of market price declines for firms adopting the plans." The effects of another twelve plans adopted by firms that were not the subject of takeover speculation were essentially nil.[53a]

Sir James Goldsmith recently gained control of Crown Zellerbach, which had implemented a rights issue similar to Household International's. Goldsmith purchased a controlling interest in the open market after Crown's board opposed his tender offer and refused to recall its rights issue. In this situation the acquirer must either tolerate the costs associated with leaving the minority interest outstanding and forsake the benefits of merging the assets of the two organizations, or incur the costs of the premium required by the rights on execution of the second-step closeout merger. The Crown case revealed a loophole in the Household/Crown version of the pill (which has been closed in newly implemented versions). Although Goldsmith could not complete a second-step merger without paying the high-premium required by the rights, he could avoid it by simply liquidating Crown.

Rights issues like Household's and Crown Zellerbach's harm shareholders. They will fundamentally impair the efficiency of corporations that adopt them, and for this reason they will reduce

---

52. Moran v Household Intl., and Unocal v Mesa.
53. See Office of the Chief Economist of the SEC, "The Economics of Poison Pills," (March 5, 1986), and Corporate Control Alert, (February, March and April, May and June, 1986).

53a. Ibid.

productivity in the economy if widely adopted.[53b]

A broad interpretation of the business judgment rule is important to the effectiveness of the corporation because a system that puts the courts into the business of making managerial decisions will generate great inefficiencies. The court has erred, however, in allowing the Household board, under the business judgement rule, to make the fundamental change in the structure of the organization implied by the rights issue without votes of its shareholders. It is unlikely the court would allow the board to decide unilaterally to make the organization a closed corporation by denying shareholders the right to sell their shares to anyone at a mutually agreeable price without the permission of the board. The Household International rights issue places just such a restriction on the alienability of shares, but only in the case of a subset of transactions—the control-related transactions so critical for protecting shareholders when the normal internal board-level control mechanisms break down. Several other poison pill cases have been heard by the courts with similar outcomes, but a New Jersey and two New York courts have recently ruled against poison pills that substantially interfere with the voting rights of large-block shareholders.[54] An Illinois District Court recently voided a poison pill (affirmed by the Seventh Circuit Court of Appeals) and two weeks later approved a new pill issued by the same company.[55]

The problem with these special securities and the provision they contain is not with their appropriateness (some might well be desirable), but with the manner in which they are being adopted—that is, without approval by shareholders. Boards of directors show little inclination to refer such issues to shareholders.

One solution to the problems caused by the Household decision is for shareholders to approve amendments to the certificate of incorporation to restrict the board's power to take such actions without shareholder approval. This is not an easy task, however, given the pressure corporate managers are bringing to bear on the managers of their pension funds to vote with management.[56] Even more problematic is the provision in Delaware law that requires certificate amendments to be recommended to shareholders by the board of directors.[57]

Exclusionary Self Tenders: The Unocal v. Mesa Decision[58]

The Delaware Supreme Court surprised the legal, financial, and corporate communities in the spring of 1985 by giving Unocal the right to make a tender offer for 29 percent of its shares while excluding its largest shareholder, Mesa Partners II, from the offer. This decision enabled the Unocal management and board to avoid loss of control to Mesa. The decision imposed large costs on Unocal shareholders and, if not reversed, threatens major damage to shareholders of all Delaware corporations.

The Unocal victory over Mesa cost the Unocal shareholders $1.1 billion ($9.48 per post-offer share). This is the amount by which the $9.4 billion Mesa offer exceeded the $8.3 billion value of Unocal's "victory."[59] This loss represents 18 percent of Unocal's pre-takeover value of $6.2 billion. The $2.1 billion net increase in value to $8.3 billion resulted from Unocal's $4.2 billion debt issue which, contrary to assertions, benefits its shareholders. It does so by effectively bonding Unocal to pay out a substantial fraction of its huge cash flows to shareholders rather than to reinvest them in low-return projects, and by reducing taxes on Unocal and its shareholders.

For his services in generating this $2.1 billion gain for Unocal shareholders, T. Boone Pickens has

53b. Another study of the effects of poison pills (Paul H. Malatesta and Ralph A. Walkling, "The Impact of Poison Pill Securities on Stockholder Wealth," (unpublished, University of Washington, 1985) also indicates they have a negative effect on stock prices. On average, stock prices fell by a statistically significant 2 percent in the 2 days around the announcement in the *Wall Street Journal* of adoption of a poison pill for a sample of 14 firms that adopted these securities between December 1982 and February 1985. This price decline, however, was smaller than the average 7.5 percent increase in price that occurred in the 10 days prior to the adoption of the pill. Firms adopting pills appear to be those in which managers and directors bear a substantially smaller fraction of the wealth consequences of their actions. In all but three of the firms the percentage of common shares owned by officers and directors was substantially below the industry average ownership of shares. The average ownership of firms in the same industry was 16.5 percent and for the firms adopting pills it was 7.5 percent.

54. Ministar Acquiring Corp. v AMF Inc., 621 Fed Sup 1252. So Dis NY, 1985, Unilever Acquisition Corp. v Richardson-Vicks, Inc., 618 Fed Supp 407. So Dist. NY 1985, Asarco Inc. v M.R.H. Holmes a Court, 611 Fed Sup 468. Dist Ct of NJ,

1985, and Dynamics Corp. of America v CTS Corporation.

55. Dynamics Corp. of America v. CTS Corp., *et al.* U.S. District Court, Northern District of Illinois, Eastern Division, No. 86 C 1624, (April 17, 1986), affirmed Seventh Circuit Court of Appeals Nos. 86-16-1, 86-1608, and Dynamics Corp. of America v. CTS Corp., *et al.* (May 3, 1986).

56. See Joe, Koleman, "The Proxy Pressure on Pension Fund Managers", Institutional Investor, (July, 1985), pp. 145-147, and Investor Responsibility Research Center, Inc., Corporate Governance Service: Voting by Institutional Investors on Corporate Governance Questions, 1985 Proxy Season, pp. 19-25.

57. 8 *Del. C.* 242(c)(1).

58. This discussion is based on my article, "When Unocal Won over Pickens, Shareholders and Society Lost," *Financier,* V. IX, No. 11 (Nov., 1985), pp. 50-53.

59. The $8.3 billion value of Unocal securities held by its shareholders is calculated as $4.1 billion in stock (116 million shares at $34 7/8 on May 24, the first trading day after close of the offer), and $4.2 billion in Unocal debt trading at $73.50.

In addition to Mesa's losses, shareholders of all Delaware corporations lose because the court's decision gives management a weapon so powerful it essentially guarantees that no Delaware corporation that uses it will be taken over by a tender offer.

been vilified in the press, and Mesa Partners II has incurred net losses before taxes—obviously a perversion of incentives.

In addition to Mesa's losses, shareholders of all Delaware corporations lose because the court's decision gives management a weapon so powerful it essentially guarantees that no Delaware corporation that uses it will be taken over by a tender offer. A determined board could, in the extreme, pay out all the corporation's assets and leave the acquirer holding a worthless shell. Because of this new power, shareholders are denied the benefits of future actions by Pickens and others to discipline managers whose strategies are wasting resources.

Society also loses. The decision will have a chilling effect on takeovers, blocking the productivity increases that are the source of the takeover gains and thereby handicapping Delaware corporations in the competition for survival.

Unocal's self-tender for 29 percent of its shares at $72 per share ($26 over the market price) was designed to defeat Mesa's $54 per share cash offer for 50.4 percent of Unocal's shares plus $54 per share in debt securities for the remaining 49.6 percent. The Unocal offer would have paid 59 percent of Unocal's pretakeover equity to other shareholders while denying participation to the 13.6 percent minority holding of Mesa Partners II. This would transfer about $248 million from Mesa's holdings to other Unocal stockholders—a classic case of corporate raiding that contrasts with the beneficial effects of the actions of takeover specialists like Pickens, Carl Icahn and Irwin Jacobs on other shareholders.

Faced with the threat of legalized expropriation of $248 million, Mesa accepted a settlement in which Unocal backed off from the Mesa exclusion. The settlement involved repurchase of part of Mesa's shares at the terms of the tender offer, a 25-year standstill agreement, a promise to vote its shares in the same proportion as other shares are voted, and constraints on Mesa's rights to sell its remaining shares.

The essential characteristics of Unocal's exclusionary repurchase defense are now incorporated in newly popular poison pill plans called back-end plans.[60] These plans give shareholders a right to tender their shares for securities worth more than the

market value of their stock when a shareholder exceeds a certain maximum limit of stock ownership that ranges from 30 to 50 percent. As with Unocal's exclusion of Mesa, the large shareholder is denied the same right to tender his shares. This threatens a shareholder who violates the holding limit with potentially large dilution of his holdings. It thereby limits the existence of large stock holdings.

"Protection" From Two-Tier Tender Offers. The court ruled that the objective of Unocal's offer was to protect its shareholders against "a grossly inadequate and coercive two-tier, front-end-loaded tender offer" and against greenmail. This assessment of the situation was upside down. Paradoxically, the court's ruling imposed on Unocal shareholders exactly the evil it purported to prevent. Unocal defeated Mesa's $1.1 billion higher offer precisely because Mesa's offer was a level $54 offer and Unocal's offer was an extreme front-end loaded two-tier offer—$72 for 29 percent of its shares in the front-end with a back-end price of $35 for the remaining 71 percent of the shares. (The back-end price was implicit, but easy to calculate and reported in the press at the time of the offer.) The effective price of the Unocal offer was therefore only $45.73 per pre-offer share (the weighted average of the front- and back-end prices).

Comparing the Unocal offer with SEC estimates of average minimums in two-tier tender offers indicates the extreme nature of the Unocal two-tier offer. Historically the average back-end premium on outside two-tier offers is 45 percent higher than the stock price measured 20 trading days prior to the offer.[61] This contrasts sharply with the *negative* back-end premium on Unocal's self tender of -25 percent. That is, the $35 back-end price was 25 percent below the Unocal market price of $46 3/8 twenty days before the offer.

The negative back-end premium on Unocal's offer means the holders of 20 million Unocal shares who failed to tender to the first tier of the Unocal offer were particularly hurt. As of the close of the offer they suffered total losses of $382 million, $215 million from the loss of $37.12/share on 29 percent of their shares,[62] plus a loss of $167 million from being denied the $54 in debt securities they would have received in

---

60. See Office of the Chief Economist of the SEC, "The Economics of Poison Pills" (March 5, 1986).

61. See Comment, Robert, and Gregg A. Jarrell, "Two-Tier Tender Offers: The Imprisonment of the Free-Riding Shareholder," (unpublished manuscript, March 1, 1986); an earlier version appeared as Office of the Chief Economist,

Securities and Exchange Commission, "The Economics of Any-or-All, Partial, and Two-Tier Tender Offers," *Federal Register*, June 29, 1984, pp. 26,751-26,761.

62. Calculated as the $72 value of the Unocal debt offered in exchange for 29% of their shares less the $34.875 post-offer closing price of the shares.

the back end of the Mesa offer.[63]

Protection From Targeted Repurchases. The court also erred in its concern over greenmail. In ruling to eliminate the threat of greenmail, the court in fact authorized Unocal to make a greenmail transaction that differs from the usual variety only in that it penalized, rather than benefited, the large-block holder (i.e., reverse greenmail). In authorizing this form of targeted repurchase, the court granted large benefits to managers who desire protection from competition but harmed shareholders.

One of the great strengths of the corporation is the long-held principle that holders of a given class of securities are treated identically in transactions with the corporation. The Unocal decision threatens to turn the corporation into a battleground where special-interest groups of shareholders fight over the division of the pie much as special interests in the public sector do. The result will be a much smaller pie.

Responsible boards of directors interested in the welfare of shareholders and the survival of the corporation as an organizational form will implement procedures to ban all targeted repurchases that carry premiums over market value

Conclusion

Although economic analysis and the evidence indicate the market for corporate control is benefiting shareholders, society, and the corporation as an organizational form, it is also making life more uncomfortable for top-level executives. This discomfort is creating strong pressures at both the state and federal levels for restrictions that will seriously cripple the workings of this market. In 1985 there were 21 bills on this topic in the Congressional hopper, all of which proposed various restrictions on the market for corporate control. Some proposed major new restrictions on share ownership and financial instruments. Within the past several years the legislatures of numerous states have passed antitakeover laws. This political activity is another example of special interests using the democratic political system to change the rules of the game to benefit themselves at the expense of society as a whole. In this case the special interests are top-level corporate managers and other groups who stand to lose from competition in the market for corporate control. The result will be a significant weakening of the corporation as an organizational form and a reduction in efficiency.

---

63. See Michael Bradley and Michael Rosensweig, "The Law and Economics of Defensive Stock Repurchases and Defensive Self-Tender Offers, (Unpublished manuscript, University of Michigan, 1985) for a thorough discussion of the issues involved in self tender offers.

APPENDIX: Evidence From Financial Transactions in Support of the Free Cash Flow Theory of Mergers

Free cash flow theory helps explain previously puzzling results on the effects of various financial transactions. Smith [1986]* summarizes more than twenty studies of stock price changes at announcements of transactions that change capital structure as well as various other dividend transactions. These results are summarized in Table 2.

For firms with positive free cash flow, the theory predicts that stock prices will increase with unexpected increases in payouts to shareholders and decrease with unexpected decreases in payouts. It also predicts that unexpected increases in demand for funds from shareholders via new issues will cause stock prices to fall. In addition, the theory predicts stock prices will increase with increasing tightness of the constraints binding the payout of future cash flow to shareholders and decrease with reductions in the tightness of these constraints. These predictions do not apply, however, to those firms with more profitable projects than free cash flow to fund them.

The predictions of the agency cost of free cash flow are consistent with all but three of the 32 estimated abnormal stock price changes summarized in Table 2. Moreover, one of the inconsistencies is explainable by another phenomenon.

Panel A of Table 2 shows that stock prices rise by a statistically significant amount with announcements of the initiation of cash dividend payments, increases in dividends, and payments of specially designated dividends; they fall by a statistically significant amount with decreases in dividend payments. (All coefficients in the table are significantly different from zero unless noted with an asterisk.)

Panel B of Table 2 shows that security sales and

---

*See Cliff Smith, "Investment Banking and the Capital Acquisition Process," *Journal of Financial Economics* 15 (1986) for references to all studies cited in this Appendix.

TABLE 2
The Stock Market Response to Various Dividend and Capital Structure Transactions

Summary of two-day average abnormal stock returns associated with the announcement of various dividend and capital structure transactions.

Returns are weighted averages, by sample size, of the returns reported by the respective studies. All returns are significantly different from zero unless noted otherwise by .*

Type of Transaction	Security Issued	Security Retired
PANEL A: Dividend changes that change the cash paid to shareholders		
Dividend initiation[1]		
Dividend increase[2]		
Specially designated dividend[3]		
Dividend decrease[2]		
PANEL B: Security sales (that raise cash) and retirements (that pay out cash) and simultaneously		
Security sale (industrial)[4]	debt	none
Security sale (utility)[5]	debt	none
Security sale (industrial)[6]	preferred	none
Security sale (utility)[7]	preferred	none
Call[8]	none	debt
PANEL C: Security sales which raise cash and bond future cash flow payments only minimally		
Security sale (industrial)[4]	conv. debt.	none
Security sale (industrial)[7]	conv. preferred	none
Security sale (utility)[7]	conv. preferred	none
PANEL D: Security retirements that pay out cash to shareholders		
Self tender offer[9]	none	common
Open market purchase[10]	none	common
Targeted small holdings[11]	none	common
Targeted large block repurchase[12]	none	common
PANEL E: Security sales or calls that raise cash and do not bond future cash flow payments		
Security sale (industrial)[13]	common	none
Security sale (utility)[14]	common	none
Conversion-forcing call[20]	common	conv. preferred
Conversion-forcing call[20]	common	conv. debt
PANEL F: Exchange offers, or designated use security sales that increase the bonding of payout of		
Designated use security sale[15]	debt	common
Exchange offer[16]	debt	common
Exchange offer[16]	preferred	common
Exchange offer[16]	debt	preferred
Exchange offer[17]	income bonds	preferred
PANEL G: Transaction with no change in bonding of payout of future cash flows		
Exchange offer[18]	debt	debt
Designated use security sale[19]	debt	debt
PANEL H: Exchange offers, or designated use security sales that decrease the bonding of payout		
Security sale[19]	conv. debt	debt
Exchange offer[16]	common	preferred
Exchange offer[16]	preferred	debt
Security sale[19]	common	debt
Exchange offer[21]	common	debt

[1] Asquith and Mullins (1983).
[2] Calculated by Smith (1986, Table 1) from Charest (1978), and Aharony and Swary (1980).
[3] From Brickley (1983).
[4] Calculated by Smith (1986, Table 1) from Dann and Mikkelson (1984), Eckbo (1986), Mikkelson and Partch (1986).
[5] Eckbo (1986).
[6] Calculated by Smith (1986, Table 1) from Linn and Pinegar (1985), Mikkelson and Partch (1986).
[7] Linn and Pinegar (1985).
[8] Vu (1986).
[9] Calculated by Smith (1986, Table 1) from Dann (1981), Masulis (1980), Vermaelen (1981), Rosenfeld (1982).
[10] Dann (1980), Vermaelen (1981).
[11] Bradley and Wakeman (1983).
[12] Calculated by Smith (1986, Table 4) from Dann and DeAngelo (1983), Bradley and Wakeman (1983).
[13] Calculated by Smith (1986, Table 1) from Asquith and Mullins (1986), Kolódny and Suhler (1985), Masulis and Korwar (1986) Mikkelson and Partch (1986), Schipper and Smith (1986).

retirements that raise cash or pay out cash and simultaneously provide offsetting changes in the constraints bonding the payout of future cash flow are all associated with returns insignificantly different from zero. The insignificant return on retirement debt fits the theory because the payout of cash is offset by an equal reduction in the present value of promised future cash payouts. If the debt sales are associated with no changes in the expected investment program, the insignificant return on announcements of the sale of debt and preferred also fits the theory. The acquisition of new funds with debt or preferred

Average Sample Size	Average Abnormal Two-Day Announcement Period Return	Sign Predicted by Free Cash Flow Theory	Agreement with Free Cash Flow Theory?	Agreement with Tax Theory
160	3.7%	+	yes	no
281	0.9	+	yes	no
164	2.1	+	yes	no
48	−3.6	−	yes	no

provide off-setting changes in the constraints bonding future payment of cash flows.

248	−0.2*	0	yes	no
140	−0.1*	0	yes	no
28	−0.1*	0	yes	yes
249	−0.1*	0	yes	yes
133	−0.1*	0	yes	no
74	−2.1	—	yes	no
54	−1.4	—	yes	no
9	−1.6	—	yes	no
147	15.2	+	yes	yes
182	3.3	+	yes	yes
15	1.1	+	yes	yes
68	−4.8	+	no**	no**
215	−3.0	—	yes	yes
405	−0.6	—	yes	yes
57	−0.4*	—	no	yes
113	−2.1	—	yes	yes

future cash flows

45	21.9	+	yes	yes
52	14.0	+	yes	yes
9	8.3	+	yes	no
24	3.5	+	yes	yes
18	1.6	+	yes	yes
36	0.6	0	no	no
96	0.2*	0	yes	yes

of future cash flows

15	−2.4	—	yes	yes
23	−2.6	—	yes	no
9	−7.7	—	yes	yes
12	−4.2	—	yes	yes
81	−1.1	—	yes	yes

[14] Calculated by Smith (1986, Table 1) from Asquith and Mullins (1986), Masulis and Korwar (1986), Pettway and Radcliffe (1985).

[15] Masulis (1980).

[16] Masulis (1983). These returns include announcement days of both the original offer and, for about 40 percent of the sample, a second announcement of specific terms of the exchange.

[17] McConnell and Schlarbaum (1981).

[18] Dietrich (1984).

[19] As calculated by Smith (1986, Table 3) from Eckbo (1986), Mikkelson and Partch (1986).

[20] Mikkelson (1981).

[21] Rogers and Owers (1985, Peavy and Scott 1985, Finnerty 1985).

* Not statistically different from zero.

** Explained by the fact that these transactions are frequently associated with the termination of an actual or expected control bid. The price decline appears to reflect the loss of an expected control premium.

is offset exactly by a commitment bonding the future payout of cash flows of equal present value.

Panel C shows that sales of convertible debt and convertible preferred are associated with significantly negative stock price changes. These security sales raise cash and provide little effective bonding of future cash flow payments for the following reason: when the stock into which the debt is convertible is worth more than the face value of the debt, management has incentives to call them and force conversion to common.

Panel D shows that, with one exception, security

retirements that pay out cash to shareholders increase stock prices. The price decline associated with targeted large block repurchases (often called "greenmail") is highly likely to be due to the reduced probability that a takeover premium will be realized. These transactions are often associated with standstill agreements in which the seller of the stock agrees to refrain from acquiring more stock and from making a takeover offer for some period into the future.

Panel E summarizes the effects of security sales and retirements that raise cash and do not bond future cash flow payments. Consistent with the theory, negative abnormal returns are associated with all such changes. However, the negative returns associated with the sale of common through a conversion-forcing call are statistically insignificant.

Panel F shows that all exchange offers or designated-use security sales that increase the bonding of payout of future cash flows result in significantly positive increases in common stock prices. These include stock repurchases and exchange of debt or preferred for common, debt for preferred, and income bonds for preferred. The two-day gains range from 21.9 percent (debt for common) to 2.2 percent (debt or income bonds for preferred).

Panel G of Table 2 shows that the evidence on transactions with no cash flow and no change in the bonding of payout of future cash flows is mixed. The returns associated with exchange offers of debt for debt are significantly positive, and those for designated-use security sales are insignificantly different from zero.

Panel H of Table 2 shows that all exchanges, or designated-use security sales that have no cash effects but reduce the bonding of payout of future cash flows result, on average, in significant decreases in stock prices. These transactions include the exchange of common for debt or preferred or preferred for debt, or the replacement of debt with convertible debt. The two-day losses range from −9.9% (common for debt) to −2.4% (for designated-use security sale replacing debt with convertible debt).

In summary, the results in Table 2 are remarkably consistent with free cash flow theory, which predicts that, except for firms with profitable unfunded investment projects, prices will rise with unexpected increases in payouts to shareholders (or promises to do so) and will fall with reductions in

payments or new requests for funds from shareholders (or reductions in promises to make future payments). Moreover, the size of the value changes is positively related to the change in the tightness of the commitment bonding the payment of future cash flows. For example, the effects of debt-for-preferred exchanges are smaller than the effects of debt-for-common exchanges.

Tax effects can explain some of these results, but not all—for example, the price changes associated with exchanges of preferred for common or replacements of debt with convertible debt, neither of which which have any tax effects. The last column of Table 2 denotes whether the individual coefficients are explainable by these pure corporate tax effects. The tax theory hypothesizes that all unexpected changes in capital structure which decrease corporate taxes increase stock prices and vice versa.[34] Therefore, increases in dividend and reductions of debt interest should cause stock price to fall and vice·versa.[35] Thirteen of the 32 coefficients are inconsistent with the corporate tax hypothesis. Simple signaling effects, where the payout of cash signals the lack of present and future investments that promise returns in excess of the cost of capital, are also inconsistent with the results—for example, the positive stock price changes associated with dividend increases and stock repurchases.

If anything, the results in Table 2 seem too good. The returns summarized in the table do not distinguish firms that have free cash flow from those that do not have free cash flow. Yet the theory tells us the returns to firms with no free cash flow will behave differently from those which do. In addition, only unexpected changes in cash payout or the tightness of the commitments bonding the payout of future free cash flows should affect stock prices. The studies summarized in Table 2 do not, in general, control for the effects of expectations. If the free cash flow effects are large and if firms on average are in a positive free cash flow position, the predictions of the theory will hold for the simple sample averages. If the effects are this pervasive, the waste due to agency problems in the corporate sector is greater than most scholars have thought. This helps explain the high level of activity in the corporate control market over the last decade. More detailed tests of the propositions that control for growth prospects and expectations will be interesting.

The Market for Corporate Control: A Review of the Evidence

by Peter Dodd,
University of Chicago

Introduction

From even the most casual reference to the popular financial press, it is clear there is an active market where the *control* of public corporations is traded. Headlines regularly announce proposals of corporate mergers and acquisitions. Tender offers have become a widespread, much publicized means of changing corporate control—and the size of the targets is becoming ever larger. Along with these fairly recent developments, the old-fashioned proxy fight now appears to be undergoing a dramatic revival. Once a phenomenon associated almost exclusively with small companies, proxy challenges have just succeeded in ousting directors of companies as large as Superior Oil and GAF. All these events, together with the less frequent, though increasingly common news of divestitures, spin-offs, and leveraged buyouts, are signs of the vigorous workings of a market for corporate control.

The existence of a well-functioning market for transferring corporate control has important economic implications. To many disinterested viewers, and no doubt to most incumbent managements whose jobs are threatened by such developments, the wave of mergers, acquisitions, and tender offers may seem to reflect the spectacle of managerial empire building, in which stockholders' interests are routinely sacrificed in a general management design to enlarge its own corporate domain. And boards of directors doubtless view proxy fights as an unwelcomed and unjustifiable nuisance, interfering with their efforts to run the company. But although this skepticism about acquiring managements and dissident stockholders may be justified in some — and perhaps many—cases, the market for corporate control provides the mechanism by which corporate assets can be channeled to those most efficient in using them. And this, as most economists would agree, is essential to the functioning of the economy as a whole.

The threat of takeover is also a crucial means of disciplining inept management, and of curbing the inevitable self-interest of those corporate managers who would prefer to pursue more private goals at their stockholders' expense. In this sense, the existence of an active market for corporate control is perhaps the best reply to the the popular corporate criticism declaiming against the "separation of ownership and control." Such a market provides — ideally, at least, if not always in practice — a self-regulating, monitoring mechanism which ensures that management's interests cannot diverge too far from those of stockholders. In so doing, an efficient market for changing corporate control increases the wealth of all stockholders.

Such a market also contributes to the general economic welfare by providing the opportunity for firms to combine to form more efficient and profitable entities. Whether through economies of scale, improved access to capital markets, combination of complementary resources, or any of the value-creating strategies that come under the term "synergies," mergers and acquisitions hold out the possibility of gains to stockholders of both acquired and acquiring firms. Critics of "big business" continue, of course, to view mergers and acquisitions as a net drain on the economy, wasting capital that could be channeled into more "productive" investment. But academic studies have demonstrated conclusively that such transactions—even after the expense of engaging the apparently "non-productive" services of lawyers, accountants, and investment bankers — significantly increase the net wealth of stockholders.

A more controversial issue, both on Wall Street and in academic finance circles alike, concerns the pricing, and thus the profitability of corporate acquisitions to buying companies. The dramatic increase in acquisition purchase premiums over the past few years has raised questions about both (1) the efficiency of the market in pricing stocks and (2) the motives of managements of acquiring companies. If stock prices have not significantly understated the value of corporate assets, it is difficult to imagine how DuPont's recent acquisition of Conoco — at a price that represents a premium of over 100 percent above Conoco's pre-offer price — can turn out to be a profitable investment. More generally, in an efficient market in which current market prices reflect an unbiased estimate of companies' market values, is there an economic justification for the large acquisition premiums over market that are being paid?

This controversy has a direct bearing on larger questions about the effectiveness of the market for corporate control. How successful is the threat of events like tender offers and proxy fights in maintaining a reasonable unity of interest between management and stockholders? Some finance scholars have interpreted the large and growing purchase premiums as strong evidence that managements of acquiring companies systematically sacrifice the interests of their own stockholders. Acquisitions and tender offers are viewed as a management strategy to expand its own prestige, increasing their corporate fiefdoms at the expense of their own stockholders. Others have argued that the premiums are justified by the increase in value that can be realized by consolidating control of the assets of the acquiring and acquired firms. According to this view, the premiums paid to the stockholders of acquired companies represent their "fair share" of the increase in value created by the combination.

In addition to the widespread skepticism about such large acquisition premiums, financial academics have expressed concern about the spread of the relatively new management strategies for warding off potential takeovers through "porcupine" amendments, "shark repellants," "standstill agreements," "golden parachutes," and targeted buybacks. Investment bankers are vigorously promoting such antitakeover "packages," and are finding that market receptive. Although purportedly designed to protect stockholders from "corporate raiders," it is hard to refrain from viewing such measures as a means of insulating management from the operation of this market for corporate control.

To be sure, corporate managements have never willingly acquiesced to hostile tender offers, even though they appear to hold out such benefits to their own stockholders. And in many cases, their resistance appears to have been justified by their willingness to accept higher offers down the road. But, the recent adoption of "antitakeover" measures, besides raising academic eyebrows, now appears to be provoking stockholder unrest. The successful proxy challenge at Superior Oil, which was aimed specifically at removing those barriers insulating management from the discipline of the market, may be only the most visible expression of stockholder disapproval, marking the beginning of a new era of stockholder activism.

Partly because of these relatively new developments, the market for corporate control has increasingly become the focus of research efforts in the U.S. The purpose of this article is to review the academic research bearing on questions like those introduced above: What are the real corporate motives for mergers and acquisitions, and who benefits from such transactions? What happens to the stock prices of companies resisting takeovers? What are the stock price consequences of proxy fights? Do they genuinely benefit current stockholders by threatening or displacing management, or are they merely obstructionist sound and fury, generated by opportunists and malcontents? What is the effect of the newly popular management "entrenchment" procedures on stock prices?

This article will provide a brief overview of the large and growing body of research on such questions, as well as suggesting directions in which the market for corporate control is evolving.

The Economics of the Market for Corporate Control

Control of the corporation is a nebulous concept. There is a longstanding debate in law and economics about the relative roles of management and stockholders in controlling the public corporation. Critics of unfettered corporate enterprise like John Kenneth Galbraith have leveraged the premise of "separation of ownership and control" into the claim that the form of the public corporation effectively confers absolute decision-making power on corporate managers, insulating them from all responsibilities to stockholders. The very couching of the debate in terms of this "separation" is partly responsible for the proliferation of corporate and securities laws that now limit corporate actions.[1]

Such critics rightly point out that the form of the corporation has changed greatly from the days of the 18th-century "joint stock companies" described by Adam Smith. Although the 19th century saw a rapid growth in the numbers of corporations, they were mostly closely-held concerns, organized around and financed by a single entrepreneur or a small group of private investors. And, of course, when "insiders" hold a large fraction of the outstanding shares, ownership and control are effectively united, thus ensuring a strong commonality of interest.

To this day, there are still many corporations where the firm is owned and managed by a particular individual, or an influential group of investors, who clearly dictate the policies of the organization. For most large public corporations, however, the proportion of shares owned by insiders is small, and establishing who *ultimately* controls the firm is far from straightforward.

Beginning with the well-known arguments of Adolf Berle and Gardner Means,[2] many commentators have leaped from the observation that management holds only small proportions of shares to the conclusion that shareholders are therefore at the mercy of management. From there it is but a short step to the prescription that corporate activities be regulated by the federal government.

The most glaring inadequacy of this reasoning is its complete failure to consider why the public corporation has survived, indeed prevailed, as the form of organization of American business enterprise. In "Reflections on The Corporation as a Social Invention," William Meckling and Michael Jensen observe that

Critics of the corporation are confronted by a striking historical phenomenon not readily reconciled with their views. The corporation has come to dominate production and commerce, not only in the United States, but in all of the world's highly developed nations. If the corporation is such a defective institution, how do we explain its chronicle of success? Freedom to choose among organizational forms provides an "organizational" test of survival just as markets provide a survival test for individual firms. . . . The organizational forms that survive and prosper will be those that satisfy consumer demands at lowest cost.

Wherever competition among organizational forms is open and unfettered, the large corporation has demonstrated its strength and durability.[3]

In proposing various forms of government control of the corporation, critics of "big business" almost invariably ignore the costs—in the form of reduced economic efficiency — of government-mandated changes of long-established institutional arrangements. Such institutions have evolved over time in response to a variety of market pressures, and they are in large part responsible for the corporation's success.

Corporate critics are right, of course, to insist that the traditional legal view of the corporation as a collection of assets "owned" by stockholders is grossly simplistic. In fact, the large modern corporation is an elaborate legal fiction, a complicated network of contracts binding a *number* of different parties to the production activities of the firm.[4] Stockholders are perhaps best represented as suppliers of capital, whose principal economic function is risk-bearing. They contract to be "residual" claimants, receiving the value of the remaining outputs only after the other inputs, or "factors of production," have been compensated. Their principal concerns are that the inputs of the firm are combined efficiently, and that the outputs are distributed scrupulously according to the specifics of the contracts. The individual stockholder, who typically holds an investment portfolio diversified across a number of firms, generally does not know much — nor perhaps even much care—about the day-to-day operations of the company.

1. Richard Posner, the University of Chicago's erstwhile Professor of Law (now a Justice), makes this point in his *Economic Analysis of Law,* New York: Columbia University Press, 1972.

2. Adolf Berle and Gardner Means, *The Modern Corporation.* See also Berle, "Functions of the Corporate System," *Columbia Law Review,* Vol. 62, pp. 433-449.

3. In *Controlling the Giant Corporation: A Symposium,* published by the University of Rochester's Center for Research in Government Policy and Business, 1982, p.84.

4. See Michael C. Jensen and William J. Meckling, "Theory of the Firm: Managerial Behavior, Agency Costs, and Capital Structure, *Journal of Financial Economics* 3 (1976): 305-60. See also Eugene Fama, "Agency Problems and the Theory of the Firm," *Journal of Political Economy,* 88, 288-307.

*The primary mechanism that constrains corporate management to
be efficient and scrupulous is the managerial labor market.*

Corporate decision-making, then, is primarily the province of professional managers hired to run the firm. But, as suggested above, and as most financial economists would agree, this specialization of functions has developed because of its efficiency. Although it has no doubt allowed some managers to exploit their stockholders, we can conclude that the benefits of such a development to the economy as a whole have far exceeded the costs.

Viewed in this light, then, "the separation of ownership and control," once the interventionist slogan of corporate critics, is transformed into a positive step in the evolution of the corporation toward greater economic efficiency.

But while it is undeniably more efficient to have professional managers controlling the day-to-day decisions of the corporation, stockholders and other contracting parties, such as employees, still require protection of their "investments." Part of this monitoring of management is accomplished through the board of directors, who are supposed to oversee corporate decision-making. But another part of this protection is provided through the contracts that bind stockholders, management, employees, and other parties. The level of protection provided by the contract determines the price at which different parties are prepared to invest. In the case of employees, this means the total level, form, and certainty of compensation that induces them to commit their "human capital" to the firm. In the case of stockholders, it refers to the price they will pay for the shares issued by the corporation.

One of the interesting implications of this analysis is that the *initiative* for providing monitoring devices, such as audited financial statements, comes not from investors, but rather from those entrepreneurs who wish to persuade potential investors to provide the funds for taking the firm public. The stronger the guarantees, the higher the price investors will pay for a given issue. And once the firm has become public, it remains in the interest of management to offer convincing promises of self-regulation, and to make good on them—at least up to the point that the benefits of added investor confidence outweigh the costs of providing such guarantees.[5]

Besides such specific contractual provisions, stockholders are also protected against mismanagement by a variety of institutional arrangements that have developed. Eugene Fama, the University of Chicago's well-known financial economist, argues forcibly that the primary mechanism that *constrains* corporate management to be efficient and scrupulous is the managerial labor market. Individuals both inside and outside the firm compete for management positions, and the existence of this market provides corporate managers with a powerful incentive to act in the interests of their stockholders. Although the precise mechanisms by which managers signal their value in this market is unclear, reference to the *Who's News* column in the *Wall Street Journal,* together with the proliferation of executive recruitment firms, suggests that this market is constantly at work.

The initiative for such management reshuffling, however, comes from the board of directors within the corporation. Typically composed of both top management and outside directors, the board is required to oversee the decision-making of management, and to replace managers or restructure the firm when it is being poorly run. Corporate boards also create compensation committees whose function is to design bonus schemes which furnish management with the proper incentives. Such programs offer stock options, or are tied to accounting measures of performance, and thus serve to unify the interests of management with those of stockholders.

But, if management does not respond to such incentives, and the board fails to respond to pressures for change, the market for corporate control then serves as a discipline of last resort. It is in this sense, as a protector of stockholder's wealth, that a freely functioning market for corporate control is an integral part of the corporate system. It is the operation of this market, together with well-designed compensation contracts and the labor market for management, that ensures that management's interests cannot diverge too far, and for too long, from the interests of their stockholders.

---

5. Ross Watts and Jerold Zimmerman have developed this idea in their writings, which will be synthesized in their forthcoming book, Positive Theories of Accounting.

Transferring Corporate Control

I will assume throughout the rest of this discussion that ultimate responsibility for decision-making rests with the board of directors and, more precisely, with the coalitions of members which control that board. The mechanisms for transferring control of the corporation are those that effectively change the composition of the board. This allows us to concentrate on those transactions that transfer control of the board: mergers, tender offers and proxy contests.

Before considering the similarities and differences between these transactions, it is important to note that many of the benefits of taking control of a corporation can be achieved without mounting a formal takeover campaign. For instance, it is possible to achieve synergistic benefits by designing joint ventures, which in effect are new business entities created by the corporate partners. It is also possible to negotiate long-term contracts to ensure the productive cooperation of two firms. The existence of these alternatives suggests that actual *voting control* of corporations must hold out benefits to acquiring firms that go beyond the operating synergies or cost savings provided by cooperative ventures and long-term contracts.

The most prominent mode of transferring control of corporate assets is, of course, the merger. Recall that a merger is a transaction in which one corporation (the acquirer) secures title to the stock or assets of another (the acquired). Consummation of a merger requires the approval of the acquired firm's board. If the board approves the transaction, it puts the merger proposal to a stockholder vote. Depending on the percentage of favorable votes required by the state corporate code, the merger is approved or rejected.

In effect, though, management has a veto power over all merger proposals and can refuse to put any proposal to a stockholder vote. Tender offers, by contrast, do not require the explicit approval of the incumbent management. A tender offer is a public offer made by the management of one firm (the bidder) to purchase a block of another (the target) firm's outstanding common stock. Ten-

der offers are made directly to the target's stockholders. If enough stockholders tender, control of the corporation changes hands.

Proxy fights are a direct attempt by dissident stockholders to remove directors through a stockholder vote. It is a formalized voting procedure in which one or more parties oppose the re-election of the incumbent directors. Although the contestants often attempt to purchase blocks of the outstanding shares prior to the election, the outcome of the contest itself has no effect upon the distribution of ownership of the firm. Unlike mergers or tender offers, where control passes to those who can convince stockholders to trade their shares, in proxy contests most stockholders do not transfer ownership of their shares. Their incentive is simply to elect the management team that will enhance the value of their investment.

Changes in the Market for Corporate Control: 1950s to the Present

The merger has long been and continues to be the most popular method of changing control. Beginning in the late 1960s, however, the number of tender offers per annum began to rival that of mergers (see Table 1). Prior to the 1960s, however, proxy fights were clearly the predominant means of *contesting* control of the corporation. In fact, the SEC files contain no record of tender offers prior to 1956.[6] Now, of course, the recent flurry of proxy fights aside, tender offers are much more commonly used for taking control of a corporation than proxy contests.

There is no completely convincing rationale for the eclipse of the proxy fight by tender offers, but changes in the regulatory climate provide a clue. My best guess is that, in the late 50s and 60s, the costs of waging a proxy war rose relative to those of making a tender offer (and the costs of tender offers then also included braving the social stigma attached to them), generating in effect a "demand" for tender offers as a substitute. In 1955, the SEC revised its proxy rules to require pre-examination of proxy materials, full disclosure of the identity of partici-

---

6. The most extensive and complete data base on tender offers is that of the Managerial Economics Research Center at the University of Rochester. It was developed by Michael Bradley, Peter Dodd, and Richard Ruback.

pants in the contest, and filing of proxy materials sent to stockholders. These rules became effective in January 1956, and were expanded in the Securities Act Amendment of 1964. Both of these regulations made proxy contests more costly, especially as the probability of litigation arising out of a contest increased with the broader disclosure requirements.

The emergence of tender offers is also associated with a significant change in the court's attitude to transactions transferring control. In a dramatic reversal of precedence, the court ruled in Perlman v. Feldman (1955) that proceeds from the sale of controlling interest in a corporation must be shared equally among all shareholders. This ruling effectively designated *control* an asset of the corpora-

tion. As early as 1952, one forward-looking commentator predicted the emergence of tender offers as a direct consequence of such a change in precedence:

If a seller can be sued by other stockholders when he makes a sale in which they have not been included, he will probably insist that an offer be made to all stockholders of the corporation. [7]

In light of this evidence, then, it can be conjectured that the rise of tender offers in the late 1950s and early 1960s reflects the increase in the costs, both actual and potential, of proxy fights brought about by regulatory and legal changes. And, as I shall suggest later, the present resurgence of the proxy fight may well reflect a fairly large and recent increase in the costs of making tender offers.

TABLE 1		Mergers	Tender Offers	Proxy Contests
New York and American Stock Exchange Firms Acquired in Mergers or Tender Offers or Involved in Proxy Contests in the Period January 1963 through June 1982	1963	16	6	7
	1964	27	4	6
	1965	26	7	5
	1966	35	10	3
	1967	56	12	8
	1968	14	23	4
	1969	6	6	4
	1970	19	4	3
	1971	6	1	9
	1972	14	3	5
	1973	13	14	4
	1974	9	21	2
	1975	7	14	3
	1976	9	11	4
	1977	17	17	1
	1978	26	21	1
	1979	44	30	NA
	1980	35	20	NA
	1981	23	21	NA
	June 1982	10	9	NA
	Total	419	254	71
	% of Population of Firms	9.5	5.7	1.6

7. Comment, *University of Chicago Law Review*, vol. 19 (1952), pp. 870.

The continuous presence of "risk" arbitrageurs provides a good illustration of how and why an efficient market works.

The Evidence on Mergers and Acquisitions

Corporate critics have long contended that unregulated financial markets are incapable of ensuring that boards of directors effectively monitor corporate managements. A corollary of this view holds that mergers and acquisitions, far from being motivated by management's desire to increase stockholder wealth, are initiated by corporate managements acting in their own self interest to the detriment of stockholders.

One of the most vocal of corporate critics, Adolf Berle, argued as early as 1932 that the market for corporate control exhibited the "megalomania" of corporate tycoons struggling to devour one another. The recent highly publicized billion dollar takeover battles for Conoco, Cities Service, Marathon Oil and Martin Marietta have rekindled these old arguments.

But while case studies are fascinating in their own right, they provide at best shaky foundations for generalizing — whether such generalizations apply to the natural sciences or the behavior of corporations. Responsible statements about the effectiveness of the market for corporate control should be based upon reasonably scientific evidence. And there is now a large and rapidly growing body of empirical evidence on the economic effects of mergers and acquisitions.

The Methods

Before summarizing the conclusions of this research, however, it is important to start with a basic understanding of its methods, and the assumptions underlying their use.

The problem faced by researchers is finding a method for evaluating the effect of a corporate merger or acquisition on stockholder wealth. At first glance, it might appear that the success of an acquisition can be judged only by observing the performance of the combined firm over a long period of time; and that only by poring over masses of accounting data (including income statements and balance sheets for competitors as well as for the firms involved) compiled over, say, a five-year period can such a determination be reached.

The relationship between accounting and market values, however, is often a tenuous one. Modern finance theory says that the most reliable way of measuring the real economic performance of a company is to track its stock price against the performance of the market as a whole (and adjusted for risk). And, in measuring the economic value added (or subtracted) by an acquisition, we would ideally like to measure the market value of the corporation both with and without the acquired firm, and then compare.

Of course, once the acquisition is accomplished, it is impossible to know and thus to track what the value of the firm would have been *without* the acquisition. But modern theory enables us to get around this problem, maintaining that we need not wait for five years to pass in order to evaluate the market consequences of corporate deals. In an "efficient market," the expected value of an acquisition — to buying and selling stockholders alike — will be *estimated* by the market in changes in stock prices *immediately upon the announcement of the transaction* (and, because of leakage, some of that value will have been captured even before).

This is not to suggest that the market's immediate response never turns out, with hindsight, to be wrong. Both our theory and the evidence suggest, however, that there is a roughly 50-50 probability that the market's assessment will fall on the low or high side in estimating the eventual success of the transaction.[8] Such price reactions therefore should be interpreted as carrying investors' "unbiased" assessment of the future economic consequences of that acquisition. They express the collective judgment of the market.

Those already skeptical about the "efficiency" of the market might argue that because of the strong speculative influence of arbitrageurs following merger proposals and tender offers, there is even less reason to rely on market pricing to judge acquisitions. But the continuous presence of such "risk" arbitrageurs, driven by the lure of profits, provides a good illustration of how and why an efficient market works. When a proposed acquisition is first publicly announced, there is a good deal of

---

8. Richard Ruback and I showed that for a large sample of tender offers the market's initial assessment was unbiased: *over the five years following the transactions,* bidding firms earned on average *zero* abnormal returns. See "Tender Offers and Stockholder Returns: An Empirical Analysis,) *Journal of Financial Economics,* vol. 5, 351-74.

uncertainty as to the eventual outcome of the transaction. In some cases the initial offer is completed as proposed, while in others competing higher bids materialize and the transaction is completed at a substantially higher price. In still other cases, the transaction is unsuccessful, the target firm is not acquired, and the target stock price usually falls dramatically. Arbitrageurs betting on the outcome of the transaction provide an active market for such stocks. Those target stockholders wanting to avoid the risk of the transaction failing can sell their shares in the market after the offer has been made.

Modern finance, as well as common sense, predicts that the target's stock price will adjust at the time of the first public announcement of the offer to reflect the probability that higher competing bids will materalize — as well as the probability that the transaction will fall through completely. In some cases, the market guesses correctly and in others it does not. In each case, however, if the market's price reflects an "unbiased" guess about the outcome of the deal, there should be no evidence of mispricing when averaging across a large sample of transaction.

A study I performed in 1981 confirms that this, in fact, is what happens.[9] For a sample of 324 *proposed* mergers, the average market-adjusted return from buying a portfolio of all the target firms' stocks one day after the first public announcement, and holding for 60 trading days, was −0.2 percent. For 268 announced tender offers, the return was a little higher —0.31 percent. If an investor had purchased shares in each of the 592 target firms the day after the offer was announced, he would have earned a market-adjusted return of 0.03 percent. From these results, I conclude that "arbitraging" the outcome of acquisitions is a "fair game" (i.e., the chances of winning and losing are roughly equal). Without access to private information on the outcome of specific proposals, the expected return to this investment strategy is zero.

Extending this reasoning to the problem of evaluating the success of acquisitions, our tests assume that the market's immediate response — to buying companies and selling companies alike — contains an unbiased assessment of the net present value of that acquisition to stockholders. It impounds immediately those cash flow consequences that will only be realized in the future. For any given firm, of course, the market's response may be

wrong. But all the players in the market have a powerful incentive to be right. If the market penalized Dupont too heavily for what it viewed as too good a deal for Conoco, then those stockholders who sold misread the long view. The short-run price response contains the market's best guess about the long-run view. If this were not so, then there would be opportunities for large profits to investors buying the Duponts and U.S. Steels of this world.

It is also possible that there are other events affecting the company's stock price at the time of the acquisition. Across a large sample of firms, however, with acquisitions spread well over time, we can be fairly confident that such random effects will cancel out, and that no one set of events, whether good or bad, will confound the analysis.

The Evidence on Target Firms

The evidence on the effects of acquisitions on target firm stocks is quite consistent across different studies. Both a study I conducted with Richard Ruback, as well as later tests by Michael Bradley, found that target shares rise dramatically on the announcement of a proposed tender offer. This is no surprise, of course, since the acquisition is always at an offer price above the current market price. For those transactions that are successfully completed, the stock price rises further over the interim as uncertainty about the outcome is resolved. Similarly large gains to target stocks in merger proposals have been documented in studies by Paul Asquith and myself.

Both Ruback's and my study of tender offers, and Asquith's study of mergers, report an interesting finding on target firms: over the periods 2 and 3 years *prior* to the acquisition, these target stocks experienced average abnormal *negative* returns of up to 15 percent. The marked failure of target firms to keep pace with the market suggests that, on average, such firms had not been performing up to their potential. And this further suggests that acquisitions, provided the price is right, offer profitable investment opportunities for acquiring firms with more efficient managers or more profitable uses for the target's assets. (By contrast, the abnormal returns to shareholders of acquiring companies *prior* to the merger were consistently positive. Acquiring companies had apparently achieved good track records

---

9. In Peter Dodd, "The Effect on Market Value of Transactions in the Market for Corporate Control," *Proceedings of Seminar on the Analysis of Security Prices,* Center for Research on Security Prices, University of Chicago, May 1981.

prior to their acquisitions, and their merger activity was the manifestation of a demonstrated ability to manage assets and growth.) Such evidence is consistent with our conception of the the market for corporate control as imposing a discipline on management, and transferring corporate assets to more profitable uses.

Another striking result of our studies is that unsuccessful merger proposals and tender offers are associated with permanent positive revaluations of target shares. For 53 unsuccessful tender offers I examined, the average excess return over the 121 days around the transaction was 15.6 percent. It is clear that the attempted transfer of control has revealed information that results, on average, in a significant increase in the market value of a corporation's shares. Over two-thirds of these firms are subsequently acquired within five years and the revaluation could reflect the market's anticipation of these acquisitions. Alternatively the revaluation could reflect expectations of improved managerial performance following the attempted takeover.

The 108 cancelled merger proposals I studied were also associated with a positive overall revaluation. The gains to target stockholders were smaller than those in tender offers, but they were nevertheless significant.

Whether such a revaluation takes place, however, is very definitely a function of the type of cancellation. As noted earlier, merger proposals occur in a different institutional setting than tender offers. The management of the target firm can decide not to submit any proposal to a stockholder vote, and thus has effective veto power over any merger proposal. But not all cancellations are the result of target management's veto. It is possible for the bidding firm to reconsider its proposal (perhaps after getting access to "insider" information about the target during the negotiations) and to decide that the merger is no longer a good investment.

Of the 108 cancelled merger proposals, it is clear from the cancellation announcements that 34 were the result of vetoes by target management. For the remaining 74, the source of the cancellation cannot be determined. The overall impact of the transactions are vastly different for the two categories. In those proposals vetoed by target management, the excess returns to target stockholders over the 121 day period around the initial public announcement averaged 16.3 percent. In the 74 cases where either the bidder withdrew or the source of cancellation could not be determined,

target stockholder returns were a -0.2 percent. From these results, we can conclude that there is a permanent revaluation associated with an average takeover bid rejected by the target management. This higher price reflects the fact that an unsuccessful acquisition attempt is often followed at a later date by a different, but successful bid. When the bidding firm withdraws, however, the target's stock price generally falls back to its level prior to the proposal.

The Evidence on Bidding Firms

The evidence on bidding firms is not nearly as conclusive, and studies using different samples have come up with conflicting results. Most studies have reported that the average abnormal return to bidding firms is close to zero, and that therefore the lion's share, if not all, of the gains from the transactions are earned by target stockholders. This would suggest that the market for corporate control is a competitive one, in which profits to buying firms are effectively bid to "zero" — that is, acquisitions earn on average "normal" rates of return for their stockholders, but no more.

In most cases the bidding firm is much larger than the target, and thus a comparison of *percentage changes* in the value of the acquiring and the acquired firm's stock might not be appropriate. In order to measure the division of gains among buyers and sellers with greater sensitivity, researchers also estimated the *total dollar gains* (and losses) to both stockholder groups. Calculated in this fashion, the gains from acquisitions appear to be divided fairly evenly, on average, between buyers and sellers.

What these broad statistical averages conceal, however, is that announcements of acquisitions are associated with a surprising number of stock price declines. The results reported by both Bradley and Asquith show over 40 percent of bidding companies' stock prices falling on the announcement of the acquisition proposal. For some samples, such as the one I used in my 1980 study of mergers of NYSE firms over the 1972-1977 period, these negative returns to bidders are accentuated.

Recently, of course, some of the largest takeovers resulted in dramatic declines in stock price. Dupont's market value fell by almost 10 percent during its negotiations with Conoco. Similar declines were experienced by Gulf in their attempt to acquire Cities Service, and by U.S. Steel when acquiring Marathon Oil.

These well-publicized cases, together with the spectacle of Bendix's bid for Martin Marietta, have given new life to the old arguments for limiting management's autonomy. Some members of Congress and the SEC have also expressed concern that the market for corporate control is being abused by corporate managements. Such concern has magnified to the extent that a task force investigation has been initiated.

Mergers and Acquisitions: 1979-1982

Implicit in this concern is the assumption that the market for corporate control has fundamentally changed in recent years. If this is the case, interpretation of the existing research must be cautious since most studies to date have looked at acquisitions that took place no later than 1977.

In order to determine whether the market for acquisitions has in fact changed, I attempted to update the existing evidence by examining returns to stockholders during the most recent wave of mergers and tender offers. Between January 1979 and June 1982, almost 200 New York and American Stock Exchange firms were acquired. For each of these transactions, I measured the returns (net of market movements) to buying and selling firms' stockholders over the period extending from 10 trading days before the first public announcement of the proposed acquisition through the day after the announcement.

The story for acquired firms is pretty much the same as reported for earlier periods: over this 11-day period target stockholders earned, on average, 27 percent in mergers and 39 percent in tender offers. The primary difference is that the premiums offered over market price, which have been increasing since the late 1960's, have become even larger. While some of the early increase in premiums was found to be associated with the passage of the Williams Act in 1968, and the various state tender offer laws that came after, the continued increase is difficult to explain.

This sharp and ever increasing growth of acquisition premiums seems to be reflected in the returns to bidding firms' stockholders. The average returns—which were slightly negative but still close to zero — are still fairly consistent with those of studies of earlier periods. But the percentage of bidding firms experiencing abnormal stock price declines rose sharply to 61 percent of firms bidding for mergers, and to 66 percent of companies making tender offers. On closer inspection, the results for bidding firms are quite revealing. Concentrating on just the week prior to (and including the day of) the public announcement of proposed acquisitions (i.e., −4 through 0), the negative abnormal returns to bidders in both tender offers and mergers are statistically significant (with t statistics of −2.3 and −2.2 respectively). Again, over 65 percent of both bidder samples recorded declines in stock price.

Thus, the stock market has clearly pronounced its judgment that a large proportion of tender offers have not served the best interest of the bidding companies' stockholders. And, the pervasiveness of negative stock price effects of acquisitions on bidding firms in the 1979-1982 period represents a marked change from the earlier evidence, providing ammunition for the critics of the market. The results are consistent with the notion that acquiring firms, on average, are paying too high a price.

TABLE 2 Percentage Abnormal Returns to Target and Bidder Stocks in Tender Offers and Mergers Between January 1979 and June 1982 (t Statistics in Parentheses)	Tender Offers		Mergers	
Days	Targets	Bidders	Targets	Bidders
−10 through 0	38.99 (7.0)	−1.04 (−1.2)	27.09 (6.6)	−0.73 (−1.1)
−4 through 0	33.76 (9.0)	−1.36 (−2.3)	23.48 (8.4)	−1.31 (−2.2)
−1 through 0	22.01 (9.2)	−1.87 (−4.9)	21.78 (12.4)	−0.16 (−0.4)

Contrary to the claims of critics, total economic value is increased by mergers and acquisitions.

Why more than half of bidding companies are willing to pay such high premiums over market — high, at least, in the market's collective judgment — to consummate these corporate unions is a mystery. Perhaps, of course, the stock market's response over the past three years has a significant downward bias to it. But if this is true, then there are profit opportunities which investors can systematically exploit by buying the shares of companies like DuPont and U.S. Steel. Both common sense, and a great deal of evidence accumulated about the way the market works, says that this is very unlikely.

On net, however, both mergers and tender offers have served to increase the wealth of stockholders as a whole. For even though bidding firms are larger than the targets on average, we also find that the dollar losses to bidding firms are far outweighed by the dollar gains to targets. This finding, substantiated by all past and present tests to date, implies that the assets of the combined firms are more valuable than when held by the individual firms prior to the acquisition. Contrary to the claims of those critics who argue that acquisitions and tender offers represent a net drain on the economy, total economic value is increased by mergers and acquisitions; and this suggests that the market for corporate control is fulfilling a valuable economic function by channeling corporate assets to more productive uses, or more efficient users.

Proxy Fights

A purer test of the effectiveness of the market for corporate control, as well as stronger testimony to its role in preserving stockholder value, is provided by a study of the stock price consequences of proxy contests.

Jerry Warner and I examined a sample of 96 proxy contests involving New York and American Stock Exchange firms between 1962 and 1977.[10] We found that these contests result, on average, in a positive stock price revaluation of over 8 percent. These returns are measured over the period extending from 60 days prior to the first public announcement of the contest until the results of the election are announced.

We began our study by classifying the 96 proxy contests into two groups, designated "control" and "participation," according to whether the dissidents proposed candidates for 50 percent or more of the available board seats. Of the 96 contests, 71 were for control of the board and 25 involved elections for less than 50 percent of the seats. In 56 of the 96 contests, dissidents won at least one seat. In 18 (or roughly 25 percent) of the "control" contests, dissidents won a majority. And in 45 (or 63 percent) of such contests, dissidents won at least one seat. In "participation" contests, dissidents won at least one seat in only 44 percent of the contests.

Proxy contests are often waged by former "insiders." In 37 of the 71 "control" contests, and in 4 of the 25 "participation" contests, the dissidents included either former board members or former high ranking officials of the firm. Such individuals typically leave the firm after a policy dispute with incumbent directors, and then later initiate the challenge.

Also, 16 of the proxy fights in the sample were led by outside firms (and 3 of these 16 contests were preceded by tender offers). The presence of either insiders or another firm seems to have a marked impact on the likelihood that the dissidents will be successful in winning seats. For example, in 29 of the 37 contests for control involving insiders, and in 10 of the 12 involving outside firms, dissident stockholders won seats. By contrast, dissidents won seats in only 7 of the 23 contests not involving either insiders or other firms.

The results of our tests of the effects of proxy fights on stockholder wealth can be summarized as follows:

Even though dissidents stockholders actually capture control in only 25 percent of the contests, over 75 percent of firms are more highly valued after the contest. On average, stockholders earn an 8.2 percent excess return over the duration of the contest.

The significant positive abnormal returns are found in both control and participation contests. In control contests, stockholders earn 8.8 percent excess returns and in participation contests they earn 6.3 percent.

The positive stock price performance over the duration of the contest does not appear to be affected by

10. Peter Dodd and Jerold B. Warner, "On Corporate Governance: A Study of Proxy Contests," *Journal of Financial Economics*, vol. 11, 1983.

the outcome of the contest. In contests where dissidents win seats, the mean excess return is 8.1 percent, and in contests where dissidents win no seats, the average return is 8.2 percent.

Whether dissidents win a majority or not, however, has a striking effect on the size of the positive revaluation. When dissidents win a majority of the board seats, the excess return is 12.8 percent on average, and for contests where they fail to win a majority, it is 7.7 percent.

The positive excess returns are earned prior to the public announcement of the contest, and most occur over the previous 40 days. The timing of the excess returns reflects the institutional mechanics of proxy contests, which require the dissidents to organize their team of experts (including lawyers, accountants, and public relations personnel) and to prepare the solicitations materials prior to public announcement. The results of our study suggest that news of the contest is known in the stock market well before the public announcement of the challenge.

The overall finding of positive abnormal performance is consistent with the proposition that proxy fights benefit stockholders by transferring corporate resources to more highly valued uses.

This positive share price performance is also found even in those contests where incumbents win all seats. Apparently, the fact of a challenge to management is associated with expectations of improved corporate performance. The outcome of the contest, however, does appear to influence stock prices somewhat. Upon the announcement of the election results, there is evidence of a small positive share price reaction when dissidents win seats, and a small negative reaction when they do not. Such evidence is consistent with the view that dissident representation was expected to improve profitability and increase stockholder wealth.

Antitakeover Strategies: Protection of Stockholders or Management Entrenchment?

In response to the wave of takeovers in the late 70's, many corporations have adopted by-law and charter amendments which make it more difficult for potential acquirers to gain control. And even more recently, senior executives have also begun to grant themselves large bonus payments in the event their firm is acquired. These "porcupine amendments" (also known as "shark repellants") and "gol-den parachutes" have become standard components of comprehensive antitakeover strategies designed and marketed by investment bankers.

The widespread adoption of such measures has further fueled the debate about the genuineness of management's service to its stockholders. Such actions clearly increase the costs of changing corporate control, reducing the profitability and thus, presumably, the probability of takeovers.

Both the SEC and NYSE have severely criticized the introduction of the amendments, objecting that they effectively entrench existing management at the expense of their stockholders. Those corporations adopting the amendments have defended themselves by pointing to the apparent vulnerability of current stockholders who become minority holders when control is transferred by fractional tender offers. Although the Williams Act and state statutes offer these stockholders some protection, charter amendments further restrict the actions that can be taken by a potential acquirer, thus increasing target management's power to control the outcome of any such proposal.

Also, because all proceeds from a successful tender offer are now required by law to be distributed equally among all tendering stockholders — regardless of which bid they initially accepted — all individual stockholders have an incentive to tender to the first bid, and not risk losing their gain. The antitakeover amendments allow target management to counteract this incentive to tender their shares (possibly) too soon by allowing them to negotiate on behalf of all stockholders for a higher price. And if the company is actually taken over, such amendments govern the dealings of the acquiring firm with remaining minority stockholders through "anti-squeeze out" provisions and "escape" clauses.

In defense of the practice of instituting "golden parachutes," it has been argued that guaranteed compensation agreements strengthen the incentive for target managers to act in their stockholders' best interests when faced with an acquisition proposal. There is some justification for this argument. But such provisions clearly increase the costs of acquiring the firm, thus reducing the expected profitability (and presumably the price paid for) the acquisition. And to the extent that potential bidding companies are deterred by such additional expenses, "golden parachutes" may be worth less to stockholders as a correction of management incentives than the loss resulting from the reduced probability of takeover.

The Evidence

Researchers have collected data on the market's response to *announcements* of both charter amendments and guaranteed compensation contracts, and the evidence seems to refute the claim that either action harms stockholders. Scott Linn and John McConnell studied over 300 firms that introduced so-called antitakeover amendments and found slightly *positive*, though insignificant abnormal returns. Harry DeAngelo and Ed Rice found similar results for a sample of over 100 firms adopting supramajority voting rules, staggered boards, fair price and lock-up provisions.

In the case of "golden parachutes," Laureen Maines identified 93 firms that introduced severance compensation plans for executives within the past five years, and found no evidence of any negative stock price effects associated with the introduction of these plans. Similar results were obtained by Richard Lambert and David Larcker.

Partially Successful Transfers of Control: Standstill Agreements and Targeted Buybacks

Two other relatively new management practices have added to the managerial "entrenchment" controversy and, in these cases, the evidence appears to *support* the claims of critics.

Bidding firms often gain a large block of a target's outstanding shares but not enough to control the board. In an increasing number of these cases the bidder (now a substantial stockholder) and target managements enter into a voluntary contract, known as a "standstill agreement," which limits the former's ownership of target shares to some maximum (less than controlling) percentage for a stipulated number of years. Such contracts also often prevent the bidding firm from participating in a proxy contest against the incumbent board.

Standstill agreement are also often accompanied by repurchases of the bidder's block at a premium above the market price. And, in many cases, such "targeted buybacks" take place without standstill agreements.

Larry Dann and Harry DeAngelo (1981) recently studied 81 of these agreements and repurchases during 1977-1981. They find that both are associated with negative abnormal returns to the other target stockholders. Even those standstill agreements not accompanied by negotiated stock repurchases are associated with significant declines in target stock prices.

The evidence thus provides strong support that such actions serve only to insulate incumbent management from the threat of removal. By interfering with the workings of the market for corporate control, such entrenchment appears clearly to reduce the market value of remaining stockholders' shares. Although both standstill agreements and negotiated purchases are currently within the bounds of corporation law, the obviously detrimental effects of such practices on remaining stockholders can be expected to generate legal challenges, and possibly further battles for control.

New Directions for the Market for Corporate Control

The evidence reviewed in these pages provides overwhelming support for the argument that the existence of a market for corporate control benefits stockholders. Simply by holding out the possibility that control can change hands, and by providing the means for transferring assets to more profitable users or uses, this market increases the efficiency, and hence the wealth, of the economy as a whole.

Let me summarize this evidence briefly. First, the transfer of control achieved through mergers and tender has provided stockholders of acquired firms with large abnormal returns. Acquired companies tend to have underperformed the market, while acquiring companies tend to have outperformed the market, over the period 2 to 3 years prior to acquisitions. This is consistent with our conception of the market for control as disciplining inept management, and transferring assets to higher-valued uses. Furthermore, *unsuccessful* tender offers and mergers are often accompanied by permanent increases in target firms' stock prices (although not in those cases where bidding firms withdraw their bid), suggesting that the mere possibility of a company being sold increases stockholder value.

Proxy challenges, too, have resulted in significant increases for stockholders. This increase occurs whether the contests are successful or not—though increases are significantly larger in those contests where dissidents win majority control. Thus, the mere threat of stockholder challenge appears to create market expectations of improved managerial performance.

These findings regarding mergers, tender offers, and proxy fights hold fairly consistently over the different time periods examined in our studies. But, more recent research suggests that the market for corporate control may be undergoing some important changes. As pointed out earlier, the operation of this market is profoundly affected by federal and state regulations, and many of the changes observed over the 50s and 60s can be explained by regulatory changes. For example, the substitution of the tender offer for the proxy fight as the predominant means for contesting corporate control in the 60s was in part attributable to restrictive legislation governing proxy fights. Such legislation greatly increased the costs, both out-of-pocket and expected, from waging proxy wars.

The recent flurry of proxy fights suggests, however, that the pendulum may have begun to swing the other way. Since the passage of the Williams Act in 1968, and the proliferation of state statutes governing tender offers, the size of acquisition premiums has become ever larger, thus increasing the costs of making tender offers. In fact, the size of the premiums have been increasing steadily through out the 70s — a fact which cannot be explained by further regulatory and legal changes.

My own study of the most recent wave of acquisitions over the period 1979-1982, shows that the premiums paid over market to acquire companies have reached unprecedented levels. The stock market's response to buying companies was significantly negative in over 60 percent of the mergers and tender offers consummated during this period. Thus, the skepticism of finance theorists about the size of such premiums is being reinforced by the collective judgment of the market.

One plausible cause of this increase in acquisition premiums is an apparent stiffening of management resistance to takeovers. Increasingly popular "antitakeover" packages now feature "porcupine"

amendments, "golden parachutes," defensive acquisitions, new stock issues to dilute control, privately negotiated repurchases, and standstill agreements. Although some of these provisions seem clearly intended to increase the costs — or, alternatively, to reduce the profitability — of takeovers, the market's response to announcements of charter amendments and guaranteed compensation contracts has been neutral. Furthermore, stockholders seem to endorse such measures directly by voting for them. In the case of "standstill agreements" and targeted repurchases, however, where the management motive of entrenchment seems to be pursued unambiguously at the expense of stockholders, the market's response has been decidedly negative. There seems to be little doubt that such provisions interfere with the operation of the market for control, and this clearly reduces the firm's value.

The spread of these relatively new antitakeover procedures, then, may have a great deal to do with the current size of acquisition premiums. And this further significant increase may in large part explain the recent series of proxy contests. Two of these contests unseated directors of very large companies. And, perhaps just as significant, they succeeded by enlisting, for the first time, the support of large institutions, which have invariably backed management during proxy contests.

Although clearly arising out of stockholder dissatisfaction with current management, such proxy activity can be interpreted as an indirect response by stockholders to the rising costs, and thus the reduced probability, of changes in control achievable through tender offers. The challenge to Superior Oil was aimed specifically at removing antitakeover amendments, calling for the establishment of an independent committee of stockholders to evaluate all bids for over 45 percent of the company. To the extent that stockholders feel themselves increasingly shut off by management from recourse to the market for corporate control, this recent reawakening of the proxy war could well turn into a general resurgence.

Observations on the Merger Phenomenon and a Review of the Evidence

Baruch Lev,
Tel Aviv University

The major objective of this opening presentation is to establish some common denominator or unified framework, if you will, for all the subsequent talks to be given here in the next two and a half days. I will start by examining broad trends in mergers in the United States. I'll then consider the main theories of mergers—hypotheses about the corporate motives for mergers and acquisitions (M & A). Next, I will review the available empirical evidence on the consequences of M & A, and then conclude briefly with some general comments summarizing what we know and don't know about mergers.

Trends in Mergers and Acquisitions

Merger activity in the United States has long been described as occurring in "waves." In Exhibit 1 below you can see depicted the well-known "three waves" of American M & A. (Actually, the most recent merger wave, beginning in the late 70's and extend-ing into the early 80's, constitutes a fourth one.)

The first one began at the close of the 19th Century and ran over into the beginning of the 20th; the second took place in the 1920's; and probably the largest of all (excluding the most recent one) occurred in the 60's.

The recent Nobel Prize laureate, George Stigler, has characterized the first of these waves as creating "monopolies" and the second as creating "oligopolies." After this second wave in the 20's, government intervened strongly to discourage mergers which could increase "concentration" or "market power." The merger wave of the 60's avoided this legislation by creating "conglomerates." This, of course, leads us to ask: What did the fourth wave, our most recent one, create? I believe it created many rich, but frustrated executives who used those "golden parachutes" to descend, mainly into obscurity. (And this might not be such a bad thing from society's point of view, but more about this later).

EXHIBIT 1
Merger Movements

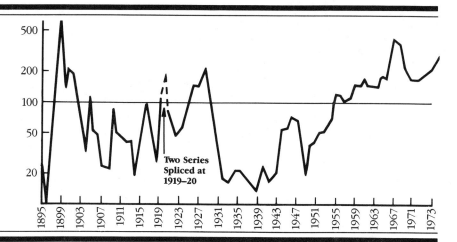

Two Series
Spliced at
1919–20

Not only am I forced to doubt the theories of merger waves, I am also inclined to doubt the existence of the waves themselves.

The appearance of these merger waves led to various theories of merger which were established largely in the 40's and 50's. According to the most prominent of such theories, mergers were somehow associated with booms in the economy and in the stock market. Probably the strongest evidence supporting this theory—although purely circumstantial—was provided by the merger wave of the early 60's, which took place when the market was very strong. And this apparent vindication of the theory then gave rise to all kinds of hypotheses which purported to explain why strong markets and a strong economy would induce such a large increase in mergers.

However, as T. H. Huxley once said, "The great tragedy of science is the slaying of a beautiful hypothesis by an ugly fact." And the ugly fact, of course, is the most recent merger wave of the 70's and early 80's. This latest merger wave is inconsistent with the earlier popular theory of mergers because it came, as you all know, with the economy in recession and with a very depressed stock market. In short, the merger theories elaborated in the 40's and 50's never made much sense—at least not to me. Because if mergers are really motivated, as many have suggested, by undervaluation of stocks or by the existence of inefficient managements or to avoid bankruptcy or to save taxes—if all these explanations are to some extent valid—there is really no reason why these motives will be more important when the market is strong than when the market is depressed. I would even argue to the contrary; that is, when the stock market is depressed, there are surely more bankruptcies than in a strong economy,

probably more widespread undervaluation of stocks (if such a thing can exist in an efficient stock market), and management inefficiencies are more clearly revealed in a weak economy than in a strong one. So I would expect a comprehensive theory of mergers to work the other way. In sum, the conventional merger-wave theory is not only inconsistent with the data of the 70's and 80's, it is also inconsistent with most of the motives for mergers we will hear discussed today.

In fact, not only am I forced to doubt the theories of merger waves that have been offered to date, but I am also inclined to doubt the existence of the waves themselves. From the end of the Depression of 1934–35 to the present, I really don't see distinct waves, but rather (as suggested by Exhibit 2) an almost continuous increase in merger activities which—with the ups and downs that we have come to expect from economic phenomena in the real world—suggests to me that mergers are here to stay for a long time.

Some characteristics of mergers, however, have changed, and they have changed quite dramatically. The trend toward conglomerate mergers, for example, is a significant new development. While only about 40 to 50 percent of all mergers during the 40's and 50's were of the conglomerate type, currently about 80 percent of all mergers are conglomerate. In fact, horizontal mergers have become almost an endangered species because of very strong FTC and Justice Department objection.

There has also been a very significant increase in the size of acquired firms. Acquisitions these days of firms with total assets of a billion dollars, and

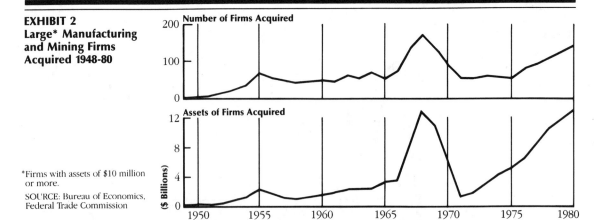

EXHIBIT 2
Large* Manufacturing and Mining Firms Acquired 1948-80

*Firms with assets of $10 million or more.

SOURCE: Bureau of Economics, Federal Trade Commission

even more, are not uncommon. But they were extremely rare, almost non-existent, during the 50's and the 60's.

However, there has *not* been a significant change in corporate investment in M & A as a percentage of total corporate new investment in the U.S. economy. That's a very important point, especially from a broad social perspective. Recently, we heard a call for legislation or some kind of government intervention into the merger process because M & A allegedly substitutes for "real" or "productive" corporate investment in new assets. Historically, corporate investment through M & A has constituted about 20 percent of total corporate investment in the economy. Of course, this represents a significant percentage of total investment. But this figure has not risen much since earlier decades, remaining fairly constant throughout the 60's and 70's.

But, by far the most dramatic increase in a merger-related statistic has been in the size of the percentage premiums over market prices paid to acquired firms. The premium is measured by dividing the price per share actually paid by the stock price just prior to the relevant announcement date. From the rather modest merger premiums of about 15 or 20 percent paid on average during the 60's, the average premium during the 70's has jumped to around 50 percent, perhaps even higher. Individual premiums have, in many cases, been substantially larger. This I find surprising. It is particularly disturbing to those of us who are strong believers in market efficiency. But, again, we will hear more about this today.

So, those are my comments on the historical development of mergers. My principal conclusion is that mergers are really not a transient phenomenon, at least not as I read the last 40 years. It has been very persistent and, except for a few periods of inactivity, steadily on the rise.

And for this reason alone, the great amount of interest in mergers exhibited by both researchers and practitioners is not really surprising. The main focus of the research on M & A has been on the motives for, and the consequences of, these transactions. So let me start with the motives.

Merger Motives

Those unfortunate enough among us to have had to muddle through the merger literature—particularly that of the 40's and the 50's—were probably struck by the diversity and abundance of different motives and explanations for merger. As Professor Stewart Myers has succinctly stated, "There appears to be a rationale for merging any firm with any other firm in the economy." Nevertheless, to provide a feel for this kind of literature (which can serve as background for further discussion), I will offer a quick overview of some such motives.

In Exhibit 3, I have attempted to summarize most of the merger motives to be found in the literature.

Basically, they can be classified into three groups. The first consists of those motives that deal with synergy; that is, those which claim to create real net gains to the merged firm, causing the value of the two firms combined to be greater than the sum of the two parts. The second group of motives are

EXHIBIT 3 **Merger Motives**	**Synergy (Neoclassical Motives)**		
	• **Short-Term Financial Synergy** –EPS or PE Effects –Improved Liquidity –Tax Effects	• **Long-Term Financial Synergy** –Increased Debt Capacity –Improved Capital Redeployment –Reduction in Debt, Bankruptcy Costs –Stabilizing Earnings	• **Operating Synergy** –Economics of Scale –No-Growth in Own Industry –Limit Competition –Acquiring Technological or Managerial Knowledge –Product or Market Extension –Reduction in Risk and Uncertainty
	Target Undervaluation		
	• **Market Inefficiency** **(Economic Disturbances)**	• **Inside Information**	• **Superior Analysis**	• **Displacing** **Inefficient Managers**
	Managerial Motives		
	• **Power Needs,** **Size, Growth**	• **Executive** **Compensation**	• **Insider Trading**	• **Human Capital** **Risk Diversification**

If capital markets are functioning well, there would seem to be little value in acquiring cash-rich companies just to fund investment in the buyer's existing businesses.

premised on the "undervaluation" of the target firm. In such cases, presumably, no new value is created through the combination; rather value is simply transferred from the selling to the buying firm from the acquisition of undervalued assets. The motives falling under this heading are largely possible "explanations" why target firms are undervalued by the market, and thus represent "good buys" to acquiring firms. The third set of motives consists of special managerial motives for mergers, and these are premised on the idea that the self-interest of corporate managers may cause them to take actions which do not harmonize with stockholder interests. I will only say a few words about each of these motives listed here, since I am sure we will return to many of them again and again during the next two and a half days.

Let's first look briefly at the "synergistic" or "neo-classical" motives, which I have further classified into three categories: short-term financial, long-term financial, and operating. Perhaps the most notorious among short-term financial strategies was the use (or the alleged use) of acquisitions to boost EPS by acquiring companies with lower P/E ratios. Such EPS manipulation was prominent, or is said to have been prominent, during the 60's. The assumption underlying this strategy is that the market mechanically applies the buying firm's P/E ratio to the articially increased EPS, thus increasing stock price.

A second short-term financial consideration is improved liquidity. Companies often acquire other firms with excess cash or stable earnings in order to improve their own liquidity—or so they have claimed. But, this motive, like the EPS manipulation described above, seems to run against the grain of efficient markets theory. If capital markets are functioning well, there would seem to be little value in acquiring cash-rich companies to fund investment in the buyer's existing businesses. Presumably, the same objective can be accomplished, and considerably more cheaply, by going directly to capital markets to raise capital.

There are also often tax benefits associated with acquisitions. Tax loss carryforwards may provide a tax shield for the acquiring firm. Also, in cases where the market value of corporate assets far exceeds book values, accounting conventions often allow acquiring firms to write up the value of acquired assets significantly. This increases the depreciation tax shield, and thus the after-tax cash flow, of the acquired firm's operations. Note that, unlike the first two motives discussed—EPS bootstrapping and

cash transfer—the effect of increased tax shields appears to us "efficient markets" academics to be a legitimate or "real" motive: the after-tax *cash* profitability of the total firm increases, and thus there appears to be real financial synergies here.

Turning to longer-term financial synergy, another way in which mergers are thought to increase the combined value of two firms is to increase debt capacity (or, although this is not a synergistic motive, to make use of the target's unused debt capacity). Presumably, the larger size of the combined entity provides lenders with greater protection, thus allowing the combined firm to have a larger debt-to-capital ratio. Also contributing to greater debt capacity is the diversification provided by conglomerates—the fact that the variability of two firms' total cash flows is stabilized (provided the two streams are not perfectly correlated).

Related to the above argument is a much more recent explanation for merger, one premised on bankruptcy costs and so-called "agency theory." Agency theory, in brief, holds that conflicts of interest between various groups—between lenders and stockholders, for example—affect the pricing of corporate securities. To the extent that such conflicts can be reduced (without undue cost), corporate securities will sell at higher prices, and the cost of issuing new securities is reduced. The prospects of companies with unstable earnings series—those subject to lots of "random shocks"— create a great deal of uncertainty for investors, both actual and potential. *Real* reductions in the variability of corporate earnings (and this is to be distinguished simply from accounting "smoothing" techniques) should reduce certainty. Mergers, especially conglomerate mergers, generally result in more stable operating earnings; and it has been argued that this stabilized earnings stream is easier for outsiders—especially lenders—to "monitor" and evaluate. This in turn should result in lower borrowing costs, or perhaps increased debt capacity.

It has also been argued that buying firms can add value by improving the target's access to capital markets, or perhaps even eliminating the need for the target to raise capital on its own. The larger firm or conglomerate can avoid having to resort to capital markets during inopportune moments, thus avoiding the costs of entering and exiting capital markets. Buying firms also may feel they can improve the efficiency of the target's management in allocating capital internally, channeling funds from

Short of preventing bankruptcy or acute financial distress, paying large premiums to diversify out of a firm's basic industries should not benefit stockholders.

less profitable to more profitable business units. And this, of course, can add economic value.

Most of the more conventional, "classical" motives for mergers fall under the heading of "operating" synergy. (I will be very brief here because, as a financial academic, I know very little about such operating synergies, while at the same time I suspect that such motives are probably among the most important explanations for merger.) Economies of scale, for example, was often the rationale for horizontal mergers. As output increases, the burden of fixed costs per unit falls, increasing margins and profitability in general. Mergers were also used to consolidate market power and limit competition. The need to acquire complementary product or market extension has also often been used to justify business-related acquisitions.

In the case of conglomerate mergers, however, where economies were not so evident, diversification seems to be a more important motive. Companies would use acquisitions to divert assets from their own industry, which they perceived to be without much potential for growth, and attempt to branch into others. The problem with this explanation, from a financial economist's standpoint, is that, short of preventing bankruptcy or acute financial distress, paying large premiums to diversify out of a firm's basic industries should not benefit stockholders. They achieve diversification much more efficiently simply by diversifying their own portfolios. And, consequently, they are not likely to pay a premium to hold the shares of a diversified company. (But, again, there will much more about this later in the conference.)

That brings us to the second group of corporate motives for acquisitions—those assuming target undervaluation. The undervaluation of corporate assets was undoubtedly among the most popular explanations offered for the merger wave of the late 1970s. And this explanation, of course, challenges our central notion of market efficiency.

James Tobin and Roger Marris claimed to document large differences between the market value of a firm's stock and the current, replacement cost value of its assets. Under certain capital market conditions, they argued, the liquidation value of the firm's net assets could be considerably higher than the market value of the firm's common stock. In such cases, you could buy the stock of the firm (and thus control of the firm's assets) far more cheaply than by going to the "real" market and buying directly the

machines, land, capacity and so on.

These arguments, to repeat, are premised on an identifiable, exploitable inefficiency in stock market pricing. But there is another explanation for target undervaluation, one which is *not* inconsistent with the tenet of market efficiency. And that has to do with "inside information." The buying firm may have inside information about the prospects of the target that the market as a whole doesn't have. This is often cited as a motive in "friendly" mergers, especially those in which besieged target firms voluntarily provide information to "white knights." So, if the buyer has inside information which indicates that the stock of the target firm is undervalued, then this seems a legitimate motive for an acquisition— one that can be reconciled with the premise of an efficient market.

A somewhat related argument is that the managements of certain buying firms have developed a capability for superior analysis, which means not that they necessarily have inside information about individual targets, but rather that they are somehow able to scan a large number of potential targets in the economy, and have become adept at identifying bargains. But, again, we have to exercise our skepticism and wonder what special abilities allow corporate management to outperform the market on a reliable, systematic basis.

A final explanation that falls under "target undervaluation" is, I think, by far the most important and interesting one—both from a private and social point of view. And this undervaluation is caused by the failure of management to manage assets efficiently. Clearly management inefficiency would be reflected in relatively depressed stock prices—depressed, that is, relative to stock prices of comparable firms run by more efficient managers. In such cases, there is thus an opportunity to acquire poorly managed firms at relatively low prices, replace the management, and improve performance and stock price. The importance of this argument—to the extent that it's really a widespread motive—from society's point of view is great because acquisitions are potentially an important mechanism in the market for re-allocating resources to more efficient corporate users.

This brings us to the third group of motives, which focuses the spotlight on corporate managers themselves. More specifically, it concerns the extent to which managers pursue their own interest at the expense of their companies' stockholders. This one

525

was very popular in the literature of the 50's and 60's. According to such explanations, management sometimes deviates from the classical economic objective of maximization of stockholders' wealth. Instead it pursues private goals: growth, empire-building, power, prestige, and so on.

The forms of executive compensation that now prevail may explain part of this divergence of managerial from stockholder interests. This argument begins with the idea that mergers are conducted in order to increase the compensation of managers (and we'll hear more about this today from Dave Larcker). Another very spicy topic: there is some indirect, and even some direct, evidence (which I will return to later) that one of the motives of managers, at least in some acquisitions, has been the chance to get hold of inside information for trading.

There is one last managerial motive I would like to mention, one which I think is a very plausible one: acquisitions allow the buying firms' managers in effect to diversify the risk that attaches to their own human capital. During the 1950's and 1960's, as I mentioned, one of the main arguments for conglomerate mergers was risk diversification. But as I also said, this doesn't make much sense when one realizes investors can achieve any degree of risk they want on their own, simply by adjusting their own portfolios. But the story is probably different when it comes to corporate managers. Their major asset, their human capital, their reputation, is at risk, and there are no markets in which this risk can be diversified. The only way to diversify this risk is to diversify the firm. And, again, this diversification benefits managers, often at the expense (to the extent the firm pays a premium just to diversify) of stockholders.

Okay, that's basically a quick sketch of some of the major motives offered for mergers, and I hope it proves helpful in organizing the literature, and in organizing our thinking about the subject. Unfortunately, it doesn't really carry us far in understanding the phenomenon of M & A partly because, as I said before, there seem to be almost as many motives as mergers. This reminds me of one of the basic laws of nature, which says, "The number of different hypotheses erected to explain a given phenomenon is inversely proportional to the available knowledge about this phenomenon." While many of these motives seem to be reasonable, they can not all be equally valid for all different merger types, all periods of time, and all economic conditions.

So, what we have really got to do is to tackle the basic question: Can we somehow develop a parsimonious theory or model—that is, one based on relatively few common factors—which retains its predictive power equally over time and economic conditions? This of course is what theory construction is all about: generalization across seemingly disparate observations. And, in order to conserve effort, energy, and time, we would prefer to develop this theory within the confines of established or well-accepted economic theory. We do not want to invent the wheel each time anew.

The prime candidate, in the case of M & A, is really the classical paradigm of the investment decision which states that managers will undertake investments (and a merger of course is just another investment) with positive risk-adjusted net present values, thereby increasing the value of the firm and the welfare of the firm's investors. So, the first question we have to resolve, then, is: Are mergers conducted in order to maximize the present value of the acquiring firm? If the answer is yes, then the exploration of all theoretical and practical issues concerning mergers can approach them as just another corporate investment.

The Evidence

This question has been investigated in basically two different ways. The first we can call the "disaggregated" approach. The aim of this approach is to determine whether certain *professed* motives for mergers have any validity. For example, do mergers lead to significant tax savings? Do they result in large increases in debt capacity? Are there significant operating synergies achievable through mergers? and so on. The alternative approach is the overall or "aggregated" approach. Here the researcher looks at the effect of the merger on the total market value of the firm, without any attempt to ascertain whether specific motives are at work. One simply wants to find out whether the total market value of firms is increased or decreased by merger.

There are, of course, advantages and disadvantages to each of these two approaches. In the case of the "disaggregated" approach—the one where you look at individual motives or arguments for mergers—you run the risk of not seeing the forest for the trees. (The aggregated approach, however, runs the opposite risk of not seeing the trees for the forest.) The disaggregated approach generally uses a classical approach in statistics, one that begins by matching merged firms with a control sample of unacquired firms in the same industry, of comparable size, and with similar financial characteristics. Then, the researcher compares the test variables between the two samples, e.g., profitability ratios, leverage ratios, depending on the motives being tested for. Hopefully everything except for the event of merger is controlled for by this matched sample design. If so, any differences in risk, profitability, debt capacity, or tax savings can be attributed to the event of merger.

Some mildly—and I would say really not more than mildly—interesting results came out of this line of research. For example, target firms were found, on average, to have lower P/E ratios than acquiring firms. And this appears to support the "high P/E buys low P/E" hypothesis, at least in the 60's. Acquired firms, again, had on average lower profitability than similar firms in the industry, which again seems to provide some support for the notion that acquisitions "weed out" inefficient managers. Acquired firms were also more liquid than the control firms. Not surprisingly, acquiring firms were growing quickly relative to similar non-acquiring firms. Another finding is that mergers were usually associated with increased leverage (though again the evidence is somewhat indirect), mildly supporting the argument that some mergers increase debt capacity.

This is all, as I said, mildly interesting. But I would say the most important fact emerging from this research—maybe surprising to some, and even disturbing—is the almost complete *absence* of any finding attesting to an increase in the efficiency or profitability of the combined firm relative to a control group of similar firms. There are a few exceptions. In some studies, they have managed to identify relatively small, statistically insignificant increases in profitability. But there is no study I know of that found a strong, statistically significant increase in profitability due to acquisitions.

Having failed, then, to identify clear synergies in merger, or to come up with strong support for the existence of synergies, we have really no support for the value maximization hypothesis, for the classical economic argument for mergers. The question now is why? Is it because the data those people were using, basically accounting or financial statement data, contain errors in measurement, or fail to reflect market or "real economic" values? Or is it because there is really an absence of synergies in mergers?

Stockholder Wealth Effects: The Market's Response to M & A

One way to resolve this question is to look at an entirely different source of data. Stock prices, in line with efficient markets theory, are expected to provide a more reliable means of evaluating corporate performance. And in the early 70's, as efficient markets theory was beginning to dominate business school faculties, there was almost a complete shift from looking at financial statement data to examining stock market reactions to mergers. The dominance of efficient markets theory, combined with the great convenience of working with stock market data from the CRSP [the University of Chicago's Center for Research in Security Prices] tapes, caused an almost complete shift in research methods. The earlier studies that looked at financial statement data to determine longer-term effects of M & A are now almost extinct. And I regard this as really very unfortunate.

Because research based on this technique of looking at stock market reaction is going to be presented here again and again throughout this conference, I think it's worthwhile briefly to outline the method here, and to explain it's underlying assumptions. So let me briefly describe the mechanics of researchers in examining the market's reaction to mergers & acquisitions.

The aim of this line of research is to isolate the so-called "abnormal return"—that part of a company's stock price change which can be attributed to the market's learning of an impending merger. The first step, then, is to establish a firm's "normal" or "expected" rate of return. This process begins by determining the historical relationship between an examined stock's rate of return and the return on the market as a whole. This is done by using the well-known "market model" to calculate the "beta" of the firm. The beta is then multiplied by the realized rate of return on the market during the examination period (a period of days or weeks surrounding the announcement of the merger) to obtain an "expected" return. Then we determine the "abnormal" return on the stock by subtracting the expected rate of return from the actual or realized rate of return (price appreciation plus any dividends paid) over the relevant period. The abnormal rate of return is interpreted as the market's response to the announcement of a merger.

*Stock price changes are thought to reflect the market's
immediate, unbiased assessment of the long-term
profitability of M & A.*

This technique is a reasonable one, but there are two important assumptions which underlie its use. The crucial one is market efficiency. Reliance on this method of assessing the value added (or lost) through acquisitions is based on strong beliefs in market efficiency. It is based on a belief that information is very quickly, if not instantaneously, impounded in stock price changes. Stock price changes are thought to reflect in an unbiased way changes in the underlying value of the company. They represent the market's immediate assessment of the long-term profitability of the investment. Only given this assumption can you deduce the long-term consequences of events like mergers from observed changes in stock prices.

Some people have objected that corporate management often gains access to inside information during the merger process. This argument was made, for example, when DuPont came in as a "white knight" to acquire Conoco. It is a known fact that DuPont's management had inside information about Conoco. Now if—and these are very big "ifs"— if DuPont didn't release all the information that it had (some people argued that they didn't release such information because it might have encouraged Conoco's shareholders to hold out), then the strong negative market reaction to the Conoco deal may not have correctly assessed the value of the Conoco deal to DuPont's shareholders. So, to repeat, stock price reactions in response to announcements of mergers must be good (or at least unbiased) predictors of the long-term value of the corporate acquisitions to the acquiring firms.

The second assumption underlying this line of research is that the capital asset pricing model provides a good measure of expected corporate returns to stockholders. The basic purpose of employing the CAPM is to adjust expected returns for the level of risk. A key assumption of the CAPM is the constancy of the risk measure "beta"; that is, beta is estimated statistically over a period running from, say, five years prior to the acquisition up to the acquisition, and the relationship is then assumed to hold over the examination period. If beta is either not constant, or for any number of other reasons fails to measure stockholder's perception of risk, then you don't get a reliable measure of abnormal returns.

In sum, then, it is difficult to say whether our current use of stock market data is unambiguously a good or bad method of gauging the success of corporate acquisitions. It is probably the only reason-able technique that we have available if you want to use market information. When using the technique, or evaluating its results, one should be aware of the major assumptions, and the resulting limitations, of the method. As I stated earlier, I think this extreme shift from looking at financial statement data to an almost complete reliance—as I read the literature—on market data is really very unfortunate. Our current stock price methods, because of remaining problems, may not be giving us a complete picture. It is a very useful and important methodology, but it should not be the only one used to investigate M & A.

The Results

Now let's move to the third part of my survey, which is a review of the empirical literature on the market consequences of M & A. Most of the studies use the technique described above, and I intend here only to give a brief summary of the results of a very large number of studies. More specifically, I will try to summarize the "abnormal returns" to stockholders of both acquiring and acquired firm. The testing periods covered by the various studies range from several years before the announcement—sometimes five, six, even seven years before announcements—to very short-term periods, sometimes just a few days surrounding the announcement. (There is some controversy, about which you will hear more today, over what the relevant announcement date is.) And then there are a few studies which have calculated stock returns over long periods *after* the merger. So long-term before, around, and long-term after are the three testing periods.

In Exhibit 4 I try to offer some kind of a coherent picture of what goes on here.

In the case of *acquired* firms, the targets, there is little difficulty in interpreting the empirical findings. Over a long-term period *prior* to the announcement of mergers, researchers uniformly find that acquired firms' stockholders earn *negative* abnormal returns; that is, the stock price performance of acquired firms is on average below the average risk-adjusted performance of the market as a whole. This finding is quite consistent with one of the major motives for mergers I mentioned before, the role of acquisitions in weeding out inefficient managers. So there is some evidence here that acquired firms were relatively inefficient—at least as the market perceived them. And, again, if this finding can be relied upon, it is a very important result for society

Practically all the gain from mergers seems to go to the acquired firms' stockholders.

as a whole. It suggests M & A activity may serve as a valuable mechanism for replacing inefficient managers, reallocating the economy's resources to more efficient users or uses.

Around the announcement date, there are of course very large gains to stockholders of acquired firms. We saw earlier that acquisition purchase premiums over market averaged around 50 percent and, in individual cases like DuPont-Conoco, ran as high as 100 percent. Now these stock price gains, as well as the premiums paid by the acquirers, may reflect expectations that significant improvements in the efficiency of operations will raise the value of the acquired firm. But, it seems somewhat surprising, as we will hear today, that practically all the gain that results from mergers seems to go to the acquired firms' stockholders. Acquiring firms' stockholders don't seem to share the benefits. Some have justified this finding by arguing that because of the great competition in the acquisitions market, selling firms are able to command far more than a "fair share" of the total synergistic gains—of the entire increase in the market value of the firm—from the combination.

When we move to the stock market's reaction to *acquiring* firms, the situation is much less clear, and here we will have to entertain all kinds of alternative hypotheses. The long-term stock price performance of buying companies prior to acquisitions—measured, again, 5, 6, or 7 years preceding the acquisition—is basically positive. Significant positive abnormal rates of return. And this of course can be interpreted in several ways. One interpretation is that these returns have nothing to do with mergers. In fact it could even be argued the other way: mergers are the result of this superior performance. The argument is that those firms who were very fortunate, very successful over a period of time accumulated cash, accumulated reserves. Or, as some cynics might say, managers after a long period of success become so bored that they look for excitement. Hence, mergers & acquisitions. But whether the real explanation is managerial boredom or the need to redeploy accumulated excess cash, the argument here is that the long-term positive abnormal returns are the reflection of great success, and one of the results of this success is venture into M & A.

There are some other arguments that might also be consistent with these findings. One of them comes from a paper by Katherine Schipper and Rex Thompson which suggests that the market reacts not to a specific announcement of a merger, but rather to an announcement or declaration by management that they are going to embark on an acquisitions program. Now such announcements were probably quite popular in the 60's. I doubt whether managers these days will make such an announcement, given the frequently negative market reaction to mergers. But, in those days the reaction was somewhat more favorable. So if this study is correct, then some of the gains to buying companies from M & A might have been captured and reflected in stock prices well before the merger was actually consummated.

Some people claim that the finding of long-term abnormal gains to stocks of acquiring firms before a specific acquisition is also consistent with a successive series of mergers. That is, firms establish a record of being acquirers, and the market reacts in anticipation of forthcoming mergers. (This establishment of a record of successive mergers always reminds me of Samuel Johnson's definition of successive marriages as "the triumph of hope over experience.")

This brings us to the market reaction to buying companies around the announcement of the transaction. And in this case, the studies are not that consistent, and the evidence is much more difficult to interpret. The studies are consistent in the sense that most indicate that the abnormal returns to buying companies' stockholders are very small—though some find negative and others find positive average gains. So, the way I read the evidence, there are no great surprises, no dramatic effects of acquisitions on stockholder wealth.

But this result is subject to a number of interpretations. One mentioned earlier is that most of the gains from mergers to buyers are already reflected in stock prices well before announcements were made. Stated differently, the market had anticipated the event, and thus there was little or no response to the actual announcement. Another explanation is that the market for corporate control (the market in which companies are bought and sold) is so competitive that there is practically no gain (no "monopoly rents") to the acquiring firm. Buying companies expect simply to earn a normal or average rate of return on their investment in the acquired firm. They paid the "right price," the acquisition represents a zero NPV investment and there is no value added (or lost) for stockholders.

Others, however, would interpret the results as indicating a rejection of the value-maximization hypothesis. Corporate managers conducting mergers

I think we are justified in doubting the argument that mergers are done to maximize stockholders' wealth.

EXHIBIT 4 **Stockholders' Abnormal Returns: Summary of Empirical Findings**	**Long-Term Before Announcement**	**Around Announcement**	**Long-Term After Merger**
Acquiring Firms	Positive	Small Positive to Small Negative	Zero to Negative
Acquired Firms	Negative	Large Positive	——

often instead pursue their own interests without regard for their stockholders. But we should temper this hypothesis by remembering never to attribute to malice that which is adequately explained by incompetence. Which means that the result of no gains to stockholders of acquiring firms could be due simply to some bad decisions by managers. For some reason, I hardly ever find this explanation in the literature. But to me it makes some sense.

Now, let's turn to results measured after acquisitions—studies examining the long-term performance of acquiring companies four or five years down the road. Several studies show that the risk-adjusted abnormal rates of return to buying firms' stockholders have been zero to somewhat negative on average. And this also, of course, casts a shadow on mergers.

But there are two other interesting findings which are germane here. All studies of mergers that I am aware of show on average significant *aggregate* gains to both buying and selling firms' stockholders. That is, even in those cases—like the Dupont-Conoco deal—where the buying company experiences large losses in market value, the gains to the selling firm's stockholders appear on average to outweigh the losses to the buyer. The second interesting finding, about which we will hear more today, is the market's strongly favorable response to "reverse merger" phenomena like spin-offs, divestitures, and leveraged buyouts.

Managerial Motives

Now, if, on the basis of the research just summarized, I were forced to make a choice among the various hypotheses about motives for mergers & acquisitions, I would lean away from the value-maximization hypothesis and toward the managerial preferences explanation. The evidence is not unambiguous, and there is no strong support for this suspicion of mine. But, nevertheless, if one looks at the picture as a whole—if you look at the mostly negative market consequences around and after acquisitions together with the positive market reaction to spin-offs and leveraged buy-outs, I think we are

justified in doubting, if not actually rejecting, the value-maximization explanation of managerial behavior in mergers—the argument that mergers are done to maximize stockholders' wealth.

The argument that the private interests of managers prevail over stockholder interests is, of course, not a new one. It was advanced in the 50's and the 60's. But academics, myself included, didn't pay serious attention to these arguments, but rather continued to accept the value-maximization premise until very recently. Our disregard for those early, if you will, warnings about the managerial role always reminds me of Churchill's comment: "Man," he said, "will occasionally stumble over the truth, but most of the time he will pick himself up and continue on." While the managerial line of research is really in its infancy, we have some interesting results—results which Dave Larcker will discuss today more fully.

One expected finding of this research is that we find substantial increases in the size of acquiring firms. I would prefer to describe this increase not as "growth" but as "expansion." My distinction here is that "growth" comes from new investment that provides a rate of return greater than the firm's cost of capital—that is, *bona fide* profitable growth. Expansion, by contrast, is simply an increase in the size of the firm without a commensurate increase in profits.

What we seem to be witnessing in the rise of conglomerate firms is mostly "expansion" or "growth-for-growth's sake." And this of course is consistent with all those managerial motives of power, prestige, empire-building, etc., which come with managing larger firms. Although the empirical evidence makes it very difficult to make a clear distinction between the "managerial" and value-maximization motives, we do know that managers of target firms almost always resist acquisitions. One must doubt whether managers have investors' welfare at heart whenever they do this. When you couple this evidence with those incredible golden parachutes and other benefits that managers provide for themselves in the event of takeovers, this tends to reinforce our suspicions about the role of managerial self-interest in the case of mergers and acquisitions.

If the tools we thought were efficient in exerting control over managers are really inadequate, then what is left to ensure stockholder interests are served?

Economists, of course, can be counted on to devise explanations consistent with their own beliefs for almost any phenomena. Some have made the argument that managers of acquired firms resist acquisitions in order to extract the best bargain for their stockholders. While this may be true of some cases, I don't find this explanation very compelling. I personally think it is really stretching the point. We have the evidence of many cases, particularly in recent years, in which managers changed the by-laws of their firms and instituted all kinds of anti-takeover amendments and stand-still agreements, basically to entrench their own position in the firm. Although studies have failed to detect statistically significant negative market responses to these changes, such practices certainly give you something to wonder about. Then there is some circumstantial evidence of insider trading. Studies by Peter Dodd and others show there is an unusual volume of trade in the stocks of acquired firms prior to announcement—well before the announcement of the acquisition. There is also direct evidence that officers of acquired firms are net purchasers of the stock of their own firms during the three months prior to announcement of acquisition.

So, although I don't regard this evidence as extremely strong, it points in the same direction. There is also evidence that firms in which managers are relatively free from stockholder control—those firms where stock holdings are widely dispersed—engage in many more conglomerate mergers than managers more tightly controlled by owners. And this of course brings us to the arguments of the relatively new "agency theory," which looks explicitly at the conflicts of interest between management and stockholders. Finally, there is evidence of an association between negative stock market reactions to acquisition announcements and the form of management compensation (which Dave Larcker will discuss later, and I don't want to preempt him).

If it is true that managers are often pursuing their own interest to the detriment of stockholders, this is extremely disturbing. The separation of ownership from control in the large public corporation—unless counteracted by effective controls, vigilant boards of directors, well-designed incentive programs, or a well-functioning managerial labor market where corporate executives are given their just rewards (and punishments)—really hits at the heart of the free-enterprise system. If the tools we thought were efficient in exerting control over managers

turn out to be inadequate, then what is left to ensure stockholder interests are served, and thus to ensure that stockholders continue to commit their savings as capital for American industry? If all else fails, then the last resort is government intervention. And while I don't advocate this solution in the M & A case, I nevertheless find the current developments disturbing.

Summary: Winners and Losers

So, let me bring this talk to a close by summarizing what I believe we know and don't know about mergers and acquisitions. Perhaps the best way of doing this is to group all merger participants into two general classes: "winners" and "losers." On the winner's side are clearly the stockholders of acquired firms. There is no doubt about it. Managers of acquiring firms are also probably beneficiaries, especially insofar as they use acquisitions for private ends, such as prestige, diversification of human capital, etc. Some of these managers no doubt live to regret these deals. Managers may be gaining, in the short run at least, at the expense of their stockholders. But the labor market may catch up with them in the longer-term. As Oscar Wilde said, "In this world there are only two tragedies. One is not getting what you want, and the other is getting it."

Society at large is a beneficiary of the merger process to the extent that mergers are an efficient mechanism for replacing less efficient by more efficient managers. But, if the markets for executive labor and for corporate control are not functioning well enough to guarantee that management acts in stockholder interest, then society could be counted among the losers. If the market values of acquiring firms are systematically reduced by acquisitions, then investors will be less likely to commit their savings to corporate capital investment. And the system as a whole may suffer.

Other big winners undoubtedly include investment bankers, lawyers, accountants—and, of course, organizers of seminars on mergers and acquisitions.

Who are the losers? Clearly, the managers of acquired firms who lose their jobs. And, at the risk of placing too strong a construction on the evidence, I think the stockholders of acquiring firms are also losers—or, if not losers, at best unharmed "bystanders." Even if the evidence suggests that they do not lose much in market value, they must lose indirectly when the time and attention of executives is wasted in these huge, mostly futile takeover battles.

Managerial Incentives in Mergers and Their Effect on Shareholder Wealth

David Larcker,
Northwestern University

We have been talking a lot today about redistributions of wealth among security holders in mergers: who wins, who loses. But we have talked relatively little about why managers undertake mergers, and whether they win or lose. In my presentation, I will provide some analysis of management incentives in mergers and the effect of incentive compensation contracts on managerial decisions and, ultimately, on shareholder value.

By way of outline, I will first provide a very general framework for looking at some of the managerial motives for mergers. It's a framework that has become popular in the literature of accounting and financial economics, and is typically referred to as the "agency" model. Next I'll consider the question: Do compensation contracts really matter? That is, does the existence and design of these kinds of contracts influence corporate investment in general and merger decisions in particular? And how does this influence translate into changes in shareholder wealth? Then I'll look specifically at managerial incentives on both sides of the merger. First, I'll consider the managers of the buying firms—those executives making the major investment decisions—to determine whether certain kinds of compensation contracts are associated with the characteristics of these mergers (including the expected profitability, as reflected in the market's reaction to the deal). Finally, I'll look at the managers of selling firms, focusing primarily on anti-takeover amendments and golden parachutes.

Agency Theory

The basic premise of agency theory is rather simple: managers and owners, that is, shareholders, have potentially contradictory motivations. Managers, one could argue, are interested primarily in maximizing the utility derived from their compensation and non-pecuniary items, whereas owners are primarily interested in maximizing stock price. Consequently, the decisions of managers can diverge from stockholder interests in several respects. For example, because managers can leave the firm or be fired (or because they may be evaluated according to short-term performance), managers may have a shorter-term decision-making horizon than shareholders. To the extent that stock prices (and thus shareholder value) reflect the longer-term prospects of corporations, shareholders are likely to have a stronger interest in the longer-term outlook and the longer-term expected profitability of investments made by managers.

Agency theory, then, concerns the potential conflicts of interest between managers and stockholders. It also concerns itself with corporate practices which have been designed to overcome, or at least mitigate, such "agency" problems. One development aimed specifically at this problem is the widespread use of incentive compensation contracts, especially at the senior level within the corporation. The most common of these are bonus contracts, which are generally based on annual performance. Another common form of incentive compensation is stock options, which of course are tied directly to stockholder value. The purpose of such contracts is to reduce so-called "agency" costs by aligning, as closely as possible, the interests of management with those of shareholders.

Over the past few years, the financial press has taken a rather dim view of corporate investment policies. Management has been repeatedly chastized for taking a short-term view of the world, and much of the blame has been directed at corporate compensation practices. It has also been charged that prevailing incentive plans have influenced managers to undertake "unproductive" mergers rather than "productive" long-term capital investment. Also, the

> *There was a significant positive stock market reaction to **announcements** of the adoption of performance plans.*

resistance to acquisition proposals by managers of target firms, together with the proliferating adoption of "porcupine amendments" and golden parachutes, has caused many to question management's service to its shareholders.

But whether, or to what extent, management pursues its own interest to the detriment of shareholders is really an empirical question, one that we don't as yet have enough evidence to answer with confidence. However, we do have some evidence, and I will be discussing that part of this body of evidence which bears on the effectiveness of compensation contracts in bringing together the interests of management and stockholders.

Do Compensation Contracts Matter?

The main focus of my presentation, then, will be on the questions: Do different compensation contracts seem to induce different choices by the managers involved in mergers? And do these choices have any significant, systematic effect on shareholder wealth?

But before I attempt to address this issue, I want to review some evidence which suggests that compensation contracts affect corporate decisions *in general*. I would like to talk about two studies I've done which ask very generally: When companies make major changes in compensation contracts with their managers, do we see changes in managerial decisions—particularly in investment or expenditure patterns? Furthermore, do we see any systematic market response to announcements of such changes in compensation programs?

In the first of these studies, I examined the adoption of long-term contracts, typically referred to as "performance plans." These performance plans generally defer a fairly certain amount of compensation sometime into the future, and this amount is tied to accounting-based yardsticks like growth in EPS and return on shareholders' equity. The important aspect of these contracts is that the compensation is deferred into the future, and the manager receives payment only if certain longer-run targets are met.

In this paper, I argue that if a manager has an important deferred compensation contract, this may lengthen his or her decision-making horizon. Since capital investments typically have negative earnings and cash flows in "early" time periods and positive earnings and cash flows in "later" periods, capital

investment will be most desirable to a manager who evaluates the financial consequences of the investment over a "long" decision-making horizon. Therefore, my expectation was that capital investment would increase for those firms adopting such performance plans. The results indicate that there are substantial changes in the level of corporate investment for the set of firms adopting these longer-range incentive contracts relative to a set of firms not using performance plans.

I also examined the stock market response to corporate announcements of performance plan adoption. Using a methodology very similar to the one we've been talking about throughout the day, I found there was a significant positive stock market reaction to the *announcement* of the contractual change. It was on the order of one percent.

A second study I did looked at expenditure decisions by bank executives when their banks introduced short-term accounting-based compensation contracts. These contracts were in effect profit-sharing arrangements. I reasoned that these executives, because they were now getting part of the profits, would be less willing to make expenditures which would not increase the profits of the firm. And in fact, I find that when banks' adopt such short-term incentive plans, the level of expenditures on "discretionary" (non-pecuniary) items tends to decrease.

Thus, the results of these two studies tend to confirm our suspicion that compensation contracts do affect managerial investment decisions. Furthermore, the market even seems to anticipate the beneficial effects of deferred compensation contracts by responding favorably to the announcement of such long-term incentive plans.

Management Incentives in Mergers

Now, however, we want to ask a more specific question: Do compensation contracts also explain some of the results we observe with mergers? There has been relatively little work done with respect to mergers. Baruch Lev, the chairman of this session, performed a study which attempted to determine whether the reduction of the risk associated with the managers' human capital and "fixed" compensation claims was really an important motive for mergers. Baruch's hypothesis was that if managers are risk-averse, then holding other things constant, they will prefer investments which reduce firm risk and, in so doing, reduce the risk associated with their

To the extent that acquiring firms have paid large premiums over market simply to diversify, this diversification has come at the expense of shareholders.

own future compensation. To the extent a manager is compensated through salary alone, he has fixed claims on the firm which are very similar to those of a bondholder. Viewed in this light, it makes sense for managers to choose the same kind of investments as those which would benefit the firm's bondholders. That is, if the manager has substantial fixed claims on the firm, we'd expect to see him take on investments which decrease cash flow variability. Of course, one of the most obvious variance-reducing investments is a conglomerate type of acquisition.

Baruch's study reasoned that this kind of agency problem—that is, the problem of management undertaking investments which are inconsistent with shareholder objectives—will occur most frequently in companies where managers don't own much of the stock, and where there are no large blocks of stock outstanding such that a few large investors would have the incentive to closely monitor and control the actions of management. Such companies are typically referred to as "manager-controlled" firms. Baruch's hypothesis was that managers are more likely to seek conglomerate mergers (and thus diversify their human capital and the various fixed claims that they hold on the firm) in manager-controlled than in owner-controlled firms.

The empirical results of this study provide support for the operation of this risk reduction motive in corporate mergers. Baruch finds that the operations of manager-controlled firms are more diversified than those of owner-controlled firms, and that manager-controlled firms engage in more conglomerate type of acquisitions—that is, those acquisitions which tend to be diversifying investments. To the extent that these acquiring firms have paid large premiums over market simply to diversify (that is, when there are no expected synergies), this diversification comes at the expense of shareholders. This kind of diversification strategy may account for much of the adverse market reaction to announcements of mergers.

I've also taken a look at this issue in a little bit more detail. Some of the questions I attempted to answer in one of my own studies were these: Do compensation contracts or performance "scorecards" faced by managers seem to influence merger activities and shareholders' wealth? In particular, does the structure of the merger deal appear to be related in any way to the provisions of the buying firm's management compensation contracts? For example, is there any relation between the compensa-

tion contract and the effect of the merger upon pro-forma EPS?

The second major question I consider is: Does the market respond differently to announcements of acquisitions by companies with different compensation contracts? For example, if we have a merger undertaken by a management compensated largely by stock options, do we find a different market reaction than the reaction to acquiring companies whose managers are compensated largely in terms of salary and annual bonus?

I looked at 43 merger proposals, both successful and unsuccessful, that occurred between 1976 and 1979. (About 70 percent of these deals were successful.) In each of these mergers, the board of directors of the bidding company owned less than 5 percent of the outstanding shares, so I would tend to classify them all as *manager-controlled* firms. As I suggested, if there's an agency problem related to mergers as diversifying investments, it will tend to be most pronounced when the management or directors don't own much of the outstanding equity.

I also restricted my sample to those mergers in which there was only a single bidder for the target firm. These were all basically friendly deals. I wanted to abstract away from the multiple bidder problem. The average acquisition premium paid by this sample of bidding companies was about 60 percent. Also, all the acquired firms were either traded on the New York or American Stock Exchange. The average size of the acquisition was about 16 percent of the market value of the buyer. Thus, these were fairly substantial acquisitions.

Well, to add to some of the controversy we discussed this morning, I came up with results very similar to Peter Dodd's negative findings on mergers. I found that the cumulative abnormal return to bidding companies was a negative one percent over the period extending from roughly two days before until three days after the merger announcement. This result, together with the negative results of Dodd's study of the 1971–1977 period, leads me to believe that the mergers that have been done in the 70s are fundamentally different from the mergers done in the 60s. I think that if we looked at the *Wall Street Journal* over the 70s and 80s, most of the *big* mergers have been greeted with a negative share price reaction.

One other point: I discovered from reading *Wall Street Journal* articles about these bidding firms that announcements of dividend and earnings

There is not much longer-term, market-based incentive provided for the managements engaged in these large M & A deals.

increases sometimes come on the same day in which mergers are announced. In fact, in my sample of 43 bidding firms, there were four firms that announced fairly substantial dividend increases along with the announcement of an impending merger. If I remove those four firms from the sample, the negative response to the bidders is much larger than that reported here. The winners and losers among these acquiring firms appear to be split fairly equally. But, on average, the losers lost far more than the winners won.

The Effects of Differences in Compensation Contracts

Let's now turn to the more specific questions about how compensation contracts seem to influence the kinds of mergers we see, and how the market responds to these deals. I have adopted the following framework for classifying compensation contracts: (1) whether they were short term— that is, paying off on a yearly basis—or deferred; and (2) whether they were based on accounting or market measures of performance. Short-term, accounting-based forms of compensation include things like yearly bonus plans, profit sharing plans, and dividend units (although these are not very common). Typical long-term, market-oriented contracts are stock options, stock appreciation rights (which are just like stock options except you don't have to exercise the option to get the appreciation), and restricted stock, which are simply stock grants. Finally, the one that's really new are the long-term accounting-based measures, typically referred to as "performance units" or "performance shares." There are some important contracts I ignore in this study, and some of them are potentially important. They include employment contracts guaranteeing executives a specified salary, golden parachutes (which we'll talk about a little later), pension plans, consulting arrangements, and various perquisites. However, I think the contracts I do consider encompass enough of management compensation to make my results meaningful.

In terms of data collection, I went through about 200 proxy statements to obtain information about the compensation plans of my sample of 43 bidding firms, and found what I think are some rather surprising results. First of all, I found that almost all the compensation for the executives of these firms was based on short-term, accounting measures. Although the ratio of short-term, accounting compensation to total compensation ranged anywhere from 50 percent all the way up to 100 percent, the average for this sample of firms was 90 percent. However, there is an upward bias to these percentages because I valued the stock options at their theoretical *lower* bound (as opposed to a value obtained from an option pricing model). The important point is that there is not much longer-term, market-based incentive provided for the managements engaged in these large M & A deals.

Some Results

Let's look at the preliminary results of my study. The research hypotheses were admittedly somewhat exploratory. It's hard to build very rigorous models to handle these kinds of questions. The first thing I attempted to answer was whether the characteristics of the merger are related in some way to the compensation contract. For example, I would expect that managers would be more likely to undertake mergers which increase pro-forma EPS when most of their remuneration comes from accounting-based sources. I also predicted that as the percentage of remuneration tied to accounting measures goes up, the stock market's reaction to the merger would be more adverse. I base this expectation on the fact that there are a lot of ways to increase earnings without benefiting—and, in some cases, while even penalizing—shareholders. This is the well-known incompatibility between earnings and the cash flows of interest to shareholders. And I think as we move more to an accounting-based type of contract, we may be motivating the manager to take investment projects that are less consistent with maximizing shareholder value.

One result of my study is that as the percentage of accounting-based compensation increases, managers are more likely to use cash in doing the deal than managers with more market-oriented compensation contracts. However, the most interesting result is that the more accounting-oriented the compensation plan, the more negative, on average, the market's reaction to the merger.

These results suggest that, at least for this specific decision, this sample of firms, and this time period, the management incentive contracts may not be consistent with the objectives of the owners of the corporation. This is not to say that such con-

*The more accounting-oriented the compensation plan,
the more negative, on average, the market's reaction
to the merger.*

tracts are globally inappropriate—because, after all, we're only looking at one specific decision made by the manager. Such accounting-based contracts may be great for other decisions, but they don't appear to be great for mergers.

The implication of this I think is clear. The type of contract used to compensate managers seems to be associated with the characteristics of mergers, and also with changes in the wealth of buyer companies' shareholders that result from these deals. I would thus argue that managerial motives arising from the structure of compensation contracts appear to be an important explanatory variable for understanding merger activity.

The Sellers

Let's move now to the other side of the merger transaction, to the incentives and responses of the target companies' management. Here I'm going to confine my comments to studies of "anti-takeover" amendments and golden parachutes.

Anti-takeover charter amendments, also known as "shark repellents," are shareholder-approved changes in the corporate charter, including things like super-majority voting and staggered election of boards of directors. There is a study recently published by Harry DeAngelo and Ed Rice which attempts to explain why these anti-takeover amendments are introduced, and what effect they have on the wealth of target shareholders. One of their hypotheses is the so-called managerial entrenchment hypothesis. They argue that managers propose anti-takeover amendments in order to increase their expected job security and compensation. If that's the case, then we would expect the market to respond negatively to these amendments because they can be used to shelter inefficient managers from the discipline of the takeover market.

DeAngelo and Rice find about a one percent negative stock market reaction in the period surrounding the proxy release disclosing that there's going to be a vote on the adoption of anti-takeover amendments. I don't think this result is statistically significant, although it's hard to tell from their study. However, it provides at least weak support for the managerial entrenchment hypothesis. I think the interesting question, here, is: If these anti-takeover amendments are associated with adverse changes in the wealth of shareholders, then why do target shareholders vote for them? In fact, a recent study

by John McConnell and Scott Linn suggests that anti-takeover amendments are associated with an increase in shareholder wealth. Thus, the shareholder wealth effects of anti-takeover amendments certainly deserve further study.

Golden Parachutes

I want to move on to "golden parachutes," the compensation contracts that have recently been chastized by the financial press. Golden parachutes are simply employment contracts, or changes to the existing employment contracts, that provide substantial compensation to executives in the event their firm undergoes some type of change of control. If you read the proxy statements, they're about that nebulous in stating the triggering mechanism and payout provisions.

My colleague, Rick Lambert, and I have examined the market's reaction to the adoption of golden parachutes by a sample of 90 companies. These were basically Fortune 1000 firms—some OTC firms, but for the most part New York and American Stock Exchange companies. The golden parachutes that we observed were *not* approved by shareholders; they simply show up in the proxy statements. Golden parachutes, furthermore, are not necessarily trivial in dollar magnitude. On average, they are about 2 percent of the market value of the firm's equity (as calculated when the golden parachutes go in). In some cases, however, they're over 10 percent of the market value of the firm. In a typical golden parachute, 10 executives are covered. However, this number ranges anywhere from one up to the 250 executives covered by the much publicized Beneficial Corporation contract.

The traditional view of golden parachutes in the financial press is that they're bad news for stockholders since they deter potential buyers. In defense of golden parachutes, it has been argued that these compensation contracts strengthen the incentives for target management to act in the interest of stockholders (by relinquishing control) when faced with an acquisition proposal. So, at first glance, it isn't clear whether or not this realignment of management incentives is worth more to shareholders than the deterrent to takeover provided by golden parachutes.

Our study of the market's response to announcements of golden parachutes in proxy statements finds that, on average, golden parachutes are "good news" for the firm. For our sample of 90, we find

*When golden parachutes are explicitly part of an anti-takeover package, there is a significantly **negative** market reaction to their announcement in proxy statements.*

that the share price goes up 2 percent on average. (We excluded from this sample firms like Bendix and Martin Marietta, where they put these contracts in during the acquisition period. Obviously that would drive up the share price artificially.) Using a "cleaned-up" sample (which made adjustments for earnings and dividend announcements and unusual proposals in the proxy statements) of about 60 firms, we find the market response to be a little over 3 percent.

The interesting issue concerns whether it is possible to discriminate among those firms where the market goes up, those firms where it doesn't go up at all, and those firms where it actually goes down. So, we attempted to determine whether there was some way of segregating our sample of firms to explain why the market responded favorably to some golden parachutes and unfavorably to others.

We began this attempt to classify the firms by considering three different explanations why companies might adopt golden parachutes. First, we hypothesized that, in some cases, golden parachutes are put in as part of an overall anti-takeover package. In fact, this is explicitly stated in about in about 10 percent of the proxies in our sample. In such cases, where the motive is to fight off a takeover and entrench the incumbent management, we would expect the effect of golden parachutes on shareholder wealth to be negative.

Second, we considered a kind of managerial risk-sharing or insurance argument. This has a sort of ambiguous effect on the value of the firm. By insuring a manager's compensation against the loss which he would incur if his firm was taken over and he were subsequently fired, golden parachutes may stop the manager from doing things to make the firm unattractive to potential bidders. (And we have seen these "scorch the earth" policies.) To the extent that golden parachutes prevent this kind of behavior, or otherwise strengthen the incentive of target management to act in stockholder interests, golden parachutes may be good news for the firm and thus have a positive effect on shareholder wealth.

The other side of this argument, however, is that once we insure the target manager's compensation, we also decrease the ability of the market to discipline the target manager. In that case, the protected manager may over-consume perks or discretionary expenditures, or whatever. And that can have a negative effect on the value of the firm.

A third possibility is that golden parachutes

may signal to the market that a takeover is likely. The argument is that when managers attempt to protect their compensation in this way, this may convey some private information to the market that the probability of a takeover has increased. To the extent the market bids up the price of the firm in anticipation of a large acquisition premium, we would expect this effect of golden parachutes to be positive.

So, given these three possible effects, we attempted to separate our sample of firms into three groups, according to which of these three effects would be expected to prevail. We started by establishing some measures of "takeover risk" designed to distinguish likely from less likely takeover candidates. The variables we used as proxies for takeover risk were the size of the firm (the larger the firm, the lower the risk of takeover), large block holdings of a company's stock by another corporation (as evidenced in 13-D filings), past acquisition bids, and recent substandard performance (losses). We then reasoned that, for those firms with higher takeover risk, the adoption of a golden parachute would be more likely to convey positive information to the market. In fact, we found that there is a positive correlation between higher takeover risk and the size of the market's positive response to golden parachute, but the relationship was not statistically significant. So there's no strong support for the explanation that the positive market response to these contracts is related to the information released about the possibility of takeover.

However, we do find that when it's mentioned that these golden parachutes are part of an anti-takeover package, there is a significantly *negative* market reaction to the announcement of the golden parachute. This is consistent with the managerial entrenchment hypothesis.

At the same time, we also find that the "managerial insurance" or "risk-sharing" hypothesis has the most statistical explanatory power. We reasoned that this risk-sharing effect would be strongest in cases where the golden parachutes are largest (relative to the market value of the firm and relative to the number of executives covered). We find that as takeover risk goes up, management tends to put in bigger golden parachutes—that is, offers managers more insurance; and as we insure the manager more, we find that the security price reaction is more favorable.

To summarize our study on golden parachutes, then, we find that golden parachutes are associated with a positive, statistically significant security market reaction. We also find that differences in the market's reaction to the adoption of these contracts can be partially explained by differences in variables which proxy for different motives. Specifically, in those cases where resistance to takeover is explicitly stated as the motive, the market responds negatively to this evidence of managerial entrenchment. But, in those cases where the contracts seem designed to provide management with the incentive to act in shareholder interest in the event of a takeover bid, the market response is significantly positive.

QUESTION: Isn't there some sort of settling up in the labor market when these executives put in large compensation contracts to protect themselves against dismissal?

LARCKER: That's something we don't know very much about. We don't know much about compensation contracts in general, but we know even less about the labor market for top managers. If we believe that there's going to be some kind of settling up to give managers their just deserts, then it's going to tend to reduce the conflicts of interest between managers and shareholders. This should also help to solve the problem—to the extent that this is really a problem—of overly aggressive managers building conglomerate empires at the expense of their stockholders.

QUESTION: Don't you think that some of the differences in these contracts might reflect differences among firms as to how much of a manager's human capital is tied to the firm, and how much is transferable?

LARCKER: Yes, I think you're right. The story that I've often heard is that firms tend to underpay their managers relative to their marginal product in the early years, and then overpay them in later years. It's kind of an implicit deferred compensation arrangement. But, in the case of a merger, particularly a hostile merger, the new firm has really no obligation to honor that kind of implicit contract. So these golden parachutes may essentially be giving managers what they're entitled to by these implicit compensation contracts that have been built up over the years. This is certainly consistent with sort of the insurance effect that the evidence seems to support.

Summing Up

In closing, I would like to just run through what are probably the most important findings of our work attempting to trace the effects of incentive compensation on managerial decisions (including mergers, of course) and on shareholder value. Although it's probably a little premature, I will venture the following statements.

First, the structure of compensation contracts— that is, whether short- or long-term, accounting- or market-oriented—appears to affect managerial decision-making. For example, those managers compensated on a deferred basis appear to choose to undertake more investment. Furthermore, the market seems to have acknowledged this because it responds favorably to contractual switches to deferred compensation policies.

Second, we find that diversifying or conglomerate acquisitions are much more prevalent among large, manager-controlled firms (those with broadly dispersed stock ownership) than owner- or shareholder-controlled firms. This suggests that the managers of acquiring or bidding firms in M & A act as if they desire to decrease the total cash flow variability, although it is by no means clear that such variance reduction benefits shareholders. In fact, to the extent companies acquire other firms simply to diversify their risks (and pay a large premium to do so), they may be penalizing their stockholders. The greater use of stock options, or some other market-based compensation scheme, might be useful in overcoming the risk aversion of management which may be driving much of this unprofitable diversification.

Third, compensation contracts appear to influence some of the characteristics of the merger. For example, managers of firms whose compensation is more accounting-oriented tend to engage in cash transactions.

Fourth, and perhaps most important, the stock market's response to the acquisitions by accounting-oriented firms has been significantly less favorable than to acquisitions by firms whose managers are compensated according to longer-term, market-based incentive plans. Thus, the adoption of more market-oriented compensation plans may furnish management with better incentives with respect to merger decisions.

Finally, anti-takeover charter amendments seem to have a slight negative impact on the wealth of target shareholders. This provides at least some support for the argument that these measures entrench existing management at the expense of shareholders. But, golden parachutes, except when adopted as part of an explicit antitakeover package, seem to have a positive impact on the wealth of target shareholders.

Divestitures: Mistakes or Learning

by Fred Weston, *University of California at Los Angeles*

A divestiture is the sale of part of a company to a third party. Assets, product lines, subsidiaries, or divisions are sold for cash or securities or some combination thereof. The buyers are typically other corporations or, increasingly, investor groups together with the current managers of the divested operation.

Divestitures have represented a substantial fraction of M & A activity for decades. In the 1980s, some 35 to 40 percent of the mergers and acquisitions reported annually by W. T. Grimm were divestitures by other firms; and this is down from peak years of over 50 percent in 1975 and 1976, when M & A volume was considerably lower.[1] The stock market has responded favorably to these transactions. Companies announcing the sale of assets accounting for more than 10 percent of their total market value have experienced price increases of some 3 percent on average. And the larger the piece sold off, the more emphatic the market's sign of approval.

What are the causes and consequences of this high rate of divestiture activity? Some observers have argued that the high rates of divestitures are incontrovertible evidence of the failure of past acquisition programs. Others have been more cautious, suggesting that the pattern of acquisitions and divestitures reflects evolving corporate strategies that attempt to match perceived competitive advantages and internal capabilities to accelerating changes in the external market environment. Corporate combinations, they suggest, that may once have made sense can lose their justification over time; and thus even acquisitions and subsequent divestitures of the same businesses may, in many cases, be "rational" transactions both in coming and going.

The evidence that I present in this article provides some support for both of these positions; that is, it appears that both mistakes and learning are involved in divestiture activity. On balance, shareholder values have probably been increased in this overall process of buying and selling companies. And, even though acquisition and divestiture programs have not always made positive contributions to the values of individual companies, I would nevertheless argue that such transactions perform an important economic role in increasing the mobility of economic resources—one that is essential to the proper functioning of an enterprise system.

*The suggestions of Kwang Chung, Stan Ornstein and Richard Roll, and the research assistance of Dan Asquith and Susan Hoag are gratefully acknowledged.

1. W. T. Grimm *Mergerstat Review*, 1987, pp. 2, 9, 63. Purchase prices are available on only about half of the transactions, with divestitures in recent years running at about 35% of the dollar value of transactions.

REASONS FOR DIVESTITURES

Like M & A activity in general, corporate divestitures reflect continuing efforts by companies to adjust to changing economic and political environments. Much M & A activity has involved the movement by companies from industries with less favorable opportunities to those with better prospects. Many companies have also tried to take advantage of strengths in their existing product market areas to combine with capabilities in new product areas.[2] A related strategy was to establish at least a toehold in new product market areas. The hope was that initial entry could be a beachhead for further growth and development.

Other firms have felt less pressure to diversify outside their core businesses. For some this represented good prior strategic planning. For others it reflected shifts in the external economic and financial environment that turned out to be favorable for particular industries and firms.

The pressures for overcoming a firm's "strategic planning gap" or "aligning more effectively" with the changing environments have varied from industry to industry and during different time periods. And, like the circumstances besetting firms at different times in different industries, the motives for divestiture activity are many and diverse. Here is a short list of the ones I think most important.

1. *Dismantling Conglomerates.* The 1960s marked the height of conglomerate merger activity. In part it stemmed from "defensive" diversification out of the aerospace and natural resource industries. In part it represented the philosophy that general managerial capabilities could be profitably transferred to diverse businesses. Many such conglomerates have proven to be inefficient combinations over time. Divestitures have been used to reduce the number and diversity of activities that had been assembled in firms such as Gulf & Western (Paramount) and ITT.

2. *Abandoning the Core Business.* The sale by a company of its original business cannot be attributed to a diversification mistake, but to changing opportunities or circumstances. In 1987 Greyhound sold its bus business. In 1988 Du Pont divested its original commercial explosives business, Wurlitzer sold its basic piano and electric keyboard business (to Baldwin piano), and B. F. Goodrich Co. sold its remaining stake in the tire business.

3. *Changing Strategies or Restructuring.* A change in strategic focus may reflect mistakes, learning, or realignment with the firm's changing environments. In 1983 Warner-Lambert sold its successful bakery unit, Entenmann's, to General Foods. In 1982, General Dynamics divested its telecommunications switching business to concentrate on defense business. In 1987 and 1988, Allegis Corp. sold its hotel and car rental units to become UAL Corp. and concentrate on operating United Air Lines, a reversal of a previous strategic plan. Alco Standard Corp. sold off distribution businesses and most manufacturing units after 1987 to focus on paper distribution, office products, and food service equipment. Between 1985 and 1988, TRW divested about $1 billion worth of lower-technology businesses in favor of the high-technology segments of aerospace and defense, automotive components, and information systems and services. Household International sold its manufacturing units to concentrate on financial services. IBM sold Rolm's manufacturing and development operations to Siemens AG, with whom a joint venture was formed for U.S. sales and service operations for Rolm's switchboard business.

4. *Adding Value by Selling into a Better Fit.* Dow Jones divested its textbook business to concentrate on business publishing and regional newspapers by selling its Richard D. Irwin unit to Times Mirror, a newspaper company which was seeking to expand in textbook and professional publishing. In 1986 IBM sold 81 IBM Products Centers, its U.S. retailing operations, to Nynex, one of the regional telephone companies created in the AT&T court-directed divestiture. In 1988 IBM sold most of its U.S. copier business to Eastman Kodak. Such sales may reflect different capabilities, different strategic philosophies, or different expectations.

5. *Large additional investment required.* Sometimes remaining in a business requires additional investments that a firm is unable or unwilling to make. Thus in 1988 Eaton sold its defense electronics business, including the B-1B electronics system, to focus on two other major business areas. For similar reasons, Gould sold its antisubmarine warfare business to Westinghouse Electric.

6. *Harvesting Past Successes.* Some divestitures represent the harvesting of successful investments, often stimulated by favorable market conditions. Here the purpose is to make financial and managerial

---

2. The strategy literature urged them to attempt to do so. See the pioneering book by H. Igor Ansoff, *Corporate Strategy* (New York: McGraw-Hill, 1965).

resources available for developing other opportunities. Such divestitures represent successes rather than failures (or mistakes). Hanson PLC is said to make a business of this activity. Other examples are hotel sales by Hilton and Marriott.[3]

7. *Discarding Unwanted Businesses from Prior Acquisitions.* Some divestitures of the type that involved selling to a value-increasing buyer were planned at the time of prior M & A activity. Such divestitures may have been pre-planned because they represented a poor fit with the acquiring firm. Sometimes such divestitures could be turned at a profit, sometimes they involved a loss that was offset by the good segments retained. Examples are Pullman's sales of Bruning Hydraulics and Waterman Hydraulics to Parker Hannifin in 1988 following its acquisition of Clevite Industries in 1987.

8. *Financing Prior Acquisitions.* A number of divestitures also regularly follow major acquisitions or LBOs for financing reasons. Campeau Corp., which acquired Allied Stores in 1986, stated that it would sell 16 Allied divisions to pay down bank debt. Similarly, after its $6.5 billion acquisition of Federated Department Stores, Campeau engaged in a program of divestitures beginning in late 1988. Other similar patterns followed Beazer PLC's acquisition of Koppers Co. and Maxwell Communications' takeover of Macmillan Inc. Earlier Du Pont, which acquired Conoco in 1981, had sold off $2 billion of Conoco's assets by 1984.

9. *Warding Off Takeovers.* Divestitures have functioned as a takeover defense by removing the "crown jewel" that attracted the takeover threat. A clear example was the sale by Brunswick Corp. of its medical division in 1982 to American Home Products when facing a takeover threat from Whittaker. The proceeds to Brunswick from the sale of the division were $100 million more than Whittaker had offered for the entire company. Ironically, faced with a similar threat in 1989, Whittaker sold its chemical and technology operations.

10. *Meeting Government Requirements.* Divestments are a common requirement for obtaining government approval of a combination. Baker Hughes was required to divest its Reed Tool Co. subsidiary to comply with the Justice Department conditions for approval of its merger. Similarly, in 1988 Santa Fe Southern Pacific Corp. was required by the ICC to sell one of its railroads. In general, the government may require divestitures as a condition for approval when a combination includes segments with competing products. This holds for LBOs as well. KKR was required to sell off some RJR Nabisco product segments that overlapped with KKR's prior holdings.

11. *Selling Businesses to their Managers.* Corporate sales of divisions or business units to operating management are increasing both in number and size. W. T. Grimm reported in 1987 that LBOs and other going private transactions represented "a consistent 11% of total corporate divestitures."[4]

12. *Taking a Position in Another Firm.* Divestitures may be used to finance an investment in another firm. An example is the sale in 1989 by Emerson Electric of 5 units for $149 million to BSR International PLC for a 45% stake in the U.K. firm.

13. *Reversing Mistakes.* Exxon's acquisition of Reliance Electric and Mobil's purchase of Montgomery Ward are widely cited as failed attempts at diversification. Both sales were management buyouts.

14. *Learning.* Successful companies may divest businesses after learning more about them. Merck & Co., whose growth has been mainly internal, divested Baltimore Aircoil Co. and part of a Calgon Corp. acquisition after its experience and review process indicated that the businesses "no longer fit its basic long-range strategy."[5] ARA Services, which grew principally by acquisition, eventually divested a construction management business because of lack of fit. Also it divested a management consulting firm because it found that the business depended on key individuals while ARA was built on systems and controls.[6]

This list of motives for divestitures is not meant to be exhaustive, but only to illustrate the variety of factors that may be at work. Strategic planning, to be sure, is a difficult exercise in uncertainty; and corporate executives typically do not have a wealth of experience in getting into unfamiliar businesses that will serve them well in new situations. Consequently, given the many economic forces and corporate motives driving divestiture activity, it is very difficult to determine whether divestitures as a whole represent "successes" or "failures" for the divesting firms.

3. This motive for divestiture is highlighted in the headline of the February 1989 issue of *Corporate Restructuring*: "A Seller's Market for Divestitures: Competitive Auctions, Multitude of Buyers Sustain High Prices for Corporate Sell-offs."

4. W. T. Grimm, 1987, p. 70.

5. See the presentation by its former chairman and CEO, John J. Horan, "Merck & Co.: Study in Internal Growth," *Mergers & Acquisitions Handbook*, M. L. Rock, ed. (New York: McGraw-Hill, 1987), p. 88.

6. As described by [an ARA executive,] William Fishman, the divested construction management business "was a good business, but not under our management. It continues to succeed under the original owner-management, which bought it back from us." The divested management consulting business was also described as "not a business we belonged in, and it took us about four years to find that out." See William S. Fishman, "ARA Services: Seeking a Common Thread," *Mergers & Acquisitions Handbook*, M. L. Rock, ed. (New York: McGraw-Hill, 1987), p. 67.

IN FACT, THE PORTER DATA COULD ALSO BE INTERPRETED AS EVIDENCE OF
STRONG AND CONTINUING RESTRUCTURING ACTIVITY BY U.S. CORPORATIONS
THE PORTER DATA, RATHER THAN A "STARK INDICATION OF FAILURE," COULD
WITH EQUAL PLAUSIBILITY BE ATTRIBUTED TO A VIGOROUS AND PROFITABLE
INTERACTION BETWEEN CORPORATE STRATEGISTS AND SHIFTING MARKET
FORCES.

ANALYSIS OF DIVESTITURE/ACQUISITION PERCENTAGES

As mentioned earlier, the high rates of divestitures have been judged by some as conclusive evidence of the failure of acquisition and diversification strategies. This view has been expressed most strongly by Michael Porter, as follows:

The track record of corporate strategies has been dismal. I studied the diversification records of 33 large, prestigious U.S. companies over the 1950-1986 period and found that most of them had divested many more acquisitions than they had kept. The corporate strategies of most companies have dissipated instead of created shareholder value.[7]

Porter's conclusion is based on a compilation of data on 33 companies over the period 1950-1986. Each company entered, on average, 27 new "fields" (e.g., financial services) and 80 new "industries" (e.g., insurance) within those "fields." About 70 percent of these entries into new fields and industries were accomplished by means of acquisition.

In order to test the success of these forays into new areas, Porter calculated the ratios of divestitures to acquisitions for each company. On average, these 33 companies ended up divesting 53% of acquisitions in new industries and 60% of acquisitions in new fields. When the acquisitions were in fields unrelated to the companies' existing fields, the rate of divestitures was 74%.

Porter then went on to calculate divestiture ratios for each of the 33 companies over various time periods—for example, the percentage of a company's acquisitions in new industries made by 1980 and then divested by 1986—as a means of ranking their performance. The range of this divestiture ratio among the 33 companies falls between 17% for the "best" corporate strategies and 87% for the "worst," with over 60% of the companies divesting more acquisitions than they kept.

Porter characterizes these results as "startling" and "sobering." But his results are not unexpected in view of the data on divestitures (regularly reported by W. T. Grimm and *Mergers and Acquisitions*) that show them ranging from 35 to 54 percent of acquisi-

tions over the years 1975 to 1988. His data are for "entries" into new fields and industries, which are clearly more difficult than expansion programs. In fact, the Porter data could also be interpreted as evidence of strong and continuing restructuring activity by U.S. corporations. His sample of 33 large, relatively mature corporations made an average of 115 new entries per company during the 1950-1986 period, constituting somewhat over three new entries per year. They were thus far from passive in coping with the challenges of almost four decades of economic change. Hence, Porter's data, which he pronounces a "stark indication of failure," could with equal plausibility be attributed to a vigorous and profitable interaction between corporate strategists and shifting market forces.

Issues of Method

Apart from this uncertainty about what divestiture ratios really tell us about past acquisition programs, there are also some fundamental weaknesses with the way such ratios have been calculated. First, all acquisitions and divestitures are given equal weight. A billion dollar transaction is given no more weight than the sale of a million dollar asset. What if most of the divestitures that enter into Porter's calculations were small and the acquisitions not divested were the larger ones? Or what if a large acquisition aimed at acquiring one particular segment was followed by the sell-offs of all the other segments judged in advance to be unattractive? The resulting divestiture-to-acquisition ratio would be well over 100 percent even though, by any reasonable financial or strategic tests, the acquisition and subsequent divestitures added to the value of the firm.[8]

Second, as Porter himself recognizes, divestitures may play a useful role in implementing successful strategies. For example, he cautions management against delaying divestitures after they have improved an acquired operation to the point where scarce financing and managerial resources could better be shifted to new activities with greater potential for improvements. Many other types of divestitures also represent successes rather than mistakes

7. Michael Porter, "From Competitive Advantage to Corporate Strategy," *Harvard Business Review*, (May-June 1987), p. 43.,

8. A second area of ambiguity in Porter's procedures is that he does not give criteria for defining "fields" or "industries." To replicate the study as a scientific test or to understand what Porter actually did and what his data really mean, we would need to have more objective criteria. The U.S. Government Standard Industrial Classification (SIC) Manual [1987] would be a helpful referent. Porter's illustration of "field" seems related to the SIC Code at the "division" level (e.g., D. Manufacturing); his designation of "industry" could be at the two-digit level (e.g., Major Group 20.—Food and Kindred Products); or at the three-digit level (e.g., 201 Meat Products); or at the four-digit level (e.g., 2015 Poultry Slaughtering and Processing). Without linking to a systematic classification system, Porter's groupings involve considerable subjectivity which could influence his results and make scientific retesting impossible.

or failures. As suggested in my survey of divestiture motives, some divestitures occur after purchases of underperforming or undervalued firms, or after probing new product-market areas with controlled investments. Some divestitures were planned at the time of acquisition because of poor fit or because they could contribute to financing. Therefore, divestiture rates cannot be interpreted as unambiguous measures of failure.

Porter's divestiture ratios, in short, do not allow us to distinguish reliably between those firms that performed well and those that did not. Even if such measures were free of statistical infirmities, how would we know whether one firm's 200 percent divestiture ratio was worse than another firm's 20 percent ratio? Curiously, after laboriously ranking the companies in his sample, he declares the performance of all 33 companies "dismal" and sweepingly extends his conclusions to the "corporate strategies of most companies.""My data," he concludes, "give a stark indication of the failure of corporate strategies. . . Only the lawyers, investment bankers, and original sellers have prospered in most of these acquisitions, not the shareholders."[9]

EFFECTS ON SHAREHOLDER VALUE

The real test of corporate performance is in the returns to shareholders provided over time. Porter's conclusions presumably imply that most of the companies in his sample achieved below-average stockholder returns.

As I stated at the beginning of this article, tests of the immediate market reaction to announcements of divestiture typically show significant gains to the selling firm. Porter himself does not subject his assessments to the stock price test because, he argues, stock price movements—at least over the short run—are unreliable indicators. "The short-term market reaction," he says, "is a highly imperfect measure of the long-term success of diversification, and no self-

respecting executive would judge a corporate strategy this way."[10] Porter's casual dismissal of the standard "event study" method ignores the findings of a vast body of research in financial economics supporting the methodology.[11]

Porter also argues that measuring the success of corporate diversification by its effects on shareholder value "works only if you compare the shareholder value that *is* with the shareholder value that *might have been* without diversification."[12] One could add the even stronger requirement that all other influences would have to be held constant as well. But many factors go into corporate strategic planning processes. Diversification is only one dimension and is interdependent with many others.[13] Given the many dimensions of corporate strategy, it is neither necessary nor informative to attempt to determine the impact on shareholder value of individual aspects of corporate strategy such as diversification alone. Hence analysis of shareholder returns over a long period is a meaningful exercise to which we shall return below.

Third, Porter also argues that the shareholder returns measure is defective because some companies start from a "strong base." Here he appears to confuse accounting and shareholder returns. Porter must have accounting returns in mind when he states that bad decisions can still produce good returns to shareholders because of a strong base. Stock prices, unlike accounting data, are forward looking; they already reflect the existence of a strong base. Thus, poor decisions coming after good performance will cause the stock price to decline in fairly short order—in some cases, upon the moment the bad decision is merely announced. If the company does not continue to meet the expectations of investors, stock returns will be lower than normal. To sustain above-normal market returns requires continuous improvement.

Therefore, it is useful to examine the event-study findings and then to look at the evidence on shareholder returns.

9. Porter, 1987, p. 46.
10. Ibid., p. 45.
11. To characterize event studies as measuring "short-term market reactions" reflects a rather gross misunderstanding of the method and its underlying assumptions. The methodology measures stock price changes in relation to total market movements for samples of firms at different calendar time periods but centered with reference to the abnormal event measured. The measurement of the impact of an event in relation to total market movements is thus best viewed as an estimate of the market's assessment of the long-term effects of the "unusual" event being studied. Random influences are averaged out by the use of relatively large samples, and consistent results are obtained in a large number of studies.

12. Porter, 1987, pp. 45-46.
13. Porter's own writings convey the many dimensions of corporate strategies. In his earlier book, *Competitive Strategy* (New York: Free Press, 1980), Porter presented 134 checklists and checklist-like diagrams—one about every three pages. In his later book, *Competitive Advantage* (New York: Free Press, 1985), the number had expanded to 187—one about every 2½ pages.

The Market Reaction to Divestitures

There are three fairly similar "event studies" of divestitures that all reported similar results: namely, that companies announcing divestitures experienced (statistically significant) 1 to 2 percent average stock price increases (adjusted for general market movements) in the two-day period surrounding the announcement. The effects on the buying firms in these transactions were not significant.[14]

A later, more detailed study[15] found that when the selling firms do not disclose the transaction price when the sell-off is initially announced, there is no statistically significant effect on the seller's share price. But when companies do mention the price in the announcement, the size of stock price effect is a positive and increasing function of the percentage of the firm divested.[16] For example, when the percentage of the equity sold is less than 10%, there is no significant price effect. When the percentage of equity sold is between 10% and 50%, abnormal returns to the seller average a positive 2.5%. When the percentage of the equity sold is greater than 50%, the percentage abnormal return is over 8%.

When the abnormal gains to sellers from divestitures are aggregated, the totals represent substantial dollar amounts. A study by SEC economists published in this journal estimated that, over the period 1981-1986, the stock price gains to sellers in corporate divestitures could be conservatively placed at $27.6 billion.[17]

These gains to sellers do not, of course, resolve our central question: Do divestitures represent the reversal of strategic "mistakes" or do they reflect a valuable on-going process of restructuring? The positive market response to divestiture announcements could reasonably be interpreted as the market's positive response to the correction of previous mistakes. The next issue, then, is how acquiring firms have performed when the earlier acquisitions were made.

The Market Reaction to Acquisitions: Some New Evidence

In the case of acquisitions, there is little doubt that consistently large premiums are earned by selling firms. There is much less agreement, however, about the effects on acquiring firms. But the most recent large-scale study of acquisitions, published in 1988 by Michael Bradley, Anand Desai, aneeeed E. Han Kim, tells a plausible story.[18]

This study begins by dividing M & A transactions into three distinct time periods. The first period runs from 1963 to 1968, the year in which the Williams Amendment gave the SEC increased power over tender offers and which also saw the beginning of state takeover legislation. The third period begins with 1981, when antitrust restrictions were reduced, the financing of takeovers was expanded, and takeover defenses were strengthened. The findings of the study are summarized below:

- Average gains to targets increased sharply from about 18% prior to 1968 to approximately 36% thereafter.
- Acquiring firms earned positive average returns of about 4% during the first period (1963-1967); positive, but insignificant returns during the second period (1968-1980); and negative 3% returns, on average, during the third period (1981-1984).
- When transactions involved only single bidders, the acquiring firms had significant gains in the first two periods and insignificant returns for the third period.
- When transactions involved more than one bidder the acquiring firms had insignificant returns for the first two periods and highly significant negative returns for the third period.
- Among multiple bidders, first-bidder acquirers had insignificant returns while late-bidder acquirers ("white knights") had significant negative

---

14. The three studies are as follows: Gordon J. Alexander, P. George Benson, and Joan M. Kampmeyer, "Investigating the Valuation Effects of Announcements of Voluntary Corporate Selloffs," *Journal of Finance*, (June 1984), pp. 503-517; Prem C. Jain, "The Effect of Voluntary Sell-off Announcements on Shareholder Wealth," *Journal of Finance*, (March 1985), pp. 209-224; and Scott C. Linn and Michael S. Rozeff, "The Corporate Sell-off," *Midland Corporate Finance Journal*, (Summer 1984), pp. 17-26. For a good, non-technical summary of the evidence on divestitures, see especially the last of these three articles.

15. April Klein, "The Timing and Substance of Divestiture Announcements: Individual, Simultaneous and Cumulative Effects," *Journal of Finance*, (July 1986), pp. 685-697.

16. As measured by the price of the sell-off divided by the market value of the equity on the last day of the month prior to the announcement period.

17. Bernard S. Black and Joseph A. Grundfest, "Shareholder Gains from Takeovers and Restructurings Between 1981 and 1986: $162 Billion is a Lot of Money," Journal of Applied Corporate Finance, Vol. 1, No. 1 (Spring 1988), pp. 5-15.

18. Michael Bradley, Anand Desai, and E. Han Kim, "Synergistic Gains from Corporate Acquisitions and their Division Between the Stockholders of Target and Acquiring Firms," *Journal of Financial Economics*, 21, (1988), pp. 3-40.

TABLE 1
SHAREHOLDER RETURNS
FOR PORTER'S SAMPLE
1950-86*

Company	% Compound Average Annual Return to Shareholders 1950-86	Company	% Compound Average Annual Return to Shareholders 1950-86
Beatrice (1950-85)	28.91	General Mills	12.49
Gulf & Western (1965-86)	18.96	RCA (1950-85)	12.46
Rockwell	17.36	Procter & Gamble	12.26
Sara Lee	16.13	Borden	12.05
IBM	15.67	MARKET RETURN	11.96
Exxon	15.56	Westinghouse	11.61
Mobil	15.11	Continental Group (1950-83)	11.23
IC Industries (1964-86)	14.80	General Foods	11.21
CBS	14.79	Signal (1969-84)	10.62
Raytheon (1953-86)	14.79	Scovill (1951-84)	10.61
Johnson & Johnson	14.78	Xerox (1962-86)	10.11
United Technologies	14.38	Du Pont	9.59
TRW	14.22	Grace, W.R. (1954-86)	9.42
3M	14.20	Tenneco (1959-86)	7.99
ITT	13.87	Allied (1950-84)	6.86
Alco Standard (1970-86)	13.31	Cummins Engine (1965-86)	5.66
GE	13.01	Wickes**	—

* Based on CRSP monthly geometric returns converted to an annual basis. When data for the full period were not available from the CRSP tapes, the years provided are shown in parentheses following the company name.
**Wickes was not included because data were available on the CRSP tapes for only one year.

returns, prompting Bradley et al. to conclude: "Clearly, the evidence is consistent with our contention that white knights, on average, pay 'too much' for the targets they acquire."[19]

This detailed evidence on acquisitions suggests that it was not so much that the strategies of acquiring firms were flawed, but that the victors in multiple bidding contests have increasingly been afflicted with what Richard Roll has called the "winner's curse."[20]

Some Evidence on "Long-Term" Shareholder Returns

Porter reports that he measured shareholder returns to his 33 sample companies over the period of his study (1950-1986) and compared them with divestment rates. He notes that "companies near the top of the list have above-average shareholder returns."[21] This statement is misleading because, in fact, most of the firms in his rankings outperformed the long-run market average. As shown in Table 1, the shareholder returns (dividends plus capital gains) from 1950-1986 for 21 of the 33 (64%) companies in his sample exceeded the market return. Another eight companies were within three percentage points of the market return; and only four firms substantially underperformed market averages. These findings, as well as others which break down the period 1950-1987 into smaller segments, are clearly inconsistent with Porter's statement that "the corporate strategies of most companies have dissipated instead of created shareholder value."[22]

I also devised a simple test to examine Porter's

19. Ibid, p. 30.
20. See Richard Roll, "The Hubris Hypothesis of Corporate Takeovers," *Journal of Business*, (April 1986), pp. 197-216.
21. Porter, 1987, p. 45.
22. Ibid, p. 43.

TABLE 2
PORTER RANKING
RELATIVE TO
SHAREHOLDER RETURNS
1981-86*

Company	Percent Shareholder Returns 1981-86*	Porter Ranking	Company	Percent Shareholder Returns 1981-86*	Porter Ranking
Sara Lee	39.92	18	Cummins Engine	18.65	30
Borden	39.21	10	Du Pont	18.59	8
Scovill	34.49	20	3M	17.14	5
Westinghouse	30.27	25	ITT	16.92	14
Gulf & Western	30.03	29	Rockwell	16.42	15
General Mills	29.33	28	Johnson & Johnson	14.94	1
Continental Group	27.12	27	IBM	14.47	7
Beatrice	26.62	13	United Technologies	11.51	4
IC Industries	26.38	11	TRW	9.94	6
General Electric	23.53	24	Mobil	7.52	9
General Foods	23.51	19	Xerox	6.90	26
CBS Inc.	22.67	32	Raytheon	6.71	3
Alco Standard	20.79	22	Signal	5.71	21
RCA	20.25	31	Allied	4.66	16
Procter & Gamble	19.51	2	Grace, W. R.	2.98	23
Exxon	18.95	17	Tenneco	2.68	12

The Spearman rank correlation coefficient is $-.3574$ with a t-statistic of -2.10 which is significant at the 5% level.
*Based on CRSP monthly returns converted to an annual basis. The market return for 1981-1986 was 15.03%.

claim that the most successful companies were those with the lowest percentage of acquisitions made by 1980 and then divested by 1986. In Table 2, I ranked the 33 companies in Porter's sample according to their stock price performance over the period 1981-1986, and then compared these shareholder return rankings against Porter's rankings to see if Porter's divestiture criterion had a strong correspondence with changes in shareholder value.

Using a form of analysis known as the Spearman rank correlation coefficient, I discovered that the relationship between Porter's acquisition/divestiture ratio and shareholder returns, far from being positive, was actually significantly negative! This negative relationship (which is statistically significant at the 5% level) suggests in fact that the lower the ranking by Porter (or the higher the divestiture rate), the higher the returns to shareholders.

I also used other time periods and other samples of companies in performing further tests of the relationship between divestiture rates and company performance. Sometimes the relationship was negative, as above; but in other cases, the relationship was positive or unreliably different from zero. In short,

the evidence suggests no consistent relationship between rankings on divestiture/acquisition ratios and the success or failure of diversification programs or other aspects of strategic planning.

CONCLUSIONS

Divestiture/acquisition ratios do not provide unambiguous evidence on the success or failure of corporate strategies. Divestitures seem as likely to reflect past successes as mistaken attempts at diversification. Some are pre-planned for good business reasons. Some represent harvesting of sound investments. And some reflect organizational learning that contributes to improvements in future strategies.

Studies of the market reaction to divestitures report significant positive gains to sellers and normal returns to buyers. These results could, of course, be interpreted as the market's positive response to the correction of previous errors in strategy. But stock market studies of takeovers and mergers also consistently report net gains to shareholders. The returns to acquiring firms in single-bid takeovers were positive until 1980. In multiple bidder takeover contests, however, the winners may have paid too much, earning only normal returns before 1980 and experiencing negative announcement returns thereafter.

My own research demonstrates that the long-term (1950-1987) returns to shareholders have been well above the average market-wide return for a large fraction of companies with high rates of divestitures. Although such evidence does not *prove* that acquisition/divestiture programs *per se* have increased shareholder value, it should give us pause before accepting sweeping indictments of past corporate strategies.

In short, the data on divestiture/acquisition rates portray a healthy and dynamic interplay between the strategic planning of U.S. companies and continually shifting market forces. Divestitures are an important means of allowing firms to follow their perceived comparative advantages. Divestitures succeed in moving corporate resources to higher-valued uses or more efficient users; and, as a result, overall corporate efficiency increases. Although some sell-offs clearly represent efforts to correct previous acquisition mistakes, many others reflect modifications of initially good strategic decisions that required adjustments in response to changes in the external environment. Regardless of which version one accepts as the dominant explanation for divestitures—"mistakes" or "learning"—the persistently high numbers and values of such transactions constitute reliable evidence that the market system is working, ensuring the mobility of resources essential to the effective operation of an enterprise economy.

Comments on M & A Analysis and the Role of Investment Bankers

George Foster,
Stanford University

Based on conversations with investment bankers, the strong impression gained is that very few mergers and acquisitions reduce the long run value of the acquiring firm. This evening I am going to attempt to restore a balance of perspective by telling a somewhat different story. The story is about the acquisition by Chock Full O'Nuts of Rheingold. It is anecdotal evidence in its more extreme form.

This story is all public record, taken from the annual reports of the acquiring company. It starts off in 1973 with Chock Full O'Nuts having not yet acquired Rheingold. In their annual report, the Chairman addresses his stockholders as follows: "If you look at our Balance Sheet, you'll see that we're in an excellent cash position. We're seeking acquisitions for cash. We're in the midst of negotiations."

In 1974 the Company's annual report reads: "To Our Stockholders: I have quite a few items this year that should be explained. I thought that I could explain them better if they were put in question-and-answer format. Question: Why did we buy Rheingold when other big companies turned it down? Answer: We would not buy it either on the terms that it was offered to the others. Question: How come Standard & Poors listed our long-term debt as $33 million? Answer: They made a mistake. Question: Standard & Poors reported that Chock Full O' Nuts acquired the beer operations of Rheingold for a token dollar payment. Is that true? Answer: That's a half truth. What they did not say is that we got $10 million of current assets for $10 million of current liabilities with the dollar. Question: I also read that the Rheingold losses may break Chock Full O'Nuts. What do you have to say to that? Answer: Chock Full O'Nuts has never had a losing year in its more than 40 years of existence. Since it went public in 1958, it has earned $72 million dollars before income taxes. That's an average of $4.5 million a year. I'm using earnings

before income taxes because we won't pay income taxes if Rheingold should lose what Chock makes."

The report then closes with: "I've saved the good news for last . . . Unlike the gadflies who know all there is to know about a business as soon as they buy a few shares of stock in it, and then travel around the country telling General Foods how to run their business one day and U.S. Steel the next, I find that after eight months I still know next to nothing about the beer business. We needed a top brewery man—desperately. We found him. His name is Robert Spiller. Bob Spiller is a dynamic, astute executive. He knows the beer business. Now that I've worked with him, I'm convinced he's the Joe Namath of our team. With him on it, I've great confidence in the future of Chock Full O' Nuts." In 1974, Chock Full O'Nuts lost $660,000 on their Rheingold operations.

The 1975 Annual Report commenced thus: "To Our Stockholders: This has been a very unusual year for us. We've had some notable successes and also some great disappointments. This has been an outstanding year in coffee. We sold 30 percent more coffee than last year, with twice the profit of the year before. Our frozen pound cake and marble cake are selling well in the supermarkets. Our cake sales are neck and neck with Sara Lee's."

"However, all this went down the drain in the beer business. When we acquired Rheingold about a year and a half ago, we figured it would lose some money in the first year and we'd be breaking even now. Whether it didn't happen that way because of the general economy, we don't know. But it didn't happen. We're still losing very heavily. We have entirely too much capacity for the beer business we're doing. We cannot go on this way. We know that something must be done about it. We are doing something about it." In 1975, Chock Full O'Nuts lost $5.69 million on their Rheingold operations.

In 1976, the company reported the following in their Annual Report: "When we acquired Rheingold we figured that the worst that could happen was that we'd lose what we made in the coffee and restaurant business. We were wrong. We lost more in the beer business than we made in the other business. On the other hand, we're doing well in our other businesses—coffee, restaurants, and frozen pound cakes. As to Rheingold, we'd like to point out that there are still quite a few regional brewers who are very successful. We feel that we can now turn Rheingold around. We've made some changes in the top management of Rheingold. We've got confidence in the new team." (Joe Namath has been benched.)

"We'd like to point out that our actual losses at Rheingold were considerably reduced. That's because the losses of Rheingold offset the profits of our other businesses, and we paid no income taxes since we acquired Rheingold. In addition, the government returned taxes to us that we paid on profits before our acquisition." In 1976 Chock Full O' Nuts lost $8.77 million on their Rheingold operations.

In their 1977 Annual Report they wrote: "We sold Rheingold. Our Rheingold acquisition was a very serious mistake. It taught us two things: never to acquire a business that we know nothing about, and never to take on a business unless it has capable, experienced management to go with it. We now have a substantial loss carry-forward, which is good for seven years. Our aim is to concentrate on the expansion of businesses we know: fast-food restaurants, coffee, frozen cakes, and possibly the nut business." And that's the end of this anecdote.

Now, if you look at the empirical evidence presented by Mike Bradley today, the story of Chock Full O'Nuts may not be as representative as I once thought. But if the message isn't as extreme as that, neither do I think it's as rosy as the picture painted by the investment banking community.

One of the distressing things about the merger literature so far is that we have not made much progress in empirically probing the underlying motives for these transactions—whether it be synergy, undervaluation, managerial motives, etc. The undervaluation issue is especially important because it really gets at just about all the theoretical and empirical problems that modern finance can throw at us. We're trying to use some fundamental data and determine what the intrinsic value of the firm is—independently of what the market is saying the price is. Most of the valuation models we have don't really specify with any level of detail the crucial variables being used. They simply say something like $V = X/R$, where X is some generic measure of income. We don't know whether it's earnings, cash flow, or whatever. And that's not very helpful. Often we use discounted cash flow analysis, but it's not clear at the moment how discounted cash flow analysis maps into some of the multi-period equity valuation models found in the literature.

I often supervise projects in this area, and one of the things that amazes me is just how easy it is to come up with any number under the sun in pricing an acquisition target. And these estimated values range far afield from the current listed price. Last quarter I was supervising some projects on the acquisition of a silver company called Rosario Resources by Amax—a company which had silver interests in Central America and oil and gas interests in Canada. If you looked at the multiples of comparable companies, you'd come up with a price of around $40. But, if you looked at discounted cash flows, depending upon what you thought silver prices were doing (and unfortunately this merger was consummated in January 1980 when silver was at the top), you could justify a price of up to about $120. The price of the stock before the merger was $30, and the merger was done at $75. Students, in doing their project, could justify any price between about $40 and $120. I've seen investment banking reports on this merger, and they came up with a similar range of values. What this means, of course, is that you may be able to hire "experts" to justify any figure within a very wide range.

In terms of managerial motivation, the evidence that Mike Bradley presents is that acquiring firms have a small increase in price. But there are some individual instances when the buying firm's stock price has a big drop at the time of merger. The one we're most familiar with is the case of U.S. Steel, whose stock price dropped by about 9 percent—an enormous drop in the wealth of the company—when it acquired Marathon Oil. Fluor had a very significant drop when it took over St. Joe Minerals as a white knight. Signal-Ampex was a very interesting merger case. Signal came in the first time in February 1980 and announced the merger bid at $415 million. The price of Signal dropped on this announcement. They pulled out of the merger in April 1980. Then, six months later, Signal came back and offered $560 million for Ampex; again Signal's stock price dropped on the new announcement date. My

There have been many cases where an investment banker's most valuable contribution to its client would have been to advise them to drop out of these takeover battles.

question is: What's going on? How does the institution advising the client on the merger react when they see a drop in the stock price?

There's a couple of ways you can approach it. One is to say: "Well, we just gave bad advice. The capital market is telling us that they are far more pessimistic about the stream of profits from the deal." The other way is to adopt the position that the market has irrational spurts (in the short run at least). I have spoken to investment bankers about this. They often tell me that large drops such as 9 percent are due to market irrationality. If you adopt that perspective, then you have to call into question most of the empirical research that has been presented today. That assumption is just completely at odds with the assumptions underlying our research and the inferences drawn from that research.

But, I find the evidence of these studies fairly persuasive. And it confirms certain suspicions about managerial motives exposited elsewhere in the literature and that I have sensed from glancing at the annual reports of companies which have had some merger experience. One case, which I subjected you to earlier, was Chock Full O' Nuts. And I'd like to go briefly through one other here. This is one from Berkshire Hathaway's Annual Report. Berkshire Hathaway is a company run by Warren Buffett and Buffett has a policy that, as a general rule, it's far better to take an equity interest in a company than to make a 100 percent acquisition.

In their 1981 Annual Report, Buffett states: "We suspect three motivations to be, singly or in combination, the important ones in most high-premium takeovers. One: leaders, business or otherwise, seldom are deficient in animal spirits and often relish increased activity and challenge. At Berkshire, the corporate pulse never beats faster than when an acquisition is in prospect." The second one, which I won't give you verbatim, alludes to a managerial desire to be in the Fortune 500. The third one—which is the one I treasure most—says, "Many managements apparently were over-exposed in impressionable childhood years to the story in which the imprisoned, handsome prince is released from the toad's body by a kiss from the beautiful princess. Consequently, they are certain that the managerial kiss will do wonders for the profitability of the target company. Such optimism is essential. Absent that rosy view, why else should the shareholders of company A want to own an interest in B at a takeover cost that is two times the market price they'd pay if they

made direct purchases on their own? In other words, investors can always buy toads at the going price for toads. If investors instead bankroll princesses who wish to pay double for the right to kiss the toad, those kisses better pack some real dynamite. We've observed many kisses, but very few miracles. Nevertheless, many managerial princesses remain serenely confident about the future potency of their kisses, even after their corporate backyards are knee-deep in unresponsive toads." Buffett has a very nice way of phrasing things, but I think there's a little bit of experience there, too.

I have one last comment, and that concerns the role of investment bankers in the merger and acquisition process. My understanding is that there are two roles—one is to give advice on the merger itself, and the other one is to do the transaction (to negotiate the deal, put the deal through, arrange financing, and things like that).

Now, I think the evidence supports the transaction-based rationale as being far more important than the financial advisory role of giving advice about whether, in fact, this is a good merger or not. I'll give a couple of pieces of evidence on that. One is that the fee is a percentage of the transaction. I think this practice clearly puts the incentives of the investment banker in the wrong place in giving quality advice, especially when they approach a white knight. There's every incentive to oversell the value of a company to the white knight. My second piece of evidence is that advertisements by investment bankers tout *completed* transactions, but never *failed* transactions—even though there may be very good economic reasons for pulling out of a transaction.

Consider the case of Seagram in the Conoco deal. If you look at the press's treatment of the deal, and the way it's been described by some of the investment bankers I've spoken with, Seagram and the investment banker associated with Seagram were the big "losers" in that transaction. But, based on what we've heard today, I'm not quite sure whether that's the appropriate characterization. Certainly the transaction didn't go through for Seagrams, but maybe the investment banker said, "Pull out, it's not worth $7.5 billion." But that's not the way it's represented in either investment bankers' advertising or the press. Now, though that's a very difficult thing to document, I think there have been many cases where an investment banker's most valuable contribution to its client would have been to advise them to drop out of these takeover battles.

The Evaluation of an Acquisition Target

Stewart Myers,
Massachusetts Institute of Technology

Over the past two days, we have been talking about mergers in two different senses. At times, we have put our scientific hat on, and tried to develop some theory which would explain what's really going on. At other times we've concentrated on the institutional or practical side. Most of my talk will be concerned with this practical side. But, just for a moment, let's keep our scientific hat on and remember that the list of things we actually know about mergers is pretty short. We know that sellers win; we know that buyers—at least buying stockholders— win sometimes and lose sometimes, but probably not very much in either direction on average. We know that merger activity is volatile. I could go on for a little while, but it still would be a relatively short list. On the other hand, the list of the things we don't know about mergers is probably sufficient to fill up a two-and-a-half-day conference. But, fortunately, not this one.

Occasionally, though, there is a little flash of insight that comes through. I want to tell you about a flash that came to me last Fall when I spent a day as a token academic at a roundtable populated mostly by high-priced merger lawyers, anti-trust people from Washington, and investment bankers who were big in the merger business. This was right after the Bendix-Martin Marietta-Allied brouhaha; and that take-over battle, along with similar kinds of fun and games, was the main topic of conversation all day. I kept trying to put up my hand and say, "Yeah, those are interesting cases but, remember, Mike Bradley and Rick Ruback have shown that mergers, *on average*, benefit buying as well as selling companies' stockholders." But they just weren't interested in the averages. And it finally came to me that, in mergers, the ratio of "noise" to "signal" is very high, and that the noise is a helluva lot more fun. All of the things that make Bendix interesting are noise and not signal. They're idiosyncratic things that happen in a particular case, once people get into it, and once people start trying to win.

As we move back to the subject of this talk and take the manager's point of view, I think that the lesson about noise and signal is really very important. If we pose the problem as one of valuing a merger candidate, what you want to do is find the signal and avoid the noise. The great danger is that you start out trying to be rational and end up as a noisemaker. What you'd like to do is get a net reduction in noise, but I'm afraid that some analyses lead to a net increase. People start out trying to be rational but they end up making mistakes in the analysis; they end up getting carried away in the heat of the battle, and they lose the kind of rationality, the kind of power, that financial analysis can bring to this kind of a problem. As Pogo used to say, "We've met the enemy and he is us."

Now if I were faced with the problem of evaluating a merger candidate, armed with that warning, armed with the idea that I wanted to do everything possible to make sure that I don't end up creating more noise than I eliminate, I would want to arm myself with some pretty clear rules. I would want to impose some discipline on myself. I would want to set up a structure that ensures that I ask the right questions. And I think that's the secret of it all: ask the right questions, don't make mistakes, and get the answer approximately right.

I'm going to start out by talking about how to define benefits and costs. That may seem to be a pedestrian thing to do, but I personally think it's critical. Because if you define the benefits and costs correctly, you end up asking the right questions. Next, I will talk about how to *value* the benefits that may come out of a merger. The main point I'm making here is that the benefits, the incremental cash flows, that come out of merger are of different types. The stream is not just one pure flow, but a mixture of different flows; and the best way to value those flows is to look at the different types and try to value them separately. The phrase that my colleague Don Lessard has been using lately is "valuation by components." That is, you break up the total stream into similar pieces, and then evaluate each of the pieces

If you assume that the valuation of a merger target is simply another discounted cash flow calculation, you're effectively ignoring some very valuable information.

separately. When you do break them up, you will see that the evaluation techniques you use for each of these three categories is different.

The Benefits and Costs of Merger

The first thing, then, is to define benefits and costs. Let's begin with a simple illustration, and suppose that a Firm A, which has a value V_A, wants to acquire a Firm B, with a value V_B. I want to define the benefits of the merger as the *gain in value from putting these two firms together*. In other words, I'm going to compare the value of the combined firm, V_{AB}, with the sum of what the two firms are worth separately. That difference is what we normally think of as the present value of expected synergy—the value of whatever it is that makes the two firms worth more together than apart.

If we define the benefit purely in terms of the expected synergy, then we have to define the cost as the *value given up by A's shareholders to B's shareholders*. I would measure this economic cost as the price paid for B minus V_B, where V_B is what the target is worth as a separate organization. For example, if it is a merger for cash, you would simply take the amount of cash and subtract what you think B is worth standing alone.

It is possible, of course, that A could pay less than the value of B (if B were significantly undervalued) to acquire its assets. In such a case, even if the expected gains from synergy were zero, we could still have a rationale for a merger. That is, even if the firms are not worth more together than apart, A's stockholders can still come out ahead if you're able to strike a deal at B's expense, get B for less than it's worth. In this case, the "cost" of the merger would be negative.

Let me pause here to say that my definitions and classifications of benefits and costs probably seem to complicate things needlessly. So let me explain why I like to do it this way. First of all, on the benefits side, the exercise of calculating the benefits from merger is important because it forces management to ask the right question. It forces them to ask whether the two firms really are worth more together than apart. It forces you to look at the synergy "incrementally," so to speak; it forces you to identify the addition to economic value.

For example, let's suppose that the rationale for the merger is that the firm wants to enter a new business and believes it may be cheaper to do so by buying a going concern rather than starting from scratch. If we define and segregate the expected benefits this way, it more or less forces the manager to ask, "How much would it cost us to enter that new line of business from scratch? If we went ahead with the merger and bought a going concern, how much more would we have to put into that going concern to get where we want to be? How much will we end up saving by buying the going concern?"

The second reason for recommending this approach is that it takes the existing values of the firm as a starting point for the analysis. It's often said that merger analysis is just another capital investment problem. In a sense that's absolutely true. But I personally don't like to say that because I think it gives the wrong impression. Merger analysis is different from standard capital budgeting in at least one very important way. The market gives you starting values for the pieces. And if you assume that the valuation of a merger target is simply another discounted cash flow calculation, you're effectively ignoring some very valuable information.

In fact, this point is so important that I'm going to digress even a little further on it. One of the problems with the MBAs that we send out into the world is their almost Pavlovian reliance on discounted cash flow. You tell them, "How much is this worth?" And they say, "Aha, value equals discounted cash flow. Let's project the cash flows. Tell me what the beta is, tell me what the discount rate is. Calculate NPV. Stop." There are lots of cases in which that's the worst thing you can do, lots of cases where you should try to restrict the application of discounted cash flows to only those parts of the problem where you really need it.

Let me give you a trivial example. Let's suppose that we were told that gold had been discovered (and only we knew this) under some piece of Weyerhaeuser timberland. And that we're sort of scribbling around in the back room of some investment banking house, trying to figure out what the value of Weyerhaeuser will be when news of that gold discovery comes out.

Now there's two different basic approaches you could take. One approach (and this is the one I have in mind when I think of the Pavlovian reliance on discounted cash flow) would be just to start from scratch and say, "Okay, the problem is to value Weyerhaeuser, which happens to have this gold deposit." So you start with an analysis of the lumber business and the paper business and everything else they do.

You try to forecast capital expenditures, forecast everything under the sun, including how much it's going to take to develop the gold mine, how many ounces you're going to get out of it, etc. In so doing, you come up with some forecast of free cash flow for Weyerhaeuser. Finally you discount these cash flows using risk-adjusted estimates of cost of capital, and you come up with a number. Let's call that the "start from scratch" approach.

The second approach would be to start with what Weyerhaeuser is actually worth, which we can look up in the paper, and then just do an incremental analysis of the gold business. As a matter of fact, we might not even have to do a discounted cash flow analysis of how much that gold deposit is worth. We might be able get people who are really expert in the gold business to say, "With these chemical characteristics, that depth, and so on, we know that people in general are willing to pay so many dollars per ounce of recoverable gold," and thereby come up with a number in a process that doesn't ever use a discount rate. In any event, if we did use discounting and a discount rate, we'd apply it to the gold deposit separately and we'd add that to the observed market value of Weyerhaeuser. I call that the "incremental" approach.

Now which do you think would be likely to give you more accurate answers, the "incremental" approach or the "start from scratch" approach? Most of you, I hope, would vote for the incremental approach. It seems to me that there are really two separate issues. One, what is that gold deposit worth? We can think of the gold deposit as analogous to the value of synergy in the evaluation of an acquisition target. The second question would be: Is the market making a mistake about Weyerhaeuser?

The purpose of my approach is to separate those two questions. If the market is indeed making a mistake about Weyerhaeuser, and we're going to take it over, it would be appropriate to look at that when we're trying to figure out the cost of the takeover.

What I see happen more often than I'd like, however, is the situation where people just merge these two questions. Suppose we're going to take over Weyerhaeuser, and we make no attempt to separate these two issues. Essentially what you're doing is just to "start from scratch" in valuing the company. You throw in the analysis of the synergy together with the analysis of whether the market is right about Weyerhaeuser. Trouble is, you're going to make random errors in analyzing what Weyerhaeuser is worth

as a separate business. Since that separate business is so much bigger than our gold deposit, or so much bigger than the synergy we might get out of a merger, your estimate of the incremental value of the gold deposit to Weyerhaeuser is going to be "swamped" by the errors in analyzing Weyerhaeuser as it exists.

To repeat, then, my suggested approach is designed to force people to focus on the synergies first, to focus on the incremental benefits, and then weigh those benefits against the incremental costs of the deal.

Valuing the Benefits of Merger

Let's now talk for a while about valuing the benefits. I'm not going to go down a list of the sources of possible merger benefits. Instead I'm just going to give you three possible motives to illustrate the threefold classification of cash flow benefits that I think can be useful in merger analysis.

Let's suppose that your motive for a merger is to make use of a tax-loss carryforward you couldn't use otherwise. A good example of this is one of my favorite companies, Penn Central, which is now a healthy, reorganized company. It is sitting with about a billion dollars of tax-loss carryforwards. To nobody's surprise, Penn Central has been out shopping for companies that are paying lots of taxes.

If that's the benefit you're seeking, tax savings, then you have a relatively simple problem in valuation. Tax savings generally turn out to be relatively safe, nominal flows. I don't mean to imply always, but when you think of something like the cash benefit of a depreciation tax shield you could not otherwise use, that is a relatively safe, nominal flow. I am calling such expected flows "debt equivalents," and such relatively safe, relatively certain nominal flows are fairly easy to value. If such flows are an important source of value in a prospective merger, they should be split off, put in a separate category.

The next category of merger benefits, operating cash flows, might come from, say, economies of scale. If there are economies of scale, the synergy benefits generated would be reflected in production cost savings. Those cost savings are real flows subject to business risks, and it's these kinds of uncertain or risky flows that we want to use our standard discounted cash flow technique to value.

A third motive might be growth opportunities provided by merger that you couldn't get otherwise: some intangible, some strategic advantage. Such opportunities do not promise a cash flow of the same kind that comes out of an established product or an established business. Instead, these growth opportunities are contingent on a lot of things and, in a rough way, have many of the qualities of options. The inadequacy of DCF becomes especially apparent in cases offering "real" options like these. My experience is that when people try to use discounted cash flow to value these kinds of intangible assets, these kinds of contingent flows, they generally don't get it right. They don't get it right for the same reason that you wouldn't get very far if you naively tried to value a call option using a discounted cash flow approach.

Valuing the Debt Equivalents

So what I propose to do now, in the next 10 or 15 minutes, is to go quickly through each category and just make a few comments. Let's take the "debt equivalent" flows first. If you really do have a flow that's safe and nominal (by "safe" we don't mean absolutely certain, but roughly as predictable as the payment of interest on a corporate bond), then you would simply discount that flow at the after-tax borrowing or lending rate. Whether you use the borrowing or lending rate depends upon exactly which question you ask, and I'll return to that shortly. The rationale is this: let's suppose that we have a safe, nominal inflow—cash coming in as a result, say, of being able to use a depreciation tax shield or investment tax credit that we would not otherwise be able to use. We could ask: How much could the firm borrow today if it used that inflow for debt service? The answer to that question can be obtained by discounting that inflow at the company's after-tax borrowing rate. It's as simple as that.

We could also ask the question in a slightly different way. How much would I have to spend to get this same inflow if I wanted to lend money to do it? In a way the logic is equivalent. You're simply changing the base point that you do your calculation from. In the first case, you're assuming you have the flow and are asking, "How much could I cash it in for?" In the second case you're thinking of the reproduction cost, in a sense, of that cash flow. If the cash flow was safe, nominal, but maybe a little bit risky, then this second one might be the more appropriate method. This way you could assume, "Well, I'll lend it with the same degree of risk as the cash flow itself." So, depending upon how you ask

the question, you could use either the after-tax borrowing or the after-tax lending rate to value the expected inflows.

Now, suppose instead we wanted to value an outflow. Again you could ask the question in two ways. You could ask, "How much would I have to set aside today to cover the outflow?" In this case, it would be like having a liability and then setting up a sinking fund or an escrow account to—I believe the word is—"defease" the liability. In other words, just to cancel it out so you don't have to worry about it any more. In that instance, you'd end up calculating the present value of that outflow using the after-tax lending rate. On the other hand, you could ask, "How much could I borrow today if the outflow were available for debt service?" In that case you'd think about it in terms of a borrowing rate.

This last question, you may recognize, is exactly the logic that people use to analyze financial leases. If you're thinking about signing a lease contract, you want to calculate the value of the cash obligations, of that series of future outflows to which you're obligated if you sign. Then you say to yourself, "Suppose I don't sign the lease contract. How much could I borrow today if those flows were available for debt service?" In leasing terminology, that amount is called the "equivalent loan." Now the rule in leasing is that, with a given set of future cash obligations, if you could borrow more by an equivalent loan through regular channels than you could get with a financial lease, then you might as well borrow. On the other hand, if the lease is giving you more money up front than you could get through regular channels, given the same future outflows, then you take the lease.

Valuing Operating Flows

This sort of analysis breaks down when flows get risky, because we can't set up a clean, hypothetical transaction to either cash in the future value or to cover it in some way by borrowing or lending. This leads to my next topic: the evaluation of risky, operating cash flows. What do you do there? Well, that's the hard one. We know just enough about the problem to make it complicated. I'm not going to go into all the complications, but I thought I'd offer a few observations.

The first tip I'd have is that managers don't always have a very good sense of what normal rates of return really are. You hear the most outlandish numbers quoted as cost of capital estimates. So, if any of

Series	Arithmetic Means of Annual Returns	Standard Deviation of Annual Returns
Common Stocks	11.4	21.9
Small Stocks	18.1	37.3
Long-Term Government Bonds	3.1	5.7
Long-Term Corporate Bonds	3.6	5.6
US Treasury Bills	3.1	3.1
Consumer Price Index	3.0	3.1
Risk Premia on Common Stocks	8.3	22.0
Maturity Premia on Long-Term Gov't. Bonds	0.2	6.5
Default Premia on Long-Term Corp. Bonds	0.5	3.2
Real Interest Rates	0.1	4.5

Source: Roger G. Ibbotson and Rex A. Sinquefield, *Stocks, Bonds, Bills, and Inflation: The Past and the Future*, 1982 Edition, Financial Analysts Research Federation, Charlottesville, VA.

your companies are thinking about going on a program of buying other companies, one of the first things I think you ought to do is to educate yourself about what's a reasonable required rate of return on corporate investment.

Fortunately, we do have some useful historical information on corporate rates of return. I'm going to show you two sets of charts. The first one, which is probably familiar to a lot of people, comes from Roger Ibbotson and Rex Sinquefield's computations of rates of returns on corporate stocks, bonds, and government bonds and bills.

The only way you're going to get a reliable estimate of normal rates of return from historical evidence is to look at a very long time period. Ibbotson and Sinquefield's results are based on returns that go back to 1926 and run up through 1981. Over this period, the mean risk premium on common stocks (their average excess return over risk-free Treasury bills) has been 8.3 percent. If you calculate this premium over the post-war period alone—which many people are more comfortable with—you get virtually the same answer. If you do it for much shorter periods, you get answers all over the place. But these have no statistical significance.

To get an estimate of normal, *nominal* rates of return on common stocks at any given time, it's not at all a bad rule of thumb to take this historical risk premium and add it to some measure of the current risk-free rate of interest. For example, let's suppose we want to know what investors expect today to earn on a market portfolio of common stocks. Presumably we'd want to take advantage of our knowledge of what interest rates are today. The risk-free rate of

interest today [March 23, 1983] is about 10 percent. That's above current Treasury bill yields, but because I'm assuming we'd be using this number to evaluate investments promising longer-lived cash flows, I'm using a medium-term government obligation instead.

So, you've got a 10 percent risk-free rate plus about 8 percent as a general market-wide risk premium. That gives you a normal or expected rate of return on common stocks of about 18 percent. And I don't think that's a bad number. The reason I'm giving you these numbers, again, is that people quote numbers like 30 percent without thinking about it. The Ibbotson-Sinquefield averages are a kind of antidote to people who throw crazy numbers around.

But there are a few intermediate steps before these data can be applied directly as a hurdle rate in merger analysis. The stock market returns reflected in Ibbotson and Sinquefield's numbers are computed using the Standard & Poor's composite index. Thus, the 8 percent risk premium I just showed you would apply only to assets with the same risk as the average company trading in the stock market. Also, we know that this number does not simply reflect operating or business risk. Because companies in the market on average have debt, that market risk premium of 8 percent also reflects some financial risk.

Now, when you're evaluating a merger candidate, and you want to establish the minimum required rate of return on your investment, you want to begin by looking at business risk alone. You want to look only at what's coming out of the *operations* of the company, and exclude the effects of financing. So as a first step we want to ask: how do you remove

TABLE 2 **Long Run After-Tax Real Rates of Return on Capital**	National Income Accounts	1926–1981	1946–1981
	All Nonfinancial Corporations (NCFs).	6.5%	6.7%
	All NFCs; Assets expanded to include land and net noninterest-beraring monetary liabilities.	——	5.2%
	All manufacturing corporations	——	7.7%
	Capital Market Data		**1947–1981**
	All NCFs	——	5.8%
	All manufacturing	——	8.7%

Source: D.M. Holland and S.C. Myers, "Profitability and Capital Costs for Manufacturing Corporations and all Nonfinancial Corporations," *American Economic Review*, May 1980. Averages updated through 1981.

the effect of financial risk from the observed market risk premium? One way you can try to do that is by constructing a *portfolio* of all the securities of U.S. corporations, stocks and bonds, and then calculate the average rate of return earned on that portfolio over a long period of time. You take all the securities issued to finance corporate assets. The return on that portfolio has to be equal to the return on those assets from the point of view of the investors who hold those assets by holding corporate securities.

Dan Holland and I have constructed such a portfolio. Here are the numbers you get over the post-war period. From 1946–1981, the mean *real* rate of return on the securities of all non-financial corporations was 5.8 percent. This number, again, is a weighted average of rates of return on corporate bonds and corporate stocks, where the weightings are designed to get a portfolio which matches, as closely as possible, the underlying assets of the companies. If we split out the manufacturing corporations from the entire sample, you get a number that's 2 to 3 percent points higher, about 8.7 percent. (Incidentally, the reason why the manufacturing corporations appear to have a higher rate of return is that they're riskier. Their profits are much more sensitive to the business cycle than the profits of the larger aggregate, which includes not just manufacturing, but industries like utilities and retail trade, transportation, services, and so on.)

So, if you take 6 percent as a good estimate of the normal *real* rate of return on corporate assets in the aggregate, then to get the *nominal* rate of return today you'd have to add your own long-term forecast of inflation—say, 6 to 7 percent? If it's 6 to 7 percent, you are talking today about an expected nominal rate of return on assets of 12 to 13 percent for the average company—and, say, 15 percent for the average manufacturing firm.

In addition to our calculations, and Ibbotson and Sinquefield's data, we also have one other source of data on historical corporate rates of return available to us. This is the National Income Accounts, which are compiled by the Department of Commerce. Using all its elaborate machinery, the Department of Commerce has calculated after-tax *accounting* rates of return (on an inflation-adjusted basis) for all non-financial corporations going back to 1926.

Let me just mention some of these numbers. Over the period 1926–1981, the average real rate of return (after corporate taxes) on assets for all non-financial corporations has been about 6.5 percent. Over the post-war period, that number was 6.7 percent. These results are actually a little bit high because the published definition of capital does not include things like land and net trade credit—assets necessary to run a business, but which for some historical reason are not included in capital stock as the Department of Commerce measures it. To adjust for this problem, Dan Holland and I got some approximate estimates of the value of land, of net trade credit, and of non-interest-bearing monetary liabilities, and we added that extra capital to the denominator in the rate of return calculation. This addition to the capital base tends to knock the estimates down by about one-and-a-half percent.

While these estimates may be somewhat controversial, the important thing here is that we have two numbers (6.7 and 5.2 percent) which bracket, and thus reinforce, the 6 percent estimate we get from capital market data. If we do the same calculation for just manufacturing corporations, we get about 7.7 percent, which is close to the estimate of 8.7 percent we got from capital market data. (But that calculation does not include the land and non-interest bearing monetary liabilities, so that's undoubtedly an overstatement.) But, again, what I find

Anytime somebody leverages up an asset, but then doesn't also adjust its discount rate, the investment always looks better than it is.

very interesting is that if you compare these two completely independent sets of data, you get just about the same number. In other words, somebody who wanted to judge normal, inflation-adjusted corporate rates of return by measuring aggregate profitability as an accountant would measure it would come out somewhere around 6 percent for all corporations, and 7 to 8 percent for the smaller aggregate of manufacturing corporations. When you do the same calculation using returns on stocks and bonds, again you get roughly 6 to 8 percent real returns.

So, if somebody asked me, "Quick, what is the cost of capital?," I would say that, on the basis of historical evidence, the average, overall *real* cost of capital seems to be 6 to 8 percent, depending on the risk of the assets you're talking about. Obviously there are some assets in the economy which are safer than average and, therefore, would require less than 6 percent. Some no doubt are much riskier, and they should be required to return more than 8 percent.

But, having said this, let me just mention some of the other problems we run into in arriving at required rates of return for specific investments. Even if you have some sense about what normal rates of return are—whether from Ibbotson and Sinquefield, current interest rates, or the accounting rates of return I just showed you—you still have to worry about adjusting for risk. And there, of course, you can get very fancy. You can try to compute industry betas. You can try to look at the cyclicality or variance of the asset's return, and thus try to get proxies for the betas of the assets you're looking at. But, even if you do know how to measure and adjust for risk, you've got a variety of risk-return theories to choose among. You could use the standard capital asset pricing model (CAPM), or maybe some so-called empirical capital asset pricing model that adjusts for the fact that low beta stocks have done better, at least over the very long run, than the standard CAPM would have predicted. You could, I suppose, go to some arbitrage pricing theory, although I don't think that's much help at this point in this kind of calculation. And we could also end up arguing about "small firm" effects; that is, do small deserve a higher cost of capital? We can't answer any of these questions with complete assurance at this point.

Another thing I think is important in merger analysis is not to confuse return on equity with return on assets. One famous case where I understand

this happened was Kennecott's takeover of Carborundum. According to some of the documents that later came out publicly, one of the things that Kennecott's analysts did was this: they had internal forecasts for Carborundum which showed cash flows, earnings, etc. over a 10-year period. But, before they actually did the present value calculation, they assumed that after Kennecott bought Carborundum, Carborundum would borrow (I believe it was) $100 million. Carborundum was then assumed to take the cash thus raised, and pay it back as a special dividend to Kennecott, the new parent. For purposes of calculating NPV, that dividend was assumed to reduce Kennecott's investment in Carborundum. They then applied a standard discount rate to get an NPV and they got what seemed to be a number justifying the price they paid.

But what they did in effect was to lever up the cash flow without raising the discount rate to reflect the increased leverage. Kennecott was really borrowing the money to buy the business. Thus, they were looking at a more leveraged asset than was there before. In so doing, they were jacking up the promised rate of return, but they forgot to jack up the discount rate. And therefore the investment looked good. It was a kind of "magic in leverage" argument. Anytime somebody leverages up an asset, but then doesn't also adjust its discount rate, the investment always looks better than it is. Simple things like that can turn out to be very important.

Valuing Real Options

I'm getting a little bit short on time, so let me skip back and make a comment or two on the third category of benefits: the evaluation of growth opportunities. This is the really tough one. The reason it's tough is that typically when a decision about a merger has to be made, after you've gone through and valued all the debt equivalents and operating flows, you're still likely to be faced with the following question: Do the intangibles or future opportunities that I can't put a number on justify the price I've got to pay?

So what are future opportunities worth? To my mind that's one of the greatest growth areas in the finance field. But it's an area, at the moment, where we can't go very far beyond saying they're like options, in principle, and therefore we ought to be able to value them with the same tools. I think in practice what people do when they are faced with this decision is one of two things. First, they may look at a

Obviously one of those markets was going to be wrong. But it wasn't clear to me why people leaped to the assumption that it had to be the stock market.

sample of comparable companies to infer the value the market is placing on such opportunities. Often, however, the search for comparable projects or firms with publicly available market values is difficult, if not impossible. And in such cases, companies must resort finally to calling in their strategy people—or strategy consultants—to see whether the strategic case for the merger is sufficient to justify the price.

Undervaluation as a Motive for Merger

Now, I want to touch on one last issue, a most interesting one and a good one to end with. When is Firm A justified in buying firm B only because the target appears to be a bargain? I have four comments here. First, think back to our "start from scratch" analysis of Weyerhaeuser. I guarantee you that even the best discounted cash flow analysis of Weyerhaeuser or any other company is going to produce random errors. If I do an evaluation of a sample of companies in order to figure out which one is a bargain, and I do it right, then I know beforehand that half of them will appear to be bargains after I finish. In some cases I will be making a positive error and in other cases a negative error. And even if I take the one out of my sample which appears to be the greatest bargain, I still don't know whether that's a random error or not. That's trap number one.

Sometimes people say, "Well, it has to be a bargain because the company can be liquidated for more than its market price." Again I'm cautious for two reasons: one is that it isn't easy to liquidate a big company; and by the time you go through the process of getting it liquidated, you may not end up with as much cash as it looked at first glance you could get out of it.

Second, in cases like that, what you're often doing is just forcing yourself to make a choice between two market prices. At the time people were saying that all the oil companies were undervalued by the stock market, they were comparing prices of companies in the stock market with (estimates of) the price of oil in another market: namely, the price for oil deposits. Now, obviously one of those markets was going to be wrong. But it wasn't clear to me why people leaped to the assumption that it had to be the stock market. Right now it appears that the stock market was right. (But it's probably not fair to rely so much on hindsight here.)

One final point, and this is the one that, I think,

clinches the argument. If you really thought there were no synergistic benefits to a merger but that you had found a bargain, you could get a lot more mileage out of that bargain by just buying the shares as a passive investor rather than paying a premium to take the firm over.

Concluding Comment

Finally, just by way of summing up: I suppose I tend to approach merger analysis from a very conservative point of view. I'm demanding to be shown that the merger generates some positive net benefits before I would give it my imprimatur. But I think this is really a very conservative approach, perhaps even too conservative. A company which comes to mind is Seagrams—not Seagrams when it finally made the offer for Conoco, but Seagrams over the two or three years prior to that. It had gotten the cash from selling off its previous oil properties, and announced that it was going to use that cash to buy another company. So it set out in a rational way to find the company that made the most economic sense.

The revealing thing was that I honestly think they tried hard to be rational and careful and conservative. They did not let themselves get carried away with these kinds of biases I've been inveighing against. But, it took them two or three years to make a major move, which was finally to go after Conoco. So, when you think about what I have been saying, if you were really going to adopt my approach and demand proof of positive benefits before you went ahead, you could see it would be hard to justify many mergers—particularly considering the price you have to pay in today's market.

QUESTION: Are you suggesting, then, that the price is irrelevant, and that the most important criterion for good acquisitions is, say, the strategic fit?

MYERS: I've never understood those words, "good fit." But maybe it refers to the strategic opportunities. They are very hard to value by discounted cash flow. If that's what "good fit" means, and if you truly have one, it may override the kinds of benefit calculations that you can put numbers on. But, the attempt to quantify the value of such opportunities should be made; and, as I suggested earlier, we are making some progress in learning how to value these strategic opportunities.

To return to the first part of your question, however, I don't think anybody would ever say—at least I hope they wouldn't—that the price is irrelevant.

Why Corporate Raiders Are Good News for Stockholders

Clifford G. Holderness
and Dennis P. Sheehan,
University of Rochester

The controversy over "corporate raiding" has become front-page news. It rages in corporate boardrooms, animates Wall Street investors, and has even been examined by Senate subcommittees. In the process, a handful of investors, branded "corporate raiders," have become perhaps the most visible of all participants in the market for corporate control. However, despite the scope and intensity of what now amounts to a national debate over the consequences of corporate raiding, little in the way of serious economic analysis or systematic evidence has been offered as a means of resolving the controversy.

Much of the media's attention to the takeover market tends toward the emotional. The opening statement of a recent article on corporate takeovers is representative: "As the American economic environment changed, predators emerged from under rocks and began to prey on healthy businesses. Is there no stopping them? Will they devour us all?"[1] Another article on the same subject is entitled "The Wasteful Games of America's Corporate Raiders."[2] The takeover process, as it has been portrayed by many financial journalists, Congressmen, and corporate executives, is simply a financial "shell game" in which unscrupulous raiders exploit helpless companies and their powerless stockholders. The perceived role of managers of target companies is ambiguous; they are viewed, alternatively(and sometimes simultaneously), as

victims of the raiders and as co-conspirators in the process. About one thing, however, there seems to be little uncertainty: namely, that the profits generated from the "raiding" process are all short-run gains, illusory "paper profits" which come at the expense of the long-run value of American corporations. The statement of a chairman of a major corporation aptly sums up the prevailing popular view of takeover challenges: "Disruption by raiders . . . is a horrible wrong. It's hurting the country. It's hurting the economic system."[3]

Although the popular press is seemingly unaware of its existence, there has been a substantial amount of academic research on corporate takeover and restructuring activity.[4] None of this research, however, has focused specifically on "corporate raiders." We decided therefore to study in a systematic way the investment activities of six well-known investors often cited as corporate raiders. They are Carl Icahn, Irwin Jacobs, Carl Lindner, David Murdock, Victor Posner, and the late Charles Bluhdorn. We arrived at this list of six after consulting with members of the financial community and reviewing news articles. Our goal was to identify those investors most widely perceived to be corporate raiders. One can reasonably argue that others should have been included in this list, but we are confident about the credentials of our chosen six.[5]

For example, an article in *Institutional Investor*

1. *Forbes*, March 11, 1985, p. 134.
2. *The Economist*, June 1, 1985, p. 73.

3. Andrew C. Sigler, Chairman of Champion International, as quoted in *Business Week*, March 14, 1985, p. 82.
4. For a summary of this research, see Michael C. Jensen and Richard S. Ruback, "The Market for Corporate Control: The Scientific Evidence," *Journal of Financial Economics*, Vol. 11, pp. 5 – 50(1983).
5. The most glaring omission from this list is, of course, Boone Pickens. Our reason for excluding Pickens is that he was not very active in acquiring stock in other firms when we began our research.

stated that Carl Icahn has been called a "'notorious corporate opportunist' and 'a racketeer, an unprincipled predator who will stop at nothing in his search for a quick buck.'"[6] Irwin Jacobs, to his critics, is "a corporate raider who has shown little talent for running the public companies he has acquired."[7] A former business partner was even less kind, calling Jacobs "a liar of the worst kind."[8] David Murdock comes off best in this cast of "villains," having been portrayed as a "usually friendly Los Angeles raider."[9] When Charles Bluhdorn was CEO of Gulf & Western, the company acquired the nickname Engulf & Devour.[10] Fellow stockholders brought suit against Carl Lindner alleging that he illegally borrowed corporate funds and then made unauthorized purchases of securities at "prices far above market value."[11]

The most notorious raiding reputation, however, belongs to Victor Posner. According to a *Barron's* article, he "is rarely identified without the tag 'corporate raider'."[12] Moreover, "few businessmen have suffered more abuse in recent years than Victor Posner."[13] To his numerous critics Posner has "all the talent of an accomplished raider: boldness, ferocity, tenacity and greed. He may not be a promising candidate for charitable work, but for the provision of loot his credentials are excellent."[14]

As mentioned earlier, however, no systematic evidence has to our knowledge been offered to support such bald assertions. In fact, given the harshness of the accusation, one would at least have expected a clear, consistent definition of what it is that "corporate raiders" are supposed to do to those companies in which they buy an interest. But this is not the case. With a willing imagination, however, one can construct from news reports a sense of what is intended. Amongst the welter of negative connotations, the common implication appears to be that "corporate raiding" is an activity which reduces the long-run value of the "raided" companies and,

thus presumably, of their stockholders' shares.

The most extreme form of raiding apparently centers around the "looting" of the corporate treasury. For example, following Victor Posner's acquisition of stock in Foremost-McKesson, a lawsuit was filed against him alleging that his goal was "to prey upon and defraud stockholders of a carefully chosen series of corporations by means of a corruptly conceived and maliciously executed strategy of corporate warfare."[15] It was further alleged that Posner had "taken over and looted at least eight corporations in approximately as many years."[16]

Another, perhaps less drastic, definition of raiding is that raiders use their corporate voting power to award themselves "excessive" compensation and perquisites. This possibility was raised by some when in 1978 Victor Posner earned at least $1.5 million in salary, bonus, and benefits from Sharon Steel Corporation,[17] and when Posner's daughter, who is a director of some of his companies, was provided an apartment at corporate expense.[18]

One could also define raiding to encompass instances where firms repurchase, typically at a premium over the market price, only the shares held by the so-called raider, the practice that has become known as "greenmail." Under this definition of raiding, it is not even necessary for an investor to gain a voting majority to effect transfers to himself from other stockholders.[19] A number of the six investors have had their shares repurchased in this manner. For example, Kaiser Steel Corporation repurchased shares held by Irwin Jacobs at $52 a share, while other Kaiser stockholders received only $40 a share.[20] And Carl Icahn is suspected of having sold shares at large premiums back to Marshall Field & Co., Hammermill Paper Co., American Can Co., Owens-Illinois Inc., Phillips Petroleum Co., and Uniroyal Inc., among others.[21] Such "greenmail" repurchases, perhaps more than any other practice of corporate raiders, have prompted calls for legislative action.

6. *Institutional Investor*, October 1982, p. 147.
7. *Wall Street Journal*, October 27, 1982, p. 35.
8. *Fortune*, September 19, 1983, p. 160.
9. *Forbes*, March 4, 1985, p. 83.
10. *Forbes*, March 15, 1982, p. 31.
11. *Wall Street Journal*, January 9, 1980, p. 2.
12. *New York Times*, February 26, 1984, p. 6F.
13. *Barron's*, November 19, 1979, p. 55.
14. *Barron's*, November 19, 1979, p. 55.

15. Quoted in the *Wall Street Journal*, June 23, 1981, p. 1.
16. *Wall Street Journal*, June 23, 1981, p. 1.
17. *Forbes*, October 29, 1979, p. 34.
18. *Barron's*, November 19, 1979, p. 5.
19. To be sure, there is evidence, which we discuss later, that targeted repurchases in general tend to reduce the wealth of stockholders who are not offered the same opportunity. See Larry Dann & Harry DeAngelo, "Standstill Agreements, Privately Negotiated Stock Repurchases, and the Market for Corporate Control," *Journal of Financial Economics*, Vol. 11, pp. 275-300 (1983); Michael Bradley & Lee Wakeman, "The Wealth Effects of Targeted Share Repurchases," *Journal of Financial Economics*, Vol. 11, pp. 301-328 (1983).
20. *Wall Street Journal*, October 28, 1983, p. 6.
21. *Wall Street Journal*, May 28, 1985, p. 6.

In efficient capital markets expected reductions in the value of corporate assets should be reflected in stock prices when it is first announced that a corporate raider has been accumulating stock.

Presented, then, with this uncertainty about just what "corporate raiding" is, we began our investigation of the six investors by posing two general questions: (1) Does the evidence support the hypothesis that the six are corporate raiders who systematically reduce the wealth of other shareholders? (2) If the evidence is not consistent with this claim, what market role do the six play?

As a first approach to resolving these questions, we measured the stock price changes associated with initial public announcements of stockholdings by any of the six investors from 1977 to 1982. Stock price changes were measured for both the firms the six were buying into ("target firms") as well as the firms used to make those purchases ("filing firms").

Why are the initial market reactions to these announcements useful indicators of anything? Regardless of how it is defined, "corporate raiding" seems to imply that stock acquisitions by the raider ultimately reduce the long-term wealth of other stockholders of target firms. In efficient capital markets like the New York and American Stock Exchanges, expected reductions in the value of corporate assets should be reflected in stock prices when it is first announced that a corporate raider has been accumulating stock in the firm. The evidence uncovered by our inquiry reveals, to the contrary, that stockholders of target firms earned statistically significant positive stock returns, on average, when it was first announced that one of our six controversial investors was accumulating stock.

To obtain additional insights into the long-run impact of the six investors on target firms, we also followed the market performance of, and the six investors' activities in, the target firms over a two-year period following their initial stock purchases. The evidence from this inquiry is likewise inconsistent with the hypothesis that the six have reduced the value of their target companies.

In short, our study finds no evidence that these six investors actually raid companies and thereby systematically reduce long-term stockholder wealth. If anything, based on our findings, they are far more

deserving of the designation "corporate saviors." That much is clear. What is less clear is how these six controversial investors succeed in increasing long-run stockholder wealth. In the pages that follow, we explore this question and describe our study in more detail.

The Investigation
Initial Stock Price Changes

Most of our analysis of the investments of the six controversial investors is based on information contained in filings required by the Securities and Exchange Commission (SEC). Under Regulation 13(d) any individual or company must file with the SEC within ten days of acquiring any security in a publicly traded firm if, after that acquisition, the individual or company owns more than 5 percent of the outstanding class of security.[22] These initial 13(d)s are available almost immediately in the SEC's public records room and are shortly thereafter published in the *SEC News Digest*.[23] It is through the filing of 13(d)s that the investing public presumably first learns of large new securities investments by any major investor. This seems a reasonable assumption because filings of 13(d)s are closely followed by several investor service firms and are often reported by the financial press.

To measure the stock market's response to the first announcement of large stock purchases by the six, we collected from the *SEC News Digest* all initial 13(d)s filed from 1977-1982 by any of the investors, or by any company with whom they were affiliated. We identified affiliated companies (listed in the Appendix) by searching two computer-based information services, the Dow Jones Free Text Search and the ABI/INFORM Data Base.[24] Together these services contain over 360,000 entries, including the text (from 1979 to present) of the *Wall Street Journal, Barron's,* and the *Dow Jones New Service,* plus abstracts of articles (from 1971 to present) from more than 500 journals, including *Business Owner, Busi-*

---

22. Securities are broadly defined in the regulations to include bonds and stocks (both voting and non-voting).

23. Subsequent 13(d)s must be filed with each 2% increase in the holdings of any security. Unless otherwise specified, references in this paper to 13(d)s are to initial filings.

24. The computer searches were also used to double-check the *SEC News Digest* for announcements of 13(d) filings and to search for expressions of intent by any of the six investors to acquire securities.

TABLE I
Number of Initial 13(d)s Filed by the Six Investors or by Affiliated Companies*

*During the Period 1977–1982 and a Random Sample of Initial 13(d)s From the Period 1977–1981.

		Individual Investor						Aggregate– The Six Investors	Random Sample
		Icahn	Jacobs	Lindner	Murdock	Posner	Bluhdorn		
All Initial 13(d)'s From SEC News Digest		8	8	47	16	40	36	**155**	689
Target Firm Not on CRSP File or Insufficient Data (Deletion)		3	3	26	6	9	9	**56**	534
Final Sample of Target Firms		5	5	21	10	31	27	**99**	155
Filing Firm Not on CRSP File or Insufficient Data (Deletion)		5	5	21	7	—	—	**38**	125
Final Sample of Filing Firms		—	—	—	3	45[a]	24	**72**	30

[a]There are many observations for Posner because he often used multiple companies to buy stock in a single target firm. This was not true of the other investors.

ness Week, Financial Analysts Journal, Forbes, Fortune, Institutional Investor, and *Mergers and Acquisitions.* In this manner we identified 35 companies that were publicly known to be affiliated with, if not controlled by, one of the six investors for at least some period between 1977 and 1982. It is possible, of course, that any of the six investors might have had "hidden" interests in other companies that were used as vehicles to acquire stock. But because our study concerns the market's reaction to activities known to involve the six investors, no attempt was made to examine stock acquisitions by "hidden" affiliates.

From the initial sample of 155 13(d)s gathered from the *SEC News Digest*, we eliminated target companies not listed on either the New York or American Stock Exchanges; this allowed us to use computer listings of daily stock prices. The final sample of target firms contained 99 observations: 5 for Icahn, 5 for Jacobs, 21 for Lindner, 10 for Murdock, 31 for Posner, and 27 for Bluhdorn (see Table I for this

data presented both by individual investor and for the six in aggregate).

We also measured the stock price changes of the firms filing these 13(d)s. Starting with the target firm sample of 99 observations, we again eliminated all observations when the filing firm was not listed on the New York or American Stock Exchanges. The final sample used to measure the stock price changes of the filing firms consisted of 72 observations: 3 for Murdock, 45 for Posner, and 24 for Bluhdorn.[25]

To obtain a benchmark against which to evaluate our so-called raiders, we also examined the market's response to initial stockholdings by a group of "average," presumably less controversial, investors. To this end we collected a random sample of 689 13(d)s filed during 1977-1981, which resulted, after exclusions, in observations on 155 target firms. The final sample of random filing firms consists of 30 observations. The data for both the six investors and the random sample are summarized in Table I.

25. There are many observations for Posner because he often used multiple companies to buy stock in a single target firm. This was not true of the other investors.

Short-sighted investors selling out because of temporary earnings declines would be systematically providing their more far-sighted counterparts with profit opportunities.

The Event Study Methodology

We then used this data to determine what impact the six investors had on the stock prices both of their target and filing firms. The methodology we employed to make this determination is known as an "event study," and has been widely used by economists for many years. Because it is so well known and accepted, we provide only a brief overview here.[26]

The goal in our investigation, as in any event study, is to isolate the impact of a specific event on a firm—in this case, the first public announcement of major stockholdings by any of the six investors. To this end, we measured the stock price changes, either positive or negative, associated with the initial public announcement that our six investors had been accumulating stock in the firm.

Because returns of individual firms tend to move with returns to the market as a whole, the first step in any event study is to adjust the individual stock return in question to remove this influence of covariance with the market return. The resulting stock price return is called the "market-adjusted" return and constitutes our best estimate of the impact of one of the six investors on a given firm.

We calculated market-adjusted returns for each of the 99 target firms in our sample and then summed the results to obtain a portfolio return. Lastly, we employed standard tests to see whether the market-adjusted returns of this portfolio were statistically significant or merely reflected the variation inherent in all stock prices.

We should also explain why, like so many other economists, we focused on stock price changes. A basic proposition of financial economics is that stock prices are the net present value of the market's current estimation of *all* future cash flows of the firm. Studies have shown that, contrary to some popular claims, stock prices do not focus exclusively on the short run but also reflect longer-term prospects.

For example, a recent study by John McConnell and Chris Muscarella showed that the market responds favorably to announcements of planned increases in capital expenditures and investments in R&D.[27] If the market were concerned only with the short run, stock prices would decline because such investment typically increases expenditures in the short run, thereby depressing short-term earnings. The benefits from capital spending programs generally do not show up in higher earnings until several years thereafter. The fact that stock prices increase on average with the announcement of such long-term investments is evidence that the market is quite capable of taking the long view of a company's prospects. In fact, it has every incentive to do so, for short-sighted investors selling out because of temporary earnings declines would be systematically providing their more far-sighted counterparts with profit opportunities.

It is on the basis of this logic, then, and the extensive body of empirical work on which the theory rests, that we began with the proposition that the stock price reaction to announcements of 13(d) filings by the six reflects the market's best estimate of the long-term impact these investors will have on the value of the target firm.

Follow-up Activities of the Six

Most event studies end at this point. In this case, however, we followed the activities of our six investors in their target firms for a period of two years following the initial 13(d). Of course, even two years may be considered less than the long run. But, given that market prices are forward-looking, this extension of the time horizon of our tests provides much more perspective on how the six investors affected the value of the target firms.

Our follow-up investigation had a number of components. From the *SEC News Digest* we determined how many amended 13(d)s were filed by the six for each target firm. (Amended 13(d)s must be filed with each 2 percent increase in the holdings of any security.) In addition, the Wall Street Journal Index and the Dow Jones Free Text Search were reviewed for three categories of corporate activity: First, we investigated how often the investor's shares were repurchased by the target firm ("greenmail"). Second, it was determined how often the target firm

---

26. Readers interested in a more complete review of the event study methodology are urged to see G. William Schwert, "Using Financial Data to Measure the Effects of Regulation," *Journal of Law and Economics*, Vol. 24, pp. 121-58 (1981).

27. John McConnell and Chris Muscarella, "Corporate Capital Expenditure Decisions and the Market Value of the Firm," forthcoming in the *Journal of Financial Economics* (Vol. 14, No. 3, 1985).

TABLE II **Summary of Activities By the Six Investors In Target Firms For the Two Years After the Filing of 13(d). 1977–1982.**		Icahn	Jacobs	Lindner	Murdock	Posner	Bluhdorn	Aggregate/ The Six Investors
	Number of Target Firms Followed For Two Years After Initial 13(d)	3	4	16	9	26	15	**73**
	Number of Target Firms Repurchasing Investor's Shares	2	2	—	1	3	4	**12**
	Reorganization of Target Firm[a] • Number of Attempted Reorganizations by Investor	—	2	1	2	—	1	**6**
	• Number Completed	—	—	—	2	—	1	**3**
	• Number of Attempted Reorganizations by Third Party	1	—	4	—	5	2	**13**
	• Number Completed	1	—	4	—	3	2	**10**
	Number of News Reports of Investor Involvement in Management of Target Firm	2	0	3	3	2	0	**10**
	Number of Target Firms Where Amended 13(d)s Were Filed	3	0	11	6	18	12	**50**
	Average Number of Amended 13(d)s Per Target Firm Followed	3.6	0	2.1	1.8	3.3	5.2	**2.7**
	Number of Firms Where No Indication of Any Activity After Initial 13(d)[b]	0	1	3	0	5	1	**9**

[a]Reorganizations are defined in this paper to include mergers, tender offers, and going private transactions.
[b]This means that for a target firm there were no repurchases of the investors' shares, no attempts to reorganize, no news reports of management by the investor, and no amended 13(d)s filed.

was involved in a corporate "reorganization"—by which we mean mergers, takeovers, and going private transactions. Third, we attempted to determine whether the proposed reorganization was completed. We also searched for press reports that the six became active in the management of the target firm. (A summary of these follow-up activities can be found in Table II.)

Event Studies on Follow-up Activities In Target Firms

To measure the market's reaction to the various follow-up activities by the six investors in the target firms, we divided the firms into four categories according to outcome: (1) target firms that were successfully reorganized (whether by the investor or by a third party) within two years of the initial 13(d); (2) those where a reorganization effort failed within the two years; (3) those where the target firm repurchased at least some of the investors' shares (greenmail), again within two years; and (4) all other target firms where we had two years of observations after the initial 13(d).

We then used the same event study methodology discussed earlier to evaluate each of these categories. For the first three categories, we measured market-adjusted returns to target firm stockholders associated with three types of events: 1) the announcement of the initial stock purchase, 2) "significant" intermediate events, and 3) the final event. Significant intermediate events are those instances (in the authors' opinion) when the investor revealed significant information about his future intention with respect to the target firm, or when the target firm's management revealed how they planned to respond to an investor's proposals for changes. (The announcement, on January 21, 1980, that Carl Icahn asked the President of Saxon Industries to either repurchase his shares or face a proxy fight is an example of an intermediate event.) The final event is defined as follows: for the successful reorganization category, it is the day on which the target firm's board announced its approval of a reorganization; for unsuccessful reorganizations, the day on which the reorganization offer was publicly withdrawn; for repurchases, it is the day on which the target firm announced it would repurchase the investor's shares.

Finally, we calculated a measure of the net "event" returns to stockholders in target firms attributable to the controversial investors' stockholdings over the entire two-year period. This is the summation of stock price changes associated with the initial, intermediate, and final events for each category.

The Empirical Findings

The Myth of Corporate Raiding

The findings of our investigations, whether from the stock price changes associated with initial stock purchases by the six or from those over the two-year follow-up period, provide no support for the widely-held view that the six are corporate raiders. As stated earlier, if the six investors in fact systematically reduced the wealth of other stockholders through corporate raiding, one would anticipate a negative market reaction, on average, to the first public announcements of stockholding. These negative stock price changes would reflect the market's expectation that the six investors would expropriate corporate assets for their own purposes, or that these transfers had already been effectuated. But the initial stock price changes were, on average, significantly *positive* for target firms. And this is true no matter how

When the six investors are viewed as a group, perhaps the most striking finding is that over the day of and the day following the first public announcement of initial stockholding by any of the six investors, other stockholders in those target firms earned a positive return of 1.8 percent on average.[28] This, of course, does not mean that all firms experienced a stock price increase of 1.8 percent above the market return for that period: some had larger increases, some smaller, and for some firms the stock price changes were negative. (The range of market responses, in fact, was from a −10 percent change, in the worst case, to a positive 16 percent.) What our findings do indicate, however, is that the positive returns outweigh the negative, resulting in a portfolio return for the 99 target firms of 1.8 percent.

Table III and Figure 1 also indicate that stockholders in target firms realized large gains during the days immediately *preceding* the public announcements of initial stock purchases by the six investors. Stock price increases have been documented for the days preceding other corporate transactions, including mergers, tender offers, proxy contests, and going private reorganizations. As with these other corporate transactions, the stock price increases prior to the announcements suggest that the event-day returns underestimate the wealth increases of stockholders.

Accordingly, we measured the cumulative abnormal returns commencing forty days prior through forty days after the announcements of initial purchases. We also measured the abnormal returns over the period from ten days before through the announcement. Both findings are reported in Table

---

28. The t-statistic for this finding is 3.7; the null hypothesis of a zero mean return can, therefore, be rejected at the .01 significance level.

FIGURE 1
**Cumulative
Market-Adjusted
Returns For Target Firms
Six Investors and
Random Sample***

*From Forty Days Before
Through Forty Days After The
First Public Announcement of
Stockholding For The Six
Investors (n = 99) (1977–1982)
and for The Random Sample
(n = 155) (1977–1981).

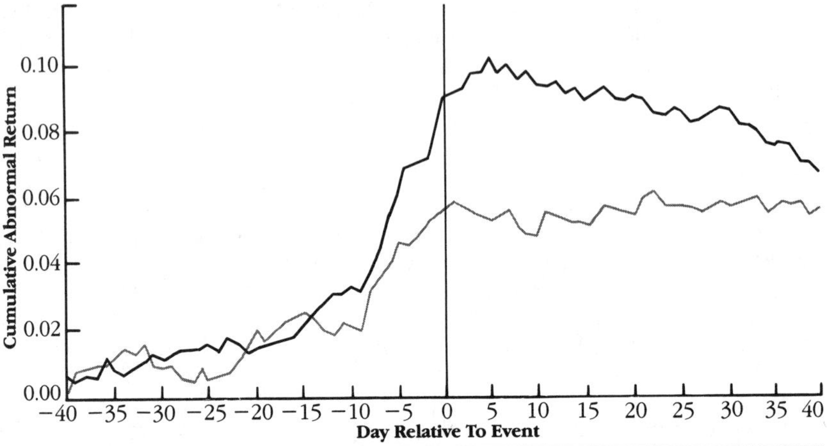

——— Six Investors
Random Sample

TABLE III
**Market Adjusted
Returns in Target Firms
for Various Parts of the
Event Period Associated
With The First Public
Announcement of
Stockholding***

*By The Six Investors
Collectively, By A Random
Sample of Investors, and By
Individual Investor (t-statistics
are given in parentheses;
sample sizes are denoted by
"N=").

	Event Period		
	Ten Days Before Through the First Public Announcement of Stockholding	**First Public Announcement of Stockholding**	**Forty Days Before Through Forty Days After the First Public Announcement of Stockholding**
All Six Investors N = 99	**5.9%** (5.2)	**1.8%** (3.7)	**6.7%** (2.2)
Random Sample N = 155	3.4% (3.8)	0.4% (1.1)	5.8% (2.4)
Icahn N = 5	7.2% (1.5)	2.4% (1.2)	21.1% (1.6)
Jacobs N = 5	9.6% (1.9)	3.8% (1.8)	20.6% (1.5)
Lindner N = 21	1.8% (0.7)	−1.7% (−1.6)	0.1% (.02)
Murdock N = 10	9.9% (3.7)	3.0% (2.7)	12.2% (1.7)
Posner N = 31	7.0% (3.8)	3.3% (4.2)	3.3% (0.7)
Bluhdorn N = 27	4.9% (3.1)	1.8% (2.7)	7.9% (1.9)

III and confirm that announcements of initial stock purchases by the six investors are associated with gains for target firms' stockholders. Finally, it should be noted that the downward drift in stockholder returns from the event day through the end of the event period is statistically insignificant.

When the six are viewed individually, we again found no support for their raider image. On average there were no negative returns that are significant for any of the six investors when measured over any of the following periods: (1) the ten days preceding and the day following the 13(d) filing; (2) the day of the filing itself; and (3) over the eighty days surrounding the filing. (These findings are summarized in Table III.)

566

The empirical evidence on the random sample of 13(d)s makes for an interesting comparison with the evidence on our six controversial investors. The six investors are associated with target firm announcement day returns that are statistically significantly larger than target firm returns associated with filings by random investors (1.8 percent for the six, 0.4 percent for the random sample). Over the eighty days surrounding the announcement of initial stockholding, the wealth increases associated with the six investors are larger than, although statistically indistinguishable from, those associated with random investors (6.7 percent for the six, 5.8 percent for the random sample). Hence, for stockholders in target firms, involvement by the six investors is, from some perspectives, more desirable—in the sense of being associated with larger wealth increases—than the presence of other, apparently less controversial, investors.

The Evidence on Filing Firms

As indicated earlier, we also measured stock price changes for firms controlled by or affiliated with one of the six investors purchasing stock in other companies and thus filing a 13(d) (hereafter "filing firms"). These returns are summarized in Table IV and plotted in Figure 2. Although the event-day returns for the six are strongly positive, the cumulative returns are slightly negative (though the downward drift in cumulative returns after the event date lacks statistical significance). Table IV and Figure 2 also contain findings for the random sample of filing firms, which serve as a benchmark to evaluate the findings on the six investors. All of these findings indicate that the six do not reduce the wealth of stockholders of firms that are used to acquire ownership positions in other companies. Perhaps the major conclusion to be drawn from these findings is that the six are not, as sometimes

FIGURE 2
Cumulative Market-Adjusted Returns For Filing Firms Six Investors and Random Sample*

*From Forty Days Before Through Forty Days After the First Public Announcement of Stockholding for the Six Investors (n = 72) (1977–1982) and for the Random Sample (n = 30) (1977–1981).

———— Six Investors
———— Random Sample

TABLE IV
Market-Adjusted Returns for Filing 13(d)'s*

*For Various Parts of the Event Period For Both the Six Investors (n = 72) (1977–1982) and for the Random Sample (n = 30) (1977–1981) (t-statistics are given in parentheses).

	Event Period		
Sample	Ten Days Before Through the First Public Announcement of Stockholding	First Public Announcement of Stockholding	Forty Days Before Through Forty Days After the First Public Announcement of Stockholding
All Six Investors N = 72	1.9% (1.4)	1.7% (3.0)	−2.2% (−0.6)
Random Sample N = 30	−0.8% (−0.6)	0.4% (0.8)	−2.0% (−0.6)

Although no love is lost between "raiders" and incumbent management in contests for control, some target firm managers have grudgingly admitted that attempted takeovers changed their outlook on what management course was best.

TABLE V Average Event Day Market-Adjusted Returns for Initial, Intermediate, and Final Announcements for Target Firms of the Six Investors	Type of Public Announcements	Successful Reorganization N = 13	Unsuccessful Reorganization N = 5	Repurchase N = 12	Other N = 39
	Initial Stock Purchase	−0.3% (−0.2)	0.5% (0.3)	4.1% (3.0)	1.8% (2.8)
	Intermediate Events	15.8% (3.5)	12.8% (3.7)	−0.4% (−0.1)	
	Final Events	−1.2% (−0.7)	−3.4% (−1.9)	−1.3% (−1.5)	
	Total Returns	**13.0%** **(3.1)**	**4.1%** **(1.0)**	**3.2%** **(1.8)**	

claimed, paying "too much" for the stock of other companies.

The Evidence on the Longer-Term

We found more empirical evidence inconsistent with the raiding hypothesis after reviewing the follow-up activities of the six investors in target firms. Regardless of what eventually happens to the target firm within the two years following an initial 13(d)—whether it is reorganized, a reorganization fails, the controversial investor's shares are repurchased, or even nothing at all happens—target firm stockholders, on average, earned positive returns (see Table V).

Of particular relevance for the raiding hypothesis are the findings of our event study on targeted repurchases ("greenmail") involving the six investors. Like other studies, we found that the *announcements* of targeted repurchases are associated with negative stock price changes for the firms making the repurchases.[29] These findings are certainly consistent with the widely-held view that targeted repurchases harm non-participating stockholders. However, the initial stock purchases that eventually led to those repurchases were on average associated with positive stock price changes of 4.1 percent over the two days surrounding the announcement of the initial purchase. And when the relevant initial stock purchases and significant intermediate events, as well as the "greenmail" repurchase itself, are all con-

sidered in aggregate, the total, net returns to target firm stockholders were a positive 3.2 percent.

Our findings on the total returns of those cases that terminate with repurchases are similar to those of Wayne Mikkelson of the University of Oregon and Richard Ruback of the Massachusetts Institute of Technology, who studied repurchases in general over the period 1978-1980.[30] Using a different and larger sample, they found that the aggregate of the returns associated with the initial purchase, intermediate events, and the repurchase was a positive 2.0 percent. Our evidence, combined with that of Mikkelson and Ruback, casts a new light on "greenmail."[31]

If Not Raiders, Then What?

Given that we found no evidence that these six investors are corporate raiders in the sense of systematically reducing the wealth of other stockholders, we turn to the second of our two questions: If the evidence is inconsistent with raiding, what market role do the six play? Although our investigations failed to identify one precise role, there are two hypotheses that are consistent with some, if not all, of our findings.

Improved Management?

One hypothesis is that the six improve the management of target firms. This explanation, which stands directly opposed to the raiding hypothesis,

29. As reported in Table V, announcements of repurchases were associated with returns of −1.3%, t=−1.5. Equivalent results on the announcement of repurchases from other more general studies are as follows: Dann and De-Angelo (1983) (−1.8%, t=−3.6); Bradley and Wakeman (1983) (−1.2%, t=−3.3); Mikkelson and Ruback (1984) (−1.7%, t=−4.2).

30. Wayne Mikkelson and Richard Ruback, "Corporate Investments in Common Stock," forthcoming in *Journal of Financial Economics* (Vol. 14, No. 4, 1985).

31. Of course, the existence or non-existence of positive returns for shareholders in not the only point on which the "greenmail" debate will be decided. For example, one might argue that firms should not be empowered to create classes of shareholders who hold the same type of stock yet have different claims on the firm.

The prospect of a takeover may be sufficient to induce management changes that benefit stockholders.

holds that the six investors help bring about management changes that increase the target firm's expected net cash flows and hence increase its value. In fact, there are some that would argue that investors such as our six function, as a *Business Week* article put it, as "healthy whips over 'fat and complacent management'."[32]

These improvements in the management of target firms could result from either a change in corporate personnel (a new CEO, for example) or from a change in corporate policy (say, a decision to abandon a previously announced acquisition or to stop investing corporate capital to maintain unprofitable operations). In a number of cases, we found that the six investors became directly involved in the management of a target firm. A few examples of direct involvement by the six follow.

After David Murdock purchased stock in Cannon Mills Company, he "moved quickly to cut costs at Cannon, which he says had archaic management. He fired dozens of front-office employees one Friday on a half-hour's notice, laid off an estimated 2,000 millworkers, and warned the rest in a videotaped speech to work harder or lose their jobs."[33]

After Irwin Jacobs bought Watkins Company, he "brought in new managers who doubled sales to around $50 million and made Watkins profitable."[34]

Carl Lindner bought stock in Penn Central, was then elected to its board, and one year later became its chairman (before eventually selling his stock). This appears to be in keeping with the Lindner management approach, which purportedly is "to keep his finger on as many details as possible and be contemptuous of management depth."[35]

Carl Icahn is open about his potential involvement in management changes: "Critics can call me what they want—corporate raider or predator. But I believe that I have functioned as catalyst for change..."[36] This might provide an insight into Icahn's attempt to gain control of TWA. In the face of TWA's management claims that he would dismantle the company, Icahn responded that "while he had considered selling TWA's planes, cutting routes and adding to TWA's debt, he now says he wants control to operate the airlines for the long term and even

expand it." "TWA has a great future," he said in an interview.[37] He did announce, however, that if his attempted takeover was successful, he would fire TWA's president.[38]

In some cases, one of the six did not institute the management change himself, but instead backed proposals for changes by other stockholders. When Irwin Jacobs bought stock in Walt Disney Productions, for example, he did not become directly involved in management, but he did announce his opposition to a planned acquisition which had already been opposed by several other major Disney stockholders and by some directors.[39]

Although no love is lost between "raiders" and incumbent management in contests for control, some target firm managers have grudgingly admitted that attempted takeovers changed their outlook on what management course was best for the firm. Raymond Watson, Disney's chairman during its recent takeover attempt by Irwin Jacobs, said that the challenge to management by stockholder dissidents "woke us up, though I hate to give credit to something like that. I think the company is stronger."[40] Thomas Pownall, chairman of Martin Marietta during the celebrated Bendix-Martin Marietta battle, later characterized that battle as "useful." "It became apparent to us that we really did need to shed some less productive operations."[41] Thus, the prospect of a takeover may be sufficient to induce management changes that benefit stockholders.

Perhaps the strongest evidence that these six investors improve the management of target firms comes from the positive market response to the first public announcement of stockholding by one of the six investors. This favorable response is consistent with the argument that the market expects the six to improve the management of target firms and thereby increase net cash flows. Additional empirical evidence consistent with the improved management hypothesis comes from the activities of the six investors following their initial stock purchases. If they were expected by the market to bring about management changes, then we would look for them to play some management role, or somehow "be heard from," after their initial stock purchases. In

32. *Business Week*, March 4, 1985, p. 83.
33. *Wall Street Journal*, March 2, 1983, p. 1.
34. *Fortune*, September 19, 1983, p. 160.
35. *Fortune*, January 1977, p. 130.
36. *Business Week*, December 12, 1983, p. 116.
37. *Wall Street Journal*, May 28, 1985, p. 6.
38. *Wall Street Journal*, June 10, 1985, p. 4.
39. *Wall Street Journal*, July 30, 1984, p. 4.
40. *Business Week*, March 4, 1985, p. 82.
41. *Forbes*, March 11, 1985, p. 44.

In only ten target firms out of the 73 in our sample was there no public indication of any activity during the two years following an initial stock purchase.

other words, they should not be "passive" investors.

That our six investors generally take some kind of active role is consistent both with the general impression we received from examining financial press reports and with the empirical evidence reported in Table II. In only ten target firms out of the 73 in our sample was there no public indication of any activity during the two years following an initial stock purchase. Moreover, in at least ten (again, out of 73) target firms, one of the investors assumed a direct and publicly-visible management role. In six other cases, one of the investors attempted to reorganize a target firm, while in 13 other instances a third party attempted the reorganization after one of the six became a stockholder. Overall, 13 target firms were successfully reorganized within the two years following an initial stock purchase by one of the investors.

Management *changes*, to be sure, do not necessarily guarantee improvements in the sense of increasing a target firm's expected net cash flows and thus its market value. The findings from our event studies on the follow-up activities, however, are consistent with the hypothesis that the majority of the management changes in our sample were in fact improvements. Successful reorganizations, which could be a prelude to the introduction of a new management team, are associated with the largest wealth gains (measured as total announcement-day returns) for target firms' stockholders (13.0 percent).[42] On the other hand, when it was announced that a reorganization effort was withdrawn, target firm stockholders suffered wealth losses of 3.4 percent—perhaps because management changes proposed by the controversial investor, and anticipated by the market, had been rejected. (Nevertheless, the total, net return to stockholders from the three events was still a positive 4.1 percent on average.) Lastly, even the 12 cases of "greenmail" repurchases could be consistent with the improved management hypothesis if the initial purchase and the subsequent repurchase increased the scrutiny of the target firm's management. This scrutiny, in turn, could have resulted in more effective monitoring of management, and perhaps even in a subsequent reorganization attempt (as happened with Disney).

Thus, our empirical evidence is consistent with the hypothesis that the six are associated with improved management of target firms. But what are the implications of the empirical evidence for filing firms? In particular, do stockholders of firms filing 13(d)s suffer wealth losses perhaps because of diseconomies of scale in management caused by these stock investments? The empirical evidence is inconsistent with this view. For those filing firms affiliated with one of the six investors, statistically significant negative returns were not observed over the eighty-day event period. Indeed, the event day abnormal returns are both positive (1.7 percent) and larger than the returns for a random filing firm (0.4 percent).

Superior Security Analyst?

An alternative, though not mutually exclusive, hypothesis holds that the six investors systematically identify and purchase undervalued stocks. This superior security analyst hypothesis is occasionally reflected in statements by and about the six. Carl Lindner, for example, has been described as an "an 'asset player' who has a nose for undervalued situations and guts to buy when other people are scared."[43] Victor Posner "says he prefers to buy stocks that are 'low multiples of earnings, never above 10 times (earnings)'."[44] Irwin Jacobs' investor groups "look for undervalued situations. [Says Jacobs] 'I like to buy dollars for 50 cents...I'm an asset-oriented individual. Intangibles carry zero on the balance sheet for me'."[45]

Stock purchases by the six could be based either on non-public information about target firms or on skills they have in interpreting publicly-available information about target firms. The positive abnormal returns to stockholders in target firms associated with the first public announcements of stockholding by the six are consistent with either version of this hypothesis. Moreover, it is possible that some investors systematically possess more valuable private information than others or have greater skills at interpreting publicly-available information on target firms. If the market is aware of this, then the hypothesis could explain the observed differences in initial stock price changes for different investors filing the 13(d).

Other findings, however—most notably the direct involvement of the six investors in

---

42. Jensen and Ruback, cited in note 4, suggest this possibility.
43. *Fortune*, January 1977, p. 138.
44. *Wall Street Journal*, June 23, 1981, p. 1.
45. *Wall Street Journal*, January 28, 1985, p. 6.

The undervaluation of assets may reflect a failure by management to put corporate assets to their highest-valued use..."Corporate raiders" may be the catalyst necessary to allow potential asset values to be realized.

management and the targeted repurchases of their shares—cannot be explained by the superior security analyst hypothesis. This explanation has relevance only for stock purchases and does not address follow-up activities in target firms. It should be noted, however, that the evidence on the follow-up activities is not inconsistent with the superior security analyst hypothesis. Indeed, it is possible, given all of the empirical evidence uncovered by our investigations, that the "improved management" and the "superior security analyst" hypotheses work best together in explaining the success of these six investors in raising stockholder values.

The improved management and superior security analyst hypotheses describe mechanisms by which the six investors were able to generate positive returns. Clearly, both hypotheses require the existence of undervalued firms, but, equally clearly, neither explains why firms are undervalued. Perhaps the most plausible explanation for the undervaluation of assets is a failure by management to put the assets at its disposal to their highest-valued use. As long as the market expects management to employ assets in a suboptimal manner, then investors lower their assessment of the market value of a company. This potentially explains why some firms sell below their book value or even below the liquidation value of their net assets.

Thus, in one sense, our two mechanisms are connected. The six investors studied here, as well as other "corporate raiders," may be the catalyst necessary to allow potential asset values to be realized. They can do this by being active investors and taking a direct role in the management of the firm, or they may be able to do this simply by spotting stocks that are undervalued and investing, thereby giving a signal to the market that increased scrutiny of the target firm may yield benefits.

Conclusion

No sensible person would argue that these six investors are not pursuing their own self-interest by accumulating stock in a given firm. They are by their own admission. The key question is: Does that

pursuit of self-interest increase the wealth of other individuals? Is Adam Smith's invisible hand at work here? Our investigations into the activities of six controversial investors show the answer to be an unequivocal yes.

Specifically, our investigations show that announcements of initial stock purchases were associated with statistically significant increases in the wealth of target firms' stockholders. Moreover, these increases, at least for the announcement day, exceeded the increases associated with initial stock purchases by random (typically less controversial) investors.

The activities of the six in target firms over a two-year period after they file an initial 13(d) are likewise consistent with wealth increases for other stockholders. Even in those cases when the investors' shares were repurchased by the target firm (so-called "greenmail"), target firms' stockholders experienced statistically significant wealth increases when events from the initial purchase through the repurchase are examined. In short, if "corporate raiding" implies the reduction in wealth of other stockholders, the empirical evidence reported in this paper lends no support to the corporate raider image attached to these six investors.

While the empirical evidence is inconsistent with the raiding hypothesis, the precise market role of the six is less clear. One reasonable interpretation of the evidence is that the six investors help bring about management changes that increase the value of corporate assets. Although our investigation of the follow-up activities of the six sheds some light on these management changes, more research is needed to identify their precise nature, and to ascertain whether the investors helped cause these changes or whether they merely anticipated them. Additional research is also needed to see to what extent, if any, the positive returns resulted because these investors are able to identify undervalued stocks. Finally, additional research is needed to answer what is arguably the biggest mystery uncovered by our investigations: Given that the six investors are on average associated with increases in the wealth of other stockholders, how did they ever obtain the label of "corporate raider," and why has that label persisted?

Mergers & Acquisitions/Selected Bibliography

Aranow, E. and H. Einhorn, *Proxy Contests for Corporate Control* (New York: Columbia University Press, 1968).

Asquith, P., "Merger Bids, Uncertainty, and Stockholder Returns," *Journal of Financial Economics* 11 (April, 1983).

Asquith, P., R. Bruner, and D. Mullins, Jr., "The Gains to Bidding Firms from Merger," *Journal of Financial Economics* 11 (April, 1983).

Bradley, M., "Interfirm Tender Offers and the Market for Corporate Control," *Journal of Business* 54 (1980), 345-76.

Bradley, M. and L. M. Wakeman, "The Wealth Effects of Targeted Share Repurchases," *Journal of Financial Economics* 11 (April, 1983).

Bradley, M., A. Desai, and E. H. Kim, "The Rationale Behind Interfirm Tender Offers: Information or Synergy?," *Journal of Financial Economics* 11 (April 1983).

Bradley, M., A. Desai, and E. H. Kim, "Specialized Resources and Competition in the Market for Corporate Control," University of Michigan Working Paper.

Dann, L., and H. DeAngelo, "Standstill Agreements, Privately Negotiated Stock Repurchases, and the Market for Corporate Control," *Journal of Financial Economics* 11 (April, 1983).

DeAngelo, H. and E. Rice, "Anti-takeover Charter Amendments and Stockholder Wealth," *Journal of Financial Economics* 11 (April, 1983).

Dodd, P., "Merger Proposals, Management Discretion and Stockholder Wealth," *Journal of Financial Economics* (June, 1980).

Dodd, P. and J. Warner, 1982, "On Corporate Governance: A Study of Proxy Contests," *Journal of Financial Economics* 11 (April, 1983).

Dodd, P. and R. Leftwich, "Trading on Private Information Prior to the Announcement of Tender Offers," Unpublished Research, University of Chicago, 1982.

Dodd, P. and R. Leftwich, "Corporate Charter Amendments: Management Entrenchment or Protection of Stockholders," Unpublished Research, University of Chicago, 1982.

Eckbo, B., "Horizontal Mergers, Collusion, and Stockholder Wealth," *Journal of Financial Economics* 11 (April, 1983).

Fama, E. F., "Agency Problems and the Theory of the Firm," *Journal of Political Economy* 88, 288-307.

Jarrell, G. and M. Bradley, "The Economic Effects of Federal and State Regulations of Cash Tender Offers," *Journal of Law and Economics* (October, 1980), 371-407.

Jensen, M. C. and R. S. Ruback, "The Market for Corporate Control: The Scientific Evidence," *Journal of Financial Economics* 11 (April, 1983).

Lease, R., J. McConnell and W. Mikkelson, "The Market Value of Control in Publicly-Traded Corporations", *Journal of Financial Economics* 11 (April, 1983).

Linn, S. and J. McConnell, "An Empirical Investigation of the Impact of 'Anti-takeover' Amendments on Common Stock Prices," *Journal of Financial Economics* 11 (April, 1983).

Malatesta, P. H., "The Wealth Effect of Merger Activity and the Objective Functions of Merging Firms," *Journal of Financial Economics* 11 (April, 1983).

Manne, Henry G., "Mergers and the Market for Corporate Control," *Journal of Political Economy* 73 (April, 1965), 110-120.

Ruback, R., "Assessing Competition in the Market for Corporate Acquisitions," *Journal of Financial Economics* 11 (April, 1983).

Schipper, Katherine and Rex Thompson, "Evidence on the Capitalized Value of Merger Activity for Acquiring Firms," *Journal of Financial Economics* 11 (April, 1983).

Part VIII: Corporate Restructuring

INTRODUCTION

In recent years, and in the 1980s especially, we have seen an unprecedented wave of "reverse mergers." The increasing number and size of divestitures, spin-offs, and leveraged buyouts are bringing about striking changes in the product mix and organizational structure of American corporations. This massive "redeployment" of corporate assets has received considerable attention in the popular business press. In the academy, however, finance scholars have only recently begun to turn their attention away from mergers and acquisitions and toward these relatively new corporate phenomena.

In a series of six articles, we present the results of the academic finance community's initial explorations in the field of corporate restructuring. The findings of this preliminary research, however tentative as yet, suggest that we may be witnessing a new phase in the evolution of the public corporation into a more efficient vehicle for building and storing stockholder wealth. The market's early endorsement of this restructuring also suggests that some forms of corporate organization — most notably, the large, sprawling conglomerate — may now be under serious challenge from increasingly activist investors, perhaps even in earliest stages of obsolescence.

In their introductory "Overview" of this slight but growing body of new research, Gailen Hite and Jim Owers view these developments as part of a "general corporate trend toward more streamlined, decentralized, entrepreneurial organizations." They announce, furthermore,

that a new kind of arithmetic has come into play. Whereas corporate management once seemed to behave as if 2 + 2 were equal to 5, especially during the conglomerate heyday of the 60s, the wave of reverse mergers seems based on the counter proposition that 5 – 1 is 5. And the market's consistently positive response to such deals seems to be providing broad confirmation of the "new math."

The article goes on to document the triumph of this "new math" and attempts to explain the market's favorable response to divestitures, total corporate liquidations, spin-offs, and leveraged buyouts.

This initial "Overview" of corporate restructuring is then fleshed out in three articles which follow, one each devoted to divestitures, spin-offs, and going private transactions.

The corporate motives for divestiture, together with the causes for the market's positive response to divestiture announcements, are explored more fully by Scott Linn and Mike Rozeff in "The Corporate Sell-Off." According to the authors, a successful divestiture is one which transfers corporate assets to a higher-valued use, or to a more efficient user. Viewed slightly differently, a divestiture may also create value by eliminating a business which interferes with the functioning of the remaining operations, a business which, in the parlance of corporate planners, has a poor "strategic fit." Linn and Rozeff argue, furthermore, that the most reliable outward signs of an economically sensible divestiture are increases in the market values of both the buying and selling companies in response to the announcement of the deal.

In "The Corporate Spin-Off Phenomenon," Katherine Schipper and Abbie Smith attempt to explain the market's prevailingly positive response to so-called "pure," voluntary spin-offs. Many observers have argued that spin-offs increase stock values by enabling analysts properly to evaluate divisions otherwise buried within a conglomerate structure. Professors Schipper and Smith express skepticism about this popular argument for spin-offs, suggesting that the market's positive response is more likely based on expected improvements in managerial accountability and incentives from separating unrelated businesses units. The authors point out that spin-offs, besides often providing divisional management with greater decision-making authority, also result in much more visible evaluation criteria (including a separate stock price) for the spun-off entity. Significant improvements in profitability may be expected from a more direct linking of managerial rewards with performance.

Similar expectations of improvements in managerial incentives and performance also seem to underlie the recent proliferation of leveraged buyouts. In "Going Private: A Study of the Effects of Changes in Corporate Ownership Structure," authors Harry DeAngelo, Linda DeAngelo, and Ed Rice present evidence dispelling the popular notion that management buyouts benefit managements at the expense of public stockholders. The authors' own research demonstrates that public stockholders benefit handsomely from proposals to take companies private.

Given that the average premium paid to take a company private exceeds 50 percent of the pre-proposal stock price, few should find this surprising. More remarkable, however, is management's willingness (and, in the case of leveraged buyouts, the desire of third-party professional investors) to pay such large premiums to buy out public stockholders and take companies private. This development raises two important questions: What are the expected benefits to going private? Furthermore, what do these multi-billion dollar leveraged buyout proposals suggest about the efficiency of the public corporation as a form of business organization?

Recent developments in finance theory—most notably, Michael Jensen and William Meckling's formulation of "agency" theory—have drawn attention to the potential loss in the value of the public corporations caused by the conflict of interest between management and its stockholders. Most finance scholars, including Jensen and Meckling, have concluded that the "agency costs" of separating ownership from control in the public corporation cannot be very great for two reasons: the existence of a market for executive labor should curb the natural tendency of corporate managements to pursue their own interests at the expense of their public stockholders, and management incentive contracts are designed to mitigate this potential conflict of interest. But the recent flurry of ever larger leveraged buyout proposals may be telling us that the "agency costs" of public equity ownership are far greater than finance scholars have suspected.

The popularity of going private no doubt reflects, in large part, the large tax and regulatory burden imposed on the public corporation. But it may also suggest that management compensation committees of public corporations could be doing far more to strengthen management incentives to perform—or that the legal impediments to adopting more effective management compensation schemes in public corporations are very great. For, besides providing significant stock ownership for a number of key managers, leveraged buyouts often strengthen managerial incentives by designing compensation agreements that tie management bonuses more closely to increases in a company's profitability (often measured interms of cash flow rather than acccounting earnings). In addition, the large amounts of leverage supported in these deals contain the suggestion either that some public companies may be significantly underleveraged or that the private corporation per se has considerably more debt capacity than its public counterpart—perhaps because of the improved management incentive structure, but also because of the intermediation of reputable third-party professional investors between management and lending institutions.

In "Equity Carve-Outs," Katherine Schipper and Abbie Smith describe a transaction that was popular throughout much of the 1980s, and which has continued to be widely used in the 1990s. Such equity carve-outs, which amount to sales to the public of minority interests in subsidiaries, are the only kind of equity offering that elicits a positive response from the market. Whereas announcements of conventional corporate equity offerings depress stock prices by about 3% on average, companies offering partial interests interests have experienced an almost 5% increase in the value of the shares in the month surrounding announcement of the offering.

The popular explanation for the positive market reaction to equity carve-outs is that they allow investors to evaluate exceptional growth opportunities on a stand-alone basis, which in turn increases the value of the parent (which typically retains a majority interest). Such an argument appears, at least at first glance, to be premised on an exploitable inefficiency in stock market pricing. While the authors concede that providing investors with more extensive financial disclosure on an involuntary, periodic basis may affect the market's assessment of a subsidiary's value, and while such securities in some cases may even have scarcity value to investors unable to find "pure plays," they also offer other suggestions. For one thing, by separating an unambiguously profitable project from the parent, a carve-out may help overcome the information problem that attends conventional equity offerings.

If such is the case, the subsidiary might obtain funding on better terms alone than as part of a large organization. Perhaps equally important, the fact that carve-outs are parts of large, diversified conglomerates suggests that one of the motives for carve-outs may be expected improvements in operating efficiency. Carve-outs, as the authors point out, are often accompanied by major changes in the responsibilities and incentives of subsidiary management; for example, stock options in the newly-trading subsidiary's shares are almost always provided the top managers.

In "The Quiet Restructuring," John Kensinger and John Martin reinforce Jensen's argument that much corporate restructuring activity represents the return by management of corporate reinvestment decisions to the marketplace. The once popular model of the large corporation as a self-financing, self-perpetuating entity (promoted by the Boston Consulting Group and other strategists) has gone into eclipse. Drawing on Jensen's "debt control" hypothesis, the authors argue that the pressures exerted by heavy debt financing, combined with greater concentrations of equity ownership by management, has led to widespread corporate downsizing along with dramatic improvements in managerial accountability and incentives.

But even as this general pressure to return capital to investors is causing many Fortune 500 companies to shrink, much of this released capital is finding its way into small, start-up ventures and growing middle market companies. This massive recycling of capital from the moribund to the vital is seen by the authors as part of a "downsizing" process in which business functions are increasingly being performed as parts of smaller, independent firms and tax-advantaged partnerships. Corporate America, they suggest, has become the site of an ongoing market test weighing the benefits of scale economies and access to public capital against what increasingly appear to be the inefficiencies of large, especially conglomerate organizations.

DHC

The Restructuring of Corporate America: An Overview

Gailen L. Hite,
Southern Methodist University,

and James E. Owers,
University of Massachusetts

Until fairly recently, modern corporate finance theory has rested securely on the premise that managers of public corporations act, on the whole, so as to maximize the wealth of their stockholders. In 1976, however, two finance professors at the University of Rochester, Michael Jensen and William Meckling, raised important questions about this foundation of financial economists' thinking. In a paper entitled "Theory of the Firm: Managerial Behavior, Agency Costs, and Ownership Structure," Jensen and Meckling pointed a new direction for research in finance by exploring the potential conflict of interest between management and stockholders—and the resulting loss of value—in the large, widely-held public corporation.

The intent of the Jensen-Meckling paper, to be sure, was not to challenge, much less to overturn, this fundamental assumption about corporate management's behavior. In fact, the standard conception of management as stewards of stockholder savings has served, and continues to serve, the academic finance profession remarkably well. It has been upheld by the findings of all but a handful of the studies that now swell the body of finance literature.

The real contribution to finance scholarship of the Jensen-Meckling argument was to draw attention to matters of corporate organization—matters which, up to that point, had been largely neglected by financial economists. In the course of re-examining this old problem of the "separation of ownership from control," Jensen and Meckling redirected our focus by viewing the corporation as a "nexus of contracts" among stockholders, managers, employees, regulators, and others. The resulting change in finance scholars' way of looking at the corporation has given rise to a new line of research attempting to explain how and why certain features (read "contracts") of the modern corporation have evolved into their present form.

In the real world, meanwhile, a host of changes —ever larger divestiture waves, the revival of the proxy war, the growing popularity of leveraged buyouts, wholesale corporate liquidations, and the proliferation of new varieties of spin-offs and split-ups—all this seems to be confirming the appropriateness of this new direction in financial research. For much of this "restructuring" activity can be explained only by looking more carefully at the contractual relationships, both explicit and implicit, among management, stockholders, regulators, and other corporate constituencies. Such restructurings seem to be making profound changes in existing corporate "contracts"—contracts which themselves have evolved and are continuously evolving through time. And, on the basis of the market's enthusiastic endorsement of these restructuring transactions, such changes promise to make the corporation a more efficient vehicle for creating and storing stockholder value.

The recent divestiture activity, for example, suggests in part an unraveling of much of the conglomerate activity of the 60s. The emphasis of strategic planning has fallen increasingly on sharpening the "corporate focus" by identifying a company's strengths or comparative advantages, and by eliminating those businesses that do not offer a good "strategic fit." (There has also, of course, been a large merger wave in recent years. But, with the glaring exception of a few very large, highly-publicized, diversifying takeovers, we suspect that most strategic acquisitions have been combinations of firms with complementary resources, prompted by prospects of real business "synergies.")

The growing number of divestitures also provides evidence of what seems to be a general corporate trend toward more streamlined, decentralized, "entrepreneurial" organizations. This trend is probably even more clearly illustrated, however, by the

576

recent flurry of spin-offs and split-ups. Such transactions, which simply divide a corporation into a number of separate firms with no change in proportional ownership, suggest that a new kind of arithmetic has come into play. Whereas corporate management once seemed to behave as if 2 + 2 were equal to 5, especially during the conglomerate heyday of the 60s, the wave of reverse mergers seems based on the counter proposition that 5 − 1 is 5. And, as suggested, the market's consistently positive response to such deals seems to be providing broad confirmation of the "new math."

Even more radical restructurings have enriched their stockholders not by concentrating the focus of corporate operations, but rather by completely dissolving the current organizational structure. In choosing total liquidation, such companies have decided they are worth more "dead than alive" and have accordingly self-destructed, selling off their assets piecemeal.

Last, and perhaps most surprising, the growing number and size of companies going private suggest that even the very form of the public corporation is being tested. The proliferation of leveraged buyouts may be telling us that management compensation committees of public corporations could be doing far more to strengthen management incentives to perform. Also, the large amounts of leverage supported in these deals contain the suggestion that either (1) some public companies may be significantly underleveraged or (2) the private corporation per se has considerably more debt capacity than its public counterpart.

To return to our earlier statement, we feel that much of the underlying corporate motivation for such widespread restructuring can only be understood by looking more closely at how management and stockholders (and regulators) are linked in the structure of the public corporation. To understand *how* and *why* the organizational structure changes through time, it is important to address five key questions: (1) How do the composition and responsibilities of the management team change as a result of the restructuring? (2) How do the managerial compensation and incentive structure change? (3) How does the ownership of the residual equity claims change? (4) If assets are exchanged, as in the case of a sell-off, how are the new assets employed? (5) What factors lead to the obsolescence of the old and the adoption of the new, presumably more efficient, contractual structures.

We will explore some of these issues in this discussion of sell-offs, liquidations, spin-offs, and leveraged buyouts. But first we present a case study of Dillingham Corporation, a company which executed each of these four transactions in a massive reorganization. The following account is based on reports published in *The Wall Street Journal*.

The Dillingham Case

From late 1978, when Dillingham began to sell off some of its properties, through 1983, when management took the company private in a leveraged buyout, the company went through a remarkable series of structural changes. In orchestrating these changes, management brought about a dramatic increase in the value of its stockholders' claims.

Before undertaking this general restructuring, Dillingham was a diversified firm involved in real estate, energy, maritime, and construction activities. In December 1978, the press carried a report that Dillingham was selling its Fabri-Value unit to the Grinnell division of IT&T and its Reef Cattle Management unit to an Australian investor. The latter operation had been losing money, but losses on such foreign operations were not deductible against U.S. taxable income. The capital loss on the sale, however, was deductible.

To assess the effect of these announcements on Dillingham's stockholders, we computed the rate of return on the shares on the day of the announcement and on the following day when the press carried the report. Adjusted for general stock market movements over that two-day period, Dillingham's stock price increased 7.8 percent.

In July 1979, management announced the suspension of its coal mining activities at its Cainmore mines in Canada due to operating losses. The market's response was to raise Dillingham's stock price by 5.1 percent (again, adjusted for market movements).

Ten days later, management initiated a continuing tender offer at the prevailing market price for all blocks of its Dillingham stock owned by holder of 50 shares or less. Management cited the disproportionate costs of servicing small accounts as the justification for the repurchase offer. While less than 1 percent of the outstanding shares were eligible, the announcement of the potential elimination of 2000–3000 small accounts generated an abnormal return of 3.5 percent for shareholders.

In orchestrating a remarkable series of structural changes, Dillingham's management brought about a dramatic increase in the value of its stockholders' claims.

In April 1980, Harry Weinberg, a private Honolulu investor owning 10 percent of Dillingham's outstanding shares, sought representation on Dillingham's board. It was rumored that Mr. Weinberg would try to bring about a merger of Dillingham with Alexander and Baldwin, a company in which he held a 13 percent stake. Dillingham's board postponed the annual meeting to prepare a proposal to reduce the board from 15 to 3 seats, according to which the unseated directors would assume new roles on an advisory council. The share price rose 9.3 percent at the time of the announcement of this anti-takeover move, and 3.2 percent more when the shareholders approved the plan denying Mr. Weinberg representation on the board (unless he upped his stake to 25 percent of the outstanding shares).[1]

Although unsuccessful in his bid to gain minority representation on the board, Mr. Weinberg did raise questions about whether Dillingham's stockholders were benefiting to the fullest extent possible from the company's extensive real estate holdings in Hawaii. After a careful study of the real estate operations, management proposed a partial liquidation of the Hawaiian properties on March 17, 1981. In the week of this announcement, Dillingham stock rose a market-adjusted 39.4 percent!

Two weeks later, when the board expanded the plan to sell nearly all the Hawaiian land holdings, the price jumped another 9.6 percent. The plan called for the following series of moves: the transfer of the properties to a newly formed limited partnership, Ala Moana Hawaii Properties; the spin-off of the limited partnership interest to existing stockholders; the liquidation of the properties; and the distribution of the cash proceeds to the limited partners (that is, the original Dillingham stockholders).

Even after Dillingham disposed of the Ala Moana shopping center, its "crown jewel," the stage had been set for a battle for control of the firm. On April 29, 1981, a group of Singapore investors bought a 5.7 percent stake, triggering a stock price rise of 4.7 percent. On September 25 the stake was increased to 9.6 percent and prices jumped another 7.5 percent.

The following day management announced a cash repurchase tender offer for 3 million shares, about 20 percent of the total then outstanding, at the then current market price of $12⅜. Although a spokesman for the board denied that the offer was related to the purchases of the Singapore investors, the board announced that only 1.6 million had been tendered. During the offer period, share prices fell 11 percent as the probability of a premium takeover bid declined.

On December 29, 1981, the board approved a change in the by-laws that provided for limitations on the rights of foreign owners. The board noted that U.S. maritime law required a minimum of 75 percent U.S. ownership to secure Maritime Administration-guaranteed financing and to retain the right to trade between U.S. ports. The change gave the directors the right to suspend voting rights and dividend payments on foreign holdings in excess of 20 percent on the outstanding shares. The by-law change left share prices unchanged.

In May of 1982 the firm repurchased all 1.5 million shares owned by the Singapore investors in a privately negotiated transaction at $14 per share when the current market price was $11.50 per share. The agreement included a "standstill" provision under which the selling group agreed not to acquire additional shares in Dillingham. The block repurchase and standstill agreement were greeted with a market-adjusted price decline of 3.3 percent.

Then, in September 1982, management announced a continuing plan to buy back additional shares in open market and private transactions in the following year. The market price of Dillingham shares jumped 3 percent upon this announcement and continued to climb another 17 percent through the middle of November.

On November 17, 1982 management announced a plan to take the company private in a deal arranged by Kohlberg, Kravis, Roberts & Co. The offer to public shareholders was made at $25 per share when the market price was $17 5/8. The return to stockholders was more than 25 percent at the time of the announcement (and roughly 40 percent by the time the deal was actually consummated). The leveraged buyout provided equity positions for senior management and no plans to dispose of any lines of business. Lowell Dillingham, chairman and a member of the founding family (which held 20 percent of the outstanding shares),

---

1. That Mr. Weinburg was unable to obtain a board seat and yet stock prices rose is not atypical. In a study of proxy contests, Dodd and Warner found that stock prices tend to rise upon the announcement of these contests, regardless of whether the dissidents are successful in acquiring board representation.

Even after the 160 percent abnormal price run-up, management expected enough additional gain from going private to be willing to pay a 40 percent premium.

described the proposal as a "unique opportunity to serve the best interests of all the company's constituencies, particularly shareowners and employees."

Summing Up Dillingham

Over this four-year period in Dillingham's history, we found that the company's public stockholders earned an *abnormal* return of 185 percent (which excludes the effect of the general market appreciation over this period). Of this total gain, more than 160 percent preceded the announcement of the leveraged buyout proposal. There can be little doubt that this restructuring of Dillingham greatly increased stockholder wealth. What seems even more remarkable, though, is that even *after* the 160 percent abnormal price run-up, management expected enough additional gains from going private to be willing to pay a 40 percent premium over the already dramatically increased market value of the company.

While the restructuring of Dillingham is an interesting case, we do not wish to imply that such gains accompanied most—or even the majority—of such restructuring transactions in recent years. To make general statements, we must examine data from larger samples of transactions. But before turning to this larger body of evidence, it is worthwhile noting two important features of the Dillingham case study. First, the stock price reactions to restructuring announcements have often been quite large, suggesting large expected gains from changes in corporate organizational structure and productive activities. Second, restructuring transactions—sell-offs, liquidations, spin-offs, and management buyouts— do not always occur as separate, isolated events but sometimes as a sequence of actions in a major restructuring plan.

Sell-offs

Over the last decade mergers and acquisitions have captured the imagination and focused the energy of many academic researchers in finance. The financial press has been equally preoccupied with business combinations and their potential effect on the economy and financial markets. With all this attention on multi-billion dollar acquisitions, it has been easy to overlook the extent of divestiture activity—the massive paring and shedding by American conglomerates of their divisions, subsidiaries, and smaller business units. In 1983, for example, W. T. Grimm reported 2533 mergers and acquisitions. What is less well known is that 932, or more than one-third of this total, were sales of operating assets from one corporation to another. As can be seen from Table 1, while total acquisition activity has increased since 1980, divestitures have increased slightly faster than the total.

A "sell-off" of assets in exchange for cash or securities is simply a "reverse" merger from the point of view of the divesting firm. From previous academic research we know that mergers, on average, create value for stockholders, though the lion's share of the gains generally go to the stockholders of the acquired firms. Divestitures also typically result in significant, positive abnormal returns for sellers and positive, but insignificant, gains for buyers. (For a more detailed discussion of studies of divestitures, see Scott Linn and Mike Rozeff's article immediately following). But this finding begs the question: if the merger of corporate assets increases the combined value of the two operations, how can the divestiture of previously acquired assets also create new value?

For the sale of a business unit to benefit existing shareholders, the selling price must exceed the

TABLE 1 Acquisition and Divestiture Trends: 1980–83*		Total Number of Transactions	Divestitures Included in Totals	Divestitures as a Percent of Totals
	1980	1,886	665	35%
	1981	2,395	830	35%
	1982	2,346	875	37%
	1983	2,533	932	37%

Source: W.T. Grimm & Co., Chicago

present value of the cash flows the unit will generate if retained within the organization. That is, the assets must be more valuable to the buyer than to the seller. This difference in value can result from synergies, the creation of scale economies for the buyer, or superior management. Alternatively, to the extent that the operations no longer "fit" with the seller's other activities, a sale may also create value by eliminating negative synergies (or what Linn and Rozeff call "anergies").

Our rationale for sell-offs might appear to be at odds with press reports of divestitures motives. For example, in 1974 Motorola announced the sale of its TV business to Matsushita Electric, a Japanese consumer electronics firm. The stockholders of Motorola enjoyed a market-adjusted gain of 21.9 percent. Management explained that the TV unit "hadn't achieved appropriate profit objectives in recent years." But how does simply selling a "loser" benefit shareholders? Shareholders don't escape losses by selling—they simply receive lower prices for the assets of losing operations.

A more plausible explanation is that Matsushita expected to turn the division into a "winner." But competition in the acquisition market forced Matsushita to share the expected gains with Motorola's stockholders. In fact, Matsushita's stock price actually declined when the deal was announced—though by a barely detectible 0.2 percent.

Another possible explanation is that divestitures represent corrections of prior acquisition mistakes. Linn and Rozeff find that divestiture "waves" follow one to two years after merger waves. This finding, however, should not necessarily be interpreted as challenging the value of merger activity. A firm may acquire another company with the intention of reorganizing the acquired firm, and getting rid of those businesses that don't complement the primary business lines. Also, changes in technology and product markets may cause combinations which were once valuable to become inefficient. A sell-off may simply indicate that the divested resources now have higher values in other uses.

Our point here is that the divestiture of previously acquired businesses may be consistent with many explanations besides the "admission of prior mistakes" hypothesis. At the current time we have no systematic evidence on why firms acquire and then divest business units. Nor do we have reason to believe that a single, simple explanation will cover all such cases.

In summary, our general finding is that the change of ownership and control in corporate sell-offs increases the wealth of the shareholders of divesting companies. We view the sell-off of a subsidiary, division, line of business, or other operating assets as a mechanism for transferring assets to higher-valued uses in other corporations. The gains may result from synergies or economies of scale offered by the buyer. Or the management of the buying firm may have a comparative advantage in monitoring and controlling the management of the subsidiary.

Liquidations

An extreme form of sell-off is the liquidation of assets. A liquidation represents a sale of assets and should not be confused with a decision to "shutdown" or abandon an operation. The assets are sold to another firm, and the proceeds are distributed to stockholders instead of being re-invested in new operating assets. Liquidations may be either partial or total. In the latter case the original firm ceases operations. We confine our attention here to total liquidations.

The interesting feature of total liquidations is the recognition by management that the existing organizational structure is no longer viable. In short, the firm is "worth more dead than alive." Not only do the assets have a higher-valued use elsewhere, but they are more valuable after being divided and sold off in a piecemeal fashion.

We examined a sample of 25 total liquidations occurring between 1963 and 1982. All 25 cases were voluntary dissolutions—that is, none of the firms were in bankruptcy. Although one might expect that these firms were performing poorly just before liquidation, this was not the case. During the period from 50 trading days through 5 trading days prior to the liquidation proposal, these firms experienced no abnormal price movements on average. That is, they did as well as expected given the general stock market performance.

In the trading week ending with the liquidation proposal, the average market-adjusted return was 9.0 percent, a statistically significant result. While the average gain was substantial there was wide variation among the sample. For example, the list of 16 gaining firms was topped by a 58.6 percent gain for National Silver in 1980 and a 56.7 percent gain for Reeves Telecom in 1979. At the other extreme were

The interesting feature of total liquidations is the recognition by management that the existing organizational structure is no longer viable.

losses of 12.5 percent for Telecor in 1978 and 11.5 percent for Reliance Manufacturing in 1964. Both Telecor and Reliance are special cases, however, since both had previously announced plans to find a merger partner. Their stock prices had initially risen in anticipation of a takeover. When the takeover plans fell through, the companies announced their intentions to liquidate. Presumably, their liquidation values were below the market's expectation of their value as a takeover candidate.

The market's strongly positive response to these corporate self-liquidations suggests that, in most of these cases, the current organizational structure was not leading to the most efficient use of the firm's assets and that dissolution was a higher-valued strategy. Management presumably recognized that continued operations would produce a substandard return on assets—one lower than the opportunity cost of capital. Concluding, furthermore, that the business was no longer viable as a going concern and could not profitably be sold as such to another corporate bidder, it elected to sell off its assets in parts and distributed the proceeds to stockholders.

Spin-offs

In its purest form, a spin-off involves a separation of the operations of a subsidiary from its parent into separate corporations, with no change in ownership of the equity claims. For example, a firm may form a subsidiary corporation and transfer assets to the new entity in return for all the stock certificates. The new shares are then distributed to the original stockholders of the parent on a pro-rata basis.[2] The two firms separate, and the subsidiary's management is vested with autonomous decision-making authority.

The distinctive feature of pure spin-offs is that parent company management gives up control of the subsidiary operations while shareholders maintain their proportional ownership of both operations. The interesting questions raised by such transactions are these: What can be accomplished with two separate, free-standing units that cannot be achieved under a unified organizational structure? Why can subsidiary management be more effective

as heads of an independent unit than as subordinates reporting to parent company management?

In an article which appears later in this issue, Katherine Schipper and Abbie Smith document a significantly positive market reaction to such spin-offs. In speculating about the reasons for this positive investor response, they state that expected tax savings and the ability to avoid regulatory interference seem clearly to have motivated a number of these transactions. But for the majority of spin-offs, the answer seems to lie in the diversity of operations within the firm. Schipper and Smith suggest that there may be large expected gains from simplifying a complicated conglomerate structure, decentralizing decision-making, and replacing an original set of compensation contracts which governed the conglomerate with two different sets of contracts, each tailored to the specific circumstances of the separate unit.

In our own work we found three reasons for spin-offs frequently given by management. The most common was a desire to "get back to basics, to the lines of business we know best." An organizational structure that is well-suited to certain operations may not profitably accommodate other, different business units. For one thing, compensation arrangements tied to the stock price of the parent may have little effect on the incentives of managers of a small division. If the division is spun off, new contracts tied directly to the stock price of the unit may be used to provide a much more effective means of motivating managers.

A second common motive was to circumvent implicit contracts with outside regulatory agencies by separating regulated and unregulated lines of business. For example, having a bank subsidiary may bring non-bank operations under the eye of banking authorities. Or in the case of rate-of-return regulated industries, such as public utilities, regulators may effectively "tax" income of profitable unregulated operations by figuring subsidiary returns into the allowable rate-of-return calculations for regulated operations.

The desire to reduce tax liabilities seems to have provided the impetus for the formation and spin-off of royalty trusts, particularly in the oil and gas industry. The strategy is most often associated

---

2. Occasionally the term "spin-off" is used to refer to the initial public offering of the stock of a subsidiary. If less than 100% of the subsidiary shares are sold, the remainder is typically distributed to parent company stockholders at a later date.

The stock price reactions to restructuring announcements have often been quite large, suggesting large expected gains from changes in corporate structure.

with Boone Pickens and Mesa Petroleum, and figured prominently in the recent proxy fight to restructure Gulf Oil. The ostensible motivation was to remove the double layer of taxation (first at the corporate level and then at the stockholder level on dividends) on distributed oil and gas income.

As a matter of curiosity we looked at the market reaction to the two Mesa spin-off announcements. For the two days surrounding the first spin-off proposal in 1979, the price of Mesa rose 9.7 percent after adjustment for general market movements. Surprisingly, however, when Mesa announced the offshore trust in 1982, the market-adjusted price declined by 14.4 percent upon the announcement. If both of these spin-offs were truly motivated by the desire to reduce taxes paid on oil and gas revenues, then we are at a loss to explain the recent bid by Mesa to reacquire the properties spun off in the 1979 transaction. It would seem that bringing the revenues back under the corporate umbrella would result in higher tax liabilities.[3]

A third reason for spin-offs was to facilitate mergers. In such cases, either the parent or a subsidiary was the target of a friendly takeover bid. The bidding company seeking only part of the target's assets arranged for the spin-off to precede the merger consummation. As an example, the spin-off of Houston Oil Trust by Houston Oil & Mineral was part of its plan to be acquired by Tenneco. The idea came out of a disagreement between the two companies' managements about the amount of "proven" gas reserves in Houston's U.S. producing wells.[4] The royalty trust was spun off to Houston's stockholders. Tenneco lowered its bid from $1.6 billion to $422 million in Tenneco stock because it was acquiring a much smaller fraction of the original asset base.

Another, and perhaps the most common, motive for spin-offs relies on the inability of investors to recognize the value of "hidden" corporate assets—those assets whose market values, though substantially above book values, are not reflected in corporate financial statements. Companies with valuable real estate holdings are often held to be undervalued for this reason, and are thus cited as prime candidates for spin-off. This line of reasoning

is presented by Dan Palmon and Lee Seidler of New York University:

Properties are shown at constantly declining historical cost net book values on the balance sheet, when they are often worth considerably more than cost. Reported income is understated because of the same requirement. These two [effects] combine to mislead investors in the opinion of managements, and tend to cause share prices to be unduly depressed.

As the popular story goes, spinning off the real estate operations will get rid of the "real estate discount."

In a crude test of this hypothesis, we looked at a sample of spin-offs of real estate subsidiaries.[5] In six cases in which *real estate firms* announced spin-offs of real assets, we found two-day abnormal returns of 0.3 percent—that is, virtually no response. But when we examined a sample of 20 *industrials* spinning off real estate subsidiaries, we found two-day average, market-adjusted returns of 9.1 percent.

When viewed together, these two sets of results do not seem to support the notion of a "real estate discount," of a systematic failure by investors to recognize the underlying cash profitability of real estate operations. The fact that the market does not appear to reward real estate companies spinning off real estate properties suggests that investors *are* capable of establishing the value of real assets within a larger corporate structure. It is only when the real assets are part of a diverse or conglomerate structure that the market responds positively. (Also, remember that the upward revaluation of the common stocks occurs when the spin-off plan is first *announced*. The subsidiary is not yet reporting separate financial information allowing investors to revise their valuations. Under the real estate discount story, it seems the revaluation would occur later, after investors see the separated operating results.)

Our findings do provide support, however, for our contracting-based argument presented earlier: namely, that the potential gains from spin-offs are larger when the divested unit consists of operations not closely related to the parent company's primary lines of business. Different operating units may not operate as efficiently as possible under a single, all-encompassing set of contracts. Such diversity of

---

3. Perhaps Mesa is anticipating tax write-offs from exploration and drilling in excess of other production income. If so, Mesa could be "purchasing" taxable income to fully use the excess write-offs. This would be comparable to U.S. Steel's acquisition of Marathon prior to taking substantial write-offs for discontinued operations.

4. See the recent article, "How a Royalty Trust Proved a Leaky Shelter and Angered Investors," *The Wall Street Journal*, April 6, 1984, p. 1.

5. See Hite, Owers, and Rogers (1983).

businesses may create the economic rationale for separating the operations into more homogeneous units with specialized contracts.

Stated more plainly, spin-offs seem part of a growing corporate design to promote decentralized, "entrepreneurial" management decision-making—while at the same time preserving a large, overarching diversified corporate structure.

Going Private[6]

In recent years, many large U.S. public corporations have transformed themselves into private companies. W. T. Grimm reports that in 1979 there were 16 buyouts of major firms totalling $600 million. By 1983, the number of transactions reached 36, and the dollar magnitude exceeded $7 billion. Many Wall Street analysts are predicting an even larger dollar volume in 1984 as the size of the deals becomes ever larger.

The term "going private" covers a wide range of transactions, all of which result in a new organizational structure with closely-held or private ownership. The ownership claims of a diverse group of outside stockholders are replaced by equity claims concentrated in the hands of a small group of investors, including the managers of the restructured firm.

In a "pure" going private transaction, management or a dominant owner-manager purchases the ownership rights of outside stockholders and reorganizes the firm as a closely-held operation. In such cases, the purchase of outside equity is accomplished by the management team without participation of a third-party equity investor.

In their published study of such management buyouts, Harry DeAngelo, Linda DeAngelo, and Ed Rice (henceforth DDR) report that for their sample of 45 buyouts, insiders typically owned just over half the total number of shares prior to the going private bid. Although management may borrow on personal account to effect the purchase, corporate leverage generally increases very little in these deals. DDR examined the financing mix of 13 transactions and found that the median debt-to-assets ratio increased modestly from .26 before to .30 after the buyout.

Several explanations of the potential gains from going private have been offered. Most obvious is the savings from eliminating the registration, listing, and other stockholder-servicing costs associated with outside ownership. Especially for companies with relatively small capitalization, the direct costs of public ownership can be significant.

Perhaps most important, though, are the incentive effects of combining ownership and control in the management team purchasing the firm. As owners, the managers have a much greater stake in corporate profitability. Furthermore, besides increased equity ownership, compensation contracts can be restructured with greater flexibility in the absence of outside shareholders.

Consider a simple case in which a key operating executive owns 10 percent of the firm's shares and receives a fixed salary. Suppose an opportunity arises that would increase current cash flow by $1.00 but would require longer hours for the manager in question. With a fixed salary, the manager must trade off his 10¢ share in the gain against the personal value of the extra leisure forgone. If he values his leisure at more than 10¢ he will not have the incentive to undertake the action. Increasing that manager's percentage ownership is likely to induce extra effort, and thus to align management's interests more closely with those of stockholders.

Another possible means of resolving this potential conflict between management and stockholders is to provide the manager with an incentive compensation contract that allows him to capture the gains from his extra effort. Of course, in the real world, conditions will be far more complicated than those in our simple example; and it will be a difficult task to determine the extent of any single executive's contribution to actual results. But there is probably an even greater impediment to adopting such a compensation scheme in the public corporation: namely, that a disproportionate share of cash flows going to a single executive will probably appear "excessive" to some stockholders, leading to costly legal actions in which the judicial system is asked to determine the "fairness" of such compensation. (The costs of such litigation aside, the courts are not likely to view an executive's marginal contribution to the value of his or her firm as their principal criterion of "fairness.")

The advantages of going private in such situations include, then, additional flexibility in compen-

---

6. This discussion is based in large part on the De Angelo, DeAngelo, and Rice (1983) paper and private discussions with the authors and Terry Smith.

sation contracting and a reduction in monitoring costs. In a private corporation, a manager can contract for a "disproportionate" share of the cash flows—one more closely matched to his marginal contribution to firm value—without fear of costly legal interference from outside shareholders. Also, the fact that other equity participants are typically insiders, too, should reduce the costs of determining the direct linkage between performance and results.

In short, we would expect to see very detailed contracts among the new owner-managers in companies going private, with the distribution of operating profits linked more closely to managerial performance than to ownership proportions.

The Leveraged Buyout

Unlike the "pure" going private deals we have been discussing, leveraged buyouts involve participation by third-party equity investors and substantial amounts of borrowings. In a sample of 23 leveraged buy-out proposals, DDR report far smaller management ownership fractions than in pure going private transactions. In their profile of the average firm acquired through a leveraged buyout, management owns just over $13 million of a total market value of $83 million (these market values are calculated 40 trading days prior to the proposals). From DDR's data one gets the impression, not surprisingly, that insider ownership proportion declines as the size of the deal increases. Furthermore, for five transactions for which they had detailed financial information, they report an increase in the median debt-to-assets ratio from .11 to .86.

Leveraged buyouts are thus different from "pure" going private transactions by virtue of their third-party equity participation, lower management ownership fractions before the buyout, and significantly larger increases in debt after the reorganization.

Henry Kravis of Kohlberg, Kravis, Roberts & Co., a pioneer in arranging leveraged buyouts, provides some insight into the typical contractual structure. Kravis and his partners put up equity, sell an interest to the target firm's management, and arrange loans for the balance of the purchase price. The existing management remains in place, while Kravis and his partners provide financing and control the board of directors. As he puts it,

Our approach is that we do not know how to run a company. We know that we are very good at financing, we are financially oriented. We know how to control a company and we know when it is getting off course. We know how to set long-range goals for companies and we know how to maximize value in a company. But the day-to-day running of a company is not in our interest.[7]

The buyout specialist plays a key role as an intermediary among management, equity investors, and lenders. Management no longer needs to deal with a diverse group of small stockholders, but instead with the specialist as a representative of outside equity. The advantage of this arrangement is that specialized management incentive contracts, which would be very expensive for a diverse stockholder group to enforce, can now be efficiently monitored by the specialist.

One of the most visible aspects of leveraged buyouts is the dramatic increase in debt ratios. In some cases, once conservatively leveraged public companies (or their divisions) lever their private equity as high as 10 to 1. What can explain this turning "upside down" of corporate capital structures?

One argument holds that buyout candidates typically have low amounts of debt. Perhaps they are underleveraged, and the restructuring takes advantage of unused "debt capacity." While we do not have a precise theory of optimal capital structure, we seriously doubt that such a dramatic increase in debt usage could arise *solely* from a previous failure to make the maximum use of debt financing. In fact, some finance theorists would argue that going private reduces corporate debt capacity because managements holding a large equity stake have even stronger incentives than otherwise to take actions which benefit themselves, as stockholders, at the expense of lenders.

A second possible explanation for the extensive use of debt financing is that interest payments offer a tax advantage. One wonders, however, why management did not exploit this advantage as a public company. Also, the additional depreciation write-offs provided by the step-up of assets after the buyout should make the tax deductions from interest payments less valuable as a tax shield.

There is one other very important reason why we find both the unused "debt capacity" and "tax advantage" explanations to be implausible—or cer-

---

7. See "The Entrepreneur Series: Henry R. Kravis," *Hermes*, Fall, 1983.

tainly not exhaustive: the first order of business after the company goes private is to start paying down the debt.[8] The arguments citing the tax advantage of debt and the unused debt capacity of public companies both imply that not only will debt be advantageous at the time of the takeover, but it will continue to be valuable after the firm is private. If large amounts of debt are taken on during the buyout and reduced shortly thereafter, then it seems that leverage has no longer-range purpose, but functions principally as part of the *mechanism* to take the company private. Remember that part of the expected gains from the buyout comes from the elimination of shareholders. The use of large amounts of debt may simply be the means of achieving the desired concentration of ownership among a small group of equity participants, who in turn exercise control through the buyout specialist.

At the same time, however, such high debt ratios also provide the potential for management to take actions that are harmful to lenders. The extensive restrictive covenants in leveraged buyout loan agreements are themselves strong evidence of this potential conflict.

How are these conflicts of interest resolved? Here again, the buyout specialist plays a key role. Because he intends to return to the debt market for future buyouts, the specialist has strong incentives to monitor the contracts. He must be sensitive to lenders' interests if he is to maintain his "reputation." Also, should the leveraged firm violate any of the specific provisions of the covenants, the costs of renegotiating the covenants should be reduced by having a specialist who serves as intermediary among a relatively small group of lenders.

Clearly, the set of contracts among managers, outside equity participants, lenders, and the buyout specialist is more complex than we have indicated. But because the firms are taken private, the actual contracts are not readily available to financial researchers. As the details of these contracts come to light, they should provide a wealth of data for improving our understanding of incentive contracting.

Conclusion

As we have seen, many corporations are streamlining their operations by selling certain lines of business. Others are creating free-standing companies out of subsidiaries and divisions. Some companies are simply calling it quits and liquidating their assets piecemeal. Still others are converting from public to private ownership and increasing the ownership of managers.

This massive corporate restructuring may simply be a fad, the brainchild of a few enterprising investment bankers foisted upon impressionable corporate managements. However, the empirical findings summarized here, and more fully in the articles which follow, suggest that these restructuring transactions create significant value for stockholders. Such widespread changes may in fact reflect a major development in the evolution of the corporate form—an evolution toward greater efficiency, toward a corporate structure more effective in generating and storing value for stockholders.

To understand the potential gains from restructuring, it is useful to focus on the conflicts of interest that can arise among the different constituencies of the corporation. For example, operating managers in large conglomerates may be poorly motivated. Divestiture may provide a means of improving the new owner's ability to motivate and monitor management performance. Spin-offs may also help to motivate management by providing operating management with greater autonomy, market recognition, and financial rewards than was possible as a united conglomerate.

More drastic alterations, such as management and third-party leveraged buyouts, suggest that the loss of value arising from the separation of ownership and control in the public corporation may be significant. Given the large premiums paid in such restructurings—premiums voluntarily offered by managements—there seems little doubt that corporate values are expected to increase in the process.

---

8. Ibid.

The authors would like to thank Don Chew, the editor of this journal, for his editorial assistance and safeguarding of the English language.

The Corporate Sell-Off

Scott C. Linn and Michael S. Rozeff,
The University of Iowa

Introduction

For decades the glamor, wealth and suggestion of economic power that attend corporate mergers and acquisitions have captured the attention of the media, academics and, inevitably of course, regulators. But while the spotlight has been focused principally on mergers and acquisitions, the divestiture has quietly become an important phenomenon in the management of corporate resources. In fact, the recent prominence of the divestiture is probably the most visible sign of that massive reallocation of corporate assets that has come to be known as "the restructuring" of corporate America.

The rising importance of the divestiture or "sell-off"—by which we mean the sale of a subsidiary, division or product line by one company to another—is seen most readily in the growing volume of such deals. In 1983 alone there were some 932 divestitures of more than $500,000 in assets. And in every year since 1971 sell-offs have amounted to at least 35 percent of the number of mergers.[1] Besides the increasing volume and dollar value of these transactions, the roster of well-known companies selling off large businesses also attests to the divestiture's rising favor among corporate strategists. In 1983, for example, General Electric sold its metallurgical coal business, RCA Corp. its finance company, and Dun & Bradstreet its television stations.

While academic studies have provided extensive documentation of the valuation consequences of mergers and acquisitions, it is only recently that studies of corporate divestitures have begun to appear in the corporate finance literature. Partly because financial economists have scanted divestitures, but also no doubt because of the strong hold of the "conventional wisdom" on Wall Street thinking, myth and unexamined assertion are rife in published commentaries on sell-offs. The popular accounts of Esmark's sale of Vickers Energy Company are a case in point. Esmark's common stock gained significantly in price when this sale was announced. Why? Echoing a Wall Street commonplace, Eugene Brigham (in the most recent edition of what is perhaps the most widely distributed finance text ever published)[2] argued that the market was thinking of Esmark as primarily a meat packing and consumer products company. Investors thus collectively overlooked Esmark's large holdings of oil reserves, resulting in a significant undervaluation of Esmark stock. Once the sale was announced, however, the market came to its senses.

This explanation is inconsistent, of course, with the central premise of modern finance theory: the efficiency of capital markets. In an efficient stock market, a company's current stock price reflects the market's unbiased estimate, using all publicly available information, of future expected cash flows from the company's operations. In the case of Esmark, there seems no reason to doubt that many people knew about the company's ownership of Vickers, and were aware of the value of Vickers if it were sold to another company. What the market did not know was *if* and *when* the sale would take place. The revaluation of Esmark occurred only when it became clear that Vickers would be sold.

But if market ignorance and a resulting undervaluation of Esmark's stock was not the reason why the stock price rose on the announcement of the sale, then what was? Our answer is simply that Vickers was worth more to several potential buyers than to Esmark, and that Esmark took advantage of this discrepancy in value by selling Vickers in a competitive market. Through the sale Esmark captured at least a portion of Vickers' increased value.

---

1. See the *Mergerstat Review* published by W. T. Grimm & Co.

2. *Financial Management*, (Chicago: Drysdale Press, 1982).

Two Cases of Successful Sell-Offs

A small amount of economic analysis should help place in perspective the two examples which follow, as well as serving as prologue to further discussion of the basic questions: Why do companies divest? and what are the market consequences of so doing?

If the selling company is rational, then it should certainly not expect to lose anything by the sale. A subsidiary will therefore not be sold for any price less than its current worth to the seller. Of course, some companies do make mistakes, so that the best we can hope to observe is that *on average* selling companies do not lose as a result of the sales.

Stated more positively, we assume that corporate managements sell off subsidiaries in order to strengthen their companies and add value for their stockholders. If management's plans are fulfilled (on average), and if the market is reasonably efficient, then this should show up in an upward revaluation of the selling company's shares *at the time the market learns of the sale*. In sum, economic logic tells us that we should observe sell-offs accompanied by gains (or at worst no losses) in the prices of selling company shares. Were we consistently to see price decreases in response to divestiture announcements, we would seriously have to wonder why managements en masse were taking actions that seemed to harm their shareholders.

A similar logic obtains for the buying company. If the buying company pays a price for the subsidiary that is reasonable in view of the returns that can be earned on its investment, then at the very least the buying company should not lose from the purchase. But if the buyer's operations form an especially good "fit" with the operation, such that the divested subsidiary is worth far more to the buyer than to the seller (and provided competing bids don't drive the subsidiary's price too high), then the market may expect significant gains to the buyer to result from the combination. Under this set of circumstances, the stock of the buyer will also rise.

A prime example of a well-structured sell-off— one in which the buyer as well as the seller appeared to benefit—was the sale by Warner-Lambert of Entenmann's, the bakery business, to General Foods. The price was $315 million. The sale was announced on October 6, 1982, and the stock price of Warner-Lambert closed up $2 to $24⅜ on that day.

General Foods' stock increased $2⅛ to $41⅜. After accounting for market price movements, the wealth increase to General Foods' stockholders was about $44 million. The gain to Warner-Lambert shareholders was approximately $101 million.

We can draw several inferences from these market responses. Since Warner-Lambert was paid a total of $315 million for Entenmann's and since the stock increased by roughly $100 million in value, the implied value of the subsidiary to Warner-Lambert prior to the sale was about $215 million. This means that the percentage "premium" paid by General Foods Corp. was about $100/$215, or 47 percent, above its value to Warner-Lambert.

Even with such a large premium, the stock market apparently approved of the acquisition. In fact, the $44 million gain in the value of General Foods' stock suggests that the market believed the present value of Entenmann's (future expected cash flows) as part of General Foods was some $359 million, or $44 million greater than the cost of $315 million. Stated another way the implicit value of the benefit/cost ratio to General Foods was $359/$315 or 1.14.

What accounts for these wealth increases? Why was the market valuing Entenmann's more highly as part of General Foods than Warner-Lambert? Security analysts noted that General Foods would be able to reduce the materials and manufacturing costs of Entenmann's. The President of General Foods, Philip Smith, stated that General Foods would increase the distribution of Entenmann's products, providing coverage of up to about 60 percent of the country (a marked increase from the 36 percent coverage prior to the sell-off). He was also quoted as saying that the bakery would very clearly earn a rate of return above its cost of capital. Hence it is understandable that General Foods' stock went up.

What about Warner-Lambert, why did its stock price rise? Entenmann's was a profitable company for Warner-Lambert, one which it had nurtured from its start as a regional baker. Despite its current level of profitability, it had the potential to become even more profitable in someone else's hands, someone that could take advantage of buying, manufacturing and distribution economies. Because of competition among potential buyers, Warner-Lambert was able to capture some of the potential gains that would come from the buyer's more efficient handling of the company.

Another plausible reason for the gain in Warner-Lambert's stock was that the market viewed its exit

In cases where a business is worth no more to any prospective buyer than the liquidation value to the seller, then closing down the unit and selling off the assets may be the best solution.

from the baking business as a signal that it possessed profitable investment opportunities that it wished to pursue in the health-care area. It is possible that the presence of Entenmann's was somehow interfering with these plans.

A second example of a sell-off benefiting both buyer and seller was the sale by INA Corp. of Hospital Affiliates International to Hospital Corp. of America. When this sale was announced on April 20, 1981, INA common rose $1⅞ to $45¾, while Hospital Corp. increased $2¾ to $42½. In dollar terms the wealth increase of the INA common was about $75 million while the market value of Hospital Corp. rose by $126 million. The subsidiary was sold for $650 million. In this case the implicit premium paid by the buyer was only 13 percent ($75/$575).

Both companies gave clues as to why their stocks rose. Hospital Corp. pointed out that economies of scale resulting from the acquisition would provide substantial savings in overhead and operating expenses. It noted that the company would now be able to enter four new states and extend operations in several others.[3] INA Corp.'s chairman and chief executive officer made it clear that the sale now made it possible for INA Corp. to allocate more resources, both management and capital, to its strategic plan to expand various insurance lines. This suggests not only that the subsidiary was worth more to someone else, but that its presence in the selling company was interfering with the pursuit of more profitable opportunities.

Why Divest?

One popular corporate motive for divestitures is that they are a means of raising capital. But such an explanation does not tell us very much. Obviously sell-offs do not increase a company's *sources* of capital since they simply exchange one set of assets for another. A sell-off does, however, increase the company's working capital in that long-term assets are usually exchanged (at least in part) for cash. For example, the sale by International Harvester Co. of its Solar Turbines International division to Caterpillar Tractor Co. may have been motivated by such a reason. The proceeds of the sale ($505 million) were used to cut Harvester's short-term debt by half. Because the division sold had been consistently profitable, the problem apparently was an asset/liability structure in which fixed assets were financed by too much short-term debt.

But however logical this explanation might seem, it really relies on the existence of some unexplained capital market "imperfection" that prevented Harvester from otherwise (and more cheaply) reorganizing its financing. The sale of fixed assets to increase working capital seems an expensive way of obtaining cash as compared with borrowing or an equity issue. Thus we strongly doubt that this motive for divestiture is a pervasive one.

Our review of sell-offs indicates, moreover, that the great majority involve healthy companies that have adequate access to the capital markets. Even in the Harvester case there are signs that the sale of the unit was not simply out of distress. Harvester had found that the use of turbines for its vehicles was impractical. Meanwhile there were active bidders for the division and Harvester was able to realize a sale price of almost 2.5 times its book value.

One sometimes reads that a sell-off is undertaken in order to repay debt and strengthen the balance sheet. But, as with divestitures undertaken to raise working capital, we find it implausible that this is a widespread motive for sell-offs. For one thing, this seems an expensive way to change one's debt/equity ratio. The sale of assets obviously involves a disinvestment decision. Like the case for sell-offs as a means of increasing working capital, this explanation seems to confuse the results of a sale with its cause. The real cause may simply be that the seller feels it can obtain a good price for the subsidiary. The fact that the newly liquid assets are used to pay down debt is merely a secondary, an incidental effect—one, at any rate, that should not be expected to increase stock value.

Divesting companies also sometimes offer as their motive the desire to get out of capital-intensive businesses. Gulf & Western, for example, cited the capital intensity of its cement subsidiary when it was

---

3. Another possibility is that the market expects Hospital Corp.'s acquisition to confer some monopolistic advantage. We do not believe, however, that an increase in monopoly power explains the gains to Hospital Corp. For one thing, its share of the market was small even after the purchase. Secondly, it did not buy hospitals in the same locations as its own hospitals. Third, the stock price of its largest rival (Humana) did not change when the acquisition was announced.

It is only when the selling company is able to locate a buyer who expects to restore the unit's profitability, or to take advantage of some other unexploited feature that real gains should be expected from selling out.

sold. It is clear, however, that excessive capital requirements per se do not explain sell-offs. Obviously the buying company is willing to undertake the capital requirements of the subsidiary. And if the subsidiary were actually or potentially profitable, the seller could obtain financing for it. We are thus inclined to regard this explanation as a way of saying that the subsidiary does not fit with the remaining operations of the company and is causing a real diseconomy of some sort.

A fourth prominent reason for sell-offs is that the unit is "losing money." We interpret this more broadly to mean that the rate of return from the unit's activities is less than the required rate of return. A lack of profitability in this sense may be signaled by more readily available indicators, such as disappointing sales volume, a slowdown in the sales growth rate, a decline in market share, or a technological change which lowers profit margins and makes a unit unprofitable.

In all of these instances, however, a sell-off is not necessarily the optimal response to the problem. There are any number of alternatives to divestiture of a sub-performing business. Profitability might be restored through changes in product pricing, alterations in product line, further investment in the operation, or cost reduction. And, in cases where a business is worth no more to any prospective buyer than the liquidation value to the seller, then closing down the unit and selling off the assets may be the best solution.

The important point here is that getting rid of an unprofitable business should not necessarily increase the market value of the company. In an efficient market, the presence of a unit that is detracting from stockholder value (that is, not earning its required rate of return) should already be reflected in the value of the parent company's shares. The stock price should already be marked down such that, at that reduced value, new or prospective shareholders expect to earn a normal rate of return on their investment in the company's shares. If at this point the company is able to sell the unit for exactly its value (to the seller), there should be no gain or loss in the value of the selling company's shares. It is only when the selling company is able to locate a buyer who expects to restore the unit's profitability, or to take advantage of some other unexploited feature of the subsidiary, that real gains should be expected from selling out.

In other words, selling a subsidiary *merely* because it is "unprofitable" or "losing money" should benefit the selling company only if it receives more than the unit's present worth as part of that company. When companies use this language to justify sell-offs, it probably means that they are unable to restore profitability, and that the assets are worth more when put to different uses or in the hands of more efficient users. The other possibility is that the presence of the money-losing subsidiary is somehow interfering with the remaining operations of the company. Casting off this corporate albatross, so to speak, may allow the remaining units to operate more profitably, and this too should cause the seller's shares to increase in price.

A fifth rationale for sell-offs is that the seller wishes to sell unrelated units or units that do not fit with its strategic plan. Or, put slightly differently, the seller wants to concentrate its resources in areas of operations that it knows best. This kind of explanation can also be interpreted as saying that the unit is producing diseconomies that would be removed if the unit were sold. Since these diseconomies are present only when the unit is run in conjunction with the other units of the company, they constitute "negative synergies," or what we have elsewhere termed "anergies."[4] Ridding the company of such "negative synergies" should cause the share price to rise.

Sixth, and finally, we come to the motive which we think prompts the majority of corporate divestitures (as well as explaining the market's positive response to them): namely, that the divested unit is worth more as part of another company (or even as a stand-alone unit) than as part of its present organization. We presented two cases earlier. But as additional examples, consider the sales by U.S. Steel and Holiday Inns of their shipping subsidiaries. Both operations were sold to maritime companies, and both transactions were probably motivated by the ability of the buyers to operate the subsidiaries more economically.

Of this list of common motives for sell-offs, then, only two make economic sense: removal of diseconomies and the presence of buyers willing to purchase the unit for more than its value to the seller. The sale of an unprofitable unit per se should

4. See our paper "The Effects of Voluntary Spinoffs on Stock Prices: The Anergy Hypothesis."

The immediate stock price reaction to a sell-off announcement can be seen as conveying the market's perception of the long-run cash flow consequences of the sell-off.

not be expected to add to stockholder value. Only if the sale is to a bidder who expects to restore profitability, or if the sale removes diseconomies, would we anticipate a stock price increase (although the market may interpret even uneconomical sales as part of a general restructuring plan, reflecting management's long-run commitment to improving profitability). Finally, those motives that view a sell-off solely as a means of raising capital (or increasing working capital) or strengthening the balance sheet should not, in and of themselves, have a significant effect on stockholder value.

The Evidence on Sell-Offs

Methods of Study

We earlier described two instances of divestiture in which the capital market clearly perceived that both the buyer and the seller added value for their stockholders. Although case studies help us to understand the market consequences of some individual events, broad generalizations about the market's response to sell-offs must rely upon studies that have examined large samples. It is to the findings of those studies that we now turn.

Studies of divestiture, like most research in modern finance, attempt to measure the effects on stock prices of *announcements* of the event in question—in this case, sell-offs. Assuming that the current price of a company's stock reflects the market's assessment of its prospective cash flows and that the market reacts quickly and unbiasedly to news, the immediate stock price reaction to a sell-off announcement can be seen as conveying the market's perception of the *long-run* cash flow consequences of the sell-off. That perception may not prove to be accurate, but it will be "unbiased"—that is, neither too high nor too low on average. A rise in the selling company's stock price carries, of course, the market's seal of approval and a decline signals its skepticism. The same logic holds for the buying company as well.

There are two factors, however, which tend to obscure the market's true reaction to a sell-off: (1) our inability to determine precisely when the market first learns that a sell-off has been decided upon,

and (2) the daily movements of the market itself that tend to sweep along individual stocks. In practice, these problems are overcome by (1) relying upon the earliest dates on which the sell-offs are publicly announced and by (2) removing statistically that part of a stock's price movement that can be accounted for by market movements. The studies discussed below use various benchmark models to calculate the expected percentage change in a divesting or buying firm's stock price, conditional on the general market return, both on and around the day on which the divestiture is announced in the financial press. The difference between a company's actual and its expected return on the announcement date is called the "abnormal return" to stockholders, and it is interpreted as the market's assessment of the expected cash flow consequences of the forthcoming sell-off.

Involuntary Sell-Offs

Divestitures are generally voluntary, but sometimes they are forced upon the firm as the result of some regulatory action. James Ellert, Donald Kummer, and Peggy Wier have each studied the impact on firms of divestitures forced by Federal antitrust actions. They all conclude that involuntary divestitures tend to reduce the value of the stocks of the affected firms. Ellert, for example, finds that the average abnormal percentage change in the market value of the equity of 205 defendants in antitrust merger cases was −1.86 percent during the month that the merger complaint was filed. Furthermore this result was significantly different from zero.[5]

Why do these declines in market value occur? Three main possibilities come to mind. The first is that the market expects that in a forced sale the seller will not obtain a fair price. Although this might be reasonable if the sale is hurried or if the assets find no ready market, we do not expect such conditions to be pervasive. As a general rule there should be enough competition among buyers to ensure a fair price for the subsidiary.

A second possibility is that the regulators are right, and that the forced sale actually takes away some monopolistic advantage possessed by the selling company. If this were the case, though, we would expect the stock prices of *rival* companies to

---

5. Kummer finds that for the period covering one month before through one month after the complaint filing, firms involved in horizontal, and horizontal-vertical mergers lose −1.63% and −1.55%, both statistically significant.

A third, and to us most likely, possibility is that forced divestitures destroy generally efficient asset structures.

fall as well, since the break-up of monopolies is supposed to result in generally lower industry prices. Studies by Robert Stillman and Bjorn Eckbo have addressed this issue by examining the effects of antitrust complaints on the shares of rival firms, and both find no evidence to support this claim.

A third, and to us the most likely, possibility is that forced divestitures destroy generally efficient asset structures—ones built up over the years to take advantage of synergies and economies of combination. In this case, forced divestitures would be expected to increase costs and decrease cash flows, thereby causing stock prices to decline.

Voluntary Sell-Offs

The results of the most recent available academic studies of *voluntary* sell-offs are summarized in Table 1. Each of the five studies finds that during the two-day period ending with the day on which the announcement of the sell-off is printed in the *Wall Street Journal*, the stocks of the sellers gain on average relative to the market. The average price increase is about one to two percent, a result which is statistically significant.[6] These findings probably understate the positive effect of sell-offs because most of the studies also indicate that the selling firm's shares rise by an additional one to three percent in the month prior to the sell-off announcement.

On balance, then, the market appears to feel that divestiture decisions by management serve stockholder interests.

In an attempt to learn more about why the market responds positively to divestitures, April Klein divided her sample according to whether the sell-off announcement contained information about the price of the sale. She found that only the group of firms that announced sale prices of the divested assets experienced average gains (of 2.41 percent). Those companies that announced sell-offs but did not provide a transaction price showed virtually no stock price movement (–.06 percent). We checked this finding on our own sample and found similar results. Those companies announcing prices rose about 2.95 percent while prices of those that did not rose only 0.49 percent.

What is the meaning of these findings? Klein contended that the revelation of the sales price to

the market was

a way to convey favorable information about the market value of the divested assets, and hence the firm. The information can be either that the value of the assets increases on transfer of ownership or that the firm sells assets undervalued by the market.[7]
As suggested earlier, the latter explanation is inconsistent with the premise of efficient markets. And, again, with so much evidence testifying to the sophistication of markets, we should certainly be reluctant to rely upon pervasive undervaluation of assets as an explanation of the market's systematically positive responses to sell-offs.

We fully agree that providing a transaction price to the market fixes the increase in value that arises from a transfer of ownership. But why is publication of a price *necessary* for the market to raise the value of the selling company's shares? Once the stock market learns that a sale is contemplated, its knowledge of the market for those real assets should enable it to make an educated guess about the value of the assets in an open-market sale. Recently, for example, Esmark's announcement of a potential leveraged buyout was accompanied in the *Wall Street Journal* by analysts' estimates of the market values of Esmark's subsidiaries. If analysts are generally capable of making such estimates (and there seems little reason to doubt this capability), then there should be some form of stock market reaction regardless of whether the sale price is announced.

One possible explanation of this result is that companies choose not to announce selling prices when they are unable to obtain a selling price that exceeds the divested unit's worth to the seller. Since we see no reason why companies should behave in this way, however, this explanation does not seem persuasive.

A second possibility is that the presence of a sales transaction price is a "proxy" for one or more other variables. For example, many of the divestiture announcements contain statements of motive as well as the price of the sale. To test whether the disclosure of motive also influences the market's response, we read all the announcement articles in our sample and classified them into four categories according to the presence or absence of a transaction price and the presence or absence of a motive for the sale. Table 2 contains the results.

---

6. The study of Gordon Alexander et al is an exception in this regard.

7. "Voluntary Corporate Divestitures: Motives and Consequences," University of Chicago, 1983, p. 31.

TABLE 2	Price Announced	Motive Announced	
The Effects of Announcing the Sale Price and the Motive for the Sale on the Seller's Stock Value (Average Abnormal Daily Returns Over Days –1 through 0)		yes	no
	yes	3.92% (N = 14)	2.3% (N = 21)
	no	.70% (N = 15)	.37% (N = 27)

It is clear that although the publication of the sales price is still highly correlated with abnormal returns to shareholders, a published statement of the motive for divestiture also plays an important role. The abnormal returns roughly double when the announcement discloses a motive for the sell-off—regardless of whether a sales price is given. For those cases when the sales price is given, the abnormal return increases from 2.3 percent to 3.92 percent when a motive for the sale is also announced.

Pursuing a somewhat different approach to this question, Gailen Hite and James Owers found that when previously announced proposals for sell-offs are cancelled, the divesting firms' stocks give up all of their earlier gains. Hite and Owers interpret this evidence as inconsistent with the hypothesis that the announced sell-off and sales price convey new information to the market about the subsidiary's true worth. If such information truly caused the market to revalue the shares, the selling company's stock would retain its price gain.

On the other hand, however, we find it somewhat hard to understand why *all* the gains are lost. For this seems to suggest that the market has ruled out almost all possibility of a sale in the future. At a minimum the market has learned from the proposal that the selling company is willing to sell the subsidiary. Perhaps the company's unsuccessful testing of the market demand for its assets means that a sale is simply a dead issue for the foreseeable future.

The explanation of this puzzle, as well as that posed by Klein's findings, will have to await further research.

Some Aggregate Data on Sell-Offs

Before concluding, let's look briefly at some general patterns of divestiture activity to see what such patterns suggest, if anything, about the corporate motives for selling off businesses.

Sell-offs, it turns out, can be divided into two

If the rate of mergers jumps we expect that the rate of divestitures will rise sharply within one to two years thereafter.

EXHIBIT 1
Numbers of Mergers and Divestitures, 1963–1983.

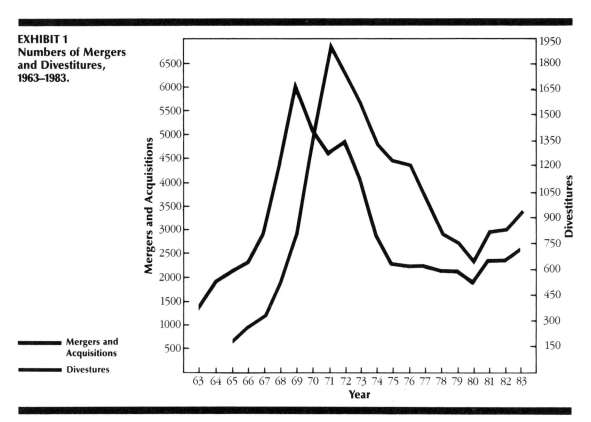

categories: those associated with a previous merger and those that are not. We believe this breakdown is a useful one because of the evidence that so many divestitures are associated with previous mergers. As stated earlier, the ratio of divestitures to mergers has been about one to three. Exhibit 1 shows a plot of major combinations—mergers and acquisitions—and divestitures since 1963.[8] These data show clearly the famous merger wave of the late 1960s, with a peak of over 6,000 mergers in 1969. There also is a divestiture wave that peaks in 1971 at almost 2,000 divestitures.

The fact that the divestiture curve has roughly the same shape as the merger curve, but displaced by several years, is no statistical accident. We converted the data to annual percentage changes (or rates of change) for each series and found a strong statistical relationship between the annual rate of change in merger activity in any given year, and the annual rate of change in divestitures *two years after*.

In other words, if the rate of mergers jumps we expect that the rate of divestitures will rise sharply within one to two years thereafter. Conversely, if the merger rate declines we can predict that the divestiture rate will fall several years later.

One can also point to specific cases in which companies active in the merger area have also been active in the divestiture area. In the five years ending with 1982, such prominently acquisitive companies as ITT, Genesco, Beatrice Foods, and W.R. Grace had each no less than 12 divestitures.

The performance of the stock market also appears to have a marginal relationship to the divestiture rate. Buyers and sellers of subsidiaries seem to transact more frequently when the market is high relative to historical levels. Using regression analysis, we found that in years when the stock market fell—such as 1966, 1969 and 1973–1974—the rate of divestiture fell below what one would have predicted given the previous merger rates; and when

---

8. The source is W.T. Grimm & Co.

The fact that sell-offs increase within such a short time period after mergers suggests that acquiring companies quickly decide to "prune down" the companies they have bought.

stocks performed well there was a tendency for more divestitures to occur. This relation was very strong during the period 1966–1977, but did not appear to hold during 1978–1982.[9] On balance, though, the data seem to show that the stock market environment, or perhaps the overall business environment as represented by the stock market, influences the rate of divestiture.

What does the relationship between divestitures and mergers tell us? On an aggregate basis, the fact that sell-offs increase within such a short time period after mergers suggests that acquiring companies quickly decide to "prune down" the companies they have bought or merged with. Indeed it is quite possible that they have the intention to do this even at the time of the merger. In other words, they may really wish to acquire only a part of the company they buy. And, for one reason or another, purchase of the entire company may have been the least costly way of obtaining the portion they wanted. Alternatively, merging companies may buy another firm with the idea that restructuring it will increase its productivity. The buyer's management may intend to carry out a reorganization that the previous management was unwilling to undertake. Still another possibility is that the bidder discovers after the acquisition that some pieces do not "fit" and would be worth more as part of some other company.

Conclusion

The evidence suggests that voluntary sell-offs, on average, create value for divesting companies' stockholders. Some analysts explain the stockholder gains to selling firms by arguing that divestitures force the market to recognize the value of previously undervalued assets. But, while the jury may still be out on this question, the abundant testimony of modern finance to the efficiency of the market in pricing assets should cause us to view this argument with some skepticism.

A more plausible explanation of the stock price increases is that the divested assets are worth more to someone else than to the current owner, and that competition among firms for those assets allows the selling firm to obtain "economic rents" from the sale. Stockholder value may also be created, in some cases, by selling a unit whose continued presence is causing diseconomies or "negative synergy" in the selling firm.

A value-enhancing corporate policy, therefore, calls for continual review of the assets of the firm, assessing both the internal effects of a unit's continued presence and the external market for these assets. The rules to guide such strategic thinking are fairly simple:

1. If an operation is worth more as part of some other company or companies, then management should consider selling it.

2. Selling an unprofitable operation does not necessarily add value for stockholders. Buyers can be expected to come forth only if they see the opportunity to restore profitability, and earn a rate of return on their investment—the acquisition price—equal to or greater than their cost of capital. Although the sale itself may provide a positive signal to the market that management is paying greater attention to profitability, the economic value of the firm increases only if the sale price is greater than the value of the expected cash flows to the seller.

3. If no buyers are found, and the prospects for future profitability are dim, then the piecemeal liquidation of the operation's assets may be the best solution. In fact, as some of the research cited earlier by Gailen Hite suggests, some entire companies have proved to be worth more "dead than alive." There may be many others which would best serve their stockholders' interest by either partially or, in extreme cases, totally liquidating their assets.

---

9. Despite the fact that the stock market has risen in four of the last five years, the rates of divestiture have been less than what one would expect given the changes in the numbers of mergers. Perhaps this is just an artifact of the current depressed levels of both mergers and divestitures.

The Corporate Spin-Off Phenomenon

Katherine Schipper and Abbie Smith,
University of Chicago

Introduction

With a frequency that seems ever increasing, the financial press reports shareholder or management proposals based on the premise that some companies are worth more divided than whole. Trans World Corporation and Gulf Oil Corporation offer two recent examples. In February 1984, after shareholders rejected a proposal to split Trans World Corporation into as many as five companies, the airline business (TWA) was separated from the rest of the firm through a public offering of a minority interest in TWA, followed by a spin-off of the remaining shares. One motive offered for the spin-off was that the airline's losses might otherwise "swamp" Trans World's profitable units—which include Hilton International, Canteen Corporation and Century 21.[1] Several analysts also predicted that both Trans World Corporation and TWA would be more valuable apart than combined. Two reasons were given. First, because the airline's unions would henceforth not be able to point to the profits of other divisions as a source of subsidies to airline operations, the airline would be better able to extract concessions from its unions. Second, it was argued that some of the other divisions were in industries that command relatively high price-earnings multiples, and that association with the airline was causing the earnings from these industries to be capitalized at a lower multiple.[2]

In the case of Gulf Oil, the proposal was to create a royalty trust and spin off the shares to the current owners of Gulf. The proposal was based on a study that claimed the royalty trust might result in a package of securities with market value nearly 60 percent larger than Gulf's then current equity value.[3]

It is probably too soon to evaluate the effects on shareholders of the spin-off of TWA by Trans World. And, given the defeat of Boone Pickens's proposal for a royalty trust (not to mention the recent takeover of Gulf by SOCAL), we will never know how the Gulf proposal would have worked out. Nevertheless, there have been enough corporate spin-offs in the last twenty years to allow us an at least preliminary answer to the question: Is the whole ever worth *less* than the sum of its parts? And if the answer is yes, then the obvious question arises: Why? What are the benefits to shareholders from such "negative mergers?"

On the basis of three empirical studies of the shareholder wealth effects of voluntary spin-off announcements, the answer to the first question appears to be yes.[4] The real cause of this consistently positive market reaction, however, is not always clear. Some spin-offs hold out the promise of significant tax or regulatory advantages. But, for the majority of these transactions, the benefits are much more elusive. A spin-off, after all, merely creates two (or more) companies where before there was one, generally without any obvious major operating or managerial changes (the kind of changes that financial economists like to designate as "real" as opposed, say, to changes produced by financial or accounting sleights of hand). Some analysts have argued that spin-offs enable the market to assess the real worth of assets whose value have become obscured by the complexities of conglomerate corporate structures. But, to believers in efficient markets, the systematic gains to shareholders at the time of spin-off announcements continue to be something of a mystery.

In this article, we review the available evidence documenting the market's response to spin-offs. But before turning to the results of the studies, and the

1. See "Trans World Corporation's Plan to Spin-off TWA was Prompted by Fears on Losses," *Wall Street Journal*, October 28, 1983.

2. See "Trans World, Soon to be Shorn of its Airline, Appears to Offer More Attractive Prospects," *Wall Street Journal*, December 30, 1983.

3. See "Pickens' Mesa Group, Gulf Wage Stiff Campaigns for Proxy Victory," *Wall Street Journal*, November 23, 1983.

4. See G. Hite and J. Owers, "Security Price Reactions around Corporate Spin-off Announcements," *Journal of Financial Economics*, December 1983; J. Miles and J. Rosenfeld, "The Effect of Voluntary Spin-off Announcements on Shareholder Wealth," *Journal of Finance*, December, 1983; K. Schipper and A. Smith, "Effects of Recontracting on Shareholder Wealth: The Case of Voluntary Spin-offs," *Journal of Financial Economics*, December, 1983.

light they cast on this market enigma, we start by explaining what a spin-off is, and how it differs from the other forms of corporate restructuring that have recently begun to proliferate. Then we discuss some of the professed corporate motives for spin-offs, offering what we believe are the most plausible explanations for the market's positive reaction. Finally, we present and interpret the results of our own study of the stock market's response to 93 voluntary spin-off announcements between 1963 and 1981.

What is a Spin-Off?

There are several ways in which a firm can be partly or completely separated into two or more parts. We will restrict our focus here to "pure" voluntary corporate spin-offs. In such spin-offs management distributes shares of a subsidiary, usually pro rata, to the shareholders of the parent company as a dividend in kind. Hence the spin-off does not alter shareholders' proportional ownership of the subsidiary and the parent. The spin-off does, however, separate the common stock of the parent and subsidiary companies for subsequent trading.

The term "spin-off" is also sometimes used by the business press to describe a variety of corporate structural changes which differ from the spin-off as defined above. Spin-offs are often confused, for example, with divestitures. In a divestiture (as described in the article immediately preceding), the divesting firm sells a set of net assets to another firm, and is generally paid in cash or marketable securities (sometimes including stock of the buying firm).

Spin-offs should also be contrasted with "split-ups," in which a firm separates into several parts, distributes the stock of these parts to its shareholders and ceases to exist. And both spin-offs and split-ups can be further distinguished from "split-offs," in which stock of a subsidiary is distributed to one or more of the parent firm's shareholders in exchange for their parent company stock. A "split-up" can be structured to have the same consequences as a spin-off; that is, the emergence of two separate firms with the same owners. A "split-off," however, alters ownership because some shareholders exchange ownership of the parent for ownership of the subsidiary.

Finally, the term "spin-off" is also sometimes applied to financing arrangements in which a parent firm offers a percentage of the shares of a subsidiary for public sale. These public offerings generally differ from spin-offs in that effective control of the subsidiary is maintained by the parent. Also unlike spin-offs, such partial public offerings generate a cash inflow from the sale of the minority interest.

Spin-offs can be either taxable as dividends or tax-free. By "tax-free" we mean that shareholders receive shares of the subsidiary but pay no tax until the shares are sold. For a spin-off to be tax free, Section 355 of the tax code requires that there be a business purpose, as opposed to tax avoidance, for the spin-off. It also requires that both the subsidiary and parent be actively engaged in some business for at least five years preceding the spin-off, that the subsidiary be at least 80-percent owned by the parent, and that the parent distribute all its subsidiary securities without a pre-arranged plan for these securities to be resold.

Because a spin-off can be regarded as simply another form of stock dividend, the SEC has not always required registration of the stock distributed in a spin-off. But during the late 1960s, there were allegations that private companies were using "shell corporations" and spin-offs to go public without SEC registration. Specifically, a private company could merge with a public "shell" and then arrange to have its stock distributed to the shareholders of the "shell." Through this process, the once private firm could have its shares traded in the over-the-counter market without registration. The popularity of this mechanism was evidenced by the appearance in the *Wall Street Journal*, between July 15 and October 10 of 1969, of 25 advertisements to buy, and 19 advertisements to sell, such corporate shells.[5]

The SEC responded by effectively requiring registration of stock issued in spin-offs. Furthermore, the Commission suspended trading and even sued certain firms for violations of the Securities Acts. Thus, there was a shift in the regulatory environment during 1969–70 which resulted in more disclosure about firms engaged in spin-offs. This shift was probably most noticeable in the over-the-counter market.

Our attention, however, will be directed mainly to spin-offs by American and New York Stock Ex-

---

5. See A. Hershman, "The Spin-off: One Minus One Equals Three?" *Dun's Review*, March 1969, and L. Orlanski, "Going Public Through the Back Door and the Shell Game," *Virginia Law Review*, 1972.

change companies. The motive for spin-off described above, and the resulting regulatory reaction, do not seem to be central to the resurgence of spin-offs we have witnessed in the past few years. Nor do they appear to have influenced the market response to spin-offs by NYSE and ASE firms reported in academic studies.

Possible Sources of Shareholder Gains from Spin-Offs

Several explanations have been offered for the stock price increases associated, on average, with voluntary spin-off announcements. One of the most straightforward is that shareholder gains arise from creditor losses. As developed by Dan Galai and Ron Masulis,[6] this hypothesis contends that parent firm bondholders lose in a spin-off because they have no claim on the assets which are spun off solely to stockholders. This reduction in bondholders' collateral implies a transfer of wealth from bondholders to stockholders.

Galai and Masulis point out, however, that any redistribution of wealth from bondholders to stockholders would be reduced to the extent that spin-offs are anticipated by bondholders. In fact, contractual arrangements existing prior to the spin-off may make the Galai-Masulis argument irrelevant. If the spun-off entity is legally separate from the parent (that is, a subsidiary as opposed to, say, a division), the debts of the parent and the entity to be spun-off are also legally separate *before* the spin-off. Creditors of one legal entity thus have no claim on the assets of the other, unless such a claim is provided for in the indenture agreement.

Also casting doubt on Galai and Masulis's hypothesis is their implicit assumption that debt is *not* assigned to the spun-off entity. In practice, debt is often transferred to the subsidiary in a spin-off. Depending on what debt is spun off, the original creditors of the parent may actually benefit from—or at worst will be unaffected by—such a spin-off. For example, what was junior debt of the total company before the spin-off sometimes becomes senior debt of either the spun-off company or the parent. In such a case, bondholders would have a claim with higher priority, but on a smaller asset base, than

before. The expected net effect of such a spin-off on the value of that debt would be uncertain—possibly negative, possibly positive. Most important, however, many bond covenants contain provisions which limit dividends and forbid asset dispositions of any kind. Because spin-offs are dividends in kind and are also considered asset dispositions, they are subject to the usual constraints that creditors write into debt covenants.

Tax and Regulatory Advantages

A second possible source of shareholder gains from spin-offs lies in their expected effects on taxes, and on regulatory or legal constraints that bind the firm. Three examples follow.

1. After a spin-off, one or both of the "new" companies' tax or regulatory status may differ from that of the original firm. Companies with certain types of assets can take advantage of the tax code by spinning off those assets. Prime examples include the formation and spin-off of REIT's and natural resource royalty trusts. These trusts pay no income taxes and pay 90 percent of their income as dividends to shareholders. The 1980 Annual Report of Southland Royalty, for instance, makes the statement that its royalty trusts "were created in order to afford shareholders a more advantageous method of participating in ownership of Southland's long-lived producing oil and gas properties," and goes on to describe the tax-saving mechanism in some detail. Royalty trusts thus allow oil and gas producers to shelter much of their income from taxation while, at the same time, allowing them to retain direct ownership of the oil and gas reserves (which, of course, allows shareholders to benefit from unexpected increases in oil and gas prices).[7]

2. If a parent spins off a regulated utility subsidiary, ratemaking commissions may grant rate increases sooner, or grant larger rate increases, than otherwise because the spun-off utility can no longer be subsidized by cash flow from unregulated operations. This motive was explicitly stated in the 1980 Annual Report of the Philadelphia Suburban Corporation:

First of all, we think there has been some confusion on the part of the public and the regulatory au-

6. D. Galai and R. Masulis, "The Option Pricing Model and the Risk Factor of Stock," *Journal of Financial Economics*, 1976.

7. See D. Levin, "Royalty Trusts, an Issue in the Gulf Oil Dispute, Seen Drawing Those Who Expect Oil Price Rise," *Wall Street Journal*, October 21, 1983.

By reducing the number annd complexity of operations under a single management group, spin-offs may promise major improvements in management's efficiency in employing assets.

thorities over the needs of the water company when viewed against the success of the unregulated portions of the company. There have been repeated suggestions that the water company derives significant benefits from its association with [the unregulated portion of the business]—benefits which should be reflected in lower rates.

Southern Union offers another example of a firm spinning off a poorly performing regulated business to prevent cross-subsidization by profitable business lines. In 1982, the company's New Mexico gas utility was earning as low as 2.5 percent on its equity base, and there was speculation that the utility would be spun off to strengthen the utility's appeal for rate relief.[8]

3. A parent that spins off a foreign subsidiary enables that subsidiary to circumvent restrictions placed by Congress on U.S. firms operating abroad. For example, Sea Containers' 1975 Annual Report described its reason for the spin-off of a foreign subsidiary as follows:

We do not pay bribes nor do we conceal the true nature of our expenses. We do pay our agents commissions and fees in 41 countries in connection with the business they generate for us. We are genuinely concerned that the outcome of the current revelations of questionable payments abroad by U.S. companies will be regulation by Congress of companies which operate the way we do, and this could again make us uncompetitive with foreigners . . . We feel the best defense is to segregate out a portion of our foreign activities and separate [that portion] from Sea Containers Inc. to allow the former to grow in overseas markets without interference by the whims of the U.S. government.

Changes in Managerial Focus, Accountability and Incentives

The tax and regulatory advantages described above are probably significant for only a small portion of the companies spinning off business units. What accounts, then, for other spin-offs—those which seem to have been prompted neither by taxes nor regulatory concerns?

Among the most popular explanations for the positive stock market reaction to spin-offs is the no-

tion that investors have a predilection for the "pure play." That is, investors are better able to understand and evaluate single-industry stocks; accordingly, they pay higher prices for companies as separate entities than as parts of diversified firms. Or, put somewhat differently, investors have a positive distaste for the complexity of conglomerates, and thus systematically discount their values.[9]

Such an argument, however, seems to run against the grain of efficient markets theory. In a sophisticated market, with its incentives to identify undervalued companies, there are enough analysts adept at untangling consolidated financial statements to ensure that conglomerates will trade at fair value. We shouldn't expect diversified companies to sell consistently below a value which reflects the sum of the values of their component businesses *simply* because the market is incapable of understanding them.

There may indeed be a systematic investor preference for "pure plays." But such a preference, we suspect, reflects less the inability of analysts to comprehend conglomerates than the markets' skepticism about the quality of management decision-making, controls and incentives in large, sprawling organizations. In short, investors may be unsure about how well diversified firms are being managed. If there are management inefficiencies that result from the conglomerate form *per se*, then the market may systematically assign higher prices to the parts when separated than combined. This explanation, moreover, is completely consistent with the information efficiency of the stock market.[10]

Some recent work in accounting and finance has focused attention on the potential improvements in managerial incentives from "disentangling" the performance of the segments of a company. This line of research highlights management incentive and performance problems that can arise when managers are spread too thin, are trying to operate several highly disparate segments, or when the exceptional performance of a given segment is lost in the consolidated financial statements. And, as this research would suggest, spin-offs may offer the most direct solution to these problems. By reducing the number and complexity of operations under a single management group, spin-offs may promise ma-

---

8. See G. Anders, "Southern Union Draws Investor Interest on Belief Utility Spinoff Will Boost Parent's Earnings," *Wall Street Journal*, April 14, 1982.

9. See M. Greenebaum, "Making the Most of Unnoticed Assets," *Fortune*, June 15, 1981.

10. "Information efficiency" means that the stock price of a firm fully reflects all public information.

A systematic investor preference for "pure plays" may reflect the market's skepticism about the quality of management decision-making, controls and incentives in large, sprawling organizations.

jor improvements in management's efficiency in employing assets. The simplification of information flows may allow managers to exert tighter control over existing operations, and to allocate the resources of the firm more effectively.

Some Casual Evidence

In the course of our own research, we found that 19 of the 93 companies in our sample offered explanations for their spin-offs which support the idea that removing a poor business "fit" and sharpening the corporate focus is expected to improve management's productivity. For example, in 1981 Itek Corporation spun off its eyeglass-manufacturing business, Camelot Industries Corporation, from its defense electronics and graphics business. The attention Itek's management devoted to the struggling eyeglass division prior to the spin-off apparently detracted from Itek's other operations. Mistakes such as gross overstocking of inventory in its graphics division and cost overruns in its government-contract business might have been avoided in the absence of the demands placed on management by the vision products division.[11] In the 1981 Annual Report, Itek's management reported:

With the separation of vision products, Itek is once again entirely a high technology company. While the separation of vision products was costly, we are now in a position to totally dedicate our efforts and resources where Itek has expertise and leadership.

Besides eliminating some of the distractions inherent in a diversified enterprise, a spin-off may also improve efficiency by strengthening managers' incentives to act in the shareholders' interests. Because a spin-off separates the parent and the spun-off subsidiary, it allows for a more effective evaluation and control of managerial performance in each business. For example, a spun-off subsidiary, as an independent public firm, will issue complete, audited financial statements. Before the spin-off the subsidiary's operating results are buried in consolidated statements or, at most, given only partial disclosure as a business segment.

The other gauge of performance that a spin-off makes possible is the stock price of the spun-off subsidiary. Stock prices reflect the collective judgment of investors about management's effectiveness in employing corporate assets. To the extent that executives' rewards can be linked to their companies' stock prices, the capital market can be used to monitor executives' actions.[12]

Some kind of incentive scheme, whether tied to stock prices or, more likely, to accounting results, was found to exist in most of the firms spinning off subsidiaries *before* the spin-off was announced. But the incentive effects of such compensation arrangements are typically diluted in diversified firms. The influence of a particular segment's operations on corporate income and share price is presented together with the results of other units, often operating in different industries. By "unbundling" these effects, a spin-off can improve managerial accountability. And stock options and stock purchase plans can provide a very effective means of motivating subsidiary management by providing a much more direct link between managerial performance, share prices, and management rewards.

The improvement of managerial incentives as a motive for spin-off was stated explicitly by six of the firms in our sample. For example, the president's letter to shareholders in the 1980 Annual Report of Peabody International describes the incentive effects of Peabody's spin-off of GEO International:

Speaking from personal experience, one of the most exciting benefits has been a rekindling of the entrepreneurial spirit and initiative within both Peabody and GEO. Managers in both companies now feel that their individual efforts can make a significant difference in bottom line results.

Similarly, the management of Valmac Industries cited the improvement of incentives in both firms as a motive for spinning off Distribuco, its food distribution subsidiary:

The poultry processing business has been subject to seasonal and cyclical fluctuations and the cotton merchandising business is subject to cyclical fluctuations also, some of which are beyond the control of management, while the food division business is somewhat more constant and is not subject to such external factors.

The corporate separation will enable the manage-

---

11. See "Itek: Shedding Its Eyeglass Division and Focusing on High-Tech Lines," *Business Week*, November 8, 1982.

12. The importance of stock price as a measure of performance in contracting with managers is discussed in E. Fama and M. Jensen, "Separation of Ownership and Control," *Journal of Law and Economics*, June, 1983 and in D. Diamond and R. Verrecchia, "Optimal Managerial Contracts and Equilibrium Security Prices," *Journal of Finance*, May, 1982.

ment of both companies to more clearly measure results of efforts of employees of each company, and to provide an incentive, through stock options, stock purchase plans, and through direct payments to reward the efforts. —1974 Annual Report—

The Evidence on the Shareholder Effects of Spin-Offs

To measure the effects of spin-offs on shareholders, we estimated the "abnormal return" (the return over and above that expected from market movements) to common stock of 93 firms that announced voluntary spin-offs between 1963 and 1981. Over the two-day period including the day before and the day of the spin-off announcement, shareholders earned abnormal positive returns of 2.84 percent. (Standard statistical tests indicate a confidence level of 99 percent associated with this result.) Sixty-one announcements were associated with positive abnormal returns, 51 with returns of at least 1.0 percent. Moreover, the size of the abnormal return was associated with the relative size of the subsidiary being spun off; that is, larger spin-offs (relative to the size of the company) resulted in larger abnormal returns. Similar results were also obtained by Gailen Hite and Jim Owers (1983) for a sample of 123 spin-offs, and by Jim Miles and Jim Rosenfeld (1983) for a sample of 55 spin-offs. Both of these studies also report that larger shareholder gains are associated with the spin-off of larger subsidiaries (where size is measured in terms of equity values relative to the parent firm).

The Bondholder Rip-off Revisited

As suggested, one potential source of these gains are the bondholder losses resulting from the wealth transfer mechanism described earlier. A transfer of wealth from bondholders to shareholders would be caused by an unanticipated reduction in bondholders' collateral. A wealth transfer upon a spin-off announcement is much less likely, however, if (1) the spun-off firm already exists as a legal subsidiary; (2) bondholders' collateral is protected by a debt covenant constraint on dividends; or (3) debt is allocated to both parent and subsidiary.

We attempted to determine the extent to which these conditions were present in our sample of companies, and our findings were as follows:

- Of 82 spun-off subsidiaries for which there was information available, 27 were created at the time of the spin-off from divisions that had not been legally separate. The rest were subsidiaries established or acquired more than a year in advance, or formed from existing subsidiaries.
- General dividend constraints or specific requirements that lenders approve spin-offs were known to exist for 34 sample firms. However, the nature of debt covenants could not be identified for about half the sample.
- Finally, debt was assigned to subsidiaries in at least 64 of the 93 sample spin-offs. The mean ratio of the book value of debt to total assets for 45 of these 64 spun-off subsidiaries (again, those for which information was available) was .51. The range of debt to assets for this subsample was from .03 to .89.

To gain more direct evidence on the effect of spin-offs on bondholders, we also examined bond price and bond rating changes around spin-off announcements. If the market's positive reaction to spin-offs was the result of wealth transfers from creditors to shareholders, then we would expect spin-off announcements to lead to declines in both bond prices and ratings. Of the 62 spin-off announcements associated with gains to shareholders, we were able to obtain price data for 26 bonds of 13 firms. For only 11 of these 26 bonds was there evidence of a decline in value upon the announcement.

We found ratings for 19 bonds of 16 firms. Only two bonds (both of the same firm) experienced a decline in bond rating during the year after the spin-off announcement.

Needless to say, our results are not suggestive of a widespread reduction in bondholder collateral caused by spin-offs. Furthermore, this finding is supported by results of Gailen Hite and Jim Owers, who actually find *positive* risk-adjusted returns (though not statistically significant) to bondholders at the time of spin-off announcements.

The Evidence on Tax- and Regulatory-Motivated Spin-Offs

Eighteen, or nearly 20 percent, of our 93 sample firms stated motives for spin-offs consistent with the realization of tax or regulatory advantages. The average abnormal return to shareholders of these 18 firms was a positive 5.07 percent, nearly twice that of the entire sample. These spin-offs, however, do not

To the extent that executives' rewards can be linked to their companies' stock prices, the capital market can be used to monitor executives' actions.

account for the total gains to the sample; that is, they are not "driving" the average results. (This statement is based on a standard test for differences in shareholder gains between the "tax-regulatory" subsample of 18 announcements, and the rest of the sample). While regulation and taxation provide powerful motives for certain companies to spin off a subset of their net assets, relatively few firms have the special characteristics necessary to realize tax and regulatory benefits from a spin-off. To repeat, such tax and regulatory benefits arise primarily from the special tax treatment accorded real estate investment trusts and royalty trusts; from removing the possibility that a rate-regulated utility may be subsidized by the operations of a nonregulated business; and from removing legal and tax restrictions on the actions of U.S. firms operating abroad.

Some Indirect Evidence on the Management Efficiency Hypothesis

We have also speculated that separating a firm into two or more segments may increase management efficiency by allowing managers to concentrate on a single line of business. The opportunity for such efficiency gains would be most likely to exist in companies with complex operations. In order to provide a crude test of this hypothesis, we reasoned that, among our sample of spin-off companies, we should expect to find a disproportionate number where there has been a past increase in the complexity of the firm's operations, as measured by the number and diversity of businesses to be managed. In fact, we found that our sample of spin-off firms is characterized both by diversity of operations and by recent expansion. For the average firm, over the five years before the spin-off announcement, sales (adjusted for inflation) grew at an annual rate of 20 percent, and the number of employees grew at a rate of 19 percent.[13] Also, more significantly, in 72 of the 93 spin-offs we examined, the parent and its spun-off subsidiary were in different industries. This is perhaps the strongest evidence we have that the desire to segregate distinct business lines, presumably for reasons of improved management efficiency (although the possibility of market under-

valuation of conglomerate assets cannot be ruled out), is behind the recent spin-off movement.[14]

Closing Remarks

We have documented a statistically significant positive average share price reaction for a sample of 93 voluntary spin-off announcements on the American and New York Stock Exchanges between 1963 and 1981. There are, we think, three plausible explanations of this favorable market response: (1) tax savings; (2) loosening of regulatory constraints; and (3) improvements in managerial efficiency, accountability and incentives brought about by reducing the number and diversity of operations under one management. We also consider, though mainly to dismiss, the explanation that such gains to shareholders represent wealth transfers from bondholders. There is little evidence to suggest that spin-offs consistently cause unanticipated reductions in bondholder collateral.

A good number of the spin-offs in our sample (at least 18 of the 93) seem clearly to have been motivated by expected tax or regulatory advantages. The most common tax advantages arise from the formation and spin-off of REITs and natural resource royalty trusts, both of which continue to be exempt from corporate income tax (though legislative rumblings about such "loopholes" are now faintly audible).

Finally, spin-offs may improve management efficiency by sharpening focus and strengthening incentives. Breaking off a single segment from a diversified enterprise frees the segment managers and the parent firm managers to concentrate on fewer lines of business. The segment can operate and be evaluated independently of the parent's operations. Spin-offs also allow for a much more direct link between segment managers' efforts and corporate results, whether measured in terms of reported net income or, perhaps more important, the share price of the spun-off business. Investors' apparent willingness to pay more for the firm divided than whole may, in many cases, reflect their judgment that each of the parts, because simpler, will be better managed.

---

13. As a benchmark, we computed growth rates in inflation-adjusted sales and number of employees for a random sample of non-spin-off firms (over the same time periods as for the spin-off sample). The growth rates are 13 percent (sales) and 7 percent (employees).

14. Nine of the twenty-one "similar" parent-subsidiary spin-offs were probably intended to relax regulatory or tax constraints. Of these, three spun off a foreign subsidiary. An additional six separated a natural resource royalty trust from an operating company or separated a regulated natural resource firm from an unregulated one.

Going Private: The Effects of a Change in Corporate Ownership Structure

Harry DeAngelo and Linda DeAngelo,
University of Rochester and

Edward M. Rice,
University of Washington

Introduction

In a "going private" transaction, the entire equity interest in a public corporation is purchased by a small group of investors that includes members of the incumbent management team. In some of these management buyouts, current managers obtain 100 percent equity ownership of the newly private company. In others, management shares equity ownership with a small group of outside investors, which typically places representatives on the private company's board of directors. Besides contributing equity capital, these outside investors generally arrange other financing for the acquisition of the publicly held stock. Deals with third-party investors almost always involve substantial borrowing by the private company and thus are commonly known as "leveraged buyouts."

Whether structured as a leveraged buyout or otherwise, going private transactions simply rearrange the ownership structure of a single operating entity. They involve no obvious "synergies"—no economies of scale or vertical integration—of the kind that potentially characterize, and are often used to justify, a business combination of two operating companies. Because there is no possibility for the usual "synergistic" gains, critics of management buyouts argue that going private cannot possibly create sufficient value *both* to provide public stockholders adequate compensation for their ownership interest in the firm and to make the transaction profitable from management's perspective. Furthermore, because management is itself the purchaser of its company's publicly-held shares, it has an ob-

vious incentive to place its own interest ahead of the welfare of its public stockholders. And, therefore, if management buyouts leave the size of the corporate "pie" unchanged, and if we assume that management benefits from the deal (which seems reasonable since they propose it), then public stockholders are bound to lose.

Our own study of going private transactions, however, does not support this argument. Rather, it indicates that public stockholders benefit substantially from the typical buyout. In the average buyout proposal, the management group bids a price for the outstanding shares that significantly exceeds the market price prior to (and immediately after) the announcement of the offer. Therefore, at least according to the market's assessment, public stockholders appear to be getting a good deal. Furthermore, the willingness of corporate management to buy out the public stockholders at a premium over market suggests that going private may actually increase the size of the corporate "pie" for some companies. This possibility raises a related question: what expected benefits underlie these value increases?

There appear to be several potential advantages from a management buyout which, taken together, may create sufficient new value to enrich *both* managers and public stockholders in the process. For one thing, going private can result in significant savings by eliminating the costs of registration, listing, and stockholder servicing incurred by publicly traded companies. Second, and perhaps more important, management's increased ownership interest after the buyout provides it with stronger incentives to perform, which can lead to significantly greater firm profitability. Furthermore, private companies seem to have more flexibility in adopting compensation packages which recognize and thus stimulate individual effort.

In the past few years, the number and size of public companies (or their divisions) receiving leveraged buyout proposals seem to have increased dramatically. This leveraged buyout phenomenon suggests that going private *per se* may increase debt capacity. The typically heavy reliance on debt financing in these deals, together with the "step-up" of largely depreciated assets, may provide significant tax benefits. Also potentially valuable in leveraged buyouts is the fact that largely passive public stockholders are replaced by knowledgeable investors who, with their substantial interest in the resulting private firm, often participate in the financial management of that firm. Moreover, the monitoring service provided by these buyout specialists may also add significant value by increasing managerial productivity.[1]

Public Stockholder Returns from Going Private: The Evidence

We recently completed a study of 72 companies that proposed to go private during the period 1973–1980. We identified these firms by inspecting each issue of *The Wall Street Journal* over that period. Forty-nine of these proposals were by companies listed on the AMEX at the time of the proposal, and the other 23 were by firms listed on the NYSE. Of the 72 proposals, 45 involved no third-party equity participation, 23 were leveraged buyouts with outside equity investors, and four were withdrawn before the precise structure of the deal was announced.

In the median firm in our sample, management held 50.9 percent of the common stock, and there were a total of 1,890 stockholders. The median size of these companies was $70.9 million in annual revenues and $53 million book value of total assets. The median ratio of long-term debt to total assets was 12.6 percent. The median market value of the public stock interest totaled $6.3 million as of two months before the proposal.

This profile of companies proposing to go private suggests that they have generally been fairly small companies, with concentrated management ownership and low leverage ratios. But, while we have no systematic evidence, our general impression is that firms proposing to go private since 1980 have tended to be considerably larger on average, have had greater third-party participation, and have been financed with greater amounts of debt. (In the largest leveraged buyout bid to date, Esmark's management recently offered $2.4 billion to buy out its public stockholders.) Not surprisingly, companies proposing buyouts in recent years also appear to be characterized by smaller proportional management ownership than firms proposing to go private during 1973–1980.

To assess whether going private proposals tend to benefit public stockholders, we used open market stock prices as an index of stockholder welfare. Specifically, we examined the average stock price changes associated with two events: (1) initial proposals to go private made by the 72 firms in our sample and (2) withdrawals of the proposal by the 18 firms for which we could clearly identify a withdrawal announcement. Our statistical method isolates the impact of a management buyout proposal (or its withdrawal) on a particular stock's value by controlling for the effects of the time value of money, risk (or beta), and overall market movements.

Proposals to Go Private

Our empirical analysis indicates that, on average, initial proposals to go private are associated with substantial increases in stock prices. This finding holds at high levels of statistical significance using a variety of methods and time periods for measuring stockholder wealth changes. For example, the average company's share price increased 22.3 percent (net of risk-adjusted market movements) over the two days surrounding a proposal announcement. Furthermore, within this sample average, virtually all of the firms (68 of 72) experienced positive changes in share value.

The data also suggest that the market anticipates going private proposals. In the period immediately prior to formal announcement, the shares of many firms increase substantially in value. Anticipatory stock price runups also characterize other ma-

---

1. A more thorough discussion of these issues (as well as a detailed statistical analysis) can be found in our earlier paper (DeAngelo, DeAngelo, and Rice (1984)).

*Going private offer premiums and stock value increases
are comparable to those associated with arm's-length
acquisition bids.*

jor corporate transactions, such as interfirm tender offers and mergers. Thus, if we measure the impact of the going private proposal over the two months immediately prior to, and including the announcement, we are likely to obtain a more accurate assessment of the impact of the proposal on public stockholder wealth. This measure shows a 30.4 percent average rise in share price, after adjustment for general market movements. Again, almost all (65 of 72) sample firms experienced value increases in this two-month period.

These large price increases reflect the premiums over market value that managers offered public stockholders in going private proposals. We calculated offer premiums for the subsample of 57 proposals in which public stockholders were offered strictly cash compensation. These premiums averaged 56 percent when measured relative to the share price two months prior to the proposal announcement.

As mentioned earlier, going private transactions are usually viewed with suspicion because of the conflict of interest when management seeks to buy out the public stockholders. It is thus worth noting that going private offer premiums and stock value increases are comparable to those associated with arm's-length acquisition bids. For example, during roughly the same period that going private offer premiums were averaging around 56 percent, the average premiums in cash tender offers ranged from 49 to 56 percent, depending on the sample studied. Also, the 30.4 percent stock value increase associated with the average buyout offer is comparable to the 24 percent average increase in target firm value associated with merger announcements and the 40 percent increase for targets of tender offers.[2]

Insider Information Effects

Our evidence indicates, then, that public stockholders typically experience large wealth increases when managers propose to take a firm private. But does this evidence really mean that going private *per se* is the cause of this wealth increase? After all, wouldn't managers be most likely to seek to increase their ownership interest when they foresee better prospects for the company, *even as a public*

concern, than those reflected in the pre-offer market price? And wouldn't an insider proposal to go private therefore reveal favorable, previously inside, information to outside market participants? If the answers to these two questions are yes, then the positive price impact may arise solely from the possibility, implicitly communicated by management's proposal, that the company's prospects are better than previously thought.

Further analysis suggests, however, that the price impact at the time of proposal is not due solely to the implicit release of favorable inside information. How did we determine this? We examined each firm's stock price *after* its proposal announcement —that is, after the market had the opportunity to capitalize the expected value of any inside information revealed by the fact that management wants to buy the firm. After announcement of the buyout proposal, one would expect the price to reflect roughly a weighted average of the values expected for the stock under two possible outcomes: (1) the going private offer succeeds, or (2) the offer fails and the stock continues to be publicly traded, at least for now.

For the offers that involved strictly cash compensation, the offer price exceeded the market price five days *after* the proposal announcement in 51 of the 57 cases, and by an average of approximately 14 percent. This price disparity suggests that the market considered the company worth more as a private than as a public enterprise. In other words, going private had a higher value to security holders than remaining public even *after* any favorable information implicit in the proposal announcement was capitalized into the stock price.

This 14 percent disparity reflects both the probability that the deal would not go through (which would harm public stockholders) and the expected delay in receipt of the offer price. It is unlikely that the full 14 percent difference could be explained completely by the delay in payment. For our sample, the average delay was about 7.3 months (6.3 months median). It would take an unrealistically high 22 percent annual riskless interest rate to explain the price disparity solely on the basis of payment timing. Moreover, the 14 percent figure understates the

---

2. In all cases, the premium and stock value statistics mentioned in the text are measured relative to open market stock prices observed two months prior to announcement. The tender offer statistics are based on studies by Michael Bradley and by Gregg Jarrell and Michael Bradley. The merger returns are reported in a study by Peter Dodd.

Going private had a higher value to security holders than remaining public even after any favorable information implicit in the proposal announcement was capitalized into the stock price.

true price disparity to the extent that the market anticipates that managers will raise the bid above the initial offer price. Such increases in the offer price are, in fact, quite common: 21 of the 57 cash bids in our sample were subsequently raised while only two were lowered.

Withdrawals of Going Private Proposals

For our sample of 18 proposal withdrawals, the announcement that managers were rescinding the offer was associated with a substantial reduction in stock prices. During the two-day period surrounding the withdrawal announcement, the open market stock price (net of market-wide effects) fell by an average of 8.9 percent. Regardless of the particular statistical method employed, we found the average wealth drop to be statistically significant at very high levels. In addition, a decline in stock price occurred for almost all (16 of 18) sample firms in which managers withdrew a going private offer, and the only two price increases were trivially small (less than 0.1 percent). Thus, according to the stock market's valuation, public stockholders would have been made better off had the going private proposal not been withdrawn.

The withdrawal price impact is smaller in percentage terms than the proposal price impact. This observation can be potentially explained by two factors. First, withdrawals are likely to be better anticipated by, and thus less surprising to professional traders who closely watch firms with going private bids outstanding. A second reason is that withdrawal often signifies only a temporary removal of an offer. (We identified nine offers during the 1973–80 period that were revived from earlier offers in the same period.) The possibility that managers will renew the bid, perhaps at more favorable terms, should act to dampen the market's assessment of any loss in public stockholder wealth at withdrawal, as should the possibility that a competing bid will emerge.

Just as a going private proposal may reveal implicit good news about firm profitability, withdrawal of the bid may reveal bad news that is unrelated to the going private transaction itself. In other words, managers have an incentive to withdraw a proposal when they learn that the future prospects of the company (whether it remains public or goes private) are worse than they previously thought. Thus,

a stock price decline at withdrawal could be primarily due to the implicit release of negative inside information about company profitability.

While we cannot rule out this possibility, two considerations suggest that implicit negative information is unlikely to explain the full stock price decline observed at withdrawal. First, managers have an incentive to disclose any "bad news" as it arrives (that is, while a proposal is outstanding) since it may lead public stockholders to view management's offer in a more favorable light. Second, as an empirical matter, we found no systematic indication of explicit negative information disclosure in the financial press reports of proposal withdrawals. In fact, we found several cases in which the withdrawal announcement was accompanied by explicit good news—for example, by competing bids or expressions of interest by other potential purchasers of the firm's shares.

Summary of the Evidence

Our data indicate that, on average, public stockholders experienced substantial stock value gains at the time of proposal to go private (see rows (1) and (2) of Table 1), were offered substantial premiums above market value in initial cash offers (see row (3)), and experienced substantial losses at proposal withdrawal (row (4)). Moreover, for almost every firm in the sample, the direction of change in value was the same as that of the sample average. Based on our statistical analysis of average wealth changes, it seems reasonable to conclude that, for our sample firms, the typical going private proposal made public stockholders better off.

The Role of Market Forces and the Legal/Regulatory System

What factors enable public stockholders to gain from these buyouts in which managers have an obvious incentive to pay as little as possible for publicly held shares? One factor is competition from other bidders. If managers of a given firm attempt to buy out public stockholders at a price perceived to be "too low," competing bids should emerge. And, indeed, we do observe them in at least some cases.

As an example, the management of Norton Simon recently proposed to buy out their public stockholders at $29.00 per share. This proposal was

The rights accorded public stockholders under the current legal and regulatory system give them substantial bargaining power with managers seeking to take the firm private.

TABLE 1		Percentage Rates of Return			
Public Stockholder Returns Associated with Going Private Proposals by 72 NYSE/AMEX Firms During 1973–1980		**Mean**	**Median**	**Maximum**	**Minimum**
	(1) Market value change in the two-day period surrounding initial proposal (72 firms)	22.27%	18.89%	89.94%	−22.12%
	(2) Market value change over the 40 trading day period prior to and including initial proposal (72 firms)	30.40	28.62	137.53	−41.87
	(3) Cash offer premium measured relative to the open market share price 40 trading days prior to proposal (57 firms)	56.31	50.00	200.00	−8.91
	(4) Market value change in the two-day period surrounding proposal withdrawal (18 firms)	−8.88	−7.33	0.07	−28.58

met by a series of competing bids by outside parties, and the firm was eventually acquired by Esmark at $35.50 per share. Esmark's own proposal to go private was just topped by an offer from Beatrice Foods. And when the management of Stokely Van Camp attempted to buy out their public stockholders at $50.00 per share, a number of competing bids emerged and the company was eventually acquired by Quaker Oats Company at $77.00 per share.

In many firms which seek to go private, managers already own a substantial block of stock. (As stated earlier, management's pre-offer ownership interest was 50.9 percent for the median company in our sample.) Such concentrated managerial holdings will deter some potential bidders from competing with management's proposal to go private. But even in this situation, stockholders are not powerless when faced with a management bid that is "too low," since they can challenge the proposal in a legal forum.

The rights accorded public stockholders under the current legal and regulatory system give them substantial bargaining power with managers seeking to take the firm private. Both the courts and the SEC provide strong incentives for management to waive its voting rights in going private transactions. Moreover, public stockholders can seek appraisal of their shares and can challenge the transaction in both state and federal courts. During our sample period (1973–1980), public stockholders in Delaware firms could challenge a going private transaction on a variety of grounds, including fraud and

inadequate compensation. (A recent Delaware decision curtailed stockholder rights to sue in state courts on grounds of inadequate compensation, but expanded the scope of admissible arguments in an appraisal proceeding.)

The important implication is that the threat of private litigation to block or delay a buyout provides public stockholders with a significant bargaining tool—one that enables them to extract concessions from management. In fact, going private transactions typically meet serious legal challenge from public stockholders. According to Arthur Borden, a corporate lawyer, "almost every going private transaction to date has been met by a suit." In our sample, we found evidence of stockholder suit in 86 percent (31 of 36) of the going private proposals for which we had a relatively complete legal summary, and which did not involve third-party participation. Transactions with third-party participants were challenged by stockholders in only 12 percent (3 of 24) of the cases for which we had access to legal data. These observations suggest that third-party involvement in these buyouts may help avert legal challenge because such involvement mitigates the appearance of managerial "self-dealing."

A dramatic example of the role played by the legal system is provided by one of our sample firms that proposed to go private via cash merger. In this case, management owned sufficient stock to approve the merger unilaterally (under statutory voting rules for arm's-length acquisitions) and announced its intention to do so. The courts enjoined the transaction in the form proposed by management and the offer was subsequently withdrawn. The market price immediately prior to withdrawal was 217 percent above the offer price and remained well above after the withdrawal announcement. In this case, a successful buyout would have benefited management, but it would be difficult to argue that it would have benefited public stockholders at the specified offer price. As this example suggests, it would clearly be inappropriate to conclude from our analysis of sample averages that *every* buyout proposal benefits public stockholders.

The Gains from Going Private

It seems reasonable to assume that managers benefit from the typical going private transaction since they voluntarily propose the buyout. If one accepts our evidence which suggests that public stockholders also benefit from the average transaction, it follows that going private must generate significant real gains.[3] In other words, if public stockholders and managers both benefit from the typical going private deal, the size of the corporate "pie" must increase. This brings us back to the question we posed earlier: What are the expected benefits of this change in corporate ownership structure?

Savings in Stockholder-Servicing Costs

Because going private results in a substantial reduction in the number of stockholders, a clear potential source of gain is the avoidance of registration, listing, and other stockholder-servicing costs incurred by public companies. Such direct costs of public ownership include the additional legal and accounting fees necessary to satisfy SEC reporting requirements. Other direct costs include those associated with the preparation and mailing of annual reports and proxy statement materials, as well as stock exchange listing and registration fees. Public stock ownership also entails additional salary expenditures for investor and public relations personnel

—those people responsible for handling stockholder inquiries and related communications with the investment community and the financial press.

These direct costs of public ownership can be substantial. For example, in its 1976 proxy statement, Barbara Lynn Stores, Inc. estimated the annual cost of public ownership to be $100,000. When capitalized in perpetuity at a conservative real interest rate of 10 percent, this figure implies a total cost saving of $1 million from going private. When set against the market value of Barbara Lynn Stores' publicly held stock, which was roughly $1.4 million just before the announcement of management's proposal to go private, this capitalized cost saving appears to be substantial.

In a published guide for firms seeking to go public, Schneider, Manko, and Kant (1981) advise companies to expect the costs of public ownership to add up to $30,000 to $100,000 per year (not including management's time). Arthur Borden estimates that the direct costs of public ownership are "$75,000 to $200,000 annually for an average public company of AMEX size and considerably more if special problems should arise." These estimates, again, seem especially significant when translated into a capitalized cost saving and compared to $6.3 million, the total market value of publicly held shares for the median firm in our sample.

Although ignored in all of these cost estimates, the time required of top management can also represent a significant cost of maintaining public ownership status. A recent news article explored this issue with Byron C. Radaker, CEO of Congoleum Corporation, a company that went private in 1980. According to the article, Mr. Radaker claims that as CEO of a private company, he is "the envy of fellow executives, who often wish they too could forego meetings with securities analysts, hearings before government bureaucrats, and other time-consuming duties faced by heads of publicly traded corporations." According to Radaker, the avoidance of annual reports, SEC filings, and similar requirements enables employees to concentrate on more productive tasks and generates savings to Congoleum of between $6 and $8 million.[4]

---

3. An alternative explanation is that these gains simply represent wealth transfers from senior claimants. This latter explanation seems implausible since, for our sample, we found no evidence of systematic senior claimant litigation revealed in proxy disclosures and/or financial press reports. Moreover, one might expect such wealth transfers to be relatively more important for publicly-traded senior claims, and only a handful of our companies had such issues.

4. *Rochester Democrat and Chronicle*, November 7, 1982.

*An increase in leverage following the buyout may be
made possible in part by changes in managerial incentives.*

The Effect on Managerial Incentives

Another potential source of gain from a change from public to private status comes from an improvement in the incentives faced by corporate management. Because increased ownership implies that managers stand to benefit more from their own effort, managerial productivity would be expected to increase when management's equity ownership in the firm increases. In cases where management acquires 100% stock ownership in the subsequent private firm, their equity ownership necessarily increases. Management's residual claim interest also typically increases following a transaction involving third-party investors, both through increased stock ownership and, indirectly, through employment agreements that tie managerial income more closely to firm profitability.

In general, productive gains from a pure organizational structure change can be expected when such a change enables managerial rewards to be more closely linked to managerial performance. For example, some profitable investment projects require a disproportionate effort by management and will therefore be undertaken only if management can capture a corresponding (disproportionate) share of the gains from these projects. In these cases, management compensation arrangements that deviate from strictly proportionate sharing of investment returns among all (public and management) stockholders can generate overall profitability increases. Such compensation schemes, however, are difficult to implement in public firms because outside stockholders may view them as "overly generous" to management, and can challenge their legality in the courts. For this reason, going private can generate productive gains to the extent that private ownership facilitates compensation arrangements that induce managers to undertake more of these profitable projects.

Casual empiricism does suggest that a return to private ownership enables managers to be compensated in ways that would be quite difficult to accomplish in a publicly-traded company. The July 24, 1976 proxy statement for the buyout of Big Bear Stores Company provides an example of such a managerial compensation scheme. This particular agreement covers a time period of 15 years, and provides for an incentive profit fund in addition to managerial salaries and fringe benefits. According to the proxy material, the incentive profit fund will be earned only to the extent that future operating earnings exceed a base earnings figure (specified to be approximately \$12.7 million). The incentive profit fund will equal 100% of pre-tax earnings above \$12.7 million, up to the point that pre-tax earnings total \$15 million. Additionally, managers will receive 15% of earnings in excess of \$15 million. Such a generous compensation plan would, of course, be exposed to possible legal challenge by outside stockholders if the company remained public. And yet, this and similar compensation agreements potentially yield material gains in managerial productivity, for at least some companies.[5]

The Role of Third-Party Investors

Another source of the value potentially created through leveraged buyouts comes from replacing a dispersed, largely passive public stockholder population with a small group of new investors who play a more active role in managing the firm. These third-party investors typically take a substantial equity position in the private firm and, therefore, have a greater incentive to monitor management (and allocate rewards appropriately) than do the typical stockholders of a public corporation. The new investors usually place representatives on the board of directors who oversee the operations of the private company following the buyout. The more active role taken by the new equity holders may therefore increase managerial productivity through increased monitoring of managerial decisions.

Third-party investors in leveraged buyouts must, of course, receive additional compensation to induce their active participation in the newly-private company. The realized returns to these investors have in fact been substantial. A recent *Fortune* article states that the leveraged buyout specialists Kohlberg, Kravis, Roberts, and Co., have earned an average annualized return of 62 percent on the equity invested in their deals.[6] And in the "Discus-

5. Big Bear Stores is one of three sample firms that went private with third-party participants and have since returned to public ownership status. The observation that some firms subsequently go public suggests that the benefits of going private discussed here are not always permanent for all companies.

6. *Fortune*, January 23, 1984.

sion" which immediately follows this article, Carl Ferenbach, another buyout specialist, states that his firm expects an annual return of 50 percent on their equity investments. Such returns include compensation not only for the commitment of equity capital, but also for the buyout specialist's role in arranging the initial financing and helping with financial management of the private firm. There is no reason to expect that equally high returns would (or should) have been earned by passive outside stockholders had the firm remained public.

Financial Leverage

Any additional financial leverage introduced by the transaction implies that equity holders in the newly private firm bear additional risks and, for this reason, should also expect to earn a higher rate of return than did the former public stockholders. An increase in leverage following the buyout may be made possible in part by changes in managerial incentives. For example, the private company's debt capacity can be greater due to the higher profits expected because managers own a greater residual claim interest or because their performance is now monitored by buyout specialists. This effect is reinforced by the increased borrowing itself to the extent that it provides managers with additional incentives to work harder in order to pay down the debt. Many newly private companies attempt to reduce their debt rapidly, which indicates that the initial borrowing is not introduced simply for its interest tax shield. Another explanation for the heavy leverage is that it is employed as a means of concentrating equity ownership when managers' personal wealth is small relative to the scale of operations.

Buyouts with third-party equity participants appear to be associated with a greater increase in financial leverage, perhaps because the value of the public stock interest tends to be larger in these deals (and managers' personal wealth is limited). For the small sample of firms for which we could obtain pro forma financial data, the increase in the debt-to-assets ratio was substantially more pronounced for those transactions involving third-party equity investors. For these buyouts, the median firm's debt-to-assets ratio increased from .11 under public ownership to a planned .86 under private ownership, which compares to an increase from .26 to .30 in transactions without third-party equity participation.

These figures suggest that the costs of debt financing may be lowered because third-party investors have long-term relationships with institutional lenders. Such relationships would be jeopardized should the new equity holders take actions for a given firm that materially increase the credit risk borne by institutional lenders. Thus, these long-term relationships may serve as a form of collateral against potential damage to lenders and, consequently, may allow additional borrowing.

Corporate Tax Savings

Like cash acquisitions in general, going private transactions can yield income tax benefits at the corporate level, such as the additional depreciation deductions made possible by an asset value "write-up." In our sample, most going private transactions were structured as cash mergers with (or sales of assets to) a shell corporation, newly created and wholly owned by the incumbent management group. (Public stockholders received cash for their shares and the management group acquired full equity ownership of the operating company, or its assets, by virtue of its ownership of the acquiring shell corporation.) And, as mentioned above, the increase in interest deductions created by additional borrowing will provide corporate tax savings while the debt remains outstanding.

Summary

Our study offers empirical evidence about the impact of going private on public stockholder wealth. For our sample of 72 AMEX/NYSE firms that proposed to go private during 1973–1980, a variety of statistical methods and measures of average stockholder wealth changes indicate that the typical buyout proposal made public stockholders better off. Specifically, we find that public stockholder wealth increased approximately 30 percent, on average, upon the announcement of a going private proposal (when pre-proposal leakage of information is included in the return). We also find that public stockholder wealth decreased an average of 9 percent when managers withdrew a going private proposal. Managers offer substantial premiums (averaging about 56 percent for cash offers) to public stockholders in these buyouts.

Managers are willing to pay a premium over

The median firm's debt-to-assets ratio increased from .11 under public ownership to a planned .86 under private ownership.

the value of the firm as a public company, presumably because going private transactions generate overall productive gains for these companies. Potential sources of these gains include improved managerial incentive arrangements, superior monitoring expertise provided by non-management stockholders in the subsequent private firm, savings in stockholder-servicing costs, and leverage-related benefits made possible by some buyouts. Public stockholders share in the gains from going private, presumably because of competition from other bidders and because, under the current legal/regulatory system, significant bargaining power is granted public stockholders in non-arm's-length acquisitions.

While our analysis suggests that the gains from going private may be substantial, it does not follow that all companies should be privately owned. We have emphasized the benefits of private ownership or, more precisely, the costs of public ownership that could be avoided by going private. But there are also important benefits to public ownership—most notably, the access to large amounts of equity capital on advantageous terms that reflect the benefits of risk reduction through diversification. For many, if not most, large companies the benefits of having access to public capital markets will remain the dominant factor in their decision to continue to operate as a public company. For other companies, including those we studied, the cost-benefit tradeoff apparently dictates a private ownership structure.

In principle, of course, companies should change from public to private ownership in response to changes in the underlying cost-benefit tradeoff. Unfortunately, we do not have the means of predicting such changes. (If we did, we would be heavily invested in going private candidates!) We can, however, offer one conjecture which might prove useful: namely, that companies will tend to find going private more attractive when they face a shrinkage of profitable growth opportunities which, in turn, reduces the value of access to the public capital markets. While we have no hard evidence to support (or refute) this speculation, it is worth noting the conventional wisdom that "dull," "stodgy" manufacturing companies make good buyout prospects.

Equity Carve-Outs

by Katherine Schipper and Abbie Smith,
University of Chicago

Late in 1981 Condec Corporation filed a prospectus describing a plan to sell to the public slightly over 20 percent of the equity in its wholly-owned subsidiary, Unimation, Inc. In this "equity carve-out" (also known as a "partial public offering"), Condec sold 1.05 million common shares of Unimation at $23 each, thereby raising $22.5 million in new equity capital (after fees and expenses). The purpose of the offering, as stated in the prospectus, was to use "$19.4 million to repay all [of Unimation's] outstanding long-term indebtedness to Condec, and the remainder to provide working capital." The market's response to Condec's announcement resulted in a 19 percent stock price increase (after taking account of market movements).

Why did Condec choose this relatively unusual method of raising capital instead of, say, selling more of its own common equity? Why, furthermore, did the market respond so favorably to the announcement of the offering—especially since announcements of common stock offerings generally signal bad news to investors?

In this article, we attempt to provide answers to these questions based on our own recently published study of 76 equity carve-out announcements by New York and American Stock Exchange companies over the period 1965-1983.[1] Our study finds, in brief, that the stockholders of parent companies earn on average almost 2 percent positive market-adjusted returns during the five-day period surrounding announcements of the carve-outs—and almost 5 percent if an additional two weeks preceding the announcement are included. In contrast, the stock prices of companies announcing seasoned equity offerings fall some 3 percent or more, on average, around the time of announcement; and announcements of convertible debt offerings provoke an average negative reaction of 1 or 2 percent. Thus,

according to the findings of recent research, equity carve-outs represent the only form of new equity financing by public companies which results, on average, in an increase in shareholder wealth.

The Popular Argument

One popular explanation for the positive market reaction to equity carve-out announcements is that carve-outs allow investors to evaluate exceptional corporate growth opportunities on a stand-alone basis. This explanation would imply that Condec, a large, defense-oriented conglomerate, decided to carve out 20 percent of Unimation, a robot manufacturer, to reinforce the market's perception of the value of that subsidiary and thus, presumably, to increase the market's valuation of Condec as a whole. As another example, MGM/UA's 1982 carve-out of its Home Entertainment Group has been described as a means of "cash[ing] in on the craving of investors for a share in what may become an enormous market for pay television and home videos."[2] Commenting on this same transaction, an analyst at Bear Stearns stated that such a partial public offering provided "a way for studios to enhance their own valuations and for investors to get a piece of the fast-growing market [for home video]."[3]

The assumption underlying this explanation seems to be that investors are attracted to subsidiary growth opportunities when these are isolated from the consolidated entity (that is, available for separate purchase). By creating a separate public market for Unimation's common stock, the popular argument seems to run, the carve-out allowed Condec to benefit by allowing direct investment in the growth opportunities of the robot subsidiary.

A variant of this popular argument holds that investors might value a specific investment opportu-

1. See Katherine Schipper and Abbie Smith, "A Comparison of Equity Carve-outs and Seasoned Equity Offerings: Share Price Effects and Corporate Restructuring," *Journal of Financial Economics* 15 (1986), pp. 153-186.

2. From "The Old Razzle-Dazzle," *Forbes*, February 14, 1985, pp. 43-44.
3. From "MGM/UA Movie-distributing Unit's Rise Has Other Studios Studying Its Strategy," *Wall Street Journal*, October 21, 1983.

nity more highly when set apart from a conglomerate if and when it offers them a scarce commodity: that is, a so-called "pure play." It might be difficult for investors to invest in, say, stand-alone public robotics manufacturers. (Such an advantage is likely to last only as long as there are few "pure plays" around.) This variant is illustrated, in the case of Unimation, by the following analysis:

The Unimation offering is among the first opportunities for substantial investment in the growing robot industry and it attracted considerable interest when it was announced last month. Most robotics companies that are publicly traded over the counter are too small to attract major investors. (Wall Street Journal, *November 27, 1981)*

In this article, we argue that although equity carve-outs may indeed create securities which have scarcity value, there are also other explanations for the market's positive response to partial public offerings. First of all, equity carve-outs may overcome the problem of the information gap between insiders and investors that attends all seasoned equity offerings (for a discussion of this problem, see Clifford Smith's article, "Raising Capital," immediately preceding). They may also provide more information to the market about the subsidiary, thereby stimulating new investor demand (not to mention the interest of potential corporate acquirers). Perhaps more important, however, is that although the parent company generally retains a majority interest in the "carved-out" subsidiary, equity carve-outs are often accompanied by important changes in management responsibilities and incentive contracts. Expected improvements in performance from changes in managerial accountability and incentives may partially explain the market's positive reaction.

In the pages that follow we shall explain more precisely what an equity carve-out is, and how it differs from and resembles both spin-offs and seasoned equity offerings. We then review our own recent research on carve-outs, and discuss differences between equity carve-outs and conventional parent equity offerings that might account for the systematically negative response to the latter and the generally positive response to the former. Last, we take a look at what happens to subsidiaries after they have had partial public offerings. Seldom do carved-out subsidiaries remain unchanged for very long, with the public simply maintaining its minority interest in the firm. Instead they are generally either reacquired by the parent, completely spunoff, acquired by management through an LBO, or acquired by some other firm. We attempt to make sense of these developments.

The Market Reaction to Related Events: Seasoned Equity Offerings and Spin-Offs

An equity carve-out resembles a primary offering of seasoned stock in that cash is received from the investing public. Several recent studies of the market's response to seasoned equity offerings have confirmed average negative returns to stockholders of 2 to 3 percent over the two-day period surrounding the announcement of the issue.[4] In addition, our own study of carve-outs found that for those companies which had a seasoned common stock offering within five years of a carveout, the average price reaction to the parent stock offering was −3.5 percent over the five-day period ending with the announcement.

Many of the features which distinguish a subsidiary equity offering from a seasoned equity offering represent similarities with a voluntary spin-off.[5] In a spin-off, distinct equity claims of a wholly-owned subsidiary are distributed as a dividend to the consolidat-

4. The share price reaction of NYSE and ASE listed firms to an announcement of a public offering of seasoned common stock is the subject of the following published studies, all of which appeared in Volume 15 (1986) of the *Journal of Financial Economics*: Ronald Masulis and Ashok Korwar, "Seasoned Equity Offerings: An Empirical Investigation"; Paul Asquith and David Mullins, "Equity Issues and Offering Dilution"; and Wayne Mikkelson and Megan Partch, "Valuation Effects of Security Offerings and the Issuance Process." The share price reactions to public offerings of convertible debt claims on NYSE and ASE listed firms were examined by Larry Dann and Wayne Mikkelson in "Convertible Debt Issuance, Capital Structure Change and Financing-Related Information: Some New Evidence," *Journal of Financial Economics* 13 (1984). The results of these studies are as follows: For offerings by industrial firms, a statistically significant negative average abnormal stock return of 2 or 3 percent is documented in the two-day period ending with the *Wall Street Journal* announcement date. In the case of equity offerings by public utilities, the return is smaller (less than one per cent), but still negative and statistically significant. Furthermore, a negative average share price effect of an increase in outstanding common equity through exchange offers

and conversions of debt to common stock is documented by the following studies: Ron Masulis, "The Effects of Capital Structure Changes on Security Prices," Unpublished doctoral dissertation, University of Chicago, 1978; and Wayne Mikkelson, "Convertible Calls and Security Returns," *Journal of Financial Economics* 9 (1981).

Conversely, evidence exists that an increase in share price is associated with a *reduction* in outstanding common equity through repurchases of shares and exchange offers: Larry Dann, "Common Stock Repurchases: An Analysis of Returns to Bondholders and Stockholders," *Journal of Financial Economics* 9 (1981); Ron Masulis, "Stock Repurchase by Tender Offer: An Analysis of the Causes of Common Stock Price Changes *Journal of Finance* 35 (1980), 305-319, (as well as the Ph.D. dissertation cited above); and Theo Vermaelen, "Common Stock Repurchases and Market Signalling: An Empirical Study," *Journal of Financial Economics* 9 (1981). Thus, the evidence suggests that an increase in outstanding equity is associated on average with a decrease in stock price, and a decrease in equity is associated with an increase in stock price.

In an equity carve-out, the parent company typically does not relinquish control over the subsidiary; instead a public minority interest is created.

ed entity's shareholders and begin to trade in public equity markets. Thus, in both spin-offs and equity carve-outs, a subsidiary's equity claims begin to trade separately from equity claims on the consolidated entity. Studies of the market reaction to announcements of corporate spin-offs all document positive abnormal returns of about 3 percent in the two-day period ending with the *Wall Street Journal* announcement date.[6]

A subsidiary equity offering differs in two respects from a corporate spin-off. First, as mentioned, whereas in a spin-off the subsidiary stock is distributed to the existing shareholders of the consolidated entity, the equity carve-out is a sale of subsidiary stock which raises new capital. Second, in a spin-off the parent company typically relinquishes control over the subsidiary by distributing all of the subsidiary stock. In an equity carve-out, the parent company typically does not relinquish control over the subsidiary; instead a public minority interest is created. Because a subsidiary equity offering partly resembles both a seasoned equity offering (associated with a negative share price reaction) and a corporate spin-off (associated with a positive reaction), it was not obvious ex ante what the market's reaction to carve-outs would be.

The Market Reaction to Equity Carve-Outs

Our study examined the stock market's response to 76 announcements of equity carve-outs by 63 NYSE and ASE firms over the period 1965 to 1983.[7] These announcements were clustered in the late 1960s through 1972 and in the early 1980s; there were no announcements in the five years 1973-1977.[8] This pattern differs from the pattern of seasoned common stock offerings reported in three recent studies; in these samples about one-fourth to one-third of common stock offerings over the same 19-year period occurred in the five-year period 1973-77.[9] The pattern of equity carve-outs does, however, conform roughly to that of initial public offerings.[10]

In our sample of 76 carve-out announcements, 37 of the announcements state that the firm "has proposed" or "is considering" offering a portion of a subsidiary to the public. The remaining 39 report that an offering has been filed with the SEC. Some of these provide no details, while others describe what is being offered, when and why. Regardless of the nature of the announcement, our share price reaction tests are based on the date the earliest announcement about the subsidiary equity offering appears in the *Wall Street Journal*. To increase the likelihood that the test period captures the first public disclosure of information about the subsidiary equity offering, the test period is defined as the five trading days ending with the day of the *Wall Street Journal* announcement.

Seventy-three percent of the carve-out offerings were underwritten. The percentage of the subsidiary's equity offered ranged from 4 percent to 75 percent, with 81 per cent of the sample with available data falling between 10 percent and 50 percent. The proceeds of the offerings ranged from $300,000 to $112,200,000. Carve-out proceeds as a percentage of the parent's common equity value ranged from .3 per cent to 69 per cent, with a median of about 8 per cent.[11]

A subset of 26 sample firms also made a total of 39 public offerings of their own common stock or convertible debt (hereafter called "parent equity") within five years of their subsidiary equity offerings. Parent equity issues of sample firms were identified by searching the *Wall Street Journal* Index for each of the five years prior to, the year of, and, where possible, the

5. A subsidiary equity offering also resembles a divestiture in that cash is received. However, a divestiture does not in general initiate the trading of subsidiary stock. Two studies (G. Alexander, P. Benson and J. Kampmeyer, "Investigating the Valuation Effects of Announcements of Voluntary Corporate Selloffs," *Journal of Finance* 29 (1984); and April Klein, "Voluntary Corporate Divestitures: Motives and Consequences," Unpublished doctoral dissertation, University of Chicago, 1983) both report positive abnormal returns of about 1 per cent or less in a three-day period (Klein) and a two-day period (Alexander et al.) ending with the announcement of the divestiture in the *Wall Street Journal*.

6. See Katherine Schipper and Abbie Smith, "Effects of Recontracting on Shareholder Wealth: The Case of Voluntary Spin-offs," *Journal of Financial Economics* 12 (1983); Gailen Hite and James Owers, "Security Price Reactions around Corporate Spin-off Announcements," *Journal of Financial Economics* 12 (1983); and J. Miles and J. Rosenfeld, "An Empirical Analysis of the Effects of Spin-off Announcements on Shareholder Wealth," *Journal of Finance* 38 (1983).

7. Although there are 76 carve-out announcements, there are actually 81 subsidiaries in the sample because four announcement dates account for nine subsidiaries. That is, three announcement dates involve two subsidiaries each and one date involves three subsidiaries. The number of parents (63) is also less than

the number of announcements because of multiple carve-outs by the same firm. The largest number of carve-out announcements by a single firm is three (by W.R. Grace); ten firms announced at least two carve-outs. Of the 81 subsidiaries in the announcement sample, eight were not carved-out during the sample period, which ends in December 1983. Thus, carve-outs of eight subsidiaries were announced and later cancelled. Details of the sample selection procedures can be found in Schipper and Smith [1986], cited in footnote 1.

8. While it is possible that a number of carve-outs occurred during 1973-1977 that we were not able to find, we do not think this is likely. Every initial public offering on the SEC's *Registrations and Offerings Statistics* tape for the years 1973-77 was checked and none was a carve-out by an NYSE or ASE listed firm.

9. See footnote 4 for full citations of the three studies of the market's response to announcements of seasoned equity offerings.

10. See Jay Ritter, "The 'Hot Issue' Market of 1980," *Journal of Business* 57 (1984).

11. The market value of parent common equity is measured by share price multiplied by the number of outstanding common shares at the end of the month preceding the carve-out announcement.

five years following that firm's announcement of a subsidiary equity offering. The share price reactions to these 39 announcements are measured by the abnormal stock returns (percentage price changes adjusted for general market movements) over the five-day period ending with the date of the *Wall Street Journal* announcement.

The market reactions to the 76 equity carve-out announcements in our sample were estimated by calculating abnormal stock returns over the five-day period leading up to the *Wall Street Journal* announcement.[12] In addition to measuring five-day returns, we also measured cumulative average abnormal stock returns for the 76 carve-out announcements over an 85-day period beginning 44 days before the *Wall Street Journal* announcement and ending 40 days after. (These returns are shown in Figure 1.) During the period starting 13 days before the announcement, the cumulative abnormal return drifts upward at an increasing rate from +0.8 percent to +4.95 percent at the announcement day. The cumulative abnormal return is nearly level in the subsequent eight weeks, ending with a value of +4.45 percent 40 trading days after the announcement.

In the case of the 39 sample firms which issued either seasoned equity or convertible debt within five years of the carve-outs, the cumulative return drops from +0.2 percent four days before the announcement of the offering of parent equity to −3.3 percent on the announcement day (see Figure 1). In the eight weeks following the announcement of the parent equity offering, the return drifts downward to −4.7 percent by 40 trading days after the announcement.[13]

The variation in the market reaction to both the sample of carve-out announcements and the sample of parent equity offering announcements is considerable. Abnormal returns at carve-out announcements range from −12.1 percent to +19.5 percent, with a median of +1.6 percent. About two-thirds of these returns (50 of 76) are positive. In contrast, about 69 percent of abnormal returns (27 of 39) at the announcement of parent equity offerings are negative. The median abnormal return for this sample is −2 percent, and the range is from −16 percent to +17.5 percent.[14]

Why, Then, The Different Market Response to Equity Carve-outs?

There are three differences between equity carve-outs and parent equity offerings which might account for the market's positive response to the former: (1) the separation of subsidiary investment projects from those of the parent firm for external financing; (2) the creation of a public market for subsidiary common stock; and (3) the restructuring of asset management and incentive contracts.

Separate Financing for Subsidiary Investments

An offering of seasoned parent equity simply increases the number of outstanding equity claims on the consolidated assets. In contrast, an initial subsidiary equity offering "carves out" the assets of the subsidiary from the assets of the original entity. Thus, an equity carve-out allows a subsidiary to obtain separate funding for subsidiary growth opportunities.[15] The equity securities publicly offered represent claims on the cash flows of the subsidiary projects only.

---

12. For details of the procedures used to compute abnormal returns and to perform statistical tests, see the appendix to Schipper and Smith [1986], cited in footnote 1.

13. t-tests for the significance of abnormal returns do not imply rejection at the .05 level (two-tailed) of the null hypothesis that the abnormal return is zero within the periods before or after the carve-out announcement. However, the t-statistic of +2.55 in the five-day announcement period leads to rejection of the null hypothesis of zero abnormal returns at better than the .02 level (two-tailed). Similarly, the abnormal returns before and after the announcement of the parent equity offerings are not significantly different from zero at the .05 level (two-tailed). However, the abnormal return of −3.5 percent in the five-day event period is significantly different from zero at better than the .01 level (two-tailed).

The difference in the cumulative abnormal returns over the event period for the announcement of 76 subsidiary equity offerings versus 39 parent equity offerings is +5.3 percent, significant at better than the .005 level (one-tailed). The average difference in the cumulative abnormal returns in the five-day event period for 26 matched pairs of subsidiary and parent equity offerings by the same firm is +5.5 percent, also significant at better than the .005 level (one-tailed). For these pairwise comparisons, each subsidiary equity offering announcement is matched, if possible, with a parent equity offering announcement by the same company. If more than one parent equity offering was available for matching, priority was given to common stock over convertible debt offerings, and to proximity to the subsidi-

ary equity offering announcement date.

14. Previous tests of share price reactions to announcements of offerings of seasoned equity have used a two-day event period (e.g., Asquith and Mullins [1986], Dann and Mikkelson [1984], Masulis and Korwar [1986], and Mikkelson and Partch [1986], all cited earlier in footnote 4. Because many of our announcements refer to SEC filings, we use a five-day event period. A two-day period, however, is reasonable for the 37 *Wall Street Journal* announcements of intentions to undertake an equity carve-out. For this subsample, the average two-day abnormal return is +1.2 per cent (t = 1.91) and the median two-day abnormal return is +1.7 per cent. A binomial test of the null hypotheses of an equal portion of positive versus negative two-day event period abnormal returns results in a z-statistic of +2.48, which is significant at the .007 level. In the entire sample, however, the two-day event period does not appear to capture the initial information release. For the entire sample of 37 intention announcements and 39 announcements that a registration statement has been filed, the two-day abnormal return is +.7 per cent (t = 1.59). These significance tests should be interpreted with caution, as they are not independent.

15. Other mechanisms for separate financing of investment projects include spin-offs and sales of limited partnership interests to finance research and development. In some cases, the tax code provides special incentives for the latter financing mechanism.

FIGURE 1
The Stock Market Response to Announcements of Equity Carve-Outs and Parent Equity Offerings

Cumulative abnormal returns for 76 equity carve-out announcements made during the period 1965-1983 are shown by the solid line. Cumulative abnormal returns for 39 seasoned equity offering announcements made by the same firms are shown by the broken line. Market model parameters are estimated for each sample firm over trading days -280 to -161 relative to the announcement in the *Wall Street Journal*.

If parent equity had instead been offered to finance the subsidiary's investment projects, the offered securities would represent a joint claim on both the parent and subsidiary projects. By separating the subsidiary projects from those of the parent, a carve-out may reduce the asymmetry of information between managers and investors about the asset base underlying the securities offered.[16]

The separate financing of subsidiary projects by an equity carve-out is expected to have a positive share price effect under either of two circumstances: (1) information is publicly revealed about the subsidiary's planned investment in a positive net present value project without negative implications about the value of the other assets of the consolidated firm; (2) separate financing implies that management will not forgo *future* positive net present value projects.

Support for viewing some carve-outs as a means of financing growth opportunities of the subsidiary apart from the parent company is found in the stated motives for our sample carve-outs. In the case of 59 of the 81 subsidiaries whose carve-outs were announced, we were able to find stated motives by reading annual reports, 10-Ks, registration statements, prospectuses and articles in the financial press. For 19 of these 59, at least part of the declared motivation was

to enable the subsidiary to obtain its own financing for expected growth.

Additional support for viewing some carve-outs as a means of financing growth opportunities of the subsidiary is found in the nature of some of the carve-outs. In six cases, registration statements or prospectuses described a specific growth opportunity to be funded with the proceeds of the subsidiary equity offering. For example, Interferon Sciences was formed by National Patent Development in 1981 to develop its interferon program. The parent contributed basic technology and patents, which were reported as having a book value of about $600,000 or $.20 per share. Shortly thereafter, 25 percent of Interferon Sciences was offered to the public at $10 a share; the proceeds were $10 million. The stated purpose of the offering was to finance the development of the interferon technology transferred by the parent to its subsidiary. Thus, Interferon Sciences represented primarily a growth opportunity, with virtually no assets-in-place. Other projects included investments in Atlantic City casinos, Hawaiian condominiums, oil drilling, and bioengineering products. In each case, the parent firm apparently rejected the option of funding the project by issuing parent equity and chose to offer separate equity claims on the growth

16. For a discussion of the information asymmetry financing problem, and why it may pay to fund growth opportunities separately from assets-in-place, see Stewart Myers and Nicholas Majluf, "Corporate Financing and Investment Decisions When Firms Have Information That Investors Do Not Have," *Journal of Financial Economics* 9 (1984).

opportunity by means of a carve-out.

Assuming that one purpose of a carve-out is to finance investment projects, a measure of the relative size of those projects is the proceeds of the carve-out offering as a percentage of the market value of parent equity. This size measure, it turns out, is positively correlated with the share price reactions of parent firms; that is, the larger the carve-out as a percentage of the total equity of the consolidated company, the larger in general was the positive market reaction.[17]

To provide evidence of the anticipated growth of carved-out subsidiaries, we computed the P/E ratios of 70 subsidiaries with available data at the time of or immediately after the carve-out. Relative to their parent firms, the carved-out subsidiaries had high P/E ratios. The median subsidiary P/E ratio was 21.7 (after excluding negative values caused by losses). In contrast, the median contemporaneous P/E ratio of the parent firms was 15. For the 58 parent-subsidiary pairs with available P/E ratios, the subsidiary had the higher P/E ratio in 43 cases (74 per cent).[18]

Creation of a Public Market for Subsidiary Stock

An equity carve-out initiates public trading of the common stock of the previously wholly-owned subsidiary. The subsidiary is thus subject to all financial and other reporting requirements of public companies (for example, 10-Q and 10-K reports and proxy statements filed with the SEC, and annual reports issued to stockholders). These requirements can impose considerable costs on the parent company's stockholders. These costs consist of the direct costs of preparing audited financial statements and other required reports for the subsidiary, as well as any indirect costs of disclosing proprietary information to subsidiary competitors.

Such costs, however, may be more than offset by the benefits to parent stockholders of the increased supply of and demand for information about the

subsidiary's growth opportunities. The carve-out of subsidiary stock *commits* the subsidiary to supply audited periodic financial reports prepared in accordance with prescribed measurement and disclosure rules, as well as other nonfinancial information about firm activities (such as the information in proxy statements). By making possible an equity investment in the subsidiary alone, the carve-out also increases the incentives of both individual investors and potential acquiring firms to gather and analyze information about subsidiary activities. The increase in both the supply of and demand for information about the subsidiary may increase the perceived value of subsidiary stock to individual and corporate investors.

Such an improvement in investor understanding is cited as a motive for 14 equity carve-outs in our sample. It is also cited in a recent announcement by Perkin-Elmer Corporation of its plan to carve out and sell to the public up to 19 percent of its minicomputer business, which was named Concurrent Computer Corporation. According to a *Wall Street Journal* report, the chairman of Perkin-Elmer said the carve-out plan "is intended to improve the visibility of Perkin-Elmer computers and thus improve sales and help attract investors."[19]

Perkin-Elmer completed the equity carve-out in January 1986 and described its advantages to parent company shareholders in a full-page *Wall Street Journal* advertisement with the following copy:

Higher visibility and a sharp, singular focus will help Concurrent Computer Corporation attract and retain a strong, motivated management team. And lead to increased recognition in the financial community where shareholders will be able to benefit from its full potential.

As the Perkin-Elmer Data Systems Group, our computer business was not accorded its true value. Yet, in just one week after its initial offering, the market has placed Concurrent Computer Corporation's worth at nearly a quarter of a billion dollars— enriching Perkin-Elmer's ownership as the major shareholder.[20]

17. The Spearman rank correlation between our size measure and the five-day abnormal returns associated with carve-out announcements is .27, which is significant at better than the .05 level (two-tailed).

18. A Wilcoxon test of the null hypothesis that the two samples are drawn from populations with the same median generates a t-statistic of 3.83, leading to rejection of the null hypothesis at better than .01 probability level. Hence, subsidiary P/E ratios tend to exceed the P/E ratios of the corresponding parent firms. Furthermore, these high subsidiary P/E ratios cannot be explained by low levels of risk. Of the 23 sample subsidiaries with returns on the CRSP Daily Excess Returns Tape within two years after the equity carve-out, 14 (61 per cent) belong to the three highest of ten beta portfolios (6,5,3 respectively). It also is unlikely that the high P/E ratios can be attributed to the use of highly conservative accounting methods

to measure subsidiary earnings. Through 1982, earnings figure reported in subsidiary registration statements were not required to include such corporate costs as interest, taxes, amortization of purchased goodwill, and certain administrative costs. It was not until 1983 that the SEC issued "carve-out accounting" rules that require proportionate allocation of these corporate costs to the subsidiary's earnings statement. Hence it is likely that the high subsidiary P/E ratios in our sample are indicative of high anticipated growth in subsidiary earnings. However, the high P/E ratios may also reflect the low earnings figures of young firms due to high research and development expenses and depreciation charges.

19. From "Perkin-Elmer Organizes New Computer Firm," *Wall Street Journal*, November 14, 1985.

20. *Wall Street Journal*, February 19, 1986.

Of the 63 sample carve-out subsidiaries for which data are available, 59 (that is, 94 per cent) adopted incentive compensation plans based on the subsidiary's stock—generally stock option plans.

The Restructuring of Asset Management and Incentive Contracts

Many carve-outs are associated with a major restructuring of managerial responsibilities and incentives. Divisions are often regrouped into a new subsidiary for the public offering with a consequent realignment in the responsibilities of various managers. Furthermore, the incentive contracts of subsidiary managers are usually revised to incorporate subsidiary share prices and profits as measures of performance. Such internal structural shifts are seldom associated with seasoned equity offerings.

Stated motives for 11 of 59 sample subsidiaries mentioned a change in corporate focus through a restructuring program or a reduction by the parent of investment in the line of business of the carved-out subsidiary. Also worth noting is that 38 of the 73 carved-out subsidiaries (52 per cent) had been formed as little as one year before the carve-out.[21] The formation of the new subsidiaries typically involved combining the operations of existing units, divisions or subsidiaries under a single management. Finally, management responsibilities in 12 cases were changed to the extent that one or more persons resigned a top management position with the parent to become president or CEO of the subsidiary.

Two pieces of qualitative evidence suggest that changes in the incentives of subsidiary managers are important considerations in carve-outs. The first is 10 statements of motive which focus on the improvements in managerial incentives associated with a public market for subsidiary shares. For example, in W.R. Grace's explanation of its decision to carve out a 27 per cent interest in its El Torito restaurant chain, Charles Erhart, vice-chairman of Grace, said the environment at Grace inhibited the entrepreneurial style of El Torito's management. "These are people-sensitive businesses. They [El Torito management] are independent cats who need a piece of the action to motivate them."[22]

The second piece of evidence concerns the use of subsidiary share prices and profit figures in contracts with subsidiary managers. Of the 63 sample carve-out subsidiaries for which data are available, 59 (that is, 94 per cent) adopted incentive compensation plans based on the subsidiary's stock—generally stock option plans. Most of these adoptions occurred within one year of the carve-out. In addition, at least 23 subsidiaries adopted incentive plans based on subsidiary net income.

This evidence suggests that restructuring of managerial responsibilities and incentives is frequently associated with equity carve-outs. To the extent the market expects such restructuring to lead to improvements in management's efficiency in using corporate assets, we would expect a favorable share price reaction.[23]

After the Carve-Out

Carved-out subsidiaries often experience some form of change in ownership following the carve-out. For our entire sample of 73 carve-outs, all but 14 of the subsidiaries as of February 1986 had undergone further changes since the initial public offering.[24]

One common fate of carved-out subsidiaries is complete separation from the parent by one of the

---

21. Of the 32 subsidiaries in existence at least 1 year before the equity carve-out announcement, 17 had been previously acquired, 4 had been formed as part of a joint venture, and 11 were formed from existing divisions.

22. *Business Week*, December 19, 1983, contains additional information.

23. The principle of "informativeness," as developed by Shavell and Holmstrom (See S. Shavell, "Risk Sharing and Incentives in the Principal and Agent Relationship" and B. Holmstrom, "Moral Hazard and Observability," both in the *Bell Journal of Economics* 10 (1979)), maintains that any (costless) variable which is marginally informative about an agent's actions can be used to increase the efficiency of the contract with the principal. Hence, if the subsidiary share price contains additional information about subsidiary management's actions, agency theory suggests that the efficiency of managers' contracts can be improved by linking compensation to the subsidiary stock price performance.

This requirement does not appear to be overly restrictive. The aggregation of the parent company with the subsidiary company for purposes of equity market valuation and financial reporting (i.e., presentation of consolidated financial statements) is likely to result in loss of information about the subsidiary's management's production, investment, and financing decisions. The contracting gains which may result from disaggregating agent performance measures for unrelated operations is discussed in the context of responsibility accounting in the following study: S. Baiman and J. Demski, Economically Optimal Performance Evaluation and Control Systems," *Journal of Accounting Research* 18 (1980),

Supplement, 184-220. Although the performance of the subsidiary and the parent company may be measured separately with internal (managerial) accounting procedures even before the equity carve-outs, in general such "divisional" accounting measures are unlikely to contain all the information contained in the subsidiary share price with respect to subsidiary management's actions. On this last point, see D. Diamond and R. Verrecchia, "Optimal Managerial Contracts and Equilibrium Security Prices," *Journal of Finance* 37 (1982), 275-287.

24. At the time of the original carve-out announcement, the market does not appear to respond differently to those carve-outs which later undergo some kind of restructuring. For carve-outs announced before 1983, a Mann-Whitney test for differences in abnormal returns at announcements of carve-outs that were later restructured versus those that remain unchanged results in a z-statistic of .82, which is not significant at conventional levels. Thus, there is not an ex ante perceived difference, in terms of impact on shareholder wealth, between carve-outs that were later reacquired, divested, spun-off or liquidated and those that have not undergone some further ownership or structural change.

Parent firm share price reactions to announcements that subsidiaries are being divested or reacquired are small and positive. For a sample of eight divestiture announcements, the two-day average abnormal return is 2.8 percent (t = 1.88). For a sample of 13 reacquisition announcements, the two-day average abnormal return is 0.6 percent (t = .55). These results are consistent with little or no revision in market expectations associated with restructuring announcements.

following means: spin-off, purchase by the subsidiary of its stock held by the parent, leveraged buyout, sale to another firm, and bankruptcy/liquidation. Of the 73 carve-outs in our sample, 30 had separated from their parents by one of the above means as of February 1986 (see Table 1). Fifteen of these 30 separations involved the outright sale of the subsidiary to another firm. Four were acquired by management in leveraged buyouts (though all of these occurred after November 1984, reflecting the newness of the LBO phenomenon).

The length of the period between the carve-out and the separation varies considerably within our sample. Some separations occurred almost immediately (that is, within one or two years), while one divestiture occurred 19 years after the carve-out. The average period, however, is approximately four or five years for most of these changes.

The fact that so many carve-outs are followed by complete separation suggests that management may have originally intended the carve-out as a way of advertising the subsidiary—that is, as an intermediary stage in a process whose final goal was divestiture. The parent may have expected that the disclosure associated with a public market for subsidiary shares would eventually lead to a greater understanding (and thus willingness to pay a higher price) on the part of the potential acquirers.[25] For example, some insurance executives speculated that the 1985 carve-out of 49 per cent of Fireman's Fund by American Express was "a way to attract higher bids for a sale of its entire interest in Fireman's Fund."[26]

Only slightly less common than complete separation, however, is the reacquisition of carved-out subsidiaries by the parent. In our sample, 26 subsidiaries were reacquired and another reacquisition is pending. Why do companies reacquire carved-out subsidiaries? One possible explanation is that the original carve-out decision was a mistake. An alternative explanation, however, is that reacquisition is attractive if the objectives of the carve-out can be accomplished with only a temporary public market for sub-

sidiary shares. For example, the need for external equity financing of subsidiary growth will decline if the subsidiary's investment projects mature to the point where they generate sufficient profits for internal equity financing. The objective of informing individual investors and potential acquirers about a subsidiary's growth potential through audited subsidiary financial statements and other reports, as well as the increased incentives for private information collection, may be achieved by a temporary public market for subsidiary stock. Even the contracting gains associated with incorporating subsidiary stock price in the incentive contracts of subsidiary managers may be temporary.

One example of a carve-out followed quickly by a reacquisition proposal is the case of First Data Resources. American Express sold 25 per cent of First Data for $14 a share in September 1983, and announced a plan to reacquire the shares for $36 a share (27 times earnings) in August 1985. The reacquisition was announced as part of a plan to narrow the corporate focus on consumer financial services. While some analysts speculated that the reacquisition might imply that the original carve-out was a mistake, the president of American Express, Louis Gerstner, Jr. disputed this point by saying that the equity ownership taken by First Data management as part of the 1983 carve-out offering helped stimulate the subsidiary's rapid growth. (In the first six months of 1985, First Data's income was nearly 50 per cent higher than in 1984.)[27]

The MGM/UA carve-out of its Home Entertainment Group mentioned earlier in this article was also followed by a reacquisition. Late in 1984 MGM/UA proposed a reacquisition at $28 in notes or MGM/UA stock; the carve-out offering price was $12. It might be concluded from this proposal that the original purpose of the carve-out had been served and there was no longer a need for a public market for HEG stock.[28]

Subsequent ownership changes are easier to accomplish if the parent retains control of its carved-out subsidiary. In our sample, parent firms typically offered only a minority interest to the public, while

25. As stated in footnote 24 earlier, parent firm share price reactions to announcements that subsidiaries are being divested are small and positive. For a sample of eight divestiture announcements, the two-day average abnormal return is 2.8 percent (t = 1.88).

26. See "Fireman's Fund Stock Offer Set by Parent Firm," *Wall Street Journal*, June 26, 1985. The carve-out offering was completed in October 1985 at $27.75 a share. By February 25, 1986, Fireman's Fund stock was selling at about $37.75 a share; to capitalize on this gain, American Express announced a plan to offer as many as 10 million shares plus warrants for another 10 million shares. (See "American Express Plans to Reduce Stake in Fireman's Fund by Second Offering," *Wall Street Journal*, February 26, 1986).

27. See "American Express Seeks Rest of Concern," *Wall Street Journal*, August 22, 1985.

28. These reacquisitions often involve premia over the current market price of subsidiary shares or lawsuits by minority stockholders to increase the reacquisition price, or both. In the case of the Home Entertainment Group, settlement of a shareholder suit resulted in a reacquisition for $28 in cash (*Wall Street Journal*, April 24, 1985).

As mentioned in footnote 24, parent firm share price reactions to announcements that subsidiaries are being reacquired are small and positive. For a sample of 13 reacquisition announcements, the two-day average abnormal return is 0.6 percent (t = .55).

**TABLE 1
Ownership Changes for
73 Subsidiaries
Carved-Out During
1965–1983[1]**

Reacquisition by parent	Number	Number of Years Between Carve-out and Event	
		Average	Range
Transaction complete	26	5.1	2–12
Proposal pending	2	5.5	5–6
Transaction proposed but failed	1	3	NA
Separation from parent			
Spin-off or purchase by subsidiary of its shares held by parent	7	5	1–12
Leveraged buyout complete or pending	4	3.5	1–5
Sale to another firm	15	6.7	1–19
Bankruptcy or liquidation	4	3.75	1–7
	59[2]		

[1] These data cover the period from the carve-out announcement through February 1986.
[2] We found no information for five subsidiaries. Nine subsidiaries (of which eight were carved-out in 1983) have had no ownership changes.

retaining a majority or supermajority interest. Some of the parent companies in our sample also maintain control over the carved-out subsidiary by creating a special class of stock which increases the parent's voting power. For example, the parent might create and hold 100 per cent of class B common stock carrying four votes while issuing common stock with one vote in a carve-out. These kinds of special stock arrangements were found in 15 of the 73 subsidiaries in our sample.

Besides facilitating ownership changes, there are two other advantages to the parent of maintaining a majority or supermajority voting interest in a carved-out subsidiary. First, effective control allows any existing operating and/or financial synergies to be maintained (although it is possible that the absence of operating synergies, in many cases, is an important motive for the carve-out in the first place). Second, 80 per cent voting control of the subsidiary is required if the subsidiary is to be consolidated for tax purposes. Tax consolidation is beneficial if operating losses or tax credits which would otherwise go unused by either the parent or subsidiary can be used to offset taxable income of the more profitable firm, thereby reducing taxes to the consolidated entity.

The benefits of tax consolidation were cited in the case of Trans World Corporation's 1983 carve-out of its airline subsidiary. After the carve-out, public ownership was 19 per cent of the common stock and 5 per cent of the voting control (the parent retained preference shares with 10 votes apiece). Because the airline subsidiary generated both tax losses and investment tax credits that could be used to shield earnings of other units from taxation (as long as a consolidated tax return was filed), this arrangement was described as "having cake and eating it too."[29] Presumably, the "cake" came from the $78 million cash generated by the offering, which permitted the subsidiary to purchase new equipment, especially Boeing 767's.

Summary and Conclusions

We recently completed a study of 76 equity carve-out announcements by public companies traded on the New York and American Stock Exchanges. Our results indicate that in the five-day period culminating with the announcement of such carve-outs, the stock prices of parent companies announcing the carve-outs outperformed the market by almost 2 percent on average; the size of the average reaction is a positive 4 to 5 percent if an additional two weeks preceding the announcement are included.

In contrast, announcements of public offerings of parent common stock and convertible debt by a subset of the same companies have been associated

---

29. See "Let Them Eat Stock," *Forbes,* April 25, 1983.

with average shareholder losses of over 3 percent. Such a negative reaction to announcements of *parent* equity offerings is consistent, furthermore, with prior research on the stock price effects of changes in outstanding equity through public sale or repurchase of common stock and convertible debt, debt conversion, and exchange offers to current security holders.[30] Initial public offerings of subsidiary stock are thus the only means of raising outside equity capital (of which we are aware) which appear to communicate a positive signal to the stock market.

How do we account for this difference in the market's response to announcements of carve-outs and seasoned equity offerings?

An equity carve-out, first of all, allows public investment in subsidiary growth opportunities apart from an investment in the parent's assets. Such a security, by offering investors a "pure play," may have scarcity value if such opportunities are typically buried within a conglomerate structure.

A partial public offering also appears to offer an effective means of overcoming the financing problem caused by the potential information gap between insiders and public investors which appears to make conventional equity offerings quite expensive. Still another possibility is that the equity carve-out may improve public understanding of the subsidiary's growth opportunities. By making the subsidiary a public company, the carve-out may increase the supply of and demand for information about the subsidiary. Periodic, audited financial statements prepared by the subsidiary in accordance with regulations are issued to the public. Investors accordingly may have added incentives to analyze publicly available data and to search for private information about the subsidiary because of the new opportunity to trade subsidiary stock. Also, the readily observable market price of subsidiary stock may attract an acquiring firm and facilitate negotiations concerning the purchase price. If such an increased flow of information increases the perceived value of subsidiary stock to individual or corporate investors, it may partially explain the more favorable share price response to equity carve-outs than to parent equity offerings.

Alternatively, the market may be saying that the conglomerate is an inefficient organizational structure for capitalizing on such growth opportunities, and for providing the entrepreneurial climate necessary to do so. Equity carve-outs often are associated with a major restructuring of managers' responsibilities and incentive contracts, and the market may associate such restructuring with improvements in management's efficiency in putting corporate assets to their most valuable uses.

---

30. See footnote 4 earlier for a review of this research, or see Clifford Smith's "Raising Capital," which appears at the beginning of this issue.

The Quiet Restructuring

by John Kensinger, *University of North Texas*, and John Martin, *University of Texas at Austin*

E very individual, therefore, endeavors as much as he can both to

employ his capital in the support of domestic industry, and so to

direct that industry that its produce may be of the greatest value

... and he is in this, as in many other cases, led by an invisible

hand to promote an end which was no part of his intention.

— Adam Smith, 1776[1] —

While the spotlight of the financial press has been turned squarely on "corporate raiders," other less dramatic manifestations of the same market forces are accomplishing a "quiet restructuring" of corporate America—without fanfare and largely unnoticed by politicians and the press. Even if the raiders were suddenly to oblige their critics and disappear, the "invisible hand" would continue subtly but relentlessly prodding management to seek out more efficient forms of organization and better uses for corporate assets.[2]

For, even as troubled sectors of American industry are being made to shrink, the abundance and variety of investment opportunities offered in today's economy have never been greater. For an entrepreneur just setting out, there are venture capitalists and business incubators to help in the birthing process. For a promising technology start-up company, there are billions of dollars available through mezzanine loans, joint ventures, project financing, and public stock offerings. For an established corporate giant, there are not only concerns about hostile takeovers and flak from militant stockholders, but also attractive opportunities—such as converting the treasury function into a profit center through securities trading and international financial arbitrage, or securitizing assets (or even entire subsidiaries) and turning them into ready cash. Then, too, there is the prospect of dramatically enlarging management's own risk-reward profile by means of a leveraged buyout.

The good news is that the financial markets have evolved to the point where capital can flow quickly to start-up companies to develop new products and technologies. The unfortunate part is that some of this money must come from the process of cutting big companies apart and wringing cash from uneconomic operations. When the capital released by these often difficult decisions reaches investors, it is *they* who decide where to reinvest in new businesses.

This widespread return of the corporate reinvestment decision to the marketplace is a relatively new development. Established tradition is that investors, in contributing capital to public corporations, voluntarily relinquish control of their funds to the managements of those corporations. In ceding such control to management—which can be reclaimed by unhappy stockholders only through the extremes of proxy contest or hostile takeover—the market effectively agrees to the substitution of management fiat for the "invisible hand" in directing the flow of capital from old to new enterprises.[3]

Not long ago, in fact, it was widely accepted that the ideal corporation consisted of a portfolio of projects at various stages of development which was balanced so that the cash flows from the mature activities were used to nourish fledgling projects. In the parlance of the Boston Consulting Group, "cash cows" were milked to feed the "rising stars." As they grew old, "stars" and "cows" became "dogs," which were harvested to feed more "rising stars" for the company.

Over this menagerie stood the corporate managers, who performed "strategic planning," deciding which new projects to finance. If their own organization was not generating enough cash to support its rising stars, they would even go out into the market to buy someone else's cash cow. If, on the other hand, they had lots of cash cows but too few deserving new projects, they might buy another company's rising star.

This approach has not stood the test of time, however, because today's investors have a much broader spectrum of opportunities than do corporate managers investing internally. Stockholder discontent with this old model has in fact played a major role in stimulating takeovers in the 1980s (which, unlike those of the 60s and 70s, represent a movement away from conglomerate structures and toward horizontal consolidations). Simply put, investors have declared their preference to milk the cash cows themselves.

If an organization runs out of natural growth opportunities when its industry matures, it no longer has such a need for cash. At this point investors legitimately demand a return of control to their own hands. And when control over resource allocation is returned to the marketplace, investors get to make all of the reinvestment decisions because *they* have first claim to the cash flows. With cash in hand, investors can choose among venture capital funds, initial public offerings (IPOs), real estate, energy explora-

1. Vol.1, *The Wealth of Nations* (edited by Edwin Cannan), The University of Chicago Press, reprinted 1976, p.477.

2. A play on Adam Smith's words, the "visible foot," has been used to describe the tactics and consequences of raiders. See William A. Brock and Stephen P. Magee, "The Invisible Foot and the Waste of Nations: Redistribution and Economic Growth," in *Neoclassical Political Economy* (David C. Colander, ed.), Ballinger, 1984.

3. See A. M. Spence, "The Economics of Internal Organization: An Introduction," *Bell Journal of Economics* (Spring 1975), pp. 163-72. Spence views the firm as a "mini capital market" with internal investment selection which parallels the activities of external capital markets.

tion partnerships, R&D project pools, or any other investment vehicle. Investors regain direct control over their money, and managers of corporations thereby give way to investment bankers in the role of guiding funds from the cash cows into the rising stars.

Corporate managements, needless to say, are not happy about this trend and often try to perpetuate the growth (or just the independence) of their firm—often at large costs to their own stockholders. But why would managers try to keep the firm going beyond its useful life, past the point where it has an economic advantage that justifies its control over resources? Management understandably feels commitments to many other corporate stakeholders than just the investors who contributed capital.[4] It often has far stronger ties to the corporation's employees, for example, and to the community which houses the corporation than to a faceless and widely dispersed group of public investors.

It can be very difficult, therefore, for professional managers to envision a future in which their corporation does not exist in some form. After the purpose for which it was conceived has been served, there are still strong pressures, both emotional and political, to extend the firm's life by redirecting its resources into some new set of activities, even though they may not be the most highly-valued use for the resources. Managers who are trying their best to be good citizens and to do what they perceive to be right for their employees and local communities may have interests which are very much at odds with those of investors and the economy at large. This sort of conflict can present some very tough decisions. But it ultimately demands resolution of the question of whether to let the marketplace achieve the highest-valued uses for the world's resources—or try to slow down economic progress and avoid making difficult decisions.

While this debate proceeds in Congress and the courts, however, the "invisible hand" remains at work, nudging management into voluntarily releasing control over resource allocation decisions in a variety of ways. Now, through various means that limit management control over the reinvestment of corporate cash flows, the give and take of the marketplace is creating a new kind of cash cow.[5] The cash flow

from mature operations is being channeled back into the marketplace for reinvestment—often into unknown start-up ventures. And even though it may not be part of management's conscious intention, this process is leading to better resource allocation and an improvement in corporate America's competitive position.

THE URGE TO USE LEVERAGE

Whoever has discretionary power over the reinvestment of a firm's operating cash flows has fundamental power over its future. The extreme use of debt—in leveraged share repurchases, leveraged buyouts (LBOs) and, most recently, leveraged recapitalizations—substantially reduces management's control over the deployment of cash flows generated by a firm's mature operations.

Consider the effect of leveraged share repurchases such as those Boone Pickens forced on Phillips Petroleum and Unocal. (Something like it also happened with Gulf, in that Chevron was forced to borrow heavily in order to buy out the Gulf stockholders.) These events all had something very basic in common: stockholders came away with a substantial wealth increase—in cash. (Also, it came in the form of capital gains for most of them, so the maximum tax rate anyone had to pay was 20 percent—these things happened, of course, before the Tax Reform Act of 1986.) These shareholders were then free to choose how to reinvest their wealth, selecting from the full array of opportunities in the marketplace.

Where did this wealth increase for the stockholders come from? Part of it came from the tax benefits of leverage, but that is not the whole story. Besides any possible tax effect, the leverage fundamentally constricted the scope of managerial discretion.

Michael Jensen recently formulated his "debt control hypothesis" to explain this constructive effect of leverage, and has applied this explanation to the oil industry as follows: When highly leveraged, an oil company's operating cash flows become committed to interest and debt retirement for a significant period into the future. New projects thus have to compete for external funding rather than be sustained by the

---

4. For a discussion of these other corporate constituencies, see Bradford Cornell and Alan Shapiro, "Corporate Stakeholders and Corporate Finance," *Financial Management* 16, (Spring 1987), pp. 5-14.

5. For a longer discussion of this development than appears here, see our earlier article, "Royalty Trusts, Master Partnerships, and other Organizational Means of 'unfirming' the Firm," *Midland Corporate Finance Journal*, Vol.4 No.2 (Summer 1986), pp. 72-80.

cash flows from the oil fields. Besides the tax effect, then, the leverage brings with it a change in the processes by which management actions are monitored, and thus a change in managerial incentives. The mountain of debt forces the cash to flow out of the firm, rather than circulate within it.[6]

If there is any danger that management might not be as demanding as the marketplace in scrutinizing internal investments, then this change increases the probability that the cash flows will find their way to the highest-valued uses. After the leveraged share repurchases, there was much less of a chance that Phillips or Unocal might buy a Reliance Electric or a Montgomery Ward or a Kennecott Copper. Nor would their managements be able to follow up on any temptation to get into the office products business, as did Exxon with such poor success. With cash flows committed to debt service, management had their wings clipped and stockholders had their money. As one would expect, managers were less happy about it than were the stockholders.

Some people raise the concern that diverting cash flows from oil and gas production into the marketplace might be detrimental in the long run. That is, the oil may eventually be depleted without replacement of reserves. Phillips' management, for example, lamented the impact of the "crushing mountain of debt" upon their exploration efforts, claiming that pleasing the financial marketplace requires short-run maximization of cash flows at the expense of long-run economic viability.

The marketplace, however, is the ultimate source of resources for commitment to any venture. When investors put a high enough value on oil and gas exploration, new drilling partnerships can be formed quickly. Meanwhile, there are opportunities in electronics, robotics, artificial intelligence, and bioengineering that hold more promise for investors. And the fact, incidentally, that investors are willing to commit themselves to ventures years in advance of their producing a penny in revenues should be sufficient answer to those protesting the market's short-term focus.

Also relevant to this issue, a recent study of the effect of new internal investments upon corporate stock values found strong evidence contradicting the claims of Phillips' management. The study found that, on average, the announcements of new capital expenditures by corporations resulted in increased stock values across a variety of different industries. The only exception was the petroleum industry, where announcements of increased expenditures on oil drilling and exploration have been greeted with systematic stock price declines since the beginning of the 1980s.[7]

LEVERAGED BUYOUTS

What was accomplished through leveraged share repurchases at Phillips Petroleum and Unocal has been done in other industries through LBOs. There have been many explanations offered for the LBO phenomenon, each of which may have some element of truth. Without claiming to offer the definitive explanation, however, it is possible to make some general observations.

First of all, stockholders are able to sell their stock for cash, at a premium over the market value, and are immediately free to reinvest the cash in the most attractive opportunities available anywhere in the marketplace.

Second, managers gain a shot at ownership and, without changing jobs, go to work for new bosses—themselves. They are free of the burden of reporting to a large group of public shareholders.

In place of the shareholders, however, management must answer to the LBO specialist, whose group generally takes a strong position on the board of directors. Also, in place of a host of public shareholders demanding ever-increasing earnings and dividends, the managers have to placate a small group of creditors who demand that every stray penny be applied to a speedy repayment of the debt used to finance the buyout.

In a buyout, then, managers do not escape monitoring; they merely exchange one form of monitoring for another. Nor do they escape pressure. In fact, it might seem that the pressure on them increases as a result of the leverage. They have the advantage, to be sure, that the bite taken from cash flows by income tax is reduced, giving them more to work with. But they are not "their own men" until the debt is taken care of. With cash flows committed to debt support, new projects will not have access to the

6. Michael C. Jensen, "Agency Costs of Free Cash Flow, Corporate Finance and Takeovers," *American Economic Review* (May 1986).

7. John J. McConnell and Chris J. Muscarella, "Corporate Capital Expenditure Decisions and the Market Value of the Firm," *Journal of Financial Economics*, (Sept 1985), pp. 399-422.

milk from the old cash cow, and any growth plans must face the test of the marketplace.

Critics of LBOs protest that the pressure of all this leverage stifles the economy, but it must not be forgotten that the stockholders got an infusion of cash at the very beginning. They will be reinvesting in growth opportunities elsewhere. In addition, the creditors of the newly-private company will be receiving regular installments of milk from the cash cow, which they will be able to reinvest in the best available opportunities. Only when the debt is repaid will the managers, at that point certainly older and perhaps wiser, once again have access to the cash spigot to finance internal expansion projects. Then it will be their own money they are spending and they may be more demanding in evaluating potential projects than when they were employees of a public corporation.

ESOPS

Besides the garden-variety LBO, there is another new player on the scene. Leveraged Employee Stock Ownership Plans (ESOPs) have been the vehicle for several buyouts in recent years. Through such an arrangement it is possible for the corporation to eliminate income tax completely, and make the entire pretax cash flow of the corporation available for debt retirement. Only if the corporation retains earnings for new investment is there be any need to pay income tax—which represents a significant turning of the tax tables. Not long ago, income tax laws had the effect of keeping cash inside a company since paying dividends resulted in double taxation. In the case of a buyout by a leveraged ESOP under current tax rules, the tax penalty is instead levied against retention of earnings for reinvestment. Instead of retaining earnings, then, the best way for an ESOP-owned corporation to raise expansion capital is by selling new stock to the ESOP; and when this requires the ESOP to go to the market for loans, the growth plans must meet outside scrutiny.

Besides giving employees a chance to own their companies, then, the new ESOPs do two other important things. First, they put cash into the hands of stockholders, who then make the reinvestment decisions themselves. Second, leveraged ESOPs commit the firm's cash flows to debt retirement, thereby returning capital to the marketplace where it can be used to fund the highest-valued new ventures.[8]

THE URGE TO SELL PIECES OF THE COMPANY

There are several means available to "securitize" a specialized pool of assets. It is now commonplace for financial institutions to sell insured mortgages in the form of securities. Credit card receivables and auto and truck loans are likewise packaged into high-denomination securities for resale. Receivables can also be held by a corporation's financial subsidiary, and a portion of the subsidiary sold to the public. Whole divisions may also be set up as parent-controlled subsidiaries, with a portion of stock offered to the public.

In addition, there are now more than ninety publicly-traded master limited partnerships (MLPs). Originated in the oil and gas industry, they have spread to timberland properties, cable television systems, real estate, mortgages, restaurant services, and mortgage loan servicing. Non-listed partnerships also own large scale hydro and geothermal power-generating plants, cogeneration facilities, and even oil refineries. All sorts of income-producing operations which require little more than caretaker management have been separated from corporations, organized as partnerships, and sold. Management-intensive operations such as R&D projects have also been financed as separate projects.[9]

The choice of organizational form used for securitizing assets is sensitive to the tax environment. Because the 1987 tax act ended favored tax treatment for some publicly-traded partnerships, a corporate subsidiary or a nontraded partnership may be the organizational form chosen as the reposi-

---

8. In these arrangements a special trust is formed to purchase stock and credit it to the accounts of individual employees. The Tax Reform Act of 1984 added two very attractive new sweeteners for leveraged ESOPs. Since January 1985, dividends paid to stock owned by an ESOP have been tax deductible. In addition, lenders need pay income tax on only half of the interest paid to them by an ESOP. Thus ESOPs are able to borrow at low interest rates, in order to buy stock in the employer corporation. Finally, employer corporations are allowed to make tax-deductible contributions of cash or stock to ESOPs, and through 1987 may even earn tax credits in addition. With these incentives, an ESOP can borrow the money to finance a buyout of an employer's stock, with the employer's guarantee on the loan.

Debt support payments would come from dividends and employer cash contributions, so the entire amount—both principal and interest—can be tax-deductible.

9. For a review of project financing for R&D and a discussion of its contribution to the set of organizational possibilities, see our article, "An Economic Analysis of R&D Limited Partnerships," *Midland Corporate Finance Journal* Vol.3 No.4 (Winter 1986), pp. 33-45. We also updated our analysis in a subsequent article, "R&D Limited Partnership Financing and the New Tax Law," *Midland Corporate Finance Journal* Vol.4 No.4 (Winter 1987), pp. 44-54.

tory for the assets to be sold. One certainly should not underestimate, however, the ability of innovative financial professionals to cope with changes in the tax environment. On the real estate front, for example, they are turning once again to trusts. This continual give-and-take between innovative financial engineers and the taxing authorities reflects the "regulatory dialectic" at work; that is, as fast as the authorities close one avenue, innovators find new ways to carry on.[10]

Managements of many large corporations have welcomed the infusion of capital that comes from securitizing assets, perhaps without noticing an important effect on managerial incentives. The sale of a corporation's real estate holdings to a trust or limited partnership, for example, has the side-effect of returning resource allocation decisions to the marketplace.

Consider the following example. When a company owns its operating space, it serves as its own landlord—and thus part of its profit really represents rent. If the property is sold to a specialized subsidiary, there is the obvious tax benefit: when the corporation's reported profit drops because it begins paying explicit rent, the corporation's income tax drops accordingly. (When the subsidiary is carefully constructed, its income can escape taxation at the corporate level altogether.)

At the same time, however, something else happens that may not have been intended: the corporation becomes subject to eviction. When it owned the property, the corporation could weather a bad year or two without having to confess that it was losing money. Without the necessity of writing rent checks, the management could ignore the fact that the company was not earning enough to justify the space it occupied. After the sale of the company's real estate, however, the management would have to give an accounting if the company could not pay its rent.

In the traditional model of the corporation, as we have seen, managers are expected not only to run existing operations efficiently, but also to take primary responsibility for deciding how to reinvest the cash flows. They may decide to pay cash dividends, which the stockholders are then free to reinvest as they see fit, yet managers have first crack at the money. But when assets are sold to special-purpose subsidiaries, things often work on a different basis. These subsidiaries frequently involve high financial leverage and often take the organizational form of the limited partnership. Management is charged with the efficient operation of existing enterprises but, once again, the need to make debt service payments restricts management's role in the reinvestment decision. In the case of limited partnerships, moreover, the managing partner's discretion in dividend and reinvestment matters is further restricted because revenues and expenses are credited directly to the partners' individual accounts according to a fixed contractual formula. Once the accounting decisions are made, the individual partners receive their pro rata share of the cash produced by the partnership assets, and the reinvestment decisions are their own.[11]

In some cases, however, the general partner may enjoy considerable discretion in the early years of the partnership. Boone Pickens has even parlayed this kind of discretion into takeover attempts.[12] As time passes, however, that discretion is progressively returned to the limited partners.

CHANGING TREASURY ROLES

As a recent study noted, "The decisions made by corporate treasurers have a potential impact on corporate profits which is often as large as the earnings from operations."[13] At first this statement might conjure up images of bond refunding or treasury stock transactions, but there is much more involved. In a growing number of companies, the corporate

---

10. For more on the regulatory dialectic, see Andrew Chen and John Kensinger, "Innovations in Corporate Financing: Tax-Deductible Equity," *Financial Management* 15 (Winter 1985) pp. 44-51. See also, Kane, "Good Intentions and Unintended Evil: The Case Against Selective Credit Allocation," *Journal of Money, Credit, and Banking* (February 1977) pp. 55-69.

11. Limited partnerships are very flexible organizational forms which convey to investors the corporate advantage of limited liability, but without double taxation (except when they are publicly traded). There is wide latitude possible in the terms that can be stated in the partnership agreement. After the agreement is entered into, however, the general partners' discretion over the use of partnership assets is bound by its terms. These partnerships are finite-lived, with a well defined set of conditions for their demise. Although limited partners give up day-to-day control of the enterprise in exchange for limited liability, they still have access to the partnership ledgers to monitor compliance with the agreement and can vote in

extraordinary circumstances (e.g., the removal of a general partner). Furthermore, the partnership agreement spells out explicitly how the partnership profits are to be paid out to the partners.

12. For example, Mesa Partners II was the major stockholder in Unocal during the recent takeover attempt. Then in January 1986, Mesa Limited Partnership made a run at KN Energy, the Colorado-based natural gas concern. Typically such partnerships are structured to take maximum advantage of the tax situation. By recomputing the tax basis of depletable properties, for example, the partnership may generate large losses in the early years. These losses are credited to the individual partners' accounts according to the partnership agreement. Subsequent profits must be credited up to a predefined point before cash payments begin to flow to limited partners.

13. Ian Cooper and Julian Franks, "Treasury Performance Measurement," *Midland Corporate Finance Journal*, Vol.4 No.4 (Winter 1987), pp. 29-43.

treasury no longer serves simply as a means to raise funds in support of operations; and many financial executives are discovering the possibilities for transforming the treasury into a profit center for securities trading. In October 1984, for example, Exxon Capital Corporation (a wholly owned subsidiary of Exxon Corporation), issued twenty-year Eurobonds with principal of $1.8 billion, and invested the proceeds in U.S. Treasury securities. The transaction was arranged in such a way that Exxon realized a substantial riskless profit after taxes, by taking advantage of tax differentials and international restrictions on capital flows.[14]

On the surface this may seem like an aberration, an occasional incursion by an oil company onto the turf of bankers. But it has an important implication. When the treasury itself becomes a profit center, alternative internal investments must compete with *it* for funding. As it grows, the trading function offers employment for more and more of the corporation's internal cash flow. Thus, potential investments in operations must compete with the array of opportunities in the full external capital market. If for example the rate of return on an investment in new plant or capital equipment, taking risk into account, is not competitive with outside investments, such internal projects will languish.

This, of course, is how things are *supposed* to have been done all along, at least according to our theory of capital budgeting. But there often needs to be a practical incentive to get management to adopt the perspective of its stockholders. Aggressive outside investment by the treasury, with the potential of investing in the full range of opportunities available in the marketplace, is likely to provide such an incentive for change. With an outward-looking treasury channeling funds into external markets, a corporation is less likely to view itself as an isolated, selffunding portfolio of businesses.

OPPORTUNITIES IN NEW TECHNOLOGIES

Major industrial research traditionally has been conducted within the confines of large integrated corporations, financed by the cash flows from established operations. The idea of the product life cycle, which came into vogue some sixty years ago, provides the foundation for the traditional concept of an integrated corporation that exploits products through all phases of their life cycles. *The heart of such a traditional integrated corporation is R&D.* As old products decline so that reinvesting cash flows in the associated production processes no longer pays, the excess cash flow is channeled to research and development of new products; and this process ensures continual renewal of the corporation.

Entrepreneurship, however, can be very attractive to today's scientists, who are likely to work harder (or at least in a more focused manner) when they have a chance to get rich as a result. In the not too distant past, though, entrepreneurship was the exception among researchers. Scientists generally remained content to enjoy the safety of a "good job" in a solid corporation. Patents added to one's prestige and job security, but the employer kept the lion's share of their value. Today, however, due to better access to venture capital, it is a quantum leap easier for a bright researcher to convert an idea into the seed of a new company. Lured by the prospect of riches, and prodded by the prospect of failure, the modern entrepreneur is exposed to far stronger incentives than was his "company-man" father.

Large corporations which cannot keep their brightest researchers happy within the salary structures of hierarchical organizations must find ways to cooperate with start-ups.[14] Dupont and Monsanto, for example, have learned the advantages of letting small, young organizations conduct research and then stepping on stage themselves when products are ready for manufacturing and marketing. DuPont has recently been buying up new companies which have developed biotechnology products in agrichemicals and pharmaceuticals, areas in which its own research efforts have come up short. The company is also trying joint ventures, which it traditionally shunned in order to keep its research efforts confidential.[15]

Monsanto, too, is sampling the benefits of cooperation with new ventures. In a recent interview CEO Richard J. Mahoney stated, "Monsanto decided it wanted to be in the biotechnology and pharmaceutical business many years ago...In fact, we were helping start up a number of these companies with venture capital. We bought Continental Pharmaceutical last year because we had a number of leads that had to be developed, and we didn't have anybody to develop

---

14. For a detailed analysis of the Exxon transaction, see John D. Finnerty, "Zero Coupon Bond Arbitrage: an Illustration of the Regulatory Dialectic at Work," *Financial Management* 14, (Winter 1985) pp. 13-17.

15. See C.S. Eklund and A.L. Cowan, "What's Causing the Scratches in DuPont's Teflon," *Business Week*, December 8, 1986, pp. 60f.

them."[16] Lacking the necessary in-house capability, Chrysler also turned to a joint venture—in this case with a Silicon Valley artificial intelligence start-up firm to bring expert systems into Chrysler cars in the 1990s.

DuPont, Monsanto, and Chrysler are not alone in seeking outside help for new product development. Indeed, one of Silicon Valley's latest contributions to the vocabulary of business is the "wizard shop." For example, Schlage Lock Company, the leading maker of mechanical locks, turned to San Franscisco's Theta Resources for the design work on an electronic lock system for hotels. Schlage's own internal R&D efforts had come up dry after a five-year effort. Theta Resources completed the job in just 18 months, and Schlage now has two patents plus a backlog of orders for its system.[17]

SRI International, a contract-research laboratory headquartered in Menlo Park, California, may be on its way to becoming the granddaddy of all wizard shops. General Electric recently *gave* its Sarnoff Laboratory to SRI. The Sarnoff Lab, which developed color television, the liquid crystal display and the VCR, to name a few of its achievements, came to GE in its merger with RCA. Sarnoff's New Jersey facilities give SRI a strong presence on both coasts, and make it a formidable factor in research circles.[18]

In sum, then, increasing opportunities in the financial markets for young, vigorous technology start-up companies spell an erosion of competitive advantage in R&D for large, integrated corporations—while stimulating the development of new technologies. Very simple changes in financing "technology" are stimulating changes in the way businesses organize themselves to do business. "Smaller," it seems, is now not only prettier but, in a growing number of cases, more efficient.

DYNAMIC NETWORK ORGANIZATIONS

We have painted a picture of a process which is grinding firms down to ever-finer, smaller, more focused entities. Old, mature corporations are returning resources to the marketplace, which in turn nurture young start-ups. This development is leading to temporary, project-specific liaisons known as "dynamic networks."[19] Dynamic networks thrive in fast-changing environments such as consumer electronics and apparel. One of them, the sports shoe marketer, Nike, has become quite well-known. Nike contracts its manufacturing to offshore factories, itself serving as developer and marketer of products.[20]

As product life cycles contract in response to continuing advances in computer-assisted design (CAD) and computer integrated manufacturing (CIM), more of the business world is being transformed into the natural habitat of the dynamic networks. Even in auto manufacturing, the bastion of traditional industrial organization, product life cycles are shrinking. It used to take five years or more to bring a new automobile to market. Ford Motor Company has cut that to two years, and it will keep getting shorter.

In networks of the future, the work might be done by professional firms specializing in research, product design, or marketing. Manufacturing is likely to be contracted out to offshore factories, or to flexible automated factories near the final market. Finally, the key role of putting all the pieces together would go to specialized brokers, perhaps a new breed of merchant bankers.

Recent experiments with partnership forms of organization may be laying the foundations of a new way of financing dynamic networks. Only time, of course, will tell the extent to which it will displace integrated corporations. But in this alternative form, investors still retain their limited liability while relinquishing much less power to managers. Investors are the direct recipients of cash flows from mature operations. They are then free to choose whether or not they wish to provide funding for the development of new products by participating directly in R&D project financing. If development

---

16. "Richard J. Mahoney Reshapes Monsanto for the Future," *DH&S Review*, Deloitte Haskins & Sells, December 9, 1985, pp. 1-3.

17. Theta Resources is not alone, and the list of customers contains some surprises. David Kelley Design of Palo Alto, for example, designed the mouse that is so familiar to users of the Macintosh computer. Stephen Beck and Edward Goldfarb of BeckTech designed the innards of an electronic hand puppet, Talking Wrinkles, for Coleco Industries' 1986 Christmas toy line. Burt Rutan, himself a "wizard" in aviation circles (his Mojave, California firm builds exotic flying prototypes for aerospace firms such as Raytheon's Beech Aircraft Division) turned to Robert Conn's Connsult Inc. to design a microelectronic monitor to record continuously the airspeed and altitude of the Voyager on its historic round-the-world flight. (See Michael Rogers, "Silicon Valley's Newest Wizards," *Newsweek*, January 5, 1987, pp. 36-7.)

18. See Otis Port, Evert Clark, and James Norman, "GE Gift-Wraps a Landmark Lab," *Business Week*, February 16, 1987, p.35.

19. For a detailed description of dynamic network organizations and predictions for their future role, see Raymond E. Miles and Charles C. Snow, "Network Organizations: New Concepts for New Forms," *California Management Review* (Spring 1986), pp. 62f.

20. See *Business Week* (March 3, 1986).

efforts are successful, the rights may be sold or licensed to a manufacturer/marketer. Alternatively, investors may choose to participate in manufacturing and marketing by means of still other partnerships.

Recently, with strong encouragement and support from the U.S. Department of Commerce, a few firms have experimented with limited partnerships formed for the purpose of promoting and marketing a specific product. Energy Sciences Corporation offers an example. It developed a data networking system which sends data via low-frequency radio signals over existing phone or power lines, while leaving normal utility services undisturbed. The development was funded through project financing.

Now the company is preparing a marketing campaign financed by what it calls "technology marketing partnerships."[21] These marketing partnerships are in essence very simple. They are business organizations formed for the purpose of bringing a specific product or group of products to market. The general partner may manufacture the product itself, or contract the manufacturing to a third party. The general partner also contracts with third parties for advertising and promotion. The partnership owns the trademark and brandname supported by its advertising, and has an exclusive distributorship for the product. It earns revenues from royalties or commissions paid out of sales by the manufacturer. In some cases they are set up with an option for the manufacturer to buy out the distributorship for a lump sum.

There can be tax advantages from such arrangements, but they also provide a project-specific organizational alternative to the corporation. It is possible for a product to be developed by a partnership and brought to market by another partnership, with heavy reliance upon capital raised in the public market. In such a complex of small, specialized organizations, the primary role of managers would be to run existing operations efficiently. In order to increase the assets under their

management, however, they would have to compete by continually creating attractive new opportunities to be offered in the marketplace for capital.

OPPORTUNITIES FOR LARGE CORPORATIONS

All is not lost, however, for big established companies. Whenever they have strong competitive advantages from economies of scale in production or marketing, they have much to gain by cooperating with start-ups or design consultants which have new technologies to offer. It seems that large corporations have the opportunity to benefit from letting small, nimble, low-cost organizations develop new products and technologies, so long as they themselves have strengths to offer in manufacturing or marketing.

No less than the giant IBM has recently undertaken a massive shift in focus, redeploying its resources from design and manufacturing to marketing and customer service.[22] When the large organizations have an edge in manufacturing or marketing, they may continue to prosper despite declining in-house R&D. The integrating core, however, will no longer be a common technological base, but instead a common manufacturing, distribution, or marketing base.

Yet the long term may bring continuing pressure upon large corporations because these advantages, too, will melt away for some companies as automated manufacturing spreads and as mass markets fragment. For example, the advent of practical computer integrated manufacturing (CIM) systems in widespread use, on the horizon perhaps as early as the mid-90s, will erode the advantages of large size in many areas of manufacturing, since such systems erase economies of scale and in their place bring tremendous economies of scope.[23] Even one of today's somewhat primitive CIM cells can produce any one of several hundred different parts, at the same cost per unit whether the production run is for a hundred units or only one unit.[24] As such CIM cells

---

21. For more details, see *Financial Planning* (October 1985), pp. 181-188.

22. See Dennis Kneale, "Tough Choices—Cutting Output, IBM Tells Some Workers: Move, Retire, or Quit," *Wall Street Journal*, April 8, 1987, p.1. See also Geoff Lewis, "Big Changes at Big Blue," *Business Week*, February 15, 1988, pp. 92f.

23. Economies of scope derive from cost reduction as a result of applying assets to the production of a variety of different products. Economies of scale, in contrast, derive from cost reduction as a result of applying assets intensely to the high-volume production of a small range of products. For the earliest development of ideas about economies of scope, see J. Panzar and R. Willig, "Economies of Scale and Economies of Scope in Multi-Output Production," and "Economies of Scope," Bell Laboratories Economic Discussion Papers No.33 (1975) and No.197 (1981), respectively.

24. The CIM cell at General Dynamics in Fort Worth, for example, can produce any of over 500 different aircraft parts, with "retooling" accomplished merely by selecting a different computer program. The automated assembly operation at the IBM plant in Austin, Texas offers another mind-stretching example. There, the PC Converible production is done entirely by robots. Machines sort the components, assemble them into finished computers, perform all systems tests, and pack the new computers in their boxes. Human workers don't enter the scene until it is time to load the finished computers onto trucks for shipment. The assembly system could be readily reprogrammed for a variety of new products.

become widespread and the bugs are smoothed out, the cost advantage will no longer be with large centrally-located factories, but instead with networks of small geographically-dispersed flexible factories that are close to final markets.[25] These flexible factories, moreover, will be capable of producing a broad range of goods under license to different designers.

Thus, the familiar specialized product-specific factories of today will give way to generalized factories that are the new-age analogue of the village blacksmith. Such factories will produce many of our basic goods locally, and in fact the local factory may well not be owned by any particular product designer. Such factories will really be more like utilities. With quality (that is, conformity to design specifications) assured within tight tolerances, competition will be on the basis of product design, where the edge seems to belong to organizations that are small enough to be flexible and provide an environment that is conducive to creativity.

The advantages of mass marketing are also eroding, with the fragmentation of the media. Cable and satellite television, VCR technology, and specialization within the print media have reduced the value of a blanket advertising appeal to the mass market, and enhanced the value of focusing on a particular audience. To take one prominent example, Campbell's Soup, a pioneer in mass marketing during the early days of radio, has recently begun shifting to a regional and ethnic focus in its product line.

CONCLUDING REMARKS

The financial marketplace is maturing rapidly, well on its way to attaining a truly world-wide scope, and the array of opportunities offered to investors is proliferating at a breakneck pace. The optimist sees opportunity in this and, indeed, the opportunities for people with good ideas have never been more abundant. Nor have the opportunities for those with cash ever seemed more promising.

To make way for these new opportunities, however, mature corporations in shrinking industries are now facing pressure to return their capital to the marketplace; and this contraction (in extreme cases, disappearance) of large firms will have unfortunate consequences for many. But, so long as vigorous new enterprises step in to replace declining operations, the net result is a stronger economy overall. Thus, where critics see only the lifeblood draining from venerable institutions, economists perceive the workings of the "invisible hand," leading to a more creative and competitive American industry with no formal central planning.

Perhaps the hardest realization for many to accept is that decisions which once fell indisputably within the province of an elite corps of corporate and regulatory minds are increasingly being made in the faceless, apparently chaotic marketplace. But in the end, of course, this is a major step toward greater democracy in economic affairs.

---

25. Recent research leads to the disquieting conclusion that many of the "bugs" now troubling some of the American pioneers in CIM are the fault of management rather than the systems themselves. It seems that American managers often try to force CIM into working the "old fashioned way," with large production runs and little variety. Their Japanese competitors, in contrast, play to the strengths of CIM by utilizing the inherent flexibility in short production runs for a variety of products. In time, U.S. management will either learn to use the flexible systems effectively, or fall by the wayside. (See Ramachanran Jaikumar, "Postindustrial Manufacturing," *Harvard Business Review*, Vol.64 No.6 (November-December 1986) pp. 69-76.)

Besides flexibility and low cost, furthermore, the new systems offer superior quality. Because of this Robert Kaplan recently warned that companies which choose not to invest in the new manufacturing technologies may find themselves in the unenviable position of being high-cost producers of inferior products. (See Robert Kaplan, "Must CIM Be Justified by Faith Alone?" *Harvard Business Review*, Vol.64 No.2 (March-April 1986), pp. 87-97.)

Corporate Restructuring/Selected Bibliography

Alexander, G., P. Benson, and J. Kampmeyer, "Investigating the Valuation Effects of Voluntary Corporate Sell-offs," *Journal of Finance* 39 (1984), 503-517.

Baiman, S. and J. Demski, "Economically Optimal Performance Evaluation and Control Systems, *Journal of Accounting Research* 18 (1980), Supplement, 184-220.

Borden, A. M., "Going Private — Old Tort, New Tort or No Tort?" *New York University Law Review* 49 (1974), 987-1042.

Bradley, M., "Interfirm Tender Offers and the Market for Corporate Control," *Journal of Business* (October, 1980), 345-376.

DeAngelo, H., L. DeAngelo, and E. Rice, "Going Private: Minority Freezouts and Stockholder Wealth," *Journal of Law Economics* (October, 1984).

Diamond, D. and R. Verrecchia, "Optimal Managerial Contracts and Equilibrium Security Prices, *Journal of Finance* 37 (May, 1982), 275-287.

Dodd, P., and J. Warner, "On Corporate Governance: A Study of Proxy Contests," *Journal of Financial Economics* 11 (April, 1983), 401-438.

Fama, E. and M. Jensen, "Separation of Ownership and Control," *Journal of Law and Economics* (June, 1983), 301-325.

Hearth, D., and J. Zaima, "Voluntary Divestitures and Value," *Financial Management* (1984).

Hite, G., and J. Owers, "Security Price Reactions around Corporate Spin-off Announcements," *Journal of Financial Economics* 12 (1983), 409-436.

Hite, G., and J. Owers, "Sale Divestitures: Implications for Buyers and Sellers," unpublished manuscript, Southern Methodist University, Dalls, TX 1984,.

Hite, G., J. Owers, and R. Rogers, "Separation of Real Estate Assets by Spin-off," unpublished manuscript, Southern Methodist University, Dallas, TX, 1984.

Jensen, M. and W. Meckling, "Theory of the Firm: Managerial Behavior, Agency Costs, and Ownership Structure," *Journal of Financial Economics* 3 (1976), 305-360.

Jensen, M. and R. Ruback, "The Market for Corporate Control: The Scientific Evidence," *Journal of Financial Economics* 11 (1983), 5-50.

Klein, A., "Voluntary Corporate Divestitures: Motives and Consequences," Unpublished Ph.D. dissertation, University of Chicago, 1983.

Kummer, Donald R., ."Valuation Consequences of Forced Divestiture Announcements," *Journal of Economics and Business* (1978), 130-136.

Linn, S., and M. Rozeff, "The Effects of Voluntary Spinoffs on Stock Prices: The Anergy Hypothesis," *Advances in Financial Planning and Forecasting* 1 (1984).

Linn, S., and M. Rozeff, "The Effects of Voluntary Selloffs on Stock Prices," Unpublished manuscript, University of Iowa, Iowa City, IA, 1984.

Miles, J., and J. Rosenfeld, "The Effect of Voluntary Spin-off Announcements on Shareholder Wealth," *Journal of Finance* 38 (1983), 1597-1606.

Mishkin, W., ed., *Techniques in Corporate Reorganization* (New York: Presidents Publishing House, 1972).

Palmon, D., and L. Seidler, "Current Value Reporting of Real Estate Companies and a Possible Example of Market Inefficiency," *The Accounting Review* 53 (1978), 776-790.

Rosenfeld, J. D., "Additional Evidence on the Relationship Between Divestiture Announcements and Shareholder Wealth," Emory University (1984).

Schipper, K., and A. Smith, "Effects of Recontracting on Shareholder Wealth: The Case of Voluntary Spin-offs," *Journal of Financial Economics* 12 (1983), 437-467.

Schneider, Carl W., Joseph M. Manko, and Robert S. Kant, "Going Public: Practice, Procedure and Consequences," *Villanova Law Review* 27 (November, 1981), 1-48.

Index of Names